CRITICAL SURVEY
OF
SHORT FICTION

Fourth Edition

CRITICAL SURVEY
OF
SHORT FICTION
Fourth Edition

World Writers

Editor
Charles E. May
California State University, Long Beach

SALEM PRESS
Ipswich, Massachusetts   Hackensack, New Jersey

Cover Photo: V.S. Naipaul © (Getty Images)

Some of the essays in this work, which have been updated, originally appeared in the following Salem Press publications, *Critical Survey of Short Fiction* (1981), *Critical Survey of Short Fiction, Supplement* (1987), *Critical Survey of Short Fiction, Revised Edition*, (1993; preceding volumes edited by Frank N. Magill), *Critical Survey of Short Fiction, Second Revised Edition* (2001; edited by Charles E. May).

The paper used in these volumes conforms to the American National Standard for Permanence of Paper for Printed Library Materials, X39.48-1992 (R1997).

LIBRARY OF CONGRESS CATALOGING-IN-PUBLICATION DATA

Critical survey of short fiction / editor, Charles E. May. -- 4th ed.

    p. cm.

Includes bibliographical references and index.
ISBN 978-1-58765-789-4 (set : alk. paper) -- ISBN 978-1-58765-790-0 (set, american : alk. paper) --
ISBN 978-1-58765-791-7 (vol. 1, american : alk. paper) -- ISBN 978-1-58765-792-4 (vol. 2, american : alk. paper) --
ISBN 978-1-58765-793-1 (vol. 3, american : alk. paper) -- ISBN 978-1-58765-794-8 (vol. 4, american : alk. paper) --
ISBN 978-1-58765-795-5 (set, british : alk. paper) -- ISBN 978-1-58765-796-2 (vol. 1, british : alk. paper) --
ISBN 978-1-58765-797-9 (vol. 2, british : alk. paper) -- ISBN 978-1-58765-798-6 (european : alk. paper) --
ISBN 978-1-58765-799-3 (world : alk. paper) -- ISBN 978-1-58765-800-6 (topical essays : alk. paper) --
ISBN 978-1-58765-803-7 (cumulative index : alk. paper)

1. Short story. 2. Short story--Bio-bibliography. I. May, Charles E. (Charles Edward), 1941-
PN3321.C7 2011
809.3'1--dc23

2011026000

First Printing

Printed in the United States of America

CONTENTS

PUBLISHER'S NOTE

World Writers is part of Salem Press's greatly expanded and redesigned *Critical Survey of Short Fiction* Series. The *Critical Survey of Short Fiction,* Fourth Edition, presents profiles of major short-story writers, with sections on other literary forms, achievements, biography, general analysis, and analysis of the writer's most important stories or collections. Although the profiled authors may have written in other genres as well, sometimes to great acclaim, the focus of this set is on their most important works of short fiction.

The *Critical Survey of Short Fiction* was originally published in 1981, with a supplement in 1987, a revised edition in 1993, and a second revised edition in 2001. The Fourth Edition includes all writers from the previous edition and adds 145 new ones, covering 625 writers in total. The writers covered in this set represent 44 countries and their short fiction dates from antiquity to the present. The set also offers 53 informative overviews; 24 of these essays were added for this edition. In addition, six resources are provided, one of them new. More than 400 photographs and portraits of writers have been included.

For the first time, the material in the *Critical Survey of Short Fiction* has been organized into five subsets by geography and essay type: a four-volume subset on *American Writers*, a two-volume subset on *British, Irish, and Commonwealth Writers*, a single-volume subset on *European Writers*, a single-volume subset on *World Writers*, and a single volume subset of *Topical Essays*. Each writer appears in only one subset. *Topical Essays* is organized under the categories "Theories, Themes, and Types," "History of Short Fiction," and "Short Fiction Around the World." A *Cumulative Indexes* volume covering all five subsets is free with purchase of more than one subset.

WORLD WRITERS

The single-volume *World Writers* contains 77 writer profiles, arranged alphabetically. For this edition, 15 new essays have been added, and 3 have been significantly updated with analysis of recently published books or stories. The volume begins with a list of contents and a key to pronunciation. The writer essays follow. The back of the volume contains the "Resources" section, which features a glossary, bibliography, guide to online resources, time line, major awards, and chronological list of writers, providing guides for further research and additional information on world writers; comprehensive versions appear in *Cumulative Indexes*. The guide to online resources and time line were newly created for this edition.

World Writers contains a categorized index of writers, in which writers are grouped by culture or group identity, literary movement, historical period, and forms and themes; a geographical index of writers; and a subject index. The "*Critical Survey of Short Fiction* Series: Master List of Contents" identifies writers profiled in *World Writers* as well as writers profiled in other *Critical Survey of Short Fiction* subsets. The *Cumulative Indexes* contains comprehensive versions of the categorized, geographical, and subject indexes.

UPDATING THE ESSAYS

All parts of the essays in the previous edition were scrutinized for currency and accuracy: The authors' latest works of short fiction were added to front-matter listings, other significant publications were added to back-matter listings, new translations were added to listings for foreign-language authors, and deceased authors' listings were rechecked for accuracy and currency. All essays' bibliographies—lists of sources for further consultation—were revised to provide readers with the latest information.

The essays in *World Writers* that required updating by academic experts received similar and even fuller attention: All new publications were added to listings, then each section of text was reviewed to ensure that recently received major awards are noted, that new biographical details are incorporated for still-living authors, and that analysis of works includes recently published books or stories. The updating experts' names were added to essays. Those original articles identified by the editor, Charles E. May, as not needing substantial updating were nevertheless reedited by Salem Press editors and checked for accuracy.

ONLINE ACCESS

Salem Press provides access to its award-winning content both in traditional, printed form and online. Any school or library that purchases *World Writers* is entitled to free, complimentary access to Salem's fully supported online version of the content. Features include a simple, intuitive interface; user profile areas for students and patrons; sophisticated search functionality; and complete context, including appendixes. Access is available through a code printed on the inside cover of the volume, and that access is unlimited and immediate. Our online customer service representatives, at (800) 221-1592, are happy to help with any questions. E-books are also available.

ORGANIZATION OF ESSAYS

The essays in *World Writers* vary in length, with none shorter than 2,000 words and most significantly longer. The profiles are arranged alphabetically, under the name by which the writer is best known. The format of the essays is standardized to allow predictable and easy access to the types of information of interest to a variety of users. Each writer essay contains ready-reference top matter, including full birth and (where applicable) death data, any alternate names used by the writer, and a list of "Principal short fiction," followed by the main text, which is divided into "Other literary forms," "Achievements," "Biography," and "Analysis." A list of "Other major works," a bibliography, and bylines complete the essay.

Principal short fiction lists the titles of the author's major collections of short fiction in chronological order, by date of original appearance. Most of the writers in *World Writers* wrote in a language other than English. The foreign-language title is given in its entirely, followed by the first English publication and its date of publication, if a translation has been made.

Other literary forms describes the author's work in other genres and notes whether the author is known primarily as a short-story writer or has achieved equal or greater fame in another genre. If the writer's last name is unlikely to be familiar to most users, phonetic pronunciation is provided in parentheses after his or her name. A "Key to Pronunciation" appears at the beginning of all volumes.

Achievements lists honors, awards, and other tangible recognitions, as well as a summation of the writer's influence and contributions to short fiction in particular and literature in general, where appropriate.

Biography provides a condensed biographical sketch with vital information from birth through (if applicable) death or the author's latest activities.

Analysis presents an overview of the writer's themes, techniques, style, and development, leading into subsections on major short-story collections, stories, or aspects of the person's work as a writer. As an aid to students, those foreign-language titles that have not yet appeared in translation are often followed by a "literal translation" in roman and lowercase letters in parentheses when these titles are mentioned in the text. If a collection of stories has been published in English, the English-language title is used in the text. Single stories that have not been translated are followed by a literal translation in parentheses. Those that have been translated are referred to by their English-language title, although the original title, if known, is also provided.

Other major works contains the writer's principal works in genres other than short fiction, listed by genre and by year of publication within each genre. If the work has been translated into English, the date and title under which it was first translated are given.

Bibliography lists secondary print sources for further study, annotated to assist users in evaluating focus and usefulness.

Byline notes the original contributor of the essay. If the essay was updated, the name of the most recent updater appears in a separate line, and previous updaters appear with the name of the original contributor.

APPENDIXES

The "Resources" section provides tools for further research and points of access to the wealth of information contained in *World Writers*.

Terms and Techniques is a lexicon of literary terms pertinent to the study of short fiction.

Bibliography identifies general reference works and other secondary sources that pertain to world writers.

Guide to Online Resources, new to this edition, provides Web sites pertaining to world short fiction and its writers.

Time Line, also new to this edition, lists major milestones and events in world short fiction and literature in the order in which they occurred.

Major Awards lists the recipients of major short fiction-specific awards in the areas covered by *World Writers* and general awards where applicable to writers of short fiction, from inception of the award to the present day.

Chronological List of Writers lists all 77 writers covered in *World Writers* by birth, in chronological order.

INDEXES

The "Geographical Index of Writers" lists all writers covered in *World Writers* by country or region. The "Categorized Index of Writers" lists the writers profiled in *World Writers* by culture or group identity, literary movements and historical periods, and forms and themes. The "*Critical Survey of Short Fiction* Series: Master List of Contents" lists not only the writers profiled in *World Writers* but also those in other subsets, allowing users to find any writer covered in the complete series. The subject index lists all titles, authors, subgenres, and literary movements or terms that receive substantial discussion in *World Writers*.

ACKNOWLEDGMENTS

Salem Press is grateful for the efforts of the original contributors of these essays and those of the outstanding academicians who took on the task of updating or writing new material for this set. Their names and affiliations are listed in the "Contributors" section that follows. Finally, we are indebted to our editor, Professor Charles E. May of California State University, Long Beach, for his development of the table of contents for the *Critical Survey of Short Fiction, Fourth Edition* and his advice on updating the original articles to make this comprehensive and thorough revised edition an indispensable tool for students, teachers, and general readers alike.

CONTRIBUTORS

A. Owen Aldridge
University of Illinois

Bryan Aubrey
Fairfield, Iowa

L. Michelle Baker
The Catholic University of America

Thomas Banks
Ohio Northern University

David Barratt
Montreat College

Ben Befu
University of California, Los Angeles

Alvin K. Benson
Utah Valley University

Richard P. Benton
Trinity College

Cynthia A. Bily
Macomb Community College

Carol Bishop
Indiana University, Southeast

Elizabeth Blakesley
Washington State University Libraries

Jo-Ellen Lipman Boon
Buena Park, California

Gerhard Brand
California State University, Los Angeles

Keith H. Brower
Salisbury State University

Mitzi M. Brunsdale
Mayville State College

Susan Butterworth
Salem State College

John Carpenter
University of Michigan

John Carr
Original Contributor

Balance Chow
San Jose State University

Julian W. Connolly
University of Virginia

Marcia B. Dinneen
Bridgewater State University

John W. Fiero
University of Louisiana at Lafayette

Earl E. Fitz
Penn State University

Lydia Forssander-Song
Trinity Western University

David W. Foster
Arizona State University

Trevor Le Gassick
University of Michigan

Natalie Harper
Simon's Rock College of Bard

David V. Harrington
St. Peter, Minnesota

Stephen M. Hart
University College London

Alan C. Haslam
Sierra College

Farhad B. Idris
Frostburg State University

Shakuntala Jayaswal
University of New Haven

Ronald L. Johnson
Northern Michigan University

Rebecca Kuzins
Pasadena, California

Linda Ledford-Miller
University of Scranton

Victor Lindsey
East Central University

R. C. Lutz
CII Group

Laurie Lykken
Century College

Paul Marx
University of New Haven

Charles E. May
California State University, Long Beach

Hugh McLean
University of California, Berkeley

Vasa D. Mihailovich
University of North Carolina, Chapel Hill

Paula M. Miller
Biola University

S. S. Moorty
Southern Utah State College

Sherry Morton-Mollo
California State University, Fullerton

Susan Nagel
New York, New York

Susana Perea-Fox
Oklahoma State University

R. Craig Philips
Michigan State University

Allene Phy-Olsen
Austin Peay State University

Susan L. Piepke
Bridgewater College

Victoria Price
Lamar University

Norman Prinsky
Augusta State University

Richard Rice
University of Tennessee at Chattanooga

Mary Rohrberger
New Orleans, Louisiana

Ruth Rosenberg
Brooklyn, New York

Harry L. Rosser
Newton Center, Massachusetts

Chaman L. Sahni
Boise State University

Barry Scherr
Dartmouth College

Barbara Kitt Seidman
Linfield College

Maria Eugenia Silva
Universidad Finis Terrae, Chile

Genevieve Slomski
New Britain, Connecticut

Judith L. Steininger
Milwaukee School of Engineering

Roy Arthur Swanson
University of Wisconsin-Milwaukee

Christine D. Tomei
Columbia University

Jon S. Vincent
University of Kansas

Shawncey Webb
Taylor University

James Whitlark
Texas Tech University

Anna M. Wittman
University of Alberta

Qingyun Wu
California State University, Los Angeles

KEY TO PRONUNCIATION

To help users of *Critical Survey of Short Fiction* pronounce unfamiliar names of profiled writers correctly, phonetic spellings using the character symbols listed below appear in parentheses immediately after the first mention of the writer's name in the narrative text. Stressed syllables are indicated in capital letters, and syllables are separated by hyphens.

VOWEL SOUNDS
Symbol: Spelled (Pronounced)

a: answer (AN-suhr), laugh (laf), sample (SAM-puhl), that (that)

ah: father (FAH-thur), hospital (HAHS-pih-tuhl)

aw: awful (AW-fuhl), caught (kawt)

ay: blaze (blayz), fade (fayd), waiter (WAYT-ur), weigh (way)

eh: bed (behd), head (hehd), said (sehd)

ee: believe (bee-LEEV), cedar (SEE-dur), leader (LEED-ur), liter (LEE-tur)

ew: boot (bewt), lose (lewz)

i: buy (bi), height (hit), lie (li), surprise (sur-PRIZ)

ih: bitter (BIH-tur), pill (pihl)

o: cotton (KO-tuhn), hot (hot)

oh: below (bee-LOH), coat (koht), note (noht), wholesome (HOHL-suhm)

oo: good (good), look (look)

ow: couch (kowch), how (how)

oy: boy (boy), coin (koyn)

uh: about (uh-BOWT), butter (BUH-tuhr), enough (ee-NUHF), other (UH-thur)

CONSONANT SOUNDS
Symbol: Spelled (Pronounced)

ch: beach (beech), chimp (chihmp)

g: beg (behg), disguise (dihs-GIZ), get (geht)

j: digit (DIH-juht), edge (ehj), jet (jeht)

k: cat (kat), kitten (KIH-tuhn), hex (hehks)

s: cellar (SEHL-ur), save (sayv), scent (sehnt)

sh: champagne (sham-PAYN), issue (IH-shew), shop (shop)

ur: birth (burth), disturb (dihs-TURB), earth (urth), letter (LEH-tur)

y: useful (YEWS-fuhl), young (yuhng)

z: business (BIHZ-nehs), zest (zehst)

zh: vision (VIH-zhuhn)

CRITICAL SURVEY
OF
SHORT FICTION
Fourth Edition

A

CHINUA ACHEBE

Born: Ogidi, Nigeria; November 16, 1930

PRINCIPAL SHORT FICTION

"Dead Men's Path," 1953
The Sacrificial Egg, and Other Stories, 1962
Girls at War, and Other Stories, 1972

OTHER LITERARY FORMS

In addition to his short-story collections, Chinua Achebe (CHEE-noo-ah ah-CHAY-bay) is known for essays, poetry collections, and children's literature. He is best known, however, for his novel *No Longer at Ease* (1960), which became a modern African classic. The book is the second in a trilogy about change, conflict, and personal struggle to find the "New Africa." The first is *Things Fall Apart* (1958) and the third is *Arrow of God* (1964). Achebe's fourth novel, *A Man of the People* (1966), was followed twenty-one years later by *Anthills of the Savannah* (1987), his fifth novel. In 1984 he became the founder and publisher of *Uwa Ndi Igbo: A Bilingual Journal of Igbo Life and Arts.* Achebe edited volumes of African short fiction, including *African Short Stories* (1985) and *The Heinemann Book of Contemporary African Short Fiction* (1992), both with C. L. Innes.

ACHIEVEMENTS

Chinua Achebe received awards or award nominations for each of his novelistic works, from the Margaret Wrong Memorial Prize for *Things Fall Apart* to a Man Booker Prize nomination for *Anthills of the Savannah.* He was also awarded a Rockefeller travel fellowship in 1960 and the United Nations Educational, Scientific, and Cultural Organization (UNESCO) Fellowship for creative artists in 1963. In 1979, he received the Nigerian National Merit Award and was named to the Order of the Federal Republic of Nigeria.

In addition, he was awarded the Man Booker International Prize in 2009 and the Dorothy and Lillian Gish Prize the following year. Achebe has also received honorary doctorates from universities around the world, including Dartmouth College in 1972 and Harvard University in 1996.

BIOGRAPHY

Chinua Achebe, christened at birth Albert Chinualumogu Achebe, was born in Ogidi in eastern Nigeria on November 16, 1930, near the Niger River. His family was Christian in a village divided between Christians and the "others." Achebe's great-grandfather served as the model for Okonkwo, the protagonist of *Things Fall Apart.* Because he was an Ibo and a Christian, Achebe grew up conscious of how he differed not only from other Africans but also from other Nigerians. Achebe was one of the first graduates of University College at Ibadan in 1953. In 1954, he was made producer of the Nigerian Broadcasting Service and in 1958 became the founding editor of Heinemann's African Writers series; this position and the publication, in that series, of *Things Fall Apart,* account for his vast influence among writers of his and the following generation.

Achebe married Christie Chinwe Okoli in 1961 and the couple had four children. When a civil war began in Nigeria in 1966 with the massacre of Achebe's fellow tribesmen in the northern part of the country, Achebe returned to the east, hoping to establish in the new country of Biafra a publishing house with other young Ibo writers. One of this band was the poet Christopher Okigbo, killed later that year in action against federal forces. After Biafra's defeat in the civil war, a defeat which meant for many of his compatriots imprisonment in camps and "reeducation," Achebe has worked as an educator as well as a writer. He traveled to the United States on several occasions to serve as a guest lecturer or visiting professor, and he visited many countries throughout the world. In addition, his interest in politics led to his serving as the deputy national president of the People's Redemption Party in 1983 and then as the president of the town union in Ogidi, Nigeria, in 1986.

Achebe served as visiting professor on an international scale. Universities at which he taught include Cambridge University, the University of Connecticut, and the University of California, Los Angeles. A 1990 car accident injured Achebe's spine, confining him to a wheelchair. He spent six months recovering, then accepted an endowed professorship at New York's Bard College. In the fall of 2009, he became the David and Marianna Fisher University Professor and professor of Africana studies at Brown University.

ANALYSIS

Chinua Achebe is an African English-language writer. As an author, Achebe uses the power of English words to expose, unite, and reveal various aspects of Nigerian culture. His subjects are both literary and political. In general, Achebe's writings reflect cultural diversity in twentieth century African society. He focuses on the difficulty faced by Africans who were once under the rule of British colonials but later had to struggle with issues of democracy, the evils of military rule, civil war, tribal rivalries, and dictatorship.

Achebe seeks to preserve the proverbs and truths of his Ibo tribal heritage by incorporating them into his stories, whether they be in his contemporary novels or his children's tales. His works do more, however, than entertain; they reveal truths about human nature and show the destruction of power corrupted. Achebe's writing does not cast blame but delivers a message to his readers concerning unity and the necessity for political stability in Nigerian culture.

"VENGEFUL CREDITOR"

Achebe's "Vengeful Creditor" is a story that seems to be about what a misconceived government decree guaranteeing free education to all can lead to, including some rather comic developments. It appears to be a story about class struggle, and then, as the reader sees layer after layer of meaning stripped away and one theme leading directly to another, it seems to be--and is--about something really quite different from either education or the class system.

Mr. and Mrs. Emenike are part of the Nigerian upper class: He is a parliamentary secretary, and he and his wife own a Mercedes and a Fiat and employ servants from the still-uneducated masses, most of them from the village of their birth, to which the Emenikes return periodically to shower largesse upon the populace. At the beginning of the story, a free-education bill has caused a mass desertion of servants, even those of college age, all of whom wish to go back to their villages and qualify for an education. Apparently many others have the same idea, for the turnout for free schooling is double what the government statisticians had predicted. The reader sees Emenike and his running buddies at the cabinet meeting at which it is decided to make everyone pay, after all, because the army might have to be called out if new taxes are announced to pay for the unexpected costs of the program.

The Emenikes, finding themselves with this "servant problem," return to their native village and ask Martha, a village woman known to them, if her daughter Vero will be their baby nurse for the princely sum of five pounds per year. Martha has led a rather sad life: She was educated at a Christian school whose reason for being was the education of African girls up to the standards expected of the wives of native pastors. The woman in charge of her school, however, by way of furthering her own romantic aspirations, persuaded Martha to marry a carpenter being trained at an industrial school managed by a white man. Carpentry never came into its own, however, at least not as much as preaching and teaching, and Martha had a "bad-luck marriage," which eventually left her a widow with no money and several children to support, although she was a Standard Three (beginning of high school) reader and her classmates were all married to prosperous teachers and bishops.

The withdrawal of the free-education decree has cast Martha's daughter, Vero, back onto the streets. When Mr. Emenike says that one does not need education to be great, Martha knows he is patronizing her; she knows exactly what the fate of an uneducated person usually is, but she needs the money from this job. Mr. Emenike rounds out his recruiting pitch by saying he thinks there is plenty of time for the ten-year-old girl to go to school. Martha says, "I read Standard Three in those days and I said they will all go to college. Now they will not even have the little I had thirty years ago." Vero turns out to be quick, industrious, and creative, but there also begins to be a connection between her charge's maturing and her own chance of an education. Finally, as she comes to realize the child will need care until hope of an education has past her, she tries to poison him by making him drink a bottle of red ink.

Mrs. Emenike, one of the least sympathetic Africans in any short story ever written by an African, beats Vero unmercifully. They drive back to the village where they were all born and pull her out of the car. Martha hears from Vero that she has been fired, sees the blood on her daughter, and drags her to the Emenikes. Called one who taught her daughter murder, she retorts to Mrs. Emenike that she is not a murderer. Mr. Emenike, trying to break up this confrontation, says, "It's the work of the devil. . . . I have always known that the craze for education in this country will one day ruin all of us. Now even children will commit murder in order to go to school."

Chinua Achebe (AP Photo/Axel Seidemann)

"UNCLE BEN'S CHOICE"

"Uncle Ben's Choice" is a ghost or magical story that involves the element of human choice. A succubus-goddess known as the Mami-Wota, capable of many disguises, is both a seducer and a betrayer. She makes it possible for a young girl who offers herself to a man to guarantee not only sexual relations but also success, riches, and whatever material things the man desires. The only condition is that the Mami-Wota prevents the man from marrying her.

"Uncle Ben's Choice" is a monologue told by Uncle Ben in a tone that is skeptical yet simultaneously sincere and ingenuous. Uncle Ben is a clerk determined not to marry, whose passions are scotch, a brand-new phonograph, and his bicycle. His affluence brings him to the attention of the Mami-Wota because he not only lives better than the average African but also is much more concerned with the material rewards of life than even his fellow clerks.

A "light" girl who is Roman Catholic falls for him, and he tries to stay out of her way. However, he comes home one night after some heavy drinking and falls into bed, only to find a naked woman there. He thinks at first that it is the girl who has been making a play for him, then he feels her hair--it feels European. He jumps out of bed, and the woman calls to him in the voice of the girl who has a crush on him. He is suspicious now and strikes a match, making the most fateful decision of his life: to abjure wealth gotten from being the exclusive property of the Mami-Wota, her lover and her slave. "Uncle Ben's Choice" is about the innate morality of men in society. Uncle Ben honors his society by suppressing his own urges and fantasies in favor of remaining a part of his family, clan, and tribe, whose rewards he values more than riches.

"GIRLS AT WAR"

"Girls at War" is a story about the war between the seceding state of Biafra and Nigeria, and both the theme and the plot are foreshadowed in the spare sentence introducing the principal characters: "The first time their paths crossed nothing happened." The second time they meet, however, is at a checkpoint at Akwa, when the girl, Gladys, stops Reginald Nwankwo's car to inspect it. He falls back on the dignity of his office and person, but this fails to impress her, which secretly delights and excites him. He sees her as "a beautiful girl in a breasty blue jersey, khaki jeans and canvas shoes with the new-style hair plait which gave a girl a defiant look." Before, in the earlier stages of the war, he had sneered at the militia girls, particularly after seeing a group recruited from a high school marching under the banner "WE ARE IMPREG-NABLE." Now he begins to respect them because of the mature attitude and bearing of Gladys, who seems both patriotic and savvy, knowing and yet naïve.

The third time they meet, "things had got very bad. Death and starvation had long chased out the headiness of the early days." Reginald is coming back to Owerri after using his influence as an official to obtain some food, unfortunately under the eyes of a starving crowd who mock and taunt him. He is something of an idealist, and this embarrasses him, but he has decided that in "such a situation one could do nothing at all for crowds; at best one could try to be of some use to one's immediate neighbors." Gladys is walking along in a crowd, and he picks her up, but not because he recognizes her. She has changed: She is wearing makeup, a wig, and new clothes and is now a bureaucrat and no doubt corrupt. She reminds him that she was the one who searched for him so long ago; he had admired her then, but now he just wants her, and as soon as they get into town he takes her into an air-raid bunker after Nigerian planes fly over, strafing.

Later, they go to a party, where in the midst of Biafran starvation there is scotch, Courvoisier, and real bread, but a white Red Cross man who has lost a friend in an air crash tells them all that they stink and that any girl there will roll into bed for a fish or a dollar. He is slapped by an African officer who, all the girls think, is a hero, including Gladys, who begins to appear to the protagonist--and to the reader--as the banal, improvident child she really is. Finally, Gladys goes home and to bed with Reginald, who is shocked by the coarseness of her language. He has his pleasure and writes her off. Then he begins to think she is nothing but a mirror reflecting a "rotten, maggoty society" and that she, like a dirty mirror, needs only some cleaning. He begins to believe she is under some terrible influence. He decides to try to help her; he gives her food and money, and they drive off together to her house. He is determined

to see who is there and who her friends are, to get to the bottom of her life of waste and callousness.

On the way he picks up a soldier who has lost part of one leg. Before, he would not have picked up a mere private, not only sweaty but also an inconvenience with his crutches and his talk of war. Then there is another air raid. He pushes past Gladys, who stops to go back to help the crippled soldier, and, terrified, goes into the timberline, where a near-miss knocks him senseless. When he awakes, he finds the driver sobbing and bloody and his car a wreck. "He saw the remains of his car smoking and the entangled remains of the girl and the soldier. And he let out a piercing cry and fell down again." With Gladys's horrible death, the protagonist understands the potential for nobility within the heart and soul of even the most banal and superficial of human beings. "Girls at War" confirms Achebe's faith in humanity and in Africa.

"CIVIL PEACE"

Because of their remarkable portrayal of Nigerian culture, Achebe's works, like the three stories analyzed above, are frequently anthologized. Achebe himself edited and published the collection *African Short Stories*. It is subdivided by regions of the African continent. In the West African section, Achebe included his own work "Civil Peace," originally published in *Girls at War, and Other Stories*.

This story takes place in the time period just after the Biafran War. It points out with the ironic title that there may not be much difference between civil war and civil peace. Jonathan Iwegbu feels fortunate that he, his wife, and three of their four children have survived the war. As an added bonus, so has his bicycle, which Jonathan had cleverly buried in his yard to keep it from the marauding troops. After the war, Jonathan's entrepreneurial instincts can flourish because he has the bicycle.

His business ventures do well and, in addition, he receives a cash payment of Nigerian money (called the *ex-gratia* award or egg-rasher by the Nigerians struggling with the foreign term) for turning in rebel money coined during the conflict. Unfortunately, a band of thieves, many of them former soldiers, armed with machine guns and other weapons, learn of his windfall and terrorize Jonathan and his family in a way reminiscent of wartime until Jonathan gives them the money. Fatalistically, yet realistically, Jonathan realizes he is back to square one, and, at the end of the story, he and his family are once again preparing to go out and start all over again. In Jonathan's own words, "I say, let egg-rasher perish in the flames! Let it go where everything else has gone."

This story illustrates one of Achebe's major themes, a portrayal of both the problems or weaknesses and the strengths of the Nigerian people. The society has been vicious and cruel to itself, yet the strength and spirit of individuals will carry it onward.

OTHER MAJOR WORKS

LONG FICTION: *Things Fall Apart*, 1958; *No Longer at Ease*, 1960; *Arrow of God*, 1964; *A Man of the People*, 1966; *Anthills of the Savannah*, 1987; *The African Trilogy*, 2010 (includes *Things Fall Apart*, *No Longer at Ease*, and *Arrow of God*).

POETRY: *Beware, Soul Brother, and Other Poems*, 1971, 1972 (pb. in U.S. as *Christmas in Biafra, and Other Poems*, 1973); *Collected Poems*, 2004.

NONFICTION: *Morning Yet on Creation Day*, 1975; *An Image of Africa*, 1977; *The Trouble with Nigeria*, 1983; *Hopes and Impediments*, 1988; *Conversations with Chinua Achebe*, 1997 (Bernth Lindfors, editor); *Home and Exile*, 2000; *The Education of a British-Protected Child*, 2009.

CHILDREN'S LITERATURE: *Chike and the River*, 1966; *How the Leopard Got His Claws*, 1972 (with John Iroaganachi); *The Drum*, 1977; *The Flute*, 1977.

EDITED TEXTS: *Don't Let Him Die: An Anthology of Memorial Poems for Christopher Okigbo, 1932-1967*, 1978 (with Dubem Okafor); *Aka weta: Egwu aguluagu egwu edeluede*, 1982 (with Obiora Udechukwu); *African Short Stories*, 1985 (with C. L. Innes); *Beyond Hunger in Africa*, 1990 (with others); *The Heinemann Book of Contemporary African Short Stories*, 1992 (with Innes).

MISCELLANEOUS: *Another Africa*, 1998 (poems and essay; photographs by Robert Lyons).

BIBLIOGRAPHY

Achebe, Chinua. "The Art of Fiction CXXXIX: Chinua Achebe." Interview by Jerome Brooks. *The Paris Review* 36 (Winter, 1994): 142-166. In this interview, Achebe discusses his schooling, work as a broadcaster, and views on other writers, as well as the nature of his writing process and the political situation in Nigeria.

Bolland, John. *Language and the Quest for Political and Social Identity in the African Novel*. Accra, Ghana: Woeli, 1996. Examines Achebe's novel *Anthills of the Savannah*, among other works, but it is valuable for its examination of African fiction and history, touching on themes found in Achebe's short stories.

Dameron, Charles. "Chinua Achebe." In *A Reader's Companion to the Short Story in English*, edited by Erin Fallon et al., under the auspices of the Society for the Study of the Short Story. Westport, Conn.: Greenwood Press, 2001. Aimed at the general reader, this essay provides a brief biography of Achebe followed by an analysis of his short fiction.

Ezenwa-Ohaeto. *Chinua Achebe: A Biography*. Bloomington: Indiana University Press, 1997. This work reveals information about Achebe's later years. Includes bibliographical references and an index.

Hunter, Adrian. "James Kelman and Chinua Achebe." In *The Cambridge Introduction to the Short Story in English*. Cambridge, England: Cambridge University Press, 2007. An analysis of postcolonial fiction, which includes discussion of Achebe's stories, including "Vengeful Creditor," "The Sacrificial Egg," and "The Madman" and his collection *Girls at War*.

Innes, Catherine Lynette. *Chinua Achebe*. Cambridge, England: Cambridge University Press, 1990. Innes's book concentrates on the entire body of Achebe's work. Background information concerning African culture is also included.

Joseph, Michael Scott. "A Pre-Modernist Reading of 'The Drum': Chinua Achebe and the Theme of the Eternal Return." *Ariel* 28 (January, 1997): 149-166. In this special issue on colonialism, postcolonialism, and children's literature, Achebe's "The Drum" is discussed as a satirical attack on European colonial values and a text dominated by nostalgia for a lost Golden Age.

Lindfors, Bernth, ed. *Conversations with Chinua Achebe*. Jackson: University Press of Mississippi, 1997. Twenty interviews with Achebe in which he discusses African oral tradition, the need for political commitment, the relationship between his novels and his short stories, his use of myth and fable, and other issues concerning his writing.

Mezu, Rose Ure. *Chinua Achebe: The Man and His Works*. London: Adonis & Abbey, 2006. Mezu, a Nigerian-born scholar and literary critic, analyzes Achebe's novels and other writings, comparing them with other works of literature by African and African American authors, including Olaudah Equiano and Zora Neale Hurston.

Morrison, Jago. *The Fiction of Chinua Achebe*. New York: Palgrave Macmillan, 2007. Analyzes Achebe's major novels, focusing on *Things Fall Apart*, as well as his short fiction, outlining areas of critical debate, influential approaches to his work, and the controversies his work has engendered.

John Carr
Updated by Paula M. Miller and
Judith L. Steininger

CHIMAMANDA NGOZI ADICHIE

Born: Enugu, Nigeria; September 15, 1977
Also known as: Amanda N. Adichie

PRINCIPAL SHORT FICTION

The Thing Around Your Neck, 2009
Birdsong, 2010
Ceiling, 2010
Quality Street, 2010

OTHER LITERARY FORMS

In addition to her prolific short-story writing, Chimamanda Ngozi Adichie (chihm-ah-MAHN-dah ehn-GOH-zeh uh-DEE-chay) has written highly reputed novels. However, she began her publishing career as a poet and playwright under the name Amanda N. Adichie. Apart from fiction, she also contributes nonfiction articles to various newspapers and magazines.

ACHIEVEMENTS

Chimamanda Ngozi Adichie's first short-story collection, *The Thing Around Your Neck*, was shortlisted for the 2009 John Llewellyn-Rhys Memorial Prize and the 2010 Commonwealth Writers' Prize. Her second novel, *Half of a Yellow Sun* (2006), won the 2007 Orange Broadband Prize for Fiction. It also was a *New York Times* Notable Book, a *People* and a *Black Issues* *Book Review* Best Book of the Year, and a finalist for the National Book Critics Circle Award. Her first novel, *Purple Hibiscus* (2003), won the 2005 Commonwealth Writers' Prize and the Hurston/Wright Legacy Award. It also was shortlisted for the 2004 Orange Prize for Fiction and 2004 John Llewellyn Rhys Memorial Prize. Awards for short stories include the 2002 David Wong Award and the 2003 O. Henry Prize. Adichie received a 2008 MacArthur Foundation Fellowship and was a 2005-2006 Hodder Fellow at Princeton University.

BIOGRAPHY

Born in Enugu, Nigeria, Chimamanda Ngozi Adichie, who considers herself first an Igbo (Nigerian ethnic group) and second a Nigerian citizen, grew up with a middle-class, Roman Catholic background in the university town of Nsukka, where her parents worked at the University of Nigeria. Her Igbo father from Abba, James Nwoye Adichie, was a professor of statistics in the Department of Mathematics, and Chimamanda Ngozi Adichie's Igbo mother from Umunnachi, Grace Ifeoma Adichie, was a registrar at the same university. Chimamanda Ngozi Adichie's father completed a B.S. in mathematics at the University College of Ibadan (now called the University of Ibadan, then included as a college of the University of London) from 1957 to 1960 and a Ph.D. in statistics at the

University of California, Berkeley, from 1963 to 1966. His educational background reflects Nigeria's ties to a colonial past, as a previous British colony, and to a contemporary dream of opportunity in the United States. Her parents had six children (three girls and three boys), and Adichie is the youngest girl as well as the fifth out of the six offspring. Her parents chose Igbo as the first language for their children, but all the children were educated in English. Both her grandfathers died during the Biafran war in Nigeria in the 1960's.

Adichie lived in the same house that Chinua Achebe, the highly acclaimed Nigerian writer and professor of English literature, occupied in Nsukka. She began studies in medicine and pharmacy at the University of Nigeria before switching to communications and political science in the United States, where she moved at the age of nineteen. She started studying communications at Drexel University in Philadelphia before graduating with a B.A. (summa cum laude) from Eastern Connecticut State University in communications and political science in 2001. She acquired an M.A. in creative writing from The Johns Hopkins University in 2003 and another M.A. in African studies from Yale University in 2008. In addition to pursuing her own writing, Adichie has taught creative writing in both the United States and Nigeria. She resides in both countries at different times of the year.

ANALYSIS

Many critics note Chimamanda Ngozi Adichie's connection to and rewriting of Achebe, the elder statesman of Nigerian literature. They share a profound love for their Igbo heritage and a keen interest in Nigerian politics. They also favor a realistic narrative style and exhibit a deep appreciation for complex characterization. Both writers come from middle-class, Christian backgrounds (Achebe from a Protestant background and Adichie from a Catholic background) and were educated in the English language in Nigeria, although they have Igbo as their first language. However, in terms of age, educational background, and career path, Achebe has more in common with Adichie's father than with Adichie. In addition, Adichie's birth after the Biafran war, her university education in the United States, and her gender set her apart from

Chimamanda Ngozi Adichie (Writer Pictures/Steve Bisgrove via AP Images)

Achebe. The major themes of her stories include home and identity, political unrest, immigration, growing up, and marriage.

THE THING AROUND YOUR NECK

Adichie's first collection of short stories, *The Thing Around Your Neck*, consists of twelve stories, all previously published in various journals, such as *The New Yorker* ("Cell One" and "The Headstrong Historian"), *Granta* ("On Monday of Last Week" and "Jumping Monkey Hill"), *Iowa Review* ("The Arrangers of Marriage"), *Other Voices* ("Imitation"), *Prism International* ("The American Embassy"), *Prospect* ("The Thing Around Your Neck" and "Tomorrow Is Too Far"), *The Virginia Quarterly Review* ("A Private Experience"), and *Zoetrope* ("Ghosts"), except for "The Shivering." Two of these stories were previously published under different titles: "A Private Experience" was "Scarf" and "The Thing Around Your Neck" was "You in America."

Most of the stories in this collection focus on the themes of home and identity, political unrest, immigration, and marriage rather than on growing up, except for "Tomorrow Is Too Far," which is about childhood relationships and memories set in both Nigeria and the United States. Other notable stories published elsewhere based on childhood and adolescence include "Real Food," which is about a nine-year-old Igbo girl's refusal to eat her native food *garri*; "Peppers," which is about a teenage girl's experience of puberty; and "Operation," which is about a female high school student's romantic relationship with a fellow student who subsequently dies in an armed robbery (also called an "operation"). In addition, Adichie's first novel, *Purple Hibiscus* has Kambili, a fifteen-year-old Igbo Catholic girl, as its narrator. All these stories are set in Nigeria.

Apart from the theme of growing up, the theme of home and identity is prominent in "Jumping Monkey Hill" and "The Headstrong Historian." Both stories engage postcolonial identity from two different angles: the position of an African writer in "Jumping Monkey Hill" and the position of an Igbo wife and subsequent widow and grandmother from the early days of colonization until after Nigeria's independence from the British in "The Headstrong Historian." In "Jumping Monkey Hill," an autobiographical short story, Ujunwa, a young Nigerian woman writer, resists the sexual, paternalistic, and colonialist suggestions of an old British scholar, Edward Campbell, in a writers' workshop setting in South Africa. In "The Headstrong Historian," Nwamgba, to some extent, is a female re-writing of Ezeulu, the village priest and protagonist in Achebe's *Arrow of God* (1964). Like Ezeulu the priest, Nwamgba the widow sends her son (in her case, her only child) to learn the English language and British ways from Christian missionaries. Unlike Ezeulu, Nwamgba finds redemption (instead of madness) in her granddaughter's respect of and relationship with her at the end of her life.

Following from the theme of home and identity, the theme of political unrest features in "Cell One," "A Private Experience," "Ghosts," and "The American Embassy." "Cell One," set on the Nsukka campus and in the Enugu police station during the time of the university cults (or gangs), depicts both campus and police violence experienced by the family of one of the university professors. "A Private Experience" portrays the brief relationship between a Catholic Igbo medical student and a Muslim Hausa trader, while they are hiding in a store during a street riot in Kano, Nigeria. "Ghosts" captures the thoughts and experiences of a retired Nigerian university professor in Nsukka, when he encounters an old colleague who had gone missing during the Biafran war. Ironically, the ghost of the protagonist's dead wife is more real than the seeming resurrection of a long-presumed-dead colleague. "The American Embassy" relates the heartbreaking story of the wife of an outspoken journalist, whose articles incited the wrath of the Nigerian government. Consequently, Nigerian government agents, who were sent to find her husband in Nigeria, kill her four-year-old son after her husband had already fled the country. The story takes place in the line to apply for a visa to go to the United States for those needing political asylum (which she never gets).

Other stories based on political unrest include her previously published short story "Half of a Yellow Sun" and her second novel of the same name, comprising a previously published short story, "The Master." Both these stories take place during the Biafran war. Adichie's gift of storytelling not only lies in her ability to describe real-life events through her sharp focus on refreshing and relatable details but also in her ability to render accurately complex human characteristics and emotions in dynamic personal relationships that continue to take place during these political upheavals. She is able to balance a sense of history with a sense of humanity.

In addition to her stories set in a politically unstable Nigeria, Adichie also sets several of her stories in the United States, her second home. Consequently, the theme of immigration is one of the highlights of this collection of short stories because the title story, "The Thing Around Your Neck," and the previously unpublished story "The Shivering" are in this category. Other stories about immigration in this collection are "Imitation," "On Monday of Last Week," and "The Arrangers of Marriage." In "The Thing Around Your Neck," the protagonist is a Nigerian girl who has just become an American immigrant. Her burden (the "thing" around her neck) as an American immigrant includes molestation by her Nigerian uncle who sponsored her immigration, financial support of her family in Nigeria and economic survival after she runs away from her uncle, cultural differences and power imbalances in her relationship with a white American man, and the death of her father in Nigeria. In "The Shivering," two Nigerian neighbors in Princeton, New Jersey, share a cultural and religious bond in the face of lost love. The open homosexuality of one of the main characters in this story only is hinted at in another story, "On Monday of Last Week," which showcases a Nigerian wife who finally reunites with her Nigerian husband in the United States after about five years of waiting in Nigeria until he gets his green card. The long separation makes them strangers to each other, and the protagonist becomes attracted to her Jewish employer's African American wife.

"Imitation" and "The Arrangers of Marriage" are about the theme of marriage as well as immigration. These stories feature wives from Nigeria who have moved to the United States because of their Nigerian husbands but who are trapped in these marriages. Nkem in "Imitation" finds out that her husband, who lives in Nigeria most of the time while she is in the United States with their children, has a girlfriend in Nigeria. Chinaza Okafor, subject of an arranged marriage who is forced to become Agatha Bell by her husband in "The Arrangers of Marriage," discovers that her husband is still legally wed to an American woman whom he married in order to obtain a green card.

"The Grief of Strangers," "Quality Street," "Ceiling," and "Birdsong"

Other stories on this theme of marriage include "The Grief of Strangers" (published in *Granta*), "Quality Street" (published in *New Statesman*), "Ceiling" (published in *Granta*), and "Birdsong" (published in *The New Yorker*). Like "The Arrangers of Marriage," "The Grief of Strangers" is about relatives arranging the marriage of a young Nigerian woman to a Nigerian man who lives overseas. Unlike "The Arrangers of Marriage," the prospective husband lives in England instead of the United States, and the prospective wife is an American resident instead of a local Nigerian woman. "Quality Street,"

"Ceiling," and "Birdsong" were all published in 2010 after *The Thing Around Your Neck*. Like "Imitation," "Birdsong" presents an adulterous husband, this time from the point of view of his Nigerian girlfriend who lives in Nigeria while his wife and children live in the United States. Like "Ghosts," "Ceiling" is a story told from a male point of view. In "Ceiling," the main protagonist, Obinze, feels trapped in his career and marriage when he receives an e-mail from an ex-girlfriend from his university days. "Quality Street," which is the brand name of a tin of candy, reveals the conflict based on social expectations between a Nigerian mother, Mrs. Njoku, and her American-educated daughter, Sochienne, over the daughter's wedding party in Nigeria.

Adichie presents the realities of immigration and marriage in a harsh light that is, nevertheless, humane and honest. She is unafraid to speak up for the women (and men) who are victimized by institutions and bureaucracies. Adichie is also eager to dispel social, sexual, and religious conventions, heroic ideals, romanticized notions, and cloying oversentimentality. She writes from a well-educated, socially privileged, and politically informed position.

Other major works

LONG FICTION: *Purple Hibiscus*, 2003; *Half of a Yellow Sun*, 2006.

PLAYS: *For Love of Biafra*, pb. 1998 (as Amanda N. Adichie).

POETRY: *Decisions*, 1998 (as Amanda N. Adichie).

Bibliography

Adichie, Chimamanda Ngozi, and Michael Ondaatje. "In Conversation." *Brick* 79 (Summer, 2007): 38-48. A conversation from the PEN World Voices festival.

Boehmer, Elleke. "Achebe and His Influence in Some Contemporary African Writing." *Interventions: International Journal of Postcolonial Studies* 11, no. 2 (2009): 141-153. Discusses Adichie's novels with a greater focus on *Half of a Yellow Sun*.

Collins, Walter P., ed. *Emerging African Voices*. New York: Cambria Press, 2010. Chapter 2 by Pauline Ada Uwakweh, "'Breaking Gods': The Narrator as

Revelator and Critic of the Postcolonial Condition in *Purple Hibiscus*," gives insight into Adichie's writing. Chapter 9 by R. Victoria Arana, "Fresh 'Cultural Critiques': The Ethnographic Fabulations of Adichie and Oyeyemi" looks at Adichie's body of work.

Franklin, Ruth. "Things Come Together." *New Republic* 240, no. 17 (2009): 52-55. A review of Adichie's *The Thing Around Your Neck* that also includes a discussion of *Purple Hibiscus* and *Half of a Yellow Sun*.

Hewett, Heather. "Coming of Age: Chimamanda Ngozi Adichie and the Voice of the Third Generation." *English in Africa* 32, no. 1 (2005): 73-97. Contextualizes Adichie's *Purple Hibiscus* within Nigerian literature.

Skidelsky, William. "The Interview: Chimamanda Ngozi Adichie." *The Observer*, April 5, 2009, p. 7. An interview following the publication of *The Thing Around Your Neck*.

Strehle, Susan. *Transnational Women's Fiction: Unsettling Home and Homeland*. New York: Palgrave Macmillan, 2008. Includes a chapter entitled "The Decolonized Home: Chimamanda Ngozi Adichie's *Purple Hibiscus*."

Walder, Dennis. *Postcolonial Nostalgias: Writing, Representation and Memory*. New York: Routledge, 2011. Contains a chapter entitled "Remembering 'Bitter Histories': From Achebe to Adichie."

Lydia Forssander-Song

Shmuel Yosef Agnon

Born: Buczacz, Galicia, Austro-Hungarian Empire (now Buchach, Ukraine); July 17, 1888
Died: Rehovoth, Israel; February 17, 1970
Also Known As: Shmuel Yosef Czaczkes

Principal short fiction

"Agunot," 1909 (English translation, 1970)
"Vehaya he-'akov lemishor," 1912
Me-az ume-'ata, 1931
Sipure ahavim, 1931
"Ha-mitpahat," 1932 ("The Kerchief," 1935)
Sefer hama'asim, 1932 (reprints 1941, 1951)
"Pat Shelema," 1933 ("A Whole Loaf," 1957)
Beshuva vanachat, 1935
Elu ve'elu, 1941
Shevu'at emunim, 1943 (*Betrothed*, 1966)
Ido ve'Enam, 1950 (*Edo and Enam*, 1966)
Samukh venir'e, 1951
Ad hena, 1952 (*To This Day*, 2008)
Al kapot hamanul, 1953
Ha-Esh veha'etsim, 1962
Two Tales, 1966 (includes *Betrothed* and *Edo and Enam*)

Selected Stories of S. Y. Agnon, 1970
Twenty-one Stories, 1970
'Ir u-melo'ah, 1973
Lifnim min hachomah, 1975
Pitche dvarim, 1977
A Dwelling Place of My People: Sixteen Stories of the Chassidim, 1983
A Book That Was Lost, and Other Stories, 1995

Other literary forms

Although it is for his more than two hundred short stories that he has gained worldwide renown, Shmuel Yosef Agnon (shmoo-EHL YOH-sehf AHG-nahn) is also a talented novelist. Three of his novels--*Hakhnasat kala* (1931; *The Bridal Canopy*, 1937), *Bi-levav yamin: Sipur agadah* (1935; *In the Heart of the Seas: A Story of a Journey to the Land of Israel*, 1947), and *Oreach nata lalun* (1939, 1950; *A Guest for the Night*, 1968)--have been published in a twelve-volume set. English translations of his other novels include *T'mol shilshom* (1945; *Only Yesterday*, 2000), *Sipur pashut* (1935; *A Simple Story*, 1985), and *Shirah* (1971; *Shira*, 1989). In collaboration with Martin Buber, he collected Hasidic tales; among his nonfiction works are *Yamim nora'im* (1938; *Days of Awe*, 1948), a compilation of learned commentaries on the holidays, and *Atem re'item* (1959; *Present at Sinai: The Giving of the Law*, 1994). In 1916, he copublished a book of Polish legends, and later he founded and coedited a journal in Berlin.

ACHIEVEMENTS

Shmuel Yosef Agnon's influence on the development of modern Hebrew literature is unparalleled. His contributions to literature earned the Bialik Prize for Literature in 1934 and in 1950, the Ussishkin Prize in 1950, the Israel Prize for Literature in both 1954 and 1958, and the Nobel Prize in Literature in 1966, shared with German-Swedish poet Nelly Sachs.

BIOGRAPHY

Shmuel Yosef Agnon derived his pen name from the novella *Agunot*, which he published in 1909. He was born Shmuel Yosef Czaczkes, the eldest of the five children of Shalom Mordecai and Esther Czaczkes. From his father, an ordained rabbi and merchant with whom he studied Talmudic commentaries, he learned Hebrew scholarship; from his mother, he gained an appreciation of German literature. He had no formal education beyond six years in private hadarim and a short period at the Baron Hirsch School, although he was given honorary doctorates by the Jewish Theological Seminary (1936) and the Hebrew University of Jerusalem (1959). In 1903, when only fifteen, he had his first poems published. At eighteen he moved to Lvov to work on a newspaper. In 1908, he became the first secretary of the Jewish court in Jaffa, Palestine, and secretary of the National Jewish Council. After two years in Jerusalem, he moved to Berlin, where he taught, wrote, and met his future publisher. Salman Schocken tried from 1916 to 1928 to have his friend's stories printed and gave him an annual stipend so he could continue writing. Finally, Schocken founded his own publishing firm, which he moved to Tel Aviv in 1938 because of the outbreak of World War II. He opened a New York branch in 1945. Agnon married Esther Marx on May 6, 1919. When his home in Germany burned down in 1924, he lost not only his library of some four thousand volumes but also his seven-hundred-page manuscript

of an autobiographical novel called "Eternal Life." Agnon returned to Jerusalem in 1924. From 1950 to 1970, he was president of the society for the publication of ancient manuscripts; he was also fellow of Bar-Ilan University. Agnon died after suffering a heart attack on February 17, 1970. Some eighty-five of Agnon's works have been published in translation in eighteen languages.

ANALYSIS

To read Shmuel Yosef Agnon's stories is to become immersed in the emerging Jewish state, Eastern Europe at the beginning of the twentieth century, the Jews in Germany during the Holocaust and throughout history, and individual people struggling to find their niche in these different places and situations. Agnon's sentences are often formed around allusions to Jewish texts and traditions, and the reader benefits from exploring the layers of meaning implied by these references. Agnon frames his stories in a way that begs the reader to struggle with the fine line between fact and fiction.

Much of Agnon's work relies on historical elements for its realism. Its combination of fact and fantasy reveals the breadth of his imagination. His connection to Israel, he said, made him feel as if he had been born in Jerusalem. Agnon, considered the greatest Hebrew writer of the twentieth century, also was inspired by past writers. Although his first book collection was destroyed, before he died he had amassed an even greater collection at his home in Jerusalem. His work, as critic Harold Fisch has said, "reflects the ongoing processes of Jewish life in his time." As a catalog of modern Jewish history and experience, Agnon's work is definitive of, as well as being defined by, its context. His influence on the development of modern Hebrew literature is unparalleled.

"FABLE OF THE GOAT"

In "Fable of the Goat," one of his earliest stories, Agnon established his genre, the medieval ethical tale, through his titles, his rhetorical devices, his use of anonymous, stereotyped figures, and his narrative stance. In 1925, he published a cycle of fourteen legends, the most frequently anthologized of which is the "Fable of the Goat." The figures are flat and unindividuated, a nameless father and his son. The mode of narration is traditional. The pose of transmitting, orally, a story that has been handed down from previous tellers is established by the passive voice of the opening sentence: "The tale is told of an old man who groaned from his heart." The diction is folkloric in its simplicity. Clauses are linked by coordinating rather than subordinating conjunctions; the sentences are compound rather than complex. Events are strung together in a similar fashion, one simply following the other, naïvely oblivious to cause and effect. Magical happenings are taken for granted.

Having set up the folkloric frame through these devices, Agnon persuades his reader to accept the enchantment on the same terms. The old man is cured of his unspecified ailment by the milk of a goat that periodically disappears. When the son offers to follow her by means of a cord tied to her tail, she leads him through a cave to the land of Israel. Desiring his father to follow him there, the son inserts a note in her ear. He assumes that his father will stroke the goat on its return and that, when it flicks its ears, the message will fall out. The father, however, assumes that his son has been killed, and the goat that led him to his death is slaughtered; not until

Schmuel Yosef Agnon (©The Nobel Foundation)

the goat is being flayed does he discover the note. Not only has he deprived himself of joining his son in the Holy Land, because, from that time on, the cave that had afforded his son access has been sealed, but also he has slain the source of the milk "which had the taste of paradise."

The meaning is conveyed stylistically, and the characters indicate their spiritual states by biblical allusions. The son shows that he has attained salvation through a simple leap of faith, by speaking in the language of the Song of Solomon. He sees "pleasant fruits," "a well of living waters," and "a fountain of gardens." He says that he will sit beneath a tree "until the day break, and the shadows flee." This love song between God and Israel is traditionally recited just before the Sabbath evening prayers. When he asks the passersby where he is, he says, "I charge you . . ."; they tell him he is close to Safed, a town which from the sixteenth century has been famous as the center of Jewish mysticism. He sees "men like angels, wrapped in white shawls" going to pray. They are carrying myrtle branches, a Midrashic symbol for a student of the Torah. When he writes his note, it is with ink made from gallnuts, with which the Torah scrolls are inscribed.

The son urges his father to adopt the same simple faith. He writes him not to ask questions but just to hold onto the cord, "then shalt thou walk in thy way safely." The father cannot read this message, however, because it is concealed from him by his own spiritual condition. His speeches echo the dirges of fathers over sons in the Bible; like David mourning Absalom, he laments, "Would God I had died for thee." Like Jacob grieving for Joseph, he cries "an evil beast hath devoured him; Joseph is without doubt rent in pieces." His lack of faith leads him to slay his one hope of redemption. When he finds the note telling him how to attain salvation "with one bound," it is too late. With the father's realization that he has condemned himself to live out his life in exile, the tale closes, intensified by the ironic contrast with the believing son from whom the father has by his own actions forever separated himself. The closing words quote the Psalm of the Sabbath, the son "shall bear fruit in his old age; full of sap and richness"; that he will live "tranquil and secure" refers to Jeremiah's prophecy of the end of exile.

The goat, whose milk is as sweet as honey, personifies the traditional epithet of Israel as "the land of milk and honey." By drinking the hope of returning to Zion, the old man heals the bitterness of his life. The concealed message sent out from the Holy Land, inscribed like a Torah scroll and promising redemption, reinforces the personification and turns it into a symbol; the words of the Torah are said to be "like milk and honey." The skeptic who deprives himself of this sustenance kills his only link with salvation. The theme, succinctly rendered in three and a half pages through subtle adjustments of biblical overtones, requires an extended explication of those allusions to readers who no longer study the Bible, and that irony is also part of the point of this brief fable.

"THE KERCHIEF"

"The Kerchief," which is also included in *A Book That Was Lost, and Other Stories*, shows the changed narrative stance in Agnon's next period, when he turned from the impersonal rendering of folkloric material to the lyrical rendition of subjective experience. The story uses the dual perspective of memoir: The child's initiation is framed by the adult's remembrance. The narrator recalls how he had given his mother's kerchief to a beggar on the day of his Bar Mitzvah; this induction into the adult congregation occurs on his thirteenth birthday. (The story is divided into thirteen episodes, and the first edition was privately issued in thirteen copies.) "The Kerchief" was composed as a Bar Mitzvah present for Gideon Schocken, the son of Agnon's patron. The tale of how a boy becomes a man opens and closes with the same tableau of the mother waiting at the window. The two scenes are informed by this difference: At the beginning she is waiting for her husband's return and at the end she is waiting for her son's.

The time scheme relates the events to the liturgical calendar and mythicizes them. The narrator says that the week of his father's absence was like Tisha B'av, a midsummer period of mourning for the destruction of both the first and the second Temples on the ninth of Av. At this lowest ebb of the year, legend says, the Messiah will be born; he will be found as a ragged pauper, binding his wounds outside the city gates. This event is introduced in a dream of the narrator, who falls asleep

thinking of the Messiah's advent and then dreams that a bird has carried him to Rome. There, among a group of poor men, sits a man binding his wounds. The boy averts his eyes from so much suffering. A few days after this dream, his father returns from his trip with presents for the family. His mother opens her gift, a kerchief, and strokes it lovingly, gazing silently at her husband. Because she wears it only on holidays, it becomes associated with family harmony. After she lights the Sabbath candles, the narrator imagines that angels' wings cause it to flutter. He feels a blessing flow into him as she silently strokes his head.

All these elements subtly converge in the climax of the story. On the day of his Bar Mitzvah, his mother has bound her kerchief around his neck. On his way home from the service he encounters a ragged beggar sitting on a pile of stones, tending his open sores; he seems to be the same figure the narrator saw in his dream. Now, having just been initiated into manhood, he does not avert his gaze, and his exchanged glance with the beggar is described with the same phrase used earlier for his parents' looks when the kerchief was first given. With a rush of feeling, the narrator hands him the kerchief, and the beggar bandages his feet and vanishes. The narrator stands for a moment before the now-empty pile of stones, which seem to dazzle, and feels the sun stroke his neck in blessing. Wondering how he can explain the loss of her kerchief, he turns homeward to find his mother waiting at the window with such affectionate acceptance that his apologies are unnecessary.

"A WHOLE LOAF"

The twenty stories in the collection *Sefer hama'asim* (book of deeds) are ironically entitled. The first-person protagonists share an inability to act effectively. Their failed missions, most of them lapses in ritual observance, induce a pervasive anxiety. They are menaced by uncanny figures who seem to be externalizations of their own psyches. "A Whole Loaf," also included in *A Book That Was Lost, and Other Stories*, has been the most frequently reprinted of these ambiguous tales. Set in twentieth-century Jerusalem on the weekend before Purim, the story, like its indecisive narrator, circles back on itself, concluding with the same passage with which it began. The speaker, having made no preparations for the Sabbath, must go out to eat because his family is abroad. It is required to bless a braided white bread in honor of the Sabbath. He is intercepted by Dr. Yekutiel Ne'eman (both of whose names are epithets for Moses, who, according to legend, died on that day, the seventh of Adar). The narrator is asked to mail some registered letters for him. The Hebrew word for "registered" is *ahrayut*, which means "obligation." Thus, he has been allegorically charged with the responsibility of carrying out the Mosaic commandments. The narrator is prevented from entering the post office by Mr. Gressler. An arsonist whose name is derived from the German word for "hateful" (grässlich), Gressler sets fire to a textile shop to get the insurance, and the narrator's entire library goes up in flames. The narrator is both attracted to and repelled by Gressler. Shortly after he enters Gressler's carriage, it overturns; both men fall into the street and grapple in the dust. Bruised and dirtied, the narrator cleans himself off, makes sure that he has not lost the letters, and decides that he had better appease his hunger before mailing them. Entering a restaurant, he orders "a whole loaf," which most likely symbolizes the protagonist's greedy nature. Many times the waiter seems to be approaching him with trays of food, but these are always for some other customer. He begins to reproach himself for having ordered a whole loaf, when he would have been satisfied with just a single slice. He sees a child eating the saffron-flavored bread his mother used to bake for Purim and longs for a mouthful. The clock strikes, reminding him that the post office will soon close, so he jumps up, knocking down the waiter who is finally bringing his order. He is asked to wait; everyone leaves, and he is locked in for the night. A mouse begins gnawing on the bones, and he fears that it will soon start gnawing him.

In the morning the cleaners ask who this fellow is lying on the littered floor, and the waiter identifies him as the one who had asked for a whole loaf. The narrator heads home in a hunger sweat, in dirty clothes, with a parched throat and heavy legs. Again he cleans himself and sets out once more on his quest for spiritual sustenance. The story closes in *t'shuvah*, which means "return," as it returns to its initial paragraph. The narrator, although he has twice fallen, arises again to seek his

tradition (symbolized by the whole hallah and the whole family). Although he is besmirched by life, he cleanses his sins (which is the second meaning of *t'shuvah*, "repentance"). As he is locked in the empty restaurant, his soul is locked in this world for a time. Soon his body and bones will be gnawed away in death, so he must make preparations for the world that is to come. There is a rabbinic saying that the Sabbath is a foretaste of Paradise, so humans must prepare themselves. Although it is Sunday when the story ends, and the post office is closed, he plans to fulfill his commitment. Alienated though he is, he still hungers for the whole loaf of life, even though he has not yet been granted even a crumb.

A BOOK THAT WAS LOST, AND OTHER STORIES

A Book That Was Lost, and Other Stories is a very readable collection of Agnon's short fiction. Named after one of the included stories, "A Book That Was Lost," the collection follows Agnon's life chronologically and geographically, providing a broad sampling of his many moods, voices, and themes, from pietistic folktales to stark modernism. The literary scope in this collection ranges from coming-of-age tales in "The Kerchief," to magical fables in "Pisces," to accounts of modern alienation in "A Whole Loaf" and "At the Outset of the Day."

The central theme of three stories, "A Book That Was Lost," "The Tale of the Menorah," and "Buczacz," focuses on the significance of Judaism in relation to political turmoil and exile endured throughout history. Other themes in this collection of short fiction include the relationship between the individual and the community, the inability to realize one's ambitions, the alienation of the individual from the community, destruction and redemption, the struggle of the individual in Israel, the intersection of religious and secular life, and human determination versus divine intervention. Throughout the collection, Agnon probes the Jewish condition, his narrators always seeking a balance and understanding between estrangement and community, antiquity and modernity, and destruction and rebirth. "A Book That Was Lost" centers on a book that is actually lost twice. At the beginning of the story, the narrator finds it in an obscure place in the Eastern European village of Buczacz. At the end of the story, the narrator is at the National Library in Israel awaiting the arrival of this same lost book. Jewish history and unity are reiterated throughout the story, bridging the gap from two thousand years ago to present Jewish identity.

"The Tale of the Menorah" and "Buczacz" can be profitably read together. In "The Tale of the Menorah," the symbol of the Menorah is used to relate the history and adaptation of the Jews of Buczacz, the eastern European village where Agnon was born. Throughout the story, the Jews of Buczacz struggle to cope with the challenges faced in understanding life in their Eastern European land of residence. In "Buczacz," Agnon expresses his abiding affection for his hometown village, a community that was swept away during the Holocaust. During the story, Agnon relates his deep feelings for such a great tragedy. By portraying the epic life of this town, Agnon reveals his hope that a single coherent community may become a model for all humankind to someday live together in peace.

OTHER MAJOR WORKS

LONG FICTION: *Hakhnasat kala*, 1931 (*The Bridal Canopy*, 1937); *Bi-levav yamim: Sipur agadah*, 1935 (*In the Heart of the Seas: A Story of a Journey to the Land of Israel*, 1947); *Sipur pashut*, 1935 (*A Simple Story*, 1985); *Oreach nata lalun*, 1939 (reprint 1950; *A Guest for the Night*, 1968); *Temol shilsom*, 1945 (*Only Yesterday*, 2000); *Shirah*, 1971 (*Shira*, 1989); *Bachanuto shel Mar Lublin*, 1974.

POETRY: *Agnon's Alef Bet: Poems*, 1998.

NONFICTION: *Sefer, sofer, vesipur*, 1938; *Yamim nora'im*, 1938 (*Days of Awe*, 1948); *Atem re'item*, 1959 (*Present at Sinai: The Giving of the Law*, 1994); *Sifrehem shel tsadikim*, 1961; *Meatsmi el atsmi*, 1976; *Korot batenu*, 1979.

MISCELLANEOUS: *Kol sippurav shel Shmuel Yosef Agnon*, 1931-1952 (11 volumes); *Kol sippurav shel Shmuel Yosef Agnon*, 1953-1962 (8 volumes).

BIBLIOGRAPHY

Aberbach, David. *At the Handles of the Lock: Themes in the Fiction of S. J. Agnon*. New York: Oxford University Press, 1984. Aberbach sets out the major patterns in Agnon's writing on a work-by-work basis. Much discussion of Agnon's short fiction is included, and the notes and references are detailed. Includes an index.

Band, Arnold J. *Nostalgia and Nightmare: A Study in the Fiction of S. Y. Agnon*. Berkeley: University of California Press, 1968. This comprehensive study covers Agnon's literary development text by text. It is also very useful for the historical background to, and context of, Agnon's work. Band discusses Agnon's life and his career as a writer. The book includes both primary and secondary bibliographies, appendixes, and a general index.

_____. *Studies in Modern Jewish Literature*. Philadelphia: Jewish Publication Society, 2003. This anthology of Band's essays from the 1960's to the early twenty-first century includes the section "Modern Hebrew Literature," which features four essays devoted to Agnon, including "A Jewish Existentialist Hero: Agnon's 'A Whole Loaf.'"

Ben-Dov, Nitza. *Agnon's Art of Indirection: Uncovering Latent Content in the Fiction of S. Y. Agnon*. New York: E. J. Brill, 1993. Discusses a number of themes in Agnon's work and includes a chapter entitled "The Web of Biblical Allusion." Also includes aBibliography and index.

Fisch, Harold. *S. Y. Agnon*. New York: Frederick Ungar, 1975. Part of a series on great writers, this work includes a useful chronology and a brief biography of Agnon's life. An in-depth discussion of individual writings follows the biographical section. Supplemented by notes, primary and secondary bibliographies, and an index.

Fleck, Jeffrey. *Character and Context: Studies in the Fiction of Abramovitsh, Brenner, and Agnon*. Chico, Calif.: Scholars Press, 1984. Fleck places Agnon's work alongside that of his contemporaries, especially in the first chapter, "Modern Hebrew Literature in Context." Individual stories such as "The Banished One," "And the Crooked Shall Become Straight," and "Legends" are discussed in detail. Fleck has included notes at the end of each chapter, as well as a list of reference works consulted for each author at the end of the book. Includes an index.

Hochman, Baruch. "An Afternoon with Agnon." *The American Scholar* 57 (Winter, 1988): 91-99. A biographical sketch and an account of a meeting with Agnon in Jerusalem. Notes how his work elegizes the traditional Eastern European Jewish world, which he saw disappearing through cultural erosion and then through the Holocaust. Claims that loss in Agnon's works is counterbalanced by miraculous transformations and restorations; a pervasive self-mockery similarly undercuts whatever the author idealizes.

_____. *The Fiction of S. Y. Agnon.* Ithaca, N.Y.: Cornell University Press, 1970. Hochman presents a detailed interpretation of Agnon's major works, placing them in the context of the time and place in which they were written. A primary bibliographical note is included for locating translations of the original works. Notes on all the chapters are supplied at the end of the book, as is an index.

Negev, Eilat. *Close Encounters with Twenty Israeli Writers.* London: Vallentine Mitchell, 2003. Negev, a literary correspondent for the Israeli journal *Yedioth Achronot*, presents twenty profiles of prominent contemporary Israeli writers, including Agnon, based on her interviews with the writers and other research.

Ozick, Cynthia. "Agnon's Antagonisms." *Commentary* 86 (December, 1988): 43-48. Ozick analyzes Agnon's story "Edo and Enam," discussing the relationship between translation and redemption and the oppositions of safety and obliteration, redemption and illusion, and exile and return.

Patterson, David, and Glenda Abramson, eds. *Tradition and Trauma: Studies in the Fiction of S. J. Agnon.* Boulder, Colo.: Westview Press, 1994. A collection of papers presented at a conference on the centenary of the birth of Agnon. A number of essays focus on such stories as "Forever," "Pat Shlemah," "Friendship," and "The Doctor's Divorce."

Shaked, Gershon. *Shmuel Yosef Agnon: A Revolutionary Traditionalist.* New York: New York University Press, 1989. Shaked details Agnon's progression as a writer, including biographical events that influenced his development. Chapter 5 addresses Agnon's short stories in particular. Contains notes on the chapters and an index.

Yudkin, Leon, ed. *Agnon: Texts and Contexts in English Translation: A Multi-Disciplinary Curriculum, Bibliographies, and Selected Syllabi.* New York: M. Wiener, 1988. A critical study of Agnon's works and their English translations. Includes aBibliography.

Ruth Rosenberg
Updated by Jo-Ellen Lipman Boon
and Alvin K. Benson

AMA ATA AIDOO

Born: Abeadzi Kyiakor, Gold Coast (now Ghana); March 23, 1942

PRINCIPAL SHORT FICTION

No Sweetness Here, 1970
The Girl Who Can, and Other Stories, 1997

OTHER LITERARY FORMS

The first work of Ama Ata Aidoo (AH-mah AH-tah ah-EE-dew) was a play, *The Dilemma of a Ghost* (1964), written when she was an undergraduate. Another drama was *Anowa* (1970). She has published two volumes of poetry: *Someone Talking to Sometime* (1985) and *An Angry Letter in January, and Other Poems* (1992). Her novels are *Our Sister Killjoy: Or, Reflections from a Black-Eyed Squint* (1977) and *Changes: A Love Story* (1991). Aidoo also has written a number of critical articles and edited *African Stories* (2006), a book of essays by African female authors.

ACHIEVEMENTS

Ever since writing a play that was produced before she graduated from college, Ama Ata Aidoo has been attracting attention as a writer. She won a short-story prize in a Mbari Press competition and was awarded another prize from Black Orpheus for "No Sweetness Here." Aidoo won a Fulbright Scholarship in 1988 and spent the following year at the University of Richmond, Virginia, as a writer in residence. Her second novel, *Changes*, won a Commonwealth Writers Prize in 1992.

BIOGRAPHY

Ama Ata Aidoo was born Christina Ama Aidoo, the daughter of Nana Yaw Fama, a chief of the Fanti tribe, and Maame Abba Abasema. Raised in the royal household, she was taught the traditions and folklore of her tribe. Her father regarded education as important for all Africans, particularly women. Consequently, she attended the Wesley School for Girls in Cape Coast, Ghana. In 1964, Aidoo, who had wanted to be a writer since age fifteen, graduated from the University of Ghana, Legon, with a B.A. in English. While a student, she participated in writers' workshops that resulted in a play, presented in the Students' Theater. Following graduation she became a research fellow at the University of Ghana and later received a creative writing fellowship to study at Stanford University in California. Aidoo traveled throughout the United States as well as Europe and East Africa, returning to Ghana in 1969. She taught at a number of universities and published her first novel, *Our Sister Killjoy*, in 1977. An oppressive military regime curtailed Aidoo's writing, censoring it, but she continued to teach literature at the University of Ghana, Cape Coast. Aidoo served as Ghana's minister of education from January, 1982, to June, 1983, until she was forced to resign because of her "radical" views. Aidoo left Ghana, and in 1983 began to live in Zimbabwe and the United States. She has continued to teach and to lecture at universities in the United States and Africa. In 1994, she cofounded of the Women's World Organization for Rights Development and Literature, to promote the rights of women. Aidoo has one child, a daughter.

ANALYSIS

Ama Ata Aidoo's work has two central themes: the role of women in contemporary African society and the effects of independence from Great Britain. Ghana, formerly named Gold Coast, became a British crown colony in 1874 and achieved independence in 1957. Colonial influence promoted the role of men in educational advancement and economic advancement. Such influence is also apparent in neocolonial Ghana. However, traditionally Ghana was a matrilineal society, tracing descent through the female line and stressing the importance of women in the communities. Such a society conflicted with colonial ideals of a society dominated by males, a patriarchy. However, women were not viewed as disadvantaged in traditional Ghanaian society, and a woman who depended on her husband economically was looked down upon. In Aidoo's short stories women may be portrayed as vulnerable to men, but the women do not play a subordinate role. Although the concerns of women are significant to her writing, to label Aidoo a feminist is a simplification. Her type of feminism not only combats a patriarchal view of society but also re-creates a society in which women are valued as the moral, and often the economic, centers of a community.

The stories also focus on the plight of women after Ghana gained independence from Great Britain. Male characters are generally not central and often are the cause of distress for women. Often men are separated from their families by the need to find work; other times men in polygamous marriages cause hurt, competition, and often rejection among the wives. Other male characters are abusive or unfaithful to their wives. Women, particularly mothers, are viewed as caretakers not only of their families but also of tribal traditions. Some women cave in to new lifestyles; others remain the anchors of their communities. However, despite the tragedies in their lives, the women endure through perseverance and celebrate their victories.

In addition, Aidoo's writing shows her strength as a dramatist as she creates scenes with a minimal number of words and effectively uses dialogue to develop her stories. Aidoo once said in an interview that her stories are meant to be told orally. In fact, they are a part of the oral tradition because each delivers a moral lesson. Her stories are generally about change, the result of a society becoming independent from colonial rule. However, independence is not always a positive thing because something is lost. Rather than embracing their culture, many want to be like the white people, stressing the value of studying abroad, purchasing appliances, and, for males particularly, wearing Western clothes.

No Sweetness Here

The eleven short stories in this collection were written over a period of five years and focus mainly on the plight of women in the "new" Africa. The stories are about change and the loss of traditions that affect the characters, mainly women. All the stories save one are set in Africa, some in the country, others in the city. The title is indicative of the situation in Africa as described by Aidoo. The lives of the characters are not filled with sweetness but with loss, longing, and disconnection. Following independence, rather than embracing cultural traditions, people attempted to imitate Western ways, glorifying education, particularly of men, and embracing alien values. Things, such as cars, become symbols of status and prestige. Those in power, the "new masters," have, in many ways, become like those colonial "masters" who are not concerned with the lives of ordinary people.

The first story in the collection, "Everything Counts," is about a woman who has just returned to Africa after studying abroad. Once home, she is astounded to see the differences in the people, particularly the women, who wish to ape white people, particularly by wearing wigs. African men travel abroad and marry Westernized women; women in Africa attempt to look and behave "white." The continuing belief that "white" is best is illustrated in a beauty pageant. All the contestants wear wigs, but it is the wigless, straight-haired mulatto woman, whose skin is almost white, who wins. This story illustrates how a foreign culture affects people who, consequently, look down on their own image and way of life. Aidoo begins the collection by stressing the negativity of change and follows with a longer story on the same subject: "For Whom Things Did Not Change." A young educated black man is seen as the master by the old houseboy. Independence has resulted in a new class of elite, educated blacks, who resemble the former white "masters"

in their abuse of the native population. As the old black man states, "some of us still have to be slaves." The story "In the Cutting of a Drink" presents another problem in the "new" Africa: how the development of cities has affected people. City people see villagers as beneath them, and villagers, as represented by the narrator, are amazed and confused by the behavior of city people. The narrator is so bewildered by this new world that he fails to recognize the sister for whom he is looking. She had left the village and gained "work" in the city as a dance-hall girl. The subtext of the story illustrates lack of economic opportunities for women and how some women have degraded themselves by moving to the city and, in effect, becoming prostitutes.

Other stories in the collection illustrate the disconnection between the old, tribal ways and the new ways of the modern world. In "The Message," a telegram completely confuses a grandmother, who assumes that her granddaughter's cesarean delivery means both she and the child are dead. How could it be otherwise if a child is cut from its mother? Economic issues are a constant concern in the stories as are the positions of women. The title story, "No Sweetness Here," describes a mother who is looked down upon by her husband and his other wives. Her only pleasure in life is her son, but when the husband divorces her, her son, against traditional ways, is given to the husband. Children represent security for their mothers. A double tragedy in the mother's life is the death of the son; truly her life has no sweetness now.

Some of the stories are told in a matter-of-fact style, some are sad, and others have a type of humor, such as "Two Sisters." Both sisters live in the city; they represent different lifestyles, yet both are dominated by men. The parents, who are dead, did not have time to impart Christian teachings and values to Mercy, the younger sister. Connie, the older sister, tries to convince Mercy that sleeping with older married men for favors is not right, but at the same time Connie is suffering from the activities of her philandering husband. Both women are victimized by men.

The final story in the collection, "Other Versions," has a different point of view, a male narrator. However, Kofi's experience as a student in the United States illustrates the vital importance of mothers in Ghanaian society. Kofi reflects on his mother's sacrifice for his well-being and thinks of his father, who takes but does not give: a representation of many males in Aidoo's fiction.

THE GIRL WHO CAN, AND OTHER STORIES

This collection was published originally in1997; the revised edition, published in 2002, has three additional stories. The fourteen stories all center on women and their lives. As in the previous collection, Aidoo writes about everyday people and their struggle with changes after independence. However, this collection is more affirming of what women can do, despite social and economic pitfalls. The writing is more engaging, smoother, and has a stronger sense of oral storytelling. As in the first collection, this book begins with a story about wigs, "Her Hair Politics." The hairdresser advocates a wig that would change the narrator's life. However, when it is stressed that the wig is real human hair, the narrator tries not to vomit, thinking of how a woman must have been truly in need to sell her hair. The following story, "Choosing," is about work, money, the wisdom of mothers, and their relationship with their daughters, a theme in Aidoo's work.

The title story, "The Girls Who Can," concerns a seven-year-old with long legs. Popular belief says a woman does not need schooling, only legs with "meat" to support her hips for childbearing. The narrator believes girls should be able to do other things with legs rather than going through childbirth and becomes a runner at school, winning an award. Her mother and grandmother, having continuously worried about the length of her legs, are proud (the grandmother) and speechless (the mother). The story concerns traditional limitations on women, as expressed by the grandmother and mother, and the increasing possibilities for women, as evidenced by the girl. As contrasted with the title story of Aidoo's first collection, this title story shows a positive outlook for women in Ghana.

"Comparisons" reflects on the life of a woman, as a child and later as a wife and mother. Like many of the women in Aidoo's stories, the narrator works at a professional but low-paying job (bank clerk). Her husband also has a poorly paying position. She thinks back to her childhood and family; her life as a child seemed easy compared to the constant busyness of life as

mother, wife, and wage earner. Her husband is unfaithful, a not-uncommon occurrence in Aidoo's work. Aidoo continuously asserts the strength of women. Her story "She-Who-Would-Be-King" is set in the future. Africa has become a Confederation of States (CAS) after fifty years of "hell," acquired immunodeficiency syndrome (AIDS), and drought. Amazingly, a woman has become president. "Heavy Moments" celebrates women who have joined the Ghana Air Force Academy and become pilots. The narrator of the story, who never belonged anywhere and had passed from town to village and back again, finds her home in the sky. "Some Global News" is a humorous story that focuses on clothes, and on how where a person lives, north or south, dictates what that person wears. Aidoo astutely states that nothing is the same for everyone in "this global village." The difference is particularly acute for Africans living in and going to university in the United States and Europe, who discover their differences extend beyond skin color.

One story, "Male-ing Names in the Sun," consists of three tales; the first is autobiographical. One tale describes Aidoo's language Fanti, defined in English-language dictionaries as native, wild, untamed, and tells of her grandfather, who was sent to prison for disturbing the "King's peace." He subsequently was tortured and killed. "Newly Opened Doors" is another story about the effects of independence. Supposedly since the whites are leaving, things should be better; but the whites do not leave, and things are not better. Before independence nothing was confusing. People knew what was expected of them under British rule, and they had their own traditions. However, independence did not improve the economic situation or provide more opportunities. Aidoo makes the point that Ghana is still under the control of "big men," who are black, and nothing much has changed.

OTHER MAJOR WORKS

LONG FICTION: *Our Sister Killjoy: Or, Reflections from a Black-Eyed Squint*, 1977; *Changes: A Love Story*, 1991.

PLAYS: *The Dilemma of a Ghost*, pr. 1964; *Anowa*, pb. 1970.

POETRY: *Someone Talking to Sometime*, 1985; *An Angry Letter in January, and Other Poems*, 1992.

CHILDREN'S LITERATURE: *The Eagle and the Chickens, and Other Stories*, 1986; *Birds, and Other Poems*, 1987.

EDITED TEXTS: *African Stories*, 2006.

BIBLIOGRAPHY

Azodo, Ada Uzoamaka, and Gay Wilentz, eds. *Emerging Perspectives on Ama Ata Aidoo*. Trenton, N.J.: Africa World Press, 1999. Includes a number of essays on Aidoo, several focusing on her short stories.

Chew, Shirley. "Ama Ata Aidoo." In *African Writers*, edited by C. Brian Cox. New York: Charles Scribner's Sons, 1997. An overview of Aidoo's publications, including *No Sweetness Here*.

Crawley-Rochette, Susan. "Ama Ata Aidoo." In *A Reader's Companion to the Short Story in English*, edited by Erin Fallon et al. Westport, Conn.: Greenwood Press, 2001. Some biography but predominantly critical analysis of stories in *No Sweetness Here*.

Dingwaney, Anuradha. "An Interview with Ama Ata Aidoo." *Massachusetts Review* 36, no. 1 (Spring, 1995): 123-133. In an interview conducted in 1992, Aidoo discusses feminism and the portrayal of cultural conflicts in her work, particularly the role of women in neocolonial Ghana.

Odamtten, Vincent O. *The Art of Ama Ata Aidoo*. Gainesville: University Press of Florida, 1994. The chapter on *No Sweetness Here* is particularly helpful in analyzing the stories and seeing the relationships between them.

Marcia B. Dinneen

RYŪNOSUKE AKUTAGAWA

Born: Tokyo, Japan; March 1, 1892
Died: Tokyo, Japan; July 24, 1927
Also Known As: Ryūnosuke Niihara

PRINCIPAL SHORT FICTION

"*Rashōmon,*" 1915 (*Rashomon, and Other Stories,* 1952, 1964)

"*Yabu no naka,*" 1922 ("In a Grove," 1952)

Aru ahō no isshō, 1927 (*A Fool's Life,* 1971)

Kappa, 1927 (English translation, 1970)

Tales Grotesque and Curious, 1930

Jigokuhen, 1946 (*Hell Screen, and Other Stories,* 1948)

Japanese Short Stories, 1961

Exotic Japanese Stories: The Beautiful and the Grotesque, 1964

The Essential Akutagawa: "Rashomon," "Hell Screen," "Cogwheels," "A Fool's Life," and Other Short Fiction, 1999

OTHER LITERARY FORMS

Ryūnosuke Akutagawa (rioo-noh-suh-kay ahk-ew-tah-gah-wah) is known mainly for his short stories, most of which were based on Japanese tales from the twelfth and thirteenth centuries, but he also wrote poetry and essays on literature.

ACHIEVEMENTS

Ryūnosuke Akutagawa gained attention even as a student in English literature at Tokyo University, publishing a short story about a priest with an enormous nose in 1916. Natsumi Sōseki, the foremost novelist of the day, wrote Akutagawa praising his concise style and predicting that if he could write twenty or thirty more such stories he would become famous. He was well recognized as a literary figure by 1918, an unusual accomplishment for such a young writer. Such was his fame that in 1935 the Akutagawa Prize was established in his name. It recognizes promising new writers and is one of the most prestigious literary awards in Japan. Akutagawa is generally considered to be one of the outstanding literary figures in the prewar era, along with Sōseki and Mori Ōgai, and he achieved this in spite of a brief career. His stories are considered classics in modern Japanese literature.

BIOGRAPHY

Ryūnosuke Akutagawa was the son of a dairyman named Niihara Toshizo. Akutagawa's mother went insane seven months after his birth, and she remained so until her death in 1902. At a time when insanity was assumed to be hereditary, Akutagawa feared it most of his life. In fact, he referred to his mother in his suicide note in 1927. Akutagawa was adopted by his mother's brother and reared by his foster mother and a maiden aunt. He was a good student, well read in both Japanese and European literature, including Guy de Maupassant, Anatole France, August Strindberg, and Fyodor Dostoevski.

In 1913, Akutagawa entered the English literature department at Tokyo Imperial University, where he published his writing in a university literary magazine. His first important short story, "Rashōmon," appeared in November of 1915, and other modern versions of ancient Japanese tales followed. Akutagawa was graduated in 1916 and briefly held a teaching job, but he soon quit to devote his full time to writing short stories, some of which already had given him fame.

Akutagawa married Tsukamoto Fumiko in 1918, and in the next few years, well established as a writer, he wrote some of his best stories. These stories were based on old tales from Chinese, Japanese, and Western literature. In 1922, however, he left this genre behind him. It may be that his literary transition and the psychological problems he had were related to his seeming loss of imagination in the early 1920's.

By 1923, Akutagawa's health was deteriorating, and he complained of nervous exhaustion, cramps, and other ailments. Despite his earlier criticisms of the self-confessional I-novel, after 1924 his writing underwent a profound change as he stopped writing imaginative period pieces and turned to contemporary subjects and his own life, especially his childhood. Possibly, he was too ill to muster the creative energy to continue his storytelling. Critics and even some friends had long urged him to reveal himself in his writing, but perhaps he feared facing the insanity that had separated him from his mother when he was a young boy.

From 1923 until his suicide in 1927, Akutagawa turned to contemporary themes that reflected his deteriorating health and increasing depression. In February, 1927, he began a famous literary dispute with Jun'ichirō Tanizaki that lasted until his death in July that year. This "plot controversy" started in a literary magazine where Akutagawa questioned the artistic value of a plot in novels. Tanizaki had denounced unstructured confessional writing in which the author describes his state of mind, ironically a position with which Akutagawa would have agreed in his early career. Month by month in the spring of 1927, they debated structure versus a quality Akutagawa called "purity," but in truth there was little lucidity in the debate, although it aroused great interest in literary circles. The debate ended with Akutagawa's death, which helped make it a turning point in Japanese fiction as writers sought new forms of expression.

With his own artistic shift in 1924, Akutagawa sensed more keenly than most writers the end of his era. He left the brilliant storytelling and plot structure behind in his last three years as he turned to gloomy autobiography that traced his descent into despair and self-destruction. He had become the tormented artist in "Jigokuhen" ("Hell Screen"), one of his most poignant works. Physically and mentally broken, he committed suicide by poisoning in 1927, leaving behind a long, depressing suicide note that has become a classic in itself.

ANALYSIS

Ryūnosuke Akutagawa has come to typify the Taishō era (1912-1926) in Japanese literature because of his challenge to the confessional and revealing I-novels that prevailed before World War I and the fact that his suicide seemed to end the era, paving the way for prewar proletarian literature. Akutagawa, perhaps influenced by his wide reading of Western authors such as Edgar Allan Poe, used the short-story genre from the start. I-novelists also wrote short stories, and in fact the Japanese term *shōsetsu* is used for both the novel and the short story, but Akutagawa rejected self-disclosure and stressed the narrative element. He saw the writer as a storyteller, and his own stories are twice removed from reality, for they are eclectic, based on other stories in classical Japanese and Chinese literature and stories by Western authors. Frequently, many elements from other works are carefully brought together in new combinations to create a self-contained structure, as Akutagawa let the story define reality in his work. Using old tales allowed him to define reality in symbolic terms and to apply the insights of modern psychology without dealing with the issue of the self.

Mining older literature was a tradition in Japanese literature, a tradition that had disappeared in the confessional novels that dominated early twentieth century Japanese literature. Akutagawa's concise polished style emerged precociously in the stories he published while a student of English literature at Tokyo Imperial University.

"Rashōmon"

One of these stories, "Rashōmon," appeared in November, 1915, in a university literary magazine, *Teikoku Bungaku* (imperial literature). Akutagawa borrowed from a twelfth century tale and other sources, setting the story in Kyōto during a period of social and economic chaos. The story begins at a dilapidated gate (the Rashōmon of the title) during a rainstorm. A man seeking shelter from the storm encounters an old woman who is plucking the hair from corpses to use as wigs that she will sell. He, too, descends into depravity as he steals her clothes to sell. Akutagawa mined literature for details that evoke the decadent spirit of the age, adding psychological elements to give the story a modern relevance. In this syncretism, he did not seek to re-create the past but to use it to symbolize a modern theme of social breakdown and the disappearance of universal values.

"The Nose"

Although many of his early stories contain sickening details, not all are morbid. His first popular success, "Hana" ("The Nose"), is a story about a Buddhist priest who has an enormous drooping nose that people pity. Embarrassed, he discovers a difficult treatment that shortens it, only to find that those who had previously taken pity on his plight now openly ridicule him for his vanity.

When the nose swells again to its former size one night, the priest is pleased that no one will laugh at him again. This grotesque but humorous story caught the attention of Sōseki, who praised it for its unusual subject and clear style. "The Nose" was reprinted in *Shinshōsetsu* (new fiction), a major literary review, and Akutagawa became a recognized new writer.

"The Spider's Thread"

Akutagawa enhanced his reputation with nearly one hundred stories between 1916 and 1924. One of his most famous, "Kumo no ito" ("The Spider's Thread"), explores the theme of self-interest. A robber, Kandata, has been sent to hell for his crimes. The all-compassionate Buddha, however, can save even criminals. Because Kandata had once spared a spider, it spins a thread that drops into hell. Kandata begins to climb up on it, but looking below, he sees other sinners following him. Selfishly, he yells at them to let go lest the thread break. This self-centered thought indeed does break the thread, and he falls back into hell with the others, a victim of selfishness. In this story, as in many others, Akutagawa used a variety of sources, causing some critics to doubt his creativity.

"Hell Screen"

Such criticism is unfair because Akutagawa, while eclectic in his sources of inspiration, recasts tales into a new, more evocative form. An excellent example of his inspired adaptations is "Hell Screen." This powerful story is about an artist, Yoshihide, who puts his art before his family, striving for an inhuman perfection. In the story, Yoshihide is commissioned by his lord to paint a series of screens depicting hell. A slave to accuracy, Yoshihide has his models tortured in varied ways to depict their agony. The last scene requires the burning of a court lady inside a carriage. The lord agrees to stage the hideous scene, but he places Yoshihide's only daughter inside because she has spurned his advances. Horrified, Yoshihide nevertheless finishes the screen. He hangs himself, however, in remorse. The screen is recognized as a masterpiece, as was Akutagawa's moral tale.

"In a Grove"

Another well-known story from this period is "Yabu no naka" ("In a Grove"), which was made into a famous film by director Akira Kurosawa in 1950, using the title "Rashōmon" from the earlier story and blending the two tales. Again using an old story, Akutagawa gives conflicting versions of a rape-murder, leaving the reader to guess which is true. The story illustrates the difficulty of finding absolute truth, as each individual describes the incident from a different self-serving perspective. A samurai and his wife encounter a bandit in the forest who, according to the dead samurai speaking through a medium, ties him up and forces him to witness the rape of his wife, who appears to be a willing victim, urging the bandit to kill her weak husband. According to the samurai, the bandit is shocked at the woman's intensity, and he runs off. Humiliated, the samurai uses his wife's dagger to kill himself. Both the bandit and the wife then give their testimony, which glorifies their own actions and contradicts the original version. All the versions of the incident are left unresolved.

In 1924, Akutagawa made a major shift in his writing that signaled a new literary viewpoint. It also coincided with a personal crisis as he fell in love with a poet and began to experience long episodes of depression, trying to reconcile his family commitment with artistic creativity. In 1926, he published a volume of poetry that, for the first time, dealt directly with his

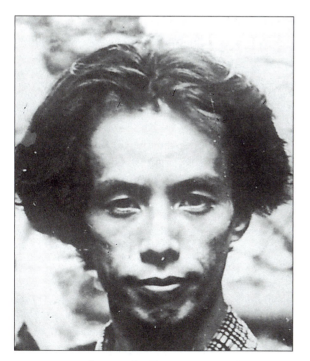

Ryunosuke Akutagawa (Kyodo/Landov)

own feelings. It marked his turn from stories to the realistic and biographical fiction that characterizes the last years of his life. His literary conversion and death were interpreted as the end of an era and a reflection of the modern debate about plot and expression and the relationship of the narrator to the novel.

Akutagawa's most important fictional work in his last year was *Kappa*, a satire about elves who appear in Japanese folklore, although the long story is similar to Anatole France's novel *L'Île des pingouins* (1908; *Penguin Island*, 1914). The grotesque kappa--part human, bird, and reptile--seem to reverse the human order of things, but they also have human problems, such as war and unemployment. Some of these problems have bizarre solutions; for example, the unemployed are eaten. Akutagawa's other stories describe mental breakdown and physical decline, reflecting his deepening gloom.

One of the best of Akutagawa's autobiographical works, "Haguruma," was published posthumously. He wrote of his mental tension and schizophrenic fears of imaginary cogwheels that blocked his vision. In his story, it is difficult to tell reality from hallucination, a reflection of his mental state. It ends with the demented plea, "Will no one have the goodness to strangle me in my sleep?" Another posthumous story written in his final days describes corpses, ennui, and death.

Akutagawa's suicide note itself is well known in Japan. Entitled "Aru kyuyu e okuru shuki" ("Memories Sent to an Old Friend"), it was addressed to Kume Masao. Akutagawa described his reasons for suicide, revealing that for two years he had constantly thought of killing himself, debating the way to carry it out with the least trouble to his family. He ruled out a gun since it would leave an untidy mess, and he did not have the courage for the sword. In the end, he took an overdose of sleeping medicine and ended his tormented life on July 24, 1927. His death shocked the literary world but was no surprise to those knew him well, for he had often talked of suicide.

Akutagawa was the first modern Japanese writer to attract wide attention abroad, and his personal literary conversion and dispute with Jun'ichirō Tanizaki reflect the modern debate over the direction of the novel. Akutagawa, the consummate storyteller, sensed the weakness of his own writing in his last years, and his dramatic death drew attention to the literary controversy he had begun with Tanizaki. His death signified the end of a period of Japanese literature when writers thought they could balance and reconcile life and art through aesthetic control. Because he was so famous and talented, most of his fellow writers were stunned by his death, and many were forced to reexamine their assumptions about literature. His last works are tragic, and the brutal honesty of his charting of his own demise has gained for him fame in modern Japanese literature. This fame is institutionalized in the Akutagawa Prize, the most sought-after source of recognition for young writers in Japan.

OTHER MAJOR WORKS

MISCELLANEOUS: *Akutagawa Ryūnosuke zenshū*, 1995-1998 (24 volumes).

BIBLIOGRAPHY

Gerow, A. A. "The Self Seen as Other: Akutagawa and Film." *Literature/Film Quarterly* 23 (1995): 197-203. Discusses the influence of film on Akutagawa's fiction. Argues that cinema affects the central conflict between East and West and traditional and modern in his work and that Akutagawa's use of film suggests the loss of traditional Japanese culture and an effort to create a new national identity.

Hibbett, Howard. "Akutagawa Ryūnosuke and the Negative Ideal." In *Personality in Japanese History*, edited by Albert M. Craig and Donald H. Shively. Berkeley: University of California Press, 1970. Hibbett notes the general conclusion that Akutagawa's suicide is generally interpreted as that of a martyr to the times, and thus symbolic. As the writer's development and various works are discussed, their relationship to his mental condition at various periods is well analyzed. Includes a table of contents and an index.

Hiraoka, Toshio. *Remarks on Akutagawa's Works: With American Students' Opinions*. Tokyo: Seirosha, 1990. Analyses of Akutagawa's works. Includes English translations of some of the fiction.

Karlsson, Matts. "Writing Madness: Deranged Impressions in Akutagawa's "Cobwheels" and Strindberg's *Inferno*." *Comparative Literature Studies* 46, no. 4 (2009): 618-644. Compares the literary styles of the two works, focusing on their authors' confessional styles and the common theme of random associations.

Keene, Donald. "Akutagawa Ryūnosuke." In *Dawn to the West: Japanese Literature of the Modern Era*. Vol. 1. New York: Holt, Rinehart and Winston, 1984. Keene's comprehensive volume devotes a chapter to Akutagawa and mentions him in other relevant chapters. Provides an overview of many major stories, as well as historical, cultural, and literary context. Includes an appendix, glossary, and index.

Lippit, Seiji M. "The Disintegrating Machinery of the Modern: Akutagawa Ryūnosuke's Late Writings." *The Journal of Asian Studies* 58 (February, 1999): 27-50. Discusses Akutagawa's relationship to Japanese modernist concepts. Challenges the critical assumption that he represents aestheticized literary practices and clarifies his advocacy of "pure" literature. Focuses on issues of representation and cultural identity in his late writings.

Peace, David. "Last Words: Haunted by His Mother's Madness, Insomnia, and Self-Loathing, Ryunosuke Akutagawa, One of Japan's Leading Literary Figures, Killed Himself at Thirty-five, but Not Before a Final Creative Outpouring. *The Guardian*, September 8, 2007, p. 22. Focuses on the work Akutagawa produced during the final months of his life, including the short stories "Genkakusanbo" ("The Villa of Genkaku"), "Shinkiro" ("Mirage"), "Aru Aho no Issho" ("The Life of a Stupid Man"), and "Haguruma" ("Spinning Gears").

Rosenfeld, David. "Counter-Orientalism and Textual Play in Akutagawa's 'The Ball' ('Buto-kai')." *Japan Forum* 12, no. 1 (April, 2000): 53-63. Akutagawa wrote "The Ball" in 1920 in response to the 1889 story "Un Bal à Yaddo," by French writer Pierre Loti. Loti's story is about a state ball that the Japanese government has staged for foreign visitors; Akutagawa rewrites Loti's story from the point of view of one of the Japanese women whom Loti describes. Rosenfeld argues that Akutagawa's story reveals a political sensibility not usually associated with this writer and compares "The Ball" to more recent works of postcolonial literature.

Ueda, Makoto. "Akutagawa Ryūnosuke." In *Modern Japanese Writers and the Nature of Literature*. Stanford, Calif.: Stanford University Press, 1976. Chapter 5 treats Akutagawa's development as a writer, relates his philosophy of literature to several of his works, and comments on the relationship of Akutagawa's work to his suicide. Includes notes, a selectBibliography, and an index.

Yamanouchi, Hisaaki. "The Rivals: Shiga Naoya and Akutagawa Ryūnosuke." In *The Search for Authenticity in Modern Japanese Literature*. New York:

Cambridge University Press, 1978. A study of twelve Japanese writers. Includes a chapter on comparing the works of Shiga Naoya and Akutagawa Ryūnosuke. Contains notes and a selectBibliography.

Yu, Beongcheon. *Akutagawa: An Introduction*. Detroit: Wayne State University Press, 1972. Follows the life and literary development of Akutagawa. Provides a helpful chronology, notes, a list of the works translated into English, and an index.

Richard Rice
Updated by Victoria Price

DANIEL ALARCÓN

Born: Lima, Peru; 1977

PRINCIPAL SHORT FICTION

War by Candlelight: Short Stories, 2005
El rey siempre está encima del pueblo, 2009

OTHER LITERARY FORMS

Daniel Alarcón (all-ahr-KOHN) has produced an award-winning novel titled *Lost City Radio* (2007) and is the creator and editor of a self-help literary manual titled *The Secret Miracle: The Novelist's Handbook* (2010). This guidebook contains interviews with renowned authors, who give advice to aspiring writers about how to produce fiction. In July, 2010, Alarcón launched *Ciudad de payasos* (*City of Clowns*), a visual novel produced in partnership with Peruvian graphic artist Sheila Alvarado. Alarcón is associate editor of *Etiqueta Negra* (*Black Label*) magazine, a Peruvian publication that blends journalism with literature. Alarcón's influential commentary "Uncover What Violence Begets in *Art of Political Murder*," a critical article about Francisco Goldman's book *The Art of Political Murder: Who Killed the Bishop?* (2007), appeared in the *San Francisco Chronicle* in 2007.

ACHIEVEMENTS

Daniel Alarcón began publishing in 2004 with great success. He writes in English, and his works are translated to Spanish and other languages. His works have received international recognition. He was finalist in the PEN USA Award for *Lost City Radio*, and for the same book he received the International Literature Award in 2009 from Haus der Kulturen der Welt (House of World Cultures). This is a significant European acknowledgment granted mainly to non-European artists. This novel made the list for best fiction in 2007 in publications such as the *Los Angeles Times*, the *Chicago Tribune*, *The Financial Post* (London), *The Christian Science Monitor*, and *The Washington Post*. Alarcón received many honors for *The King Is Always Above the People*, including the Whiting Writers' Award in 2004 and the Lannan Literary Fellowship the same year. Alarcón is a recipient of the Guggenheim Fellowship and the Fulbright scholarship. Because of his dual background, Peruvian and American, he was named one of the Twenty-one Young American Novelists in 2007 by the British literary magazine *Granta* and was considered among the thirty-nine best Latin American novelists under age thirty-nine in 2007 by the Hay Festival in Bogota, Colombia. Moreover, in 2007, he was selected one of thirty-seven under age thirty-six Young American Innovators in the Arts and Sciences by *Smithsonian Magazine.*

BIOGRAPHY

Daniel Alarcón was born in 1977 in Lima, Peru. His family moved to the United States when he was three years old. His parents were professionals, and the family could afford to live in a wealthy neighborhood in Birmingham, Alabama. Alarcón attended the Indiana Springs School in Shelby County, where he was an outstanding student. He was selected in his senior year to participate in the Telluride Association Summer Program, a project founded in 1911 that fosters groups learning self-governance and intellectual inquiry with the purpose of becoming leaders in public service. Among Alarcón's high school alumni are film director and author John Badham; the president of the Federal Reserve Bank of Philadelphia, Charles I. Plosser; writer Sally Nemeth; screenwriter Michael McCullers; chairman of the board, president and chief executive officer of MetLife, Robert Henrikson; and award-winning author John Green.

Alarcón continued his education at Columbia University in New York, where he earned a degree in anthropology. As an undergraduate he visited China and West Africa to conduct anthropological studies. In 1999, he went to Peru to teach photography in an impoverished district of Lima called San Juan de Lurigancho, where he stayed for two years. In 2001, he returned to the United States to begin graduate school. He obtained a master of arts degree from the University of Iowa and attended the distinguished Iowa Writers' Workshop. In 2007, he was invited to be part of the United States Cultural Section, with the mission to visit the Middle East to present his works.

Alarcón became associate editor of the Peruvian magazine *Etiqueta Negra* (*Black Label*), a publication founded by renowned journalist Julio Villanueva. The journal has received and continues to receive submissions by reputable "accomplices," the nickname given to anyone who has been published in it. Among them are Guillermo Cabrera Infante, Mario Vargas Llosa, Susan Orlean, Jorge Luis Borges, Jaime Bayly, Ivan Thays, Alberto Fuguet, and Oliver Sacks. Alarcón selects works that rigorously fulfill the originality and quality standards established by this magazine, for which it is known in many parts of the world.

Alarcón produces interesting nonfiction pieces as well. They relate to a variety of topics, such as "What Kind of Latino Am I?," an article that appeared in the prestigious digital journal Salon in 2005. In it Alarcón expresses the annoyance he felt during a fund-raiser as an elderly woman constantly asked him questions related to his background. This brief piece brings to the forefront certain preconceived notions people have about what it is to be Latino in the United States. Alarcón also has published his works in *The New Yorker*, *Granta*, and *The Virginia Quarterly Review*. One of his most significant articles, "Let's Go, Country: The New Latin Left Comes to Peru," appeared in *Harper's* in 2006 and generated positive feedback.

Alarcón settled in Oakland, California, where he has been a visiting writer at Mills College and at the California College of Arts. In 2010, he was visiting scholar at the Center for Latin American Studies at the University of California, Berkeley.

ANALYSIS

Although Daniel Alarcón did not experience in person the political violence his native country (Peru) endured in the 1980's and 1990's, his short stories and novel contain details of those events as if he had lived through them. This is because, although his parents moved to the United States in 1977, they constantly received news of the guerrilla war initiated in 1980 by the Sendero Luminoso (Shining Path). Shining Path was a Communist Maoist group that originally belonged to Peru's Communist Party, but it was led to rebellion by Abimael Guzman, a philosophy professor who believed in Maoism. He maintained that in order to rid the country of the bourgeoisie and the elites who controlled the nation's wealth, a stronger movement had to be created. Shining Path's method included recruiting impoverished farmers and other alienated groups in order to conduct raids on wealthy land owners and to kill business speculators. The reaction by the Peruvian government was to repress terrorism with force and to crush many supposedly dissident groups without determining whether they were or were not true Shining Path followers. Violence escalated when Shining Path

Daniel Alarcon (Tobias Kleinschmidt/dpa/Corbis)

started slaughtering government figures and individuals the group considered "enemies of the revolution." The end result of the actions of Shining Path and the government's repression was an unstable and violent Peruvian society.

Alarcón captures this brutality both in his short stories and in his novel *Lost City Radio*. *Lost City Radio* unfolds in a nameless country that is coming out of a ten-year war. There is a strong effort being made by this unidentified nation's citizens to overcome the madness left by the war. The events of the novel revolve around the only radio in the city. There is an announcer, Norma, who takes on the task of broadcasting reports, with the purpose of reuniting people. She becomes the only support for the mountain inhabitants and for the people in the poor suburbs. In the aftermath of the struggle, Norma reads the names of those who have disappeared and those who have been found. Her husband is missing, and she has no idea where he might be. Suddenly, a boy who had been living in the forest brings news about people who have been killed in the jungle or who still are alive. Norma's life is

turned inside out when she learns her husband had been assassinated. The narrator in this novel demonstrates a sharp attention to detail. The reader gets the feeling that the author personally knows the characters because of the remarkable nuances he uses in presenting them. Alarcón again makes use of flashbacks to bring about an understanding of the horrors of war, and he skillfully exposes the self-centeredness of both sides of the confrontation, showing how neither side ever cared about the victims of the clash. This novel makes readers think about how it is to live in the middle of a war, how a society can be devastated and altered by senseless violence, and how men and women are marked by destruction. However, this novel is also a tale of hope and resilience, as survivors make another attempt at normal life after such a brutal conflict.

Alarcón's prose style has been shaped by his education and his reading. As a student in the United States, he was exposed to major American writers, and he has expressed admiration for two artists in particular: Tobias Wolff and Carson McCullers. His favorite international authors are Ryszard Kapuscinski and Mario Vargas Llosa. Alarcón also has confessed love for historical and sociological texts, in particular those related to the Peruvian conflict of the 1980's and 1990's. Carlos Tapia, Gustavo Gorriti, and Carlos Ivan Degregori are considered by Alarcón to be brilliant analysts and faithful reporters of what took place during the Peruvian upheavals of the past decades.

Perhaps his interest in objective historical readings explains his choice of words and his masterful creation of direct and clean phrases in his tales. The quality of his prose has been acclaimed and rewarded with highly regarded prizes, such as the Whiting Writers' Award. Alarcón's work reflects journalistic impartiality and profound understanding obtained through observation and research of the places and people portrayed in his narrations.

WAR BY CANDLELIGHT

Alarcón puts together nine vibrant stories in this collection. There is no predictable narrative arc or chronological order in the arrangement of the tales. Alarcón leads readers into perplexing situations where poverty reigns and where there is no sign of democracy. With a

clever use of metaphor and allegory, Alarcón ingeniously underlines humanity under dreadful economic
and sociopolitical conditions, without naming ideologies. The stories rise above a sense of location because
events move from a remote Peruvian forest to a Lima
suburb and to an apartment in New York.

Characters usually are marginalized individuals,
people who have been exiled or who have no future. The
tales' protagonists cannot control their destinies because
they are extremely poor or because they are victims of
war or natural disasters. Nevertheless, they exhibit a
particular strength against the difficulties of their life
circumstances, possessing a kind of goodness and a
marked sense of dignity. Alarcón makes brilliant use of
the flashback technique to bring up the past that haunts
his characters, a past that normally constitutes the essence of the story.

In the tale "City of Clowns" a young journalist
named Oscar is the son of a nanny and a thief. Oscar
decides to dress as a clown in order to walk the streets
of Lima. He needs to gather information for an article
he is writing, yet as he walks he begins to remember
the sad episodes of his young life. Among the memories is
the time when he had to help his father break into his
best school friend's house to steal something. The narrator shows precision in describing not only the city but
also the emotional state of the clown.

The themes in "Suicide," "Florida," and "Absence"
refer to the sufferings and troubles of immigrants in
New York. The writing style in these tales shows
American literary influences in the sense that the topics
of loneliness and exile felt by the characters are presented skillfully without pretentiousness and artifice.

In the story "War by Candlelight," Fernando, a
guerrilla fighter, must carry out several subversive missions. As he goes to perform his revolutionary tasks, he
remembers several episodes of his past. Mainly he recalls how poor he was, the many family problems he
had to endure as a child, the social and political injustices he had to abide. There is no prejudice in Alarcón's
presentation of the characters, regardless of their background. What he manages to show are the individual's
feelings and the difficulties he or she must confront. In
"Huayco" and "The Visitor," Alarcón remarkably depicts the misery and abandonment suffered by the poor

Peruvian population when struck by natural disaster.

Alarcón's personal experience as a Peruvian raised
in America provides him with a particular outlook. In
War by Candlelight, the reader gets a sense that the narrator understands both worlds, relating with precision
the despair experienced by second-class citizens in
Peru and in the United States. Writing about it seems to
be a kind of authorial pursuit for identity.

"LIMA, PERU, JULY 28, 1979"

This story is part of the *War by Candlelight* compilation. The events take place in Lima, Peru, on July 28,
1979, a date that marks the dawn of Shining Path's
guerrilla warfare actions. The story is narrated in the
first person through the memories of Pintor (Painter), a
Shining Path activist. He begins by explaining that he
and a squad of ten men are assigned to find and kill
black dogs in order to hang them from street posts in
the city of Lima. They also have to attach a sign over
the suspended animals with the slogan "Die Capitalist
Dog." Pintor explains that they were running out of
black dogs, so they decided to kill any color dog and
paint them black. In a satirical twist, Pintor takes on the
task because it is supposed he knows about paint after
studying art at the university. As Pintor and his comrades search the streets for more mutts, Pintor sees out
of the corner of his eye a big black dog. Catching it and
killing it become an obsession. Pintor follows the dog
and feels victorious when he finally stabs it. As he does,
he travels back in time to remember the harsh conditions in which he grew up. He recalls how his father
became blind and how hard he worked in his leather
workshop in order to provide for his family. Pintor recollects how his father's hands were worn out by the
tools he employed to create saddles and other rawhide
products. Pintor recollects the sacrifices his family had
made so he could study philosophy and art in college.
He remembers the moment he learned of the thousands
of people who died in an earthquake that swept away a
whole mountain town, how helpless he was before the
tragedy, and how unfair it was that the survivors did not
receive any help. He then recalls his activities as a
guerrilla fighter in the jungle. When he comes back to
the present, he is confronted by a police officer, Manuel
Carrion, for having killed the dog. Pintor lies about it,
saying that he had to do it because the dog had bitten

his brother and he was certain that it had rabies. The policeman, in spite of the fact that he is drunk, is a bit skeptical, but in the end he buys the fib. However, as he is leaving, he sees one of Pintor's comrades killing a white dog. The policeman instantly realizes that they are guerrilla fighters, and so he strikes Pintor with the butt of his gun, knocking Pintor unconscious, and pursues the other insurgent. As Pintor awakens, he speaks about his feelings of emptiness, of nothingness, and he vows revenge on Carrion, who will be killed by other revolutionaries in the city. Pintor closes the story with the first and only sign of regret toward the fate of the dog he had enjoyed killing. This complex tale penetrates the thinking and the emotions of its protagonist, as he remembers his miserable adolescence in a deprived home and later his life as a failed painter turned guerrilla fighter.

OTHER MAJOR WORKS

LONG FICTION: *Lost City Radio*, 2007.

EDITED TEXTS: *The Secret Miracle: The Novelist's Handbook* (2010).

MISCELLANEOUS: "Uncover What Violence Begets in *Art of Political Murder*," 2007.

BIBLIOGRAPHY

Hernandez, Daniel. "Between the Lost and the Found: Daniel Alarcón and His Novel of the Disappeared." *LA Weekly*, March 21, 2007. A long interview with Alarcón, in which he talks about the power the topic of immigration wields over his works. Although this article refers to his novel, the themes discussed are reflected in his short stories.

Romero, Simon. "Past War and Cruelty, Peru's Writers Bloom." *The New York Times*, October 29, 2006. Puts Alarcón and his works in the historical and social context of Peru.

Upchurch, Michael. "Vibrant Stories by Peruvian-Born Writer." *Seattle Times*, May 20, 2005. When one says "Dublin," James Joyce comes to mind. Say "Lima, Peru," however, and Alarcón fulfills the promise. This review of *War by Candlelight* notes that the "sights and sounds and tensions" come alive in Alarcón's stories.

Maria Eugenia Silva

SHOLOM ALEICHEM

Born: Pereyaslav, Russia (now Pereyaslav-Khmel-
nitsky, Ukraine); March 2, 1859
Died: Bronx, New York; May 13, 1916
Also known as: Sholom Naumovich Rabinowitz

PRINCIPAL SHORT FICTION

Tevye der Milkhiger, 1894-1914 (*Tevye's Daughters,*
1949; also known as *Tevye the Dairyman and
Railroad Stories,* 1987)
Menakhem-Mendl, 1895 (*The Adventures of Men-
achem-Mendl,* 1969)
Der farkishnefter Shnayder, 1900 (*The Bewitched
Tailor,* 1960)
Mottel, Peyse dem Khazns, 1907-1916 (*The Adven-
tures of Mottel, the Cantor's Son,* 1953)
Jewish Children, 1920
The Old Country, 1946
Inside Kasrilevke, 1948
Selected Stories of Sholom Aleichem, 1956
Stories and Satires, 1959
Old Country Tales, 1966
Some Laughter, Some Tears, 1968
Holiday Tales of Sholem Aleichem, 1979
The Best of Sholom Aleichem, 1979 (Irving Howe
and Ruth R. Wisse, editors)
Tevye the Dairyman and the Railroad Stories, 1987
The Further Adventures of Menachem-Mendl, 2001

OTHER LITERARY FORMS

Sholom Aleichem (SHOL-ehm ah-LAY-kehm) was
a prolific writer throughout a career that spanned thirty-
six years. His total output comprises more than forty
volumes, but much is unavailable in English and would
be of little pertinence to most modern readers. Early
writings from his rabbinical period, including Hebrew
essays on Jewish education, are curiosities but lack
originality. His social criticism, never cruel and always

mitigated by humor, remains valuable to understanding
the now-vanished milieu in which he lived and worked.
Journalistic essays, satires, autobiographical sketches,
and rhapsodic meditations on biblical and folk themes
are often indistinguishable from his short stories and
therefore difficult to classify. Though he was less impressive in long narratives and dramas, he did produce
several novels still interesting to read. His plays were
never total popular and critical successes, but several
remain significant for their exploration of themes especially important to Jewish life.

ACHIEVEMENTS

Sadly, Sholom Aleichem's chief legacy is his richly
detailed delineation of the world destroyed by Nazi
genocide and the Soviet repression of all religious cultures. Read by thousands of Jews dispersed throughout
the world, Aleichem evokes nostalgically the society
that Jewish ancestors knew; the thick tapestry of Jewish
life in czarist Russia--messianic claimants, holy fools,
idealistic youth, merchants, scholars, revolutionaries-
-is resurrected in his sketches. His major achievement
may have been his decisive establishment of Yiddish,
however briefly, as a worthy vehicle for literary expression. He has been credited with the virtual creation of
modern Yiddish literature. Before him and his writing
contemporaries, Yiddish was "the tongue without tradition." Only sentimental romances were written in
"the jargon," along with simplistic books of scriptural
explication and devotional verses for women, who, unlike men, did not read Hebrew.

Aleichem became a godfather to subsequent Yiddish writers. Isaac Bashevis Singer was perhaps the last
of international significance. However, an entire generation of Jewish fiction writers, whose language is
English, must also trace its lineage to Aleichem. In the
early 1990's in Ukraine, the Society of Jewish Culture
began moving ahead with plans to establish a museum
in the house where Aleichem lived. A special library of

mementos and writings, all in Hebrew translation, is maintained in Tel Aviv, Israel. The American stage and screen have far extended the gentile audience of this most characteristic of Yiddish masters. *The World of Sholom Aleichem*, an off-Broadway production written by Arnold Perl and inspired by the writings of Aleichem and Issac Leib Peretz, debuted in 1953, while *Fiddler on the Roof*, a musical based on his stories, had a long run on Broadway and in motion picture theaters throughout Europe and the United States. Music for the Broadway production, which debuted in 1964, was written by Jerry Bock with lyrics by Sheldon Harnick; the film, produced in 1971, was directed by Norman Jewison.

BIOGRAPHY

Much of Sholom Aleichem's life is detailed in his writings, only thinly fictionalized. Born Sholom Rabinowitz, in the Ukrainian town of Pereyaslav, he was the son of a merchant of some education and means. He lost his mother the year of his Bar Mitzvah, only to have her quickly replaced by an unfavored stepmother whose sole contribution to his well-being was a vivid vocabulary of Yiddishisms he would use profitably in his writing. Reversals in family fortune sent the young man in search of employment as a "crown rabbi" (half religious functionary and half Russian bureaucrat) and as a tutor. By marrying Olga Loyev, his pupil, he acquired a loving life companion, a substantial dowry, and inspiration for lyrical narratives. Moving to Kiev, Aleichem wrote novels and short stories and, through the annuals that he published and the banquets that he hosted, became a patron of Yiddish writers. Financial problems again dislocated him, however, this time to Odessa, another flourishing center of Jewish life. It was finally the social turmoil following the assassination of Czar Alexander II that drove him abroad to Geneva and New York.

Despite the fame that preceded him to the New World, Aleichem had difficulty supporting his increasingly large family from the proceeds of his writings and theatrical ventures. Through public readings in Western Europe and even Russia, he was still able to earn a living. Remaining a part of the intellectual life of his homeland, he made friends with leading Zionists,

corresponded with Leo Tolstoy and Anton Chekhov, and met Maxim Gorky. During his last years, though beset by bereavement and tuberculosis, Aleichem was a revered international man of letters. His funeral in New York, attended by thousands of mourners, became the occasion for an affirmation of the Yiddish culture he had done so much to dignify.

ANALYSIS

It is nearly impossible to summarize the plot of a Sholom Aleichem story. There is no linear, causally enchained sequence in his fiction. The type of plot to which readers have become accustomed in Western fiction--that which moves through clearly defined stages to a predetermined end--is not readily found in Aleichem's work. The reason for this lies in the milieu which is embodied there. Logic and the laws of cause and effect require a stable, orderly world to function. The world of the Russian pale at the close of the nineteenth century was a turbulent chaos of pogroms, revolution, wars, cholera epidemics, starvation, overcrowding, and perpetual hunger.

Except for the few years when he was able to be a patron of letters and to pay his fellow Yiddish writers well for their contributions to his annual, in which he attempted to establish a canon, Aleichem himself was continually in debt. His prodigious output was necessitated by his need to provide for his many dependents. These pressures, the outward instability, and the haste in which he was forced to compose contributed to the absurdist, surrealistic situations he depicted. His plots, rather than moving from explication to complication to resolution, begin in complication and accumulate further complications with ever-increasing momentum to the pitch of madness and then abruptly stop without having been resolved; the story is simply interrupted. One can say that a typical Aleichem plot is a succession of calamities and misfortune, followed by disaster, followed by tragedy.

Aleichem's reputation is nevertheless that of one of the world's greatest humorists. In England, he was compared to Charles Dickens; in America, to Mark Twain. How could he fashion comedy from such dark materials? The answer lies in the authorial stratagems he evolved. He invented a persona, Sholom Aleichem, who is present not as a speaker but only as a listener, to whom others tell their stories. Thus, the act of speech itself is foregrounded, not the events that are related. The linguistic surface predominates. Its exuberance and charm, its wit, its pleasure in homely proverbs and folk wisdom, and its eccentric digressions shield the pain and provide a compensatory pleasure.

TEVYE STORIES

This quality is exemplified in the nine Tevye stories. The first published in 1894 and the last in 1914, they appeared separately over the period of twenty years. They have, however, enough structural similarity to be read as a family chronicle. What gives them their coherence is the voice of Tevye. Each episode begins with Tevye meeting Sholom Aleichem somewhere. After greeting Aleichem, Tevye recapitulates what has happened to him since their last encounter and then relates his most recent catastrophe. Each story closes with farewells and the promise of more stories to come at future meetings.

Sholem Aleichem (Library of Congress)

The events related are a series of disasters: loss, early death, revolution, apostasy, suicide, pogroms, and exile. These are so successfully distanced by the mode of narration that they are perceived as comedy. It is Tevye's humane, sardonic voice that is heard, quarreling with God about how He runs the universe, using His Own Word against Him with such vigorous audacity and such mangling of the texts that one cannot help laughing. The monologue form focuses readers' attention on Tevye's moral resiliency and on his defiant debate with an invisible antagonist. It subordinates the tragic fates of the seven dowryless daughters by keeping these at the periphery. In the foreground is the poor milkman who is their father, with his rickety wagon drawn by a starving horse, punctuating his speech with lines from the prayer book. For example, when he wishes to indicate that no more need be said on any subject, he announces: "Here ends the service for the first Sabbath before Passover." It is his way of saying, "period." He tells how daughter Tzeitl has refused a match with the rich butcher, not because he is widowed and has several children her own age, but because she is already engaged, secretly, to a poor tailor. She marries Motel and is left with orphans when he dies of tuberculosis. The next daughter, Hodel, marries a revolutionary who is arrested soon after the wedding; Hodel follows him into exile. The third daughter, Chava, is converted by a priest in order to marry a Gentile. According to religious law, Tevye must declare her dead, so he tells his wife Golde that they must "sit shiva" for her (observe the customary period of mourning for the deceased).

The next time they meet, Tevye tells Sholom Aleichem that his hair has turned white because of what has happened to his daughter Schprintze. He says, "God wanted to favor his chosen people, so a fresh calamity descended upon us." The irony of having been especially elected to endure the privilege of suffering permeates these stories.

One of Tevye's customers, a widow summering in Boiberik, asks his advice about her spendthrift son. Having inherited a million rubles he has lived in idleness. Tevye complies: "I sat down with him, told him stories, cited examples, plied him with quotations and drummed proverbs into his ears." Here in this self-description is the essence of Tevye's mode of speech.

Aarontchick, the son, is invited for blintzes on Shavuos. When Tevye wants Golde to bring in another platterful, he says it, as he does everything, in liturgical metaphors. "What are you standing there for, Golde? Repeat the same verse over again. Today is Shavuos and we have to say the same prayer twice."

Schprintze and the handsome idler fall in love. Tevye, always ready with a quotation, sums it up from the Psalms. "Don't we say in the Psalms: 'Put your trust in God?'--Have faith in Him and He will see to it that you stagger under a load of trouble and keep on reciting: 'This too is for the best.'"

Tevye is summoned to the widow's. He thinks that it is to arrange the details of the wedding. He is asked "How much will this affair cost us?" He answers that it depends on what sort of a ceremony they have in mind. It turns out that they want to buy him off and end the engagement.

Mother and son leave without saying good-bye and still owing for their milk and cheese. Schprintze wastes away from sorrow. One night as Tevye is driving home, "sunk in meditation, asking questions of the Almighty and answering them myself," he sees a crowd gathered at the pond. Schprintze has drowned herself.

Beilke marries a war-profiteer so that she can provide for her father's old age, but he loses his fortune and they are forced to flee to America. Tevye's wife dies and he is driven into exile by Russian peasants, but he remains good-humored and spiritually indestructible. That dignity and self-respect can be sustained under such extreme conditions is the secret of the immense popularity of these stories. It is the narrative strategy that permits this revelation. The monologue form allows an impoverished milkman to reveal the humaneness of his character and the grandeur of his soul without any authorial intervention.

MENACHEM-MENDL LETTERS

Another way of presenting a speaking voice without meditation is the epistolary form. In 1892, Aleichem began the Menachem-Mendl letters, which he continued to publish until 1913. This correspondence constitutes another famous short-story cycle. The hero's name has become synonymous with a *Luftmensch*, someone who builds castles in the air. He is the archetype of Bernard Malamud's luckless businessmen, like Salzman, whose office is "in his socks," and Sussman, whose enterprises are negotiated "in the air." He is the prototype of Saul Bellow's Tommy Wilhelm, who loses his last cent on the stock exchange under the influence of a confidence man. He is also the projection of the author's own financial disaster at the Odessa stock exchange and his subsequent bankruptcy.

Each comic episode follows the same repetitive pattern. The husband writes from the city, feverishly detailing his latest scheme for getting rich. His skeptical wife responds from the village, urging him, with innumerable quotations from her mother's inexhaustible store of proverbs, to come home. His next letter always confirms his mother-in-law's forecasts with its news of his most recent disaster. His inevitable failures, however, have taught him nothing about economic realities because he has already flung himself enthusiastically into yet another doomed enterprise. The comedy derives from the repetition of this formula. He is flat, neither aging nor changing; rigid, driven by a single obsessive notion; he is the eternal loser whose hopes are never dimmed.

Menachem-Mendl fails as an investor. He fails as a currency speculator. He fails as a broker in houses, and forests, and oil. He fails as a writer, as a matchmaker, and as an insurance agent; but his irrepressible flow of rhetoric never fails. He says, "The most important thing is language, the gift of speech." He can "talk against time; talk at random; talk glibly; talk himself out of breath; talk you into things; talk in circles." In the pleasure of verbalizing his experiences, relishing his own eloquence, he compensates for them. The comic effect derives precisely from his overvaluation of language. The limited protagonist deludes himself that he has masked the facts in highflown words; the reader penetrates this verbal screen.

To be successful, comedy must sustain a rapid pace. If the events move slowly enough for readers to think about them, their essential sadness is exposed. Thus, Menachem-Mendl is kept rushing. He is presented as always in a hurry. His gestures indicate frenzy, accelerated to a dizzying pace. The irony that his busyness is stasis, that his frantic activity is inert because he is speeding only to another dead end, contributes to the comic effect.

Both in these early works and in his later short-story cycles, such as the *Railroad Stories*, the children's Stories, the festival Stories, and the Kasrilevke cycles, Aleichem shows his unparalleled mastery of the extended monologue, which he employs with such virtuosity.

OTHER MAJOR WORKS

LONG FICTION: *Natasha*, 1884; *Sender Blank und zayn Gezindl*, 1888; *Yosele Solovey*, 1890 (*The Nightingale*, 1985); *Stempenyu*, 1899 (English translation, 1913); *Blondzne Shtern*, 1912 (*Wandering Star*, 1952); *Marienbad*, 1917 (English translation, 1982); *In Shturm*, 1918 (*In the Storm*, 1984); *Blutiger Shpas*, 1923 (*The Bloody Hoax*, 1991).

PLAYS: *A Doktor*, pr. 1887 (*She Must Marry a Doctor*, 1916); *Yakenhoz*, pr. 1894; *Mazel Tov*, pr. 1904; *Tsuzeyt un Tsushpreyt*, pr. 1905; *Die Goldgreber*, pr. 1907; *Samuel Pasternak*, pr. 1907; *Stempenyu*, pr. 1907; *Agenten*, pb. 1908; *Az got Vil, Shist a Bezem*, pb. 1908; *Konig Pic*, pb. 1910; *Shver tsu zein a Yid*, pb. 1914; *Dos Groyse Gevins*, pb. 1915 (*The Jackpot*, 1989); *Menshen*, pb. 1919; *Der Get*, pr. 1924; *The World of Sholom Aleichem*, pb. 1953; *Fiddler on the Roof*, pr. 1964.

NONFICTION: *Fun'm yarid*, 1916 (*The Great Fair: Scenes from My Childhood*, 1955); *Briefe von Scholem Aleichem und Menachem Mendl*, 1921.

BIBLIOGRAPHY

Aarons, Victoria. *Author as Character in the Works of Sholom Aleichem*. Lewiston, N.Y.: Edwin Mellen Press, 1985. An exploration of Aleichem's interesting literary technique and the use of himself as "naïve auditor." Religious insights in his fiction are also given suitable attention.

Butwin, Frances, and Joseph Butwin. *Sholom Aleichem*. Boston: Twayne, 1977. The best single introduction in English to the life and writings of Aleichem. Sound, scholarly, and concise.

Finkin, Jordan. "Jewish Jokes, Yiddish Storytelling, and Sholem Aleichem: A Discursive Approach." *Jewish Social Studies* 16, no. 1 (Fall, 2009): 85-110. Explores the relationship between Jewish jokes and the development of modern Yiddish literature. Describes how Aleichem used humor as a means of expanding the forms and genres of that literature.

Frieden, Ken. *Classic Yiddish Fiction: Abramovitsh, Sholom Aleichem, and Peretz*. Albany, N.Y.: State University of New York Press, 1995. Examines the works of Shalom Jacob Abramovich, Aleichem, and Isaac Leib Peretz.

Howe, Irving. *The World of Our Fathers: The Journey of the Eastern European Jews to America and the Life They Found and Made*. New York: Harcourt Brace Jovanovich, 1976. A superbly readable account of the Yiddish culture reflected in Aleichem's writing. This classic study of Jewish immigrant life in the United States gives ample attention to newspapers, journals, and theater, the usual forums for Yiddish literary expression.

Howe, Irving, and Aliezer Greenberg, eds. *A Treasury of Yiddish Stories*. New York: Viking Press, 1954. This volume is not only an enjoyable collection of stories that illustrate Aleichem's proper place within the stream of Yiddish fiction but also a fine survey of the genre. The editor's introduction is the best brief discussion of Yiddish writing that exists in English.

Katz, Michael R. "'Go Argue with Today's Children': The Jewish Family in Sholem Aleichem and Vladimir Jabotinsky." *European Judaism* 43, no. 1 (May, 2010): 63-77. Analyzes Aleichem's stories about Tevye and Jabotinsky's novel *The Five*, both of which are about children growing up during a time of transition. Katz compares the fates of children in both authors' works and the authors' treatments of the issues of assimilation and modernity.

Miron, Dan. *The Image of the Shtetl and Other Studies of Modern Jewish Literary Imagination*. Syracuse, N.Y.: Syracuse University Press, 2000. Miron describes how Aleichem and other Jewish writers recreated the world of the shtetls, the small towns in which the Eastern European Jews resided. Four of the chapters are devoted to Aleichem, including analyses of the short stories contained in *The Adventures of Menachem-Mendl*; *The Adventures of Mottel, the Cantor's Son*; and the *Railroad Stories*.

Roskies, David G. *A Bridge of Longing: The Lost Art of Yiddish Storytelling*. Cambridge, Mass.: Harvard University Press, 1995. Places Aleichem in the context of Eastern European Yiddish storytelling as the best loved of all Yiddish folklorists. Examines his creation of Tevye, the Milkman as a way to explore life's ironies. Discusses Tevye as a Jewish everyman who embodies the invented tradition of storytelling that came to be more authentic than the orthodox rabbinic tradition it replaced.

Sherman, Joseph. "Holding Fast to Integrity: Shalom Rabinovich, Sholom Aleichem, and Tevye the Dairyman." *Judaism* 43 (Winter, 1994): 6-18. Discusses narrative strategy in the Tevye stories, arguing that Aleichem tests the validity of traditional Jewish teaching in the stories through the

monologues of the Jewish characters. Suggests that the narratives compel readers to ask questions, which Tevye answers with incomplete, inappropriate, or irrelevant traditional theology.

Waife-Goldbert, Marie. *My Father, Sholom Aleichem.* New York: Simon & Schuster, 1968. This volume is valuable because it is the first complete biography in English and because of its use of Aleichem's own unfinished autobiography. This is a family memoir, lovingly idealized, rather than an objective evaluation of accomplishments.

Ruth Rosenberg
Updated by Allene Phy-Olsen

ISABEL ALLENDE

Born: Lima, Peru; August 2, 1942

PRINCIPAL SHORT FICTION

Cuentos de Eva Luna, 1990 (*The Stories of Eva Luna,* 1991)

OTHER LITERARY FORMS

Isabel Allende (ahl-YEHN-dee) has published a number of novels, including *La casa de los espíritus* (1982; *The House of the Spirits*, 1985), which established her reputation, *De amor y de sombra* (1984; *Of Love and Shadows*, 1987), *Eva Luna* (1987; English translation, 1988), *El plan infinito* (1991; *The Infinite Plan*, 1993), and *Hija de la fortuna* (1999; *Daughter of Fortune*, 1999). She has also published an account of her daughter's death in *Paula* (1994; English translation, 1995), as well as a collection of children's stories entitled *La gorda de Porcelana* (1984; *The Porcelain Fat Lady*, 1984), and a collection of humorous pieces poking fun at machismo, originally published in the magazine *Paula*, entitled *Civilice a su troglodita: Los impertinentes de Isabel Allende* (1974).

ACHIEVEMENTS

Isabel Allende has been the recipient of numerous prestigious literary prizes, including the Panorama Literario Novel of the Year (1983), Author of the Year in Germany (1984 and 1986), the Grand Prix d'Évasion in France (1984), the Colima prize for best novel in Mexico (1985), the Donna Citta di Roma literary award from Italy (1998), and the Dorothy and Lillian Gish Prize from the United States (1998). In 1994, she was named a Chevalier of the French l'Ordre des Arts et des Letters. A 1993 film version of *La casa de los espíritus*, directed by Bille August, was a box-office success.

BIOGRAPHY

Though Chilean by nationality, Isabel Angelica Allende was born in Lima, Peru, on August 2, 1942. The niece of the former Chilean president Salvador Allende, who died in September 1973, during the military coup d'état engineered by Augusto Pinochet, Allende attended a private high school in Santiago, Chile, from which she graduated in 1959. She worked as a secretary at the United Nations Food and Agricultural Organization until 1965. She married Miguel Frías in 1962, and the couple had a daughter, Paula, and a son, Miguel. In Santiago, she worked as a journalist, editor, and advice columnist for *Paula* magazine from 1967 to 1974 and as an interviewer for a television station from 1970 to 1975. She was also an administrator for Colegio Marroco, in Caracas, from 1979 to 1982. Isabel divorced her husband in 1987 and married William Gordon in 1988. Her daughter died in 1993, and this event formed the basis of the book named after her.

ANALYSIS

Isabel Allende's literary career is notable in that it stands outside the shifting fashions of the Latin American literary scene. Since the 1960's in Latin America the literary fashion has tended to favor intricate, self-conscious novels that test the reader's interpretative powers. Flying in the face of this trend, however, Allende's novels favor content over form, reality over novelistic devices. Though her fiction has been dismissed by some critics as simply an imitation of Gabriel García Márquez's work, especially his so-called Magical Realist style, it is clear that Allende enjoys unparalleled popularity. Her novels and short stories have attracted an enormous readership in Spanish as well as languages such as English, French, and German. Allende tends to write plot-centered, reader-friendly fiction. Her stories often focus on love and sex as seen from a feminine perspective.

THE STORIES OF EVA LUNA

The short-story collection *The Stories of Eva Luna* is essentially a sequel to her novel *Eva Luna* (1987), published three years earlier; thus the narrator of *The Stories of Eva Luna* is the Eva Luna who appeared in the earlier novel, that is, a resourceful, bright young woman who, though born to poverty, rises to riches as a result of becoming a famous soap-opera writer. Two of the stories provide a direct link to *Eva Luna* the novel. "El huésped de la maestra," for example, finishes a story that was left unresolved in the novel. The novel describes how Inés, the schoolmistress of Santa Agua, saw her son brutally murdered at the hands of a local man who caught him stealing mangoes in the garden. Riad Halabí, by an ingenious plan, managed to force the murderer to leave town. In the short story, the reader learns that the murderer returns many years later to Santa Agua and is then killed by Inés in an act of revenge; much of the short story is taken up by a description of the ingenious way in which Halabí disposes of the body. Also related to the novel is the short story "De

barro estamos hechos." The novel introduces the reader to Rolf Carlé, a cameraman, who eventually becomes Eva's companion. Here the reader sees firsthand his experience of the floods that ravaged the country and that caused a young girl called Azucena to die slowly and painfully, even while he was filming her. The short story focuses on how this experience has changed Rolf's life. These two short stories can be seen as sequels to Allende's long fiction and show continuity of theme and character.

There are twenty-three short stories in *The Stories of Eva Luna* and only two of them, as described above, use the same characters that the novels do. In other words, above all, they are new stories that Eva Luna has invented for the enjoyment of her lover, Rolf Carlé. The overriding structure is provided by the theme of *Alf layla wa-layla* (fifteenth century; *The Arabian Nights' Entertainments*, 1706-1708), in which the female narrator, Scherezade, must tell a story each night in order to avoid being executed by the king. The collection of short stories opens, indeed, with Rolf Carlé asking the narrator, who, though unnamed, is

Isabel Allende (AP Photo/Peter Morgan)

obviously Eva Luna, to tell him a story that has never been told to anyone else. The first story, "Dos palabras," explores the same theme. Here the protagonist, Belisa Crepusculario, wrote a speech for a man who wanted to become president, and she also gave him two secret words. The speech was an enormous success, but the Colonel soon discovers that he is fatally attracted to Belisa as a result of the linguistic spell she has cast over him.

There are a number of themes that run through the stories. The most obvious one is that of sexuality and love, which forms the focus for nineteen out of the twenty-three stories in the collection. Love is often presented as occurring purely through chance. In "Tosca," for example, a love relationship begins in this short story as a result of the apparently insignificant fact that Leonardo is seen by Laurizia reading the score of the work *Tosca* by the famous Italian composer Giacomo Puccini. From this chance encounter a passionate affair develops. Of the nineteen stories that focus on love and sexuality, ten focus on illicit sex. A good example is "Si me tocaras el corazón," which tells the story of Amadeo Peralta, who, while on a visit to Santa Agua, seduces a fifteen-year-old girl called Hortensia; when he tires of her, he decides to lock her up permanently in the basement of a sugar refinery. Years later, some children hear monstrous noises coming from the basement, and Hortensia is discovered, diseased and at the brink of death, which leads to Amadeo's discomfiture. The moral of this short story seems to be that unbridled sexual passion can have disastrous consequences. Some of the stories, such as "Boca de sapo," "María, la boba," and "Walimai," explicitly allude to prostitution.

Other themes covered in the stories include vengeance, as in "Una venganza," in which revenge for rape is enacted on the rapist; the clash between cultures, as in "Walamai," which describes the struggles between the tribe of the Sons of the Moon and the white man, told from an Indian perspective; the miracle, as in "Un discreto milagro," which tells how Miguel, a priest, has his sight restored by a local saint, Juana de los Lirios; as well as predestination, as in "La mujer del juez," a well-written, suspense story which focuses on the protagonists, Nicolás Vidal and Casilda Hidalgo, who conduct an illicit affair even though they

know beforehand that it will lead to their deaths. One particularly powerful story, "Un camino hacia el norte," contains a strong social critique. It describes how Claveles Picero, and her grandfather, Jesás Dionisio Picero, are tricked into giving up Claveles's illegitimate son Juan to a United States adoption agency, which is later discovered to be a front for a contraband agency that sells human organs. The story ends with a description of their journey to the capital in an attempt to discover Juan's fate; they, like the reader, fear the worst. The message is that poverty leads to exploitation and death.

A common technique in the stories involves the story opening with a scene (whose import is not understood) and then cutting to the past, at which point the narrative of the lives of the main protagonists is told. This occurs in a number of stories, including "El camino hacia el norte" and "El huésped de la maestra." Most of the stories are told in the third person, although some, such as "Walimai," are told in the first person.

OTHER MAJOR WORKS

LONG FICTION: *La casa de los espíritus*, 1982 (*The House of the Spirits*, 1985); *De amor y de sombra*, 1984 (*Of Love and Shadows*, 1987); *Eva Luna*, 1987 (English translation, 1988); *El plan infinito*, 1991 (*The Infinite Plan*, 1993); *Hija de la fortuna*, 1999 (*Daughter of Fortune*, 1999); *Retrato en sepia*, 2000 (*Portrait in Sepia*, 2001); *Zorro*, 2005 (English translation, 2005); *Inés del alma mía*, 2006 (*Inés of My Soul*, 2006); *La isla bajo el mar*, 2009 (*Island Beneath the Sea*, 2010).

NONFICTION: *Civilice a su troglodita: Los impertinentes de Isabel Allende*, 1974; *Paula*, 1994 (English translation, 1995); *Conversations with Isabel Allende*, 1999; *Mi país inventado*, 2003 (*My Invented Country: A Nostalgic Journey Through Chile*, 2003); *La suma de los días*, 2007 (*The Sum of Our Days*, 2008).

CHILDREN'S LITERATURE: *La gorda de porcelana*, 1984 (*The Porcelain Fat Lady*, 1984); *Ciudad de las bestias*, 2002 (*City of the Beasts*, 2002); *El reino del dragón de oro*, 2003 (*Kingdom of the Golden Dragon*, 2004); *El bosque de los Pigmeos*, 2004 (*Forest of the Pygmies*, 2005).

MISCELLANEOUS: *Afrodita: Cuentos, recetas, y otros afrodisíacos*, 1997 (*Aphrodite: A Memoir of the Senses*, 1998).

BIBLIOGRAPHY

De Carvalho, Susan. "The Male Narrative Perspective in the Fiction of Isabel Allende." *Journal of Hispanic Research* 2, no. 2 (Spring, 1994): 269-278. Shows that "Walimai" is different from the other short stories in *Los cuentos de Eva Luna* in that it is written in the first person and from a male perspective. Argues that the first-person, male perspective in this story represents the ideal narrative voice.

García Pinto, Magdalena, ed. *Women Writers of Latin America: Intimate Histories.* Austin: University of Texas Press, 1991. Contains an excellent interview with Allende in which she provides a great deal of insight into the way she views her writing. It is here that Allende mentions that she sees herself as a troubadour going from village to village, person to person, talking about her country.

Hart, Patricia. *Narrative Magic in the Fiction of Isabel Allende.* Toronto: Associated University Presses, 1989. A good overview of Allende's fiction up to 1987; it has a chapter on Magical Realism and a clearly written, helpful section on the novel *Eva Luna*, which is useful background for the analysis of the short stories. Argues that Allende parodies rather than imitates García Márquez.

Hart, Stephen M. *Isabel Allende: "Eva Luna" and "Cuentos de Eva Luna."* London: Grant & Cutler, 2003. A student guide to Allende's short-story collection and a related novel.

_____. *White Ink: Essays on Twentieth-Century Feminine Fiction in Spain and Latin America.* London: Tamesis, 1993. Sets Allende's work within the context of women's writing in twentieth century Latin America. Examines the ways in which Allende fuses the space of the personal with that of the political in her fiction and shows that, in her work, falling in love with another human being is often aligned with falling in love with a political cause.

Levine, Linda Gould. *Isabel Allende.* New York: Twayne, 2002. An introductory overview of Allende's life and works. Chapter 5 focuses on *The Stories of Eva Luna.* Includes bibliographical references and index.

Rodden, John, ed. *Critical Insights: Isabel Allende.* Pasadena, Calif.: Salem Press, 2011. Collection of original and reprinted essays providing critical readings of the key themes and contexts of Allende's work, including *The Stories of Eva Luna.* Also includes a biography, a chronology of major events in Allende's life, a complete list of her works, and aBibliography listing resources for further research.

Swanson, Philip. *The New Novel in Latin America: Politics and Popular Culture after the Boom.* Manchester: Manchester University Press, 1995. Chapter 9 contains a discussion of the use of popular culture in Allende's fiction, showing that the people and popular culture are seen to challenge official culture and patriarchy in her work. Also has a good introduction which sets Allende's work in the context of other postboom novelists of Latin America.

Umpierre, Luz Maria. "Unscrambling Allende's 'Dos palabras': The Self, the Immigrant/Writer, and Social Justice." *MELUS* 27, no. 4 (Winter, 2002): 129. Examines the short story "Dos palabras," placing it in historical context, analyzing its main character and story line, and pointing out the connections between the realities of the protagonist and of Allende.

Williams, Raymond L. *The Postmodern Novel in Latin America: Poltics, Culture, and the Crisis of Truth.* New York: St Martin's Press, 1996. Williams is one of Allende's most vigorous critics, who argues that Allende's fiction simply imitates García Márquez's and that it is not postmodern in any real sense.

Stephen M. Hart

JUAN JOSÉ ARREOLA

Born: Zapotlán (now Ciudad Guzmán), Jalisco,
    Mexico; September 21, 1918
Died: Guadalajara, Mexico; December 3, 2001

PRINCIPAL SHORT FICTION

Varia invención, 1949 (*Various Inventions*, 1964)
Confabulario, 1952 (*Confabulary*, 1964)
Bestiario, 1958 (*Bestiary*, 1964)
Punto de Plata, 1958 (*Silverpoint*, 1964)
Confabulario total, 1941-1961, 1962 (*Confabulary,
    and Other Inventions*, 1964)
Palindroma, 1971
Confabulario personal, 1980
Narrativa completa, 1997

OTHER LITERARY FORMS

Primarily known for his short stories, fables, and experimental literary sketches, Juan José Arreola (wahn
hoh-SAY ahr-ee-OHL-ah) also wrote the novel *La
feria* (1963; *The Fair*, 1977), some one-act plays, and
several essays. Known for his prodigious memory and
a legendary ability to talk eloquently and entertainingly
about a variety of topics, the best of Arreola's "oral
prose" from lectures, round-table discussions, interviews, and radio and television talks shows over the
years has been carefully edited by Jorge Arturo Ojeda
and published as *La palabra educación* (1973; the
word education) and *Y ahora, la mujer. . .* (1975; and
now, woman . . .).

ACHIEVEMENTS

Juan José Arreola has a special place in Latin American literature for successfully experimenting with fictional modes and techniques. A cosmopolitan man of
letters, he pushed the genre of the short story in new
directions. At the core of his creative representations is
the interaction between rational, objective reality and
idiosyncratic, subjective perceptions of it. His work includes more than one hundred short prose pieces: stories, fables, parables, biographical portraits, diary entries, advertisements, articles, science-fiction reports,
and many sketches best classified as microtexts.

Acclaimed for steering Mexican literature beyond
traditional realism with its emphasis on political and
socioeconomic problems, Arreola deals imaginatively
with the nature of human values in the face of twentieth
century materialism. He probes the perverse ways in
which alienated people behave when confronted with
matters of love, life, and death. Like Jorge Luis Borges,
he delights in making philosophical speculations and
devising scenarios, although in a more playful manner,
in which the line between the real and the unreal is
blurred.

Arreola's irreverent humor, clever use of language,
prodigious vocabulary, and vast repertoire of images
are hallmarks of a unique and stimulating style. Writers
from several generations have acknowledged his influence on their work, among them such prominent figures at Rosario Castellanos, Salvador Elizondo, Carlos
Fuentes, Luisa Josefina Hernández, José Agustín, Vi-
cente Leñero, Carlos Monsiváis, and Gustavo Sainz.

BIOGRAPHY

Born in 1918 in Zapotlán, Jalisco, Juan José Arreola
saw the destruction wrought by warring factions during
the Mexican Revolution, which had begun eight years
earlier. The fourth of fourteen children, Arreola was neglected by his parents, who could barely provide for
the family. He was a mischievous schoolboy, but it was
also clear that he was very bright. Blessed with an
amazing memory, he could recite huge amounts of literary material to astounded audiences. Strongly influenced by José Ernesto Aceves, an inspiring teacher,
Arreola read a number of literary anthologies with
samples of the works of authors from around the world.
The short story being of particular appeal, he read

thousands of these during his early years. His formal schooling ended at the age of twelve, when the local school closed. For several years, he worked at various jobs, including bookbinding and printing, always gravitating toward the cultural life that Guadalajara offered.

At the age of eighteen, he moved to Mexico City, where he held odd jobs and studied acting. His first serious literary attempts resulted in three short theatrical pieces that never circulated. He continued to educate himself by reading constantly in various disciplines. When his theater group failed and a love affair fell apart, Arreola suffered a nervous breakdown, leading him to return to Jalisco. There, in the early 1940's, he tried to settle down by teaching school and getting married to a local woman, but the relationship soon ended in divorce. He spent a considerable amount of his time writing, and he succeeded in having several stories published in local newspapers and literary reviews such as *Pan* and *Eos*, the latter of which he founded with friends. An early piece called "Hizo bien minetras vivió" ("He Did Good While He Lived") drew national attention as an excellent story, bringing the emerging writer a host of contacts. Among them was a prominent French actor who helped Arreola win a scholarship in 1945 to study theater in Paris. Arreola has said that his life can be divided into "before and after" that stimulating sojourn, which he had to abandon after a year as a result of another physical collapse.

Arreola moved back to Mexico City permanently to work at the Fondo de Cultura Económica, a reputable publishing company. There, he met Alfonso Reyes, the world-renowned Mexican scholar and writer who in 1948 gave Arreola a scholarship to the prestigious Colegio de México, a center for humanistic studies, which Reyes headed. Arreola, who was by this time writing in earnest with his new mentor's encouragement, published his first collection of short stories, *Various Inventions*, the following year. Since it largely dealt, although imaginatively, with existential concerns, some critics expressed their disapproval for its lack of "Mexicanness," a reaction that fostered much debate in literary circles. Undaunted, Arreola responded in 1952 with a second collection of stories, *Confabulary*, considered by some critics to be his best for its surprising existential vignettes reminiscent of Jean-Paul Sartre and Franz Kafka.

By now a recognized presence on the literary scene, Arreola joined the Center for Mexican Writers, where he continued writing and where he began tutoring students who would follow him in incorporating imagination and fantasy into Mexican fiction. Another book of stories, *Silverpoint*, appeared in 1958, dazzling readers with whimsical portraits of animals with human traits. Then, in 1962, Arreola issued a new edition of some of his earlier texts, calling it *Confabulario total, 1941-1961*, but added significant new selections that clearly established him as one of Mexico's major writers. During this productive period, he also wrote *The Fair*, his first novel, which appeared in 1963, bringing mixed reviews with a modicum of praise for its multilayered, kaleidoscopic representation of life in a Mexican village. *Palindroma* (palindrome), Arreola's fourth collection of brand-new stories, appeared in 1971. Included in this collection was a theatrical piece, which suggested to some critics that the author's strength was not as a playwright.

In his later years, Arreola continued encouraging young writers, teaching at the University of Mexico, appearing on radio and television talk shows, and writing critical essays, some of which have been occasionally published, such as those in the collection *Inventario* (1976; inventory). His active career consistently reflects his commitment to find new ways through the art of fiction to express the universal conflicts, concerns, and ironies of life, never losing sight of his mission as a writer to challenge and entertain in an aesthetic fashion.

Arreola received numerous awards for his work, including the National Prize in Letters in Mexico City (1979), the Jalisco Prize in Letters (1989), the Literatura Latinoamericana y del Caribe Juan Rulfo Prize (1992), the Alfonso Reyes Prize (1997), and the Ramón López Velarde Prize (1998). In 1999, he was named favorite son of Guadalajara, where he died two years later.

ANALYSIS

The complex fiction of Juan José Arreola, Mexico's acknowledged master of the fantastic, is so unique and varied in its content, forms, tones, and strategies that it practically defies classification. Critics have an easier time defining what his texts are not rather than what they actually are. Arreola's work is definitely not within the current of social realism, which is so characteristic of the bulk of the writing associated with Mexico over the centuries. He eschews the conventional mode that depicts socioeconomic and moral injustices in objectified fashion with its focus on verifiable events and the delineation of typically realistic characters. Like Reyes and Julio Torri, predecessors who also marched to a different drummer, Arreola is an innovator. He looks at reality through a different prism in order to represent its multidimensionality, its irrational side, its unexpectedness, its ambiguity.

It is clear from his short prose fiction that, like a growing number of Mexican and Latin American writers in the years since he began experimenting with writing, Arreola's interest lies in representing the personal experience of reality. In his variegated texts, he seeks ways to present what has not yet necessarily been sensed, creating mental images of things unseen, yet to be done, unreal. He chooses to experiment with the short story to show the power of imagination and fantasy as well as the flexibility of the genre itself. Texts as he imagines them include previously established possibilities as well as transformations of those possibilities. In his hands, texts stretch limits and change the rules of the literary game.

Short stories, fables, parables, miniportraits, microtexts, literary miniatures, reveries, diary entries, announcements, essays, advertisements, pseudoreports, prose poems, science-fiction pieces, sketches--Arreola writes all of these and more. Their commonality is their creator's brilliant use of language, penchant for parody, eye for the absurd, outrageous imagery, and relentless sense of humor. Readers are introduced to such figures as a consummate businessman who turns into a bull, a poet who marries a blue whale, a manic-depressive who buys a huge poisonous spider and deliberately loses it in the house, and a man who argues with an angel standing beside him at a urinal, to mention a few of the more memorable. All Arreola's literary inventions serve as scenarios for calling attention to the nature of value, to perverse and hypocritical behavior, to a world whose very survival is threatened by rampaging materialism. His pessimism, however, is not absolute. Arreola does believe that within every human being lies the potential of becoming a better person, even if the odds are against it. His idea of progress lies in the self-realization of human beings as opposed to scientific breakthroughs or technological achievements. This, in fact, is the underlying message of practically all he has written.

"THE SWITCHMAN"

One of the most widely read stories by Arreola is "El guardagujas" ("The Switchman"). In it, he develops one of the main themes and preoccupations that he plays out in a number of other stories: the condemnation of a dehumanized world where human dignity is at the mercy of organized technology. An anonymous traveler meets a gnomelike switchman in an empty train station and inquires about a train to T--, discovering through a lengthy and entertaining dialogue the peculiarities of the railway system: There is no guarantee that the train will ever go to a particular destination; passengers are often left in remote areas to fend for themselves; some immobile trains have moving pictures in the windows to convince the passengers that they are going somewhere; sometimes the tracks end at a river's edge with no bridge, requiring that the train be dismantled and carried to the other side; in some stretches, there is only one rail, and it is on the side of the first-class ticket holders; some passengers end up living in special cars and are taken to a prison car if they misbehave or to a funeral car if they die; spies who work for the company roam throughout the train in disguise; and so on. The lone traveler's train finally arrives, and the miniature switchman goes hopping down the tracks with his little red lantern, laughing as the man's answer to his question about his destination rings in his ears. "I'm heading for X--!" Critics have praised this curious story because it lends itself to interpretation on at least three levels: as a criticism of the railway system, as a satire of social institutions in general, and as an exploration of the nature of reality per se. The irony is that the traveler does not know before boarding the train if what he has heard is all imagined, made up by the little man, or real. In this dreamlike story, Arreola, like Franz Kafka, suggests that everything--family, friends, work--is part of the imagination and nothing more.

"The Prodigious Milligram"

In "El prodigioso miligramo" ("The Prodigious Milligram"), Arreola continues to work with metaphors in the form of a modern allegorical fable involving an ant colony. Like the previous story, it is one of the author's best-known and cleverest pieces. Arreola's main concern is with human social behavior and the nature of human values. A nonconformist ant known for wandering out of line at work time discovers "a prodigious milligram" (it is never defined otherwise) and joyfully carries it back to the colony. There, she is greeted with derision, suspicion, and disapproval for disrupting the routine and introducing something unusual of her own free will, an act that would have led to her execution but for the intervention of a psychiatrist who promptly declares her mentally incompetent and suggests that she be locked up in a cell. The ant dies in her cell while admiring the splendid, glowing milligram. Legends begin to spread about her, and hundreds, then thousands of ants give up their assigned tasks to go out and find prodigious milligrams as she had, carrying them back to a central room in the colony. Conflicts arise between different groups of ants over the quality of the milligrams and their safeguarding. Wealthy ants form private collections. Thievery becomes rampant. War erupts and many ants are killed. Famine follows, for no one has been storing food for the winter. At the end of the story, the entire species is on the verge of extinction.

As in a good fable, ambiguity abounds in this one. Arreola plays with the notion of how arbitrary value can be, starting from an absurd premise and carrying it logically to its extreme conclusion in a convincing fashion. Readers can think about this story in terms of politics, religion, and economics, exploring with the author the tragic consequences to society when people behave in ways that stifle originality, creativity, independence, and human dignity. In many ways, the story is open-ended, for it easily lends itself to myriad interpretations. Whichever conclusions readers may draw, there is a clear sense that definite truths about human nature are represented here.

"Baby H. P."

On an entirely different note, Arreola carries on the theme of the way that human beings allow themselves to be degraded in their embrace of the progress presumably brought by technology in a bizarre short piece written in the form of an advertisement that bears the title in English of "Baby H. P." This is meant as a dig at the capitalist model par excellence of the United States, with its emphasis on utilitarianism and a more comfortable life made possible by the ingenious uses of practical contraptions. Arreola has come up with a "Made in U.S.A." device that is strapped to babies and small children in order to harness their natural energy when they kick, thrash, and run about, funneling their "horse power" into a special transformer that can then be used for operating small appliances such as blenders and radios. An accompanying warning label downplays the possibility that the baby can electrocute itself; as long as the parents carefully follow the directions for proper use, there is no risk. This is Arreola's way of criticizing the excessive interest that people have in functionalism, especially when their self-worth is subordinated to its pursuit.

"Small Town Affair"

A more controversial theme that at times seems to consume Arreola is presented in several of his stories, which dramatize the difficulty that men and women have in maintaining harmonious relationships, whether married or not, because of the human tendency toward infidelity and what the author sees as a basic fear that men have of women. In "Pueblerina" ("Small Town Affair"), a husband who discovers that his wife has a lover decides to encourage the affair rather than try to block it. The upshot is that the passion and excitement quickly fade for the lovers when they are no longer stimulated by the risk of getting caught by the husband. In "Eva" ("Eve"), Arreola represents the notion that originally the platonic human being was complete and bisexual until a primordial split occurred that left male and female feeling incomplete ever since. The flesh component was distributed to the woman, while the man received the spirit. The male, being most vulnerable, seeks to reunite with the woman, an impossible and tragic dream that can end only when a new species is formed through the female reincorporation of the male spiritual component.

"The Bird Spider"

A kind of existentialist horror story, "La migala" ("The Bird Spider") shows Arreola's skill at creating and maintaining a suspenseful mood in a condensed text. Rejected by the woman he loves, a lonely and insecure man copes with his despair by purchasing a huge spider with a poisonous bite. Deliberately letting it loose in the house, he distracts himself from his despair over his lost love by substituting for it the threat of immediate death, wandering about the house in his bare feet, never knowing when the spider will strike. Arreola's depiction of the strange coping mechanisms that human beings devise for themselves is a grim commentary on the lives of quiet desperation that people are both driven to lead and to which they allow themselves to succumb.

Finally, in another type of text that allows the author to deal more whimsically with his existential concerns, animals are cleverly used to display human traits and weaknesses. Modeled after traditional beast books from medieval times, Arreola's psycho-zoological portraits allow him to unleash his imagination once again as he pokes fun by focusing on what he sees as human in such diverse animals as the hyena, the toad, the monkey, the boa, the seal, the rhinoceros, and a bevy of other creatures. Most of these pieces are a tour de force for their penetrating symbolism, startling use of language, and acerbic wit.

Clearly, a reading of only a sampling of Arreola's texts reveals creative instincts that are unique and multifaceted. A true artisan, he makes skillful use of structure, point of view, brevity, and the power of suggestion in a minimalist fashion, providing readers with just enough detail to trigger their own imaginations so that they will follow his in several possible directions and beyond. His obsession with the threat to the human spirit that excessive materialism and technological progress represent has driven Arreola to display this main theme in kaleidoscopic fashion in a variety of experimental, and for the most part highly effective, literary texts. His success is owed largely to his imaginative approach to reality; his highly creative use of the Spanish language; his colorful imagery; and his bizarre, daring, and even scandalous sense of humor. In the long run, Arreola seems to suggest, the line between the real and the unreal may be just as tenuous as the line between laughing and crying when one contemplates the psychodrama of the human condition.

Other Major Works

LONG FICTION: *La feria*, 1963 (*The Fair*, 1977).

PLAYS: *La hora de todos*, pb. 1954; *Tercera llamada ¡Tercera! O empezamos sin usted*, pb. 1971.

NONFICTION: *La palabra educación*, 1973 (Jorge Arturo Ojeda, editor); *Y ahora la mujer . . .*, 1975 (Arturo Ojeda, editor); *Inventario*, 1976; *Prosa dispersa*, 2002 (Orso Arreola, editor).

EDITED TEXT: *Lectura en voz alta*, 1968 (anthology).

MISCELLANEOUS: *Estas páginas mías*, 1985; *Obras*, 1995.

Bibliography

Brescia, P. "A 'Superior Magic': Literary Politics and the Rise of the Fantastic in Latin American Fiction." Forum for Modern Language Studies44, no. 4 (October, 2008): 379. An examination of Latin American fantastic literature. Brescia argues that between 1930 and 1950, Arreola and Jorge Luis Borges "actively engaged in a promotion of the fantastic," not only in fiction but also in other genres, such as essays, prologues, and lectures."

Gilgen, Read G. "Absurdist Techniques in the Short Stories of Juan José Arreola." *Journal of Spanish Studies: Twentieth Century* 8, no. 1/2 (1980): 67-77. This concise treatment of the notion of the absurd focuses on techniques that help explain Arreola's artistic philosophy. The notes provide references to a few other studies on the absurd as well as on Arreola's work.

Larson, Ross. *Fantasy and Imagination in the Mexican Narrative*. Tempe: Arizona State University Center for Latin American Studies, 1977. A systematic survey of the substantial, although somewhat neglected, body of literature of fantasy and imagination written in Mexico over the years. Arreola is viewed as a major contributor to the movement away from literature with an explicit social purpose. Several of his stories are dealt with, although in somewhat cursory fashion. Contains an extensiveBibliography and a useful index.

McMurray, George R. "The Spanish American Short Story from Borges to the Present." In *The Latin American Short Story: A Critical History*, edited by Margaret Sayers Peden. Boston: Twayne, 1983. Argues that "The Switchman" is an excellent example of Albert Camus's philosophy of the absurd. Suggests that the railway journey is a metaphor for life and that the act of boarding the train means accepting life's challenges and uncertainties.

Menton, Seymour. "Juan José Arreola and the Twentieth Century Short Story." *Hispania* 42, no. 3 (September, 1959): 295-308. This study of Arreola by a critic who became his close friend remains the classic introduction to the man and his early work. Arreola is credited with developing the fantastic as a viable way to represent the conflicts and concerns of people trapped under the pressures of modern society. Attention is given to his place within the surrealist movement, his major themes, techniques, and worldview.

_____, comp. *The Spanish American Short Story: A Critical Anthology*. Berkeley: University of California Press, 1980. This collection of Spanish American stories translated into English includes information on the literary movements and tendencies that have shaped the genre in Latin American countries from the 1830's to the "Boom" period of the 1960's and 1970's. Thumbnail sketches introduce Menton's choices as the best and most representative stories available at the time. Brief critical commentaries assist with interpretation of the texts. Arreola's "The Switchman" is included.

Schade, George. Introduction to *Confabulario, and Other Inventions*. Austin: University of Texas Press, 1964. This excellent English translation largely follows the text and arrangement of the 1962 edition of *Confabulario total*. Excluded is the one-act play *La hora de todos*, which Schade deems ineffectual and out of place in this collection. Provides a brief but incisive introduction to the stories.

Washburn, Yulan. *Juan José Arreola*. Boston: Twayne, 1983. The most thorough study of Arreola and his work available in English. Drawing on a variety of critical studies in both Spanish and English, as well as on a series of personal interviews with the writer himself, Washburn carefully analyzes most of Arreola's major stories, his novel, *The Fair*, and the overall preoccupations reflected in his work as a whole. Detailed plot summaries are followed by scrupulous textual analyses. Included is an extensive discussion of Arreola's life and times and a substantial selectBibliography of primary and secondary sources, most of which are available only in Spanish.

Harry L. Rosser

Miguel Ángel Asturias

Born: Guatemala City, Guatemala; October 19, 1899
Died: Madrid, Spain; June 9, 1974

Principal short fiction

Leyendas de Guatemala, 1930
Week-end en Guatemala, 1956
El espejo de Lida Sal, 1967 (*The Mirror of Lida Sal,* 1997)
Novelas y cuentos de juventud, 1971
Viernes de dolores, 1972

Other literary forms

The first published works of Miguel Ángel Asturias (mee-GEHL AHN-hehl ah-STEWR-yahs) were translations of Mayan Indian lore whose influence is strongly present in his own writings. His first and most famous novel, *El Señor Presidente* (1946; *The President,* 1963) is a subjective account of the Manuel Estrada Cabrera dictatorship in Guatemala. His "Banana Trilogy" of novels deals with the imperialistic excesses of the United Fruit Company. Because of their use of intense visual images to appeal to the audience's subconscious, his dramas have been regarded as highly experimental. Asturias also wrote poetry, essays, children's stories, and newspaper articles.

ACHIEVEMENTS

Miguel Ángel Asturias sought to give a universal consciousness to the problems of Latin America in his writings. He is best known for fusing native legends, folklore, and myths with harsh reality and even Surrealism in his novels.

In 1923, the University of San Carlos in Guatemala awarded Asturias the Premio Galvez for his law degree dissertation on the sociocultural problems of the Indian; he won the Chavez Prize that same year. The Prix Sylla Monsegur was bestowed upon him in 1931 for his collection of Indian tales entitled *Leyendas de Guatemala*. The Prix du Meilleur Roman Étranger was awarded to him in 1952 for his first novel, *El Señor Presidente*. The International Lenin Peace Prize from the Soviet Union was awarded to him in 1966 for the three works in the "Banana Trilogy." Asturias's most prestigious award was the Nobel Prize in Literature from the Swedish Academy in 1967.

BIOGRAPHY

Miguel Ángel Asturias was born in 1899 in Guatemala City, Guatemala, only one year after the country succumbed to the dictatorship of Manuel Estrada Cabrera. Asturias's father, a supreme court magistrate, lost his position in 1903, when he refused to convict students who protested against Estrada Cabrera's totalitarian regime. Consequently, Asturias's family was forced to leave the city for a rural area in Guatemala, where the young Asturias's interest in his country's Indian and peasant customs began to develop.

After attending secondary school, Asturias entered the University of San Carlos to study law. There he was politically active, participating in demonstrations that helped to depose Estrada Cabrera. Asturias also helped to found both a student association of Guatemala's Unionist party and the Universidad Popular de Guatemala, an institution providing free evening instruction for the country's poor. In 1923, Asturias earned his law degree and shortly thereafter founded the weekly newspaper *Tiempos Nuevos*. Later that year Asturias fled the country; his political writings began to

endanger his life. After living in London for the next five months, Asturias moved to Paris, where he worked as European correspondent for Mexican and Central American newspapers. He also studied ancient Central American Indian civilizations at the Sorbonne. There he completed a dissertation on Mayan religion and translated sacred Indian texts.

It was in Paris that Asturias began his literary career. There he was introduced to the techniques and themes of the Surrealist literary movement; this movement was to have a significant effect on his writing style. In 1925, Asturias privately published a book of poetry and a prizewinning collection of Indian stories. Asturias returned to Guatemala in 1933 and spent the next ten years working as a journalist and a poet while Guatemala was governed by the military dictatorship of Jorge Ubico Castañeda. Between 1935 and 1940, Asturias published several more volumes of poetry. He entered politics in 1942 with his election as deputy to the Guatemalan national congress. Three years later, after the fall of the Castañeda regime, he joined the Guatemalan diplomatic service. He served in several ambassadorial posts in Mexico and Argentina for the next ten years. During this time, he published several novels and worked on the three novels in his "Banana Trilogy"--a portrait of the real-life United Fruit Company.

Stripped of his Guatemalan citizenship in 1954 for supporting president Jacobo Arbenz Guzmán, he lived in exile for the next twelve years in Argentina, Venezuela, and Italy. During this period he continued to write. Regaining his Guatemalan citizenship in 1966, he accepted a position as ambassador to France, which he held until 1970. He died in Madrid, Spain, in 1974.

ANALYSIS

It is likely that, in general terms, Miguel Ángel Asturias is most known for his literature of social denunciation. Indeed, there are those who would claim that he was awarded the Nobel Prize primarily because his fiction attacked political oppression in Latin America, particularly the deleterious influence of American capitalism. Nevertheless, Asturias is notably prominent in Latin American literature for what one may loosely call a highly "poeticized" fiction, that is, a fictional texture that proposes the dissolution of conventional distinctions between poetic and prosaic registers. Nowhere is this aspect of his writing more apparent than in his first book of short fiction, *Leyendas de Guatemala* (legends of Guatemala).

Like many Latin American writers, Asturias spent his culturally formative years in France. This French experience was doubly significant. Not only was it the opportunity to enter into contact with the most important writers, artists, and intellectuals of the ebullient *entreguerre* period in Paris, but also it was the transition from a feudal Latin American society of his youth to the free-wheeling, liberal if not libertine society of postwar Europe. The result for many writers like Asturias is the fascinating conjunction of traditional, autochthonous, and folkloric--and even mythic--Latin American material and themes and a mode of literary discourse shaped by Surrealism and the other vanguard modernist tendencies of the 1920's and 1930's in the "sophisticated" centers of the West. Surrealism maintained a prominent interest in the primitive and the antirational and had as one of its primary goals the demythification of the primacy of so-called high culture in Western society. Thus it is only natural to find a continuity among the intellectuals of the 1920's and 1930's of the interest in Latin American materials that dates back to early anthropological and archaeological studies of the nineteenth century.

In the case of Asturias, what is particularly significant was his opportunity to work in Paris with Georges Raynaud, who was engaged at that time in preparing a scholarly translation of the *Popol Vuh*, the sacred texts of the Quiché Indians of Guatemala. That is, Asturias, in moving from Guatemala to Paris, exchanged a context of the oppression of indigenous culture for one of scholarly and intellectual interest in the cultural accomplishments of the native population of his own country. In *Leyendas de Guatemala*, Asturias attempts to stand as a mediator between the Western and Quiché cultures. It is a mediation consisting of both linguistic and cultural "translations" of indigenous materials into cultural idioms or codes of twentieth century literary discourse. This does not mean ethnographic or folkloristic transcription of indigenous legends, nor does it mean the re-creation of indigenous narratives and their

rearticulation in terms of homologous modern myths. Rather, it means the semantic reformulation of indigenous materials in terms of the linguistic and cultural symbologies of the modern writer. The representation in Spanish, either directly or indirectly, of indigenous myths can never be only a translation. The rhetorics, styles, and modes of writing of a modern Western language such as Spanish, although they may be influenced by the poetic attempts to incorporate the modalities of an indigenous language such as Quiché, can never be the anthropologically faithful or scientific re-creation of the original materials because of the enormous distance that separates the two linguistic and cultural systems.

The so-called poetic language of Asturias in the *Leyendas de Guatemala*, or in the novel *Hombres de maíz* (1949; *Men of Maize*, 1975) is not, therefore, a translation into Spanish of Quiché materials, nor is it an attempt to write in Spanish as though one were in reality writing in Quiché. Rather, it is the attempt to attain an independent discourse that, on the one hand, will suggest the melding of the two cultures into an idealized sociohistoric reality and, on the other hand, will attest the role of the artist and writer as the mediating bridge between two cultures that deplorable but all-too-present circumstances keep separate by a virtually unbreachable abyss.

The influence of Surrealism in Latin American literature has meant not merely the recovery of the subconscious and the unconscious as it has in European culture. More significantly, it has meant the recovery of indigenous cultures and the aspects of those cultures that may be seen as prerational or authentically mythic. The discovery by the Latin American of his subconscious reality is, therefore, not simply a psychological discovery; it is the discovery of those mediating cultural elements--usually indigenous but often creole--which were repressed by nineteenth century liberal and Europeanizing ideologies.

"LEYENDA DEL SOMBRERÓN"

"Leyenda del sombrerón" (legend of the big hat) is an excellent example of the elaboration in a fictional text of the aforementioned principles. Superficially, it reminds one of those nineteenth century narratives by such writers as Peru's Ricardo Palma or Colombia's

Miguel Ángel Asturias (©The Nobel Foundation)

Tomás Carrasquilla--narratives that represent an ironic, urbane retelling of traditional or legendary material of a quasi-documentary nature, lightly fictionalized by a somewhat partronizing narrator who claims to have either discovered his material in an out-of-the-way corner of a dusty library or heard it on the lips of gossipy washerwomen and garrulous mule drivers. These narratives were part of the Romantic and prerealist fiction of Latin America and represented that area's version of local color and the discovery of an idealized past and an idealized *Volkspoesie*.

Asturias's story is like these antecedents in that it deals with quasi- or pseudolegendary material: the origin of the devil's big hat. The legend as Asturias tells it concerns a monastery built by the Spanish conquerors of Central America, a monastery inhabited by devout monks, specifically by one monk who spends his time in appropriately devotional readings and meditation. One day, the monk's exemplary otherworldliness is broken by a ball that comes flying through the window, the lost toy of an Indian boy playing outside the walls of the monastery. At first, the monk is entranced by this

unknown object, which he takes in his hands, imagining that so must have been the earth in the hands of the Creator. Thus distracted from his saintly preoccupations, the monk begins to play with the ball with almost childish joy. A few days later, however, the child's mother comes to the door of the monastery to ask that her son be given religious instruction; it seems that he has been heartbroken since the loss of his ball in the area of the monastery, a ball claimed popularly to be the very image of the devil. Suddenly possessed by a violent rage, the monk runs to his cell, picks up the ball, and hurls it beyond the walls of the monastery. Flying through the air, the ball assumes the form of the black hat of the devil. The story ends with: "And thus is born to the world the big hat."

The superficial resemblance of Asturias's text with its nineteenth century ironic predecessors is borne out by an overt narrator who obliquely addresses himself to the reader. This narrator assumes the function of telling the reader what happened and sharing with him the unusual, surprising, and notable event. Thus, the text is characterized by a number of rhetorical ploys to be seen as markers of this conventional form of ironic storytelling: the explicit allusions to the recovery of the story from antiquarian sources; the fact that the event narrated concerns a remote time and place that, because of its strangeness for the reader, makes the story all the more notable; the heavy-handed condescension toward the simplicity of manner and ingenuous behavior of the participants--the monk, the Indian child, and his humble mother; and, finally, the explicit allusions to the fact that someone is telling a story. These allusions take the form of phatic formulas such as "Let us continue," "Let us go on," "And thus it happened," "And thus it was," as well as frequent references to the noteworthiness of the event being related, toward confirming the value of the narrative as narrative and as a form of privileged discourse.

It must be stressed that all these features are only superficial characteristics of nineteenth century ironic, local-color literature. Indeed, the fact that they are superficial echoes in Asturias's text becomes a wholly different sort of irony, an irony at the expense of a reader willing to take them as indicative of peasant superstitions recounted in a straightforward fashion by a narrator slightly amused at folk superstitions. To understand the way in which Asturias's story is much more than such a retelling of a local superstition, it is necessary to keep in mind the presence of two systems of cultural reference in the text. In the first place, it is necessary to recall the enormous sociocultural impact of the activities of religious orders in Latin America during the colonial period. The conquest was accompanied by religious orders charged with the establishment in the New World of Christianity and the conversion of the indigenous population. In the case of the area known today as Guatemala, this imperative meant the wholesale destruction of the artifacts of indigenous culture, so that by the twentieth century less than a half dozen of the Quiché codices were the survivors of the Christian priests' destructive zeal. It would be no exaggeration to say that, as a consequence, the sort of monastery described with much detail in Asturias's text dominated the daily lives of the conquered indigenous peoples.

Second, ballplaying enjoyed a ritual and religious status in Quiché culture. Indeed, one of the cultural contributions of the Quichés to their conquerors was the ball, an artifact of leisure. Thus, in Asturias's text the encounter between the priest and the ball--and through the ball, between the former and indigenous culture--may be a circumstantial occurrence. In terms, however, of the cultural system represented on the one hand by the pious monk and the fortress-like monastery he occupies, and on the other hand by the system represented by the Indian boy's ball are posited by the story as antagonistic forces. The ball becomes a token in a pattern of cultural invasion and expulsion. In the event narrated, the cultural space of the monk is "penetrated" or "invaded" by the alien object, just as the cultural space of the Quichés had been invaded by the Spanish conquerors and their representatives of an alien religion. The indigenous culture, however, cannot displace the invading culture. The priest's almost hysterical realization of the "diabolical" meaning of the ball with which he has played with such childish abandon is the acknowledgment that the ball is much more than a child's toy. In casting the ball away from the monastery, he is expelling indigenous culture from the fortress

of Christianity and reaffirming the primacy and the dominion of the latter. The miraculous transformation of the ball into the devil's hat is not really a fantastic but a phenomenological circumstance. At issue is not a superstitious belief in such occurrences (although an antirational ideology may well affirm them) but rather the perception of the symbolic importance of the object the priest flings away from him with words that recall the "Vade retro, Satanas" commonplace.

It is significant that the narrator of Asturias's story does not end his description of the monk's expulsion from his sanctuary of the artifact of indigenous culture with an explanation of the meaning of that gesture, particularly since, in the opening segments of the text, he takes great pains to describe the setting of the religious community concerned and the monk's initial distraction with the child's stray toy; yet it is the abrupt end of the text that most confirms the significance of the symbolic interplay between the cultures here described. By not appending an explanatory conclusion, the narrator runs the risk of his reader's taking the event at face value--that is, as a miraculous or fantastic event, the authenticity of which is maintained by conventional and ingenuous superstition. Nevertheless, to the extent that the conventions of serious twentieth century literature preclude the telling of superstitious material for shock effect, the reader is obliged, when confronted with such material, to attribute to it some profound, if only vaguely perceived, semiological value. Such is the case with the encounter between the monk and the ball.

The reader need not endorse the overwhelming significance here implied of the religious community on the one hand and the ritual value of the child's ball on the other to appreciate how the story concerns conflicting antagonistic forces. In terms of the most elemental cultural values in the story one sees the ball interpreted in a conflicting manner by the monk: He sees it first as a symbol of God's creation, and it is only with the appearance of the peasant woman and her casual reference to the ball as the image of the devil that he suddenly becomes enraged with its offending presence. It crosses the monk's mind initially that the ball may be bewitched; nevertheless, he sees in it something less worldly that his books cannot explain. In giving himself over to its humble simplicity, he is, to a certain extent, escaping the treacheries of a bookish culture. Thus there is a subsystem of oppositions whereby on the larger level of the narrative there is a contrast between the monk and the ball, between Christian and indigenous sociocultural values, and there is in the monk's own world a contrast between signs of the devil and signs of God's grace. Before he realizes that the ball is the symbol of the devil, to the extent that it is an artifact of the culture that Christianity is dedicated to eradicating, he considers the errant toy a sign of God's simple grace against the potential treachery of the books with which he surrounds himself. The opposition between grace and evil that the monk perceives in his cell with the appearance of the ball is projected onto the larger plane of the opposition between two alien cultures.

In the world evoked by Asturias's story, there is an impenetrable barrier between two cultures given objective representation by the walls of the monastery. Asturias's text is nevertheless a mediator between these two cultures in the sense that they are brought together as opposing and interdependent elements in a narrative system. Without either one, there would be no story; because both are necessary for this narrative to exist, the text then becomes a form of mediation between the two of them, confirming the unique status of the text as a form of unifying cultural discourse. Asturias's text is unquestionably ideological, but not in the sense of sociopolitical denunciation. Rather, it is ideological by virtue of the implied conception of the praxis of narrative art as a form of mediation between two cultures often condemned to an oppressor/oppressed relationship. Writing such as that of Asturias provides the attempt at mediation with a coherence and purpose that is singularly distinctive.

OTHER MAJOR WORKS

LONG FICTION: *El Señor Presidente*, 1946 (*The President*, 1963); *Hombres de maíz*, 1949 (*Men of Maize*, 1975); *Viento fuerte*, 1950 (*The Cyclone*, 1967; better known as *Strong Wind*, 1968); *El papa verde*, 1954 (*The Green Pope*, 1971); *Los ojos de los enterrados*, 1960 (*The Eyes of the Interred*, 1973); *El alhajadito*, 1961 (*The Bejeweled Boy*, 1971); *Mulata de tal*, 1963 (*Mulata*, 1967); *Maladrón*, 1969.

PLAYS: *Cuculcán*, pb. 1930, pr. 1955; *Soluna*, pb. 1955; *La audiencia de los confines*, pr., pb. 1957; *Chantaje*, pr., pb. 1964; *Dique seco*, pr., pb. 1964; *Teatro*, pb. 1964.

POETRY: *Sien de alondra*, 1949; *Bolívar*, 1955; *Clarivigilia primaveral*, 1965.

NONFICTION: *Sociología guatemalteca: El problema social del indio*, 1923 (*Guatemalan Sociology: The Social Problem of the Indian*, 1977); *La arquitectura de la vida nueva*, 1928; *Rumania: Su nueva imagen*, 1964 (essays); *Latinoamérica y otros ensayos*, 1968 (essays); *Tres de cuatro soles*, 1977.

MISCELLANEOUS: *Obras completas*, 1967 (3 volumes).

BIBLIOGRAPHY

Brotherston, Gordon. *The Emergence of the Latin American Novel*. Cambridge, England: Cambridge University Press, 1977. This scholarly work is intended as an introduction to the Latin American novel, particularly from the 1950's to the 1970's. The chapter on Asturias discusses the author's work in the light of his politics, culture, and literary influences. Contains a generalBibliography of secondary works on Latin American literature, as well as a list of works by and on the major authors mentioned in the text. Accessible to the general reader.

Brushwood, John S. "The Spanish American Short Story from Quiroga to Borges." In *The Latin American Short Story: A Critical History*, edited by Margaret Sayers Peden. Boston: Twayne, 1983. A brief discussion of Asturias's appropriation of legends to use as story material. Includes a brief discussion of "The Legend of the Tattooed Woman."

Callan, Richard J. *Miguel Ángel Asturias*. New York: Twayne, 1970. Callan seeks to acquaint English-speaking readers with Asturias works and ideas and to outline the substructure of his work--the depth psychology of Carl Jung. Beyond sketching the historical and cultural context of Asturias's writings, Callan plunges into its essential depths. Supplemented by an annotatedBibliography, a chronology, and notes.

_____. "Miguel Ángel Asturias: Spokesman of His People." *Studies in Short Fiction*, no. 1 (1971): 92-102. Focuses on both the formal and thematic concerns of Asturias's fiction. Particularly emphasized are the means by which the author represents the Indian culture of Guatemala through myths, legends, and supernatural events.

Gonzalez Echevarria, Roberto. *Myth and Archive: A Theory of Latin American Narrative*. Cambridge, England: Cambridge University Press, 1990. A helpful volume in coming to terms with Asturias's unusual narratives.

Harss, Luis, and Barbara Dohmann. "Miguel Ángel Asturias: Or, The Land Where the Flowers Bloom." In *Into the Mainstream: Conversations with Latin-American Writers*. New York: Harper & Row, 1967. Based on interviews, the section devoted to Asturias offers useful information on the author's thought. The commentary on the novels and plays, however, reveals an extremely cursory reading of his works.

Henighan, Stephen. *Assuming the Light: The Parisian Literary Apprenticeship of Miguel Angel Asturias*. Oxford, England: Legenda, 1999. Focuses on Asturias's literary apprenticeship in Paris in the 1920's and 1930's to describe how the writer developed his concepts of Guatemalan cultural identity and Spanish-American modernity from a French vantage point. Examines his short fiction, particularly the stories in *Leyendas de Guatemala*, and other early works as a means of understanding how Asturias eventually created his contemporary Spanish-American novels.

_____. "Bearded Self/Heroic Love: M. A. Asturias' 'La barba provisional' and Robert Desnos's *La Liberté ou l'amour*." *Comparative Literature Studies* 33 (1996): 280-296. Claims that Asturias's story is an imaginative transformation of Desnos's novel. Argues that the story also suggests Asturias's unconscious concern that his connection with French writers would affect his successful use of Spanish-American materials. Shows how Asturias reworks themes in Desnos's novel.

Lund, Joshua, and Joel Wainwright. "Miguel Angel Asturias and the Aporia of Postcolonial Geography." *Inventions: The International Journal of Postcolonial Studies* 10, no. 2 (July, 2008): 141-157. A postcolonial reading of Asturias's "Mayanist" works, focusing on the novel *Men of Maize* but also mentioning Leyendas de Guatemala.

Peden, Margaret Sayers, ed. *The Latin American Short Story*. Boston: Twayne, 1983. The essays in this insightful collection chart the main currents and principal figures of the historical mainstream of the Latin American short story, suggesting the outlines of the great depth and breadth of the genre in these lands. The section devoted to Asturias focuses on *Leyendas de Guatemala*. Contains a selected list of authors, collections in English, and critical studies in English.

Prieto, Rene. *Miguel Ángel Asturias's Archaeology of Return*. Cambridge, England: Cambridge University Press, 1993. The best available study in English of the novelist's body of work. Prieto discusses both the stories and the novels, taking up issues of their unifying principles, idiom, and eroticism. In his measured introduction, Prieto carefully analyzes Asturias's reputation and identifies his most important work. Includes very detailed notes and Bibliography.

David W. Foster
Updated by Genevieve Slomski

B

Isaac Babel

Born: Odessa, Ukraine, Russian Empire (now in Ukraine); July 13, 1894

Died: Butyrka prison, Moscow, Russia, Soviet Union (now in Russia); January 27, 1940

Principal short fiction

Rasskazy, 1925

Istoriia moei golubiatni, 1926

Konarmiia, 1926 (*Red Cavalry,* 1929)

Odesskie rasskazy, 1931 (*Tales of Odessa,* 1955)

Benya Krik, the Gangster, and Other Stories, 1948

The Collected Stories, 1955

Isaac Babel: The Lonely Years, 1925-1939, Unpublished Stories and Private Correspondence, 1964, 1995

Izbrannoe, 1957, 1966

Lyubka the Cossack, and Other Stories, 1963

You Must Know Everything: Stories, 1915-1937, 1969

Other literary forms

Although Isaac Babel (BA-byihl) spent most of his career writing short stories, he tried his hand at other genres without making significant contributions to them. He wrote two plays: *Zakat* (1928; *Sunset,* 1960) and *Mariia* (1935; *Maria,* 1966). He also wrote several screenplays, most of which remain unpublished. Babel was known to have worked on several novels, but only a few fragments have been published. If he ever completed them, either he destroyed them or they were confiscated by police when he was arrested in 1939, never to be seen in public again. Because of their fragmentary nature, the tendency among critics is to treat them as short fiction. He also wrote a brief autobiography, a diary, reminiscences, and newspaper articles.

Achievements

Isaac Babel's greatest achievement lies in short fiction. From the outset, he established himself as a premier short-story writer not only in Russian but also in world literature. He achieved this reputation not only through his innovative approach to the subject matter--the civil war in Russia, for example, or the Jewish world of his ancestry--but also through his stylistic excellence. His mastery of style earned for him, early in his career, a reputation of an avant-garde writer--a model to be emulated, but at the same time difficult to emulate. He elevated the Russian short story to a new level and attracted the attention of foreign writers such as Ernest Hemingway, who read him in Paris. At the same time, it would be unjust to attribute his greatness only to the uniqueness of his subject matter or to his avant-garde style. Rather, it is the combination of these and other qualities that contributed to his indisputably high reputation among both critics and readers, a respect that seems to grow with time.

Biography

Isaac Emmanuilovich Babel was born in Odessa on July 13, 1894, into a Jewish family that had lived in southern Russia for generations. Soon after his birth, the family moved from this thriving port on the Black Sea to the nearby small town of Nikolayev, where Babel spent the first ten years of his life. His childhood was typical of a child growing up in a colorful Jewish environment and, at the same time, in a Russian society replete with prejudices against Jews. In his stories, Babel describes the difficult lessons of survival that he had to learn from childhood on, which enabled him not only to survive but also to keep striving for excellence against all odds. He was a studious child who read under all conditions, even on his way home, and his imagination was always on fire, as he said in one of his stories. Among many other subjects, he studied

Hebrew and French vigorously, becoming more proficient in them than in Russian.

After finishing high school in Odessa--which was difficult for a Jewish child to enter and complete--Babel could not attend the university, again because of the Jewish quota. He enrolled in a business school in Kiev instead. It was at this time that he began to write stories, in French, imitating his favorite writers, François Rabelais, Gustave Flaubert, and Guy de Maupassant. In 1915, he went to St. Petersburg, already thinking seriously of a writing career. He had no success with editors, however, until he met Maxim Gorky, a leading Russian writer of the older generation, who published two of his stories and took him under his wing. This great friendship lasted until Gorky's death in 1936. Gorky had encouraged Babel to write and had protected him but had published no more of his stories, and one day Gorky told Babel to go out into the world and learn about real life. Babel heeded his advice in 1917, setting off on a journey lasting several years, during which he volunteered for the army, took part in the revolution and civil war, married, worked for the secret police, was a war correspondent, and finally served in the famous cavalry division of Semyon Mikhaylovich Budenny in the war against the Poles. Out of these dramatic experiences, Babel was able to publish two books of short stories, which immediately thrust him into the forefront of the young Soviet literature. The period from 1921 to 1925 was the most productive and successful of his entire career.

By the end of the 1920's, however, the political climate in the Soviet Union had begun to change, forcing Babel to conform to the new demands on writers to serve the state, which he could not do, no matter how he tried. His attempts at writing a novel about collectivization never materialized. His inability (or, more likely, unwillingness) to change marks the beginning of a decade-long silent struggle between him and the state. Refusing to follow his family into emigration, he tried to survive by writing film scenarios, unable to publish anything else. In May, 1939, he was arrested and sent to a concentration camp. On January 27, 1940, he was shot for espionage. His confiscated manuscripts--a large crate of them--were never found.

ANALYSIS

Isaac Babel's short stories fall into three basic groups: autobiographical stories, tales about Jews in Odessa, and stories about the Russian Revolution and Civil War. Even though the stories were written and published at different times, in retrospect they can be conveniently, if arbitrarily, classified into these three categories. A small number of stories do not fall into any of these groups, but they are exceptions and do not figure significantly in Babel's opus.

While it is true that many of Babel's stories are autobiographical, even if indirectly, a number of them are openly so. Several refer to his childhood spent in Nikolayev and Odessa. In one of his earliest stories, "Detstvo: U babushki" ("Childhood: At Grandmother's"), Babel pays his emotional due to his kind grandmother, who kept quiet vigil over his studying for hours on end, giving him her bits of wisdom every now and then: "You must know everything. The whole world will fall at your feet and grovel before you. . . . Do not trust people. Do not have friends. Do not lend them money. Do not give them your heart!" Babel loved his childhood because, he said, "I grew up in it, was happy, sad, and dreamed my dreams--fervent dreams that will never return." This early wistful realization of the inevitable transience of all things echoes through much of his writings. The mixture of happiness and sadness is reflected in one of his best stories, "Istoriia moei golubiatni" ("The Story of My Dovecot"), where a child's dream of owning a dovecote is realized during a pogrom, but the dove, which his father had promised him if he was accepted to high school, is squashed against his face. The trickling of the dove's entrails down his face symbolizes the boy's loss of innocence and a premature farewell to childhood.

Babel's discovery of love as the most potent feeling of humankind came to him rather early. As he describes in "Pervaia liubov" ("First Love"), he was ten years old when he fell in love with the wife of an officer, perhaps out of gratitude for her protection of Babel's family during the pogrom in Nikolayev. The puppy love, however, soon gave way to fear and prolonged hiccuping--an early indication of the author's rather sensitive nervous system that accompanied him all his life. This innocent, if incongruous, setting points to a sophisticated sense of humor and to irony, the two devices used by Babel in most of his works. It also foreshadows his unabashed approach to erotica in his later stories, for which they are well known.

As mentioned already, Babel lived as a child in a world of books, dreams, and rampant imagination. In addition, like many Jewish children, he had to take music lessons, for which he had no inclination at all. He had little time for play and fun and, as a consequence, did not develop fully physically. He was aware of this anomaly and tried to break out of it. During one such attempt, as he describes it in "Probuzhdenie" ("Awakening"), he ran away from a music lesson to the beach, only to discover that "the waves refused to support" him. Nevertheless, this experience made him realize that he had to develop "a feel for nature" if he wanted to become a writer. Another experience of "breaking out" concerns Babel's awareness of his social status, as depicted in the story "V podvale" ("In the Basement"). In the story, he visits the luxurious home of the top student in his class and has to use his power of imagination to convince the rich boy that socially he

Isaac Babel (Hulton Archive)

is on equal footing with him. When the boy visits the apartment of Babel's family, "in the basement," however, the truth becomes obvious, and the little Isaac tries to drown himself in a barrel of water. This realization of the discrepancy between reality and the world of dreams and the need and desire to break out of various imposed confines were constant sources of aggravation in Babel's life. Other autobiographical stories, as well as many other stories seemingly detached from the author's personal life, attest this perennial struggle.

TALES OF ODESSA

The stories about the life of Jews in the collection *Tales of Odessa* demonstrate Babel's attachment to his ethnic background, as well as his efforts to be objective about it. In addition to being an economic and cultural center, Odessa had a strong underground world of criminals made mostly of Jews, which fueled the imagination of the growing Isaac; later, he used his reminiscences about the Jewish mafia in some of his best stories. He immortalized one of the leaders, Benya Krik, alias the King, in "Korol" ("The King"). Benya's daring and resourcefulness are shown during the wedding of his elderly sister, whose husband he had purchased. When the police plan to arrest Benya's gang during the wedding celebration, he simply arranges for the police station to be set on fire. He himself married the daughter of a man he had blackmailed in one of his operations.

An old man who saw in Babel a boy with "the spectacles on the nose and the autumn in the heart" told him the story of Benya's rise to fame in "Kak eto delalos v Odesse" ("How It Was Done in Odessa"). Here, Benya orders the liquidation of a man who did not give in to blackmail, but Benya's executioner kills the wrong man, a poor clerk who had very little joy in life. Benya orders a magnificent funeral for the unfortunate clerk and a lifelong financial support for his mother, thus showing his true nature and revealing that it is not crime that attracted him to the underground life but rather a subconscious desire to right the wrongs and help the downtrodden. Through such characters and their motives, Babel is able to lend his stories a redeeming grace, neutralizing the mayhem saturating them.

Loyalty is another quality that binds these law-breakers, as illustrated in the story "Otec" ("The Father"), where Benya helps an old gangster, who had given him his start, to marry off his daughter to the son of a man who had rejected the marriage. They are assisted by another legendary figure, Lyubka, known also from the story "Liubka Kazak" ("Lyubka the Cossack"). Lyubka, a middle-aged shop and whorehouse keeper, reigns supreme in her dealings with customers, who, in turn, help her wean her baby from breastfeeding. This interdependency in a life fraught with danger and risks gives Babel's characters a human face and his stories a patina of real drama.

Not all stories about Jews in Odessa deal with the underground world, as "Di Grasso," a colorful tale about theater life in Odessa, shows. Di Grasso, a Sicilian tragedian, and his troupe flop the first night of the show. After a favorable newspaper review praising Di Grasso as "the most remarkable actor of the century," the second night the theater is full and the spectators are so enthralled that the wife of the theater "mogul," to whom the fourteen-year-old Isaac had pawned his father's watch, makes the husband return the watch, sparing Isaac much trouble. Babel's uncanny ability to intertwine high aspirations and small concerns, pathos with bathos, turns seemingly insignificant events into genuine human dramas. This is even more evident in the story "Konets bogadel'ni" ("The End of the Old Folks' Home"), where the inmates of a poorhouse near the Jewish cemetery make a living by using the same coffins again and again, until one day the authorities refuse to allow a used coffin for the burial of a revolutionary hero. The ensuing rebellion by the inmates leads to their dispersal and to the end of their life-sustaining scheme. Thus, what began as a clever business proposition turns into tragedy, making Babel's story a timeless statement of the human condition.

Red Cavalry

Babel uses a similar technique in the collection *Red Cavalry*. Although the stories here are based on Babel's real-life experiences in the war between the Russian revolutionaries and the Poles, their real significance lies beyond the factual presentation of a historical event, as the author endows every gesture, almost every word, with a potential deeper meaning. It is not

coincidental that the entire campaign is seen through the eyes of, and told by, a baggage-train officer named Liutov (a persona standing for Babel), not by a front-line participant. Readers learn about the general nature of the conflict, recognize the place names, and even follow the course of the battles, but they cannot piece together the exact history of the conflict simply because that was not the author's intention. Babel gives readers single episodes in miniature form instead, like individual pieces of a mosaic; only after finishing the book are readers able to take in the complete picture.

The first story, "Perekhod cherez Zbruch" ("Crossing into Poland"), sets the tone for the entire collection. The opening lines reveal that a military objective has been taken, but Liutov's baggage train that follows sinks into a hazy, dreamy, impressionistic atmosphere, as if having nothing to do with the campaign:

> Fields flowered around us, crimson with poppies; a noontide breeze played in the yellowing rye; on the horizon virginal buckwheat rose like the wall of a distant monastery. The Volyn's peaceful stream moved away from us in sinuous curves and was lost in the pearly haze of the birch groves; crawling between flowery slopes, it wound weary arms through a wilderness of hops. . . .

This passage shows a poetic proclivity of Babel, but it is also his deliberate attempt to take his readers away from the factual course of events and move them to what he considers to be more important--the human perception of the events. Many of the stories in the collection bear the same trademark.

Although many stories deserve detailed comment, several stand out for their "message" or meaning that can be culled from the story. Nowhere is the brutal nature of the civil war depicted more poignantly than in "Pis'mo" ("A Letter"). A young, illiterate Cossack, Vasily, dictates to Liutov a letter to his mother. He inquires about his beloved foal back home, and only after giving detailed advice about handling him does he tell how his father, who is on the other side, killed one of his sons and was then killed in return by another. This most tragic piece of news is relayed matter-of-factly, as if to underscore the degree of desensitization to which all the participants have fallen prey through endless killing.

The cruelty of the civil war is brought into sharp focus by an old Jewish shopkeeper in "Gedali." Gedali reasons like a legitimate humanitarian and libertarian: "The Revolution--we will say 'yes' to it, but are we to say 'no' to the Sabbath? . . . I cry yes to [the Revolution], but it hides its face from Gedali and sends out on front naught but shooting." He understands when the Poles commit atrocities, but he is perplexed when the Reds do the same in the name of the revolution. "You shoot because you are the Revolution. But surely the Revolution means joy. . . . The Revolution is the good deed of good men. But good men do not kill." Gedali says that all he wants is an International of good people. Liutov's answer that the International "is eaten with gunpowder," though realistic, falls short of satisfying the old man's yearning for justice, which, after all, was the primary driving force of the revolution. It is interesting that, by presenting the case in such uncompromising terms, Babel himself is questioning the rationale behind the revolution and the justification of all the sacrifices and suffering.

A similar moral issue is brought to a climactic head in perhaps the best story in *Red Cavalry*, "Smert' Dolgushova" ("The Death of Dolgushov"). Dolgushov is wounded beyond repair and is left behind the fighting line to die. He is begging Liutov to finish him off because he is afraid that the Poles, if they caught him alive, would mutilate his body. Liutov refuses. The commander gallops by, evaluates the situation, and shoots Dolgushov in the mouth. Before galloping away, the commander threatens to kill Liutov, too, screaming, "You guys in specks have about as much pity for chaps like us as a cat has for a mouse." Aside from the revolutionaries' mistrust of Liutov (alias Babel) and the age-old question of euthanasia, the story poses a weighty moral question: Has a human being the right to kill another human being? Even though Babel seems to allow for this possibility, he himself cannot make that step, making it appear that he is shirking his responsibility (after all, he is fighting alongside the revolutionaries). More likely, he is hoping that there should be at least someone to say no to the incessant killing, thus saving the face of the revolution (as if

answering Gedali's mournful plea). More important, this hope hints at Babel's real attitude toward the revolution. Babel was severely criticized for his "misunderstanding" of the revolution, and it is most likely that through such attitudes he sowed the seeds of his own destruction two decades later.

Not all stories in *Red Cavalry* are weighed down with ultimate moral questions. There are stories of pure human interest, colorful slices of the war, and even some genuinely humorous ones. In "Moi pervyi gus'" ("My First Goose"), Liutov is faced with the problem of gaining the respect of the illiterate Cossacks in his unit. As a bespectacled intellectual ("a four-eyed devil," as they called him), and a Jew at that, he knows that the only way to win them over is by committing an act of bravery. He thinks of raping a woman, but he sees only an old woman around. He finally kills a goose with his saber, thereby gaining the respect of his "peers." Only then are they willing to let him read to them Vladimir Ilich Lenin's latest pronouncements. With this mixture of mocking seriousness and irony, Babel attempts to put the revolution in a proper perspective. His difficulties at adjusting to military life are evident also in the story "Argamak," where he ruins a good horse by not knowing how to handle it.

The Jews are frequently mentioned in these stories because the war was taking place in an area heavily populated by them. Babel uses these opportunities to stress their perennial role as sufferers and martyrs, but also to gauge his own Jewish identification. In "Rabbi" ("The Rabbi"), he visits, with Gedali, an old rabbi, who asks him where he came from, what he has been studying, and what he was seeking--typical identification questions. Later, they and the rabbi's son, "the cursed son, the last son, the unruly son," sit amid the wilderness of war, in silence and prayers, as if to underscore the isolation of people threatened by an alien war. In "Berestechko," a Cossack is shown cutting the throat of an old Jewish "spy," being careful not to stain himself with blood. This one detail completes the picture of a Jew as an ultimate victim.

Many characters are etched out in these miniature stories. There is Sandy the Christ in the story by the same title ("Sashka Khristov"), a meek herdsman who at the age of fourteen caught "an evil disease" while carousing with his stepfather and who later joined the Reds and became a good fighter. There is Pan Apolek ("Pan Apolek"), an itinerant artist who painted church icons in the images not of the saints but of local people. There is Afonka Bida ("Afonka Bida"), the commander who almost shot Liutov because of Dolgushov, who loses his horse Stepan and disappears hunting for another. After several weeks, he reappears with a gray stallion, but the loss of Stepan still makes him want to destroy the whole world. In "So" ("Salt"), a woman carrying a bundled baby uses him to gain sympathy and hitch a train ride. It turns out that the bundle is nothing but a two-pound sack of salt; she is thrown out of the moving train and then shot from the distance. The man who killed her pronounces solemnly, "We will deal mercilessly with all the traitors that are dragging us to the dogs and want to turn everything upside down and cover Russia with nothing but corpses and dead grass," which is exactly what he has just done. Finally, in one of the best stories in the book, "Vdova" ("The Widow"), a lover of the dying commander is bequeathed all of his belongings, with the request that she send some of them to his mother. When the widow shows signs of not following the will of the deceased, she is beaten, and, if she forgets the second time, she will be reminded again in the same fashion. These stories are perfect illustrations of Babel's ability to create unforgettable but credible characters, to set up dramatic scenes, and to conjure a proper atmosphere, while endowing his creations with a truly human pathos--qualities that characterize most of his stories but especially those in *Red Cavalry*.

Among the stories outside the three groups, several are worth mentioning. An early story, "Mama, Rimma, i Alla" ("Mama, Rimma, and Alla"), resembles an Anton Chekhov story in that the domestic problems in a family (a mother finds it difficult to cope with her daughters in absence of her husband) are not solved and the story dissolves in hopelessness. "Iisusov grekh" ("The Sin of Jesus") is a colorful tale of a woman whose husband is away at war and who goes to Jesus for advice about loneliness. When Jesus sends her an angel, she accidentally smothers him to death in sleep. She goes again to Jesus, but now he damns her as a slut, which she resents, for it is not her fault that she

lusts, that people drink vodka, and that he has created "a woman's soul, stupid and lonely." When finally Jesus admits his error and asks for forgiveness, she refuses to accept it, saying, "There is no forgiveness for you and never will be." The story displays Babel's exquisite sense of humor, along with a keen understanding of human nature and the complexities of life. A variant, "Skazka pro babu" ("The Tale of a Woman"), another Chekhovian story, again depicts the plight of a widow who, in her loneliness, asks a friend to find her a husband. When she does, he mistreats her and walks out on her, which causes her to lose her job. Finally, "Ulitsa Dante" ("Dante Street") is a Paris story in the tradition of Guy de Maupassant, showing Babel's versatility and imagination.

Babel's stylistic excellence has been often praised by critics. His style features a Spartan economy of words, and he is known to have spent years reworking and revising his stories. Babel's attention to detail, especially to line and color, often result in fine etchings. There is a pronounced poetic bent in his stories, whether they are located in a city milieu or in the countryside. This is reinforced by a prolific use of images and metaphors in the style of the following passages, quoted at random:

> A dead man's fingers were picking at the frozen entrails of Petersburg. . . . The gentleman had drooping jowls, like the sacks of an old-clothes man, and wounded cats prowled in his reddish eyes.

One finds in Babel also a surprising amount of humor, as if to offset the cruelty and gruesome injustice of his world.

Babel's artfulness is especially noticeable in his treatment of irony as his strongest device. He refuses to accept reality as one perceives it. He also plays games with the reader's perceptions, as he says openly, "I set myself a reader who is intelligent, well educated, with sensible and severe standards of taste. . . . Then I try to think how I can deceive and stun the reader." This cool intellectual approach, coupled with the strong emotional charge of his stories, gives his stories an aura of not only skillfully executed works of art but also pristine innocence of divine creation.

OTHER MAJOR WORKS

PLAYS: *Zakat*, pb. 1928 (*Sunset*, 1960; also known as *Sundown*); *Mariia*, pb. 1935 (*Maria*, 1966).

SCREENPLAYS: *Benia Krik: Kinopovest'*, 1926 (*Benia Krik: A Film Novel*, 1935); *Bluzhdaiushchie zvezdy: Kinostsenarii*, 1926.

POETRY: *Morning in the Burned House*, 1996.

NONFICTION: *1920 Diary*, 1995.

MISCELLANEOUS: *The Complete Works of Isaac Babel*, 2001 (short stories, plays, screenplays, and diaries).

BIBLIOGRAPHY

Avins, Carol J. "Kinship and Concealment in *Red Cavalry* and Babel's 1920 Diary." *Slavic Review* 53 (Fall, 1994): 694-710. Describes how a diary that Babel kept during his service in the 1920 Polish campaign was a source of ideas for his collection of stories *Red Cavalry*. Claims that Babel's efforts to conceal his Jewishness, recounted in the diaries, is also reflected in the stories.

Babel, Isaac. *Isaac Babel's Selected Writings: Authoritative Texts, Selected Letters, 1926-1939, Isaac Babel Through the Eyes of His Contemporaries, Isaac Babel in Criticism and Scholarship*. Selected and edited by Gregory Freidin, translated by Peter Constantine. New York: W. W. Norton, 2010. In addition to containing some of Babel's short stories, this volume also reprints some of the letters he wrote to his sister and mother; reminiscences by Maxim Gorky and other contemporaries of Babel; and four major assessments of Babel's legacy by Viktor Shklovsky, Lionel Trilling, Efraim Sicher, and Gregory Freidin.

Bloom, Harold, ed. *Isaac Babel*. Philadelphia: Chelsea House, 2004. One in a series of books about short-story writers, this volume features a biography of Babel, extracts from major critical essays discussing important aspects of some of his short stories, a list of characters and thematic analysis for each short story that is analyzed, a bibliography of critical works about the short stories covered in the book, and an index of themes and ideas in Babel's work.

Carden, Patricia. *The Art of Isaac Babel*. Ithaca, N.Y.: Cornell University Press, 1972. In this discerning study of Babel's art, Carden combines biography and analysis of his main works and themes, especially his search for style and form, and philosophical, religious, and aesthetic connotations. The meticulous scholarship is accompanied by keen insight and empathy, making the book anything but cut-and-dried. Includes a select bibliography.

Charyn, Jerome. *Savage Shorthand: The Life and Death of Isaac Babel*. New York: Random, 2005. Offers an overview of Babel's life, as well as a discussion of his short fiction. Features an introduction by literary critic and writer Cynthia Ozick.

Ehre, Milton. "Babel's *Red Cavalry*: Epic and Pathos, History and Culture." *Slavic Review* 40 (1981): 228-240. A stimulating study of Babel's chief work, incorporating its literary, historical, and cultural aspects. No attention to detail, but rather a sweeping overview.

Falen, James E. *Isaac Babel, Russian Master of the Short Story*. Knoxville: University of Tennessee Press, 1974. Falen's appraisal of Babel is the best overall. Following the main stages of Babel's life, Falen analyzes his works in minute detail, emphasizing the short stories. Lucidly written and provided with the complete scholarly apparatus, the study also offers an exhaustive bibliography.

Luplow, Carol. *Isaac Babel's Red Cavalry*. Ann Arbor, Mich.: Ardis, 1982. This detailed, full-length study of Babel's most famous collection focuses on the narrative perspective of the stories, the basic dialectic between the spiritual and the physical which they embody, their style and romantic vision, and the types of story structure and epiphanic vision they reflect.

Maguire, Robert. "Ekphrasis in Isaak Babel ('Pan Apolek,' 'My First Goose')." In *The Russian Twentieth-Century Short Story: A Critical Companion*, edited by Lyudmila Parts. Brighton, Mass.: Academic Studies Press, 2010. Analyzes two of the short stories in *Red Cavalry*.

Mendelson, Danuta. *Metaphor in Babel's Short Stories*. Ann Arbor, Mich.: Ardis, 1982. A scholarly discussion, drawing from linguistic and psychological studies as well as structuralist studies of narrative. Analyzes *Red Cavalry* as an episodic novel in the modernist tradition, rather than as a strictly linear realist work. Makes clear how the action of the book takes place on several poetic planes at once.

Rubin, Rachel. "Imagine You Are a Tiger: A New Folk Hero in Babel's Odessa Tales." In *Jewish Gangsters of Modern Literature*. Urbana: University of Illinois Press, 2000. Examines how Babel and other left-wing Jewish writers featured gangster characters in their work in order to create a vernacular literature, to craft a virile Jewish masculinity, and to explore the fate of Jews in the Soviet Union and the United States.

Shcheglov, Yuri K. "Some Themes and Archetypes in Babel's *Red Cavalry*." *Slavic Review* 53 (Fall, 1994): 653-670. Discusses initiatory and other-worldly thematic patterns in "My First Goose," showing how Babel used archetypes subtly and selectively. Concludes that "My First Goose," with its density reinforced by archetypal connotations, is an emblematic prototype of later works of Soviet fiction that focus on similar themes.

Sicher, Efraim. *Style and Structure in the Prose of Isaak Babel*. Columbus, Ohio: Slavica, 1986. Primarily a formalist study of the style of Babel's stories. In addition to discussing Babel's lyrical prose, the book analyzes setting, characterization, narrative structure, and point of view in Babel's stories.

Terras, Victor. "Line and Color: The Structure of I. Babel's Short Stories in *Red Cavalry*." *Studies in Short Fiction* 3, no. 2 (Winter, 1966): 141-156. In one of the best treatments of a particular aspect of Babel's stories, Terras discusses his style in terms of line and color and of his poetic inclination.

Zholkovskii, A. K. "How a Russian Maupassant Was Made in Odessa and Yasnaya Polyana: Isaak Babel and the Tolstoy Legacy." *Slavic Review* 53 (Fall, 1994): 671-693. Examines the influence of Leo Tolstoy on Babel, arguing that although both sought to liberate the individual from impersonal routine, Babel's approach is the opposite of Tolstoy's; whereas for Tolstoy finding the self meant relinquishing falsehood and society and returning to truth and childlike innocence, for Babel, one finds the self through erotic contact, culture, art, and invention.

Vasa D. Mihailovich

MARÍA LUISA BOMBAL

Born: Viña del Mar, Chile; June 8, 1910
Died: Santiago, Chile; May 6, 1980

PRINCIPAL SHORT FICTION

La última niebla, 1934 (*The Final Mist*, 1982; previously revised and translated as *The House of Mist*, 1947)
New Islands, and Other Stories, 1982

OTHER LITERARY FORMS

María Luisa Bombal (bohm-BAHL) is the author of wo influential novels, *La amortajada* (1938; revised and translated as *The Shrouded Woman*, 1948) and *La historia de María Griselda* (1977).

ACHIEVEMENTS

María Luisa Bombal was the Chilean representative to the International PEN Conference in the United States in 1940; she received Chile's Academy of Arts and Letters Prize in 1977 for *The Story of María Griselda*.

BIOGRAPHY

María Luisa Bombal was born in Viña del Mar, Chile, on June 8, 1910. She moved to Paris in 1922 with her widowed mother and attended the École Notre Dame de l'Assomption and the Lycée La Bruyère; she then studied philosophy and literature at the Sorbonne, University of Paris, where she became involved with the avant-garde movement in the arts. She returned to Chile in 1930 and became associated with a literary group that included Jorge Luis Borges, Victoria

Ocampo, and Pablo Neruda. In 1935, her first work, *La última niebla* (*The Final Mist*), was enthusiastically received because of its narrative experimentalism.

In 1940, after she shot Eulogio Sanchez Errázuriz, either because of unrequited love or because she imagined him to represent all that was wrong with her life, Bombal moved to the United States and married. Her husband helped her begin writing screenplays. She continued to write and translate until her husband died, after which she moved back to Chile, where she lived until her death on May 6, 1980.

ANALYSIS

Although her output is relatively small, María Luisa Bombal has been hailed as one of the most important Latin American writers of the twentieth century. Part of the reason for this high praise is that she explored the inextricable mixture of fantasy and reality called Magical Realism before its more famous practitioners, Jorge Luis Borges, Julio Cortazar, Carlos Fuentes, and Gabriel García Márquez. The fact that she was female and wrote about the sexual liberation of women in a patriarchal culture that had long suppressed them has added to her fame in late twentieth century criticism.

Bombal more likely learned her narrative technique from the avant-garde of 1920's France than from her Latin American compatriots, for the European gothic tradition that inspired that literary trend is much in evidence in her fiction. The women in her stories, caught in a trap created for them by males, who force them to be either submissive wives or sexual objects, yearn to escape; however, the only means they have to do so is through dreams and fantasies, as they romantically yearn for dark, mysterious men, who turn out to be phantoms, or as they embody darkly mysterious sexual creatures, primevally as much animal as human.

THE FINAL MIST

A number of gothic romance conventions characterize Bombal's novella *The Final Mist*. The female protagonist marries a childhood friend who tells her he knows every inch of her body without her having to take her clothes off. Moreover, she feels she has to imitate his first wife, who, according to him, was a perfect woman before she died an untimely death, and, typical of such romances, the narrator, herself quite young, is

unaware of her physicality, never having dared to look at her own breasts.

Throughout the story, a mist or fog hangs over everything, giving the external world the warm intimacy of a closed room, muffling all sound. This dreamlike real world is so permeated by the narrator's dreams and fantasies that when a young man of almost supernatural aspect appears and kisses her she feels she has been waiting for him and must surrender to his power; her sexual encounter with the stranger is described as an ultimate romantic fantasy in a single magical and dreamlike night.

As ten years go by, in typical romantic fashion, she never sees him again, does not know where he is, but feels that it is enough to know that somewhere he exists. However, when her sister-in-law shoots herself in her lover's house, she feels she is a "casualty" of her own invention, her life a "charade performed in shadows." The ultimate gothic fantasy element is played out in the story when the protagonist locates the house of her dream lover, only to discover that the man who lived there was blind and died of a fall fifteen years earlier. The story ends with her envy of her sister-in-law, who may have died for love; she considers suicide, but settles for living and dying correctly, while the mist settles over everything like a "shroud."

"THE TREE"

Bombal's best-known story is perhaps "El árbol" ("The Tree"), a self-conscious narrative manipulation of the interaction between past and present. The story begins in present tense as the protagonist, Brigida, who, while listening to an opening Wolfgang Amadeus Mozart piece at a concert, recalls allowing herself to be led into marrying a friend of her father. The second concert piece, by Ludwig von Beethoven, leads her back to her marriage and the tree outside her dressing room window, with its foliage reflected in her mirrors, creating the illusion of an infinite forest. As she listens to the third piece, by Frédéric Chopin, the music intermingles in her memory with rain hissing through the leaves of the rubber tree.

Brigida's husband Luis knows she does not love him, but says it is not convenient for them to separate. Although she realizes "that [i]s life," she feels that underneath the mediocrity of experience there is a melody of "grave and slow words that transfixed her." Just when she feels an unexpected sense of fulfillment and placidity, knowing she can live without hope or fear, she hears a thunderous noise. At this point the reader is made aware of the simultaneity of the past and present by the line "The Intermission? No. The rubber tree." The concert hall is ablaze with light and the audience files out, but she is imprisoned in the "web of her past," trapped in her dressing room, which has been flooded by a terrifying white light. Because her husband has had the rubber tree outside her window chopped down, the light reveals all the ugliness and shabbiness of things. Feeling he has stolen her intimacy, her secret, she leaves him.

The thematic focus of the story is a childlike mode of perception that is poetic and atemporal, lost in the shadows of desire and the imagination. Brigida's preference for the shadowy romantic world of her dressing room over the brightly lit external reality makes her unfit for practical experience. However, the story does not suggest that Brigida's obsession with the shadows made by the tree is an escape but rather that her desire for romantic love and loss of self in dream or passion is justifiable.

"BRAIDS"

The two shortest stories in *New Islands, and Other Stories* are similar in their essayistic and folklorish qualities. "Trenzas" ("Braids") begins like an essay on modern women, who cut off their braids and thus sever their ties with "magic currents that issue from the very heart of the earth." Examples of the supernatural power of woman's hair are cited from the stories of Tristram and Isolde, Queen Mélisande, and Bluebeard. After this essayistic preface, Bombal tells a fabulistic story of two sisters and the identification of braids with the primeval forest to illustrate why women, having renounced their braids, have lost their prophetic power and no longer have their old magnetism.

"Lo secreto" ("The Unknown") is a conventional fable about a pirate ship trapped centuries ago in a whirlpool and sent spinning to the bottom of the sea. When the pirate captain awakens, he thinks he has landed on a deserted island, but he sees his sails billowing without wind and an inverted image of his beached ship above him. When he and his crew realize

that their feet leave no tracks and their sails throw no shadow, they know they are a thousand fathoms beneath the sea and damned. The fable ends with the captain's terrifying moan-- "a cry of affliction from someone desperate, burning with desire for something irrevocably lost."

"NEW ISLANDS"

"Las islas nuevas" ("New Islands"), the title story of Bombal's short-fiction collection, climaxes the slender volume by making its heroine Yolanda not merely the psychologically desirous female figure but also the psychological archetype of desire itself. Imaged as a beautiful serpent and as a seagull, she is ageless, lost in a world of dreams, while at the same time the object of the dreams of others, particularly the male hunter Juan Manuel. Of the many metaphors that characterize the primitive nature of Yolanda, the central one is that of the new islands that have erupted in the lake, for just as the male hunter desires to explore and conquer the islands, so also does he wish to conquer Yolanda.

The magical nature of Yolanda is revealed most emphatically when Juan Manuel, in a typical romantic convention, peeks in her window and sees a "fairy tale unfold," for on her right shoulder he sees either the beginning of, or the atrophy of, a wing--an image Bombal uses to suggest that Yolanda, as a magical female creature, is earthbound, with only vestigial remnants of her lost winged freedom--much like a mermaid who has lost her fishlike ability to live under the sea. Juan Manuel flees from the incomprehensible vision, "incapable of soaring into the intricate galleries of Nature in order to arrive at the mystery's origin."

OTHER MAJOR WORKS

LONG FICTION: *La amortajada*, 1938 (revised and translated as *The Shrouded Woman*, 1948); *La historia de María Griselda*, 1977.

MISCELLANEOUS: *Obras completas*, 2005.

BIBLIOGRAPHY

Agosin, Marjorie. "María Luisa Bombal: *O el lenguaje alucinado*." *Symposium* 48 (Winter, 1995): 251-256. In this special issue on Latin American women writers, Agosin argues that Bombal challenged the conventional writing of her time by creating a language that moved back and forth between hallucination and daydream. Describes how Bombal's female characters are marginalized women who seek the meaning of their lives through imagination and memory.

Debicki, Andrew P. "Structure, Imagery, and Experience in María Luisa Bombal's 'The Tree'." *Studies in Short Fiction* 8 (Winter, 1971): 123-129. Discusses how Bombal uses imagery and descriptive detail to explore the theme of illusion and the conflict between illusory and matter-of-fact realities. Argues that the patterns of the story heighten the reader's experience of the protagonist's plight while simultaneously placing that plight within a more universal scheme.

Diaz, Gwendolyn. "Desire and Discourse in María Luisa Bombal's *New Islands*." *Hispanofila* 112 (September, 1994): 51-62. Discusses the stories in *New Islands, and Other Stories* as examples of Bombal's experimentation with a new language that reflects a woman's point of view and thought. Argues that the heroine of the stories struggles to place her own perceptions in a world of phallocentric social structures. Discusses how Bombal wants to create a new rhythm that reflects a more complete view of a world previously divided by sexual hierarchies.

Kostopulos-Cooperman, Celeste. *The Lyrical Vision of María Luisa Bombal*. London: Tamesis Books, 1988. A brief monograph on the lyrical and poetic qualities of Bombal's fiction. Discusses Bombal's central thematic preoccupation of women in relationship to their surrounding worlds. Argues that both technically and thematically Bombal was clearly ahead of her time. Provides detailed discussions of "New Islands" and "The Tree."

Llanos, Bernardita M. "María Luisa Bombal, or the Feminine Writer." In *Passionate Subjects/Split Subjects in Twentieth-Century Literature in Chile: Brunet, Bombal, and Eltit*. Lewisburg, Pa.: Bucknell University Press, 2009. Analyzes the work of Bombal and two other women writers to describe how they developed a "counternarrative" to the Chilean literary canon. Argues that these writers point out the flaws in Chile's patriarchal ideology and show how motherhood and womanhood challenge masculinity and the process of modernization.

Long, William R. "Latina Writers Are Silent No Longer." *Los Angeles Times*, November 11, 1994, p. A1. Notes that books by Latin American women have become best sellers in what many have called a new "boom" in Latin American literature, reminiscent of the explosion of talented male writers in the 1960's. Quotes several writers, scholars, and critics who argue that the most original work being produced in the 1990's in Latin America is by women who are talking about themselves in an open and daring way, a trend that reflects the breakdown of gender bias throughout Latin America.

Mendez Rodenas, Adriana. "Narcissus in Bloom: The Desiring Subject in Modern Latin American Narrative, María Luisa Bombal and Juan Rulfo." In *Latin American Women's Writing: Feminist Readings in Theory in Crisis*, edited by Anny Brooksbank Jones. New York: Oxford University Press, 1996. Mendez Rodenas applies psychoanalytic theory and a feminist approach to Bombal's fiction, especially focusing on her novel *La amortajada*, translated as *The Shrouded Woman*. Compares Bombal's use of the Narcissus theme with Juan Rulfo's use of this myth.

Rivero, Isel. "Among Generals, Bishops, and Guerillas." *Ms.* 1 (May/June, 1991): 70-72. An article on Latin American women writers, noting that while they still wrestle with the process of day-to-day living, their stories are breaking the silence their sisters have endured for so long. Discusses the work of several writers, including Bombal, Isabel Allende, and Victoria Ocampo.

Weldt-Basson, Helene Carol. "Paradoxical Silence, Part II: Silence/Narrative Voice in the Works of María Luisa Bombal." In *Subversive Silences: Nonverbal Expression and Implicit Narrative Strategies in the Works of Latin American Women Writers*. Madison, N.J.: Fairleigh Dickinson University Press, 2009. Describes how Bombal and six other twentieth- and twenty-first-century Latin American women writers invert the notion of "submissive silence" to create a sign of women's rebellion against the silence that a patriarchal society has imposed upon females. Analyzes Bombal and the other writers' use of hyperbole, irony, parody, and other narrative devices.

Charles E. May

JORGE LUIS BORGES

Born: Buenos Aires, Argentina; August 24, 1899
Died: Geneva, Switzerland; June 14, 1986
Also known as: F. Bustos, H. Bustos Domecq, B. Suárez Lynch

PRINCIPAL SHORT FICTION

Historia universal de la infamia, 1935 (*A Universal History of Infamy,* 1972)

El jardín de senderos que se bifurcan, 1941

Seis problemas para don Isidro Parodi, 1942 (with Adolfo Bioy Casares, under joint pseudonym H. Bustos Domecq; *Six Problems for Don Isidro Parodi,* 1981)

"Tres versiones de Judas," 1944 ("Three Versions of Judas," 1962)

Ficciones, 1935-1944, 1944 (English translation, 1962)

Dos fantasías memorables, 1946 (with Bioy Casares, under joint pseudonym Domecq)

El Aleph, 1949, 1952 (translated in *The Aleph, and Other Stories, 1933-1969,* 1970)

La muerte y la brújula, 1951

La hermana de Eloísa, 1955 (with Luisa Mercedes Levinson)

Cuentos, 1958

Crónicas de Bustos Domecq, 1967 (with Bioy Casares; *Chronicles of Bustos Domecq,* 1976)

El informe de Brodie, 1970 (*Doctor Brodie's Report,* 1972)

El matrero, 1970

El congreso, 1971 (*The Congress,* 1974)

El libro de arena, 1975 (*The Book of Sand,* 1977)

Narraciones, 1980

OTHER LITERARY FORMS

Though most famous for his short fiction, Jorge Luis Borges (HOR-hay luh-EHS BAWR-hays) also holds a significant place in Latino literature for his work in poetry and the essay. In fact, Borges would be considered a major writer in Latino letters for his work in these two genres (the vast majority of which was produced before the Argentine writer branched into short fiction) even had he never written a single short story. Borges's early poetry (that for which he earned his reputation as a poet) is of the ultraist school, an avant-grade brand of poetry influenced by expressionism and Dadaism and intended by its Latino practitioners as a reaction to Latino modernism. Borges's essays, as readers familiar with his fiction might expect, are imaginative and witty and usually deal with topics in literature or philosophy. Interestingly, because of the writer's playful imagination, many of his essays read more like fiction than essay, while, because of his propensity both for toying with philosophical concepts and for fusing the fictitious and the real, much of his fiction reads more like essay than fiction. It seems only fitting, however, that for a writer for whom the line between fiction and reality is almost nonexistent, the line between fiction and essay should be almost nonexistent as well.

ACHIEVEMENTS

It is virtually impossible to overstate the importance of Jorge Luis Borges within the context of Latino fiction, for he is, quite simply, the single most important writer of short fiction in the history of Latino literature. This is true not only because of his stories themselves, and chiefly those published in *Ficciones, 1935-1944* and *El Aleph,* but also, just as important, because of how his stories contributed to the evolution of Latino fiction, both short and long, in the latter half of the twentieth century.

Borges was the father of Latino's "new narrative," the type of narrative practiced by the likes of Julio Cortázar, Gabriel García Márquez, Carlos Fuentes, Mario Vargas Llosa, and others. Latino fiction prior to Borges was chiefly concerned with painting a realistic and detailed picture of external Latino reality. Borges's imaginative *ficciones* (or fictions) almost single-handedly changed this, teaching Latino writers to be creative, to use their imaginations, to treat fiction as fiction, to allow the fictional world to be just that: fictional. Borges's works also taught Latino writers to deal with universal themes and to write for an intellectual reader. Without Borges, not only would the literary world be without some superb stories, but also Latino narrative in the second half of the twentieth century would have been radically different from what it evolved to be.

BIOGRAPHY

Jorge Luis Borges was born on August 24, 1899, in Buenos Aires, Argentina, the first of two children born to Jorge Guillermo Borges and Leonor Acevedo de Borges. (His sister, Norah, was born in 1901.) Borges's ancestors included prominent Argentine military and historical figures on both sides of his family and an English grandmother on his father's.

"Georgie," as Borges's family called him, began reading very early, first in English, then in Spanish. Tutored first by his English grandmother and later by a private governess, and with access to his father's library (which contained numerous volumes in English), young Borges devoured a wide range of writings, among them those of Robert Louis Stevenson, Rudyard Kipling, and Mark Twain, as well as works of mythology, novels of chivalry, *Alf layla wa-layla* (fifteenth century; *The Arabian Nights' Entertainments*, 1706-1708), and Miguel de Cervantes's *El ingenioso hidalgo don Quixote de la Mancha* (1605, 1615; *Don Quixote de la Mancha*, 1605, 1615).

Borges finally entered school at age nine, and at age thirteen he published his first story, a dramatic sketch entitled "El rey de la selva" (the king of the jungle), about his favorite animal, the tiger. Borges and his family traveled to Europe in 1914. World War I broke out while they were visiting Geneva, Switzerland, and they remained there until 1918. During his time in Geneva, Borges began to take an interest in French poetry, particularly that of Victor Hugo and Charles Baudelaire, as well as the poetry of Heinrich Heine and the German expressionists. He also began to read the

works of Walt Whitman, Arthur Schopenhauer, and G. K. Chesterton, and he maintained his literary connection to his native Argentina by reading *gauchesca* (gaucho) poetry.

In 1919 Borges and his family moved to Spain, living for various lengths of time in Barcelona, Majorca, Seville, and Madrid. While in Spain, Borges associated with a group of ultraist poets and published some poetry in an ultraist magazine. In 1921, Borges and his family returned to Buenos Aires. His return to his native city after a seven-year absence inspired him to write his first volume of poetry, entitled *Fervor de Buenos Aires* (fervor of Buenos Aires) and published in 1923. During this same period (in 1922), he collaborated on a "billboard review" entitled *Prisma* (prism) and edited the manifesto "Ultraísmo" (ultraism), published in the magazine *Nosotros* (us). He also helped found a short-lived magazine entitled *Proa* (prow). Following a second trip with his family to Europe (1923-1924), Borges continued to write poetry during the 1920's, but he began to branch out into the essay genre as well, publishing three collections of essays during this period: *Inquisiciones* (inquisitions) in 1925, *El tamaño de mi esperanza* (the size of my hope) in 1926, and *El idioma de los argentinos* (the language of the Argentines) in 1928. One of his collections of poetry, *Cuaderno San Martín* (1929; San Martín notebook), won for him second prize in the Municipal Literature Competition in 1929. The prize carried an award of three thousand pesos, which Borges used to buy an edition of the *Encyclopædia Britannica*.

Borges continued writing both poetry and essays in the 1930's, but this decade would also bring his first (though unconventional) steps into fiction. He began contributing to the magazine *Sur* (south) in 1931, through which he met his friend and future literary collaborator Adolfo Bioy Casares; later, in 1933, he became the director of *Crítica* (criticism), a Saturday literary supplement for a Buenos Aires newspaper. As a contributor to the supplement, Borges began to rewrite stories that he took from various sources, adding his own personal touches and reworking them as he saw fit. He finally wrote, under a pen name, a wholly original piece entitled "Hombres de las orillas" (men from the outskirts), which appeared on September 16, 1933, in the supplement. This story and his other *Crítica* pieces were well received and published together in 1935 in a volume entitled *Historia universal de la infamia*.

Borges's foray into fiction writing continued to follow an unconventional path when in 1936 he began writing a book-review page for the magazine *El Hogar* (the home). Each entry carried a brief biography of the author whose work was being reviewed. Once again, Borges could not leave well enough alone. To the author's true biographical facts, Borges began to add his own "facts," even including apocryphal anecdotes from the author's life and supplementing the author's bibliography with false titles. This mix of fact and fiction, with no regard or concern for which was which, would come to be one of the trademarks of Borges's fiction.

Borges took a job as an assistant librarian in a suburban Buenos Aires library in 1937, a position in which the workload and setting afforded the writer ample time and resources to read and write. In December,

Jorge Luis Borges (©Washington Post; reprinted by permission of the D.C. Public Library)

1938, however, the Argentine writer suffered a near-fatal accident, slipping on a staircase and striking his head while returning to his apartment. The resulting head injury developed into septicemia, and Borges was hospitalized for more than two weeks. While still recovering in early 1939, Borges decided that he would abandon poetry and the essay (though he would later return to these genres) and dedicate his literary efforts to short fiction. Though it is somewhat unclear as to precisely why he made this decision (there are various accounts), it is speculated by some (and Borges's own comments have supported such speculation) that he did so because after his head injury he was not sure that he could write poetry and essays of the quality for which he had been known before the accident. Short stories, for which he was virtually unknown at this point, would not allow anyone to compare an old Borges with a new, and potentially inferior, Borges. Again, this is only one suggestion as to why the Argentine writer made the decision he did; what is most important, however, is that he made it, and this decision, and the accident that seems to have caused it, would change the face of Latino fiction of the twentieth century.

Almost immediately, Borges began to produce a series of short stories that would make him the most important writer in Latino fiction and that would eventually make him famous. The first of these stories was "Pierre Menard, autor del *Quijote*" ("Pierre Menard, Author of the *Quixote*"), which appeared in *Sur* in May, 1939. This story was followed in 1940 by "Tlön, Uqbar, Orbis Tertius" ("Tlön, Uqbar, Orbis Tertius") and the collection *El jardín de senderous que se bifurcan* (the garden of forking paths) in 1941. Six stories were added to the eight collected in *El jardín de senderos que se bifurcan*, and a new collection, entitled *Ficciones, 1935-1944*, one of the most important collections of short fiction in Latino literature, appeared in 1944. Another landmark collection, *El Aleph*, followed in 1949.

During this time, the height of his literary career up to this point, Borges, who was anti-Peronist, fell into disfavor with the government of Argentine president Juan Perón. He was dismissed from his position at the library in 1944 and appointed inspector of poultry and eggs in the municipal market. He resigned, but he did return to public service in 1955 when, following the fall of Perón, he was named the director of the National Library. Ironically, in the same year, he lost his sight, which had been declining for several years.

Despite the loss of his sight, Borges continued to write (through dictation), though less than before. At the same time, his two collections of stories from the 1940's had made him a household name among Latino literati. Worldwide recognition came in 1961, when he shared the Formentor Prize (worth ten thousand dollars) with Samuel Beckett. The fame that this award brought Borges changed his life. That fall, he traveled to the United States to lecture at the University of Texas, and between 1961 and his death in 1986, he would make numerous trips to the United States and elsewhere, teaching and speaking at colleges and universities, attending literary conferences on his works, collecting literary awards, and otherwise serving as an international ambassador for Latino literature.

Borges married for the first time (at age sixty-eight) in 1967, the same year that he accepted an invitation to teach at Harvard University as a Charles Eliot Norton lecturer. The marriage dissolved in 1970, with Borges, according to one popular anecdote, leaving the home he shared with his wife and taking only his prized *Encyclopædia Britannica* with him. Perón returned to the Argentine presidency in 1973, and Borges resigned as director of the National Library. His mother died at age ninety-nine in 1975.

Borges continued to write during the 1970's and until his death, working in short fiction, poetry, and the essay, having returned to these last two genres in the 1950's. The bulk of his fame, however, and particularly that specifically related to short fiction, had come from his two collections of stories from the 1940's. He was nominated repeatedly for the Nobel Prize in Literature but never won it. In 1986, he married his companion María Kodama and shortly thereafter died of cancer of the liver on June 14, 1986, in Geneva, Switzerland.

ANALYSIS

Jorge Luis Borges may be, quite simply, the single most important writer of short fiction in the history of Latino literature. The stories he published in his collections *Ficciones, 1935-1944* and *El Aleph*, particularly

the former, not only gave Latino (and world) literature a body of remarkable stories but also opened the door to a whole new type of fiction that would be practiced by the likes of the above-mentioned Julio Cortázar, Gabriel García Márquez, Carlos Fuentes, and Mario Vargas Llosa, and that, in the hands of these writers and others like them, would put Latino fiction on the world literary map in the 1960's.

Prior to Borges, and particularly between 1920 and 1940, Latino fiction, as stated previously, was concerned chiefly with painting a realistic and detailed picture of external Latino reality. Description frequently ruled over action, environment over character, and types over individuals. Social message, also, was often more important to the writer than was narrative artistry. Latino fiction after Borges (that is, after his landmark collections of stories of the 1940's) was decidedly different in that it was no longer documentary in nature, turned its focus toward the inner workings of its fully individualized human characters, presented various interpretations of reality, expressed universal as well as regional and national themes, invited reader participation, and emphasized the importance of artistic--and frequently unconventional--presentation of the story, particularly with respect to narrative voice, language, structure (and the closely related element of time), and characterization. This "new narrative," as it came to be called, would have been impossible without Borges's tradition-breaking fiction.

This is not to say that Borges's stories fully embody each of the characteristics of the Latino "new narrative" listed above. Ironically, they do not. Borges's characters are often far more archetypal than individual, his presentation tends to be for the most part quite traditional, and reader participation (at least as compared to that required in the works of other "new narrativists") is frequently not a factor. The major contributions that Borges made to Latino narrative through his stories lie, first, in his use of imagination, second, in his focus on universal themes common to all human beings, and third, in the intellectual aspect of his works. In the 1940's, Borges, unlike most who were writing so-called Latino fiction, treated fiction as fiction. Rather than use fiction to document everyday reality, Borges used it to invent new realities, to toy with philosophical concepts, and in the process to create truly fictional worlds, governed by their own rules. He also chose to write chiefly about universal human beings rather than exclusively about Latinos. His characters are, for example, European, or Chinese, frequently of no discernible nationality, and only occasionally Latino. In most cases, even when a character's nationality is revealed, it is of no real importance, particularly with respect to theme. Almost all Borges's characters are important not because of the country from which they come but because they are human beings, faced not with situations and conflicts particular to their nationality but with situations and conflicts common to all human beings. Finally, unlike his predecessors and many of his contemporaries, Borges did not aim his fiction at the masses. He wrote instead, it seems, more for himself, and, by extension, for the intellectual reader. These three aspects of his fiction--treating fiction as fiction, placing universal characters in universal conflicts, and writing for a more intellectual audience--stand as the Argentine writer's three most important contributions to Latino fiction in the latter half of the twentieth century, and to one degree or another, virtually every one of the Latino "new narrativists," from Cortázar to García Márquez, followed Borges's lead in these areas.

Given the above, it is no surprise that Borges's *ficciones* (his stories are more aptly called "fictions" than "stories," for while all fit emphatically into the first category because they contain fictitious elements, many do not fit nearly so well into a traditional definition of the second because they read more like essays than stories) are sophisticated, compact, even mathematically precise narratives that range in type from what might be called the "traditional" short story (a rarity) to fictionalized essay (neither pure story nor pure essay but instead a unique mix of the two, complete, oddly enough, with both fictitious characters and footnotes, both fictitious and factual) to detective story or spy thriller (though always with an unmistakably Borgesian touch) to fictional illustration of a philosophical concept (this last type being, perhaps, most common). Regardless of the specific category into which each story might fall, almost all, to one degree or another, touch on either what Borges viewed as the labyrinthine

nature of the universe, irony (particularly with respect to human destiny), the concept of time, the hubris of those who believe they know all there is to know, or any combination of these elements.

As stated above, most of Borges's fame as a writer of fiction and virtually all of his considerable influence on Latino "new narrative" are derived from his two masterpiece collections, *Ficciones, 1935-1944* and *El Aleph*. Of these two, the first stands out as the more important and may be the single most important collection of short fiction in the history of Latino literature.

Ficciones, 1935-1944 contains fourteen stories (seventeen for editions published after 1956). Seven of the fourteen were written between 1939 and 1941 and, along with an eighth story, were originally collected in *El jardín de senderos que se bifurcan* (the garden of forking paths). The other six stories were added in 1944. Virtually every story in this collection has become a Latino classic, and together they reveal the variety of Borges's themes and story types.

"DEATH AND THE COMPASS"

"La muerte y la brújula" ("Death and the Compass") is one of the most popular of the stories found in *Ficciones, 1935-1944*. In it, detective Erik Lönnrot is faced with the task of solving three apparent murders that have taken place exactly one month apart at locations that form a geographical equilateral triangle. The overly rational Lönnrot, through elaborate reasoning, divines when and where the next murder is to take place. He goes there to prevent the murder and to capture the murderer, only to find himself captured, having been lured to the scene by his archenemy, Red Scharlach, so that he, Lönnrot, can be killed.

This story is a perfect example of Borges's ability to take a standard subgenre, in this case the detective story, and give it his own personal signature, as the story is replete with Borgesian trademarks. The most prominent of these concerns irony and hubris. Following the first murder and published reports of Lönnrot's line of investigation, Scharlach, who has sworn to kill Lönnrot, constructs the remainder of the murder scenario, knowing that Lönnrot will not rest until he deciphers the apparent patterns and then--believing he knows, by virtue of his reasoning, all there is to know--will blindly show up at the right spot at the right time for Scharlach to capture and kill him. Ironically, Lönnrot's intelligence and his reliance (or over-reliance) on reasoning, accompanied in no small measure by his self-assurance and intellectual vanity, which blind him to any potential danger, bring him to his death. Other trademark Borgesian elements in the story include the totally non-Latino content (from characters to setting), numerous references to Jews and things Jewish (a talmudic congress, rabbis, and Cabalistic studies, to name only a few), and an intellectual content and ambience throughout not typical of the traditional detective story. (Lönnrot figures out, for example, that the four points that indicate the four apparent murders--there are really only three--correspond to the Tetragrammaton, the four Hebrew letters that make up "the ineffable name of God.")

"THE GARDEN OF FORKING PATHS"

"The Garden of Forking Paths" is another story from *Ficciones, 1935-1944* that in the most general sense (but only in the most general sense) fits comfortably into a traditional category, that of spy thriller, but like "Death and the Compass," in Borges's hands it is anything but a story typical of its particular subgenre. In this story, Dr. Yu Tsun (once again, a non-Latino character), a Chinese professor of English, working in England (a non-Latino setting as well) as a spy for the Germans during World War I, has been captured and now dictates his story. Yu tells of how he had needed to transmit vital information to the Germans concerning the name of the town in which the British were massing artillery in preparation for an attack. Yu's superior, however, had been captured, thus severing Yu's normal lines of communication. Identified as a spy and pursued by the British, Yu tells how he had selected, from the phone directory, the only man he believed could help him communicate his message, one Stephen Albert (though the reader at this point is not aware of exactly how Albert could be of help to Yu). Yu tells of how he traveled to Albert's house, hotly pursued by a British agent. Yu had never met Albert, but Albert mistook him for someone else and invited Yu into the house. The two talked for an hour about Chinese astrologer and writer Ts'ui Pêen (who happened to be one of Yu's ancestors) and Ts'ui's labyrinthine book *The Garden of Forking Paths* (which, given its content,

gives Borges's story a story-within-a-story element) as Yu stalled for time for the British agent to catch up with him. Yu says that as the agent approached the house, Yu killed Albert and then allowed himself to be captured by the agent. The final paragraph of the story reveals that Yu had chosen to kill Albert and then be arrested so that news of the incident would appear in the newspaper. He knew that his German colleagues would read the small news item and would divine Yu's intended message: that the British had been massing artillery near the French town of Albert--thus Yu's reason for having chosen Stephen Albert.

"THE CIRCULAR RUINS"

"Las ruinas circulares" ("The Circular Ruins") is one of a number of examples in *Ficciones, 1935-1944* of Borges's frequent practice of using a story to illustrate (or at least toy with) philosophical concepts, in this particular case, notably, the Gnostic concept of one creator behind another creator. In this story, a mysterious man travels to an equally mysterious place with the intention of creating another person by dreaming him. The man experiences great difficulty in this at first, but eventually he is successful. The man instructs his creation and then sends him off. Before he does, however, the man erases his creation's knowledge of how he came to be, for the man does not wish him to know that he exists only as the dream of another. Soon after the man's creation has left, fire breaks out and surrounds the man. He prepares for death, but as the flames begin to engulf him, he cannot feel them. He realizes then that he too, ironically, is but an illusion, not real at all but simply the dream of another.

"PIERRE MENARD, AUTHOR OF THE *QUIXOTE*"

"Pierre Menard, autor del *Quijote*" ("Pierre Menard, Author of the *Quixote*"), also from *Ficciones, 1935-1944*, is one of Borges's most famous stories that may be classified as a fictionalized essay, for it is clearly not a story: a fiction, yes, but a story (at least by any traditional definition of the term), no. In it, a pompous first-person narrator, a literary critic, in what is presented as an essay of literary criticism, tells of the writer Pierre Menard (fictional in the real world but completely real in Borges's fictive universe). After considerable discussion of Menard's bibliography (complete with titles and publication dates, all fictional but with titles of real literary journals--once again, an example of Borges's practice of fusing the fictive and the real), as well as other facts about the author, the critic discusses Menard's attempt to compose a contemporary version of Cervantes's *Don Quixote de la Mancha*. Menard accomplishes this not by writing a new *Don Quixote de la Mancha* but simply by copying Cervantes's original text word for word. The critic even examines identical passages from the two versions and declares that Menard's version, though identical to Cervantes's, is actually richer. The critic pursues the reasons and ramifications of this fact further. The result is, among other things, a tongue-in-cheek send-up of scholars and literary critics and the snobbish and often ridiculous criticism that they publish.

"THE SOUTH"

Finally, "El Sur" ("The South"), from *Ficciones, 1935-1944* as well, is a classic Borges story that demonstrates the author's ability to mix reality (at best a relative term in Borges's world and in Latino "new narrative" as a whole) with fantasy and, more important, to show that the line between the two is not only very subtle but also of no real importance, for fantasy is just as much a part of the universe as so-called reality. This story, which Borges once said he considered his best, concerns Johannes Dahlmann, a librarian in Buenos Aires. Dahlmann, the reader is told, has several heroic, military ancestors, and though he himself is a city-dwelling intellectual, he prefers to identify himself with his more romantic ancestors. In that spirit, Dahlmann even maintains a family ranch in the "South" (capitalized here and roughly the Argentine equivalent, in history and image, to North America's "Old West"). He is, however, an absentee landowner, spending all of his time in Buenos Aires, keeping the ranch only to maintain a connection, although a chiefly symbolic one, with his family's more exciting past. Entering his apartment one night, Dahlmann accidentally runs into a doorway (an accident very similar to that which Borges suffered in 1938). The resulting head injury develops into septicemia (as also was the case with Borges), and he is sent off to a sanatorium. Finally, he recovers well enough to travel, at his doctor's suggestion, to his ranch in the South to convalesce. His train trip to the South is vague to him at best, as he slips in and out of sleep. Unfamiliar with the region, he disembarks one stop too early and waits in a general store for transportation. While there, he is harassed by a group of ruffians. He accepts the challenge of one among them, and as the story ends, he is about to step outside for a knife fight he knows he cannot win.

If that were all there were to "The South," the story would be interesting, perhaps, but certainly nothing spectacular, and it would probably fit fairly comfortably into the type of Latino narrative popular before Borges. There is more, however, and it is this "more" that places the story firmly within the parameters of Latino "new narrative." The story is, in fact, the literary equivalent of an optical illusion. For those who can perceive only one angle, the story is essentially that described above. For those who can make out the other angle, however, the story is completely different. There are numerous subtle though undeniably present hints throughout the second half of the story, after Dahlmann supposedly leaves the sanatorium, that suggest that the protagonist does not step out to fight at the end of the story. In fact, he never even leaves the sanatorium at all but instead dies there. His trip to the South, his encounter with the ruffians, and his acceptance of their challenge, which will lead to certain death, are all nothing but a dream, dreamt, it seems, in the sanatorium, for death in a knife fight is the death that he, Dahlmann--the librarian who likes to identify himself with his heroic and romantic ancestors--would have preferred compared to that of the sanatorium. This added dimension, as well as the rather subtle manner in which it is suggested (an attentive reader is required), separates both the story and its author from the type of fiction and fiction writer that characterized Latino fiction before Borges. It is this type of added dimension that makes Borges's fiction "new" and makes him a truly fascinating writer to read.

Borges continued to write short fiction after *Ficciones, 1935-1944* and *El Aleph*, but the stories produced during this period never approached the popularity among readers nor the acclaim among critics associated with the two earlier collections. This is attributable in part to the fact that most of the stories the Argentine writer published in the 1960's, as well as the 1970's and 1980's, lack much of what makes Borges

Borges. Most are decidedly more realistic, often more Argentine in focus, and in general less complex--all in all, less Borgesian and, according to critics, less impressive. Some of this, particularly the change in complexity, has been explained as attributable to the fact that because of his loss of sight, Borges turned to dictation, which made reediting and polishing more difficult. Regardless of the reason, most of Borges's fiction after his two landmark collections of the 1940's has been largely ignored.

OTHER MAJOR WORKS

LONG FICTION: *Un modelo para la muerte*, 1946 (with Adolfo Bioy Casares, under joint pseudonym B. Suárez Lynch).

SCREENPLAYS: *"Los orilleros" y "El paraíso de los creyentes,"* 1955 (with Bioy Casares); *Les Autres*, 1974 (with Bioy Casares and Hugo Santiago).

POETRY: *Fervor de Buenos Aires*, 1923, 1969; *Luna de enfrente*, 1925; *Cuaderno San Martín*, 1929; *Poemas, 1923-1943*, 1943; *Poemas, 1923-1953*, 1954; *Obra poética, 1923-1964*, 1964; *Seis poemas escandinavos*, 1966; *Siete poemas*, 1967; *El otro, el mismo*, 1969; *Elogio de la sombra*, 1969 (*In Praise of Darkness*, 1974); *Para las seis cuerdas: milongas*, 1970 (illustrations by Héctor Basaldúa); *El oro de los tigres*, 1972 (translated in *The Gold of Tigers: Selected Later Poems*, 1977); *La rosa profunda*, 1975 (translated in *The Gold of Tigers*); *La moneda de hierro*, 1976; *Historia de la noche*, 1977; *Sonetos a Buenos Aires*, 1979; *Antologia poética, 1923-1977*, 1981; *La cifra*, 1981; *Los conjurados*, 1985; *Obra poética, 1923-1985*, 1989; *Selected Poems*, 1999; *Poems of the Night*, 2010 (Efrain Kristal, editor); *The Sonnets*, 2010 (Stephen Kessler, editor).

NONFICTION: *Inquisiciones*, 1925; *El tamaño de mi esperanza*, 1926; *El idioma de los argentinos*, 1928; *Evaristo Carriego*, 1930 (English translation, 1984); *Figari*, 1930; *Discusión*, 1932; *Las Kennigar*, 1933; *Historia de la eternidad*, 1936; *Nueva refutación del tiempo*, 1947; *Aspectos de la literatura gauchesca*, 1950; *Antiguas literaturas germánicas*, 1951 (with Delia Ingenieros; revised as *Literaturas germánicas medievales*, 1966, with Maria Esther Vásquez); *Otras Inquisiciones*, 1952 (*Other Inquisitions*, 1964); *El*

"Martin Fierro," 1953 (with Margarita Guerrero); *Leopoldo Lugones*, 1955 (with Betina Edelberg); *Manual de zoología fantástica*, 1957 (with Guerrero; *The Imaginary Zoo*, 1969; revised as *El libro de los seres imaginarios*, 1967, *The Book of Imaginary Beings*, 1969); *La poesía gauchesca*, 1960; *Introducción a la literatura norteamericana*, 1967 (with Esther Zemborain de Torres; *An Introduction to American Literature*, 1971); *Prólogos*, 1975; *¿Qué es el budismo?*, 1976 (with Alicia Jurado); *Cosmogonías*, 1976; *Libro de sueños*, 1976; *Siete noches*, 1980 (*Seven Nights*, 1984); *Nueve ensayos dantescos*, 1982; *This Craft of Verse*, 2000; *The Total Library: Non-Fiction, 1922-1986*, 2001 (Eliot Weinberger, editor).

TRANSLATIONS: *Orlando*, 1937 (of Virginia Woolf's novel); *La metamórfosis*, 1938 (of Franz Kafka's novel *Die Verwandlung*); *Un bárbaro en Asia*, 1941 (of Henri Michaux's travel notes); *Bartleby el escribiente*, 1943 (of Herman Melville's novella *Bartleby the Scrivener*); *Los mejores cuentos policiales*, 1943 (with Bioy Casares; of detective stories by various authors); *Los mejores cuentos policiales, segunda serie*, 1951 (with Bioy Casares; of detective stories by various authors); *Cuentos breves y extraordinarios*, 1955, 1973 (with Bioy Casares; of short stories by various authors; *Extraordinary Tales*, 1973); *Las palmeras salvajes*, 1956 (of William Faulkner's novel *The Wild Palms*); *Hojas de hierba*, 1969 (of Walt Whitman's *Leaves of Grass*).

EDITED TEXTS: *Antología clásica de la literatura argentina*, 1937; *Antología de la literatura fantástica*, 1940 (with Adolfo Bioy Casares and Silvia Ocampo); *Antología poética argentina*, 1941 (with Bioy Casares and Ocampo); *El compadrito: Su destino, sus barrios, su música*, 1945, 1968 (with Silvina Bullrich); *Poesía gauchesca*, 1955 (with Bioy Casares; 2 volumes); *Libro del cielo y del infierno*, 1960, 1975 (with Bioy Casares); *Versos*, 1972 (by Evaristo Carriego); *Antología poética*, 1982 (by Franciso de Quevedo); *Antología poética*, 1982 (by Leopoldo Lugones); *El amigo de la muerte*, 1984 (by Pedro Antonio de Alarcón).

MISCELLANEOUS: *Obras completas*, 1953-1967 (10 volumes); *El hacedor*, 1960 (*Dreamtigers*, 1964); *Antología personal*, 1961 (*A Personal Anthology*, 1967); *Labyrinths: Selected Stories, and Other Writings*,

1962, 1964; *Nueva antología personal*, 1968; *Selected Poems, 1923-1967*, 1972 (also includes prose); *Adrogue*, 1977; *Obras completas en colaboración*, 1979 (with others); *Borges: A Reader*, 1981; *Atlas*, 1984 (with María Kodama; English translation, 1985).

BIBLIOGRAPHY

Bell-Villada, Gene H. *Borges and His Fiction: A Guide to His Mind and Art*. Chapel Hill: University of North Carolina Press, 1981. An excellent introduction to Borges and his works for North American readers. In lengthy sections entitled "Borges's Worlds," "Borges's Fiction," and "Borges's Place in Literature," Bell-Villada provides detailed and very readable commentary concerning Borges's background, his many stories, and his career, all the while downplaying the Argentine writer's role as a philosopher and intellectual and emphasizing his role as a storyteller. A superb study.

Boldy, Steven. *A Companion to Jorge Luis Borges*. Rochester, N.Y.: Tamesis, 2009. Focuses on Borges's short stories from the 1940's and 1950's, particularly those collected in *Ficciones, 1935-1944* and *El Aleph*, which Boldy considers the Argentine writer's most significant works. Analyzes the short stories of this period text by text, charts Borges's intellectual development, and places his work in the wider context of Argentine literature.

Butler, Rex. *Borges's Short Stories: A Reader's Guide*. New York: Continuum, 2010. Analyzes ten of Borges's short stories, examines his narrative strategies, and sets his work within wider literary, cultural, and intellectual contexts.

Christ, Ronald. *The Narrow Art: Borges' Art of Allusion*. New York: New York University Press, 1969. An important study of how Borges relinquishes circumstantial reality to reach the primordial world of myth. For Borges, the fantastic is not characteristic of another world but rather is the covert essence of this world. Shows how Borges's fiction is intertextually related to the mythic, fantastic, and literary tradition.

Frisch, Mark F. *You Might Be Able to Get There from Here: Reconsidering Borges and the Postmodern*. Madison, N.J.: Fairleigh Dickinson University Press, 2004. Careful study of the meaning of the term "postmodernism" in relation to Borges and his fiction, describing how the symbols, techniques, parody, irony, and ambiguity in his writings force readers to question what they can know with certainty.

Harss, Luis, and Barbara Dohmann. "Jorge Luis Borges: Or, The Consolation by Philosophy." In *Into the Mainstream: Conversations with Latin American Writers*. New York: Harper & Row, 1967. This piece combines and intertwines personal biography, literary biography, critical commentary, and interview to produce a multifaceted look at Borges's life, his works, and his philosophical beliefs, and, most of all, how his philosophical beliefs are reflected in both his poetry and, more so here, his prose. A classic piece of the body of criticism written on Borges in spite of its publication date.

McMurray, George R. *Jorge Luis Borges*. New York: Frederick Ungar, 1980. Intended by the author as "an attempt to decipher the formal and thematic aspects of a synthetic universe that rivals reality in its almost overwhelming complexity," namely, Borges's universe. An incisive and well-organized study of Borges's dominant themes and narrative devices, with many specific references to the Argentine author's stories. Includes an informative introduction on Borges's life and a conclusion that coherently brings together the diverse elements discussed in the book.

Nunez-Faraco, Humberto. "In Search of *The Aleph*: Memory, Truth, and Falsehood in Borges's Poetics." *The Modern Language Review* 92 (July, 1997): 613-629. Discusses autobiographical allusions, literary references to Dante, and cultural reality in *The Aleph*. Argues that Borges's story uses cunning and deception to bring about its psychological and intellectual effect.

Rodríguez Monegal, Emir. *Jorge Luis Borges: A Literary Biography*. New York: E. P. Dutton, 1978. A biography of Borges by one of the Argentine writer's (and contemporary Latin American literature's) most prominent critics. Particularly interesting for its constant blending of facts about Borges's life and literary text by him concerning or related to the events or personalities discussed. Detailed, lengthy, and highly informative; useful for anyone seeking a better understanding of Borges the writer.

Soud, Stephen E. "Borges the Golem-Maker: Intimations of 'Presence' in 'The Circular Ruins.'" *MLN* 110 (September, 1995): 739-754. Argues that Borges uses the legend of the golem to establish authorial presence in the story. Maintains that Borges did not seek to deconstruct literature but to "re-sacralize" it and to salvage the power of the logos, the Divine Word.

Stabb, Martin S. *Borges Revisited*. Boston: Twayne, 1991. An update of Stabb's *Jorge Luis Borges*, published in 1970 and listed below. Though Borges's early works, including those from the 1940's and 1950's, are discussed and analyzed here, the emphasis is on his post-1970 writings, how the "canonical" (to use Stabb's term) Borges compares to the later Borges, and "a fresh assessment of the Argentine master's position as a major Western literary presence."

_____. *Jorge Luis Borges*. New York: Twayne, 1970. An excellent study of Borges intended by its author "to introduce the work of this fascinating and complex writer to North American readers." Includes an opening chapter on Borges's life and career, followed by chapters on the Argentine writer's work in the genres of poetry, essay, and fiction, as well as a concluding chapter entitled "Borges and the Critics." A superb and very readable introduction to all aspects of Borges's literary production through 1968; particularly useful when read in tandem with Stabb's 1991 revision.

Wheelock, Carter. *The Mythmaker: A Study of Motif and Symbol in the Short Stories of Jorge Luis Borges*. Austin: University of Texas Press, 1969. Argues that Borges has a superb conceptual grasp of mythic reality as described by anthropologists and philosophers Mircea Eliade, Ernst Cassirer, and Sir James Frazier. Discusses Borges's stories as allegories of the construction of metaphor, the imaginative apprehension of reality, and the nature of thought.

Williamson, Edwin. *Borges: A Life*. New York: Viking, 2004. Drawing on interviews and extensive research, Williamson provides a comprehensive and well-reviewed Borges biography.

Wreen, Michael J. "Don Quixote Rides Again." *Romanic Review* 86 (January, 1995): 141-163. Argues that Pierre Menard is not the new Miguel de Cervantes in Borges's story "Pierre Menard, Author of the *Quixote*," but rather the new Quixote. Asserts that in the story Borges pokes fun at himself and that a proper interpretation of the story requires readers to understand that Menard's *Quixote* is simply Cervantes's Quixote, although Menard thinks it is a new and important work.

Zubizarreta, Armando F. "'Borges and I,' a Narrative Sleight of Hand." *Studies in Twentieth Century Literature* 22 (Summer, 1998): 371-381. Argues that the two characters in the sketch are involved in the implementation of vengeance. Maintains that the character Borges, driven by a compulsive pattern of stealing, unsuspectingly takes over the I character's grievances against him through his own writing.

Keith H. Brower

IVAN BUNIN

Born: Voronezh, Russia; October 22, 1870
Died: Paris, France; November 8, 1953

PRINCIPAL SHORT FICTION

"Na kray sveta" i drugiye rasskazy, 1897
Pereval: Rasskazy, 1892-1902, 1912
Sukhodol: Povesti i rasskazy, 1911-1912, 1912
Sukhodol, 1912 (novella; *Dry Valley,* 1935)
Izbrannyye rasskazy, 1914
Zolotoye dno: Rasskazy, 1903-1907, 1914
Chasha zhizni: Rasskazy, 1913-1914, 1915
The Gentleman from DSan Francisco, and Other Stories, 1922
The Dreams of Chang, and Other Stories, 1923
Fifteen Tales, 1924
Mitina lyubov', 1925 (novella; *Mitya's Love,* 1926)
Sny Changa: Izbrannyye rasskazy, 1927
Delo korneta Yelagina, 1927 (*The Elaghin Affair,* 1935)
Grammatika lyubvi: Izbrannyye rasskazy, 1929 (*The Grammar of Love,* 1934)
The Elaghin Affair, and Other Stories, 1935
Tyomnyye allei, 1943, 1946 (*Dark Avenues, and Other Stories,* 1949)
Petlistyye ushi i drugiye rasskazy, 1954
Rasskazy, 1955
The Gentleman from San Francisco, and Other Stories, 1975
In a Far Distant Land: Selected Stories, 1983
Sunstroke: Selected Stories of Ivan Bunin, 2002
The Elagin Affair, and Other Stories, 2005
Night of Denial: Stories and Novellas, 2006

OTHER LITERARY FORMS

In addition to more than one hundred short stories, Ivan Bunin (BEWN-yihn) published in his sixty-six-year writing career several books of poetry, novels, memoirs, essays, travelogues, and translations. His collected and selected works have been published several times.

ACHIEVEMENTS

Ivan Bunin came on the literary scene in the 1890's, after the so-called Golden Age of Russian literature, dominated by the straightforward, realistic approach. Along with Maxim Gorky, Leonid Andreyev, and others, he wrote in the neorealistic vein, for which his poetically tinged prose was well suited. With his short stories, novels, and, to a lesser degree, poetry, he upheld the high standards of Russian literature as the world came to know it. It was therefore fitting that he would be the first Russian writer to receive the Nobel Prize, as "the incomparable painter of the vast and rich beauty of the Russian land." Despite his enmity toward the regime in the Soviet Union, his collected works have been published there twice posthumously (1956 and 1965-1967), and in 1973 two volumes of *Literaturnoe nasledstvo* (literary inheritance) were devoted to him.

BIOGRAPHY

Ivan Alexeyevich Bunin was born on October 22, 1870, in the central Russian town of Voronezh, in a cultured but impoverished family of landowning gentry. He grew up in rural Russia, and his love and understanding of it enabled him to write about the countryside with authority. He left school at the age of fifteen and never finished his formal education. He started writing and contributing to leading literary journals at an early age. His first book of poems was published in 1891 and his first collection of short stories in 1897. Bunin developed a yen for traveling and in 1900 began visiting many countries in Asia, Africa, and Europe, especially those along the Mediterranean. Many stories that came out of these travels were enriched by a peculiar exotic flavor. He was recognized early as one of the leading young writers in Russia, a reputation that remained relatively constant throughout his life. In fact, Gorky considered him in 1911 to be "the best contemporary writer."

The turning point in Bunin's life came during the revolution. Opposed to the Bolsheviks, he took part in the campaign against them, survived eight months of their rule, and in 1920 emigrated rather than live under them. After a brief stay in several countries, he settled in Paris in 1920, continuing to fight against the Bolsheviks. He also resumed his writing and published some of his best works. In 1933, he reached the pinnacle of his literary career as he received the Nobel Prize. As time passed, however, he withdrew increasingly from public life, cutting ties with fellow émigrés and living in poverty. During World War II, yearning for his homeland, he rooted for the victory of the Soviet Union over its enemies, yet he refused to return afterward. He died in Paris on November 8, 1953, in poverty but writing to the very end.

Ivan Bunin (©The Nobel Foundation)

ANALYSIS

Ivan Bunin wrote poetry, novels, and literary essays, but it was in short fiction that he was most successful. His stories employ a wide range of themes, but he returned to three themes time and again: the life of landed gentry and peasantry, love, and death. There are many other themes and subthemes, but those mentioned above constitute the main features of Bunin's profile as a writer.

In his early stories and novels, Bunin showed great interest in the fate of the landed gentry and peasantry and in their role in the society. His first novel, *Derevnya* (1910; *The Village*, 1923), depicts the anarchy, squalor, and drunkenness in Russian villages and the bleak prospects for the future. It is the gloomiest of Bunin's works. He continued in the same vein in his novella *Dry Valley*, which is quite naturalistic in tone. With its meager plot, its story is more of a chronicle of decay, moral degradation, spiritual emptiness, and even physical degeneration of the gentry and the peasants, both driven by irrational forces and equally doomed. The story also represents the author's vain attempt to recapture the glory of the old days, of the *temps perdu* of Russian rural life. In this

sense, *Dry Valley* is a statement of Bunin's social philosophy of sorts and a revelation of his thinking about the state of both the gentry and the peasantry. His artistic acumen, especially the verbal mastery, lifts the story above the level of social tract, however, exemplified by the symbolism of the peasants dredging ponds in the bed of a river that has dried out.

Dry Valley is not the only work about the decay of Russian rural life. Stories such as "Nochnoi razgovor" ("A Nocturnal Conversation"), "Ermil," "Ignat," and "Vesennii vecher" ("A Spring Evening"), show similar features. A series of "mood paintings," "Antonovskie iabloki" ("Antonov's Apples"), more than any other story, conjures the nostalgic atmosphere of Bunin's world.

To be sure, not all the stories paint such bleak pictures of Russian life. Stories such as "Sverchok" ("Cricket") and "Veselyi dvor" ("A Gay Farmhouse") show that the peasants are capable of selfless love and that they possess spiritual values that might help them regenerate themselves. Still, the predominant effect in Bunin's early stories is bleakness and despair.

To escape such an atmosphere, Bunin undertook between 1900 and 1917 several journeys to the Mediterranean, the Middle East, and the Far East, out of which came some of his best stories: "Brat'ia" ("Brethren"), "Sny Changa" ("The Dreams of Chang"), "Syn" ("The Son"), and "Gospodin iz San Frantsisko" ("The Gentleman from San Francisco"). The changed mood of these stories, buoyed by the abundant life and exotic settings, could not fully repress Bunin's pessimistic outlook, but it sublimated it to artistic perfection. The stories with Asian settings manifest also his interest in the Buddhist tenet that suffering results from desire and that peace comes only when desire ceases.

For Bunin, love is one of the primary manifestations of human experience. He shows different types of love--love for the opposite sex, for one's family, and for other human beings--and various reactions to love. There is one constant in all these relationships: Love is basically an unhappy, even tragic experience. In "Brethren," for example, the father of the family, in his love and care for his dear ones, "was moved by earthly love, by that which, from the start of time, summons all creatures into being." This love, however, also multiplies his earthly sorrows. His beloved son, upon finding out that the woman he loved had betrayed him and run away to the city where she was giving pleasure to other men, allows a poisonous snake to bite him to death. A sudden death of a beloved woman in "Grammatika liubvi" ("Grammar of Love") forces her lover into total seclusion and degeneration because he is unable to cope with her death. In his virtual paralysis, all he hears and sees reminds him of her as he realizes that memories are all that is left to him. A young couple in the story "Meteor" ("Meteor") experiences only thirty minutes of amorous bliss before the inevitable return to harsh reality. In "Solnechny udar" ("Sunstroke"), a brief night of bliss is replaced by forlorn agony and despair after the parting. Thus, even though Bunin allows for the possibility of a true love, it almost invariably ends in unhappiness.

It is a harsh reality that dooms all these loves to unhappy endings. The presence of animalistic passion also contributes to degradation and eventual failure of erstwhile promising love relationships. A prince in "Gautami" takes advantage of a local beauty, who

mistakes his passion for sincere love; when a child is born, he spurns her, relegating her to a distant corner on his estate. A young woman in "Lyogkoe dukhanie" ("Light Breathing") seduces an older man and promises to marry him, only to be murdered by him when she reneges. A tragic passion here is derived from both love and hatred. Ignat, a character in the story by the same title, resigns himself to a life with a half-witted woman because his love for his former wife was unfulfilled. He turns into a cruel man, capable of extreme violence. In perhaps the most dramatic illustration of love feelings gone astray, Mme Marot in "The Son" attempts to compensate for the vanished love of her husband with a love for her friend's young son, the physical consummation of which leads her to suicide and him to severe depression. Finally, in "Tyomnye allei" ("Dark Paths"), a man chances upon the woman he had abandoned long ago and realizes belatedly that he has squandered the opportunity for happiness. In all these stories, Bunin shows that unhappiness in love, no matter what the cause, changes the characters from sincere, well-meaning persons into bearers of unhappiness and tragedy.

The preponderance of such pessimistic attitudes toward love does not mean that Bunin denies the sublime nature of pure love and its fulfillment. Even in the death throes of the son in "Brethren," Bunin admits to "that ultimate, all-embracing thing that is called love, the yearning to encompass within one's heart all the universe, seen and unseen, and to bestow it anew upon some other." When pure, sincere love ceases to exist, be it because of harsh reality, impure passion, misunderstanding, or missed opportunity, unhappiness and sorrow invariably result, leading to degeneration. Thus, Bunin's lovers are capable of experiencing only fleeting moments of love. Bunin cannot seem to free himself from a belief that "all the torments of this universe, where everyone is either a slayer or slain, that all its sorrows and plaints, come from love."

"THE GENTLEMAN FROM SAN FRANCISCO"

The theme of death also plays a prominent--perhaps the most prominent--role in Bunin's opus. It is present in many stories, either as a primary objective or as a by-product. Nowhere is this theme more sharply focused than in his best story, "The Gentleman from San

Francisco." It is a tale of a fifty-eight-year-old American millionaire who has worked hard all of his life and is now making a trip around the world with his unmarried daughter, in a belated attempt to make up for all the enjoyment that he has missed. They make a stop at Capri, the isle of beauty and joy, and while there, he is fatally stricken by a heart attack. The same ship that brought him to Capri takes him back home. The simple plot is fraught with philosophical and symbolic meanings. No one on the ship or at Capri remembered his name (he was known simply as the gentleman from San Francisco), as though he represented all humankind, making the story a morality play with the Everyman theme. There is an irony in the fact that, just as he was ready to enjoy the fruits of his labor for the first time, he meets death. The covert philosophical overtones compel the reader to think about the true meaning of life, and the horror of the gentleman's loneliness at the time of death, despite his daughter's presence, makes the thinking even more poignant. The transience of life devoid of a spiritual meaning is underscored by the sight of the casket in the boiler room of the ship, while on the way to Capri the gentleman enjoyed the journey on the deck.

A comparison with Leo Tolstoy's *Smert' Ivana Il'icha* (1886; *The Death of Ivan Ilyich*, 1887) imposes itself. Although the basic premises are the same, the difference lies in the approach to the principle of life and death. While Tolstoy muses over the moral question of death, Bunin refrains from overt philosophizing and from analyzing his characters beyond the artistic framework. He is interested primarily in the physical aspect of things and the emotional responses that they provoke. The Marxist interpretation of the story is even more out of place, for the fact that the gentleman is an American millionaire is a sheer coincidence; he could have been anyone else and the moral of the story would have been the same.

Death is depicted in many other stories, each time with a slightly different emphasis. In "Chasha zhizni" ("The Cup of Life"), death reveals the darker side of human nature. In "Petlistye ushi" ("Gnarled Ears"), it is tied directly to crime, and in "A Nocturnal Conversation," it comes as veritable horror visits upon the characters. Death is also often connected with love in

Bunin's novellas, as in *Mitya's Love*, where death comes from unrequited love, and in *The Elaghin Affair*, where death is caused by jealousy. No matter what the reason is, Bunin's fascination with death is matched only by his preoccupation with the theme of love.

Among the chief characteristics of Bunin's style are economy of expression and full-bodied texture; a fine attention to detail; a leisurely pace and slow plot development; irony and understatement; "physical lyricism," rich imagery, and mood evocation; and a "classical," pure, precise, and concrete language. All these characteristics have made him one of the best writers in Russian literature.

OTHER MAJOR WORKS

LONG FICTION: *Derevnya*, 1910 (*The Village*, 1923); *Zhizn Arsenyeva: Istoki dney*, 1930 (*The Well of Days*, 1933); *Zhizn Arsenyeva*, 1939 (includes *Zhizn Arsenyeva: Istoki dney* and *Lika*; *The Life of Arseniev: Youth*, 1994).

POETRY: *Stikhotvoreniya, 1887-1891*, 1891; *Pod otkrytym nebom: Stikhotvoreniya*, 1898; *Listopad: Stikhotvoreniya*, 1901; *Stikhotvoreniya*, 1912; *Izbrannyye stikhi, 1900-1925*, 1929; *Stikhotvoreniya*, 1961.

NONFICTION: *Okayannyye dni*, 1935 (*Cursed Days: A Diary of Revolution*, 1998); *Osvobozhdeniye Tolstogo*, 1937 (*The Liberation of Tolstoy: A Tale of Two Writers*, 2001); *Vospominaniya*, 1950 (*Memories and Portraits*, 1951); *O Chekhove: Nezakonchennaya rukopis'*, 1955 (*About Chekhov: The Unfinished Symphony*, 2007); *Pos serpom i molotom*, 1975; *Ustami Buninykh*, 1977-1982 (3 volumes).

MISCELLANEOUS: *Stikhi i rasskazy*, 1900; *Sobraniye sochineniy*, 1902-1909 (5 volumes); *Rasskazy i stikhotvoreniya, 1907-1910*, 1912; *Sukhodol: Povesti i rasskazy, 1911-1912*, 1912; *Ioann Rydalets: Rasskazy i stikhi, 1912-1913*, 1913; *Polnoye sobraniye sochineniy*, 1915 (6 volumes); *Gospodin iz San Frantsisko: Proizvedeniya, 1915-1916*, 1916; *Sobraniye sochineniy*, 1934-1939 (12 volumes); *Sobraniye sochineniy*, 1956 (5 volumes); *Sobraniye sochineniy*, 1965-1967 (9 volumes); *Sochineniya*, 1982 (3 volumes).

BIBLIOGRAPHY

Bayley, John. "The Backward Look." *The New York Review of Books* 42 (August 10, 1995): 31-33. Notes that Bunin expressed a genuine Russian sympathy and versatility in his writing. Calls him a master of a detailed and pitiless realism, which he applied to the backwardness and barbarity of provincial Russia. Provides a biographical background to Bunin's writing.

Connolly, Julian W. *Ivan Bunin.* Boston: Twayne, 1982. An introduction to Bunin's art for the general reader, focusing on his primary ideological positions and charting his evolution as a writer. The study includes a brief biographical sketch but is primarily organized around thematic discussions of Bunin's major prose works in chronological order.

Cravens, Gwyneth. "Past Present." *The Nation* 256 (February 8, 1993): 173-174. Claims Bunin's short stories are marked by acute and objective observations, surprising details caught by his artist's eye, and a crystalline style. Notes that Bunin focused on the enigmas of nature, love, death, and the soul with a passion that would be unique among contemporary authors. Discusses several of his works.

Gross, S. L. "Nature, Man, and God in Bunin's 'The Gentleman from San Francisco.'" *Modern Fiction Studies* 6, no. 2 (1960): 153-163. A perceptive analysis of "The Gentleman from San Francisco," focusing on its alleged pessimistic outlook. Gross takes exception to those critics who see it as a prevalently pessimistic story and counters with the image of two pipers from Abruzzi offering the vision of grace.

Karshan, Thomas. "Between Tolstoy and Nabokov: Ivan Bunin Revisited." *Modernism/Modernity* 14, no. 4 (November, 2007): 763-769. A lengthy review of two collections of Bunin's short fiction: *The Elagin Affair, and Other Stories* (2005), translated by Graham Hettlinger,and *Night of Denial: Stories and Novellas* (2006), translated by Robert Bowie.

Kryzytski, Serge. *The Works of Ivan Bunin.* The Hague: Mouton, 1971. In this standard work on Bunin, Kryzytski combines biographical and critical approaches. He follows Bunin's career chronologically, commenting on each important work and its themes, influences, and overall significance. This valuable book concludes with a good bibliography.

Marullo, Thomas Gaiton. "Crime Without Punishment: Ivan Bunin's 'Loopy Ears.'" *Slavic Review* 40, no. 4 (1981): 614-624. Marullo compares "Loopy Ears" with *Crime and Punishment* of Fyodor Dostoevski, to whose works Bunin had a strong aversion. Sokolovsky of "Loopy Ears" experiences neither recrimination nor remorse for his crime. Marullo does not see Bunin as being in the "classical" tradition of Russian literature but as redirecting the Russian short story from the urban realism of the nineteenth century to the modernistic probing of the twentieth.

_____. *If You See the Buddha: Studies in the Fiction of Ivan Bunin.* Evanston, Ill.: Northwestern University Press, 1998. Part of the Studies in Russian Literature and Theory series, this is a perceptive examination of Bunin's works. Includes bibliographical references and an index.

_____. *Ivan Bunin, from the Other Shore, 1920-1933: A Portrait from Letters, Diaries, and Fiction.* Chicago: Ivan R. Dee, 1995.

_____, ed. *Ivan Bunin, Russian Requiem, 1885-1920: A Portrait from Letters, Diaries, and Fiction.* Chicago: Ivan R. Dee, 1993.

_____. *Ivan Bunin, the Twilight of Emigré Russia, 1934-1953: A Portrait from Letters, Diaries, and Memoirs.* Chicago: Ivan R. Dee, 2002. Three-volume biography, in which Marullo has interwoven excerpts from Bunin's letters, diaries, and fiction; the writings of family, friends, and critics; and recollections of Bunin's wife to create a detailed portrait of the Russian writer.

Minot, Susan. "Ivan Bunin." *The Paris Review* 37 (Winter, 1995): 152-153. A brief discussion of Bunin by a noted short-story writer, praising Bunin's short stories and commenting on his life and writing. Asserts that Bunin's memoir of his friend Anton Chekhov is the most elegant tribute one writer has ever written about another.

Reeve, F. D. "The Achievement of Ivan Bunin." *Sewanee Review* 116, no. 4 (Fall, 2008): 654-660. In his review of a collection of Bunin's short stories, Reeve provides his opinions of Bunin's writing ability, analyzes Bunin's creation of plot and theme, and comments on Bunin's literary achievement.

Struve, Gleb. "The Art of Ivan Bunin." *Slavonic and East European Review* 11, no. 32 (1933): 423-436. In this excellent introductory essay on Bunin, Struve, an expert on emigré Russian literature and a translator of Bunin's work, offers a cogent chronological analysis of the author's works, summarizing his most important features. Written two decades before Bunin's death, the essay could not assess his later works.

Vygotsky, Lev. "Bunin's 'Gentle Breath.'" In *The Russian Twentieth-Century Short Story: A Critical Companion*, edited by Lyudmila Parts. Brighton, Mass.: Academic Studies Press, 2010. Provides a critical reading of this story.

Woodward, James B. *Ivan Bunin: A Study of His Fiction*. Chapel Hill: University of North Carolina Press, 1980. As the name implies, this study has a specific aim and scope, yet it is very thorough and scholarly; in fact, it is the most detailed and comprehensive study of Bunin's fiction. Woodward treats all important aspects of Bunin's fiction chronologically, combining critical examination and description and reevaluating earlier judgments on Bunin, which may be the book's most salient feature. An extensive bibliography and a thorough index make this book useful.

Vasa D. Mihailovich

C

ALEJO CARPENTIER

Born: Havana, Cuba; December 26, 1904
Died: Paris, France; April 24, 1980

PRINCIPAL SHORT FICTION

Guerra del tiempo, 1958 (*War of Time,* 1970)

OTHER LITERARY FORMS

In contact with avant-garde groups in Havana and Paris, Alejo Carpentier (ah-LAY-ho kahr-pehn-TYAYR) wrote poetry as well as opera libretti and texts for other theatrical enterprises in his early years. Involved in publishing, broadcasting, and film for virtually all his life, he contributed hundreds of articles of criticism on literature and the fine arts, especially music, some of which have been republished in book form. He is best known for his novels, which have been widely translated and studied.

ACHIEVEMENTS

Considered a pioneer and a continuing advocate of the New Novel in Latin America, Alejo Carpentier contributed a steady stream of fiction from the early 1930's until his death in 1980. His wide scope of interests, which range from politics and botany to the mythology and music of primitive Native American civilizations, is evident in his highly complex novels.

In his famous and influential essay, "De lo real maravilloso americano" (1962; "On the Marvelous Reality of America"), which grew out of the prologue to his novel *El reino de este mundo* (1949; *The Kingdom of This World,* 1957), Carpentier provides an alternative to the realistic "nativismo" style then popular in Latin American fiction and describes his theory of the quality of Latin American literature, which depicts a reality infused with magic and myth. In 1977, he was awarded the Cervantes Prize for literature by the Royal Academy of Spain.

BIOGRAPHY

Alejo Valmont Carpentier, the son of French and Russian parents, was educated in France, as well as Cuba, studying architecture and music. A journalist during the 1920's, he became fascinated with Afro-Cuban culture, publishing his first novel, which dealt with this theme, shortly after being exiled for political activities. During the 1930's he moved among avant-garde coteries in Paris, including the Surrealists, although he later rejected doctrinaire Surrealism. His re-encounter in 1939 with the Caribbean--Venezuela, Mexico, and Haiti--initiated his finest years of literary production. In 1959, he began serving the government of Fidel Castro in a wide assortment of cultural offices, and he was without question the most prestigious Cuban to lend it such support. Carpentier died in Paris, France, on April 24, 1980.

ANALYSIS

Alejo Carpentier's "Semejante a la noche" ("Like the Night") is indicative of one of the prominent alternatives for sociological literature in the mid-twentieth century, an alternative that has had an enormous impact on the so-called new Latin American narrative. This is a mode of writing that is depersonalized, structurally geometric, and virtually allegorical in its thematic otherness. Unlike the social realism of the 1930's and 1940's in Latin America that shared with American and European counterparts a sentimentality and idealization that often bordered on kitsch and the trite, the committed literature represented by Carpentier's stories aspires, by eschewing all rhetoric of empathy, to a Brechtian intellectual and analytical contemplation. The goal may be to prevent contaminating the object'--the verbal message and its sociopolitically definable meaning--with trivial emotional responses, but the artistic effect is equally to render ostensible "propositional" meaning less transparent and to increase the density of the symbolic texture. In short, fiction like Carpentier's, as properly ideological as it may be, is more complex and, therefore, less assimilable to reductionary meanings than are its ancestors in a literature of sociopolitical commitment.

"LIKE THE NIGHT"

"Like the Night" deals with the oppressively ideological myths of war. Three separate time frames and three separate nuclei of incident and event are seamlessly worked together to project a holistic image of war as an enterprise that engulfs a certain class of young men in convenient commonplaces concerning adventure, ennobling sacrifice, and righteous strife. Men subscribe to these ideological myths in a gesture of unconscious self-betrayal to the interests of power structures that use war not only as a means of conquest and subjugation but also as an instrument for self-serving lies that provide the masses with a unifying and "noble" cause.

The three time frames are the Trojan War, the Spanish Conquest, and the French conquest of the New World. In each case, an innocent youth

Alejo Carpentier (Getty Images)

prepares to embark by ship on an adventure that has been justified for him by his superiors. In each case, the explanation of the just cause is an ideological cliché that the reader associates with the particular culture at issue. "I breathe in deeply the breeze that came down from the olive tree groves, thinking how beautiful it would be to die in such a just cause, in the very cause of reason." These are the words of the young Trojan warrior. The Spanish sailor thinks:

> They were millions of souls that we would win for our holy religion, thereby fulfilling Christ's mandate to his Apostles. We were soldiers of God at the same time we were soldiers of the king, and through those Indians baptized and claimed, freed of their barbarous superstitions by our work, our nation would know the prize of an unbreakable greatness that would give us happiness, riches and power over all of the kingdoms of Europe.

Finally, the French legionnaire claims:

> We were going to carry out a great civilizing task in those immense wooded territories that extended from the burning Gulf of Mexico to the regions of Chicagúa, teaching new skills to the nations that lived there.

In each case the youth utters these self-serving commonplaces of an imperialistic ideology as he takes leave of a familiar and comforting personal reality: the familiar sounds and smells of his hometown, his betrothed.

Thus, from a semiological point of view, the four segments of the story (one for each of the three settings; the last returns to close the cyclical pattern) arrange an opposition for the reader, in the persons of a series of innocent and uncritical youths, between familiar and comforting knowns and the threatening unknowns of exploration, war, and conquest explained and given importance by patriotic slogans. To be sure, the story depends on the reader's accepting for himself a greater perceptivity than that of the three overlapping narrators. That is, it is the reader who must realize that the thoughts of the youths that so stir their minds and hearts are so many political bromides by which governments seek to ennoble the ignoble slaughter and subjugation of their military campaigns.

The cyclical nature of the narrative is an important ingredient in the rhetorical demand for such a perception on the part of the reader. In the first place, the contemporary reader--aware (thanks to historical interpretations and popular legends) that the three campaigns described by Carpentier's story were not the heroic gests that the protagonists believed them to be--is asked to perceive the thoughts of the youths as ideological clichés. In the second place, the repetition of a nucleus of narration--the preparations for a heroic adventure, the excitement of the hustle and bustle, the heightened emotions, and the patriotic claims for the adventure--in a variety of times and places serves to suggest, rather than its unique transcendence, its quality as commonplace.

This dual semiological strategy--the appeal to the reader's cultural knowledge and the repetition of a commonplace--is enhanced by what in the original Spanish is a subtle linguistic parody. If readers recognize the key thoughts of the one-in-three narrators as political commonplaces, they also recognize the texture of the three first-person narrations as kitschy recreations of the expressive style of the different periods and cultures. Thus, the text of the Trojan has a neutral "Attic" quality that stresses, in a way reminiscent of passages of Homer, the cumulative details of epic campaigns. The text of the Spanish youth abounds in the archaisms of fifteenth century Spanish, in the pithy and earthy proverbs of the peasant, and in references to the clamorous sounds and pungent smells of late-medieval Mediterranean locales. By contrast, the text of the French warrior is characterized by the *sermo gravis*, the measured periods, and the self-sufficient cultural superiority characteristic of French classicism; it is also the longest of the three narrations.

In order to confirm the demythificational, anti-ideological reading suggested to the reader by the three strategies mentioned, the conclusion is "revisionist" in that the Trojan narrator, to whom Carpentier returns in the fourth and final segment, suffers a moment of sudden critical reflection:

Now it would be the bugles, the mud, the wet bread, the arrogance of the chiefs, the blood spilled in error, the gangrene smelling of infected syrups. I was no longer so sure that my courage would increase the greatness and fortunes of the long-haired Achaeans. An older soldier going off to war as a job, with no more enthusiasm than the shearer of sheep heading for the stables, was telling anyone who cared to listen how Helen of Sparta was very happy in Troy and how when she lay with Paris her groans of pleasure reddened the cheeks of the virgins who dwell in Priamos's palace. It was said that the whole story of the sad captivity of Leda's daughter, offended and humiliated by the Trojans, was merely the propaganda of war, spread by Agamemnon with Menelaus' consent.

Thus Carpentier ensures his reader's "proper reading" of the separate but overlapping narrations. Carpentier's rhetoric strategies are not simply a clever artistic device for structural originality, although whatever aesthetic reaction that may derive from contemplating the neatness of the meshing narrations is certainly a legitimate response to the story. Rather, these strategies are elements in an overall narrative configuration in which Carpentier's story is in semiologically productive clash with the stories of the narrator participants. This irony vanishes suddenly in the closure of the text, when the naïveté of the young warrior, challenged by the hardened soldier's cynicism, yields suddenly to a shock of recognition that confirms in a demythifying "reading" of the events and slogans surrounding the military preparations the demythifying reading of the individual narrations that the structure of Carpentier's text sets out to encourage in the reader. It is in this subtle and complex narrative texture that "Like the Night" is eminently paradigmatic of alternatives for Marxist and committed fiction in the new Latin American narrative that eschews the broadside approach of classical social realism.

OTHER MAJOR WORKS

LONG FICTION: *¡Ecué-Yamba-O! Historia Afro-Cubana*, 1933; *El reino de este mundo*, 1949 (*The Kingdom of This World*, 1957); *Los pasos perdidos*,

1953 (*The Lost Steps*, 1956); *El acoso*, 1956 (*Manhunt*, 1959); *El siglo de las luces*, 1962 (*Explosion in a Cathedral*, 1963); *El derecho de asilo*, 1972; *Concierto barroco*, 1974 (*Concert Baroque*, 1976); *El recurso del método*, 1974 (*Reasons of State*, 1976); *La consagración de la primavera*, 1978; *El arpa y la sombra*, 1979 (*The Harp and the Shadow*, 1990).

POETRY: *Dos poemas afro-cubanos*, 1930; *Poèmes des Antilles*, 1931.

NONFICTION: *La música en Cuba*, 1946 (*Music in Cuba*, 2001); *Tientos y diferencias*, 1964; *Afirmación literaria latinoamericana*, 1978; *La novela latinoamericana en vísperas del nuevo siglo y otros ensayos*, 1981; *Conversaciones con Alejo Carpentier*, 1998.

MISCELLANEOUS: *El milagro de Anaquillé*, 1928 (ballet scenario); *Obras completas de Alejo Carpentier*, 1983-1990 (14 volumes).

BIBLIOGRAPHY

Adams, M. Ian. *Three Authors of Alienation: Bombal, Onetti, Carpentier*. Austin: University of Texas Press, 1975. The intent of this work is to study alienation as a literary theme in the works of these three authors, each of whom modifies traditional literary forms in order to present different aspects of the theme. The section devoted to Carpentier is subtitled "Alienation, Culture, Myth, and 'Marvelous Reality.'" Select bibliography.

Brotherston, Gordon. *The Emergence of the Latin American Novel*. Cambridge, England: Cambridge University Press, 1977. Intended as an introduction to the Latin American novel, particularly from the 1950's to the 1970's, this is a scholarly work that is also accessible to the general reader. The chapter on Carpentier discusses the historical, cultural, and mythic dimensions of his work. Contains a general bibliography of secondary works on Latin American literature, as well as a list of works by and on the major authors mentioned in the text.

Cacheiro, Adolfo. "Utopian Possibilities and the Play Drive in 'Viaje a la Semilla.'" *Confluencia* 21, no. 1 (Fall, 2005): 27-41. Asserts that the short story "Viaje a la Semilla," originally published in 1944, is one of Carpentier's best works from the 1940's.

Demonstrates how the story is a modernist work and places Carpentier in the larger context of the global modernist movement.

Figueredo, Danilo H. "Beyond the Boom: García Márquez and the Other Latin American Novelists." *Wilson Library Bulletin* 69 (February, 1995): 36-40. Notes that, although Gabriel García Márquez is the most famous Latin American novelist, many of his predecessors and contemporaries, such as Jorge Luis Borges, Juan Rulfo, and Carpentier, refined *belles lettres* and invented a literature that did not wish to duplicate reality. Notes that Borges, Rulfo, and Carpentier sought universality and employed experimental literary techniques.

González Echevarría, Roberto. *Alejo Carpentier: The Pilgrim at Home*. Austin: University Press of Texas, 1990. A good introduction to Carpentier's writings. Offers a sustained consideration of his works and their overall significance, both within the field of Latin American literature and in the broader context of contemporary literature. Comes to terms with the basic question posed by his fiction, as well as with the larger theoretical questions about literary modernity and history.

Hart, Stephen M., and Wen-chin Ouyang. *A Companion to Magical Realism*. Rochester, N.Y.: Tamesis, 2005. Includes two essays that discuss Carpentier's "reinvention" of Latin America as "real and marvelous" and the presence of myth in the work of Carpentier and several other Spanish-language writers.

Harvey, Sally. *Carpentier's Proustian Fiction: The Influence of Marcel Proust on Alejo Carpentier*. London: Tamesis, 1994. Examines the themes and style in Carpentier's work that are derived from Proust. Includes bibliographical references and an index.

Peden, Margaret Sayers, ed. *The Latin American Short Story*. Boston: Twayne, 1983. The essays in this insightful collection chart the main currents and principal figures of Latin American short-story writing, suggesting the great depth and breadth of the genre in this region. The section devoted to Carpentier focuses on the story "Like the Night." Includes a select list of authors and collections and critical studies in English.

Shaw, Donald L. *Alejo Carpentier*. Boston: Twayne, 1985. The first adequate critical work in English dealing with the entire body of Carpentier's writing. The work's primary aim is to present an overview of Carpentier's entire fictional production. Offers a balanced appraisal of Carpentier's development from his earliest work, through his discovery of "marvelous realism," to his last, apparently Marxist, stance. Supplemented by an annotated bibliography and a chronology.

Unruh, Vicky. "The Performing Spectator in Alejo Carpentier's Fictional World." *Hispanic Review* 66 (Winter, 1998): 57-77. Argues that Carpentier uses the concept of performance to explore subjectivity and identity. Maintains he was interested in performance because of his interest in switching identities.

Claims his theater activity is a key to understanding his fictional world, in which spectatorship is an important way of experiencing the world.

Wakefield, Steve. *Carpentier's Baroque Fiction: Returning Medusa's Gaze*. Rochester, N.Y.: Tamesis, 2004. Traces the origins of Carpentier's literary style to his interest in Spanish baroque architecture and the Spanish Golden Age. Explains how Carpentier's historical fiction seeks to create the ambience of this period through descriptions of architecture and the visual arts and parodies of Spanish Golden Age writers. Although Wakefield focuses on the novels, his observations also pertain to Carpentier's short fiction.

David W. Foster
Updated by Genevieve Slomski

VIKRAM CHANDRA

Born: New Delhi, India; July 23, 1961

PRINCIPAL SHORT FICTION
   Love and Longing in Bombay, 1997

OTHER LITERARY FORMS

Vikram Chandra (VEE-krahm CHAHN-drah) is probably best known for his novels, though the short-story collection *Love and Longing in Bombay* gained him similar critical praise. Chandra is also a screenwriter, having penned the series *City of Gold*, which was produced in Mumbai, India, in 1996. His work also has appeared in *The New Yorker*, *The New York Times Book Review*, *The Paris Review*, *The Village Voice*, *Time*, and *Boston Review*, among others.

ACHIEVEMENTS

After he was awarded several prizes for creative writing while an undergraduate in India, Vikram Chandra had his story "Shakti" published in *The New Yorker* in 1994, followed by the publication of "Dharma" in *The Paris Review* later that year;

"Dharma" also was awarded a Discovery Prize. Chandra's first novel, *Red Earth and Pouring Rain* (1995), was awarded both the David Higham Prize in 1995 and the Commonwealth Writers Prize for Best First Book in 1996. Chandra was awarded the Commonwealth Writers Prize for Best Book of the Year (South Asia and Europe Region) for *Love and Longing in Bombay* in 1997. Chandra's 2006 novel, *Sacred Games*, was awarded the Vodafone Crossword Book Award in India and was nominated for a National Book Award the same year in the United States.

BIOGRAPHY

Vikram Chandra was born to Kamna Kavshik Chandra, a prolific screenwriter, playwright, and author, and Navin Chandra, a businessman, in New Delhi, India, on July 23, 1961. After attending St. Xavier's College in Bombay, Vikram Chandra moved to the United States to attend Pomona College in Claremont, California, where he graduated magna cum laude with a B.A. in English in 1984. Then Chandra moved to Baltimore, Maryland, to pursue an M.A. in creative writing at The Johns

Hopkins University, which he completed in 1987. Early in his college career, Chandra supported himself by working in technology, founding the consulting firm Letters and Light, and teaching literature and writing. Chandra entered film school at Columbia University in New York, where he was influenced by the autobiography of Colonel James "Sikander" Skinner, a nineteenth century Anglo-Indian soldier, which led him to drop out of film school and pursue writing a novel that would eventually become *Red Earth and Pouring Rain.* Chandra believed he could finish his novel in a relatively short time and benefit from the environment of a university writing program, so he moved to Texas, enrolled in the University of Houston's M.F.A. program, and worked as an adjunct professor. While in Houston, Chandra was awarded a writing grant from the Cultural Arts Council of Houston, and he had the good fortune to work with the respected writer Donald Barthelme. Although *Red Earth and Pouring Rain* was not yet complete when Chandra finished his M.F.A. in 1992, two of his short stories produced during that time, "Dharma" and "Shakti," were both published. Chandra then moved to Washington, D.C., and worked as a visiting writer at George Washington University. *Red Earth and Pouring Rain* was published shortly thereafter in 1995, and the book was a critical and popular success. Chandra continued to maintain residences in both the United States and India, dividing his time between the two. In the years following publication of *Red Earth and Pouring Rain*, Chandra published stories and integrated them into the acclaimed collection *Love and Longing in Bombay* in 1997. Chandra secured a large advance for his next novel, *Sacred Games*. Chandra and his wife, novelist Melanie Abrams, divide their time between Berkeley, California, where Chandra has taught creative writing at the University of California, Berkeley, and Mumbai, India, where his family still lives. He has two younger sisters, Tanuja Chandra, a successful director and screenwriter, and Anupama Chopra, a noted author and film critic who works for India's NDTV and the newsmagazine *India Today*.

ANALYSIS

Vikram Chandra's fiction is often categorized by critics and scholars as both postmodern and postcolonial, terms that often go hand-in-hand. The features of Chandra's text that could easily be labeled postmodern include his many intertextual references, the exploration of binary oppositions through his characters, and his preference for metafiction, or, as it is often utilized in Chandra's work, simply stories within stories. Metafiction is central in Chandra's first novel and in *Love and Longing in Bombay*. *Red Earth and Pouring Rain* is narrated by a monkey with a typewriter, who is the reincarnation of a fictional eighteenth century poet named Sanjay, which provides several layers of storytelling. In *Love and Longing in Bombay*, the narrator is an unnamed young Indian man who hears the other five stories from an old man, named Subramaniam, the narrator meets in a bar; in some of those stories are other stories within stories as well. Another hallmark of postmodern fiction that Chandra frequently employs is intertextuality, the references limited not only to text but also to the Bollywood sensibilities of Indian cinema,

Vikram Chandra (Getty Images)

which some critics argue is a major influence in *Sacred Games* (2006) and which play a part in *Love and Longing in Bombay*, especially the genres of ghost story, mystery, and detective story. In addition to the different genres present in *Love and Longing in Bombay*, the yarns Subramaniam spins to the bar patrons--essentially fables, though with modern lessons --are reminiscent of the stories Scheherazade tells in *Alf layla wa-layla* (fifteenth century; *The Arabian Nights' Entertainments*, 1706-1708), the famous collection of ancient East Indian folktales. These postmodern features in Chandra's fiction flow from an impulse to marry old storytelling traditions to new, specifically, an impulse to reconcile traditional stories, values, and meanings with the stories of a newer culture, one imposed upon or superseding the existing culture. This attempt at making meaning is a central feature of what critics refer to as postcolonial fiction. Chandra is interested in characters who exist in two worlds, between opposing points on a continuum. Often, the characters have difficulty knowing who they are, between the Eastern influences of India and the Western influences of their British colonizers. Chandra is interested in the conflict characters feel between the Old India, the spiritual, mystical India of previous centuries, and the New India, built on commerce, entertainment, and loose morals. Chandra's characters are often of the New India and come to value the memory and wisdom of the Old India. Other binary oppositions are explored as well, which grow naturally from the Old/New India conflict: The New India values material wealth, has only perfunctory use for religion, relies heavily on logic and reason, is the playground of the young, changes and adapts quickly, and is vital and growing. Conversely, the Old India is poor and sees no use for material riches, still holds tradition sacred, puts value in faith, is deeply religious, is slow to change, and is ultimately becoming extinct. In spite of the rather complex structure and aims of his novels and short stories, and in spite of the densely woven references and cultural allusions, Chandra creates work that is humorous, warm, and accessible, attributes that critics and general readers alike have praised. At his core, Chandra is a storyteller, and he does not let literary conceits supersede a good story or his characters'

searches for elusive human truths.

LOVE AND LONGING IN BOMBAY

The collection *Love and Longing in Bombay* collects five stories, "Dharma," "Shakti," "Kama," "Artha," and "Shanti," into one volume. Three of the four stories are named for Hindu *purusarthas*, which in traditional Hinduism are the goals or aims of human existence. "Dharma" means righteousness, "Kama" means pleasure, and "Artha" means wealth. The fourth *purusartha*, which Chandra omits, is "Moksa," which translates to freedom. Chandra replaces freedom with "Shakti" and "Shanti," which represent "strength" and "peace," respectively. These are perhaps appropriate substitutions, given Chandra's stories; according to Chandra, in these stories there is no true freedom, although that fact can be mitigated by inner strength and peace. The reference to classical Hinduism is an important one. India is a predominantly Hindu country, and modern Hinduism is as open to interpretation as any ancient religion in the world and as ripe with competing interpretations. Each of the stories in *Love and Longing in Bombay* corresponds to its namesake, seeking to answer the question of how Indian men and women can live in modern Bombay and reconcile the oppositions of the Old India and the New India in terms of seeking righteousness, pleasure, wealth, strength, and peace. Embodying these challenging questions is the first-person narrator of *Love and Longing in Bombay*, a lonely young man, who is very much enmeshed in the New India as a software designer in a large office. The narrator meets an old retiree at a bar, an ex-Ministry of Defense joint secretary named Subramaniam, who spins the long tales that make up *Love and Longing in Bombay*. Each chapter begins with a brief scene at the bar, during which the narrator and the other men talk about some local issue, and Subramaniam questions their "modern" views before showing them, through his fables, the wisdom of older, traditional values. Thus, *Love and Longing in Bombay* is a frame tale, like Chandra's novel *Red Earth and Pouring Rain* and *The Arabian Nights' Entertainments*.

"KAMA"

The third and longest story in *Love and Longing in Bombay* is the novella "Kama," the style, scope, and themes of which are broadly representative of the others in the collection. "Kama" opens with a short introduction, in which the young narrator socializes with Subramaniam and the other men in a bar. The narrator in this case describes himself as "heartbroken," after a happy relationship unexpectedly ends. As he silently drinks, he overhears the locals talking about a recent unsolved murder and wants to hear more. One of the men posits that the murder was probably over something "simple and stupid," such as property, money, or politics, and Subramaniam disagrees, suggesting that it was perhaps instead about "the most complicated thing of all." This piques the narrator's curiosity, and he listens as Subramaniam spins another tale.

"Kama" is a detective story, and its protagonist is detective Sartaj Singh, a Sikh living and working in Bombay, himself heartbroken over the recent divorce filed against him by his wife, Megha. Sartaj thinks often of Megha and has been procrastinating about filing the divorce papers. Sartaj is working to solve the murder of Chetanbhai Ghanhyam Patel, whose body has been found in a ditch in the city. Sartaj has a lead in the case based on Patel's Rolex, found on a transient named Shanker Ghorpade. He is a reasonable suspect, but it soon becomes clear that there is much more to the case than simple robbery and murder. Sartaj visits Patel's house, where his teenage son, Kshitij, and the son's mother, Asha, live. Kshitij accompanies Sartaj to the morgue, where he identifies his father's body. Ghorpade's conviction should proceed without a great deal of fuss, but, in spite of this, Sartaj uncovers several clues that dissuade him from an open-and-shut case. The clues lead Sartaj to suspect the involvement of Kshitij or Asha in Patel's murder, though Sartaj's suspicions are never spoken explicitly. Sartaj discovers that Chetanbhai and his wife habitually have extramarital encounters together in a hotel outside the city, though the exact nature of these encounters and who is involved (men, women, or both) are unclear. Sartaj eventually learns from Asha that this arrangement is consensual to everyone involved, knowledge that confounds his assumptions. Sartaj additionally discovers that Kshitij is involved in a conservative youth movement and belongs to a gang called the *Rakshaks*, whose value system abhors such an antitraditional view of marriage, a view

which Kshitij seems to share. Under questioning and even minor torture, however, Kshitij will not reveal any personal involvement in the murder. During Sartaj's investigation, Ghorpade dies while being held in prison, and thus Sartaj decides to close the case, leaving it essentially unsolved.

"Kama" refers to pleasure or desire, specifically romantic or sexual, and the novella contains many explorations of the subject, which is a central one to *Love and Longing in Bombay* as a whole, as the title would suggest. Sartaj himself struggles with desire for his estranged wife, and late in the story he even gives in to a final tryst with her, though on some level he knows it will only make the separation more painful. In spite of that, their final sexual act enables him finally to sign the divorce papers and move on at the end of the story. The idea of *Kama* and its place within a marriage is also put into question when the Patels' extramarital sex life is revealed. Such sexual behavior is controversial in the modern culture of Bombay, much as it is in modern America. Sartaj exemplifies Chandra's typical characters in that he is caught between the opposing poles of a binary opposition: in this case the promiscuity and relative sexual freedom of Westernized India versus the traditional Indian ideal that sexual relations are sacred and should take place only in marriage. Though Sartaj is scandalized by the Patels' actions, he is curious and intrigued to know more and not entirely for professional reasons. His in-between state is further illustrated when he thinks back to his adolescence, when he would nervously fantasize about sex but be afraid to "go all the way" with his girlfriend, in contrast to his former brother-in-law, Rahul, who as a young man had so much sex with so many different girls that he is already bored with it. Based on Sartaj's generally more traditional views of sex, he at first believes Asha could only have been coerced into the extramarital acts she and her husband take part in, but he later discovers she was complicit. The Patels' expression of desire and the fact that they allowed such a taboo practice into their lives together have profound effects on Sartaj: that their lives could look so normal on the outside yet conceal a vastly different private life casts a light on his defunct relationship and gives him strength. Through his investigation into these other lives, and through searching for explanations and finding none, he moves toward becoming comfortable in his own uncertainty and accepts some of the inexplicable events in his own life.

OTHER MAJOR WORKS

LONG FICTION: *Red Earth and Pouring Rain*, 1997; *Sacred Games*, 2006.

TELEPLAY: *City of Gold*, 1996 (series).

BIBLIOGRAPHY

Agarwal, Ramlal. "Review of *Love and Longing in Bombay* by Vikram Chandra." *World Literature Today* 72, no. 1 (Winter, 1998): 206-207. This mixed review discusses the function of the narrator and views the titles as "ironic," ultimately concluding that the convoluted plots detract from the overall experience of the stories.

Oindrila, Mukherjee. "'Ruthless Patience': A Conversation with Vikram Chandra." *Gulf Coast: A Journal of Literature and Fine Arts* (Summer/Fall, 2008): 271-277. Chandra discusses his biography, themes, and creative process in this informative interview.

Shukla, Sheobhusan, et al., eds. *Entwining Narratives: Critical Explorations into Vikram Chandra's Fiction.* New Delhi: Sarup, 2010. This volume contains ten highly theoretical, scholarly essays on Chandra's work as well as a detailed introduction and a bibliography.

Alan C. Haslam

ANTON CHEKHOV

Born: Taganrog, Russia; January 29, 1860
Died: Badenweiler, Germany; July 15, 1904
Also known as: Anton Tchekhov, Anton Tchehov, Anton Chekov

PRINCIPAL SHORT FICTION

Skazki Melpomeny, 1884
Pystrye rasskazy, 1886
Nevinnye rechi, 1887
V sumerkakh, 1887
Rasskazy, 1888
The Tales of Tchehov, 1916-1922 (13 volumes)
The Undiscovered Chekhov: Forty-three New Stories, 1999 (revised and expanded, 2001)

OTHER LITERARY FORMS

The literary reputation of Anton Chekhov (CHEHK-awf) rests as much on his drama as on his stories and sketches, despite the fact that he was a far more prolific writer of fiction, having written only seventeen plays but almost six hundred stories. *Chayka* (1896, rev. 1898; *The Seagull*, 1909), *Dyadya Vanya* (1897; *Uncle Vanya*, 1914), *Tri sestry* (1901; *Three Sisters*, 1920), and *Vishnyovy sad* (1904; *The Cherry Orchard*, 1908), Chekhov's chief dramatic works, are universally considered classics of modern theater. Chekhov was also an indefatigable correspondent, and his letters, along with his diaries and notebooks, form an important segment of his writing. He also wrote numerous journal articles and one long work, *Ostrov Sakhalin* (serialized in 1893 and 1894), a scholarly exposé of an island penal colony that Chekhov visited in 1890.

ACHIEVEMENTS

In his lifetime, Anton Chekhov gained considerable critical acclaim. In 1888, he won the Pushkin Prize for his fiction, and in 1900, he was selected to honorary membership in the Russian Academy of Sciences for both his fiction and his drama.

Chekhov's fiction departs from the formulaic, heavily plotted story to mirror Russian life authentically, concentrating on characters in very ordinary circumstances that often seem devoid of conflict. A realist, Chekhov treads a fine line between detachment and a whimsical but sympathetic concern for his subjects. In his mature work, he is perhaps the most genial of Russian masters, compassionate and forgiving, seldom strident or doctrinaire. Equally important, that mature work reflects very careful artistry, worthy of study for its technique alone.

BIOGRAPHY

Anton Pavlovich Chekhov, the third of six Chekhov children, was born on January 29, 1860, in Taganrog, a provincial city in southern Russia. His father, Pavel Egorovich Chekhov, son of a serf, ran a meager grocery store, which young Anton often tended in his neglectful father's absence. A religious fanatic and stern disciplinarian, Pavel gave his children frequent beatings and forced them to spend long hours in various devotional activities. For Anton, who did not share his father's zeal, it was a depressing, gloomy childhood.

Although the family was poor and Pavel's marginal business was slowly failing, Anton was able to get some schooling, first at a Greek parochial school, then at the boys' *Gymnasium*, or high school. In 1875, after a bout with acute peritonitis, young Chekhov decided to become a physician. His future brightened when, in 1876, his father, trying to evade his creditors, secretly moved the family to Moscow, leaving Anton to finish school.

In 1879, Anton moved to Moscow, entered the medical school of the University of Moscow, and almost immediately began publishing stories in various magazines and newspapers. A very prolific apprentice, by 1884, when he was graduated from medical school, he had published his first collection of short fiction. By 1886, Chekhov had begun his long association and friendship with A. S. Suvorin, the owner of an influential conservative newspaper to which Chekhov contributed dozens of pieces. Recognized as a significant new author, Chekhov devoted more time to writing and less and less time to his medical practice, which he eventually would abandon.

His greatly improved finances allowed Chekhov to buy a better Moscow house and gave him time to travel, which he frequently did, despite ill health. In 1887, he journeyed to the Don Steppe, and two years later crossed Asia to visit the Russian penal colony on Sakhalin Island. The next year he traveled to Europe with Suvorin. In 1892, Chekhov purchased Melikhovo, an estate outside Moscow that became a gathering place for family, relatives, and associates. There, too, Chekhov practiced medicine, more as a human service to poor villagers than as a necessary source of income.

In 1896, Chekhov had his first theatrical success with *The Seagull*, although the reaction of the opening-night audience greatly distressed the author. Suffering from tuberculosis, by the mid-1890's he began coughing up blood, and in 1897 he had to be hospitalized. In 1898, Chekhov began his propitious association with the newly formed Moscow Art Theater and its great director, Konstantin Stanislavski. He also met Olga Leonardovna Knipper, a young actress. Despite his ill health and his frequent sojourns to Yalta, they carried on a love affair and were married in 1901.

The last six years of Chekhov's life, from 1898 to 1904, brought him as much recognition as a dramatist as his earlier career had brought him as a writer of fiction. *Uncle Vanya*, *Three Sisters*, and *The Cherry Orchard*, his last significant work, were all major successes. In 1904, in one last attempt to stay the course of his disease, Chekhov and his wife went to Germany, where, at Badenweiler, he died on July 15.

ANALYSIS

Anton Chekhov published his earliest stories and sketches in various popular magazines under pseudonyms, the most often used being "Antosha Chekhonte." As that pen name hints, he was at first an unassuming and relatively compliant "hack," willing to dash off careless pieces fashioned for the popular reader. Most are light, topical studies of social types, often running less than a thousand words. Many are mere sketches or extended jokes, often banal or cynical. Some are farces, built on caricatures. Others are brief parodies of popular genres, including the romantic novel. Few display much originality in subject. Still, in their technique, economy of expression, and themes, the early pieces prefigure some of Chekhov's most mature work. In them, Chekhov experimented with point of view and particularly the use of irony as a fictional device. He also established his preference for an almost scientific objectivity in his depiction of character and events, an insistence that, in the course of his career, he would have to defend against his detractors.

Chekhov's penchant for irony is exemplified in his very first published story, "Pis'mo k uchenomu sosedu" ("A Letter to a Learned Neighbor"), which appeared in 1880. The letter writer, Vladimirovich, is a pompous, officious oaf who makes pretentious statements about science and knowledge with inane blunders in syntax, spelling, and diction, inadvertently revealing his boorish stupidity while trying to ingratiate himself with his erudite neighbor.

As does this sketch, many of Chekhov's first pieces lampoon types found in Russian society, favorite satirical targets being functionaries in the czarist bureaucracy and their obsequious regard for their superiors. One sketch, "Smert' chinovnika" ("The Death of a Government Clerk"), deals with a civil servant named Chervyakov who accidentally sneezes on a general and is mortified because he is unable to obtain the man's pardon. After repeated rebukes, he resigns himself to defeat, lies down, and dies. His sense of self-worth is so intricately bound up in his subservient role that, unpardoned, he has no reason to continue living.

In another story, "Khameleon" ("The Chameleon"), Ochumelov, a police officer, vacillates between placing blame on a dog or the man whom the dog has bitten until it can be confirmed that the dog does or does not belong to a certain General Zhigalov. When it turns out that the dog belongs to the general's brother, the officer swears that he will get even with the dog's victim. Like so many other characters in Chekhov's fiction, Ochumelov is a bully to his subordinates but an officious toady to his betters.

Other stories, not built on irony or a momentous event in the central character's life, are virtually plotless fragments. Some chronicle the numbing effects of living by social codes and mores rather than from authentic inner convictions, while others record human expectations frustrated by a sobering and often grim reality. In several stories, Chekhov deals with childhood innocence encountering or narrowly evading an adult world that is sordid, deceitful, or perverse. For example, in "V more" ("At Sea"), a man decides to provide a sex education for his son by having him observe a newly married couple and a third man through a bulkhead peep hole. Presumably to satisfy his own puerile interest, the father peeps first and is so mortified by what he sees that he does not allow his son to look at all.

Sometimes severely restricted by magazine requirements, Chekhov learned to be direct and sparse in statement. Many of his early stories have little or no exposition at all. The main character's lineage, elaborate details of setting, authorial incursions--all disappear for economy's sake. In his precipitous openings, Chekhov often identifies a character by name, identifies his class or profession, and states his emotional condition, all in a single sentence. Others open with a snippet of conversation that has presumably been in progress for some time. When he does set a scene with description, Chekhov does so with quick, deft, impressionistic strokes, with only the barest of details.

Chekhov also learned the value of symbols as guides to inner character. In "Melyuzga," a pathetic clerk named Nevyrazimov is trying to write a flattering Easter letter to his superior, whom, in reality, he despises. Hoping for a raise, this miserable underling must grovel, which contributes to his self-loathing and self-pity. As he tries to form the ingratiating words, he spies a cockroach and takes pity on the insect because he deems its miserable existence worse than his own.

Anton Chekhov (Library of Congress)

After considering his own options, however, and growing more despondent, when he again spies the roach he squashes it with his palm, then burns it, an act that, as the last line divulges, makes him feel better. The destruction of the roach is a symbolic act. It seems gratuitous and pointless, but it reveals the dehumanizing effect that *chinopochitanie*, or "rank reverence," has on the clerk. In destroying the roach, Nevyrazimov is able to displace some of the self-loathing that accompanies his self-pity. His misery abates because he is able, for a moment, to play the bully.

Despite the limitations that popular writing imposed, between 1880 and 1885 there is an advance in Chekhov's work, born, perhaps, from a growing tolerance and sympathy for his fellow human beings. He gradually turned away from short, acrid farces toward more relaxed, psychologically probing studies of his characters and their ubiquitous misery and infrequent joy. In "Unter Prishibeev" ("Sergeant Prishibeev"), Chekhov again develops a character who is unable to adjust to change because his role in life has been too rigid and narrow. A subservient army bully, he is unable to mend his ways when returned to civilian life and torments his fellow townspeople through spying, intimidation, and physical abuse. His harsh discipline, sanctioned in the military, only lands him in jail, to his total astonishment.

By 1886, Chekhov had begun to receive encouragement from the Russian literati, notably Dmitrí Grigorovich, who, in an important unsolicited letter, warned Chekhov not to waste his talents on potboilers. The impact on Chekhov was momentous, for he had received the recognition that he desired. Thereafter, he worked to perfect his craft, to master the *literature nastroenija*, or "literature of mood," works in which a single, dominant mood is evoked and action is relatively insignificant.

This does not mean that all Chekhov's stories are plotless or lack conflict. "Khoristka" ("The Chorus Girl"), for example, is a dramatic piece in method akin to the author's curtain-raising farces based on confrontation and ironic turns. The singer, confronted by the wife of one of her admirers, an embezzler, gives the wife all of her valuables to redeem the philanderer's reputation. His wife's willingness to humble herself before a chorus girl regenerates the man's love and admiration for his spouse. He cruelly snubs the chorus girl and, in rank ingratitude, leaves her alone in abject misery.

Other stories using an ironic twist leave the principal character's fate to the reader's imagination. "Noch' pered sudom" ("The Night Before the Trial") is an example. The protagonist, who narrates the story, makes a ludicrous blunder. On the eve of his trial for bigamy, he poses as a doctor and writes a bogus prescription for a woman. He also accepts payment from her husband, only to discover at the start of his trial that the husband is his prosecutor. The story goes no further than the man's brief speculation on his approaching fate.

In yet another, more involved story, "Nishchii" ("The Beggar"), a lawyer, Skvortsov, is approached by a drunken and deceitful but resourceful beggar, Lushkov, whom he unmercifully scolds as a liar and a wastrel. He then sets Lushkov to work chopping wood, challenging him to earn his way through honest, hard work. Before long, Skvortsov persuades himself that he has the role of Lushkov's redeemer and manages to find him enough work doing odd jobs to earn a meager livelihood. Eventually, growing respectable and independent, Lushkov obtains decent work in a notary's office. Two years later, encountering Skvortsov outside a theater, Lushkov confides that it was indeed at Skvortsov's house that he was saved--not, however, by Skvortsov's scolding but by Skvortsov's cook, Olga, who took pity on Lushkov and always chopped the wood for him. It was Olga's nobility that prompted the beggar's reformation, not the pompous moral rectitude of the lawyer.

In 1887, when Chekhov took the time to visit the Don Steppe, he was established as one of Russia's premier writers of fiction. With the accolades, there inevitably came some negative criticism. A few of his contemporaries argued that Chekhov seemed to lack a social conscience, that he remained too detached and indifferent to humanity in a time of great unrest and need for reform. Chekhov never believed that his art should serve a bald polemical purpose, but he was sensitive to the unjust critical opinion that he lacked strong personal convictions. In much of his mature writing, Chekhov worked to dispel that misguided accusation.

For a time Chekhov came under the spell of Leo Tolstoy, his great contemporary, not so much for that moralist's religious fervor but for his doctrine of nonresistance to evil. That idea is fundamental to "The Meeting." In this tale, which in tone is similar to the didactic Russian folktales, a thief steals money from a peasant, who had collected it for refurbishing a church. The thief, baffled by the peasant's failure to resist, gradually repents and returns the money.

"THE STEPPE"

In 1888, Chekhov wrote and published "Step'" ("The Steppe"), inspired by his journey across the Don Steppe. The story, consisting of eight chapters, approaches the novella in scope and reflects the author's interest in trying a longer work, which Grigorovich had advised him to do. In method, the piece is similar to picaresque tales, in which episodes are like beads, linked only by a common string--the voyage or quest.

The main characters are a merchant, Kuznichov, his nine-year-old nephew, Egorushka, and a priest, Father Christopher, who set out to cross the steppe in a cart. The adults travel on business, to market wool, while Egorushka is off to school. The monotony of their journey is relieved by tidbits of conversation and brief encounters with secondary characters in unrelated episodes. Diversion for young Egorushka is provided by various denizens of the steppe. These minor characters, though delineated but briefly, are both picturesque and lifelike.

Some of the characters spin a particular tale of woe. For example, there is Solomon, brother to Moses, the Jewish owner of a posting house. Solomon, disgusted with human greed, has burned his patrimony and now wallows in self-destructive misery. Another miserable figure is Pantelei, an old peasant whose life has offered nothing but arduous work. He has nearly frozen to death several times on the beautiful but desolate steppe. Dymov, the cunning, mean-spirited peasant, is another wretch devoid of either grace or hope.

The story involves a realistic counterpart to the romantic quest, for the merchant and the priest, joined by the charming Countess Dranitskaya, seek the almost legendary figure, Varlamov. Thus, in a quiet, subdued way, the work has an epic cast to it. Its unity depends on imagery and thematic centrality of the impressions

of Egorushka, whose youthful illusions play off against the sordid reality of the adult world. The journey to the school becomes for Egorushka a rite of passage, a familiar Chekhovian motif. At the end of the story, about to enter a strange house, the boy finally breaks into tears, feeling cut off from his past and apprehensive about his future.

"The Steppe" marks a tremendous advance over Chekhov's earliest works. Its impressionistic description of the landscape is often poetic, and though, like most of Chekhov's fiction, the work is open plotted, it is structurally tight and very compelling. The work's hypnotic attraction comes from its sparse, lyrical simplicity and timeless theme. It is the first of the author's flawless pieces.

"A BORING STORY"

Another long work, "Skuchnaia istoriia" ("A Boring Story"), shifts Chekhov's character focus away from a youth first encountering misery in the world to an old man, Nikolai Stepanovich, who, near the end of life, finally begins to realize its stupefying emptiness. The professor is the narrator, although, when the story starts, it is presented in the third rather than the first person. It soon becomes apparent, however, that the voice is the professor's own. The story is actually a diary, unfolding in the present tense.

The reader learns that, although Stepanovich enjoys an illustrious reputation in public, of which he is extremely proud, in private he is dull and emotionally handicapped. Having devoted his life to teaching medicine, the value of which he never questions, the professor has sacrificed love, compassion, and friendship. He has gradually alienated himself from family, colleagues, and students, as is shown by his repeated failures to relate to them in other than superficial, mechanical ways. He admits his inability to communicate to his wife or daughter, and although he claims to love his ward, Katya, whom his wife and daughter hate, even she finally realizes that he is an emotional cripple and deserts him to run off with another professor who has aroused some jealousy in Nikolai.

The professor, his life dedicated to academe, has become insensitive to such things as his daughter Liza's chagrin over her shabby coat or her feelings for Gnekker, her suitor, who, the professor suspects, is a fraud. Unable to understand his family's blindness to Gnekker, whom he perceives as a scavenging crab, Nikolai sets out to prove his assumption. He goes to Kharkov to investigate Gnekker's background and confirms his suspicions, only to discover that he is too late. In his absence, Liza and Gnekker have married.

Bordering on the tragic, "A Boring Story" presents a character who is unable to express what he feels. He confesses his dull nature, but, though honest with himself, he can confide in no one. Detached, he is able to penetrate the illusions of others, but his approach to life is so abstract and general as to hinder meaningful interpersonal relationships. Near the end of life, he is wiser but spiritually paralyzed by his conviction that he knows very little of human worth. "A Boring Story" reflects Chekhov's fascination with the fact that conversation may not ensure communication, and his treatment of that reality becomes a signatory motif in his later works, including his plays. Characters talk but do not listen, remaining in their own illusory worlds, which mere words will not let them share with others.

"THE DUEL"

"Duel" ("The Duel"), a long story, is representative of Chekhov's most mature work. Its focal concern is with self-deception and rationalization for one's failures. It pits two men against each other. The one, Laevsky, is a spineless, listless, and disillusioned intellectual who has miserably failed in life. The other, Von Koren, is an active, self-righteous zoologist who comes to despise the other man as a parasite.

In his early conversations with his friend Dr. Samoilenko, Laevsky reveals his tendency to place blame on civilization for human failings, a notion espoused by Jean-Jacques Rousseau and a host of other Romantic thinkers. The doctor, whose mundane, pragmatic values simply deflect Laevsky's lament, cannot understand his friend's ennui and disenchantment with his mistress, Nadezhda Feydorovna. Laevsky perceives himself as a Hamlet figure, one who has been betrayed by Nadezhda, for whom he feels an increasing revulsion, which he masks with hypocritical sweetness. He envisions himself as being caught without purpose, vaguely believing that an escape to St. Petersburg without Nadezhda would provide a panacea for all of his ills.

Laevsky's antagonist, Von Koren, is next introduced. Von Koren is a brash, outspoken, vain man who believes that Laevsky is worthy only of drowning. He finds Laevsky depraved and genetically dangerous because he has remarkable success with women and might father more of his parasitical type. During their encounters, Von Koren is aggressive and takes every chance to bait Laevsky, who is afraid of him.

Laevsky's situation deteriorates when Nadezhda's husband dies, and she, guilt ridden, looks to him to save her. Laevsky wants only to escape, however, and he runs off to Samoilenko, begging the doctor for a loan so he might flee to St. Petersburg. After confessing his depravity, he swears that he will send for Nadezhda after he arrives in St. Petersburg, but in reality he has no intention of doing so.

Caught up in his own web of lies and half truths, Laevsky must deal with those of Nadezhda, who is carrying on affairs with two other men and who has her own deceitful plans of escape. Convinced that Samoilenko has betrayed him through gossiping about him, Laevsky starts an argument with him in the presence of Von Koren, who supports the doctor. The heated exchange ends with a challenge to a duel, gleefully accepted by Von Koren. The night before the duel, Laevsky is extremely frightened. He is petrified by the prospect of imminent death, and his lies and deceit weigh upon him heavily. He passes through a spiritual crisis paralleled by a storm that finally subsides at dawn, just as Laevsky sets out for the dueling grounds.

The duel turns into a comic incident. The duelists are not sure of protocol, and before they even start they seem inept. As it turns out, Laevsky nobly discharges his pistol into the air, and Von Koren, intent on killing his opponent, only manages to graze his neck. The duel has a propitious effect on both men. Laevsky and Nadezhda are reconciled, and he gives up his foolish romantic illusions and begins to live a responsible life. He is also reconciled to Von Koren, who, in a departing confession, admits that a scientific view of things cannot account for all life's uncertainties. There is, at the end, a momentary meeting of the two men's minds.

"The Duel" is representative of a group of quasi-polemical pieces that Chekhov wrote between 1889 and 1896, including "Gusev" ("Gusev"), "Palata No.

6" ("Ward Number Six"), and "Moia zhizn" ("My Life"). All have parallel conflicts in which antagonists are spokespersons for opposing ideologies, neither of which is capable of providing humankind with a definitive epistemology or sufficient guide to living.

"ROTHSCHILD'S FIDDLE"

Other mature stories from the same period deal with the eroding effect of materialism on the human spirit. "Skripka Rotshil'da" ("Rothschild's Fiddle") is a prime example. In this work, the protagonist is Yakov Ivanov, nicknamed Bronze, a poor undertaker. Yakov, who takes pride in his work, also plays the fiddle and thereby supplements his income from making coffins.

For a time, Yakov plays at weddings with a Jewish orchestra, the members of which, inexplicably, he comes to hate, especially Rothschild, a flutist who seems determined to play even the lightest of pieces plaintively. Because of his belligerent behavior, after a time the Jews hire Yakov only in emergencies. Never in a good temper, Yakov is obsessed with his financial losses and his bad luck. Tormented by these matters at night, he can find some respite only by striking a solitary string on his fiddle.

When his wife, Marfa, becomes ill, Yakov's main concern is what her death will cost him. She, in contrast, dies untroubled, finding in death a welcome release from the wretchedness that has been her lot married to Yakov. In her delirium, she does recall their child, who had died fifty years earlier, and a brief period of joy under a willow tree by the river, but Yakov can remember none of these things. Only when she is buried does Yakov experience depression, realizing that their marriage had been loveless.

Sometime later Yakov accidentally comes upon and recognizes the willow tree of which Marfa had spoken. He rests there, beset by visions and a sense of a wasted past, regretting his indifference to his wife and his cruelty to the Jew, Rothschild. Shortly after this epiphany, he grows sick and prepares to die. Waiting, he plays his fiddle mournfully, growing troubled by not being able to take his fiddle with him to the grave. At his final confession, he tells the priest to give the fiddle to Rothschild, in his first and only generous act. Ironically, the fiddle for Rothschild becomes a means of improving his material well-being.

As "Rothschild's Fiddle" illustrates, Chekhov continued his efforts to fathom the impoverished spirit of his fellow man, often with a sympathetic, kindly regard. Most of his last stories are written in that vein. Near the end of the 1890's, Chekhov gave increasing attention to his plays, which, combined with his ill health, reduced his fictional output. Still, between 1895 and his last fictional piece, "Nevesta" ("The Bride"), published in 1902, he wrote some pieces that rank among his masterpieces.

As in "Rothschild's Fiddle," Chekhov's concern with conflicting ideologies gives way to more fundamental questions about human beings' ability to transcend their own nature. He examines characters who suffer desperate unhappiness, anxiety, isolation, and despair, experienced mainly through the characters' inability either to give or to accept love. He also, however, concerns himself with its antithesis, the suffocating potential of too much love, which is the thematic focus of "Dushechka" ("The Darling").

"THE DARLING"

In this story, Olenka, the protagonist, is a woman who seems to have no character apart from her marital and maternal roles. She is otherwise a cipher who, between husbands, can only mourn, expressing her grief in folk laments. She has no important opinions of her own, only banal concerns with petty annoyances such as insects and hot weather. She comes to life only when she fulfills her role as wife and companion to her husband, whose opinions and business jargon she adopts as her own, which, to her third husband, is a source of great annoyance.

Ironically, alive and radiant in love, Olenka seems to suck the life out of those whom she adores. For example, her love seems to cause the demise of her first husband, Kukin, a wretched, self-pitying theater manager. Only in the case of her last love, that for her foster son, Sasha, in her maternal role, does Olenka develop opinions of her own. Her love, however, ever suffocating, instills rebellion in the boy and will clearly lead to Olenka's downfall.

"THE BRIDE"

By implication, the comic, almost sardonic depiction of Olenka argues a case for the emancipation of women, a concern to which Chekhov returns in

"Nevesta" ("The Bride"). This story deals with a young woman, Nadya, who attempts to find an identity independent of roles prescribed by traditional mores and the oppressive influence of her mother, Nina, and her grandmother.

Nadya, at twenty-three, is something of a dreamer. As the story begins, she is vaguely discontent with her impending marriage to Andrew, son to a local canon of the same name. Her rebellion against her growing unhappiness is encouraged by Sasha, a distant relative who becomes her sympathetic confidant. He constantly advises Nadya to flee, to get an education and free herself from the dull, idle, and stultifying existence that the provincial town promises.

When Andrew takes Nadya on a tour of their future house, she is repulsed by his vision of their life together, finding him stupid and unimaginative. She confides in her mother, who offers no help at all, claiming that it is ordinary for young ladies to get cold feet as weddings draw near. Nadya then asks Sasha for help, which, with a ruse, he provides. He takes Nadya with him to Moscow and sends her on to St. Petersburg, where she begins her studies.

After some months, Nadya, very homesick, visits Sasha in Moscow. It is clear to her that Sasha, ill with tuberculosis, is now dying. She returns to her home to deal with her past but finds the atmosphere no less oppressive than before, except that her mother and grandmother now seem more pathetic than domineering. After a telegram comes announcing Sasha's death, she leaves again for St. Petersburg, resolved to find a new life severed completely from her old.

As well as any story, "The Bride" illustrates why Chekhov is seen as the chronicler of twilight Russia, a period of stagnation when the intelligentsia seemed powerless to effect reform and the leviathan bureaucracy and outmoded traditions benumbed the people and robbed the more sensitive of spirit and hope. While the contemporary reader of Chekhov's fiction might find that pervasive, heavy atmosphere difficult to fathom, particularly in a comic perspective, no one can doubt Chekhov's mastery of mood.

With Guy de Maupassant in France, Chekhov is rightly credited with mastering the form, mood, and style of the type of short fiction that would be favored by serious English language writers beginning with Virginia Woolf and James Joyce. His impact on modern fiction is pervasive.

OTHER MAJOR WORKS

LONG FICTION: *Drama na okhote*, 1884-1885 (*The Shooting Party*, 1926).

PLAYS: *Platonov*, wr. 1878-1881, pb. 1923 (English translation, 1930); *Ivanov*, pr., pb. 1887 (revised pr. 1889; English translation, 1912); *Medved*, pr., pb. 1888 (*A Bear*, 1909); *Leshy*, pr. 1889 (*The Wood Demon*, 1925); *Predlozheniye*, pb. 1889, pr. 1890 (*A Marriage Proposal*, 1914); *Svadba*, pb. 1889, pr. 1890 (*The Wedding*, 1916); *Yubiley*, pb. 1892 (*The Jubilee*, 1916); *Chayka*, pr. 1896 (revised pr. 1898, pb. 1904; *The Seagull*, 1909); *Dyadya Vanya*, pb. 1897, pr. 1899 (based on his play *The Wood Demon*; *Uncle Vanya*, 1914); *Tri sestry*, pr., pb. 1901 (revised pb. 1904; *The Three Sisters*, 1920); *Vishnyovy sad*, pr., pb. 1904 (*The Cherry Orchard*, 1908); *The Plays of Chekhov*, pb. 1923-1924 (2 volumes); *Nine Plays*, pb. 1959; *The Complete Plays*, pb. 2006 (Laurence Senelick, editor).

NONFICTION: *Ostrov Sakhalin*, 1893-1894; *Letters on the Short Story, the Drama, and Other Literary Topics*, 1924; *The Selected Letters of Anton Chekhov*, 1955.

MISCELLANEOUS: The Works of Anton Chekhov, 1929; *Polnoye sobraniye sochineniy i pisem A. P. Chekhova*, 1944-1951 (20 volumes); *The Portable Chekhov*, 1947; *The Oxford Chekhov*, 1964-1980 (9 volumes).

BIBLIOGRAPHY

Bartlett, Rosamund *Chekhov: Scenes from a Life*. New York: Simon & Schuster, 2006. Bartlett's biography describes not only Chekhov's life but also the geography and history of the Russian empire in which he lived.

Evdokimova, Svetlana. "Chekhov's 'The Darling': Femininity Scorned and Desired." In *The Russian Twentieth-Century Short Story: A Critical Companion*, edited by Lyudmila Parts. Brighton, Mass.: Academic Studies Press, 2010. Provides a critical reading of this story.

Flath, Carol A. "The Limits to the Flesh: Searching for the Soul in Chekhov's 'A Boring Story.'" *Slavic and East European Journal* 41 (Summer, 1997):

271-286. Argues that "A Boring Story" affirms the value of art and offers comfort against the harshness of the truth about ordinary life and death.

Gottlieb, Vera, and Paul Allain, eds. *The Cambridge Companion to Chekhov*. New York: Cambridge University Press, 2000. Although the essays in this collection focus on Chekhov's drama, the article by Chekhov scholar Donald Rayfield, "Chekhov's Stories and the Plays," analyzes how Chekhov's drama was influenced by the characters, situations, techniques, and language of his short stories.

Hardwick, Elizabeth. "The Disabused." *The New Republic*, November 27, 2000, 24-27. Reviews a collection of thirty of Chekhov's short stories translated by Richard Pevear and Larissa Volokhonsky. Discusses, among other subjects, Chekhov's use of language and tone, his depiction of Russian peasants, and the influence of the Russian Orthodox Church upon his fiction.

Johnson, Ronald J. *Anton Chekhov: A Study of the Short Fiction*. New York: Twayne, 1993. An introduction to Chekhov's short stories, from his earliest journalistic sketches and ephemera to his influential stories "Gooseberries" and "Lady with a Dog." Discusses Chekhov's objective narrative stance, his social conscience, and his belief in the freedom of the individual. Includes excerpts from Chekhov's letters in which he talks about his fiction, as well as comments by other critics who discuss Chekhov's attitude toward religion and sexuality.

Kirk, Irina. *Anton Chekhov*. Boston: Twayne, 1981. This study in the Twayne series offers a good departure point for serious further inquiry. In addition to provocative interpretations of selected fictional and dramatic works, it includes a useful chronology and select bibliography. The study is most helpful in delineating the guiding principles of Chekhov's art.

Lantz, K. A. *Anton Chekhov: A Reference Guide to Literature*. Boston: G. K. Hall, 1985. Lantz offers an indispensable tool for the researcher. The work provides a brief biography, a checklist of Chekhov's published works with both English and Russian titles, chronologically arranged, and a useful annotated bibliography of criticism through 1983.

Malcolm, Janet. *Reading Chekhov: A Critical Journey*. New York: Random House, 2001. With Chekhov as a guide, Malcolm draws on her observations as a tourist and journalist to compose a melancholy portrait of post-Soviet Russia. She weaves her encounters with contemporary Russians with biographical and critical analyses of Chekhov and his writings.

Martin, David W. "Chekhov and the Modern Short Story in English." *Neophilologus* 71 (1987): 129-143. Surveys Chekhov's influence on various English-language writers, including Katherine Mansfield, Virginia Woolf, James Joyce, Sherwood Anderson, and Frank O'Connor. Compares selected works by Chekhov with pieces by those he has influenced and discusses those Chekhovian traits and practices revealed therein. Credits Chekhov with showing how effete or banal characters or circumstances can be enlivened with the dynamics of style. A good departure point for further comparative study.

McSweeney, Kerry. "Aesthetic Readings of Chekhov's Stories." In *The Realist Short Story of the Powerful Glimpse: Chekhov to Carver*. Columbia: University of South Carolina Press, 2007. McSweeney provides "aesthetic readings" of Chekhov's stories, in which he treats them as "realist works of art."

Pritchett, V. S. *Chekhov: A Spirit Set Free*. New York: Random House, 1988. A critical biography and a solid general introduction to Chekhov. Himself a writer of fiction, Pritchett has a readable, engaging style. However, his discussions of selected works, though helpful, are prone to summary rather than extensive analysis.

Prose, Francine. "Learning from Chekhov." *Western Humanities Review* 41 (1987): 1-14. An appreciative eulogy on the enduring influence of Chekhov's stories as models for writers. Notes that while Chekhov broke many established rules, his stress on objectivity and writing without judgment is of fundamental importance.

Rayfield, Donald. *Anton Chekhov: A Life*. New York: Henry Holt, 1998. A detailed and highly documented biography by a noted Chekhov scholar. Comments on Chekhov's relationship with his family, discusses the sources of his work, describes his literary friendships, and provides a context for his work in prerevolutionary Russia.

Troyat, Henri. *Chekhov.* Translated by Michael H. Heim. New York: E. P. Dutton, 1986. Troyat's biography, drawing heavily on Chekhov's letters, is a much more detailed and comprehensive study of Chekhov's life than is V. S. Pritchett's (above). It is less a critical biography, however, and is mainly valuable for its intimate portrayal of Chekhov the man. It is well indexed and documented by Chekhov's correspondence. Illustrated with photographs.

John W. Fiero

MICHELLE CLIFF

Born: Kingston, Jamaica; November 2, 1946

PRINCIPAL SHORT FICTION

Bodies of Water, 1990
The Store of a Million Items, 1998
Everything Is Now: New and Collected Stories, 2009

OTHER LITERARY FORMS

Michelle Cliff is recognized for her contributions as a writer of fiction and poetry and as a literary critic. It was in response to an article about Jamaica, which she felt presented a false image, that she wrote her first creative works. In her long fiction, poetry, and essays, she particularly treats issues of growing up in Jamaica as a mixed-blood and of the effects of colonialism and postcolonialism on the lives of Jamaicans. In addition, as in her short fiction, she addresses prejudice and intolerance in regard to skin color, race, sex, and sexual orientation and the resulting oppression and discrimination. Her novels emphasize the importance of rewriting "official" or mainstream history, which she believes neglects, ignores, or misrepresents the history of the oppressed and the ostracized. In her works, she recovers their lost oral history.

ACHIEVEMENTS

Michelle Cliff is one of the most significant writers who explore themes of colonialism; of problems of identity for those of mixed blood; of feminism; and of race, color, and sexual orientation. In her writing, she retrieves the lost history of marginal and oppressed segments of society and has made a significant contribution to "rewriting" history. She is also highly respected as a literary critic. She held the position of the Allan K. Smith Professor of English Language and Literature at Trinity College. Cliff has received several fellowships and awards. In 1982, she was awarded two fellowships, one from the National Endowment for the Arts and one from MacDowell College. In 1984, she was given a Massachusetts Artists Foundation Award and was selected as an Eli Kantor Fellow.

BIOGRAPHY

The daughter of a mixed marriage, an American father and a Jamaican mother, Michelle Cliff was born on November 2, 1946, in Kingston, Jamaica. A light-skinned Creole, she grew up in a family that attached great importance to skin color; this emphasis on skin color, in both her immediate and extended family, heavily affected her life. Her younger sister, dark-skinned like their mother, was considered her mother's child, while Cliff, light-skinned like their father, was considered his child. Her extended family constantly insisted that she pass for white. This rejection of her black heritage became objectionable to Cliff as she grew up.

As a child, Cliff lived in Jamaica and the United States. Her family moved to New York City when she was three. She was left in Jamaica with relatives for a time, but soon she went to live with her parents and her sister in a Caribbean neighborhood in New York City. During the late 1940's and early 1950's, the family visited Jamaica often. In 1956, Cliff moved back to Jamaica to attend boarding school.

After completing her secondary education, she moved back to the United States to attend Wagner College. She became involved in the feminist movement, in politics, and in protests against the war in Vietnam. She graduated from Wagner College in 1969 with a bachelor of arts degree. She worked in various capacities in the publishing field, including as a reporter, a researcher, and an editor. In 1974, she received a master of philosophy degree and then a Ph.D. from the Warburg Institute, University of London. While she had been at boarding school in Jamaica, Cliff had found herself attracted to a female classmate, but it was not until she was studying in London that she realized that her sexual orientation was lesbian rather than heterosexual. In 1976, she began a relationship with the poet Adrienne Rich.

As Cliff matured, she became concerned about reclaiming the black heritage she had been denied by her family. Then she read an article portraying Jamaica in a way totally opposed to the Jamaica of her childhood. Prompted by her desire to reclaim her black heritage and to present the Jamaica of her childhood, she began to write prose poetry. Her first book of poetry, *Claiming an Identity They Taught Me to Despise*, was published in 1980. She was coeditor of the multicultural lesbian journal *Sinister Wisdom* with Rich from 1981 to 1985. Her second collection of poetry, *The Land of Look Behind*, appeared in 1985. In these poems, she continued to reclaim her identity and to portray the real Jamaica as she knew it.

In 1985, Cliff published her first fictional work, the novel *Abeng*, and followed it with a sequel, *No Telephone to Heaven*, in 1987. Based on her personal experiences, these two narratives explore the oppression, segregation, and discrimination that are part of everyday life in a multicultural, multiracial society intolerant of difference. Cliff published her first collection of short stories, *Bodies of Water*, in 1990. In 1993, she returned to long fiction with the novel *Free Enterprise*. In 1998, her second collection of short fiction, *The Store of a Million Items*, appeared. In 2009, she published her third collection, *Everything Is Now: New and Collected Stories*. In 2010, she published a fourth novel, *Into the Interior*. Cliff has continued to write, lecture, and teach, and she has translated Spanish and Italian poetry into English.

ANALYSIS

Michelle Cliff has published three collections of short fiction. *Bodies of Water* includes ten stories; only one of the stories, "Columba," uses a Jamaican setting, and all of the rest are set in the United States. *The Store of a Million Items* contains eleven stories, which compare and contrast American life during the 1950's and 1960's, a period of prosperity but also of intense racism, with life in Jamaica. *Everything Is Now* includes all of the stories from the two previous collections and adds fourteen new stories to Cliff's short fiction. The narratives address the same themes and issues that Cliff investigates in her long fiction and in her prose poetry. She recounts stories of marginalization of individuals because of difference. Skin color, nationality, social class, being female, and sexual orientation all bring about ostracism and oppression. The stories present a rigid social structure, whether in Jamaica or in America, which refuses to admit any deviation from its norm. Prejudice, racism, and colonialism permeate the stories. The short fiction is part of her search for her identity as well as a means of recovering lost oral history and making it a part of "official" history.

Stylistically, Cliff's writing is a mixture, drawing on and combining elements of poetry and prose. In her short fiction, as in all of her writing, language plays an important role. The choice of words and their placement on the page contribute to the meanings of the stories. Images and descriptions not only create atmosphere but also develop the plot of the narratives. With these elements, she fills her stories with allusions and suggestions that carry along the plot. Although the stories often contain violence, there is little action. The details of what happens are presented in short, matter-of-fact sentences. The stories are dominated by the characters, their inner thoughts, reactions, and memories. The narratives rely heavily on stories retold and memories recollected and shared. The past and the present blend into one. The past can be neither forgotten nor erased. The narratives are well brought together under the title *Everything Is Now: New and Collected Stories*.

"WHILE UNDERNEATH"

"While Underneath" is the story of a fraternity gang rape at an upper-class private college and its cover-up.

The story is being told by a new English faculty member (probably Cliff), who is curious about the woman sitting in the Rooster's Nest, talking to stuffed animals. In the narrative, Cliff attacks many beliefs ingrained in a society divided by social class and affluence. After the rape and a subsequent suicide, the college president suggests that they plant rosebushes around the fraternity house because bad things do not occur in beautiful places. The rape incident is dismissed as being fabricated by a young woman seeking attention or instigated by her. She should not have gone into the tunnels; by so doing she asked for what happened, if it happened. The fault is hers. Her parents "put her away" because she is disturbed. Paying hundreds of dollars a day for twenty years is preferable to admitting the rape happened. Rape does not happen to people of their social standing, only to "other" people.

Cliff uses irony and satire extensively in the story. The professor sees the students in her experimental fiction seminar, with the exception of Jean (a student from Mount Holyoke), as embodiments of J. Crew and L. L. Bean catalogs. Her seminar is a dialogue between her and Jean, with the uninterested, half-asleep, hung-over catalogs as the audience. Everything at the college is false, a sham and a pretense. When the college became coeducational in 1970, "Wo" is added to "Men" on signs and tampon machines are installed beside urinals. The college handbook points out that the tunnels under the college are evidence of participation in the Underground Railroad. The tunnels were actually used for menservants to rush hot food from the college kitchen to their masters' rooms. The college takes pride in its concern about equality for all, yet it operates on a strict separation of faculty, staff, and workers.

Cliff uses multiple narrators in the narrative. Dorothy, the department secretary, tells the rape story as she knows it to the professor. The professor next talks to a colleague, Tom Maxwell, who was a student there when the rape and suicide happened. Maxwell denies any knowledge and then addresses the reader saying he lied. He tells the reader the suicide was committed by his roommate, who left a letter revealing his desires for Maxwell. Although having the same desires, Maxwell admitted nothing. He became an English professor, studying the work of Thomas Bowdler who removed

all improper words from texts while leading his own bowdlerized life. Ellen, the girl who was raped, then takes up the narrative to the reader. She explains her innocence, her parents' betrayal, her stuffed animals, and her need to talk to people, such as the cafeteria workers. She cannot say why she returns to the campus. The narration returns to the professor. The story ends with her looking at an open yearbook on a mahogany table showing the "catalogs" recreating. Scratched on the table is "while underneath."

"BODIES OF WATER"

"Bodies of Water" introduces two main characters--Anne Dillon, an old woman, and Jess, a younger woman--both of whom live alone on a lake in a region of changing seasons. The lake supposedly is inhabited by the ghosts of dead women. As the narrative begins, it is winter, the lake is frozen, and Anne is ice fishing. Jess is watching her through the window of her brother's cottage, where she has come to live. In the first two chapters of the story, which primarily focus on Anne, Cliff weaves in brief bits of information about Jess and her brother, Bill, foreshadowing the narrative of the other seven chapters of the fiction. Together the narratives deal with prejudice and intolerance of anything that challenges accepted social practices and ways of being, especially sexual orientation. Given the time during which the remembered stories took place, Jess's in the late 1950's, Anne's earlier, neither the word "lesbianism" nor the word "homosexuality" appears. Cliff emphasizes the propriety, secretiveness, and refusal to face reality prevalent in the social system

The juxtaposition of Anne and Jess both living alone and recalling the past adds an intriguing complexity to the story. At the end, the reader wonders if Jess will one day be like Anne--self-accepting and content. Cliff includes many small details of similarity between the two women in the beginning of the story. Both live alone; once inside their homes, they are warm and safe. Anne feeds a stray cat, which accepts the food she offers but not the shelter; Jess feeds a cardinal and wonders why he is alone. Both women are surrounded by the past through physical objects and memories. Anne, who has come to terms with the past, is in control of her well-ordered life. Her routine provides her with contentment. Jess, in contrast, is at war with the past.

Anne was an only child; her mother died at Anne's birth. Anne spent her childhood reading in the waiting room of her father's law office. As a young girl, she met Isabella Straniere (Bessie). Friendship became a love affair. They shared the home by the lake and their lives until Bessie died. Cliff reveals the lesbian relationship of the two women through a few brief sentences scattered throughout Anne's reminiscences.

Anne's story is touched by a bitter and ironic humor. Her niece constantly threatens to put Anne in a nursing home. Anne swears she will not be taken alive; she has money hidden and a plan to flee west and change her name. Cliff includes Anne's thoughts about a sign in front of a nursing home, admonishing guests not to leave keys in cars, as though the elderly residents pose a dangerous threat if they escape.

Jess's story develops as she reads a letter from her brother and remembers their childhood. The brother's diary, marked private property, has been read by his parents; this is taken from Cliff's personal experience. The diary reveals his suspicion that he may be homosexual. The parents, devastated and enraged, call the minister, lock Bill in a glass-enclosed porch on an Indian summer day, and, taking Jess with them, go to consult the doctor. Bill is subjected to shock treatments, sent to a tough place, and eventually leaves home. The family is destroyed. Jess blames herself for not fighting for her brother. She tries to write to him, first in the winter, then in the spring. She cannot. The story ends as she tears up the letter.

"THE STORE OF A MILLION ITEMS"

In "The Store of a Million Items," Cliff brings the world of children into collision with the world of adults. The hostility between adults and children is a recurring theme in her work. It represents the conflict between natural reactions and learned reactions, between acceptance/tolerance and learned prejudice, between life freely lived and life bound by social restriction. Children buy yo-yos without worrying about who made them. Adults speak of the danger of items made in Japan. At school, children learn how horrible life is in Russia, but the murder of Emmett Till for whistling at a white woman is not mentioned.

Adults insist upon order; the children live in a chaotic world of yo-yos, water pistols, and Flexible Flyers (sleds). Pandemonium reigns. There is an airplane crash supposedly caused by a kid who kept playing with a radio when told to stop. A father recounts the story in a berating manner to his daughter. The story ends with recollection of the X-ray machine in the shoe department of the Store of a Million Items; parents thought it let them see through their children.

OTHER MAJOR WORKS

LONG FICTION: *Abeng*, 1985; *No Telephone to Heaven*, 1987; *Free Enterprise*, 1993; *Into the Interior*, 2010.

POETRY: *Claiming an Identity They Taught Me to Despise*, 1980; *The Land of Look Behind: Prose and Poetry*, 1985.

NONFICTION: "History as Fiction, Fiction as History," 1994;

If I Could Write This in Fire, 2008.

EDITED TEXTS: *The Winner Names the Age: Collection of Writings*, 1982 (Lillian Smith).

BIBLIOGRAPHY

Adisa, Opal Palmer. "Journey into Speech, a Writer Between Two Worlds: An Interview with Michelle Cliff." *African American Review* 28, no. 2 (1994): 273. Cliff on color issues, oppression and racism in Jamaica, resistance as a community, and the importance of women in resistance history.

Cliff, Michelle. *Abeng*. New York: Penguin, 1995. Cliff's fiction based on her own experiences and reactions elucidates her motivation to write.

Elia, Nada. *Trances, Dances, and Vociferations: Agency and Resistance in Africana Women's Narratives*. New York: Garland, 2001. Examines Cliff's use of alternative and oral history, sexual disguise, and racial passing.

MacDonald-Smythe, Antonia. *Making Homes in the West/Indies: Constructions of Subjectivity in the Writing of Michelle Cliff and Jamaica Kincaid*. New York: Garland, 2001. A thorough investigation of how and why Cliff and Kincaid create an identity in which race, nationality, and sex play important roles.

Paravisini-Gebert, Lizabeth. *Literature of the Caribbean*. Westport, Conn.: Greenwood Press, 2008.

Good for historical background on Cliff's writings. Places her in context with other Caribbean writers.

Walters, Wendy. *At Home in Diaspora: Black International Writing*. Minneapolis: University of Minnesota Press, 2005. Examines the works of Cliff and other displaced black writers in regard to the effect of displacement on their writing and their search for an identity.

Shawncey Webb

JULIO CORTÁZAR

Born: Brussels, Belgium; August 26, 1914
Died: Paris, France; February 12, 1984
Also known as: Julio Denís

PRINCIPAL SHORT FICTION

Bestiario, 1951

Final del juego, 1956

Las armas secretas, 1959

Historias de cronopios y de famas, 1962 (*Cronopios and Famas,* 1969)

End of the Game, and Other Stories, 1963 (also known as *Blow-Up, and Other Stories,* 1967)

Todos los fuegos el fuego, 1966 (*All Fires the Fire, and Other Stories,* 1973)

Octaedro, 1974 (included in *A Change of Light, and Other Stories,* 1980)

Alguien que anda por ahí, y otros relatos, 1977 (included in *A Change of Light, and Other Stories,* 1980)

Un tal Lucas, 1979 (*A Certain Lucas,* 1984)

A Change of Light, and Other Stories, 1980

Queremos tanto a Glenda, y otros relatos, 1980 (*We Love Glenda So Much, and Other Stories,* 1983)

Deshoras, 1982

OTHER LITERARY FORMS

Besides his short stories, Julio Cortázar (HOO-lee-oh kohr-TAH-sahr) published novels, plays, poetry, translations, and essays of literary criticism. In his essay on short fiction entitled "Algunos aspectos del cuento" ("Some Aspects of the Short Story"), Cortázar studies the varying role of the reader with regard to different literary forms. Cortázar's first book, *Presencia* (1938), was a collection of poetry that he published under the pseudonym Julio Denís. He translated authors as diverse as Louisa May Alcott and Edgar Allan Poe into Spanish and considered French Symbolist poetry to be of enormous influence on his prose writing. He experimented with a form of collage in his later works of short fiction.

ACHIEVEMENTS

An antirealist, Julio Cortázar is often grouped with Gabriel García Márquez as one of the foremost proponents of the Magical Realism movement and, during his lifetime, one of the most articulate spokespersons on the subject of Latin American fiction.

Although Cortázar is most admired for his short stories (his short story "Las babas del diablo" was made into a classic film in 1966 called *Blow-Up* by director Michelangelo Antonioni), it was the publication of the novel *Rayuela* (1963; *Hopscotch,* 1966) that placed the author among the twentieth century's greatest writers. *The Times Literary Supplement* called *Hopscotch* the "first great novel of Spanish America."

BIOGRAPHY

Julio Cortázar was born in Brussels, Belgium, in 1914, during the German occupation. His Argentine parents were stationed there while his father was on the staff of a commercial mission. Cortázar's antecedents came from the Basque region of Spain, as well as France and Germany, and they had settled in Argentina. When Cortázar was four years old, his parents returned to Argentina, where he would grow up in Banfield, a suburb of Buenos Aires. His father abandoned the family, and he was reared by his mother and an aunt.

Cortázar attended the Escuela Norman Mariano Acosta in Buenos Aires and earned a degree as a public schoolteacher in 1932. In 1937, he accepted a high school teaching post and shortly thereafter published *Presencia*, a collection of poems, under the pseudonym Julio Denís. In 1940, he published an essay on Arthur Rimbaud, under the same pseudonym, and began to teach a class on the French Symbolist movement at the University of Cuyo in Mendoza. In 1946, Jorge Luis Borges, at that time the editor of the literary journal *Anales de Buenos Aires*, published "Casa tomada" ("House Taken Over")--the first work that Julio Cortázar penned under his own name.

A writer with outspoken political beliefs, Cortázar was defiantly anti-Peronist. He was arrested and as a result was forced to relinquish his academic career in Argentina. Instead, however, he became a translator, and in 1951 he went to Paris, where he soon established permanent residency. Much of his best short fiction, including "Bestiary" and "End of the Game," was published in the 1950's and reveals his experience as an expatriate--a Latin American living in Paris.

In Paris, Cortázar got a job as a translator for the United Nations Educational, Scientific and Cultural Organization (UNESCO), which he kept for the rest of his life, despite his international success as an author. In 1953, he married Aurora Bernandez, with whom he translated Poe's prose works into Spanish while they lived briefly in Rome. In 1963, he published *Hopscotch* and, after a visit to Cuba, became a powerful figure on both the literary and the political scenes.

His audience grew wider during the 1960's and 1970's with the translation of *Rayuela* into dozens of languages and the appearance of the film *Blow-Up*. He also traveled extensively to such diverse places as Chile, New York, and Oklahoma to attend conferences, receive awards, and participate in political tribunals. In 1981, he finally became a French citizen. He died in Paris on February 12, 1984, of leukemia and heart disease. He is buried in the Montparnasse cemetery in Paris.

ANALYSIS

Influenced by the European movements of nineteenth century Symbolism and twentieth century Surrealism, Julio Cortázar combines symbols, dreams, and the fantastic with what seems to be an ordinary, realistic situation in order to expose a different kind of reality that exists in the innermost heart and mind of modern human beings. Like Edgar Allan Poe, Cortázar is fascinated by terror. He uses human beings' worst nightmares to explore which fears control them and how phobias and dreams coexist with seemingly rational thought. Using symbols and metaphors for subconscious obsessions, Cortázar's short fictions, unlike those of the Surrealists, are carefully constructed. His journey into the irrational is not a free-flowing adventure; rather, it is a study of a particular corner of the mind that is common to all people.

"BESTIARY"

"Bestiary," an early story published in 1951, contains many of the elements of poesy and mystery that are characteristic of the nineteenth century Symbolists so admired by Cortázar. The story is told by a child whose scope of understanding and point of view are limited, thereby leaving certain details vague and confusing. Isabel is sent to the country for the summer to

Julio Cortázar (Library of Congress)

stay in a home inhabited by another child, Nino, and three adults: Luis, Nino's father; Rema, who may or may not be Nino's mother, Luis' wife or sister, Nino's sister, or the housekeeper; and the Kid, who is not a kid but Luis' brother. The information given about the family is not specific in those terms, but it is quite specific in Isabel's feelings about each person. The overwhelming oddity about this summer home is that a tiger is allowed to roam freely about the house and grounds. The people are advised as to the location of the tiger each day, and they go about their business as usual by simply avoiding the room or part of the fields in which the tiger happens to be.

Life seems to be filled with very typical activities: Luis works in his study, the children gather an ant collection, and Rema supervises meals. Isabel is especially fond of Rema but not of the Kid. Events are relayed that expose Isabel's true feelings about the Kid and the kind of person she believes him to be. He is surly at the dinner table. Once, after Nino has hit a ball through the window leading to the Kid's room, the Kid hits Nino; the most disturbing moment, however, is a scene between Rema and the Kid during which Isabel acts as a voyeur, revealing some sort of sexual abuse on the part of the Kid toward Rema. Because of Isabel's admiration for Rema, she decides to take revenge on the Kid. The culmination of the story is that Isabel lies to the family about the whereabouts of the tiger, sending the Kid into the room where the animal is. Screams are heard, and it is clear that the Kid has been mauled to death. Isabel notices that Rema squeezes her hand with what the child believes to be gratitude.

Many critics have speculated about the meaning of the tiger. Cortázar, in true Symbolist fashion, has himself said that the reader receives a richer experience if no specific symbol is attributed to the animal in this story. As in the works of Poe, constant tension and terror pervade the work, and the tiger's meaning becomes a relative one--a personal nightmare for each character and each reader.

"LETTER TO A YOUNG LADY IN PARIS"

"Letter to a Young Lady in Paris" begins on a charming note. It is a letter from a young man to his girlfriend, who is visiting Paris. She has asked him to move into her apartment, and, through very delicate language, he tries to convince her that he would disrupt her very orderly and truly elegant apartment. He succumbs to her wishes, however, and moves his belongings, but on the way up in the elevator he begins to feel sick. Panic ensues when he vomits a bunny rabbit, and, while living in the apartment, each wave of anxiety produces another. Soon, he is sequestering ten bunny rabbits in an armoire. The rabbits sleep in the daytime and are awakened at night; he manages to keep his secret from his girlfriend's nosy maid. The nocturnal insomnia and the constant production of bunny rabbits drive him to jump out the window along with the last one regurgitated. The charming letter is really a suicide note, and the seemingly eccentric but sweet story becomes a horrific account of phobia and insanity.

"AXOLOTL"

Cortázar seems particularly fascinated with the unusual placement of animals in these stories. In "Bestiary" and "Letter to a Young Lady in Paris," animals take over the lives of people. In another short story, "Axolotl," the man who visits the aquarium every day to see the axolotl swim becomes the axolotl. The narrative point of view switches back and forth between the man and the sea creature, telling the story from both points of view, but since there is no regular pattern or warning when the point of view changes, it is often difficult to determine inside whose skin readers are. The nightmare of being trapped inside the body of a beast is the human's experience, and the panic of being abandoned by the man is the axolotl's final cry. The only hope, as noted by the axolotl, is the creation of art where the writer can become another and communicate on behalf of all creatures--expressing the feelings of all creatures so that none may feel the terror of isolation and imprisonment.

"ALL FIRES THE FIRE"

The shifting of narrative point of view, as well as the alternation of time and place, is a technique that Cortázar developed during his career as an author. A later story, "All Fires the Fire," revolves around two unhappy love triangles. One takes place in modern times and one during a gladiator fight in an ancient coliseum. Again, Cortázar uses animals to provide a menacing tone to what seem to be ordinary failures in romance.

In both cases, raging blazes burn the lovers to death. No clear delineation is made when the story shifts scenes. The reader begins to sense these changes as the story unfolds; the scenes are different, but the tension never desists. The author creates deliberate ambiguity so that the reader, who is being intentionally confused by the author, nevertheless receives signals at the same time. Like the Symbolist writers whom he admired, Cortázar, in "All Fires the Fire," understands the power of the suggestive image and insists that readers use their own senses to feel the intensity of hate, lust, and love in both triangles. Through smell, sound, and sight, the reader gets two complete and distinct pictures that have similar endings. Like the Surrealist writers who unraveled the varying layers of the mind, Cortázar here projects two events that occur at two different times in two different places yet at the same moment in the reader's consciousness.

"BLOW-UP"

Through fractured narration, Cortázar is able to examine how the mind can appropriate different personalities and points of view. The games of the mind are a constant theme in the works of Cortázar, and it is for that reason that a journey into his fictive world is an opportunity to explore the relationship between what seems to be real and what seems to be illogical. Cortázar confounds the reader's system of beliefs with his manipulation of discourse. He begins the story "Blow-Up," for example, by stating: "It'll never be known how this has to be told, in the first person or in the second, using the third person plural or continually inventing modes that will serve for nothing." He continues by telling readers how he writes--by typewriter--making them absolutely aware of the fact that they are going to enter the world of fiction. Although "Blow-Up" begins on this self-conscious trial, which seems to draw an obvious distinction between art and life, its actual theme is the interchangeability of the two. The narrator introduces the reader to the story's hero, a French-Chilean photographer named Robert Michel, and then becomes him. The story is narrated alternatively in first-person "I" and third-person "he" and becomes a collage of identities.

Out for a stroll on a pleasant November day, the photographer happens by chance upon a scene that disturbs him. Chance is an essential component of the world of magic, the fantastic and the illogical in Cortázar's short fiction. Chance rearranges preexisting order and creates a new future, past, and present for Cortázar's characters. The photographer/narrator witnesses a brief moment among a young man, a woman, and an older man sitting in a car--another love triangle with menacing undertones--and creates a history of what might have brought all three to the quay near the Seine. After the particular episode, he creates a future of what might happen to each of them afterward. Later, when he himself reflects on the episode, he studies his photographs as if the moments were frozen in time. Strangely, the more he studies his enlargements, the more his memory alters. Because he creates a fiction about each of the people involved, the photo and his involvement in their little dramas also become fiction, and he is not at all certain of what he has witnessed. The whole episode develops into a dream, a game of the mind.

The photographs that he had taken, which were supposed to reproduce reality with exactitude, become a collage of suggestions. Magnified, the photographs reveal even less about what he thought had occurred. The photographer believes that his camera is empowered with precision and with accuracy; he discovers, however, that the artwork has a life of its own that is constantly re-creating itself.

The search for truth in art is the pervading theme in Julio Cortázar's short fiction. He attempts to break with realist attitudes to force the reader to look beyond that which is ordinary and comfortable in order to explore the realms that seem, on the surface, incomprehensible and fearful. Cortázar believes that as human beings, people must recognize the inexplicable as just that and must admit that they do not have control over everything. The characters in "Bestiary" do not have control over the tiger. The young man in "Letter to a Young Lady in Paris" does not have control over the rabbits that he regurgitates. "All Fires the Fire" depicts the characters involved in passionate love triangles whose emotions are out of control. Finally, in "Blow-Up," the artist's work has a life of its own.

It was the Symbolist movement that gave Cortázar his stylistic signature and the Surrealists who divulged the irrational to later artists. Cortázar combined his appreciation for both movements and consolidated them with his own voice to create exciting and challenging short fiction.

OTHER MAJOR WORKS

LONG FICTION: *El examen*, wr. 1950, pb. 1986 (*Final Exam*, 2000); *Los premios*, 1960 (*The Winners*, 1965); *Rayuela*, 1963 (*Hopscotch*, 1966); *62: Modelo para armar*, 1968 (*62: A Model Kit*, 1972); *Libro de Manuel*, 1973 (*A Manual for Manuel*, 1978).

POETRY: *Presencia*, 1938 (as Julio Denís); *Los reyes*, 1949; *Pameos y meopas*, 1971; *Salvo el crepúsculo*, 1984.

NONFICTION: *Buenos Aires Buenos Aires*, 1968 (English translation, 1968); *Viaje alrededor de una mesa*, 1970; *Prosa del observatorio*, 1972 (with Antonio Galvez); *Fantomas contra los vampiros multinacionales: Una utopía realizable*, 1975; *Literatura en la revolución y revolución en la literatura*, 1976 (with Mario Vargas Llosa and Oscar Collazos); *Paris: The Essence of Image*, 1981; *Los autonautas de la cosmopista: O, Un viaje atemporal Paris-Marsella*, 1983 (with Carol Dunlop; *Autonauts of the Cosmoroute: A Timeless Voyage from Paris to Marseille*, 2007); *Nicaragua tan violentamente dulce*, 1983 (*Nicaraguan Sketches*, 1989); *Cartas*, 2000 (3 volumes).

TRANSLATIONS: *Robinson Crusoe*, 1945 (of Daniel Defoe's novel); *El inmoralista*, 1947 (of André Gide's *L'Immoraliste*); *El hombre que sabía demasiado*, c. 1948-1951 (of G. K. Chesterton's *The Man Who Knew Too Much*); *Vida y Cartas de John Keats*, c. 1948-1951 (of Lord Houghton's *Life and Letters of John Keats*); *Filosofía de la risa y del llanto*, 1950 (of Alfred Stern's *Philosophie du rire et des pleurs*); *La filosofía de Sartre y el psicoanálisis existencialista*, 1951 (of Stern's *Sartre, His Philosophy and Psychoanalysis*).

MISCELLANEOUS: *La vuelta al día en ochenta mundos*, 1967 (*Around the Day in Eighty Worlds*, 1986); *Último round*, 1969; *Divertimiento*, 1986.

BIBLIOGRAPHY

Alazraki, Jaime, and Ivan Ivask, eds. *The Final Island*. Norman: University of Oklahoma Press, 1978. *The Final Island* is a collection of essays, including two by Cortázar himself, about the role of magic or the marvelous as it works alongside what appears to be realism in Cortázar's fiction. In a more general way, the history of fiction is approached with the theory that the fabulous is itself more revealing about human truth than is the so-called realism. Contains a chronology and an extensive bibliography that offers data on Cortázar's publications in several languages.

Alonso, Carlos J., ed. *Julio Cortázar: New Readings*. New York: Cambridge University Press, 1998. The essays in this collection examine some of the short stories; the titles of these stories are listed in the index.

Bloom, Harold, ed. *Julio Cortázar*. Philadelphia: Chelsea House, 2004. Focuses on the short fiction, featuring plot summaries, lists of characters, and critical essays about the stories "Axolotl," "Bestiary," "Blow-Up," "End of the Game," and "The Night Face Up."

Garfield, Evelyn Picon. *Julio Cortázar*. New York: Frederick Ungar, 1975. Garfield begins and ends her study with personal interviews that she obtained with Cortázar at his home in Provence, France. She studies the neurotic obsession of the characters in Cortázar's fiction and offers firsthand commentary by Cortázar on his methods of writing and his own experiences that helped create his work. Cortázar's philosophies, his preferences, and even his own personal nightmares are expounded upon, illuminating much of the symbolism found in his work. Includes chronology, analysis, complete bibliography, and index.

Harris, Mark D. "Existence, Nothingness, and the Quest for Being: Sartrean Existentialism and Julio Cortázar's Early Short Fiction." *Latin American Literary Review* 37, no. 74 (July-December, 2009): 5-25. Analyzes Cortázar's short fiction from the perspective of Jean-Paul Sartre's existential philosophy. Notes that in many of the stories the protagonists' outlooks and experiences are existentialist.

Hernandez del Castillo, Ana. *Keats, Poe, and the Shaping of Cortázar's Mythopoesis*. Amsterdam: John Benjamins, 1981. Studies the influence of John Keats and Edgar Allan Poe on the work of Cortázar; the author states that of these two poets, whose works Cortázar translated, Poe had the greater influence on Cortázar. Studies the role of archetypes in mythology and psychology and how they have been used in the works of all three writers. Contains an excellent index, which includes references that have had an enormous impact on trends in the twentieth century.

Palmer, Julia. "Verbs, Voyeurism, and the Stalker Narrative in Cortázar's 'Continuidad de los parques.'" *Romance Quarterly* 56, no. 3 (Summer, 2009): 207-216. Describes the story as a stalker narrative in two senses: It is a story about a homicidal stalker, as well as a story "in which the reader is turned into a stalker." Examines how the use of verb tenses enables Cortázar to shape the narrative.

Peavler, Terry J. *Julio Cortázar*. Boston: Twayne, 1990. Divides Cortázar's short fiction into four categories--the fantastic, the mysterious, the psychological, and the realistic--in order to show how he used these genres as games to study discourse. Argues that studying any of Cortázar's works as merely "psychological" or "political" offers a superficial understanding of his intent, which is really to study the nature of fiction itself. That is why Cortázar's narrative often changes voice, undermines itself, and even offers a choice of endings. Includes a chronology and a through bibliography, and offers intelligent analysis.

Schmidt-Cruz, Cynthia. *Mothers, Lovers, and Others: The Short Stories of Julio Cortázar*. Albany: State University of New York Press, 2004. Analyzes the conception of the feminine in Cortázar's short fiction, arguing that his obsession with the mother is the source of his uneasiness with femininity.

Standish, Peter. *Understanding Julio Cortázar*. Columbia: University of South Carolina Press, 2001. An analytical overview of Cortázar's life and works, including the posthumous publications. Chapter 3 focuses on the short stories.

Stavans, Ilan. *Julio Cortázar: A Study of the Short Fiction*. New York: Twayne, 1996. A study of Cortázar's short fiction that shows how his art reflects his life and his life is affected by his art. Stavans calls his book an "autobiography" of Cortázar's short fiction that attempts to trace the sources of his short stories in biographical information. Divides Cortázar's work into two creative periods of his life: 1945 to 1966 and 1967 to 1983.

Sugano, Marian Zwerling. "Beyond What Meets the Eye: The Photographic Analogy in Cortázar's Short Stories." *Style* 27 (Fall, 1993): 332-351. Summarizes and critiques Cortazar's analogy between the short story and photography in his essays "Some Aspects of the Short Story" and "On the Short Story and Its Environs." Explains how Cortázar dramatizes this analogy in "Blow-Up" and "Apocalypse at Solentiname."

Susan Nayel

D

Osamu Dazai

Born: Kanagi, Aomori, Japan; June 19, 1909
Died: Tokyo, Japan; June 13, 1948
Also known as: Shūji Tsushima

PRINCIPAL SHORT FICTION

Bannen, 1936
Tokyo hakkei, 1941
Kajitsu, 1944
Otogizōshi, 1945
Shinshaku shokoku banashi, 1945
Fuyu no hanabi, 1947
Dazai Osamu: Selected Stories and Sketches, 1983
Crackling Mountain, and Other Stories, 1989
Self Portraits: Tales from the Life of Japan's Great
   Decadent Romantic, 1991
Blue Bamboo: Tales of Fantasy and Romance, 1993

OTHER LITERARY FORMS

The international fame of Osamu Dazai (oh-sahm-ew dah-zi) is based largely on a short novel, *Shayō* (1947; *The Setting Sun,* 1956). Translations also exist of a defensive fictional autobiography, *Ningen shikkaku* (1948; *No Longer Human,* 1958), and an equally personal travelogue, *Tsugaru* (1944; English translation, 1985; also as *Return to Tsugaru: Travels of a Purple Tramp,* 1985). Dazai published two plays, as well as a number of essays, and like all Japanese authors, he experimented with the haiku. His total literary output is, with regard to genre, almost as versatile as it is prolific.

ACHIEVEMENTS

During his life, Osamu Dazai was much more of a cult figure than an institutional model, and for this reason he did not receive the major awards available in his milieu. After his death, however, he was accorded widespread homage. A literary journal has instituted an annual Osamu Dazai prize, televised memorial services at Dazai's graveside take place annually, and at least three memorial sites have been established throughout Japan.

BIOGRAPHY

All forms of autobiographical fiction are popular in Japan, especially the "I" novel, and Osamu Dazai's fictional reenactment of his own life has become the hallmark of his style. Indeed, his personal entourage, including his wives, mistresses, intimate friends, and members of his immediate family, repeatedly turn up in his fiction under their own names or thinly disguised pseudonyms. A bare chronology of the principal events in Dazai's life would be a somewhat sordid account of sexual encounters, family disputes, drugs, drinking, and attempted suicides. Only when accompanied by introspective analysis, artistic reflections, and literary parallels, as they are in the author's fiction, do these events become material of universal human interest.

Dazai was a poor little rich boy born Shūji Tsushima in the northernmost district of the main island of Japan. At the age of nineteen, shortly after meeting a geisha, Hatsuyo, he unsuccessfully attempted suicide. Four months later, he began the study of French literature at Tokyo University. In the same year, he made a joint suicide attempt with a waitress; he recovered, but she died. In the following month, he married Hatsuyo. Along with magazine editing and short-story writing, he engaged in leftist political activities. In 1933, he used for the first time his pen name, Osamu Dazai, with a story that won a newspaper prize. Three years later, he published his first collection of stories and entered a mental hospital. In 1937, he again unsuccessfully attempted suicide, this time with Hatsuyo; shortly thereafter, their union was dissolved, and he entered into an arranged marriage with a woman from his own social class. During World War II, he was disqualified by ill health from active military service, but he engaged in various noncombatant activities while continuing to write. For some time, he carried on a correspondence with a young woman, Ota Shizuko, on literary subjects, and, shortly after their initial meeting in 1941, she became his mistress. In 1947, while writing *The Setting Sun*, he established a liaison with a beautician, Yamazaki Tomie, while still involved with and living with his wife. Shortly after completing *No Longer Human*, the most explicit of his confessional fiction, Dazai committed suicide with Tomie by drowning, leaving behind several notes, including one to his wife.

ANALYSIS

Osamu Dazai's longer narratives are easier than his stories for Western readers to approach. In the blending of autobiography and fiction, he resembles Marcel Proust and Thomas Wolfe. The protagonist of most of his fiction is perennially the same character, a loser in society who, nevertheless, wins the sympathy of the reader. As such, he has been compared to Tom Sawyer and Holden Caulfield. He has equal resemblance to a stock character in classical Russian fiction, the useless man. Since Dazai knew the work of Ivan Goncharov, who portrayed this type in the novel *Oblomov* (1859; English translation, 1915), it would not be farfetched to describe Dazai's perennial persona as a decadent Oblomov. He is, however, a greater misfit in society, and he never succeeds in solving his problems. In *No Longer Human*, Dazai describes himself as a man "who dreads human beings," and in reference to city crowds in "Tokyo Hakkei" ("Eight Views of Tokyo"), he is reminded of the question posed by a Western author, "What is love?" and the answer, "To dream of beautiful things and do dirty ones." He is placed by critic Phyllis I. Lyons in "the school of irresponsibility and decadence." All this makes him appeal to youth both in Japan and elsewhere. As a rebel against convention, he highlights the antagonism between rich and poor and the clash between parents and children. In his youth, he had frequently acted the part of a buffoon, and he sometimes portrays this aspect of his personality in his fiction. His tone varies between self-dramatization and self-satire. In two of his works based on

plots from William Shakespeare and Friedrich Schiller, however, he radically departs from his ostensible autobiographical mold. Although various episodes in Dazai's fiction treat human debasement, there is nothing prurient in his descriptions, which are frequently laconic or subtle. Occasionally, he resembles Honoré de Balzac with endless references to crude and minor details of life, debts, expenditures, and financial waste.

"AN ALMANAC OF PAIN"

In one of his stories, "Kuno no nenkan" ("An Almanac of Pain"), Dazai suggests that he does not have thoughts, only likes and dislikes, and that he wants "to record in fragmentary form just those realities I cannot forget." Because of writing these personal fragments instead of formal history or philosophy, he describes himself in the same work as "a writer of the marketplace." In *Return to Tsugaru*, he remarks that "the gods spare no love for a man who goes burdened under the bad karma of having to sell manuscripts filled with details of his family in order to make a living." One of his themes is the problems of family life, but he frequently maintains that only individuals count. Translator Edward Seidensticker regards Dazai as "a superb comic writer," but little of this comic genius is apparent in translation. It consists in caricature of himself, as well as others, and the portrayal of absurd situations rather than satire. Dazai is perhaps the outstanding example in any literature of solipsistic intertextuality or the constant quotation of previous works from his own pen. In *Return to Tsugaru*, for example, he quotes frequently and extensively from his own stories, as well as from histories and guidebooks by other authors. Indeed, key passages from his early stories reappear over and over in his later works.

Despite the wide variety of style and subject matter in Dazai's short stories, they may be divided into two main categories, fantasy and autobiography. The latter group belongs to a special Japanese genre, shishōsetsu, or personal fiction. In stories about his own physical and psychological development, Dazai adheres closely to historical fact but arranges details to suit his aesthetic purpose. Among his recurring themes are the individual and the family, friendship, the search for identity, class barriers and distinctions, and the ambivalence of personality. "Omoide" ("Recollections") embodies all these themes in a Proust-like, somewhat lugubrious reminiscence of childhood. Blending the tones of irony and confession, he describes such episodes as sexual initiation and the trading of books for bird eggs and such feelings as loneliness and longing for parental love. A later story, "Gangu" ("Toys"), concerns his return home after a long absence. Here, he uses a narrative artifice of taking the reader into his confidence while assuming that the action takes place at the moment he is speaking or thinking. He goes back to the early stages of infancy and introduces one of his common scatological motifs of making water. His fantasies seem more real than his actual surroundings. In "Anitachi" ("My Older Brothers"), he portrays his histrionic involvement with French satanism and the role of a dandy, which he defines as a handsome, accomplished man loved by more than one woman. This and other narratives of his behavior with women do not measure up to the level of rakishness associated with contemporary France or even with the known details of his own activities. He portrays himself as bashful, inept, and inadequate in his sexual relationships, nearly all of which are with women of a lower social class.

"PUTTING GRANNY OUT TO DIE"

Dazai several times describes his abortive suicide attempts. The title of the translation of "Ubasute" ("Putting Granny out to Die"), refers to an ancient custom of exposing old people to the elements when they are no longer able to cope with life, but the story itself concerns his attempted suicide with Hatsuyo. En route to a mountain inn, he rehashes various derogatory terms that have been applied to him-- "liar, swellhead, lecher, idler, squanderer"--and then makes a sincere prayer in the toilet, a typical combination of incongruous elements. Dazai suggests that, although he represents a composite of unsavory qualities, he is still superior to the common lot. The reader wonders, however, whether Dazai's life story would have been worthy of attention if he had not belonged to a wealthy and influential family and whether a proletarian would have written it in the same style. His "Eight Views of Tokyo" is another example of a title not descriptive of the contents. Although it promises an account of urban life in the manner of Charles Dickens or Balzac, the

work itself consists of further true confessions. It mentions only casually a project to write about Tokyo that was never carried out. Dazai includes an epigraph, "For one who has suffered," and introduces the marketplace theme by referring to his ten volumes of "mediocre writings" already published. He bids farewell to his youth, denies the accusation that he has joined the ranks of the philistines, and vaguely alludes to his radical political activities. Most important, he announces a spiritual crisis in the form of a "serious aspiration to become a writer." He affirms that his autobiographical style is inseparable from his art, an unambiguous declaration that the first-person narrator in most of his works is indeed himself. Striking a pose like Balzac, he observes that he himself has become one of the sights of Tokyo.

In the realm of fantasy, Dazai draws on native classical sources. "Gyofukuki" ("Transformation") combines the thoughts of a young girl about the death of a young man in a mountain pool with a folktale about a man who turned into a serpent after eating several trout. After her drunken father attempts to rape her, the girl commits suicide in the pool, fantasizing in the process that she has been transformed into a carp. The story has no connection with Franz Kafka's *Die Verwandlung* (1915; *The Metamorphosis*, 1936) but has some resemblance to Ovid's retelling of classical legends. "Sarugashima" ("The Island of Monkeys") is more like Kafka and has an outlook less gloomy. The narrator engages in dialogue with a group of monkeys after a sea voyage. Looking back on his own childhood, he seems to interpret his present incarnation as a sign of immortality or transmigration. Suddenly he realizes that people are coming to gape at him. He agrees with the most compatible of the monkeys that it is better to choose unknown dangers over boring regularity. The story concludes with a news item that two monkeys have escaped from the London Zoo. Another simian tale, "Saruzuka" ("The Mound of the Monkey's Grave"), resembles a Voltairean *conte philosophique*. A young couple flee from their parents because religious differences in the two households have kept them from marrying. They are accompanied by a monkey who acts as their servant. When a child is born, the monkey demonstrates an affection equal to that of the father and mother. One day, in the absence of the parents, the monkey, in giving the child a bath, immerses it in boiling water, not realizing the fatal consequences of the deed. He later commits suicide at the child's grave, and the parents abandon the world for religion. Dazai, intervening in the narrative, asks which sect they have chosen. The tragic story loses its point, he observes, if the original faith of either parent must be adopted by the other.

"CURRENCY"

"Kohei" ("Currency") conforms to an extensive Western genre, the thingaresque, a form of narrative in which the protagonist, either an animal or inanimate object, provides an intensely realistic portrayal of the social conditions in which it exists. The genre derives from Lucius Apuleius's Metamorphoses (second century C.E.; *The Golden Ass*, 1566) and was also used by Dazai's forerunner Natsume Sōseki in his *Wagahai wa Neko de aru* (1905-1906; *I Am a Cat*, 1961). Dazai's story concerns the experiences of a one-hundred-yen note as it is passed from hand to hand in Tokyo in the aftermath of World War II. The story is exceptional in having absolutely nothing to do with the personal life of the author, but it does illustrate an aspect of Dazai's style described by James O'Brien as ironic reversal: Much of the story illustrates a woman's greed, but it concludes with the noble sacrifice of a prostitute. "Kobutori" ("Taking the Wen Away"), based on an ancient tale, describes a Rip Van Winkle situation in which an old man with a large wen climbs a hill at night in a drunken condition and encounters ten red demons, contentedly drunk like himself. As the old man joins them in a delirious dance, they insist that he return another time and let them take his wen with them as a pledge. A rich old man also with a wen, hearing this story, goes to the same place, but his measured cadences displease the demons and they prepare to leave. He catches one of them, entreating that his wen be removed, but they think he is asking for its return. They give him the wen of the first man, and he then has two. Dazai concludes that the story has no moral except to point up the currents of comedy and tragedy in life.

"DAS GEMEINE"

Dazai's two streams of autobiography and fantasy are brought together in "Das Gemeine" ("Das Gemeine"), whose title is the German word for "vulgarity"; however, the strands are interwoven in such a way that no coherent plot structure can be discerned. For this reason, the story, one of Dazai's most difficult, is sometimes considered as an example of Dadaism or deliberate mystification. It is both a pastiche of Western literature and an account of the efforts of Dazai and his collaborators to establish a literary journal. It begins humorously with the narrator, Sanojiro, contemplating a double suicide until jilted by his paramour. He then becomes involved with a waitress at a sake stand. As a means of expressing spring joy, he composes a poem opposite in tone to the *ubi sunt* theme of French Renaissance poetry. Later, Dazai himself, as a character in the story, intones, "The rain falls on the town," paraphrasing a famous line by Arthur Rimbaud. He asks his fellow editors whether they prefer strawberries prepared for the market or purely natural ones, an allegory for literary works as well as a reflection of his theme of the marketplace. At the end of the story, the narrator, while questioning his identity, is run over by a train and records his death in the manner of the protagonist of "Transformation." Here, as in the rest of Dazai's works, the emphasis is on the individual rather than society. His stories, as well as his longer fiction, use his own personality to portray various contradictions in the human condition.

OTHER MAJOR WORKS

LONG FICTION: *Shin Hamuretto*, 1941; *Seigi to bishō*, 1942; *Udaijin Sanetomo*, 1943; *Pandora no hako*, 1945; *Sekibetsu*, 1945; *Shayō*, 1947 (*The Setting Sun*, 1956); *Ningen shikkaku*, 1948 (*No Longer Human*, 1958).

PLAYS: *Fuyu no hanabi*, pb. 1946; *Haru no kaeha*, pb. 1946.

NONFICTION: *Tsugaru*, 1944 (English translation, 1985; also as *Return to Tsugaru: Travels of a Purple Tramp*, 1985).

MISCELLANEOUS: *Dazai Osamu zenshu*, 1955-1956 (12 volumes).

BIBLIOGRAPHY

Cohn, Joel R. "Dazai Osamu." In *Modern Japanese Writers*, edited by Jay Rubin. New York: Charles Scribner's Sons, 2001. Provides an introductory overview of Dazai's life and works.

_____. *Studies in the Comic Spirit in Modern Japanese Fiction*. Cambridge, Mass.: Harvard University Press, 1998. Examines humor in the works of Dazai, Masuji Ibuse, and Hisashi Inoue. Includes bibliographical references and an index.

Keene, Donald. *Landscapes and Portraits: Appreciations of Japanese Culture*. Tokyo: Kodansha International, 1971. Of particular relevance is the section on Osamu Dazai in chapter 4, "Three Modern Novelists," which focuses on the difference between Western and Japanese responses to Dazai's fiction, the strongly autobiographical elements in his works, and the style and major themes of his narrative. Supplemented by illustrations and a short reading list.

Kirkup, James. "Now Out of Japan Something New." *The Times*, December 13, 1990. A brief biographical sketch, followed by comments on Dazai's short stories and autobiographical essays. Focuses on Dazai's collection *The Crackling Mountain, and Other Stories*. Discusses Dazai's variations on the title story, one of the best-known folktales in Japan.

Lyon, Phyllis I. *The Saga of Dazai Osamu: A Critical Study with Translations*. Stanford, Calif.: Stanford University Press, 1985. Provides various critical perspectives of Dazai's work. Includes aBibliography and index.

Motofùji, Frank T. "Dazai Osamu." In *Approaches to the Modern Japanese Short Story*, edited by Thomas E. Swann and Kinya Tsuruta. Tokyo: Waseda University Press, 1982. Provides analyses of two short stories, "Villon's Wife" and "A Sound of Hammering," written in 1947, one year before the author's suicide. The two stories are seen as reflections of the dilemma of the writer in postwar Japan, overwhelmed by the chaos of a ruined past.

O'Brien, James. *Dazai Osamu*. Boston: Twayne, 1975. An introductory overview that combines a biography with a chronologically based study of Dazai's creative output. Includes a chronological summary and a select bibliography.

Rimer, J. Rhomas. "Dazai Osamu: The Death of the Past, The Setting Sun." In *Modern Japanese Fiction and Its Traditions: An Introduction*. Princeton, N.J.: Princeton University Press, 1978. Views the novel *The Setting Sun* as a reflection of the tensions in Japan before, during, and after the war years. The characters and situations relentlessly probe the realities of a transitional period.

Starrs, Roy. "Nation and Region in the Work of Dazai Osamu." In *Tsugaru: Regional Identity on Japan's Northern Periphery*, edited by Nanyan Guo et al. Dunedin, New Zealand: University of Otago Press, 2005. This collection of essays examining the distinctive life and culture in Tsugaru includes a discussion of Dazai's travelogue *Return to Tsugaru*.

Ueda, Makoto. "Dazai Osamu." In *Modern Japanese Writers and the Nature of Literature*. Stanford, Calif.: Stanford University Press, 1976. Focuses on the literary concepts of Dazai as revealed within his fiction. Underlying his "expansive, emotional, and spontaneous" prose style, with its seeming artlessness, is a view of literature as a "food for losers." Includes references to the Japanese originals of the texts discussed and aBibliography focusing on Dazai.

Vachon, John. "An Overly Sensitive Heart." *Daily Yomiuri*, November 25, 1990, p. 7. A review of Dazai's *Self-Portraits: Tales from the Life of Japan's Great Decadent Romantic*. Provides a brief biographical sketch and comments on Dazai's style in the eighteen pieces of this early work. Notes that he is a better writer of short stories than of novels.

Westerhoven, James, trans. Preface to *Return to Tsugaru: Travels of a Purple Tramp*. Tokyo: Kodansha International, 1985. An overview of the developments of the novel, viewing it as the journal of a quest for love, founded on the premise that acceptance and love require the shedding of all affection. Includes a brief biography with background material to the novel (a family tree and a map of Dazai's journey through the Tsugaru peninsula).

Wolfe, Alan Stephen. *Suicidal Narrative in Modern Japan: The Case of Dazai Osamu*. Princeton, N.J.: Princeton University Press, 1990. An insightful study. Includes bibliographical references and an index.

A. Owen Aldridge
Updated by Anna M. Wittman

ANITA DESAI

Born: Mussoorie, India; June 24, 1937
Also Known As: Anita Mazumbar

PRINCIPAL SHORT FICTION
"Tea with the Maharani," 1959
"Grandmother," 1960
Games at Twilight, and Other Stories, 1978
Diamond Dust, 2000

OTHER LITERARY FORMS

Anita Desai (ah-NEE-tah deh-SI) is best known as a novelist. Three of her novels have been shortlisted for the Booker Prize; others have won various awards. The early ones are set entirely in India; later ones have more cosmopolitan settings, such as *The Zig Zag Way* (2004), set in Mexico.

ACHIEVEMENTS

Anita Desai is among the first wave of Indian writers to write in English to emerge after Indian independence. She quickly established a reputation as a chronicler of the urban and suburban middle-class world, with its nostalgia for its colonial past, its hopes for a new India, and its growing disillusionment that the modern was not as good as the past. She especially achieved a close depiction of the women of this middle class, their lives in conflict between their family duties and obligations and their desire for freedom and independence.

In her short stories, Desai manages to catch for the first time little cameos of such women, as in "The Rooftop Dwellers." However, she depicts the men, too, such as the little civil servant of "Diamond Dust" and the successful doctor in "A Devoted Son." Some of her short stories parallel the settings of the novels. Mexico features in "Tepoztlan Tomorrow," as it does in *The Zig Zag Way*, as an alter ego for India. Although not as heavily awarded as her novels, the short stories point to an able and articulate writer, who pushes the boundaries of the traditional Western short story.

BIOGRAPHY

Anita Desai was born Anita Mazumbar in the Indian hill station of Mussoorie to Dhiren Mazumbar, a businessman, and his German wife, Antoinette Nime. Desai was brought up in Old Delhi, with her brother and two sisters. Both parents were fierce opponents of the British Raj, whose presence in nearby New Delhi, the capital of India, was manifest until Indian independence in 1947. Desai was educated at Queen Mary's Higher Secondary School, which was run by British Catholic nuns, though most of the girls were Hindu and Muslim, fairly equally divided.

At independence, the Muslim students disappeared, Desai's first experience of the partition of the country into India and Pakistan. She could speak German, English, and Hindi, though some of her school education was in Urdu, the language of culture in the old empire, spoken especially by the Muslims but shortly replaced by Hindi as the official language in the new secular India. Desai used English as her language of choice.

During this time, Desai began to write stories, her first written as early as seven years old. She became known as the writer of the family and a voracious reader. Unsurprisingly, she studied English literature for her B.A., at Miranda House, a women's college attached to Delhi University. While attending college in 1957, her short story "Circus Cat, Alley Cat" was published in a New Delhi journal. After winning the university's Pershad Memorial Prize for English, she graduated and went to work for the German Cultural Institute in Calcutta, where she met and married Ashuin Desai, a businessman, in 1958. By him she had four children. The young family moved frequently, from Calcutta to Bombay (now Mumbai), Kalimpong, Chandigarh, back to Delhi, and then to Pune. She continued writing short stories. "Tea with the Maharani" was published in London in 1959 and "Grandmother" in Calcutta in 1960. However, the milieu she moved in was far from literary, and she wrote clandestinely.

Her first novel, *Cry, the Peacock*, appeared in 1963. Influenced by Virginia Woolf's interior monologue, it traces the heroine killing her husband then herself after four years of marriage. It depicts the emerging modern urban India and brought to Anglo-Indian fiction a new symbolic and imagistic technique and style. The emphasis was on husband-wife relationships rather than political and social identity.

A series of novels then flowed, bringing Desai her first recognition. *Fire on the Mountain* (1977) won the Winifred Holtby Prize of the Royal Society of Literature in 1978 from England, and from India came the National Academy of Letters Award in the same year and the Sahitya Akademi Award the next year. Her first collection of short fiction, *Games at Twilight, and Other Stories*, was published in 1978 and well reviewed in England. One of its stories, "The Accompanist," became the basis for the novel *In Custody* (1984), shortlisted for the Booker Prize, and later it was made into a film, for which she wrote the script in 1993.

With her family grown, Desai felt free to move abroad and take up various academic positions offered to her. In 1986-1987 she was Helen Cam Fellow at Girton College, Cambridge, followed by stays at Smith College in Connecticut, Mount Holyoke in Massachusetts, and Barnard College in New York. She then traveled back to Cambridge in England, before becoming a Rockefeller Foundation scholar in Italy and Visiting Professor in Cairo, Egypt. She finally put down anchor in 1993 at the Massachusetts Institute of Technology (MIT), where she remained John Burchard Professor of Writing for a number of years.

Desai stayed in Massachusetts, in retirement from teaching activities, when she became Professor Emerita at MIT. In 2003, she received the Benson Medal from the Royal Society of Literature, of which she was by then a fellow. Her papers are at the Harry Ransom Humanities Research Center at the University of Texas, Austin.

ANALYSIS

Most of Anita Desai's short stories are contained in two volumes published twenty-two years apart. Although this suggests her long fiction took most of her energies, themes and settings found in her long fiction are encapsulated in the short fiction.

Desai is a natural storyteller, mainly in the Western tradition of H. G. Wells and E. M. Forster in the British tradition and Guy de Maupassant in the French tradition. However, she is aware of the older traditions in Indian literature. Like her Western predecessors, she explores clashes of culture, whether of class, of modernity, or of city life versus rural life. In her early short stories, she confines these clashes to Indian middle-class life, such as she experienced as a girl in Old Delhi, basically colonial in feel. In the later volume, the clashes expand to those between East and West and even take in Western perspectives on the newly emerging India.

Typically her stories revolve around female characters, seeking some form of identity and significance, but a number involve male leads. These stories are diverse, exploring the nature of success, the need to emigrate, and even touching on the male psyche in a middle-class society that is rule-bound and limiting.

"GAMES AT TWILIGHT"

This is the opening story of *Games at Twilight, and Other Stories*, Desai's first collection. As in her novel *Clear Light of Day* (1980), the story evokes the Old Delhi of her youth, with its fading suburban streets and gardens housing the respectable civil servants who used to work for the British Raj and at the present serve the Indian government in New Delhi, a few miles down the road.

The story centers on the youngest boy in a game of hide-and-seek. Desai brilliantly evokes the heat of an Indian summer, when it is too hot to play outside during the day, and the gradual coming of the evening. The boy finds a brilliant hiding place and remains undiscovered. Time passes, and he fears he is forgotten, as indeed he has been. Rushing out, he finds his intrusion in a new game ignored. His sense of his own identity is fragile and insecure. He suddenly realizes just how insignificant he is.

The story highlights one of Desai's concerns: that of finding significance in old social structures, especially for women who want to break out of their invisibility. As girls, they seem to matter, be educated and instructed; thereafter they disappear as wives and mothers. However, this story suggests boys face the same problem, not only in Indian society but also in the society of universal childhood.

"THE ACCOMPANIST"

This story also has a male protagonist, this time one who traces his feelings of identity through adolescence into manhood. His sense of significance emerges starkly as a willingness to subordinate his music, career, and even personality to a charismatic virtuoso sitar player. The protagonist remains an almost unheard player on a three-stringed instrument, played merely to keep the soloist within certain traditional limits. Desai presumes her (Western) readers know enough of Indian music to understand the point. When the accompanist is challenged by some school friends that he is wasting his talents, he runs away, unable to bear examining the truth of what they say. Desai leaves the story open: Does he find himself by losing himself in the greater art, or is he really feeding on the greater man's personality as a leech or parasite? Desai took this theme and developed it in a later novel, *In Custody.*

"THE FAREWELL PARTY"

Several stories expose the petty hypocrisies of the Indian bourgeoisie, which in turn reveal the universality of bourgeois mentality and society as a whole. "Pineapple Cake" reveals the pretensions and lies of the lower middle class in a way reminiscent of the work of Wells or Maupassant. "A Dutiful Son" shows the insensitivity of the successful son, who has become a top surgeon. In "The Farewell Party," a commercial representative and his wife hold a farewell party as they are moved by the firm to a new city. They are treated as if they have been an indispensable part of small-town society, whereas in fact Desai makes clear they have been complete nonentities. The lack of lighting at the evening garden party symbolizes the lack of truth in the human relationships enacted. The husband and wife have no real friends. The reader wonders if anyone at the party has any real friends, so deep run the social falsities.

"DIAMOND DUST"

Although not standing first in Desai's later collection, *Diamond Dust*, "Diamond Dust" is one of the most dramatic of the stories and makes an easy bridge to the earlier volume. Subtitled "A Tragedy," it is a pathetic, even comic, domestic tragedy for a civil servant from Delhi. Mr. Das becomes obsessed with the black dog he acquires, even though the dog is totally unsocial and almost untameable. Das's reputation as a respectable citizen plummets because the dog runs wild, biting all comers. Das pathetically looks for the dog when it breaks out of its compound on one of its amorous orgies. Finally, Das finds the animal in the dogcatcher's van, about to be put down. He chases the van, collapsing and dying with a heart attack. What emerges is the strength of passion beneath the most respectable of men. The dog becomes symbolic of the inner psyche. Das's erstwhile companions are all shown with their inner urges manifesting in bizarre behaviors, but they can be contained within society. However, they have no patience with Das, who cannot control his.

Anita Desai (Getty Images)

"THE ROOFTOP DWELLERS"

By contrast, "The Rooftop Dwellers" deals with a slight and inexperienced girl, Moyna, who is determined to become one of India's "new women"--independent career girls. She moves from a rural background through college to a literary job in Delhi, working for a magazine. Most of her energies are spent, however, in just surviving, first in a dreadful women's hostel, which is like a prison, then in a rooftop apartment, miles out in the suburbs. The story relates her various adventures. Moyna has a stubborn streak, and she refuses to be ground down by discomfort, prejudice, and poor pay. Her mother brings some family comforts and encourages Moyna to make a respectable marriage. However, when she receives a letter from her mother inviting Moyna to meet a suitable prospective husband, she finally resolves to stay where she is. Anything, it would seem, is better than being a nonentity of a wife in rural India.

The human resilience Moyna shows in the last story is one thread that Desai traces through nearly all her stories. No matter how bad conditions or relationships are, most of her characters survive, even if on a reduced scale. Life goes on, despite heat, poverty, tradition, and lack of apparent purpose. When Desai uses a foreign setting, be it England, Mexico, or Canada, the same lesson comes through: India is perhaps a more interesting and diverse microcosm, but its humanity is not ultimately different from humanity elsewhere.

OTHER MAJOR WORKS

LONG FICTION: *Cry, the Peacock*, 1963; *Voices in the City*, 1965; *Bye-Bye Blackbird*, 1971; *Where Shall We Go This Summer?*, 1975; *Fire on the Mountain*, 1977; *Clear Light of Day*, 1980; *In Custody*, 1984; *Baumgartner's Bombay*, 1988; *Journey to Ithaca*, 1995; *Fasting, Feasting*, 1999; *The Zig Zag Way*, 2004.

SCREENPLAY: *In Custody*, 1993.

NONFICTION: "Indian Fiction Today," 1989; "Women and Fiction in India," 1992.

CHILDREN'S LITERATURE: *The Peacock Garden*, 1974; *The Village by the Sea: An Indian Family Story*, 1982.

BIBLIOGRAPHY

Afzal-Khan, Fawzia. *Cultural Imperialism and the Indo-English Novel: Genre Ideology in R. K. Narayan, Anita Desai, Kamala Markandaya, and Salman Rushdie*. University Park: Pennsylvania State University Press, 1993. A postcolonial literary study based on poststructuralist tenets. Advanced analysis of Desai.

Ahmad, Hena. *Postnational Feminisms: Postcolonial Identities and Cosmopolitanism in the Works of Kamala Markandaya, Tsitsi Dangarembga, Ama Ata Aidoo, and Anita Desai*. New York: Peter Lang, 2009. A feminist analysis of Desai's work, comparing it with that of other postcolonial women writers.

Bande, Usha. *The Novels of Anita Desai: A Study in Character and Conflict*. New Delhi: Prestige, 1988. One of a number of critical texts by Indian scholars. This details in a straightforward way Desai's bourgeoisie and their characterization.

Jain, Jasbir. *Stairs to the Attic: The Novels of Anita Desai*. Jaipur, India: Printwell, 1987. Although not dealing directly with the short stories, the past-present conflicts identified form typical thematic material in the stories.

Prasad, Madhusudan. *Anita Desai: The Novelist*. Allahabad, India: New Horizon, 1981. An early full-length study of Desai's fiction, recognizing the potential of her novels. A good introduction.

Sengupta, Jayita. *Refractions of Desire: Feminist Perspective in the Novels of Toni Morrison, Michele Roberts, and Anita Desai*. Delhi: Atlantic, 2006. Compares the portrayal of family relationships and gender representation across three different cultures.

David Barratt

JOSÉ DONOSO

Born: Santiago, Chile; October 5, 1924
Died: Santiago, Chile; December 7, 1996

PRINCIPAL SHORT FICTION

Veraneo y otros cuentos, 1955
Dos cuentos, 1956
El Charlestón, 1960 (*Charleston, and Other Stories,* 1977)
Los mejores cuentos de José Donoso, 1965
Cuentos, 1971
Tres novelitas burguesas, 1973 (novellas; *Sacred Families,* 1977)
Cuatro para Delfina, 1982
Seis cuentos para ganar, 1985
Taratuta; Naturaleza muerta con cachimba, 1990 (novellas; *"Taratuta" and "Still Life with Pipe,"* 1993)

OTHER LITERARY FORMS

José Donoso (hoh-ZAY doh-NOH-soh) is best known for his novels, among which *El obsceno pájaro de la noche* (1970; *The Obscene Bird of Night,* 1973) stands out internationally as his signature masterpiece. In the 1990's he published *Donde van a morir los elefantes* (1995) and *El mocho* (1997). He also wrote a number of autobiographical works, one of which is the significant *Historia personal del "boom"* (1972; *The Boom in Spanish American Literature: A Personal History,* 1977), as well as a play based on one of the novellas in *Cuatro para Delfina* and a volume of poetry.

ACHIEVEMENTS

Receiving his B.A. at Princeton University with the aid of a Doherty Foundation Fellowship, José Donoso went on to win the Santiago Municipal Short-Story Prize for *Veraneo y otros cuentos;* the William Faulkner Foundation Prize for his first novel, *Coronación* (1957;

Coronation, 1965); two John Simon Guggenheim Memorial Foundation Fellowships (1968, 1973); and a Woodrow Wilson Fellowship (1992). His other awards include the Chile-Italia Prize for journalism, the National Prize for Literature (Chile), the Prize for Criticism (Spain), the Mondello Prize (Italy), the Roger Caillois Prize (France), and, in 1990, the Grand Cross of Civilian Merit, granted by Spain's Cabinet of Ministers.

BIOGRAPHY

José Donoso Yañez was born in Santiago, Chile, on October 5, 1924. He specialized in English during his early education and majored in English literature at Princeton University, where he published his first two short stories, both written in English: "The Blue Woman" (1950) and "The Poisoned Pastries" (1951). Returning to Chile, he published "China," his first short story written in Spanish, in 1954. The seven stories of his prizewinning first volume of short stories, published at his own expense, include the outstanding "El Güero" ("The Güero") and "Una señora" ("A Lady"). During a biennium in Buenos Aires (1958-1960) he met an artist, also from Chile, María del Pilar Serrano, whom he married in 1961. His travels subsequently took him to Mexico; to the University of Iowa, where he lectured for the Writers' Workshop; to Mallorca, where he and his wife adopted an infant girl; to Colorado State University for a lectureship terminated by illness; to Spain again in 1973; to a post at Princeton University in 1975; back to Spain in 1976; and, finally, home to Chile in 1981.

Literary history identifies Donoso with the "boom" in Spanish American literature that occurred during the 1960's and 1970's, comprising such notable writers as Julio Cortázar, Carlos Fuentes, Gabriel García Márquez, Juan Rulfo, and Mario Vargas Llosa. Donoso's critical contribution to this movement is his *The Boom in Spanish American Literature.*

His last years in Chile, following the global fame he had received for *The Obscene Bird of Night* and his other novels, were clouded by political opposition to his antigovernment writings. Along with many Spanish American artists, intellectuals, and writers, he was bitterly opposed to the military overthrow of President Salvador Allende and the installation of the dictator Augusto Pinochet. Donoso died on December 7, 1996, at the age of seventy-two.

ANALYSIS

José Donoso, like Marcel Proust, William Faulkner, and the stream-of-consciousness writers, gave literary testament to the belief that ultimate human reality is disclosed not in rational observation, historicity, or scientific proof but in the workings of human emotion and imagination. For Donoso, as for Proust, the reality of an event is not its actual occurrence but the subjective recollection and reexperience of it. This view of reality is shared, in general, by writers of the Spanish American "boom," whose fiction tends to be cyclic, discontinuous, intertextual, and indiscriminately narrated, as opposed to conventionally linear, plot-oriented, and fixedly narrated.

If a story by Donoso starts with conventional narration of sequential and explicable actions, it will eventually challenge the reader with either a narrator who exposes himself or herself as androgynous or an undemarcated plurality of narrators and with events that defy rational explication or analysis. In his novels *El lugar sin límites* (1966; *Hell Has No Limits*, 1972) and *The Obscene Bird of Night*, for example, a male narrator experiences life as a woman; in his short stories "The Güero" and "Santelices" a creative imagination vitally exceeds ordinary existence and then fatally exceeds itself: The güero (fair-haired male) follows a sorceress's path of jungle mystery in preference to the normal activities of his European heritage and meets a magical death; Santelices, an office worker, deprived of the pictures that have provided him with a life of fully imagined bestial ambience, feeds his subsequently uncontrolled imagination to the point of leaping to his death from his office window to rescue an imaginary female from an imaginary horde of beasts.

Three characteristic elements of Donoso's fiction are surrealism (his presentation of the superrealism of imagination), existentialism (in his major characters' unrelenting exercise of personal and authentic choice), and a kind of deconstruction or introverted semiotics (by which language appears to speak about itself).

"A LADY"

One of the shortest of Donoso's short stories is also one of his most typical. "A Lady" seems to be quite straightforward in its simple first-person narration of a man who catches sight of a fiftyish lady, ordinary but not unattractive, and continues to see her around town, always from a distance. His imagination details her way of life and her role in life, until, after her appearances cease, he culls her name from an obituary and attends her funeral. The story has the quality of a Joycean epiphany, except for the narrator's confession of feeling a "special tranquillity" after his walk home from the funeral. The satisfying calm, instead of sadness or sympathy, translates the burden of the story from incidence and coincidence to concerted hunting, finding, and disposing--the result of his perversely creative imagination.

The narrator's first, and perhaps only, proximity to the lady is on a streetcar, where he sees her "knee covered with a green raincoat" next to his knee and then glances at her figure. All that follows is the narrator's construction of a satisfied desire to destroy a female, the psychological transference having resulted, possibly, from either hatred of his mother or loss of a potential (or actual) mate, or both. The streetcar, the obituary, and the funeral are real; all else is in the narrator's imagination, which is not necessarily false, because it is the narrator's own reality. Such reality, because it inheres in the narrator, constitutes the narrator: It is not self-deception.

GASPARD DE LA NUIT

Orchestration of the various aspects of imagination, as the development and projection of one's individual reality, is perfected in the novella *Gaspard de la nuit*. The novella concludes *Sacred Families*, a trilogy of three novellas with recurrent themes and characters. In the first of the novellas, *Chattanooga Choo-Choo*, characters control their lovers and partners by disassembling and reassembling their body parts; the second novella, *Atomo verde número cinco* (*Green Atom Number Five*), concerns the reality of art. Each novella begins prosaically and quickly develops into a phantasm.

In *Gaspard de la nuit*, the third novella, Mauricio, a sixteen-year-old reared by his paternal grandmother after his parents' separation, is to spend a trimester with his mother and her current consort. Mauricio's eerily unconventional behavior disturbs and offends his mother. He has no interest in food, sports, record players, motor scooters, rock music, or any of the usual preoccupations of teenagers. He spends his time walking and whistling the three movements--*Ondine* (water nymph), *Le Gibet* (the gallows), and *Scarbo* (scarab, or Punch and Judy clown)--of Maurice Ravel's *Gaspard de la nuit* (1908), the title of which ("casper of the night") is an epithet of Satan. Existentialistically, Mauricio refuses to find his essence in material possessions or bourgeois mentality.

The first three sections of the novella correspond to the three movements of Ravel's composition, which Mauricio whistles flawlessly, following the interpretation of Ravel's friend, the pianist Robert Casadesus. In the fourth section, Mauricio loses his ability to whistle impeccably the composition as he finds his essence by transferring himself into the life and freedom of a raggedly dressed vagrant coeval, the vagrant thereby taking on the life, whistling talent, and bourgeois accoutrements of Mauricio. Having become Mauricio, the former vagrant delights the mother by eating upon invitation, asking for a motor scooter, and readily agreeing to go on a trip with the mother and her consort. Having become a vagrant, Mauricio, refusing to be identified by those among whom he might remain for too long, walks off "toward other things." The walk away from the constrictions and identity determinations of middle-class life are also strikingly dramatized in Donoso's short story "The Walk."

"THE WALK"

Like *Gaspard de la nuit*, "Paseo" ("The Walk") consists of five sections, or movements, in the last two of which occur pronounced changes of situation and personal identity.

In the first section, a mature narrator recalls from his childhood the saddened mien of his father and two uncles. In the next two sections, the narrator describes the household of his widowed father, himself, his two uncles, and his unmarried aunt, Matilde. The members of the household follow a comfortable but inflexible routine, presided over by Aunt Matilde, who keeps house, takes care of clothing, supervises the servants and cooks, and directs the evening billiard games, telling each of her brothers when to shoot. The routine continues even after a sick, runty white dog appears as the narrator and his aunt are returning from church, and his "aunt's and the dog's eyes" meet.

In the concluding sections, the dog becomes part of the household. Matilde nurses it to health, cares for it, and regularly walks it. Her attention shifts from the males of the house to the white dog; and one day she takes the dog for a walk and is never seen again. The narrator supposes that Aunt Matilde "got lost in the city, or in death, or in a place more mysterious than both." The reader familiar with Donoso's fiction may understand that whatever Matilde's course may have been, it was indisputably her own.

"THE CLOSED DOOR"

If there is any heaven or bliss of pure blessedness in human existence, it is to be discovered, outside religious faith, only at the supremely tenuous intersection of dreams and death. The dream is the vital imagination, uninhibited and uncontrolled by physical objectivity, and sleep is a minor mode of death. This is the notion developed by Donoso in "La puerta cerrada" ("The Closed Door"). Sebastián Rengifo spends most of his time sleeping, to the consternation of his mother and the irritation of his employer. His dreams take him to a world of light and of ineffable happiness, which an oneiric closed door will not permit him to bring into his waking state. He is so certain that he will one day breach the door that he makes a bet with his employer: If he dies with an expression of bliss on his face, it will be proof of his success, and the employer will provide a proper funeral for him; if not, the employer will inter him in a pauper's grave. The bet continues, even after Sebastián resigns his position to devote himself to sleep. He becomes a vagrant, sleeping at will, and eventually returns to his employer's home, where he dies with such an expression of joy on his face that the employer concedes and provides the proper funeral. The story contains the qualification that one has to be alive in order to dream and the suggestion that the reality of life is fatally explicit in the passage of the unfettered imagination through the door of death.

GREEN ATOM NUMBER FIVE AND
STILL LIFE WITH PIPE

The distance between the falseness of material life and the reality of the dream is measured in these two novellas, published, respectively, in 1973 and 1990, as the distance between art as material possession and art as living imagination. The earlier novella, the second story of the Sacred Families trilogy, shows the disintegration of a married couple whose mass of trendy possessions disappears through theft and mysterious loss. Their concern with the husband's painting *Green Atom Number Five* is not a matter of its inherent value but of its value as a gift to his wife. When the painting disappears, they search for it, taking the painting's material weight designation, "Pound-Ounces 204" (that is, 12.5 pounds), to be the address of its location. Their futile search culminates in their tearing off each other's clothing.

Donoso's last novella, *Still Life with Pipe*, is the obverse of *Green Atom Number Five*. The still life is a painting that Marcos Ruiz Gallardo comes more and more to experience rather than to understand. The deepening experience is directly proportional to his coming to love Hilda Botto, to whom his incapacity for love had hitherto rendered him indifferent. The fully developed situation incorporates the lovers, as Marcos sees Hilda and himself, into the painting, which is newly entitled *The Gentleman Marcos Ruiz Gallardo and His Lady*. Marcos learns that art, unpossessed by and alien to rational comprehension, substantiates those viewers who see it outside the contexts of monetary value or semantic interpretation.

OTHER MAJOR WORKS

LONG FICTION: *Coronación*, 1957 (*Coronation*, 1965); *Este domingo*, 1965 (*This Sunday*, 1967); *El lugar sin límites*, 1966 (*Hell Has No Limits*, 1972); *El obsceno pájaro de la noche*, 1970 (*The Obscene Bird of Night*, 1973); *Casa de campo*, 1978 (*A House in the Country*, 1984); *La misteriosa desaparición de la Marquesita de Loria*, 1980; *El jardín de al lado*, 1981; *La desesperanza*, 1986 (*Curfew*, 1988); *Donde van a morir los elefantes*, 1995; *El Mocho*, 1997.

PLAYS: *Sueños de mala muerte*, pb. 1985; *Este domingo: Versión teatral de la novela homónima*, pb. 1990.

POETRY: *Poemas de un novelista*, 1981.

NONFICTION: *Historia personal del "boom,"* 1972 (*The Boom in Spanish American Literature: A Personal History*, 1977).

BIBLIOGRAPHY

Carbajal, Brent J. *The Veracity of Disguise in Selected Works of José Donoso: Illusory Deception*. Lewiston, N.Y.: Edwin Mellen Press, 2000. Examines Donoso's use of masks, both literal and metaphorical, in his novels.

Friedman, Mary Lusky. *The Self in the Narratives of José Donoso: Chile, 1924-1996*. Lewiston, N.Y.: E. Mellen Press, 2004. Argues that the most important theme in Donoso's work is the peril of establishing a self. Traces this theme in his late writings, including the novella *Taratuta*.

González Mandri, Flora. *José Donoso's House of Fiction: A Dramatic Construction of Time and Place*. Detroit: Wayne State University Press, 1995. Contains chapters on all of Donoso's major fiction, in which González Mandri explores the treatment of history and of place. Focuses on Donoso's incorporation of masks and houses in his fiction, the latter implicating allusions to Henry James. Although the study is chiefly of the novels, it includes searching attention to the short story "Santelices" and the novella *Taratuta*.

King, Sarah E. *The Magical and the Monstrous: Two Faces of the Child-Figure in the Fiction of Julio Cortázar and José Donoso*. New York: Garland, 1992. Pages 63-73 examine Donoso's short fiction, including "The Walk." Informative, although the short citations in Spanish are not translated into English, and the "white dog" (*perra blanca*) in "The Walk" is identified as "the human-like yellow dog." Despite the minor obstacles for the non-Spanish reader, this comparative study of two figures of the Spanish American "boom" is valuable.

Magnarelli, Sharon. *Understanding José Donoso*. Columbia, S.C.: University of South Carolina Press, 1993. Thoroughgoing study of Donoso's works. The second chapter is devoted to the short stories, with lengthy analyses of "The Walk" ("one of Donoso's most superbly crafted stories") and "Santelices," a story leading the writer to consider that artistic imagination may be the original sin. Chapter 7 analyzes the novellas of *Sacred Families*, calling special attention to the semiotics of the trilogy.

McMurray, George R. *José Donoso*. Boston: Twayne, 1979. Readable and informative account of the life and work of Donoso, especially the chapters entitled "The Short Stories" and "*Sacred Families:* Middle-Class Reality and Fantasy." Unmatched in its depth of insight. McMurray, a prominent expert on Spanish American literature, was personally acquainted with Donoso and gained much firsthand knowledge about the author's work. His analyses of the existentialism, surrealism, and Freudianism that inform the fiction are valid and edifying.

Roy Arthur Swanson

Fyodor Dostoevski

Born: Moscow, Russia; November 11, 1821
Died: St. Petersburg, Russia; February 9, 1881
Also known as: Feodor Dostoyevsky, Feodor Dostoevsky

Principal short fiction

Sochineniya, 1860 (2 volumes)
Polnoye sobraniye sochineniy, 1865-1870 (4 volumes)
Povesti i rasskazy, 1882
The Gambler, and Other Stories, 1914
A Christmas Tree and a Wedding, and an Honest Thief, 1917
White Nights, and Other Stories, 1918
An Honest Thief, and Other Stories, 1919
The Short Novels of Dostoevsky, 1945

Other literary forms

In addition to short fiction, Fyodor Dostoevski (FYAW-dur dahs-tuh-YEHF-skee) wrote novels, nonfiction, criticism, and *Yevgeniya Grande* (1844), a translation of Honoré de Balzac's novel *Eugénie Grandet* (1833). In his own time, Dostoevski was exceptionally influential, especially through *Dnevnik pisatelya* (1876-1877, 1800-1881; *The Diary of a Writer*, 1949), a series of miscellaneous writings that he published occasionally in St. Petersburg. Dostoevski also wrote a series of essays on Russian literature, some feuilletons, and the well-known travelogue "Zimniye zametki o letnikh vpechatleniyakh" (1863; "Winter Notes on Summer Impressions," 1955). His most famous contribution in his own time was his speech in Alexander Pushkin's honor, given on the occasion of the dedication of a monument to Pushkin in 1880.

Achievements

In the world literature of the nineteenth century, Fyodor Dostoevski has few rivals. Some of his characters have penetrated literary consciousness and produced a new generation in the works of prominent twentieth century authors, such as Jean-Paul Sartre and Jorge Luis Borges. He initiated psychological realism, inspiring both Friedrich Nietzsche and Sigmund Freud. His novels are read in translation in twenty-six languages. Dostoevski was originally suppressed in the Soviet Union, only to reemerge as even more influential in the second half of the twentieth century, finding a whole new generation of admirers in his transformed homeland. Even though his style is markedly nineteenth century, Dostoevski still seems quite modern even in the twenty-first century.

BIOGRAPHY

Fyodor Mikhailovich Dostoevski was born on November 11, 1821, in a small Moscow public hospital, where his father, physician Mikhail Andreevich Dostoevski, worked. Fyodor was the second son to the doctor and Marya Fyodorovna (née Nechaeva). One year after his mother's death, in 1837, Fyodor enrolled in the St. Petersburg Academy for Military Engineers. He completed his studies at the academy even after his father had died of a stroke in 1839, thanks to the inheritance of the Dostoevski estate.

Like many writers, Dostoevski's first foray into the literary world was through translation--in his case, of Balzac's *Eugénie Grandet*, appearing in print in 1844. His first original work was a novel in letters, *Bednye lyudi* (1846; *Poor Folk*, 1887), which met with immediate success, creating quite a literary sensation even before its publication. The great critic Vissarion Belinsky hailed it with such enthusiasm that the novice writer was propelled into early fame.

Dostoevski followed this initial success with *Dvoynik* (1846; *The Double*, 1917). This novel was met more coolly, was considered an artistic failure, and was generally unpopular. The failure of *The Double* is quite ironic because it contains many of the thematic occupations that eventually made Dostoevski famous. His next novel, *Netochka Nezvanova* (1849; English translation, 1920), was never completed. Most novels then appeared in journals and were serialized; this was the case with all Dostoevski's novels. After the first three installments of *Netochka Nezvanova* appeared in 1849, Dostoevski was arrested for participating in a secret anticzarist society, the Petrashevsky Circle. He and thirty-two of his associates were arrested, imprisoned for eight months, and sentenced to death. At precisely the moment that his comrades were facing the firing squad, the sentence was commuted to hard labor. Dostoevski spent four years in hard labor at Omsk, followed by three years of exile from the Russian capital.

Dostoevski married Marya Isaeva in 1857, while still in Siberia. He was beginning to suffer from epilepsy, however, and she was also sickly. They returned to St. Petersburg in 1859, and shortly thereafter his works began again to appear in print. Life, however, did not return to normal. In 1864, his brother died,

leaving him a second family to support. His wife, too, died the same year. Strapped financially, Dostoevski accepted an advance payment, agreeing to deliver a novel to a publisher that same year, or forfeit the profits from all his subsequent works. He succeeded in completing *Igrok* (1866; *The Gambler*, 1887), satisfying this publisher thanks to his stenographer, Anna Snitkina, whom he married in 1867. They left Russia for a few years, returning in 1871. The novels that he wrote while abroad established him as an important writer but not as a popular or successful one. In fact, during his life, he received very little recognition.

The one shining exception to this neglect came at the dedication of a monument to Pushkin, in 1880. Thousands of people greeted his speech enthusiastically. He died only a few months later, in 1881, when an even larger crowd attended his funeral.

ANALYSIS

Fyodor Dostoevski's works fall into two periods that coincide with the time before his imprisonment and following it. The seven-year hiatus in his creative output between 1849 and 1857 corresponds to the four years that he spent in prison and the three subsequent years during which he was banished in Siberia. During the first period he primarily produced shorter novels and short stories, many of which have never been translated into English; the latter period is represented more by the great novels, the epithet denoting both significance and size, as well as by *The Diary of a Writer*, which also contains several new short stories.

In Dostoevski's works, complex structures are created that introduce fundamentally antipodal constructs and that produce, among other effects, a mythologization of the antagonistic elements. Thus, the city, often the St. Petersburg of Dostoevski's present, contrasts with the countryside. The squalor of poverty permeates St. Petersburg with sounds and smells in Dickensian realistic fashion, as opposed to the quaint, provincial quiet of the country. Usually problems or actual troublemakers come from the city, or if one leaves the provinces for the city, one may become "infected" with urban discontent and return to plague the countryside. In another prevalent dichotomy, the "man of the forties" (that is, the optimistic believer in the Enlightenment) often clashes with the "man of the sixties" (that is, the atheistic and/or nihilistic revolutionary). This conflict often is positioned generationally, and it is seldom clear whether the representative of either generation should prevail.

Often throughout Dostoevski's works men of a higher social class, although not necessarily a very high class, interact most significantly with women who are socially inferior, usually powerless or "compromised." The relationship takes on many different attitudes in the various works, but in almost every case the woman turns out to be of greater virtue or higher moral and spiritual constitution than the man, who from his privileged position in society nevertheless fares better than the woman.

Perhaps most important of all the themes in his work is the belief in God versus atheism. If there is no God, many of Dostoevski's characters realize, then either every human being is a God or every human being is nothing at all. This conflict can, and sometimes does, take place within a single person as

Fyodor Dostoevski (Library of Congress)

well as between two characters. Atheism usually appears in its most extreme state--that is, in the belief that, since there is no God, the human being must be God. While Dostoevski's proponents of atheism are strong-willed, disciplined, and morbidly dedicated, in Dostoevski's world they need to accept the existence of God as their only chance for peace or, in the final analysis, for existing in the world at all. While free will is interpreted by these radical proponents as the ability to become gods, the submission to the will of the divine God is the only means toward happiness. Those who fail to redeem themselves through God either perish or are subject to enormous spiritual and psychological torment. Such conflict forms the crux of more than one novel in Dostoevski's latter period, and his treatment of this conflict later earned him recognition as the founder of existentialism in literature. Ironically from the point of view of Dostoevski's beliefs, it is his existential writings rather than his metaphysical ones that constitute his most profound influence on world literature in the twentieth century.

Most of Dostoevski's short stories are simpler works than the novels, both in terms of the psychology of the characters and in terms of structure.

"WHITE NIGHTS"

One of his best-known short stories, "Belye nochi" ("White Nights"), is subtitled "A Sentimental Story from the Diary of a Dreamer." The unnamed protagonist of this work meets a young woman, Nastenka, by chance one evening along the embankment. When they have the opportunity to speak to each other, they find that they have much in common: Neither of them is able to enjoy a life of his or her own, and both of them, because of varying circumstances, are confined to their own abodes, occupied most of the time in daydreaming. Nastenka is physically restrained by her grandmother by being pinned to her skirt; the male protagonist is confined by his abject poverty and the inertia of unsociability to his quarters, with the green wallpaper and the spiderwebs. At the end of the story, Nastenka, nevertheless, is able to escape her fate thanks to the offices of the young boarder, who has taken pity on her, but she has had to wait an entire year; it is precisely at the end of this year that she meets the protagonist, whom, she claims, she would certainly love, and does in fact love, but as she truly still loves the other, she must relinquish. Nastenka leaves, imploring the protagonist not to blame her, knowing that he cannot blame her because he loves her. The protagonist feels that, somehow, this "moment" that they have shared is enough love to sustain him for a lifetime of dreaming. This story, unusual in the oeuvre of Dostoevski, does not involve the motif of the abused young woman, and the rejected young man seems quite content with his fate. Unlike most of Dostoevski's women, Nastenka has succeeded in meeting an honorable man who seemingly keeps his word, making her a singular female in the works of Dostoevski.

"A CHRISTMAS TREE AND A WEDDING"

More in keeping with Dostoevski's image of the abused, victimized woman is the young girl in "Elka i svad'ba" ("A Christmas Tree and a Wedding"). The first-person narrator relates how he notices the indecent attention of a "great man" of society toward an eleven-year-old girl playing with dolls, who has been promised a huge dowry during one family's Christmas party. The "great man" is interested only in the fabulous dowry and bides his time. Five years later, the narrator notices a wedding taking place in the church and focuses on the face of the very young bride, "pale and melancholy," her eyes perhaps even red from "recent weeping" and her look of "childish innocence," where could be detected "something indescribably naive . . . mutely begging for mercy." He recognizes the young girl of a few years before and also the "great man," who is now the groom. The narrator concludes that it was a "good stroke of business." In this story, the theme of the helpless woman completely at the mercy of rapacious, evil men plays a major role, and the fate of the young girl in "A Christmas Tree and a Wedding," for all her money, bodes much worse than that of the impoverished Nastenka.

"THE DREAM OF A RIDICULOUS MAN"

Perhaps Dostoevski's best-known short story, "Son smeshnogo cheloveha" ("The Dream of a Ridiculous Man"), presents more of the most typical Dostoevskian philosophy of any short story. In it, a petty clerk who has realized that he has no reason to live believes that he should commit suicide to put an end to his ridiculous existence. Just when he decides to do so, a young girl accosts him and seemingly tries to engage his assistance. He pushes her aside, but his action causes him great shame, and he feels deep pity for the young girl. The experience of these two emotions causes him to postpone his suicide, if only for a few hours. Meanwhile, he falls asleep, and in his dream he shoots himself. Then, after he is dead and buried, he is transported to an Earth-like planet inhabited by people who only love. Unfortunately, he corrupts the entire population, causing wars, antipathies, and alienation. Upon awakening, the man feels that he has undergone a revelation and must preach his new religion, trying to convince people that it is possible to live in harmony together and to love sincerely people other than oneself.

In "The Dream of a Ridiculous Man," many themes from Dostoevski's mature novels appear: whether one is nothing or a human being, whether there is an afterlife, suffering as the only condition for the possibility of love, and suicide as a means of investing significance to human action, as well as many more. It is in his great novels that the complex world wherein the actions of all Dostoevski's creations take place, including the short works. To read his short stories without a fundamental background in other seminal works, such as the novel *Zapiski iz podpolya* (1864; *Letters from the Underworld*, 1913, better known as *Notes from the Underground*), would likely lead to a trap that could trivialize what are, by themselves, minor works. If, however, the short stories are contextualized within the entire oeuvre of Dostoevski over both his major periods, they form several interesting transitional points between many of his philosophical designs.

The young girls, usually victimized by poverty and evil men, seem to be an outgrowth of an early novel, *Poor Folk*, and a continuing motif throughout the later period. Here, an orphan serf girl is pressured into a marriage that will doubtless cause her endless degradation and possibly physical harm. The paradoxical "spiteful man" of *Notes from the Underground* is the model of the "little clerk" who, nevertheless, has been influenced by German romantic philosophy and against logical positivism. His voice and "spite" reverberate almost palpably in the short stories as well as in the great novels. The theme of life as suffering and love or compassion as life's greatest suffering is developed throughout the great novels, which, when used as a backdrop for the short works, provides a glimpse into the motivations of many of the protagonists.

Dostoevski's short stories clearly have a place of their own in Russian literature. Together, they form a miniature portrait of the most compelling people in Dostoevski's world. Reading them, along with the longer works, gives the discriminating reader an insight into one of the most powerful and intricate minds of the nineteenth century.

OTHER MAJOR WORKS

LONG FICTION: *Bednye lyudi*, 1846 (*Poor Folk*, 1887); *Dvoynik*, 1846 (*The Double*, 1917); *Netochka Nezvanova*, 1849 (English translation, 1920); *Unizhennye i oskorblyonnye*, 1861 (*Injury and Insult*, 1886; also known as *The Insulted and Injured*); *Zapiski iz myortvogo doma*, 1861-1862 (*Buried Alive: Or, Ten Years of Penal Servitude in Siberia*, 1881; better known as *The House of the Dead*); *Zapiski iz podpolya*, 1864 (*Letters from the Underworld*, 1913; better known as *Notes from the Underground*); *Igrok*, 1866 (*The Gambler*, 1887); *Prestupleniye i nakazaniye*, 1866 (*Crime and Punishment*, 1886); *Idiot*, 1868 (*The Idiot*, 1887); *Vechny muzh*, 1870 (*The Permanent Husband*, 1888; also known as *The Eternal Husband*); *Besy*, 1871-1872 (*The Possessed*, 1913; also known as *The Devils*); *Podrostok*, 1875 (*A Raw Youth*, 1916); *Bratya Karamazovy*, 1879-1880 (*The Brothers Karamazov*, 1912); *The Novels*, 1912 (12 volumes).

NONFICTION: "Zimniye zametki o letnikh vpechatleniyakh," 1863 ("Winter Notes on Summer Impressions," 1955); *Dnevnik pisatelya*, 1876-1877, 1880-1881 (2 volumes; *The Diary of a Writer*, 1949); *Pisma*, 1928-1959 (4 volumes); *Iz arkhiva F. M. Dostoyevskogo: "Idiot,"* 1931 (*The Notebooks for "The Idiot,"* 1967); *Iz arkhiva F. M. Dostoyevskogo: "Prestupleniye i nakazaniye,"* 1931 (*The Notebooks for "Crime and Punishment,"* 1967); *F. M. Dostoyevsky: Materialy i issledovaniya*, 1935 (*The Notebooks for "The Brothers Karamazov,"* 1971); *Zapisnyye tetradi F. M. Dostoyevskogo*, 1935 (*The Notebooks for "The Possessed,"* 1968); *Dostoevsky's Occasional Writings*, 1963; *F. M. Dostoyevsky v rabote nad*

romanom "Podrostok," 1965 (*The Notebooks for "A Raw Youth,"* 1969); *Neizdannyy Dostoyevsky: Zapisnyye knizhki i tetradi 1860-1881*, 1971 (3 volumes; *The Unpublished Dostoevsky: Diaries and Notebooks, 1860-1881*, 1973-1976); *F. M. Dostoyevsky ob iskusstve*, 1973; *Selected Letters of Fyodor Dostoyevsky*, 1987.

TRANSLATION: *Yevgeniya Grande*, 1844 (of Honoré de Balzac's novel *Eugénie Grandet*).

MISCELLANEOUS: *Polnoe sobranie sochinenii v tridtsati tomakh*, 1972-1990 (30 volumes).

BIBLIOGRAPHY

Catteau, Jacques. *Dostoevsky and the Process of Literary Creation*. Translated by Audrey Littlewood. Cambridge, England: Cambridge University Press, 1989. Excellent book offering detailed textual analysis and factual information on Dostoevski. Provides a thematic overview of the pressures and inspirations that motivated Dostoevski. Includes ninety-five pages of notes, aBibliography, and an index.

Frank, Joseph. *Dostoevsky: The Seeds of Revolt, 1821-1849*. Princeton, N.J.: Princeton University Press, 1976. *Dostoevsky: The Years of Ordeal, 1850-1859*. Princeton, N.J.: Princeton University Press, 1983. *Dostoevsky: The Stir of Liberation, 1860-1865*. Princeton, N.J.: Princeton University Press, 1986. *Dostoevsky: The Miraculous Years, 1865-1871*. Princeton, N.J.: Princeton University Press, 1995. *Dostoevsky: The Mantle of the Prophet, 1871-1881*. Princeton, N.J.: Princeton University Press, 2002. Frank's critically acclaimed biography began as an examination of Dostoevski's fiction, but Frank eventually realized that he could not properly analyze the writer's work without attaining a better understanding of his life and of the cultural and political movements in mid- and late-nineteenth century Russia. Frank's five-volume biography attains his goal by integrating discussions of Dostoevski's work, including his short fiction, within the context of the writer's life and times. Princeton University Press has released a one-volume, abridged version of this biography, *Dostoevsky: A Writer in His Time* (2010), edited by Mary Petrusewicz.

Grossman, Leonid. *Dostoevsky: A Biography*. Translated by Mary Mackler. New York: Bobbs-Merrill, 1975. Grossman was himself a good writer, and his critical work reads well. There are moments of suspense and drama in Grossman's biography of Dostoevski, but most of all one senses the care and consideration he has taken on Dostoevski's behalf. Covers Dostoevski's life and works, creative product, and critical reception. Includes detailed notes and an index.

Jackson, Robert Louis, ed. *Dialogues with Dostoevsky: The Overwhelming Questions*. Stanford, Calif.: Stanford University Press, 1993. Chapters on the writer's relationships with Ivan Turgenev, Leo Tolstoy, Anton Chekhov, Maxim Gorky, Nikolai Gogol, William Shakespeare, and Friedrich Nietzsche.

Kjetsaa, Geir. *Fyodor Dostoevsky: A Writer's Life*. Translated by Siri Hustvedt and David McDuff. New York: Viking, 1987. A through biography in which Kjetsaa definitively debunks the myth of Dostoevski's father's murder; Kjetsaa's access to archives closed to previous scholars provides him with unambiguous evidence. His viewpoint is, appropriately, to shed light on the creation of Dostoevski's fiction, citing letters and notes as artistic points of departure. Includes a thorough Bibliography of thirty pages, illustrations, and index.

Leatherbarrow, W. J., ed. *The Cambridge Companion to Dostoevskii*. New York: Cambridge University Press, 2002. Collection of essays by Dostoevski scholars providing various interpretations of his works. Includes examinations of Dostoevski and the Russian folk heritage, money, the intelligentsia, psychology, religion, the family, and science. Although it focuses on the novels, the topics discussed can apply to the short stories.

Miller, Robin Feuer. *Dostoevsky's Unfinished Journey*. New Haven, Conn.: Yale, 2007. Examines Dostoevsky's literary influences, including the ways in which other authors had an impact on his work, and the role that his religious conversion played in his writing. Provides analysis of some of the short stories that can be located by using the comprehensive index.

Mochulsky, K. V. *Dostoevsky: His Life and Work*. Translated by Michael Minihan. Princeton, N.J.: Princeton University Press, 1967. This book's title may slightly mislead the reader into thinking that the author is somehow isolating Dostoevski's life from his work. Mochulsky, however, informs the reader in his preface that "the life and work of Dostoevsky are inseparable. He lived in literature." Mochulsky interweaves biography and literary analysis brilliantly and writes in an engaging and accessible style. This book is regularly recommended for undergraduates by many teachers of courses on Dostoevski.

Straus, Nina Pelikan. *Dostoevsky and the Woman Question: Rereadings at the End of a Century*. New York: St. Martin's Press, 1994. Like most books on Dostoevski, this study centers on the novels, but it is helpful in understanding his work generally. Argues that Dostoevski's compulsion to depict men's cruelties to women is a constitutive part of his vision and his metaphysics. Claims that Dostoevski attacks masculine notions of autonomy and that his works evolve toward "the death of the patriarchy."

Wasiolek, Edward. *Dostoevsky: The Major Fiction*. Cambridge: Massachusetts Institute of Technology Press, 1964. In this interesting and comprehensive work, Wasiolek not only addresses virtually all Dostoevski's fiction but also introduces much of the political polemics of Dostoevski's times. Includes a well-balanced assessment of many important subsequent literary critical opinions, which is interwoven in Wasiolek's analysis of the individual works. Contains notes about the first publication of Dostoevski's works, as well as a detailedBibliography presenting both general subject headings and information apropos an individual work.

Christine D. Tomei

SERGEI DOVLATOV

Born: Ufa, Soviet Union (now in Russia); September
3, 1941
Died: Brooklyn, New York; August 24, 1990

PRINCIPAL SHORT FICTION

Solo na Undervude: Zapisnye knizhki, 1980
Kompromiss, 1981 (*The Compromise,* 1983)
Zona: Zapiski nadziratelia, 1982 (*The Zone: A
Prison Camp Guard's Story,* 1985)
Nashi, 1983 (*Ours: A Russian Family Album,* 1989)
Zapovednik: Povest', 1983 (novella)
Remeslo: Povest' v dvukh chastiakh, 1985 (novella)
Chemodan, 1986 (*The Suitcase,* 1990)
Inostranka, 1986 (novella; *A Foreign Woman,* 1991)
Filial, 1987 (novella)
Predstavlenie, 1987

OTHER LITERARY FORMS

Sergei Dovlatov (sir-GAY DAWV-lah-tawv) was a
respected journalist in his native country before being
forced to emigrate. He also published in several Soviet
underground journals. His major works are all entitled
"novels," although they read much more like short-
story collections. His "considerable talent" is cited by
The Christian Science Monitor as "best suited to the
short story and the sketch." Dovlatov was also an editor, a contributor, and a cofounder of *New American,* a
newspaper expressly for Russian émigrés.

ACHIEVEMENTS

Dovlatov is primarily recognized as one voice
among a bevy of Soviet emigrant writers that includes
Joseph Brodsky, Edward Limonov, Vassily Aksyonov,
Yuz Aleshkovsky, Vladimir Voinovich, and Dmitri
Savitsky, compatriots in the fact that they either were
not published in their native homeland or were defamed in Soviet Russia as potential enemies of the

state. In addition to cofounding *New American,* Dovlatov focused his attention on the intrinsic problem of
the Soviet writer: the forced choice between country
and intellectual freedom. *Contemporary Authors*
quotes Dovlatov as stating, "I can live in freedom
without my native land, but I'm physically incapable of
living without freedom." He was a member of the International Association of Poets, Playwrights, Editors,
Essayists, and Novelists (PEN).

BIOGRAPHY

Sergei Dovlatov was born to Donat Mechik, a theater director, and Nora Dovlatov, a proofreader. He attended the University of Leningrad for two years,
dropped out, and was ultimately drafted into the Soviet
army, where he served as a guard for high-security
prison camps. This latter experience was the basis for
Zona: Zapiski nadziratelia (*The Zone: A Prison Camp
Guard's Story*), which purports to be the written documents of an inmate that have been smuggled out to the
Western world. In 1963, Dovlatov married Elena
Ritman, and the couple had two children, Katherine
and Nicholas.

Dovlatov began to work as a journalist in 1965, initially in Leningrad, then in Tallinn, Estonia. During
this period and until 1978, he was the subject of intense
governmental harassment. Despite his position as a respected journalist, he was unable to obtain publication
for his fictional works via official means. Undaunted,
he began to publish in unauthorized and underground
sources, including the Russian-language edition of
Kontinent. He also involved himself in smuggling his
manuscripts to the West because of his disappointment
with the official censor. The Soviet authorities' harassment of him culminated in a dismissal from the journalists' union, an arrest, and finally a release, prompted
by Western pressure and publicity. Dovlatov immi-
grated to the United States in 1979.

His first published work in the United States (and in English translation) was *Nevidimaia kniga* (1977-1978; *The Invisible Book: Epilogue*, 1979), a recounting of his journalistic struggles and attempts at publishing his fictive work. This recounting, however, is not a straightforward narration but rather an opportunity for the author to hold forth on topics that interest him--including his opinions on publishing, censorship, and the tribulations of a thwarted writer. Dovlatov followed *The Invisible Book* with several more "novels," including *The Compromise* in 1981; *The Zone*, appearing in Russian in 1982 and published in English translation in 1985; and *Ours: A Russian Family Album* (also known as *Nashi*, or "the clan" in some sources) in 1983.

Dovlatov died on August 24, 1990. The translation of his novel *Chemodan* (1986) appeared earlier in 1990 and is entitled *The Suitcase*, an apt symbol for his traveling spirit and his artistic life.

ANALYSIS

Many of Sergei Dovlatov's short stories have been combined and loosely gathered together into "novel" form. In fact, three of his major novels are in reality compilations of his short stories, grouped generally by theme and specifically by tone. *Ours: A Russian Family Album*, for example, includes eight short stories; these stories originally appeared in national magazines, such as *Harper's, The New Yorker*, and *Partisan Review*. While purporting to be a novel, *The Zone* is really a series of sketches about prison life and different characters' responses to it. Dovlatov's last "novel," *The Suitcase*, has been described as a "volume of interconnected tales" and "episodes" that "are in fact short stories."

According to a 1986 article in *The Christian Science Monitor*, "Dovlatov's considerable talent is best suited to the short story and the sketch. His first novel, 'The Compromise,' was a brilliant satire of Soviet journalism that really amounted to an ingeniously connected string of short pieces." Similarly, noting Dovlatov's talent for implying much through terse, abbreviated glimpses into Russian life, *Newsweek* stated in a review of *Ours: A Russian Family Album*:

Famous for their long books, Russian writers can startle us with a brief one, as Sergei Dovlatov does in this deftly economical gallery of family portraits. An émigré living in New York, Dovlatov is witty in the Russian manner--which is a kind of farce played out against an open cellar door, the darkness yawning just beyond the actors' nimble feet.

"UNCLE ARON"

This sense of "farce" is evident throughout Dovlatov's stories, in probability a function of the short-story form, which is motivated by, and infused with, the need for brevity and sharp focus. Dovlatov always describes poignantly and yet sardonically the machinations of people who display the inherent contradiction of living in a Soviet state while remaining unique, individual human beings. In "Uncle Aron," Dovlatov relates how he and his aunt's husband would wage verbal political battles that were in reality name-calling stances of personal opinion. This same Uncle Aron unwittingly displays the paradox of ideology pitted against personal preference. After years of favoring Soviet heroes who were repeatedly defamed and removed from power, Uncle Aron decides to play it safe and idolize Lenin: "Lenin had died long ago and could not be removed from power. It was close to impossible even to smear his name. This meant the love could not be endangered." After the years of disillusioning disappointment with a government that continually changes its mind, Uncle Aron himself comes apart, the seams of Soviet party lines and propagandist constructions unraveling in one singular life.

> At the same time, though, my uncle somehow came loose ideologically. He fell in love with Lenin but also with Solzhenitsyn. Sakharov, too--mainly because he had helped develop the hydrogen bomb in the Soviet Union and then hadn't become a drunk but fought for the truth.

> In the last years of his life, my uncle was practically a dissident, but a moderate one. He never for an instant tolerated the anti-Communist, pro-Nazi Vlasovites; he revered Solzhenitsyn selectively.

It has been asserted that Russian literature in general is "dense" with ideological import and that this trait distinguishes Russian and Soviet writers from their "freer confreres in the West." If the concern for ideology is indeed a large part of the impetus for Russian literature, and, if Western writers are enabled to write without its heavy-handed influence, then Dovlatov is caught somewhere in the middle, in the margin, between East and West in his philosophical stance. For although Dovlatov may not exhibit the emotionalism and transcendent mysticism of Fyodor Dostoevski or the wide historical perspective of Leo Tolstoy, his stories and "sketches" exist as precious insights into both the basic humanness and ordinariness of the average Soviet citizen and the absurdities created when ideology conflicts dramatically with ordinary human concerns.

In other words, ideology, for Dovlatov, is subordinate to those elements that make human beings human, and is, in turn, often debunked in his stories by the mere interaction of the human with the supposedly acceptable state-induced attitude. What emerges as inviolable and paramount in Dovlatov's "brief glimpses" is the sense of the unique, individual, independent (as far as one was able to gain independence in the Soviet Union), and salient human being. The individual is always coupled with the dramatic, the nonindividual with the bland, gray colorlessness of the bureaucrat or Party member. Being part of the accepted Soviet Union is being part of something deadened, shameful, and yet something necessary.

"MOTHER"

In "Mother," Dovlatov reveals how at the age of six he knew the score, the true nature of living in modern Russia:

> By the age of six, I myself knew that Stalin had been responsible for the death of my grandfather, and by the time I finished school, I knew most everything else. I knew that the newspaper printed lies. That ordinary people abroad lived better lives, were materially better off and more carefree. That to be a Party member was shameful but to one's advantage.

This is the central issue and question that runs through Dovlatov's text, like a subliminal motif or subtext in every description, observation, or satiric wisecrack: How can people live like this? How do they?

Dovlatov's "heroes" (or antiheroes) somehow manage to rebel in either blatant or quietly subversive ways. Aunt Mara, from the story "Aunt Mara," is a literary editor for the state and has volume after volume of "officially" accepted books from sanctioned authors of her day but, in the end, hoards by her bed books of "Akhmatova, Pasternak, Baratynski. . . . " Officially, her life is aligned to the state facade; unofficially, she treasures the banned and the dissident. Ironically, her "official" books with handwritten inscriptions must be censored by her relatives, who ripped out the pages of inscriptions.

"MY FIRST COUSIN"

In "My First Cousin," Dovlatov's cousin Boris is a blatant rebel who tailors the system to his own inner and psychic needs. A born achiever, he engages in self-sabotage as a means of both living in *and* out of the Soviet system. Here too, Dovlatov cannot resist the potshot at a system that he both understands and abhors: "Life turned my first cousin into a criminal. It seems to me he was lucky. Otherwise, he would inevitably have become a high-ranking Party functionary." The terrors of

Sergei Dovlatov (Alexander Saverkin /Landov)

Dante's hell hold not a candle to the yawning abyss of Party machinations.

Boris, the reader discovers, was an "exemplary" Soviet citizen, consistently held up to the young Sergei as a role model. Readers learn of his exploits, his good grades, his dogged adherence to a Party image: "In the drama club he always played the Young Guard." Then, as if in dawning awareness, Boris strikes out on his own particular path of deviance from political acceptance, for which the narrator-author almost has "no words." What would be an insult and schoolboy prank in the United States becomes a most serious crime (and unheard of scandal) in Russia: Cousin Boris has urinated on a school official:

> Whereupon, my cousin climbed up onto the windowsill, asked the girls to turn around, skillfully calculated his trajectory. And doused Chebotaryov from head to foot.

This incredible stunt, however, does not stop Boris from a meteoric rise within the state film industry, at the height of which he again destroys his immediate future by committing twelve robberies. Years later, after prison camp, he again rises in his field and again subverts himself--all, it is implicitly suggested, because of the need to rebel, to have a self, to be an independent agent in a land of manipulated cogs. For Dovlatov, his cousin needed drama and "extreme situations." He "was a natural-born existentialist," able to "build a career only in prison, fight for life only on the edge of the abyss."

"UNCLE LEOPOLD"

This need for drama in the lives of individuals in an inherently dramaless state is a subtheme of Dovlatov's writing. Early in *Ours: A Russian Family Album*, he describes the price for revolt or rebellion against a capricious system in the story "Uncle Leopold." For Grandpa Isak, the price was nothing short of eradication; arrested as a spy for Belgium, Grandpa is shot.

> Specific grounds for this charge were not cited. It was enough to have relatives living abroad. Though maybe it mattered that Grandpa was not enthusiastic about the sweep of Stalin's five-year plans. Then, too, he was a little too noticeable--tall, angry, and

loud-voiced. Under dictators, people who stand out do not fare well.

Grandpa's conspicuousness, however, is preferable to the gray, colorless, monotonous uniformity of state-dictated norms. The Soviet Union in which the adult Dovlatov finds himself may be freed of a singular, personal dictator, but in Joseph Stalin's stead stands an impersonal, vapid vacuum of mediocrity: "Life was becoming increasingly lacklustre and monotonous. Even villainy took on a kind of banal, abject quality. Goodness was transformed into apathy. People would say 'So-and-So is a good person, he doesn't inform on anyone.'"

The universe of the Soviet Union in Dovlatov's fiction is a universe that demands uniformity (and therefore loss of individuality) and a certain voicelessness. People have no power and no means by which to assume personal responsibility for their own actions. Thus, Dovlatov can claim that goodness metamorphoses into apathy in Russia. Interestingly enough, Dovlatov, with his omnipresent ability to reverse his perceptions and wring every drop of irony from a situation, shows how the human spirit, even under these repressive conditions, still can manage to triumph--even if only unobtrusively and covertly. When Aunt Mara palpably confronts the Russian condition of voicelessness, Dovlatov shows how the writer Mikhail Zoshchenko maintains a silent ability to assume personal responsibility for the tribulations of his life:

> She happened to meet Mikhail Zoshchenko on the street. The difficult time of official disfavor had already begun for him. Zoshchenko turned his head and quickly walked past her.
> My aunt caught up with him and asked, "Why didn't you say hello to me?"
> Zoshchenko grinned and said, "Forgive me. I'm trying to make it easy for my friends not to talk to me."

THE COMPROMISE

Dovlatov's style, impact, topics, and format are inextricably woven from his personal history as a writer. Not only do his books describe the process of writing and attempting to publish what is considered "dissident" material, but also they assume the format of a hounded, forbidden artist smuggling out the truth to the rest of the world. In *The Compromise*, each of the eleven chapters (displaying Dovlatov's predilection for the short, interlocking tale) is a news story narrated by a journalist named Dovlatov, followed by a true account of what occurred. Censorship is simultaneously revealed and debunked; the hypocrisy of Soviet news propaganda is exhibited and ridiculed; and finally, the larger theme, made possible by eleven separate tales, is exposed: All truth is always somehow compromised.

THE ZONE

In *The Zone*, almost every chapter is punctuated with a letter to Dovlatov's "editor," a pose that promotes the fiction of an actual manuscript being smuggled out of the Soviet Union in pieces, bit by bit, on microfilm. (The editor was in reality Dovlatov's editor for the Russian-language edition of this novel published in the United States.)

The book becomes at once an analogy for the process of writing in Russia and, in a larger framework, an analogy for the process of writing itself--prismatic, revealing the author bit by bit. The opening letter to the publisher highlights the three reasons why Dovlatov is having difficulty getting this particular work published:

> The prison camp theme is exhausted. The reader is tired of endless prison memoirs. After Solzhenitsyn, the subject ought to be closed.
>
> This idea does not stand up to critical examination. It goes without saying that I am not Solzhenitsyn. But does that deprive me of a right to exist?
>
> Also, our books are completely different. Solzhenitsyn describes political prison camps. I--criminal ones.
>
> Solzhenitsyn was a prisoner. I--a prison guard. According to Solzhenitsyn, camp is hell. Whereas I think that hell is in us ourselves.

With this bit of introduction, Dovlatov, without any disparagement of Aleksandr Solzhenitsyn, defines his position (hell is personal, not a social or political construction) and presents a subtle critique of all types of censorship--that is, the structure of a literary canon that precludes his publication because he is too similar to an already established literary giant.

Finally, Dovlatov's stories have an insightful wit that subtly comments on the action of his narrative and allows for both the ridiculous, ludicrous side of human beings and their defiant, triumphant side. Nestled within his short stories are nuggets of wisdom, pearls of perception that enable the reader to look newly on what is often considered the ordinary or commonplace. His stories include observations, characterizations, and ideas that apply universally to humankind (whether Western or Eastern) and furtively ask the reader to think:

> Our memory is selective, like a ballot box.
> Punctuation is something every writer invents for himself.
> Father . . . looked like a cross between Pushkin and an American on unemployment.
> Apparently, people at the bottom of the social ladder don't care much for others like them. They prefer to love the masters, or if worst comes to worst, themselves.
> Silence is an enormous power. It ought to be banned by law, like biological warfare.

Dovlatov, who emigrated in 1979, was crucially aware of the differences (and inherent likenesses) between Russians and Americans. Besides the need for drama in humdrum Soviet lives, however, and the desperate desire to express oneself both individually and as part of a coherent nation, Russians, according to Dovlatov, lack the ability to be dreamers or idealists and are totally given over to the sense of a positivism about life.

> "Freedom?" one [KGB officer] said. "You give a Russian freedom. The first thing he'll go and do is slit his mother's throat. . . . "
>
> "Sakharov reasons like a child," another said. "His ideas are useless. What is all this nonsense about human rights? A Russian needs only one right: the right to get over his hangover." ["Glasha"]

For this Soviet writer, the most obvious characteristic of Americans is not their professed democracy (after all, as a system it has its corruptions) but rather a more basic innate sense of freedom--a freedom of being that allows total unselfconscious-ness--an ability simply to be and enjoy it:

> What is the main quality of Americans? I immedi-ately decided it was their optimism. In the courtyard of our building there was a man who got around in a wheelchair. If you asked him, "How are things?" he answered, "Fine," without the slightest trace of self-consciousness. Or else you saw a girl on the street, pale, disheveled, heavy-legged, wearing a T-shirt that said, "I'm Ursula Andress." Again, not the least bit self-conscious. ["Glasha"]

In stories such as "Driving Gloves," "The Photo Album," and "The Colonel Says I Love You," Dov-latov satirizes Soviet life and pretensions but also moves onto a personal level that asks relevant ques-tions about the nature and meaning of human life--out-side political systems and cultural values. In "The Photo Album," the narrator (Dovlatov as himself) stumbles on an old album of photographs accumulated by his wife. Suddenly his life slaps him in the face, and he knows that his life is here and now, and real in tan-gible terms.

> But I was morbidly agitated. . . . I saw that every-thing going on in our lives was for real. If I was feel-ing that for the first time only now, then how much love had been lost over the long years?

It is only after this internal revelation that Dovlatov admits that his wife will emigrate without him. The story ends on a questioning note, suspended in a reality that no longer applies to the author. His wife leaves him an imported Rumanian shirt. Dovlatov ends the story, ruminating: "But where would I go in it? Really, where?"

OTHER MAJOR WORKS

LONG FICTION: *Nevidimaia kniga*, 1977-1978 (*The In-visible Book: Epilogue*, 1979).

NONFICTION: *Marsh odinokikh*, 1983; *Not Just Brodsky*, 1988; *Maloizvestnyi Dovlatov*, 1995 (correspondence).

MISCELLANEOUS: *Sobranie prozy v trekh tomakh*, 1993 (3 volumes).

BIBLIOGRAPHY

Galloway, David J. "Sergei Dovlatov's *Zona* as Metatextual Memoir." *Canadian Slavonic Papers* 50, no. 3/4 (September-December, 2008): 325-340. Argues that The Zone: A Prison Camp Guard's Sto-rycontains many of the elements of the metafictional novel. Describes the book as a record of Dovlatov's "developing need to write as it tracks the transfor-mation of the guard Boris Alikhanov, Dovlatov's alter-ego."

Grimes, William. "A Novel of Crime and Freezing Punishment in Russia." *The Christian Science Mon-itor*, January 21, 1986, p. 26. An insightful glimpse into Dovlatov's style and intent in *The Zone: A Prison Camp Guard's Story*. Although *The Zone* is a moving account of prison life, Grimes states that the book is not too disheartening: "It would take more than prison to blunt Dovlatov's comic edge."

Prescott, Peter S. "Actors, Uncles, Existentialists." Re-view of *Ours: A Russian Family Album*, by Sergei Dovlatov. *Newsweek*, April 24, 1989, 26. In this brief review, Prescott selects a few of the book's characters who demonstrate human failings and shows Dovlatov's compassion in regard to their ac-tions and his uneasiness in regard to the Communist Party and the state.

Shragin, Boris, et al. "Writers in Exile: A Conference of Soviet and East European Dissidents." *Partisan Re-view* 50, no. 4 (1983): 487-525. A discussion of dis-sident writers including Dovlatov, Boris Shragin, Stanisław Baránczak, Erazim V. Kohak, and Yuz Aleshkovsky.

"Soviet Émigrés." *The Christian Science Monitor*, Oc-tober 2, 1987. Discusses Dovlatov's position on glasnost and perestroika in terms of the reasons why he and Soviet émigrés are not published in the So-viet Union. Despite the literary freedoms that fol-lowed glasnost, Dovlatov believes that the outlook for Soviet émigré writers is not very positive and that total glasnost cannot be achieved by a state con-trolled by one party.

Toker, Leona. *Return from the Archipelago: Narratives of Gulag Survivors*. Bloomington: Indiana Univer-sity Press, 2000. Dovlatov is included in this study of politically dissident Soviet writers.

Young, Jekaterina. "Dovlatov's *Compromise:* Journalism, Fiction, and Commentary." *Slavonica* 6, no. 1 (2000): 44-68. Analysis of Dovlatov's anthology *The Compromise* that focuses on the role of the Soviet press in ideological struggle.

_____. *Sergei Dovlatov and His Narrative Masks*. Evanston, Ill.: Northwestern University Press, 2009. Introductory overview that places Dovlatov's life and work within the context of contemporary Soviet society, literature, and émigré culture. Devotes chapters to discussions of *The Zone: A Prison Camp Guard's Story*, *The Compromise*, *Ours: A Russian Family Album*, and some of the other short fiction.

Sherry Morton-Mollo

E

Shūsaku Endō

Born: Tokyo, Japan; March 27, 1923
Died: Tokyo, Japan; September 29, 1996
Also known as: Paul Endō

PRINCIPAL SHORT FICTION

Aden made, 1954

Endō Shūsaku shū, 1960

Aika, 1965

Endō Shūsaku yūmoa shōsetsu shū, 1969-1973 (2 volumes)

Gekkō no domina, 1972

Endō Shūsaku misuteri Shōsetu shū, 1975

Juichi no irogarasu, 1979 (*Stained-Glass Elegies,* 1984)

The Final Martyrs, 1993

Five by Endo: Stories, 2000

OTHER LITERARY FORMS

Although Shūsaku Endō (shew-sah-kew ehn-doh) wrote first-rate short fiction, he is better known as the leading Roman Catholic writer of Japan and as a novelist and essayist. Of his novels, the best known are *Obakasan* (1959; *Wonderful Fool,* 1974), *Kazan* (1959; *Volcano,* 1978), *Chimmoku* (1966; *Silence,* 1969), *Kuchibue o fuku toki* (1974; *When I Whistle,* 1979), *Samurai* (1980; *The Samurai,* 1982), *Sukyandaru* (1986; *Scandal,* 1988), *Fukai kawa* (1993; *Deep River,* 1994), and *Shukuteki* (1995). Two of these, *Silence* and *The Samurai,* are historical, the rest contemporary. In addition to these important works, Endō wrote plays, biographies, essays, diaries, interviews, and accounts of his travels. As for essays, he wrote on morality, religion, art, literature, and history; specifically, he focused on Jesus, Christian martyrs, medieval castles, women and the family, and love.

ACHIEVEMENTS

Shūsaku Endō wrote several volumes of short stories, about twenty novels, some plays, and numerous essays. He is regarded in Japan not merely as its leading Catholic author but also as one of its most important literary figures. Western critics have compared Endō with the British authors Graham Greene and Evelyn Waugh and with the French writers François Mauriac and Georges Bernanos. Such comparisons, however, are misleading: as a Japanese Catholic, Endō's ethos is quite different from any of theirs. In Japan, Catholics are an insignificant minority, and Endō himself held that Japanese culture and Christianity are incompatible.

Endō received virtually every important literary prize awarded in Japan: the Akutagawa Prize, the Sincho Award, the Mainichi Press Cultural Award, the Tanizaki Prize, and the Noma Prize. These prizes were awarded, respectively, for the following novels: *Shiroi hito* (1954; white man), *Umi to dokuyaku* (1957; *The Sea and Poison,* 1972), *Silence,* and *The Samurai.* These and other basically serious works are often infiltrated with humor. Endō has also written straight comic novels such as *Taihen da* (1969; good grief). His biography of Christ represents Jesus as a maternal and compassionate figure. Endō was editor of the literary journal *Mita bungaku.* His *Iseu no Shōgai* (1973; *A Life of Jesus,* 1973) won the Dag Hammarskjöld Prize in 1978. He was scheduled to receive the Culture Prize from the emperor in 1995 but was too ill to attend the ceremonies at the Imperial Palace and was awarded the prize in absentia. Nominated for the Nobel Prize more than once, he was expected to win in 1994, but lost to his colleague Kenzaburō Ōe.

BIOGRAPHY

Shūsaku Endō, the future Catholic convert and prominent writer, was born in Tokyo, Japan, on March 27, 1923. Four years later, his parents moved to Dairen, a city in southern Manchuria. Six years later, Endō's mother, a domineering woman, left her husband and returned with Endō and his elder brother to Japan. She and her family took up residence with her Catholic sister in Tokyo. After his mother became a Catholic convert, Endō was persuaded at the age of eleven to be baptized in the Catholic faith. For a long time, however, he felt uncomfortable with this foreign religion. To him, as Van C. Gessel has written, Catholicism felt like "an ill-fitting suit of Western-style clothes," which he attempted through his future writing "to retailor . . . into native Japanese attire."

Pleurisy kept Endō out of World War II. Later in life, he was often hospitalized for respiratory ailments, culminating in the removal of a lung. His hospital experiences often figure in his fiction. In 1945, he entered Keio University, a prestigious private institution in Tokyo, where he majored in French literature. In 1950, he went to France, the first Japanese citizen to study abroad after the war. There, he attended the University of Lyons, specializing in French Catholic authors such as Paul Claudel, Mauriac, and Bernanos. In Europe, Endō hoped to recover from the "anguish of an alien," which he had felt since his religious conversion. His entry into an environment in which Christianity was both dominant and pervasive, however, only increased the tension that he felt between East and West. He decided to become a novelist and, in his writings, to attempt to reconcile the two selves that divided him.

In 1953, Endō left France and returned to Japan in a mood of discouragement and depression. His desire to write and to express himself in regard to his inner conflicts, however, served to sustain him and to reshape his life. His first book, *Furansu no Daigakusei* (a French collegian), was published in 1953. His first fiction, the novella *Aden made* (to Aden), came out the following year, causing no stir. His first novel, however, *Shiroi hito*, won the Akutagawa Prize, which is awarded to promising Japanese writers. As a writer of imaginative literature, Endō was on his way. The conflict within him of his ideals, on the one hand, and of his obligations, on the other, continued, acerbated at the same time by his poor health, the result of lung disease. Bogged down in what he referred to as his Japanese "mudswamp," he sought escape by carrying a banner

on which was pictured his own *imago Christi*. In addition, he felt an absolute obligation not to betray his Catholic mother by abandoning her faith or by leaving the house of the wife whom she had arranged for him to marry, even though he had no love for this woman. According to Jean Higgins, it was not until the writing of his prizewinning novel *Silence* that he began to reconcile himself with himself, with the cosmos, and with Christ. His well-known contemplative biography of Jesus, *A Life of Jesus*, has had a considerable impact on Western theologians and the church. His fiction has received the praise of his own compatriot Yukio Mishima and also of the Western writers Graham Greene and John Updike. Having suffered poor health all his life, Endō died on September 29, 1996, in Tokyo, of kidney ailments. He was survived by his wife and son.

Analysis

Shūsaku Endō's writings in general reflect his Roman Catholic beliefs and his peculiarly Japanese attitude toward the foreign religion to which he was converted at the age of eleven by virtue of his mother's will. For years, a conflict simmered within him: Feeling betrayed by his mother, he also felt guilty because of his own arrogant but silent disobedience. For years, he also felt uncomfortable wearing his Western "monkey suit" while tramping about the "mudswamp" that he considered modern Japan to be. As time went on, however, his commitment to Roman Catholicism gradually crystallized and became hard-core, yet the hallmarks of his writings are wisdom, tolerance, and compassion.

Endō's short stories have been collected principally in two volumes: *Aika* (elegies) and *Juichi no irogarasu* (eleven stained-glass windows). Van C. Gessel has translated twelve stories selected from these volumes into English under the title *Stained-Glass Elegies*. The protagonists, who are usually observers rather than actors, tend to be personae--that is, masks that the author himself has donned to disguise his own identity, whatever pseudonyms he has conferred on them. Most of Endō's short stories treat themes similar to those found in his novels: sickness, fear of dying, the changes brought about in a person from growing old, alienation from society, religious doubt and faith, treason, apostasy, good and evil, failure, disappointment, the gulf between Eastern and Western ideals, torture and physical suffering, Christian conscience and sin, the Christian life--especially of monks and priests--the Japanese view of Jesus, and the many Christian martyrs of the times of proscription, as well as the trials of the *kakure Kirishitan* (clandestine Christians)--Japanese Christians who managed by a subterfuge to escape the prohibition edicts during successive waves of persecution. Apart from those persons who have followed Saint Paul's admonition to become "fools for Christ," there are no heroics in Endō's fiction, and apart from the short stories that recall historical events of the seventeenth century, most of them are contemporary or recall the World War II period. Most of the stories are set in Japan, mainly in Tokyo and its environs, although one is set in the prefecture of Nagasaki; another in Manchuria; and a third in Lyons, France.

In a good number of short stories--at least seven or eight--Endō has created a protagonist named Suguro who is very much like his creator: He has been troubled by lung disease, has been hospitalized, and has had an operation. He has a dumpy wife whom he does not love but to whom he remains loyal. After the war, he studied in France. He returned home to become a Catholic novelist interested in the problems of contemporary Japanese Christians and in the historic sufferings of Christian martyrs during the periods of persecution. He is a keen observer of human life and of the characters of human beings, especially of troubled persons, for whom he has compassion in respect to their loneliness. He feels that the sad eyes of birds and dogs express these creatures' sympathy for the human condition. Realizing that he himself is a mixture of good and evil, that every man has an evil doppelgänger as a constant companion, he shrugs his shoulders at others' sins, his Christ having urged Judas to do quickly what he was bent on doing; it is his Jesus who kisses the lips of the Grand Inquisitor in Fyodor Dostoevski's *Bratya Karamazovy* (1879-1880; *The Brothers Karamazov*, 1912).

"A FORTY-YEAR-OLD MAN"

In the story "Shi-jū sai no dan" ("A Forty-Year-Old Man"), Suguro is the middle-aged man who is hospitalized and operated on for lung disease. Depressed and fearing physical suffering and possible death, he is also racked by guilt, having committed sins of adultery and abortion. He is unable to confess these sins to a priest, and he is unable to communicate his feelings to other persons, neither to his wife, to whom he sticks despite his lack of love for her, nor to his sister-in-law, who has been his mistress and has aborted his child. He does think that he will be able to communicate with, and get solace from, a pet bird, so he requests that his wife purchase a mynah bird for him because such a bird has the ability to mimic human speech. Although such a bird is expensive, his wife fulfills his request. He tries to get the bird to say "Good morning" (*O hayō gozaimasu*), but it cannot say this any more than he can confess his sins and ask God's forgiveness. The ending of this story is an ironical tour de force.

"RETREATING FIGURES"

In "Rashiroshi" ("Retreating Figures"), Endō, through his surrogate Suguro, seeks to evoke a tragic sense of life--a perception, according to Suguro, that becomes especially evident after a man passes into his fifties. On a sleepless night, Suguro recalls several casual acquaintances whom he knew only briefly before they departed; he never saw them again. One such person is Mrs. Horiguchi, a patient in the room next to Suguro when, fifteen years previously, he was hospitalized to undergo a third operation. She is a frail, pale-faced, middle-aged invalid of ten years and the wife of a famous Kabuki actor. She decides to leave the hospital to benefit her husband despite her doctor's warning that absence of further treatment would soon result in her death. When she bids Suguro good-bye, he watches her walk away "with her head bowed down the long, silent corridor," but "even after she was gone, the afterimage of her retreating figure remained before" Suguro's eyes. She died three years later.

In several other stories, the narrator or protagonist is not identified by name but is referred to simply as "I," "he," or "the man." In these cases, however, the text strongly suggests that the unidentified person can be no one other than Endō's persona Suguro.

"THE DAY BEFORE" AND "THE SHADOW FIGURE"

In "The Day Before," the narrator is hospitalized, and it is "the day before" his third and most serious operation. He has sent his friend, Father Inouye, to Nagasaki to fetch back an antique *fumie*, a copper engraving of the crucified Christ on which Christians were obliged to stamp their feet as proof of their apostasy, which had been used during the persecutions at Urakami during the second half of the nineteenth century. While the narrator is waiting anxiously to view the image of Jesus before facing his operation, a peddler of pornographic photographs drops into his room seeking to interest him in buying sex pictures. Also, having read a Catholic tract about the fourth siege of Urakami, the narrator tells the story of the apostate Tōgorō, who was ashamed of his treason but could not help himself.

"The Shadow Figure" is written in epistolary form. A Catholic novelist explains his attitude toward a former Spanish priest whom he has just seen (without being seen) for the first time in years. He knew this priest well when a schoolboy because the priest was his mother's spiritual adviser. His mother revered the priest--a handsome, impeccably dressed, vigorous man--and considered him a model for her son to follow. After the writer's mother died, however, the priest became the lover of a Japanese woman--much to the writer's disillusionment--and married her. Hence the priest was defrocked and became separated from the Christian community.

Endō's persona Suguro is the protagonist of his novel *Scandal*. Here, Suguro finds his reputation as a Catholic novelist is on the line by virtue of allegations that he is in the habit of indulging in sordid sex. At first, he thinks that some unknown enemy is seeking to scandalize him, but after visiting Tokyo's pleasure quarters in an effort to discover the impostor, he concludes that his supposed double is none other than himself, his face of innocence having masked his inner depravity.

"DESPICABLE BASTARD"

Endō's short stories that do not present or suggest the author's surrogate Suguro include "Hiretsuna-kan" ("Despicable Bastard") and "Kusuteki kokai" ("Incredible Voyage"). In "Despicable Bastard," the bastard and contemptible fellow is Egi. He is a university student in Tokyo during World War II and lives in a dormitory occupied mostly by Christians. The classes at the school are not being held because the students are being required to work in a war factory that is under military discipline. Egi is a noncooperative type, a

slacker. Not respectful enough to satisfy a military police officer, he is beaten and his knee is wounded.

Every year, the Christian students organize a program at the leper asylum in Gotemba. Part of the program consists of a baseball game with the healthier lepers. Egi is asked to take part in the game, but he does so with considerable trepidation. He is particularly fearful of being infected because of his wounded knee. Having gone up to bat, he hits a fair ball and rounds first base to find himself trapped between first and second. Egi stops and fearfully awaits the tag of the ball in the hand of the leper. The leper baseman's eyes, however, flicker plaintively, and the patient says softly: "Go ahead. I won't touch you." When Egi was by himself, he felt like crying. By contrast, this story echoes Gustave Flaubert's legend of Saint Julian the Hospitaler who, having granted a leper a kiss, found himself face to face with Jesus.

"INCREDIBLE VOYAGE"

"Incredible Voyage" is generally a Rabelaisian parody of science fiction, but specifically it is a parody of a 1966 American science-fiction film called *Fantastic Voyage*. Like the film, the story is set in the twenty-first century, after it has become possible to miniaturize any object to microscopic size. As in the film, a team of doctors and a boat are miniaturized and injected into the bloodstream of a patient needing critical surgery. In the film, the patient is a scientist important to the defense establishment, and the complication is that one of the doctors is a traitor. In the story, the patient is also the fiancé of one of the doctors, and the complication is that in exiting after the operation, the doctors mistakenly get into the girl's intestines, where they discover that her attendants have neglected to give her an enema prior to her operation. The story is therefore broadly and coarsely humorous.

"THE FINAL MARTYRS"

The title story of Endō's collection *The Final Martyrs* is a moral exemplum told in a simple narrative fashion. Set in the nineteenth century during a time of persecution of Japanese Christians, the story focuses on son Kisuke, a giant of a man, who is clumsy, ineffectual, and easily frightened. When his village is raided by government agents seeking to punish anyone who has violated the prohibition against Christianity,

Kisuke's cowardice makes him quickly recant his religion, an act that transforms him into a Judas figure who has betrayed his savior. Unable to bear the guilt of his betrayal, two years later, Kisuke, now a beggar, returns to the prison where his friends, who held firm to their religion, are kept, for he has heard a voice telling him what he has to do to be with the others. Kisuke's return, in spite of his terror, reaffirms to the others that they have been right to uphold their faith, for it reflects the power of Christian forgiveness. Thus Kisuke becomes one of the most beloved of all the final martyrs because he came back even though he was the most frightened.

"THE BOX"

"The Box," a mystical treatment of Christian eschatology, focuses on a central symbolic object and takes place in a world that is at once both real and in the realm of desire. The central theme is stated emphatically when, after relating an anecdote about talking to his plants, the narrator says that humans and animals are not the only ones that have hearts and language and faculties; even things humans think of as simple objects--sticks and stones--have some kind of power living inside them. The story begins when the narrator, a writer, finds an old wooden box in an antique shop containing a Bible with some postcards and a photograph album. The narrator evinces a writerly curiosity about the postcards addressed to a Mademoiselle Louge and some photographs of an old deserted road. He learns that the woman has been tortured by the Japanese military police for not agreeing to spy for them. When the narrator notices that the return addresses of the postcards are actually references to passages in the Bible, which are in turn allusions to the war and peace efforts sent to Mademoiselle Louge and then passed on to others, he believes the postcards have taken on a will of their own, waiting for someone like him to reveal their truth. He explains that this is why he speaks to plants, for he thinks that plants must talk to each other and that trees and rocks and even postcards are saturated with the thoughts of people.

Although Endō held himself a Catholic and clung stubbornly to his Christianity, his faith was flavored with intellectual doubt and was neither doctrinaire nor fanatical. He was ever humble and compassionate.

Without arrogant pride, he realized that all humans are to some degree a compact of good and evil and that they all need forgiveness, whether its source be Jesus or the universe.

OTHER MAJOR WORKS

LONG FICTION: *Shiroi hito*, 1954; *Kiiroi hito*, 1955; *Umi to dokuyaku*, 1957 (*The Sea and Poison*, 1972); *Kazan*, 1959 (*Volcano*, 1978); *Obakasan*, 1959 (*Wonderful Fool*, 1974); *Watashi ga suteta onna*, 1963 (*The Girl I Left Behind*, 1994); *Ryugaku*, 1965 (*Foreign Studies*, 1989); *Chinmoku*, 1966 (*Silence*, 1969); *Taihen da*, 1969; *Kuchibue o fuku toki*, 1974 (*When I Whistle*, 1979); *Samurai*, 1980 (*The Samurai*, 1982); *Sukyandaru*, 1986 (*Scandal*, 1988); *Hangyaku*, 1989 (2 volumes); *Kessen no tiki*, 1991; *Otoko no issho*, 1991; *Yojo no gotoku*, 1991; *Aio chiisana budo*, 1993; *Fukai kawa*, 1993 (*Deep River*, 1994); *Shukuteki*, 1995.

PLAY: *Ogon no kuni*, pr. 1966, pb. 1969 (*The Golden Country*, 1970).

NONFICTION: *Furansu no Daigakusei*, 1953; *Gūtara seikatsu nyūmon*, 1967; *Iesu no shōgai*, 1973 (*A Life of Jesus*, 1978); *Shikai no hotori*, 1973; *Seisho no naka no joseitachi*, 1975; *Tetsu no kubikase*, 1976; *Watakushi no Iesu*, 1976; *Kirisuto no tanjō*, 1977; *Ningan no naka no X*, 1978; *Jū to jūjika*, 1979; *Watakushi no ai shita shōsetsu*, 1985; *Haru wa basha ni notte*, 1989 (essays); *Honto no watakushi o motomete*, 1990; *Iesu ni atta onnatachi*, 1990; *Ihojin no tachiba kara*, 1990 (essays); *Kirishitan jidai: Junkyo to kikyo*, 1992; *Kokoro no sunadokei*, 1992 (essays).

MISCELLANEOUS: *To Friends from Other Lands: A Shūsaku Endō Miscellany*, 1992.

BIBLIOGRAPHY

Beverly, Elizabeth. "A Silence That Is Not Hollow." *Commonweal* 116 (September 22, 1989): 491-494. Maintains that Endō's writing is inspired by two elemental aspects of his identity: the Japanese culture and Catholicism. Argues that Endō's embrace of both has often made his life difficult and perilous, but the labor of fiction has made it bearable.

Cavanaugh, William T. "The God of Silence: Shūsaku Endō's Reading of the Passion." *Commonweal* 125 (March 13, 1998): 10-12. Argues that Endō's work can be seen as a profound exploration of the twisted logic of the Incarnation--the trajectory of God from heaven to earthly flesh and the assumption of weakness by omnipotence. Maintains that Endō weaves together the spiritual anguish of his characters with an embattled and paradoxically orthodox theology.

Gessel, Van C., trans. Introduction to *Stained-Glass Elegies: Stories by Shūsaku Endō*. New York: Dodd, Mead, 1984. An explanation of Endō's talents and position as a writer in Japan and the West, plus a brief but comprehensive rundown on each of the stories translated in the volume: dates of composition, sources or occasions inspiring the stories, and analyses of their themes.

_____. "The Voice of the Doppelgänger." *Japan Quarterly*, no. 38 (1991): 198-213. Gessel examines four postwar Japanese novelists, including Endō, and notes how the postwar fiction differs from the prewar tradition of the "I story," in which author and persona are one. He selects Endō's *Scandal* as a model of the new treatment in which the doppelgänger actually mocks the protagonist who represents the novelist, thus introducing aesthetic distance and irony.

Higgins, Jean. "The Inner Agon of Endō Shūsaku." *Cross Currents*, no. 34 (1984/1985): 414-416. Higgins seeks to explain the conflicts that have made Endō the writer he is. One conflict is the guilt and sense of betrayal Endō felt toward the mother who persuaded him to become a Christian and his lack of a full acceptance of Christianity; the other conflict is the confusion and dismay he felt in attempting to absorb the extent and richness of Western culture, which works against the Japanese grain.

Mase-Hasegawa, Emi. *Christ in Japanese Culture: Theological Themes in Shusaku Endo's Literary Works*. Boston: Brill, 2008. Analyzes Endō's central works from a theological perspective, viewing them as documents that demonstrate the inculturation of Christianity in Japan. Argues that *koshinto*, a traditional Japanese ethos, plays a central role in Endō's ideas about inculturation.

Mathy, Francis. "Endō Shūsaku: White Man, Yellow Man." *Comparative Literature Studies* 23, no. 1 (1967): 58. A Jesuit, Mathy explores Endō's fiction and essays and produces a clear and comprehensive treatment of the cultural conflict between Japan and Western Europe, especially as this conflict relates to religion and notions of beauty and morality. Mathy shows how Endō has experienced strong opposition between his Japanese heritage and the Christian view of life that he was taught by his mother and by Christian missionaries.

_____. "Shūsaku Endō: Japanese Catholic Novelist." *America* 167 (August 1-8, 1992): 66-71. A biographical account of Endō's life, from his childhood and his education through the development of his most important works. Surveys Endō's work and analyzes the themes presented in two early essays, "God and Gods" and "The Problems of a Catholic Writer."

Netland, John T. "From Resistance to Kenosis: Reconciling Cultural Difference in the Fiction of Shūsaku Endō." *Christianity and Literature* 48 (Winter, 1999): 177-194. Discusses Endō's translation of the polemics of cultural difference into art. Argues that his works replace a simple binary, postcolonial tension with a three-dimensional configuration of Christianity, Easter, and European perspectives.

Pinnington, Adrian. "Yoshimitsu, Benedict, Endō: Guilt, Shame and the Post-War Idea of Japan." *Japan Forum* 13, no. 1 (April, 2001): 91-105. Traces the origins and evolution of the belief that Japan is a "shame culture" and that Japanese people have a week sense of sin. Describes how Endoō expressed this concept in his novels and how his views on Japanese shame and weakness changed as his career proceeded.

Quinn, P. L. "Tragic Dilemmas, Suffering Love, and Christian Life." *Journal of Religious Ethics* 17 (1989): 151-183. A comprehensive description and analysis of Endō's *Silence*, in which the life of Sebastian Rodrigues, the Portuguese priest who became an apostate by trampling on an image of Christ to save his parishioners from torture and death by the governmental authorities, is reflected upon in the hope of enriching ethical thought.

Reinsma, Luke M. "Shūsaku Endō's River of Life." *Christianity and Literature* 48 (Winter, 1999): 195-211. In this special issue on Endō, Reinsma discusses the natural world, particularly the river, as a metaphorical backdrop for his work. Claims that Endō has shifted from landscapes and waters ravaged by a Father God in his early work to the lush vegetation of his later.

Richie, Donald. *Japanese Literature Reviewed*. New York: ICG Muse, 2003. Reprints Richie's critiques of the works of numerous Japanese writers, including Endō.

Williams, Mark. *Endō Shūsaku: A Literature of Reconciliation*. New York: Routledge, 1999. An interesting study of Endō's fictive technique. Includes bibliographical references.

Richard P. Benton
Updated by Charles E. May

F

CARLOS FUENTES

Born: Panama City, Panama; November 11, 1928

OTHER LITERARY FORMS

Known primarily as a novelist, Carlos Fuentes (KAHR-lohs FWEHN-tays) also has written plays and has collaborated on several screenplays. His numerous nonfiction works include political tracts, essays on Mexican life, and literary criticism. He has been a frequent contributor to periodicals in the United States, Mexico, and France.

ACHIEVEMENTS

Carlos Fuentes is regarded by many as Mexico's foremost contemporary novelist. Perhaps the most valuable contribution of Fuentes's writing is that it introduced innovative language and experimental narrative techniques into mainstream Latin American fiction. His concern for affirming a viable Mexican identity is revealed in his allegorical and thematic use of his country's legends and history, from the myths of the Aztecs to the events of the Mexican Revolution.

Fuentes has won many literary awards. These include the Biblioteca Breve award (1967) for *Cambio de piel* (1967; *A Change of Skin*, 1968), the Rómulo Gallegos prize (Venezuela) in 1977 for *Terra nostra* (1975; English translation, 1976), the Alfonso Reyes Prize (Mexico) in 1979 for the body of his work, the National Award for Literature (Mexico) in 1984 for *Orquídeas a la luz de la luna* (1982; *Orchids in the Moonlight*, 1982), the Miguel de Cervantes Prize from the Spanish Ministry of Culture in 1987, and the Rubén Darío Order of Cultural Independence (Nicaragua) and the literary prize of Italo-Latino Americano Institute, both in 1988.

Fuentes received the Capita Maria Medal (1991), the Chilean Order of Merit (1992), the French Legion of Honor (1992), and the Menendez Pelayo International Award from the University of Santander (1992). He was named honorary citizen of Santiago de Chile, Buenos Aires, and Veracruz (1993), received the Principe de Asturias Prize (1994), and in 2008 he became the first recipient of Spain's new International Don Quixote Prize in recognition for his outstanding career. He was a candidate for the Neustadt International Prize for Literature (1996) and received honorary degrees from Bard College, Cambridge University, Columbia College, Chicago State University, Dartmouth College, Harvard University, Georgetown University, Essex University, and Washington University.

BIOGRAPHY

Carlos Fuentes was born into a Mexican family that he later characterized as typically petit bourgeois. Son of Rafael Fuentes, a career diplomat, and Berta Macias Rivas, Carlos Fuentes traveled frequently and attended the best schools in several of the major capitals of the Americas. He learned English at the age of four while living in Washington, D.C. After he graduated from high school in Mexico City, he studied law at the National University and the Institut des Hautes Études Internationales in Geneva, Switzerland. Fuentes also lived in Santiago, Chile, and Buenos Aires, Argentina.

From 1950 to 1952, Fuentes was a member of the Mexican delegation to the International Labor Organization in Geneva. Upon his return to Mexico, he became assistant head of the press section of the Ministry of Foreign Affairs in 1954. While he was head of the department of cultural relations at the Ministry of Foreign Affairs (1957-1959), he founded and edited *Revista mexicana de literatura* (Mexican review of literature). He later edited or coedited the leftist journals *El espectador, Siempre*, and *Política*.

In 1954, Fuentes published his first book, a collection of short stories, entitled *Los días enmascarados* (the masked days). About this time, Fuentes devoted himself to writing full time--novels, book reviews, political essays, screenplays (for director Luis Buñuel, among others), and plays.

La muerte de Artemio Cruz (1962; *The Death of Artemio Cruz*, 1964), a novel that treats the Mexican Revolution and its betrayal in modern Mexican society through the memories of Cruz, as he lies dying, is generally regarded as Fuentes's most successful work and has been translated into fifteen languages. For several years after its publication, Fuentes lived primarily in Paris. He moved back to Mexico in 1969 and joined with his literary colleague Octavio Paz, among others, in an attempt to challenge the monopoly of Mexico's official political party (the Partido Revolucionario Institucional) and to advocate for more responsive democratic governmental structures. From 1975 to 1977, Fuentes served as Mexico's ambassador to France. In 1989, he became president of the Modern Humanities Research Association. Fuentes also became a member of the Mexico's National Human Rights Commission. After his diplomatic duties, Fuentes moved to the United States, where he has continued to lecture at universities and professional meetings.

ANALYSIS

Fundamentally a realist, Carlos Fuentes found that his search for the quintessence of Mexican reality often led him to its mythological roots. For him, Mexico's Aztec, Christian, and revolutionary past is not merely a literary theme but a powerful force to be dealt with when representing contemporary society. The foremost concern of his fiction is the Mexican Revolution and its eventual betrayal, a subject that has earned for him both the hostility of the Mexican establishment and the admiration of new generations looking to him for ideological leadership. The form of this literary search for Mexico's past has been termed Magical Realism. Fuentes states that he has "always attempted to perceive behind the spectral appearance of things a more tangible, more solid reality than the obvious everyday reality."

Fuentes began his literary career with a collection of six short stories, *Los días enmascarados*, published in 1954. In this work, the author denounces customs and primitive modes of life that he views as burdensome to modern Mexican life. The stories are fantastical. Like *Aura*, Fuentes's 1962 magical novella about the desire for eternal youth, the stories contain eruptions of the fantastic into everyday life and can be included in the category of Magical Realism.

"CHAC MOOL"

"Chac Mool," the first story in *Los días enmascarados* (and also in a later collection, *Burnt Water*), records the "takeover" of the protagonist, Filiberto, by a statue of the ancient rain god--the Chac Mool--that he buys at a flea market. The Chac Mool reemerges into the twentieth century, but with this rebirth come old age and presumably death. This story illustrates well the major themes and styles of Fuentes's fiction because it combines the author's penchant for fantasy and joins two periods of time, demonstrating how the past continues to be a vital element of the present. The story describes the residual impact of the primitive gods on the subconscious mind of a man born of Mexican heritage who must come to terms with that heritage.

CANTAR DE CIEGOS

The seven stories contained in the volume *Cantar de ciegos*, published in 1964, portray various psychological or social deviations; they are not magical but often are bizarre. In the ten years between the two collections, the development of the writer and artist is significant. Although Fuentes has denied any close connection between these stories and the scriptwriting that he was doing at the time, several of the stories appear to be conceived in cinematic terms. The attitude common to these stories is that modern society is decadent and that the few "decent" individuals encountered are eventually destroyed by this decadence.

The first story, "Las dos Elenas" ("The Two Elenas"), is a subtle study in amorality. It is a triple character sketch constructed around a young wife, the first Elena, her husband, Victor, and her mother, the second Elena. The wife, a very modern young woman, attempts to persuade her husband of the theoretical acceptability of a ménage à trois as a way of life. The irony is that the husband is already carrying on an affair with his mother-in-law, the second Elena. The true decadent element is that the wife is naïvely honest in her approach to the problem of marital boredom, while her husband and her mother play the game of adultery furtively, in the age-old dishonest and traditional way. The author seems to imply that so-called modern morality may actually be an innocent sort of naïveté when compared with the old dishonesty. Fuentes's incongruous realism produces a chillingly controlled effect.

"Vieja moralidad" ("The Old Morality"), often considered the most accomplished story of the collection, again echoes the theme of loss and innocence, as it recounts the disruption of an eccentric but happy household by traditionally moral but inwardly corrupt meddlers. The provincial atmosphere, with its moral and sexual hypocrisy, links this story to the novel *Las buenas conciencias* (1959; *The Good Conscience*, 1961). In this story, the presentation is much more straightforward than in "The Two Elenas," and amorality is again seen to be more honest than the "old morality" of the title, although the old morality is presented not as decadent but rather as a form of psychological ignorance. The characters are tortured into perversion and incestuous outlet because of an unreasonable adherence to the old, hypocritical ethics of Mexican Catholicism.

AURA, HOLY PLACE, AND CUMPLEAÑOS

Aura, *Holy Place*, and *Cumpleaños* (birthday) are a trilogy of novellas. In *Aura*, Fuentes displays less concern with social criticism than in previous works and makes greater use of bizarre images and fantastic developments. The novella's use of witchcraft and archaic rituals and its defiance of chronological time all contribute to making it one of Fuentes's most fascinating stories. Clearly, it is structured around two sets of doubles, Consuelo de Llorente as Aura and Felipe Montero as the long-dead General Llorente. Through her satanic rituals, Consuelo creates a double, an alternative personality, identical to herself when younger, which she controls and through which she has sexual intercourse with Montero. In an obscure fashion, however, Montero is also a re-creation of the general. In some way, Montero is identical to Llorente, just as Aura is to Consuelo.

This amazing identity cannot be attributed to some sort of ritual practice of Consuelo, as is the case with Aura. Although she conducts an erotic ritual akin to a black mass, it is never indicated that Felipe has been altered physically. Possibly he is a reincarnation of the general.

The fragmentation of time is one of Fuentes's favorite themes, and something close to reincarnation or at least continuing consciousness across time is a major thread in *Cumpleaños*. There is no real indication, however, of this concept in *Aura*. One critic suggested that *Aura* may be a subjective experience, either a dream or something close to it. Another maintains that the story is narrated by a madman, an unreliable narrator. Thus, the doubling in the story is not only a structural device but also a thematic one. *Aura* may be read as the record of one man's delusion.

Holy Place is, in one sense, a series of scenes from a descent into madness, a graphic voyage into hell. There are a number of resemblances to *Aura*. Aside from the doubling technique is the mythic structure, here carried to an extreme degree of complexity, embodying both pre-Hispanic and Greek mythological constructions. Significant also is the characteristic flight from chronological time. In addition, the protean structure of the novel reflects the attempts of the characters to re-create and thus perpetuate themselves through constant change. They seek to defy the corrupting course of chronological time that will lead them inevitably toward decay and death.

One of the chief resemblances to *Aura* is the unreliable narrator, trapped in a destructive Oedipal conflict. His beloved apartment, his sacred place, is something out of a fin de siècle dream. The protagonist, Mito, is obsessed by incestuous desires, potentially homosexual; he is a sadist as well. Finally, he is reduced to total dissociation as he adopts the role of a dog, completing the sadomasochistic compulsion that animates him. To accept the version of reality offered by Mito is to ignore the fact that he is incapable of anything resembling objective narration. His tale is hopelessly suspect. His vision is of a disturbed world created by his own psyche.

Of the three novellas, *Cumpleaños* is the most dense and difficult. Like *Aura*'s, the atmosphere is magical, but the narrative does not build toward a climax in the same way. It is more fragmented and experimental. A birthday marks the passage of time: The stark one-word title accentuates the work's abstract focus on time without a mitigating social context. The conspicuous absence of "happy," most frequently modifying "birthday," suggests the inexorable rather than the joyful nature of birthdays and reflects the longing for eternal life that appears in the novel. *Cumpleaños* is a total fiction that abandons rational, chronological, and causal progression in favor of a dreamlike multiplication and conflation of times, places, and figures. Contradictions and paradoxes are often recounted with the dreamer's mixture of acceptance and puzzlement.

Within the narration, which seems to have no clear beginning or end, times are reversed: George, the dreamer-narrator, sees himself as an old man--and perhaps also as a boy. The labyrinthine house is simultaneously itself, the city of London, and a Henry James-like house of fiction. The whole narration, dreamlike as it is, finds itself confirmed and recorded in the mind of Siger de Brabant, a polemical thirteenth century philosopher. In this novella, Fuentes has constructed narrative analogues for Siger's theses, and, like those theses, whose notions of multiple times and souls were heretical, Fuentes's text, with its plurality of times and voices, constitutes a kind of narrative heresy.

THE CRYSTAL FRONTIER

Subtitled *A Novel in Nine Stories*, this is a collection of related stories that focus somewhat nebulously on Don Leonardo Barroso, a Mexican millionaire "Godfather," who symbolizes what Fuentes has called the "scar" of the Mexican-American border. Although the book falls short of the politically complex novel of ideas that Fuentes perhaps intended it to be, it does explore a variety of controversial issues--drug trafficking, immigration restrictions, and government corruption--that plague the transparent but inflexible frontier between the two countries.

"A Capital Girl," which many reviewers recognize as the strongest story in the collection, focuses on Don Barroso's ruthlessness in getting what he wants, even to the extent of grooming his beautiful young goddaughter to be the wife of his bookish son so that Barroso himself can have her as a lover. Other stories deal with more political issues, such as factory workers on the border, the importing of cheap labor into the United States, and blacklisted union organizers. In some of these "issue" stories, Fuentes's effort to create a political novel that criticizes both Mexican and American officials, who ignore the real lives of ordinary people, often leads him to didactic excesses, stick-figure stereotypes, and stilted dialogue.

Two stories have been singled out for praise by critics. "Pain" is about a young medical student, Juan Zamora, for whom Barroso has provided a scholarship to Cornell. While there, Juan, whose homosexuality makes him feel doubly alienated, pretends to be rich for his American hosts, who have no idea of the poverty in Mexico. The title story, "Crystal Frontier," focuses on Lisandro Chavez, a young man from Mexico City who is brought to New York to work as a janitor. To manifest the "crystal frontier" between Mexico and America, Fuentes creates a delicate scene in which Chavez, while washing windows at a Manhattan skyscraper, sees Audrey, an advertising executive, catching up on work alone. After communicating through the window by pantomime, they put their lips to the glass: "Both closed their eyes. She didn't open hers for several minutes. When she did, he was no longer there."

The final "chapter" in the collection is Fuentes's lyrical attempt to pull the various strands of the stories together by presenting a poetic summary of Mexican history, situating himself within the story in the persona of José Francisco, a writer stopped by Mexican and American guards for taking literature across the border. The resultant image is a central metaphor for Fuentes's efforts to create a cultural meeting point between two nations:

> The manuscripts began to fly, lifted by the night breeze like paper doves able to fly for themselves. They . . . went flying from the bridge into the gringo sky, from the bridge to the Mexican sky . . . and José Francisco gave a victory shout that forever broke the crystal of the frontier.

HAPPY FAMILIES

Happy Families consists of sixteen short stories and sixteen "Choruses." The short stories take place mainly in Mexico, either in the countryside or in the cities, and narrate the stories of dysfunctional families and individuals. As a preamble to the collection, Fuentes begins by quoting Leo Tolstoy's famous line from *Anna Karenina* (1875-1877; English translation, 1886): "Happy families are alike; every unhappy family is unhappy in its own way." The second part of this sentence brings the reader close to the content of these stories. The first story, "A Family Like Any Other," perhaps the most experimental, begins with a mysterious "wink," that can be interpreted as confidential, ironic, burlesque, or even complicit to the reader.

The stories parade a variety of characters and themes. The characters represent types, even though they have first and last names, such as Leonardo Barroso, or just first names, such as José or Lucila. In the first story, for example, each member is introduced by his or her title: "The Father," "The Mother," "The Daughter," and "The Son." They reappear, in the same cyclical order, and "dialogue" with the other members of the family until "The Boss" interrupts the circle. "The Boss" represents a rich tyrant, who denigrates his workers. "The Father" devotes his life to the ungrateful "Boss," who fires him and later hires "The Son," with the purpose of subjecting him to the same treatment. Like *Anna Karenina*, these stories deal with the topic

of love or, more accurately, with the lack of love. This theme is re-created as solitude, lack of communication, juvenile behavior, eroticism, pessimism, and violence. In the story "The Disobedient Son," without a discussion a father decides that his three sons will become priests to honor his father's Cristero involvement; instead of obeying him, each one decides his own destiny. "The Gay Divorcee" humanizes the plight of homosexuals, presenting the tribulations that a couple has to endure to live a normal life. Using an epistolary style in "Mater Dolorosa," a woman befriends her daughter's killer in order to find out about her last minutes alive.

The "Choruses" seem to have as their objective to comment on themes and represent the general population, just as choruses in classical tragedies do. The subject matter varies from the tragic to the mundane. Tragic choruses include the vicious cycle of life of street babies and their mothers, and the horror of a woman who kills herself to protect her family from drug dealers, and the senseless death of a man racing his best friend on the highway, and even the "perfect" wife who suffers in silence the abuses of her husband. Using a stream-of-consciousness style, Fuentes presents the mundane, for example in the conundrum of a couple who lose their luggage on the way to their honeymoon. The collection offers Fuentes's understanding of "family" as individuals who hurt each other and later, after they repent, hurt themselves. The last chorus, "Choruscodaconrad," may summarize it all: "the violence, the violence."

OTHER MAJOR WORKS

LONG FICTION: *La región más transparente*, 1958 (*Where the Air Is Clear*, 1960); *Las buenas conciencias*, 1959 (*The Good Conscience*, 1961); *La muerte de Artemio Cruz*, 1962 (*The Death of Artemio Cruz*, 1964); *Cambio de piel*, 1967 (*A Change of Skin*, 1968); *Terra nostra*, 1975 (English translation, 1976); *La cabeza de la hidra*, 1978 (*The Hydra Head*, 1978); *Una familia lejana*, 1980 (*Distant Relations*, 1982); *Gringo viejo*, 1985 (*The Old Gringo*, 1985); *Cristóbal nonato*, 1987 (*Christopher Unborn*, 1989); *La campaña*, 1990 (*The Campaign*, 1991; first volume of trilogy *El tiempo romantico*); *Diana: O, La Cazadora Solitaria*, 1994

(*Diana, the Goddess Who Hunts Alone*, 1995); *Los años con Laura Díaz*, 1999 (*The Years with Laura Diaz*, 2000); *Instinto de Inez*, 2001 (*Inez*, 2002); *La silla del águila*, 2003 (*The Eagle's Throne*, 2006); *La voluntad y la fortuna*, 2008; *Adán en Edén*, 2009.

PLAYS: *El tuerto es rey*, pb. 1970; *Todos los gatos son pardos*, pb. 1970; *Orquídeas a la luz de la luna*, pb. 1982 (*Orchids in the Moonlight*, 1982); *Ceremonias del alba*, revised edition pb. 1991.

SCREENPLAYS: *El acoso*, 1958 (with Luis Buñuel; adaptation of Alejo Carpentier's novel); *Children of Sanchez*, 1961 (with Abbey Mann; adaptation of Oscar Lewis's work); *Pedro Páramo*, 1966 (adaptation of Juan Rulfo's novel); *Tiempo de morir*, 1966; *Los caifanes*, 1967.

NONFICTION: *The Argument of Latin America: Words for North Americans*, 1963; *Paris: La revolución de mayo*, 1968; *El mundo de José Luis Cuevas*, 1969; *La nueva novela hispanoamericana*, 1969; *Casa con dos puertas*, 1970; *Los reinos originarios: Teatro hispano-mexicano*, 1971; *Tiempo mexicano*, 1971; *Cervantes: O, La crítica de la lectura*, 1976 (*Cervantes: Or, The Critique of Reading*, 1976); *Myself with Others: Selected Essays*, 1988; *Valiente mundo nuevo: Épica, utopía y mito en la novela*, 1990; *El espejo enterrado*, 1992 (*The Buried Mirror: Reflections on Spain and the New World*, 1992); *Geografía de la novela*, 1993; *Tres discursos para dos aldeas*, 1993; *Nuevo tiempo mexicano*, 1994 (*A New Time for Mexico*, 1996); *Latin America: At War with the Past*, 2001; *En esto creo*, 2002 (*This I Believe: An A to Z of a Life*, 2005); *Viendo visiones*, 2003; *Contra Bush*, 2004; *Los 68: París-Praga-México*, 2005; *Los caballeros del siglo XXI*, 2005.

EDITED TEXT: *The Vintage Book of Latin American Stories*, 2000 (with Julio Ortega).

BIBLIOGRAPHY

Abeyta, Michael. *Fuentes "Terra Nostra,"and the Reconfiguration of Latin American Culture*. Columbia: University of Missouri Press, 2006. Analyzes how gift-giving, excess, expenditure, sacrifice, and exchange shape the novel. Reveals the relevance of this theme in the relationship between art and the gift.

Bloom, Harold, ed. *Carlos Fuentes's "The Death of Artemio Cruz."* New York: Chelsea House, 2006. A collection of essays that analyzes different aspects of *The Death of Artemio Cruz*, including structure and theme, the relationship between father and son, and the expression of memory and time.

Brody, Robert, and Charles Rossman, eds. *Carlos Fuentes: A Critical View*. Austin: University of Texas Press, 1982. This well-written collection of essays takes various critical approaches to Fuentes's major works of prose, drama, and literary criticism. The work also includes bibliographical references and a chronology.

Brushwood, John S. *Mexico in Its Novel*. Austin: University of Texas Press, 1966. This book takes account of a nation's search for identity through an examination of its fiction. The section devoted to Fuentes discusses the author's major works (published before 1966). Brushwood underscores Fuentes's belief that Mexico has accepted realities that prevent the realization of its potential. Contains a chronological list of Mexican novels and a select bibliography.

Duran, Gloria. *The Archetypes of Carlos Fuentes: From Witch to Androgyne*. Hamden, Conn.: Archon Books, 1980. The first work in English to deal exclusively with the body of Fuentes's novels that have been translated into English. Duran maintains that an examination of the place of witchcraft and occultism is critical to an understanding of Fuentes's work as a whole. Contains biographical data, an appendix, and a bibliography.

Fainaru, Steve. "Poisoned Pen." *The Boston Globe*, November 4, 1997, p. E1. A detailed account of the bitter feud between Fuentes and Paz; discusses the origin of the feud in the 1980's over an attack on Fuentes that Paz allowed to be published in a journal he helped establish.

Faris, Wendy B. *Carlos Fuentes*. New York: Frederick Ungar, 1983. Faris's book offers both biographical information and an insightful critical assessment of Fuentes's early novels, short fiction, and plays. Complemented by a useful bibliography, a chronology, and an index.

Guzmán, Daniel de. *Carlos Fuentes*. New York: Twayne, 1972. The author provides a brief but insightful view on the historical context (specifically, the Mexican

Revolution) of Fuentes's fiction. Guzman's book also includes a select bibliography, an appraisal of the author's works, a historical and sociocultural background, and a chronology of Fuentes's works.

Gyurko, Lanin. *Lifting the Obsidian Mask: The Artistic Vision of Carlos Fuentes*. Potomac, Md.: Scripta Humanistica, 2007. Analyzes Fuentes's short stories, novels, essays, and plays from the early mythic and fantastic short stories to *La silla del águila*, 2003 (*The Eagle's Throne*, 2006) and his unique autobiographical dictionary *En esto creo*, 2002 (*This I Believe: An A to Z of a Life, 2005*).

_____. *Magic Lens: Transformation of the Visual Arts in the Narrative World of Carlos Fuentes*. New Orleans: University Press of the South, 2010. Explores the influence of visual arts, particularly world film from the silent era through film noir to the present, in the works of Fuentes.

Helmuth, Chalene. *The Postmodern Fuentes*. Lewisburg, Pa.: Bucknell University Press, 1997. Examines the postmodern features in Fuentes's novelistic production, particularly since 1975. According to Helmuth, the postmodern novels hold a nonmimetic view of the textual representation of reality, which becomes evident when considering the continual reminders of the artificial nature of the written word that Fuentes scattered in his later narratives.

Ibsen, Kristine. *Author, Text, and Reader in the Novels of Carlos Fuentes*. New York: Peter Lang, 1993. A reader-oriented analysis of four major novels: *A Change of Skin*, *Terra Nostra*, *Distant Relations*, and *Christopher Unborn*.

Morton, Adam David. "The Social Function of Carlos Fuentes: A Critical Intellectual or in the 'Shadow of the State'?" *Bulletin of Latin American Research* 22 (January, 2003): 25-51. Explores the role of intellectuals in Latin American society, using Fuentes as a model.

O'Connor, Anne-Marie. "The Sum of Unequal Parts." *Los Angeles Times*, October 24, 1997. An extended discussion, based on an interview with Fuentes, of his treatment of the border between Mexico and the United States in *The Crystal Frontier*. Fuentes talks of Latin American writers and intellectuals, criticizes the news media for ignoring the plight of the poor, and comments on his efforts to reflect the changes that have taken place in Mexican society.

Van Delden, Maarten. *Carlos Fuentes, México, and Modernity*. Nashville, Tenn.: Vanderbilt University Press, 1998. Analyzes the ongoing tension in Fuentes's works between nationalism and cosmopolitanism, which stands in a complex relationship to the problem of Latin American modernization.

Weiss, Jason. "At the Frontier." Review of *The Crystal Frontier*, by Carlos Fuentes. *The Boston Globe*, November 16, 1997, p. L1. A review of Fuentes's collection, praising especially "Rio Grande, Rio Bravo"; criticizes the frequent didactic message in many of the stories.

Williams, Raymond Leslie. *The Writings of Carlos Fuentes*. Austin: University of Texas Press, 1996. Considering *Terra Nostra* a keystone in Fuentes's narrative production, Williams maintains that the early novels contained all major themes and topics later developed by Fuentes and, by the same token, that the later novels are reworkings and expansions of many of the motifs found in Fuentes's masterpiece.

Genevieve Slomski; Charles E. May
Updated by Susana Perea-Fox

G

Gabriel García Márquez

Born: Aracataca, Colombia; March 6, 1927
Also known as: Gabo

OTHER LITERARY FORMS

Besides his short fiction, including short stories and
novellas, Gabriel García Márquez (gahb-ree-EHL
gahr-SEE-ah MAHR-kays) has also written full-length
novels, such as his masterpiece and best-known novel,
Cien años de soledad (1967; *One Hundred Years of
Solitude,* 1970). In addition, during his long career as a
journalist he has written numerous articles, essays, and
reports on a variety of topics, particularly relating to
Latin American life and politics. Among his nonfiction
works is *Noticia de un secuestro* (1996; *News of a Kidnapping,* 1997), an account of the nefarious activities
of drug lord Pablo Escobar in 1990.

ACHIEVEMENTS

In 1967, Gabriel García Márquez's highly acclaimed novel *One Hundred Years of Solitude* appeared and was immediately recognized by critics as
a masterpiece of fiction. As a work of high literary
quality, this novel was unusual in that it also enjoyed
tremendous popular success both in Latin America
and in translation throughout the world. This work
made García Márquez a major figure--perhaps *the*
major figure--of contemporary Latin American
literature.

García Márquez's work has been praised for
bringing literary fiction back into contact with real
life in all of its richness. His combination of realism
and fantasy known as Magical Realism (*realismo
mágico*) sets the stage for a full spectrum of Latin
American characters. His stories focus on basic
human concerns, and characters or incidents from
one work are often integrated into others, if only with
a passing reference.

García Márquez won the Colombian Association
of Writers and Artists Award in 1954 for the story
"Un dia despues del sabado." The novel *One Hundred Years of Solitude* garnered the French Prix de
Meilleur Livre Étranger, the Italian Chianciano
Award, and the Venezuelan Rómulo Gallego Prize.
Awarding him the Nobel Prize in Literature in 1982,
the Nobel committee compared the breadth and
quality of his work to that of such great writers as

William Faulkner and Honoré de Balzac. In 1988 García Márquez won the *Los Angeles Times* Book Award, for *El amor en los tiempos del cólera* (1985; *Love in the Time of Cholera*, 1988).

BIOGRAPHY

Gabriel José García Márquez was born in Aracataca, a town near the Atlantic coast of Colombia, on March 6, 1927. His parents, Luisa Santiaga and Gabriel Eligio Márquez, sent him to live with his maternal grandparents for the first eight years of his life. He attended school in Barranquilla and Zipaquirá and went on to law studies at the Universidad Nacional in Bogotá.

His first short story was published in 1947 in the Bogotá newspaper *El Espectador*. The literary editor praised the work, and in the next five years several more short fictions were also published. When his studies were interrupted by political violence in 1948, García Márquez transferred to the Universidad de Cartagena, but he never received his degree. Instead, he began his career as a journalist, writing for *El Universal*. He soon had a daily column and became friends with the writers and artists of the "Barranquilla group." In 1950, he moved to Barranquilla and in 1954 to Bogotá, continuing his work as a journalist. During this time, he also published *Leaf Storm, and Other Stories* and received a prize from the Association of Artists and Writers of Bogotá.

In 1955, he was sent to Geneva, Switzerland, as a European correspondent. When *El Espectador* was closed down in January, 1956, García Márquez spent a period of poverty in Paris, working on the novel *La mala hora* (1962; *In Evil Hour*, 1979) and writing some freelance articles. In the summer of 1957, he traveled through Eastern Europe before moving to Caracas, Venezuela, as a journalist. With the prospect of a steady job, he married Mercedes Barcha in March, 1958.

Interested since his university days in leftist causes, García Márquez worked for the Cuban news agency Prensa Latina in Bogotá after Fidel Castro came to power in 1959, and he later worked in Havana, Cuba, and New York. After leaving the agency, he moved to Mexico City, where he worked as a journalist and screenwriter with Carlos Fuentes during the period 1961-1967. In 1962, *In Evil Hour* was published and

won the Esso Literary Prize in Colombia. That same year, a collection of stories, *Los funerales de la Mamá Grande*, also appeared. Then, in a spurt of creative energy, García Márquez spent eighteen months of continuous work to produce his best-selling novel *One Hundred Years of Solitude*, which won book prizes in Italy and France in 1969. In order to be able to write in peace after the tremendous success of this book, he moved to Barcelona, Spain, where he met Peruvian author Mario Vargas Llosa. In 1972, he won both the Rómulo Gallego Prize in Venezuela and the Neustadt International Prize for Literature. The money from both prizes was donated to political causes.

García Márquez left Barcelona in 1975 and returned to Mexico. That same year, *El otoño del patriarca* (1975; *The Autumn of the Patriarch*, 1975), about the life of a Latin American dictator, was published, and in 1981, his novella *Crónica de una muerte anunciada* (*Chronicle of a Death Foretold*, 1982), appeared. His news magazine, *Alternativa*, founded in 1974 in Bogotá to present opposing political views, folded in 1980, but García Márquez continued his activism by

Gabriel Garcia Márquez (©The Nobel Foundation)

writing a weekly column for Hispanic newspapers and magazines. His Nobel Prize speech in 1982 made a strong statement about conditions in Latin America yet sounded the note of hope in the face of oppression.

García Márquez continued his literary production after receiving the Nobel Prize, publishing, among other works, *El general en su laberinto* in 1989 (*The General in His Labyrinth*, 1990), based on the life of South American revolutionary leader Simón Bolívar. He also continued his political work, appearing at conferences with, variously, Colombian, Venezuelan, Mexican, and U.S. presidents on such issues as civil war and drug trafficking. In 1999 he fell ill in Bogotá, in one of his seven houses, and was diagnosed with and treated for lymphatic cancer. His illness went into remission, and he continued to write, publishing the novel *Memoria de mis putas tristes* (2004; *Memories of My Melancholy Whores*, 2005) and the first volume in a proposed trilogy of memoirs, *Vivir para contarla* (2002; (*Living to Tell the Tale*, 2003).

ANALYSIS

Gabriel García Márquez's fiction is characterized by a thread of common themes, events, and characters that seem to link his work together into one multifaceted portrayal of the experiences of Latin American life. From the influences of his early childhood, when he learned from his grandmother how to tell the most fantastic stories in a matter-of-fact tone, to his later observations of the oppression and cruelties of politics, García Márquez captures the everyday life of the people of coastal Colombia, with its Caribbean flavor, as well as the occasional resident of the highlands of Bogotá. He has an eye for the details of daily life mixed with humor and an attitude of acceptance and wonder. His characters experience the magic and joy of life and face the suffering of solitude and isolation but always with an innate dignity. García Márquez's vision touches real life with its local attitudes and values, and in the process it also reveals a criticism of politics, the church, and U.S. imperialism, as they contribute to the Latin American experience.

García Márquez's body of work portrays a complete reality breaking out of conventional bounds. Characters from one story regularly show up or are mentioned in another, while his complex mix of fantasy and reality reveals a consummate storyteller capable of bringing to his work the magic of his non-European world. His impact as a writer lies in the fact that, although his work describes the Latin American experience of life, it also goes beyond to reveal a universal human experience.

OJOS DE PERRO AZUL

García Márquez's earliest stories have a bizarre, almost surreal tone, reminiscent of Franz Kafka. Collected in *Ojos de perro azul*, these stories represent an experimental phase of García Márquez's development as a writer. They exemplify his new, or strange, realism, extending the reality of life into and beyond the experience of death. "La tercera resignación" ("The Third Resignation"), for example, deals with the thoughts and fears of a young man in his coffin. "Nabo, el negro que hizo esperar a los ángeles" ("Nabo, the Black Man Who Made the Angels Wait") tells of a man who is locked in a stable because he goes insane after being kicked in the head by a horse.

In *Isabel viendo llover en Macondo* (*Monologue of Isabel Watching It Rain in Macondo*), García Márquez captures the atmosphere of a tropical storm through the eyes of his protagonist. Here, the world of Macondo, also used in his novella *Leaf Storm* and made world-famous in *One Hundred Years of Solitude*, is presented amid the suffocating oppressiveness of tropical weather. Here, as later, nature itself is often a palpable force in the fiction of García Márquez--often exaggerated and overwhelming in order to reflect the reality of Latin American geography and the natural forces within it. The repetition underscores the monotony of the continuing deluge, and the theme of solitude is reflected in the imagery, as well as in the personal relationship of Isabel and Martin: "The sky was a gray, jellyish substance that flapped its wings a hand away from our heads."

NO ONE WRITES TO THE COLONEL

After demonstrating his ability to capture the tropical atmosphere, García Márquez shows himself capable of capturing a portrait in words with his well-structured novella *No One Writes to the Colonel*. The central character is a dignified man with a deep sense of honor who has been promised a military pension.

Every Friday, he goes to the post office to wait for mail that never comes, and then he claims that he really was not expecting anything anyway. He is a patient man, resigned to eternal waiting and hope when there is no reason to expect that hope to be fulfilled. "For nearly sixty years--since the end of the last civil war--the colonel had done nothing else but wait. October was one of the few things which arrived." His other hope is his rooster, which belonged to his son, who was executed for handing out subversive literature, but since he is too poor to feed the rooster, some townspeople work out an arrangement to provide food until after the big fight. The political background is introduced subtly as the story opens with the funeral of the first person to die of natural causes in this town in a long time. Violence, censorship, and political repression are a given, as is the pervasive poverty. The colonel continues passing out the literature in his son's place and waiting for his pension. His dignity sustains him in the face of starvation.

The dialogues between the colonel and his practical wife of many years are woven through the novella and reach a climax at the very end of the story. She presses him to sell the rooster, asking plaintively and persistently what they will eat:

> It had taken the colonel seventy-five years--the seventy-five years of his life, minute by minute--to reach this moment. He felt pure, explicit, invincible at the moment when he replied: "S--!"

LOS FUNERALES DE LA MAMÁ GRANDE

The image of dignity is developed again in the first story of *Los funerales de la Mamá Grande*, entitled "La siesta del martes" ("Tuesday Siesta") and also set in Macondo. Said to be García Márquez's favorite story, it tells of a woman and her young daughter who arrive by train in the stifling heat at siesta time. The woman asks the priest to be allowed to visit her son in the cemetery. The young man was shot for being a thief, but she proudly claims him as her own with quiet self-control: "I told him never to steal anything that anyone needed to eat, and he minded me."

The title story, "Los funerales de la Mamá Grande" ("Big Mama's Funeral"), still set in Macondo, breaks the tone of the other stories into a technique of

hyperbole, which García Márquez later used in *One Hundred Years of Solitude* to good effect. The opening sentence sets the tone:

> This is, for all the world's unbelievers, the true account of Big Mama, absolute sovereign of the Kingdom of Macondo, who lived for ninety-two years, and died in the odor of sanctity one Tuesday last September, and whose funeral was attended by the Pope.

The panorama and parody of the story mention Mama's power and property in high-sounding phrases, many from journalism. The pageantry is grandiose to the point of the absurd for this powerful individual, a prototype of the patriarch who appears in García Márquez's later work. She is a legend and local "saint," who seemed to the local people to be immortal; her death comes as a complete surprise. The story criticizes the manipulation of power but also skillfully satirizes the organized display or public show that eulogizes the holders of power with pomp and empty words. The story ends when the garbage men come and sweep up on the next day.

INNOCENT ERÉNDIRA, AND OTHER STORIES

Fantastic elements characterize the collection *Innocent Eréndira, and Other Stories*. Two of the stories, "Un señor muy viejo con unas alas enormes" ("A Very Old Man with Enormous Wings") and "El ahogado más hermoso del mundo" ("The Handsomest Drowned Man in the World"), have adult figures who are like toys with which children, and other adults, can play. With the second story, García Márquez also tries a technique of shifting narrators and point of view to be used later in the novel *The Autumn of the Patriarch*.

A political satire is the basis for another story, "Muerte constante más allá del amor" ("Death Constant Beyond Love"). The situation that forms the basis for the satire is also incorporated into the longer "Innocent Eréndira." Geographically, in this collection García Márquez has moved inland to the barren landscape on the edge of the Guajiro desert. Here, he sets a type of folktale with an exploited granddaughter, a green-blooded monster of a grandmother, and a rescuing hero named Ulises. Combining myth, allegory, and references from other works, García Márquez weaves a story in which "the wind of her misfortune" determines the life of the extraordinarily passive Eréndira. Treated as a slave and a prostitute by her grandmother, Eréndira persuades Ulises to kill the evil woman--who turns out to be amazingly hard to kill. Throughout the story, García Márquez demonstrates the ability to report the most monstrous things in a matter-of-fact tone. Some critics have pointed out that the exaggeration that seems inherent in many of his tales may have its roots in the extraordinary events and stories that are commonplace in his Latin American world.

CHRONICLE OF A DEATH FORETOLD

In *Chronicle of a Death Foretold*, García Márquez blends his experience in journalism with his mastery of technique to tell a story based on an actual event that took place in 1955 in Sucre, where he lived at the time. Using records and witness testimony, he unfolds his tale on the lines of a detective story. The incident is based on the revenge taken by Angela Vicario's brothers on their friend Santiago Nasar, who supposedly took Angela's virginity, although some doubt is cast on this allegation. The story is pieced together as the townspeople offer their memories of what happened, along with excuses for not having warned the victim. Tension builds as the reader knows the final outcome but not how or why it will occur. The use of dreams (ironically, Nasar's mother is an interpreter of dreams), the feeling of fatalism, and submission to the code of honor, all of which form a part of this society's attitudes, play a central role in the novella, as do García Márquez's use of vision and foreshadowing. Although the basis for the story is a journalistic report of a murder, the actual writing captures the themes of love and death, as well as the complex interplay of human emotions and motives in a balanced and poetic account, which reveals García Márquez's skill as a writer.

STRANGE PILGRIMS

Strange Pilgrims picks up the Magical Realism of the earlier short stories, organizing twelve works written between 1976 and 1982 so that seven stories, having to do with the death-force of life are followed by five stories that evoke the vitality of death. The opening story portrays a septuagenarian former president whose imminent death proves to be illusory; the seventh story depicts a septuagenarian woman, to whom the approach of death also proves to be illusory. In both stories, dying is detailed as a form of intensified living. The second and sixth stories deal with the supernatural, one through a corpse that does not putrefy and the other through a haunted bedroom, and both include Italian settings. The third and fifth stories carry fairy-tale variations: a sleeping beauty who, unkissed, awakes of her own volition, and a lady in distress who, imprisoned in a madhouse, transcends her incarceration. In the fourth story, the umbilicus of the seven, a woman, whose life consists of dreaming, awakens from her dreams only through death. The concluding five stories present, first, two stories of murder--between which is a story of suicide--and two stories dealing with strange fatalities. In one, the wave function of light drowns persons without diving gear; in the other, an apparently negligible rose-thorn prick on a young bride's ring fingertip inexorably causes her death.

OTHER MAJOR WORKS

LONG FICTION: *La mala hora*, 1962 (revised 1966; *In Evil Hour*, 1979); *Cien años de soledad*, 1967 (*One Hundred Years of Solitude*, 1970); *El otoño del patriarca*, 1975 (*The Autumn of the Patriarch*, 1975); *El amor en los tiempos del cólera*, 1985 (*Love in the Time of Cholera*, 1988); *El general en su laberinto*, 1989 (*The General in His Labyrinth*, 1990); *Collected Novellas*, 1990; *Del amor y otros demonios*, 1994 (*Of Love and Other Demons*, 1995); *Memoria de mis putas tristes*, 2004 (*Memories of My Melancholy Whores*, 2005).

NONFICTION: *La novela en América Latina: Diálogo*, 1968 (with Mario Vargas Llosa); *Cuando era feliz e indocumentado*, 1973; *Chile, el golpe y los gringos*, 1974; *Crónicas y reportajes*, 1976; *Operación Carlota*, 1977; *De viaje por los países socialistas*, 1978; *Periodismo militante*, 1978; *Obra periodística*, 1981-1999 (5 volumes; includes *Textos costeños*, 1981; *Entre cachacos*, 1982; *De Europa y América, 1955-1960*, 1983; *Por la libre, 1974-1995*, 1999; *Notas de prensa, 1961-1984*, 1999); *El olor de la guayaba: Conversaciones con Plinio Apuleyo Mendoza*, 1982 (*The Fragrance of the Guava: Plinio Apuleyo Mendoza in*

Conversation with Gabriel García Márquez, 1983; also known as *The Smell of Guava*, 1984); *La aventura de Miguel Littín, clandestino en Chile*, 1986 (*Clandestine in Chile: The Adventures of Miguel Littín*, 1987); *Noticia de un secuestro*, 1996 (*News of a Kidnapping*, 1997); *Por un país al alcance de los niños*, 1996 (*For the Sake of a Country Within Reach of the Children*, 1998); *Vivir para contarla*, 2002 (*Living to Tell the Tale*, 2003).

BIBLIOGRAPHY

Bell-Villada, Gene H. *García Márquez: The Man and His Work*. Chapel Hill: University of North Carolina Press, 1990. This well-written book traces the forces that have shaped the life and work of García Márquez and analyzes his short fiction, as well as his novels. Includes an index and a fine selected bibliography of sources in English and Spanish, as well as a listing of works by García Márquez and of available English translations.

Bloom, Harold, ed. *Gabriel García Márquez*. Updated ed. New York: Chelsea House, 2007. Collection of essays, including three that focus on the short fiction: "Hemingway's Presence in the Early Short Fiction (1950-1955)," by Harley D. Oberhelman, "The End of Eréndira's Prostitution," by Diane E. Marting, and "From Mystery to Parody: (Re)readings of García Márquez's *Crónica de una Muerte Anunciada*," by Isabel Alvarez-Borland. Also includes an interview with García Márquez and an overview of his life.

Byk, John. "From Fact to Fiction: Gabriel García Márquez and the Short Story." *Mid-American Review* 6 (1986): 111-116. Discusses the development of García Márquez's short fiction from his early imitations of Franz Kafka to his more successful experiments with Magical Realism.

Gerlach, John. "The Logic of Wings: García Márquez, Todorov, and the Endless Resources of Fantasy." In *Bridges to Fantasy*, edited by George E. Slusser, Eric S. Rabkin, and Robert Scholes. Carbondale: Southern Illinois University Press, 1982. Argues that the point of view of "A Very Old Man with Enormous Wings" makes readers sympathize with the old man by establishing his superiority over the villagers.

Hart, Stephen M. *Gabriel García Márquez: "Crónica de una Muerte Anunciada."* London: Grant & Cutler, 1994. A thorough critical guide to *Chronicle of a Death Foretold*.

Martin, Gerald. *Gabriel García Márquez: A Life*. New York: Knopf, 2009. The product of seventeen years of research, this biography takes a comprehensive look at García Márquez's personal life, as well as his writing. Provides insightful analysis of his novels and stories. Essential for anyone interested in his life and works.

McMurray, George R., ed. *Critical Essays on Gabriel García Márquez*. Boston: G. K. Hall, 1987. A collection of book reviews, articles, and essays covering the full range of García Márquez's fictional work. Very useful for an introduction to specific novels and collections of short stories. Also includes an introductory overview by the editor and an index.

McNerney, Kathleen. *Understanding Gabriel García Márquez*. Columbia: University of South Carolina Press, 1989. An overview addressed to students and nonacademic readers. After an introduction on Colombia and a brief biography, the five core chapters explain García Márquez's works in depth. Chapters 1 through 3 discuss three novels, chapter 4 focuses on his short novels and stories, and chapter 5 reviews the role of journalism in his work. Includes a select, annotated bibliography of critical works and an index.

McQuirk, Bernard, and Richard Cardwell, eds. *Gabriel García Márquez: New Readings*. Cambridge, England: Cambridge University Press, 1987. A collection of twelve essays in English by different authors reflecting a variety of critical approaches and covering García Márquez's major novels, as well as a selection of his early fiction: *No One Writes to the Colonel, Innocent Eréndira*, and *Chronicle of a Death Foretold*. Also includes a translation of García Márquez's Nobel address and a select bibliography.

Minta, Stephen. *García Márquez: Writer of Colombia*. New York: Harper & Row, 1987. After a useful first chapter on Colombia, the book traces García Márquez's life and works. Minta focuses his discussion on the political context of the *violencia* in *No*

One Writes to the Colonel and *In Evil Hour*. Includes two chapters on Macondo as García Márquez's fictional setting and another chapter with individual discussions of *The Autumn of the Patriarch, Chronicle of a Death Foretold*, and *Love in the Time of Cholera*. Includes a select bibliography by chapter and an index.

Oberhelman, Harley D. *Gabriel Gárcia Márquez: A Study of the Short Fiction*. Boston: Twayne, 1991. Argues that García Márquez's short fiction is almost as important as his novels. Suggests that his stories have the same narrative pattern as his novels. Includes five interviews with García Márquez and essays by four critics.

Stevans, Ilan, ed. *Critical Insights: Gabriel García Márquez*. Pasadena, Calif.: Salem Press, 2010. Collection of original and reprinted essays providing critical readings of García Márquez's works. Three essays are particularly pertinent to the short stories

and novellas: "The Master of Short Forms," by Gene H. Bell-Villada, "Magical Realism and García Márquez's Eréndira," by Moylan C. Mills and Enrique Grönlund, and in "'The Paralysis of the Instant': The Stagnation of History and the Stylistic Suspension of Time in Gabriel García Márquez's *La hojarasca*,'" by Deborah Cohn.

Swanson, Philip, ed. *The Cambridge Companion to Gabriel García Márquez*. New York: Cambridge University Press, 2010. A collection of twelve essays about García Márquez's life and works, including Steven Hart's piece "García Márquez's Short Stories." Other essays examine the writer's life and times, his critical reception, his novels and nonfiction works, and "García Márquez, Magical Realism, and World Literature."

Susan L. Piepke
Updated by Roy Arthur Swanson

NIKOLAI GOGOL

Born: Sorochintsy, Ukraine, Russian Empire (now in Ukraine); March 31, 1809

Died: Moscow, Russia; March 4, 1852

PRINCIPAL SHORT FICTION

Vechera na khutore bliz Dikanki, vol. 1, 1831, vol. 2, 1832 (*Evenings on a Farm near Dikanka*, 1926)

Arabeski, 1835 (*Arabesques*, 1982)

Mirgorod, 1835 (English translation, 1928)

The Complete Tales of Nikolai Gogol, 1985 (2 volumes; Leonard J. Kent, editor)

OTHER LITERARY FORMS

Nikolai Gogol (nyihk-UH-li GAW-guhl) established his reputation on his remarkable short stories, but he is often better known in the West for his play *Revizor* (pr., pb. 1836; *The Inspector General*, 1890) and for the first part of his novel *Myortvye dushi* (1842; *Dead Souls*, 1887). Still the subject of much debate and

criticism, his *Vybrannye mesta iz perepiski s druzyami* (1847; *Selected Passages from Correspondence with Friends*, 1969) represents a range from literary criticism to tendentious and presumptuous evaluation of Russia as seen from abroad.

ACHIEVEMENTS

In Russian literature of both the nineteenth and the twentieth centuries, it is impossible to overstate the importance of Nikolai Gogol as an innovator in style and subject matter. He created a great and enduring art form composed of the manners of petty officials, small landowners, and the fantastic and all-too-real people who inhabit the three worlds that he describes: the Ukraine, St. Petersburg, and the Russian heartland.

Outside Russia, his influence can be detected most noticeably in Franz Kafka's *Die Verwandlung* (1915; *The Metamorphosis*, 1936), which centers on a conceit not unlike the hapless titular councillor in Gogol's "Nos" ("The Nose"). Inside Russia, Fyodor Dostoevski is reputed to have begun the saying that "we all came from under Gogol's 'Overcoat,'" meaning that Gogol's stories originated the themes, social and spiritual anguish, and other literary preoccupations of the rest of Russian literature.

BIOGRAPHY

Nikolai Vasilyevich Gogol was born in the Ukraine on March 31, 1809, to a Ukrainian landowner, Vasily Afanasievich Gogol-Yanovsky, and his young wife, Mariya Ivanovna. Vasily Afanasievich wrote plays in Ukrainian and sponsored artistic evenings at his home. Nikolai would write almost nothing in Ukrainian throughout his life. On his father's estate, Nikolai would absorb the manner and, significantly, the pace of provincial life, which would flavor his works from his early stories through *Dead Souls*.

At school and later in the *Gymnasium*, Nikolai remained something of a loner. He participated in activities, especially in drama performances, where he is said to have excelled. His classmates called him "the mysterious dwarf," though, for his predilection to aloofness and his unassuming stature.

Gogol's first work, *Hans Kuechelgarten* (1829), which he published at his own expense, was received so poorly that he bought all the unsold copies, burned them, and never wrote in verse again. He fled the country (in what was to become a characteristic retreat) and took refuge in Germany for several weeks. When he returned, he occupied a minor post in the civil service in St. Petersburg and began writing the stories that would begin to appear in 1831 and subsequently make him famous. His first collection of stories, *Evenings on a Farm near Dikanka*, met with great critical and popular acclaim and set the stage for the series of successes that his later stories were to have.

In 1836, however, his play *The Inspector General* premiered, was produced most outlandishly in Gogol's mind, and created a minor scandal. Although this initial reaction was reversed and, through the intercession of the czar himself, the play was to continue its run, Gogol was nevertheless mortified at the antagonism he had aroused in the audience. He again left the country, only this time--with the exception of two rather short trips back to Russia--forever.

His last and most enduring works, "Shinel" ("The Overcoat") and *Dead Souls*, were thus written abroad. The irony of the profound resonance that his writing enjoyed at home was not lost on him. He began to doubt his ability to convey the "truth" to the Russians from such a distance and began to search for artistic inspiration. His self-doubt gave birth to his last literary production, *Selected Passages from Correspondence with Friends*. This product of his doubt was met with indignation and even anger in Russia. Vissarion Belinsky wrote his famous letter excoriating Gogol for his "fantastic book" and for writing from his "beautiful distance." Had Gogol forgotten the misery of Russia, its serfdom and servility, its "tartar" censorship, its totalitarian clout? Belinsky believed that the public was justified in its censure of this work; the public has the right to expect more from literature.

Gogol spent the last six years of his life fighting depression and artistic barrenness, trying to reach the "truth" in the second part of *Dead Souls*. Unfortunately, he failed to finish this work and, shortly before his death, burned what he had written. Physically ill, spiritually empty, and emotionally depleted, he died in pain in Moscow on March 4, 1852.

ANALYSIS

Nikolai Gogol combines the consummate stylist with the innocent spectator, flourishes and flounces with pure human emotion, and naturalism with delicate sensitivity. He bridges the period between Romanticism and realism in Russian literature. He captures the "real" against the background of the imagined and, in the estimation of at least one critic, the surreal. Frequently, the supernatural or some confounding coincidence plays a major role in his works. His heroes of the "little man" variety imprinted the most profound impression on his readers and critics alike. These petty clerks, all socially dysfunctional in some major respect, nevertheless explore the great depth of the human soul and exhibit certain personality traits characteristic of the greatest heroes in literature.

Gogol focuses his major creative occupation on the manners of his characters; his creative energy is nowhere more apparent than in the "mannerizing" in which he describes and characterizes. His genius

Nikolai Gogol (Library of Congress)

does not dwell in philosophical dialogues, allegory, or involved interior monologue as do the realist novels of the latter half of the century, nor does he engender his heroes with abandon and ennui, as do his near contemporaries Alexander Pushkin and Mikhail Lermontov. The depth of his psychological portraiture and the sweep of his romantic apostrophes, however, remain powerful and fascinating. In his plays, speech is swept aside from its characteristic place in the foreground; the dramatic foreground is given over to the manner or mannerisms of the characters. The actions literally speak louder than words. The social satire, deeply embedded in the manners of the characters, unfolds without special machinations and with few unnatural speech acts, such as asides. It is a tribute to Gogol's skill that his characters do not necessarily become superficial or unidimensional as a result but are imbued with certain attributes that display a wide range of human passion, particularly human dignity and the cognizance of the injustices created in social stratification.

One of Gogol's favored narrative devices can be called the chatty narrator. This narrator, seemingly prolix and sometimes random, will supply the reader with most of the information that will ever be revealed about a character. In a typical passage, the reader will encounter a character who might say something utterly commonplace, such as: "I won't have coffee today, Praskovia Osipovna, instead I will take some hot bread with onions." The character says little that can be used to describe himself. The reader's attention, however, is then directed to the information supplied by the narrator: "Actually, Ivan Yakovlevich would have liked to take both, but he knew it was utterly impossible to ask for two things at the same time since Praskovia Osipovna greatly disliked such whims." Thus Ivan Yakovlevich is described by his manners--he speaks to his wife in a formal tone that relates very little information to the reader--but the narrator, in his chatty, nosy fashion, reveals much about this individual and describes Ivan's wife, his subordinate position at home, and his struggle for dignity within this relationship at the same time. Thus, from a seeming excess of information, the reader becomes familiar with a character who might otherwise remain nondescript.

Gogol's narratives abound in descriptions, and these tend to be humorous. Many times, humor is created by the device of metonymy, whereby a part stands for the whole. Thus, women become "slender waists" and seem so light that one fears that they will float away, and men are mustaches of various colors, according to their rank. Another humorous effect might be created by the chatty narrator's remark about some individual in a very unfavorable light. This information that he, for some reason, knows in regard to the character informs the reader's opinion of that character and often lends either a humorous or a pathetic tone to his or her person. Also humorous is the effect created through realized metaphors, another favorite technique of Gogol. Thus, instead of "he ate like a pig," the person is actually transformed into a pig with all the attributes of a perfect pig, at least temporarily. In general, Gogol's works abound with descriptions packed with colors, similes, and wayward characterizations by his narrator or actors.

Gogol's works fall roughly into three categories, which in turn correspond approximately to three different periods in his creative life. The first period is represented solely by short stories that exhibit lush local color from the Ukraine and Gogol's own mixing of devils and simple folk. Seven of the eight stories from the collection *Evenings on a Farm Near Dikanka*, which appeared in 1831 (with the second part following in 1832), belong in this category, as well as the stories in *Mirgorod*, first published in 1835.

The second major period of Gogol's literary life features works either centered on a locus in the imperial center of Russia, St. Petersburg itself, or surrounding the bureaucrats and petty officials ubiquitous in the provinces of the empire. This period stretches roughly from 1835 to 1842 and includes the short stories "Nevsky Prospekti" ("Nevsky Prospect"), "Zapiski sumasshedshego" ("The Diary of a Madman"), "The Overcoat," "The Nose," the play *The Inspector General*, and the novel *Dead Souls*. The short story "Portret" ("The Portrait"), although definitely a product of this period, is singular for its strong echoes of the devil tales in the early period.

The last period can claim only one published work, *Selected Passages from Correspondence with Friends*, and is typically interpreted as a reversal in Gogol's creative development. If the analyst, however, can keep in mind Gogol's rather fanatic attachment to his artistic life as a devotional to God, then perhaps this otherwise unexplainable curve in his creative evolution might seem more understandable.

The two volumes of *Evenings on a Farm Near Dikanka* contain eight stories. However atypical they were to become in terms of setting and subject matter, these tales of the Ukraine, with various elements of the supernatural adding terror, exhibit many of the qualities found in the mature writer of the second period. They are magical and engaging, heroic and base, simply enjoyable to read and quite poignant.

"A MAY NIGHT"

An excellent example of these tales is "Mayskaya Noch: Ili, utoplennitsa" ("A May Night: Or, The Drowned Maiden"). The plot is a simple love story in which the lovers are not allowed to wed because of the objection of the man's father. The seeming simplicity,

however, is overwhelmed by acts of Satan, witches, and *rusalki*. (In folk belief, *rusalki* are female suicides who endlessly inhabit the watery depths of ponds, tempting men and often causing their deaths.) When the antics of Ukrainian cossack youths do not by themselves bring the matter to resolution, the *rusalka* puts a letter into the young man's hand, which secures for him his marriage.

The characters are depicted in ways highly reminiscent of the oral folktales. Levko, the hero, sings to his beloved to come out of her house. He speaks of his "brighteyed beauty," her "little white hands," and her "fair little face." All these figures of speech are fixed epithets common in folklore. He promises to protect her from detection-- "I will cover you with my jacket, wrap my sash around you, or hide you in my arms--and no one will see us,"--forfending the possible intrusion three ways. Likewise, he promises to protect her from any cold-- "I'll press you warmer to my heart, I'll warm you with my kisses, I'll put my cap over your little white feet"--that is, a threefold protection. The reinforcement of images in threes is also quite common in folklore. Thus, Gogol is clearly invoking folklore in his artistic works. Nevertheless, there are hints of the mature Gogol in the landscape descriptions. Even the intervention of the supernatural to produce, in this case, the successful outcome of the story belongs to the second period, as well as to the first.

"IVAN FYODOROVICH SHPONKA AND HIS AUNT"

One story, in retrospect, however, stands out clearly from the others. "Ivan Fyodorovich Shpon'ka i ego tetushka" ("Ivan Fyodorovich Shponka and His Aunt") certainly presages the later works that will come to be regarded as Gogol's most characteristic. Set in the Ukraine, the story begins with an elaborate frame involving the following: The original storyteller of the tale wrote the story entirely and gave it to the narrator (for reasons that are not explained), but the narrator's wife later used the paper to wrap her pies, so the end of the story was unfortunately lost. The readers are assured, however, that should they so desire, they may contact the original storyteller, who still lives in that village and who will certainly oblige in sharing the ending.

There are many details in this frame alone that are very typical of the mature Gogol. First, the narrator does not take responsibility for the story--that is, that it is left unfinished; the abrupt end is presented as something over which he has no control. Second, the woman is the undoing of the man, although, in this case, the undoing is caused by her illiteracy and not by an inherent evil. Moreover, the narrator could have rectified the situation himself, but, seemingly, he was fated to forget to ask the storyteller for another copy of the ending. Most of all, the story in the frame abounds with chatty, seemingly irrelevant details that serve to characterize the narrator, his wife, and the storyteller but that, ultimately, motivate the plot and occasion the sometimes precipitous changes in the course of the narrative.

The motifs described above reappear in forms both changed and unchanged throughout Gogol's work. A woman will appear in many guises in three of the four stories in *Mirgorod*. In "Taras Bulba," a long story with the color and force of an epic, a Polish beauty causes the son, Andrei, to defect to the enemy. Later, the traitor will be murdered by his father's own hands, described in the father's own words as a "vile dog."

"VIY"

In another story from this collection, "Viy," a young student, Khoma Brut, meets an old woman on his way home on vacation. When he stays for the night in her barn, she comes after him with outstretched arms. Khoma tries to avoid her three different ways, but she persists and, to his amazement, he loses the use of his arms and legs. The old woman turns out to be a witch who wickedly torments and then rides on the back of the young philosopher. Remembering some exorcisms, however, he renders her harmless and, in fact, exchanges places with her, now riding on her back. Khoma makes an incredible trek in this fashion until she falls in a faint. Now, watching her prone form, he is amazed to find not a witch or an old woman but a fair young maiden. Khoma races off, making it all the way to Kiev, but is called back to watch over her corpse for three nights, which was the last request of the dying maiden. During the third night, he is overcome by the supernatural devil, Viy, who emanates from the dead woman and thus brings his own doom.

"THE TALE OF HOW IVAN IVANOVICH QUARRELED WITH IVAN NIKIFOROVICH"

Another story from this collection, "Povest o tom, kak possorilsya Ivan Ivanovich s Ivanom Nikiforovichem" ("The Tale of How Ivan Ivanovich Quarreled with Ivan Nikiforovich"), also revolves around the same motif of the evil woman, although almost imperceptibly. Here, it is a "stupid" woman who sets out the gun while cleaning the house, which causes Ivan Ivanovich to envy this possession of his neighbor Ivan Nikiforovich. This seemingly insignificant act is the very act that causes an ensuing argument and that in turn builds into a lasting enmity between the former friends and then lasts in the courts for a decade. In Russia, this story is often invoked when people quarrel over imagined improprieties or insignificant trifles.

"NEVSKY PROSPECT"

In the collection *Arabesques*, the two most famous stories, "Nevsky Prospect" and "The Diary of a Madman," similarly feature the demonic power of women over men. "Nevsky Prospect" indeed centers on this "demonic" nature of women. Two tales are told, one of the "sensitive young man," the artist Piskarev, and the other of a rather older, down-to-earth lieutenant named Pirogov. The artist, perhaps fooled by the falling darkness, is stunned by the dazzling beauty of a woman walking by on Nevsky Prospect, a main avenue in St. Petersburg. At the same moment, Pirogov notices and blindly takes off after a blond woman, "convinced that no beauty could resist him." Piskarev, almost overwhelmed at his own audacity, meekly follows his beauty to her "home," only to find out that she is, indeed, a prostitute. This development soon becomes the undoing of the poor artist as he falls into daytime and nighttime dreaming in a vain attempt to rescue his former exalted vision and save her image from the reality of her vile lifestyle. He takes to opium and, finally, emboldened, decides on the desperate act of proposing marriage to her. When she rebuffs him, he goes mad and takes his own life. Pirogov, on the other hand, for all of his self-confidence and experience, fares only slightly better after following his blond beauty home--to her husband. He blindly but cunningly continues his pursuit of her, only to end up being humiliated and physically abused. Indignant, he sets out to put his case before the court, but, somehow, after eating a little and spending some time rather pleasantly, he becomes diverted and seemingly forgets the whole thing. The narrator then closes the story with the admonition not to trust Nevsky Prospect because nothing there is as it seems, especially not the ladies.

"The Diary of a Madman"

"The Diary of a Madman" appears to be the personal journal of Popryshchin, whose name sounds very much like "pimple." The story is written as a series of entries with the chronology becoming entirely skewed at the end in accordance with the degree of dementia within the protagonist. The appearance of Popryshchin, the poor government clerk, marks the introduction of a new incarnation of the meek Shponkin type who will populate many of Gogol's works thereafter and enter the world of Russian literature as a prototype for many writers, notably Dostoevski. Popryshchin, a rather older, undistinguished man, adores the director's daughter but recognizes that pursuing her is useless. Moreover, he sees that his infatuation for her will be his doom: "Dear God, I'm a goner, completely lost!" Virtually at the same moment that he admits his futile position, his attention is drawn to the thin voice of Madgie, the young lady's dog, who is speaking to Fido. This rather fantastic conversation is centered on the letter that poor Fido seemingly never received from Madgie. Popryshchin's delusions continue to build up, with him even reading the canine correspondence. It is actually through Madgie's letters that Popryshchin learns of the young lady's love for, and engagement to, a handsome young chamberlain. Moreover, Popryshchin finds the young man's description unflattering. The sentence, "Sophie always laughs at him," becomes the crowning blow to his sanity. Shortly thereafter he goes mad, imagining himself to be the king of Spain. He is committed to Spain, more accurately, to a mental hospital, where he is constantly tormented. The pathos of the "little man" is palpable, conveyed through the evocation of a beautiful image--a troika coming to fly to him and rescue him--juxtaposed to the hateful attendants dousing him repeatedly with cold water.

"The Overcoat"

Another "little man" follows closely in Popryshchin's footsteps. In "The Overcoat," Akaky Akakievich, whose humorous name is a reminder of fecal matter (kaka), represents such a meek and orderly person that he can perform only one duty: copying papers. This duty he discharges perfectly and with great pleasure, sometimes so much so that he occasionally brings the document home and, in his spare time, copies it again. Akaky Akakievich lives in St. Petersburg, victim of almost unimaginable poverty with barely enough means to keep himself alive. It was, indeed, a terrible day when he could no longer convince his tailor to have his overcoat remade; he would have to buy a new one. The physical privations that were necessitated by this desperate position are reminiscent of saintly asceticism. However, Akaky begins to sublimate his anguish and dreams of the great overcoat as though of a wife. With the mention of the word "wife," the reader who is accustomed to Gogol might immediately suspect the potential danger of this coat because women in Gogol's fiction are almost always the undoing of a man. True to form, after withstanding all the hardships, enduring all the misgivings and new sensations, Akaky wears the new coat only once before he is mugged and the coat stolen from him. Dazed and exposed in the cold of St. Petersburg, he musters the courage to petition a "Person of Consequence" who dismisses him pompously. Akaky then falls into a fever from which he will not emerge alive. The tale, however, takes on a fantastic ending. Akaky comes back from the dead, intimidates and robs the Person of Consequence of his overcoat, and then, apparently satisfied, leaves the scene forever.

The supernatural revenge makes "The Overcoat" quite singular in Gogol's work. The fantastic element, however, appears again in another story of the same period, "The Nose." A barber, Ivan Yakovlevich, takes a roll for breakfast and finds, much to his alarm, a human nose in it, and he recognizes the nose as that of the Collegiate Assessor Kovalyov. Ivan Yakovlevich tries to rid himself of the nose. Meanwhile, its erstwhile owner wakes up to find a completely smooth area where his nose and incipient pimple had been the previous evening. He sets out on foot with the empty spot concealed by a handkerchief, only to witness his own former nose walking about freely, moreover in the uniform of a civil councillor--that is, a higher-ranking individual than Kovalyov himself. He accosts the nose very deferentially, but the nose claims to be an independent individual and not part of Kovalyov at all. In desperation, he sets out for the police department but, thinking better of it, decides to place an advertisement in the local newspaper. There, the clerk, thinking about it, decides against publishing such an advertisement to avoid potential scandals for the paper. Luckily for Kovalyov, the nose is returned to him by a police officer, but to his horror, it will not stick to his face. Then, as absurdly as the story began, it ends. Kovalyov wakes up with the nose back in its former place, goes to Ivan Yakovlevich and has a shave (the barber now not touching the olfactory organ), and it is as though nothing happened.

Many of Gogol's characters have penetrated into everyday Russian speech. If someone works hard at a brainless job, he is called an "Akaky Akakievich," for example, a testament to how well the writer created a type of Russian "little man" who, however uncreative, still captures the hearts and alliances of readers. There is something real about these absurd, impossible characters, something in their unidimensionality that transcends their locus and becomes universal. Gogol, while embroidering in highly ornate circumlocution, directly touches the wellspring of humanity in even the lowliest, most unattractive character. In his descriptions, there are simultaneously resonances of slapstick humor and the depths of human misery and social injustice.

Gogol left quite an imprint on the course of Russian literature; very few subsequent writers would produce anything that did not at all reverberate the Gogolian legacy. Even in the twentieth century, writers incorporated his artistic ideas or emulated his style to a degree.

OTHER MAJOR WORKS

LONG FICTION: *Taras Bulba*, 1842 (revision of his 1835 short story; English translation, 1886); *Myortvye dushi*, part 1 1842, part 2, 1855 (*Dead Souls*, 1887).

PLAYS: *Vladimir tretey stepeni*, wr. 1832, pb. 1842; *Zhenit'ba*, wr. 1835, pr., pb. 1842 (*Marriage: A Quite Incredible Incident*, 1926); *Revizor*, pr., pb. 1836 (*The Inspector General*, 1890); *Utro delovogo cheloveka*, pb. 1836, pr. 1871 (revision of *Vladimir tretey stepeni*; *An Official's Morning*, 1926); *Igroki*, pb. 1842, pr. 1843

(*The Gamblers*, 1926); *Tyazhba*, pb. 1842, pr. 1844 (revision of *Vladimir tretey stepeni*; *The Lawsuit*, 1926); *Otryvok*, pb. 1842, pr. 1860 (revision of *Vladimir tretey stepeni*; *A Fragment*, 1926); *Lakeyskaya*, pb. 1842, pr. 1863 (revision of *Vladimir tretey stepeni*; *The Servants' Hall*, 1926); *The Government Inspector, and Other Plays*, pb. 1926.

POETRY: *Hanz Kuechelgarten*, 1829.

NONFICTION: *Vybrannye mesta iz perepiski s druzyami*, 1847 (*Selected Passages from Correspondence with Friends*, 1969); *Letters of Nikolai Gogol*, 1967.

MISCELLANEOUS: *The Collected Works*, 1922-1927 (6 volumes); *Polnoe sobranie sochinenii*, 1940-1952 (14 volumes); *The Collected Tales and Plays of Nikolai Gogol*, 1964.

BIBLIOGRAPHY

Bloom, Harold, ed. *Nikolai Gogol*. Philadelphia: Chelsea House, 2004. Focuses on Gogol's short fiction. Contains a biography of Gogol; extracts from major critical essays discussing important aspects of the short stories "The Portrait," "Nevsky Prospect," "The Nose," "The Overcoat," and "Ivan Fyodorovich Shponka and His Aunt"; a list of characters and thematic analysis for each short story that is analyzed; a bibliography of critical works about the short stories covered in the book; and an index of themes and ideas in Gogol's work.

Erlich, Victor. *Gogol*. New Haven, Conn.: Yale University Press, 1969. For nonspecialists, this book may be the most accessible and evenhanded. Erlich concentrates on Gogol's oeuvre without shortchanging the generally disavowed *Selected Passages from Correspondence with Friends*. He deals with much of the "myth" of Gogol and supplies interesting background to the making of Gogol's works.

Fanger, Donald L. *The Creation of Nikolai Gogol*. Cambridge, Mass.: Belknap Press of Harvard University Press, 1979. Fanger presses deeply into the background material and includes in his purview works both published and unpublished in his effort to reveal the genius of Gogol's creative power. This book is worthwhile in many respects, particularly for the wealth of details about Gogol's life and milieu. Includes notes and an index.

Frazier, Melissa. *Frames of the Imagination: Gogol's "Arabesques" and the Romantic Question of Genre.* New York: Peter Lang, 2000. Describes how Arabesques was part of a philosophical debate among Gogol's contemporaries, who sought to create a uniquely Russian literature from the ideas of European Romanticism. Shows how Gogol's text adapted Romantic aesthetics in order to structure Russian history, nationality, and personal identity.

Gippius, V. V. *Gogol.* Translated by Robert Maguire. Ann Arbor, Mich.: Ardis, 1981. Originally written in 1924, this famous monograph supplies not only the view of a fellow countryman but also a vast, informed, and intellectual analysis of both the literary tradition in which Gogol wrote and his innovation and contribution to that tradition. Vastly interesting and easily accessible. Contains notes and a detailed list of Gogol's works.

Hart, Pierre R. "Narrative Oscillation in Gogol's 'Nevsky Prospect.'" *Studies in Short Fiction* 31 (Fall, 1994): 639-645. Argues that the story is a commentary on the author's development of strategies to deal with reality. Discusses the urban scene in the story, suggesting that the city forces the protagonist into a final defensive position.

Koropeckyj, Roman, and Robert Romanchuk. "Ukraine in Blackface: Performance and Representation in Gogol's Dikan'ka Tales, Book I." *Slavic Review: Interdisciplinary Quarterly of Russian, Eurasian, and East European Studies* 62, no. 3 (Fall, 2003): 525-547. Focuses on the depiction of Ukraine in the first volume of *Evenings on a Farm near Dikanka.* Discusses the book's plot, its cultural and social significance, and Gogol's writing style.

Maguire, Robert A. *Exploring Gogol.* Stanford, Calif.: Stanford University Press, 1994. The most comprehensive study in English of Gogol's entire writing career. Includes a chronology, detailed notes, and an extensive bibliography.

_____, ed. *Gogol from the Twentieth Century: Eleven Essays.* Princeton, N.J.: Princeton University Press, 1974. This collection of essays, with a lengthy introduction by the editor and translator, represents some of the most famous and influential opinions on Gogol in the twentieth century. Some of the most problematic aspects of Gogol's stylistics, thematics, and other compositional elements are addressed and well elucidated. Features a bibliography and index.

Rancour-Laferriere, David. *Out from Under Gogol's "Overcoat": A Psychoanalytic Study.* Ann Arbor, Mich.: Ardis, 1982. Much of the discussion in this specialized study focuses on Gogol's particular use of words. Even students with no command of Russian will find the explication understandable because the examples are clear and self-defining. Contains a bibliography that includes many background works.

Robey, Judith. "Modelling the Reading Act: Gogol's Mute Scene and Its Intertexts." *Slavic Review* 56 (Summer, 1997): 233-250. Discusses scenes in which viewers look at paintings in Gogol's fiction and essays. Argues that these moments correspond to a metanarrative in Gogol's works in which reading is depicted as a process that can lead to redemption and salvation.

Setchkarev, Vsevolod. *Gogol: His Life and Works.* Translated by Robert Kramer. New York: New York University Press, 1965. Still often recommended in undergraduate courses, Setchkarev's monograph concentrates on both the biography and the works, seen individually and as an artistic system. Very straightforward and easily readable, this work might be perhaps the best place for the student to begin.

Tosi, Alessandra. "Andrei Kropotov's 'Istoriia o Smurom Kaftane': A Thematic Source for Gogol's 'Shinel'?" *Slavonic and East European Review* 76 (October, 1998): 601-613. Compares Gogol's "The Overcoat" with Kropotov's earlier story; in both stories a trivial garment takes on significance for the main characters and ultimately causes their ruin. Discusses the similarity in the twists in the plots. Suggests that Kropotov's story may have been a source for Gogol's.

Troyat, Henri. *Divided Soul.* Translated by Nancy Amphoux. Garden City, N.Y.: Doubleday, 1973. This study provides perhaps the most information on Gogol's life and demonstrates masterfully how Gogol's life and work are inextricably intertwined. Troyat does not neglect the important role that "God's will" played in Gogol's life, the thread that lends the greatest cohesion to the diverse developments in his creative journey. The

volume contains some interesting illustrations, a bibliography, notes, and an index.

Christine D. Tomei

NADINE GORDIMER

Born: Springs, Transvaal, South Africa; November 20, 1923

PRINCIPAL SHORT FICTION

Face to Face: Short Stories, 1949

The Soft Voice of the Serpent, and Other Stories, 1952

Six Feet of the Country, 1956

Friday's Footprint, and Other Stories, 1960

Not for Publication, and Other Stories, 1965

Livingstone's Companions: Stories, 1971

Selected Stories, 1975

A Soldier's Embrace, 1980

Something out There, 1984

Reflections of South Africa, 1986

Crimes of Conscience, 1991

Jump, and Other Stories, 1991

Why Haven't You Written? Selected Stories, 1950-1972, 1992

Loot, and Other Stories, 2003

Beethoven Was One-Sixteenth Black, and Other Stories, 2007

OTHER LITERARY FORMS

Nadine Gordimer (NAY-deen GOR-dih-mur) is known for several novels, including *A World of Strangers* (1958), *The Conservationist* (1974), *Burger's Daughter* (1979), and *The House Gun* (1998), as well as the acclaimed *My Son's Story* (1990). She has published heavily in nonfiction, especially contributing to South African scholarship with such books as *Lifetimes Under Apartheid* (1986), with David Goldblatt, and *Living in Hope and History: Notes from Our Century* (1999). Gordimer has also published essays and edited a study of the literature of her homeland. Gordimer's novel, *The*

Pickup, was published in 2001; her novel *Get a Life* was published in 2005. *Telling Times: Writing and Living, 1954-2008,* a collection of essays covering more than fifty years of her career, was published in 2010.

ACHIEVEMENTS

As a courageous chronicler of life in South Africa, Nadine Gordimer is known throughout the world. She received the W. H. Smith and Son Prize in 1971 for *Friday's Footprint, and Other Stories.* Two years later she won the James Tait Black Memorial Prize for *A Guest of Honour* (1970). The next year, *The Conservationist* shared with Stanley Middleton's *Holiday* (1974) the prestigious Booker Prize. Gordimer was also a recipient of France's Grand Aigle d'Or, and in 1991 she won the Nobel Prize in Literature.

Gordimer rejected candidacy for the Orange Prize in 1998 because it was restricted to female writers. She is the vice president of PEN International and an executive member of the Congress of South African Writers. Gordimer has been honored with the Modern Literature Association Award and the Bennett Award in the United States and the Chevalier de l'Ordre des Arts et des Lettres in France. Her short fiction has been published in such magazines as *The New Yorker.*

One American reviewer summed up Gordimer's importance in literature, writing: "Gordimer is in the great mainstream of the short story--(Guy de) Maupassant, (Anton) Chekhov, (Ivan) Turgenev, (Henry) James, (Ernest) Hemingway, (Katherine Anne) Porter." Most of Gordimer's fiction has been published in paperback form, enabling a great number of readers and critics to recognize and enjoy her work.

BIOGRAPHY

Nadine Gordimer grew up a rebel. Both parents were immigrants to South Africa: Her mother was

English; her father was an Eastern European Jew. In Springs, the gold-mining town near Johannesburg where she spent her early years, Gordimer frequently played hooky from her convent school. When she did attend, she would sometimes walk out of classes. She found it difficult to tolerate all the pressures to conform.

In the middle-class environment in which Gordimer grew up, a girl could aspire only to marry and rear a family. After leaving school and working at a clerical job for a few years, she was singled out as a prospective wife by a young man who had come from a family very much like her own. Within months, she realized the great dream of young womanhood: She had an engagement party, a linen shower, a wedding ceremony, and a first child. None of these dreams were served by her education; books, in perhaps leading her mind astray, interfered with the years of her preparation to fit the mold.

At an early age, Gordimer wanted to break out of the mold--she became an avid reader. By nine, she was already writing, and at fourteen she won a writing

Nadine Gordimer (©The Nobel Foundation)

prize. Her favorite authors were Chekhov; W. Somerset Maugham; Maupassant; D. H. Lawrence; and the Americans Porter, O. Henry, and Eudora Welty. As Gordimer matured, she increasingly became interested in politics and the plight of black South Africans. She did not, however, launch her writing career as a way to bring about change.

A male friend, who was an important influence, told her that she was ignorant and too accepting of society's values. Gordimer wrote, "It was through him, too, that I roused myself sufficiently to insist on going to the university." Since she was twenty-two at the time and still being supported by her father, her family did not support her desire to attend the university.

She commuted to Johannesburg and the University of Witwatersrand. While at the university, she met Uys Krige, an Afrikaans poet who had shunned his Afrikaner heritage, lived in France and Spain, and served with the International Brigade in the Spanish Civil War. He, too, was a profound influence on her. She had been "a bolter," as she put it, at school; she was in the process of bolting from her family and her class and the culture of white South Africa, and Krige gave her a final push. She became committed to honesty alone. She began to send stories to England and the United States. The stories were well received, and she began to build her reputation as a short-story writer and novelist.

In the 1950's, Gordimer married her first husband, Reinhold Cassirer, a German Jew who had fled Berlin. They had a son, Hugo, with whom she collaborated in the mid-1990's on a documentary about Berlin and Johannesburg. A second marriage produced another child.

In the 1980's Gordimer turned to a new medium. She wrote teleplays of four of her stories--*Praise, Oral History, Country Lovers*, and *A Chip of Glass Ruby* (all 1985); she also participated in the production of others. Taken together, the films present a compelling vision of Gordimer's South Africa. A filmed interview of Gordimer by Joachim Braun often accompanies the showing of her films. In this interview, Gordimer said many interesting things about her work and the tragic state of her country. Always passionate about politics, Gordimer was a member of the African National Congress during the 1990's.

ANALYSIS

Nadine Gordimer is a distinguished novelist and short-story writer. About *Selected Stories*, drawn from her earlier volumes of stories, a reviewer said,

> the stories are marked by the courage of moral vision and the beauty of artistic complexity. Gordimer examines, with passionate precision, the intricacies both of individual lives and of the wide-ranging political and historical forces that contain them.

About the stories in *A Soldier's Embrace*, a reviewer wrote, "Their themes are universal: love and change, political transition, family, memory, madness and infidelity, to name a few. . . . What makes Nadine Gordimer such a valuable--and increasingly valued--novelist and short-story writer is her ability to meet the demands of her political conscience without becoming a propagandist and the challenges of her literary commitment without becoming a disengaged esthete." Over the course of her career, three of her books were banned in South Africa.

It would be easy for Gordimer to declare self-exile. Unlike James Joyce, however, she chose not to abandon the inhospitable country of her birth, accepting the obligation of citizenship to help make her country better. She did this by practicing her art, for it is an art that enables her diverse compatriots to understand better themselves and one another.

The settings and characters in Gordimer's stories cut across the spectrum of South African life. She writes about black village life and black urban experiences. She writes about the Afrikaans-speaking whites, English-speaking whites, Indians, and others. Her protagonists are as likely to be males as females, and reviewers have commented on her uncanny ability to fully realize her male characters. In *The House Gun* (1998), Gordimer ponders the deeply personal question of whether parents can even trust their own child not to commit murder. With amazing range and knowledge, she sheds light on the intricacies of individual lives and on the historical and political forces that shape them.

Reading Gordimer's stories is always exciting because one does not know what will have caught her interest--urban or rural blacks, urban or rural Boers, leisured or working or revolutionary whites, an African or a European setting. It is a great surprise, for example, to discover a story in the form of a letter from a dead Prague father to the son who predeceased him. It is a made-up letter in which Hermann Kafka tells off the ungrateful, congenitally unhappy Franz.

As she has demonstrated again and again during more than thirty years of writing, Gordimer does not restrict her focus to people and scenes that are familiar. In reading "A City of the Dead, a City of the Living," for example, one marvels at what the author, a well-off white woman, knows of black-township life, at the total credibility of characters Samson Moreke and his wife, Nanike. Gordimer's knowledge and credibility are characteristic of all of her short fiction. "A City of the Dead, a City of the Living," "Sins of the Third Age," and "Blinder" could easily be included among the twenty best short stories of the twentieth century.

In 2004, Gordimer organized a group of writers to contribute short stories for a collection entitled *Telling Tales*, to raise funds for a group that lobbies for government funding for the prevention of human immunodeficiency virus (HIV) and acquired immunodeficiency syndrome (AIDS) and for the care of sufferers. In 2005, when Fidel Castro became ill, Gordimer and six other Nobel Prize winners urged the United States not to take advantage of the illness to try to destabilize Cuba's communist government. In 2006, Gordimer was attacked in her home by robbers and locked in a storeroom; her injuries were not serious.

"IS THERE NOWHERE ELSE WHERE WE CAN MEET?"

Among Gordimer's most gripping stories are those in which blacks and whites are at cross-purposes. From *The Soft Voice of the Serpent, and Other Stories*, "Is There Nowhere Else Where We Can Meet?" is one of the best of this group. On a country road, a young white woman's handbag is torn from her by a passing local, whose bedraggled condition had evoked the woman's pity. The day is very cold, yet he is shoeless and dressed in rags. When she attains safety and has brought her fear under control, she decides not to seek aid or inform the police. "What did I fight for?" she asks herself. "Why didn't I give him the money and let him go? His red eyes, and the smell and those cracks in his feet, fissures, erosion."

"Six Feet of the Country"

The title piece of Gordimer's 1956 collection, *Six Feet of the Country*, is another exceptional story. A young black laborer walks from Rhodesia to find work in South Africa, where he has family employed on a weekend farm of a white Johannesburg couple. When he arrives at the farm, the illegal immigrant becomes ill and dies. There ensues a prolonged entanglement with the authorities, who insist on having the body so that it can be examined and the bureaucratic requirement for a statement of the cause of death can be fulfilled. With great reluctance, the family surrenders the body. When at last the casket is returned to the farm for burial, they discover that the body in it is that of a stranger. In the course of spinning out a plot about the fate of a corpse, Gordimer provides great insight into the lives of the farm laborers, the proprietors, and the police official, and she also reveals the relative inability of the laborers to deal with illness and the bureaucracy.

"A Chip of Glass Ruby"

"A Chip of Glass Ruby," in *Not for Publication, and Other Stories*, is about an Indian family in the Transvaal. The wife and mother is loving and unassuming and a very competent manager of a household that includes nine children. To the chagrin of her husband, Bamjee, she is also a political activist. It makes no sense to him that she takes grave risks for blacks, who are regarded as lower even than Indians. During the course of the story, she is arrested and imprisoned and participates in a prison hunger strike. Bamjee, a poor, small-time fruit and vegetable dealer, cannot understand any of this. He asks, "'What for?' Again and again: 'What for?'" His birthday comes, and he does not even remember. The eldest daughter brings word from her mother, in the prison, however, that his birthday must not be forgotten. Bamjee is moved and begins to have a glimmer of understanding of the wonderful woman who is his wife. As the daughter explains: "It's because she always remembers; remembers everything--people without somewhere to live, hungry kids, boys who can't get educated--remembers all the time. That's how Ma is."

"The Intruder"

"The Intruder," which appears in *Livingstone's Companions*, focuses on the decadence of an upper-class man of English descent. After shedding his wife, hard-drinking, stay-out-late James Seago takes up with the beautiful teenage daughter of Mrs. Clegg, a woman of his age who affects a bohemian morality. Seago refers to the daughter, Marie, whom he uses sexually and enjoys having in his lap as he drinks, as his teenage doll, his marmoset, his rabbit. Because he has financial problems, Seago is plausibly able to postpone committing himself to her in marriage. Once they are married, Seago's irresponsible life of nightly partying does not change. Having married his pet, however, he must live with her, and so they set up housekeeping in an unpleasant flat. Marie becomes pregnant. The arrival of a child will force changes in Seago's way of life: For one thing, they will have to find living quarters more suitable for a child; for another, his wife-pet will have to give her primary attention to the child, not him. Arriving home early one morning after a night of partying, they fall into bed exhausted. A few hours later, Marie awakens hungry. She wanders out of the bedroom and finds the rest of the flat a wreck. All the kitchen staples have been spilled or thrown about; toothpaste is smeared about the bathroom. In the living room, on one of the sofa cushions, is "a slime of contraceptive jelly with haircombings--hers." Gordimer only hints at the perpetrator. It seems more than likely, though, that it is Seago, who again is rebelling at the prospect of being forced into a responsible mode of life.

"Abroad"

In "Abroad," the main character is an Afrikaner. Manie Swemmer is a likable, middle-aged widower who has worked hard his entire life at construction and with cars. His grown sons have moved to neighboring black-run Zambia, known as Northern Rhodesia while still a British colony. Manie decides to take the train up to Zambia and visit his sons. Arriving in Lusaka, the capital, Manie is met by his younger son, Willie. Expecting to stay with Willie, Manie is surprised to learn that Willie does not have quarters of his own but is staying at a friend's, where there is no room for his father. To his dismay, Manie learns that all the local hotels are booked. The irrepressible Manie, though, manages to talk the manager of the Regent into placing him in a room that already has been rented as a single. The problem is that it is rented to an Indian, although an educated Indian. Manie is given a key to the room and places his belongings inside, but when he returns later, the Indian has bolted the door and locked out the Afrikaner. Manie then is offered a bed in a room intended for black guests. The blacks have not yet arrived, and Manie uses the door bolt to lock them out. "Abroad" is a beautiful story about a well-meaning Afrikaner who is excited by the racial mixing of the new nation and who wants to stretch himself to his liberal limit. His feelings toward blacks, though, are still conditioned by his South African base, where all blacks are automatically regarded as inferior. "I've only just got here, give me a bit of time," Manie tells the desk clerk. "You can't expect to put me in with a native, right away, first thing."

"A SOLDIER'S EMBRACE"

Upon gaining its independence from Portugal in 1975, Mozambique became another black-ruled neighbor of South Africa. "A Soldier's Embrace," the title story of Gordimer's 1980 collection, is about the changeover, the exultation, and the disillusionment of a liberal white couple. The story begins with a brilliant scene of the celebration of the victory of the guerrillas who have been fighting the colonial power. Swept up by the street crowd, the woman finds herself embraced by two soldiers, one a white peasant youth, the other a black guerrilla. She puts an arm around each and kisses each on the cheek. Under the new regime, one is certain, a human being will be a human being; all groups will be treated equally. Although many whites take flight to Europe, the woman and her husband, a lawyer, are eager to participate in building the new nation. Weeks and months pass, however, and, despite the friends the lawyer has among highly placed blacks, the government does not ask the lawyer for his services. There is an atmosphere of hostility toward whites. There is looting and violence. When a friend in nearby Rhodesia, soon to be Zimbabwe, offers the lawyer a position in that country, with reluctance and relief he and his wife pack and go. The couple wanted the country in

which they spent their adult years to be black-run; when that comes about, they find that there is no role for them.

SOMETHING OUT THERE

In the novella that provides the title for Gordimer's volume of short fiction *Something out There*, a race war looms but has not yet erupted. Acts of violence are taking place; any one of them might well precipitate a war. In the novella, the "something out there" is a baboon. Gordimer's intention is to suggest that the response of white South Africans to the baboon corresponds to the irrational way they have been responding to the carefully planned symbolic acts of violence by guerrillas. Those acts of violence are handwriting on the wall, announcing the coming of race war, which still could be prevented if the writing were read intelligently.

All that the whites want, however, is to be left alone. They want the animal "to be confined in its appropriate place, that's all, zoo or even circus." They want South African blacks to be confined to their appropriate places--locations and townships, black homelands, villages in the bush. As the baboon is "canny about where it was possible somehow to exist off the pickings of plenty," so, too, is the South African black majority, before the cataclysm, somehow able to exist off pickings of white wealth. That wealth will not be shared, only protected, "while charity does not move those who have everything to spare, fear will"--the fear of the baboon, the fear of the guerrilla.

What is the fate of the baboon? It is finally shot and slowly bleeds to death from its wounds. The implication is clear: A similar fate awaits the guerrillas. Gordimer's prime minister speaks: "This government will not stand by and see the peace of mind of its peoples destroyed. . . . We shall not hesitate to strike with all our might at those who harbour terrorists. . . . " The four guerrillas who are the novella's human protagonists, in counterpoint to the movements of the baboon, succeed in blowing up a power station; three escape and it is made clear that they will carry out further attacks. The meaning in this plot--though not in all Gordimer plots on this subject--is that a ruthless government will be a match for those attempting to destroy it.

That the white population is greatly outnumbered makes no difference. They have the honed intelligence, the technology, the will to defend to the death what they have. Racial justice is an idea with which only a few whites--the man and woman on the power-station mission--are concerned. Protecting privilege and property is what most whites care about. They cannot understand the few who act from disinterested motives. A minor character in "Something out There" is a decent white police sergeant. He is totally mystified by the white guerrillas whom he interrogates:

> "There's something wrong with all these people who become enemies of their own country. . . . They're enemies because they can't enjoy their lives the way a normal white person in South Africa does."

One of the black guerrillas is dispassionate, determined, fearless Vusi, whose life is dedicated to bringing about black majority rule. Vusi says, "They can't stop us because we can't stop. Never. Every time, when I'm waiting, I know I'm coming nearer." A Vusi, however, is rare. "At the Rendezvous of Victory," another story in this volume, looks ahead to the ultimate black victory. It is about the man who served as commander in chief of the liberation army, known as General Giant. As a warrior, he was invaluable; as a cabinet minister after victory, he is a great burden to his prime minister. He led his people to victory and freedom; in freedom, his chief interest is women.

"A City of the Dead, a City of the Living"

In "A City of the Dead, a City of the Living," a young black man on the run from the police who has committed illegal acts for his people's liberation is given shelter by a township family. With their small house already overcrowded, the family is inconvenienced, but the husband knows his duty. His wife, nursing her fifth child, does not like the idea of taking in a stranger, but the man is pleasant and helpful, and she softens. She begins to feel attracted to him. Frightened, she goes to the police to inform on him, thus betraying the cause of her people's liberation.

"Sins of the Third Age"

"Sins of the Third Age," surprisingly, is not a political story. It is about a couple who survived World War

II as displaced persons. Nothing remains of their pasts. They meet and in a strange country begin to build their lives together. Gordimer is wonderfully evocative as she suggests the passing of years and the deepening of their love. The wife's job as an interpreter takes her on frequent trips, many times to Rome and Milan. On one of her trips, she gets the idea that they should buy a home in Italy for their retirement, near a Piedmontese village. The husband retires first and goes to Italy to prepare the house. After several months, he appears suddenly and announces, "I've met somebody." His affair eventually ends, but the betrayal destroys the vitality of the marriage. To have done otherwise than to take her husband for granted would have been betrayal on her part. She trusted, and she loses.

"Blinder"

"Blinder" is still another fine story in the 1984 volume. It is about an aging servant woman's loss of her lover, a man who was the main consolation of her life. Ephraim's first loyalty, however, was to his wife and children in his home village; the wife got his earnings, and after his death, her children get his bicycle. When Ephraim suddenly dies, Rose's white family expected her to increase her drinking, to go on a "blinder." Instead, she plays hostess to Ephraim's wife, who has come to the city to see about a pension.

"The Defeated"

"The Defeated" was originally published in the collection *Why Haven't You Written? Selected Stories, 1950-1972* and was reprinted in 1993. It is a first-person narrative concerning a European Jewish family that runs a concession store for black South Africans in a forbidden, filthy part of town. The narrator, a young girl, befriends Miriam Saiyetovitz, whose immigrant parents work long hours selling goods to indecisive customers. The shop they live above is across from an eating establishment teeming with the smells of slaughtered animals. Mrs. Saiyetovitz, "ugly, with the blunt ugliness of a toad; the ugliness not entirely at home in any element--as if the earth were the wrong place, too heavy and magnetic for a creature already blunt," and her dull husband devote their lives to giving their daughter everything they possibly can. When Miriam describes all the birthday gifts her friend received, her mother assures her they will throw her a huge party. As the two girls grow up together and it comes time for university, Miriam's parents labor to send her to a good college. Miriam grows apart from them, moving into the upper classes as she attends pool parties and eventually marries a doctor. Ultimately, she abandons the two people who made her comfortable life possible. When the narrator, now a grown woman, goes to visit Mr. and Mrs. Saiyetovitz, she learns that they hardly see their daughter and her baby son.

In "The Defeated," Gordimer conjures an evocative variety of discordant but powerful moments: the sweaty smell of the black Africans mingling with the odor of bloodied meat, the toadlike mother juxtaposed with her blossoming daughter, the quiet, rage-filled father who takes terrible advantage of his status as a white man to humiliate his black customers. Noticeable is the contrast between the narrator's relatively benign home life and the concession area where black South Africans are forced to shop among the refuse. "The Defeated" deftly envelops class differences, the burgeoning of female sexuality, and the tragedy of wasted lives, both of immigrants and of dispossessed indigenous peoples. Gordimer does not openly judge Miriam, but it is clear through the telling of her growing alienation that Miriam is only one of the upwardly mobile Afrikaners whose sights are set on material gain and not on remaining true to those who sacrificed happiness for them.

LOOT, AND OTHER STORIES

Because some of the freedoms that Gordimer has always bravely fought for in South Africa have now been realized, the stories in the collection *Loot, and Other Stories* may not seem as politically pointed as her previous works. However, the brief title story, although more than a little fantastic, is perhaps a cautionary parable of the danger facing the post-apartheid world of South Africa. When an earthquake tips a continental shelf and draws the ocean back, revealing secret treasures, people rush in to loot, only to have the sea sweep back to add them to its treasury.

The two conventional stories in the collection have nothing to do with racial tensions in South Africa, but rather they examine, in Gordimer's tight ironic style, familiar themes. "The Generation Gap" explores how grown-up children react when their sixty-seven-year-old father leaves their mother for a younger woman. It's a wonderfully wistful and cleverly comic exploration of the hard fact that whereas young people cannot imagine what it is like to be old, old people can never quite forget what it was like to be young. "The Diamond Mine" is a story that has been told many times before, about a sixteen-year-old girl who is seduced in the back seat of her parents' car by a young soldier they are taking to camp. While her father, oblivious as fathers often are, prattles on about diamonds, the soldier's exploring hands, concealed by a blanket, are invasive but not entirely unwelcome. In the novella-length "Mission Statement," forty-six-year-old Roberta Blayne, who works for an international aid agency, falls in love with a deputy director of land affairs, who happens to be a native African. Rather than a simple polemical story of racial divides in a post-apartheid world, this syntactically demanding fiction concludes with an abrupt reminder of cultural divergence, as she turns down his proposal that she become his simultaneous second wife. "Karma," defined as "the sum and the consequence of a person's actions during the successive phases of his existence," is another novella-length piece that examines the Eternal Return of a single existence in different reincarnations--male and female, young and old--to atone for previous errors, to right past wrongs, and to complete acts previously left undone.

Although she is optimistic about South Africa's future, Gordimer is not so naïve as to think that the fall of apartheid signals a rosy utopia. She knows that the residue of racial intolerance and the clash of disparate cultures cannot be eradicated by a simple regime change. Nonetheless, a collection of stories by a committed writer, for whom politics is inevitably part of the human condition, is always welcome, especially when told by a fine artist such as Gordimer.

Beethoven Was One-Sixteenth Black, and Other Stories

With her former subject, South African apartheid, mostly history, Gordimer seems to have made history her new focus. In the title story of her tenth collection, a biology professor hears a radio presenter announce that Ludwig von Beethoven was one-sixteenth black and ponders the seeming paradox that while once blacks wanted to be white, now there are whites wanting to be black. Exploring his own antiapartheid past and his possible black ancestry, the man recognizes that the past is valid only if the present recognizes it. In "A Frivolous Woman," when "a grandmother who had never grown up" dies, her family finds a trunk filled with fancy dress costumes she brought from Berlin as a refugee from Nazi extermination. Although they laugh at her frivolity, Gordimer shows that the costumes are not the grandmother's whole story, quoting L. P. Hartley's memorable line, "The past is a foreign country." The story "Beneficiary" also examines haunting remnants of the past, beginning with the warning that caches of old papers are graves that one should not open. When a woman's actor mother dies, the woman discovers a letter revealing that she is the child of an actor with whom her mother had had an affair. At the end of the story, when the man she thought to be her father hugs her, she knows that love has nothing to do with biology.

The dangers of exploring the foreign country that is the past is also central to "Allesverloren," which means "everything lost." A history teacher whose husband dies searches out a man with whom he had had a homosexual affair years before. However, not all of Gordimer's stories are serious explorations of the past. For example, "Tape Measure" is a silly little allegory of the processes of life told by a tapeworm that proceeds through someone's digestive system. "Gregor," with apologies to Franz Kafka's dung beetle, is a trivial *jeu d'esprit* about a writer finding a small cockroach behind the plastic window of her word processor, until it consumes itself and becomes a hieroglyph to be decoded. In "Safety Procedures," when the narrator experiences terrifying air turbulence, he is astonished when his calm seat partner assures him that he will be safe, for she has tried to kill herself three times this year and

failed. These are just mischievous finger exercises and concept pieces, showing that even a Nobel Prize winner has the right to fool around a little. Gordimer's literary playfulness is more serious in the three stories collectively entitled "Alternative Endings," which she self-reflexively introduces by announcing that she wishes to try out three different endings to what is basically the same story. Somewhat artificially structured on the senses of sight, hearing, and smell, each explores her favorite nonpolitical subject: love affairs and infidelity. Although *Beethoven Was One-Sixteenth Black* is more a miscellany than an even-textured short-story collection, even when Gordimer is playing around, she is a pleasure to read.

Other major works

LONG FICTION: *The Lying Days*, 1953; *A World of Strangers*, 1958; *Occasion for Loving*, 1963; *The Late Bourgeois World*, 1966; *A Guest of Honour*, 1970; *The Conservationist*, 1974; *Burger's Daughter*, 1979; *July's People*, 1981; *A Sport of Nature*, 1987; *My Son's Story*, 1990; *None to Accompany Me*, 1994; *The House Gun*, 1998; *The Pickup*, 2001; *Get a Life*, 2005.

TELEPLAYS: *A Chip of Glass Ruby*, 1985; *Country Lovers*, 1985; *Oral History*, 1985; *Praise*, 1985.

NONFICTION: *On the Mines*, 1973 (with David Goldblatt); *The Black Interpreters: Notes on African Writing*, 1973; *Lifetimes Under Apartheid*, 1986 (with Goldblatt); *The Essential Gesture: Writing, Politics, and Places*, 1988 (Stephen Clingman, editor); *Conversations with Nadine Gordimer*, 1990 (Nancy Topping Bazin and Marilyn Dallman Seymour, editors); *Three in a Bed: Fiction, Morals, and Politics*, 1991; *Writing and Being*, 1995; *A Writing Life: Celebrating Nadine Gordimer*, 1999 (Andries Walter Oliphant, editor); *Living in Hope and History: Notes from Our Century*, 1999; *Telling Times: Writing and Living, 1954-2008*, 2010.

EDITED TEXTS: *South African Writing Today*, 1967 (with Lionel Abrahams); *Telling Tales*, 2004.

Bibliography

Bazin, Nancy Topping, and Marilyn Dallman Seymour, eds. *Conversations with Nadine Gordimer*. Jackson: University Press of Mississippi, 1990. The scope of this volume renders it invaluable. It reveals some of Gordimer's insights and attitudes toward her works and their origins, in conversations spanning thirty years. Supplemented by an index and a bibliography.

Cooke, John. *The Novels of Nadine Gordimer: Private Lives, Public Landscapes*. Baton Rouge: Louisiana State University Press, 1985. Cooke discusses Gordimer's development as a writer of fiction, tracing the shift in Gordimer's identity from colonial writer, to South African writer, and, even further, to African writer. Cooke provides valuable interpretation of, and critical insight into, Gordimer's work. Complemented by useful bibliographies and an index.

Ettin, Andre Vogel. *Betrayals of the Body Politic: The Literary Commitments of Nadine Gordimer*. Charlottesville: University Press of Virginia, 1995. Ettin examines all Gordimer's genres of writing and discovers recurring themes: betrayal, politics of family, concept of homeland, ethnicity, and feminism.

Haugh, Robert F. *Nadine Gordimer*. New York: Twayne, 1974. Haugh provides the first book-length study of Gordimer's work and places her among the masters of short fiction (he finds her novels less impressive). His analysis stops with *A Guest of Honour* and *Livingstone's Companions*. Includes bibliographical references and an index.

Lazar, Karen. "Feminism as 'Piffling?' Ambiguities in Nadine Gordimer's Short Stories." In *The Later Fiction of Nadine Gordimer*, edited by Bruce King. New York: St. Martin's Press, 1993. Examines a number of Gordimer's short stories in terms of her changing attitudes toward women's oppression and feminism, ranging from her early view that many women's issues are "piffling" to views that reveal Gordimer's politicization on the question of gender.

Lomberg, Alan R. "Once More into the Burrows: Nadine Gordimer's Later Short Fiction." In *The Later Fiction of Nadine Gordimer*, edited by Bruce King. New York: St. Martin's Press, 1993. An analysis of how Gordimer continues to examine concerns raised in early stories in her later ones. After discussing how two early stories are developed into a later novella, Lomberg analyzes other stories that Gordimer has written again and again, particularly those that treat love affairs.

Roberts, Ronald Suresh. *No Cold Kitchen: A Biography of Nadine Gordimer*. Johannesburg: STE, 2005. An informal but detailed and analytical biography based on access to Gordimer's private papers.

Smith, Rowland, ed. *Critical Essays on Nadine Gordimer*. Boston: G. K. Hall, 1990. An excellent selection of essays on Gordimer's works. Includes bibliographical references and an index.

Temple-Thurston, Barbara. *Nadine Gordimer Revisited*. New York: Twayne, 1999. Part of Twayne's World Authors series, this is a good updated study of the author and her works. Bibliographical references and an index are provided.

Trump, Martin. "The Short Fiction of Nadine Gordimer." *Research in African Literatures* 17 (Spring, 1986): 341-369. Argues that in her best stories Gordimer describes the hardships of South Africans, particularly women, who suffer social inequality; summarizes a number of stories that illustrate this focus.

Paul Marx; Carol Bishop
Updated by Charles E. May

MAXIM GORKY

Born: Nizhny-Novgorod, Russia; March 28, 1868
Died: Gorki, near Moscow, Soviet Union (now
  Nizhny Novgorod, Russia); June 18, 1936
Also known as: Maksim Gorky, Aleksey Maksimov-
  ich Peshkov

PRINCIPAL SHORT FICTION

"Makar Chudra," 1892 (English translation, 1901)
"Chelkash," 1895 (English translation, 1901)
"Byvshye lyudi," 1897 ("Creatures That Once Were
  Men," 1905)
Ocherki i rasskazy, 1898-1899 (3 volumes)
"Dvadtsat' shest' i odna," 1899 ("Twenty-six Men
  and a Girl," 1902)
Orloff and His Wife: Tales of the Barefoot Brigade,
  1901
Rasskazy i p'esy, 1901-1910 (9 volumes)
Skazki ob Italii, 1911-1913 (*Tales of Italy,* 1958?)
Tales of Two Countries, 1914
Chelkash, and Other Stories, 1915
Po Rusi, 1915 (*Through Russia,* 1921)
Stories of the Steppe, 1918
Zametki iz dnevnika: Vospominaniia, 1924 (*Frag-
  ments from My Diary,* 1924)
Rasskazy 1922-1924 godov, 1925
Selected Short Stories, 1959
A Sky-Blue Life, and Selected Stories, 1964
The Collected Short Stories of Maxim Gorky, 1988

OTHER LITERARY FORMS

Maxim Gorky (mahk-SEEM gawr-KEE) wrote in
many genres, including several novels, of which *Foma
Gordeyev* (1899; English translation, 1901), *Mat*
(1906; *Mother*, 1906), *Delo Artamonovykh* (1925;
Decadence, 1927),and *Zhizn Klima Samgina* (1927-
1936; *The Life of Klim Samgin*, 1930-1938) are the best
known. He also wrote several plays, among which the

most acclaimed is *Na dne* (pr., pb. 1902; *The Lower
Depths*, 1912). His three-part autobiography, *Detstvo*
(1913; *My Childhood*, 1915), *V lyudyakh* (1916; *In the
World*, 1917), and *Moi universitety* (1923; *My Universities*, 1923), is perhaps his most moving work. His
reminiscences of literary friends, as well as his letters,
are valuable documents for the literary history and atmosphere of his time.

ACHIEVEMENTS

Maxim Gorky appeared at the end of the nineteenth
century and of the Golden Age of Russian literature.
Thus he spent most of his career writing in the shadow
of the giants. Caught in the revolutionary spirit, he
spent his entire life fighting for a better lot for his
people, mostly through his writings. He was the
founder of the new realistic trend best suited for that
purpose. To that end he wrote many works depicting
the depth of social injustice and poverty of his people,
as best illustrated in his play *The Lower Depths*. During
the revolution, he strove to preserve Russian culture
threatened by the wanton destruction, and he did his
best to help young writers. In the last years of his life,
he was revered as the doyen of Soviet literature, even
though he distanced himself from the excesses of the
revolution. Some of his stories, novels, and plays are
considered to belong to the best works in twentieth
century Russian literature.

BIOGRAPHY

Maxim Gorky was born Aleksey Maksimovich
Peshkov on March 28, 1868, in Nizhny-Novgorod, a
central Russian town, into a small-merchant family.
The family became impoverished in his childhood, and
when Gorky was three, his father died and his mother
remarried. After she died, he went to live with his
grandparents but left home at fifteen, looking for work.
He wandered through Russia for several years. At one
time, he attempted suicide because of his hard life. He

later met one of the leading Russian writers, Vladimir Korolenko, and his life was changed forever, as he discovered an ability and urge to write. He published his first story, "Makar Chudra," in 1892, under the pseudonym of Maxim Gorky ("Maxim the Bitter"), a name that he kept throughout his career. He continued to write at a steady pace for the rest of his life.

He was arrested as a political activist in 1898, an event that foreshadowed a lifetime of revolutionary activity. The publication in 1899 of his first novel, *Foma Gordeyev*, established him as a leading younger writer and brought him the friendship of Leo Tolstoy, Anton Chekhov, and other well-known writers. He was arrested again but released at Tolstoy's intervention. He fled to Finland, visited the United States in 1906, and settled on the Italian island of Capri, where he met Vladimir Ilich Lenin and other Russian luminaries, who flocked to him as on a pilgrimage. He returned to Russian in 1913, continued the revolutionary struggle, and was arrested several more times before the revolution of 1917. During the revolution, he lent total support to the Bolshevik cause. At the same time, he was appalled by the excesses and brutality of the civil war, and he tried to save what he could of Russian culture threatened by the revolution. He also helped established writers to survive by organizing, translating, and publishing activities, and he also encouraged the younger ones to write.

By then, he was a world-famous figure, his works having been published in many countries. In 1921, he left Russia for Capri, where he stayed for seven years, ostensibly for his health but more likely because of his disagreement with the developments in postrevolutionary Russia. In 1928, he made peace with the country's leaders and returned to Russia. He spent the rest of his life being revered as the patriarch of Soviet letters, yet, strangely enough, he never wrote anything with the Soviet reality as a subject matter. His health, which was poor throughout his life, deteriorated severely, and he died in 1936 from tuberculosis, although rumors about foul play persist to this day. He was buried in the Kremlin as a national figure; at that time, his hometown had been renamed for him, but it later assumed its former name.

ANALYSIS

Maxim Gorky's short stories offer a composite portrait of a writer dedicated not only to his craft but also to the solution of the pressing problems of his society. The main features of this portrait reveal Gorky as an idealist, a humanitarian, a revolutionary, and a realist. Often, several of these traits are combined. There is a distinct constancy in his views and attitudes and in his desire to lend his talent to the service of both his literary vocation and the bettering of the lives of his compatriots.

"THE SONG OF THE FALCON"

Gorky's idealism is best illustrated by the short-short story, actually a poem in prose, "Pesnia o sokole" ("The Song of the Falcon"). In this early story, his belief in human beings' dignity, yearning for freedom, and lofty aspirations is manifested by the glorification of a stately bird, a falcon, which soars majestically through vast blue expanses. At the same time, a snake on the ground is bound to its low-level existence, and when it tries to imitate the falcon, it falls from a cliff from which it attempted to fly. With the help of these symbols, Gorky expresses a notion that human beings' destiny can resemble the soaring flight of a falcon if they strive for it; if not, theirs is the lot of a snake. It is an act of faith on his part, perhaps more of a hope, that humankind can realize its lofty aspirations. This faith or hope reveals Gorky's tendency to romanticize human potential, prompting some critics to call him a romantic idealist.

Further examples of this romantic idealization are found in three other early stories, "Makar Chudra", "Starukha Izergil" ("Old Woman Izergil"), and "Chelkash." Makar Chudra tells a story of a young Gypsy who kills the girl he loves rather than submit to her demand that he crawl before her if he wants to be her lover. Here, Gorky extols human beings' determination to preserve freedom and dignity, sacrificing all other considerations. In the second story, "Old Woman Izergil," based on Russian folklore, Danko is leading his people out of a dark forest by taking his heart out of his chest and using it as a torch. Freedom, Gorky preaches, is not cheap and often requires the ultimate sacrifice, like that of the Gypsy in the preceding story. Gorky's admiration for bravery and boldness is brought to a head in "Chelkash," where the characters of two vagabonds, a thief and a peasant, are contrasted. The thief Chelkash acts like a rapacious beast, whereas the peasant is driven by common greed. Gorky's sympathies are clearly on the side of Chelkash because he follows blindly his instincts, thereby displaying character strength, while the peasant is moved by low, selfish interests.

"Twenty-six Men and a Girl"

Gorky also believes that yearning for freedom and a better life, no matter how sincere and justified, is futile if it is not accompanied by resolute action. In perhaps his best story, "Dvadtsat'shest' i odna" ("Twenty-six Men and a Girl"), he confronts twenty-six bakery workers with an opportunity to satisfy their yearning for freedom and beauty in the person of pretty, sixteen-year-old Tanya, who purchases baked goods in their shop every day. To them, Tanya is like a sun, a symbol of life, beauty, and freedom which they crave in their wretched lives but cannot obtain because of their position but also their passivity. When a dashing soldier takes advantage of Tanya's infatuation with him, the

Maxim Gorky (Library of Congress)

workers feel betrayed and leer at her humiliation. Gorky chastises, in symbolic fashion, the passivity of an entire class that, even though it knows what it needs and deserves, will remain frustrated without decisive action.

"A Man Is Born"

This story points at other characteristics of Gorky: his humanitarianism, his revolutionary spirit, and his interest in social issues. Love for human beings and belief in their sanctity have always been the cornerstones of his creed. Nowhere is this better depicted than in his short story "Rozhdenie cheloveka" ("A Man Is Born"), in which a traveler, a persona representing Gorky, assists a mother in delivering her baby in the bushes, amid the bleak background of famine and hopelessness. By ushering a new man-child into the world, Gorky expresses hope that better days are in store if human beings are willing to help one another.

The revolutionary spirit, which informs many of Gorky's stories and novels, is best manifested in his prose poem "Pesnia o Burevestnike" ("The Song of the Stormy Petrel"). He again resorts to nature to symbolize the feelings of human beings, in this case their determination to solve their problems by force, if necessary. While other birds are cowering in the storm, the stormy petrel flies majestically (like the falcon in the earlier prose poem), "laughing at the storm-clouds," which will never obliterate the sun, and crying out, "like a prophecy of triumph": Let the storm break in all its fury. This poem in prose has been adopted by revolutionaries as the hymn of the revolution, prophesying the victory.

"One Autumn Night"

Preoccupation with social themes pervades many of Gorky's works. Such stories, written in a straight, realistic style, show, more than any others, the quintessential Gorky: not only his love and respect for humankind and his concern for social injustice but also his realization that poverty and injustice have lowered some human beings to the level of beasts. At times, Gorky is preaching, but most of the time he depicts settings and simple characters to act out his messages, as in the story "Odnazhdy osen'iu" ("One Autumn Night"), in which two young, hungry, cold, and ill people console each other under an overturned boat; the woman warms the man with her body, a few minutes after she has expressed hatred for another man who has grieved her. Not all stories of this kind are sentimental; sometimes they show callousness and brutality precluding any hope. Such is the story "V stepi" ("In the Steppe"), in which three young tramps (from Gorky's gallery of vagabonds), tortured by hunger, strangle a sick man who has given them food because they want more food and money. As the oldest among them explains, "Nobody is to blame for anything, because we are all beasts." Such pessimistic stories are not common with Gorky; his granite faith in a better life usually prevails.

A good number of Gorky's stories are devoid of moral preaching and ideological colorations. They are concerned mainly with human characters and situations, with an interesting plot for its own sake, and with whatever it is that urges a writer to write a story. Most of such stories are from Gorky's later years. In an early one, "Na plotakh" ("On the Rafts"), a father takes over his son's wife, regretting that he had not met her before. "Suprugi Orlovy" ("Orlov Married Couple") presents a drunken husband who beats his wife until they both go to work in a hospital. There, she finds her vocation, while he is incapable of mending his ways and leaves in rage and defiance. "Varen'ka Olesova" ("Varenka Olesova"), the only story by Gorky that is favorable to the landowning class, presents a landowner who despises Russian novels because of their overly realistic depiction of daily life, exhibiting weak, timid characters, while the woman in the story prefers the adventurous heroes of the French novels, who take her out of the miserable life surrounding her.

In his later stories, Gorky showed that he could rise above mundane topics, as in "Golubaia zhizn'" ("Sky-Blue Life"), in which the character copes with approaching insanity but eventually recuperates. "O pervoi liubvi" ("First Love") is an autobiographical story of lovers who part after realizing that they are not meant for each other. Such stories prove that Gorky was a true artist. It is this artistry that built and preserved his reputation as one of the best Russian writers.

OTHER MAJOR WORKS

LONG FICTION: *Goremyka Pavel*, 1894 (novella; *Orphan Paul*, 1946); *Foma Gordeyev*, 1899 (English translation, 1901); *Troye*, 1901 (*Three of Them*, 1902); *Mat*, 1906 (serial), 1907 (book) (*Mother*, 1906); *Ispoved*, 1908 (*The Confession*, 1909); *Zhizn Matveya Kozhemyakina*, 1910 (*The Life of Matvei Kozhemyakin*, 1959); *Delo Artamonovykh*, 1925 (*Decadence*, 1927; better known as *The Artamonov Business*, 1948); *Zhizn Klima Samgina*, 1927-1936 (*The Life of Klim Samgin*, 1930-1938; includes *The Bystander*, 1930, *The Magnet*, 1931, *Other Fires*, 1933, and *The Specter*, 1938).

PLAYS: *Meshchane*, pr., pb. 1902 (*Smug Citizen*, 1906); *Na dne*, pr., pb. 1902 (*The Lower Depths*, 1912); *Dachniki*, pr., pb. 1904 (*Summer Folk*, 1905); *Deti solntsa*, pr., pb. 1905 (*Children of the Sun*, 1906); *Varvary*, pr., pb. 1906 (*Barbarians*, 1906); *Vragi*, pb. 1906, pr. 1933 (*Enemies*, 1945); *Posledniye*, pr., pb. 1908; *Chudake*, pr., pb. 1910 (*Queer People*, 1945); *Vassa Zheleznova* (first version), pb. 1910, pr. 1911 (English translation, 1945); *Falshivaya moneta*, wr. 1913, pr., pb. 1927; *Zykovy*, pb. 1914, pr. 1918 (*The Zykovs*, 1945); *Starik*, wr. 1915, pr. 1919, pb. 1921 (*Old Man*, 1924); *Yegor Bulychov i drugiye*, pr., pb. 1932 (*Yegor Bulychov and Others*, 1937); *Dostigayev i drugiye*, pr., pb. 1933 (*Dostigayev and Others*, 1937); *Vassa Zheleznova* (second version), pr., pb. 1935 (English translation, 1975); *Seven Plays*, pb. 1945; *Five Plays*, pb. 1956; *Plays*, pb. 1975.

NONFICTION: *Detstvo*, 1913 (*My Childhood*, 1915); *V lyudyakh*, 1916 (*In the World*, 1917); *Vozpominaniya o Lev Nikolayeviche Tolstom*, 1919 (*Reminiscences of Leo Nikolaevich Tolstoy*, 1920); *Moi universitety*, 1923 (*My Universities*, 1923); *Vladimir Ilich Lenin*, 1924 (*V. I. Lenin*, 1931); *Reminiscences of Tolstoy, Chekhov and Andreyev*, 1949; *Untimely Thoughts: Essays on Revolution, Culture, and the Bolsheviks*, 1968; *Selected Letters*, 1997 (Andrew Barratt and Barry P. Scherr, editors); *Gorky's Tolstoy and Other Reminiscences: Key Writings by and About Maxim Gorky*, 2008 (Donald Fanger, editor).

MISCELLANEOUS: *Polnoe sobranie sochinenii*, 1949-1955 (30 volumes); *Polnoe sobranie sochinenii*, 1968-1976 (25 volumes); *Collected Works of Maxim Gorky*, 1979-1981 (8 volumes).

BIBLIOGRAPHY

Barratt, Andrew. *The Early Fiction of Maksim Gorky: Six Essays in Interpretation*. Nottingham, England: Astra Press, 1993. Excellent essays on Gorky's early works. Includes bibliographical references and an index.

Borras, F. M. *Maxim Gorky the Writer: An Interpretation*. Oxford, England: Clarendon Press, 1962. One of the more astute interpretations of Gorky's works, especially his novels and plays. Unlike many other books that concentrate either on biography or political issues, Borras's book emphasizes Gorky's artistic achievements. Chapter 2 analyzes his short stories.

Figes, Orlando. "Maxim Gorky and the Russian Revolution." *History Today* 46 (June, 1996): 16-22. Argues that Gorky's journalism and correspondence revealed in Soviet archives shows Gorky was not a devout Bolshevik and had doubts concerning the revolution and the course it took after 1917, all of which forced him into exile in 1921.

Gorky, Maxim. *Gorky's Tolstoy and Other Reminiscences: Key Writings by and About Maxim Gorky*. Translated, edited, and introduced by Donald Fanger. New Haven, Conn.: Yale University Press, 2008. A compendium of material by and about Gorky. Contains Gorky's reminiscences about prominent Russian literary figures, selected stories from his collection *Fragments of My Diary*, and portraits of Gorky written by two literary critics and a Russian poet and novelist.

_____. *Maxim Gorky: Selected Letters*. Edited and translated by Andrew Barratt and Barry P. Scherr. New York: Oxford University Press, 1997. A collection of letters beginning in 1889 and ending with Gorky's death in 1936. The letters reveal Gorky's life story in his own words, shed light on many writers, including Anton Chekhov and Leo Tolstoy, and are representative of the development of Russian literature.

_____. *Untimely Thoughts: Essays on Revolution, Culture, and the Bolsheviks, 1917-1918*. Translated by Herman Ermolaev. New Haven, Conn.: Yale University Press, 1995. A collection of critical articles that denounce the Bolshevik system of government, depict the Russian national character, and render a vision of the future.

Hare, Richard. *Maxim Gorky: Romantic Realist and Conservative Revolutionary*. London: Oxford University Press, 1962. The first substantial study of Gorky in English since Alexander Kaun's book (below). Hare combines the political aspects of Gorky's biography with critical analyses of his works, with the latter receiving the short end. Contains some interesting observations obtained from anonymous people who knew Gorky well.

Kaun, Alexander. *Maxim Gorky and His Russia*. New York: Jonathan Cape and Harrison Smith, 1931. The first book on Gorky in English, written while Gorky was still alive and supported by firsthand knowledge about him. It covers literary and nonliterary aspects of Russian literary life and the political atmosphere in Gorky's time. Still one of the best biographies, despite some outdated facts, corrected by history.

O'Toole, L. Michael. "'Twenty-six Men and a Girl.'" In *Structure, Style, and Interpretation in the Russian Short Story*. New Haven, Conn.: Yale University Press, 1982. A structuralist analysis of Gorky's story.

Peterson, Dale E. "Richard Wright's Long Journey from Gorky to Dostoevsky." *African American Review* 28 (Fall, 1994): 375-387. Discussion of the influence of Gorky and Fyodor Dostoevski on Richard Wright. Notes similarities between Gorky and Wright's writing, but claims that Wright moved away from Gorky's faith in collectivist culture and social engineering.

Weil, Irwin. *Gorky: His Literary Development and Influence on Soviet Intellectual Life*. New York: Random House, 1966. The most scholarly book on Gorky in English, skillfully combining biography with critical analysis. Valuable especially for the discussion of Soviet literary life and Gorky's connections with, and influence on, younger Soviet writers. Contains select but adequate bibliography.

Yedlin, Tova. *Maxim Gorky: A Political Biography*. Westport, Conn.: Praeger, 1999. Biography focusing on Gorky's complicated relationship to the Soviet Union, including his early support for the Bolshevik revolution, his later disavowal of the Communist government, and the scrutiny he encountered when he went to the Soviet Union during the regime of Joseph Stalin.

Vasa D. Mihailovich

JOÃO GUIMARÃES ROSA

Born: Cordisburgo, Minas Gerais, Brazil; June 27,
  1908
Died: Rio de Janeiro, Brazil; November 19, 1967

PRINCIPAL SHORT FICTION

Sagarana, 1946, 1966

Corpo de Baile, 1956 (subsequent editions in three
  volumes: *Manuelzão e Miguilim*; No
  Urubùquaquá, no Pinhém; and *Noites do Sertão*)

Primeiras Estórias, 1962, 1968 (*The Third Bank of
  the River, and Other Stories*, 1968)

Tutaméia, 1967

Estas Estórias, 1969

Ave, Palavra, 1970

The Jaguar, and Other Stories, 2001

OTHER LITERARY FORMS

The first work of João Guimarães Rosa (ZHWAH-
oh gee-mah-RAYS ROH-sah), a collection of poems
entitled *Magma*, has never been published, even though
it won an important prize in 1937. *Grande Sertão:
Veredas* (1956; *The Devil to Pay in the Backlands*,
1963), his masterpiece, is considered the most significant Brazilian novel of the twentieth century.

ACHIEVEMENTS

João Guimarães Rosa's fiction is generally regarded
as the watershed work of the twentieth century Brazilian short story and novel, much as the fiction of Joaquim Maria Machado de Assis in the nineteenth century prompted critics to label every work of fiction as
either "before" or "after" that writer. Guimarães Rosa
was not only a master teller of tales but also a doctor, an
amateur naturalist, and a polyglot. All of his stories reflect his fascination with the physical and natural world
and the ways language might be bent to describe that
world. His fiction always contains an element of moral

or spiritual inquiry, and most of it is set in the interior of
Brazil. All of his works are characterized by a highly
original and perverse diction, which helps account for
the paucity of translations. Guimarães Rosa was also a
diplomat, having achieved the rank of ambassador in
the Brazilian diplomatic service.

BIOGRAPHY

João Guimarães Rosa was a quiet, myopic child
with a taste for natural history and a formidable talent
for learning languages. After studying medicine, he
practiced in a small town in the *sertão*, acquiring there
a profound knowledge of the land and the people. He
divided his subsequent years between various government posts and the diplomatic corps, ending his career
with the rank of ambassador. He was elected unani-
mously to the Brazilian Academy of Letters in 1963,
and in 1965 he served as vice president at the first Latin
American Writers Conference in Mexico City. He died
in November, 1967, of a brain hemorrhage.

ANALYSIS

Latin American literature is filled with narratives
that represent the awareness of the physical reality of
Latin America and the adoption of an emotional position toward literature. Indeed, the stereotypic caricature of the Latin American narrative, in the eyes of both
Latin Americans and their foreign readers, is that of W.
H. Hudson (born and reared in Argentina) in *Green
Mansions* (1904) or of reductionist readings of classics
such as Ricardo Güiraldes's *Don Segundo Sombra*
(1926), José Eustasio Rivera's *La vorágine* (1923), or
Rómulo Gallegos's *Doña Bárbara* (1929). At its worst
this strain of Latin American literature is a blend of romantic ideals (the Pampas and the Andean highlands)
and bizarre exotica (the jungles and feudal oppression).
At its best, however, as exemplified in the novels of
contemporary masters such as Gabriel García Márquez,
Juan Rulfo, Mario Vargas Llosa, Augusto Roa Bastos,

and Alejo Carpentier, it represents the attempt to come to grips with the paradoxes and the anomalies of a complex sociocultural tradition that seems to defy its Western roots without really opting out of the modern world nourished by those roots. The fiction of Guimarães Rosa clearly belongs to this view of Latin America as an unstable amalgam of modern Western myths and a sense of experiential reality as something far richer and more profound than nationalism is capable of recognizing or explaining. Hence there appeared terms such as Magical Realism, or the "marvelous real," that have been applied to writings exemplified by the aforementioned writers. It is a groping for the much-desired terminological exactitude of academic criticism in the attempt to identify a texture of event and experience in modern Latin American fiction that depends on the reader's recognizing it as not consonant with the everyday rational description of reality purveyed by official ideologies.

"THE THIN EDGE OF HAPPINESS"

Guimarães Rosa's "As Margens da Alegria" ("The Thin Edge of Happiness") is deceptively simple, yet its semiological richness is what makes it so indicative of the sort of fiction described above. Five narrative segments that break up the barely five-page story into microtexts seem to describe no more than a young child's sadness over realizing that his initial, spontaneous happiness with a newly beheld nature can be so suddenly shattered by the inexorable needs of human society. Taken by an aunt and uncle to visit a new city being carved out of the wilderness (probably the futuristic capital of Brasília, one of the symbols of the mid-twentieth century economic boom of capitalism in Brazil), "the boy" (he remains nameless throughout the story) is thrilled, amazed, and awestruck by the new reality he discovers at the end of a mere two-hour plane trip from his home. This reality includes the hustle and bustle of a veritable frontier city, a big city being built almost overnight by powerful machines, and the lush and seductive flora and fauna of the wilderness literally at his doorstep. Suddenly, however, one of the wondrous creatures he sees, a prancing turkey, is killed for a birthday party. Just as suddenly, the boy is treated to what the adults intend as a marvelous display of the power of the machines being used to carve the

new metropolis out of the jungle: A sort of juggernaut machete slashes down a tree so efficaciously that the boy does not even see it fall. One minute it stood in understated beauty, then the machine leapt, and the tree lay on the ground, reduced to kindling. Rather than amazement at the machine's prowess, the boy feels sick as he contemplates the "astonished and blue" sky, exposed so brutally by the slash of the machine.

It would be an impoverishment of Guimarães Rosa's text to read it as a brief sketch of a child's loss of innocence in the face of the implacable and mindless destruction of what he has held as beautiful and to which he has reacted with spontaneous, childlike joy. To be sure, Guimarães Rosa's text, particularly when one senses the vignettelike effect of the internal divisions, is somewhat of an inverted narrative haiku (Guimarães Rosa was profoundly influenced by Asian culture): A series of spare images describes not the independent glory of nature as perceived by a neutral and respectful observer but the sudden and irrevocable destruction of a sense of the integrity of natural beauty as perceived by an innocent witness. What increases the depth of sociocultural meaning of this story is precisely the nature of the controlling consciousness described by the narrator, the "privileged" status of the consciousness vis-à-vis the situation or reality portrayed and the conjunction of different orders, the mechanical-industrial and the natural-physical, that are arrayed antagonistically.

Guimarães Rosa's narrator tells his story in a tone that is virtually a parody of children's once-upon-a-time tales: "This is the story: A little boy went with his aunt and uncle to spend a few days in a place where the great city was being built." The narrative goes on to describe in a matter-of-fact, short-sentence fashion how the boy leaves behind his parents and the city to fly with his aunt and uncle to the unknown frontier, how the plane trip is a child's delight of new sensations provided by the indulgent and solicitous adults, and how the place where he arrives is a veritable fairyland: "The boy looked around and breathed deeply, wishing with all his heart that he could see even more vividly everything that presented itself in front of his eyes--so many new things!" One of these new things is a spectacular turkey, an animal unknown in the city, but no sooner is the boy's delight with the pompous and lo-quacious animal described than it "disappears," slaugh-tered for a birthday meal. The boy's awe turns to terror: The turkey's absence foregrounds the threatening wil-derness from which the animal's strutting had dis-tracted him. Just as quickly the narrator moves to the scene of the mechanized machete felling the simple tree.

In rapid succession the narrative juxtaposes implied opposites: known experiences versus unknown de-lights, childlike and exuberant joy versus unfocused anxiety, wild nature versus "wild" machines, the wil-derness versus civilization and progress, childlike wonderment versus adult matter-of-factness, and the comforting versus the terrifying.

More than an anecdote concerning the brutal shat-tering of youthful and innocent happiness, Guimarães Rosa's text foregrounds, through the boy's mediating consciousness, a paradigmatic Latin American con-flict: the natural versus the mechanical, spontaneous sentiment versus artificial power, what is human versus what is artificial and therefore destructive. Whereas United States society might typically see the union of the mechanical and the human as bringing the greater comfort of the latter, a text such as Guimarães Rosa's sees the two as irremediably antagonistic. The boy's loss of innocence is not the product of any routine pro-cess of maturation, whereby the child comes to harmo-nious terms with modern mechanized society. Rather, it is the result of the brutal imposition of the new mech-anized society (the adult representatives of progress and their machines, for whom the beauties of nature discovered by the boy are at best food and at worst a nuisance) on an awesome nature. It is only when the boy's perception of his new surroundings has been "conditioned" by the attitudes and action of the adults that he sees the new reality as no longer a fairyland but a threatening and dark void: "The boy could not under-stand it. The forest, the black trees, were much too much, they were the world."

In the view of one metatheory of contemporary an-thropology, acculturation is a process of acquiring a socially conditioned way of seeing unordered events and situations and of giving them structure and meaning. Guimarães Rosa's story proposes the clash of two processes of acculturation, one the unfettered spontaneity of childlike innocence, whereby the world is a garden of delightful marvels, and the other the harsh dominance of nature by humans' mechanized so-ciety, whereby the world is a threatening enemy to be conquered, swept away in the name of civilized prog-ress. While the child cannot adequately assess the clash between these two processes and while the essentially laconic narrator refrains from doing so, the spiritual de-struction of the boy evokes more than a mythic loss of innocence. It bespeaks the semiologically productive clash between two processes of acculturation that un-derlies much of Guimarães Rosa's writing, making it characteristic of the literary exploitation of a funda-mentally unresolved conflict of Latin American society.

"THE THIRD BANK OF THE RIVER"

Guimarães Rosa's most anthologized story is a first-person narrative in which a son recounts how his fa-ther, a dutiful, orderly, straightforward man, one day takes a boat out on the river and never returns; he just floats around, going nowhere. The father gives no ex-planation for his action, and the son, who secretly pro-vides him with food, cannot understand how his father endures the hardship. Only when the son shouts to the father that he will take his place does the old man agree to come home. However, the son, terrified, runs from his father, who seems as if he has come from another world, and the son is unable to take his father's place. The son's only desire is that when he dies, his body will be put in a little boat and launched down the river.

In order to understand the puzzling behavior of the father in "The Third Bank of the River," it is necessary to recognize the story as a fable. Characters in fables often do things because they must; there seems to be a strong element of unmotivated compulsion in their be-havior. If one were able to ask characters in a fable why they do what they do, they probably could not tell you because their behavior is built into their determinate being as fictional characters. In realistic fictions, char-acters seem to control the story; in fables, story domi-nates over characters.

In "The Third Bank of the River" the father is nothing more than the role he plays. All the reader knows is that he is a father and that he goes out on to the river. Therefore, the only cause the reader can postulate for his action is his status as a father. The fact that the effect of this act on the son is the story's central element supports this hypothesis. The questions the reader might ask are: What does a father communicate to his son by floating aimlessly on the river? Why does the father want the son to take his place? Why is the son unable to do so?

The reader can only guess at answers to these questions within the framework of the story as fable. If the river is understood to be a traditional metaphor for time that is simultaneously timeless or for change that is also permanence, the father's action is a metaphor for escaping time by remaining in one place as the river constantly flows by. It is the central task of human beings to try to transcend time; this is an heroic task because it marks the refusal to accept the passing of time as inevitable. Human beings at their most heroic, or, some would say, at their most insane, are never willing to accept that life is contained, as within two banks of a flowing river; they insist on transcending these limitations and seeking the timeless third bank of the river instead of allowing the river to sweep them on until they die. This is the central task that every father passes on to every son, but because this often means casting oneself off alone, only a few are willing to attempt it.

OTHER MAJOR WORKS

LONG FICTION: *Grande Sertão: Veredas*, 1956 (*The Devil to Pay in the Backlands*, 1963).

BIBLIOGRAPHY

Coutinho, Eduardo F. "João Guimarães Rosa." In *Latin American Writers*, edited by Carlos A. Solé and Maria Isabel Abreu. 3 vols. New York: Charles Scribner's Sons, 1989. An excellent introduction to the complete works, including remarks on language, causality, regionalism and universality, the use of myth, the importance of emotion, and the unusual position in Guimarães Rosa's works of madmen, poets, and children.

Daniel, Mary L. "João Guimarães Rosa." *Studies in Short Fiction* 8 (Winter, 1971): 209-216. This essay provides a useful discussion of the oral nature of the narrative and linguistic novelty.

Englekirk, Allan. "The Destruction of Realism in the Short Prose Fiction of João Guimarães Rosa." *South Atlantic Review* 47 (1982): 51-61. Argues that the father's efforts in "The Third Bank of the River" to define truth and reality other than the way it is defined by the majority sets him apart as an heroic figure.

Foster, David William, and Virginia Ramos Foster, eds. *Modern Latin American Literature*. 2 vols. New York: Frederick Ungar, 1975. Contains translations and reproductions of sixteen critical studies, some translated from Portuguese, French, or German, and some in the original English, which give a feel for the reception of the works at or near the time of publication.

Hamilton, Russell G., Jr. "The Contemporary Brazilian Short Story." In *To Find Something New: Studies in Contemporary Literature*, edited by Henry Grosshans. Pullman: Washington State University Press, 1969. An overview of the importance of the short-story genre in Brazil, useful for contextualizing Guimarães Rosa's work. The only work studied in detail is *Tutaméia*.

Harss, Luis, and Barbara Dohmann. *Into the Mainstream: Conversations with Latin American Writers*. New York: Harper & Row, 1967. A fascinating and sometimes illuminating interview with Guimarães Rosa.

Martins, Wilson. "Structural Perspectivism in Guimarães Rosa." In *The Brazilian Novel*, edited by Heitor Martins. Bloomington: Indiana University Press, 1976. Though focusing largely on *The Devil to Pay in the Backlands*, this study is relevant to the short fiction for its discussion of Guimarães Rosa as both a radical innovator of style and a "classic" writer in the traditions of Brazilian regionalism.

Perrone, Charles A. "Guimarães Rosa Through the Prism of Magic Realism." In *Tropical Paths: Essays on Modern Brazilian Literature*. New York: Garland, 1993. Discusses some of Guimarães Rosa's short stories from the perspective of their Magical Realism; analyzes their relationship to modernity.

Romano, James V. "Structure and Mysticism in 'The Third Bank of the River.'" *Luso-Brazilian Review* 20 (1983): 93-103. Discusses three pairs of opposites in the story: river versus shore, sanity versus insanity, freedom versus bondage. These antitheses are synthesized or transcended by the father but not by the son.

Valente, Luiz Fernando. "Against Silence: Fabulation and Mediation in João Guimarães Rosa and Italo Calvino." *Modern Language Studies* 19 (Fall, 1989): 82-92. Compares Guimarães Rosa's treatment of the fable generic form with that of Calvino.

Vessels, Gary M. "The Search for Motives: Carnivalized Heroes and Paternal Abandonment in Some Recent Brazilian Fiction." *Luso-Brazilian Review* 31 (Summer, 1994): 57-65. Discusses the carnivalesque element in the heroes of such Brazilian writers as Jorge Amado and Guimarães Rosa; also discusses the mystery of motivation in Guimarães Rosa's theme of the abandonment by the father.

Vincent, Jon S. *João Guimarães Rosa.* Boston: Twayne, 1978. The first study of the complete works in any language. This critical study contains a brief summary of Guimarães Rosa's life and is divided into seven chapters, one on each of the short fiction books and one on the novel. The bibliography is, however, dated.

David W. Foster; Jon S. Vincent
Updated by Charles E. May

H

BESSIE HEAD

Born: Pietermaritzburg, South Africa; July 6, 1937
Died: Serowe, Botswana; April 17, 1986
Also known as: Bessie Amelia Emery

PRINCIPAL SHORT FICTION

*The Collector of Treasures, and Other Botswana
    Village Tales,* 1977
Tales of Tenderness and Power, 1989
The Cardinals, with Meditations and Stories, 1993

OTHER LITERARY FORMS

Bessie Head's reputation was established by her novels *When Rain Clouds Gather* (1969), *Maru* (1971), and *A Question of Power* (1973). After that, she shifted her attention to historical chronicles of her adopted country, Botswana, producing Serowe: Village of the Rain Wind(1981) and *A Bewitched Crossroad: An African Saga* (1984). In 1991 Head published *A Gesture of Belonging: Letters from Bessie Head, 1965-1979.*

ACHIEVEMENTS

Bessie Head's *A Question of Power* was a finalist for the Booker McConnell Prize in 1973. Her short-story collection *The Collector of Treasures, and Other Botswana Village Tales* was nominated for the Jock Campbell Award for literature by new or disregarded talent from Africa or the Caribbean in 1978.

BIOGRAPHY

The career of Bessie Amelia Head (née Emery) falls naturally into three parts: first, her childhood and youth in South Africa; second, her exile in the neighboring country of Botswana; and third, her life there as a citizen of that country, tragically cut short at the age of forty-eight by hepatitis. Head's mother was a rich white woman, who was committed to a mental hospital at the time of her birth. The insanity was real but also covered the fact that Head's father was a black stableman. Head was thus "colored"--the South African term for being of mixed race. She was fostered with a white couple, then passed on to a colored couple, whom she thought of as her natural parents. Her foster father died when she was six, and the family's situation deteriorated to the extent that, at thirteen, she was sent away to a mission school. There, the principal told her the truth of her birth at the traumatic end of her first term.

She was a good scholar and finally graduated in 1955 with a Natal Teachers' Senior Certificate. She taught briefly in Durban, then entered journalism, writing for the Post. In 1960, she left for Cape Town and then Johannesburg, writing for *The New African* and *Drum,* radical literary and political journals. This brought her to the notice of the apartheid authorities. In 1961 she was briefly married to a fellow journalist, Harold Head, by whom she had one child, a son, Harold.

In 1964 she left for Botswana on an exit visa to become an exile. She taught for two years and then devoted herself again to writing, living very simply, recovering from a mental breakdown, and adjusting gradually to the rural life of Serowe, the largest village in South Africa. Gradually her novels won her recognition, and after one refusal she gained citizenship in 1979.

She turned her attention to the history of her new country, which had never been fully colonialized, and produced several remarkably conceived books. She began to travel to writers' conferences and had just embarked on her autobiography when she died.

ANALYSIS

Although Bessie Head's reputation was based initially on her long fiction, her short fiction has confirmed it. Although some of the short stories date back to her days as a journalist in South Africa, most derive from her period in Botswana, when she interviewed people to compile her two chronicle histories. This activity generated so much material from the personal testimonies of her subjects and their own stories that she had plenty left over to fashion into short stories. In fact, much of the material is not fiction at all but oral history written down. Head dissolves genre boundaries between documentary, traditional tale, folklore, memories, and fiction in a unique style.

Journalism had taught her to write economically. Her style and subject matter are deceptively simple. Her themes are universal, although the setting is emphatically local, rural, and everyday. They deal with the harshness of nature, especially ever threatening drought, the tension between newer ways and tribal traditions (a universal African theme), the position of women, and the abuse of power. Ordinary people are dealt with sympathetically, but in celebrating their ordinariness, she avoids the simplicities of good (peasant, rural, traditional, black) against bad (white, modern, urban).

Although Head apparently avoids political statement or stance, her short stories can be fully analyzed in terms of a liberal and humane politics, unlike many of her black South African contemporaries. Similarly, while avoiding religious belief statements, her beliefs in the power of love to overcome are tautly idealistic in the way religious fiction at its best demonstrates.

As a writer of short stories, it is her own humility and self-effacement that come through, even while she is working out her own life traumas in her fictions of powerless women. Such tensions between objective and subjective stance produce a delicate counterpoint that eschews the big rhetoric in which other contemporaries engage. It would not be too much to suggest parallels with the short fiction of her white South African contemporary, Nadine Gordimer.

THE COLLECTOR OF TREASURES, AND OTHER BOTSWANA VILLAGE TALES

This volume consists of thirteen short stories of village life, specifically of the village life Head observed during thirteen years of exile in Serowe. They partly chronicle the social history of the village, although that is much more systematically done in *Serowe: Village of the Rain Wind*; more particularly, they explore the conflicts

around the changing status and identity of women in rural African society. They are thus susceptible to a thorough-going feminist analysis, even though Bessie Head denied she was a feminist. The resulting sophisticated analyses often seem at odds with the studied simplicity of Head's technique, which is closely modeled on traditional oral storytelling.

The title story is perhaps the best known of this carefully arranged collection. Dikeledi is a model wife married to a ne'er-do-well. Even while unhappily married, she manages to collect "treasures" of love, friendship, community, and good deeds from the women of the neighborhood. The real shock of the story is her desperate act of killing her husband by castrating him. The judicial system shows little mercy for her, and she is sentenced to life in prison. While in prison she meets other women who have also killed their husbands, and a new community of suffering is set up.

The story is crisscrossed with all sorts of issues with wider ramifications than the purely domestic. Head presents the ideal marriage of Paul Thebolo and his wife as a paradigm for the future. Paul becomes the ideal husband--clearly Head is trying to point the way ahead for men also. Dikeledi's husband has lost his own identity in his oppression by both tribal custom and colonial exploitation. His abuse of Dikeledi is the one act of power he can make.

Another story, "Life," contrasts interestingly with this one. The heroine, Life, is a "good-time girl" returning from the bright lights of South African city life to set herself up as a prostitute. She is quite open about the economic power and independence this brings her. The husband she takes, a simple shepherd, kills her. This time, the courts are merciful--it is a crime of passion. This slanting of the justice system is a token of the whole male-dominated society, whether tribal or colonial.

Other stories in the collection deal with religion, especially the clash of tribal religion and Christianity, as in "Heaven Is Not Closed" and "Witchcraft." Head's anti-Christian bias is muted here as she does not wish to appear supportive of tribal religion either. Both are part of a wider conflict between tradition and modernity, yet other stories deal with love and marriage and the conflict between traditional arranged marriage and romantic marriage.

"The Lovers"

This story appears in her second collection, *Tales of Tenderness and Power*. It has parallels with the story "The Deep River: A Story of Ancient Tribal Migration" of the first collection. Both are mythic, placed in a legendary past; both portray the conflict between romantic love and arranged marriage. In "The Lovers," the young man, Keaja, is already an independent thinker, willing to step out of the collective mentality of the tribe. The girl, Tselane, is mesmerized by such freethinking and by Keaja's proposal of marriage, whether her parents approve of it or not. They do not, and neither do his; eventually the lovers are forced to flee. The legend has it that the earth was so offended by their behavior that the hill where they had their meetings opened up and swallowed them. Head delicately describes passion and desire in Tselane, despite the fact that there is no language, let alone any model, for such emotions.

"The Prisoner Who Wore Glasses"

The story represents a move away from the village tales. It is set in a prison camp, presumably in South Africa, and involves a group of political prisoners apparently powerless against the oppression of the white prison guard yet managing to control him and break his dominance. The hero, Brille, is so called because he wears glasses. He is an older man, whose spirit has not been broken mainly because the prisoners of "Span One" work as a team. This theme of solidarity and community is an important one for Head. It is not the same as the tribal collective, however, which she questions. It is much more a willed community of support and respect working in a highly democratic way, not easily subverted. This is what the warder, Hannetjie, discovers. He is brought into line by the determination of the prisoners and his own need to survive in an oppressive regime. At the end, roles are reversed in a "live and let live" cooperation.

"The Coming of the Christ-Child"

This is another exceptional story for Head. It is again set in South Africa but this time makes very explicit political and religious comments. The hero, known only as "the young man," comes from a long line of black African pastors, but the social injustices of apartheid and the inability of his father to withstand them make him feel that God is dead.

His academic education resembles the political education of many young black Africans of the 1960's and 1970's--the young man could be a young Nelson Mandela in his struggles, as he absorbs socialism and a hatred of racial oppression. He sees the limits of the peaceful protest of the African National Congress. His protests lead to imprisonment, exile, and eventually death.

However, in this apparently bleak ending, Head sounds a note of optimism: The "winds of change" blowing over the rest of Africa will eventually reach South Africa, and the Christ-Child, the Messiah, will eventually come to deliver his people.

Other major works

LONG FICTION: *When Rain Clouds Gather*, 1968; *Maru*, 1971; *A Question of Power*, 1973.

NONFICTION: *Serowe: Village of the Rain Wind*, 1981; *A Bewitched Crossroad: An African Saga*, 1984; *A Woman Alone: Autobiographical Writings*, 1990 (Craig Mackenzie, editor); *A Gesture of Belonging: Letters from Bessie Head, 1965-1979*, 1991 (Randolf Vigne, editor).

Bibliography

Abrahams, C., ed. *The Tragic Life: Bessie Head and Literature in Southern Africa*. Trenton, N.J.: Africa World Press, 1990. This collection of essays is one of the best available studies of Head. Includes chapters dealing with the short stories, a bibliography, and an index.

Brown, Coreen. *The Creative Vision of Bessie Head*. Madison, N.J.: Fairleigh Dickinson University Press, 2003. Examines how Head's writing was her response to her personal life, demonstrating how she used her work to subvert the oppression she encountered in South Africa and Botswana, to create a utopian haven in Botswana, and to understand the nature of good and evil after she suffered a mental breakdown. Devotes individual chapters to analyses of the short-fiction works *The Cardinals* and *The Collector of Treasures, and Other Botswana Village Tales*.

Chapman, Michael. *Southern African Literatures*. New York: Longman, 1996. One of the fullest overviews of South African literature. Sets Head well into context in the section "Writing in the Interregnum." Includes an excellent chronology and a full bibliography of individual authors.

Eilersen, Gillian Stead. *Bessie Head: Thunder Behind Her Ears, Her Life and Writing*. 2d ed. Johannesburg: Wits University Press, 2007. Discusses the relationship between Head's life and her writing.

Ibrahim, Huma. *Bessie Head: Subversive Identities in Exile*. Charlottesville: University Press of Virginia, 1996. A feminist analysis of Head, dealing with powerlessness and marginality in terms of actual exile. *The Collector of Treasures, and Other Botswana Village Tales* forms the subject of the chapter "Women Talk: A Dialogue on Oppression."

_____, ed. *Emerging Perspectives on Bessie Head*. Trenton, N.J.: Africa World Press, 2004. Collection of essays written by contributors from Africa, Asia, Europe, and the United States. Some essays focus on issues of biography and autobiography in Head's works, her influence on South African literature, the critical reception of her works, and her life in Botswana. Two articles analyze her short fiction: "Taboo, a Positive Transgression? A Study of Bessie Head's *The Cardinals*," by Sisi Maquagi, and Robert Cancel's comparison of short stories by Head and Ghanian writer Ama Ata Aidoo.

Johnson, Joyce. *Bessie Head: The Road of Peace of Mind--A Critical Appreciation*. Newark: University of Delaware, 2008. Johnson concentrates her study on the public's perception of Head and on Head's mental illness and its effect on her writing. She places Head's writing in biographical context and offers an insightful and easy-to-read analysis of her works, including *The Cardinals* and *The Collector of Treasures, and Other Botswana Village Tales*.

Lionnet, Francoise. "Geographies of Pain: Captive Bodies and Violent Acts in the Fictions of Gayl Jones, Bessie Head, and Myriam Warner-Viegra." In *The Politics of (M)Othering: Womanhood, Identity, and Resistance*, edited by Obioma Nnaemeka. New York: Routledge, 1997. Deals specifically with *The Collector of Treasures, and Other Botswana Village Tales* from a generally feminist point of view.

Mackenzie, Craig. "Short Fiction in the Making: The Case of Bessie Head." *English in Africa* 16, no. 1 (May, 1989). Mackenzie is one of the leading South African exponents of Bessie Head, having edited her book A Woman Alone. He traces the interweaving of the making of *Serowe: Village of the Rain Wind*, and *The Collector of Treasures, and Other Botswana Village Tales*.

_____. "The Use of Orality in the Short Stories of A. C. Jordan, Mtutuzeli Matshoba, Njabulo Ndebele, and Bessie Head." *Journal of Southern African Studies* 28, no. 2 (June, 2002): 347-358. Explores how four South African writers use elements of orality in their written stories, including an analysis of Head's collection *The Collector of Treasures, and Other Botswana Village Tales*. Concludes that Head is the most successful "oral stylist" of the four because she is able to bridge the gap between oral and literary forms.

Ola, Virginia Uzoma. *The Life and Works of Bessie Head*. Lewiston, N.Y.: The Edwin Mellen Press, 1994. One of the most useful introductions to Head's work. In seven chapters, Ola deals with the topics of good and evil, women's roles, nature, and Head's ability to tell stories. She concludes by comparing Head to other African women writers.

Olaussen, Maria. *Forceful Creation in Harsh Terrain: Place and Identity in Three Novels by Bessie Head*. New York: Peter Lang, 1997. An overview of three of Head's novels.

Sample, Maxine, ed. *Critical Essays on Bessie Head*. Westport, Conn.: Praeger, 2003. Some of the essays discuss Head's life, her novels, and her short-fiction works *The Cardinals* and *The Collector of Treasures, and Other Botswana Village Tales*.

David Barratt

LAFCADIO HEARN

Born: Levkás, Ionian Islands, Greece; June 27, 1850
Died: Tokyo, Japan; September 26, 1904

PRINCIPAL SHORT FICTION

Stray Leaves from Strange Literature, 1884
Some Chinese Ghosts, 1887
Kotto: Being Japanese Curios, with Sundry Cob-webs, 1902
Kwaidan: Stories and Studies of Strange Things, 1904
The Romance of the Milky Way, 1905
Fantastics and Other Fancies, 1914

OTHER LITERARY FORMS

Lafcadio (lahf-KAHD-ee-oh) Hearn's travel sketches include *Glimpses of Unfamiliar Japan* (1890), *Two Years in the French West Indies* (1894), and *In Ghostly Japan* (1899). He is also remembered for his more comprehensive assessments of Japan. His numerous other nonfiction works and his long fictions have been less influential.

ACHIEVEMENTS

The author of more than sixty books (if one includes posthumous collections and translations), Lafcadio Hearn was one of the most successful travel writers in history, known during his lifetime as Japan's principal interpreter to the Occident.

BIOGRAPHY

The child of Charles Hearn, a British surgeon-major, and Rosa Tessima, a Greek, Patricio Lafcadio Tessima Carlos Hearn spent his first two years on the island of Santa Maura and the remainder of his childhood in Ireland. In 1884, alienated and mentally ill, his mother abandoned him with a pious great-aunt, who fostered his fears of the supernatural. He was first educated by tutors, then at a church school in Normandy, and finally at Saint Cuthbert's College in England, which he left without receiving a degree, primarily for financial reasons but also because of the accidental loss of an eye.

In 1868, he went to America, where, after an impoverished stay in New York, he made a name for himself in Cincinnati as a reporter (1869-1877). During ten years in New Orleans, he rose to the position of literary editor of the *Times-Democrat*. The fruits of two trips to the West Indies, his travel sketches received a sufficient audience, so that his departure to Japan in 1890 was under the auspices of the publishing house of Harper and Brothers.

Entranced by Japan, Hearn married a Japanese woman, Setsu Koizumi, became a Japanese citizen, and accepted a professorship at the Imperial University of Tokyo. According to a 1903 letter first published in 1998, in his final years Hearn was lonely, alienated from most Westerners in Japan, who saw him as a religious heretic, and embittered by salary negotiations that caused him to leave his university position.

ANALYSIS

Lafcadio Hearn's apprenticeship was in the translation of French works. In translating these works, he learned how to make the exotic and the bizarre evocative in a Latinate style redolent of fin-de-siècle decadence. To achieve this mannered effect, he would often make extensive use of thesauri and etymological dictionaries, but he would also go to the opposite extreme of relying on his own unconscious. By the time *Some Chinese Ghosts* was written, his style was artificial enough that he was criticized for it and thereafter learned to moderate it somewhat, but his model was never Hemingwayesque simplicity. Rather, he admired the way William Butler Yeats retold Irish folklore in a dreamlike manner, echoing French symbolism. The brevity of Hearn's and

Yeats's tales keeps their mannerisms from being as distracting as they would be at novel length.

Hearn's Irish and French models did not mean that his work had nothing in common with American short narratives. His morbidity earned for him the nickname "The Raven" because it was reminiscent of Edgar Allan Poe; Hearn's fascination with retelling old narratives was shared by other nineteenth century Americans, such as Nathaniel Hawthorne in his *Twice-Told Tales* (1837, expanded 1842). More clearly than Hawthorne, however, Hearn adopted the traditional role of the storyteller, perpetuating what might otherwise be lost. A lifelong outsider, Hearn accepted his role as spokesman for the ghostly and exotic--what modernism excluded from the Occident. His success depended on his representing alien cultures in a form that the skeptical West could accept; thus, as mediator, he placed himself in a position in which he risked suspicion from both hemispheres.

FANTASTICS AND OTHER FANCIES

Although this collection was not published until after Hearn's death, it contains his earliest, extant short fictions, most of which are in a genre he developed--brief, impressionistic sketches. Each presents a *Liebestod* (love/death) theme, softened as in a dream or in a story for children. A whimsically described, brave, female cat in "The Little Red Kitten" adopts a kitten; they die looking for each other and are thrown by chance on the same ashes. In "The Ghostly Kiss," the narrator wishes to embrace the woman in front of him in a theater, even if he should die for it. When he succumbs to this temptation, she announces that the kiss has forged an eternal compact, and he finds himself alone in a graveyard. In "The Vision of the Dead Creole," despite serpents, bats, and vampires, a lover opens the grave of his beloved, and in his dying vision the two of them become strangely mingled with the Virgin Mary. Designed for newspaper consumption, these stories are obviously popular literature, some owing much to Poe. However, Hearn's stories are forged to create reverie, whereas Poe's comparable ones elicit terror. Hearn himself deprecated these apprenticeship pieces, yet his fusing of journalistic conciseness with what he

Lafcadio Hearn (Library of Congress)

had learned from translating French literature produced a unique style.

SOME CHINESE GHOSTS

In his preface, Hearn explains the shortness of the volume and, by implication, the brevity of the tales by quoting Sir Walter Scott's observation that, despite the inherent appeal of the supernatural, reading about it requires a stretching of credulity that soon becomes exhausting. Subsequent to J. R. R. Tolkien's *The Lord of the Rings* (1955), epic fantasies became common. Scott and Hearn, however, are speaking for a period when the fantastic was palatable only if presented as a refined version of the inherently short folktale; the folktale collection of Jacob and Wilhelm Grimm, for example, was simultaneously esteemed for its powerful portrayal of emotion and deprecated for its outgrown superstitions. The tone of Hearn's volume is set by the first story, "The Soul of the Great Bell." Because an astrologer forecasts that the bell's forging will require a human sacrifice, the daughter of a master craftsman throws herself into the molten metal, and the completed bell's sound is exceptional because of the influence of her ghost. Hearn expands and embellishes a French translation so that the details become vivid. He ends with the story being mentioned to toddlers, as if he were asking his readers themselves to return to childhood and suspend adult disbelief. The book ends with notes and a glossary of Chinese (particularly Buddhist) terms.

STRAY LEAVES FROM STRANGE LITERATURE

Similar to the previous volume but larger in scope, this is a retelling of traditional narratives from Egyptian, Polynesian, Finnish, Hindu, Buddhist, Islamic, and Jewish sources. That Buddhism is particularly noted may owe something to Hearn's having researched the subject for his previous book and to the popularity that Sir Edwin Arnold's 1879 life of the Buddha, *The Light of Asia*, enjoyed in America. Hearn adapts the tales freely, sometimes condensing, sometimes combining elements from several stories into one. For instance, by using indexes to the Talmud, he builds a character sketch of a rabbi, amalgamating anecdotes scattered throughout that tome. What holds Hearn's book together is, paradoxically, its very diversity, its exoticism--a melange of bizarre behavior, quaint turns of phrase, ghosts, demons, and miracles. On a popular level, he is continuing the work of the American Transcendentalists, showing that neglected traditions, particularly those of Asia, still have cultural value. Even while treasuring the unfamiliar, he must excise whatever seems to him too strange, too divergent from Christian morals and sentiments. Certainly, like most of Hearn's Eastern fictions, these stories may be accused of what critic Edward Said calls "Orientalism": the imperialistic appropriation of the Orient to satisfy Occidental desires, thus betraying its reality. Such a charge suits these first two volumes better than the ones written after Hearn committed himself to the East.

KOTTO

Dedicated to Sir Edwin Arnold, this collection actually diverges significantly from the orientalism of Arnold's *The Light of Asia* and Hearn's two previous collections of mostly Asian tales. In all three, the narrators are primarily modern believers in magic--a device with prejudicial implications that Easterners are perennially childlike and credulous. In contrast, the tone of *Kotto* is

set by two stories in which Hearn speaks in his own voice and emphasizes that the narrative's origins are very old. "In a Cup of Tea" makes particularly significant use of this distancing frame. He begins by comparing the reading of interrupted narratives to the act of stepping into an abyss and then gives as an example an old tale about someone who swallowed a soul (at which point, the original narrative breaks off). He adds that he could provide various endings but nothing that would please "an Occidental"; thus, he admits his difference from both the Occidental reader and Oriental author. Hearn is left in the vertiginous gulf between them, not a comfortable position but an honest one, which does not try to appropriate East or West.

KWAIDAN

Adapted by Masaki Kobayashi into the classic film *Kwaidan* (1964) and used as a source for new No plays, Hearn's book has continued to appeal to the Japanese. Perhaps one reason for this is that after much modernization, they are themselves distanced from their own heritage, making them comparable to the Western readers Hearn addressed. He comments on this situation at the book's close, where he imagines westernization as a wind stripping fairylike beauty from Japan. In the next to last story, a Japanese word reminds him of a Welsh one, and he recalls a time in his childhood when he sought fairy rings in the grass. Just as English modernism and imperialism pushed aside Celtic culture in Britain, the Occident had begun a cultural deracination in Japan. One of the most frequent themes in the stories of *Kwaidan* is making love to ghosts, for it represents the necessary and nourishing traditions of Japan, which have been reduced to that spectral condition.

OTHER MAJOR WORKS

LONG FICTION: *Chita: A Memory of Last Island*, 1888 (serial), 1889 (book); *Youma: The Story of a West-Indian Slave*, 1890.

NONFICTION: *Historical Sketch Book and Guide to New Orleans and Environs*, 1885; *Two Years in the French West Indies*, 1890; *Glimpses of Unfamiliar Japan*, 1894; *Kokoro: Hints and Echoes of Japanese Inner Life*, 1896; *Gleanings in Buddha-Fields*, 1897; *Exotics and Retrospectives*, 1898; *In Ghostly Japan*, 1899; *Some Strange English Literary Figures of the*

Eighteenth and Nineteenth Centuries, 1899; *Shadowings*, 1900; *Japan: An Attempt at Interpretation*, 1904; *Lafcadio Hearn, Japan's Great Interpreter: A New Anthology of His Writings, 1894-1904*, 1992 (Louis Allen and Jean Wilson, editors); *Inventing New Orleans: Writings of Lafcadio Hearn*, 2001 (S. Frederick Starr, editor); *Lafcadio Hearn's America: Ethnographic Sketches and Editorials*, 2002 (Simon J. Bronner, editor).

MISCELLANEOUS: *American Writings*, 2009 (Christopher Benfey, editor).

BIBLIOGRAPHY

Bisland, Elizabeth. *The Life and Letters of Lafcadio Hearn*. 2 vols. Boston: Houghton Mifflin, 1906. An authorized biography.

Cott, Jonathan. *Wandering Ghost: The Odyssey of Lafcadio Hearn*. New York: Knopf, 1991. A biography containing numerous excerpts from Hearn's writings. Particularly valuable for literary analysis.

Dawson, Carl. *Lafcadio Hearn and the Vision of Japan*. Baltimore: Johns Hopkins University Press, 1992. This book's strength is its examination of Hearn's European background.

Gale, Robert L. *A Lafcadio Hearn Companion*. Westport, Conn.: Greenwood Press, 2002. An encyclopedic guide to Hearn's life and career. Contains alphabetically arranged entries on his writings, family members, and colleagues. Many of the entries cite materials for further reading, and the volume includes a bibliography.

Hasegawa, Yoji. *A Walk in Kumamoto: The Life and Times of Setsu Koizumi, Lafcadio Hearn's Japanese Wife, Including a New Translation of Her Memoir "Reminiscences."* Folkestone, England: Global Oriental, 1997. As informant and translator, Hearn's wife Setsu Koizumi provided Hearn with many of the sources for his tale adaptations. Her reminiscences of her husband thus contain valuable accounts of Hearn's short-story production.

Hirakawa, Sukehiro, ed. *Lafcadio Hearn in International Perspectives*. Folkestone, England: Global Oriental, 2007. Hirakawa, who has written extensively about Hearn, compiled this collection of essays because he said he was intrigued by the gap between negative perceptions of Hearn in the United States and positive appreciations of his work in Japan. Among other topics, these essays discuss Hearn's "nightmares," Hearn and the sea, his retelling of Japanese folk stories, his interest in folklore studies, and the image of the mother in his work.

_____. *Rediscovering Lafcadio Hearn: Japanese Legends Life and Culture*. Folkestone, England: Global Oriental, 1997. Although quite miscellaneous, this collection includes treatment of Hearn's short fiction, including an essay assessing the influence of one of his stories on French poet Charles Baudelaire.

Murray, Paul. *A Fantastic Journey: The Life and Literature of Lafcadio Hearn*. Folkestone, England: Japan Library, 1993. This biography and account of Hearn's writings emphasizes his Irish influences.

Ronan, Sean G., ed. *Irish Writing on Lafcadio Hearn and Japan: Writer Journalist and Teacher*. Folkestone, England: Global Oriental, 1997. Ronan, a former Irish ambassador to Japan, has assembled this collection of tributes to Hearn.

Umemoto, Junko. "The Reception of Chinese Culture Reflected in Lafcadio Hearn's Retelling of Chinese Literature." *Comparative Literature Studies* 39, no. 4 (2002): 263. Describes how Hearn altered Chinese ghost stories to create his romantic love tales "The Story of Ming-Y" in *Some Chinese Ghosts* and "The Story of Ito Norisuke" in *The Romance of the Milky Way*.

Yu, Beongcheon. *An Ape of Gods: The Art and Thought of Lafcadio Hearn*. Detroit: Wayne State University Press, 1964. Assesses the degree to which Hearn managed to intuit a universal "philosophy" based on a combination of European and Japanese attitudes.

James Whitlark

I

Ihara Saikaku

Born: Ōsaka, Japan; 1642
Died: Ōsaka, Japan; September 9, 1693
Also Known As: Hirayama Tōgo

OTHER LITERARY FORMS

The best-known work of Ihara Saikaku (ee-hahr-ah si-kah-kew) is the picaresque novel *Kōshoku ichidai otoko* (1683; *The Life of an Amorous Man*, 1964). He first won fame as a poet, however, with *Ikudama manku* (1673; ten thousand verses at Ikudama), a compilation that includes *haikai* (comic linked verse) of Saikaku and more than two hundred of his associates. His solo *haikai* performances are recorded in *Dokugin ichinichi senku* (1675; solo verses, one thousand in one day), *Saikaku haikai ōkuzaku* (1677; Saikaku's haikai, a great many verses), and *Saikaku ōyakazu* (1681; Saikaku's a great many arrows). Saikaku also wrote two puppet plays, *Koyomi* (calendar) and *Gaijin Yashima* (triumphant return from Yashima), both of which were staged in 1685.

ACHIEVEMENTS

Ihara Saikaku first gained literary repute as a leading member of Ōsaka's innovative *Danrin* school of *haikai*. Like others in this group, he wrote with verve and abandon. In 1673, he was a central participant in a twelve-day poetry party that produced ten thousand verses; later, prodigious solo poetizing marathons solidified his fame as a poet. Saikaku's lasting reputation, however, would come from prose fiction. In 1682, he created a new genre, *Ukiyo-zōshi* (books of the floating world), with the publication of his novel *Kōshoku ichidai otoko*, the first of two dozen books written during his last decade. They made him--with *haiku* poet Matsuo Bashō and dramatist Chikamatsu Monzaemon--one of the three dominant figures of Tokugawa literature and earned him a place second only to Murasaki Shikibu, author of *Genji monogatari* (c. 1004; *The Tale of Genji*, 1925-1933, 1935) as a premodern Japanese writer of narrative fiction. He gave the *chonin* (townsmen) heroes and heroines from their own class and made colloquial Japanese a literary language. While his stories sometimes treated the mores of the samurai or Confucian ethics, his most enduring works chronicled with stylistic originality, detached wit, and sharp insight the chief preoccupations of Japan's new urban class: love and money.

BIOGRAPHY

Little is known of Ihara Saikaku's personal life. He was most certainly born in Ōsaka in 1642, there being sufficient indication that he considered this city to be his hometown. His given name was, according to one source, Hirayama Tōgo; Ihara was, most likely, his mother's maiden name, which he later adopted for his professional name. "Saikaku" is the last of a series of pseudonyms that he used. According to the same source, he was a merchant in an unspecified trade who could afford to leave the management of the business to trusted clerks and devote his life to literary pursuits and to travel.

He took an early interest in *haikai* and is believed to have qualified in his twenty-first year to become a *haikai* teacher (*tenja*). In the early 1670's, he became a disciple of Nishiyama Sōin (1605-1682), the head of the Danrin school of *haikai* and a major challenger to the traditional Teimon school. By 1673, when *Ikudama manku* was performed, Saikaku had established himself as a leading force under Sōin.

Traditionally, *haikai* poetry is composed in linked sequences by several poets as a ritualized social and literary activity. Saikaku was by no means the first to break from this tradition--there had been others before him, most notably Arakida Moritake (1473-1549), who is credited with *Dokugin senku* (compiled 1536-1540; a thousand verses composed by one man). Nevertheless, Saikaku was the first to compose one thousand verses in a single day in 1675. The occasion was an emotional one: a memorial tribute to his young wife, who had died after a brief illness. Saikaku titled the compilation *Dokugin ichinichi senku*. This effort was followed in 1677 by *Saikaku haikai ōkuzaku*, another solo performance in which sixteen hundred verses were composed in a single day and night. When rivals bested him, first with eighteen hundred verses, then with twenty-eight hundred, Saikaku returned in 1680 with a public performance of four thousand verses in a single day and night. The record of this feat was published the following year as *Saikaku ōyakazu*. When rivals reported besting him again, Saikaku was determined to put an end to all such rivalry. In 1684, he assembled an audience, and in the presence of referees and scribes he composed 23,500 verses in a twenty-four-hour period. Unfortunately, he delivered the verses so fast that the scribes could only draw hash marks for each verse.

Saikaku proved his point, and as a result the Danrin school embarked on a path of self-destruction. It was not, however, the end of Saikaku. As long as linked verse remained a group activity, fettered by the constraints of traditional versification, it allowed little room for the genius of any single individual to bloom. It is not surprising that Matsuo Bashō (1644-1694) and Saikaku, the two leading men of the Danrin school, discovered a way to free themselves from these limitations and so unleash their talents. Bashō's concentration on the opening verse (*hokku*) of the *haikai* sequence allowed him to reach unsurpassed heights in his endeavor. As for Saikaku the raconteur, performing rapid-fire solo *haikai* gave him experience in weaving together *haikai* sequences with something approaching narrative content and led the way to the development of an idiosyncratic narrative that displayed *haikai* techniques.

With the death of his teacher Sōin in 1682, Saikaku was emboldened to proceed with the publication of his first attempt at fiction, *The Life of an Amorous Man*. The work was so well received that publishers encouraged him to continue; he was thus embarked on a brief but prolific career as a writer of fiction, producing more than two dozen novels and collections of short stories in the last decade of his life. When he died in 1693, one of his disciples moved into his residence as a caretaker; he edited and possibly made additions to the unfinished manuscripts he found before he had them published. Saikaku's enormous popularity can be seen in that a succession of works purporting to be sequels or written in a style and vein emulating Saikaku's began to appear almost immediately and continued to be published for decades after his death.

Saikaku's last words summarize his attitude toward life. Noting that he had exceeded man's allotted span of fifty years, he gave thanks in this deathbed poem:

> The moon of this Floating World
> I have enjoyed a surplus
> These last two years

ANALYSIS

Ihara Saikaku was a poet who turned to writing prose fiction late in his life. As a *haikai* poet he had distinguished himself as a daredevil maverick with his rapid-fire performances, although his focus in *haikai* was the real world of the commoner's life. Unlike the poems of his contemporary Matsuo Bashō, which tend to be sublimated, Saikaku's poems deal squarely with the diurnal activities of the men and women of the cities. When he turned to fiction, he continued to draw his materials directly from the commercial, urban society of his day.

Saikaku was a consummate storyteller who told his stories with relish. He was also a supreme stylist who wrote in a terse, innovative style that was emulated by his contemporaries and followers. To a large extent, Saikaku's style derived from his training as a *haikai* poet whose medium required communication by splashes of imagery rather than articulated narrative. (Unfortunately, such matters of style are usually lost in translation and can be seen only in the original text.) Saikaku's genius lay in the brilliant insight with which he wrote about sex and money in the life of the townsmen. His earliest work was imbued with optimism and an exuberant air, while his later works turned increasingly pessimistic. However, throughout his writing career, Saikaku displayed a rare talent for intermingling the comic with the tragic.

Five Women Who Loved Love

Five Women Who Loved Love is generally considered to be Saikaku's masterpiece. It is a rather carefully crafted collection of five scandalous love stories. In contrast to Saikaku's other works on "love," which were in reality about mere sexual encounters, these are stories that dwell more extensively on the portrayals of men and women in love and the often tragic consequences which follow. All but the last of these love stories end tragically; the protagonists pay for their indiscretions with their lives. Punishments for crimes considered subversive to the hierarchical order were harsh in the Tokugawa period. A hired hand who had illicit intercourse with his master's daughter, for example, could have been sentenced to death. Adultery by a married woman was also punishable by death, and a husband who caught his wife in the act could kill her and her lover on the spot. Death was also often the penalty for kidnapping, or even for the embezzlement of ten *ryō* or more. These stories acquired additional poignancy as each of them was based on actual scandals, some still very fresh in the minds of Saikaku's readers. Saikaku freely altered and embellished the incidents and, in typical Saikaku style, added comical touches.

The first story is that of Onatsu, the younger sister of a shopkeeper in the regional town of Himeji, who falls in love with Seijūrō, a clerk in her brother's employ. At an outing carefully staged by Seijūrō, they fulfill their desire. The liaison cannot go unnoticed, however, and fully aware of the penalty for Seijūrō, they flee by boat to reach Ōsaka but are tracked down and brought back to face the consequences. When Seijūrō is executed, Onatsu loses her mind; at one point she tries to kill herself but is restrained. She then becomes a nun in order to care for Seijūrō's grave, and she prays for his soul day and night. Saikaku comments, "This then is my creation, a new river and a boat for the lovers to float their love downstream, like bubbles in this sad fleeting world." He makes no comment on the harshness of the punishment or the injustice of the law. However, this final line makes it clear where his sympathy lay: They had violated no moral law; they were simply two hapless lovers caught in an unreasonable legal system.

The second story is about adultery between a barrel-maker's wife, Osen, and her neighbor Chōzaemon. Osen is falsely accused of adultery by Chōzaemon's wife. Incensed, she vows to give the accuser real cause to worry. Her desire for revenge, however, soon turns to lust. One evening after a party, when Chōzaemon follows her home, she invites him in. They are no sooner in bed when the barrelmaker appears and discovers them in the act. Chōzaemon flees the scene, only to be caught and later executed. Osen chooses a more heroic path to death, plunging a carpenter's chisel-like plane into her heart. Osen had acted out of vengeance, rather than love. Chōzaemon's conduct, too, was deficient. Saikaku comments, "The scoundrel's and her corpse too were put on public display at Togano to expose their shame. Their names, through countless ballads, spread to faraway provinces; there's no escaping from one's own misdeeds. Frightful, this world of ours!" Although Osen is spared the indignity of public execution, Saikaku leaves no doubt as to his disapproval of the conduct of Osen and Chōzaemon: unmitigated adultery stemming from revenge or lust.

The third and perhaps most effective of the five stories is about Osan, the beautiful wife of an almanac maker, and Moemon, a clerk in her husband's Kyōto shop. The almanac maker has hired Moemon specifically to look after the shop and Osan while he takes an extended business trip to Edo. During her husband's absence, Osan and her maid Rin, who is attracted to Moemon, play a trick on him. The prank backfires, however, and Osan ends up in bed with Moemon. Moemon has come to Rin's bed in response to a note from her; meanwhile Osan has taken Rin's place in her bed to surprise him. Osan, however, falls asleep and is taken unaware. In the morning, when Osan realizes what has happened, she is mortified about the "shame" as well as the nature of her transgression. The only honorable way to salvage the situation, she believes, is to "sacrifice her life in order to save her honor," and she asks Moemon to "join her in her journey to death." They elope, stage a mock suicide to fool pursuers, and flee to a mountain hamlet where they find momentary bliss. One day, unable to suppress an urge to reconnoiter the situation back in the capital, Moemon slips back into the city and is spotted; the misadventure leads to their demise: They are paraded through the streets and executed.

In spite of the essentially tragic nature of the incident, the story is told with humorous turns of phrases and is sprinkled with comic interludes. In less skilled hands, it could easily have become a farce; in Saikaku's, it has been crafted into a thoroughly enjoyable tragicomedy. The adultery is unintended, but Osan has made an irrevocable mistake. To validate her good-faith effort to maintain her honor, Saikaku portrays her as an admirable woman, truly in love with Moemon. She is further portrayed as a spirited woman, full of life, who makes the most of the last days of her life and does not regret her action. Saikaku's final comment: "At dawn of the twenty-second of the Ninth Month they met their end as in a fleeting dream, an end far from dishonorable. Their story is widely known and even in the twentieth century the name of Osan is remembered as vividly as her lovely figure in the pale-blue robe she wore to her death."

The fourth story unfolds with a greengrocer's family taking temporary refuge in a temple when their shop is destroyed by fire. As they await the rebuilding of the shop, an adolescent love affair develops between Oshichi, the fifteen-year-old daughter, and Kichisaburō, a temple page from a samurai family. When the shop is rebuilt and the family returns to their new quarters, Oshichi yearns to see Kichisaburō again. Blinded by love, she sets fire to the new building, believing that the family will then return to the temple. The fire is stopped at an early stage, but Oshichi is paraded about the city and eventually burned at the stake. Saikaku comments, "No one should ever commit such an evil act. Heaven does not tolerate it." He continues,

> Since it was something Oshichi had done with conviction, knowing full well its consequences, she did not allow herself to waste away. Instead, each remaining day, she had her black hair done up and looked as beautiful as ever. Early in the Fourth Month, alas at sixteen she was in the spring of her youth, as the cherry blossoms were falling to the ground and even the cuckoos cried out in unison their songs of lament, she was finally told that her time had come. She remained as calm and collected as ever, ready to accept life as an illusory dream of an existence and earnestly awaited rebirth in the Land of the Buddha. How very sad!

Saikaku is emphatic in his condemnation of the grave crime of arson and does not question the harshness of the punishment. However, he also allows an outpouring of sympathy for Oshichi. Although she has been illogical and foolish, she has acted out of pure love, Saikaku seems to suggest, when the more common cause of criminal transgressions are greed, jealousy, and spite. Her motive is honorable. Furthermore, faced with death, Oshichi conducts herself with dignity. Saikaku portrays her as showing no remorse but as being sincere in her acceptance of death as the consequence of her act.

Saikaku continues the story beyond the death of the heroine, relating an aspect of the young man's life that had only been hinted at earlier: his homosexual relationship with another youth. Kichisaburō had been so weakened with lovesickness that he had not been told of Oshichi's fate. When he learns of it, he quickly reaches for his sword, but the monks restrain him from killing himself, reminding him of the pledge of homosexual love that he has made to his "sworn brother." He is torn between his obligation to his lover and what he believes is his duty to the girl he once loved. He is relieved, however, when his sworn brother releases him from the obligation, counseling him to join the priesthood to look after Oshichi.

Saikaku's aim was to cover the spectrum of love "in all its varied forms" and particularly to show how duty, honor, and dignity play key roles in the relationships among men. The homosexual segment here anticipates the fifth story, in which a handsome young man who has suffered the loss of two male lovers is relentlessly pursued by a young woman. Madly in love with him, she visits him dressed as a young boy to attract his attention. In the end, they marry, inherit a fortune, and, presumably, live happily ever after.

The success of *Five Women Who Loved Love* and Saikaku's stories in general derives from the wry humor and detachment with which he tells his stories. He maintains a distance from his characters yet manages to portray them sympathetically. The women in these stories are portrayed as independent and strong-willed, undaunted by the harsh laws of society and able to risk their lives for love.

Saikaku shokoku-banashi

Saikaku traveled extensively around the country and wrote hundreds of short stories which were published over the years as collections, usually with specific themes. Legends and tales with strong local flavor, for example, were brought together in *Saikaku shokoku-banashi* (Saikaku's tales of the provinces), a collection of thirty-five stories told with typical Saikaku-esque humor. This short-story form, rooted in the oral tradition and no more than several pages long, was to become with appropriate refinement Saikaku's favorite and most effective form in the years to come. With Saikaku's background and genius in *haikai* versification and with his talent as a raconteur, it was inevitable that he would abandon the novel in favor of the short story. In time, he began to produce collections of short stories with more distinct themes.

Honchō nijū fukō

As the Tokugawa shogunate mounted a renewed campaign to encourage filial piety in the early 1680's, Saikaku responded characteristically with the publication in 1686 of his *Honchō nijū fukō* (twenty cases of unfilial conduct in Japan), a gleeful collection of stories about the most reprehensible sort of children, sons and daughters who plot against one another and who would even murder their parents for money. Though doomed by the very odious nature of the stories, the work opened the way for Saikaku to explore the use of themes as a unifying device for other collections of stories.

Nanshoku ōkagami

Saikaku returned to the theme of male homosexuality in earnest with the publication in 1687 of *Nanshoku ōkagami* (*The Great Mirror of Male Love*). In this collection of forty stories, he focused on two groups: samurai and their "sworn brothers" and Kabuki actors and their townsmen patrons. In these stories, particularly in the former group, conflicts arise from triangular relationships, with honor and dignity playing key roles in their resolution. Samurai morality, especially as it pertained to the codified vendetta of the Tokugawa period, is the theme for the thirty-two stories in *Budō denraiki* (the transmission of martial arts), while it is the gnarled notion of samurai honor that serves as the thematic unifier for the twenty-six stories in *Tales of Samurai Honor*. These works of the samurai world are usually criticized as being inaccurate depictions of the samurai mind-set. When viewed as humorous portrayals of the strange world of the samurai, however, they are as entertaining as the bulk of Saikaku's writing.

The Japanese Family Storehouse

While Saikaku had begun his career as a novelist with an unmistakable optimism, he entered a new phase in 1688 with the publication of *The Japanese Family Storehouse*. Perhaps he had become disillusioned with life under the Tokugawa regime; certainly, the seemingly unlimited economic opportunities that were in evidence earlier were rapidly disappearing. His focus took a pragmatic turn, and he began to write stories that revolved almost exclusively around the economic life of the townsmen. The theme to which he turned for *The Japanese Family Storehouse* was the economic life of the wealthy merchants. Of its thirty stories, seventeen are lively, humorous stories on how to become a millionaire, while the remaining thirteen serve as warnings to the merchants on how easy it is to lose their fortunes. Interestingly, many of the stories were based on true stories. Here, Saikaku unabashedly exhorts his fellow merchants not to neglect their family trade and to pay close attention to their business on a daily basis, and he advises them on how to manage their household finances. The didactic tone, however, is held in check by Saikaku's skill as an effective storyteller.

WORLDLY MENTAL CALCULATIONS

While there are positive aspects of *The Japanese Family Storehouse*, the success stories are by and large based on events that had taken place decades earlier. In the late 1680's, the economic outlook was bleak; it was no longer easy to amass a fortune. Saikaku's next important work, the last to be published during his lifetime, was *Worldly Mental Calculations*, which is about the merchants' year-end struggle to settle their accounts. Here, Saikaku turns his attention to the poor merchants, portraying their struggles to escape the harangues of the bill collectors. With irony, detachment, and humor, Saikaku tells tales of the poor, who will manage, by hook or by crook, to see the New Year in even when they have no resources except their wits. To Saikaku's credit, even the bleakest story somehow ends on a light note.

SAIKAKU OKIMIYAGE

In both his earliest works, which dealt with the themes of pleasure and sensuality, and his latest, which dealt with economic realism, Saikaku had turned from the optimistic to the pessimistic. In his last memorable work, *Saikaku okimiyage* (Saikaku's parting present), published in 1693, a few months after his death, Saikaku returned to the men who squander their fortunes on the denizens of the pleasure quarters. They are portrayed as living in poverty, typically with the courtesans on whom they spent a fortune to ransom them from their indentured service. They show no remorse, and, significantly, although they are penniless in the slums, they have not lost their self-respect: They are managing their lives with dignity.

Saikaku was, above all, a raconteur who wrote to entertain. He was a highly original writer, and he wrote in a distinct individual style, a combination of the oral tradition and the ornate literary style. His use of subject matter drawn from contemporary society as well as his use of seventeenth century colloquialism for dialogue contributes to a sense of realism. Saikaku's stories, especially the novels, are weak in plot development; it must be remembered, however, that the concept of plot construction is largely alien to traditional Japanese literature. Saikaku's stories, and much of traditional Japanese literature, must be appreciated more as segments in sequence than in consequence.

OTHER MAJOR WORKS
LONG FICTION: *Kōshoku ichidai otoko*, 1683 (*The Life of an Amorous Man*, 1964); *Shoen ōkagami*, 1684; *Wankyū isse no monogatari*, 1685; *Kōshoku ichidai onna*, 1696 (*The Life of an Amorous Woman*, 1963).
PLAYS: *Gaijin Yashima*, pr. 1685; *Koyomi*, pr. 1685.
POETRY: *Ikudama manku*, 1673; *Dokugin ichinichi senku*, 1675; *Saikaku haikai ōkukazu*, 1677; *Saikaku ōyakazu*, 1681.
NONFICTION: *Yakusha hyōbanki*, 1683?

BIBLIOGRAPHY

Danly, Robert Lyons. "Ihara Saikaku and 'Opening Night in the Capital.'" *The Literary Review* 39 (Winter, 1996): 214-215. A translation of the story, accompanied by comments on the problems of translating Ihara Saikaku. Discusses the difficulty of explaining a temporally distant culture and capturing a fugitive linguistic charm.

De Bary, Wm. Theodore. Introduction to *Five Women Who Loved Love*. Rutland, Vt.: Charles E. Tuttle, 1956. An excellent introduction to both Saikaku and the urban environment of large Tokugawa cities, such as Ōsaka, against which most of Saikaku's fiction is set.

Hibbett, Howard. *The Floating World in Japanese Fiction*. New York: Oxford University Press, 1959. An excellent introduction to late seventeenth century society, including the licensed pleasure quarters, which provides the social background of much of Saikaku's fiction. A chapter is devoted to Saikaku, and a sizable portion of his *The Life of an Amorous Woman* is translated. Illustrations include block prints by artists such as Hishikawa Moronobu and by Saikaku himself.

_____. "Saikaku and Burlesque Fiction." *The Harvard Journal of Asiatic Studies* 20 (June, 1957): 53-73. Illuminates a central quality in the culture of Tokugawa Japan's new urban class: mocking irreverence toward established social and cultural norms. Contains examples from Saikaku and other writers of *Ukiyo-zōshi* and compares their use of burlesque with English authors, such as Henry Fielding and Daniel Defoe.

Keene, Donald. *World Within Walls: Japanese Literature of the Pre-Modern Era, 1600-1867*. New York: Holt, Rinehart and Winston, 1976. Part of a multivolume history of Japanese literature, this volume devotes a chapter to Saikaku's fiction, as well as one to Saikaku and others in the Danrin school of *haikai*. Beyond making perceptive critical comments, Keene summarizes many of Saikaku's stories and sets them in historical context.

Lane, Richard. "Saikaku's 'Five Women.'" In *Five Women Who Loved Love*. Rutland, Vt.: Charles E. Tuttle, 1956. An interesting interpretation of what is perhaps Saikaku's finest work. Lane reviews other accounts of the historical incidents on which the stories are based and notes what is distinctive about Saikaku's treatment of them.

Miner, Earl, Hiroko Odagiri, and Robert E. Morrell. *The Princeton Companion to Classical Japanese Literature*. Princeton, N.J.: Princeton University Press, 1985. A brief but judicious characterization of Saikaku's contribution to Tokugawa literature.

Richie, Donald. *Japanese Literature Reviewed*. New York: ICG Muse, 2003. This introductory overview of Japanese literature includes reviews of Saikaku's writings and places his work within the broader context of Edo literature.

Rimer, J. Thomas. *A Reader's Guide to Japanese Literature*. New York: Kodansha International, 1988. A brief review of Saikaku's place in Japanese fiction. Focuses on what is probably his finest work, *Five Women Who Loved Love*.

"Saikaku." In *Kodansha Encyclopedia of Japan*. 9 vols. New York: Kodansha International, 1983. A succinct summary of Saikaku's career. Includes perceptive critical comments on his major works of fiction.

Ben Befu
Updated by R. Craig Philips

J

Ha Jin

Born: Jinzhou, Liaoning Province, China;
   February 21, 1956
Also known as: Xuefei Jin

Other literary forms

Although best-known for his award-winning short fiction, Ha Jin (hah jihn) published his poetry first. His first published poem, "Dead Soldiers Talk," was submitted by his creative-writing instructor at Boston University and appeared in *The Paris Review.* After this auspicious beginning, two volumes of poetry followed before Jin's first collection of short fiction, *Ocean of Words,* came out. Following two collections of short stories, Jin turned to writing longer fiction because, he claims, one of his stories became too long to be classified as short fiction. Jin has published five novels and has continued to write both poetry and short fiction. In 2008, he added nonfiction to his list of book-length publications, with *The Writer as Migrant,* essays based on his Rice University Campbell Lecture Series.

Achievements

Ha Jin has garnered both critical praise and numerous literary awards for his work, including a Guggenheim Fellowship. His short stories have been chosen for inclusion in *The Best American Short Stories* of 1997, 1999, 2000, and 2001. His short stories also have earned three prestigious Pushcart Prizes. His first collection of short fiction, *Ocean of Words: Army Stories,* won the PEN/Hemingway Award. His second collection of short stories, *Under the Red Flag,* won the

Flannery O'Connor Award. His second novel, *Waiting,* won both a National Book Award and the PEN/Faulkner Award. His fourth novel, *War Trash* (2004), was a finalist for the Pulitzer Prize and won a second PEN/Faulkner Award. Jin's short-story collection *The Bridegroom* received the Asian American Literary Award and the Townsend Prize for Fiction. Perhaps Ha Jin's greatest achievement, however, was his 2002 return as a full professor to Boston University, where he had studied creative writing from 1991 to 1994 and the goal that drove him to become a published writer in the first place. In 2005, Jin was elected to the American Academy of Arts and Sciences.

Biography

Xuefei Jin (Ha Jin is his pseudonym) was born in China in 1956 to a military father and a mother who worked at whatever job she could find where her husband was currently stationed. "My father was transferred to different places," Jin told *The Paris Review* in 2009, so his mother "didn't have a stable profession." Jin attended an army boarding school after kindergarten, which he claims accounts for the lack of closeness he feels to his parents, his four brothers, and his sister. Jin says, "It was a fancy school, and it was very expensive." However, the Cultural Revolution (1966-1976) and, with it, the closing of schools in China cut Jin's formal education short.

Shortly before his fourteenth birthday, with his parents' approval--even though being sixteen was a requirement--Jin enlisted in the army because his older friends were enlisting and because he "wanted to leave home," where "there was nothing to do." While serving on the northeast border with Russia, Jin began educating himself by reading such works as *El ingenioso hidalgo don Quixote de la Mancha* (1605, 1615; *The History of the Valorous and Wittie Knight-Errant, Don Quixote of the Mancha,* 1612-1620; better known as

Don Quixote de la Mancha) and Walt Whitman's *Leaves of Grass* (1855, 1856, 1860, 1867, 1871, 1876, 1881-1882), presumably in Chinese.

After serving five and a half years, Jin left the army and went to work for the Harbin Railroad Company as a radio telegrapher. Having a room of his own and working night shifts gave Jin time to read the middle-school textbooks and the high-school literature books that his parents managed to send him. He also began teaching himself English by listening to the radio. Jin claims he took the name "Ha" from Harbin to acknowledge the opportunity to educate himself that this job gave him.

When the Cultural Revolution ended and the universities reopened, Jin enrolled in Heilongjiang University where he was chosen to study English, ironically last on his list of five areas of possible study. Graduating in 1981 with a bachelor's degree, Jin continued his education at Shangdong University, earning a master's degree in American literature. He married Lisha Bian, a mathematician, in 1982; their son Wen was born in 1983. Jin completed his master's degree in 1984.

Ha Jin (AP Photo/Vincent Yu)

In 1986, Jin came to the United States without his wife and son, whom he was not allowed to bring, in order to begin his doctoral work at Brandeis University with a focus in modernist poetry, the subject of his dissertation. At that time, Jin fully intended to return to China after earning his Ph.D. to teach English or become a translator. The Chinese government allowed his wife but not their son to join Jin in United States in 1987. Even more surprisingly, the Chinese government allowed their son to join them shortly after the 1989 confrontation the Tiananmen Square between students and the military. It was the Tiananmen Square incident that caused Jin to change his mind about returning to China. In his interview in *The Paris Review*, Jin says, "The massacre made me feel the country was a kind of manifestation of violent apparitions." For this reason, he could not see himself teaching in the Chinese state-run schools. Jin has said that were he to have returned to China, he would have had "to exercise caution constantly" and would have most likely suffered "mental fatigue . . . harder even than physical hardship."

As a permanent exile, Jin worried about his ability to find a job in the United States teaching American literature, what he would have taught had he returned to China as planned. He decided that the best way for him to land a teaching job in the United States was to be published first. He enrolled in the creative-writing program at Boston College with the goal of getting published in order to get hired. He also decided at this time to write in English rather than in Chinese. He has said that he chose to write in English to distance himself from "Chinese state power," which "has a lot of political jargon." Jin also has said that English is "more flexible" than Chinese and "very plastic, very shapeable, very expressive."

Following the critical success of his first collection of poems --*Between Silences: A Voice from China* (1990)--and earning his doctorate, Jin was hired by Emory University in Atlanta to teach creative writing as an assistant professor. Despite achieving his goal of landing a teaching job, Jin continued writing. To explain why he continues teaching even though his writing has been so successful, Jin has said that "it's good for me to have a regular job. A good book doesn't always sell. . . . . But because I have a job, I don't care about that."

In 2002, Jin returned to Boston University, this time as a full professor in the creative-writing department, where his extremely successful writing career began. Jin became a citizen of the United States and is not pleased about the censorship of his work in China because of its "taboo subjects: Tibet, the Korean War, the Cultural Revolution, the Tiananmen Square incident." This rejection is in sharp contrast to the enthusiastic reception Jin's work has received in the United States for bringing "Jin's distant homeland close to Western audiences." Jin's later work has focused on the experiences of Chinese immigrants in the United States. He has begun translating his work into Chinese.

ANALYSIS

Ha Jin has said that he began writing short fiction because he "realized that some of the material that didn't make it in [his poetry] would be better presented in prose." He claims he was not very serious about this shift, that he thought he could use "some leftover material [from his poems] . . . to write maybe one book of stories." Having decided to stay in the United States and not return to China, he was anxious to publish in order to help him land a university teaching job.

Successful at writing poetry, long fiction, and even nonfiction and having achieved his original goal of securing a post at a university, Jin claims that he is "more a short-story writer--most at home with short fiction." He admits that "most fiction writers think of short fiction as a minor form." For him, however, "it's the most literary form" because he "can spend a few hours a day on a story and then teach."

The first three collections of Jin's short stories are set in China and reveal not only the exotic nature of that setting for Western readers but also the common humanity Western readers share with Jin's characters, despite the differing details of their everyday life. Ha Jin later turned his attention to writing about the experience of Chinese immigrants in the United States. He credits this shift in part to his teaching about the immigrant experience in his college courses. He told *The Paris Review*, "I read and thought about a lot of immigrant issues, and that really opened me up." His novel *A Free Life* (2007) and his collection of short fiction *A Good Fall* reflect this new direction for Jin.

OCEAN OF WORDS: ARMY STORIES

Ha Jin's first collection of short fiction centers on the lives and concerns of soldiers in the People's Liberation Army (PLA), as Jin was as a teenager. The setting is the border between China and Soviet Union in the early 1970's, when the two countries seemed on the verge of war. Jin's characters are watchful for signs of enemy attack and of improper behavior, including such ordinary human emotions as love, lust, and longing in themselves and in other soldiers. Their attempts to deal with the conflicts between Communist Party ideology and basic human nature are sometimes amusing, sometimes disastrous, and sometimes both. Though all the stories in this collection have merit, the following three merit attention.

"A REPORT"

The story that opens the collection is a letter from a soldier, Chen Jun, to Divisional Commissar Lin. In the letter, Jun confesses that the men in his company have sung a song during their march through Longmen City that has made them break down and cry. It is a song about mothers worrying about their soldier sons. Jun takes responsibility for the song and vows to not allow his men to sing this song again. He offers another song that will keep them behaving less bourgeois and more in line with the party ideal for a soldier. In addition, he suggests that "the poisonous song" be banned and its composer and family be investigated. The story shows the letter writer's nervousness as he first accepts responsibility and then attempts to shift responsibility to the composer of the song.

"TOO LATE"

After winning a bet that he could somehow manage to sleep on the bed of a group of girls from Shanghai living in the Youth Home, soldier Kong Kai begins behaving strangely. He spent the night sleeping soundly, keeping on his clothes, and not touching any of the girls. Yet much to the annoyance of the narrator of the story and his company commander, Kong keeps sneaking away. At first Kong admits to no wrongdoing. Eventually, however, it becomes clear that he is meeting one of the girls in the larch woods. In a style similar to a fable or fairy tale and with comic overtones, the commander finds it impossible to stop the lovers from meeting, even after the girl's bourgeois background is revealed to Kong, to show him that this romance will cost him not only command of his unit but also his membership in the Communist Party and his parents' respect. This fails to stop Kong from meeting the girl, however, and eventually the pair elopes. A year later, the commander receives a photograph of them, looking fat and annoyingly happy, a baby perched between them. Though the narrator does not openly accept that Kong has made the right choice--the personal over the dictates of the state--the reader sees that he has.

"DRAGON HEAD"

Long Yun is Dragon Head, the commander of the local militia in Guanmen Village on the Chinese border with the Soviet Union, where the People's Liberation Army (PLA) has been stationed. Even though the commissar and the commander of the government-sanctioned unit do not like the idea of a local militia, they avoid trouble with Dragon Head because he has the hearts of the local people. The government officials look the other way when Dragon Head steals from the PLA and even forgive his playful attack on the Soviets after the tensions between the Soviets and the Chinese have cooled. All along the higher ranking commissar is more eager to avoid directly confronting Dragon Head than the commander, the narrator of the story. At each new transgression of Dragon Head, the commissar supplies reasons for looking away that the commander concedes are logical. One night while drinking together, the commissar shares his family's past with the commander. Though not classified as a landowner, the commissar confesses, he would be had it not been for his uncle, who refused to back down to the Japanese when they invaded and was beheaded as a result, thus becoming an instant folk hero. As soon as the story is out, the commander realizes that his knowing this story will not be good for him. Once sober, the commissar will regret having told the commander and will worry that the commander will reveal his landowner status. When the opportunity to take classes on the writings of Friedrich Engels is presented, the commissar insists that the commander go. The classes last several weeks. The commander is the lowest-ranking officer, and this, coupled with a warning about the commissar, creates the suspicion that the commissar is up to something.

This is borne out when the commander discovers that Dragon Head has been arrested and executed in the commander's absence. In the end, the commander is forced to leave the military. This turns out to be a good thing, because he is able to spend time with his children. Readers see more in the long and complex story than the commander does, though he seems to realize at the end that he is better off out of the army and home with his family.

UNDER THE RED FLAG

Jin's second collection of short fiction is focused on the lives of ordinary people during and shortly after the Chinese Cultural Revolution (1966-1976). Set in the small Chinese village of Dismount Fort (a creation of Jin, and not a real location), the stories reflect the difficult and often unpleasant aspects of trying to replace the old ways with the new and often just as harsh ways. Most of the stories concern male characters, but the bleak experiences of women are in evidence as well. Jin, a boy during this period, has frequently included the actions and reactions of boys to all that is happening around them. The brutal violence of the mob, easily stirred to gang up on individuals, is forcefully portrayed in these stories.

"IN BROAD DAYLIGHT"

In this story, a boy recalls the excitement surrounding the arrest of a not-young woman named Mu, who is accused by the Red Guard of being a prostitute. That Mu is indeed a prostitute--a woman who has taken money a few times after a sexual encounter--seems to be common knowledge and not surprising to anyone in town. The Red Guard insists that Mu must confess and be humiliated by having her head shaved and then being paraded around town before being let go. Though the townspeople act as an angry mob, demanding the death of Mu in the traditional way--being hung upside down above a wood fire and whipped until she dies--the Red Guard is more dispassionate. Their interest lies in making an example out of Mu. At first Mu is defiant. When her husband comes to plead for her, she blames his lack of manliness for her adulterous acts. Later, worn down and no longer defiant, she calls for her husband. However, too humiliated, he has killed himself. There is no one to comfort Mu. Perhaps death would have been the easier punishment for Mu after all.

"A Decade"

Returning to the village of Dismount Fort where she grew up, the narrator of this story, Aina, recalls a teacher she had for fourth grade ten years earlier during the Cultural Revolution. Zhu Wenli, originally a music teacher, came from a capitalist family in Shanghai. Having this kind of bourgeois origin made her suspect, especially after she is caught singing a wistful folk song and dancing too lightly and gracefully. Her students, poor peasants, workers, and cadres, watch her closely. When the students catch Wenli and another teacher flirting, the other teacher is sent to the countryside to be reeducated, and Wenli is assigned his class. She attempts to teach the concept of the metaphor to the class by using a sentence Mao has written, but the students take her lesson as a criticism of Mao and turn her in. As a result, she, too, is sent to the countryside. Home again, the adult Aina decides to look up her teacher to share a story that Aina has had published in a literary magazine. Because the times are different, Aina wants her former teacher, who is married and living in Dismount Fort, to see that she, Aina, is more cultured than she was as a child. Aina finds her former teacher, but what she finds makes her cry. While Aina has become educated and is receiving recognition for her creativity, Wenli has been reeducated to be a coarse woman.

"Man to Be"

Hao Nan is engaged to one of the pretty girls in his village. Life seems good. On the third day of the spring festival, while Nan and four other men from his militia are drinking and playing cards, Sang Zhu comes in with an outrageous proposition. He wants the men to gang-rape his wife. At first, they cannot believe he means what he is saying; Uncle Sang insists that he does. His young wife has been seeing other men, and he wants to teach her a lesson. Nan is cautious, concerned about what sort of repercussions the men will face if they do this. However, Uncle Sang promises to sign a pledge that he will not get the men in trouble for what he is asking them to do. The men go to Sang's house, wait for his wife, and overpower her when she comes in. The older men go first. When it is Nan's turn with the wife, he cannot do it because thoughts of his fiancé and a barking dog interfere. Later on, Nan

continues to suffer from erectile dysfunction. Word of his problem travels, causing his future in-laws to cancel the engagement. Nan tries every cure; none works for him. The village scorns him. Even though Uncle Sang had signed a pledge, Nan is punished for his participation in the rape. Readers see a lesson about the repercussions an individual might suffer after participating in mob violence of any kind, repercussions that do not always come from the expected sources, such as the state.

The Bridegroom

This story collection marks Jin's return to short fiction after several successful novels, and he revisits themes from his early work, such as clashes between political doctrine and basic human nature, the often whimsical nature of power, and the cruelties of everyday life. Set in the fictitious Muji City during the past and the present day, the stories in this collection portray the conflicts and contradictions of the New China at it struggles to make room for entrepreneurial undertakings (capitalism) while still maintaining good Communist Party discipline. This leads to sneaky acts of revenge, which assert the individual's resistance to the misuses of power by those put in charge.

"The Saboteur"

In this Kafkaesque story, Mr. Chiu, a professor at Harbin University, is at the station in Muji City, waiting for the train home, when two policemen toss water on his bride's shoe. Mr. Chiu confronts them and is arrested. As he is dragged from the scene, he urges his wife to use her ticket to take the train home without him. At the police station, the police bully Mr. Chiu to get him to sign a confession of sabotage. He refuses, saying if anything it is the police who are guilty of sabotaging the social order with their misuse of power. His indignation does not serve him well, even though he is clearly right. While Mr. Chiu remains locked up, the poor conditions of the jail cause his health problems to flare up. Still, Mr. Chiu stubbornly refuses to sign. Eventually, Fenjin, a former student of Mr. Chiu, arrives to help, but Fenjin is taken in and tormented within Mr. Chiu's sight. With more than himself to think about, Mr. Chiu relents and signs the confession. The police release both men. On their way of out of town, the angry Mr. Chiu makes sure to contaminate many dishes with his infection and, in this way, is a saboteur after all.

"IN THE KINDERGARTEN"

The central character in this story is five-year-old Shaona, a new arrival at a boarding kindergarten. Not quite at home yet in the room she shares with seven other children, Shaona, awake during naptime, over-hears her teacher's tearful conversation about money owed for what sounds like an abortion. That afternoon, the teacher takes the class to the turnip field instead of releasing them on the playground. She instructs them to pick the parslanes, an edible weed, that are growing in the turnip field. She promises them that they will have the parslanes for dinner and will love them. The children work hard and are proud of all that they manage to collect. That night at dinner, however, there are no parslanes, and Shaona is disappointed. The next day, the teacher once again takes the children to the field, but Shaona is not enthusiastic about collecting the parslanes. When a rabbit and the chance to catch it distract both the teacher and the rest of the class, Shaona relieves herself on the teacher's bag of parslanes. She then worries that the parslanes will be served for dinner that night. However, no parslanes are served again. Shaona is happy and, in addition, no longer homesick. Though she is too young to know that the teacher has sold the parslanes to help pay off her debt, Shaona understands she has been used by the teacher and getting revenge for this in a way that will not lead to her also getting punished is satisfying indeed.

"THE BRIDEGROOM"

This story shares its title with that of the overall collection. Old Cheng tries to understand the relationship between his adopted daughter, Beina, and her husband, Baowen, a handsome man who could have married any single woman in the factory where both work but chose to marry the homely Beina. Old Cheng worries that Baowen will divorce Beina because, after seven months of marriage, she is not yet pregnant. Then Baowen is arrested for "indecent activity," and Old Cheng sets out to discover what that means. The quest leads to the discovery of the uncertain and often conflicting ideas about homosexuality in the New China. Is

homosexuality a criminal act, a mental illness, or a natural state to which some are born? The experts he consults disagree. Even more difficult for Old Cheng to understand, however, is Beina's determination to stand by Baowen, despite his numerous arrests and the failure of doctors to "cure" him. In the end, Old Cheng decides there is a limit to love when he severs his ties with Beina so that he no longer has to think about or answer for Baowen.

"A TIGER FIGHTER IS HARD TO FIND"

In this humorous story with tragic overtones, the governor praises the television series *Wu Song Beat the Tiger* while also criticizing it. The tiger, which the hero kills, looks fake and needs to look real. To satisfy the governor, the television company obtains a tiger--a three-hundred-pounder--by not strictly legal means, but the actor Wang Huping is not ex-cited by the idea of using a real tiger in the scene. The director decides to give Huping a stiff drink for courage and the tiger a tranquilizer to make him less dangerous. The tiger is released, and the cameras roll. Huping fights the tiger, and just when it seems the tiger will win, the tranquilizer takes effect, and the tiger collapses. Huping jumps the tiger and punches him until the director calls cut. Unfortu-nately, Huping never rode the tiger, as the scene re-quires, so the director wants to reshoot. Shooting the scene has done something to Huping, however. He thinks he really is a tiger fighter. The company looks for another actor. In the end, they must use Huping. This time the tiger definitely gets the upper hand and Huping must be tranquilized to get him out of the tree he has climbed to escape the tiger. At this point the director realizes that the live tiger is too much. He has the tiger killed and talks a young truck driver into donning the tiger skin to play the part for the shoot. Huping, more disturbed than ever, attacks the man in the tiger suit and viciously beats him, thinking all the while that he is fighting a real tiger. In the end, the rather badly shot scenes are spliced together and declared acceptable. The once magnifi-cent and now dead tiger, the physically damaged truck driver, and the mentally damaged actor are the cost of this attempt to make something idealized "real."

A GOOD FALL

This collection reflects Jin's move away from stories set in China to stories set in the United States and once again is rich with the imagery that shows Jin's background in poetry. Because he had been writing novels for years, Jin claimed to have lost some feel for the short-fiction genre. In an interview for *Publishers Weekly* following the publication of his novel *A Free Life*, also set in the United States, Jin said, "I never wrote stories set in the States before; that is why I wanted to do this now . . . my subject matter is not about Asia anymore; it's about the America experience." In these stories, the characters bring the attitudes and attributes of their Chinese origins to their lives in the United States. Confusion and a sense of displacement are present in ways that border on being humorous but ultimately are not.

"THE BANE OF THE INTERNET"

In this first story of the collection, the narrator, who lives in the United States, explains the price she has had to pay to stay connected to her younger sister, Yuchin, in China. Though the narrator lives in Flatbush and works as a waitress at a sushi house ten hours a day, seven days a week, her family seems to think that living in America means being rich. Yuchin, though divorced, has a degree in graphic design. In addition, she has her own apartment, while the narrator is trying to save to buy a home for herself. At the center of the story is Yuchin's desire to have a car in China, an even more expensive item in China than it is in the United States; the narrator does not think her sister even needs a car. Seeing Yuchin's desire for a car merely as a desire for increased status, the narrator refuses to give Yuchin the money Yuchin has asked for. When Yuchin posts an ad on the Internet offering her organs for sale, however, the narrator relents on the condition that Yuchin remove the ad. In the end, the desire to save face still trumps the narrator's needs and the logic of the situation.

"BEAUTY"

Successful real estate agent Dan Feng is jealous of his beautiful wife Gina's relationship with Fooming Yu. Though Gina insists that she is just friends with Fooming, Dan begins to wonder if their baby is really Fooming's baby. After all, both Gina and Dan are good

looking, and Fooming is as homely as the homely baby they have. Supposedly, Gina and Fooming come from the same medium-sized city in China, but Dan does not think this is reason enough for them to have drinks together in the afternoon. Dan decides to hire a private detective to investigate their village connection and to spy on the pair when they meet. Though Gina does not seem to be from this village, Fooming is. In addition, Dan learns that Gina once hired the same detective to check out him. These turn out to be minor surprises, however. The biggest surprise is that Gina has had plastic surgery, and the knowledge of this has allowed Fooming to blackmail her into spending time with him. Dan realizes their baby is homely because Gina's mother was born homely, too. Though Dan gets Fooming to back off from Gina, Dan cannot bring himself to care about Gina as he did when he thought she was naturally beautiful. What is real, after all, and what is artificial? This is a question that living in the United States certainly raises. Was Dan's love of Gina real if his newfound knowledge about her altered looks affects that love?

"CHOICE"

Hired to tutor seventeen-year-old Sami so she can realize her deceased father's dream for her to attend an Ivy League college, Dave Hong soon finds himself the object of both Sami's and her mother Eileen Min's affections. Though Sami is closer in age to Dave, Dave chooses to become romantically involved with the mother. Eileen makes Dave promise not to reveal their relationship to Sami. Sami catches them in bed together one night, however. As a result, Dave is fired. Still, he continues to hope that his relationship with Eileen will resume once Sami leaves for college. Sami ruins Dave's plan by choosing to stay in New York City for college instead of attending Cornell, the Ivy League school that accepted her, thanks to Dave's tutoring. Eileen tells Dave that she has agreed with her daughter that neither of them will have anything more to do with Dave, because both of them are in love with him. It seems the choice was not Dave's to make all along, and yet he feels curiously uplifted by the whole experience, because, in a way, he was chosen by both. Again, this story touches on many things, starting and ending with the idea of choice and the multiple meanings of that word in the United States.

OTHER MAJOR WORKS

LONG FICTION: *In the Pond*, 1998; *Waiting*, 1999; *The Crazed*, 2002; *War Trash*, 2004; *A Free Life*, 2007.

PLAYS: *The First Emperor*, pr. 2006 (libretto; music by Tan Dun)

POETRY: *Between Silences: A Voice from China*, 1990; *Facing Shadows*, 1996; *Wreckage*, 2001.

NONFICTION: *The Writer as Migrant*, 2008.

BIBLIOGRAPHY

Fay, Sarah. "Ha Jin: The Art of Fiction No. 202." *The Paris Review* 191 (December, 2009):117-145. In this excellent interview, Jin answers the interviewer's questions about his life and his work in a candid and revealing manner.

Ge, Liangyan. "The Tiger-Killing Hero and the Hero-Killing Tiger." *Comparative Literature Studies* 42, no. 1 (2006): 39-56. This essay provides an in-depth exploration of the meaning of Jin's short story "A Tiger-Fighter Is Hard to Find" from his short-story collection *The Bridegroom*.

Rosen, Stanley. "The Victory of Materialism: Aspirations to Join China's Urban Moneyed Classes and the Commercialization of Education." *The China Journal* 51 (January, 2004): 27-51.Though this article is not directly about Jin's work, it touches on the themes in much of his short fiction, including the conflict between personal goals and public ideals, and in this way the article sheds light on the characters in Jin's writing.

Laurie Lykken

K

Yasunari Kawabata

Born: Ōsaka, Japan; June 11, 1899
Died: Zushi, Japan; April 16, 1972

Other literary forms

Besides approximately two hundred short stories and fictional vignettes (or short, short stories), Yasunari Kawabata (yah-suhn-ah-ree kah-wah-bah-tah) wrote both "serious" novels, which earned for him a Nobel Prize, and "popular" novels, which gained for him financial security. The latter, considered by some critics as vulgarizations, are not included in editions of his complete works. His serious works include juvenile fiction, travel accounts, journalism, letters, reviews, translations, editions, plays, and lectures.

Achievements

Known throughout the world as the first writer from his country to have received the Nobel Prize in Literature, Yasunari Kawabata was also awarded every major Japanese literary honor, including membership in the Japanese Academy of Arts (1954). In 1972, he was posthumously awarded the First Class Order of the Rising Sun. In his work, Kawabata combines universal themes with literary techniques and conventions typical of Japanese culture. His eminence as a writer of fiction is based on this characteristic of fusing contrary, although not antithetical, elements. He draws upon the East and the West, as well as the traditional and the modern; juxtaposes mimetic precision with symbolic evocation; joins the erotic and the spiritual; and fluctuates between dream and reality. In like manner, he cultivated and perfected both long and short genres of fiction and in a sense brought them into conjunction because many of his long works can be broken down into short, independent elements. His themes embrace both the mundane and the esoteric, his narrative style ranges from the graphic to the lyrical, and his highly original plots and situations touch upon fundamental moral and aesthetic issues of modern life.

Biography

Orphaned at the age of four, Yasunari Kawabata was reared by his grandparents and later by an uncle. Originally attracted by painting, he later decided to follow writing as a career, and at the age of sixteen he published in a little magazine an account of carrying his teacher's coffin. Two years earlier, he had written reminiscences of his grandfather, which he later published under the title *Jūrokusai no nikki* (*Diary of a Sixteen-Year-Old*). In 1921, he received his first payment for a literary work, a review, and published in a student literary magazine an account of a memorial day commemoration that drew the favorable attention of a prolific novelist, Kikuchi Kan, a dominating force in Japanese literary circles of the time. The themes of death and loneliness of Kawabata's mature years appeared early in his career and may have been influenced by the loss of his parents and grandparents. During his youth, he came briefly under the influence of a Japanese avant-garde clique that advocated the adoption of novel Western movements such as Dadaism, Futurism, and Surrealism. These tendencies were wrapped up in the term *Shinkankakuha*, which embraces neoperceptionism or neosensualism, but Kawabata's allegiance to this extremely many-sided coterie was only temporary and irresolute. His major work in the experimental mode, *Suishō gensō* (crystal fantasy), uses the stream-of-consciousness technique.

Kawabata established his reputation as a creative writer with the publication in 1926 of his story *Izu no Odoriko* (*The Izu Dancer*) and acquired both critical and popular acclaim with his novel *Yukiguni* (1935-1937, serial; 1947, book; *Snow Country*, 1956). In 1941, he visited Manchuria twice, spending a month in the ancient capital of Mukden and returning to Japan shortly before the outbreak of the Pacific War. Throughout the conflict, Kawabata's publications consisted in large measure of childhood recollections, and he immersed himself in the study of traditional Japanese culture. In the aftermath of his country's defeat, Kawabata announced that he would henceforth write only eulogies, a promise not fulfilled unless his major themes of death, loneliness, and opposition to the Westernization of Japan could be considered elegiac. These themes dominated the first two of his great postwar novels, *Sembazuru* (1949-1951, serial; 1952, book; *Thousand Cranes*, 1958) and *Yama no oto* (1949-1954, serial; 1954, book; *The Sound of the Mountain*, 1970), and another novel, *Kyōto* (1962; *The Old Capital*, 1987).

The Old Capital, which has as protagonists virginal twins who meet for the first time in their late teens after being separated as infants, has received relatively little critical attention in English, perhaps because of the innocence of the characters and the extensive descriptions of the woodland scenery surrounding Kyōto. Western critics have been more attracted by the novella *The House of the Sleeping Beauties*, concerning an unusual brothel in which old men spend the night with naked girls, who are voluntarily drugged into unconsciousness. The love of nature in the one and the eroticism in the other are both typical of Kawabata and are often coalesced in his other works.

In 1948, Kawabata became president of the PEN Club of Japan, a position he used to continue his perennial occupation of encouraging and promoting the careers of young writers. In 1957, he was the guiding spirit behind the twenty-ninth congress of PEN, held in Tokyo, and in 1959, he was elected vice president of that organization, attending three of its congresses in other countries.

In his Nobel Prize acceptance speech, Kawabata remarked that he neither admired nor was in sympathy with suicide. It was a great shock to his associates and to the world at large, therefore, when in April, 1972, he took his own life by inhaling gas.

ANALYSIS

The short story or the vignette is the essence of Yasunari Kawabata's literary art. Even his great novels were written piecemeal. Not only were they originally published in serial form, the parts frequently presented as separate stories, but also many segments were rewritten and revised for both style and content. Japanese tradition has applied the term *shosetsu*, loosely translated as "fiction," to both novels and short stories, and as a result, such works as "The Izu Dancer," consisting of only thirty pages, and *The House of the Sleeping Beauties*, with less than one hundred, have been treated critically as novels.

DIARY OF A SIXTEEN-YEAR-OLD

Kawabata composed his first work *Jūrokusai no Nikki* (*Diary of a Sixteen-Year-Old*) at that age and published it eleven years later. The work describes the humiliating last days and suffering of his grandfather and foreshadows the themes of aging and death in his later works. Comparing the diary with his recollections at a later date, Kawabata maintained that he had forgotten the sordid details of sickness and dying portrayed in his narrative and that his mind had since been constantly occupied in cleansing and beautifying his grandfather's image.

THE IZU DANCER

With Izu no odoriko (*The Izu Dancer*; also translated as "The Dancing Girl of Izu"), his first work to obtain international acclaim, the opposite is true. Here, he idealizes a somewhat commonplace autobiographical incident and group of characters. The story, told in the first person, concerns the encounter of a nineteen-year-old youth on a walking tour of the Izu Peninsula with a group of itinerant entertainers, including a young dancer, who appears to be about sixteen. The young man accompanies them on their way, spurred with the hope that he would eventually spend a night with the young dancer. One morning, as he prepares to enter a public bath, he sees her emerging naked from the steam

Yasunari Kawabata (©The Nobel Foundation)

and realizes that she is a mere child, and a feeling akin to a draught of fresh water permeates his consciousness. Learning that she is only thirteen years of age, he, nevertheless, remains with the players and is accepted by them as a pleasant companion until they reach their winter headquarters. There, he takes a boat back to Tokyo, and his eyes fill with tears as the dancer bids him farewell, floating in a "beautiful emptiness."

The situation of a young man joining forces with a group of itinerant entertainers resembles that in Johann Wolfgang von Goethe's *Wilhelm Meisters Lehrjahre* (1795-1796; *Wilhelm Meister's Apprenticeship*, 1824), perhaps the reason that the work was translated into German in 1942, more than twenty years before being rendered into any other Western language. Some years after the original publication, Kawabata revealed that the portrayal of his youthful journey is highly idealistic, concealing major imperfections in the appearance and behavior of the actual troupe. Presumably in real life, moreover, the young age of the dancer would have been no deterrent to his amorous inclinations, since he later portrayed a thirteen-year-old prostitute as the heroine of one of his popular novels concerning Asakusa, the amusement section of Tokyo. The longing for virginal innocence and the realization that this degree of purity is something beyond ordinary attainment is a recurrent theme throughout Kawabata's work, portraying innocence, beauty, and rectitude as ephemeral and tinged with sadness. The sentimental ending of "The Izu Dancer" is considered to symbolize both the purifying effect of literature upon life, as well as Kawabata's personal passage from misanthropy to hopefulness.

"THE MAN WHO DID NOT SMILE"

Kawabata pursues the theme of the psychological effect of art and nature in another autobiographical story, "Warawanu otoko" ("The Man Who Did Not Smile"), representing his middle years. The author of a screenplay, impressed by the beauty of the dawn in the countryside, where the script is being filmed, rewrites the last scene with the intention of wrapping "reality in a beautiful, smiling mask." The rewriting is inspired by his notion of having every one of the characters in a mental hospital, the locale of the film, wear a laughing mask. On returning to Tokyo, the author visits his own wife in a hospital, where she playfully places one of these masks on her own face. He is horrified by perceiving the ugliness and haggardness of her features in contrast with the beauty of the mask. He meditates on the commonplace that life is ugly but art is beautiful, and he concludes that everyone's smile may be artificial, but he cannot decide whether art in itself is a good thing.

"OF BIRDS AND BEASTS"

Kawabata gives another unflattering view of life and his own personality in *Kinjū* ("Of Birds and Beasts"). The misanthropic protagonist en route to attend the dance recital of a discarded mistress reflects on a pair of dead birds that he had left at home. Musing that the "love of birds and animals comes to be a quest for superior ones, and so cruelty takes root," he finds a likeness in the expression of his former mistress, at the time of her first sexual yielding, to the placid reaction of a female dog while giving birth to puppies. When he encounters the dancer as she is being made up in her dressing room, he envisions her face as it would be in the coffin. Although the story reveals, as he later admitted, that it was written in a fit of cantankerousness, it embodies the serious theme that human and animal kingdoms share the final destiny of death.

THE MOLE

In *Hokuro no nikki* (*The Mole*), Kawabata looks at life from a woman's perspective, delineating a wife's obsession with a physical flaw. Designed to reveal how the process of loving and being loved differs in men and women, *The Mole* consists of a letter from a wife to her separated husband, describing the disintegration of their marriage in which a bodily blemish acts as a catalyst. Ever since childhood, the wife had played with the mole, shaped like a bean, a female sex symbol in Japan. The habit had at first merely irritated the husband, later driven him to beat her, and eventually induced his indifference. On one occasion, the wife dreamed that the mole came off and she asked him to place it next to a mole on his own nose, wondering whether it would then increase in size. This image of gender reversal suggests what is wrong with the marriage. Her obsession with the mole represents an expression of love that proved counterproductive because the husband failed to recognize its true nature.

Although the wife's dilemma arouses the reader's sympathy, Kawabata may have had opposite intentions because he had originally given the story the title "Bad Wife's Letter."

THE MOON ON THE WATER

The feminine perspective is also dominant in *Suigetsu* (*The Moon on the Water*), a story of reciprocated love combining the themes of death, beauty, and sexuality. The story concerns a hand mirror that a dying husband uses while lying in bed to watch the processes of nature outside his window. The moon as such appears in the narrative in only two sentences, where it is seen in the mirror as itself the reflection of a reflection, thereby introducing the philosophical problem of the nature of reality. The moon in the water is without substance, but in Zen Buddhism, the reflected moon is conversely the real moon and the moon in the sky is the illusion. The moon is also a symbol of virginity, relevant to the wife's continence, enforced by the husband's illness during nearly the entire period of her marriage. After the husband dies, the woman remarries and no longer feels shy when a man praises the beauty of her body. At the same time, she realizes that human anatomy prevents her from seeing her own face, except as a reflection in a mirror. She had loved her first husband because she imagined while he was dying that he had been a child inside her, and she is puzzled because she does not feel an equal degree of devotion toward her second husband. She, nevertheless, becomes pregnant and then revisits the area where she had lived during her first marriage. At the end of the story, she asks, "What if the child should look like you?" leaving the reader with uncertainty concerning the antecedent of the pronoun. The reveries of this paradoxically innocent woman in a second marriage combine and recombine the sexual, the aesthetic, and the metaphysical.

THE HOUSE OF THE SLEEPING BEAUTIES

The same elements form Kawabata's somewhat sensational novella *The House of the Sleeping Beauties*, combining lust, voyeurism, and necrophilia with virgin worship and Buddhist metaphysics. The house is an imaginary brothel in which the patrons, old men approaching senility, sleep with naked virgins who are drugged into insensibility. The protagonist is exceptional in that he still has the physical capacity of breaking a house rule against seeking ultimate sexual satisfaction, but he resists the impulse. The circumstances of the story array the beauty of youth and purity against the ugliness of old age and death. Additional contrasts are introduced in the protagonist's subsequent visits to the house, in each of which a different girl evokes erotic passages from his early life. The various beauties could be interpreted as composite recollections or dreamlike fantasies from his past. In the three last visits, his sexual meditations are intermixed with thoughts of death, and he asks to be given for his own use the potent drug administered to the girls. The five visits as a whole suggest the human life span, the first featuring a lovely girl, representing "life itself" and giving off the "milky scent of a nursing baby," and the last portraying the death and abrupt carrying away of one of the sleeping beauties.

ONE ARM

A related story, *Kataude* (*One Arm*), can be interpreted as either more bizarre or more delicate in its eroticism. A young virgin takes off her arm and gives it to a somewhat older man, who takes it home and carries on a conversation with it as he lies in bed, a conversation that makes him recollect the sexual surrender of a previous acquaintance. Along with the erotic descriptions of the arm in contact with parts of the man's body, the narrative introduces New Testament quotations concerning pure and sacrificial love. On one level, the arm is simply a symbol of a woman giving herself sexually to a man, but it may also represent the loneliness of a man who is deprived of a companion with whom to share his thoughts.

OTHER MAJOR WORKS

LONG FICTION: *Asakusa kurenaidan*, 1930 (*The Scarlet Gang of Asakusa*, 2005); *Matsugo no me*, 1930; *Yukiguni*, 1935-1937, serial (1947, book; *Snow Country*, 1956); *Hana no warutsu*, 1936; *Meijin*, 1942-1954, serial (1954, book; *The Master of Go*, 1972); *Utsukushii tabi*, 1947; *Otome no minato*, 1948; *Sembazuru*, 1949-1951, serial (1952, book; *Thousand Cranes*, 1958); *Yama no oto*, 1949-1954, serial (1954, book; *The Sound of the Mountain*, 1970); *Asakusa monogatari*, 1950; *Hi mo tsuki mo*, 1953; *Saikonsha*, 1953;

Kawa no aru shitamachi no hanashi, 1954; *Mizuumi*, 1954, serial (1955, book; *The Lake*, 1974); *Tokyo no hito*, 1955; *Utsukushisa to kanashimi to*, 1961-1963, serial (1965, book; *Beauty and Sadness*, 1975); *Kyōto*, 1962 (*The Old Capital*, 1987); *Shōsetsu nyumon*, 1970; *Aru hito no sei no naka ni*, 1972; *Tampopo*, 1972.

NONFICTION: *Shinshin sakka no shinkeikō kaisetsu*, 1925; *Bungakuteki jijoden*, 1934; *Rakka ryusui*, 1966; *Bi no sonzai to hakken/The Existence and Discovery of Beauty*, 1969 (bilingual); *Utsukushii nihon no watakushi/Japan, the Beautiful, and Myself*, 1969 (bilingual); *Isso ikka*, 1973; *Nihon no bi no kokoro*, 1973.

TRANSLATIONS: *Ocho monogatari shū*, 1956-1958 (of ancient Japanese stories); *Isoppu*, 1968 (of Aesop's fables).

MISCELLANEOUS: *Kawabata Yasunari zenshū*, 1948-1969; *Fuji no hatsuyuki*, 1958 (8 stories and one play; *First Snow on Fuji*, 1999).

BIBLIOGRAPHY

Cassegård, Carl. *Shock and Naturalization in Contemporary Japanese Literature.* Folkestone, England: Global Oriental, 2007. Using the concepts of "naturalization" and "naturalized modernity," Cassegård analyzes how modernity has been experienced and depicted in post-World War II Japanese literature, focusing on the works of Kawabata and three other postwar writers.

Gessel, Van C. *Three Modern Novelists: Soseki, Tanizaki, Kawabata.* New York: Kodansha International, 1993. Concentrates on Kawabata's detachment from modernity. Contains excellent biographical background and detailed notes but no bibliography.

Keene, Donald. *Dawn to the West: Japanese Literature of the Modern Era.* New York: Holt, Rinehart and Winston, 1984. Fifty-nine pages by this eminent critic and translator of Japanese fiction are devoted to Kawabata. Traces many of Kawabata's themes to his childhood experiences and gives the circumstances of publication and reception of his major works. Keene believes that Kawabata's main preoccupations were Japanese landscapes, Japanese women, and Japanese art. Contains a bibliography and extensive notation.

Morris, Mark. "Orphans." *The New York Times*, October 12, 1997. A review of *The Dancing Girl of Izu, and Other Stories*, discussing the title story and the "palm-of-hand" stories in the collection. Generally praises the stories as excellent examples of Kawabata's early short fiction.

Napier, Susan J. *The Fantastic in Modern Japanese Literature: The Subversion of Modernity*. New York: Routledge, 1996. Chapter 3, "Woman Lost: The Dead, Damaged, or Absent Female in Postwar Fantasy," examines Kawabata's fiction and includes a separate discussion of "Sleeping with the Dead: Kawabata's *House of Sleeping Beauties* and *One Arm*."

New Statesman. "The Month of Cherry Blossom." 135, no. 4806 (August 21, 2006): 46-48. An examination of Kawabata's life and work, describing how his traumatic childhood influenced his writings. Discusses Kawabata's writing style and assesses his place in Japanese literature.

Palmer, Thom. "The Asymmetrical Garden: Discovering Yasunari Kawabata." *Southwest Review* 74 (1989): 390-402. Examines Kawabata's small fictions called "palm-of-the-hand stories." Argues that these stories are stylized, intuitive studies of the tension, mystery, and beauty of being alive in an "ephemeral, unfathomable universe."

Petersen, Gwenn Boardman. *The Moon in the Water: Understanding Tanizaki, Kawabata, and Mishima*. Honolulu: University Press of Hawaii, 1979. An excellent critical study, emphasizing nuances of Japanese style and culture. Includes a chronology, a bibliography, and explanatory notes.

Schmidt, Roger. "A Literary History of Teeth." *Raritan* 29, no. 3 (Winter, 2010): 23-44. Examines the fascination with teeth and the representation of teeth in literature and painting. Analyzes Kawabata's novella *The House of the Sleeping Beauties*, Death in Veniceby Thomas Mann, and the short story "Berenice" by Edgar Allan Poe.

Starrs, Roy. *Soundings in Time: The Fictive Art of Kawabata Yasunari*. Richmond, England: Japan Library, 1998. A full-length study of Kawabata's fiction, chronicling how his life impacted his writings.

Swann, Thomas E., and Kinya Tsuruta. *Approaches to the Modern Japanese Short Story*. Tokyo: Waseda University Press, 1982. Analyzes "The Izu Dancer," *The House of the Sleeping Beauties*, and *One Arm*.

Ueda, Makoto. *Modern Japanese Writers and the Nature of Literature*. Stanford, Calif.: Stanford University Press, 1976. Devoting forty-five pages to Kawabata, this distinguished Japanese scholar emphasizes the elements of positive thought and action, vitality, beauty, and purity in Kawabata's work. Complemented by a bibliography and an index.

A. Owen Aldridge

L

Nikolai Leskov

Born: Gorokhovo, Oryol, Russia; February 16, 1831
Died: St. Petersburg, Russia; March 9, 1895

Other literary forms

The most memorable works of Nikolai Leskov (ny-ihk-UH-li lyih-SKOF) were in the shorter forms of fiction, he also attempted to meet the characteristic nineteenth century demand for "major works" with several novels, including *Nekuda* (1864; no way out) and *Na nozhakh* (1870-1871; at daggers drawn). Recognizing that novels were not his forte, he also tried to develop a different long form, the "chronicle," the major result of this effort being *Soboriane* (1872; *The Cathedral Folk,* 1924). Leskov also wrote one play, *Rastochitel'* (pb. 1867; the spendthrift), and a large body of journalistic nonfiction.

Achievements

Despite the continued output over more than thirty years of much high-quality fiction and despite his popularity among Russian readers, Nikolai Leskov's immense narrative talent went largely unrecognized by the critics of his time. He was to some extent eclipsed by his great contemporaries: Ivan Turgenev, Fyodor Dostoevski, and Leo Tolstoy. He was also adversely affected by the view that only big novels really "counted." Finally, he was caught in political cross fire and early in his career was virtually read out of literature by certain radical critics for his supposed retrograde views. Nevertheless, the first twelve-volume edition of his collected works (1889-1896) was a symbolic acknowledgment of his status as a classic, and that status has been more and more widely recognized in the decades since his death. New Russian editions of his works are frequent, and there is a substantial body of scholarship dealing with him. His reputation has also spread abroad, and many volumes of translations and of books about him have been published in English, French, German, Italian, Dutch, Swedish, and other languages. He is regarded as a major narrative artist and a thoughtful critic and moralist, a keen and often caustic observer of Russian society, and an especially penetrating and well-informed commentator on Russian religious life.

Biography

Nikolai Semyonovich Leskov was born on February 16, 1831, in Gorokhovo, a village in Oryol Province. His class background was varied and unusual. His father, a priest's son, had become a government official, receiving technical membership in the hereditary gentry when he attained the required rank. His mother was the daughter of an impoverished gentleman married to a merchant's daughter. Leskov grew up partly in the country, where his father had bought a tiny estate, and partly in the town of Oryol, where he attended the *Gymnasium*. He did not complete the course, however, dropping out to take a lowly civil service job, first in Oryol and later in Kiev, where an uncle was a university professor. Though in later years, by wide and incessant reading, he educated himself enough for several university degrees, the lack of a formal degree remained a sore point for Leskov. In Kiev, he worked in an army recruiting bureau, a position that obliged him to witness and take part in some of the gross injustices and cruelties of Czar Nicholas I's regime. In 1857, Leskov took leave from the service and entered private business, working as a factotum for an uncle by marriage, a Russified Scotsman who managed the estates of some wealthy grandees. This work necessitated much travel within Russia, and Leskov drew heavily on these experiences in his later writings, which exhibit a connoisseur's knowledge of colorful nooks and crannies of Russian provincial life. The success of a few early experiments with writing convinced Leskov to move to St. Petersburg with the intention of becoming a professional journalist.

Leskov obtained a position as editorial writer for a leading newspaper, but in 1862 he fell afoul of the radicals. At issue was an article in which he suggested that a recent series of fires in the capital might actually have been set by revolutionary arsonists, as had been rumored; he urged the police to make public its list of suspects so that popular anger would be deflected from the general body of university students. The threats and attacks on him infuriated Leskov, and he retaliated with an antiradical roman à clef, *Nekuda*, which incensed the radicals against him even more. He struck again with a second novel, *Na nozhakh*, and there are also antiradical sallies in *The Cathedral Folk*. In fact, despite all the anger and name-calling, Leskov's views on society and politics were consistently progressive. He called himself a "gradualist." He hailed the reforms of Czar Alexander II, especially the abolition of serfdom, and he favored equality of all citizens before the law, freedom of speech and of the press, and an independent judiciary. He was often discouraged, as were many others, by the enormity of the country's problems and the inadequacy of the resources, human and material, it could bring to bear on them. The

age-old demons of hunger and cold still haunted the lives of all too many Russians, making other problems seem trivial luxuries.

As early as 1862, Leskov began to publish short stories, and he soon became convinced that fiction was his true calling. Some of his most famous stories date from this early period; he went through no phase of literary maturation. In the 1870's, after the termination of his long war with the radicals, Leskov produced another series of classic stories. Many were published in the organ of the right-wing ideologue Mikhail Katkov, and for some time Leskov was considered an established member of the Katkov camp. In 1874, Leskov broke with Katkov, ostensibly because of high-handed editing of one of his stories; in fact, their political differences would eventually have led to rupture anyway.

Because of *The Cathedral Folk* and other works with clerical heroes, Leskov had been typed as Russian literature's chief expert on the clergy and its most ardent proponent of Orthodoxy, but actually, by 1875 his own religious development had led him to break with the Russian Orthodox Church. Meditation, rereading of the Gospels, and contacts with Protestants during an extended trip to Western Europe in 1875 brought about this major reorientation. "I no longer burn incense to many of my old gods," Leskov wrote to a friend. His alienation from Orthodoxy only deepened during the remainder of his life. Eventually he went so far as to assert categorically that Orthodoxy was "*not* Christianity." By that time, his ideas had "coincided," as he put it, with those of Tolstoy. Though he acknowledged the brighter light cast by Tolstoy's "enormous torch," Leskov had valid reason to claim that in many respects he became a Tolstoyan even before Tolstoy did. Leskov had suffered from heart disease for several years; he died suddenly on March 9, 1895.

ANALYSIS

Early in his career, Nikolai Leskov developed a characteristic form for his short stories: the "memoir"--half fiction, half fact--with a narrating "I" who regales the reader with tales of the colorful personalities and unusual events that he has experienced in his adventurous life. The border between "fiction" and "fact" is left intentionally blurred--an adroit illusionistic stratagem in an age that claimed the

Nikolai Leskov (Library of Congress)

label "realism." In "Ovtsebyk" ("The Musk-Ox"), for example, the narrator is presumably to be equated, at least by unsophisticated readers, with the actual author. Indeed, the story contains, in a lengthy digression, a lyrical account of what are believed to be the actual pilgrimages to monasteries on which the real Leskov as a boy accompanied his grandmother. The main focus of the story, however, is on the mature narrator's encounters with a character who illustrates Leskov's conviction of the futility of the radical intellectuals' efforts to stir the peasantry to revolt.

"THE STINGER"

"Iazvitel'nyi" ("The Stinger") evokes a theme Leskov touched on many times later--the difficulties encountered by the foreigner in Russia. An Englishman working as an estate manager in Russia comes to grief and brings disaster on his peasant charges through his inability to understand their mentality. The story avoids the impression of chauvinism, however, by the narrator's clear recognition that the downfall of the humane Englishman is caused not by any Russian superiority of soul but by the peasants' stubborn barbarism and backwardness.

"THE AMAZON"

"Voitel'nitsa" ("The Amazon") remains one of the classic examples of what the Russians call *skaz*, in which a frame narrator, more or less identifiable with the author, hears and records an inner, oral narrative, which is related in picturesque, "marked" language by a folk character. In this case, the inner narrator is one of Leskov's most colorful literary offspring, a St. Petersburg procuress. Catering to the secret sexual needs of the capital, she has entrée into all levels of society, and her language is a mixture of correspondingly disparate layers, the substratum of local dialect being overlaid with upper-class words, often of Western origin, but not always perfectly understood or accurately reproduced. Her motley language is in perfect harmony with her personality: vulgar, down-to-earth, cynical, yet endlessly vital.

"LADY MACBETH OF THE MTSENSK DISTRICT"

"Ledi Makbet Mtsenskogo uezda" ("Lady Macbeth of the Mtsensk District"), though somewhat atypical in technique, remains one of Leskov's most famous stories; it was the basis for the libretto of Dmitri Shostakovich's opera. Like Turgenev's earlier "Gamlet Shchigrovskogo uezda" ("Hamlet of the Shchigrovsky District"), the title oxymoronically situates a regal Shakespearean archetype in a maximally unromantic, provincial Russian setting; the story itself demonstrates that such human universals know no boundaries of place, time, or class. Presented in a more conventional omniscient-author format than the pseudomemoirs, "Lady Macbeth of the Mtsensk District" is a lurid tale of adultery and murder in a provincial merchant milieu.

In 1866, Leskov began the most ambitious literary enterprise of his career: to encapsulate in a single artistic work, class by class, the provincial Russia he knew so well. The life of a single town would serve as its microcosm. The huge project was never completed, but the section dealing with the clergy eventually emerged in 1872 as a full-length book, the celebrated novel *The Cathedral Folk*. This volume opened up for Russian literature a hitherto unexplored social territory--the provincial clergy--presented in a highly attractive form, with a winning mixture of sentiment and humor. Leskov insisted that *The Cathedral Folk* was not a novel, a genre he considered hackneyed in form and limited in content to man-woman "romance," but rather a "chronicle," a genre already made classic in Russian literature by Ivan Aksakov. The chronicle had the advantage for Leskov of legitimizing almost unlimited structural looseness because its only explicit guiding principle is the sequence of events in time.

Leskov sustained a high level of narrative art through his works of the early 1870's.

"The Sealed Angel"

"Zapechatlennyi angel" ("The Sealed Angel") is one of his most virtuoso performances in the art of *skaz*. Its narrator is a former Old Believer whose speech combines two highly marked linguistic stocks: the religious jargon of the "ancient piety" and the technical language of icon-painting. In this picturesque language, he relates a stirring, skillfully paced tale of his comrades' struggle to recapture a confiscated icon. "Ocharovannyi strannik" ("The Enchanted Pilgrim") is the life story of a monk purportedly encountered by the "author" on a steamer plying Lake Ladoga. This character, Ivan Severyanovich Flyagin, a former serf whose life has been a kaleidoscopic series of extraordinary adventures, is made to epitomize some of the essential qualities of the Russian national character as Leskov perceived it. These generalizations, however, are incarnated in a vivid sequential narrative that grips the reader from beginning to end.

"At the Edge of the World"

In "Na kraiu sveta" ("At the Edge of the World"), Leskov explored in fictional form an issue about which he had strong personal opinions: the missionary activities of the Orthodox Church among primitive tribes in Siberia. It was a risky subject, but Leskov cleverly camouflaged his subversive message by having his tale told by a sympathetic and unimpeachably Orthodox bishop. Intense experiences in Siberia convince the bishop that there is more natural Christianity among the heathen tribesmen than among all the lazy clerics and rapacious, hard-drinking officials then engaged in bringing "civilization" to Siberia. The bishop's tale includes one of the most powerful blizzard stories in Russian literature.

"Iron Will"

Religious subjects did not occupy Leskov exclusively. "Zheleznaia volia" ("Iron Will") again takes up the theme of the difficulties of the foreigner working in Russia. This time, a German engineer who carries Teutonic discipline and self-control to the point of absurdity is vanquished by the "doughy" formlessness of Russian life. Again, Leskov avoids any impression of chauvinism by showing that it is Russian weaknesses--insouciance, irresponsibility, and hedonism--that bring the German to his doom.

"Righteous" People

Even when not dealing directly with religious themes, Leskov took very seriously his responsibility to teach morality through literary art. He produced a whole cycle of portraits of *pravedniki* or "righteous ones," people who demonstrate that moral beauty and even sainthood are still possible in the tainted modern world. For all their differences of form and style, these stories are intended to function much like medieval hagiography: While entertaining the reader, they inculcate ideas of virtue. Among the most successful are "Odnodum" ("Singlethought"), "Nesmertel'nyi Golovan" ("Deathless Golovan"), and "Chelovek na chasakh" ("The Sentry"). Leskov took pugnacious pride in his ability to depict virtuous characters. "Show me another writer who has such an abundance of positive Russian types," he demanded. In some of these latter-day moralities, to be sure, artistic performance far overshadows morality. The left-handed hero of the famous "Levsha (Skaz o tul'skom kosom lefshe i o stal'noy blokhe)" ("Lefty: Being the Tale of the Cross-Eyed Lefty of Tula and the Steel Flea") is indeed a "righteous one"--not only a craftsman of extraordinary skill but also an (unappreciated) patriot. The principal impact of this classic *skaz* comes from its manner, not its message--its marvelous display of verbal acrobatics. "The Sentry," on the other hand, is cast in a more somber key. There, an omniscient author, moving through a series of terse chapters, builds up extraordinary tension by focusing on the hour-by-hour movement of the clock.

The memoir form

The memoir form employed in many of his stories had many advantages for Leskov. The memoir at least ostensibly transposed a "story" from the realm of fiction to that of history or fact, thus not only enhancing the illusion of reality but also avoiding the charge of deception and even lying that troubled such creators of imaginary realities as Tolstoy. Furthermore, reminiscences of the past provide both philosophical perspective and didactic impetus. The memories Leskov resurrects are drawn mainly from the period of his youth, the reign of Czar Nicholas I. It was not only enlightening to show Russians how far their country had evolved since those dark days, largely through the reforms of Czar Alexander II, but also disturbing to reveal how dangerously reminiscent of the tyrannies of Nicholas's time were the reactionary tendencies prevalent under Czar Alexander III. Finally, the ultimate paradox of the memoir form lies in the nature of art: Concrete images, even explicitly dated memories of a vanished past, may be a vehicle for universal, timeless truths about human nature and fate.

"THE TOUPEE ARTIST"

From Leskov's memoir tales of the era of Nicholas I, one could construct a comprehensive sociology of Russia as it was then. The country's most egregious evil was serfdom, and in "Tupeinyi khudozhnik" ("The Toupee Artist") Leskov created one of the most searing evocations in Russian literature of the horrors of that institution, especially its corrupting effect on both master and slave. For all his abhorrence of serfdom, however, Leskov never succumbed to the populist tendency to idealize the "people." From the beginning of his career to the end, he demonstrated again and again the "darkness" of the peasant world. Characteristically, the terrible famine of 1891-1892 inspired Leskov to recollect, in "Iudol" ("Vale of Tears"), the equally terrible famine of 1840. The comparison revealed that society had measurably advanced in that interval: Relief measures were now open, energetic, and public. However, the peasants were as benighted as ever, superstitious, and prone to senseless violence. By no means, however, are all of Leskov's pieces so somber. One of the most humorous is "Grabezh" ("A Robbery"), another superb example of *skaz*, which evokes the atmosphere of the prereform provincial merchant class as a setting for comedy.

DIDACTICISM

After his "conversion" to Tolstoyanism, Leskov placed even greater stress on the didactic function of literature. He plumbed a medieval Russian translation of the ancient Greek text *Synaxarion* for materials for an entire cycle of moralistic stories, slyly doctoring their plots to fit Tolstoyan specifications. The most substantial of these stories is "Gora" ("The Mountain"). In another *Synaxarion*-based fable, "Povest' o Fedorekhristianine i o druge ego Abrame zhidovine" (the story of Theodore the Christian and his friend Abraham the Hebrew), Leskov preached a much-needed sermon of tolerance and fraternity between Christians and Jews, thus demonstratively reversing the anti-Semitic tendency of some earlier stories.

SATIRE

Perhaps the most memorable and most artistically successful works of Leskov's late years were his satires of contemporary Russian society, which he viewed with deep pessimism, seeing little but corruption and folly among the elite and savagery in the masses. "Polunoshchniki" ("Night Owls") ridicules as a fraud (though without naming him) the highly touted Orthodox thaumaturge, Father Ioann of Kronstadt; the contrasting figure is a saintly Tolstoyan girl. In "Zimnii den'" ("A Winter's Day"), Leskov depicts another pure-hearted Tolstoyan girl alone in a degenerate milieu of police informers, extortionists, and sexual delinquents. Perhaps the greatest of these satires, Leskov's swan song, is "Zaiachii remiz" ("The March Hare"). Here, beneath a humorous camouflage--the narrator is a lovable Ukrainian lunatic who relates muddled memories of his adventurous youth--Leskov ridicules the "police paranoia" so pervasive in Russia (and elsewhere) at that time and later, the mentality that sees a subversive plotter lurking behind every bush. The camouflage, however, proved insufficient; no magazine editor was brave enough even to submit the story to the censors.

In his depiction of nineteenth century Russian life, Leskov's sociological range is broader than that of any other writer before Anton Chekhov. For those who can read him in Russian, his verbal pyrotechnics are simply dazzling, and his *skaz* technique has inspired many twentieth century imitators, notably Aleksei Mikhailovich

Remizov, Yevgeny Zamyatin, and Mikhail Zoshchenko. For non-Russians, such as Walter Benjamin, Leskov remains the storyteller par excellence, a practitioner of pure, uncontaminated narrative art. This description would doubtless have surprised and perhaps annoyed Leskov, who set greater store by his efforts as a moralist, but it seems to be the verdict of history.

OTHER MAJOR WORKS

LONG FICTION: *Nekuda*, 1864; *Oboidennye*, 1865; *Ostrovitiane*, 1866; *Na nozhakh*, 1870-1871; *Soboriane*, 1872 (*The Cathedral Folk*, 1924).

PLAY: *Rastochitel'*, pb. 1867.

NONFICTION: *Velikosvetskii raskol*, 1876-1877 (*Schism in High Society: Lord Radstock and His Followers*, 1995); *Evrei v Rossii: Neskol'ko zamechanii po evreis komu*, 1884 (*The Jews in Russia: Some Notes on the Jewish Question*, 1986).

MISCELLANEOUS: *Sobranie sochinenii*, 1889-1896; *Polnoe sobranie sochinenii*, 1902-1903 (36 volumes); *Sobranie sochinenii*, 1956-1958 (11 volumes).

BIBLIOGRAPHY

Andrews, Larry R. "Hugo's Gilliatt and Leskov's Golovan." *Comparative Literature* 46 (Winter, 1994): 65-83. Compares heroes in works by Leskov and Victor Hugo. Suggests that Leskov was influenced by native experience in creating the hero of his story "Deathless Golovan." Discusses the hybrid genre that Leskov develops in which his hero represents a specifically Russian virtue.

Benjamin, Walter. "The Storyteller: Reflection on the Works of Nikolay Leskov." In *Illuminations*. New York: Harcourt, Brace & World, 1968. In this general study of the short story as an oral and written genre, Benjamin discusses Leskov and the technique of *skaz* by linking it to the oral transmittance of stories either by foreign travelers or by natives familiar with their own oral tradition.

Eekman, Thomas A. "The Genesis of Leskov's *Soborjane*." *California Slavic Studies* 2 (1963): 121-140. Eekman traces the genesis of *Soboriane*, the first great novel about the life of the

Russian clergy, and examines its relationship to some of Leskov's stories that may have been planned for future volumes of the novel.

Grimstad, Knut Andreas. *Styling Russia: Multiculture in the Prose of Nikolai Leskov*. Bergen, Norway: University of Bergen, 2007. Argues that Leskov not only was a patriot who believed in the spiritual uniqueness of the Russian people but also was a writer who depicted ethnic identity as unstable. Examines the image of Russians in five of Leskov's major works, including "The Enchanted Pilgrim" and "The Sealed Angel." A difficult book to locate but worth the effort.

Howe, Irving. "Justice for Leskov." *The New York Review of Books* 34 (April 23, 1987): 32-36. Points out that Leskov has never been widely received outside Russia because he defies the rigid expectations that Westerners impose on Russian literature. Argues that in Leskov's work the faith of the rationalist and the faith of the pietist are parallel, and both faiths are secularized as part of national culture.

Lantz, K. A. *Nikolay Leskov*. Boston: Twayne, 1979. A brief biography and a general study of Leskov's works. A useful introductory overview for quick reference.

Lottridge, Stephen S. "Nikolaj Leskov and the Russian *Prolog* as a Literary Source." *Russian Literature* 3 (1972): 16-39. A detailed discussion of Leskov's *Prolog* tales of 1886-1891, which he patterned after Russian religious legends from various sources. Describes how these legends influenced him in writing his short fiction and in his overall development as a writer. Lottridge also touches upon Russian culture and literature in the second half of the nineteenth century.

_____. "Solzhenitsyn and Leskov." *Russian Literature TriQuarterly* 6 (1973): 478-489. Although Lottridge deals primarily with Aleksandr Solzhenitsyn, by commenting on Leskov's short stories he provides valuable insights into Leskov, whom he considers Russia's greatest pure storyteller.

McLean, Hugh. *Nikolai Leskov: The Man and His Art*. Cambridge, Mass.: Harvard University Press, 1977. The standard work in English on Leskov, satisfactory in every respect. McLean presents Leskov in both scholarly and interesting fashion, making Leskov less foreign to the English-speaking reader.

Sperrle, Irmhild Christina. *The Organic Worldview of Nikolai Leskov.* Evanston, Ill.: Northwestern University Press, 2002. Examines Leskov's consistent themes of movement and transformation in an "organic manner," or a manner in which death and rebirth alternate and affect each other. Discusses his disrespect for authority and his dislike of people's efforts to establish rules defining God's message of salvation.

Wachtel, Andrew. "The Adventures of a Leskov Story in Soviet Russia: Or, the Socialist Realist Opera That Wasn't." In *Epic Revisionism: Russian History*

and Literature as Stalinist Propaganda, edited by Kevin M. F. Platt and David Brandenberger. Madison: University of Wisconsin Press, 2006. Discusses efforts to "Sovietize" Leskov's short story "Lady Macbeth of the Mtsensk District" during the reign of Joseph Stalin, beginning with composer Dmitri Shostakovich's decision to write a Soviet Realist opera based on the story.

Hugh McLean
Updated by Vasa D. Mihailovich

CLARICE LISPECTOR

Born: Chechelnik, Ukraine, Soviet Union (now in Ukraine); December 10, 1925
Died: Rio de Janeiro, Brazil; December 9, 1977

PRINCIPAL SHORT FICTION

Alguns contos, 1952
Laços de família, 1960 (*Family Ties*, 1972)
A legião estrangeira, 1964 (*The Foreign Legion*, 1986)
Felicidade clandestina: Contos, 1971
A imitação da rosa, 1973
A via crucis do corpo, 1974
Onde estivestes de noite, 1974
A bela e a fera, 1979
Soulstorm, 1989 (includes stories from *Onde estivestes de noite* and *A via crucis do corpo*)

OTHER LITERARY FORMS

Clarice Lispector (leh-SPEHKT-ur) achieved almost equal success in the short story and the novel. Her novels include *Perto do coração selvagem* (1944; *Near to the Wild Heart*, 1990), *O lustre* (1946; the chandelier), *A cidade sitiada* (1949; the besieged city), *A maçã no escuro* (1961; *The Apple in the Dark*, 1967), *Água*

viva (1973; *The Stream of Life*, 1989), and *A hora da estrela* (1977; *The Hour of the Star*, 1986). Lispector also wrote a limited number of works for children, the most famous of these being *O mistério do coelho pensante* (1967; the mystery of the thinking rabbit) and *A mulher que matou os peixes* (1968; *The Woman Who Killed the Fish*, 1982). She also wrote nonfiction prose pieces.

ACHIEVEMENTS

It is no exaggeration to suggest that Clarice Lispector was one of the most original and singular voices to be found in twentieth century Western literature. In a career that spanned more than thirty years, Lispector produced a series of novels and short stories that not only helped lead a generation of Brazilian writers away from the limitations of literary regionalism but also gave Western literature a unique body of narrative work characterized by a highly personal lyrical style, an intense focus on the subconscious, and an almost desperate concern for the individual's need to achieve self-awareness. Though her works earned for her numerous literary awards during her lifetime, including an award she received in 1976 from the Tenth National Literary Competition for her contributions to Brazilian literature, Lispector is only beginning to receive the attention she deserves from critics and readers alike as her spellbinding narratives attract a growing international audience.

Biography

Clarice Lispector was born in the tiny Ukrainian village of Chechelnik on December 10, 1925, while her family was emigrating from the Soviet Union to Brazil. The family settled in the city of Recife in northeastern Brazil before moving to Rio de Janeiro, when Lispector was twelve years old. A precocious child, Lispector began composing stories as early as age six, even attempting to have them published in a local newspaper. A voracious reader in general and a devotee of writers such as Hermann Hesse and Katherine Mansfield in particular, it was a well-read Lispector who entered the National Faculty of Law in 1940, from which she was graduated in 1944. While in law school, she first took a job on the editorial staff of the Agência Nacional (a news agency) and then as a reporter for the newspaper *A noite*. It was while working for the newspaper that Lispector began writing her first novel, *Near to the Wild Heart*. It was during this period that she met Lúcio Cardoso, an innovative novelist who would serve as her mentor.

Lispector married Mauri Gurgel Valente in 1943 and, after being graduated from law school, accompanied him to his diplomatic post in Naples, Italy. She followed her husband to Berne, Switzerland, and to Washington, D.C., before separating from him in 1959 and returning with the couple's two children, Pedro and Paulo, to Rio de Janeiro, where she lived and wrote until she died of inoperable cancer only one day before her fifty-second birthday, in 1977.

Analysis

Although Clarice Lispector achieved fame as a novelist, as well as a writer of short stories, most critics agree that it is the shorter genre to which the author's storytelling talents, writing style, and thematic concerns are more suited. The bulk of Lispector's stories (particularly those published before 1970, for which the author is most famous) are intense and sharply focused narratives in which a single character (almost always female) is suddenly and dramatically forced to deal with a question concerning an integral part of her existence, and, by extension, on a thematic level, human existence itself. Save for a single act that prompts the character to look inward, there is little action in Lispector's stories, as the author seeks not to develop a plot but instead to capture a moment in her character's life. The central event of each story is not nearly so significant as the character's reaction to it, as he or she is shocked out of complacency and forced into a situation that will lead to self-examination and, in most cases, self-discovery.

Because Lispector's stories focus on the rarefied world of her characters' subconscious, many of the short narratives possess a dreamlike quality. Adding to this quality is the lyrical prose in which the stories are written, a prose in which not only every word but also the syntax seems to have been very carefully selected, frequently making the reading of the pieces more like reading poetry than prose.

In spite of the emphasis on the inner world of her characters and the subjective and highly metaphorical language, Lispector's stories still maintain contact with the world that exists beyond the confines of her characters' minds. While the characters' reaction to a given situation is intensely personal, the theme dealt with in that reaction is always a universal one, such as frustration, isolation, guilt, insecurity, uncertainty, or the coming-of-age, in other words, fundamental questions of human existence. Also, the events that trigger these questions in the characters' minds are everyday events of modern society. In this way, Lispector manages to examine both private and universal human concerns while still keeping her stories grounded firmly in reality.

Alguns contos

Lispector's first collection of short stories, *Alguns contos* (some stories), appeared in 1952 and was immediately praised by critics. In fact, this one collection not only placed the author among the elite of Brazil's writers of short fiction of the time but also showcased her as a leader among the new generation of writers in this genre.

Alguns contos contains six stories: "Mistério em São Cristóvão" ("Mystery in São Cristoóvão"), "Os laços de família" ("Family Ties"), "Começos de uma fortuna" ("The Beginnings of a Fortune"), "Amor" ("Love"), "A galinha" ("The Chicken"), and "O jantar" ("The Dinner"). All six narratives are lyrical pieces that focus on the act of epiphany--that is, a single moment of crisis or introspection from which the character emerges transformed. The story most representative not only of this collection but also of all Lispector's short fiction is "Love." Its central character, Ana, is a basically satisfied, middle-class wife whose world is stable, controlled, predictable. Taking the tram home from shopping one afternoon, however, she spots a blind man chewing gum. For some reason, Ana's world is totally and inexplicably shaken by the sight of him. Disoriented, she gets off the tram well past her stop and finds herself in the relatively primitive and hostile setting of a botanical garden. Feeling out of place and even threatened, she makes her way home and attempts to resume her normal patterns, but while she is happy to be back in the security of her predictable domestic lifestyle, she has been profoundly affected by her brief and confusing excursion into a world foreign to her own, and she wonders if she can ever be as happy in her world as she was before.

This story is a Lispector classic, both because it presents a single character whose normal existence is shaken by a seemingly insignificant event, an event that destroys the stable lifestyle of the character and takes him or her to a new level of awareness concerning life, and because, in large part as a result of its language, the story takes on a dreamlike quality that reflects the disoriented state of the protagonist. This story, however, is not unique; it is simply the best of a collection of six similar tales.

FAMILY TIES

As good as *Alguns contos* is, Lispector's next collection, *Family Ties*, surpasses it. In fact, this collection, the high point of Lispector's work in short fiction, is truly one of the masterpieces of Brazilian literature, regardless of period or genre.

Family Ties is composed of thirteen enigmatic stories, six of which had already appeared in *Alguns contos*, and once again the stories focus on the act of epiphany. For example, in "Preciosidade" ("Preciousness"), a girl going through puberty experiences both fear and confusion after an ambiguous encounter

with some boys. This story is particularly interesting in that the event that triggers the protagonist's reaction is never fully described to the reader. The reader sees the character's reaction to the event, however, and it is that reaction, full of anxiety and uncertainty, that constitutes the story, demonstrating that Lispector is not so concerned with the central event of her stories as she is with her characters' reactions to the event. By not providing details concerning the event in this particular story, she assumes that her reader's concerns are the same as her own. Another interesting story included in this collection is "O crime do professor de matemática" ("The Crime of the Mathematics Professor"), which recounts the story of a man who buries a stray dog he has found dead in a desperate attempt to relieve himself of the guilt he feels for having once abandoned his own dog. Finally, there is "Feliz aniversário" ("Happy Birthday"), the story of an old woman surrounded by her family on her eighty-ninth birthday. Rather than celebrate, she observes with disdain the offspring she has produced and, much to the shock of those in attendance, spits on the floor to show her lack of respect. All the stories in this collection present individual characters in turmoil and how each deals with this turmoil from the inside out.

THE FOREIGN LEGION

Lispector's preoccupation with personal growth through epiphany continues in her third collection of stories, *The Foreign Legion*. Here again, Lispector's protagonists grow as a result of some sort of circumstance in which they find themselves. There is a difference in this collection, however, as the author appears more overtly interested in an existentialist angle concerning her characters' reactions to the situations they confront. For example, in one story, "Viagem a Petrópolis" ("Journey to Petrópolis"), an old woman, told to leave the house in which she has been living, realizes that she is no longer of any use to the world and that she is not only alone but also unwanted. Her "growth," her manner of dealing with the truth surrounding her existence, is quite fatalistic, existentialist in nature: She dies. In stories in previous collections, the character might well have emerged with some sort of new insight that would have made life more interesting if not better. Here, however, the character merely dies, reflective perhaps of Lispector's growing interest in existentialist thought.

FELICIDADE CLANDESTINA

Lispector's fourth collection of stories, *Felicidade clandestina* (clandestine happiness), follows much the same track as her previous collections. The style is still lyrical, the focus is internal, and the thematic concerns are self-awareness and self-discovery. However, there are some differences between this collection and the earlier ones. In this work, for example, Lispector is more sharply ironic, at times bordering on an almost cruel humor. Also new, or at least intensified, is the author's criticism concerning the condition of both women and the elderly in modern society, concerns that are present in earlier works but never brought before the reader in such an obvious manner.

ONDE ESTIVESTES DE NOITE

After *A limitação da rosa* (the imitation of the rose), a collection of some of her best previously published stories, Lispector published *Onde estivestes de noite* (where were you last night?). While a number of the pieces included in this collection are indeed stories, fictions in the truest sense, several pieces are personal commentaries or reflections by the author, while still others seem to be a mixture of both fiction and commentary. In the pieces that are in fact stories, it is easy to see that Lispector has abandoned neither her thematic concerns nor her interior perspective. This is best seen in the story entitled "A procura de uma dignidade" (the search for dignity), which focuses on a nearly sixty-year-old woman who becomes lost in the maze of halls and tunnels that run beneath the mammoth soccer stadium of Maracanã. While wandering the halls in search of an escape route, she comes to the realization that she is not only physically lost but also psychologically lost, that it is indeed possible that her life up to this point, a life lived in large part through her husband, may have been a wasted, empty existence. By the end of the story, she is seeking an escape route from both her physical and her psychological confinements.

A VIA CRUCIS DO CORPO

A via crucis do corpo (the stations of the body) is somewhat of a departure from the stories previously published by Lispector--so much so, in fact, that it has confounded critics, most of whom admire it for its quality but nevertheless are left uncertain as to how to interpret it because it does not fit neatly into the Lispector mold. The two main differences between this collection and the others before it is that the stories in this collection contain not only eroticism but also open sexuality, as well as an ample dose of sardonic humor, neither of which is found, at least not to such a degree, in her earlier stories. There is, for example, the story "Miss Ruth Algrave," in which the protagonist is visited by an alien being from Saturn named IXTLAN. He makes love to her and in so doing raises Miss Algrave to a new level of existence. She quits her job and becomes a prostitute while awaiting her extraterrestrial lover's return. Then there is the story "O corpo" (the body), about a bigamist who is murdered by his two wives. Rather than going to the trouble of arresting the two women, the police tell them to leave the country, which they do. This collection is nothing if not entertaining.

A BELA E A FERA

Published after her death, *A bela e a fera* (the beauty and the beast) is a collection of Lispector stories put together by her friend Olga Borelli. Some of the stories included in this collection were written when Lispector was a teenager and had never been published. Given the time they were written, these stories and the collection in which they appear are potentially revealing for those interested in the evolution of Lispector the short-story writer. Unlike other collections such as *Alguns contos*, *Family Ties*, and *The Foreign Legion*, however, *A bela e a fera* is not considered a major collection of the author's stories but rather a literary curiosity piece.

Between 1952 and 1977, Clarice Lispector produced a consistent body of short narratives characterized by a sharpness of focus, a lyrical presentation, and a deep and sincere interest in the psychological growth of the individual human being. These three qualities, which pervade all the author's short stories, are the same ones which form her individual literary voice and which will guarantee that the popularity of her short fiction not only endures but also increases as more readers gain access to it.

OTHER MAJOR WORKS

LONG FICTION: *Perto do coração selvagem*, 1944 (*Near to the Wild Heart*, 1990); *O lustre*, 1946; *A cidade sitiada*, 1949; *A maçã no escuro*, 1961 (*The Apple in the Dark*, 1967); *A paixão segundo G. H.*, 1964 (*The Passion According to G. H.*, 1988); *Uma aprendizagem: Ou, O livro dos prazeres*, 1969 (*An Apprenticeship: Or, The Book of Delights*, 1986); *Água viva*, 1973 (*The Stream of Life*, 1989); *A hora da estrela*, 1977 (*The Hour of the Star*, 1986); *Um sopro de vida: Pulsações*, 1978.

NONFICTION: *Para não esquecer*, 1978; *A descoberta do mundo*, 1984 (*Discovering the World*, 1992); *Correio feminino*, 2006; *Entrevistas*, 2007; *Minhas queridas*, 2007.

CHILDREN'S LITERATURE: *O mistério do coelho pensante*, 1967; *A mulher que matou os peixes*, 1968 (*The Woman Who Killed the Fish*, 1982).

MISCELLANEOUS: *Seleta de Clarice Lispector*, 1975.

BIBLIOGRAPHY

Alonso, Cláudia Pazos, and Claire Williams, eds. *Closer to the Wild Heart: Essays on Clarice Lispector*. Oxford, England: Legenda, 2002. The essays in this collection examine autobiography, identity, gender, class, race, and nation in Lispector's works and chronicle her critical reception, including the early dissemination of her writings in the United States. One of the essays discusses "defamiliarization and deja vu" in her short-story collection *Family Ties*.

Cixous, Hélène. *Reading with Clarice Lispector*. Edited and translated by Verena Andermatt Conley. Minneapolis: University of Minnesota Press, 1990. A playfully profound deconstructionist reading of a number of Lispector's works, including the stories "Sunday Before Falling Asleep" and "The Egg and the Chicken." Argues that Lispector's texts, like Franz Kafka's, contain a secret that cannot be understood on a first reading.

Colvin, Michael. " Cannibalistic Perspectives: Paradoxical Duplication and the Mise en Abyme in Clarice Inspector's 'A menor mulher do mundo.'" *Luso-Brazilian Review* 41, no. 2 (2004): 84-95. An analysis of "The Smallest Woman in the World" that discusses the story's theme of cannibalism, its characters, and its "paradoxical duplication." Comments on Lispector's description of her character Pequena Flor (Little Flower) as the "smallest woman mature human being."

Fitz, Earl E. *Clarice Lispector*. New York: Twayne, 1985. An excellent, book-length study of Lispector's writings by the foremost authority on her works. Chapters include "Biography and Background," "The Place of Clarice Lispector in the History of Brazilian Literature," "Some Intrinsic Considerations: Style, Structure, and Point of View," "Novels and Stories," and "The Nonfiction Work." A must-read for serious readers of the Brazilian writer's fiction or for anyone seeking a deeper understanding of both Lispector and her works.

_____. *Sexuality and Being in the Poststructuralist Universe of Clarice Lispector: The Différance of Desire*. Austin: University of Texas Press, 2001. Demonstrates how Lispector's short stories, novels, and children's literature exemplify many of the issues central to poststructuralism, including the nature of language, truth, and meaning. Examines Lispector's fiction to describe how her style, structure, characters, themes, and sociopolitical conscience are influenced by poststructuralism.

Lindstrom, Naomi. "Clarice Lispector: Articulating Woman's Experience." *Chasqui* 8 (November, 1978): 43-52. Lindstrom examines the narrative voice employed in the short story "Love" (from *Family Ties*) and that voice's relationship to the emerging (and then fading) self-awareness of the protagonist, Ana. Lindstrom shows how the narrator first dominates the story, then allows Ana to speak more, before retaking the narrative in the end as the protagonist "finds no supportive response." An interesting slant on an important story in Lispector's body of work.

Marting, Diane E. "Clarice Lispector's (Post)modernity and the Adolescence of the Girl-Colt." *MLN* 113 (March, 1998): 433-444. Examines the story "Seco estudo de cavalos" in terms of poststructuralist theories. Argues that Lispector configures the unrepresentable as the Feminine and valorizes words as an approach to the object more than as a designation.

Moisés, Massaud. "Clarice Lispector: Fiction and Cosmic Vision." Translated by Sara M. McCabe. *Studies in Short Fiction* 8 (Winter, 1971): 268-281. A study of how the thematics of Lispector's short fiction reflect and support the author's "cosmic vision." Moisés discusses "the privileged moment," in which "the 'I' and the universe meet as if for the first time, framed in a halo of original 'purity,' causing the mutual discovery to become suspended in time, a vision of the most intimate part of reality, without deformation of thought or prejudice." An excellent article on the themes in Lispector's short fiction.

Moser, Benjamin. *Why This World: A Biography of Clarice Lispector*. Oxford, England: Oxford University Press, 2009. An insightful literary biography that ties Lispector's life to her works. Charts her development as a writer and discusses the various influences on her works, including what Moser argues are her "deep roots" in the Jewish mystical tradition.

Nunes, Maria Luisa. "Narrative Modes in Clarice Lispector's *Laços de família*: The Rendering of Consciousness." *Luso-Brazilian Review* 14 (Winter, 1977): 174-184. Citing several stories in *Family Ties*, Nunes examines how Lispector renders the consciousness of her protagonists, stating that the Brazilian writer employs "*style indirect libre* or narrated monologue, interior monologue, internal analysis including sensory impressions, direct discourse in the form of 'asides,' and the mixture of many of the above techniques." Nunes explains each technique and demonstrates how each is used by Lispector to reveal the inner workings of her characters. Insightful and very readable.

Peixoto, Marta. "*Family Ties*: Female Development in Clarice Lispector." In *The Voyage In: Fictions of Female Development*, edited by Elizabeth Abel, Marianne Hirsch, and Elizabeth Langland. Hanover, N.H.: University Press of New England, 1983. Peixoto focuses on the protagonists of the stories in *Family Ties*, arguing that these stories "can be read as versions of a single developmental tale that provides patterns of female possibilities, vulnerability, and power in Lispector's world." Peixoto examines the epiphanies experienced by the female protagonists of several stories, describing how these epiphanies allow the characters, although only momentarily, to break out of their "metaphoric prisons formed by their eager compliance with conforming social roles."

_____. *Passionate Fictions: Gender, Narrative, and Violence in Clarice Lispector*. Minneapolis: University of Minnesota Press, 1994. Written with a decidedly feminist bias, *Passionate Fictions* analyzes Lispector's frequently violent subject matter, juxtaposing it with her strange and original use of language. Special attention is paid to the nexus with Hélène Cixous and to the autobiographical elements of *The Stream of Life* and *A via crucis do corpo*.

_____. "Rape and Textual Violence in Clarice Lispector." In *Rape and Representation*, edited by Lynn A. Higgins and Brenda R. Silver. New York: Columbia University Press, 1991. An analysis of three short narratives focusing on how Lispector distances and naturalizes violence against women. The narratives move in a progression from a mild symbolic representation to a literal and farcical plot event, yet all three minimize violence.

Rosenberg, Judith. "Taking Her Measurements: Clarice Lispector and 'The Smallest Woman in the World.'" *Critique* 30 (Winter, 1989): 71-76. Claims that the core of "The Smallest Woman in the World" is sexual politics, a female fantasy of autonomy in competition with the male fantasy of domination. In the story, Little Flower is the object of male desire, the pure essence of femininity as refined, rare, valuable, and potent.

Keith H. Brower

Lu Xun

Born: Shaoxing, China; September 25, 1881
Died: Shanghai, China; October 19, 1936
Also known as: Chou Shu-jên, Lu Hsün, Zhou
Shuren

Principal short fiction

Ah Q zheng zhuan, 1921, serial; 1923, book (in
Nahan; The True Story of Ah Q, 1926)
Nahan, 1923 (*Call to Arms*, 1981)
Panghuang, 1926 (*Wandering*, 1981)
Gushi xinbian, 1935 (*Old Tales Retold*, 1961)
Ah Q and Others: Selected Stories of Lusin, 1941
Selected Stories of Lu Hsün, 1954, 1960, 1963
The Complete Stories of Lu Xun, 1981

Other literary forms

Lu Xun (loo shuhn) wrote prolifically throughout
his life, producing essays, verses, reminiscences, and
translations of other writers, as well as the short fiction
for which he is known in the West. The bulk of Lu
Xun's writing consists of polemical essays, written between 1907 and 1936, directed against aspects of Chinese culture and politics of which he disapproved.
These writings have been collected from time to time
and make up more than twenty volumes. Varying in
style, these essays were published in newspapers and
magazines and are journalistic in design compared to
the sensitive, imaginative, and carefully constructed
short stories.

Much of Lu Xun's writing as a whole consists of the
translations of foreign authors, a practice he continued
during his entire career. His translations were rendered
from Japanese or German, the only foreign languages
he knew. As early as 1903, he translated the science fiction of Jules Verne. In 1909, he and his brother, Zhou
Zuoren, collaborated in publishing *Yuwai xiaoshuo ji*
(collection of foreign stories). In two volumes, it

included works by Anton Chekhov, Leonid Andreyev,
Vsevolod Mikhaylovich Garshin, Henryk Sienkiewicz,
Guy de Maupassant, Oscar Wilde, and Edgar Allan
Poe. In the 1930's, Lu Xun translated works by many
other Russian authors. He and his brother also issued
an anthology of Japanese authors titled *Xiandai riben
xiaoshuo ji* (1934; a collection of modern Japanese
short stories), which included works by Mushakoji Saneatsu, Kunikida Doppo, Mori Ōgai, and Natsume
Sōseki.

Lu Xun also produced autobiographical sketches in
Zhaohua xishi (1928; *Dawn Blossoms Plucked at
Dusk*, 1976) and prose poems and reminiscences in *Ye
cao* (1927; *Wild Grass*, 1974). He composed verses in
wenyan (classical Chinese) as well as in the vernacular,
baihua. According to the late scholar and critic, Zian
Xia, Lu Xun's classical verses are superior to those in
the vernacular and are at least equal to his best *pai-hua*
prose. Lu Xun also kept copious diaries, which have
been published in facsimile in twenty-four volumes.

Lu Xun maintained a lifelong interest in graphic art.
In 1929, he published a volume of British wood engravings and another which featured the work of Japanese, Russian, French, and American artists. In 1934,
he published selected works of young Chinese artists in
Muke jicheng (the woodcut record). He also published,
in collaboration with Zheng Zhenduo, two collections
of traditional-style stationery by the seventeenth century artist Wu Zhengyan. He developed a strong interest in the wood engravings of socialist artists in
Western Europe and the Soviet Union, and he published books on the form.

Achievements

Lu Xun is generally regarded as one of the most
important of modern Chinese writers. His short
story "Kuangren riji" ("The Diary of a Madman"),
modeled on Nikolai Gogol's story of the same title,
was the first Chinese story written in the style of

Western fiction and Lu Xun's first story written in the modern vernacular. His reputation as a short-fiction writer rests primarily on two volumes of stories written between 1918 and 1925, *Call to Arms* and *Wandering*. After these, Lu Xun wrote little fiction. His best-known story is the novella *The True Story of Ah Q*.

Lu Xun developed a narrative style of pointing without commentary, allowing silence to generate meaning within the form of the short story, a method reminiscent of Poe, who may have influenced Lu Xun's sense of structure. Like many Chinese writers of short fiction, Lu Xun was influenced by Western masters of the form, especially those whom he translated. It was Lu Xun, however, who pioneered the movement in short fiction that helped launch a new literary era in China, and his assimilation of Western ideas became the new reality in Chinese fiction.

Lu Xun's tales often tend toward satire, and his sense of irony is masterful and pervasive. Reminiscent of the traditional Chinese painter, Lu Xun renders a whole person from a few deft strokes and evokes atmosphere without elaborate detail. Considered a pioneer of modern Chinese realism, he has been translated more than any other modern Chinese writer. Because he believed that the literature of a nation reflected its character or spirit, he also believed that in order for his country to emerge from centuries of torpor there must be a reawakening in its literature. The prevailing view of Lu Xun has been that he was a writer who considered literature to be propaganda for social ends; Mao Zedong called him "not only a great writer but also a great thinker and a great revolutionist." It is true that Lu Xun was fervently committed to his nation's future and the development of Chinese society, but his fiction is redeemed from didacticism by his humanism and the high quality of his art.

The communists attacked Lu Xun at first as a bourgeois writer but later accepted him as a proletarian. After they established the Chinese People's Republic in Beijing, they considered him to be the Maxim Gorky of China. Mao Zedong referred to him as a "national hero." In 1939, the Communists established the Lu Xun Academy of Arts in Yan'an. Following the fall of Shanghai to the Japanese in 1937, the magazine *Lu Zun*

Feng (Lu Xun's style) was started by a group of Communist writers. After Communist troops shattered the Chinese Nationalist defenses of Shanghai in 1949 and occupied the city, the Lu Xun Museum was established in Beijing. Lu Xun's tomb is located in northeast Shanghai.

Many books and articles have been written about Lu Xun. For his pioneering efforts in restructuring the Chinese short story and in developing vernacular speech into a new form of written prose, Lu Xun deserves to be considered the leader of the Chinese Literary Renaissance of 1917-1937. As a writer of short stories, however, he has formidable contenders in such colleagues as Chang Tianyi, Shen Congwen, and Mao Dun.

Biography

Lu Xun, the pen name of Zhou Shuren, was born on September 25, 1881, into an upper-middle-class family in the village of Shaoxing, Zhejiang Province, China. He was the eldest of the four sons of Zhou Fengyi (or Zhou Boyi), an old-style Chinese scholar, and Lu Rui, the daughter of a minor government official. Of Lu Xun's three younger brothers, Zhou Zuoren became a writer, Zhou Jianren became a scientist, and the youngest died of pneumonia at the age of five.

The Zhou family was prosperous until 1893, when Lu Xun's grandfather, Zhou Fuqing, a *jinshi* (entered scholar), was convicted of attempting to bribe a provincial examination official and sentenced to be beheaded. His execution, however, was postponed until he was fortunate enough to be released from prison under a general amnesty. This scandal and the prolonged illness and death of Lu Xun's father in 1896 brought the family to the brink of poverty.

Lu Xun's formal education began at the age of five under the tutelage of his granduncle Chao-lan, who taught him to love books. Grandfather Fuqing, always unorthodox, required him to read history but encouraged him to read popular novels as well. At the age of eleven, Lu Xun was enrolled in a private school supported by the Zhou clan, where he was obliged to study the Confucian classics known as the Four Books.

Although as late as 1898 Lu Xun was still practicing the writing of the *baguwen*, or the eight-legged essay, and the poetry required for the civil service examinations, he decided to pursue an unorthodox path to social advancement. He enrolled in the Kiangnan Naval Academy at Nanjing. Dissatisfied with the poor quality of education offered there, however, at the end of the year he returned to Shaoxing.

Deciding now to attempt the orthodox route, he presented himself at the Kuanji District examination for the *xiucai* (flowering talent) degree. Although he passed this examination, he never sat for the prefectural examination. Instead, he returned to Nanjing and transferred from the Naval Academy to the School of Mines and Railroads attached to the Kiangnan Army Academy. He was graduated in 1901.

Lu Xun obtained a government scholarship to study medicine in Japan. Arriving in Tokyo in 1902, he entered the Kōbun Institute to study the Japanese language. After being graduated from Kōbun in 1904, he enrolled in the medical school at Sendai, Honshū. In 1906, however, he received a severe shock. In

Lu Xun (Library of Congress)

viewing a newsslide of the Russo-Japanese War, he witnessed a bound Chinese man awaiting execution as a spy for the Russians while a crowd of Chinese stated indifferently at him. As a result, Lu Xun was convinced that the soul and not the body of China needed curing. Withdrawing from medical school, he returned to Shaoxing. There, he submitted to an arranged marriage to a woman he never afterward regarded as his wife. Then, in company with his brother, Zhou Zuoren, he returned to Japan, this time resolved to devote himself to literature.

The brothers spent their time reading, writing, and translating foreign literature. Although able to read German and Japanese, Lu Xun used these languages mainly to gain access to the cultures of the "oppressed peoples" of Russia, Eastern Europe, and the Balkans. He also composed essays in classical Chinese on a variety of cultural topics. Near the end of his stay in Japan, the brothers published their *Yuwai xiaoshuo ji* (collection of foreign stories), rendered in classical Chinese. Succeeding in obtaining a teaching position at the Zhejiang Normal School at Hangzhou, he returned to China in 1909.

Lu Xun quit teaching at Hangzhou in 1910 to return to Shaoxing to serve as the school principal. On October 10, 1911, the Republican Revolution, led by Sun Yat-sen, burst forth, throwing the country into turmoil. With the overthrow of the monarchy in 1911, Lu Xun composed his first short story--in classical Chinese--which was entitled "Huaijiu" ("Remembrances of the Past") when published in 1913.

When Sun Yat-sen resigned the presidency of China in favor of Yuan Shikai, Lu Xun was called to Beijing to serve in the ministry of education. Soon disgusted with reform party politics, he buried himself in the study of ancient Chinese texts and inscriptions and developed a strong interest in the history of Chinese literature. This latter interest resulted in his famous volume *Zhongguo xiaoshuo shilue* (1923-1930; *A Brief History of Chinese Fiction*, 1959).

Awakened to creative activity by the Literary Revolution of 1917, the following year Lu Xun wrote his first short story in *baihua*, or colloquial Chinese, "The Diary of a Madman," employing Western technique. From this time until 1926, he would write twenty-five such stories that would appear in two collections--fourteen stories in *Call to Arms* and eleven in *Wandering*. His novella *The True Story of Ah Q* brought him national recognition. After 1926, however, Lu Xun wrote only brief satirical tales collected in *Old Tales Retold*, devoting himself mostly to writing polemical essays.

Following the massacre of demonstrating students in Beijing on March 18, 1926, by the Duan Qirui government, Lu Xun was looked upon as a dangerous radical and was forced into hiding. Leaving Beijing, he joined the faculty of Amoy University. In 1927, he moved to Sun Yat-sen University in Guangzhou, where he taught and served as academic dean. Resigning in the spring, Lu Xun and Xu Guangping, a former student who had become his common-law wife, left Guangzhou for Shanghai.

In 1930, Lu Xun, having studied Marxism-Leninism, lent his name to the founding of the League of Left Wing Writers. He joined the International Union of Revolutionary Writers. In 1933, he became associated with the Far Eastern Conference against Imperialist War. A close friend of Chu Qiubai, former general secretary of the Communist Party, Lu Xun provided him with a safe haven from arrest and acted as a courier for the Communists. He himself lived in constant fear of arrest and possible execution.

Although by 1930 Lu Xun had apparently concluded that the Chinese Communist Party rather than the Kuomintang was the only viable force to reform China, he neither accepted Marxist-Leninist dogma fully nor became a member of the Communist Party. Although from 1927 until his death from tuberculosis on October 19, 1936, Lu Xun produced no original creative work, he has continued to be viewed by many Chinese as their nation's leading writer of short fiction in the twentieth century.

Analysis

Nearly all Lu Xun's short stories were written between 1918 and 1925. The time they deal with is from the eve of the Republican Revolution of 1911 until the May Fourth movement of 1919. The characters they present are mostly women whom Lu Xun considers victims of traditional Chinese society--he calls them "unfortunates"--whether a failed *litteratus*, a *maudit*

révolté (cursed rebel), an unlucky ricksha puller, or a young village woman plagued by widowhood. Although Lu Xun seems more comfortable as a writer when he deals with the downtrodden, he also sometimes concerns himself with certain members of the ruling class, the scholar-gentry either in or out of office, who are opportunists, compromisers, or oppressors of the common people. Although the stories usually focus on a single protagonist and expose either his or her misery or hypocrisy and cruelty, sometimes they also condemn the entire Chinese populace. This view is developed in "The Diary of a Madman," in which the protagonist goes beyond tradition and sees the people as cannibals--the weak devouring the strong. Lu Xun was a moralist who viewed contemporaneous China as a sick and degenerate society badly in need of treatment. Ironically, the young man's concern for the health of China gains for him the diagnosis of "mad."

Lu Xun is usually termed a "realist" as a writer of short fiction. Communist critics call him a "critical realist," a "militant realist," and even a Socialist Realist. Although Lu Xun sought to make his stories conform to reality as he had experienced it and wanted his readers to credit them as based on the truth, he was not realistic in the sense of the fiction of the great European exponents of nineteenth century realism and naturalism, such as Ivan Turgenev, Gustave Flaubert, and Émile Zola, in whom he never showed any interest. His realism was very personal and highly subjective. He was not interested in the material but in the spiritual. In his short stories, he probes into the human spirit as it has been affected by environment and tradition. If one considers the men he took for his intellectual mentors, Thomas Henry Huxley, Max Stirner, Søren Kierkegaard, Henrik Ibsen, Friedrich Nietzsche, Georg Brandes, Lord Byron, Gogol, and Andreyev, one sees a curious thing: The majority are associated with the anti-Romantic spirit of individualism, and only two of them, Huxley and Brandes, with the anti-Romantic spirit of positivism. Lu Xun had an ironic view of reality that was highly subjective and tempered by strong Romantic elements. It was this view that attracted him to writers such as Gogol and Andreyev, both of whom attempted the fusion of Romanticism and realism and then the fusion of realism and Symbolism, and Lu Xun adopted similar practices. Therefore, as a writer, Lu Xun might be more usefully termed a subjective realist or an expressionist rather than a social realist; he was surely not a Socialist Realist. One wonders how he would have taken Mao's Yan'an Forum Talks of 1942. A satirist must exaggerate, draw sharp contrasts between good and evil. Although he exposed the faults of Chinese society, Lu Xun never offered any remedy except that it should honor the individual and free the spirit.

Lu Xun's short stories, for the most part, grew out of his personal experience. He enhanced this subjectivity by the power of his imagination and taut artistic skill. His stories are characterized by their brevity but above all by their compactness of structure and their pithy, sharp style, in which each word is needed and apposite. His prose is strongly imagistic, especially in its visual appeal. Lu Xun seldom employs the figures of metaphor or simile; when he does use such a figure, however, it is usually highly effective. He makes use of historical and literary allusion, and one or more such allusions are to be found in the vast majority of his stories. He sometimes resorts to symbolism. Dialogue is usually kept to a minimum. Irony is a pervasive element in nearly all Lu Xun's stories, with satire a frequent weapon used in defense of individual freedom. He shows unusual skill in fusing an action with its scene. Although description is suppressed, atmosphere emerges strongly.

Lu Xun was a highly sensitive man with a strong sense of justice. He was not content to endure evil with passive indifference. A sedentary literary man (a *wenren*), he admired action more than anything else but had no heart for it himself. An acute observer of human nature, but one with a limited range, he had a special knack for sketching what he saw with deft, swift strokes of his pen and with a minimum of words. He was a very gifted writer of short fiction but a mediocre thinker. His thinking fell short of complete clarity. A "wanderer" in the wasteland of hopes and broken dreams, he was at first inspired by Charles Darwin and Friedrich Nietzsche but misunderstood both. His later excursions into Karl Marx and Vladimir Ilich Lenin curtailed his imagination, aroused in him resentment and prejudice, and ran counter to his natural instinct for

freedom, independence, and appreciation of individual worth. It was unfortunate that as a creative writer he thought that changing the face of China was more important than painting its portrait. As an individual, he could do little about the former but could have done much about the latter. He never realized this truth until the last year of his life.

Perhaps Lu Xun's major weakness as a writer of fiction is his fondness for nostalgia, his lapses into sentimentality, and his inability always to deal fairly with persons other than the downtrodden. If in his short fiction Lu Xun had depicted humanity as he found it in all its richness, splendor, and nobility together with its poverty, stupidity, and moral degeneracy--in a spirit that extended charity to all and with a sense of the kinship of all human beings that included tolerance and a readiness on his part to pardon, leaving moral lessons for others to proclaim and class distinctions for others to condemn--he might have been a great writer rather than simply a gifted one whose full potential as a creative artist was never realized.

"The Diary of a Madman"

Of Lu Xun's stories collected in *Call to Arms*, "The Diary of a Madman," although it made its author prominent, is not one of his best. The first story to be written in the Western manner, it is more clever in conception than effective as a well-constructed tale. As C. T. Hsia, a judicious critic, has pointed out, the story's weakness lies in the author's failure to provide a realistic setting for the madman's fantasies.

"Kong yiji"

The story "Kong yiji," about a failed scholar who has become a wine bibber at a village tavern, where he is the butt of jokes, is a much stronger story than "The Diary of a Madman." Kong yiji has studied the classics, but he has failed to pass even the lowest official examination. With no means of earning a living, he would have been reduced to beggary except for his skill in calligraphy, which enabled him to support himself by copying. He loved wine too much, however, and he was lazy. When he needed money, he took to stealing books from the libraries of the gentry. For such actions he was frequently strung up and beaten. After being absent from the tavern for a long time, he reappears, dirty and disheveled, his legs broken. Partaking of warm wine, he is the butt of the jokes and taunts of the tavern yokels. He departs from the tavern, but he is never seen again. It is presumed that he has died. As a commentary on the Chinese social order, the story presents a man who is a part of the detritus left by the examination system. At the same time, he must take responsibility for his own weaknesses of character. In addition, the story shows how cruel and unfeeling people can be to those who are less fortunate than they.

"MEDICINE"

"Yao" ("Medicine") is another powerful story. It shows especially careful construction and makes effective use of symbolism. The story concerns two boys who are unknown to each other but whose lives follow equally disastrous courses to become linked after their deaths. Hua Xiaozhuan is the tubercular son of a tea shop owner and his wife. The boy is dying. Anxious to save his life, the parents are persuaded to pay a packet of money for a *mantou* (steamed bread roll) soaked with the blood of an executed man, which is alleged by tradition to be a sure cure for tuberculosis. The beheaded man is young Xia You, the son of the widow Xia. A revolutionary seeking the overthrow of the Manchu or Qing Dynasty, he was betrayed to the authorities by his conservative Third Uncle, who collected a reward for his treason. Thus, the blood of a martyr and hero, a representative of the new order, is used in the service of a superstitious and useless medical cure. If the parents are ignorant and superstitious, they also truly love their son and try by all the means they know to save him, but he dies, regardless. Nobody has sought to save Xia You from execution; indeed, all the customers at the tea shop highly approve of his arrest and beheading. His widowed mother, who loved him dearly, was powerless to help her son.

Influenced by his admiration for the Russian writer Andreyev, Lu Xun sought to emphasize the story's purport through the use of symbolism. Since the two boys in the story are linked in the action purely by accident, Lu Xun reinforces the connection through their surnames, "Hua" and "Xia," which as "Huaxia" literally means "glorious and extensive"; this compound is also an ancient name for China. It is a story of the opposition between the old China--the China of darkness, superstition, and lethargy under foreign rulers--and the new China--the China trying to emerge into the light, the China of the awakened, of the revolutionary. The symbolism is especially dense at the conclusion of the story, when the two mothers meet at the graves of their sons, who are buried opposite each other. Natural flowers are growing on the grave of the Hua boy, but on Hsia Yu's grave has been placed a wreath of red and white flowers. When Xia You's mother perceives the wreath, she cannot understand its presence. She believes that her son has wrought a miracle as a sign of the wrong done to him, that he desires that his death be avenged. Perplexed, she looks around her but sees only a crow perched on a leafless bough. She tells her son that heaven will surely see that a day of reckoning will come. Uncertain of his presence, though, she requests him to make the crow fly onto his grave as a sign to her that he is really there. The crow remains still perched on its bough, as if made of iron. Mrs. Xia and Mrs. Hua have, in their mutual grief, formed a bond of sympathy. Mrs. Hua now suggests that the two of them might as well leave for home. As they depart, they hear a loud caw behind them. Startled, they turn their heads to look behind them. They see the crow stretch its wings and fly off toward the horizon.

THE TRUE STORY OF AH Q

The *True Story of Ah Q* is Lu Xun's longest and most important story. It originally appeared serially on a weekly basis in the Beijing *Chenbao* (weekly post) in its Sunday supplement; these circumstances may have been responsible for its rambling, episodic plot and other literary defects. The story made a powerful impact, however, on its Chinese audience. It saw in the protagonist, Ah Q, what Lu Xun wanted it to see: the embodiment of all the weaknesses of the Chinese national character, which just prior to the fall of the Qing Dynasty had constituted a national disease. Ah Q is a homeless peasant who lives in the temple of the tutelary god of Wei village. Because no one knows his true surname, the narrator calls him simply "Ah Q" because the foreign letter "Q" resembles a man's head with a queue, or pigtail, hanging down. Thus, "Q" is a pictograph of every Chinese man during the rule of the Manchus because the conquerors required Chinese men to shave their heads and wear queues. Ah Q is a Chinese Everyman.

Ah Q is a dunce whose foolish actions result in repeated humiliating defeats. He just as repeatedly glosses over these defeats by convincing himself that, if he has been physically overcome, he has nevertheless won a "spiritual victory." Ah Q is a perfect antihero, but he is an unusual one in that he is, as William A. Lyell, Jr., has pointed out, "victimizer as well as victim." He is bullied and mistreated by those stronger than he, but he, in turn, bullies and mistreats those who are weaker. Like the other inhabitants of Wei village, he follows the Chinese social principle: *Pa chang qiruo* (fear the strong, bully the weak). He is opposed to revolutionaries until he learns that the village power elite is terrified of them. He tries to join them, but they arrest him for thievery. He is condemned to death, not by the sword but by the rifles of a firing squad. He tries to be brave, but, his soul ripped, he is about to utter, "Help." However, as Lu Xun writes, "Ah Q never said that. Blackness had already covered his eyes. He heard the shots ring out and felt his body scatter like a heap of dust."

Ah Q may personify the Chinese social sickness of his time. According to the perceptive scholar, Lee Oufan Lee, Ah Q's life revolves around subsistence in a world that he does not understand. He is only a face in the crowd without spirit, interior self, or self-consciousness. His negative qualities combine to depict a slave mentality. He may suggest how the people of Wei village responded to the Republican Revolution of 1911. He suggests as well why the revolution eventually failed.

WANDERING

On the whole, the stories collected in Lu Xun's second volume *Wandering* are superior to those of his first. He himself favored them and pointed out the reasons for their superiority: his having outgrown his foreign influences, his more mature technique, his more incisive delineation of reality, and his having cooled his personal anger and sorrow. Of the eleven stories included in *Wandering*, three of them are particularly noteworthy: "Zhufu" ("The New Year's Sacrifice"), "Zai jiulou shang" ("Upstairs in a Wineshop"), and "Lihun" ("Divorce").

"THE NEW YEAR'S SACRIFICE"

"The New Year's Sacrifice" is the story of the tragic lot and cruel treatment accorded a peasant woman, Xiang Linsao, who, widowed at twenty-six, is forced to remarry against her will, is then widowed a second time, has her infant son carried off by a wolf, and is hired as a servant by a scholar-gentry family named Lu. The head of the Lu family, Hanlin, the neo-Confucian scholar Fourth Uncle Lu, thinks that Xiang Linsao, as a twice-married widow, is impure and unfit to touch any food or implement connected with the family ancestral sacrifices. Despite her religious efforts to atone for her "sin," she is rejected by the Lus and turned into a beggar. She dies in poverty just as the Lus are about to invoke a New Year's blessing. The news of her death annoys Fourth Uncle Lu. In anger, he berates her for dying at such an unpropitious time. He remarks to his wife, "You can tell from that alone what a rotten type she is." Thus, this renowned neo-Confucian scholar and rationalist reveals himself to be an inhumane, unfeeling, superstitious, rigid traditionalist whose narrow and inflexible morality is the executioner of a good, simple-hearted peasant woman. The twice-widowed woman is the victim of tradition and superstition. Being a widow, she must bear the stigma of carrying the ghosts of her two husbands; in fact, it may even be believed that she caused their deaths. When she asks the noncommittal narrator if he believes a person's soul goes on after death, she seems to be clutching for meaning in a realm of existence beyond the world she has known, where she can be reunited with her child who was eaten by wolves.

"UPSTAIRS IN A WINESHOP"

"Upstairs in a Wineshop" is the story of the chance reunion one winter evening of two former friends and colleagues upstairs in a village wine shop, back home after a ten-year interval. The story is obviously autobiographical and the unnamed narrator a mask for Lu Xun himself. The narrator arrives at the wine shop alone. He goes upstairs, orders wine and some dishes, and sits drinking and eating while looking out over the snow-covered courtyard outside. The atmosphere here is beautifully evoked by Lu Xun--inside warm wine and food, outside snow. The snow introduced at the beginning, the symbolism of the crimson camellias blossoming in the snow (suggesting the homeliness of the south as opposed to the strangeness of the north), and the snow and wind at the end that wash away the bittersweet taste of the remembrances of the past give to this story a special pictorial quality in respect to its text--reminiscent of those scholar-painters who did *Wenrenhua* (literary men's painting), harmonizing text with picture. When the narrator's old friend and colleague Lü Weifu appears by chance, each is surprised at meeting the other, and they greet each other warmly. Both recollect their younger days when they were avid reformers who had rejected the Old Learning in favor of the New. Now they are both middle-aged. To his dismay and disappointment, the narrator learns that his friend is changed, has lost his nerve, and has rejoined the Confucian establishment. He lives with his mother in a northern province where he tutors the children of a prosperous family in the Confucian classics. He also deceives his mother by making up white lies in order to shield her from a painful reality. Lü Weifu has given up "pulling the beards of the gods."

Perhaps the most remarkable feature of "Upstairs in a Wineshop" is Lu Xun's seeming ambivalence of his anti-Confucian position. As C. T. Xia has observed, although Lu Xun undoubtedly intended to present Lü Weifu as a weak-kneed, broken man, "the kindness and piety of Lü Weifu, however pathetic, also demonstrate the positive strength of the traditional mode of life, toward which the author must have been nostalgically attracted in spite of his contrary intellectual conviction." Xia concludes that the story, then, with an irony contrary to its author's intention, "is a lyrical confession of his own uncertainty and hesitation."

"Divorce"

"Divorce" provides a vivid portrait of a tough, uncouth, rebellious country girl as well as a picture of how the power structure of traditional Chinese society works in a rural setting to cow such a female rebel. As the story opens, a family feud has been going on for three years between the Xhuangs and the Shis. The girl, Aigu, born a Chuang, married young Mr. Shi. After a time, however, she and her husband did not get along and his parents disliked her. Soon, her husband took up with a young widow and informed his wife that he no longer wanted her. Since that time, she has been living

with her father, Zhuang Musan, and her six brothers. For the past three years, the two feuding families have entered into negotiations several times without any settlement being reached. Preferring to be an unloved wife with honor rather than a dishonored divorcée, Aigu has insisted each time that her husband take her back despite an offer of money by the Shis to effect a separation, and until now her father has supported her position. Father and daughter are now traveling by boat to the village of Pang, where another meeting between the Shis and the Zhuangs has been arranged by Old Gentleman Wei in a final effort to produce a settlement of the family feud. When they arrive, Wei announces that Seventh Master, a prestigious urban relative of the Weis, visiting him for the New Year's celebration, has agreed to preside over Aigu's case and will attempt to persuade the Zhuangs to accept the terms of divorce proposed, with which he, Wei, already agrees. To make the settlement more agreeable, Seventh Master has persuaded the Shis to add ten dollars to the sum of money already offered to the Zhuangs. Although Aigu is confident that her father will again reject the divorce proposal, she becomes alarmed when he remains silent. In desperation, she speaks out in her own defense.

Seventh Master reminds her, however, that a young person ought to be more compliant in adjusting to reality, for "compliance produces riches." Furthermore, he informs her, because her in-laws have already dismissed her from their presence, she will have to suffer a divorce, regardless of whether there is a money settlement. At this point, Young Shi takes the opportunity to remind Seventh Master that if Aigu acts in this manner here, she must have acted much worse in his father's home. He complains that at home she always referred to his father and to himself as "beasts." Indeed, she even called him a *sishengzi* (bastard). Aigu breaks in to deny this charge and counters that he called her a *pinchuan* (bitch).

At Aigu's response, Seventh Master cries out a command: "Come in!" Silence immediately follows. Aigu is thunderstruck. A servant enters and hurries up to the dignitary, who whispers some order to him which nobody can understand. The man replies: "Yes, venerable sir," and departs. Fearfully, Aigu blurts out to Seventh Master that she always meant to accept his decision. Wei is delighted. The families exchange wedding certificates and money. The servant enters and gives something to Seventh Master, who puts his hand to his nose and then sneezes; the whispered order was for snuff. Zhuang Musan and Aigu leave after refusing to take a cup of New Year's wine.

Other major works

POETRY: *Yecao*, 1927 (*Wild Grass*, 1974).

NONFICTION: *Zhongguo xiaoshuo shilue*, 1923-1930 (*A Brief History of Chinese Fiction*, 1959); *Refeng*, 1925; *Huagai ji*, 1926; *Fen*, 1927; *Huagai ji xubian*, 1927; *Eryi ji*, 1928; *Zhaohua xishi*, 1928 (*Dawn Blossoms Plucked at Dusk*, 1976); *Erxin ji*, 1932; *Sanxian ji*, 1932; *Wei ziyou shu*, 1933; *Jiwai ji*, 1934; *Nan qiang beidiao ji*, 1934; *Zhun fengyue tan*, 1934; *Huabian wenxue*, 1936; *Qiejieting zawen er ji*, 1937; *Qiejieting zawen mobian*, 1937; *Qiejieting zawen*, 1937; *Lu Xun riji*, 1951.

TRANSLATIONS: *Yuwai xiaoshuo ji*, 1909 (with Zhou Zuoren; of works by Anton Chekhov, Leonid Andreyev, Vsevolod Mikhaylovich Garshin, Henryk Sienkiewicz, Guy de Maupassant, Oscar Wilde, and Edgar Allan Poe); *Xiandai Riben xiaoshuo ji*, 1934 (of Mushakoji Saneatsu's, Kunikida Doppo's, Mori Ōgai's, and Natsume Sōseki's short stories).

EDITED TEXT: *Muke jicheng*, 1934 (2 volumes).

MISCELLANEOUS: *Selected Works of Lu Hsün*, 1946-1960 (4 volumes); *Silent China: Selected Writings of Lu Xun*, 1973.

Bibliography

Button, Peter. "Lu Xun's *Ah Q* as Gruesome Hybrid." In *Configurations of the Real in Chinese Literary and Aesthetic Modernity*. Boston: Brill, 2009. Chronicles how Chinese writers created their own form of literary modernism, beginning with Lu Xun's work *The True Story of Ah Q*.

Chang, Lung-hsi. "Revolutionary as Christ: The Unrecognized Savior in Lu Xun's Works." *Christianity and Literature* 45 (Autumn, 1995): 81-93. Discusses Lu Xun's fascination with the Christ figure, particularly as recorded in the Gospel of Matthew. Argues that by rereading his works and carefully considering their neglected aspects, such as his use of the Christ figure, readers may begin to fully understand Lu Xun and his significance for modern China.

Chen, Pearl Hsia. *The Social Thought of Lu Hsün, 1881-1936*. New York: Vantage Press, 1976. Chronicles the development of Lu Xun's thought against his cultural background, including his encounter with Western ideas, his belief in women's rights, his involvement with liberal socialism, and his reevaluation of traditional Chinese culture. The preface, by Franklin S. C. Chen, is an essay on traditional China's economic structure as it related to social thought.

Feng, Jen. "Books and Mirrors: Lu Xun and the Girl Student." In *The New Woman in Early Twentieth-Century Chinese Fiction*. West Lafayette, Ind.: Purdue University Press, 2004. Feng's book examines how male Chinese writers depicted the "new woman" in order to establish themselves as "modern" intellectuals. She analyzes the portrayal of the female heroine, Zijun, in Lu Xun's story "Regret for the Past," discussing Lu Xun's view of emotionality in literature and his use of emotion as a mark of gender and identity.

Foster, Paul B. *Ah Q Archaeology: Lu Xun, Ah Q, Ah Q Progeny, and the National Character Discourse in Twentieth Century China*. Lanham, Md.: Lexington Books, 2006. Chronicles the critical reception of *The True Story of Ah Q*, which has been considered both a representation and a critique of the Chinese national character from its initial publication through the present day. Chapter 5 summarizes the plot of the story and discusses its attack on the national character and "Chinese spiritual culture."

Hanan, Patrick. "The Technique of Lu Xun's Fiction." In *Chinese Fiction of the Nineteenth and Early Twentieth Centuries: Essays*. New York: Columbia University Press, 2004. Discusses possible influences of writers, such as Nikolai Gogol, Vsevolod Mikhaylovich Garshin, and Leonid Andreyev, as well as Lu Xun's use of symbols and different types of irony.

Lee, Leo Ou-fan. *Lu Xun and His Legacy*. Berkeley: University of California Press, 1985. This collection of essays by various scholars discusses Lu Xun's perception of traditional and modern literature, his development of form, and his intellectual and political views.

_____. *Voices from the Iron House*. Bloomington: Indiana University Press, 1987. Lee's stated purpose is to "demythify" Lu Xun with the aim of evaluating his literary accomplishments on their own ground. His discussions of Lu Xun's works include biographical information but emphasize literary analysis.

Lyell, William A., Jr. *Lu Hsün's Vision of Reality*. Berkeley: University of California Press, 1976. The first third of this book provides a biography, and the remainder is devoted to a basic discussion of Lu Xun's fiction.

Pollard, David E. *The True Story of Lu Xun*. Hong Kong: Chinese University Press, 2002. A comprehensive English-language biography.

Pusey, James Reeve. *Lu Xun and Evolution*. Albany: State University of New York Press, 1998. Explores the theme of evolution in Lu Xun's works.

Shiqing, Wang. *Lu Xun: A Biography*. Beijing: Foreign Languages Press, 1984. Traces Lu Xun's life, particularly his political and intellectual development. Includes several photographs.

Tambling, Jeremy. *Madmen and Other Survivors: Reading Lu Xun's Fiction*. Hong Kong: Hong Kong University Press, 2007. Provides detailed analyses of *The True Story of A Q*, "The Diary of a Madman," and the stories in *Call to Arms and Wandering*.

Tang, Xiaobing. "Lu Xun's 'Diary of a Madman' and a Chinese Modernism." *PMLA* 107 (October, 1992): 1222-1234. A reading of Lu Xun's short story as a modernist text, particularly in the modernist time-consciousness it introduces. Argues the story can be read as a manifesto of the birth of modern subjectivity, as well as the birth of modernist politics in twentieth century China. Discusses the nature of the madman's madness, the story as a search for meaning, and the modernism of the story as one that displaces the myth of a homogeneous nature culture.

Yn, Xiaoling. "The Paralyzed and the Dead: A Comparative Reading of 'The Dead' and 'In a Tavern.'" *Comparative Literature Studies* 29 (1992): 276-295. Shows how in both stories the theme of death undermines the theme of paralysis by the ironic nature of the protagonists.

Richard P. Benton
Updated by Mary Rohrberger

M

Joaquim Maria Machado de Assis

Born: Rio de Janeiro, Brazil; June 21, 1839
Died: Rio de Janeiro, Brazil; September 29, 1908

Principal short fiction

Contos fluminenses, 1870
Histórias da meia-noite, 1873
Papéis avulsos, 1882
Histórias sem data, 1884
Várias histórias, 1896
Histórias românticas, 1937
The Psychiatrist, and Other Stories, 1963
What Went on at the Baroness', 1963
The Devil's Church, and Other Stories, 1977
A Chapter of Hats: Selected Stories, 2008

Other literary forms

The first published works of Joaquim Maria Machado de Assis (joh-ah-KEEM mah-REE-ah muh-SHAH-dew thee ah-SEES) were poems and literary criticism, including two frequently cited studies on Brazilian literature. He wrote comedies for the theater, was master of a journalistic genre known as the *crônica* (literally, "chronicle"), and carried on an extensive correspondence, since published. He is best known for his novels, especially the last five, for which *Memórias póstumas de Brás Cubas* (1881; *The Posthumous Memoirs of Brás Cubas,* 1951; better known as *Epitaph of a Small Winner,* 1952) and *Dom Casmurro* (1899; English translation, 1953) are probably the best known outside Brazil.

Achievements

At the time of his death, in 1908, Joaquim Maria Machado de Assis was revered as Brazil's most important and influential man of letters, a distinction many critics feel he deserves. An innovator in such areas as the use of irony and of self-conscious but unreliable narrator-protagonists, Machado de Assis was instrumental in leading Brazilian literature toward an appreciation of both technical sophistication and authenticity of expression. Although he did outstanding work in all the literary genres, including poetry, drama, translation, and critical theory, it was in narrative--the novel and short-story forms especially--that he achieved his greatest successes. His extraordinary work *The Posthumous Memoirs of Brás Cubas* can, for example, be regarded as the first modern novel of either North or South America, while the text widely held to be his supreme achievement, *Dom Casmurro,* ranks as one of the outstanding novels of its time. Perhaps even more brilliant as a writer of short fiction, however, Machado de Assis is credited with having originated the modern short-story form in Brazil, where tales such as "The Psychiatrist," "Midnight Mass," "A Singular Event," "The Companion," and "Dona Paula" are still judged to be masterpieces of his laconic, metaphoric art.

Biography

A lifelong resident of Rio de Janeiro, Joaquim Maria Machado de Assis was the son of a Portuguese mother and a mulatto father. Despite humble origins, epilepsy, and a speech defect, this self-taught intellectual not only attained the highest civil service position open to him but also founded the Brazilian Academy of Letters and served as its president until his death in 1908. While still living, Machado de Assis saw himself acknowledged as Brazil's greatest writer.

Analysis

To some modern readers it may appear lamentable that Joaquim Maria Machado de Assis's works bear neither overt references to his racial heritage nor arguably even oblique ones. In this regard the Brazilian mulatto will be seen to be fully integrated with the concerns and priorities of the European-leaning dominant bourgeois society in late nineteenth century Brazil. Nevertheless, Machado de Assis wrote on the fringes of "polite" society in a way that did not specifically derive from race, although a sense of social inferiority may well have contributed to his development of a cynical and biting stance toward the higher spiritual aspirations of the socially dominant Brazilian of his day. Specifically, this stance can be seen in his critical analyses of the ambiguities of the human soul (his "Jamesian" quality) and in his dissection of the pious self-sufficiency of the ignorant bourgeoisie (his "Flaubertian" and "Tolstoyan" qualities). Like many of the great realists, Machado de Assis lends himself to a Lukacsian or Marxist analysis. His works bespeak, beneath the surface of the comings and goings of polite, ordered society, the tremendous conflicts, passions, and irreconcilable tensions of a society that fragments human experience and strives to metaphorize, in terms of a myth of spiritual transcendence, humans' carnal and materialistic nature. The patterned texture of an ordered society remains permanently at odds with fundamental aspects of the human soul which it chooses to ignore or metaphorize.

"A SINGULAR EVENT"

In this regard, Machado de Assis's story "Singular occurrência" ("A Singular Event") may be considered a metatext not only of the Brazilian's concern with ambiguities of the human experience that polite society cannot account for in terms of its own ideological construction of the world, but also of his typically nineteenth century rhetorical strategies for the framing of ambiguous narrative. The story concerns the "singular event" in the amorous relations between a young married lawyer and a woman of unspecified occupation ("she was not a dressmaker, nor a landlady, nor a governess; eliminate the professions and you will get the idea") who becomes not only his devoted lover but also his "pupil." The relationship described between the two goes beyond simply the sexual bond between a gentleman and his extramarital companion (a Latin American sociocultural cliché). The lawyer undertakes to form the woman, teaching her to read and to appreciate the "finer" things in life in the form of the high cultural artifacts of the period. Then one night the woman undertakes a sordid adventure with another man in such a way that it appears she is flaunting her perfidy. The idolizing lawyer is possessed with despair; yet she remains silent as to the reasons for her infidelity or at least for the "dramatization" of an apparent flagrant infidelity. The lovers are reconciled, she bears him a child who soon dies, he subsequently dies while out of town, and she spends the rest of her days conducting herself as a proper widow: When the story opens she is seen going to church clad in somber black.

The semantic contrasts put forth by the narrator's story of the beautiful "widow" and the singular event that colors it are the overt markers of the ambiguities of human nature involved: the intensely correct and well-bred man versus the woman of questionable occupation; her natural goodness versus his cultural refinement; her acquisition of ennobling culture versus subjugation to an all-consuming passion willing to accept even her putative fall from grace; the predictable patterns of behavior that characterize their socially acceptable liaison versus the traumatic and inexplicable flouting of the propriety that the woman seems to have gone to such lengths to accomplish; her refusal to give an accounting of her actions versus his need to reimpose the security of a proper relationship; and her past--particularly the singular event--versus her insistence on assuming the role of a dutiful widow.

There are many ways in which the foregoing semantic contrasts may be interpreted as they are given narrative form in the story. First, the woman's dramatic rebellion may be seen as a gesture of class differences: The socially inferior courtesan must affirm her status by reminding her lover of her sordid origin. Second, the singular event may be seen as a dramatic farce in a game of sexual politics: The woman ensures her dominance of her lover by threatening to deceive him with other men. Third, the relationship may be seen in feminist terms: the unstable and degrading situation of a woman who, despite the social acceptance of the man's extramarital affairs, is a social outcast, treated as an adoring child by the man-father who educates her to his own sociocultural norms. Fourth, in larger social terms, the story concerns exploitation, with sex in the guise of ennobling love the instrument of dominance on both sides. Which of these interpretations is the "true meaning" of Machado de Assis's story is less important than the reader's understanding of the text's narrative strategies for arranging semantic contrasts and for underscoring the fundamental ambiguities of the human relations these ambiguities signal. "A Singular Event" is a metatext of Machado de Assis's fiction not so much because it typifies a prominent thematic preoccupation in his works but because it is paradigmatic of the narration of an event that is strikingly ambiguous and lacking in any reductionary meaning that will make either it or the narrative about it a transparent explanation of human experience.

The narrative framing of "A Singular Event" is the direct correlative, in terms of literary *écriture*, of the paradox of ambiguity: how to explain what has no coherent explanation. The reader reads a formal literary text (with all the external trappings of literature, from title to the inclusion in a self-identified literary work, to the complete graphic array of grammatological texts) which is ostensibly the verbatim transcription of a natural narrative. By natural narrative the reader understands a tale or a story told in an oral register that does not purport to be written literary narrative. (The classic examples are natural narrative introduced by the marker "That reminds me of the story about. . . ." ; a parallel marker that has been extensively literaturized is "Once upon a time. . . .")

It is significant in this regard that Machado de Assis's interlocutors situate themselves in the street (a "natural" setting), that their narrative is triggered by the chance passing of the black-dressed mistress, and by the fact that only the "natural" interlocutors speak--that is, there is no extranatural narrative commentary by Machado de Assis as either literary author or omniscient literary narrator. Moreover, the natural narrator narrates the "singular event" not as he saw or experienced it but as it was told to him by the distraught lawyer in his desperate attempt to understand the occurrence and to know how to handle it. All these layers are a sort of interpretational deferral of meaning of the event being related, to the extent that each can and does give the particulars but none can explain them--not the lawyer, not his confidant-turned-narrator, not the silent author. The narrator can say only, "I have invented nothing. It's the pure truth."

By contrast, the one person who can explain things, the woman, not only refuses to do so in the real-life world posited by the story but also fails to have any direct or indirect speaking role in the natural narrative transmitted by the literary text (her lover does, as he is paraphrased repeatedly by the narrator). From the point of verisimilitude, one can say this silence derives from the narrator's opportunity to interview the woman. In terms of the semiological strategies of the literary text, however, her lack of voice in the story, like Machado de Assis's failure to exercise the authorial prerogative he uses elsewhere in his fiction to comment on events or others' natural narratives about those events, can be seen only to reinforce the image in the story of ambiguous, enigmatic events that are in a certain sense semantic voids. One can talk about them, with extensive reference to concrete particulars, but one can never explain them in a way that will satisfy the driving need to understand complex human experience.

OTHER MAJOR WORKS

LONG FICTION: *Resurreiãço*, 1872; *A mão e a luva*, 1874 (*The Hand and the Glove*, 1970); *Helena*, 1876 (English translation, 1984); *Iaiá Garcia*, 1878 (*Yayá Garcia*, 1977); *Memórias póstumas de Brás Cubas*, 1881 (*The Posthumous Memoirs of Brás Cubas*, 1951; better known as *Epitaph of a Small Winner*, 1952); *Quincas Borba*, 1891 (*Philosopher or Dog?*, 1954; also as *The Heritage of Quincas Borba*, 1954); *Dom Casmurro*, 1899 (English translation, 1953); *Esaú e Jacob*, 1904 (*Esau and Jacob*, 1965); *Memorial de Ayres*, 1908 (*Counselor Ayres' Memorial*, 1972).

PLAYS: *Desencantos*, pb. 1861; *Quase ministro*, pb. 1864; *Os deuses de casaca*, pb. 1866; *Tu só, tu, puro amor*, pb. 1880; *Teatro*, pb. 1910.

POETRY: *Crisálidas*, 1864; *Falenas*, 1870; *Americanas*, 1875; *Poesias completas*, 1901.

NONFICTION: *Páginas recolhidas (contos, ensaios, crônicas)*, 1899; *Relíquias de Casa Velha (contos, crônicas, comédias)*, 1906; *A semana*, 1910; *Crítica*, 1910; *Crítica por Machado de Assis*, 1924; *Crítica literária*, 1937; *Crítica teatral*, 1937; *Correspondência*, 1938.

MISCELLANEOUS: *Outras relíquias*, 1908; *Obra completa*, 1959.

Bibliography

Borges, Dain. "The Relevance of Machado de Assis." In *Imagining Brazil*, edited by Jessé Souza and Valter Sinder. Lanham, Md.: Lexington Books, 2005. Examines the significance of Machado de Assis works in the development of Brazilian identity and culture.

Caldwell, Helen. *The Brazilian Othello of Machado de Assis*. Berkeley: University of California Press, 1960. The first book-length study in English to deal with Machado de Assis. Focuses on his novel *Dom Casmurro* and shows how Machado apparently utilized a modified version of *Othello*'s plot structure. Discusses numerous other examples of the influence William Shakespeare had on Machado de Assis's work. Caldwell was the first critic to argue that the novel's heroine, Capitu, was not necessarily guilty of adultery, as generations of readers had assumed.

_____. *Machado de Assis: The Brazilian Master and His Novels*. Berkeley: University of California Press, 1970. A concise survey of Machado de Assis's nine novels and his various narrative techniques. Includes good discussions of his primary themes, a useful bibliography, and some comments on his short stories, plays, and poems.

Dixon, Paul. *Retired Dreams: Dom Casmurro, Myth and Modernity*. West Lafayette, Ind.: Purdue University Press, 1989. Though he limits his critical discussion to the novel *Dom Casmurro*, Dixon leads his readers to see Machado de Assis as cultivating a radically new style of writing, one that featured ambiguity as the most "realistic" aspect of language and that conceived of language as a system of tropes only arbitrarily connected to physical reality. Dixon also suggests that Machado de Assis was critical of his society's patriarchal codes and that, as evidenced in the relationship between the novel's two major characters (Bento and Capitu), he implies the virtues inherent in a more matriarchal approach to sociopolitical organization.

Douglas, Ellen H. "Machado de Assis's 'A Cartomante': Modern Parody and the Making of a 'Brazilian' Text." *MLN* 113 (December, 1998): 1036-1055. Discusses the story's introduction of an act of modern parody; argues that this act of parody occurs in its intertextual opening, which features a reference to William Shakespeare's *Hamlet*.

Fischer, Sibylle Maria. "Geography and Representation in Machado de Assis." *Modern Language Quarterly* 55 (June, 1994): 191-213. Argues that Machado de Assis's narratives respond to the interplay of three factors: a postcolonial nationalism with a strong desire for self-representation, a displaced "high culture" maintained through continuous transfer of literary and cultural products from Europe to Brazil, and social and economic structures unlike those of any relevant European country.

Fitz, Earl E. *Machado de Assis*. Boston: Twayne, 1989. The first English-language book to examine all aspects of Machado de Assis's literary life--his short stories, novels, poetry, theater, critical theory, translations, and nonfiction. Includes sections on his life, his place in Brazilian and world literature, his style, and his themes. Argues that Machado de Assis--largely because of his ideas about the connection between language, meaning, and reality--is best appreciated as a modernist.

Gledson, John. *The Deceptive Realism of Machado de Assis: A Dissenting Interpretation of "Dom Casmurro."* Liverpool, England: Francis Cairns, 1984. Focusing on what the majority of critics have judged to be Machado de Assis's greatest novel, *Dom Casmurro*, Gledson argues against interpreting the author either as a modernist or as a precursor of the New Novel in Latin America and in favor of regarding him as a master (if unique) realist. Sees him as a subtle and artful stylist whose work accurately reflects the prevailing social and political tensions of his time.

Graham, Richard, ed. *Machado de Assis: Reflections on a Brazilian Master Writer*. Austin: University of Texas Press, 1999. Contains essays by John Gledson, Daphne Patai, and Sidney Chalhoub, most of which focus on *Dom Casmurro*.

Jackson, K. David. "The Brazilian Short Story." In *The Cambridge History of Latin American Literature*. Vol. 3 Edited by Robert González Echevarria and Enrique Pupo-Walker. Cambridge, England: Cambridge University Press, 1996. Discusses Machado de Assis's technique of suggestions and implication within an ironic frame of reference. Suggests that his humor and irony underline the futility of human conflict in a world in which the nature of reality is illusory. Points out that he eschews naturalist explanations and uses complex narrative strategies.

Kristal, Efráin, and José Luiz Passos. "Machado de Assis and the Question of Brazilian National Identity." In *Brazil in the Making: Facets of National Identity*, edited by Carmen Nava and Ludwig Lauerhass, Jr. Lanham, Md.: Rowman and Littlefield, 2006. Examines the reception of Macado de Assis'ss novels in relation to discussions of Brazilian identity from the late nineteenth century to the present day.

Machado de Assis, Joaquim Maria. *A Chapter of Hats: Selected Stories*. Translated from the Portuguese by John Gledson. London: Bloomsbury, 2008. A selection of Machado de Assis's short stories. Gledson, a noted Machado de Assis scholar, provides an introductory overview to the stories.

Neto, José Raimundo Maia. *Machado de Assis, the Brazilian Pyrrhonian*. West Lafayette, Ind.: Purdue University Press, 1994. Part 1 explores the first phase of Machado de Assis's career (1861-1878), when he went from writing essays to writing stories and his first novels. Part 2 concentrates on his second phase (1879-1908), with separate chapters on *The Posthumous Memoirs of Brás Cubas*, *Dom Casmurro*, and later fiction. Includes detailed notes and bibliography.

Nist, John. "The Short Stories of Machado de Assis." *Arizona Quarterly* 24 (Spring, 1968): 5-22. Nist hails Machado de Assis as not only a great novelist but also perhaps the outstanding prose fiction writer of either North or South America during the late nineteenth and early twentieth centuries. Surveys a number of his most celebrated stories, including "The Psychiatrist," "A Woman's Arms," and "Midnight Mass." Nist also notes the economy of means that marks the author's style, the ironic and philosophic base of his fiction, his alleged "pessimism," and the modernist ethos inherent in his ambiguous vision of human reality.

Nunes, Maria Luisa. *The Craft of an Absolute Winner: Characterization and Narratology in the Novels of Machado de Assis*. Westport, Conn.: Greenwood Press, 1983. An excellent study of Machado de Assis's novelistic techniques, his skill at characterization, and his primary themes. Offers good summaries of his novels and shows how they compare to one another and how their author grew in sophistication and skill. Argues that the essence of Machado de Assis's genius, like that of all truly great writers, lies in his singular ability to create powerful and compelling characters.

Schwarz, Roberto. "The Historical Meaning of Cruelty in Machado de Assis." Translated by S. E. Wilson. *Modern Language Quarterly* 57 (June, 1996): 165-179. Discusses the historical meaning of cruelty as represented in Machado de Assis's novel *Memórias Póstumas de Brás Cubas*.

David W. Foster
Updated by Earl E. Fitz

Naguib Mahfouz

Born: Cairo, Egypt; December 11, 1911
Died: Cairo, Egypt; August 30, 2006

Principal short fiction

Hams al-junūn, 1939

Dunyā Allāh, 1963 (partial translation as *God's World,* 1973)

Bayt sayyi' al-sum'a, 1965

Khammārat al-qitt al-aswad, 1968 (*The Tavern of the Black Cat,* 1976)

Tahta al-mizalla, 1969 (stories and plays)

Hikaya bila bidaya wala nihaya, 1971

Al-Jarima, 1973

God's World, 1973

Al-hubb fawqa haðabat al-haram, 1979

Al-Shaytan Ya'iz, 1979

Ra'aytu fīmā yarā al-nā'im, 1982

Al-Tanzīm al-sirri, 1984

Al-Fajr al-kādhib, 1989

The Time and the Place, and Other Stories, 1991

Voices from the Other World, 2003

The Dreams, 2005

The Seventh Heaven: Stories of the Supernatural, 2005

Other literary forms

Despite his lifelong dedication to the short story, the reputation of Naguib Mahfouz (nah-HIHB mahk-FEWS) stems chiefly from the many novels he produced during his lengthy career, notably the Cairo Trilogy (1956-1957). He was also an important influence in the Egyptian cinema, having written the screenplays for many films drawn from Arabic novels, including some of his own works. He is the author of several short plays, some of which have been performed on stage. In addition, he wrote the nonfiction work *Asda' al-sirah al-dhatiyah* (1995; *Echoes of an Autobiography,* 1997).

Achievements

By the late 1950's, Naguib Mahfouz had earned recognition throughout the Arab world as one of the most sophisticated authors of the Arabic novel. While earlier Arab novelists had initiated this literary form, Mahfouz demonstrated a gift for presenting characters and situations that intimately captured the spirit of his native Egypt. His generally tragic works often center their interest on individuals in crisis and examine issues relating to class, ambition, and morality in government. They illustrate the personal faults or the incidents of fate that can bring tragedy to humankind; though didactic, they are usually nonjudgmental. Contemporary political and social issues, both of the Middle East and of the world at large, are central to his writing. The recipient of many honorary doctoral degrees from foreign universities and prestigious awards from the Egyptian government, Mahfouz received the Nobel Prize in Literature in 1988.

Biography

Though gregarious and accessible, Naguib Mahfouz disclosed little about his personal life or background. His father was apparently a shopkeeper (or perhaps a minor civil servant), and Mahfouz was the youngest of seven children. At the time of his birth, the family resided in Gamaliya, an area named after a street traversing an ancient quarter of Cairo. It is this colorful, conservative environment that provides the locale for many of his works. In his preteens, the family moved to the wealthier and more European neighborhood of Abbasiya. His early education was in public schools, and he earned a B.A. in philosophy from Cairo University in 1934. He continued studies there for an M.A. in philosophy but withdrew for undisclosed reasons to take employment in the university's administration; shortly thereafter, he joined the government bureaucracy, first working in the ministry of religious endowments. In 1971, he retired and became director of the government-controlled board of film censorship, while continuing to devote himself to his writing. He married in his early forties and had two daughters.

Mahfouz was awarded the Nobel Prize in Literature in 1988. After this recognition, he became more widely translated and read outside the Arab world. Within the Arab world he was controversial because he advocated peace with Israel. In 1994, he was stabbed in the neck outside his Cairo home, in an assassination attempt by Muslim ultraconservative extremists.

In his old age, Mahfouz became nearly blind and suffered from diabetes, kidney problems, and cardiac failure. In July, 2006, he injured his head in a fall and was taken to a Cairo hospital, where he died on August 30, 2006, at the age of ninety-four. The following day, he received a state funeral with full military honors in Cairo.

ANALYSIS

In his fiction, Naguib Mahfouz assumed the role of chronicler and conscience of Egypt in the twentieth century. Because many of his works examine issues that are common to all humanity, however, they are timeless and of universal interest. Mahfouz's works consistently expressed his interest in the role of women in society. His fiction suggests that he has generally been supportive of women exerting their personal choice. Even women who become prostitutes are viewed with equanimity and understanding, if not admiration.

Mahfouz is perhaps the best-known Arab fiction writer in the Anglophone world. Over a period of half a century he has given voice to the hopes and frustrations of his nation. Through his fiction, Egyptian and Arab-Islamic cultural heritage has become accessible to Westerners. His works illustrate the position of women in his culture, and clarify the changes and disruptions that Western ideas and culture have brought to individuals and society as a whole in Egypt.

HAMS AL-JUNŪN

Mahfouz is said to have published his first short story in an obscure Cairo journal, *Al-Siyasa*, in July, 1932. This was followed by regular publication of his short fiction in several Egyptian journals, both literary

and popular. These early stories number approximately eighty, of which more than twenty have been republished in a collection entitled *Hams al-junūn*. The stories frequently present situations in which sadness results from faults of character and immorality or from ill fortune. The situations are often domestic and the problems prosaic, such as marital infidelity or a family's descent into poverty through unemployment or the death of the wage earner.

These stories are generally didactic and sentimental and reflect the influence of the works of the then hugely popular Sheikh Mustafa Lutfi al-Manfaluti; this author's genius for archaic, sonorous, and rhythmic prose Mahfouz was, however, unable to match. Other early stories present flat and static character sketches of the lives and personalities of curious characters; these are reminiscent of the fiction of Mahmud Taymur, a prominent Egyptian writer who was himself a devotee of Guy de Maupassant. Often with characters and situations that are unconvincing and lack development, these works nevertheless suggest the pessimism and high seriousness that have characterized Mahfouz's literary production.

Naguib Mahfouz (©The Nobel Foundation)

"GOD'S WORLD"

The short stories of the late 1930's and 1940's, like the novels, still largely concern themselves with the issues and dilemmas that affect the poor, the bureaucracy, and the petit bourgeois. They emphasize the negative aspects of Egypt's class structure and demonstrate how the struggle for survival and advancement entails loss of mortality and personal happiness. They suggest a general compassion for the underprivileged and a disapproval of the values of his compatriots who enjoy wealth and power.

The whimsical "Dunyā Allāh" ("God's World"), in the collection *Dunyā Allāh* and available in various English translations, centers sympathetically on an aging man, an impoverished messenger in a department of the bureaucracy, who, having stolen the salaries of his colleagues, absconds to Alexandria with a young woman. Though his idyllic vacation ends with her rejection of him and his capture by the police, the thief has no cause for regret because he has achieved one brief period of happiness in an otherwise dismal life.

Mahfouz's writings of the 1950's and 1960's became increasingly complex in their structure and style and more political and obscure in their themes. As was the case with other Egyptian writers, such as Yusuf Idris and Ihsan 'Abd al-Quddus, his works now contained subtle expressions of discontent at the repressive nature of the rule of the country's dictator, Gamal Abdel Nasser, who had led an army coup in 1952 that had overthrown the monarchy. While viewed as generally benevolent and reformist, the Nasser regime brooked no criticism from its citizenry, and brief jail sentences were served by many intellectuals whose loyalty became suspect. Caution and obfuscation were clearly necessary to escape notice or defy interpretation by the "defenders of the revolution." The stories are therefore metaphorical and the criticisms oblique, though some do lend themselves to easy equational interpretation.

"SA'IQ AL-QITAR"

For example, his "Sa'iq al-qitar," in the collection *Bayt sayyi' al-sum'a*, presents passengers on a train; one man, reminiscent of a bear, standing for the Soviet Union, constantly challenges another, reminiscent of an "eagle,"

representing the United States, over the future of a woman who presumably stands for Egypt. The passengers realize that their train is rushing headlong into certain disaster. The train driver--clearly Nasser--locked in the engine compartment refuses all advice to slow down and seems crazed and suicidal. It is implied that the nation is helpless and headed for tragedy under his leadership.

"ZAABALAWI"

Other short stories of the period reflect the malaise and confusion widely shared by Egyptian intellectuals. While they applauded the new international attention and prestige that the regime had won for Egypt as a leader of the neutralist Third World and were pleased at the downfall of the landowning aristocracy, the nation suffered from involvement in a debilitating war in Yemen, a stagnant economy, and restrictions on travel. Intellectuals also chafed at the abolition of the country's political parties and freedoms of expression, while they disdained the Nasser worship of the powerful state-controlled media. Stories such as "Zaabalawi," in the collection *Dunyā Allāh*, clearly suggest this malaise; it involves a sick man's search for a revered healer, a holy man who embodied inherited rather than imported values and procedures of contemporary "doctors." The dissatisfaction at the root of this story is viewed by some critics as similar in its message to that of Mahfouz's extremely controversial novel *Awlād Hāratinā* (1959, serial; 1967, book; *Children of Gebelawi*, 1981), which chronicles the failures of both the religions and the governmental structures to satisfy people's needs for security and justice.

"BENEATH THE SHELTER"

In the several months following the disastrous war of June, 1967, between Israel and the Arabs, Mahfouz wrote a variety of curious and disturbing short stories and five one-act plays, which were collected and published in 1969 in the volume *Tahta al-mizalla*. These works present characters and situations that show Egyptians to be living in a Kafkaesque and chaotic world where individuals live in distress and terror. The story reflects the trauma then affecting Egyptians from two sources--the fear of death from sporadic Israeli air attacks and the repressive policies being pursued by the Nasser regime.

While the internal message in these works is constrained and camouflaged by symbolism, their intent to reveal despair and to suggest criticism is clear. While not lending themselves to full equational interpretation, unlike some of his earlier stories, they contain enough "clues" to suggest the author's purpose, which at times extended beyond the prosaic criticism of the country's leadership into the metaphysical.

For example, the story "Tahta al-mizalla" ("Beneath the Shelter") could obviously be interpreted as an expression of the tragedy and absurdity of the human experience stemming from failure to replace brutality and chaos with an order based on morality and compassion. In this story, dramatic and tragic events unfold in the street before onlookers awaiting the arrival of a bus. These incidents, occurring in an atmosphere of unrelieved gloom and downpourings of rain in increasing intensity, suggest the progression of the recent history of the Middle East as seen from an Egyptian perspective. The onlookers are reluctant to accept as reality the strange and bloody events that they witness. To justify their own fear of involvement, they convince themselves that the changing scene is merely the action of a motion picture being shot. A final horrific event, however, convinces them that they are witnessing a reality too horrible to ignore; a head gushing blood--presumably during the 1967 war--rolls down the street before them. Belatedly seeking involvement, they call out to a "policeman" who has also been an uninvolved observer of the scenes. His response, however, is to question their identity and loyalty and to shoot them all dead. While the general intent of the story is evident, its specific symbols may be variously interpreted. It is not clear, for example, whether the uninvolved spectators are Egyptian or foreign, or whether the brutal and callous policeman is Nasser or an abstraction, such as time or fate.

Such stories, for all the interest they arouse in Arabic and the speed and frequency with which they have been published in translation, have received little interpretation. Clearly, commentators have realized that it would be an act of betrayal to reveal the purposes of an author who has taken such pains to present his ideas in so obscure and circumspect a manner.

TAHTA AL-MIZALLA

The issue of commitment against injustice is clearly a major theme of Mahfouz's oeuvre, and, in works written before 1978, this theme often finds expression in relation to the Arab-Israeli conflict. In several works --for example in the story "Fijian Shayy" and the one-act play *Death and Resurrection*, both from the collection *Tahta al-mizalla* (with the play published in English translation in the1989 collection *One-Act Plays*)--Mahfouz insists on the need to redress the wrongs done to the Palestinians and to continue the Arab struggle against Israel. These works all appeared before Egypt's 1978-1979 rapprochement with Israel, following which Mahfouz was an outspoken advocate of peace and cooperation between Arabs and Israelis.

The chaotic and fast-changing nature of contemporary Egyptian society and its values and the resultant sense of disorientation and bewilderment has been the subject of several stories. In "False Dawn," in the collection *Al-Fajr al-kādhib*, the reader follows a young man's apparently logical search for an enemy only to discover that he has been suffering from paranoid schizophrenia caused by the confusion of change in modern society.

"THE ANSWER IS NO" AND "MIN TAHT ILA FAWQ"

Several of the short stories similarly center on strong-willed women; indeed, it could be maintained that Mahfouz, like many prominent Arab authors, has his female characters exemplify virtues lacking in his male figures. Mahfouz's advocacy of the right to choose or reject marriage clearly contradicts traditional male mainstream opinion in his society. For example, in the story "The Answer Is No," from the collection *Al-Fajr al-kādhib*, a young girl who is seduced by a teacher refuses to marry him despite his dutiful proposal to her as soon as she reaches the legal age for marriage. Years later, when he becomes the principal of the school where she teaches and inquires after her marital status, she expresses no regret at her unmarried state. Similarly, in "Min taht ila Fawq," also in *Al-Fajr al-kādhib*, an unmarried young woman, orphaned as a child and exploited by her family for whom she acts as an unpaid cook and housekeeper, decides to take employment as a servant in luxury Cairo apartments. Formerly sickly and depressed at home, she becomes

happy and earns a fine salary. When her health, mo-
rale, and dress improve, she marries an electrician,
whom she proudly introduces to her family; she has
married by choice, and as an equal.

OTHER MAJOR WORKS

LONG FICTION: *Abath al-Aqdār*, 1939 (*Khufu's
Wisdom*, 2003); *Rādūbīs*, 1943 (*Rhadopis of Nubia*,
2003); *Kifāh Tība*, 1944 (*Thebes at War*, 2003);
Khān al-Khalīli, 1945; *Zuqāq al-Midaqq*, 1947
(*Midaq Alley*, 1966, revised 1975); *Bidāya wa-
nihāya*, 1949 (*The Beginning and the End*, 1951);
Bayn al-qasrayn, 1956 (*Palace Walk*, 1990); *Al-Suk-
kariya*, 1957 (*Sugar Street*, 1992; previous 3 titles
collectively known as *Al-Thulāthiya* [*The Trilogy*]);
Qasr al-shawq, 1957 (*Palace of Desire*, 1991);
Awlād Hāratinā, 1959 (serial), 1967 (book) (*Chil-
dren of Gebelawi*, 1981; also known as *Children of
the Alley*, 1996); *Al-Liss wa-al-kilāb*, 1961 (*The
Thief and the Dogs*, 1984); *Al-Summān wa-al-kharīf*,
1962 (*Autumn Quail*, 1985); *Al-Tarīq*, 1964 (*The
Search*, 1987); *Al-Shahhādh*, 1965 (*The Beggar*,
1986); *Tharthara fawq al-Nīl*, 1966 (*Adrift on the
Nile*, 1993); *Mirāmār*, 1967 (*Miramar*, 1978); *Al-
Marāya*, 1972 (*Mirrors*, 1977); *Al-Karnak*, 1974
(*Karnak*, 1979; *Karnak Café*, 2007); *Hadrat al-
muhtaram*, 1975 (*Respected Sir*, 1986); *Hikāyāt
Hāratinā*, 1975 (*The Fountain and the Tomb*, 1988);
Malhamat al-harāfīsh, 1977 (*The Harafish*, 1994);
Afrāh al-qubbah, 1981 (*Wedding Song*, 1984); *Layālī
alf Laylah*, 1982 (*Arabian Nights and Days*, 1995);
Rihlat Ibn Fattumah, 1983 (*The Journey of Ibn Fat-
touma*, 1992); *Al-ā'ish fī al-haqīqah*, 1985
(*Akhenaten: Dweller in Truth*, 2000); *Yawm Qutila
al-Za'īm*, 1985 (*The Day the Leader Was Killed*,
1989).

PLAYS: *One-Act Plays*, pb. 1989.

NONFICTION: *Asda' al-sirah al-dhatiyah*, 1995
(*Echoes of an Autobiography*, 1997); *Naguib Mahfouz at Sidi Gaber: Reflections of a Nobel Laureate,
1994-2001*, 2001.

TRANSLATION: *Misr al-Qadīmah*, 1931 (of James
Baikie's *Ancient Egypt*)

BIBLIOGRAPHY

Abadir, Akef, and Roger Allen. Introduction to *God's
World*. Minneapolis, Minn.: Bibliotheca Islamica,
1973. This introduction by Abadir and Allen is followed by twenty translations selected from Mahfouz's short stories.

Beard, Michael, and Adnan Haydar, eds. *Naguib Mahfouz: From Regional Fame to Global Recognition*.
Syracuse, N.Y.: Syracuse University Press, 1993. A
collection of essays derived from a symposium recognizing Mahfouz's 1988 Nobel Prize. Includes essays on Mahfouz's image of woman, on dreams, on
the sublime, and on his critics. An essay on existential themes focuses specifically on Mahfouz's short
stories.

Coetzee, J. M. "Fabulous Fabulist." *The New York Review of Books* 41 (September 22, 1994): 30-33. Argues that it was Mahfouz's example that spurred interest in the novel in Arabic in the 1950's and 1960's.
Briefly discusses Mahfouz's fiction, describing the
world of Cairo as he depicts it.

El-Enany, Rasheed. *Naguib Mahfouz: His Life and
Times*. Cairo: American University in Cairo Press,
2007. A literary biography that assesses Mahfouz's
works and his legacy in the Egyptian and Arab literary worlds. Includes a chapter entitled "The Little
Pieces of Clay: The Novelist as Short Story Writer
and Dramatist."

Hesse, Reinhard. "Egypt's Intelligentsia Fights Back."
World Press Review 42 (February, 1995): 50. Argues
that the galvanizing moment of the culture wars
being waged to deny Egypt its rich heritage occurred
when Mahfouz was stabbed. Notes that Mahfouz's
novel *Children of Gebelaawi* had been banned by
fundamentalists as a disrespectful allegory of the
life of the Prophet.

Johnson-Davies, Denys. Introduction to *The Time and
the Place, and Other Stories*. Garden City, N.Y.:
Doubleday, 1991. Consists of twenty of Mahfouz's
short stories selected and translated, following an
introduction by Denys Johnson-Davies.

Kilpatrick, Hilary. *The Modern Egyptian Novel: A
Study in Social Criticism*. London: Ithaca Press,
1974. This academic study examines Mahfouz's
novels in the context of contemporary Egyptian

fiction. Contains appropriate literary and critical evaluations, notes, and bibliographies.

Le Gassick, Trevor, ed. *Critical Perspectives on Naguib Mahfouz*. Washington, D.C.: Three Continents Press, 1991. Eleven articles by authorities on Mahfouz, following an introduction by the editor. The articles, four of which are in translation from Arabic, range widely over Mahfouz's contributions to the short story, the novel, and the Egyptian cinema. Complemented by bibliographies of materials in English.

Mahfouz, Naguib. *Naguib Mahfouz at Sidi Gaber: Reflections of a Nobel Laureate, 1994-2001*. New York: American University in Cairo Press, 2001. Writer Mohamed Salmawy compiled more than one hundred of the short conversations and interviews that he conducted with Mahfouz during a seven-year period. In these pieces, Mahfouz reflects upon his past and present life, winning the Nobel Prize and other awards, literature generally, his own writings, "Mother Egypt," politics, and "the world of tomorrow."

Somekh, Sasson. *The Changing Rhythm*. Leiden, the Netherlands: E. J. Brill, 1973. A careful, comprehensive study of Mahfouz's major novels. Academically sound and with good bibliographies, it addresses the general reader, as well as the student of Near Eastern literatures.

Viorst, Milton. "Man of Gamaliya." *The New Yorker* 66 (July 2, 1990): 32-38. In this brief biographical sketch, Viorst discusses Mahfouz's denunciation by Muslim authorities and the death threats made against him for defending Salman Rushdie. Also comments on his later view that Rushdie should stand trial for slander.

Weaver, Mary Anne. "The Novelist and the Sheikh." *The New Yorker* 70 (January 30, 1995): 52-58. In this brief biographical sketch, the author notes that the stabbing of Mahfouz underscores the battle between the Egyptian government and Islamic militants. Discusses how Mahfouz's characters debate issues of justice and injustice, expectation and disillusionment, and belief in God.

Trevor Le Gassick
Updated by Susan Butterworth

YUKIO MISHIMA

Born: Tokyo, Japan; January 14, 1925
Died: Tokyo, Japan; November 25, 1970
Also Known As: Kimitake Hiraoka

PRINCIPAL SHORT FICTION

Hanazakari no mori, 1944 (short fiction and plays)
Kaibutsu, 1950
Tōnorikai, 1951
Manatsu no shi, 1953 (*Death in Midsummer, and Other Stories*, 1966)
Eirei no koe, 1966 (short fiction and essays)

OTHER LITERARY FORMS

Yukio Mishima (yuhk-ee-oh mee-shee-mah) wrote more than eighty short stories; twenty novels;

more than twenty plays, several in the manner of the classical No dramas, as well as plays for the Kabuki theater; several essay collections; two travel books; a bit of poetry; and a handful of works that defy clear-cut classification.

ACHIEVEMENTS

The collected works of Yukio Mishima form thirty-six volumes, more than the literary production of any other writer of his time. The Japanese writer best known outside Japan, from the viewpoint of Western critics he is the most gifted of the post-World War II writers. Mishima also combined his knowledge of classic Japanese literature and language with his wide knowledge of Western literature to produce plays for the Kabuki theater and the first truly successful modern No plays.

While uneven in some volumes, style is the most distinctive feature of Mishima's work. His writing is characterized by beautiful but rarely lyric passages. Figures of speech, notable in his later works, are also present in his juvenilia. He consistently used ornate language, though he could also write realistic dialogue.

A Nobel Prize hopeful at least two times, Mishima is among those Japanese writers closest to attaining the rank of master of twentieth century fiction.

BIOGRAPHY

Kimitake Hiraoka, who began using the pseudonym Yukio Mishima in 1941, was the son of a middle-class government official who worked in Tokyo. When Mishima was less than two months old, his paternal grandmother, Natsu, took the boy to her living quarters; his mother, Shizue, felt helpless to protest, and his father, Azusa, appeared to be totally subjected to his mother's will.

In 1931, Mishima was enrolled in the Gakushūin (the Peer's School), a school attended largely by young aristocrats. In due time, he was graduated at the head of his class and received a silver watch from the emperor personally at the imperial palace. By this time, his literary gifts had already become evident, and "Hanazakari no mori" ("The Forest in Full Bloom") was published in 1941.

In 1946, Mishima entered the Tokyo Imperial University to study law. After being employed for a time at the Ministry of Finance, he resigned in 1948 to devote full time to writing. The publication of *Kamen no kokuhaku* (1949; *Confessions of a Mask*, 1958) established him as a literary figure.

The 1950's were eventful years in Mishima's life. During this decade, he produced several novels, two of them major successes. He also traveled to the United States, Brazil, and Europe, and his visit to Greece in particular was a highlight because of its classical associations. During these years, his novel *Shiosai* (1954; *The Sound of Waves*, 1956), a best seller, was published and film rights were sold, and *Shiroari no su* (pr., pb. 1956; the nest of the white ants) established his reputation as a playwright. He also began a bodybuilding program (having been a

spare, sickly child) and married Yoko Sugiyama in 1958.

During the first half of the 1960's, writing plays occupied Mishima's time. He trained at the Jieitai (Self-Defense Forces) bases and traveled periodically. He was a strong contender for the Nobel Prize in 1968, the year that his mentor Yasunari Kawabata won. The short story "Yūkoku" ("Patriotism"), in which the hara-kiri (ritual suicide by disembowelment) of a young patriot is described, was published in 1961. He also acted in his first film, a gangster story.

By this time, Mishima's obsession with death was manifested both in word and in deed. He developed a plan for organizing a private army to be used somehow in his death, a step labeled foolish by his friends and ignored by others. During the final five months of his life, he completed the third and fourth books of his tetralogy *Hōjō no umi* (1969-1971; *The Sea of Fertility*, 1972-1974), and on November 25, 1970, he delivered the final volume to the magazine that was publishing it in installments. Later that day, following his plan and schedule implicitly, Mishima went to the Ichigaya

Yukio Mishima (Bettmann/CORBIS)

Self-Defense headquarters with a group of his Shield Society (a private legion) and, following a nationalistic speech, committed ritual seppuku (suicide).

ANALYSIS

The world will never know what course the literary career of Yukio Mishima might have taken had he not died at age forty-five. Nevertheless, he was the best known of post-World War II writers among critics and readers outside Japan, and he received a fair share of attention within his own country. Not all of his work was of equal literary merit, but a certain unevenness is almost certain for a prolific writer.

Apart from his style, usually ornate and meticulously wrought, Mishima's success stemmed in part from his effectiveness in capturing the sense of void and despair that typified many Japanese during the postwar period. Another key to his success lay in his unusual interest in Japanese cultural tradition. His abilities, unique among his peers, enabled him to write in the genre of classical Kabuki and No plays.

"THE FOREST IN FULL BLOOM"

Mishima's early works represent a period that both clarified the directions in which his talents would go and developed features that would become trademarks of his later works. He came to realize that poetry was not to be his major effort. In 1941, the year he was graduated from the Peer's School, he published his first long work, "The Forest in Full Bloom" in October, at the age of sixteen. The maturity of style in this juvenile work amazed his mentors and peers. The sophisticated word choice is noteworthy, but its maturity goes much farther; it establishes the major theme of his life's work, for he was well on his way to evolving the aesthetic formula that would distinguish his work: Longing leads to beauty; beauty generates ecstasy; ecstasy leads to death. Likewise, the sea, an important motif throughout his writing, is associated with death. Indeed, as critic Donald Keene has noted, Mishima seemed to be "intoxicated with the beauty of early death."

DEATH IN MIDSUMMER, AND OTHER STORIES

Preoccupation with death is obvious even in the title of the short-story collection that constitutes Mishima's major short fiction, *Death in Midsummer, and Other Stories*. The title story, "Death in Midsummer," takes an epigraph from one of Charles Baudelaire's poems that translates as "Death affects us more deeply under the stately reign of summer." The psychological realism of Mishima's presentation of the family's reactions to three deaths in the family is the focus of the story. Masaru and Tomoko Ikuta have two sons, Kiyoo and Katsuo, and a daughter, Keiko. Yasue, Tomoko's sister-in-law, is babysitting the children while Tomoko takes an afternoon nap. Despite warnings to the children against wandering away, during a brief moment when Yasue is preoccupied with other thoughts, two of the children disappear, leaving the three-year-old Katsuo alone, crying. When Yasue realizes what has happened, she is stricken with a heart attack and dies. Informed of Yasue's accident, Tomoko "felt a sort of sweet emptiness come over her. She was not sad." (This is only one of several passages in which a dearth of feeling is expressed.) Only then does she inquire about the children; she finds Katsuo, who informs her that "Kiyoo . . . Keiko . . . all bubbles." Tomoko is afraid; she sends her husband a telegram telling him that Yasue is dead and that the two children are missing, although by now it is clear that the children have drowned.

Masaru prepares to go down to the resort where the family was vacationing. Devoid of any emotion, he feels more like a detective speculating on the circumstances of death than a distraught father. Intuitively, he senses that the children are dead, not simply missing. When he arrives at the resort, he hears that three people have died, and his thoughts turn to how to approach his wife. Funeral preparations are made. Tomoko is conscious of the incongruity of her almost insane grief alongside her businesslike attention to detail and her large appetite at such a time. She vacillates between a feeling of guilt and her knowledge that she did not cause the deaths. Dissatisfied, she believes that Yasue is lucky to be dead because she does not have to feel that she has been "demoted and condemned" by relatives. Mishima here intrudes to comment that, although Tomoko does not know it, it is her "poverty of human emotions" that is most troubling her.

On the surface, life returns to normal, but Tomoko associates almost everything with the tragic accident, while Masaru takes refuge in his work. Tomoko questions the fact that "she was living, the others were dead. That was the great evil. How cruel it was to have to be alive." Autumn comes and goes; and life becomes more peaceful, but Tomoko comes to feel as if she is waiting for something. To try to assuage her empty feelings, Tomoko seeks outside activities. She asks herself why she had not "tried this mechanical cutting off of the emotions earlier." Winter comes. Tomoko, who is to have another child, admits for the first time that the pain of the lost children was gone, but she cultivates forgetfulness in order not to have to deal with her feelings further. After two years, one summer day, Tomoko asks Masaru to return with her to the beach. Grudgingly, he consents. Tomoko is silent and spends much of her time gazing at the sea, as if she were waiting for something. Masaru wants to ask but then realizes that "he thought he knew without asking."

As in much Japanese literature, the cycle of the seasons is prominent. Deaths come in midsummer, when things should be flourishing and in full bloom. When winter comes, the final ritual of burying the ashes of the dead is completed. Tomoko becomes pregnant, and Momoko is born the following summer. Again, it is summer when she returns to the beach. The cryptic ending is typical of some, not all, of Mishima's work. One may speculate that the return to the beach in the summer is a sign of acceptance or an effort by Tomoko to come to terms with her own identity. Possibly, her waiting represents some sense of communication with the spirits of the dead or even indicates a longing for her own death. A less gloomy interpretation of the return to the beach, however, may recall Baudelaire's line suggesting that death in summer is out of place; death is for the winter, when nature too is desolate.

"THE PRIEST OF SHIGA TEMPLE AND HIS LOVE"

More often anthologized, the story "Shigadera Shōnin no Koi" ("The Priest of Shiga Temple and His Love") manifests Mishima's familiarity with classical Japanese literature. At the same time, the central theme of the story is one that is common in the West but relatively rare in Japanese literature: the inner conflict between worldly love and religious faith. A brief account

in a fourteenth century war chronicle of an elderly priest falling in love with the imperial concubine provides the subject matter of the story.

It is the motivation of the concubine and the priest--rather than the events--that is the focus of the story. The priest is an exemplar of virtue; he is old and doddering, physically a "bag of bones"; it is unlikely that he would become infatuated with a beautiful young woman. When the concubine comes to the area to view the springtime foliage, the priest "unwittingly" glances in her direction, not expecting to be overwhelmed by her beauty. He is, however, and he realizes that "what he had imagined to be completely safe had collapsed in ruins." Never had he broken his vow of chastity, but he realizes that this new love has taken hold of him. The concubine, having forgotten their meeting, is reminded of it when she hears a rumor that an old priest has behaved as if he were crazed after having seen her. She, too, is without blemish in that, while she performed her duties to the emperor, she has never given her love to any suitor.

The priest is now tormented by the implications of this love in relation to his attaining enlightenment. He longs to see the lady once more, confident in his delusion that this will provide escape from his present feelings. He goes to her garden, but when the concubine sees him, she orders that his presence be ignored; she is frightened when he continues to stand outside all night. The lady tells herself that this is a one-sided affair, that he can do nothing to her to threaten her security in the Pure Land. Finally, she admits him, and her white hand emerges from beneath the dividing blind that separates them, as custom decrees. She waits, but the priest says nothing. Finally, he releases her hand and departs. Rumor has it that a few days later, the priest "achieved his final liberation" and the concubine begins copying rolls of religious sutras. Thus, the love story between these two who both are faithful to the tenets of *Jōdo* Buddhism focuses on the point at which the ideal world structure that each one envisioned was in this incident "balanced between collapse and survival." If nothing more, the story reflects the aesthetic formed early in Mishima's life, which holds that beauty causes ecstasy which, in turn, causes death.

"PATRIOTISM"

The story "Yōkoku" ("Patriotism"), which was adapted for film, is the first of several that focus on ideals of young military officers of the 1930's. To understand this work, it is important to grasp the meaning of the translation of the word "patriotism." The word *yōkoku* means grieving over a country rather than loving a country (*aikoku*), which is a positive emotion. Thus, it is autobiographical in that it expresses Mishima's own grief over the country that he perceived to be in disorder. "Patriotism," according to Mishima's own evaluation, contains "both the best and the worst features" of his writing. The story concerns a young lieutenant, Shinji Takeyama, who commits seppuku because he feels that he cannot do what he has been ordered to do: lead an attack on the young rebels in the Ni Ni Roku Incident, an unsuccessful coup d'état that occurred on February 26, 1936, in Tokyo. Although Mishima was only eleven years old at the time of the incident, its influence on him provided the germ for two other works, a play *Tōka no Kiku* (pr., pr. 1961; tenth-day chrysanthemums) and *Eirei no Koe* (voices of the heroic dead). These works confirm Mishima's growing dedication to imperialism. The story contains what is possibly the most detailed account of the samurai rite of seppuku in all of Japanese literature.

Almost everything spoken or written by Mishima fits into a personal cosmology that evolved and was refined throughout his life; the living out of this system led to his death: Beauty leads to ecstasy, ecstasy to death. Literature was central to Mishima's cosmos and was virtually inseparable from it. To understand one is to comprehend the other. Mishima was obsessed with death, and to create beauty in his works, in his system, led inevitably to his death.

OTHER MAJOR WORKS

LONG FICTION: *Kamen no kokuhaku*, 1949 (*Confessions of a Mask*, 1958); *Ai no kawaki*, 1950 (*Thirst for Love*, 1969); *Kinjiki*, 1951 (English translation in *Forbidden Colors*, 1968); *Higyō*, 1953 (English translation in *Forbidden Colors*, 1968); *Shiosai*, 1954 (*The Sound of Waves*, 1956); *Kinkakuji*, 1956 (*The Temple of the Golden Pavilion*, 1959); *Kyōko no ie*, 1959; *Utage no ato*, 1960 (*After the Banquet*, 1963); *Gogo no eikō*, 1963 (*The Sailor Who Fell from Grace with the Sea*, 1965); *Kinu to meisatsu*, 1964 (*Silk and Insight*, 1998); *Haru no yuki*, 1969 (*Spring Snow*, 1972); *Homba*, 1969

(*Runaway Horses*, 1973); *Hōjō no umi*, 1969-1971 (collective title for the following 4 novels; *The Sea of Fertility: A Cycle of Four Novels*, 1972-1974); *Akatsuki no tera*, 1970 (*The Temple of Dawn*, 1973); *Tennin gosui*, 1971 (*The Decay of the Angel*, 1974).

PLAYS: *Kantan*, wr.1950, pb. 1956 (English translation, 1957); *Dōjōji*, pb. 1953 (English translation, 1966); *Yoro no himawari*, pr., pb. 1953 (*Twilight Sunflower*, 1958); *Shiroari no su*, pr., pb. 1955; *Aya no tsuzumi*, pr. 1955, pb. 1956 (*The Damask Drum*, 1957); *Aoi no ue*, pr., pb. 1956 (*The Lady Aoi*, 1957); *Hanjo*, pb. 1956 (English translation, 1957); *Kindai nōgakushū*, pb. 1956 (includes *Kantan*, *The Damask Drum*, *The Lady Aoi*, *Hanjo*, and *Sotoba Komachi*; *Five Modern Nō Plays*, 1957); *Sotoba Komachi*, pb. 1956 (English translation, 1957); *Tōka no kiku*, pr., pb. 1961; *Sado kōshaku fujin*, pr., pb. 1965 (*Madame de Sade*, 1967); *Suzakuke no metsubō*, pr., pb. 1967; *Waga tomo Hittorā*, pb. 1968, pr. 1969 (*My Friend Hitler*, 1977); *Chinsetsu yumiharizuki*, pr., pb. 1969.

NONFICTION: *Hagakure nyūmon*, 1967 (*The Way of the Samurai*, 1977); *Taiyō to tetsu*, 1968 (*Sun and Steel*, 1970); *Yukio Mishima on "Hagakure": The Samurai Ethic and Modern Japan*, 1978.

EDITED TEXT: *New Writing in Japan*, 1972 (with Geoffrey Bownas).

BIBLIOGRAPHY

Keene, Donald. *Fiction*. Vol. 1 in *Dawn to the West: Japanese Literature of the Modern Era*. New York: Holt, Rinehart and Winston, 1984. Keene's section on Mishima contains both biographical data and critical evaluations of a large number of Mishima's works. He quotes important passages from various works and from conversations he had with Mishima. Includes notes, a bibliography, and a detailed index.

_____. *Landscapes and Portraits: Appreciation of Japanese Culture*. Tokyo: Kodansha International, 1971. The section on Mishima and his work comments on a variety of his works but especially on *Confessions of a Mask* because, atypically, this novel is autobiographical, providing insight into his thinking and his relation to his own work. As in most studies of Mishima, his preoccupation with death is explored. Includes a short reading list but no index.

_____. "Mishima in 1958." *The Paris Review* 37 (Spring, 1995): 140-160. Keene recalls his 1958 interview with Mishima, in which Mishima discussed influences, his delight in "cruel stories," the importance of traditional Japanese theater for him, and his novels and other writing.

Miyoshi, Masao. *Accomplices of Silence: The Modern Japanese Novel.* Berkeley: University of California Press, 1974. Chapter 6 in part 2, "Mute's Rage," provides studies of two of Mishima's major novels, *Confessions of a Mask* and *The Temple of the Golden Pavilion*, as well as comments on works that Miyoshi considers to be important. Includes notes and an index.

Napier, Susan J. *Escape from the Wasteland: Romanticism and Realism in the Fiction of Mishima Yukio and Ōe Kenzaburō.* Cambridge, Mass.: Harvard University Press, 1991. Napier uncovers shocking similarities, as well as insightful differences, in the work of Mishima and Ōe and ponders each writer's place in the tradition of Japanese literature.

Nathan, John. *Mishima: A Biography.* 1974. Reprint. Cambridge, Mass.: Da Capo Press, 2000. In this readable biography, Nathan's personal acquaintance with Mishima as one of the writer's several translators is evident. The chapters are organized according to chronological periods in Mishima's life. In addition to a chronological listing of the major plays and novels, this volume contains a helpful index. The 2000 edition features a new preface by Nathan.

Piven, Jerry S. *The Madness and Perversion of Yukio Mishima.* Westport, Conn.: Praeger, 2004. A psychological study of Mishima. While Piven focuses on an examination of Mishima's novels, there are references to the short stories, and his discussions of the novels' depictions of homoeroticism, misogyny, impotence, death, voyeurism, and other topics can also pertain to the short fiction.

Scott-Stokes, Henry. *The Life and Death of Yukio Mishima.* Rev. ed. New York: Noonday Press, 1995. After providing a personal impression of Mishima, Scott-Stokes presents a five-part account of Mishima's life, beginning with the last day of his life. The author then returns to Mishima's early life and the making of the young man as a writer. Part 4, "The Four Rivers," identifies the rivers of writing, theater, body, and action, discussing in each subsection relevant events and works. Part 5 is a postmortem. Supplemented by a glossary, a chronology, a bibliography, and an index.

Southern Humanities Review. "Editor's Comment." 36, no. 4 (Fall, 2002): 2. Discusses Mishima's short story "Death in Midsummer," including its reverence to the past and its theme of forgiveness.

Starrs, Roy. *Deadly Dialectics: Sex, Violence, and Nihilism in the World of Yukio Mishima.* Honolulu: University of Hawaii Press, 1994. A critical and interpretive look at sex and violence in Mishima's work. Includes bibliographical references and an index.

Ueda, Makoto. *Modern Japanese Writers and the Nature of Literature.* Stanford, Calif.: Stanford University Press, 1976. Mishima is one of eight Japanese writers treated in this volume. While Ueda examines certain novels in some detail, for the most part his discussion centers on philosophical and stylistic matters and suggests that Mishima's pessimism derived more from his appraisal of the state of human civilization than from his views on the nature of literature. Includes a brief bibliography and an index.

Wolfe, Peter. *Yukio Mishima.* New York: Continuum, 1989. Wolfe argues that common sense explains very little about motives in Mishima, maintaining "What makes him unusual is his belief that anything of value exists in close proximity to death."

Victoria Price

EZEKIEL MPHAHLELE

Born: Marabastad township, Pretoria, South Africa;
    December 17, 1919
Died: Lebowakgomo, Limpopo, South Africa;
    October 27, 2008
Also known as: Es'kia Mphahlele

PRINCIPAL SHORT FICTION

Man Must Live, and Other Stories, 1946
The Living and Dead, and Other Stories, 1961
In Corner B, 1967
*The Unbroken Song: Selected Writings of Es'kia
    Mphahlele,* 1981
Renewal Time, 1988

OTHER LITERARY FORMS

Although he wrote short stories and novels, Ezekiel Mphahlele (eh-ZEE-kee-uhl uhm-fuh-LAY-lay) is best known for his nonfiction works. His two-volume autobiography, *Down Second Avenue* (1959) and *Afrika My Music: An Autobiography* (1984), brought international attention to the oppression of blacks in South Africa. Mphahlele was also the author of a collection of essays, *The African Image* (1962, revised 1974), an important early discussion of the "African personality." *Es'kia: Education, African Humanism and Culture, Social Consciousness, Literary Appreciation* (2002) is a compilation of Mphahlele's essays and public addresses about African literature and literary criticism, education in a democratic South Africa, relations between Africans and African Americans, and African identity, among other subjects. He also edited or coedited important volumes, including the landmark anthology *African Writing Today* (1967), *Perspectives on South African English Literature* (1992), and *Seasons Come to Pass: A Poetry Anthology for Southern African Students* (1994).

ACHIEVEMENTS

Ezekiel Mphahlele is widely considered the most significant black South African writer of the twentieth century and the most balanced critic of African literature. His autobiographical novel *The Wanderers* (1971) was awarded the *African Arts* magazine prize in 1972. He received a Carnegie Foundation grant in 1980 and was awarded honorary doctoral degrees from the University of Pennsylvania, the University of Natal at Pietermaritzburg, the University of Denver, and the University of Cape Town.

BIOGRAPHY

Ezekiel Mphahlele was born in Marabastad township, Pretoria, South Africa, on December 17, 1919. His father left the family early in Mphahlele's life, and he was raised by his mother, a housemaid, and his grandmother, who struggled to keep him in school in spite of economic hardship and an oppressive, strictly segregated social structure. His birth name was Ezekiel, but he later changed his name to Es'kia; both names appear on his works.

In 1945, employed as a high school teacher, he married Rebecca Mochadibane. His first collection of short stories, *Man Must Live, and Other Stories*, was published in 1946. In the early 1950's, he was fired for protesting the segregation of schools, and in 1957 he chose exile from South Africa over life under apartheid. His autobiographical volume *Down Second Avenue*, describing South Africa's black townships, was an international success, but it led to the official banning of his work in that country.

For twenty years, Mphahlele moved about Africa, Europe, and the United States, teaching at various universities and writing highly acclaimed fiction and criticism. He was allowed to return to South Africa in 1977, and the ban on his writing was lifted two years later. His next several books were published in South Africa and were addressed to an African audience. After the end of apartheid in 1990, he continued to teach and write about political and cultural imperialism. He died on October 27, 2008, at the age of eighty-eight.

ANALYSIS

Ezekiel Mphahlele's fiction and other writing have been important bridges between African and Western societies. As an African in a segregated South Africa dominated by Western whites, and later as an African living in exile in Europe and the United States, Mphahlele was in a unique position to present to many Westerners a picture of black South African life that they would not otherwise have had. Because his writings were officially banned by the South African government in 1961, making it illegal for South Africans to read or even quote his work, most of his stories were not read in his own country until the ban was lifted in 1979. While Mphahlele always considered himself an African author writing for an African audience, he also recognized the opportunity to address Western oppressors at the same time that he celebrated the strength and beauty of his own people.

Trained in a European-based school system, Mphahlele had as literary models only Western fiction writers, including Charles Dickens, Miguel de Cervantes, and Fyodor Dostoevski. He wrote in *Afrika My Music* that he had never read an "artful" short story before he began writing them, "so I had no genuine models." He traced his realism to Dickens, William Faulkner, and others and his tendency to focus on a single character in a single intense situation to Scottish and English ballads. Over these European frameworks he draped the cloth of South African experience and sensibility. His stories typically focus on one African character struggling to survive.

Critics often point to Mphahlele's prevailing sense of hope and optimism, even as he wrote about racial tension. This optimism came from Mphahlele's immersion in African humanism, a belief in the essential connection between human nature and the natural world, strengthened by the presence of ancestral spirits and the spirit of community.

MAN MUST LIVE, AND OTHER STORIES

Mphahlele's first short-story collection, *Man Must Live, and Other Stories*, included five short stories

about characters struggling to survive in a difficult world. The theme of survival grew out of his own childhood in a segregated black township, always under a cloud of poverty and oppression. In the title story, a black railroad policeman named Khalima Zungu adopts a philosophy that he chants to himself, "man must live." He marries a woman of means, then treats her poorly and squanders her money, always telling himself that he is entitled to whatever he can get because "man must live." After his new family leaves him and he burns down their house out of revenge, he lives alone in a tin shack, still believing that his need to live is more important than how he treats others. Zungu's life has been a hard one, but his decline is due more to his character than to his circumstances.

Mphahlele knows that survival in a racist society is a struggle, but his underlying belief in community informs this story and many later stories. Community is a central pillar in the belief system Mphahlele has called African humanism. The seven hundred copies of *Man Must Live, and Other Stories* sold quickly in and around Cape Town, establishing Mphahlele's early reputation. As he grew as a writer, however, Mphahlele rejected most of the stories as clumsy and immature. Only "Man Must Live" retained his approval, and he included it in his next collection, *In Corner B*.

"GRIEG ON A STOLEN PIANO"

One of Mphahlele's most likable characters is Uncle, the central character in "Grieg on a Stolen Piano" from *In Corner B*. Uncle, like many black South Africans, has been shaped by a rich blend of traditional and Western cultures. He is a school inspector who moves between the white and black worlds, sometimes playing Edvard Grieg on the piano and using the services of medical doctors, sometimes playing African music and calling for a traditional herbalist and witch doctor. He shares with Zungu of "Man Must Live" a strong will to survive, but Uncle is amusing and gentle, harmful only to himself.

As the story unfolds, Uncle hatches a get-rich-quick scheme to pay off a gambling debt by coaching pretty Mary-Jane to victory in a beauty contest. His plan includes bribing the judges, but Mary-Jane loses anyway. Uncle feels no remorse for his crookedness, nor for the fact that many of his possessions, including his piano,

Ezekiel Mphahlele (AP Photo)

were bought as stolen property. "Don't we steal from each other," he asks, "lie to each other every day and know it, us and the whites?"

"IN CORNER B"

The title story of *In Corner B* shows the richness of life in South Africa's black townships, a world that is invisible to whites, who encounter blacks only as employees and know nothing of them socially. This simple story is about the recently widowed Talita and her troubled memories of her husband of nineteen years on the day of his funeral. Just before her husband's death, Talita learned that he had a mistress, Marta. Marta comes to the funeral and wails loudly but later writes Talita a letter to say that the husband never gave Marta his love. The story again shows Mphahlele's concern with community, and it includes scenes of township people laughing, drinking, and preparing for a funeral. "In Corner B" does not deal with racial tension; whites appear only in the background. Mphahlele would write later, in the essay "Renewal Time," that whites would appear less and less in black African writing because they are "simply irrelevant to the black man's understanding of himself."

"MRS. PLUM"

Mphahlele has called "Mrs. Plum" "the best thing I ever pulled off." First published in *In Corner B*, it tells the story of the black housemaid Karabo and her white employer Mrs. Plum. Told from Karabo's viewpoint, the story is one of the first pieces of fiction to feature a black African woman as the central character. Karabo is young and eager to take her place in the world. Like Zungu in "Man Must Live," she carries a refrain with her: "I learned. I grew up." What she learns is that Mrs. Plum, a typical white liberal in segregated South Africa, is as hypocritical as she is well meaning. Mrs. Plum allows herself to be arrested to protest the injustice of discriminatory laws but will not allow her daughter to marry a black intellectual, who has been a guest in their home. Additionally, she is never able to see Karabo as an equal. Gradually Karabo develops the confidence to demand fair treatment from her employer.

Mphahlele's indictment of white liberal hypocrisy and his detailed true-to-life scenes of South African domestic life are typical of his fiction. Also typical is the story's focus on one central character, struggling to survive in an oppressive society. Karabo's story is set in a real place, at a real time, and the civil injustices she faces are historically accurate.

RENEWAL TIME

Renewal Time is especially significant because it was the first collection of Mphahlele's short fiction published and reviewed outside Africa. Published in 1988 by Readers International, it made the short fiction more easily available to American and European readers who already admired Mphahlele for his autobiographical volumes and criticism. *Renewal Time* comprises the eight stories Mphahlele considers his best, including "Man Must Live," "Grieg on a Stolen Piano," "In Corner B," and "Mrs. Plum"; all of the stories were included in *In Corner B*, and most were written during Mphahlele's exile from South Africa.

Mphahlele begins and ends the volume with new essays reflecting on the stories in the context of his own exile and return. "The Sounds Begin Again--Essay, 1984" (actually the first chapter of *Afrika My Music*) is a narrative account of the author's return to South Africa, interwoven with memories of his youth. In the episodic structure and poetic language of fiction, the piece traces the educational system and the writers--mostly Western--who shaped Mphahlele's own writing. Discovering the short stories of Richard Wright in the 1940's, Mphahlele learned "how to use the short story as a way of dealing with my anger and indignation." In "Renewal Time--Essay, 1981," Mphahlele addresses the reader directly, calling for revolution and renewal.

OTHER MAJOR WORKS

LONG FICTION: *The Wanderers*, 1971; *Chirundu*, 1979, 1994; *Father Come Home*, 1984.

NONFICTION: *Down Second Avenue*, 1959 (autobiography); *The African Image*, 1962 (revised 1974); *A Guide to Creative Writing*, 1966; *Voices in the Whirlwind, and Other Essays*, 1972; *Let's Write a Novel*, 1981; *Afrika My Music: An Autobiography*, 1984; *Let's Talk Writing: Prose*, 1985; *Let's Talk Writing: Poetry*, 1986; *Poetry and Humanism*, 1986; *Es'kia: Education, African Humanism and Culture, Social Consciousness, Literary Appreciation*, 2002.

EDITED TEXTS: *Modern African Stories*, 1964 (with Ellis Ayitey Komey); *African Writing Today*, 1967; *Perspectives on South African English Literature*, 1992 (with Michael Chapman and Colin Gardner); *Seasons Come to Pass: A Poetry Anthology for Southern African Students*, 1994.

BIBLIOGRAPHY

Akosu, Tyohdzuah. *The Writing of Ezekiel [Es'kia] Mphahlele, South African Writer: Literature, Culture and Politics*. Lewiston, N.Y.: Mellen University Press, 1995. An important overview of the critical reception of Mphahlele's work and an assessment of his literary achievements. Akosu claims that aesthetic questions about African writing are inappropriate because they do not take into account the sociopolitical environment in which the work is created. He maintains that Mphahlele's work should be analyzed in terms of its value as a protest against apartheid.

Barnett, Ursula A. *Ezekiel Mphahlele*. Boston: Twayne, 1976. Although published before Mphahlele's return to South Africa from exile in 1977, this volume is still the best introduction to Mphahlele's early and middle life and work. Includes a chronology, biography, and close reading of the major writings.

Egejuru, Phanuel Akubueze. *Towards African Literary Independence: A Dialogue with Contemporary African Writers*. Westport, Conn.: Greenwood Press, 1980. Interwoven interviews with several important writers, including Mphahlele, on the importance of African literature for Africans and for Westerners. Mphahlele discusses the challenges of being both an African and an exile and of writing for an African audience but being published and read by Westerners.

Heywood, Christopher. "Fiction of Resistance and Protest: Bosman to Mphahlele." In *A History of South African Literature*. New York: Cambridge University Press, 2004. Although it focuses on works other than short fiction, this chapter provides an overview of Mphahlele's writings and their importance within the history and tradition of South African literature.

Hodge, Norman. "Dogs, Africans, and Liberals: The World of Mphahlele's 'Mrs Plum'." *English in Africa* 8 (March, 1981): 33-43. A close reading of "Mrs. Plum," emphasizing the indictment the story makes of white liberals in South Africa under apartheid. Hodge believes that "Mrs. Plum" is Mphahlele's most important piece of short fiction and demonstrates his ability to depict characters in the process of intellectual and moral development.

Manganyi, N. Chabani. *Exiles and Homecomings: A Biography of Es'kia Mphahlele*. Johannesburg, South Africa: Ravan Press, 1983. An insightful biography written by a clinical psychologist with full cooperation from Mphahlele and his family. This biography is unusual in using a first-person narrative voice.

McDonald, Peter D. "Es'kia Mphahlele's Worldly Music and the Transcendent Space of Culture." In *The Literature Police: Apartheid Censorship and Its Cultural Consequences*. New York: Oxford University Press, 2009. Examines the cultural impact of censorship by South Africa's white minority government in the period from 1948 through 1994. The chapter on Mphahlele discusses some of his works, including *In Corner B*, and his philosophy of African humanism.

Obee, Ruth. *Es'kia Mphahlele: Themes of Alienation and African Humanism*. Athens: Ohio University Press, 1999. Mphahlele has often discussed African humanism, rather than European influences, as it underlies the writings of the black consciousness movement. Obee extracts the basic values that describe African humanism and traces these values as they appear in Mphahlele's major works and in other important works of South African literature and criticism.

Pitok, Todd. "An Interview with Es'kia Mphahlele." *Poets and Writers Magazine* 22 (November/ December, 1994): 64-71. A brief overview of Mphahlele's life and career, important because of its glimpse of the author's life since the end of apartheid. Pitok discusses Mphahlele's political role in a democratic South Africa, including his missed chance to help Nelson Mandela complete an autobiography.

Ruth, Damian. "Through the Keyhole: Masters and Servants in the Work of Es'kia Mphahlele." *English in Africa* 13 (October, 1986): 65-88. An examination of the theme of the white employer and black employee in South Africa under apartheid as depicted in three of Mphahlele's short stories. In each case, the white employer is blind to the humanity of the employee, while the employee is able to see and to grow.

Cynthia A. Bily

DANIYAL MUEENUDDIN

Born: Los Angeles, California; April, 1963

PRINCIPAL SHORT FICTION

In Other Rooms, Other Wonders, 2009

OTHER LITERARY FORMS

Daniyal Mueenuddin (DAN-yuhl mween-oh-DEEN) has said that when he first went back to run his father's farm in Pakistan, he spent a great deal of time writing poetry. However, those poems were published. After the publication of *In Other Rooms, Other Wonders*, he told several interviewers that he was writing a novel set in Pakistan, a love story about the eternal triangle.

ACHIEVEMENTS

In Other Rooms, Other Wonders was a finalist for the 2009 National Book Award and the 2010 Pulitzer Prize. It won the Story Prize for 2009 and was shortlisted for the *Los Angeles Times* First Fiction Award and the 2010 Ondaatje Prize. It was listed on the "Top Ten" list and "Best Books" list for 2009 by *The Economist*, *Time*, *The Guardian*, *The New Statesman*, and *The New York Times*.

BIOGRAPHY

Daniyal Mueenuddin's father, an Oxford-educated Pakistani civil servant, and his mother, a *Washington Post* correspondent, who met in the United States during the 1950's, were living in Lahore, Pakistan, when his mother became pregnant and flew back to the United States to give birth in the Los Angeles area in April, 1963. After a couple of months, the mother and infant went back to Lahore, where Mueenuddin attended Lahore American School until he was thirteen.

In an interview, Mueenuddin said his family spent most vacations on the farm that he manages in southern Punjab. Although he went to school in Lahore with Westernized Pakistanis and some foreigners, while visiting the farm he played with the children of the village, learning the rhythms and details of the villagers' lives. At age thirteen, he was sent to a prep boarding school in Massachusetts, which he attended for five years before enrolling in Dartmouth College. By this time, he says he had been "lacquered" to such a "glossy Boston-Episcopalian sheen" that he passed as an American. After four years of writing poetry, he graduated with a degree in English literature.

At this time, his father, who was eighty and had suffered several heart attacks, asked him to return to Pakistan and take care of the family farm that was in managerial disarray. His father died soon after Mueenuddin's return, leaving him to learn about the crops, marketing, managing, and dealing with corrupt local police and politics. After six years of bringing the farm under control and achieving some financial stability--meanwhile reading voraciously and writing poetry--he went to Yale Law School, graduating in three years and working at a large New York City law firm from 1998 to 2001. During this time, he says he gradually developed confidence in the stories he had lived though on the farm, both as a child and as an adult, realizing that he was in a unique position to write about the dissolving feudal order in Pakistan. He resigned from the law firm, enrolled in the M.F.A. program at the University of Arizona in Tucson, and began writing stories, earning a degree in 2004. His first story, published in *Zoetrope: All Story* in 2006, interested a literary agent, who then placed a story in *Granta* and three stories in *The New Yorker*. This led to a contract with Norton, which published In *Other Rooms, Other Wonders* in 2009. The book was well received by reviewers and won many awards. Mueenuddin says he is working on a novel set in Pakistan.

ANALYSIS

Daniyal Mueenuddin is an inveterate storyteller. When asked to submit something to the "Contributors' Notes" for *Best American Short Stories, 2008*, for which his *New Yorker* story "Nawabdin Electrician" was chosen, and the "Writers on Their Work" section of *PEN/O. Henry Prize Stories: 2010*, for which his *New Yorker* story "A Spoiled Man" was chosen, he launched into new stories only tangentially related to the original ones, ending one with the triumphant note: "So there it is. A story glosses a story." In an interview with *The Times* of London, when he talked about his encounters with bureaucrats in Pakistan, he invariably launched into what the interviewer called "narrative mode," speaking in sentences that might very well be going into his next story.

This compulsion for storytelling was honed, Mueenuddin says, during the six years of solitude he spent reestablishing his father's farm, during which he read fiction and wrote poetry and hundreds of letters. He spent a lot of time observing the people and actions around him--the crooked deals, the power-mongering, the manipulating of the law--later realizing that he was among the very few who combined the ability to write with the things he saw and the life he lived in Pakistan.

Indeed, much of the positive critical response that greeted Mueenuddin's collection of stories is because of the fact that such a careful and scrupulous writer--powerfully influenced by his reading of Anton Chekhov and Ivan Turgenev--had an insider's knowledge of the feudal system of landlords and their serflike servants that still lingered from old colonial days. Mueenuddin was greeted by *The Wall Street Journal* as a "fresh voice" of Pakistan from within Pakistan, distinguished by his focus on class struggles within that country, offering readers a look inside a culture that is in the headlines. Although *In Other Rooms, Other*

Daniyal Mueenuddin (India Today Group/Getty Images)

Wonders is not a novelistic set of linked stories, many of the stories have at their narrative center the farm of a feudal landlord named K. K. Harouni. Harouni plays a major role in one of the stories, but even when he is in the background, he is a significant force, for his servants depend on him for their livelihood and their lives. When Mueenuddin was asked in an interview if he sees himself as a political writer, he replied that he objects to the idea of writers being too political, for while it gets them a ready-made audience, it takes something away from the writing. Mueenuddin says he does not want to be considered a spokesperson for Pakistan.

"NAWABDIN ELECTRICIAN"

A worker on the farm of his patron Harouni, Nawabdin has developed a crude technique for cheating the electric company by slowing down the revolutions of electric meters, a feat he will perform for customers for a small fee, which he will eventually need for the dowries of his twelve daughters. Having reached a point when he can no longer manage to serve all his customers and do his work for Harouni on his ancient bicycle, he pleads for a motorcycle and receives a Honda 70 and a gasoline allowance, all of which increases his status among the other workers and the community. However, Nawab's fortune takes a turn for the worse when he is accosted on the road by a man with a gun who steals his Honda and tries to drive away with it. When Nawab fights back, the man shoots him in the groin, but knowing the bike means his livelihood, Nawab fights back and is shot at five more times, getting wounded in the leg. The robber runs away when villagers arrive and is shot by one of them. Both men are taken to the pharmacist in the village, who tends to Nawab's wounds but ignores the thief, who dies.

Although Mueenuddin said in the "Contributors' Notes" to *Best American Short Stories, 2008* that he first heard the story of Nawab's being robbed and shot from the "incomparably salty mouth" of Nawabdin himself, one of the employees on his father's farm in South Punjab, Nawab's cunning magic and "superhuman efforts" to slow down electric meters, a discovery that eclipses the philosopher's stone, mark him as a "trickster," a conventional figure common in many folklores, who succeeds by cunning, craft, and supernatural abilities. When the robber pleads for Nawab to

tell the pharmacist to fix him, or at least not to let him die unforgiven, Nawab smells the good strong smell of disinfectant and ignores him. After the robber dies, Nawab thinks of the motorcycle saved and the glory of saving it. The story is about the triumph of life over death, of the right way over the wrong way, and of cunning over crassness. It is a universal fable, not a political statement.

"SALEEMA"

This is an unlikely love story of a young maidservant in Harouni's house, married to a helpless drug addict, who uses her charms to secure favors and protection from other men. Although she is currently the bedmate of the overbearing cook Hassan, she begins to think she could have greater advantage and position if she were to take up with Harouni's elderly valet Rafik. Although he, too, is married, he is seduced by her attention, and they begin an affair, which soon leads to her pregnancy. Saleema insists on having the baby, and Rafik becomes strongly bonded to the little boy. However, when his wife, who lives away from him in Lahore, begins to get suspicious and insists on coming to see him at the big house in the country, his sense of obligation is too much for him. Although he loves Saleema, and she loves him, he begins to pull away from her.

This all comes to a climax when Harouni dies and his grown daughter tells the servants and workers that she is selling the house and that they all must find other jobs and places to live. Because they are completely dependent on the patronage of Harouni, they all utter the same cry that Saleema does, "What'll become of me?" She goes to Rafik, but since Harouni has been his charge, his wealth, his whole life, there is nothing he can do for her or the child. The story ends with two brutal short paragraphs, which summarize the rest of Saleema's life. She begins taking drugs, leaves her husband, and ends up begging on a street corner, controlled by a man who takes most of her earnings. Soon, she dies, and the boy continues to beg on the streets, "one of the sparrows of Lahore," the beggar children whose stories were told in the popular 2008 film *Slumdog Millionaire*. One of the most straightforward tales in the collection, this is the kind of classic love story that Mueenuddin prefers, which, as all great love stories, ends with separation and loss.

"IN OTHER ROOMS, OTHER WONDERS"

In this story, it is the landlord who becomes involved with a young woman. Husna, a distant relative and a maidservant and companion of Harouni's wife, from whom he is estranged, comes seeking his patronage, and he agrees to provide her with typing lessons. However, this is not the kind of patronage that Husna wants, and because Harouni is lonely, they begin a flirtatious relationship that results with his inviting her to live in an annex to the big house, which soon leads to their sleeping together. Harouni's youngest daughter, Sarwat, who is married to a wealthy industrialist and lives in Karachi, disapproves of the relationship, but Harouni insists on it, and Husna enjoys privileges in the house and becomes a favorite of his elderly men friends. However, as usual in these stories, the good fortune cannot last. When Harouni complains of chest pains one night and must be taken to the hospital, the end looms near. When he dies, his daughters dismiss Husna immediately. With whatever dignity she can muster, she tells them, as all of her class ultimately must, that she has no power, that while they are important people, she is nothing and her family is nothing. The story concludes with the kind of understated ending that characterizes "Saleema," when two men load Husna's trunks onto a horse-drawn cart and carry them away to the Old City.

"A SPOILED MAN"

This story focuses on another of Mueenuddin's "little men," in this case, Rezak, who lives alone in a small boxlike shack wherever he can find a location and which he moves when necessary to whatever pickup job he can procure. When he gets a job working in the gardens at Harouni's estate, all is well, until a young man from Rezak's home village stops by and mentions that his cousin has a simpleminded daughter who can cook and sew and is young enough to bear Rezak a son, suggesting that a marriage be arranged. The girl comes to live with Rezak and soon shares his bed; again all seems well, until one day, inexplicably, she disappears. Rezak frantically seeks help from retainers in the Harouni household, but the girl cannot be found. Things get out of hand at a Christmas party, when the son of the inspector general of police hears of the disappearance and reports it to the deputy superintendent, who has Rezak arrested, interrogated, and beaten before finally being released. Rezak accepts the concept of justice usual for one of his class: He had been sheltered by the family, given money to live beyond his station in life, and granted the young girl--making him hope for too much. He then had to be punished for daring to reach too high. As usual in a Mueenuddin story, the end comes rather quickly. Rezak is found dead in his little cubicle and is buried, as he had requested, in a corner of the property. His house is placed on the big estate in a hidden corner as a sort of memorial. Gradually, it is broken into, ransacked, and stripped of everything. The door swings open, and the wind and rain scour it clean. As in all things, it is as if it never was.

Not all the stories in this collection deal with the servant class. "Provide, Provide" focuses on one of Harouni's managers, who cheats him at every opportunity. "About a Burning Girl," the only truly comic, satiric story in the collection, is about the corrupt and convoluted ways of the Pakistani justice system. "Our Lady of Paris" is about a love affair between one of Harouni's sons and a foreign woman. "Lily" is about a young party girl who marries a solid but stolid man and lives, unhappily, with him on his country estate. However, it is the stories of the little men and the helpless women that make this collection so reminiscent of those of the Russian writers Mueenuddin admires, Chekhov and Turgenev.

BIBLIOGRAPHY

Dirda, Michael. "Stories from Pakistan About Living Upstairs, Downstairs, and Everywhere in Between." *The Washington Post*, February 15, 2009, p. BW10. An important review by a noted critic, who analyzes the common narrative dynamic in Mueenuddin's stories.

Habib, Shahnaz. "The Exchange: Daniyal Mueenuddin." *The New Yorker*, March 3, 2009. A long interview with Mueenuddin, in which he discusses the reaction of Pakistanis to his stories, censorship, and how he creates his characters.

Trachtenberg, Jeffrey A. "Tales from a Punjab Mango Farm." *The Wall Street Journal*, January 31, 2009, p. W2. A lengthy profile that introduces Mueenuddin to a wide audience, emphasizing his focus on class struggles within Pakistan.

Charles E. May

BHARATI MUKHERJEE

Born: Calcutta (now Kolkata), West Bengal, India;
    July 27, 1940

PRINCIPAL SHORT FICTION

Darkness, 1985
The Middleman, and Other Stories, 1988 (includes
    "The Management of Grief")

OTHER LITERARY FORMS

Bharati Mukherjee (bah-RAH-tee MOO-kehr-jee) has written several novels, including *The Tiger's Daughter* (1972), *Wife* (1975), *Jasmine* (1989), *The Holder of the World* (1993), *Leave It to Me* (1997), *Desirable Daughters* (2002), and *The Tree Bride* (2004). She also is the author of a travel memoir, *Days and Nights in Calcutta* (1977; with her husband Clark Blaise); a nonfiction critique of Canadian racism, *The Sorrow and the Terror: The Haunting Legacy of the Air India Tragedy* (1987; in collaboration with Blaise); a political treatise, *Kautilya's Concept of Diplomacy* (1976); the nonfiction studies *Political Culture and Leadership in India: A Study of West Bengal* (1991) and *Regionalism in Indian Perspective* (1992); and several essays and articles.

ACHIEVEMENTS

Bharati Mukherjee occupies a distinctive place among first-generation North American writers of Indian origin. She has received a number of grants from the Canada Arts Council (1973-1974, 1977), the Shastri Indo-Canadian Institute (1976-1977), the John Simon Guggenheim Memorial Foundation (1978-1979), and the Canadian government (1982). In 1980, she won first prize from the Periodical Distribution Association for her short story "Isolated Incidents"; in 1981, she won the National Magazine Award's second prize for her essay "An Invisible Woman." Her story "Angela" was selected for inclusion in *The Best American Short Stories 1985*, and "The Tenant" was included in *The Best American Short Stories 1987*. Her second collection of short stories *The Middleman, and Other Stories*, won the National Book Critics Circle Award in 1988.

BIOGRAPHY

Bharati Mukherjee was born into a well-to-do, traditional Bengali Brahman family in the Calcutta suburb of Ballygunge on July 27, 1940. Her Hindu family's affluence buffered them from the political crises of independence and partition that engulfed the Indian subcontinent in the 1940's, and by the end of that troubled decade her father, Sudhir Lal Mukherjee, a chemist and the proprietor of a successful pharmaceutical company, had moved the family first to London (1948-1950) and then to Switzerland (1951) before returning them to India. Accordingly, Mukherjee explains, she and her two sisters (one older, one younger) "were born both too late and not late enough to be real Indians." Her educational experiences abroad had made her fluent in English at an early age, so that once back in India she began attending Calcutta's Loreto Convent School, an elite institution for girls run by Irish Catholic nuns, where she occasionally glimpsed Mother Teresa early in her ministry to the city's poor. At the time, Mukherjee herself followed the habits of her caste and preferred to turn away from the misery on the streets around her rather than question or reflect upon it.

Neither did she consciously plan to deviate very far from the traditional path of Indian womanhood expected of her; even her early interest in becoming a writer, fed by an ever-expanding fascination with the European novels to which her travels and education had exposed her, was tolerated because she was female--such impractical aspirations would have been quickly discouraged in a son, she believes. She has praised her mother for courageously insisting that Mukherjee receive a top-flight English education so that she, in her mother's words, "would not end up . . . as chattel to a traditional Bengali husband." Although her father intended to have his middle daughter marry a bridegroom of the family's choosing from within their own strictly defined social class, he encouraged her intellectual aspirations in the meantime, and so Mukherjee earned an honors B.A. in English from Calcutta University in 1959 and a master's degree in English and ancient Indian culture in 1961 from the University of Baroda. She then joined "the first generation of Indians who even thought of going to the United States rather than automatically to England" when she accepted a Philanthropic Educational Organization International Peace Scholarship to the University of Iowa Writers' Workshop, receiving an M.F.A. in 1963. During that time she met Clark Blaise, an American writer of Canadian descent, whom she married on September 13, 1963, in an action that, she explains, "cut me off forever from the rules and ways of upper-middle-class life in Bengal, and hurled me into a New World life of scary improvisations and heady explorations." The couple had two sons, Bart and Bernard, and over the course of their long marriage they collaborated on a number of book projects, most strikingly *Days and Nights in Calcutta*, a travel journal of their respective observations during a trip together to India.

Having already taught at Marquette University and the University of Wisconsin at Madison, in 1966 Mukherjee moved with Blaise to Montreal, Canada, where she assumed a teaching position at McGill University, which she held until 1978. She completed a Ph.D. in English at the University of Iowa in 1969 and published her first novel, *The Tiger's Daughter*, soon thereafter. In 1972, Mukherjee became a Canadian citizen but quickly grew disenchanted with her new country as she experienced the persistent racial discrimination and harassment suffered by Indians and other immigrants of color; she registered her protest in a celebrated article entitled "An Invisible Woman" and in several short stories.

After fourteen years in Canada, a period during which she published a second novel, *Wife*, along with *Days and Nights in Calcutta*, Mukherjee and Blaise brought their family to the United States and became permanent residents in 1980. In 1976-1977, she served

as director of the Shastri Institute in New Delhi, India. She became writer-in-residence and distinguished professor of English at the University of California, Berkeley. In later years she and Blaise jointly published *The Sorrow and the Terror: The Haunting Legacy of the Air India Tragedy*, which pointedly documents what she regards as Canada's refusal "to renovate its national self-image to include its changing complexion." In 1987, Mukherjee became a naturalized U.S. citizen. Over the course of her career she has taught in numerous American universities, including Emory University, Skidmore College, Columbia University, Queens College, and the University of Iowa Writers' Workshop. Since the 1980's, Mukherjee has regarded herself squarely as an "American" writer (categorically eschewing hyphenated Asian- or Indian-American labels) and describes her geographic relocation as the seminal moment in her artistic maturation. In Canada, she said, she had come to view herself, for the first time in her life, as

> a late-blooming colonial who writes in a borrowed language (English), lives permanently in an alien country, and is read, when read at all, in another alien country, the United States.

That multilayered dispossession ended in the United States as she found herself moving "away from the aloofness of expatriation to the exuberance of immigration." The ideological legitimacy of the immigrant story in American culture has in fact become one of her central literary themes, one in which she explores "America" as "an idea" and "a stage for transformation." Her impressive literary production since arriving in the United States has included a number of critically acclaimed novels centered on strong-willed American or Americanized heroines (including *Jasmine*, *The Holder of the World*, and *Leave It to Me*) and two expansive short-story collections (*Darkness* in 1985 and *The Middleman, and Other Stories* in 1988, the latter the recipient of the National Book Critics Circle Award). Her enthusiasm has not blinded her to political backlash against America's most recent newcomers; in 1997 she warned in *Mother Jones* magazine against a spreading "cultural crisis" wherein "questions such as who is an American and what is American culture are being posed with belligerence, and being answered with violence." Because she sees such polarization as having "tragic" consequences not only for its victims but also for the unique "founding idea of 'America'" itself, which rejected "easy homogeneity" for a "new version of utopia," she urges instead, "We must think of American culture and nationhood as a constantly re-forming, transmogrifying 'we' that works in the direction of both the newcomer and the culture receiving her."

ANALYSIS

Bharati Mukherjee has herself become one of the literary voices whose skillful depictions of the contemporary non-European immigrant experience in the United States she credits with "subverting the very notion of what the American novel is and of what American culture is." In Canada she kept her "Indianness" smugly intact despite--or because of--a painful awareness of her displacement in the West. She consciously regarded other immigrants, as she notes in the introduction to *Darkness*, as "lost souls,

Bharati Mukherjee (AP Photo/Marty Lederhandler)

put upon and pathetic," in contrast to the more ironically sophisticated postcolonials with whom she identified: people "who knew all too well who and what they were, and what foul fate had befallen them," and who therefore escaped the emotional turmoil of divided loyalties or assimilationist incongruities. Once in the United States she found herself drawn toward those same immigrant "outcasts" she once pitied--and not just the ones from the Indian subcontinent. In Mukherjee's two critically acclaimed short-story collections she sets out to "present a full picture, a complicated picture of America," one in which evil as well as good operates and where "we, the new pioneers, who are still thinking of America as a frontier country . . . are improvising morality as we go along." While she unblinkingly paints the bigotries that bedevil her protagonists, she resists casting them as victims

> because they don't think of themselves as victims. On the contrary, they think of themselves as conquerors. We have come not to passively accommodate ourselves to someone else's dream of what we should be. We've come to America, in a way, to take over. To help build a new culture . . . with the same guts and energy and feistiness that the original American Pilgrims had.

DARKNESS

Mukherjee's first collection of short fiction is something of a transitional work in documenting the shift in sensibility that occurred when she left Canada for the United States. Three of its twelve stories reveal a lingering bitterness about Canadian prejudice toward its Indian citizens and concern themselves with the problems that bigotry generates in the lives of individuals still wrestling with the question of whether they believe themselves to be in voluntary exile or hopeful self-transformation. The nine stories set in the United States, by way of contrast, regard the immigrant experience more dynamically and offer "a set of fluid identities to be celebrated" as a result of Mukherjee's having personally "joined imaginative forces with an anonymous, driven underclass of semi-assimilated Indians with sentimental attachments to a distant homeland but no real desire for permanent return." In this new context her own "Indianness" functions less "as a fragile identity to be preserved against obliteration" than as "a metaphor, a particular way of partially comprehending the world." The American-based Indian protagonists of *Darkness* generate stories "of broken identities and discarded languages, and the will to bond oneself to a new community, against the ever-present fear of failure or betrayal."

In an interview published in the *Canadian Fiction Magazine*, Mukherjee stated, "My stories center on a new breed and generation of North American pioneers." The "new pioneers" inhabiting her fictional world include a wide variety of immigrant characters --most of them India-born and others, increasingly, from Third World countries--who pull up their traditional roots and arrive in the New World with dreams of wealth, success, and freedom. *Darkness* focuses on immigrant Indians in North America and deals primarily with the problems of expatriation, immigration, and cross-cultural assimilation.

Mukherjee calls the three Canadian pieces "uneasy stories about expatriation" because they stem from her personal encounters with racial prejudice in this country. Among these pieces is a notably painful and uneasy story about expatriation and racial bigotry, "The World According to Hsü," which explores the diasporic consciousness of Ratna Clayton, an Indian woman married to a Canadian professor of psychology at McGill University in Montreal. Her husband, Graeme Clayton, has been offered the chair of the psychology department at the University of Toronto. Ratna dreads the thought of moving to Toronto: "In Toronto, she was not Canadian, not even Indian. She was something called, after the imported idiom of London, a Paki. And for Pakis, Toronto was hell." Hoping that a vacation would be the ideal setting to persuade his wife to move, Graeme arranges a trip to a beautiful African island. Upon their arrival, they find themselves caught in the midst of a revolution and constrained by a night curfew. The threat of violence unleashes memories of Toronto in Ratna's mind:

 A week before their flight, a Bengali woman was
 beaten and nearly blinded on the street. And the
 week before that an eight-year-old Punjabi boy was
 struck by a car announcing on its bumper: KEEP

CANADA GREEN. PAINT A PAKI.

At the dinner table, when her husband reads her an article by Kenneth J. Hsü about the geological collision of the continents, Ratna wonders why she had to move to Toronto to experience a different kind of collision --racial and cultural. Finally, she brings herself to accept her situation when she realizes that "no matter where she lived, she would never feel at home again."

Another story, "Tamurlane," depicts the lives of Indian émigrés at the opposite end of the class hierarchy from the one Ratna occupies. It dramatizes the precarious situation of illegal aliens who, lured by the dream of a better life, are smuggled into Canada, where they are forced to lead an anonymous, subhuman, underground existence, sleeping in shifts and living in constant fear of being raided by immigration authorities. "Was this what I fled Ludhiana for?" poignantly asks the narrator, an illegal Indian working as a waiter at a dingy Indian restaurant in Toronto. The title of the story (alluding to Tamerlane, a lame Mongol warrior) refers to the restaurant's chef Gupta, who had been maimed six years earlier when he was thrown on the subway tracks. During a raid on illegals at the restaurant, Gupta orders the mounted police to leave. When they refuse and threaten to use force against him, he picks up a cleaver and brings it down on the outstretched hand of one of the policemen. He then defiantly holds his Canadian passport in front of his face. "That way," the story ends, "he never saw the drawn gun, nor did he try to dodge the single bullet."

The immigrant experience dramatized in the American stories is less about the humiliations inflicted on the newcomer by New World intolerance than about the inner struggles of that newcomer in mediating between the pull of old cultural loyalties and the pressures to assimilate to a new context. Dr. Manny Patel, in "Nostalgia," is an Indian psychiatrist working at a state hospital in Queens, New York. His American Dream has come true; he lives in an expensive home, drives a red Porsche sports car, is married to an American nurse, and sends his son to school at Andover. Counting his manifold acquisitions and blessings, he regards himself as "not an expatriate but a patriot." However, he knows that despite becoming a U.S.

citizen, he will forever continue to hover between the Old World and the New. Being the only child of his parents, he feels it is his duty to return to India and look after them in their old age. Caught in a mood of remorse and longing, he drives one day into Manhattan, is smitten by the beauty of an Indian saleswoman, Padma, and invites her on a date, which she readily accepts. They go to an Indian restaurant for dinner and then to bed at an expensive hotel. The whole experience makes him so nostalgic that he wishes "he had married an Indian woman" and "had any life but the one he had chosen." At the end of their tryst, Padma's uncle enters the hotel room with a passkey and accuses Dr. Manny of the rape of his minor niece. Shocked and humiliated, Dr. Manny discovers that "the goddess of his dreams" was nothing more than a common prostitute in collusion with her uncle-pimp to deceive him for profit. The uncle extorts not only seven hundred dollars but also a physician's note on hospital stationery to secure immigration for a nephew. Afterward Dr. Manny defecates into the bathroom sink, squatting as he had done in his father's home, and writes "WHORE" on the bathroom mirror and floor with his excrement, now become "an artist's medium." Just before dawn he drives home, doubly chastened by having succumbed so foolishly to the siren's song of a culture to which he no longer truly belongs and whose gilded memories he now sees for what they are. As he approaches his home he finds the porch light still on, "glow[ing] pale in the brightening light of morning," and he decides to take his wife on a second honeymoon to the Caribbean, in effect repledging his troth to the tangible reality of America itself.

The conflict between Old World and New World takes a different form in "A Father." Mr. Bhowmick, a traditional Bengali, works as a metallurgist with General Motors and lives in Detroit with his Americanized wife and a twenty-six-year-old engineer daughter. He worships the goddess Kali in his home shrine, believes in the sanctity of Hindu superstitions, and lives in constant awe of the unseen powers he believes govern his destiny. Every day he finds himself making frequent compromises between his beliefs and the American pragmatism that surrounds him. When he discovers, to his horror, that his unmarried daughter is pregnant, his first reaction is that she should get an abortion to save the family honor. He blames his wife for this unhappy situation because coming to the United States was her idea. Then he tries to be reasonable. He pities the double life between conflicting values that his daughter must live; he hopes that maybe she has already married secretly; he prays that his hypothetical son-in-law turns out to be a white American. He even secretly enjoys the thought of having a grandson, for he is sure, in this rosier scenario, that the child must be a male.

Thus he reconciles himself to this new situation without resorting to the draconian measures a father in India would be expected to take, only to be confronted with an even more contemporary twist: His daughter reveals that she was impregnated by artificial insemination, and with all the fury of Kali herself she bluntly counters her parents' revulsion at the "animality" of such calculated procreative behavior with assurances that she has secured a sperm donor who meets all the standard bourgeois criteria for a good mate, just as they would have done in arranging a "good" marriage for her were they still in India: "You should be happy-- that's what marriage is all about, isn't it? Matching bloodlines, matching horoscopes, matching castes, matching, matching, matching." Her caustic deflation of the traditions Mr. Bhowmick still venerates defeats his effort to rise to the challenges of modernity, and he strikes out at his daughter, hitting her swelling belly with the rolling pin he has just taken away from his wife. The story ends with Mrs. Bhowmick forced into an unthinkable violation of family honor: She calls the police, thus relying on outsiders to intervene publicly in the self-destruction of her family. In the ways it pulls the reader's sympathies back and forth inconclusively among its characters, "A Father" simulates the actual see-sawing of loyalties characteristic of the multigenerational acculturation process itself.

THE MIDDLEMAN, AND OTHER STORIES

While *Darkness* focuses primarily on the experience of immigrants from the Indian subcontinent, Mukherjee's second collection, *The Middleman, and Other Stories*, is broader in range and scope, as it explores the American experience of immigrants from across the developing world, including India, Afghanistan, Iraq, the Philippines, Sri Lanka, Trinidad, Uganda, and Vietnam. Moreover, four of the eleven stories in this volume have white American protagonists who offer another perspective on the contemporary immigrant situation. (It is worth noting, however, that the concluding piece, "The Management of Grief," once more returns to Mukherjee's deep animus toward the special form of bigotry suffered by Asians in Canada; it renders fictively the same subject with which she and Blaise have dealt in *The Sorrow and the Terror*.)

Virtually all of the stories examine the compromises, losses, and adjustments involved in the process of acculturating newcomers to American life and remaking American culture to reflect the immigrants' presence: In fact, the volume virtually hums with the hustle of modern American cultural diversity played out across an equally various set of U.S. locations ranging from Atlanta to Detroit to Miami to Iowa. Most of the "new pioneers" in this collection are, in a metaphoric sense, middlemen and -women caught between two worlds and cultures (and sometimes more), as even a brief sampling of the cast of characters suggests: an Amerasian child reunited with her veteran father, a Trinidadian "mother's helper," a fully assimilated third-generation Italian American and her Afghan lover, an Iraqi Jew being chased by police in Central America, and a Filipino makeup girl. Such international pedigrees bespeak the widespread political breakdowns that on a shrinking planet increasingly link people who once inhabited completely different worlds. Mukherjee consistently uses the cross-cultural romance as a locus for the societal frictions and emotional barriers that exemplify and exacerbate the problems of communication across culturally constructed differences. The faith of the newest aspirants to the American Dream is frequently contrasted with the decadent malaise of "ugly Americans," who no longer have to travel abroad to betray or defile peoples of other lands. The vigorous immediacy of the American vernacular (to which Mukherjee confesses a delighted addiction) penetrates the speech of these characters, many of whom speak directly to the reader in the first person, and conveys the volatile excitement of the dreams ignited in them by what Mukherjee calls "the idea of America."

The volume's title story is narrated by Alfred Judah from Baghdad, an individual regularly mistaken for an Arab or an Indian. When not on the job, he lives in Flushing, Queens, and he was once married to an American, but he nonetheless feels like an eternal outsider, for "there are aspects of American life I came too late for and will never understand." As such he remains on the margins by working for an illicit border-jumper, gun smuggler Clovis T. Ransome. Judah is a middleman delivering contraband weapons when the armed uprising in the Central American country where he and Ransome had been operating, in callous indifference to the politics of their customers, violently ends their exploitative enterprise and leaves Judah (through the casual intervention of Ransome's bloodthirsty mistress and his own recent lover Maria) to negotiate his way back to "civilization" by drawing yet again upon his basic repertoire of survival in the New World: "There must be something worth trading in the troubles I've seen."

Similarly, in "Danny's Girls," a young Ugandan boy living in Flushing works as a middleman for a hustler, Danny Sahib (originally "Dinesh," a Hindu from northern India), whom the boy calls "a merchant of opportunity." Danny started out selling tickets for Indian concerts at Madison Square Garden, then worked for fixed beauty contests, and eventually went into the business of arranging green cards through proxy marriages for Indians aspiring to become permanent U.S. residents. The latter launched a business of mail-order brides, with Danny in partnership with the African boy's aunt, Lini, in selling Indian and other Asian girls to American men eager for reputedly "compliant" wives. The young narrator has always looked up to Danny and has wanted, like his hero, to attain financial independence in the big world of the United States. When he falls in love with a Nepali girl for whom Danny had arranged a green card, however, he determines to liberate both of them from Danny's clutches, accepting the challenge of becoming his own man by resisting Danny's commodifying ethic--surely American opportunity should mean more.

"Jasmine" is the story of an ambitious Trinidadian girl of that name, who, through a middleman, illegally enters Detroit over the Canadian border at Windsor.

She finds a job cleaning and keeping the books at the Plantations Motel, a business run by the Daboo family, Trinidadian Indians also trying to remake their destinies in Michigan. In picaresque fashion Jasmine later goes to Ann Arbor and works as a live-in domestic with an easygoing American family: Bill Moffitt, a biology instructor, Lara Hatch-Moffitt, a performance artist, and their little girl, Muffin. When Lara goes on the road with her performing group, Jasmine is happily seduced by her boss, and as they make love on the Turkish carpet, she thinks of herself as literally reborn, "a bright, pretty girl with no visa, no papers, and no birth certificate. No nothing other than what she wanted to invent and tell. She was a girl rushing wildly into the future." The story in many ways presages the improvisational Indian heroine of Mukherjee's full-length novel *Jasmine*, published in 1989.

Not all of the stories in *The Middleman, and Other Stories*, deal with characters struggling to move from the margins into the mainstream of American opportunity: "A Wife's Story" and "The Tenant" focus on well-educated Indian women. In the first, Mrs. Panna Bhatt, married to the vice president of a textile mill in India, has come to New York on a two-year scholarship to get a Ph.D. in special education. Haunted by memories of the oppressive gender roles imposed on her mother and grandmother, she believes that she is making something new of her life; her choice of special education as a field of study provocatively mirrors the kind of intervention in her own constricted development that she is undertaking with her radical experiment abroad. She even develops a friendship with a married Hungarian man with whom she attends the theater. When an actor makes obscene jokes about Patel women, however, she feels insulted:

> It's the tyranny of the American dream that scares me. First, you don't exist. Then you are invisible. Then you are funny. Then you are disgusting. Insult, my American friends will tell me, is a kind of acceptance. No instant dignity here.

When her husband comes for a short visit, as a reminder of the more decorous world she misses, she must feign enthusiasm for him. She tries to make up to him for her years away, pretending that nothing has changed, but finally she refuses to return to India with him. When forced to choose between the vulgar freedoms of the United States and the repressive if "safe" institutions of her homeland, she realizes she has already crossed over to another country psychologically.

"The Tenant" goes to the other extreme by showing how an attractive, middle-class, young Bengali woman becomes vulnerable when she breaks with her traditional ways and tries to become part of mainstream America. Maya Sanyal from Calcutta came to the United States ten years earlier, at age nineteen. In smooth succession she received a Ph.D., married an American, became a naturalized citizen, got divorced, and now teaches comparative literature in Cedar Falls, Iowa. During that time she has indiscriminately slept with all kinds of men, except Indians, in a seemingly ambivalent repudiation of the constrictive gender mores of her homeland. Now, afraid that her bachelor landlord might make sexual advances toward her, she calls the other Bengali professor on campus, Dr. Chatterji, and secures an invitation to tea. The traditional atmosphere of his life prompts a newly awakened longing for her homeland, even as his pathetic attempt at seduction leaves her embarrassed. Tired of the fact that her unattached status makes her vulnerable to the lust of every passing male and newly nostalgic for her homeland traditions, she responds to an *India Abroad* matrimonial advertisement from a countryman seeking "the new emancipated Indo-American woman" with "a zest for life," "at ease in USA [sic]," but still holding on to values "rooted in Indian tradition." To her surprise, as she meets Ashoke Mehta at the Chicago airport, she suddenly feels as if a "Hindu god" is descending to woo her--a handsome Indian man who has indeed merged his two cultures in ways that seem to make them destined for each other. However, witnessing his seamless acculturation also erodes her own self-confidence:

> She feels ugly and unworthy. Her adult life no longer seems miraculously rebellious; it is grim, it is perverse. She has accomplished nothing. She has changed her citizenship but she hasn't broken

through into the light, the vigor, the hustle of the New World. She is stuck in dead space.

More to the point is their mutual recognition that each carries a complicated romantic history to this moment--a history that makes each wary of the other and precludes Ashoke's contacting her again for several months. During that time she resumes her life in Cedar Falls and, when her landlord abruptly marries, moves to a new room rented to her by an armless man named Fred, whose lover she soon becomes, "two wounded people" who "settle into companionship." She also recognizes uncomfortably that this liaison speaks to some sense of her own deficiency as an rootless émigré in flight from her own past: "She knows she is strange, and lonely, but being Indian is not the same, she would have thought, as being a freak." When at last Ashoke calls and obliquely concedes the entanglements that had kept him from committing to her, she knows she will accept his invitation to join him out East--each has made peace with the contradictory emotions about their shared legacy they arouse in each other.

The Middleman, and Other Stories, like *Darkness* before it, contains many melodramatic situations and a pronounced streak of violence. Mukherjee does not always provide sufficient context for the behaviors and attitudes of her characters. Nevertheless, she imparts a potent voice to these "new pioneers" and sheds light on the dynamic world of America's newest wave of self-inventors--people often invisible to those in the mainstream. Many of them suffer from racism and prejudice; others seem welcome only in the shady underworlds of sex, crime, and drugs; and some merely scramble for a living in their struggle for survival. To adapt to their new milieu, even professional men and women have to make compromises and trade-offs between their old belief systems and the New World ethos. In the process, many suffer cultural disorientation and alienation and undergo traumatic changes --psychological, cultural, linguistic. Mukherjee, however, appears to have no doubt that such a break is desirable. As she has told journalist Bill Moyers,

America is a total and wondrous invention. Letting go of the old culture, allowing the roots to wither is natural; change is natural. But the unnatural thing is

to hang on, to retain the old world . . . I think if you've made the decision to come to America, to be an American, you must be prepared to really, emotionally, become American and put down roots. . . . In doing that, we very painfully, sometimes violently, murder our old selves. . . . I want to think that it's a freeing process. In spite of the pain, in spite of the violence, in spite of the bruising of the old self, to have that freedom to make mistakes, to choose a whole new history for oneself, is exciting.

Admittedly, the new selves that emerge from her stories are not always models of virtue, but "pioneering does not necessarily equate with virtue. . . . I like to think my characters have that vigor for possessing the land," with all the mother wit, ruthlessness, and tenacity of their predecessors. Yes, she admits,

the immigrant's soul is always at risk. . . . I have to make up the rules as I go along. No one has really experienced what the nonwhite, non-European immigrants are going through in the States. We can't count on the wisdom and experience of the past of the old country; and we can't quite fit into the traditional Eurocentric experiences of Americans.

In telling the stories of these immigrants, then, Mukherjee regards herself as "writing a fable for the times. I'm trying to create a mythology that we can live by as we negotiate our daily lives."

OTHER MAJOR WORKS

LONG FICTION: *The Tiger's Daughter*, 1972; *Wife*, 1975; *Jasmine*, 1989; *The Holder of the World*, 1993; *Leave It to Me*, 1997; *Desirable Daughters*, 2002; *The Tree Bride*, 2004.

NONFICTION: *Kautilya's Concept of Diplomacy*, 1976; *Days and Nights in Calcutta*, 1977 (with Clark Blaise); *The Sorrow and the Terror: The Haunting Legacy of the Air India Tragedy*, 1987 (with Blaise); *Political Culture and Leadership in India: A Study of West Bengal*, 1991; *Regionalism in Indian Perspective*, 1992; *Conversations with Bharati Mukherjee*, 2009 (Bradley C. Edwards, editor).

BIBLIOGRAPHY

Alam, Fakrul. *Bharati Mukherjee*. New York: Twayne, 1996. An introductory overview of Mukherjee's life and works that also looks at India, women, and East Indian Americans in literature. Includes a bibliography and index.

Ascher, Carol. "After the Raj." Review of *The Middleman, and Other Stories*, by Bharati Mukherjee. *Women's Review of Books* 6, no. 12 (1989): 17, 19. Using illustrative detail from six of the eleven short stories in this collection, Ascher shows how in dealing with the immigrant experience "the strategy of short stories has served [Mukherjee] well."

Bowen, Deborah. "Spaces of Translation: Bharati Mukherjee's 'The Management of Grief.'" *Ariel* 28 (July, 1997): 47-60. Argues that in this story, the assumption of moral universalism is a crucial precursor to the problems of negotiating social knowledge. Mukherjee addresses questions of cultural particularization by showing how inadequately translatable are institutionalized expressions of concern.

Burton, Rob. *Artists of the Floating World: Contemporary Writers Between Cultures*. Lanham, Md.: University Press of America, Inc., 2007. Looks at Mukherjee and three other writers whose works explore a "floating world" in which cultures collide and converge. The chapter on Mukherjee focuses on her depiction of "subalterns," devoting several pages to a discussion of *The Middleman, and Other Stories*.

Dascalu, Cristina Emanuela. "Bharati Mukherjee and the Exile's Constant Shuttling." In *Imaginary Homelands of Writers in Exile: Salman Rushdie, Bharati Mukherjee, and V.S. Naipaul*. Youngstown, N.Y.: Cambria Press, 2007. Demonstrates how Mukherjee's "fiction captures precisely the radical nature of exile." Focuses on an analysis of the novel *Jasmine*, which originated as a short story of that name published in *The Middleman, and Other Stories*.

Drake, Jennifer. "Looting American Culture: Bharati Mukherjee's Immigrant Narratives." *Contemporary Literature* 40 (Spring, 1999): 60-84. Argues that assimilation is portrayed as cultural looting, cultural exchange, or a willful and sometimes costly negotiation in Mukherjee's stories. Notes that Mukherjee rejects the nostalgia of hyphenated "Americans" and their acceptable stories and instead portrays settlers, Americans who want to be American--not sojourners, tourists, guest workers, or foreigners.

Gelfant, Blanche H., ed. *The Columbia Companion to the Twentieth-Century American Short Story*. New York: Columbia University Press, 2000. Includes a chapter in which Mukherjee's short stories are analyzed.

Ispahani, Mahnaz. "A Passage from India." Review of *Darkness*, by Bharati Mukherjee. *The New Republic* 14 (April, 1986): 36-39. Ispahani believes that the short stories in this collection "treat the classical theme of diaspora--of exile and emigration." She singles out five stories for analysis to demonstrate her point, and includes a brief comment on Mukherjee's style.

Morton-Mollo, Sherry. "Bharati Mukherjee." In *A Reader's Companion to the Short Story in English*, edited by Erin Fallon et al., under the auspices of the Society for the Study of the Short Story. Westport, Conn.: Greenwood Press, 2001. Aimed at the general reader, this essay provides a brief biography of Mukherjee followed by an analysis of her short fiction.

Mukherjee, Bharati. "American Dreamer." *Mother Jones*, January/February, 1997. Depicted literally as wrapped in an American flag while standing in a cornfield, Mukherjee speaks to her passionate sense of herself as an American writer and citizen.

_____. "An Interview with Bharati Mukherjee." Interview by Geoff Hancock. *The Canadian Fiction Magazine* 59 (1987): 30-44. In this important interview, Mukherjee discusses her family background, formative influences, and work. She provides illuminating comments on her fictional characters, themes, and voice.

_____. "Interview." In *Speaking of the Short Story: Interviews with Contemporary Writers*, edited by Farhat Iftekharuddin, Mary Rohrberger, and Maurice Lee. Jackson: University Press of Mississippi, 1997. Mukherjee discusses the origins of her stories and the process by which they are composed. She criticizes Marxist and other social critics who reduce stories to sociology and anthropology.

_____. *Conversations with Bharati Mukherjee.* Edited by Bradley C. Edwards. Jackson: University Press of Mississippi, 2009. A compilation of interviews with Mukherjee, including one conducted specially for this book in 2007 and a conversation with both Mukherjee and her husband Clark Blaise.

Nazareth, Peter. "Total Vision." *Canadian Literature: A Quarterly of Criticism and Review* 110 (1986): 184-191. Nazareth analyzes Mukherjee's first collection of short stories, *Darkness*, to show how she has distinguished herself by becoming "a writer of *the other America*, the America ignored by the so-called mainstream: the America that embraces all the peoples of the world both because America is involved with the whole world and because the whole world is in America."

Sant-Wade, Arvindra, and Karen Marguerite Radell. "Refashioning the Self: Immigrant Women in Bharati Mukherjee's New World." *Studies in Short Fiction* 29 (Winter, 1992): 11-17. An analysis of "The Tenant," "Jasmine," and "A Wife's Story" as stories in which immigrant women refashion themselves and are reborn. In each story the women's sense of possibility clashes with a sense of loss, yet their exuberant determination attracts the reader to them and denies them the power of pity.

Scheer-Schäzler, Brigitte. "'The Soul at Risk': Identity and Morality in the Multicultural World of Bharati Mukherjee." In *Nationalism vs. Internationalism: (Inter)National Dimensions of Literature in English*, edited by Wolfgang Zach and Ken L. Goodwin. Tübingen, Germany: Stauffenburg, 1996. Discusses Mukherjee's approach to identity and morality, a common theme of immigration literature. Describes the tensions between the monocultural self and its multiculturally transformed versions in her writing.

Chaman L. Sahni
Updated by Barbara Kitt Seidman

Haruki Murakami

Born: Kyoto, Japan; January 12, 1949

PRINCIPAL SHORT FICTION
The Elephant Vanishes, 1993
Kami no kodomotachi wa mina odoru, 2000 (*After the Quake,* 2002)
Blind Willow, Sleeping Woman, 2006

OTHER LITERARY FORMS
Haruki Murakami (hah-REW-kee mur-ah-KAH-mee) has won critical recognition worldwide for his novels, particularly *Nejimaki-dori kuronikuru* (1994-1995; *The Wind-Up Bird Chronicle,* 1997) and *Umibe no Kafuka* (2002; *Kafka on the Shore,* 2005). His popularity was established with his romantic ode to pop culture, the novel *Noruwei no mori* (1987; *Norwegian Wood,* 2000). His time abroad has led him to write travel essays and the occasional nonfiction piece, notably the interviews he conducted in the wake of the Tokyo subway attacks, *Andaguraundo,* (1997; *Underground: The Tokyo Gas Attack and the Japanese Psyche,* 2000), and his memoir *Hashiru koto ni tsuite kataru toki ni boku no kataru koto* (2007; *What I Talk about When I Talk about Running,* 2008). Murakami also translates extensively.

ACHIEVEMENTS
Haruki Murakami's first novel *Kaze no uta o kike* (1979; *Hear the Wind Sing,* 1987) was awarded the Gunzo New Writer Award. The Noma Literary Prize for new writers was bestowed upon a later installment in what was to become *The Trilogy of the Rat,* which includes *Hear the Wind Sing; 1973: nen no pinboru* (1980; *Pinball, 1973,* 1985), and *Hitsuji o meguru bōken* (1982; *A Wild Sheep Chase,* 1989). In 1995, he was presented with the Yomiuri Literary Prize for *The Wind-Up*

Bird Chronicle by one of his most strenuous critics, Japan's 1994 Nobel Prize winner, Kenzaburō Ōe. Murakami's collection *Blind Willow, Sleeping Woman*, containing English translations of short fiction written and published throughout Murakami's career, was awarded the Kiryama Prize for Fiction from the Pacific Rim.

BIOGRAPHY

Haruki Murakami was born in Kyoto, Japan, several years after the end of World War II. Although the U.S. military continued to occupy Japan during his childhood, and his college years were marked by the student protests of the late 1960's, Murakami surprisingly is apolitical. The only son of two high school English teachers, he was a voracious reader but not a good student. His failure to pass college entrance examinations on the first round led him to study literature instead of pursuing law, which he had originally intended.

At Waseda University, he met Yoko Takahashi, whom he married in 1971. Murakami's passion for music and his entrepreneurial spirit led the two of them to open a jazz club in Tokyo. They named it Peter Cat, in honor of one of Murakami's many feline friends. Despite the strain on their time and resources, they both finished college while managing the club. Not until 1978 was Murakami inspired to write, out of the blue, as he tells it, while at a baseball game. He sent his first novel to a literary magazine and won the Gunzo Award for New Writers. The recognition inspired him to continue writing and eventually to sell the club.

He began to travel in 1984, and on his first trip to the United States he was able to meet some of the authors he most admired. He has since spent much of his time in Greece, Italy, and America, to the consternation of his Japanese critics. The time abroad has given Murakami a unique perspective on the Japanese personality. His work alternates between attempts to explain the worldview of his fellow citizens and deep, often subconscious, explorations of it.

ANALYSIS

The story "Honey Pie" in *After the Quake* features a storyteller by the name of Junpei, who studies literature at Waseda University; who has been nominated repeatedly for, but has never been a recipient of, the coveted

Akutagawa Prize; and who, although a fairly successful short-story writer, cannot fathom sustaining such an effort as a novel. Despite the overt and somewhat ironic similarities between this character and Murakami, they differ in at least one key respect: Murakami has sustained the novelistic impulse to great acclaim on more than one occasion.

In his own opinion, however, Murakami's longer works offer the background for details merely visible in his short fiction. He compares the first to developing a forest, the second to creating a garden. If the character Junpei resembles Murakami the writer, he also demonstrates one of the author's central themes: the pain of alienation. When Junpei's two best friends fall in love and marry, he becomes strangely situated as both inside and outside their circle of intimacy. Murakami's translator and biographer Jay Rubin has identified the position as uniquely Japanese, a culture rooted in the group--whether it be military, political, religious, or economic--that has dissolved into a loose coalition of as-yet-undefined individuals. In a later story, "The Kidney-Shaped Stone," which also features a short-story writer named Junpei, the character finds peace inside his emotional strength and within his craft.

Even in the first-person narration that Murakami employs most often, the paradox of Japanese individualism is foregrounded. Rubin explains the difference between the more formal first-person pronouns common to Japanese literature, *watakushi* or *watashi*, and the informal and indeterminate *boku* used by Murakami. (The fact that *boku* refers exclusively to a male narrator may explain the dearth of female protagonists in Murakami's short fiction, although female characters appear in nearly every story.) The narrator creates an atmosphere that is welcoming in its informality, while revealing practically nothing about himself, thus holding the reader at arm's length.

"Slow Boat to China," one of Murakami's early efforts, reflects the use he makes of this perspective to convey themes of alienation, loneliness, and guilt. As the narrator reflects upon when he may have met his first Chinese person, he rejects the comfort of fact for the emotional and unstable "reality" of memory. He proceeds through the increasingly shameful and embarrassing encounters he has had to finally meditate upon the faraway land of China, full of mystery, that has brushed against him so few times in life. It is a powerful metaphor for the certainties and the unknowns that constitute individual personalities.

The title story to Murakami's first collection displays a deep anxiety at the theorems and structures modern humanity has constructed in its effort to interpret and control reality, while the ability to take the world at face value slowly disappears. The narrator of "The Elephant Vanishes" lives alone and is obsessed with the story of an elephant that is displaced when a zoo closes and the property is purchased by a developer. The narrator collects newspaper clippings, visits the improvised display set up by the town, and secretly spies on the elephant and its keeper late at night. He is fascinated by the fact that the evening of the elephant's disappearance he witnessed a radical shift in perspective that made the keeper seem much larger than the animal, and he relates all he knows to a woman he has just met, ensuring his continued isolation, which he describes as a fault in his perceptions, something in him having lost balance or broken down.

A prominent feature of Murakami's narration is the lack of names. Given the wealth of detail in his settings and the carefully wrought idiosyncrasies of his characters, such a frequent and significant omission seems especially important. The narrator addresses the question in "A 'Poor Aunt' Story," an allegory for the creative process. In it, the narrator thinks of writing a story about a poor aunt and then literally, comically, a poor aunt appears on his back. As he contemplates her existence, he acknowledges that all names fade, but he explains that upon death some disappear with a trite phrase memorializing their life, others burn out slowly, and for some, like the poor aunt, the name fades before the person is gone from this world. The narrator imagines a community of lost names creating a maze in which people either die in horrific ways or go on living quietly. Neither option is shaded as more preferable, a blasé approach toward human destiny and personality that characterizes Murakami's plots and his tone.

Haruki Murakami (AFP/Getty Images)

AFTER THE QUAKE

These six stories each respond in some way to the Kobe earthquake, which hit on January 17, 1995, and which devastated the busiest and most profitable of Japan's port cities and the national psyche. The tales thus cohere thematically in a way that Murakami finds antithetical to the nature of a short-story collection. Given that connection, the reader might be struck with the ways in which that event forms the periphery of the narrative in all but the first story, "UFO in Kushiro," in which a wife is so absorbed with news of the earthquake that she withdraws completely into herself and eventually leaves her husband, forcing him to discover who he is without her.

As in many works by Murakami, these tales are pervaded by a sense of loneliness, purposelessness, and the inability to "be" in any meaningful sense of the term. The first two of the collection's stories delay or deny entirely any sense of resolution. Strikingly, though, for Murakami, the final four tales close with a sense of peace and a hint that the future might include more of a communal spirit. Especially hopeful are the visions of Yoshiya Osaki's final moments dancing on a deserted baseball field under a starlit sky in "All God's Children Can Dance" and Katagiri's vigil over the six-foot Super-Frog who congratulates him for helping to save Tokyo from a similar fate as Kobe.

The connection between purpose and community is reinforced by the point of view. As opposed to the first-person voice that pervades many of Murakami's other short works, these stories are all narrated in a third person who pretends to be omniscient but who reveals only the thoughts, impressions, and feelings of the main character in each story. Ironically, the perspective thus creates a distance between the protagonist and the story's other characters, emphasizing the lack of community, which is vital for the development of the individual, even if only as something to define oneself against.

"THE SECOND BAKERY ATTACK"

In one of the early manifestations of Murakami's narrative style, a young newlywed couple wake up to a ravenous hunger so powerful they cannot return to sleep. The experience demonstrates how unsuited they are as yet to married life; the fact that they both feel the pain simultaneously suggests that their union runs quite deep. The feeling causes a sudden memory to surface for the narrator, about an escapade he and a friend had shared during their university days. Vowing not to work as a form of political protest, the two made a living stealing what they needed to survive. One evening they exchange their time for bread in an attack upon a bakery store. The experience somehow sours them on thievery, and they quit. His wife convinces him that his inability to commit to his conviction has cursed them, and they must enact a successful robbery to purge the marriage of its taint.

Comically, they drive through Tokyo in the early hours of the morning with a shotgun and ski masks but are unable to find an all-night bakery. They settle for a McDonald's, where they steal fifty Big Macs, eat as many as they can, and fall asleep peacefully in their car. Ironically, the episode demonstrates their suitability as a married couple. The narrator is surprised by his wife's acumen and at how easily they fall into tandem,

resolving his apparent anxiety about the loss of his freedom and individuality.

The story is characterized by the image of an imaginary volcano that the husband first glimpses through water so clear as to defy depth perspective. The volcano could thus be many hundreds of miles below him or directly contiguous with the surface. As the story progresses, the volcano recedes and the surrounding water becomes less of a threat and ultimately a source of peace. The image could be a symbol for the narrator's marriage, the protests in which he engaged during his youth, or the hunger he and his wife are both experiencing. The author rejects any interpretation, claiming it is literally what he sees and feels when he is hungry.

OTHER MAJOR WORKS

LONG FICTION: *Kaze no uta o kike*, 1979 *(Hear the Wind Sing*, 1987);

1973: Nen no pinbo-ru, 1980 *(Pinball, 1973*, 1985); *Hitsuji o meguru bōken*, 1982 *(A Wild Sheep Chase*, 1989); *Sekai no owari to hādoboirudo wandārando*, 1985 *(Hard-Boiled Wonderland and the End of the World*, 1991); *Noruwei no mori*, 1987 *(Norwegian Wood*, 2000); *Dansu dansu dansu*, 1988 *(Dance, Dance, Dance*, 1993); *Kokkyō no minami, taiyō no nishi*, 1992 *(South of the Border, West of the Sun*, 1999); *Nejimaki-dori kuronikuru*, 1994-1995 (3 volumes; *The Wind-Up Bird Chronicle*, 1997); *Supūtoniku no koibito*, 1999 *(Sputnik Sweetheart*, 2001); *Umibe no Kafuka*, 2002 *(Kafka on the Shore*, 2005); *Afutādāku*, 2004 *(After Dark*, 2007).

NONFICTION: *Andaguraundo*, 1997 *(Underground: The Tokyo Gas Attack and the Japanese Psyche*, 2000); *Hashiru koto ni tsuite kataru toki ni boku no kataru koto*, 2007 *(What I Talk About When I Talk About Running: A Memoir*, 2008).

TRANSLATIONS: *Za sukotto Fittsujerarudo bukku* (F. Scott Fitzgerald miscellany), 1988; *Aru kurisumasu* (Truman Capote's *One Christmas*, 1983), 1989; *Kurisumasu no omoide* (Truman Capote's *A Christmas Memory*, 1956), 1990; *Reimondo Kāvā zenshu* (*Complete Works of Raymond Carver*) 8 volumes, 1990-1997; *Saigo no shunkan no sugoku ōkina henka* (Grace Paley's *Enormous Changes at the Last Minute*, 1974), 1999; *Hitsuyō ni nattara denwa o kakete* (Raymond Carver's *Call If You Need Me*: *The Uncollected Fiction and Other Prose*, 2000), 2000.

BIBLIOGRAPHY

Giles, Jeff. "A Shock to the System: Haruki Murakami's Stories Are Set in Japan in the Month after Kobe." *The New York Times Book Review*, August, 18, 2002. Offers the historical and psychological context for *After the Quake* and mentions how Americans will surely read it in a more personal light after 9/11.

Lai, Amy Ty. "Memory, Hybridity, and Creative Alliance in Haruki Murakami's Fiction." *Mosaic* 40, no. 1 (March, 2007): 163. Surveys the use of animalistic imagery in all of his work, shedding some light on "The Elephant Vanishes," "The Kangaroo Communiqué," and "A Perfect Day for Kangaroos."

Loughman, Celeste. "No Place I Was Meant to Be: Contemporary Japan in the Short Fiction of Haruki Murakami." *World Literature Today* 71, no. 1 (Winter, 1997): 87. Defends pop culture and in particular Americanized pop in Murakami's work as a product of a thoroughly hybridized Japan. Explains that he relies on a clear, fixed setting to compensate for disappearing identities and social consensus.

Rubin, Jay. *Haruki Murakami and the Music of Words*. London: Harvill Press, 2002. Mingles biographical descriptions with large excerpts from Murakami's writings. Includes Murakami's comments in interviews about his works and his process of writing, discussion on Murakami's assessment of literature, and speculations about Murakami's influences.

Welch, Patricia. "Haruki Murakami's Storytelling World." *World Literature Today* 79, no. 1 (January-April, 2005): 55. Although Welch gives more attention to Murakami's novels than to his short stories, she discusses his characterization and offers context for the history and culture at the time of each work.

L. Michelle Baker

N

RABBI NAHMAN OF BRATSLAV

Born: Medzibezh, Poland (now in Ukraine); April 4, 1772
Died: Uman, Ukraine, Russian Empire (now in Ukraine); October 15, 1811
Also known as: Rabbi Nachman of Breslov

PRINCIPAL SHORT FICTION

Sipure Ma'asiyot, 1815 (*The Tales,* 1956)

OTHER LITERARY FORMS

Rabbi Nahman (NAH-muhn) of Bratslav's scribe, Nathan Sternhartz of Nemirov, wrote a biography, edited two volumes of the rabbi's sermons and ethical teachings and a collection of his prayers, and transcribed his stories. Nahman had ordered that his writings be destroyed in 1808; his disciples refer to this as *The Burned Book.*

ACHIEVEMENTS

Rabbi Nahman's achievement lies in the faith that his stories inspired. Powerfully spiritual, his work became the guiding force for the Bratslav sect of the Hasidim. As writer Howard Schwartz noted, Rabbi Nahman's view was that "every act, no matter how small, held potentially great significance." In many cases, Rabbi Nahman's work was not original; rather, it was often adapted from much older Russian and Ukrainian folklore. His quest was to create religious allegories that would hold deep significance to the ordinary human condition. As he wrote in the introduction to his story "The Losing of the King's Daughter," "I told this story . . . and everyone who heard it had thoughts of repentance." Ultimately, Rabbi Nahman's literary success stemmed from his use of major theological issues to stimulate thought while disguising them as entertainment.

BIOGRAPHY

Little is known about the first twenty-six years of Rabbi Nahman's life except that he was shy, ascetic, morbidly obsessed with his own sinfulness, endowed with visions, and given to praying fervently on the grave of his great-grandfather, the Baal Shem Tov, who had been the founder of Hasidism. Married at thirteen to Sosia, he lived in his father-in-law's house in Usyatin until 1790, and then they moved to Medvedevka, in the province of Kiev, where he was established as a zaddik (a charismatic leader of a group of Hasidim, literally "a righteous one"). In 1798, he left his wife and three daughters to undertake an arduous pilgrimage to the Holy Land with one of his disciples, Simeon. Beginning in 1800, he was the center of continual controversy, but he interpreted these rejections as signs of his messianic mission. Shortly before his own death from tuberculosis at the age of thirty-nine, during the period of his deepest personal tragedies--the death of his only son in 1806, and of his wife in 1807--he began to tell his stories.

ANALYSIS

The critical theory presented in the introduction to *The Tales,* culled from Rabbi Nahman's sermons, defends storytelling as a redemptive act. By engaging their imaginations, storytelling awakens listeners from their spiritual slumber. It lifts them up out of their fallen state, inspiring them to participate in the world's salvation. The interpretive strategies to be used for these charming fairy tales are anagogic; the plots are really revelations of the dynamics of the universe. The characters are figurations of the *sefirot,* the emanations of God, by means of which the world was created. The story form garbs these truths which would, in their naked form, blind and dazzle the mind, so they are "clothed" as tales.

The Lurianic myth, which gives the tales coherence, tells how the Fall and the Creation were simultaneous. God was originally coextensive with the universe. In order to clear space for the world, He contracted Himself (this is called the *tzimtzum*), and in that void where God was absent, the earth was created. In the stories this empty space is represented by a desert. The next stage of creation is called the *shevirah*, the shattering of the vessels. The Divine emanations were too overwhelming to be contained in the earthly forms into which They had been infused, so these exploded into shards and fragments (*klippot*). In the universal cataclysm, the Divine Sparks became mixed with mundane evil. It becomes human beings' task to lift up these fallen sparks by good deeds so that the cosmos can once again be restored to its primordial harmony. Until this reparation (*tikkun*) occurs, all humankind remains in a state of exile. The redemption is figured as a cosmic marriage because the lowest of the ten Divine Emanations, the *Shekina*, was expelled into the world by the violence of the *tzimtzum* and must remain in exile until the messiah, who is destined to be her bridegroom, brings salvation. This is the plot of the first of Rabbi Nahman's tales, "The Lost Princess."

"THE LOST PRINCESS"

In this tale, a king is deeply grieved that his beloved daughter has been banished from his kingdom. A viceroy offers to seek her out and bring her back. His search leads him to a desert, "the empty spot" devoid of God's presence, where she is being held captive. She tells him that he must "yearn for her mightily" and fast. He fails. Repeating Adam's sin, he is smitten with such a great craving for an apple that he cannot resist and falls into a deep sleep. She forgives him for having yielded to the evil impulse and gives him a second chance to redeem her. This time, she says, he must not drink or he will again fall into a spiritual stupor. Once again he succumbs to temptation as a spring gushes forth that looks red and smells like wine. By repeating Noah's drunkenness he is condemned to seventy years of sleep. Sadly the princess tries to rouse him, but although she shakes him vigorously, he will not arise. She unbinds the kerchief from her head and writes on it with her tears that she is being taken to an even more inaccessible place, to a pearly castle on a golden mountain.

Now determined to find her, the viceroy wanders many years through desert places, encountering, one after another, three giants. The first, who says he controls all the animals, insists that there is no pearly castle and summons the animals to testify to this; but the viceroy's faith is undaunted, and he persists, even though the second giant summons all the birds to swear that they have never seen a golden mountain. His faith remains unshaken in spite of this evidence. The more obstacles he encounters, the more convinced he is that he will ultimately find the princess. Even when the third giant summons all the winds to witness, he does not give up. Just as the giant is reproving him-- "Don't you see that they have told you nonsense?"--a final wind blows in all out of breath. It apologizes for being late because it had to carry a princess to a pearly castle on top of a golden mountain. The story does not stipulate how the viceroy finally finds the lost princess because their reunion will not occur until the redemption of the world, which is not yet. Prophecy is characteristically open-ended, and the prophetic mode usually ends with a rhetorical question. The declined closure implies that the listeners must participate in shaping the desired ending and suggests that the conclusion is up to them. The tale is meant to move them to act.

The Bratslaver Hasidim, who worship in the synagogue in the Mea Shearim sector of Jerusalem beneath a sign inscribed with Rabbi Nahman's motto, "Jews, never despair!" say that "The Lost Princess" shows that they must sustain their faith in spite of all obstacles. In spite of gigantic doubts, offered with the marshaling of evidence, provided with such certitude and with such an appearance of reason, even if everything that swims, slithers, walks, and flies should testify to the contrary, the Jew must persist in his belief.

What is so fascinating about this narrative structure is the way in which content, rhetoric, and plot all mirror one another. Narratology and theology are self-reflexive. Furthermore, the language is so full of trance-inducing repetitions that it becomes numinous. Martin Buber's 1906 German translation deleted these numinous repetitions in the interest of smoother reading that would be more appealing to impatient twentieth century readers; Meyer Levin's 1932 rendering into English also took liberties with this aspect of the text; and

Elie Wiesel's 1972 version "re-creates" the original to speed up the pace. Only the translation of Arnold J. Band in 1978 pretends to be faithful to the slowness and repetitiousness of the orally transmitted Yiddish story as it was actually told.

For example, here is the contact with the first giant, totally structured in an excruciating number of reiterations:

> The giant said to him: "Surely it does not exist at all." He rebuffed him and told him that they had deluded his mind with nonsense, that it surely did not exist at all. And the viceroy began to weep bitterly and said, "It surely, definitely exists somewhere." The wild man rebuffed him again saying that they surely had deluded him with nonsense. And the viceroy said that it surely exists.

The effect of the syntactic structures is also hypnotic. The repeated paratactic clauses with their endless chain of *and*'s is incantatory. Thus syntax, plot, and theme conspire to cast a spell upon the mind of the listener. The language, which twentieth century translators felt should be linear and forward-driving to sustain interest, is exposed as circular, mind-numbing, and repetitive, like the slow-moving circular dances to a wordless tune (*niggun*) with which the Hasidim closed their worship services.

"THE MASTER OF PRAYERS"

"The Master of Prayers" describes the role of the zaddik. Through his ability to ascend to the upper worlds like Elijah, Moses, and Enoch, he must lead men along the true path. He must be able to assume the guise of what each individual values most, to encounter him on his own terms, to speak with him in his own language, so that he can appeal to him to seek the King. Then follows a long satirical saga on the capitalist world, which, having lost touch with the King, has begun to worship money. With Swiftian satire the Master of Prayers forces humankind to recognize the stench of money. Appalled by its revolting smell, they roll, gasping and choking on the ground. In horror they exclaim that it stinks like excrement--an association that Sigmund Freud was to make a century later.

As a story within this story there appears a cabalistic cosmogony in retrospective flashback. The Holy Community was scattered by a great storm. At the tempest following the *tzimtzum*, the King, the Queen, the Princess, and her miraculous son were all dispersed, along with the Warrior and the Master of Prayers. These represent all the *sefirotic* attributes of the Lord sundered during the cataclysmic shattering of the vessels. They must be reunited by the power of the zaddik, who inspires men to this great work of reparation, the *tikkun*, after which universal harmony will be restored. The story ends: "The Master of Prayer gave them prayers of repentance and he cleansed them. And the King became ruler of the whole world, and the whole world returned to God and all engaged only in Torah, prayer, repentance, and good deeds. Amen. May it be His will."

One of Rabbi Nahman's innovations as zaddik was to stress the "cleansing" of his Hasidim. In "The Master of Prayers," he valorizes the practice of confession, both as an initiation ritual and at periodic intervals. Other autobiographical elements appear in this tale as well, showing how deeply Nahman internalized his messianic mission so that his role and his life were no longer distinguishable. For example, the fact that at the time that he told "The Master of Prayers" he was already dying of tuberculosis is reflected in the story when the King shows the Warrior a marvelous, two-edged sword:

> Through one edge all enemies fall and through the other they are afflicted with consumption. They become thin and their bodies waste away just like in the plague. Heaven help us! And with a sweep of the sword, the enemies are afflicted by the two edges and their powers, defeat and consumption.

"THE TALE OF THE SEVEN BEGGARS"

The most famous of all the stories is the last one, "The Tale of the Seven Beggars." The opening episode tells of a King who wanted to transfer his power during his own lifetime to his son. The Prince is told at the coronation ceremonies that he must always remain joyous, but he becomes learned in philosophy and is plunged into despair by his rational knowledge. It comes to pass as a result that there is a mass dispersion, and everyone flees. These are the first two steps of the cosmogonic process overlaid with Hasidic ideology. The "Ayn Sof," the primordial nothingness that is God without attributes, the ineffable cosmic substance which cannot be apprehended, wills the world into being. By contracting Itself (the tzimtzum), the transfer of power is effected. Man, who is God's heir, is instructed to worship ecstatically; but instead of dancing joyously to the hymn of praise sung by the whole of creation, man studies gloomy philosophical texts. The cataclysm which follows the transfer of power from the infinite core of pure being into the material world is the *shevirah* which causes a scattering.

The second episode tells of two children who are lost in the forest and crying with hunger. Seven beggars bring them bread. The first is blind, the second deaf, the third stutters, the fourth has a twisted neck, the fifth is hunchbacked, the sixth is handless, and the seventh is legless. Each of these apparent defects turns out to be a virtue, and each beggar, after feeding the children, blesses them with the same wish: "May you be as I am." The children are later married and each beggar comes in turn to the wedding feast to tell a marvelously intricate story showing the power inherent in his illusory defect and endowing the wedding couple with that same magical power. Thus each tale becomes a wedding gift to celebrate the *tikkun*, the cosmic marriage that takes place "in the pit" of this world which restores the rejoicing in heaven.

First, the blind beggar tells them a complicated narrative revealing that his vision can penetrate through the illusions of this world into the secrets of infinity. His sight is so keen that it can pierce the delusory outer shape into the essence. He remembers the nothingness that preexisted creation, and he bestows upon them the same power of vision. Then the deaf beggar wishes upon them his power of hearing. All the noises of this world are complaints, arguments, obscenities, and quarrels. Let their ears not be afflicted with these.

Then comes the third beggar to prove that he is not a stutterer except for worldly words which are not praises of the Holy One. He proves himself an extraordinary orator who can recite marvelous riddles and poems and songs; his enigmatic lyric about the spring and the heart is excerpted and reprinted in every Hasidic anthology. In the poised tension of its oppositions lies the vision of balanced contraries which sustains the universe. Each *sefirah* is yearning for its opposite. Turbulence and disorder would follow if either submitted to the pull of the other. The cosmos is energized by the flow of longing from one to the other; the spring at one end of the world is always longing for the heart which is at the other end. The passage, too long to quote in its entirety, ends:

> And if the heart will no longer look upon the spring, its soul will perish, for it draws all its vitality from the spring. And if the heart would expire, God forbid, the whole world would be annihilated, because the heart has within it the life of everything.

The fourth beggar proves that his twisted neck enables him to throw his voice and mimic any sound. He tells how he demonstrated his gift to a group of skeptics. He imitated the sound of a door opening and shutting and being locked with a bolt. "Then I shot a gun and sent my dog to retrieve what I had shot. And the dog struggled in the snow." The scoffers looked for all these things and saw nothing.

The fifth and sixth beggars bring their gifts of wondrously wrought tales and prove themselves also master raconteurs. Only the seventh beggar does not appear. Following the pattern of paradoxical reversals that have been established by his predecessors, he, presumably, would have danced at the wedding, since he was legless. Either Nahman was obeying the principle of declined closure he had established in his first tale about the lost princess in this last one, or, because the consummation of the sacred marriage has not yet been realized, he preferred to defer it.

The most stunning artistry links each of these fabulations with the frame narrative which encloses them. Each beggar relates another instance whose paradoxicality defies reason. This joyous sequence of illogical, irrational wonder tales to which the Prince listens should heal his melancholy. Arnold J. Band dedicated his volume on Nahman to "the Seventh Beggar, the marvelous legless dancer who never appeared at the wedding feast, but whom we all still await."

OTHER MAJOR WORKS

NONFICTION: *Likkutei Moharan*, 1806; *Likkutei Moharan Tinyana*, 1811; *Sefer Hamidot*, 1821 (*The Aleph-Bet Book: The Book of Attributes*, 1986); *Likkutei Tefillot*, 1821-1827; *Ma'gele Zedek*, 1846; *Haye Moharan*, 1874; *Yemei Moharan*, 1876; *Rabbi Nachman's Teachings*, 1973; *Rabbi Nachman's Wisdom*, 1973.

BIBLIOGRAPHY

Green, Arthur. *Tormented Master: A Life of Rabbi Nahman of Bratslav*. University: University of Alabama Press, 1979. This text is widely acknowledged as the definitive biographical work on Rabbi Nahman. It includes a chronology of his life and a special section, entitled "Excursus II: The Tales," on the stories. Green provides detailed notes, including the schema he used for the transliteration of Hebrew and Yiddish. A useful glossary is helpful for non-Yiddish or non-Hebrew speakers. Both the primary and the secondary bibliographies are extensive, and an index is included.

Kaplan, Aryeh. *Until the Mashiach: Rabbi Nachman's Biography, an Annotated Chronology*. Edited by Dovid Shapiro. Jerusalem, Israel: Breslov Research Institute, 1985. An extensive biography of Rabbi Nahman. Includes indexes.

Liebes, Yehuda. *Studies in Jewish Myth and Jewish Messianism*. Translated by Batya Stein. Albany: State University of New York Press, 1993. Includes an examination of Rabbi Nahman's mystical worldview. Includes bibliography and index.

Magid, Shaul. ed. *God's Voice from the Void: Old and New Studies in Bratslav Hasidism*. Albany: State University of New York Press, 2002. A collection of scholarly essays about Rabbi Nahman's religious beliefs that approach his ideas from literary, philosophical, and interpretive theory perspectives. Some of the essays discuss the impact of Nahman's tales on religious literature and his views on death, gender, and circumcision.

_____. "Nature, Exile, and Disability in R. Nahman of Bratslav's 'The Seven Beggars.'" In *Judaism and Ecology: Created World and Revealed Word*, edited by Hava Tirosh-Samuelson. Cambridge, Mass: Harvard University Press, 2002. Examines the short story from an ecological perspective, describing how it reflects Nahman's ideas about nature.

Mark, Zvi. *Mysticism and Madness: The Religious Thought of Rabbi Nachman of Bratslav*. New York: Continuum, 2009. Describes Rabbi Nahman's religious doctrines, placing Bratslav Hasidism in the context of other forms of Jewish mysticism.

Nahman of Bratslav. *Nahman of Bratslav: The Tales*. Edited by Arnold J. Band. New York: Paulist Press, 1978. This edition of Rabbi Nahman's stories is invaluable for the accompanying commentary and biography provided by Band. The commentary is offered for each story, and Band is scrupulous in his translations and interpretations, making this text a good English version to read and consult. A brief bibliography and a detailed index are included.

Polsky, Howard W., and Yaella Wozner. *Everyday Miracles: The Healing Wisdom of Hasidic Stories*. Northvale, N.J.: Jason Aronson, 1989. Polsky and Wozner present the cultural and theoretical background to Hasidic short fiction, including the role of the stories in Hasidic society. They use a multitude of different Hasidic stories to illustrate their points. Contains an appendix on the linguistic foundation of Hasidic stories, a glossary, a transliteration guide, references, a title list of the stories used, and an index.

Schleicher, Marianne. *Intertextuality in the Tales of Rabbi Nahman of Bratslav: A Close Reading of "Sippurey Ma'asiyot."* Boston: Brill, 2007. A scholarly analysis of the thirteen tales in *Sipure Ma'asiyot*, treating them as religious literature and seeking to find a unified theme in the stories. Schleicher maintains that Rabbi Nahman uses his stories to define his theology of redemption and to invite readers to adopt his religious views.

Wiesel, Elie. *Souls on Fire*. New York: Random House, 1972. Wiesel devotes a complete chapter to Rabbi Nahman, including in it biographical details and examples of his work. Wiesel evaluates the tales from a religious, mystical perspective within the context of Hasidism. Includes a synchronology of all the Hasidic masters profiled in the book, as well as some historical background notes.

Wiskind-Elper, Ora. *Tradition and Fantasy in the Tales of Reb Nahman of Bratslav.* Albany: State University of New York Press, 1998. Examines the themes of fantasy and tradition in the short fiction. Provides bibliographical references and an index.

Ruth Rosenberg
Updated by Jo-Ellen Lipman Boon

V. S. NAIPAUL

Born: Chaguanas, Trinidad and Tobago;
   August 17, 1932
Also Known As: Sir Vidiadhar Surajprasad Naipaul

PRINCIPAL SHORT FICTION

Miguel Street, 1959
A Flag on the Island, 1967
In a Free State, 1971

OTHER LITERARY FORMS

V. S. Naipaul (ni-PAHL) is better known for his novels and his controversial travel writings than for his short fiction. No careful consideration of colonialism in the twentieth century or of former colonies in the several decades following their independence would be complete without reference to Naipaul's travelogues and long fiction, nor would a non-Islamic consideration of Islam in the late twentieth century be complete without reference to Naipaul. For that matter, a consideration of experimental fiction in English ought to refer to Naipaul, who, in *A Way in the World* (1994), blurs the distinction between what the British publisher Heinemann called a sequence and what the American publisher Knopf called a novel. Furthermore, in early works Naipaul blurs the distinction between books labeled "novels" and books labeled "short fiction."

ACHIEVEMENTS

Determined from his childhood in colonial Trinidad to become a writer, V. S. Naipaul gained acclaim only a few years after his graduation from Oxford University in 1953. His novel *The Mystic Masseur*, published in 1957, won the John Llewellyn Rhys Memorial Prize.

Miguel Street, published two years later, won the Somerset Maugham Award. With the novel *A House for Mr. Biswas* in 1961, critics recognized Naipaul as a major author from the disintegrating British Empire. In 1963 came the novel *Mr. Stone and the Knights Companion*, which won the Hawthornden Prize. *The Mimic Men* (1967) won the W. H. Smith Award, and *In a Free State* (1971) brought Naipaul the Booker Prize. Besides the acclaim for his fiction, Naipaul received widespread attention for his travel books, such as *An Area of Darkness: An Experience of India* (1964) and *Among the Believers: An Islamic Journey* (1981); those books also brought him verbal attacks from offended Indians and Muslims and persons aligned with them. Nevertheless, other readers, as well as institutions, appreciated his work: In 1986, the Ingersoll Foundation gave him the T. S. Eliot Award for Creative Writing; in 1990, Queen Elizabeth II knighted him, and Trinidad and Tobago, by then an independent nation, gave him the Trinity Cross. There followed an honorary doctorate from Oxford (1992), the initial David Cohen British Literature Prize (1993), and in 2001 the Nobel Prize in Literature.

BIOGRAPHY

Born at Chaguanas, Trinidad, on August 17, 1932, Vidiadhar Surajprasad Naipaul was the second child and first son of English-speaking descendants of Asian Indians, who had traveled to the British West Indies to become indentured servants. His father, Seepersad Naipaul, was an impoverished Brahmin working as a sign painter when he married Droapatie Capildeo, one of the daughters of the widowed Soogee Capildeo, the matriarch of a big and prosperous family. Named for Vidyadhar, an eleventh century Hindu king who had fought Islamic invaders, "Vido," as V. S. Naipual was called, spent long periods apart from his father, who, trying to make a living, held various jobs, including that of a reporter for the *Trinidad Guardian*. Seepersad's struggles with himself and the Capildeos appear in fictional form in *A House for Mr. Biswas*.

Like his father, Naipaul was intelligent; but unlike his father, he had a formal education that helped him fulfill his ambition to write for a living. Going from one school to another as he grew older and as his immediate family moved, Naipaul enrolled in 1943 at Queen's Royal College, an academically challenging institution in Port of Spain, the principal city of Trinidad. An excellent student, he eventually received a scholarship to study abroad and, happy to leave his native island, he traveled in 1950 to Oxford University in England, where he studied English literature at University College. While at Oxford, "Vidia," as Naipaul was known there, wrote for *Isis*, a university magazine; sold stories to be read over the radio on *Caribbean Voices*, a program of the British Broadcasting Corporation (BBC); met Patricia (Pat) Hale, a fellow student; and earned a bachelor of arts in 1953.

Despite feeling alien in England, Naipaul stayed there to earn his living, rather than return to a racially troubled colony that he considered a literary backwater. At first, making money was hard, but late in 1954 he got a job with the BBC Colonial Service, for which, until 1958, he moderated discussions on the literature of the West Indies, interviewed authors and other artists, reviewed books, and, in general, gained skills that would help him as a writer. Early in 1955, he married Pat, who for his sake gave up her hope to be an actress and, early in their marriage, helped support him by teaching. He proved to be a temperamental and eventually unfaithful husband in this childless marriage, consorting with prostitutes and later conducting an on-and-off affair with Margaret Gooding, an Anglo-Argentine whom he found more sexually attractive than his wife. Shortly before Pat died of breast cancer on February 3, 1996, he passively ended his relationship with Gooding and gave an engagement ring to Nadira Khannum Alvi, a divorced Pakistani journalist, whom he married on April 15 in England.

The stories in *Miguel Street* comprise Naipaul's first book, but it was not published until 1959, after the publication of the novels *The Mystic Masseur* and *The Suffrage of Elvira* (1958). Naipaul's professional life, when he became internationally renowned, remained what it had been in his rise to fame: He used England as his base but spent long periods elsewhere, often collecting material he would use in his books, whether they would deal with the West Indies, South America, Africa, Asia, or the East Indies. By the end of 2010, nine years after he had received the Nobel Prize, he had produced thirty-one published books and many articles and reviews.

ANALYSIS

V. S. Naipaul writes unsentimentally in his short fiction about persons who are out of place: They may be descendants of indentured servants brought from poverty in northern India to work on plantations in Trinidad. They may be descendants of Africans enslaved and shipped to Trinidad or islands farther north in the West Indies. They may be Europeans or North Americans in Africa or the West Indies, or even Chinese in Italy and Egypt. Whatever their case may be, the characters are

V. S. Naipaul (Getty Images)

outsiders in an historical sense. Sometimes they are victims, sometimes victimizers, and sometimes both.

MIGUEL STREET

Whether the seventeen related stories in *Miguel Street* form a novel is a matter of opinion. Naipaul binds them through the primary location of Miguel Street in Port of Spain, through characters that appear in several stories, and through the style that the first-person narrator uses throughout the book and the comedy that overlies what, in a different treatment, would be tragic lives. The most important character of the book as a whole is the young narrator, who lives alone with his widowed mother and tells each story with a simplicity that conceals Naipaul's artistry. In all but the last story, someone other than the narrator is the main character, and most of the stories could stand apart from the others and still work well as fiction. In fact, André Deutsch, Naipaul's first British publisher, thought of *Miguel Street* as a collection of short stories and, fearing it would not sell, delayed its publication from 1955 until 1959.

For the facts behind the fiction in the book, Naipaul went back across the Atlantic in memory to his childhood in a rundown neighborhood on Luis Street and elsewhere in Port of Spain and to the neighbors he knew, most of them having Indian ancestry and speaking English in a Trinidadian dialect of the 1930's and 1940's. The stories "George and the Pink House," "His Chosen Calling," and "Titus Hoyt, I.A.," taken together, give examples of both the comedy and the despair of *Miguel Street*. In the first of those stories, the narrator tells of George, who beats his wife, daughter, and son. The wife dies; and, after George has turned their home into a brothel, the daughter marries the man of George's choice and disappears from the neighborhood. In "His Chosen Calling," the narrator focuses on George's son, Elias, a studious boy all the neighbors think will succeed in becoming a doctor, but his education in Mr. Titus Hoyt's school does not prepare the boy for the examination he must take. Despite repeated efforts to get a high score, he ends up driving a rubbish cart and trying to convince his neighbors and himself that he likes his work. In the story that bears Titus Hoyt's

name, the narrator reveals a mostly well-meaning, unintentionally funny, would-be intellectual, who succeeds more in gaining publicity for himself than in educating himself or any of the neighborhood children. The narrator, however, escapes not only the neighborhood schoolmaster but the whole of Trinidad when, unlike Elias, he receives a scholarship to study abroad. In "How I Left Miguel Street," the last story of the book, he walks toward an airplane, seeing his little shadow before him.

A FLAG ON THE ISLAND

A Flag on the Island, published in 1967, starts with ten short stories and ends with the long story that gives the book its title. Eight of the stories are set in Trinidad in the same historical period as the stories in *Miguel Street*, and four of those are narrated by someone resembling the narrator in that book, with the narrator in "The Raffle" even being named Vidiadhar Naipaul. "A Christmas Story," however, is narrated by a Trinidadian Hindu who has converted to Presbyterianism and has risen professionally in the colony's educational system before he finds himself in a legal predicament. "The Baker's Story" also contains a first-person narrative, but it is delivered by a Grenadian-born black man who succeeds in business in Trinidad by learning an important fact about ethnic expectation. In "The Heart," Naipaul uses third-person narration to tell of a middle-class schoolboy named Hari and his psychologically revealing relationships with dogs. "The Night Watchman's Occurrence Book" differs from all the other stories in the collection by being written in an epistolary style, comprising a record kept by a night watchman at a disreputable hotel in Trinidad and the interspersed notes by the demanding manager.

Two or three stories in the collection are set outside Naipaul's home island. Both "Greenie and Yellow" and "The Perfect Tenants" are narrated by one of the residents of the Cookseys' rooming house in London and show Naipaul's skill in comedy, sometimes gruesome, and his ability to present working-class London dialect as deftly as Trinidadian dialect. The longest story in the collection is "A Flag on the Island: A Fantasy for a Small Screen," set on a multiethnic West Indian island, maybe not Trinidad, that has received its independence from Britain. Frank, the narrator, makes an unscheduled stop there to avoid a hurricane, and the time goes from the present back to World War II, when he was stationed at an American naval base on the island and met various persons whom he encounters again when the story returns to the present. Among those whom he reencounters are Selma, with whom he lived awhile, and a black author called H. J. B. White, who has gained postwar fame for such works as *I Hate You: One Man's Search for Identity*. With the fantasy of the story, Naipaul blends satire and a consideration of nationality.

IN A FREE STATE

Sometimes considered a novel, the 1971 book *In a Free State* comprises a prologue (said to come from a journal), two stories of intermediate length, a long story that gives the book its title, and an epilogue (also said to come from a journal). Throughout the whole work, Naipaul honestly studies misplaced or displaced persons: persons neither emotionally nor ethnically belonging where they are, persons free from the constraints and consolations of home, if they have homes at all. The prologue, "The Tramp at Piraeus," is a Naipaul-like narrator's first-person account of travel by ship from Greece to Egypt and the strange wanderer also on board. In "One out of Many," an Indian cook raised in a village tells how he accompanies his boss from Bombay to Washington, D. C., where he fears African Americans and, after deserting his boss, also fears deportation. "Tell Me Who to Kill," also narrated in the first person by the main character, shows the widespread rage of a hard-working, psychologically traumatized Trinidadian of Indian descent who moves to England, eventually opens a roti shop, stabs a hooligan (or imagines he does), and, in the present time of the story, attends his brother's wedding to a young Englishwoman, attends, that is, with a seemingly official companion whom the narrator both admires and resents. The long story "In a Free State," narrated in the third person, presents the perilous trip by automobile that two English persons make from the capital of an African country (such as Uganda) to the foreigners' compound four hundred miles away. The relationship between Bobby, sexually attracted to African boys, and Linda, his married passenger, is tense, and so is the political situation: The country's president has just used his soldiers to seize complete political power from the country's king, the monarch of a rival tribe, and is imprisoning the king's supporters and expelling ethnic Indians. The epilogue, "The Circus at Luxor," begins in Italy and ends in Egypt, where the narrator contemplates empires, peoples, and time.

OTHER MAJOR WORKS

LONG FICTION: *The Mystic Masseur*, 1957; *The Suffrage of Elvira*, 1958; *A House for Mr. Biswas*, 1961; *Mr. Stone and the Knights Companion*, 1963; *The Mimic Men*, 1967; *Guerrillas*, 1975; *A Bend in the River*, 1979; *The Enigma of Arrival*, 1987; *A Way in the World*, 1994; *Half a Life*, 2001; *Magic Seeds*, 2004.

NONFICTION: *The Middle Passage: Impressions of Five Societies--British, French, and Dutch--in the West Indies and South America*, 1962; *An Area of Darkness: An Experience of India*, 1964; *The Loss of El Dorado: A History*, 1969; *The Overcrowded Barracoon, and Other Articles*, 1972; *India: A Wounded Civilization*, 1977; *The Return of Eva Perón* with *"The Killings in Trinidad,"* 1980; *Among the Believers: An Islamic Journey*, 1981; *Finding the Center: Two Narratives*, 1984; *A Turn in the South*, 1989; *India: A Million Mutinies Now*, 1990; *Beyond Belief: Islamic Excursions Among the Converted Peoples*, 1998; *Between Father and Son: Family Letters--Selected Correspondence of V. S. Naipaul and His Family, 1949-1953*, 2000 (pb. in England as *Letters Between a Father and Son*, 1999); *Reading and Writing: A Personal Account*, 2000; *The Writer and the World: Essays*, 2002 (Pankaj Mishra, editor); *Literary Occasions: Essays*, 2003 (Mishra, editor); *A Writer's People: Ways of Looking and Feeling*, 2007; *The Masque of Africa: Glimpses of African Belief*, 2010.

MISCELLANEOUS: *The Nightwatchman's Occurrence Book, and Other Comic Inventions*, 2002.

BIBLIOGRAPHY

Coovadia, Imraan. *Authority and Authorship in V. S. Naipaul*. New York: Palgrave Macmillan, 2009. Studies how Naipaul uses rhetoric to establish his authority as a writer and to treat authority in colonies and postcolonial countries.

Cudjoe, Selwyn R. *V. S. Naipaul: A Materialist Reading*. Amherst: University of Massachusetts Press, 1988. Attacks Naipaul as a writer who, after *The Mimic Men* (1967), let his racism and his animus against the Third World ruin his work.

Feder, Lillian. *Naipaul's Truth: The Making of a Writer*. New York: Rowman & Littlefield, 2001. Defends Naipaul as an author who uses autobiography, history, and fiction to search for truth about himself and others, especially the colonized.

French, Patrick. *The World Is What It Is: The Authorized Biography of V. S. Naipaul*. New York: Knopf, 2008. Covers the life until 1996 and relies on extensive research to present Naipaul as ambitious, talented, intelligent, hard-working, selfish, and adulterous.

Gupta, Suman. *V. S. Naipaul*. Plymouth, England: Northcote House, 1999. Gives a short chronology of Naipaul in the twentieth century and a critical introduction to his books published by 1998.

Hayward, Helen. *The Enigma of V. S. Naipaul: Sources and Contexts*. New York: Palgrave Macmillan, 2002. Outlines the life until 2001, considers Naipaul's use of his personal history and previous books, and provides a huge bibliography.

King, Bruce. *V. S. Naipaul*. 2d ed. New York: Palgrave Macmillan, 2003. Clearly examines Naipaul's books and the relevant criticism, praising Feder and refuting Cudjoe, the Palestinian scholar Edward Said, and the West Indian poet Derek Walcott.

Naipaul, V. S. "Two Worlds." In *Nobel Lectures: From the Literature Laureates 1986 to 2006*. New York: New Press, 2007. Tells in his 2001 lecture of the two worlds he sensed in his childhood and of his effort to learn, through writing, of the one beyond his grandmother's gate.

Victor Lindsey

R. K. NARAYAN

Born: Madras, India; October 10, 1906
Died: Madras, India; May 13, 2001

PRINCIPAL SHORT FICTION

Malgudi Days, 1941 (expanded 1982)
Dodu, and Other Stories, 1943
Cyclone, and Other Stories, 1944
An Astrologer's Day, and Other Stories, 1947
Lawley Road: Thirty-two Short Stories, 1956
Gods, Demons, and Others, 1964
A Horse and Two Goats, and Other Stories, 1970
Old and New, 1981
Under the Banyan Tree, and Other Stories, 1985
A Story-Teller's World, 1989 (stories, essays, and sketches)
Salt and Sawdust: Stories and Table Talk, 1993.
The Grandmother's Tale, and Selected Stories, 1994

OTHER LITERARY FORMS

A prolific writer, R. K. Narayan (nuh-RI-yuhn) published more than a dozen novels, a shortened prose version of each of the two famous Indian epics, *The Ramayana* and *The Mahabharata*, several travel books, volumes of essays and sketches, a volume of memoirs, and numerous critical essays. His novel *The Guide* (1958) was made into a successful motion picture, both in English and in Hindi.

ACHIEVEMENTS

R. K. Narayan, an internationally recognized novelist and the grand patriarch of Indo-Anglian writers (writers of India writing in English), received a number of awards and distinctions. In 1961, he was awarded the National Prize of the Indian Literary Academy (Sahitya Akademi), India's highest literary honor, for his popular novel *The Guide*. His other honors include India's Padma Bhushan Award for distinguished service of a high order, 1964; the

United States' National Association of Independent Schools Award, 1965; the English-speaking Union Award, 1975; the Royal Society of Literature Benson Medal, 1980; and several honorary degrees. In 1982, Narayan was made an honorary member of the American Academy and Institute of Arts and Letters. He was named a member of India's nonelective House of Parliament, the Rajya Sabha, in 1989.

BIOGRAPHY

Rasipuram Krishnaswami Narayan was born in Madras, South India, on October 10, 1906. Until the family moved to Mysore, he remained in Madras with his grandmother, who supervised his school and college education. In his autobiography, *My Days* (1974), Narayan admits his dislike of education; he "instinctively rejected both education and examinations with their unwarranted seriousness and esoteric suggestions." Nevertheless, in 1930, he was graduated from Maharaja's College (now the University of Mysore).

In 1933, he met a woman by the name of Rajam and immediately fell in love with her. In 1935, after overcoming almost insurmountable difficulties (to begin with, their horoscopes did not match), Narayan and Rajam were married. She was a great help in his creative work, but she lived to see publication of only three novels; she died of typhoid in 1939. Narayan's fourth novel, *The English Teacher* (1945; also known as *Grateful to Life and Death*, 1953), dedicated to his dead wife, centers on the trauma of this loss and on a hard-won sense of reconciliation. Rajam is portrayed in some detail as Sushila in that novel and, later, as Srinivas's wife in *Mr. Sampath* (1949; also known as *The Printer of Malgudi*, 1957).

Narayan had not begun his career as a writer without some false starts. Indeed, only after having worked at a number of jobs without satisfaction and success--he worked for a time in the civil service in Mysore, taught for a while, and served as a correspondent for *Madras Justice*--did Narayan finally embark upon writing as a full-time career. In the beginning, many of his writings were rejected--a traumatic experience that he bore with fortitude. He was firm in his resolve to make his living as a writer. Experiencing bitter dejection when several British publishers rejected his first novel, *Swami and Friends* (1935) Narayan instructed a friend not to mail the manuscript back to him in India but to throw it into the Thames. Instead, his friend took the manuscript to writer Graham Greene, who was successful in finding a publisher for the novel. Thus, from a frustrating experience began the literary career of an eminent Commonwealth writer whose books are known throughout the world. Narayan settled in Mysore, India, and his involvement with Indian Thought Publications led to the publication of several of his works.

Narayan continued to write and publish well into his nineties, concentrating on short fiction and essays. He experimented with "table talk," a new form of his own devising, which he described as a loosely structured reflection on any subject. Narayan died in Madras, India, on May 13, 2001.

ANALYSIS

R. K. Narayan said that he found English the most rewarding medium to employ for his writing because it came to him very easily: "English is a very adaptable language. And it's so transparent it can take on the tint of any country." Critics frequently praise the unaffected standard English with which Narayan captures the Indian sensibility, particularly the South Indian ambience. His unpretentious style, his deliberate avoidance of convoluted expressions and complicated grammatical constructions, his gentle and subtle humor--all this gives his writing an elegant, unforced simplicity that is perfectly suited to the portrayal of ordinary life, of all classes and segments of Indian society (household servants, herdsmen, saints, crooks, merchants, beggars, thieves, and hapless students).

Narayan was essentially an old-fashioned storyteller. With Addisonian wit, Twainian humor, and Chekhovian irony, he depicted everyday occurrences and moments of insight; while some of his stories are essentially sketches, quite undramatic, others feature the ironic reversals associated with O. Henry. Although Narayan's characters are imbued with distinctively Indian values, their dilemmas are universal.

MALGUDI DAYS

Malgudi's first short-story collection, *Malgudi Days*, features nineteen stories. Narayan invented for his fiction the town of Malgudi, which critics consider a literary amalgam of Mysore, where he lived for several decades, and Madras, the city of his birth. He gently asserted that "Malgudi has been only a concept but has proved good enough for my purposes." In its imaginative scope, Narayan's Malgudi is similar to William Faulkner's Yoknapatawpha County, but whereas Faulkner's vision is complex and dark-hued, Narayan's vision is simpler, ironic, sad at times, yet ultimately comic.

Two stories in *Malgudi Days*, "Old Bones" and "Neighbours' Help," are laced with supernatural elements. This volume also includes such memorable stories as "The Gold Belt," "The White Flower," "An End of Trouble," and "Under the Banyan Tree." Some of the stories may be viewed as social criticism; Narayan looks with a satiric eye on various aspects of traditional South Indian society, particularly the dowry system and the powerful role of astrology and other forms of superstition.

R. K. Narayan (Library of Congress)

One of the finest stories in the collection, "The Mute Companions," centers on the ubiquitous Indian monkey, a source of meager income for poor people and a source of delight for children. Adopting the omniscient point of view yet without moralizing or judging, Narayan portrays the life of Sami the dumb beggar, whose "very existence depended on the behavior of the monkey." Having taught the monkey several tricks, Sami is able for a time to subsist on the earnings of the clever creature, who is his "only companion." This brief story is an excellent example of Narayan's art, revealing his ability to portray a segment of society that typically goes unnoticed. The story emphasizes the passiveness characteristic of the poor Indian, his acceptance of his Karma, or fate. Narayan's gentle social criticism also emerges: "Usually he [Sami] avoided those big places where people were haughty, aloof, and inaccessible, and kept formidable dogs and servants." As in many of his stories, Narayan in "The Mute Companions" blends humor and sadness.

Malgudi Days, it should be noted, is also the title of a later collection, published in the United States in 1982. Eight of the thirty-two stories in this collection-- "Naga," "Selvi," "Second Opinion," "Cat Within," "The Edge," "God and the Cobbler," "Hungry Child," and "Emden"--were previously uncollected; the remaining stories were selected from Narayan's two earlier volumes, *An Astrologer's Day* and *Lawley Road*.

DODU, AND OTHER STORIES

In his second collection, *Dodu, and Other Stories*, Narayan concentrates on themes related to motherly love, South Indian marriages, the financial and economic frustrations of the middle class, and childhood. Among the outstanding pieces in this volume of seventeen stories are "Dodu," "Gandhi's Appeal," "Ranga," "A Change," "Forty-five a Month," and "The One-Armed Giant." (Originally published in *The Hindu*, a Madras newspaper, as most of his stories had been, "The One-Armed Giant" was the first story that Narayan wrote.) The title story, "Dodu," satirically focuses on adult attitudes toward children: "Dodu was eight years old and wanted money badly. Since he was only eight, nobody took his financial worries seriously. . . . Dodu had no illusions about the generosity of his elders. They were notoriously deaf to requests." One of the significant contributions of Narayan is his uncanny ability to portray children--their dreams, their mischief, their psychology. "Ranga," an early tale, is a moving story of a motherless child developing into a disillusioned youth. "Forty-five a Month" is a simple and tender story of the relationship of a father and his family--his wife and their young daughter. The conflict between economic security and the little pleasures of life is evocatively and movingly delineated; indeed, this depiction of a white-collar worker eking out his dreary existence reflects the experience of an entire generation in modern India.

LAWLEY ROAD

In *Lawley Road*, as in most of his fiction, Narayan is concerned more with character than with plot. He notes that he discovers "a story when a personality passes through a crisis of spirit or circumstances," but some stories present flashes of significant moments in characters' lives without any dramatic circumstances; others simply show "a pattern of existence brought to view." Many of the pieces in this collection have a reportorial quality--there are sketches and vignettes, character studies and anecdotes. Of the thirty-two stories gathered here, fourteen are reprinted from previous collections. The title story is delightful. Named after a typical thoroughfare in the fictitious city of Malgudi, the story recounts how Kabir Lane is renamed as Lawley Road. The narrator is one of Narayan's most engaging recurring characters, whom the people of Malgudi have nicknamed the "Talkative Man," or TM for short, who lends distance and historicity to the story. In another strong story, "The Martyr's Corner," the focus is on a humble seller of *bondas, dosais* (South Indian snacks), and *chappatis* (wheat-flour pancakes) rather than on the violent action. It is the character of the vendor--his dreary and drab life and his attitude toward existence--that holds the interest of the reader.

A HORSE AND TWO GOATS, AND OTHER STORIES

A Horse and Two Goats, and Other Stories comprises five stories with illustrations by Narayan's brother R. K. Laxman. The title story deals with Muni, a village peasant, and his meeting with a "red man" from the United States. The language barrier is responsible for confusion about a statue and a pair of goats, with hilarious results. The second story, "Uncle," is a

masterpiece; it slowly unfolds the mystery that teases a growing boy about his benevolent but inexplicably sinister "uncle." "Annamalai" and "A Breath of Lucifer" deal with two simple, hardworking, faithful servants. Annamalai is an eccentric gardener who attaches himself to a reluctant master; Sam in "A Breath of Lucifer" is a Christian male nurse. In the end, both Annamalai and Sam, governed by their own impulses, unceremoniously leave their masters. "Seventh House," perhaps a continuation of "The White Flower" in *Lawley Road*, dealing in astrology and superstitions, touchingly explores a husband's tender devotion to his sick wife. Each of the five stories is a character study; all the stories are embellished with picturesque native customs. The dominant tone throughout the collection is casual and understated.

UNDER THE BANYAN TREE, AND OTHER STORIES

Under the Banyan Tree, and Other Stories is a superb retrospective collection of twenty-eight tales, published specifically for American readers; almost all the stories are drawn from earlier volumes. When the collection appeared in the United States, several glowing reviews were published in the leading weeklies and periodicals. This collection further confirms Malgudi's place as a great imaginary landscape. The title story, fittingly taken from Narayan's first collection, reaffirms storytelling as a central human activity. The villagers of Somal "lived in a kind of perpetual enchantment. The enchanter was Nambi the story-teller." However, having regaled his audience for several years with his tales, Nambi spends the rest of his life in "great consummate silence."

THE GRANDMOTHER'S TALE, AND SELECTED STORIES

The Grandmother's Tale, and Selected Stories (titled *The Grandmother's Tale, and Other Stories* in the paperback edition) was the first collection of Narayan's fiction that attempted to give a comprehensive overview of his more than fifty years of productivity. Many of the stories, including "A Horse and Two Goats" and "Lawley Road," have been widely anthologized for many years. Others, including "Salt and Sawdust" and the title story, make their first North American appearance in this collection. Many of the stories feature humble but complex characters engaged in daily life in

India. As a collection, the tales demonstrate the richness of Indian life, which blends ancient tradition with Western technological modernity, but Narayan's stories do not call attention to the setting. Rather, they focus on the characters, showing with gentle humor the wonderful absurdity that makes one human and the ironic twists that shape one's life.

In "Salt and Sawdust," for example, Narayan presents a childless housewife who cannot cook--her sense of taste is so bad that she cannot tell the difference between salt and sawdust. Her poor husband is forced to take over the cooking, while his wife occupies herself with writing a novel. However, when the novel is finally completed, the publisher advises the wife to turn it into a cookbook. Narayan was a master of the small details that make domestic scenes seem true and important. Although the wife is made fun of in "Salt and Sawdust," she is a fully rounded character. The humor is good-natured, and Narayan's respect for humans with all their flaws never wavers.

"The Grandmother's Tale" is adapted from a tale Narayan's mother told him about his own great-grandmother. The story is narrated in a winding fashion by a young boy who is sent to live with his strict grandmother. Although he resents his new situation at first, he gradually comes under the spell of the story she tells him, in bits and pieces, about her own grandmother's life. The grandmother's story is set firmly in India. The heroine is married in a traditional ceremony at the age of seven, but her husband abandons her to take a new wife. The landscape she crosses to reclaim her husband is clearly the Indian subcontinent. Ironically, regaining her husband costs her her independence. "The Grandmother's Tale" is unlike many of Narayan's stories in having a strong and admirable central female character. The framing device of the boy narrator reinforces the timelessness and universality of the grandmother's story, which is equally powerful to a young Indian boy in a small village and to adult readers around the world.

As an old-fashioned storyteller, Narayan sought to convey the vitality of his native India, a land that is full of humanity, oddity, poverty, tradition, "inherited culture," picturesqueness. Narayan realized

that the short story is the best medium for utilizing the wealth of subjects available. A novel is a different proposition altogether, centralized as it is on a major theme, leaving out, necessarily, a great deal of the available material on the periphery. Short stories, on the other hand, can cover a wider field by presenting concentrated miniatures of human experience in all its opulence.

Narayan's concern was the heroic in the ordinary Indian. John Updike affirms that

all people are complex, surprising, and deserving of a break: this seems to me Narayan's moral, and one hard to improve upon. His social range and his successful attempt to convey, in sum, an entire population shame most American authors, who also, it might be charged, 'ignore too much of what could be seen.'

With dignified simplicity, honesty, and sincerity, Narayan infused his stories with charm and spontaneous humor; his narrative voice guides the reader through his comic and ironic world with an unobtrusive wit.

OTHER MAJOR WORKS

LONG FICTION: *Swami and Friends*, 1935; *The Bachelor of Arts*, 1937; *The Dark Room*, 1938; *The English Teacher*, 1945 (also known as *Grateful to Life and Death*, 1953); *Mr. Sampath*, 1949 (also known as *The Printer of Malgudi*, 1957); *The Financial Expert*, 1952; *Waiting for the Mahatma*, 1955; *The Guide*, 1958; *The Man-Eater of Malgudi*, 1961; *The Sweet-Vendor*, 1967 (also known as *The Vendor of Sweets*); *The Painter of Signs*, 1976; *A Tiger for Malgudi*, 1983; *Talkative Man: A Novel of Malgudi*, 1987; *The World of Nagaraj*, 1990.

NONFICTION: *Mysore*, 1944; *My Dateless Diary*, 1960; *Next Sunday: Sketches and Essays*, 1960; *My Days*, 1974; *Reluctant Guru*, 1974; *The Emerald Route*, 1977; *A Writer's Nightmare: Selected Essays, 1958-1988*, 1988; *The Writerly Life: Selected Nonfiction*, 2001 (includes essays from *My Dateless Diary*, *A Writer's Nightmare*, *A Story-Teller's World*, and *Salt and Sawdust*; S. Krishnan, editor).

TRANSLATIONS: *The Ramayana: A Shortened Modern Prose Version of the Indian Epic*, 1972 (of Vālmīki); *The Mahabharata: A Shortened Prose Version of the Indian Epic*, 1978.

BIBLIOGRAPHY

Bery, Ashok. "'Changing the Script': R. K. Narayan and Hinduism." *Ariel* 28 (April, 1997): 7-20. Argues that Narayan often probes limitations and contradictions in Hindu worldviews and identities. Analyzes the ways Narayan challenges Hindu doctrines, particularly those that teach that the individual self and the phenomenal world are unimportant; although Hinduism is indispensable to Narayan, it is not unchallengeable.

Holstrom, Lakshmi. *The Novels of R. K. Narayan.* Calcutta: Writers Workshop, 1973. An early study of Narayan's first ten novels in terms of his themes and narrative technique. It attempts to place him in the tradition of Indian fiction. Includes a bibliography.

Kain, Geoffrey, ed. *R. K. Narayan: Contemporary Critical Essays.* East Lansing: Michigan State University Press, 1993. A collection of essays, mostly on the novels, including feminist, cultural, postcolonial, and other contemporary approaches. Other essays focus on irony, satire, transcendence, self-reflexivity, and mythmaking in Narayan's fiction.

Knippling, Alpana Sharma. "R. K. Narayan, Raja Rao, and Modern English Discourse in Colonial India." *Modern Fiction Studies* 39 (Spring, 1993): 169-186. Using Michel Foucault's notion that discourse does not necessarily implicate human intention, Knippling contends that Narayan is not heavily influenced by English discourse and therefore not culpable in the whole Westernizing process.

Naik, M. K. *The Ironic Vision: A Study of the Fiction of R. K. Narayan.* New Delhi: Sterling, 1983. A perceptive study of Narayan's fiction demonstrating his use of irony, in its various forms, to portray human character and situations and to project his total vision of life. Devotes a chapter to the short stories and contains references, a layout of Malgudi and its surroundings, a select bibliography, and an index.

Olinder, Britta. "R. K. Narayan." In *A Reader's Companion to the Short Story in English*, edited by Erin Fallon et al., under the auspices of the Society for the Study of the Short Story. Westport, Conn.: Greenwood Press, 2001. Aimed at the general reader, this essay provides a brief biography of Narayan followed by an analysis of his short fiction.

Prasad, Amar Nath, ed. *Critical Response to R. K. Narayan.* New Delhi: Sarup and Sons, 2003. Collection of essays analyzing Narayan's works. Although many of the essays focus on his novels, others provide more general discussions of his prose fiction, including examinations of Narayan's India; myth and reality in his fiction; and Talkative Man, a recurring character in his novels and short fiction.

Sundaram, P. S. *R. K. Narayan.* New Delhi: Arnold-Heinemann, 1973. This volume's only aim, according to the author, "is to acquaint the Common Reader with the works of an outstanding writer and to suggest what makes the writing outstanding." Contains a brief study of Narayan's short stories and notes the thematic connections between many of the stories and the novels. Supplemented by notes and references, a select bibliography, and an index.

Thieme, John. *R. K. Narayan.* Manchester, England: Manchester University Press, 2007. An examination of Narayan's fiction that focuses on his novels but can also pertain to the short stories. Discusses, among other subjects, the influences on Narayan's fiction and his construction of the fictional town of Malgudi.

Urstad, Tone Sundt. "Symbolism in R. K. Narayan's 'Naga.'" *Studies in Short Fiction* 31 (Summer, 1994): 425-432. Discusses Narayan's basic technique of juxtaposing scenes from modern life with the exploits of gods, demons, and heroes in the short story "Naga." Argues that in this story Narayan creates a mythic framework in which humans act out age-old patterns and conflicts.

Venugopal, C. V. *The Indian Short Story in English: A Survey.* Bareilly, India: Prakash Book Depot, 1975. The chapter on R. K. Narayan provides a useful overview of his short fiction. Complemented by references, a select bibliography, and an index.

Walsh, William. *R. K. Narayan.* London: Longman, 1971. A booklet in the British Council Writers and Their Work series, it gives a general critical appraisal of Narayan as a novelist. Walsh discusses Narayan's novels as "comedies of sadness" and argues that "his work is an original blend of Western method and Eastern material." Includes a select bibliography.

S. S. Moorty
Updated by Chaman L. Sahni and Cynthia A. Bily

Ngugi wa Thiong'o

Born: Kamiriithu village, near Limuru, Kenya; January 5, 1938

PRINCIPAL SHORT FICTION
Secret Lives, and Other Stories, 1975

OTHER LITERARY FORMS

Ngugi wa Thiong'o (ehn-GEW-gee wah tee-ONG-goh) is the author of several major novels. Set primarily in Kenya both before and after the country's independence in 1963, these works treat a variety of complex issues, such as tradition, modernity, colonialism, postcolonialism, class, gender, and race. Ngugi has been prolific equally as a playwright and an essayist. Ngugi's nonfiction writings, especially works on politics and literature, figure prominently in postcolonial studies. Published mostly in his early career as a writer, his short stories number slightly above a dozen. Significantly, many of them have led to some of his best works of fiction.

ACHIEVEMENTS

Ngugi wa Thiong'o has held teaching positions at prestigious institutions all over the world and has received numerous awards and prizes, including seven honorary doctorates. He was a guest lecturer at Oxford University (1996), Cambridge University (1999), and Harvard University (2006). In addition, he served as a visiting professor at Yale University and at Amherst and Smith Colleges (1990-1992). He has received the Nonino International Prize for Literature (2001), the Fonlon-Nichols Prize for Artistic Excellence and Human Rights (1996), the Distinguished Africanist Award (1996), Contributor's Arts Award (1994), the

Zora Neale Hurston-Paul Robeson Award (1993), the Lotus Prize for Afro-Asian literature (1973), and many other honors.

BIOGRAPHY

Born in colonial Kenya in a Kikuyu community (its language is known as Kikuyu and Gikuyu), Ngugi wa Thiong'o was baptized James Ngugi. Son of a subsistence farmer with many children, Ngugi first went to an independent school, Mangua Karinga School, which later became Kinyogoori District Education Board School. Next he attended the prestigious residential Alliance High School for his secondary education. His parents separated in 1946; Ngugi and his five siblings were raised by their mother. When Ngugi returned home from Alliance High School during a vacation, he found his village razed in a "villagization" project and his mother detained and tortured by the colonial British administration on suspicion of aiding the Mau Mau rebels. Ngugi completed the bachelor's program at Makerere University College in Uganda from 1959 through 1964. Soon after graduation he went to the University of Leeds for a master's degree and studied under the noted Marxist scholar Arnold Kettle.

Ngugi's teaching career began at about this time. In the late 1960's and the 1970's, he taught at University College, Nairobi, University College, Dar es Salaam, and Makerere University; he also held brief visiting positions at various U.S. universities. His play *Ngaahika Ndeenda* (with Ngugi wa Mirii, 1977; *I Will Marry When I Want,* 1982) was staged in 1977. Considered politically subversive, the performance led to Ngugi's imprisonment at Kamiti Maximum Security Prison in Nairobi, the site of innumerable hangings of the Mau Mau rebels. He had started writing *Caitaani Mūtharaba-Inĩ* (1980; *Devil on the Cross,* 1982), a scathing novel on Kenya's capitalism and corruption after independence. He completed it in prison, on toilet paper smuggled into the cell. Widespread international outcry forced the government of Jomo Kenyatta to release him after a year, but Ngugi was not allowed to teach at University College, Nairobi again. Out of favor with the repressive government, Ngugi continued to write and traveled abroad widely as a guest lecturer and keynote speaker in the 1980's. He became visiting professor at Yale University in the early 1990's and concurrently held a similar position at Amherst College and Smith College. He was appointed Professor of Comparative Literature Performance Studies at New York University in 1993, a position that included also the prestigious Erich Maria Remarque Chair. In 2001, he became the Distinguished Professor of English and Comparative Literature and director of the International Center for Writing and Translation at University of California, Irvine.

Ngugi is a socially and politically engaged writer, one who questions not only the material impact of colonialism but also its more subtle cultural effects. He believes that the study of English perpetuates colonial ideology. When teaching in Africa in the late 1960's, he proposed abolishing the English Department in African universities and replacing it with a Department of African Literature and Languages, a move that took effect a few years later at University College, Nairobi, where the Department of English became the Department of Literature. Out of his dedication to this belief, Ngugi began writing in Gikuyu. Many of his English works since the late 1970's were originally written in Gikuyu and translated into English by himself. He also enacted a legal change of his name in 1977. James Ngugi became Ngugi wa Thiong'o, which includes names of both of his parents and suggests his African roots.

ANALYSIS

Written over a period of twelve years early in his career, Ngugi's short stories are collected in *Secret Lives, and Other Stories*. Ngugi indicates in the preface that the stories form his "creative biography." He also mentions the traumas of his boyhood and adolescence, some of which came from his parents' quarrels, but a lot of which arose from the turbulent history of preindependence Kenya. Recalling his mother, Ngugi notes her "struggle with the soil," so he and his siblings could have food, clothes, and education. Appropriately, the first part of *Secret Lives* is titled "Of Mothers and Children"; it contains three stories. Two of them deal with infertility and one with drought. Part 2, "Of Fighters and Martyrs," offers six stories and describes a society traumatized by colonial occupation. Conflicts are many in these stories; they are between freedom and servitude, tradition and modernity, tradition and Christianity, men and women, and so on. The last section of *Secret Lives* includes four stories; they portray Kenyan society after independence in 1963. In them, Ngugi displays remarkable perfection of techniques, such as balancing of complex points of view, deft handling of indirect free style, and intricate unfolding of plot.

"THE VILLAGE PRIEST"

Included in part 2 of *Secret Lives*, "The Village Priest" begins with a great deal of irony. After an interminably long drought that causes a severe famine, rain finally comes to Makuyu, a remote village, but the

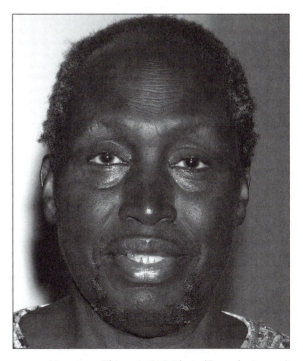

Ngugi wa Thiong'o (AP Photo/Tammie Arroyo)

priest Joshua is unhappy. He has been dreading the event, as a matter of fact. Soon the reader learns that Joshua's many prayers to God for rain were unanswered in the past. The rainmaker, a practitioner of the traditional Gikuyu religion and Joshua's rival, had sacrificed a ram that morning under a sacred tree. Despite Joshua's entreaties for a different outcome, rain comes in buckets and weakens his standing among the villagers, many of whom he has converted to Christianity. Joshua knows that his work is not going to be easy. He is upset not just by that problem alone but by the confusing turn of events. He has believed so far that the Christian God is all-powerful, but his failure to bring rain tells him otherwise. Joshua believes he should make peace with the traditional god of his people and goes to the sacred Agikuyu tree. That is when he hears a derisive laugh--from his rival, the rainmaker. The rainmaker taunts Joshua and his new-found religion but still offers him an invitation to return to the religion of the tribe through a process of atonement. Humiliated and ashamed, Joshua returns in haste. His interest in renewing his traditional roots gone, he faces another problem: his guilt for wavering. He must confess to Livingstone, the white missionary, who strangely has been absent during the entire drought but set to arrive in the village any day. When Joshua reaches the village, Livingstone is already there. Joshua's confession does not provoke a rebuke, however. Livingstone accepts Joshua's failing with sympathy and suggests that they pray together.

In their study of Ngugi, David Cook and Michael Okenimkpe indicate that before the final version of "The Village Priest" in *Secret Lives*, Ngugi published two other versions in the preceding thirteen years. Changes made in each retelling of the story witness his growth as a writer. These changes, according to Cook and Okenimkpe, also demonstrate Ngugi's increasingly hardening attitude toward Christianity. While in the early versions Joshua finds some comfort in his new faith after an overwhelming spiritual crisis, in the one published in *Secret Lives* no such solace awaits him at the end. Livingstone's role, on the other hand, remains the same in all versions. Though his physical presence is brief in the story, he occupies Joshua in each thought and deed. The reader can guess why Livingstone has

avoided Makuyu all the days of drought. Obviously, the white missionary is aware of the psychology of his African converts: They would expect him to perform a visible miracle if he shows up in the village during a disaster. However, Joshua cannot fathom this clever strategy because he, too, is one of them.

"A Meeting in the Dark"

Joshua is no ordinary convert. His privileged status is apparent in his big house with a tin roof and strong walls, which stands apart from those with roofs thatched with straw and walls made of mud. Joshua benefits materially from his conversion, as does Stanley in "A Meeting in the Dark." Unlike Joshua, on the other hand, the Calvinist Stanley never falters in his faith and rules his wife and son with an iron fist. All his words and actions, Stanley never hesitates to point out, conform to the tenets of Christianity. He even addresses his wife Susana as "Sister" because she is, after all, "Sister-in-Lord." Though an exemplary Christian, Stanley did sin once. His son John was conceived out of wedlock. This is the reason that he is extremely protective of John and watches the young man's every move like a hawk. John's excellent conduct and status as a clergyman's son earn him a scholarship to study at Makerere, an opportunity not available to just anybody. Unbeknown to nearly the entire tribe, John, on the other hand, has been living a double life. He has gotten a girl pregnant and wonders how he can get out of the fix. To complicate matters, she comes from a family still believing in the tribal ways and is circumcised. Confused and fearful of consequences, John offers her money, so she would attribute paternity of the unborn child to some other man, not an uncommon practice in this community. When she refuses, he keeps increasing the amount, hugging her passionately, which soon turns to violence. What began as a warm embrace ends in tragedy. John kills her, though perhaps not intentionally.

Two concerns drive John's action: his deep fear of his father and his dread of losing the scholarship. He has managed to conceal his secret relationship with Wamuhu from everybody except her parents, but even they do not know the level of intimacy between their daughter and her boyfriend. If they come to know of her pregnancy, they are likely to force marriage upon him. That is an option John contemplates but chooses not to pursue. Even if he survives his father's wrath for having a relationship with a woman before marriage, he knows he cannot make him accept the match. Neither Stanley nor his church would approve a marriage between John and a circumcised woman. The irony of the situation is that Stanley acted very similarly himself, but his past is hidden to John.

John is a victim as much of Calvinism as of modernity. Stanley's Christianity leaves no room for compassion, no forgiveness of human failing. He lives by the Bible and follows all its precepts. John's ambition to rise in the world through higher education works against him, as does Stanley's Christianity. Thus "A Meeting in the Dark" is a poignant reminder of the ethical dilemma at the heart of colonialism: The so-called progress it brings occurs at a huge cost.

"MINUTES OF GLORY"

Ngugi mentions the genesis of "Minutes of Glory" included in part 3 of *Secret Lives* in the book's preface. A friend told him the story of a barmaid who stole money and lived like a princess for just a day. "Minutes of Glory" describes Wanjiru, a barmaid who, ironically, goes by the name of Beatrice, Dante's divine inspiration. Wanjiru works as a barmaid during the days, a prostitute during the nights. Aging fast and losing her looks, she faces stiff competition from younger and prettier rivals. That is why she tries hard to lighten her complexion by using facial creams and ointments. While at Treetop Bar, she comes to know a trucker who hires her for nightly pleasures. He tells her his story. He has fought in the freedom struggle, but that gives him no edge over those with education in Kenya after independence. Indeed, the difference between him and those with education and money is visible in the cool reception he usually gets from the other patrons of Treetop Bar. Hard work alone has helped him all the way; he owns the truck he drives. Wanjiru identifies with him readily. She has a similar story to tell, but when she tells it, the result is different. As she tells him how she became a barmaid because of poverty, he falls asleep. Wanjiru discovers that though she took his story to heart, he paid no attention to hers. What she feels is not mere disappointment but a huge betrayal. Out of spite, she steals his money, buys expensive clothes, and

dines in an expensive Nairobi restaurant. When she returns to Treetop, she draws admiration from men who ignored her before. Evidently, her failure to attract men was not because of her looks but because of her poor attire and dull appearance. The trucker shows up with a policeman few hours later and has her arrested and removed. When he tells everybody how he has been a victim of theft, he receives a lot of sympathy. Men who spurned him before presently mingle with him. One of them proposes that laws should be written to hang all thieves, even the petty ones.

Opportunities created by independence benefit a select few, only those with money and connections. Ngugi's portrayal of such a society in "Minutes of Glory" and some of the other stories in *Secret Lives* derives from his Marxism, especially from *Black Skin, White Mask* (1952) and *The Wretched of the Earth* (1963), two influential critiques of the bourgeoisie in decolonized societies by the noted Marxist scholar Frantz Fanon. In these works Fanon suggests that independence of a colonized nation does not allow the disadvantaged to rise. On the one hand, there is the psychological baggage of racism that forces black people to accept a white identity. On the other, there is the privileged class of people left by the departed colonizer; though black, they control state power the same way their colonial masters did. To the divisions of race and class, Ngugi adds gender. It is telling that the only person with whom Wanjiru is able to connect is Nyaguthii, another barmaid. "Minutes of Glory" brings to the fore women's issues in postcolonial Kenya where women are treated the worst. The trucker who has had a hard life brutally excludes Wanjiru from his world. He, in fact, suffers no qualm in sacrificing her, claiming instead the privilege that the men in the bar provide.

OTHER MAJOR WORKS

LONG FICTION: *Weep Not, Child*, 1964; *The River Between*, 1965; *A Grain of Wheat*, 1967; *Secret Lives*, 1974; *Petals of Blood*, 1977; *Caitaani Mũtharaba-Inĩ*, 1980 (*Devil on the Cross*, 1982); *Matigari ma Njiruung*, 1986 (*Matigari*, 1989); *Mũrogi wa Kagogo*, 2004 (*Wizard of the Crow*, 2004).

PLAYS: *The Black Hermit*, pr. 1962, pb. 1968; *This Time Tomorrow: Three Plays*, pb. 1970 (includes *The Rebels*, *The Wound in My Heart*, and *This Time Tomorrow*); *The Trial of Dedan Kimathi*, pr. 1974, pb. 1976 (with Micere Githae-Mugo); *Ngaahika Ndeenda*, pr. 1977, pb. 1980 (with Ngugi wa Mirii; *I Will Marry When I Want*, 1982); *Maitu Njugira*, pb. 1982 (with Ngugi wa Mirii; *Mother, Sing for Me*, 1986).

NONFICTION: *Homecoming: Essays on African and Caribbean Literature, Culture, and Politics*, 1972; *Detained: A Writer's Prison Diary*, 1981; *Writers in Politics*, 1981 (revised 1997); *Barrel of a Pen: Resistance to Repression in Neo-colonial Kenya*, 1983; *Decolonising the Mind: The Politics of Language in African Literature*, 1986; *Writing Against Neocolonialism*, 1986; *Moving the Centre: The Struggle for Cultural Freedoms*, 1993; *Penpoints, Gunpoints, and Dreams: Toward a Critical Theory of the Arts and the State in Africa*, 1998; *Something Torn and New: An African Renaissance*, 2009; *Dreams in a Time of War: A Childhood Memoir*, 2010.

BIBLIOGRAPHY

Booker, Keith M. *The African Novel in English: An Introduction*. Portsmouth, N.H.: Heinemann, 1998. Offers an overview of Ngugi's life and works, a brief history of Kenya, and a detailed discussion of *Devil on the Cross*.

Cook, David, and Michael Okenimkpe. *Ngugi wa Thiong'o: An Exploration of His Writings*. 2d ed. Oxford, England: James Currey, 1997. Examines Ngugi's growth as a writer with chapters on his fiction, plays, and short stories.

Gikandi, Simon. *Ngugi wa Thiong'o*. Cambridge, England: Cambridge University Press, 2000. Studies Ngugi in light of Gikuyu nationalism and discusses his major short stories.

Lindfors, Bernth, and Reinhard Sander, eds. *Ngugi wa Thiong'o Speaks: Interviews with the Kenyan Writer*. Trenton, N.J.: Africa World Press, 2006. Offers a fine collection of Ngugi's interviews and comments of nearly forty years.

Farhad B. Idris

O

Kenzaburō Ōe

Born: Ōse, Shikoku, Japan; January 31, 1935

Other literary forms

Although Kenzaburō Ōe (kehn-zah-buh-roh oh-eh) first gained attention through his short stories, which are included in many anthologies of postwar Japanese writing, he has also written many novels, including: *Kojinteki na taiken* (1964; *A Personal Matter,* 1968), *Man'en gannen no futtoboru* (1967; *The Silent Cry,* 1974), *Pinchi rannā chōso* (1976; *The Pinch Runner Memorandum,* 1994), *Jinsei no shinseki* (1989; *An Echo of Heaven,* 1996), *Shizuka na seikatsu* (1990; *A Quiet Life,* 1996), *Chūgaeri* (1999; *Somersault,* 2003); *Torikaeko* (2000; *The Changeling,* 2010) and *Rōtashi Anaberu Rii sōkedachitsu mimakaritsu* (2007). In

addition, Ōe has published many essays on literature and politics, the latter reflecting his political activism. Much of this nonfiction work has been collected in *Aimai na Nihon no watakushi* (1995; *Japan, the Ambiguous, and Myself: The Nobel Prize Speech, and Other Lectures,* 1995). Ōe's memoir of his life with his mentally disabled son, *Kaifuku suru kazoku* (1995; *A Healing Family,* 1996), includes beautiful watercolor paintings by his wife Itami Yukari.

Achievements

Kenzaburō Ōe emerged in the late 1950's as one of the leading figures of the postwar generation of writers. His short story "The Catch" received the coveted Akutagawa Prize in 1958. *A Personal Matter* won the 1964 Shinchōsha Literary Prize and *The Silent Cry* won the Tanizaki Jun'ichirō Prize in 1967. As Ōe's novels continued to win major Japanese literary awards, such as the Noma Literary Prize in 1973, the Yomiuri Prize in 1982, and the Ito Sei Literary Prize in 1990, his reputation began to attract international attention.

The European community awarded Ōe the Europelia Prize in 1989, and he won the Italian Mondelosso Prize in 1993. Ōe's high standing in world literature was fully recognized in 1994, when he won the Nobel Prize in Literature. Indicative of Ōe's inner conflict with what he called the antidemocratic cult of the emperor at home in Japan, he immediately declined Japan's Imperial Order of Culture, which he received days after the Nobel Prize. In 2009, Ōe traveled to China to receive that country's Weishanhu Award for Best Foreign Novel in the Twenty-first Century for his novel *Rōtashi Anaberu Rii sōkedachitsu mimakaritsu* (the beautiful Annabel Lee was chilled and killed).

Biography

Kenzaburō Ōe was born on January 31, 1935, in a small village on Shikoku, the smallest of Japan's four main islands. The third son of seven children, he was only six when World War II erupted; he lost his father in the war. Ōe was ten when Hiroshima and Nagasaki were destroyed by atomic attack as the war ended. He entered prestigious Tokyo University in 1954, studying French literature, and burst upon the literary scene while still a student there, publishing a short story, "Shisa no ogori" ("Lavish the Dead"), in the magazine *Bungakukai* in 1957. It attracted attention, and his talent was widely recognized when he received the prestigious Akutagawa Prize in 1958 for "The Catch," which draws upon his experience as a boy in a remote rural village during World War II.

After his graduation, Ōe married Itami Yukari, the daughter of screenwriter Itami Mansaku, in February, 1960. In May of that year he was a member of the Japan-China Literary Delegation, which met with Chinese leader Mao Zedong. The next year he traveled in the former Soviet Union and Western Europe, where he met writer and philosopher Jean-Paul Sartre.

Drawing upon his childhood, Ōe dealt in his early works with alienation and people on the fringes of society, as well as political issues, contemporary society, and sexual mores. In the summer of 1963, however, his first son was born with serious brain damage, leading him to a new stage in his writing, in which he affirmed hope arising from despair. In five works written between 1964 and 1976, Ōe used the persistent theme of a father dealing with a disabled son: *A Personal Matter* and *Sora no kaibutsu Aguii* (*Aghwee the Sky Monster*) are notable examples.

In 1965, Ōe traveled to the United States, returning there for another visit in 1968. He also visited Australia, and in 1970 he toured Southeast Asia. He made frequent literary appearances and in 1975 took part in a two-day fast protesting the treatment of Korean writer and poet Kim Chi Ha. In 1976, Ōe met the Colombian writer Gabriel García Márquez after teaching for a semester at the Collegio de Mexico. Impressed by García Márquez's work, Ōe returned to Japan and published *Shosetsu no hoho* (1978; methodology of the novel), which promotes the Western literary theory of structuralism to revive Japanese writing. Indeed, many of Ōe's next writings show his fascination with structuralism and marginal existence.

Often traveling to Europe after 1980, Ōe visited the Soviet Union, where he attended a 1987 Conference on Peace in Moscow. Ōe also publicly debated authors: Germany's Günter Grass in 1990 and France's Michel Tournier in Paris in 1991.

Winning the Nobel Prize in Literature in 1994 came as a joyful surprise for Ōe. In his acceptance speech in Stockholm on December 7, 1994, Ōe claimed the prize in part on behalf of other dissident Asian writers, and he indirectly explained why he had immediately declined Japan's Imperial Order of Culture as belonging to a feudalistic past.

Back in Japan, Ōe told a stunned public that he would stop writing novels now that his mentally disabled son Hikari Ōe had become a successful composer of music. He later reversed this decision, publishing several novels from 1999 through 2007. In 1997, Ōe's ongoing political involvement led to his participation in protests against French nuclear testing in the Pacific. Having settled in Tokyo with his wife and family, Ōe gave literary lectures around the world and continued to spend time with close friends.

Kenzaburō Ōe (©The Nobel Foundation)

ANALYSIS

Prewar Japanese writers, such as Jun'ichirō Tanizaki and Yasunari Kawabata, who continued to build their literary reputations after World War II, focused on the introspective (notably in the so-called I-novel), but New Left writers emerging after the war, such as Kenzaburō Ōe, are as indebted to Western literary traditions as they are to those of Japan. Like his contemporary Kōbō Abe, Ōe writes about alienation from modern society and the loss of identity in modern Japan. He does so by using as themes his childhood in a small village, the war and subsequent occupation by Americans, and the personal tragedy of his son's birth defect.

One of the most prolific and popular writers in Japan, Ōe clearly reflects the concerns of the postwar generation, a generation that saw the fall of old symbols, such as the emperor. The war and defeat of Japan left a void in which his characters try to find themselves, groping for meaning. In "The Catch," the harmony of rural Japan is shattered as a young boy is disillusioned by the adults around him. In "The Day He Himself Shall Wipe My Tears Away," a boy sees his father's death as a sacrifice to the old values. This same hero appears in Ōe's later writing--older, but trying to escape through sex and deviant behavior. *Teach Us to Outgrow Our Madness* is a powerful tale of the importance of telling the truth, even when doing so can be painful. Ōe's unique style, heavily influenced by Western traditions and directness, is fresh and controversial, undergirding the issue addressed in most, if not all, of his fiction: the cultural disharmony that his generation has experienced as a result of World War II and its aftermath. In writing about his own personal crisis, Ōe deals with the larger themes of modernity and meaning in Japan. Like the hero in his favorite novel, Mark Twain's *Adventures of Huckleberry Finn* (1884), Ōe sees life as a quest for adventure, whether in Africa or in the back streets of Tokyo--a quest for truth.

"THE CATCH"

In "The Catch," the boy-narrator is combing the village crematory looking for bone fragments with friends when an American plane roars overhead at treetop level. The next morning, the children awaken to an ominous silence. The adults are out searching for downed American airmen. They return late in the day from the mountains, leading an enormous black man. The boy is reminded of a boar hunt as the hunters silently circle around the captive, who has the chain from a boar trap around his legs.

The enemy excites both fear and curiosity among the children. He is put into the cellar of the communal storehouse and a guard is posted. The storehouse is a large building, and the boy and his young brother live on the second floor with their father, an impoverished hunter. The boy is excited at the thought of sleeping in the same building as the exotic prisoner who has fallen into their midst.

At first the captive is treated as a dangerous animal. The boy goes with his father to town to report the capture. He is uncomfortable in the town, aware of his poverty and dirtiness. The local officials refuse to take the prisoner until they receive orders from the prefecture offices. The boy and his father return to the village at sunset with the unwelcome news.

The boy carries food down into the dark cellar, guarded by his father with shotgun ready. At first the captive only stares at the food, and the boy realizes in shame that the poor dinner might be rejected, but the black man suddenly devours the meal. Gradually the boy loses his fear of the American as they bring him food every day. The children begin to take a proprietary interest in the captive. As time passes, the adults return to fieldwork, and the children are left with the American. Noticing that the man's leg is wounded from the boar trap, the boy and his friend release him with trepidation, but they find him well behaved. Even the adults in the village accept the idea that the black man is human, coming to trust him.

Eventually the children let the captive out of the cellar to walk through the village. The adults come to accept this, and he is even allowed to wander around the village alone. The women lose their fear and give him food from their own hands. The children take him to the village spring, where they all strip naked and splash in the water. The boy considers the man a splendid animal, an animal of great intelligence.

Trust and respect evaporate, however, when an official appears on a rainy day. As the adults assemble, the prisoner senses that he is about to be taken away, and he grabs the boy and drags him to the cellar, locking the door behind them. The boy is shocked and hurt as he realizes his sudden danger and sees the airman reverting to the dangerous beast he was when first captured. The grown-ups break into the cellar, and the boy's father plunges a hatchet into the prisoner's skull. They plan to cremate the black man but are ordered to keep the body for identification.

The story ends in irony. Paying another visit, the village official notices the children using the lightweight tail of the American plane as a sled on the grass. In a playful mood, he decides to give it a try, but he hurtles into a rock and is killed. He will be cremated with the wood that villagers collected to cremate the American captive.

Although the story is set during the war years and the events occur in the context of unusual hardship, its major theme, a youth's coming-of-age, is a universal one: The young boy finds his childhood innocence and trust betrayed by the black captive and the adults who rush to rescue him in a frenzy of hatred. There are echoes of *The Adventures of Huckleberry Finn* in this story: in the young boys' spirit of adventure, in their unaffected wonder and curiosity, and in their rejection of adult attitudes. (It is not surprising that during his trip to the United States in 1965, Ōe visited Hannibal, Missouri, the birthplace of Mark Twain.) The coming-of-age theme also underscores another major concern in the story: man's (as opposed to boy's) inhumanity to man. Ōe uses juxtaposition to create a realistic yet somehow absurd view of the world; the young narrator allows him to introduce humorous elements of childish enthusiasm that make the final tragedy all the more appalling.

AGHWEE THE SKY MONSTER

In the novella *Aghwee the Sky Monster*, a young father is haunted by an imaginary baby that flies down from the sky, reminding him of his own baby, whom he killed in the false belief that it had a malignant brain tumor. The story is told through a young college student, who is hired to take care of a banker's son. The student is told that the son, a composer, is having delusions and requires supervision. Needing the money, the

student agrees to act as a chaperon to help keep the son's mind off his delusions. The student accompanies the composer on trips about Tokyo, wary of the possibility that his charge may, at any moment, be joined by the imaginary Aghwee.

He learns that Aghwee is a fat baby, dressed in a white nightgown, who is as big as a kangaroo. From time to time, the composer believes that he sees Aghwee flying down to his side; this naturally alarms the student chaperon, who worries about a possible suicide attempt. In time, the student learns to step aside to leave room for the imaginary baby as they make excursions to bars, motion-picture theaters, and swimming pools, where they invariably turn back without entering the water. When the composer gets his chaperon to take a message to a former lover in Kyōto, the student learns that the lovers were in bed together in a hotel room when a call came from the hospital informing them of the death of the baby, who had uttered only one sound, "Aghwee."

Then disaster strikes. While walking on the Ginza on Christmas Eve with the composer and Aghwee, the student is shocked as they are mysteriously pitched forward into the path of a truck; the student escapes serious harm, but the composer is fatally injured. Visiting the dying composer in the hospital later that day, the student admits that he was about to believe in Aghwee, and the composer smiles. He dies the next day.

Ten years later, the student is suddenly attacked by rock-throwing children who have been mysteriously provoked. One of the rocks hits him in the eye, and he suddenly senses a large white being the size of a kangaroo: Aghwee. He has completed his identification with the dead composer's fantasy.

"THE DAY HE HIMSELF SHALL WIPE MY TEARS AWAY"

In his lengthy short story "Mizu kara waga namida o nuguitamau hi" ("The Day He Himself Shall Wipe My Tears Away"), Ōe again writes about a man who is trying to grasp the reality of his youth, this time in an isolated farm village as World War II is ending. It is difficult and sometimes frustrating work, and the background of the story is only gradually revealed as the protagonist shifts from the present to a mythical reconstruction of events.

The story opens in a hospital room where the man is dying, or imagines he is dying (this is never resolved), of cancer. What is clear is that the narrator is grappling with a lifetime struggle to free himself from his mother's harsh and stifling influence. He is dictating a history of the events leading to his father's bizarre death in a futile uprising on August 16, 1945, the day after the Japanese surrender in World War II. He attempts to shut his mother and the rest of the contemporary world out by wearing his father's old goggles, which are masked with green cellophane. His identification with his father and his reconstruction of events that he only dimly understood as a six-year-old boy are meant to challenge his mother's sarcastic realism and allow him to relive the most important moment in his life.

The boy's father apparently was involved in right-wing political activities with the military in Manchuria in northeastern China. After Japan's military fortunes took a turn for the worse at Midway and Guadalcanal, his father was involved with an underground group that was against Prime Minister Hideki Tojo. The group's plans to change policy failed, for the father suddenly appeared in the valley on January 1, 1943, going straight into seclusion in the storehouse.

The boy's elder stepbrother was sent to war and became the valley's first war casualty. Even though he was not her own son, the narrator's mother took the death as a failure of the father and his politics. Thereafter, the father's name was never spoken in the family; throughout the story he is referred to as "a certain party," who lived by himself in a shed behind the main house. The boy's mother also shut herself off from all contact with the neighbors in the valley, ignoring everyone thereafter.

The valley was not a peaceful childhood sanctuary for the young boy, for he was subject to ridicule and hazing by the village children at school. When school bullies taunted him for his impoverished appearance, he stabbed himself in the hand with a hand sickle and threatened to slit his own throat if they attempted to harm him. Confused and appalled, the gang backed off because the boy did not react normally: "He's like a *kamikaze* pilot that didn't get to die!" In the same fashion, the narrator, now thirty-five years old, hopes to upstage his elderly mother by dying of real or imagined cancer.

He was still psychologically wounded by her actions when she caught him attempting suicide when he was almost out of high school. She took his suicide note, stole into the mimeograph room of the school, printed it, and distributed it to all of his teachers and classmates to reveal his weakness. To complete his humiliation, she noted all the incorrect characters he had written in the sentimental will. By making him the fool, she made it impossible for him to consider suicide in the future. Now he believes that cancer can get her attention.

As a boy he both feared and admired his father, wanting to be recognized and accepted, but he was ignored. His father was repugnantly fat, spending his days in semidarkness, sitting in a barber chair, wearing the green goggles. While in Manchuria he had acquired the habit of eating meat, and he had sent the boy to town to buy the only meat Japanese would not eat, oxtails and pig feet. Acquiring his loathsome burden, the boy also had to visit Korean forest workers to ask for some garlic to flavor the stew his father was going to make. His father had emerged from his dark room to cook the meat outdoors but collapsed on the boy, venting blood and urine. The doctor had been summoned and had diagnosed cancer of the bladder. From that time, the summer of 1944, his father had remained inside the storehouse, his disease slowly progressing.

The critical incident in the story is the appearance in the valley of ten soldiers who had deserted their unit when the surrender of Japan was announced. They came to the boy's house to enlist the support of the former political activist but also to get the funds that the boy's mother had inherited. That night, the soldiers made plans to go to the city the next day to get money from the bank; they hoped to capture some army planes, disguise them as American planes, and somehow fly to Tokyo and crash them into the Imperial Palace in a final attempt to get the Japanese people to rise up against the invaders. They drank sake and listened over and over to an old German record on the phonograph, a Johann Sebastian Bach cantata with the line, "His Majesty the Emperor wipes my tears away with his own hand, Death, you come ahead, you brother of Sleep you come ahead, his Majesty will wipe my tears away with his own hand. . . ." It is from this evocation of the prewar imperial ethos that Ōe chose his title.

The next morning, the ten soldiers pulled the father in a hand-built cart to a truck they had stolen and drove to town. The boy's father was bleeding from his terminal cancer and was in considerable pain, but he agreed to lead the quixotic band. The group vowed *junshi*, or death, as a sign of allegiance to the emperor. As they emerged from the bank--it was not clear whether they had robbed it or made a withdrawal on the mother's account--they encountered another band of soldiers who opened fire on them, killing all of them except the young boy.

Just as the narrator gets to this crux of the story, the mother suddenly speaks from the corner of the hospital room. She may have been there all along, taking it all in. His mother narrates a different account, describing in cynical terms the soldiers who came after the money and the futility of the make-believe uprising. She shatters the mythical reconstruction the narrator has been trying to build, once again dominating his life and reducing him to a madness that only death will relieve.

TEACH US TO OUTGROW OUR MADNESS

For a contemporary American reader, Ōe's recurrent concern with the issue of mental disability, which is also at the core of his novella *Teach Us to Outgrow Our Madness*, sheds an interesting light on another culture's handling of the subject. Although Ōe illuminates aspects of the traditional fear of disability as possibly hereditary and shameful in Japan, his fiction outspokenly opposes this view and argues for a positive attitude of compassion for the disabled. Thus, the story's father, referred to only as "the fat man," refuses to kill his love for his disabled four-year-old son, even in the face of severe social prejudice.

The story unfolds as the father gradually recovers from nearly being thrown into the pool of the polar bear exhibit at the Tokyo Zoo. As he lies in his bed alone, in a moment of existential self-introspection typical for Ōe's characters, he mentally recounts a conflict with his mother. Recently, she has unjustly accused him of having contracted syphilis in China, a sexually transmitted disease which, if not treated, can lead to brain damage and was believed to be transmitted to one's children. Thus, she viciously insists on a link between

her husband, the "fat man's" father, whom she calls mad for admiring the Chinese and mysteriously secluding himself in a storehouse for years before dying with a blood-curdling scream, and her "mad" son who passed on his illness to her grandson.

Gradually, Ōe deconstructs this convenient belief of the mother, who uses the term "madness" to explain anything which does not fit in her traditional views. She thus becomes a stand-in for those aspects of traditional Japanese culture which Ōe himself felt he rejected when he declined Japan's Imperial Order of Culture in 1994. For as the story reveals, the "fat man's" father confined himself because he let down his friends who tried to kill the emperor during World War II as a protest against Japan's war on China.

The "fat man's" probing for details about his father's actions is rejected by his mother as a mere symptom of syphilitic madness, for to acknowledge the validity of his quest would lead the mother to confront the fact of Japanese atrocities against the Chinese in the war, an issue which had met with near-unanimous silence in the Japanese postwar political debate until the 1990's. The false excuse of syphilis also serves to exonerate the mother from any societal blame for her own genes when it comes to her grandson's disability.

The "fat man" comes to repudiate all this, and Ōe offers an exquisite description of his loving, emphatic relationship with his son Mori. The father named him so after the Japanese word for forest in an allusion to his being a child of nature rather than intellect. Betraying the influence of Western writing on the author, the father also calls his son affectionately Eeyore, the name of the little donkey in A. A. Milne's English story *Winnie-the-Pooh* (1926).

In the end, the "fat man's" love for his son causes his mother to renounce the false story of her son's alleged syphilis and to tell the truth about her husband. As Ōe's story implies, the "fat man's" love finally leads his family to outgrow their real madness of lying.

OTHER MAJOR WORKS

LONG FICTION: *Memushiri kouchi*, 1958 (*Nip the Buds, Shoot the Kids*, 1995); *Warera no jidai*, 1959; *Yoru yo yuruyaka ni ayume*, 1959; *Seinenno omei*, 1960; *Okurete kita seinen*, 1962; *Sakebigoe*, 1963; *Kojinteki na taiken*,

1964 (*A Personal Matter*, 1968); *Nichyoseikatsu no boken*, 1964; *Man'en gan'nen no futtoboru*, 1967 (*The Silent Cry*, 1974); *Nichijo seikatsu no boken*, 1971; *Kōzui wa waga tamashii ni oyobi*, 1973; *Pinchi rannā chōsho*, 1976 (*The Pinch Runner Memorandum*, 1994); *Dōjidai gemu*, 1979; *Atarashii hito yo mezameyo*, 1983 (*Rouse Up O Young Men of the New Age!*, 2002); *Natsukashii toshi e no tegami*, 1987; *Jinsei no shinseki*, 1989 (*An Echo of Heaven*, 1996); *Chiryōtō*, 1990; *Shizuka na seikatsu*, 1990 (*A Quiet Life*, 1996); *Chiryōtō wakusei*, 1991; *Moeagaru midori no ki*, 1993-1995 (includes *"Sukuinushi" ga nagurareru made*, 1993; *Yureugoku "vashireshon,"* 1994; *Ōinaru hi ni*, 1995); *Chūgaeri*, 1999 (2 volumes; *Somersault*, 2003); *Torikaeko*, 2000 (also known as *Chenjiringu*; *The Changeling*, 2010); *Ureigao no doji*, 2002; *Nihyakunen no kodomo*, 2003; *Sayōnara watashi no hon yo!*, 2005; *Rōtashi Anaberu Rii sōkedachitsu mimakaritsu*, 2007.

NONFICTION: *Sekai no wakamonotachi*, 1962; *Genshuku na tsunawatari*, 1965; *Hiroshima nōto*, 1965 (*Hiroshima Notes*, 1982); *Jisokusuru kokorozashi*, 1968; *Kakujidai no sōzōryoku*, 1970; *Kowaremoto to shite no ningen*, 1970; *Okinawa nōto*, 1970; *Dōjidai to shite no sengo*, 1973; *Bungaku nōto*, 1974; *Jōkyō e*, 1974; *Kotoba ni yotte*, 1976; *Shosetsu no hoho*, 1978; *Ōe Kenzaburō dojidaironshu*, 1981; *Sengo bungakusha*, 1981; *Kaku no taika to "ningen" no koe*, 1982; *Atarashii bungaku no tame ni*, 1988; *Bungaku sainyūmon*, 1992; *Aimai na Nihon no watakushi*, 1995 (*Japan, the Ambiguous, and Myself: The Nobel Prize Speech, and Other Lectures*, 1995); *Kaifuku suru kazoku*, 1995 (*A Healing Family*, 1996); *On Politics and Literature: Two Lectures*, 1999; *"Jibun no ki" no shita de*, 2001; *Bōryoku ni sakaratte kaku: Ōe Kenzaburō ōfuku shokan*, 2003.

EDITED TEXT: *Nan to moshirenai mirai ni*, 1985 (*The Crazy Iris, and Other Stories of the Atomic Aftermath*, 1985).

BIBLIOGRAPHY

Cargas, Harry James. "Fiction of Shame." *The Christian Century* 112 (April 12, 1995): 382-383. Brief biographical sketch commenting on Ōe's theme of guilt over Japanese attraction to Western customs and rejection of their own traditions, as well as guilt about the sneak attack on Pearl Harbor, which violated the samurai code of honor.

Claremont, Yasuko. *The Novels of Ōe Kenzaburō*. New York: Routledge, 2009. Traces the path from nihilism to atonement and then to salvation in Ōe's works and discusses his use of myth. Although focusing on the novels, Clarement also examines some of the short fiction, including "The Day He Himself Shall Wipe My Tears Away" and *Aghwee the Sky Monster*; references to short fiction are listed in the index.

Gotom, Shoji. "Huck Finn and America in Kenzaburo Oe." In *Postmodernity and Cross-Culturalism*, edited by Yoshinobu Hakutani. Madison, N.J.: Fairleigh Dickinson University Press, 2002. Examines the influence of Mark Twain's *Adventures of Huckleberry Finn* on Ōe's short fiction and novels, describing the two authors' similar themes and characterizations.

Ōe, Kenzaburō. *The Art of Fiction No. 195*. Interview by Sarah Fay. *The Paris Review* 183 (Winter, 2007): 37-65. Among other subjects, Ōe discusses his political activism, the role of elaboration in art, his writing process, and his reading of William Butler Yeats's poetry.

_____. "Kenzaburō Ōe: After the Nobel, a New Direction." Interview by Sam Staggs. *Publishers Weekly* 242 (August 7, 1995): 438-439. Ōe talks about his decision to discontinue writing fiction, his lifestyle, and his relationship with Jean-Paul Sartre.

Remnick, David. "Reading Japan." *The New Yorker* 70 (February 6, 1995): 38-44. Recounts a meeting with Ōe, in which the writer talks about his life and art. Discusses Ōe's obsession with his mentally disabled son in several of his stories and his place in modern Japanese culture and literature.

Swain, David L. "Something Akin to Grace: The Journey of Kenzaburō Ōe." *The Christian Century* 114 (December 24-31, 1997): 1226-1229. Brief profile describing Ōe's sense of native place, his sense of marginalization, and his literary cosmopolitanism. Briefly discusses *An Echo of Heaven* and *A Healing Family*.

Wilson, Michiko Niikuni. "Kenzaburō Ōe." *The Georgia Review* 49 (Spring, 1995): 331-350. A biographical sketch, including a Bibliography of Ōe's work that has been translated into English. Includes the text of Ōe's 1994 Nobel Prize lecture, in which he discusses the influence of Mark Twain and Yasunari Kawabata on his work and comments on contemporary Japanese culture and literature. Ōe also used this vehicle to make his famous announcement that he would stop writing fiction.

_____. *The Marginal World of Ōe Kenzaburō: A Study in Themes and Techniques*. Armonk, N.Y.: M. E. Sharpe, 1986. An attempt at dealing with the weird, grotesque, and perverse imagination of Ōe by showing--or attempting to show--how two short stories and three novels present the relationship of a corpulent father and his mentally disabled son by establishing a unity of theme, a chronological development, and an ironic turn of events.

Yamanouchi, Hisaaki. "In Search of Identity: Abe Kōbō and Ōe Kenzaburō." In *The Search for Authenticity in Modern Japanese Literature*. New York: Cambridge University Press, 1978. Draws parallels between Abe and Ōe regarding their treatment of themes and mutual concern about the search for identity. Explains how the ideas of identity, authenticity, and alienation that Ōe attempts to use are Western themes stemming from the existentialist philosophy of Martin Heidegger and Jean-Paul Sartre; Ōe seeks to graft these themes onto a Japanese culture that, although rapidly modernized, still maintains some strong traditions. Also discusses Ōe's creation of antisocial characters, whether juvenile delinquents, sexual perverts, or vicious criminals, whom he treats as "fallen angels," while he himself dreams of a "pastoral community."

Yoshida, Sanroku. "Kenzaburō Ōe: A New World of Imagination." *Comparative Literature Studies* 22 (Spring, 1985): 80-96. Ōe is presented as the leading Japanese literary reformer, who, rejecting literary elitism and high art, holds that literature should be democratic and should appeal to the masses in didactic terms. Describes how Ōe sees literature as having an obligation to protest against social evils, which, in his view, have only political solutions; hence, he believes that political ideology has a legitimate place in literature.

_____. "Kenzaburō Ōe's Recent Modernist Experiments." *Critique: Studies in Modern Fiction* 26 (Spring, 1985): 155-164. A general view of Ōe's innovative narrative techniques, including his characterizations, recurrent themes, stylistic practices, and use of grotesque and animal imagery.

Richard Rice
Updated by Richard P. Benton and R. C. Lutz

BEN OKRI

Born: Minna, Nigeria; March 15, 1959

PRINCIPAL SHORT FICTION

Incidents at the Shrine, 1986
Stars of the New Curfew, 1988
Tales of Freedom, 2009 (poems and short stories)

OTHER LITERARY FORMS

Besides his collections of short fiction, Ben Okri (OHK-rih) has written several novels, including *Flowers and Shadows* (1980), *The Landscapes Within* (1981), *The Famished Road* (1991), *Dangerous Love* (1996), *Infinite Riches* (1998), *Phoenix Rising* (2001), *In Arcadia* (2002), and *Starbook: A Magical Tale of Love and Regeneration* (2007). He has also published the nonfiction work *A Way of Being Free* (1997) and two collections of poetry.

ACHIEVEMENTS

Ben Okri has impressed his readers with his colorful, vibrant use of the English language, the power of his words and imagery, and his control over structure and motif. He received both the Commonwealth Writer's Prize for the African region for *Incidents at the Shrine* and *The Paris Review* Aga Khan Prize for Fiction in 1987. In addition, he received the Man Booker Prize for *The Famished Road* in 1991, the Crystal Award from the World Economic Forum in 1995, Italy's Premio Palmi for *Dangerous Love* in 2000, and the International Literary Award Novi Sad from Serbia in 2008.

BIOGRAPHY

Ben Okri was born in Minna, Nigeria, in 1959, the son of Silver Oghekeneshineke Loloje Okri and Grace Okri, both of the Urhobo ethnic group of southwestern Nigeria. His father was an executive officer with the Nigerian Post and Telecommunications. After finishing his secondary education in 1972, three months before his fourteenth birthday, Okri moved to Lagos. He is the first Nigerian writer to have won the Man Booker Prize and the first to have chosen self-expatriation; he settled in London, England. He has been poetry editor of the magazine *West Africa* and a broadcaster for the British Broadcasting Corporation (BBC).

ANALYSIS

The settings in Ben Okri's stories are for the most part African, specifically Nigerian. More important, the attitudes expressed toward society and the natural world seem consistent with an African cosmology. That is to say, Okri presents a world wavering between order and chaos, an ambiguous and mysterious world, of which human beings are but a part and over which they have little control. Whatever differences may exist between Okri and his two famous countrymen Chinua Achebe and Wole Soyinka in their styles or subjects, he shares with these two writers both the awe and the comic bemusement with which they face the human condition. While offering guidance, these writers do not presume to offer solutions. While calling to account instances of irresponsible behavior, they do not expect it to cease or promise peace if it does. While not being fatalists, they accept a certain inevitability in human affairs. Like Achebe and Soyinka, Okri takes Africa as his primary subject but humanity as his theme. What his Nigerians do in exaggerated gestures, all people do in some measure.

Acknowledging the limitations of human perception, Okri does not, then, insist upon absolutes. He does, however, suggest some patterns. For example, the principle of reciprocity in Soyinka's works (for example, the play *Madmen and Specialists*, pr. 1970; rev. pr., pb. 1971) is also in those of Okri: What one sows, one also reaps. The responsibility that one has toward others and toward nature seems to be fundamental in

Okri's thought. If his stories are bleak and nightmarish, a cause may be the failure of individuals in society to observe this principle. The primary manifestation of this behavior in his collections of stories is the failure of characters to face reality. Okri presents this evasion as an escape into dreams (illusions) that, because false and evasive, become nightmares. The reader can hardly distinguish dream from reality because characters without warning, after a short sleep, step out of reality into dream. What people really need is honesty and the capacity for "terror and compassion" to face what honesty reveals. Because awareness is thus central to Okri's theme, "seeing" is a major motif in his collections. In fact, the most Okri seems to hope for in his characters or his readers is some conceptual breakthrough, some acknowledgment that much of life is pain and that life ends in death. Only then can one know sweetness and beauty.

INCIDENTS AT THE SHRINE

Okri's short-story collection *Incidents at the Shrine* opens with a story about a child being initiated into reality during the Nigerian Civil War. The nameless ten-year-old boy who narrates "Laughter Beneath the Bridge" has not as yet begun to evade reality but instead offers an objective if naïve account of what he sees and feels. He, along with two other boys, abandoned at school because of the war, survives by foraging and stealing. His mother, a member of "the rebel tribe," accompanies him on a harrowing journey home in a crowded truck; they must speak only the father's language at the barricades. The soldiers physically and mentally abuse them, partly because the boy refuses to speak at all. The boy sees, apparently for the first time, the terrors of war, as the illiterate, lascivious, and repulsive soldiers rape and kill suspicious passengers. Only the boy's sudden urge to defecate, spoken in the safe language, allows them to continue their journey. Once home, he continues to face the repulsiveness and danger of war. Beneath the bridge outside town, dead bodies begin to dam the river. His childhood girlfriend, Monica, acts even more strangely than usual. The soldiers have killed her brother, Ugo. She has been spending her time, the boy soon learns, sitting on the bank above the river, contemplating the spot where the soldiers threw his body. At that moment the boy has an epiphany: "The things on the water suddenly looked different, transformed." He "saw them as they were." The soldiers above the bridge laugh; then Monica "started to laugh. I had never heard that sort of twisted laughter before." Then he hears something unearthly: "I thought it was all the swollen corpses that were laughing."

At this point, the world of the boy begins its transition into the frenetic world of the adult, but he has not yet blocked out the reality of death and pain. During a mock Egungun (ancestral) dance, he and Monica defy the soldiers. Seizing the occasion, the soldiers take her away to be raped and killed, as the elders of the town exult because they have cleared the bloated bodies that were polluting the town's air and clogging the river. The child's awakening to death contrasts with the elders' blind, inadequate victory over pollution. The narrator cannot explain why he recalls this period in his life as "a beautiful time," but the reader speculates that beauty is in the clarity and purity of the child's seeing.

Ben Okri (Rex Features via AP Images)

In the title story, "Incidents at the Shrine," Anderson in a daze exits a museum through "the Department of Antiquities" and "the ancestral stoneworks in the museum field." He has just been fired. His resulting paranoia--people seem to be pointing at him--increases after a sleep in which he dreams of "his dead parents." The very goats in the marketplace stare at him, and a fire that breaks out seems "intent upon him because he had no power to protect himself." People call out his names, not only his English one, Anderson, but also the ones out of his past. Two rusty nails give him tetanus. Quack doctors give him injections and medicines. After three days, he has "the gaunt face of a complete stranger." At this point, he returns to his home village.

The emphasis in the first part of the story on Anderson's personal and cultural past and on an obsessive insecurity that has no observable cause suggests by juxtaposition that a cure or an answer demands a return to origins. This is the only story in the collection that holds out any such hope. What follows is a dreamlike sequence, a psychological or spiritual recovery of archetypal experiences. Each dream or trance carries him further back into the inner recesses of the self and its cultural history.

As he approaches the village on foot, "three rough forms" chase him, calling out his names and causing him to abandon his box of clothes, medicines, and gifts. He thus enters the village empty-handed. He does not recognize Mr. Abas, and the town itself seems changed. Ants carry him in a dream into the pool office, where he eventually recognizes his uncle who, Mr. Abas tells him, is the Image-maker, and who guides Anderson through this ancestral world. As the uncle grows "raw and godlike" in Anderson's mind, he utters words of wisdom and parabolic riddles: "The more you look, the less you see" and "The world is the shrine and the shrine is the world." The two men walk through "irregular rows of soapstone monoliths" (like those at the museum), which according to the uncle "were originally decorated with pearls, lapis lazuli, amethysts and magic glass which twinkled wonderful philosophies. But the pale ones from across the seas came and stole them." Clearly the uncle's cure for this "afflicted 'son of the soil'" is to reintroduce him to his African heritage. Anderson enters the shrine, where he finds "the

master Image" still sporting its jewels, in order to undergo a grotesque yet symbolic initiation. After the purification, the Image-maker assures him (what the pragmatic dreamer wants to hear) that he can with confidence collect the salary the museum owes him and can find another job. The shrine, he explains, is a meeting place for "spirits from all over the world," who come to discuss "everything under the sun." Anderson himself "must come home now and again," for it is at home that he will "derive power," whose ultimate source, a strange voice warns him, is awareness of self and the world. In his final dream, he eats of the ever-replenished master Image. He recognizes as he walks out of the village that "There is hunger where I am going" and understands Mr. Abas's parting words: "Suffering cannot kill us." The rough forms that chased him into the village, the threats of death, no longer frighten him. He continues the journey of life with a "new simplicity." This symbolic dream experience, in fact, proposes a simple solution to the nightmarish complications of modern society: an acceptance of the human condition. What the story gives, however, it also takes away. The solution comes in a dream, and dreams are not reliable. The stories that follow show little promise that human beings in a waking state are likely to be so lucid and bold.

The final story, "The Image-Vendor," with its emphasis on dreams, anticipates Okri's second collection of stories, *Stars of the New Curfew*. The main character, Ajegunle Joe, is not only a victim but also a seller of dreams. After taking "Correspondence Courses in psychology and salesmanship," he is reborn as a mystic and publishes pamphlets describing his visions--that is, quack solutions to life's problems. After two years at this job, however, he loses confidence. When he becomes sexually impotent, he himself visits a quack and undergoes a grotesque ritual cure. In his most intriguing dream, a midget offers him a gift, but when he looks, it flies away. It is wisdom, he learns. The midget then offers him a second gift, which Joe pockets on faith. When the midget returns in a later dream to reclaim the gift, Joe learns that he has been carrying around "bad luck." The midget's ironic advice is that Joe should keep his eyes open. With eyes open or closed, Joe apparently cannot win. The Image-maker has already warned Anderson, one remembers, that "the more you look, the less you see." Okri thus ends this collection on a not unexpectedly ambiguous note. Joe and his friend Cata-cata (confusion) try to escape temporarily by fishing off a pier "washed by the August rain." Joe sums up his life as "one long fever" and thinks now that he is "getting well." However, he still believes that "a man must fly," and the only vision he can muster is another quack pamphlet, "Turning Experience into Gold." This final story calls into question the efficacy and reliability of the lesson learned in the title story at the African shrine. The god of confusion, Eshu, will not permit definitive answers.

STARS OF THE NEW CURFEW

In *Stars of the New Curfew*, dream becomes nightmare. In the opening story, "In the Shadow of War," Okri once again starkly contrasts a child's innocence with the brutality of war. Repulsive soldiers again contaminate the environment with their crude manners and disrespect for human life. The boy watches them abuse and kill a woman suspected of being a spy, as corpses float down a river. However, the soldiers, with some gentleness, carry the boy back to his father, who speaks apologetically to the soldiers when the son tries to explain what has happened. The son's delirium sets the tone and theme for the remaining stories.

In "Worlds That Flourish," a nightmarish parody of the title story in the first collection, the main character, now nameless, also loses his job and his way in the world. Soldiers falsely arrest him for burglarizing his own house. His neighbors gradually disappear around him, though he does not notice until one reclusive neighbor chastises him for not "seeing." In a daze, he begins to see handwriting on faces. Then the neighbor disappears, and a two-day rainstorm turns the city into chaotic ruins. His escape, unlike Anderson's, is "without a destination." His frenzied, dreamlike journey seems to move him in circles; his car drives him. An old man at a service station warns him against going "that way": "Stay where you can be happy." As he continues into the forest, people attack his car; blood and flesh cling to broken glass. The car crashes into an anthill. If what has been happening to him is "real," he now has what might be called an out-of-body experience. His spirit enters a traditional village, where

objects are upside down, where people move backward and walk through mirrors. Oddly, they have been expecting him for some three months. Both his reclusive neighbor and his dead wife are among those welcoming him to the land of the dead. He passes the shrine, where a huge statue of a god has only holes for eyes; this is not the same sanctifying image that Anderson encounters. He escapes by running backward. Pursued to the boundary, he finds his car, reenters his body, extricates himself from the wreckage, and tries to find the old man before dying. Like Anderson, he has faced death --he had not been willing before to accept his wife's death--but Okri does not suggest any spiritual purification. At most, the nameless man has achieved awareness. His last words are a warning to another young man traveling in the same direction he had taken.

"In the City of Red Dust" and "Stars of the New Curfew" are likewise bleak extensions of a story in *Incidents at the Shrine*. In the former, two men, Emokhai and Marjomi, and a woman, Dede, are even further trapped in the world of nightmare than their counterparts in "The Dream-Vendor's August." The men survive by selling their blood to a hospital and by picking pockets. Against the suggestive background of Adamic red dust and Egyptian plagues, the military governor, hiding his "secret physical corruptions" and "his monstrosities," celebrates his fiftieth birthday with a parade and an air show. A plane crashes, causing havoc and death. Raped by five soldiers, Dede attempts suicide. The only redeeming grace is Emokhai's protective care of Dede in the hospital and of Marjomi sleeping in his room deep in the ghetto. In that room, Emokhai finds a "confusion of books" on the occult--including the one Joe contemplates writing at the end of "The Dream-Vendor's August." While Joe and Cata-cata escape by fishing, Emokhai and Marjomi smoke marijuana stolen from the governor's secret farms.

In the latter story, "Stars of the New Curfew," the narrator and main character, Arthur, is a vendor not of visionary pamphlets but of mind-altering drugs. As the drugs become more powerful in their promise to cure a multitude of ills, he and his customers enter deeper into nightmare. He is responsible for a bus accident killing seven people. His escape to his past yields only petty quarrels and struggles for power and sexual advantage.

His escape to his home village traps him in a confrontation between two wealthy power seekers, an ugly satire on Nigeria's political corruption. When he returns to the city at the end, he is aware enough to know that life is a nightmare, but he would prefer to dream and continues to sell drugs.

Okri closes this second collection with a poignant love story and a farcical allegory. "When the Lights Return" traces the fate of a young singer whose vanity, insensitivity, and neglect lead to the death of the woman he should have loved. As he watches her die, he sings like Orpheus of those victimized by life. He truly sees her, however, only after she dies, and then her image gives way to a midget girl who yells "thief," as market women stone him to death. In "What the Tapster Saw," death is again the teacher. Forewarned by a dream, the tapster falls from a tree and wakes up in the land of the dead. In this allegory, reminiscent of the fiction of Amos Tutuola, the death experience combines wisdom and nonsense, comic inversions, talking animals, and teasing proverbs--for example, "your thoughts are merely the footsteps of you tramping round the disaster area of your own mind." The herbalist who claims credit for the tapster's seven days in death had never had "a better conversation." The god of chaos does indeed rule in death, in dreams, and among the living. While Okri's language is sometimes accusatory, his tone is not, and his final utterance is a laugh.

OTHER MAJOR WORKS

LONG FICTION: *Flowers and Shadows*, 1980; *The Landscapes Within*, 1981; *The Famished Road*, 1991; *Songs of Enchantment*, 1993; *Astonishing the Gods*, 1995; *Birds of Heaven*, 1996; *Dangerous Love*, 1996; *Infinite Riches*, 1998; *Phoenix Rising*, 2001; *In Arcadia*, 2002; *Starbook: A Magical Tale of Love and Regeneration*, 2007.

POETRY: *An African Elegy*, 1992; *Mental Fight*, 1999.

NONFICTION: *A Way of Being Free*, 1997.

BIBLIOGRAPHY

Bissoondath, Neil. "Rage and Sadness in Nigeria." Review of *Stars of the New Curfew*, by Ben Okri. *The New York Times Book Review*, August 13, 1989, 12. Bissoondath calls Okri "a natural storyteller" and especially appreciates his social commentary "on a variety of issues," including politics in Nigeria. The stories respond sensitively to conditions not only in Africa but also, by inference, in the Third World generally. Only the final story, being totally imaginative rather than based in reality, is pointless and disappointing.

Costantini, Mariaconcetta. *Behind the Mask: A Study of Ben Okri's Fiction*. Rome: Carocci editore, 2002. Focuses on the metafictional aspects of Okri's works, describing how his writings reflect upon the functions and methods of art. Argues that Okri's fiction uses the recurrent paradigm of the mask as a means of reviving the artist's sense of responsibility and commitment.

Elder, Arlene A. *Narrative Shape-Shifting: Myth, Humor, and History in the Fiction of Ben Okri, B. Kojo Laing, and Yvonne Vera*. Rochester, N.Y.: James Currey, 2009. Examines the works of Okri and two other African writers, focusing on how they combine traditional oral storytelling with postmodern experimentation to explore the sociopolitical condition of postindependent Africa.

Fraser. Robert. *Ben Okri: Towards the Invisible City*. Tavistock, Devon, England: Northcote House, 2002. Examines Okri's writings to date. Argues that Okri's works are best understood in the context of his early exposure to the Nigerian Civil War of 1967-1970 because he uses his literature as a means to reconcile the conflict.

Hawley, John C. "Ben Okri's Spirit Child: Abiku Migration and Postmodernity." *Research in African Literatures* 26 (Spring, 1995): 30-39. Addresses Okri's use of the *abiku*, or child-spirit, narrator; discusses the background of the *abiku* in Nigerian culture and analyzes how Okri uses the figure as a spokesman for two worlds.

Henry, Andrea. "More Magic than Realism." Review of *Infinite Riches*, by Ben Okri. *The Independent*, August 29, 1998, p. 15. Comments on the novel's use of fantasy and folklore and its strong anticolonial message. Suggests that the fantastic sense of the magical in the book is not always satisfying.

Kakutani, Michiko. "Brave New Africa Born of Nightmare." Review of *Stars of the New Curfew*, by Ben Okri. *The New York Times*, July 28, 1989, p. C25. Kakutani interprets the stories as surreal commentary on contemporary Africa, where "social realities . . . resemble our worst dreams" and the "people live in a state of suspended animation." While the style is "fiercely lyrical," Okri's "voice . . . needs only to expand its narrative territory to fulfill its bright promise."

Moh, Felicia Alu. *Ben Okri: An Introduction to His Early Fiction*. Enugu, Nigeria: Fourth Dimension, 2001. Focuses on Okri's satirical and critical appraisal of the social and political condition of Africa generally, and of Nigeria particularly. Analyzes the tradition of satire in African oral and written literature and describes how Okri's use of satire relates to it. Discusses the targets of criticism in Okri's works, his techniques of attack, and the other literary devices he employs.

Olshan, Joseph. "Fever Dreams from Nigeria's Troubled Soul." Review of *Stars of the New Curfew*, by Ben Okri. *Chicago Tribune*, July 16, 1989, p. 6. Olshan calls *Stars of the New Curfew* a "magnificent" collection depicting Nigeria in a state of crisis. He notes Okri's "feverishly poetic" language, frenetic characters "living on the edge of extinction," and incidents hovering between nightmare and reality.

Quayson, Ato. *Strategic Transformations in Nigerian Writing: Orality and History in the Work of Rev. Samuel Johnson, Amos Tutuola, Wole Soyinka, and Ben Okri*. Bloomington: Indiana University Press, 1997. Compares the work of these Nigerian writers and discusses the Nigerian oral tradition and the Yoruba peoples. Includes a Bibliography and an index.

Ryan, Alan. "Ben Okri's Modern Fetishes." Review of *Stars of the New Curfew*, by Ben Okri. *The Washington Post*, August 7, 1989, p. 602. Ryan emphasizes the "deeply Nigerian and universal" qualities of the stories, as they depict a world without stability, where a city, without communal traditions, is a forest, and "demons dig potholes" for human travelers.

Smith, Ali. "A Treasure Beyond Dreams." A review of *Infinite Riches*, by Ben Okri. *The Scotsman*, August 22, 1998, p. 15. Suggests that the story is a masterpiece of narrative slippage, a book full of disintegration and divisions. Comments on the book's allusions to bygone English literature.

Thomas, Maria. Review of *Stars of the New Curfew*, by Ben Okri. *Los Angeles Times Book Review*, September 24, 1989, 3. Thomas sees in Okri "an updated [Amos] Tutuola," who presents "an Africa of its own myths, thronged and bewitched." Argues that despite his black humor, Okri can be wonderful and hilarious; despite the corruption, terror, and despair, he registers hope through an indestructible "vitality."

Thomas Banks

JUAN CARLOS ONETTI

Born: Montevideo, Uruguay; July 1, 1909
Died: Madrid, Spain; May 30, 1994

PRINCIPAL SHORT FICTION

Un sueño realizado, y otros cuentos, 1951

Los adioses, 1954 (novella; *Goodbyes,* 1990)

Una tumba sin nombre, 1959 (novella; better known as *Para una tumba sin nombre; A Grave With No Name,* 1992)

La cara de la desgracia, 1960 (novella; *The Image of Misfortune,* 1990)

El infierno tan temido, 1962

Tan triste como ella, 1963 (novella)

Jacob y el otro: Un sueño realizado, y otros cuentos, 1965

Cuentos completos, 1967, revised 1974

La novia robada, y otros cuentos, 1968

Cuentos, 1971

Tiempo de abrazar, y los cuentos de 1933 a 1950, 1974 (short stories and fragments of unpublished novels)

Tan triste como ella, y otros cuentos, 1976

Goodbyes, and Other Stories, 1990

OTHER LITERARY FORMS

Juan (wahn) Carlos Onetti (oh-NEHT-tee) first gained recognition with the publication of his novels, particularly *El astillero* (1961; *The Shipyard,* 1968) and *Juntacadáveres* (1964; *Body Snatcher,* 1991), which confirmed his role as an international literary figure. He has also published the novels *Dejemos hablar al viento* (1979; *Let the Wind Speak,* 1997) and *Cuando ya no importe* (1993; *Past Caring?,* 1995). In addition to his short stories and novels, Onetti has published a number of novellas, including *The Image of Misfortune* and *Tiempo de abrazar.* In 1975, a number of his literary essays were collected in the volume *Réquiem por Faulkner, y los otros artículos.*

ACHIEVEMENTS

Among Juan Carlos Onetti's many awards is the Premio National de Literatura, Uruguay's most prestigious literary prize, which he received in 1962. He received the William Faulkner Foundation Certificate of Merit that same year for his novel *The Shipyard.* His novel *Body Snatcher* was a finalist for the prestigious Rómulo Gallegos Prize, given only once every five years to the author of the best Spanish-language novel. In 1980, Onetti was nominated for the Nobel Prize in Literature and was awarded the Premio Miguel de Cervantes Prize.

BIOGRAPHY

Juan Carlos Onetti was born in Montevideo, Uruguay, on July 1, 1909, the son of a customs official. Onetti did not complete high school or attend a university; he earned a living in his early years by taking on a number of menial jobs. In 1930, he married his cousin and left for Buenos Aires to accept a job as a calculator salesman. In the late 1930's his first marriage broke up, and he married his wife's sister.

Onetti published his first short story in 1933, and in 1939 he helped found, and became chief editor of, *Marcha,* which developed into an influential cultural weekly in Latin America. After the publication of *El pozo* (1939, 1965; *The Pit,* 1991) he began working for the British news agency Reuters and edited several periodicals. His best-known novel *La vida breve* (1950; *A Brief Life,* 1976) established him as a significant literary figure in Latin America.

In 1973, when the civilian government of Uruguay was overthrown by the military, *Marcha* was closed down and many journal archives were burned; historical research was forbidden, and many European and American writers were banned. Because Onetti was a judge for a literary prize awarded to a work critical of the military regime, he was put in prison, but he was soon released because of public outcry and poor health.

Later, after he was refused permission to leave Uruguay to receive an award, he escaped to live in Madrid, Spain, where he stayed in exile until his death in 1994.

ANALYSIS

Frequently compared to William Faulkner, both for his elaborate prose style and for his creation of a postage-stamp fictional world, Juan Carlos Onetti is often praised for his modern focus on alienated human beings and his postmodern experiments with self-reflexive metafictions. Many of his characters, facing old age and death, desire to find a way to retreat into the past or to escape to an ideal fictional creation to regain what is lost. As a result, his stories often focus on the power of the imagination and feature characters who are writers, actors, and dramatists. Ultimately, this emphasis compels Onetti to examine the nature of fictionality and playacting, which finally forces many of his stories into a realm somewhere between fantasy and reality, where the nature of reality itself is questioned.

"A DREAM COME TRUE"

The narrator of the title story of Onetti's first collection is a theater producer asked by a woman to stage a play for her. The woman has in mind a single scene featuring herself, a man, and a girl who comes out of a shop to give the man a glass of beer. When pressed for a title, the woman says she will call it "A Dream Come True." She is willing to pay to see the scene enacted once for her alone. Even though the producer thinks the woman is crazy, he has had a bad season and needs the money to escape to Buenos Aires; he thus contracts an actor he knows and makes the arrangements.

The woman has a mythical ageless quality about her; although she appears to be fifty, she has a girl's air from another century "as if she had fallen asleep and only awakened now, her hair in disarray, hardly aged but seemingly at any moment about to reach her own age all of a sudden and then shatter in silence." In the dramatized scene, she sits on a curb beside a green table next to which a man sits on a kitchen stool. When the man crosses the street to get a beer the girl has carried out, she fears he will be hit by a car. The woman lies on the sidewalk as if she were a child, and the man leans over and pats her on the head. The woman wants the scene enacted because she has dreamed it; during

the dream she felt happy, and she wants to recapture that feeling.

During the enactment of the scene, while the woman lies on the stage being patted on the head by the actor, she dies, and the story ends with the producer concluding that he finally understands what it was all about, what the woman had been searching for. "I understood it all clearly, as if it were one of those things that one learns once and for all as a child, something that words can never explain." Indeed, the woman's desire is not as enigmatic as it may first appear, for by actualizing a dream, she fulfills a common human fantasy, after which she can happily die.

"HELL MOST FEARED"

The story focuses on a journalist who reports on horse racing for a newspaper. After the reporter is separated from his actress-wife, he begins to receive intimate photographs of her with other men. The first two photographs create in him a feeling that is neither hate nor pain, a feeling that he cannot name but which is "linked to injustice and fate, to the primal fears of the first man on earth, to nihilism and the beginning of faith." He thinks that although he can understand and even accept his wife's act of revenge, there is some "act of will, persistence, the organized frenzy with which the revenge was being carried out" that is beyond his comprehension.

When the estranged wife begins to send photographs to other people, even the man's young daughter in a convent school, he begins to understand, but he is no longer interested in knowing what it is that he understands. The story ends with the man, blaming himself for mistakes in his relationship and in his life, killing himself. In sending the photographs, the wife seems to be searching for her husband's weakness, until, finally, by sending a pornographic photo of herself to the husband's daughter she has found the place where he is most vulnerable.

"WELCOME, BOB"

In this early Onetti story, popular with anthologists, a middle-aged narrator gets a sadistic pleasure from observing the aging of Bob; it is his revenge for Bob's preventing his marriage several years earlier to his sister Inez because he was too old for her. At that time Bob told the narrator that he was a finished man, washed up, "like all men your age when they're not extraordinary." Bob tells the narrator that the most repulsive thing about old age, the very symbol of decomposition, is to think in terms of concepts formed by second-rate experiences. For the old, Bob says, there are no longer experiences at all, only habits and repetitions, "wilted names to go on tagging things with and half make them up."

After the sister rejects the narrator and Bob grows older, the narrator begins a friendship with him so that he can more closely watch Bob's aging process. He delights in thinking of the young Bob who thought he owned the future and the world as he watches the man now called Robert, with tobacco-stained fingers, working in a stinking office, married to a fleshy woman. "No one has ever loved a woman as passionately as I love his ruin," says the narrator, delighting in the hopeless manner in which Bob has sunk into his filthy life. The story ends with the narrator's final sad and ironic triumph: "I don't know if I ever welcomed Inez in the past with such joy and love as I daily welcome Bob into the shadowy and stinking world of adults."

OTHER MAJOR WORKS

LONG FICTION: *El pozo*, 1939, 1965 (*The Pit*, 1991); *Tierra de nadie*, 1941 (*No Man's Land*, 1994; also known as *Tonight*, 1991); *Para esta noche*, 1943 (*Tonight*, 1991); *La vida breve*, 1950 (*A Brief Life*, 1976); *El astillero*, 1960 (*The Shipyard*, 1968); *Juntacadáveres*, 1964 (*Body Snatcher*, 1991); *La muerte y la niña*, 1973; *Dejemos hablar al viento*, 1979 (*Let the Wind Speak*, 1997); *Cuando ya no importe*, 1993 (*Past Caring?*, 1995).

NONFICTION: *Réquiem por Faulkner, y otros artículos*, 1975; *Confesiones de un lector*, 1995.

MISCELLANEOUS: *Obras completas*, 1970; *Onetti*, 1974 (articles, interview).

BIBLIOGRAPHY

Adams, M. Ian. *Three Authors of Alienation: Bombal, Onetti, Carpentier*. Austin: University of Texas Press, 1975. Includes an extended discussion of Onetti's novel *The Pit*. Shows how Onetti's artistic manipulation of schizophrenia creates the sensation of participating in an alienated world.

Craig, Linda. *Juan Carlos Onetti, Manuel Puig, and Luisa Valenzuela: Marginality and Gender*. Rochester, N.Y.: Tamesis, 2005. Compares the work of Onetti and two other twentieth century Latin American writers. Devotes separate chapters to theoretical analyses of Onetti's *The Pit*, *The Shipyard*, and *Body Snatcher*, examining these novels from psychoanalytical, feminist, and other perspectives. Argues that the three writers use their fiction to explore "postcolonial emptiness, a constant questioning of realism and a love of tango."

Deredita, John F. "The Shorter Works of Juan Carlos Onetti." *Studies in Short Fiction* 8 (Winter, 1971): 112-122. Surveys Onetti's short fiction, focusing on the two ages of man--naïve youth and the age of conformity--in such stories as "Welcome, Bob" and "A Dream Come True."

Harss, Luis, and Barbara Dohmann. "Juan Carlos Onetti or the Shadows on the Wall." In *Into the Mainstream: Conversations with Latin-American Writers*. New York: Harper & Row, 1967. Claims that in Onetti's middle-aged protagonists there is a yearning for vanished youth and innocence. Discusses the collection *Un sueño realizado, y otros cuentos*, Onetti's Faulknerian style in *Goodbyes*, and Onetti's pessimism.

Lewis, Bart L. "Realizing the Textual Space: Metonymic Metafiction in Juan Carlos Onetti." *Hispanic Review* 64 (Autumn, 1996): 491-506. Discusses four Onetti works in terms of his use of metonymy as a metafictional device. Argues that the plasticity of *Goodbyes* gives it a composed, pictorial quality absent from his other works. Explores the relationship between story and storytelling.

Maio, Eugene A. "Onetti's *Los adioses*: A Cubist Reconstruction of Reality." *Studies in Short Fiction* 26 (Spring, 1986): 173-181. Shows how Onetti's novella has affinities with the aesthetic goals and structures of cubism. Argues that his narrative style has much in common with the aesthetics of contemporary art in general and cubism in particular.

Millington, Mark. *An Analysis of the Short Stories of Juan Carlos Onetti: Fictions of Desire*. Lewiston, N.Y.: Edwin Mellen Press, 1993. Looks at Onetti's short stories from a largely psychological perspective.

_____. "No Woman's Land: The Representation of Woman in Onetti." *MLN* 102 (March, 1987): 358-377. Discusses the function of the wife, prostitute, girl, and mad woman in Onetti's fiction. Argues that the subjection of women is one of the major impasses of Onetti's thinking.

_____. *Reading Onetti: Language, Narrative and the Subject.* Liverpool, England: Francis Cairns, 1985. Discusses the development of Onetti's work under the "hegemony of international modernism." Drawing on stylistics, narratology, and poststructuralism; Millington focuses on the status of Onetti's fiction as narrative discourse. Examines how *Goodbyes* problematizes the act of reading.

Murray, Jack. *The Landscapes of Alienation: Ideological Subversion in Kafka, Céline, and Onetti.* Stanford, Calif.: Stanford University Press, 1991. Focuses on alienation in Onetti's fiction, providing some background about how Uruguay has affected Onetti's ideological unconscious.

Oakley, Helen. "Aesthetics of the Game: Faulkner's 'A Rose for Emily' Plays Juan Carlos Onetti's 'La novia robada' and 'Tan triste como ella.'" In *The Recontextualization of William Faulkner in Latin American Fiction and Culture.* Lewiston, N.Y.: Edwin Mellen Press, 2002. Analyzes how the works of William Faulkner have been projected onto the works of Onetti by comparing one of Faulkner's short stories with two of Onetti's works. Places the three fictional works in the broader context of America's relationship with Latin America and the culture of Argentina and Uruguay in the 1940's and 1950's.

Richards, Katherine C. "Playing God: The Narrator in Onetti's *Los adioses.*" *Studies in Short Fiction* 26 (Spring, 1989): 163-171. Argues that the narrator has a will to power that conflicts with his role as witness-observer. Maintains the narrator's special knowledge contradicts the reader's experience of reality and literary convention.

Sullivan, Mary-Lee. "Projection as a Narrative Technique in Juan Carlos Onetti's *Goodbyes.*" *Studies in Short Fiction* 31 (Summer, 1994): 441-447. Argues that Onetti's novella is designed to draw on the projective capacity of readers. Suggests that by leaving inexplicable gaps in the narrator's version of the story, Onetti elicits readers' desires and fears within the creative space of the text.

Charles E. May

Amos Oz

Born: Jerusalem, British Mandate of Palestine (now in Israel); May 4, 1939

Also Known As: Amos Klausner

PRINCIPAL SHORT FICTION

Artsot hatan, 1965, revised edition 1976 (*Where the Jackals Howl, and Other Stories,* 1981)

Ahavah me'uheret, 1971 (*Unto Death,* 1975)

Har ha'etsah ha-ra'ah, 1976 (*The Hill of Evil Counsel: Three Stories,* 1978)

OTHER LITERARY FORMS

Amos Oz has written several novels, among them the well-known *Mikha'el sheli,* 1968 (*My Michael,* 1972), the basis of an esteemed feature film of that title; *Kufsah shehorah* (1987; *Black Box,* 1988), which received worldwide attention when it was published; *Al tagidi lailah* (1994; *Don't Call It Night,* 1995); *Oto hayam* (1999; *The Same Sea,* 2001); *Pit'om be-'omek ha-ya'ar* (2005; *Suddenly in the Depths of the Forest,* 2010); and *Haruze ha-hayim veha-mavet* (2007; *Rhyming Life and Death,* 2009). He is also the author of a children's novel, *Sumkhi* (1978; *Soumchi,* 1980).

His many nonfiction books range from collections of essays on history, politics, and society, as in *Po vasham be-Erets-Yisra'el bi-setav* (1982; *In the Land of Israel,* 1983) and *Mi-mordot ha-Levanon: Ma'amarim u-reshimot* (1987; *The Slopes of Lebanon,* 1989), to essays mixing autobiography, philosophy, literary criticism, and sociopolitical analysis, as in *Be- or ha-Techelet ha-azah: Ma'amarim ve-reshimot* (1979; *Under This Blazing Light: Essays*, 1995) and *Israel, Palestine, and Peace: Essays* (1994), to focused literary criticism in *Shetikat ha-shamayim* (1993; *The Silence of Heaven*, 2000) and *Mathilim sipur* (1996; *The Story Begins: Essays on Literature*, 1999). His autobiography, *Sipur 'al ahavah ve-hoshekh*, appeared in 2002 and was translated in 2004 as *A Tale of Love and Darkness*.

Achievements

With Avraham Yehoshua and Aharon Appelfeld, Amos Oz is among the most highly regarded writers in the earliest of the new waves in Israeli fiction. He has won not only prestigious literary prizes (Holon Prize, 1965; Brenner Prize, 1978; Bialik Prize, 1986; French Prix Femina, 1988; Israel Prize for Literature, 1998) but also political awards (Frankfurt Peace Prize, 1992; French Legion of Honor, 1997), which reflect his liberal philosophy and leadership in the Peace Now movement in Israel. He continued to receive numerous honors in the twenty-first century, including the Goethe Prize from the city of Frankfurt, Germany (2005), the Jerusalem-Agnon Prize (2006), Spain's Prince of Asturias Award for Literature (2007), the German President's High Honor Award (2008), and Italy's Primo Levi Prize (2008). His books consistently have been translated into not only English but also most Asian and European languages in worldwide publication.

Biography

Born Amos Klausner, Amos Oz left his Jerusalem home at age fifteen, breaking with the right-wing politics and Eurocentrism of his family. He changed his surname to one with biblical overtones, as many settlers in Israel have done, and he joined Kibbutz Hulda. Subsequently, he has been a kibbutz agricultural field hand, kibbutz teacher, member of an Israeli army tank crew in the 1967 and 1973 wars, writer, globe-trotting lecturer, visiting professor at Oxford University in England and Colorado Springs College in the United States, and the Agnon Professor of Literature at Ben Gurion University in the Negev.

The varied experiences of Oz's life are revealed in much of his fiction. The emphasis in the three interlinked novelettes of *The Hill of Evil Counsel* on a young boy's growing up in Jerusalem on the eve of Israel's war of independence in 1948, also paralleled in Oz's novel *Panter ba-martef* (1994; *Panther in the Basement*, 1997), reflects Oz's own experience. The kibbutz settings of five of the eight stories in *Where the Jackals Howl, and Other Stories* reflect Oz's personal knowledge of kibbutz life; the many soldiers and military characters in his short fiction likewise reflect Oz's life experiences--indeed, the main character Sergei Unger in "Late Love" (*Unto Death*) acquires a book about Israeli tank warfare. The many intellectuals and ideologues in Oz's short fiction reflect not only people Oz encountered on the kibbutz but also intellectual European immigrants to Israel, political activists, teachers, such as Oz himself, and even some of Oz's own family, including his father and grandfather.

Analysis

Amos Oz's short fiction focuses on the Jewish experience, especially in his homeland. It has, collectively, an impressive historical sweep from biblical times to the decades following the 1948 founding of the state of Israel. The main character in "Upon This Evil Earth," in *Where the Jackals Howl, and Other Stories*, is the biblical Jephthah (Judges 11-12); the main characters in "Crusade," in *Unto Death*, are the aggressively anti-Semitic members of the medieval retinue of the Count Guillaume of Touron on their way from Europe to the Holy Land in a crusade of the year 1095; the characters in the three interlinked novelettes of *The Hill of Evil Counsel* are Jerusalem inhabitants concerned about the imminent end of the British mandate and subsequent war of liberation in 1948; finally, "Late Love," in *Unto Death*, and the stories in *Where the Jackals Howl, and Other Stories* (except "Upon This Evil Earth") are set on the kibbutz, an Israeli military base, or in the cities of Jerusalem or Tel Aviv in Israel in the decade or two after the 1948 founding of the state. In all of these works, a main concern is the contrast between belonging and not belonging, between being an insider and an outsider, to the land, culture, or society.

Other themes and subjects that pervade Oz's short and long fiction, especially as connected to sociopolitical conditions, are nostalgia for European culture and ideas in the midst of harsh Middle Eastern realities, the dangers of obsession and extremism, the interrelation between humanity and the natural world, the injuries done to romantic love and marriage by a harsh physical and political environment, the problems of the parent-child relationship, the contrast between one generation and the next, and the power of language and art.

These themes are expressed in articulated form. The short stories--not shorter than twenty pages--and novelettes all have numbered sections, as well as subsections indicated by spacing. The only exception is "Longing" (in *The Hill of Evil Counsel*), which is epistolary: eight letters of Dr. Emanuel Nussbaum to his former sweetheart, Dr. Hermine ("Mina") Oswald, from September 2 to September 10, 1947. Also distinctive--beyond Oz's shifts in point of view (particularly in and out of the first-person plural mode), symbolism, figurative language, pervasive personifications, and sentence fragment notation of details--is his frequent biblical allusion. Writing in the very language of the Hebrew Bible, Oz is alert to and makes thematic use of biblical references and overtones in his stories' titles, characters' names, imagery, and plot parallels. He even has his own expanded version of a biblical narrative.

WHERE THE JACKALS HOWL, AND OTHER STORIES

Damage done to marriage and, consequently, the parent-child relationship by the pioneering life in a new, hard land, permeated by threats, is a theme of four of the stories in *Where the Jackals Howl, and Other Stories*, as well as "The Hill of Evil Counsel," "Mr. Levi," and "Longing" in *The Hill of Evil Counsel*. In "Where the Jackals Howl," what appears to be the luring of the beautiful Galila to an attempted lover's tryst in his kibbutz bachelor's quarters by the ugly workman Matityahu Damkov, using Galila's interest in art--painter's supplies Damkov got from South America--turns out to be the surprising revelation by Damkov to Galila that he is her father. Her father is not her mother's husband, Sashka, one of the kibbutz intellectuals.

Reader and child are likewise surprised at the end of "Strange Fire" (note the title's overtones of perversity from Leviticus 10:1). Lily Dannenberg has not, spurred by her Eurocentric unhappiness with Israeli culture, capriciously broken an appointment with the father of her daughter's fiancé Yosef in order to make a pass at her future son-in-law Yair Yarden. She instead pressures Yair into taking a walk around Jerusalem with her to reveal to him his father's secret: Yosef had long ago been married for several months to Lily.

Amos Oz (AP Photo/Bernd Kammerer, File)

The title "Way of the Wind"--with allusions to Genesis and Ecclesiastes--suggests the caprice of the father, Shimshon Sheinbaum, who to be strong, like his similarly unshorn biblical namesake Samson, in his devotion to country and to political writing has abandoned his wife and son Gideon. He lives apart from them on the kibbutz. The allusive title also forecasts Gideon's tragic attempt to live up to his own heroic biblical namesake to please Shimshon. The result is his becoming fatally tangled in power lines on the kibbutz when his army paratroop unit makes a jump and the wind shifts. Gideon ironically enacts his nickname, "Pinocchio," by literally hanging from lines. Furthermore, an unpleasant though athletic youngster attempts to rescue him and is surprisingly revealed at the story's end to be a half brother, one of Shimshon's rumored but unacknowledged children on the kibbutz.

In "Before His Time," the unrelenting adversities of the new land--its heat, barrenness, Arab theft or attack--are the background for Dov Sirkin's desertion of his wife and young children. Poring over maps, a recurrent symbol in Oz's short fiction, Sirkin lives in Jerusalem, leaving his family behind on the kibbutz. The story's title refers to Dov's premature desertion, the death in combat of his estranged military-hero son, and the slaughter of the kibbutz prize stud bull, Samson. Although still healthy, the bull was impotent from the bite of a poisoned jackal. Jackals are recurrent symbols in Oz's short fiction of the untamed, sometimes savage land in which a struggle for possession and belonging is continual.

In "The Hill of Evil Counsel" the unhappy, Eurocentric Ruth Kipnis, in contrast to her biblical namesake, deserts her husband and young son, Hillel. She begins an affair, at the ominously named geographical site of the story's title, with a British officer and World War II hero and leaves Israel with him. Hillel, in contrast to his self-possessed Talmudic namesake, is so upset that he eventually has to be placed on a kibbutz while his father continues to live in Jerusalem.

Another displaced boy is young Uriel ("Uri") Kolodny, in "Mr. Levi" and "Longing," who has a series of surrogate parents as he grows up. This situation partly results from his mother being somewhat incapacitated by life in the new land, while his father struggles with making a living, helping his wife, and dealing with British oppression. Uri's surrogate parents include Ephraim, a young repairman and underground agent, who is obsessed with developing a secret weapon--another recurring motif in Oz's short fiction; the old poet, Nehamkin, who speaks the obsessive language of biblical prophecy; and the seriously ill Dr. Emanuel Nussbaum, whose beloved, Mina Oswald, has left him and Israel behind.

Four other stories in *Where the Jackals Howl, and Other Stories* illustrate how, in the context of pioneering in an often hostile environment, obsession and alienation may impair romantic love. This theme is also exemplified in the stories "Crusade" and "Late Love," in *Unto Death*, and Oz's uncharacteristically brief (ten-page) "Setting the World to Rights," included in *The Penguin Book of Jewish Short Stories* (1979, edited by Emanuel Litvinoff).

In "Nomad and Viper," Geula's natural, unfulfilled sexuality and the negative relations between Israeli settlers and native Arabs cause her to have conflicting emotions about a young Arab goat-herder to whom she

is drawn. She meets him in an orchard, which, with the garden, is a recurrent, often biblical symbol in Oz's short fiction. When the young goat-herder--friendly, polite, but nervous--is frightened off by her intensity, her conflict is resolved into hatred toward Arabs and the delusion of an attempted rape.

"The Trappist Monastery" ends with the ironic revelations that the main character, Itcheh, passionately cares about Bruria, despite his exaggeratedly apparent indifference toward her. His behavior results from the strains of combat and from maintaining his image as a legendary military hero. In reality, he is just a Romanian immigrant who plans to retire from the army as soon as he can to join a soccer team or head a bus service. Unfortunately, Bruria begins to carry on affairs with other men. While pursuing Bruria on an erroneous chase, Itcheh's Jeep breaks down in Arab territory, near the landmark of the story's title, with implied fatal disaster for Itcheh and his malevolent passenger, Nahum, a military medic jealous of Itcheh.

Death in combat permanently severs the romantic relationship between the central character Batya Pinski and her husband, Abraham, in the story "A Hollow Stone." Abraham's fervor about socialism in Israel and Spain began his emotional drift from his wife even before he went to fight and die in the Spanish Civil War of the 1930's. This makes Abraham yet another deserter in Oz's short fiction. The placid existence of the fish in Batya's aquarium, a repeated symbol in the story, where the hollow stone of the title is located, differs greatly from that of the people on Batya's kibbutz.

The fifty-page novelette "Upon This Evil Earth" has a complex intertwining of themes like many of Oz's stories--the term "story" being what Oz prefers, or "prose narrative," following the Hebrew language, instead of the term "fiction." Gilead the Gileadite lives in the hard country between the fertile lands of the Ammonites and the tribe of Ephraim. Both his external surroundings and internal temperament lead to an almost existentialist alienation that is shared by his son Jephthah. As a result of this alienation, neither Gilead nor Jephthah is capable of true romantic love. Jephthah's inability to love is aggravated by his being the son of a concubine (reflecting the biblical account) from Ammon (not in the biblical account), making him only the half brother of the sons from Gilead's proper Israelite wife. Jephthah repeatedly asserts that he does not feel complete allegiance either to the Israelites or to the Ammonites, much as a liberal modern Israeli might feel when caught between obsessed Israelis and obsessed Arabs, neither willing to acknowledge the vision and values of the other.

Sergei Unger in "Late Love" represents the Israeli obsessed by an enemy, in Unger's case the Russian Communists. He is so obsessed that he frankly confesses he has given up romantic love. The story shows how he has missed his chance for this love with a constant companion on the lecture tour for much of his life, Liuba Kaganovskaya. Unger's parallel opposite in "Crusade" is the medieval Count Guillaume of Touron, whose name suggests the pride of a tower and the monument from the Crusades explained in "The Trappist Monastery": "Latrun," from "Le Touron des Chevaliers--The Tower of the Knights." The Count is an anti-Semite obsessed with exterminating Jews in general and, in particular, the Jew whom he repeatedly and paranoically imagines has infiltrated his Crusader band. Only at the end of "Crusade," when the Count has suffered tremendously, learned to empathize with all other human beings, and killed himself as a symbol of equating himself to a Jew, does he finally return to the long lost feelings of love for his wife.

Sadly, the central character of "Setting the World to Rights," whose very anonymity, being never named, is symbolic of his commonness, never modifies the mainspring of his being: his hatred of all things he is obsessively sure are wrong. He has magnified his kibbutz occupation of repairman to monstrous proportions, thinking everything in the world needs repairing but, ironically, is unable to repair himself. A bachelor, he lives alone, unable to find love or let it into his life, and at the story's end he hangs himself in the kibbutz orchard. An orchard or the Garden of Eden represents the possibilities of life, growth, and love, making the setting an ironically symbolic opposite of the repairman's suicide and life's work.

OTHER MAJOR WORKS

LONG FICTION: *Makom aher*, 1966 (*Elsewhere, Perhaps*, 1973); *Mikha'el sheli*, 1968 (*My Michael*, 1972); *Laga 'at ba-mayim, laga 'at ba-ruah*, 1973 (*Touch the Water, Touch the Wind*, 1974); *Menuhah nekhonah*, 1982 (*A Perfect Peace*, 1985); *Kufsah shehorah*, 1987 (*Black Box*, 1988); *La-da 'at ishah*, 1989 (*To Know a Woman*, 1991); *Matsav ha-shelishi*, 1991 (*Fima*, 1993); *Al tagidi lailah*, 1994 (*Don't Call It Night*, 1995); *Panter ba-martef*, 1994 (*Panther in the Basement*, 1997); *Oto ha-yam*, 1999 (*The Same Sea*, 2001); *Pit 'om be- 'omek ha-ya 'ar*, 2005 (*Suddenly in the Depths of the Forest*, 2010); *Haruze ha-hayim vehamavet*, 2007 (*Rhyming Life and Death*, 2009).

NONFICTION: *Be-or ha-techelet ha- 'azah: ma'a;amarim u-reshimot*, 1979 (*Under This Blazing Light: Essays*, 1995); *Po va-sham be-Erets-Yisra'el bi-setav*, 1982 (*In the Land of Israel*, 1983); *Mi-mordot ha-Levanon: Ma'amarim u-reshimot*, 1987 (*The Slopes of Lebanon*, 1989); *Shetikat ha-shamayim*, 1993 (*The Silence of Heaven: Agnon's Fear of God*, 2000); *Israel, Palestine, and Peace: Essays*, 1994; *Mathilim sipur*, 1996 (*The Story Begins: Essays on Literature*, 2000); *Kol ha-tikvot: Mahashavot 'al zehut Yisre 'elit*, 1998; *Sipur 'al ahavah ve-hoshekh*, 2002 (*A Tale of Love and Darkness*, 2004); *How to Cure a Fanatic*, 2006.

CHILDREN'S LITERATURE: *Sumkhi*, 1978 (*Soumchi*, 1980).

MISCELLANEOUS: *The Amos Oz Reader*, 2009 (Nitza Ben-Dov, editor).

BIBLIOGRAPHY

Aschkenasy, Nehama. "On Jackals, Nomads, and the Human Condition." *Midstream* 29 (January, 1983): 58-60. One of the more extended reviews of *Where the Jackals Howl, and Other Stories*.

Balaban, Avraham. *Between Good and Beast: An Examination of Amos Oz's Prose*. University Park: Pennsylvania State University Press, 1993. Chapter 2, "Introduction to Oz: The Early Stories," provides a detailed analysis of *Where the Jackals Howl, and Other Stories*, including some Hebrew stories left out of the revised Hebrew edition and the English translation. The novelette collections receive much less attention in this book.

Bargad, Warren. "Amos Oz and the Art of Fictional Response." *Midstream* (November, 1976): 61-64. An article focusing on *Unto Death*.

Dickstein, Morris. Review of *The Hill of Evil Counsel*, by Amos Oz. *The New York Times Book Review*, May 28, 1978, 5. The lengthiest review, surpassing by several hundred words, in its 1,850 words, the review in the *New York Review of Books* (July 20, 1978) and *The New Yorker* magazine (August 7, 1978).

Fuchs, Esther. *Israeli Mythogynies: Women in Contemporary Hebrew Fiction*. Albany: State University of New York Press, 1987. A six-page subsection of chapter 4, "Amos Oz: The Lack of Conscience," focuses on *Where the Jackals Howl, and Other Stories*, analyzed from the feminist perspective of the depiction of women from the sometimes biased male view; the other two sections discuss the image of women in Oz's novels *Elsewhere, Perhaps* and *My Michael*.

Isaksen, Runo. *Literature and War: Conversations with Israeli and Palestinian Writers*. Translated by Kari Dickson. Northampton, Mass.: Olive Branch Press, 2009. Includes an interview with Oz, in which he discusses the relationship of the Israeli-Palestinian conflict to his writings. He states that the conflict is "always in the background never in the foreground. I don't write to compete with the headlines."

Jacobson, David. *Modern Midrash: The Retelling of Traditional Jewish Narratives by Twentieth-Century Hebrew Writers*. Albany: State University of New York Press, 1987. A nine-page subsection of chapter 7, "Uses and Abuses of Power in Ancient and Modern Israel: Nissim Aloni, Moshe Shamir, and Amos Oz," examines "Upon This Evil Earth" in *Where the Jackals Howl, and Other Stories* as "midrash," a commentary and expanded parable based on biblical material.

Mazor, Yair. *Somber Lust: The Art of Amos Oz*. Translated by Marganit Weinberger-Rotman. Albany: State University of New York Press, 2002. Traces the development of Oz'a aesthetic and political vision by examining all of his writing, including the short stories and novellas. Devotes a chapter to an analysis of the story "Nomads and Viper." Concludes with an interview in which Oz discusses his work.

McElroy, Joseph. Review of *Unto Death*, by Amos Oz. *The New York Times Book Review*, October 26, 1975, 4. The lengthiest review, surpassing by several hundred words, in its eleven hundred words, the substantial review in *The New Republic* (November 29, 1975).

Mojtabai, A. G. Review of *Where the Jackals Howl and Other Stories*, by Amos Oz. *The New York Times Book Review*, April 26, 1981, 3. The lengthiest contemporary review, twenty-two hundred words long, about a thousand words longer than the substantial reviews to be found in *The New Republic* (June 27, 1981), the *Times Literary Supplement* (September 25, 1981), *Studies in Short Fiction* (1982), or *World Literature Today* (1982).

Yudkin, Leon. *1948 and After: Aspects of Israeli Fiction*. Manchester, England: University of Manchester Press, 1984. Chapter 10, "The Jackal and the Other Place: The Stories of Amos Oz," is devoted to an analysis of Oz's principal short fiction collections of 1965, 1971, and 1976.

Norman Prinsky

P

Boris Pasternak

Born: Moscow, Russia; February 10, 1890
Died: Peredelkino, near Moscow, Soviet Union (now
in Russia); May 30, 1960

Principal short fiction

"Pisma iz Tuly," 1922 ("Letters from Tula," 1945)
"Detstvo Liuvers," 1923 ("The Childhood of
Luvers," 1945)
Rasskazy, 1925
Sochineniya, 1961 (*Collected Short Prose,* 1977)

Other literary forms

Primarily a lyric poet, Boris Pasternak (PAS-tur-nak) also wrote epic poems upon revolutionary themes and translated English and German classics into Russian. Besides several pieces of short fiction, he wrote two prose autobiographies and an unfinished play, *Slepaya krasavitsa* (pb. 1969; *The Blind Beauty,* 1969), intended as a nineteenth century prologue to his single novel, *Doktor Zhivago* (1957; *Doctor Zhivago,* 1958), the first major Russian work to be published only outside the Soviet Union. Pasternak won the Nobel Prize in Literature in 1958, but Soviet governmental pressure forced him to refuse it. His lyric "The Nobel Prize" describes him "caught like a beast at bay" in his homeland.

Achievements

Boris Pasternak is best known in his native country for his poetry and abroad for his novel *Doctor Zhivago.* In both of these genres he ranks among the best in Russian literature. His short fiction, though not on the same level of excellence as his poetry and the novel, is still appreciated. Pasternak was also an accomplished translator into Russian, especially of William Shakespeare's works and of Georgian poetry. An equally important achievement on his part was his ability to project himself as an ultimate artist in a Soviet environment notably hostile to free art. During the last four decades of his life, he was able to preserve the dignity of a free individualist and to write his works according to the dictates of his conscience. It was this courageous attitude, in addition to the artistic merits of his works, that won him the Nobel Prize in 1958.

Biography

The eldest son of the celebrated Russian Jewish painter Leonid Pasternak and his wife, the musician Rosa Kaufman, Boris Leonidovich Pasternak abandoned an early interest in music for the study of philosophy at the Universities of Moscow and later Marburg, where he remained until returning to Russia at the outbreak of World War I. At this time he began to write seriously. From his literary debut in 1913 to 1914 with "The Story of a Contraoctave" and a collection of lyrics, *Bliznets v tuchakh* (1914), Pasternak devoted the whole of his creative life to literature. Most of his short fiction and both long epic poetry and shorter lyrics, compiled in the collection *Sestra moia zhizn': Leto 1917 goda* (1922; *My Sister, Life,* 1964), occupied him for the next fifteen years. His first autobiography, *Okhrannaya gramota* (1931; *Safe Conduct,* 1945), foreshadowed his personal and artistic survival through the Stalinist purges of the 1930's, when a new moral direction became evident in his work, demonstrated in fragments of a novel he never finished. Although he again wrote lyric poetry during World War II, Pasternak answered Soviet postwar restrictions on creativity by mainly supporting himself with his translations, producing versions of works by Johann Wolfgang von Goethe, Friedrich Schiller, and William Shakespeare. He also began the novel that he eventually considered his finest achievement, *Doctor Zhivago,* in which he discussed and analyzed the disintegrative reality of Russia's conversion to Communism. At the end of 1946 he met his great love, Olga Ivinskaya, the model for the heroine of the novel, and although the Soviet authorities imprisoned her in an attempt to silence Pasternak's apolitical praise of Christian values, he nevertheless completed the novel and allowed it to be published in 1957 in Italy. The Soviet regime retaliated by forcing Pasternak to refuse the Nobel Prize awarded him in 1958, the same year his autobiography, *Avtobiograficheskiy ocherk* (1958; *I Remember: Sketch for an Autobiography*, 1959), appeared in the West. Crushed by depression and fear for those he loved, Pasternak died of leukemia in early 1960, and two months later, as he had dreaded, Ivinskaya was rearrested and sentenced again to prison.

ANALYSIS

All Boris Pasternak's fiction illustrates the tragic involvement of a poet with his age. Just prior to World War I, Russian literature was dominated by the figure of Vladimir Mayakovsky, who embodied a strange combination of Symbolist mythmaking with the fierce futurist rejection of traditional forms. Bordering on the theatrical, Mayakovsky's self-dramatization pitted the gifted literary artist's elevated emotions and extreme sensitivity against his supposedly dull and unappreciative or even hostile audience, an artistic tendency that Pasternak recognized and from which he tried to liberate himself in his early stories.

"THE STORY OF A CONTRAOCTAVE"

"The Story of a Contraoctave," written in 1913, stems from Pasternak's Marburg years and his exposure there to German Romanticism. Centered upon a German organist who, caught up in a flight of extemporaneous performance, unknowingly crushes his son to death in the instrument's works, this story exhibits the Romantic artist's "inspiration," his lack of concern for ordinary life, and the guilt that society forces upon him. Pasternak's first published story, "Apellesova Cherta" ("The Mark of Apelles"), written in 1915 at the height of his admiration for Vladimir Mayakovsky, explores the problem of Pasternak's simultaneous attraction to, and dismay with, the neo-Romantic posture. In this story, two writers agree to a literary competition that quickly spills over into real life when one, clearly named for Heinrich Heine, the nineteenth century

Boris Pasternak (Time & Life Pictures/Getty Images)

German poet whose irony punctured the naïve bubble of Romantic idealism, outdoes the heavy-handed idealistic fantasy of his opponent Relinquimini by arousing and responding to genuine love in Relinquimini's mistress. A similar pair of antagonists forms the conflict in "Bezlyube" ("Without Love"), written and published in 1918 and originally intended as part of an unfinished longer work, although it actually furnished material for *Doctor Zhivago*. "Without Love" paradoxically shows an activist living in a peculiar never-never land, while a lyric dreamer's adherence to the truth of remembered experience illustrates Pasternak's inability to adapt his artistic inspiration to political service.

"LETTERS FROM TULA"

"Letters from Tula," written in 1918, again juxtaposes reality and art, but here the Russia of Pasternak's own time provides his setting. A powerful contrast develops between the reactions of a young poet and an old retired actor to a film crew working near the town of Tula. The poet, passing through on the train, is in the grasp of a violent passion for his distant lover. The mediocrity of the vulgar filmmakers appalls him, but as he tries to write to his beloved, he becomes even more disgusted with his own self-consciously arty efforts at conveying his emotion. On the other hand, the aged actor, who wholeheartedly detests the philistine cinema and the loss of tradition it caused, uses his own successful artistic representation. Made grindingly aware by them of his age and his loneliness and most of all of his need for "the human speech of tragedy," the old man returns to his silent apartment and re-creates a part of one of his performances, which in turn calls up a valid response of healing memory.

In *Safe Conduct*, his first autobiography, Pasternak wrote, "In art the man is silent, and the image speaks." The young poet's silence in "Letters from Tula" would eventually foster his creativity, but it had to be purchased at the sacrifice of his youthful arrogance and the painful achievement of humility. The old actor attains his creative silence because he is the only one in the story who could make another speak through his own lips. Thus the humble willingness to serve as the vehicle of art, allowing experience to speak through him, becomes an important stage in Pasternak's artistic development, enabling him to move beyond romantic self-absorption toward an art that needs no audience.

"THE CHILDHOOD OF LUVERS"

Pasternak wrote one of his masterpieces, "The Childhood of Luvers," from 1917 to 1919, intending it originally as the opening of a novel but finally publishing it by itself in 1923. This long short story shares the childlike innocence of *My Sister, Life*, the height of Pasternak's lyric expression, which appeared the previous year. In the first section of the story, the world of childhood impressions becomes a part of Zhenya Luvers's experience. Little by little, the shapes, colors, smells--all the sensory images to which the young child responds so eagerly--impinge upon her consciousness, are assimilated, and finally arrange into an order that becomes more coherent as she grows older. Zhenya's impressions of her surroundings also gradually give place to her emotional impressions of people and situations, as the child's comprehension of "things" progressively is able to grasp more complex relations between them. Zhenya's world is at first markedly silent, as is the world of the angry young lover and the old actor in "Letters from Tula"; Pasternak's impressionistic technique

allows few "realistic" details, preferring to let lovely and strange combinations of images flood the child's developing awareness of her life.

In the second part of this story, Pasternak shifts his attention from Zhenya's instinctive grasp of emotions through images given to her by the bewildering world of adulthood. As Zhenya matures, she begins to respond to the essential sadness of things by assuming, as children do, that she herself has committed some sin to cause her misery. When Zhenya's household is turned upside down by her mother's miscarriage and she is sent to the home of friends, she learns how to deal with adult condescension and cruelty. At the moment that Zhenya realizes her own participation in the body of humankind, her simultaneously Christian and singularly Russian consciousness of shared suffering, her childhood abruptly ceases.

One of the pervasive themes of Pasternak's work, the suffering of women, is thus treated in "The Childhood of Luvers," reflecting Pasternak's anguish at being "wounded by the lot of women" that underlay his fascination with the tragic Mary, Queen of Scots. Zhenya Luvers, however, evokes the growth into recognition of adult responsibility that is basic to the human condition, extending from fragments of sense impressions into the ability to make the only sense of her world a Christian knows: the participation in its suffering. For Pasternak, Zhenya Luvers also marks the childhood of the girl whom his great love Olga Ivinskaya called "the Lara of the future," the woman at the heart of *Doctor Zhivago*. The capacity to grow and mature through the experience of suffering makes Zhenya the personification of Pasternak's betrayed Russia, trusting and defenseless in the grip of the godless aggression that followed the 1917 Communist Revolution.

"THE STORY"

All Pasternak's works of the 1920's reveal his growing awareness of the poet's responsibility to humankind, continuing to lead him from his earlier lyric expression of romantic self-absorption toward the epic presentation of his moral impulse. "Three Chapters from a Story" and "Vozdushnye puti" ("Aerial Ways"), as well as his long narrative poetry of the decade, also illustrate Pasternak's attempt to come to grips with the cannibalistic tendency of revolutions to devour the very forces that unleashed them. By 1929, in another long short story titled simply "Povest" ("The Story"), Pasternak reached a new manifestation of his creative position. His young hero Seryosha comes to visit his sister, exhausted and dismayed by the chaos around him in the turmoil of 1916, when Russia's contribution to the struggle against Germany was faltering because of governmental ineptitude and social tensions. Pasternak's impressionistic glimpses of the disorder swirl around Seryosha like nightmarish, demonic scenes, until he lies down on a shabby cot to rest, losing himself in memories of the bittersweet prewar years when his artistic vocation had come to him.

Seryosha had been a tutor to a well-to-do family, but he saw his real mission as saving the world through art. Pasternak's "suffering women," here a sympathetic prostitute and later a widowed Danish governess trapped in poverty, awaken Seryosha's compassion and lead him to begin a story within "The Story," the tale of "Y3," a poet and musician who intends to alleviate the suffering of some of his fellow men by selling himself at auction. As Seryosha's retrospective experiences flash through his tired mind, he suddenly becomes distressingly aware of his own failure in those earlier years. At the very time when he was self-consciously creating his gloriously idealistic artistic work, he was overlooking the genuine self-sacrifice of a young acquaintance being called into the army, ignoring the man so completely that he could not even remember his name, and now, miserable himself, guilt overcomes Seryosha.

"The Story" employs Pasternak's early impressionistic technique of unprepared-for, disruptive shifts in plot, setting, and time, but at the same time, its portraiture and characterization are both more intimate and more realistic than those he had previously created. The element Pasternak had added to Zhenya Luvers's recognition of the necessity of shared suffering was now Seryosha's guilty realization of the need for self-sacrifice, a distinct shift from a passive to an active participation in the fate of Russia. By setting "The Story" in the context of the gathering revolution, whose true meaning the oblivious "artist" cannot grasp until it has swept him up, Pasternak establishes the grounds for his subsequent opposition of creative moral man to deathly political machine. "The Story" unmistakably illustrates Pasternak's growing preference for longer and more realistic prose forms, and thematically it demonstrates his tendency, increasing steadily during the period just before the Stalinist purges of the 1930's, to integrate his own experience with that of his suffering fellows, a distinct foreshadowing of the life and poems of Yuri Zhivago that Pasternak was later to create.

SECOND BIRTH

For many of Russia's artists, Mayakovsky's suicide in 1930 marked the end of faith in the ideals of the 1917 revolution. The title of Pasternak's collection of verse *Vtoroye rozhdeniye* (1932; *Second Birth*, 1964) reflects his new orientation, for in one of the poems an actor speaks: "Oh, had I known when I made my debut that lines with blood in them can flood the throat and kill!" During the decade of terror, Pasternak inclined still further toward a realistic novel of the revolution, although only six fragments of it remain, the last short pieces of fiction he wrote. "A District in the Rear" and "Before Parting," both written in the late 1930's, treat autobiographical motifs from 1916, the strange prelude to the revolution, with none of Pasternak's earlier swift flashes of impression nor any penetration of the creating artist's consciousness. "A District in the Rear," however, links family love with the stirrings of the artistic impulse because the hero senses the feelings of his wife and children as "something remote, like loneliness and the pacing of the horse, something like a book," as he approaches the decision to leave them and sacrifice his life "most worthily and to best advantage" at the front.

The four remaining story fragments, "A Beggar Who Is Proud," "Aunt Olya," "Winter Night," and "The House with Galleries," do not involve the events of 1917 but rather Pasternak's childhood reminiscences of the 1905 revolution, possibly because in the late 1930's he was as yet unable to deal fully with the poet's relation to the Communist movement and its aftermath. Only after he had lived through World War II and met Olga Ivinskaya could Pasternak express his experiences through the fictional perspective of Doctor Zhivago, binding the moral and the creative, the personal and the objective, the loving and the sacrificial elements of human life into an organic whole. While all Pasternak's short fiction are steps toward that goal, each piece also independently reflects successively maturing phases of his recognition, as he wrote toward the end of his life, that to be a great poet, writing poetry was not enough; it was also essential to contribute in a vital way to his times by willingly sacrificing himself to a lofty and lovely destiny. Accordingly, the personae of Pasternak's short fiction--the romantic poet, the lyric dreamer, the aging actor, the maturing girl, the suffering woman, the self-sacrificing husband and father--all finally coalesced into the figure of his Christian "Hamlet":

> The noise is stilled. I come out on the stage . . . The
> darkness of the night is aimed at me
> Along the sights of a thousand opera glasses.
> Abba, Father, if it be possible,
> Let this cup pass from me. . . .

OTHER MAJOR WORKS

LONG FICTION: *Doktor Zhivago*, 1957 (*Doctor Zhivago*, 1958).

PLAY: *Slepaya krasavitsa*, pb. 1969 (*The Blind Beauty*, 1969).

POETRY: *Bliznets v tuchakh*, 1914; *Poverkh barierov*, 1917 (*Above the Barriers*, 1959); *Sestra moia zhizn': Leto 1917 goda*, 1922 (*My Sister, Life*, 1964; also known as *Sister My Life*); *Temy i variatsii*, 1923 (*Themes and Variations*, 1964); *Vysokaya bolezn'*, 1924 (*High Malady*, 1958); *Carousel: Verse for Children*, 1925; *Devyatsot pyaty' god*, 1926 (*The Year 1905*, 1989); *Lyutenant Shmidt*, 1927 (*Lieutenant Schmidt*, 1992); *Spektorsky*, 1931; *Vtoroye rozhdeniye*, 1932 (*Second Birth*, 1964); *Na rannikh poezdakh*, 1943 (*On Early Trains*, 1964); *Zemnoy prostor*, 1945 (*The Vastness of Earth*, 1964); *Kogda razgulyayetsa*, 1959 (*When the Skies Clear*, 1964); *Poems*, 1959; *The Poetry of Boris Pasternak, 1917-1959*, 1959; *Poems, 1955-1959*, 1960; *In the Interlude: Poems, 1945-1960*, 1962; *Fifty Poems*, 1963; *The Poems of Doctor Zhivago*, 1965; *Stikhotvoreniya i poemy*, 1965, 1976; *The Poetry of Boris Pasternak*, 1969; *Selected Poems*, 1983.

NONFICTION: *Okhrannaya gramota*, 1931 (autobiography; *Safe Conduct*, 1945 in *The Collected Prose Works*); *Avtobiograficheskiy ocherk*, 1958 (*I Remember: Sketch for an Autobiography*, 1959); *An Essay in Autobiography*, 1959; *Essays*, 1976; *The Correspondence of Boris Pasternak and Olga Freidenberg, 1910-1954*, 1981; *Pasternak on Art and Creativity*, 1985; *Boris Pasternak: Family Correspondence, 1921-1960*, 2010 (Maya Slater, editor); *Pis'ma k gruzinskim*, n.d. (*Letters to Georgian Friends by Boris Pasternak*, 1968).

TRANSLATIONS: *Hamlet*, 1941 (of William Shakespeare); *Romeo i Juliet*, 1943 (of Shakespeare); *Antony i Cleopatra*, 1944 (of Shakespeare); *Othello*, 1945 (of Shakespeare); *King Lear*, 1949 (of Shakespeare); *Faust*, 1953 (of Johann Wolfgang von Goethe); *Maria Stuart*, 1957 (of Friedrich Schiller).

MISCELLANEOUS: *The Collected Prose Works*, 1945; *Safe Conduct: An Early Autobiography, and Other Works by Boris Pasternak*, 1958 (also known as *Selected Writings*, 1949); *Sochinenii*, 1961; *Vozdushnye puti: Proza raz nykh let*, 1982; *The Voice of Prose*, 1986.

BIBLIOGRAPHY

Barnes, Christopher. *Boris Pasternak: A Literary Biography, Volume One: 1890-1928*. New York: Cambridge University Press, 1990. A comprehensive biography, scholarly but also accessible.

Björling, Fiona. "An Analysis of 'The Childhood of Luvers' by Boris Pasternak" In *The Russian Twentieth-Century Short Story: A Critical Companion*, edited by Lyudmila Parts. Brighton, Mass.: Academic Studies Press, 2010. Provides a critical reading of this story.

Ciepiela, Catherine. *The Same Solitude: Boris Pasternak and Marina Tsvetaeva*. Ithaca, N.Y.: Cornell University Press, 2006. Ciepiela examines the ten-year love affair between Pasternak and Tsvetaeva, whose relationship was primarily limited to long-distance letters. Included in this volume is the correspondence between the two authors, along with letters from poet Rainer Maria Rilke, who completed the couple's literary love triangle. Ciepiela reveals the similarities between Pasternak and Tsvetaeva by painting a portrait of their lives and personalities.

Conquest, Robert. *The Pasternak Affair: Courage of Genius*. London: Collins and Harvill, 1961. A detailed account of Pasternak's conflict with the Soviet state on his reception of the Nobel Prize. Conquest provides much valuable information about Pasternak as a man and a writer.

De Mallac, Guy. *Boris Pasternak: His Life and Art*. Norman: University of Oklahoma Press, 1981. An extensive biography of Pasternak. The second part is devoted to De Mallac's interpretation of the most important features of Pasternak's works. A detailed chronology of his life and an exhaustive bibliography complete this beautifully illustrated book.

Erlich, Victor, ed. *Pasternak: A Collection of Critical Essays*. Englewood Cliffs, N.J.: Prentice-Hall, 1978. This skillfully arranged collection of essays covers all important facets of Pasternak's work, including short fiction, although the emphasis is on his poetry and *Doctor Zhivago*.

Gifford, Henry. *Boris Pasternak: A Critical Study*. New York: Cambridge University Press, 1977. Follows the stages in Pasternak's life and discusses works written during those stages in order to establish his achievements as a poet, writer of prose fiction, and translator. This volume contains many sharp critical remarks, and chapter 6 deals with the short fiction. Supplemented by a chronological table and a select bibliography.

_____. "Indomitable Pasternak." *The New York Review of Books* 37 (May 31, 1990): 26-31. Discusses Pasternak's courage in his defense of artistic freedom under Soviet power.

Ivinskaya, Olga. *A Captive of Time*. Garden City, N.Y.: Doubleday, 1978. Ivinskaya, Pasternak's love in the last years of his life, the model for Lara in *Doctor Zhivago*, and a staff member at the influential Soviet literary magazine *Novy mir*, provides a wealth of information about Pasternak, his views and works, and Russia's literary atmosphere in the 1940's and 1950's.

Mossman, Elliott. "Pasternak's Short Fiction." *Russian Literature Triquarterly* 3 (1972): 279-302. Mossman sees Pasternak's preoccupation with short fiction in the 1920's not as a diversion but as an alternative to poetry and a legitimate genre in his work. He discusses "Aerial Ways," "The Story," "The Childhood of Luvers," and "The Story of a Contraoctave" within Pasternak's development as a writer.

Rudova, Larissa. *Understanding Boris Pasternak*. Columbia: University of South Carolina Press, 1997. A general introduction to Pasternak's work, including both his early poetry and prose and his later work. Provides analyses of individual novels and stories.

Swift, Megan. "'The Tale' and the Novel: Pasternak and the Politics of Genre." *Canadian Slavonic Papers* 49, no. 1/2 (March-June, 2007): 111-121. An analysis of "The Story," one of Pasternak's early short stories. Notes that the story was conceived as a novel and the outline of that unfinished novel remains within the story, which accounts for its sense of noncompletion.

Mitzi M. Brunsdale
Updated by Vasa D. Mihailovich

PU SONGLING

Born: Zichuan, Shandong, China; June 5, 1640
Died: Shandong, China; February 25, 1715
Also known as: P'u Sung-ling

PRINCIPAL SHORT FICTION

Liaozhai zhiyi, 1766 (also known as *Liao-chai chih-i*; *Strange Stories from a Chinese Studio,* 1880)
Liaozhai zhiyi weikan gao, 1936
Chinese Ghost and Love Stories: A Selection from the Liaozhai Stories by Pu Songling, 1946

OTHER LITERARY FORMS

Although the literary fame of Pu Songling (pew suhng-lihng) rests solely on his collection of short fiction, *Liaozhai zhiyi* (*Strange Stories from a Chinese Studio*), a compilation of 431 stories, he was a versatile writer in both classical and colloquial Chinese. He was the author of various works, including a remarkable novel written in the vernacular titled *Xingshi yinyuan zhuan* (1870; the story of a marriage to rouse the world). Written under the pseudonym Xizhoushang (Scholar of the Western Chou Period), this novel's author remained anonymous for two centuries, until Dr. Hu Shih, in the course of his important studies in the history of Chinese vernacular literature, revealed that the real name of the author was Pu Songling. The earliest known printed edition is dated 1870, but in 1933 a punctuated edition was published to which were added some discussions of the authorship problem by various writers who were in agreement with Hu Shih's finding. Pu Songling's literary efforts were by no means confined to the writing of fiction, whether short or long. A man of parts, he wrote several kinds of poems: *Shi* poems in regular meter; folk musical narratives; drum songs; and folk songs. He wrote plays and numerous essays. He indulged in miscellaneous writings

(*tongchu*): a lexicon of colloquial expressions in daily use in the Zichuan district, a treatise on agriculture and sericulture, a treatise on grass and trees, a manual on truancy, a satire on the examination of the self, books on dealing with hungry ghosts, correspondence, and desultory and neglected pieces. Apart from the *Liaozhai zhiyi* and the novel mentioned above, all the works subsequently attributed to Pu Songling are included in the two-volume collection, *Liaozhai quanzhi* (1936; complete works from the Chinese studio).

ACHIEVEMENTS

The Ch'ing, or Manchu, Dynasty, between its establishment in 1644 and the Opium War of 1840-1842, gave birth to at least four great literary masterpieces in drama and fiction: Hongshang's *chuan qi* style opera *Zhangshang dian* (c. 1688; *The Palace of Eternal Youth,* 1955) and two great novels, Cao Xueqin's romance, *Hungloumeng* (1792; *Dream of the Red Chamber,* 1929) and Wu Ching-tzu's satire, *Ju-lin waishih* (1768-1779; *The Scholars,* 1957). Pu Songling's *Strange Stories from a Chinese Studio* is the great masterpiece of short fiction of the Ch'ing era. The American scholar Allan Barr concluded that no really precise progression in sequence of characterization, theme, and structure corresponds to the chronological sequence. Hence he proposed that readers regard the *Liaozhai zhiyi* as "falling into three phases": early (c. 1675-1683), middle (c. 1683-1705), and late (c. 1690-1705). Despite the great variety of the narrative aspects throughout the whole work, there is, according to Barr, a perceivable sense of "creative growth and technical development" from the first to last of the last volumes that can be appreciated by a close reader.

After the printing of 1766, *Strange Stories from a Chinese Studio* attracted such widespread attention that the author's fame was assured. Educated readers with some literary training recognized that his work represented the perfected culmination of a long tradition of the use of classical Chinese for fictional narrative from the *shan ji* ("records of marvels") of the Wei and Tsin dynasties to the *chuan qi* ("strange transmissions")--the short prose romances of the T'ang Dynasty, whose range of subject matter is practically identical with that of Pu's stories. His superb handling of the *guwan* style, his ability to revivify old plots that had become hackneyed and flimsy through a new "magic realism" that made the improbable and the impossible probable and supernatural creatures, such as flower or fox spirits, seem human, went far beyond what had been accomplished in the past.

His stories appealed to an unprecedented number of readers from many walks of life, not simply educated people with some literary training. Consequently, his fictions revived the *chuan qi* tradition for nearly a century. Pu's tales are admired for their masterly style, which combines terse expression with abundant literary allusions and succeeds in maintaining a contrasting yet harmonious balance between the fantastic and the realistic elements of his fiction.

BIOGRAPHY

Pu Songling was born on June 5, 1640, in Zichuan, Shandong, China. Possibly of Mongol ancestry, he was the son of Pu Pan, a merchant, who was also a man of action as well as of some learning. In this old but impoverished family of gentry there were scholars and officials such as Pu's granduncle, Pu shangwan, who held the *jinshi* ("entered scholar"), the highest, or "doctor's," degree, and was the magistrate of Youtian, in Zhili. In addition to his family name of Pu and his personal name of Songling, Pu Songling had two "courtesy names," taken at age twenty, by which he was known among his friends: Liu Xian (last of the immortals) and Jian Chan (knight-errant). He also had two "artistic names," adopted on occasion as names for his library or studio, by which he was popularly known after he became famous: Luo Chuan (willow spring) and Liao Zhai (casual studio).

In 1658, at age eighteen, Pu qualified for the lowest, or "bachelor's," degree, which required him to pass three successive sets of examinations by writing eight or ten essays on themes assigned from the "Four Books and Five Classics," as well as five poems on prescribed patterns.

Although he regularly took the provincial examinations for the next highest degree, he consistently failed. Not until 1711, at age seventy-one, did he succeed in being made a senior licentiate. Apparently his diverse interests prevented him from pursuing the traditional program of study rigorously enough.

As a result, Pu Songling spent his life in a variety of activities. In 1670, he was employed as a secretary to the magistrate at Baoying, Jiangsu. In 1672, he became secretary to a wealthy friend, Bi Jiyou, sometime department magistrate of Tongzhou, Kiangsu, a position which Pu held for nearly twenty years. The rest of his activities consisted of his employment as a licentiate to the district school from 1685 onward, private tutoring in the homes of local gentry, the management of his family affairs (he was happily married to an amiable wife by whom he had four sons, three of whom became licentiates), and the writing of short stories, poems, songs, and miscellaneous essays.

His writing of short stories apparently began as early as 1660 and extended to, and possibly beyond, 1679, when he wrote a preface to *Strange Stories from a Chinese Studio*. Although in his day his literary genius was little known beyond the circle of his friends and acquaintances, eventually his fame was to spread over China and even to foreign lands. By 1848, his stories had been translated into Manchu, and by 1880, into English. In the twentieth century they had been translated into French, Japanese, German, and Russian.

Pu Songling's preface to *Strange Stories from a Chinese Studio* reveals decided connections between his short stories and his personal life and sentiments. He begins, through references to clothes, by ridiculing the official classes and suggesting that they hold posts for which, from a literary standpoint, they are unfit. Furthermore, in his view, political intrigue in official circles is all too common. The evil machinations of bad and false men often destroy good and true men.

Evidently a man much attached to the Buddhist faith, Pu provides a Buddhist interpretation of his existence in the preface. In sum, taking the attitudes and sentiments appearing in Pu Songling's preface and the circumstances of his biography and comparing these things with the short stories--their characterizations, themes, satire, and social criticism--leads to the definite conclusion that they embrace Pu's personal philosophy: his dreams, faith, and worldview.

In his last years Pu Songling's family fortunes are said to have slightly improved. In 1713, his wife (née Liu) died. He and she had apparently led a happy but uneventful life together. His fondness for her is shown by the sketch of her life he wrote following her death and the several poems he composed dedicated to her memory. In three more years he himself died, on February 25, 1715.

ANALYSIS

In his *Strange Stories from a Chinese Studio*, Pu Songling mostly presents encounters between human beings and supernatural or fantastic creatures. The human beings may be students, scholars, officials, peasants, Daoist or Buddhist priests, fortune-tellers, magicians, maidens, wives, or concubines, among others. Some of these human beings, especially the Daoist or Buddhist priests and the magicians, may possess supernatural powers or illusionary skills of various kinds. The supernatural or fantastic creatures may be animals, birds, flowers, fairies, devils, or ghosts who have assumed human shape, or they may retain their natural forms but have the human powers of speech and understanding. Although when portraying supernatural or fantastic creatures Pu is highly imaginative, in dealing with ordinary mortals he controls his imagination to the degree that they are not exaggerated or unnatural. He appears to seek to make the extraordinary plausible and the ordinary interesting and to press home the point that the ordinary world is endowed always with extraordinary possibilities.

His favorite themes seem to be changeableness, in which animals or devils are changed into human form or vice versa; reincarnation; living humans becoming immortals; the dead being brought back to life; male students falling in love with beautiful women; exposure of corrupt or incompetent officials; and criticism of the civil service examination system and of pedantic scholarship. Although Pu imitated the classical short tales of the T'ang Dynasty, he introduced original elements in terms of his personal views and he included criminal and detective stories in his collection. Some of his stories seem to have been written from motives of pure entertainment, but the majority of them state or imply some moral lesson. The stories demonstrate Pu's sincere or facetious conviction that in this world evildoers are eventually punished and the kindhearted are in the long run rewarded for their good deeds.

"THE TIGER OF ZHAOCHANG"

"Zhaochang hu" ("The Tiger of Zhaochang") is the story of a tiger who eats the son of an elderly widow who has no relations besides her son and depends entirely on him for her support. Thus left to starve to death, the mother indignantly journeys to town, where she levels a charge against the tiger with the magistrate. Eventually, the tiger confesses to the crime of having eaten the young son. The magistrate informs the tiger that it must forfeit its own life unless it can act as the old woman's son and support her in the same manner that he did, in which case the magistrate will allow it to go free. The tiger declares that it can fulfill this obligation and does. In conclusion, the narrator warns the reader not to take the story as true; on the other hand, he says, it is not to be considered a joke. Indeed, it is a moral exemplum. Although the tiger is a, it displays human feelings. Hence it is quite unlike some human beings of the present day, who follow the practice of oppressing orphans and widows and are far from being equal to a member of the brute creation.

"THE PUPILS OF THE EYES THAT TALKED"

In "Tongran yu" ("The Pupils of the Eyes That Talked"), a young scholar, Fang Lian, a married man, has a character weakness: He likes to look at pretty women and girls other than his wife. On one occasion his ogling results in a handful of dirt thrown in his face, which blinds him. Although a variety of medical remedies are tried over a good period of time, he remains a blind man. Now very worried, he repents of his past sins. He obtains a copy of the Buddhist sutra known as the *Guangming jing* and begins to recite it daily. Although its recitation at first is boring, he eventually experiences a quietude of mind that he has never known before. He starts to hear a voice in each eye. These voices turn out to be two tiny men, who exit through Fang Lien's nose to see what is transpiring outside.

Eventually, Fang Lien hears a small voice in his left eye say, "It's not convenient for us to go and come by way of these nostrils. We had each better open a door for ourselves." The small voice in the right eye, however, declares that his wall is too thick to break through. They therefore break through the wall of the left eye. Immediately the light flows into Fang Lien's darkened orb. To his great delight, he can see again. Although he always remains blind in his right eye, he never ventures to fix his good eye on any woman other than his own wife.

In an annotation to this story, the translator implies that its plot is based partly on a folk belief widely held throughout China--namely, that each of a person's eyes contains a tiny human figure. He thinks this myth originated from one experiencing the reflection of oneself when looking into another person's eyes, or into one's own when viewing oneself in a mirror.

"THE PICTURE HORSE"

The story "Huama" ("The Picture Horse") concerns Mr. Cui, who finds a strange horse--black marked with white and with a scrubby tail--lying in the grass inside his premises. Although he repeatedly drives it away, it persists in returning to the same spot. Mr. Ts'ui decides to borrow the horse and ride it to see a friend, some distance away.

Mr. Ts'ui finds that the horse travels at an astonishingly rapid rate, and it needs no food and little rest. It is not long before Mr. Ts'ui reaches his destination. When the local prince hears of the speed and endurance of this remarkable horse, he purchases it after a long wait for its owner to appear.

After a time, the prince has business near Mr. Ts'ui and rides there on the remarkable horse. Upon his arrival, he leaves it in the custody of one of his officers. The horse breaks away from its custodian and escapes. The officer gives chase to the home of Mr. Ts'ui's neighbor, Mr. Tsâng, wherein it disappears. The officer accosts Mr. Tsâng and demands the return of the prince's horse, but Mr. Tsâng denies knowing anything about any horse, whereupon the officer bursts into Mr. Tsâng's private quarters. To his dismay, he finds no horse, but upon one wall he observes a picture of a horse exactly like the one he seeks. It becomes clear to him and to Mr. Ts'ui that the prince's horse is a supernatural horse. Since the officer is afraid to return to the prince without the horse, Mr. Ts'ui intervenes and refunds the purchase price willingly. Naturally, Mr. Tsâng greatly appreciates his neighbor's generosity, since he never knew that the

horse had been sold in the first place.

According to Pu, the picture of the horse in Mr. Tsâng's apartment was painted by the early T'ang poet and painter Chan Tzuang, who, although apparently specializing in the painting of horses, was even better known as a writer. In China a close bond existed between painting and scholarship. The object of the painting was to capture the *qi*, or the life-spirit and the vitality of a thing, and writing was regarded as "mind painting." In this case the painted thing has such powerful vitality that it leaves the picture plane and take up an existence in the real world. Such stories as Pu's "The Picture Horse" remind one of the American writer Edgar Allan Poe's tapestry horse that comes alive in his story "Metzengerstein" (1832), as well as his "The Oval Portrait" (1842), in which an artist has extracted the life-spirit from his female model and put it into her portrait, thus leaving the former living model dead.

"THE PAINTED SKIN"

In Pu's story "Huapi" ("The Painted Skin"), Mr. Wang meets a pretty girl who claims that she was sold as a concubine, cruelly abused, and has run away. Mr. Wang invites her to his home. She gratefully accepts his offer. He lets her stay in the library, and she requests him not to tell anyone where she is staying. Although he agrees to keep her secret, he tells his wife of the girl's presence as soon as he sees her.

When Wang is out walking again, he encounters a Daoist priest, who asks him if he has met any stranger recently. Wang denies that he has. Walking away from him, the priest calls him a fool and remarks that some people never know when they are in danger of dying. Although Wang thinks that the Daoist is simply trying to land a client, upon returning home he peeks in the library window. Inside he sees a hideous-looking devil with a green face and sawtooth teeth. The devil has spread out a human skin on a table and is painting it with a brush. Having completed the design it is putting on the skin, the devil picks up the skin, shakes it out like a coat, and throws it over its shoulders. To Wang's amazement, he sees that the devil is now the pretty concubine!

Terrified out of his wits, Wang finds the Daoist priest, who presents Wang with a fly-brush and prescribes that he hang it on the door of the premises occupied by the devil. Wang complies. When the devil appears, it responds to the fly-brush by gnashing its teeth and cursing. It grabs the fly-brush and tears it to pieces, then, rushing into the room occupied by Wang and his wife, the devil grabs Wang and tears out his heart. Still raging, the devil departs. Wang is dead.

Wang's wife sends his brother to report the tragedy to the Daoist priest. The priest inquires of him whether any stranger has just come to Wang's house. The brother replying that an old woman has just been hired as a maid, the priest informs him that the person must be the devil in disguise. Taking up his wooden sword, the Daoist accosts the presumed maid face-to-face, exposing her as the devil. Calling her a "base-born fiend," he demands the return of the fly-brush. His demand not met, he raises his sword and strikes her. As she falls to the ground, the human skin separates from her body to reveal her devilish hideousness. Then he cuts off the devil's head. As for the sheet of human skin, complete with eyebrows, eyes, hands, and feet, the priest rolls it up into a scroll. He is about to depart when Wang's wife tearfully pleads with him to restore her dead husband to life. He replies that he does not possess such power, and she must apply to the town maniac. Mrs. Wang finds the maniac raving by the roadside. She approaches the man on her knees and entreats him to restore her husband to life. He laughs at her. Then he gives her a thrashing with his staff. She endures this harsh treatment without a murmur. Then he hands her a distasteful looking pill and orders her to swallow it. She does so with great difficulty.

Returning home, Wang's wife mourns bitterly over her dead husband, greatly regretting the action she has taken. She undertakes to prepare the corpse herself. As she does so, she feels a great lump rising in her throat which soon pops out of her mouth straight into the open wound of the dead man. She sees that it is a human heart. Excitedly, she closes the wound over it, holding the sides together with her hands. Rubbing the corpse vigorously for a time, she then covers it over with clothes. During the night she inspects the dead man and discovers breath coming from his nostrils. By morning Wang is alive again.

Except for a number of very short stories, the stories discussed above represent a fair cross section of those in Pu Songling's collection in terms of treatment and

plot structure. Apart from the sketches which are mere anecdotes, his stories range from very simple plots, such as that found in "The Tiger of Zhaochang," to rather complicated ones, such as that of "The Painted Skin." Other tales of special interest might be added to this list: "Dou xishi" ("The Fighting Cricket"), "Laoshan daozi" ("The Daoist Priest of Laoshan"), "Zhi qingxu" ("The Wonderful Stone"), "Niaoyu" ("The Talking of the Birds"), "Zhanban" ("Planchette"), "Toutao" ("Theft of the Peach"), "Jiannuo" ("Miss Jiannuo"), and "Hua quzi" ("The Flowernymphs"). All these stories are included in Herbert A. Giles's collection of 164 of Pu's stories, *Strange Stories from a Chinese Studio*, which was reprinted in 1969, under the English titles given above. Rose Qong's collection, *Chinese Ghost and Love Stories: A Selection from the Liao-chai Stories by Pu Songling*, contains forty tales. Translations of one or several tales are scattered in various anthologies and periodicals.

Pu Songling weaves together the natural and the supernatural in a more realistic manner than the T'ang authors of *chuan qi*. In his criticism of Confucian officialdom, he introduces new moral principles. He ignores philosophical Daoism to emphasize the superstition, magic, and exorcism of the popular religion of that name. This sort of Daoism concerned itself with the alchemical promise of the prolongation of life by discovering the elixir of immortality; with communication with *xian*, or immortals; with magic pills; and with defeating devils.

In like manner, Pu favors Buddhism over Daoism, giving the Buddhist clergy more integrity, dignity, and respect than he does the Daoist priesthood or Confucian officials. He mainly ignores the intellectual, meditative Buddhist Chan sect in favor of the popular Qing Tu, or Pure Land School, which concerns itself with the worship of Buddha Amitabha, who saves into his Pure Land all those who call upon his name in faith. Adhering to the doctrine of karma and reincarnation, the followers of Qing Tu Buddhism believe in a whole pantheon of Buddhas and bodhisattvas and in a variety of celestial and terrestrial realms, including heavens and hells. Qing Tu Buddhism emphasizes right living and the value of the recitation of favored Buddhist sutras.

In sum, Pu Songling treated the natural and the supernatural in terms of Chinese popular religion, according to which men sought communication with gods and spirits primarily to obtain benefits and avoid calamities.

OTHER MAJOR WORKS

LONG FICTION: *Xingshi yinyuan zhuan*, 1870 (also known as *Hsing-shih yin-yuan chuan*; *The Bonds of Matrimony*, 1995).

MISCELLANEOUS: *Liaozhai quanzhi*, 1936 (also known as *Liao-chai ch'uan-chi*).

BIBLIOGRAPHY

Barr, Allan. "A Comparative Study of Early and Late Tales in *Liaozhai zhiyi*." *Harvard Journal of Asiatic Studies* 45 (1985): 157-202. Because a comparison of the text's narrative development with its chronological progression shows no precise relationship between them, Barr believes it best to consider the text as having progressed through early, middle, and late periods.

_____. "Disarming Intruders: Alien Women in *Liaozhai zhiyi*." *Harvard Journal of Asiatic Studies* 49 (1989): 501-517. Barr offers a new interpretation of Pu's "alien women," or women of supernatural character, such as ghosts, fox spirits, flower nymphs, and predatory femme fatale demons. He analyzes these women's relationships with their lovers and other humans and classifies them as residents, transients, and wicked predators.

_____. "The Textual Transmission of *Liaozhai zhiyi*." *Harvard Journal of Asiatic Studies* 44 (1984): 515-562. Demonstrates how a comparison of the arrangement of the extant text with the individual stories that can be dated provides a means of tracking the text's chronological development.

Chang, Chun-shu, and Shelley Hsueh-lun Chang. *Redefining History: Ghosts, Spirits, and Human Society in P'u Sungling's World, 1640-1715*. Ann Arbor: University of Michigan Press, 1998. An examination of the characters, human and nonhuman, in Pu's fiction.

Chiang, Sing-chen Lydia. *Collecting the Self: Body and Identity in Strange Tale Collections of Late Imperial China*. Boston: Brill, 2005. A Freudian interpretation of *Liaozhai zhiyi* and short-story collections by two contemporaries of Pu Songling. Examines how these stories about ghosts, animal spirits, gods, monsters, and other supernatural phenomena were a means of writing about suppressed cultural anxieties, gender issues, and the authors' self-identity.

Francis, Sing-Chen Lydia. "Body and Identity in *Liaozhao zhiyi*." *Nan Nu: Men, Women and Gender in Early and Imperial China* 4, no. 2 (October, 2002): 207-231. Focuses on Pu Songling's creation of an alternative self-identity through his depictions of the corporeal body in *Liaozhao zhiyi*.

Li, Wai-yee. "Rhetoric of Fantasy and Rhetoric of Irony: Studies in *Liao-chai chih-i* and *Hung-lou mâng*." In *Dissertation Abstracts International* 49 (August, 1988): 249A. Examines the truth, fiction, irony, and illusion in the collection of Pu's classical short stories and his vernacular novel. Focuses on the play and limitations of the structure of desire--embracing freedom, justice, and the ideal--and the structure of order--embracing morality, individual discipline, love, and the real.

Prusek, Jaroslav. "*Liao-chai chih-i* by Pu Songling." In *Chinese History and Literature: Collection of Studies*. Dordrecht, Netherlands: Reidel, 1970. A sensitive discussion of Pu's life when employed as a tutor in various rich families and while engaged in the writing of *Liaozhai zhiyi*, especially while residing with the Pi family. Prusek links certain aspects of Pu's life during this period with certain of his poems to advantage and corrects an important misinterpretation that alters those facts as given in the American collection *Eminent Chinese of the Ch'ing Period* (1976).

_____. "Pu Songling and His Work." In *Chinese History and Literature: Collection of Studies*. Dordrecht, Netherlands: Reidel, 1970. A fine general discussion of the circumstances of Pu's unfulfilled life of poverty; his personality, family life, and political philosophy; his literary achievements, especially the realism of his fantasies; and his literary importance both in the history of Chinese literature and as a world figure. This piece was originally a foreword to Prusek's volume of selections under the title *Zkazky o sestery cest osudu* (1955; tales of six different paths of destiny).

_____. "Two Documents Relating to the Life of P'u Sung-ling." In *Chinese History and Literature: Collection of Studies*. Dordrecht, Netherlands: Reidel, 1970. Two documents concerning Pu's life are presented which heretofore have never been translated into any European language: one written by Pu himself at the age of seventy-four, the other an inscription on the stela erected on Pu's grave.

Yang, Rui. "Oedipal Fantasy in Disguise: A Psychoanalytic Interpretation of *Liaozhai Zhiyi*." *Tamkang Review* 25 (Winter, 1994): 67-93. Using the psychoanalytic theories developed by Norman Holland in *The Dynamics of Literary Response*, this essay discusses Pu Songling's treatment of the Oedipal conflict.

Zeitlin, Judith T. *Historian of the Strange: Pu Songling and the Chinese Classical Tale*. Stanford, Calif.: Stanford University Press, 1993. A good study of Pu's fiction and its place in the modern short-fiction canon.

Zhou, Jianming. "A Literary Rendition of Animal Figures: A Comparison Between Kafka's Tales and P'u Songling's Stories," translated by Jerry Krauel and Dariusz Rybicki. In *Kafka and China*, edited by Adrian Hsia. Bern, Switzerland: Peter Lang, 1996. Discusses Franz Kafka and Pu Songling's treatment of animals in their fiction.

Richard P. Benton

ALEXANDER PUSHKIN

Born: Moscow, Russia; June 6, 1799
Died: St. Petersburg, Russia; February 10, 1837

PRINCIPAL SHORT FICTION

Povesti Belkina, 1831 (*Russian Romance*, 1875; better known as *The Tales of Belkin*, 1947)
Pikovaya dama, 1834 (*The Queen of Spades*, 1858)

OTHER LITERARY FORMS

Generally considered the greatest poet in the Russian language, Alexander Pushkin (POOSH-kuhn) is known not only for his lyrical and narrative poems but also for his brilliant verse novel *Evgeny Onegin* (1825-1832, 1833; *Eugene Onegin*, 1881), as well as his play *Boris Godunov* (pb. 1831, pr. 1870; English translation, 1918), which was the inspiration for the opera by Modest Mussorgsky.

ACHIEVEMENTS

Often termed the father of Russian literature, Alexander Pushkin occupies a unique position in Russian literary history. During his age, the language of the Russian aristocracy was French, not Russian, and Pushkin's literary sensibility was largely formed by French writers, particularly writers of the eighteenth century. He combined their classical approach with the Romantic elements of the English poet Lord Byron and native Russian materials, such as folktales, in a transformation that produced a number of masterpieces, primarily in poetry. Pushkin's general influence on nineteenth century Russian prose writers is immeasurable because his primary contribution was neither to character type nor to technique but to the very language of fiction itself. Precision and brevity, he believed, are the most important qualities of prose--elements that the eighteenth century French essayists also held in high regard--and his tales are characterized by a concise, plain language that set the standard for Russian prose writers who followed. Although character analysis was not Pushkin's primary achievement, his insight into the protagonist in *The Queen of Spades* is considered a precursor to the development of the psychological analysis of character, which was the hallmark of the great Russian novelists of the nineteenth century. Ivan Turgenev, Leo Tolstoy, and Fyodor Dostoevski all acknowledged the influence of various aspects of his work. Russian critics have long expected Pushkin's reputation to become more firmly established in other countries, but because Pushkin's primary achievement is in poetry, and his particular, precise language is so difficult to translate, his reputation outside Russia has remained limited.

BIOGRAPHY

Alexander Sergeyevich Pushkin was born into the Russian aristocracy and lived the relatively privileged life of a member of the nobility. One element that set him apart from other aristocrats who gathered around the czar was his heritage on his mother's side: His great grandfather was the black slave Hannibal, whom Peter the Great bought in Turkey and brought back to Russia. At an early age, Pushkin's poetic talents were recognized, but the subject of some of his poetry was the desire for liberty, and for political reasons the czar banished him from Moscow to his mother's estate when he was twenty years old. Although Pushkin eventually was called back to Moscow by the czar, for the remainder of his life he was subject to the czar's direct censorship. At the height of his literary powers, Pushkin died a tragic death. He married a woman who was in favor with many members of the czar's court because of her beauty; she was not an intellectual, however, and did not appreciate Pushkin's writing. When Pushkin discovered that she was secretly meeting a member of the court in a liaison, he challenged the man to a duel in which Pushkin was wounded in the stomach. He died two days later.

ANALYSIS

Alexander Pushkin's short fiction exhibits the classic characteristics of the Romantic tale. The focus is on event, on plot, with character portrayal subordinated to dramatic action. These cleverly plotted, entertaining stories have much in common with such early masters of the modern short story as Sir Walter Scott, Washington Irving, Edgar Allan Poe, and Honoré de Balzac. As Romantic tales, Pushkin's stories have been termed perfect. However, his reputation as one of the developers of the modern short story rests on a remarkably small body of work: the five tales that make up the collection *The Tales of Belkin* and the masterpiece *The Queen of Spades*. In addition to these completed stories, a number of fragments were published after his death that illustrate Pushkin's struggle in writing fiction. In contrast to his early achievements in poetry, his technical mastery of fiction required a long, difficult period of apprenticeship.

One of Pushkin's most challenging technical problems was the appropriate management of point of view, and in *The Tales of Belkin* he finally solved that problem. He framed the tales with an opening device, as Scott had done in a series of novels titled "Tales of My Landlord" (1816-1819) and as Irving had done in his *Tales of a Traveller* (1824), works popular in Russia at the time that Pushkin began writing fiction. Pushkin's tales are presented as stories told by various people to one Ivan Petrovich Belkin, who wrote them down; upon his death, they were passed on to a publisher. The opening section of the collection is not a story but an address to the reader by this fictitious publisher, who comments on the background of the tales in a short paragraph and then presents a letter by a friend of Belkin that describes Belkin's life. This elaborate device does function to place the tales together in a coherent arrangement wherein Pushkin's voice carries consistently from one tale to the next.

"THE SHOT"

The opening tale of the collection is "Vystrel" ("The Shot"), one of the most widely anthologized tales in short fiction. Within that single story, Pushkin exhibits a master's manipulation of point of view, with a central narrator who, in turn, relates narration by two other characters. The central narrator is a young army officer, Lieutenant I. L. P., who describes the conditions of his regiment in a small, isolated town. The young officers spend their evenings gambling at the house of a thirty-five-year-old civilian named Silvio, who is a Byronic figure--a Romantic hero, detached and proud, somewhat ironic and cynical, with an obsessive personality. When Silvio is insulted by a newcomer, everyone expects Silvio to kill the brash young newcomer in a duel, for Silvio is a renowned shot who practices daily. Silvio passes up the opportunity, however, and the incident is forgotten by everyone but the lieutenant/narrator, who secretly cannot forgive Silvio for what he considers his cowardice.

Later, however, when Silvio learns that he must leave town, he calls the lieutenant aside and explains his reason for passing up the duel by relating a series of previous events, thus becoming a second narrator in the story. Six years previously, as a hussar himself, Silvio had a duel with another young officer, a brilliant count of great social position and wealth. From the details that Silvio relates, it is obvious that subconsciously he was jealous of the man. The conditions of the duel were such that the two men drew lots for the first shot; Silvio's opponent won, but his shot missed, passing through Silvio's cap. As Silvio prepared for his shot, the young count possessed such aplomb that he ate cherries, calmly spitting out the seeds, as he waited. Angered by this show of superiority, Silvio made the strange request that he be allowed to take his shot at some future date, at any time he should choose to do so; the young count, with his great poise, agreed without any sign of apprehension. Now, Silvio has learned that the count is to be married, and Silvio is leaving to take his revenge. Because of this previous commitment to his honor, Silvio was forced to allow the recent insult to go unchallenged; consequently, the lieutenant learns that Silvio is not a coward after all. After Silvio relates these events, however, the lieutenant has strange, contradictory feelings about him: What kind of a man would do such a thing? An antihero in the Byronic tradition, Silvio is an elevated figure who believes that he is beyond the common sensibilities of society; the response of the narrator illustrates his ambivalence toward that Byronic role, an ambivalence that reflects Pushkin's own attitude.

The first section of the story ends with Silvio's departure, and the second begins four or five years later, when the lieutenant has left the army to return to his country estate. His neighbor, a Countess B., has been absent from her estate, but when she returns with her husband, the narrator visits them to relieve his boredom. In a short while, the narrator discovers that the husband is the same man whom Silvio left to kill, the brilliant young count, and he becomes the third narrator as he relates the events that followed Silvio's departure at the end of the first section of the story. Silvio indeed did appear at the estate, finding the count enjoying his honeymoon, but when Silvio claimed his shot, the count agreed. Silvio, however, in the spirit of

the duelist, determined that they should draw lots again. Once more, the count wins the first shot, but once more he misses, his stray shot striking a painting on the wall. As Silvio readies himself to fire the deciding shot, the countess rushes in and, seeing her husband in danger, throws her arms around his neck. This action is too much for the count, and he angrily demands that Silvio shoot. Silvio, now satisfied that he has broken the count's poise, fires his shot off to one side, into the same painting that the count struck. The story ends with the comment by the central narrator that Silvio was killed some years later in a military battle. The portrayal of Silvio that emerges from the separate narrators of this highly crafted tale is that of a principled, intriguing figure. There is a new twist to this tale, however, that deviates from the literary type of the day: The Byronic antihero has been bested by a straightforward, decent man. Although Pushkin actually began this story as a parody on the Byronic figure, his technical proficiency enabled him to explore the larger meanings of that figure, and "The Shot" became a masterpiece.

Alexander Pushkin (Library of Congress)

"THE BLIZZARD"

The two stories that follow "The Shot" in the collection, "Metel" ("The Blizzard") and "Grobovshchik" ("The Undertaker"), are not as complex. "The Blizzard" revolves around a case of mistaken identity, which was a popular subject for Romantic tales at the time. A young heroine, Maria Gavrilovna, who has been brought up reading French novels, falls in love and sneaks off to marry her lover at night. Without her knowledge, a blizzard causes her lover to lose his way while going to the church, and she marries a man who, unknown to her, is not her lover. She returns to her parents' home and four years later learns that her lover--whom she believes is her husband--was killed in the War of 1812. Afterward, she meets a Colonel Burmin, a veteran of the same war, and falls in love with him. He responds to her love but declares that one night on a whim he married an unknown woman who mistakenly thought he was someone else, and thus he cannot marry. The situation recalls that of Irving's "The Spectre Bridegroom," not only in its mistaken identities in marriage but also in its tone; as in Irving's story, all ends happily as the events eventually reveal the true identities: The heroine is, indeed, the unknown woman whom Colonel Burmin married that night. The events in Pushkin's story move much more quickly than those in Irving's, for they are presented without Irving's relaxed digressions; the influence of the occasional essayist was much stronger in Irving's work, and his tales, in general, do not have the quickly paced dramatic action of Pushkin, in whose stories one seldom finds superfluous material or inessential detail.

"THE UNDERTAKER"

"The Undertaker" is a humorous tale about an undertaker who is visited one night by the corpses he has buried, in response to an invitation he impulsively made at a party the previous night. The descriptions of the corpses are the highlight of this supernatural story, which ends with the undertaker waking from what proves to have been a dream. The tone and events of this story, particularly the corpses who come back to haunt the living, were to influence Nikolai Gogol--Pushkin's younger contemporary, another major prose writer of the period--in his famous "Shinel" ("The Overcoat"). Gogol had read Pushkin's collection and

thought highly of it. One specific aspect of Pushkin's "Stantsionnyi smotritel" ("The Stationmaster") influenced Gogol: the character of the "little man." The story, narrated by government official "Titular Counsellor A. G. N.," is about a poor post office stationmaster of low rank, Samson Vyrin, a "little man," who has a beautiful daughter, Dunya. When the narrator was traveling one day, he happened to stop at Samson's station for horses; there he noticed a series of pictures on the wall depicting the story of the Prodigal Son. He also first saw the girl Dunya, who was fourteen at the time. Her beauty deeply impressed him, and one day some years later, when he happens to be in the same district, he remembers her and stops at the same station. He asks about her, and the stationmaster, now a broken man, relates her story, thus becoming a second narrator.

Three years previously, the stationmaster tells the traveler, a hussar named Captain Minsky stopped at the station and, seeing the beautiful Dunya, pretended to be too ill to continue his journey. The hussar remained at the station several days, with Dunya nursing him, and then, one day when the stationmaster was away, fled with her. The stationmaster followed, until it became obvious that Dunya had willingly run off with Minsky. Later, the stationmaster takes a two-month leave and, on foot, traces the pair to St. Petersburg. There he discovers the pair living in a fancy hotel, and he confronts Minsky alone, demanding the return of his daughter before she is ruined. Minsky declares that he is in love with Dunya and that neither she nor the stationmaster could ever be happy with each other because of what has happened. The stationmaster leaves, but he returns to find his daughter, and he discovers her enjoying her elegant surroundings as she tenderly winds her fingers in Minsky's hair. When she sees her father, she faints, and Minsky drives the father away.

The stationmaster's narration at this point in the story is ended, and the original narrator, the government official, tells how the stationmaster has now taken to drink. In the closing scene of the story, some years later, the official returns once more to the station house and discovers that the stationmaster has, indeed, died from drink. In asking directions to the grave, he learns that a wealthy lady recently visited the area with her children in a coach-and-six and also asked for the stationmaster. On learning of his death, she began weeping and then visited the grave herself; the woman was the daughter Dunya.

The twist of the young daughter returning not lost and ruined but happy and in good spirits creates the dramatic irony in these events. On one level, the story is thus an attack on the sentimental tales of the day about the young daughter gone to ruin. Once again, Pushkin elevated a story begun in parody to a masterpiece--many critics consider it the finest in the collection. The foolishness of the stationmaster in drinking himself to death for his lost daughter becomes the object lesson of the events as it completely reverses the story of the Prodigal Son.

"THE SQUIRE'S DAUGHTER"

The last story in the collection, "Barishnya krestyanka" ("The Squire's Daughter"), is a lighthearted and delightful tale, related to Belkin by "Miss K. I. T.," the same source of "The Blizzard." As in "The Blizzard," events revolve around a case of mistaken identity. Two landowners are at odds; one has a seventeen-year-old daughter, Liza, and the other a young son, Alexey, home from the university, where he has picked up the Byronic posturing so common to the age. Here, Pushkin gently satirizes that behavior, in contrast to his probing of it in "The Shot." Liza seeks to meet the young man, and learning that he likes peasant girls, she dresses up one morning as such a girl and goes to a forest through which she knows he will be passing. He sees her, is attracted by her, and they begin to meet regularly at the same place in the forest, she continuing with her disguise. Meanwhile, the two landowners reconcile their differences, and Alexey's father demands that he marry the other landowner's daughter. Alexey refuses because of his love for the "peasant" girl, but at the crucial moment Liza's true identity as the landowner's daughter is revealed, and all ends happily in light comedy.

THE QUEEN OF SPADES

The Queen of Spades, written after *The Tales of Belkin* was published, remains one of the most widely known stories in the history of short fiction. In this complex story, Pushkin uses an omniscient point of view, moving from one character to another as the

situation demands; the narrative is divided into six sections and a conclusion. The story opens after an all-night game of cards with a young officer named Hermann, a Russified German, who learns that the grandmother of a fellow officer, an old countess, supposedly has special knowledge of the three cards that will appear in faro--a gambling game in which only someone with supernatural powers can predict the cards and their sequence before they appear. Hermann himself cannot play cards; he can only watch, for his financial circumstances would not allow him to lose. At heart, however, he is a gambler who feverishly longs to play, and the countess's supernatural ability fires his imagination. He begins to hang around the street where the countess lives, his imagination dwelling on her secret. One night after a compelling dream about winning at cards, he wakes and wanders the streets until he finds himself mysteriously before the house of the old countess. He sees in the window the face of a fresh, young woman, Lizaveta, and that moment seals his fate. She is the ward of the countess, and she is receptive to Hermann's advances. He uses her to gain entrance one night to the countess's bedchamber, where he surprises the countess as she is going to bed. He pleads with the countess to tell him the secret, but she insists that the story is only a joke, that there is no secret. Hermann becomes agitated, convinced that she is lying, and when she refuses to talk to him, he draws a pistol to scare her into answering. This threat is too much for her, and she suddenly collapses in death.

Hermann confesses the situation to Lizaveta, and they conceal the real events of the countess's death. At the funeral, Hermann hallucinates that the old countess is winking at him from the coffin. That night, her corpse, or "ghost," visits him, and, in exchange for the promise that he will marry Lizaveta, tells him the winning sequence: three, seven, ace. The device of the returning corpse, or ghost, has been popular in literature from William Shakespeare's *Hamlet* (pr. c. 1600-1601, pb. 1603) to Charles Dickens's *A Christmas Carol* (1843), and, as in both of those works, the returning ghost indicates an unnatural situation and a disturbed personality. In this Pushkin story, the reader is to assume that the ghost is not "real" but rather an indication of Hermann's disturbed mind. It is this aspect of the tale that was to influence the psychological analysis of character that became the hallmark of the great Russian novels, especially Dostoevski's *Prestupleniye i nakazaniye* (1866; *Crime and Punishment*, 1886). The three cards are perpetually in Hermann's mind and on his lips, and one night he takes all the money he has in the world to a famous gambling house, where he bets on the three. He wins and returns the following night to stake everything on the seven; again he wins, and the third night he returns to bet on the ace. A large crowd gathers, having heard of his previous success. This night, however, instead of the ace appearing, the queen of spades is the chosen card, and Hermann sees the face of the old countess in the figure on the card, smiling up at him. The short paragraph of the conclusion relates that Hermann is now at a mental hospital, where he simply repeats, over and over, "Three, seven, queen! Three, seven, queen!" Lizaveta, however, has married a very pleasant young man and is happy.

In the opera by Peter Ilich Tchaikovsky, based on this story, the events differ somewhat. In the opera, Hermann and Lizaveta become lovers, and when he leaves her to gamble, she throws herself into the river; after the appearance of the queen, Hermann stabs himself. During the remainder of his life, Pushkin was never to equal the dramatic intensity of this story. It remains a classic, one of those tales that helped shape the direction of modern short fiction.

OTHER MAJOR WORKS

LONG FICTION: *Evgeny Onegin*, 1825-1832, 1833 (*Eugene Onegin*, 1881); *Arap Petra velikogo*, 1828-1841 (*Peter the Great's Negro*, 1896); *Kirdzhali*, 1834 (English translation, 1896); *Kapitanskaya dochka*, 1836 (*The Captain's Daughter*, 1846); *Dubrovsky*, 1841 (English translation, 1892); *Yegipetskiye nochi*, 1841 (*Egyptian Nights*, 1896); *Istoriya sela Goryukhina*, 1857 (*History of the Village of Goryukhino*, 1966).

PLAYS: *Boris Godunov*, wr.1824-1825, pb. 1831, pr. 1870 (English translation, 1918); *Kamyenny gost*, wr.1830, pb. 1839, pr. 1847 (*The Stone Guest*, 1936); *Skupoy rytsar*, wr.1830, pr., pb. 1852 (*The Covetous Knight*, 1925); *Motsart i Salyeri*, pr., pb. 1832 (*Mozart and Salieri*, 1920); *Pir vo vryemya chumy*, pb. 1833, pr.

1899 (*The Feast in Time of the Plague*, 1925); *Stseny iz rytsarskikh vryemen*, wr.1835, pr., pb. 1937; *Rusalka*, pb. 1837, pr. 1838 (*The Water Nymph*, 1924); *Little Tragedies*, pb. 1946 (includes *The Covetous Knight*, *The Stone Guest*, *Mozart and Salieri*, and *The Feast in Time of the Plague*).

POETRY: *Ruslan i Lyudmila*, 1820 (*Ruslan and Liudmila*, 1936); *Gavriiliada*, 1822 (*Gabriel: A Poem*, 1926); *Kavkazskiy plennik*, 1822 (*The Prisoner of the Caucasus*, 1895); *Bratya razboyniki*, 1824; *Bakhchisaraiskiy fontan*, 1827 (*The Fountain of Bakhchisarai*, 1849); *Graf Nulin*, 1827 (*Count Nulin*, 1972); *Tsygany*, 1827 (*The Gypsies*, 1957); *Poltava*, 1829 (English translation, 1936); *Domik v Kolomne*, 1833 (*The Little House at Kolomna*, 1977); *Skazka o mertvoy tsarevne*, 1833 (*The Tale of the Dead Princess*, 1924); *Skazka o rybake ir rybke*, 1833 (*The Tale of the Fisherman and the Fish*, 1926); *Skazka o tsare Saltane*, 1833 (*The Tale of Tsar Saltan*, 1950); *Skazka o zolotom petushke*, 1834 (*The Tale of the Golden Cockerel*, 1918); *Medniy vsadnik*, 1837 (*The Bronze Horseman*, 1899); *Collected Narrative and Lyrical Poetry*, 1984; *Epigrams and Satirical Verse*, 1984.

NONFICTION: *Istoriya Pugacheva*, 1834 (*The Pugachev Rebellion*, 1966); *Puteshestviye v Arzrum*, 1836 (*A Journey to Arzrum*, 1974); *Dnevnik, 1833-1835*, 1923; *Pisma*, 1926-1935 (3 volumes); *The Letters of Alexander Pushkin*, 1963 (3 volumes); *Pisma poslednikh let 1834-1837*, 1969.

MISCELLANEOUS: *The Captain's Daughter, and Other Tales*, 1933; *The Poems, Prose, and Plays of Pushkin*, 1936; *The Works of Alexander Pushkin*, 1936; *Polnoye sobraniye sochineniy*, 1937-1959 (17 volumes); *The Complete Prose Tales of Alexander Pushkin*, 1966; *A. S. Pushkin bez tsenzury*, 1972; *Pushkin Threefold*, 1972; *Polnoye sobraniye sochineniy*, 1977-1979 (10 volumes); *Alexander Pushkin: Complete Prose Fiction*, 1983.

BIBLIOGRAPHY

Bayley, John. *Pushkin: A Comparative Commentary.* Cambridge, England: Cambridge University Press, 1971. Offers erudite commentaries on Pushkin's works. Chapter 7 deals with his prose and its relationship to his entire canon.

Bethea, David, and Sergei Davidov. "Pushkin's Saturnine Cupid: The Poetics of Parody of *The Tales of Belkin*." *Publication of Modern Language Association of America* 96 (1971): 748-761. This article is basically an answer to the essay by Richard Gregg (below). The authors emphasize, among other things, the parody of *The Tales of Belkin* as their most pronounced facet.

Binyon, T. J. *Pushkin: A Biography*. New York: Alfred A. Knopf, 2003. Binyon, a lecturer at Oxford University, focuses on the events of Pushkin's life, detailing the sometimes dissolute behavior and bad judgment that resulted in personal failures alongside his literary successes.

Debreczeny, Paul. *The Other Pushkin: A Study of Alexander Pushkin's Prose Fiction*. Berkeley: University of California Press, 1983. Debreczeny discusses all Pushkin's prose works, drawing upon the extensive scholarship on the subject. Pushkin's stories are discussed at length.

_____. *Social Functions of Literature: Alexander Pushkin and Russian Culture*. Stanford, Calif.: Stanford Univ. Press, 1997. Debreczeny divides his study into three parts: the first is devoted to selected readers' responses to Pushkin; the second explores the extent to which individual aesthetic responses are conditioned by their environment; and the third concerns the mythic aura that developed around Pushkin's public persona.

Emerson, Caryl. "'The Queen of Spades' and the Open End." In *Pushkin Today*, edited by David M. Bethea. Bloomington: Indiana University Press, 1993. Summarizes briefly the socioliterary, psychoanalytical, linguistic, and numerological studies of the story, and argues that what is parodied in the story is the reader's search for a system or a key. Contends that Pushkin teases his readers with fragments of codes, partial keys that do not add up.

Feinstein, Elaine. *Pushkin: A Biography*. Hopewell, N.J.: Ecco Press, 1999. An excellent, updated biography of Pushkin.

Gregg, Richard. "Pushkin's Novelistic Prose: A Dead End?" *Slavic Review* 57 (Spring, 1998): 1-27. Argues that Pushkin systematized, perfected, and pushed to its furthest limit a kind of prose that had never been practiced before with such consistency, elegance, and taste. Contends that in terms of the novel, however, which was the preeminent fictional genre by the 1840's, prose of this kind was not possible.

_____. "A Scapegoat for All Seasons: The Unity and the Shape of *The Tales of Belkin*." *Slavic Review* 30 (1971): 748-761. Gregg discusses *The Tales of Belkin* as a unified cycle within Pushkin's total output.

Kahn, Andrew, ed. *The Cambridge Companion to Pushkin*. New York: Cambridge University Press, 2006. Collection of essays providing information about Pushkin's life and works, including a discussion of his prose fiction that includes an examination of The Queen of Spadesand some of the other short fiction.

Kim, Sang Hyun. *Aleksandr Pushkin's "The Tales of Belkin": Formalist and Structuralist Readings and Beyond the Literary Theories*. Lanham, Md.: University Press of America, 2008. Focuses on Pushkin's artistic intention in this short-story collection, discussing the autobiographical, folklorist, and thematic elements of the work. Using formalist and structuralist literary theories, Kim demonstrates how the tales in the collection are structurally and thematically interrelated.

Kropf, David. *Authorship as Alchemy: Subversive Writing in Pushkin, Scott, Hoffmann*. Stanford, Calif.: Stanford University Press, 1994. A discussion of the social institution of authorship. Focuses on Pushkin's creation of an invented persona, Belkin; addresses Pushkin's author as a textual or semiotic entity. Discusses the story "The History of the Village of Foriukhino."

Lezhnev, Abram. *Pushkin's Prose*. Ann Arbor, Mich.: Ardis, 1974. In one of the rare examples of Russian scholarship translated into English, Lezhnev presents views of a native scholar on Pushkin's prose as perceived in the thought and criticism of Pushkin's contemporaries.

O'Toole, Michael L. "'The Post-Stage Master.'" "'The Pistol Shot.'" In *Structure, Style, and Interpretation in the Russian Short Story*. New Haven, Conn.: Yale University Press, 1982. A structuralist discussion of "The Post-Stage Master" in terms of a fable (fabula), and of "The Pistol Shot" in terms of plot. O'Toole bases his approach on the analytical model of Russian Formalists and on their belief that serious discussion of literature must start with the "text" itself. The result is a lively analysis of the two stories.

Rosenshield, Gary. *Pushkin and the Genres of Madness: The Masterpieces of 1833*. Madison: University of Wisconsin Press, 2003. Examines how Puskhin explores the theme of madness, including the destructive and creative aspects of insanity, in *The Queen of Spades* and two other works written around the same time. Rosenshield argues that Hermann's vulgar imagination devalorizes madness, and that in taking the queen of spades instead of the ace, Hermann chooses the right card, for it constitutes for him a victory of the imagination and thus of life over death.

Terras, Victor. "Pushkin's Prose Fiction in an Historical Context." In *Pushkin Today*, edited by David M. Bethea. Bloomington: Indiana University Press, 1993. Discusses Pushkin's importance in the ascendancy of prose fiction in Russia in the nineteenth century. Comments on the basic characteristics of Pushkin's prose style.

_____. "The Russian Short Story, 1830-1850." In *The Russian Short Story: A Critical History*, edited by Charles A. Moser. Boston: Twayne, 1986. Contends that Pushkin's tales are parodies of early nineteenth century prose fiction. Argues that parodic deconstruction, like that in Pushkin's tales, was a common feature of the Romantic tale.

Troyat, Henry. *Pushkin*. New York: Pantheon Books, 1950. This standard biography of Pushkin by the French author Troyat reads like a novel. Literary works are mentioned without extended discussion. Unfortunately, the critical discussion, as well as the extensive bibliography, have been omitted from the original.

Ronald L. Johnson
Updated by Vasa D. Mihailovich

Q

Horacio Quiroga

Born: El Salto, Uruguay; December 31, 1878
Died: Buenos Aires, Argentina; February 19, 1937

Los arrecifes de coral, 1901
El crimen del otro, 1904
Cuentos de amor, de locura y de muerte, 1917
Cuentos de la selva para los niños, 1918 (*South American Jungle Tales,* 1923)
El salvaje, 1920
Anaconda, 1921
El desierto, 1924
La gallina degollada, 1925 (*The Decapitated Chicken, and Other Stories,* 1976)
Los desterrados, 1926 (*The Exiles, and Other Stories,* 1987)
Más allá, 1935

Other literary forms

Though famous to readers of Spanish American literature exclusively for his short fiction, Horacio Quiroga (aw-RATH-you kee-ROH-gah) wrote, to a limited degree and with equally limited success, in other forms. He published two novels, *Historia de un amor turbio* (1908; story of a turbulent love) and *Pasado amor* (1929; past love), as well as one theatrical work. He included poems in his first book, *Los arrecifes de coral* (coral reefs), a work written in the fin de siècle tradition of Spanish American modernism and completely anti-Quiroga in both style and content. He also wrote literary criticism and theory. His most famous (at least among experts in Spanish American fiction) foray into this particular area was a handful of articles that he wrote for the magazine *El Hogar* (the hearth), in which he discussed the theory and practice of writing short stories.

Achievements

Horacio Quiroga holds much the same position in Spanish American literature as does Edgar Allan Poe in North American letters. Like Poe, whom Quiroga admired and who influenced the Uruguayan writer's work significantly, Quiroga dedicated his literary efforts almost entirely to the short-story genre, and in the process he not only penned some of the most famous and most anthologized stories to be found in Spanish-American literature but also wrote about the genre, even offering a decalogue of suggestions to other writers on how they should approach writing the short story. These suggestions appeared in his essay "Manual del perfecto cuentista" (manual for the perfect short-story writer), published in *El Hogar* on April 10, 1925.

Quiroga is without a doubt one of the most highly regarded and most widely read short-story writers in the history of Spanish American literature and is considered by most to be the foremost Spanish American short-story writer prior to the arrival of Jorge Luis Borges, Julio Cortázar, and other writers of the so-called new narrative on the Spanish American literary scene. While critical interest in Quiroga diminished during the Borges and post-Borges eras, the Uruguayan writer's popularity among readers did not--all of which, perhaps, is just as well, for Quiroga's stories, with rare exception the highly polished gems of a consummate short-story writer, lend themselves far more to reader enjoyment than to literary criticism.

Biography

Two elements play significant roles in Horacio Quiroga's life and also frequently find their way into some of the writer's most famous stories. These two elements are tragic violence and the Uruguayan author's fascination with the jungle-filled Misiones region of northern Argentina. The first of these elements, tragic violence, punctuates Quiroga's life--so much so, in fact, that were his biography offered as fiction, it would almost certainly be roundly criticized for being unbelievable, for no one's life in the "real world" could be so tragically violent, especially when a good portion of this violence comes through accident. The author's fascination with the harsh jungles of Misiones cost him at least one wife and possibly a second, while this unforgiving environment provided him at the same time with the setting and thematic point of departure for many of his most famous stories.

Horacio Silvestre Quiroga y Forteza was born on December 31, 1878, in El Salto, Uruguay, the youngest of four children born to Prudencio Quiroga and Pastora Forteza. Three months after Horacio's birth, don Prudencio was killed when his hunting rifle went off accidentally as he was stepping from a boat. Quiroga's mother, doña Pastora, ashore with infant son Horacio in her arms, witnessed the tragic event and fainted, dropping her son to the ground. Later the same year, doña Pastora moved the family to the Argentine city of Córdoba. She remarried in 1891, taking Ascencio Barcos as her second husband, and the family moved to Montevideo, Uruguay. On a September afternoon in 1896, don Ascencio, having suffered a cerebral hemorrhage earlier, took his own life with a shotgun. Seventeen-year-old Horacio was the first to arrive on the scene.

Personal tragedy followed Quiroga in 1901 with the death of both his brother Prudencio and his sister Pastora. Then in 1902, the budding writer, who had published his first book, *Los arrecifes de coral*, the previous year, accidentally shot and killed one of his closest friends and literary companions, Federico Ferrando. After teaching off and on for several years in Buenos Aires, in September, 1909, Quiroga married Ana María Cirés and moved with her to San Ignacio, in the Misiones section of Argentina. Quiroga had first visited this jungle hinterland in 1903 with friend and Argentine writer Leopoldo Lugones. Enamored of the region, he bought land there in 1906 and divided his time between Misiones and Buenos Aires for the rest of his life. In 1915, unable to cope with the hardships of living in the jungle, Ana María poisoned herself, leaving Quiroga a widower with the couple's two children. The following year, the writer returned to Buenos

Aires, and over the next ten years he saw the publication of his most famous collections of stories, *Cuentos de amor, de locura y de muerte* (stories of love, madness, and death), *South American Jungle Tales, Anaconda*, and *The Exiles, and Other Stories*, all the while moving periodically between the backlands and the Argentine capital. He remarried in 1927, when he was forty-nine years old, taking a nineteen-year-old friend of his daughter as his second wife. Quiroga and his new wife moved to Misiones in 1931, but she returned to Buenos Aires with their infant daughter the following year. Quiroga's health deteriorated significantly in 1934. He returned to Buenos Aires in 1936, where he was diagnosed with cancer the following year. He took a lethal dose of cyanide to end his life in February, 1937.

ANALYSIS

Horacio Quiroga published approximately two hundred short stories, many of which are considered classics within the Spanish American literary canon. Most of the author's stories, classics or not, fall within one or more of the following three general categories: Poesque stories of horror, often punctuated by madness and/or genetic defect; stories of human beings against a savage and thoroughly unromanticized nature; and Kiplingesque animal stories that frequently contain an underlying moral message. The vast majority of Quiroga's stories are dramatic, intense, even memorable tales that captivate the reader and in general reveal a true master of the genre at work.

Some of Quiroga's most popular stories come from the first of the three categories listed above, that of Poesque stories of horror, often featuring madness and/ or genetic defect. Two widely read and exemplary stories from this category are "El almohadón de plumas" ("The Feather Pillow"), first published in 1907, and "La gallina degollada" ("The Decapitated Chicken"), first published in 1909.

"THE FEATHER PILLOW"

"The Feather Pillow" is the more purely Poesque of these two stories. In it, a newlywed woman falls mysteriously ill and quickly progresses toward death. Her husband and doctor are at a complete loss as to what ails her and what to do to help her. Finally, she dies.

Shortly thereafter, a servant finds what appears to be two small punctures in her feather pillow. Further examination reveals that the pillow is inordinately heavy. The husband cuts the pillow open and in it finds a swollen creature (later identified as a bird parasite), which had been sucking the blood out of its victim for some time, literally draining the life out of her.

This story is both classic Poe and classic Quiroga. It is classic Poe in large part because of the horrific nature of its content. It is classic Quiroga for numerous elements, almost all of which have to do with the manner in which the writer presents the content. The story runs only three to five pages (depending on the print of the edition), yet in this short span the narrator takes the reader from an introduction of the characters to the conflict itself to the horrifying ending. As in most of Quiroga's stories, not a single word is wasted, as each contributes not only to the tale being told but also to the overall effect of the story. This story is also a classic Quiroga story because of the inclusion of a seemingly insignificant detail, which at the time it is mentioned is almost overlooked by the reader (the narrator mentions rather offhandedly after several paragraphs about the couple's relationship that the woman had taken ill); the dramatic and surprise ending (featuring the blood-laden anthropoid); and the foreshadowing of this ending (the narrator states that the woman had seen an "anthropoid" staring at her from the carpet, but the reader is told that this is a hallucination), even though the first-time reader is not aware that this is indeed foreshadowing at the time that he or she encounters it. Also typical of Quiroga in this story is the writer's ability to turn a tale that deals with specific characters and apply its situation to the world of the reader. Quiroga accomplishes this in "The Feather Pillow" by adding a paragraph after the action of the story has ended in which the narrator states, matter-of-factly, that such creatures, bird parasites, are frequently found in feather pillows. In this way, the narrator makes the previously distanced and protected reader a potential victim of the same fate as the woman in the story. As a result, certainly more than a few readers of "The Feather Pillow" have checked their own pillows before sleeping on the night they read this story, an effect on the reader that would please both Quiroga and his chief influence for this story, Poe, to no small degree.

"THE DECAPITATED CHICKEN"

"The Decapitated Chicken" is less purely Poesque and more in the naturalist tradition, but it is no less horrifying in content. The story opens with a couple's four "idiot" (the word used by Quiroga) sons seated on a bench on a patio, their tongues sticking out, their eyes staring off into space. The narrator recounts how, with the birth of each son, the couple had hoped for a "normal" child and how each had blamed the other for the defective genes (a naturalist element) that produced the "idiot" sons. Finally, the couple's fifth child, a daughter, is "normal." She receives all the couple's attention, while the sons are relegated to the less than loving care of a servant. One day, the four sons wander into the kitchen as the servant is cutting off the head of a chicken to prepare it for lunch. Later, by accident, both the sons and the daughter are left unattended. The daughter attempts to climb the garden wall on the patio, where her "idiot" brothers sit, her neck resting on the top as she works to pull herself up the wall. Captivated by the sight, the four sons grab the daughter, drag her into the kitchen, and behead her just as the servant had beheaded the chicken.

This story features several classic Quiroga traits that are also on display in "The Feather Pillow." Chief among them are the early and rather offhand mention of something that will be of tantamount importance later in the story (the decapitation of the chicken) and the presence of subtle foreshadowing (the narrator mentions that though believed incapable of true learning, the four sons do possess at least a limited ability to imitate things that they see--again the decapitation of the chicken), though once again this foreshadowing is almost certainly missed by the first-time reader. This story also demonstrates Quiroga's penchant for surprise and horrifying endings, endings that place Quiroga among the best writers of this type of tale.

MAN VERSUS NATURE

Some of the most famous stories from the second of the aforementioned categories--that concerning man against savage and thoroughly unromanticized nature--share many of the characteristics found in the stories referred to above: dramatic and detailed narration, the inclusion of an often seemingly insignificant detail or event that will eventually cause a character's demise, subtle though undeniably present foreshadowing, death and/or surprise in the end, and no small amount of irony, particularly as it pertains to fate (an element that, though present in "The Decapitated Chicken," is even more prominent in stories in this category). If Quiroga's stories, particularly those of this second category, are any indication of his philosophy, then he saw human beings as anything but the masters of their own destiny, particularly in the harsh and unforgiving environment of the author's beloved Misiones, where even the most careful person (and particularly the least careful) was at the mercy of the jungle. The slightest misstep or false move could spell disaster, and, in fact, it almost always did, if not in real life then at least in Quiroga's stories. In this environment, Quiroga's stories demonstrate, there is little or no room for error, and accidents befall even the most diligent of individuals. This is fairly vividly illustrated in some of the author's most famous stories, such as "A la deriva" ("Drifting"), "La miel silvestre" (wild honey), "El hombre muerto" ("The Dead Man"), and "El hijo" ("The Son").

"DRIFTING"

The first of these stories, "Drifting," tells of a man who, by accident (and in the very first sentence of the story), steps on a snake and is bitten. A few pages later, after considerable (and detailed) effort to make his way by canoe downriver for help, he is dead. Near the end of the story, briefly, it seems as though the protagonist's condition is improving, but his apparent improvement is but the illusion of a dying man, for a few sentences later he dies, another victim of the unforgiving environment in which he has lived. The protagonist of "La miel silvestre" (wild honey), an accountant, sets out to conquer the jungle, a world totally foreign to him. At one point, he stops to sample some wild honey. Within seconds, he is paralyzed, a result of the particular type of honey that he has eaten. Almost immediately thereafter, an army of carnivorous ants (skillfully foreshadowed by Quiroga earlier in the story) begins making its way toward him. His skeleton is found a few days later. The protagonist of "The Dead Man" is nearing the end of his work for the morning, clearing his banana grove with his machete and self-satisfied in his work, when suddenly, and quite by accident, he falls. He falls well,

he believes, except, he soon discovers, for one significant detail: He has fallen on his machete. For the rest of the story, he watches as the rest of the world, from which he is suddenly and unexpectedly separated, goes on as usual around him, as he, helpless and unable to seek help, slowly dies, ironically, within sight of the roof of his own house.

"THE SON"

In "The Son," a father sees his son off as the latter heads into the jungle to hunt alone. While he is gone, the father thinks of his son and even imagines what he is doing at every moment. The reader is told that the father suffers from hallucinations (an important piece of information later in the story) and has often even envisioned the violent death of his son. When the father hears two shots in the distance, he believes that his son has killed two doves. Later, when his son does not return home on time, he sets off looking for him. While searching, the father imagines finding his son dead. The narrator suggests, however, that the father has found the son safe and sound. A final paragraph, though, separated from the rest of the text, reveals that this has been a hallucination and that the son, in fact, has died, much as his father had earlier envisioned, accidentally, by his own hand, his dead body entangled in a wire fence.

While Quiroga's stories of horror seem to be intended principally for the entertainment of the reader, these stories of human beings versus the jungle unmistakably communicate the dual themes that human beings are indeed no match for nature and that life, ironically, can be whisked away not only suddenly but also by the slightest of accidents. This latter aspect of the writer's thematic intent is nowhere more apparent than in "The Dead Man," in which one moment the protagonist is working happily on his land and the next he lies dying, his life suddenly coming to an end, with neither pomp nor circumstance, as a result of a simple fall.

ANIMAL STORIES

The third and final category in which one may easily classify Quiroga's stories--that of Kiplingesque animal stories that frequently contain an underlying moral message--features, from a technical standpoint, probably some of the weakest of the Uruguayan author's most famous stories. These stories are generally far less tightly structured, narratively less compact than those found in the first two categories, and in part, as a result, do not possess the dramatic intensity present in the other stories. Even the narrative voice is frequently different from that found in most of Quiroga's other stories. While "The Feather Pillow," for example, or "The Dead Man" features a distanced, omniscient narrator, these stories often read more like fairy tales, with the narrator's voice more like that of an old storyteller. Their technical differences from Quiroga's other stories aside, however, many, and in fact some of the author's most widely read works, fit into this category and display, even more so than his other stories, the vivid imagination of their author.

ANACONDA AND "JUAN DARIÉN"

Two of the most famous stories from this category are *Anaconda*, the story (almost novella in length) of a group of snakes that band together in an attempt to kill the team of scientists who have invaded their territory and whose work to develop an antivenom serum threatens the snakes' very existence; and "Juan Darién," the story of a tiger cub that, through love, turns into a boy, a human, only to turn into a tiger once again and return to the animal world when he is rejected by humans for being different. The first of these two stories, *Anaconda*, is interesting, if nothing else, for its imaginative description of the snake world, complete with interspecies prejudice and a congress for debating issues of concern to the group. The second story, "Juan Darién," with its Christ-figure protagonist, sends an obvious moral message concerning human intolerance and cruelty and with its magical reality in some ways serves as a precursor for the works of "new narrativists" such as Borges and Cortázar.

Quiroga is one of the most widely acclaimed and most popular short-story writers in the history of Spanish American literature. He is known, for the most part, for intense, even dramatic narration, the offhand inclusion of a pivotal detail or event, skillful foreshadowing, and surprising and frequently horrific endings. If Quiroga has one significant defect, it may be that his stories are a bit too predictable. A veteran reader of Quiroga can often identify the seemingly insignificant detail and the foreshadowing and immediately thereafter discern exactly where the story is going. This

potential flaw, however, is hardly a defect at all since even if one can predict the story's direction, even its outcome, the story is still entertaining and interesting, because of how Quiroga gets the reader to the outcome. In other words, much like an old joke for which one already knows the punch line but which one never tires of hearing, Quiroga's stories, even his most predictable ones, are true pleasures to read. While literary fashion, particularly among critics, may come and go, Quiroga's stories, given both their content and their skillful presentation, will always, it seems, have a wide audience. They are, after all, plainly and simply, good stories, and as such they will probably never lose their appeal to readers.

OTHER MAJOR WORKS

LONG FICTION: *Historia de un amor turbio*, 1908; *Pasado amor*, 1929.

BIBLIOGRAPHY

Borge, Jason. "Hollywood Revisions: Cinematic Imaginary in Quiroga and Monteiro Lobato." *Journal of Latin American Cultural Studies* 10, no. 3 (December, 2001): 311-323. Examines Quiroga's writings about American cinema, focusing on his short story, "Miss Dorothy Phillips, Mi Esposa." Borge argues that in this story about an Argentine bureaucrat determined to marry a Hollywood film star, Quiroga uses the American film industry as a theme while simultaneously imitating cinematic form.

Brushwood, John S. "The Spanish American Short Story from Quiroga to Borges." In *The Latin American Short Story: A Critical History*, edited by Margaret Sayers Peden. Boston: Twayne, 1983. Brushwood dedicates most of the first four pages of this twenty-six-page chapter to Quiroga. He comments on Quiroga's place in the Spanish American short story, discusses Quiroga's decalogue for the perfect short-story writer, and considers various aspects of the stories "The Decapitated Chicken," "Juan Darién," and "The Dead Man." Contains interesting although brief commentary.

Englekirk, John. "Horacio Quiroga." In *Edgar Allan Poe in Hispanic Literature*. New York: Instituto de las Españas, 1934. In a lengthy study of Poe's influence on numerous Spanish and Spanish American writers, Englekirk devotes his longest chapter (twenty-nine pages) to the work of Quiroga. He discusses Poe's influence in some of the most obviously Poesque stories in Quiroga's repertoire but finds elements of Poe in many other works not usually considered to be influenced by the American writer. An interesting read.

French, Jennifer. "The Freedom in the Field: Empire and Ecology in the Misiones Stories of Horacio Quiroga." In *Nature, Neo-Colonialism, and the Spanish American Regional Writers*. Hanover, N.H.: Dartmouth College Press, 2005. Analyzes the short fiction of Quiroga and works by two other Spanish American writers to describe how the writers' fiction reflects the economic supremacy of Great Britain in the Misiones region from the early national period to World War I.

Gunnels, Bridgette W. "Blurring Boundaries Between Animal and Human: Animalhuman Rights in 'Juan Darién' by Horacio Quiroga." *Romance Notes* 46, no. 3 (Spring, 2006): 349-358. Explores the relationship between humans and animals in this short story.

_____. "An Ecocritical Approach to Horacio Quiroga's *Anaconda* and 'Regreso de Anaconda.'" *Mosaic: A Journal for the Interdisciplinary Study of Literature* 39, no. 4 (December, 2006): 93-110. An ecocritical analysis of these two snake stories. Gunnels argues that Quiroga's life in theMisiones region of Argentina made him conscious of ecological issues, including the Western belief that the superiority of human beings justifies the destruction of the environment. Gunnels demonstrates how Quiroga's stories contradict this belief by "decentralizing" human experience while simultaneously "humanizing" nonhuman experience.

Peden, William. "Some Notes on Quiroga's Stories." *Review* 19 (Winter, 1976): 41-43. Peden reviews the chief characteristics of Quiroga's stories and briefly refers to a number of stories that contain these characteristics. Succinct and on target, though perhaps equally if not more useful for its presentation in English translation of Quiroga's decalogue of the "Perfect Short Story Writer." Published as part of a twenty-page "Focus" section on Quiroga.

Pupo-Walker, Enrique. "The Brief Narrative in Spanish America: 1835-1915." In *The Cambridge History of Latin American Literature*. Vol. 1, edited by Robert González Echevarria and Enrique Pupo-Walker. Cambridge, England: Cambridge University Press, 1996. Provides a valuable historical and cultural context for Quiroga by charting the development of short narrative in Spanish America in the nineteenth century, from the early sketches of customs and manners and the influence of Edgar Allan Poe through the early part of the twentieth century.

Rivera-Barnes, Beatriz. "Yuyos Are Not Weeds: An Ecocritical Approach to Horacio Quiroga." In *Reading and Writing the Latin American Landscape*, by Rivera-Barnes and Jerry Hoeg. New York: Palgrave Macmillan, 2009. Examines Quiroga's relationship to the jungle, the area in which he lived and the site of many of his stories.

San Roman, Gustavo. "Amor Turbio, Paranoia, and the Vicissitudes of Manliness in Horacio Quiroga." *The Modern Language Review* 90 (October, 1995): 919-934. Discusses the theme of love in Quiroga's fiction, focusing on the novel *Historia de un amor turbio*, commenting on the links between the story and paranoia. Argues that Quiroga's texts are more the work of a victim than of a self-controlled author.

Schade, George D. "Horacio Quiroga." In *Latin American Literature in the Twentieth Century: A Guide*, edited by Leonard S. Klein. New York: Ungar, 1986. Largely a three-page version of Schade's introduction to Margaret Sayers Peden's *The Decapitated Chicken, and Other Stories* (below). Provides concise discussion of Quiroga's life, career, and chief characteristics and limited consideration of specific stories. Includes a list of Quiroga's works and a brief bibliography (with most of the entries in Spanish).

_____. Introduction to *The Decapitated Chicken, and Other Stories*. Edited and translated by Margaret Sayers Peden. Austin: University of Texas Press, 1976. In this ten-page introduction to Peden's English-language collection of twelve of Quiroga's most famous stories, Schade provides an overview to Quiroga for the uninitiated reader, discussing the writer's life and career, as well as the chief characteristics of his works. In the process, he comments briefly on the stories included in the collection, among them "The Feather Pillow," "The Decapitated Chicken," "Drifting," "Juan Darién," "The Dead Man," *Anaconda*, and "The Son."

Keith H. Brower

R

Valentin Rasputin

Born: Ust'-Uda, Siberia, Soviet Union (now in Russia); March 15, 1937

OTHER LITERARY FORMS

Valentin Rasputin (VAHL-ehn-TEEN reh-SPUHT-yihn) has written sparingly outside the short-fiction genre, but he has published a collection of essays and two nonfiction books, including one about Siberia. Some of his stories belong to what in Russian literature is called *povest'*, and there is a legitimate question whether they are long stories or short novels. They are considered abroad to be both. Because of Rasputin's strong allegiance to short fiction, they are treated here as short stories.

ACHIEVEMENTS

Valentin Rasputin belongs to the generation of Soviet writers that appeared in the mid-1960's, after Soviet literature had awakened from the nightmare of Socialist Realism. Along with Vasilit Belov, Fyodor Abramov, and others, Rasputin has written almost exclusively about village life. He has raised the village prose to a higher artistic level. He is also one of few to write about Siberia. Above all, his ability to present seemingly mundane events in a high artistic fashion and to create fine characters has made him a prominent writer in contemporary Russian literature. Rasputin has been received many honors from the former Soviet Union and Russia, including the State Prize for Literature, the Order of Lenin in 1984, and the Solzhenitsyn Prize in 2000.

BIOGRAPHY

Valentin Rasputin was born on March 15, 1937, in central Siberia, in Ust'-Uda, a small village on the Angara River, halfway between Irkutsk and Bratsk. His parents were peasants. During much of his childhood, most of which fell during and shortly after World War II, his father was away at war. After finishing elementary and high school, Rasputin enrolled at Irkutsk University to be a teacher. Before he was graduated in 1959, he started working as a journalist for the local newspaper and continued to work in that capacity after moving to Krasnoyarsk.

Rasputin published his first story, "Ia zabyl sprosit' u Lioshki" ("I Forgot to Ask Lyoshka"), in 1961, and his first novella, *Krai vozle samogo neba* (the land next to the very sky), in 1966. Between those two years, he traveled as a newspaper correspondent, covering a wide area and meeting many interesting people. These experiences served him well as sources for his stories. In 1968, he published *Money for Maria,* his second novella--a genre that would become his main mode of expression. The same year he was admitted to the Union of Soviet Writers, usually a sign that a writer "has arrived." Three more novellas followed in the next eight years--*Borrowed Time, Live and Remember*, and *Farewell to Matyora*--along with a number of short stories. In 1977, he received the State Prize for Literature in recognition of his contribution to Russian literature.

A serious accident in 1980 sidelined him for a while. He was mugged on a street in Irkutsk by four men demanding his jeans, and he underwent two operations in Moscow, having suffered a temporary loss of memory. After recuperation, he continued to publish but at a slower pace. An introspective story, "Chto peredat' vorone?" ("What Shall I Tell the Crow?"), along with several other stories and a book, *You Live and Love, and Other Stories*, were published in the early 1980's. A later novella, *Pozhar*, was published in 1985.

Rasputin is a private man, reluctant to speak about himself. For that reason, not much is known about his private life. The best sources for his biography are his stories, especially those about his childhood. He has resided in Irkutsk for much of his adult life, spending the summers in his dacha on Lake Baikal.

ANALYSIS

All Valentin Rasputin's stories take place in the area around Irkutsk and Lake Baikal in south-central Siberia. All of them are about village life or life in a small town. Most of his characters are peasants or people who have just moved into towns from villages. Almost all the events depicted are of post-World War II vintage, with sporadic flashbacks to the prewar period.

Rasputin's creativity can be divided into two distinct periods: the first phase, from the mid-1960's to the mid-1970's, and the second stage, beginning with the 1980's. The pause in his writing was caused by the serious injury to his head that he suffered in March, 1980. Apparently, the period of recuperation gave him time to take stock of his career up to that point; as a result, the stories that followed are somewhat different from those written before.

Rasputin's first stories show characteristics typical of a novice: unassuming subject matter; no stand on issues; somewhat two-dimensional characters, without

psychological probing; and a straightforward, realistic, almost journalistic style.

As his writing ability progressed, his stories gained in significance. In the first noteworthy story, "Vasilii i Vasilisa" ("Vasily and Vasilisa"), Rasputin is already more interested in the psychological makeup of his characters, while the depiction of village life is used primarily as a frame. Vasily and Vasilisa, husband and wife, at first pass for common villagers coping with daily life and beset with postwar woes and shortages. When Vasily takes another woman for a wife because Vasilisa has refused to live with him, she displays typical signs of jealousy and resentment, and she fights the intruder. However, when the new woman reveals to Vasilisa her own problems and heartaches, Vasilisa shows remarkable understanding and even willingness to help. Thus, a simple woman seemingly incapable of rising above the common meanness does exactly the opposite. She is the first of a number of remarkable women characters Rasputin has created.

"FRENCH LESSONS"

Another early story, "Uroki francuzskogo" ("French Lessons"), shows Rasputin's further progress as a writer. On the surface, it is a charming autobiographical story about Rasputin's difficult childhood and school days, when he had to play games for money to buy food and avert starvation. His young French teacher attempts to help him by inviting him to eat with her, but he refuses out of dignity. She then makes him play games with her for money and pretends to lose, losing her job in the process. Instead of a simple childhood story, "French Lessons" becomes a story of coming-of-age and of learning--in inconspicuous fashion--the value of human kindness.

MONEY FOR MARIA

Rasputin achieved great success with his novella *Money for Maria*. Not only does the plot reveal his growing preoccupation with social problems besetting the Russian peasants, but also his characters are fully credible human beings, not puppets. When Maria--another remarkable female character--faces a deficit in the shop that she manages and is forced either to repay a thousand rubles or to go to jail, the calamity gives her husband, Kuzma, a chance to show his true character. It also gives the villagers a chance to reveal what they are

Valentin Rasputin (Getty Images)

made of. Kuzma goes around the village asking for loans with varied success but eventually collects the money. What is important here is the characters' adherence to family life and the sense of solidarity among the villagers, which make up for the state's shortcomings or fate's cruel indifference. As one of the helpers says, "A person's got to have a conscience. We've got to help each other without thinking of ourselves. . . . Another time you'd do as much for me. A person's got to be decent to his neighbors if he wants to win their esteem." This statement, though potentially maudlin, rings true, coming from Rasputin's skillfully executed characters. Criticism of the state's allowing such sorry situations is muted because the characters regard the state as an unimportant agent, emphasizing their own interrelationships.

BORROWED TIME

Another novella, *Borrowed Time*, features another strong female character, Anna, in her last hours. Before she dies, she witnesses the meanness of her children, who have been summoned to her deathbed. Instead of comforting her, they argue about who has done more

for her, until Anna realizes that she and her children belong to different worlds and that her world is that of the past and will never return. Rasputin shows his growth as a writer by tackling some of the most difficult problems of Russian society--or of any society, for that matter. He bemoans the loss of family values and the disintegration of society's fabric, as illustrated by the conflict not only between the past (Anna) and the present (her children) but also among the children themselves. He also dwells on the different roles of men and women--a recurrent theme in his stories. Rasputin considers *Borrowed Time* to be his best story, out of which many others emanate. Undoubtedly, the changes in the social and moral life of his people have now become his prime concern.

Rasputin is also interested in his characters' reaction to various difficult situations. In *Live and Remember*, he makes the plight of his simple villagers universal, as a loving wife, Nastena, is compelled to hide her husband, who had deserted the army in the last days of war. When she becomes pregnant, she is faced with the dilemma of whether to reveal her husband's whereabouts or to admit publicly her infidelity to him; either way, she will suffer indignities. She drowns herself rather than face the grim reality. Rasputin posits here a host of moral questions, each one worthy of a Greek tragedy. Once again, he sidesteps criticism of society (after all, the husband's desertion had mitigating circumstances) for the sake of concentrating on fundamental human problems.

FAREWELL TO MATYORA

Farewell to Matyora turns to more mundane matters, although human concern is still the focus of Rasputin's attention. Matyora is a village, located on a river island; the village is slated for destruction in order for a dam to be built. Daria, the protagonist, leads a number of her villagers who are opposed to the destruction, without understanding the need and rationale for it. The conflict between the past and the future, played out in the present, becomes the focal point of the story. Rasputin seems to side with Daria in describing the callous burning of the village by outsiders before the flooding, symbolizing the intrusion of outside forces that do not understand the bond with nature that the villagers have enjoyed all their lives. At the end, Daria and her supporters are defeated; they stay behind until the last moment, and, because a thick fog descends upon the island, it is not clear whether they got out or drowned. This is Rasputin's favorite device--not providing the story with a clear ending, leaving it up to readers to draw their own conclusions. Another ambiguity lies in the fact that the end of Matyora signifies the end of the life that Daria and people like her used to live, while for the younger generation, it is the beginning of a new, seemingly better life. The author does not intrude upon the reader's judgment, although his sympathies lie clearly with those who want to preserve their values and their bond with nature.

RASPUTIN'S SECOND PERIOD

The second period in Rasputin's creativity, which began in the early 1980's, has yielded fewer stories. After his head injury, he became more introspective, as evidenced in several stories that he published in 1981. "Chto peredat' vorone" ("What Shall I Tell the Crow?"), "Natasha," and "Vek zhivi--vek liubi" ("You Live and Love") all show visible changes in Rasputin's approach to literature. He began mixing reality and the dream world with abandon. While he has always used dreams as a device, he now employs dreams to depict an experience of "losing oneself in oneself" and "nonbeing in oneself," for which processes dreams are a suitable vehicle. Earlier features can still be found, as critic Teresa Polowy rightly states: the altered states of consciousness and unconsciousness, the communion between human beings and nature, guilt and responsibility, and the preservation of values that are in danger of extinction. In the new stories, Rasputin stresses individuals, their emotional and mental processes, and their moral responsibilities that extend to their society. "Natasha," in particular, signals the change in Rasputin toward the inner world of his characters (all of these stories are told in the first person) as he describes the protagonist's stay in the hospital, drifting from consciousness into a dream world.

Rasputin's later novella, *Pozhar*, goes back to his previous preoccupation with social issues. The novella resembles *Farewell to Matyora* in that it depicts the same clash between the old and the new, between nature and progress, and between the individual and society. New factors here include the author's stronger, almost strident voice protesting the blind advance of technological progress at the expense of everything else, and a male character who carries the struggle for the preservation of old values, instead of a woman, as in many of Rasputin's previous stories. The message and the commitment, however, are the same.

OTHER MAJOR WORKS

NONFICTION: *Zemlia rodiny*, 1984; *Essays*, 1988; *Sibir, Sibir*, 1991 (*Siberia, Siberia*, 1996).

MISCELLANEOUS: *Sobranie sochinenii v trekh tomakh*, 1994 (3 volumes); *Sobranie sochinenii v chetyrekh tomakh*, 2007 (4 volumes); *V poiskakh berega: Povest, ocherki, stati, vystupleniia, esse*, 2007.

BIBLIOGRAPHY

Bagby, Lewis. "A Concurrence of Psychological and Narrative Structures: Anamnesis in Valentin Rasputin's 'Upstream, Downstream.'" *Canadian Slavonic Papers* 22 (1980): 388-399. Through an analysis of *Borrowed Time*, *Money for Maria*, and "Upstream, Downstream," Bagby discusses Rasputin's fascination with death, his retrospective themes and anamnestic personality, and his adherence to memory as a constructive principle.

Björling, Fiona. "When the Film Is Better Than the Book." *Russian Studies in Literature* 40, no. 3 (Summer, 2004): 64-78. Compares Rasputin's novella *Farewell to Matyora* with the Russian film *Farewell* (1982) by director Elem Klimov. Discusses the metaphysical and philosophical meaning of the novella, its open ending, and its symbolism.

Brown, Deming. "Valentin Rasputin: A General View." In *Russian Literature and Criticism*. Berkeley, Calif.: Berkeley Slavic Specialties, 1982. Brown concentrates on the settings and treatment of nature in Rasputin's stories.

Gillespie, David C. "Childhood and the Adult World in the Writing of Valentin Rasputin." *The Modern Language Review* 80 (1985): 387-395. Gillespie treats Rasputin's depiction of children and their relationship to the adult world as one of the basic themes in his works.

_____. *Valentin Rasputin and Soviet Russian Village Prose*. London: Modern Humanities Research Association, 1986. In this relatively brief study, Gillespie focuses on Rasputin's treatment of rural life and how it relates to Soviet society in general.

Lapidus, Rina. "Surrogate for Man-Woman Relations in Post-War Soviet Literature: Vasilyiev, Grossman, and Rasputin. In *Passion, Humiliation, Revenge: Hatred in Man-Woman Relationships in the Nineteenth and Twentieth Century Russian Novel*. Lanham, Md.: Lexington Books, 2008. Analyzes the male-female relationship in *Farewell to Matyora*.

Mikkelson, Gerald. "Religious Symbolism in Valentin Rasputin's Tale *Live and Remember*." In *Studies in Honor of Xenia Gasiorowska*, edited by L. G. Leighton. Columbus, Ohio: Slavica, 1983. An attempt to understand the situations, events, and characters in *Live and Remember* through the novella's symbolic structure as a modern-day Christian parable and Nastena as a suffering saint and martyr.

Polowy, Teresa. *The Novellas of Valentin Rasputin: Genre, Language, and Style*. New York: Peter Lang, 1989. The most serious treatment of the works of Rasputin. Polowy covers, in a scholarly fashion, his themes, characterization, and the formal aspects, such as plot and structure. The matters of language and style are discussed at length. A select bibliography is appended. An excellent introduction to Rasputin.

Porter, R. C. *Four Contemporary Russian Writers*. New York: St. Martin's Press, 1989. Examines the works of Rasputin, Chingiz Aitmatov, Vladimir Voinovich, and Georgii Vladimov.

Rich, Elizabeth. "Fate?" *Soviet Literature*, no. 3 (1987): 149-168. Rich examines Rasputin's treatment of women characters, their attitude toward self-sacrifice, and Rasputin's views on this moral question.

Shrayer, Maxim D. "Anti-Semitism and the Decline of Russian Village Prose." Partisan Review 67, no. 3 (Summer, 2000): 474. Shrayer argues that the Russian village prose of Rasputin and other writers features "anti-Semitic" elements, and he examines the impact of this prejudice on the writers' works and on the decline of the genre.

Vasa D. Mihailovich

JUAN RULFO

Born: Barranca de Apulco, Sayula, Jalisco, Mexico; May 16, 1918
Died: Mexico City, Mexico; January 7, 1986

PRINCIPAL SHORT FICTION
El llano en llamas, 1953, revised 1970 and 1980 (*The Burning Plain, and Other Stories*, 1967)

OTHER LITERARY FORMS
Juan Rulfo (wahn REWL-foh) is known for two major works, his novel *Pedro Páramo* (1955, rev. 1959, 1964, 1980; English translations 1959, 1994) and his collection of short stories. Rulfo also wrote screenplays and essays of literary criticism and published collections of his photographs. In 1994,

the posthumous *Los cuadernos de Juan Rulfo* was published.

ACHIEVEMENTS
Juan Rulfo's two major works hjave been translated into more than ten languages. His novel *Pedro Páramo* is widely credited with changing the course of Mexican literature. Rulfo received two fellowships to the Center for Mexican Writers (1952-1954) and was awarded Mexico's National Literature Prize in 1970. He was elected to membership in the Mexican Academy of Letters in 1980 and received the Príncipe de Asturias Prize from Spain in 1983. He was honored after death by the creation of the Juan Rulfo Latin American and Caribbean Literature Award.

BIOGRAPHY

Juan Nepomuceno Carlos Pérez Vizcaíno Rulfo was born in Barranca de Apulco, Mexico, on May 16, 1918, but his family soon moved to San Gabriel, in the same state of Jalisco, where the young Rulfo suffered the assassination of his father in 1925 and the death of his mother by heart attack two years later. In 1928, Rulfo enrolled in an orphanage in Guadalajara run by Josephine nuns, where he remained until 1932, when he entered the seminary to become a priest. He left the seminary upon the death of his grandmother, preferring to study business and law. A strike at the University of Guadalajara forestalled his higher education, and in 1935 he moved to Mexico City, where he immediately began working in the office of the Ministry of Migration. He left the ministry in 1946 to become a traveling salesman for Goodrich Tires. He married Clara Aparicio in 1948 and had four children. He worked in public relations for Goodrich, then in publishing and television before joining the Instituto Indigenista in 1962.

Rulfo published his first stories in periodicals as early as 1945. In 1952 a fellowship at the Center for Mexican Writers made it possible for him to complete and collect his stories for his first book, *The Burning Plain, and Other Stories*. A second year of fellowship allowed him to complete his novel *Pedro Páramo*. Though he continued to write, Rulfo did not produce new novels or short stories, publishing only screenplays, occasional essays of literary criticism, and collections of his photographs until his death on January 7, 1986, from lung cancer.

ANALYSIS

Juan Rulfo's international reputation rests on only two slender volumes published in his thirties. In contrast to the novel of the Mexican Revolution, with its descriptive realism and nationalism, Rulfo introduced the new Mexican narrative that would lead to what has been called the boom in Latin American literature, an outpouring of innovative fiction. Colombian novelist and Nobel Prize-winner Gabriel García Márquez claimed Rulfo as one of his greatest influences. The Mexican poet and Nobel Prize-winner Octavio Paz praised Rulfo

as "the only Mexican novelist to have provided us with an image--rather than a mere description--of our physical surroundings."

The isolation and desolation of the rural Mexican desert landscape of his stories provide a setting where human characters have as little hope or possibility as the landscape has fertility. Just as the sterility of the desert is broken only by the implied violence of snakes and buzzards, so too are Rulfo's stories studded with vengeance and violence, death and despair. Several critics have suggested that Rulfo's preoccupation with violence stems from the violent death of his father when he was only seven and the violent condition of a Mexico still in turmoil after a revolution that ended in 1920.

The journey, which is often a physical journey combined with a symbolic quest (inevitably doomed to failure), is the dominant theme and organizing principle in many of Rulfo's stories. The relationship between father and son, or the absence of a father, is a recurring motif. Other recurring themes include poverty and power, such as the poor versus the government, or the poor versus the local *cacique*, or landowner-boss.

"BECAUSE WE ARE SO POOR"

Like all of Rulfo's stories, "Es que somos muy pobres" ("Because We Are So Poor") reveals much about the lives of Mexico's poor *campesinos*, or rural people. A first-person narrator, the boy in a poor family, tells his story in the present tense to an unnamed listener, which creates a sense of immediacy, as if events are unfolding along with the narrative. A series of disasters has affected this family: Aunt Jacinta just died and was buried; the rains came unexpectedly, without giving the family time to salvage any of their rye harvest, which was stacked outside to dry in the sun; and now the cow his father gave his sister Tacha for her twelfth birthday has been swept away by the newly overflowing river. Tacha is the last of three sisters. The other two "went bad" and became prostitutes. Tacha's cow was her only hope for a better life; without her cow she has nothing to attract a man to marry her. Tacha's dowry and the only bank account she will ever have has washed away in the floodwaters of the river. As the boy observes his sister crying, he notes that her "two little breasts bounce up and down . . . as if suddenly they were beginning to swell, to start now on the road to ruin." Tacha is devastated by the loss of her cow, but she does not yet understand the depth of her loss nor what seem to be the inescapable consequences of that loss. These people, like so many of Rulfo's characters, are helpless victims of poverty and all it entails.

"TALPA"

"Talpa" combines some of Rulfo's common themes, using the physical journey as the means to a frustrated quest. Natalia and the anonymous first-person narrator agree to take Natalia's husband Tanilo to the religious center of Talpa so he can pray to the Virgin there for a cure for the weeping wounds on his arms and legs. Tanilo's quest is for a miracle--the miracle of renewed health. The narrator and Natalia agree to take him because they hope he will die en route.

It is a long journey on foot. Every night along the way Natalia and the narrator, who is Tanilo's brother, steal off to make passionate love. Tanilo's condition worsens, and he asks to go home, but the lovers push him onward, not wanting an end to their freedom from societal restrictions. They arrive at Talpa with Tanilo in serious condition. After rallying briefly to dance to the Virgin with other pilgrims, he dies, his quest for new health unsatisfied. Even though Tanilo's death is the desired object of his brother's quest, his brother regrets Tanilo's passing. After burying Tanilo, Natalia and the narrator-brother make the long trip home in silence. Upon arriving home and seeing her mother, the hitherto stoic Natalia breaks down in inconsolable sobbing. The love and passion between the narrator and Natalia are forever quenched by guilt. In death Tanilo exercises more power than in life.

"TELL THEM NOT TO KILL ME!"

Rulfo considered "Diles que no me maten!" ("Tell Them Not to Kill Me!") his best story. Unlike most of Rulfo's stories, an anonymous first-person narrator does not relate "Tell Them Not to Kill Me!" Rather, dialogue between Juvencio Nava, the sixty-year-old protagonist, and his son Justino opens the story, followed by third-person narration from Juvencio's point of view, followed by dialogue between Juvencio and the Coronel who orders his death, and closing with a brief dialogue between Justino and the corpse of his father.

Juan Rulfo (AP Photo)

Thirty-five years ago Juvencio Nava killed Don Lupe Terreros in a dispute over livestock. Lupe refused to let Juvencio use his pastures. Juvencio cut a hole in Lupe's fence, Lupe killed one of Juvencio's yearlings, and Juvencio killed Lupe in a particularly violent manner, hacking him with a machete. As a result of his rash act, Juvencio loses everything: He killed Luce to save his cows, but they go to pay a corrupt judge; his wife leaves him; and he lives a hidden life with his son. The unnamed Coronel who captures Juvencio is Lupe's son and is determined to avenge his father's death. Juvencio pleads for his life, saying he has already paid many times over. In an act of mercy, the Coronel instructs his men to give Juvencio plenty to drink "so the shots won't hurt him." Violence begets violence.

"LUVINA"

"Luvina" is set in two locations and two times: in the present time of the inn, where an anonymous storyteller is talking to an unknown listener, and in the past Luvina of the narrator's memory. The narrator is a teacher who went to San Juan Luvina many years ago. He explains his experience to his listener, who intends to go there. As he describes it, Luvina is a ghost town of ghostly inhabitants. There is no restaurant, no inn, and no school. It is a town full of women dressed in black, who move among the shadows like otherworldly shades. Occasionally husbands return with the winds, remaining long enough to beget another child, then they disappear again. The children leave as soon as they are able. When the teacher suggests to Luvina's inhabitants that they move somewhere else with the help of the government, they laugh. The government only remembers Luvina when it kills one of its sons, they say, and besides, the dead "live here and we can't leave them alone." The narrator keeps drinking and telling his tale, saying, "I left my life there--I went to that place full of illusions and returned old and worn out." He describes Luvina as if it were a dream, an illusion rather than a reality, but a frightful illusion, a nightmare rather than a dream. The phantasmagoric landscape takes on near-human characteristics and, along with the listener, the reader seems to be transported to purgatory.

OTHER MAJOR WORKS

LONG FICTION: *Pedro Páramo*, 1955, revised 1959, 1964, 1980 (English translation, 1959, 1994).

SCREENPLAY: *El gallo de oro, y otros textos para cine*, 1980 (partial translation, "The Golden Cock," *Review* 46, 1992).

NONFICTION: *Juan Rulfo: Autobiografía armada*, 1973 (compiled by Reina Roffé); *Inframundo: El México de Juan Rulfo*, 1980 (*Inframundo: The Mexico of Juan Rulfo*, 1983).

MISCELLANEOUS: *Toda la obra*, 1992 (critical edition); *Los cuadernos de Juan Rulfo*, 1994.

BIBLIOGRAPHY

Burton, Julianne. "A Drop of Rain in the Desert: Something and Nothingness in Juan Rulfo's 'Nos han dado la tierra' ('They've Given Us the Land')." *Latin American Literary Review* 2, no. 3 (Fall/Winter, 1973): 55-62. Analyzes Rulfo's use of absences ("nothingness"), such as barrenness, poverty, and isolation, in combination with the presence ("something") of elements like the buzzards that symbolize death and magnify the sterility of the locale and the people's lives.

Ekstrom, Margaret V. "Frustrated Quest in the Narratives of Juan Rulfo." *American Hispanist* 2, no. 12 (November, 1976): 13-16. Discusses "No Dogs Bark," "Talpa," "The Burning Plain," and "Macario" in relation to the actual journeys and symbolic quests undertaken by Rulfo's characters, who are "unsuccessful" heroes on frustrated quests.

Janney, Frank, ed. and trans. *Inframundo: The Mexico of Juan Rulfo*. New York: Ediciones del Norte, 1983. Collection of critical articles by major Latin American authors like the Nobel Prize-winning Gabriel García Márquez, along with Rulfo's story "Luvina" and nearly one hundred of his stunning black and white photographs illustrating the Mexico described in his works.

Jordan, Michael S. "Noise and Communication in Juan Rulfo." *Latin American Literary Review* 24, no. 27 (January-June, 1996): 115-130. Excellent analysis of several short stories and *Pedro Páramo*, investigating the presence of noise and abundance of "speech acts" in a narrative universe in which real communication is ultimately impossible.

Leal, Luis. *Juan Rulfo*. Boston: Twayne, 1983. The first full-length study in English of Rulfo's work. Relates Rulfo's first unpublished novel, "The Son of Affliction," to Rulfo's difficult childhood. Divides Rulfo's writing into the first prose work, the early stories, and the later stories, then focuses on the novel *Pedro Páramo* by examining "Context and Genesis" and "Structure and Imagery." Also includes a brief chapter on Rulfo's screenplays and the films made from them, as well as his public lectures. Excellent bibliography.

_____. "Juan Rulfo." In *A Luis Leal Reader*. Edited by Ilan Stavans. Evanston, Ill.: Northwestern University Press, 2007. Leal was an internationally recognized authority on Mexican, Chicano, and Latin American literature. This collection of his essays includes a short piece about Rulfo.

Lyon, Ted. "Ontological Motifs in the Short Stories of Juan Rulfo." *Journal of Spanish Studies: Twentieth Century* 3 (Winter, 1973): 161-168. Examines all fifteen stories of *The Burning Plain, and Other Stories* according to four motifs: walking, memory, futility of effort, and vision impeded by darkness.

Ramírez, Arthur. "Juan Rulfo: Dialectics and the Despairing Optimist." *Hispania* 65 (December, 1982): 580-585. Argues that despite the tensions between the dualities of life and death, love and hate, hope and despair, heaven and hell, and reality and unreality in Rulfo's fiction, the overall effect is cohesiveness rather than polarity. Concludes that Rulfo's pessimism contains a kind of affirmation: a preoccupation with death underscores the importance of life and love.

Reinhardt-Childers, Ilva. "Sensuality, Brutality, and Violence in Two of Rulfo's Stories: An Analytical Study." *Hispanic Journal* 12, no.1 (Spring 1991): 69-73. Discusses "At Daybreak" and "The Burning Plain" from the perspective of the extreme and unpredictable violence they contain, perhaps because Rulfo witnessed violence while growing up during the aftermath of the Mexican Revolution.

Rulfo, Juan. *Juan Rulfo's Mexico*. Washington, D.C. Smithsonian Institution Press, 2002. A compilation of 175 of Rulfo's photographs of rural Mexico, the majority of which were taken between 1945 and 1955. Includes six essays about the photographs and Rulfo's life and writings, including one by Carlos Fuentes and another by Rulfo himself; these essays were translated by Margaret Sayers Peden.

Thakkar, Amit. "Ambivalence and the Crisis of the Mimic Man: Centrifugal Irony in Juan Rulfo's 'Luvina.'" *Journal of Iberian and Latin American Studies* 11, no. 1 (April, 2005): 65-89. Analyzes Rulfo's short story from the perspective of events in postrevolutionary Mexico. Discusses how the story reflects the attitudes of the Spanish crown and the Roman Catholic Church in relation to colonial society, the social activities of education reformers after the Mexican Revolution, and efforts to fill the vacuum created by the departure of the Church with the "revolutionary self of the urban state."

Linda Ledford-Miller

SALMAN RUSHDIE

Born: Bombay (now Mumbai), India; June 19, 1947

PRINCIPAL SHORT FICTION
East, West: Stories, 1994
"The Firebird's Nest," 1997
"Vina Divina," 1999

OTHER LITERARY FORMS

Best known for *The Satanic Verses* (1988), other novels by Salman Rushdie (SAHL-mehn ROOSH-dee) include *Grimus* (1975), *Midnight's Children* (1981), *Shame* (1983), *The Moor's Last Sigh* (1995), *The Ground Beneath Her Feet* (1999), *Fury* (2001), *Shalimar the Clown* (2005), *The Enchantress of Florence* (2008), and *Luka and the Fire of Life* (2010). He also has written a children's fable, *Haroun and the Sea of Stories* (1990); a monograph on cinema, *The*

Wizard of Oz: A Short Text About Magic (1992); and three nonfiction books: *The Jaguar Smile: A Nicaraguan Journey* (1987), *Imaginary Homelands: Essays and Criticism, 1981-1991* (1991), and *Step Across This Line: Collected Nonfiction, 1992-2002* (2002).

ACHIEVEMENTS

Salman Rushdie received the James Tait Black Memorial Prize in 1982 and was made a Fellow of the Royal Society of Literature in 1983. *Shame* won the Prix du Meilleur Livre Étranger in 1984; *The Satanic Verses* and *The Moor's Last Sigh* received Whitbread Literary Awards in 1988 and 1995, respectively. *Midnight's Children* garnered the 1981 Man Booker Prize; in 1993, this novel received the Booker of Bookers Prize as the best novel to win the Man Booker Prize during the award's first twenty-five years of existence; similarly, *Midnight's Children* won The Best of the Booker Prize in 2008 to celebrate the fortieth anniversary of the award. In addition, Rushdie was knighted for his services to literature during the Queen's Birthday Honours on June 16, 2007.

BIOGRAPHY

After early schooling at Bombay's Cathedral School (1954 to 1961), Ahmed Salman Rushdie was sent by his nominally Moslem but Anglophile parents to England for an even more British education at Rugby (1961 to 1964) and King's College, Cambridge (1965 to 1968). After traveling to Pakistan, he was forced to return to England because his production of Edward Albee's *The Zoo Story* (pr., pb. 1959) mentioned "pork," thereby inciting Moslem protests. He tried acting, worked as an advertising copywriter, and composed the poorly received novel *Grimus*. Not until his success with *Midnight's Children* in 1981 could he earn a living from his fiction.

In 1988, his life changed radically with the publication of *The Satanic Verses*. Even though its references to Muhammad are part of a dream sequence, conservative Moslems were outraged. Protests against it included one in Islamabad, Pakistan, where five rioters were killed and more than one hundred injured. In Iran, Ayatollah Khomeini issued a fatwa (religious decree) condemning Rushdie and his publishers to death for blasphemy. Rushdie himself has had to live under police protection and in hiding. Casualties of the fatwa include the assassination of the Japanese translator and the serious injury of the Norwegian publisher. The fatwa may have contributed to the collapse of Rushdie's year-long marriage (1988-1989) to the novelist Marianne Wiggins. Despite the threats, Rushdie continued to publish nonfiction, short stories, and novels. In 1998, the Iranian government declared that it would not continue to enforce the fatwa.

ANALYSIS

Because of their shared love of puns and allusions, Salman Rushdie often compares himself to James Joyce, a predecessor Rushdie also resembles in the fate of his reputation. Their humorous, vertiginous, multicultural mixture of erudition and popular culture might never have reached large audiences if they had not had

works condemned for blasphemy and pornography, respectively. Rushdie's texts are more erotic than Joyce's and Joyce's more blasphemous than Rushdie's, so their public images are largely a misunderstanding. Both are best seen as postcolonial authors, Joyce condemning the web of British oppression that stagnated Ireland, while Rushdie has satirized vestiges of it in India, Pakistan, and émigré communities.

A significant difference, however, divides the importance short stories have played in the careers of each. Joyce learned his craft through writing his collection of stories, *Dubliners* (1914), which marked a major advance for the genre; the interconnecting stories focus on a single locale. Rushdie's works of short fiction, the casual fruits of the middle period of his career, although skillful in their dazzling ironic twists and word play, signal only a refinement, not a major change in the genre. Instead, each work functions largely within some past tradition (such as those of Tom Stoppard or Donald Barthelme). With the exception of "Vina Divina" (an extension of one of his novels), they do not have an original voice that would give them the

Salman Rushdie (Lefteris Pitarakis/AP/dapd)

importance of his larger works. The latter, however, have a rambling, episodic movement that makes them sometimes resemble short-story collections (such as *Harmoun and the Sea of Stories*); thus, in a sense, Rushdie has followed the lead of *Dubliners* by eroding further the distinction between short-story collection and novel.

"GOOD ADVICE IS RARER THAN RUBIES"

The title conflates Middle Eastern sayings about the preciousness of wisdom, which the biblical book Proverbs likens to a woman as desirable as rubies. Consequently, this title seems to predict a story about useful information or feminine beauty. It concerns both, but in an ironic manner, and it is meant to make a political statement. Its protagonist is an advice wallah (specialist), cheating "Tuesday" women who come nervously on that day for visas from India to Britain, as if their salvation depended on escaping their homeland. However, because of the beauty of one woman, Miss Rehana, the wallah dispenses with his usually perfidious counsel and offers her a forged passport. She refuses, lest she confirm the British in their assumption that all Indians are liars, a dishonesty forced on them by English oppression. When he sees her smile upon exiting the embassy, he assumes that her beauty has also triumphed over the "Sahibs"--what he calls the British because they are still to him the lords and masters of the land. Nonetheless, she has received no visa; therefore, she will avoid marrying a man old enough to be her father. Without disobeying her parents (who arranged the match), she avoids being pulled into their and the wallah's folly. A slave to the colonial past, the wallah deludes both others and himself with such obsolete notions as the desirability of immigrating to racist Britain because he has found nothing in modern India to love. Miss Rehana, though, enjoys being the governess of three children. Of virtue and wisdom like hers, Proverbs contends, "her price *is* far above rubies."

"THE PROPHET'S HAIR"

Another of the narratives from the Asian third of *East, West*, this tale is the kind of satire that has caused Rushdie so much trouble--his subjecting Moslem influence in India to a critique almost as severe as he addresses against the British. "The Prophet's Hair" is based on a real incident: A relic is stolen from a Kashmir mosque and then recovered. Rushdie, however, imagines the circuitous path of its return as it works a series of miracles, all of them disastrous. Held illegally by a moneylender (a profession condemned by Islam), the hair, nonetheless, makes him hypocritical enough to force Moslem rigors upon his family, beating them and wishing to cut off the hand of one of his debtors. To escape this religiosity, his son tries to restore the hair to the mosque, but it miraculously returns to the moneylender. Then, risking their lives, the son and daughter hire a violent thief, who like the moneylender has previously led a tolerable life because it was free from religion. The supernatural power of the hair, however, cures his children (whom the thief kindly crippled), and they will thus starve because their income from begging is thereby cut by 75 percent. Death or madness destroys practically everyone else who comes anywhere near the hair. Ironically, the story concludes that Kashmir is closer to Paradise than any other spot on earth--a depressing revelation in a story of widespread horror. D. C. R. A. Goonetilleke compares the story to Robert Louis Stevenson's *The New Arabian Nights* (1882) in their borrowing rapid action from the Oriental folktale but reversing its characteristic optimism. One might also read "The Prophet's Hair" as a parable of the misfortune of recovering faith, based on Rushdie's own experience--he publicly returned to Islam in 1990 only to renounce it again in 1992.

"AT THE AUCTION OF THE RUBY SLIPPERS"

Author of a monograph-length study of the film *The Wizard of Oz* (1939), Rushdie employs the Barthelme-like Magical Realism of this story to evoke what that film means to a culture looking to cinematic fantasies as its past and auctioning even these away. The bidders are expected to go insane. One of them schizophrenically interweaves the auction and his love affair with his cousin Gale, whose name is linked through a pun to the film's tornado. The Ruby Slippers, preserved behind bulletproof glass, are the ones that Dorothy used to return home. In Rushdie's erotic subplot, however, "home" is given obscene meaning, and that subplot is acknowledged to be itself at least partly hallucination, so there seems to be no real, untainted home in a world of migrants and delusion--one with which Rushdie is very familiar. Significantly, fundamentalists threaten to purchase the slippers in order to burn them because they insist on having a complete monopoly on hope.

"THE COURTER"

In a 1994 interview, Rushdie revealed that this tale was partly autobiographical. Demonstrating skill at depicting a cross-cultural world that Rushdie knows so well, this nostalgic reminiscence of the narrator's teen years in London portrays his family's elderly ayah (nurse) and her romance with Mecir, a porter. The porter, whose title the ayah mispronounces as "courter," courts her by teaching her chess, a game of which he is a grand master, a status in obvious contrast to the humble occupation forced on him as an émigré from Eastern Europe. Violent racism leaves the ayah torn between East and West and marks the end of the narrator's innocence. Telling the tale many years later, he realizes that his youthful impertinence in nicknaming Mecir as "Mixed Up" was itself racist, foreshadowing the forces that bring the romance to tragedy. The story concludes the intercultural third of *East, West* (whose middle portion was Occidental, including "At the Auction of the Ruby Slippers").

"VINA DIVINA"

Released a month before Rushdie's six-hundred-page novel *The Ground Beneath Her Feet*, this *New Yorker* story is the novel's first chapter retitled and reworked just enough so that it constitutes a relatively self-contained unit. Both fictions take place in an alternative world where the greatest rock celebrities are Ormus Cama and Vina Apsara, modeled on the mythical Orpheus and Eurydice. An alternative version of the novel's introductory section, this tale is an instance of how Rushdie's short fiction has been engulfed by epic projects (undertaken to distract him from the fatwa). As in the novel, the tale is told by Rushdie's persona, the photographer Rai, who engages in long diatribes against religious fanaticism and is worried about being assassinated by terrorists. He is famous for his photograph of Vina's descent into the earth, "The Lady Vanishes." This title echoes not only Rushdie's disappearance but also "The One Who Vanished," Franz Kafka's title for a work of fiction that, like "Vina Divina," evokes a dreamlike version of the United States.

OTHER MAJOR WORKS

LONG FICTION: *Grimus*, 1975; *Midnight's Children*, 1981; *Shame*, 1983; *The Satanic Verses*, 1988; *The Moor's Last Sigh*, 1995; *The Ground Beneath her Feet*, 1999; *Fury*, 2001; *Shalimar the Clown*, 2005; *The Enchantress of Florence*, 2008; *Luka and the Fire of Life*, 2010.

PLAY: *Midnight's Children*, pr., pb. 2003 (adaptation of his novel; with Simon Reade and Tim Supple).

NONFICTION: *The Jaguar Smile: A Nicaraguan Journey*, 1987; *Imaginary Homelands: Essays and Criticism, 1981-1991*, 1991; *The Wizard of Oz: A Short Text About Magic*, 1992; *Conversations with Salman Rushdie*, 2000 (Michael Reder, editor); *Step Across This Line: Collected Nonfiction, 1992-2002*, 2002.

CHILDREN'S LITERATURE: *Haroun and the Sea of Stories*, 1990 (fable).

EDITED TEXT: *The Best American Short Stories, 2008*, 2008 (with Heidi Pitlor).

BIBLIOGRAPHY

Ahsan, A. R. *Sacrilege Versus Civility: Muslim Perspectives on "The Satanic Verses" Affair*. Markfield, Leicester: Islamic Foundation, 1993. Among the more than seventy books that have been written about the fatwa, this is one of many that are largely critical of Rushdie.

Brennan, Timothy. *Salman Rushdie and the Third World: Myths of the Nation*. London: Macmillan, 1989. This sociopolitical study was the first book-length analysis of Rushdie's art.

Burton, Rob. *Artists of the Floating World: Contemporary Writers Between Cultures*. Lanham, Md.: University Press of America, Inc., 2007. Looks at Rushdie and three other writers whose works explore a "floating world" in which cultures collide and converge. The chapter on Rushdie devotes several pages to a discussion of *East, West*.

Cundy, Catherine. *Salman Rushdie: Contemporary World Writers*. Manchester, England: Manchester University Press, 1996. Although it gives very little attention to *East, West*, this is a readable overview of Rushdie's work.

Fletcher, M. D., ed. *Reading Rushdie: Perspectives on the Fiction of Salman Rushdie*. Amsterdam: Cross/Cultures, 1994. A collection of essays, most previously published.

Gonzalez, Madelena. Fiction after the Fatwa: Salman Rushdie and the Charm of Catastrophe. New York: Rodopi, 2005. Analyzes what Rushdie achieved after the Iranian government declared its fatwa against the author on February 14, 1989. Gonzalez argues that since the fatwa, Rushdie has continued to question fictional form and the use of language, opening up new possibilities for late twentieth and early twenty-first century writing. Devotes a chapter to "*East, West*: The Dislocation of Culture."

Goonetilleke, D. C. R. A. *Salman Rushdie*. 2d ed. New York: Palgrave Macmillan, 2010. Includes a chapter examining the stories in *East, West*.

Gurnah, Abdulrazak, ed. *The Cambridge Companion to Salman Rushdie*. Cambridge, England: Cambridge University, 2007. Collection of essays analyzing Rushdie's works, including an examination of "The Shorter Fiction" by Deepika Bahr. Other essays explore some common themes and ideas in his writing and discuss his private life, including his early occupations, his four marriages, and his break from Islamic fundamentalism.

Ifterharuddin, Farhat. "Salmon Rushdie." In *A Reader's Companion to the Short Story in English*, edited by Erin Fallon et al., under the auspices of the Society for the Study of the Short Story. Westport, Conn.: Greenwood Press, 2001. Aimed at the general reader, this essay provides a brief biography of Rushdie followed by an analysis of his short fiction.

Morton, Stephen. *Salman Rushdie: Fictions of Postcolonial Modernity*. New York: Palgrave Macmillan, 2008. Places Rushdie's fiction in historical and theoretical context. Includes a chapter analyzing *East, West*, *The Satanic Verses*, and *Haroun and the Sea of Stories*.

Parameswarn, U. *The Perforated Sheet: Essays on Salman Rushdie's Art*. New Delhi: Affiliated East-West, 1988. Despite some heterogeneity to the essays, this collection offers insight into Rushdie's Indian context.

Rushdie, Salman. *Salman Rushdie Interviews: A Sourcebook of His Ideas*. Edited by Pradyumna S. Chauhan. Westport, Conn.: Greenwood Press, 2001. A selection of Rushdie's many interviews that illuminates his thinking, writing, and life experience.

James Whitlark

S

Olive Senior

Born: Troy, Trelawny, Jamaica; December 23, 1941

OTHER LITERARY FORMS

In her quest to define Jamaica--its history, its culture, and what it means to be Jamaican--Olive Senior writes poetry and nonfiction, as well as short stories. Her four collections of poetry span her career as a writer; poetry is an important means of expression for her. In her poetry, she portrays Jamaica as a geographical area of beauty and mystery, and she depicts the multifaceted culture and ethnicity of the country. Her nonfiction works deal with Jamaica's history and culture. *Working Miracles: Women's Lives in the English-Speaking Caribbean* (1991) addresses the role of women and how that role has changed.

ACHIEVEMENTS

Olive Senior writes poetry, short stories, and nonfiction, and she is recognized as an authority on Jamaican history and culture. She is respected as a major Caribbean writer, for both her poetry and her short fiction, which explore and reveal the complexity of the Jamaican identity. Senior shares her knowledge of Jamaica and what it means to be Jamaican as a writer, as a lecturer, as a workshop leader, as a writer-in-residence, and as a visiting professor at international universities and conferences. Her collection of short fiction *Summer Lightning, and Other Stories* has been used as a textbook in literature classes in Caribbean schools, and her works are taught in literature classes in

universities worldwide. She has received awards for both her poetry and her short fiction, including the 1987 Commonwealth Writers' Prize and the 1994 F. G. Bressani Literary Prize for Poetry. In 2005, Senior was awarded the Musgrave Gold Medal for her contribution to literature by the Institute of Jamaica.

BIOGRAPHY

Olive Marjorie Senior was born in Jamaica on December 23, 1941, in the small village of Troy in the parish of Trelawny. One of ten children, she spent her childhood in rural Jamaica but lived in two strongly contrasting environments; she stayed part of the time with her parents and siblings in Trelawny and the rest of the time as an only child with relatives in Westmoreland. The middle-class Westmoreland relatives were far more affluent than her parents, so Senior experienced Jamaica at opposite ends of a social system based on race, color, and class. At home she spoke Creole but at school only English was permitted. She attended Montego Bay High School for Girls. While she was still a student, she worked part time for *The Daily Gleaner*, a newspaper. After graduating from high school, she became a full-time reporter for the newspaper in Kingston. After attending a journalist-training course in Cardiff, Wales, Senior received a scholarship to Carleton University in Ottawa, Canada. She majored in journalism but also took liberal arts courses and began writing poetry and short stories. She received her bachelor of arts degree in 1967 and returned to Jamaica, where she worked as an information officer with the Jamaica Information Service. In 1969, she became a public relations officer with the Jamaica Chamber of Commerce and editor of the organization's journal.

In 1972, Senior joined the Institute of Social and Economic Research at the University of the West Indies, where she worked as editor of the institute's journal, *Social and Economics Studies*. She published her first book, a nonfiction work, *The Message Is Change* (1972), dealing with the election of Michael Manley as priminister of Jamaica. In 1977, she left the institute; she worked independently as a freelance writer, consultant, and speechwriter. In 1980, seven of her poems were included in *Jamaica Woman: An Anthology of Poems*. In 1982, Senior returned to working as an editor, joining the Institute of Jamaica as managing editor of publications and the editor of the *Jamaica Journal*. Working with the institute, she published *A-Z of Jamaican Heritage* (1984), an encyclopedia of Jamaican culture and history. During this time, she continued to write poetry and short stories. In 1985, she published her first poetry collection, *Talking of Trees*, and the following year her first short-story collection, *Summer Lightning, and Other Stories*, for which she was awarded the Commonwealth Writers' Prize.

In 1988, finding herself living without electricity and running water as a result of Hurricane Gilbert, Senior decided to move to Europe, and she lived in Portugal, the Netherlands, and England. In 1989, she published her second collection of short stories, *Arrival of the Snake-Woman, and Other Stories*. She then moved to Toronto, Canada. Her creative work continued, however, to focus on Jamaica and the Jamaican experience. In 1991, she published *Working Miracles: Women's Lives in the English-Speaking Caribbean*. In 1994, she published her collection of poetry *Gardening in the Tropics*. In 2004, she republished *A-Z of Jamaican Heritage* in an expanded form as the *Encyclopedia of Jamaican Heritage*. In 2005, her third collection of poetry, *Over the Roofs of the World*, and her third collection of short stories, *Discerner of Heart*, both dealing with Jamaica, appeared. In 2007, she published her fourth collection of poetry, *Shell*. Senior has remained closely attached to her homeland, returning to Jamaica every year and spending time there, particularly in Kingston.

ANALYSIS

Olive Senior has published three collections of short stories; in her short fiction, as in her poetry, she is concerned with expressing what it means to be Jamaican and to have a Jamaican identity. Although Senior is not an autobiographical writer, her short stories draw heavily upon her experiences growing up in Jamaica. Recognizing the Creole patois of rural Jamaica as a viable language, she considers herself bilingual and uses both Creole and English in her works, thus emphasizing the importance of authentic language to the creation of realistic stories. Senior's writing is heavily influenced by the oral storytelling tradition with which she grew up. She draws the reader into the story and at times, as in "Ballad," directly addresses the reader. Her short fiction is composed of stories that could be told by women working or chatting or within the family circle at the end of the workday. Senior portrays the beliefs, mores, problems, and experiences of Jamaicans living everyday lives.

Female voices dominate Senior's short fiction. Her narrators are primarily female, either women or young girls. The stories concentrate on female characters and how they create their identities and lives. She does occasionally use a young boy as her narrator, as in "Arrival of the Snake-Woman"; however, even in this story, the main character is female. Senior also addresses the issues resulting from colonialism, which established hierarchies of race and color. The stories depict the problems and dilemmas faced by individuals who grow up in a strictly class-stratified milieu in which ancestry, skin color, and race matter highly and are accepted readily as social classifiers. Dark-skinned, uneducated, rural, and poor contrasts sharply with light-skinned, educated, urban, and middle class. The close ties of country Jamaicans to their African heritage in contrast with the assimilation of English ways by the urban Jamaicans is a central theme of her fiction. The child who is sent by a rural, poor, uneducated family to live with a better educated, more affluent, and urban relative is a recurring character in her stories. The issues of skin color, hair texture, and language appear throughout the stories. She poignantly describes the alienation, loneliness, and fear experienced by these children, yet her stories are most often enhanced by compassionate humor.

Senior also treats the importance of religion and the Bible in the Jamaican community. She considers organized Christianity, the religion of the English masters, as the strongest and most influential of the elements that brought about the oppression of the African slaves and their freed descendants, both economically and culturally. In "Bright Thursdays," "Confirmation Day," and "Do Angels Wear Brassieres?"--three of the stories included in the *Summer Lightning* collection--she satirizes the Christianity forced upon them by the English. For the child in each story (two of them narrators), the God-Jesus figure is a frightening creature that chases her in the clouds and comes to judge and punish sinners. Each child rebels against the religious dogma of the Church, and the sky becomes cloudless. Refusal to accept Christianity is liberation. In "Confirmation Day," Senior describes the Church as wet, moldy, and smelly, with bats living in the rafters. In "Do Angels Wear Brassieres?" the child protagonist Beccka reads the Bible assiduously in order to ask puzzling and improper questions of the pastors.

"ARRIVAL OF THE SNAKE WOMAN"

In "Arrival of the Snake-Woman," an Indian woman, known as a Coolie-Woman or a Snake-Woman, comes to live in the rural community where the narrator lived as a boy. The story recounts how, although she is at first shunned and feared, she creates a central role for herself in the community and has positive effects on the community. Senior begins by creating an aura of mystery around the Snake-Woman: She is from the Bay, the other side of the mountain, and the community, while fascinated, fears anyone or anything from the outside. Their fear is intensified by Parson Bellow's fanatical preaching against her as a daughter of Babylon. Then the children of the community, including the Snake-Woman's child, become ill. Bellows and his wife Miss Rita give the children medicine; however, Bellows refuses to treat the Snake-Woman's child. She returns with the child to the Bay, where he is treated, and then comes back to the village. The parson's refusal to help her weakens his influence on the community; when she returns, she begins to be accepted, eventually sets up a small business, and becomes a commercial link between the community and the Bay.

One of the main themes of the story is the oppressive power of the Church on the people. Senior portrays the parson as using his religion to control the people by threatening them with eternal damnation. The narrator speaks at length of his dilemma because he believes the Snake-Woman is a good, kind person, and he does not understand the parson's condemnation of her. In addition, the parson threatens to prevent the narrator from receiving a scholarship to school if he befriends her.

The story also develops the feminist theme of a woman's ability to overcome obstacles and create her own identity through determination and perseverance. The Snake-Woman becomes the richest, most respected member of the community. It is her advice and encouragement that result in her son becoming a lawyer and the narrator becoming a doctor.

"THE TWO GRANDMOTHERS"

In "The Two Grandmothers," Senior depicts the sharp contrast between the life in rural Jamaica, where the people are poor and dominated by religion, and the importance of respectability and the materialistically oriented life of the urban, middle-class Jamaicans. She also addresses the problem of the loss of heritage and identity, as Jamaicans become better educated, more affluent, and more cosmopolitan. The story is told by a girl to her mother in a series of loosely connected talks or letters, which span the period of her childhood and adolescence. The girl's parents are not of the same social class. Her father is a black-skinned man from a rural family. Since he was a bright child, he was able to obtain an education and become a member of the middle class. Her mother's family is urban, light-skinned, and affluent. The conversation or correspondence is one sided, as the mother never responds. Senior provides only the girl's impressions and reactions to the different lives of her two grandmothers, Grandma Del and Grandma Elaine (who prefers to be called Towser).

As a child, the girl is fascinated by her Grandma Del, who lives without electricity in the country, lets the girl help with cooking and baking, makes her dresses, and tells her stories. As the girl grows up, Grandma Del becomes less interesting and Grandma Elaine more interesting. Eventually, the girl tells her mother she does not want to visit Grandma Del anymore, because it would interfere with the girl going to charm school. Finally, she suggests that the family visit Grandma Del for a few hours on a Sunday so that they can forget about her for a year.

Senior underlines the way in which social status based on shade of skin, hair texture, and money creates a barrier between members of families. As the girl grows up, she develops discriminatory attitudes. There are only black people where Grandma Del lives, and they are boring and ask stupid questions. They wear ragged, dirty clothes and have babies all the time. The girl is ashamed to tell her friends she is going to the country for the summer.

"DISCERNER OF HEARTS"

The two main characters in "Discerner of Hearts" are Theresa Randolph and Cissy. Cissy works for the Randolphs as a household domestic and cook. Theresa is the middle of the three Randolph daughters and the one Cissy prefers. Senior uses the character of Theresa to move the action of the story forward. Theresa's self-discovery through her concern and efforts to help Cissy is the subplot that frames Cissy's story.

In Cissy's story, Senior treats the traditional African beliefs in magic, spells, vengeful curses, and ceremonies to ward off bad spirits and bring good ones. Cissy has consulted Mister Burnham, a balman, to help her "tie" Fonso, the man she wants to father her baby. Mister Burnham will, as long as the man is not Fonso. Cissy lies about the man's identity. Fonso has a woman Ermine. Cissy succeeds but believes Ermine has set an obeah, curse, on her, and she will not have her baby. Cissy is desolate; if she does not have a baby, she will be worth no more than a mule. Theresa visits Mister Burnham, who tells Cissy he knows what has happened and can help her. Cissy returns to him and arranges a bath and a feast with drumming, for which she pays in silver sixpence, the only coin he accepts.

OTHER MAJOR WORKS

POETRY: *Talking of Trees*, 1985; *Gardening in the Tropics*, 1994; *Over the Roofs of the World*, 2005; *Shell*, 2007.

NONFICTION: *The Message Is Change*, 1972; *A-Z of Jamaican Heritage*, 1984, republished in expanded form as *Encyclopedia of Jamaican Heritage* 2004; *Working Miracles: Women's Lives in the English Speaking Caribbean*, 1991.

EDITED TEXTS: *The Journey Prize Anthology: Short Fiction from the Best of Canada's New Writers*, 1996;. *Jamaica Portraits, 1995-1998*, 1998, by Maria LaYacona, 1998; *Go Tell It on the Mountain, and Related Readings*, 1998, by James Baldwin.

BIBLIOGRAPHY

Donnell, Alison. "The Short Fiction of Olive Senior." In *Caribbean Women Writers: Fiction in English*, edited by Mary Condé and Thorunn Lonsdale. New York: St. Martin's Press, 1999. Good analysis of Senior's use of narrators, especially child narrators, to critique the polarized Jamaican society.

Patteson, Richard F. "The Fiction of Olive Senior: Traditional Society and the Larger World." *ARIEL: A Review of International English Literature* 24, no. 1 (1993): 13-33. Discusses how Senior uses accounts of family relationships and language (Creole and standard English) to address the oppression inherent in colonialism.

Pyne-Timothy, Helen. "The Double Vision: Ethnic Identity and the Caribbean Woman Writer." In *The Woman, the Writer, and Caribbean Society: Essays in Literature and Culture*, edited by Helen Pyne-Timothy. Los Angeles: UCLA Center for African American Studies, 1999. Places Senior in context of Caribbean women who write and discusses the importance of the feminist movement in their decision to write.

Rowell, Charles H. "An Interview with Olive Senior." *Callaloo*, 3, no. 11 (Summer, 1988): 480-490. Senior talks about her hostility toward the Christian Church and her belief that the Church affirms and perpetuates oppression of Jamaicans.

Smith-Allen, Paula. "*Summer Lightning*: Olive Senior's Jamaican Redemption." In *Beyond the Cane Break: West Indian Women Writers in Canada*, edited by Emily Williams. Laurenceville, New Jersey: Africa World Press, 2007. Discusses the influence on Senior's work of her being born in Jamaica but living in Canada. Looks at identity and levels of discourse.

Shawncey Webb

VARLAM SHALAMOV

Born: Vologda, Russia; July 1, 1907
Died: Moscow, Soviet Union (now in Russia); January 17, 1982

PRINCIPAL SHORT FICTION

Kolymskie rasskazy, 1978 (*Kolyma Tales*, 1980, and *Graphite*, 1981)

OTHER LITERARY FORMS

Varlam Shalamov (vahr-LAHM SHAH-lahm-uhf) was primarily a writer of short stories, although the particular nature of the genre he developed is unique. His stories are a blend of fiction and nonfiction. Shalamov was also a poet, and his only works to be published in the Soviet Union were poems. A collection of poems titled *Shelest List'ev* (rustling of leaves) was published in 1964, and *Tochka kipeniia: Stikhi* (boiling point: poems) appeared in Moscow in 1977. Shalamov also wrote essays, in particular *Ocherki prestupnogo mira* (n.d.; essays on the criminal world).

ACHIEVEMENTS

Varlam Shalamov's achievements cannot be measured by ordinary standards or norms. Certainly, his greatest achievement was to stay alive during his seventeen years in what he calls the "death camps"--as opposed to ordinary camps--in Kolyma in northeastern Siberia. He survived: Although he was indelibly marked by the experience, it did not break him.

The quality of his short stories, which are a subtle blend of fiction and nonfiction, is extraordinarily high. John Glad, who translated most of the *Kolymskie rasskazy* into English in two volumes, *Kolyma Tales* and *Graphite,* claimed in 1981 that Shalamov was "Russia's greatest living writer." Although this might seem excessively enthusiastic, particularly in view of the achievements of Aleksandr Solzhenitsyn, the claim is

not to be lightly dismissed. The stories are strikingly original in their use of the short-story form. Solzhenitsyn himself had the highest regard for Shalamov's talent. When he first read Shalamov in 1956, he later recalled, he felt as if he had "met a long-lost brother" and believed that in some ways Shalamov's experience surpassed his own. "I respectfully confess," Solzhenitsyn wrote, "that to him and not to me was it given to touch those depths of bestiality and despair towards which life in the camps dragged us all." Solzhenitsyn writes relatively little about the mining camps of Kolyma in *Arkhipelag Gulag* (1973-1975; *The Gulag Archipelago,* 1974-1978) or about the infamous "numbered" death camps that had no names but only numbers to designate them.

The critic Grigori Svirski has well described the shock experienced by Russian readers when Shalamov's first stories were circulated in samizdat form in the 1960's:

> It was truth and not perfect style that was required of Shalamov, and in each new story he uncovered new pages of truth about convict life with such power, that even former political prisoners who had not witnessed such things were struck dumb. The truth revealed by Shalamov shocks because it is described by an artist, described with such skill, as they used to say in the nineteenth century, that the skill is invisible.

BIOGRAPHY

Varlam Tikhonovich Shalamov was born and reared in Vologda, a town in north-central European Russia. Shalamov's adult life was largely spent in prisons and camps, but ironically even his childhood was spent in a region affected by the Russian penal system. He has written of Vologda that "over the centuries as a result of the banishment to the area of so many protesters, rebels, and different critics of the tsars, a sort of sediment built up and a particular moral climate was formed which was at a higher level than any city in Russia." In 1919, Kedrov, the Soviet commander of the northern front, had two hundred hostages shot in Vologda. Little is known of Shalamov's life, but he says in a story that one of the hostages killed was the local chemistry teacher--as a result, Shalamov never learned chemistry or even the formula for water.

Shalamov was married, and in 1937, he was arrested for declaring that Ivan Bunin, the winner of the 1933 Nobel Prize in Literature, was "a Russian classic." Shalamov spent the next seventeen years in labor camps, mostly in Kolyma, in northeastern Siberia, where the prisoners worked in gold mines. The Soviet Union was the second largest producer of gold in the world, largely because of these mines, which utilized prison and slave labor; it is estimated that more than three million people died there from cold, hunger, and overwork. In *The Gulag Archipelago*, Solzhenitsyn calls Kolyma "the pole of cold and cruelty"; the British author Robert Conquest argues in *Kolyma: The Arctic Death Camps* (1978) that these killings were the conscious result of a policy of extermination.

Shalamov was released in 1954 and returned to Moscow. His stories were first circulated in manuscript form in the Soviet Union and were later published in Russian in the émigré journals *Grani* and *Novyi Zhurnal*. Some authors in the Soviet Union at the time were establishing regular contact with Western journalists and even obtaining Western lawyers to protect their rights, but Shalamov, old and ill, could do nothing to ensure more adequate publication of his works. A French version of his stories was published in 1969. It was not until 1978, however, that a complete Russian edition of the stories was brought out by Overseas Publications Interchange in London. The Soviet authorities forced Shalamov to denounce publicly the publication of his stories.

Shalamov was ill during the last decades of his life. A contemporary observer described Shalamov in Moscow: "On the speaker's rostrum stood a man with a completely fixed expression on his face. He appeared dried up and curiously dark and frozen like a blackened tree." Shalamov died on January 17, 1982.

ANALYSIS

It is natural to compare Varlam Shalamov's work to that of Aleksandr Solzhenitsyn; there are similarities in their subject matter, and they had great respect for each other. Solzhenitsyn was among the first to recognize Shalamov's talent in the early 1960's, when Shalamov's brief sketches of life in the Kolyma labor camps began to trickle into the embryonic network in Moscow, Leningrad, and a few other cities. Recognizing their importance, Solzhenitsyn invited Shalamov to share the authorship of The Gulag Archipelago, the multivolume "experiment in literary investigation" on which he was working. Shalamov was too ill, however, to accept Solzhenitsyn's invitation.

Unlike Solzhenitsyn, Shalamov does not aim at a panoramic view of the camp world. Also, his language is quite different from that of Solzhenitsyn. On the surface, at least, he does not appear to maintain a high pitch of passionate indignation and invective; he adheres to a deliberately cool and neutral tone. In contrast to the passionately self-righteous, not-to-be-intimidated Solzhenitsyn, with his steely courage and seemingly infinite capacity for resistance, Shalamov appears chilly, remote, preferring a miniature canvas that is fragmentary and almost incomplete. Rhetoric is left behind, the writer taking refuge in a kind of passive quietism. This first impression, however, is almost entirely false.

If Shalamov lowers his voice, it is to be even more direct, precise, and telling. His experience was quite different from that of Solzhenitsyn. Arrested in 1937, Shalamov was in Kolyma throughout World War II and observed the war only by means of the new arrivals of prisoners. Solzhenitsyn was arrested at the war's end, in 1945. Shalamov's camp experience was twice as long and harsher; he knew no *sharashka*, or special projects camp, like that described in Solzhenitsyn's *V kruge pervom* (1968; *The First Circle*, 1968). Instead, Shalamov was designated for extermination and according to all expectations should have died.

It is difficult for the Western reader, with current notions of history and modernity, to understand Kolyma. In the United States, slavery ended with the Civil War; in Russia, the serfs were emancipated at about the same time. Though readers may think of themselves as skeptical and as not believing in unabated progress, still, old habits die hard; many realities of the contemporary world and of foreign countries appear to be impossible. In the mid-1930's, the Soviet government began to exploit its underground gold seams by means of slave labor of an unprecedented kind. Slaves, as is well known, are relatively unproductive; the People's Commissariat of Internal Affairs (NKVD), however, resolved to overcome the reluctance of their prisoners to work through the goad of hunger by deliberately undernourishing them unless they achieved high production norms. The result was that most of the prisoners died. Then again, the NKVD paid nothing for its captives and could always replace dead ones by enslaving new people. Kolyma was the ultimate pole of this murderous system, cut off from continental Russia yet attached to it by its need for laborers.

Shalamov was arrested for calling Ivan Bunin a "Russian classic"; others were arrested for still more trifling reasons--for example, writing to a fiancé. Once in Kolyma, the captives' immediate overseers would be thieves and common criminals, officially described by the Soviet government as "friends of the people" or "socially friendly elements." In the story "Esperanto," Shalamov describes one of his jobs: "On the very first day I took the place of a horse in a wooden yoke, heaving with my chest against a wooden log." Shalamov observes wryly that man has more endurance than any other animal. In the story "Zhitie inzhenera Kipreeva" ("The Life of Engineer Kipreev"), a prisoner, Kipreev, declares that "Kolyma is Auschwitz without the ovens"; the inscription over the prison gates--strikingly similar to the German "Arbeit macht frei" at Auschwitz--is "Labor is honor, glory, nobility, and heroism." Few survived the first three years in Kolyma; the narrator observes in the story "Kusok mysa" ("A Piece of Meat"), "two weeks was a long time, a thousand years." The area contained innumerable mass graves. In the frozen taiga, dead bodies did not decompose; in the chilling story "Po Lend-licu" ("Lend Lease"), a recently arrived bulldozer--a gift from the United States government--has as its first task to cut a trench to hold a mass grave of bodies that is slowly sliding down the frozen side of a mountain.

In conditions such as these it would be unrealistic to expect a sustained attitude of vituperation like that of Solzhenitsyn. The prison conditions described by Fyodor Dostoevski in *Zapiski iz myortvogo doma* (1861-1862; *Buried Alive: Or, Ten Years of Penal Servitude in Siberia*, 1881; better known as *House of the Dead*) were considered to be almost luxurious in comparison with those of the camps in Kolyma, and the same applied to Anton Chekhov's 1894 description of the penal colony on Sakhalin Island. In one of Shalamov's stories, a general, sent to Kolyma at the close of World War II, notes that the experience of the front cannot prepare a man for the mass death in the camps. One character, informed that the Soviet Union has signed the United Nations resolution on genocide in 1937, asks with caustic irony, "Genocide? Is that something they serve for dinner?" ("The Life of Engineer Kipreev"). The conditions were closer to those described by Bruno Bettelheim in *The Informed Heart: Autonomy in a Mass Age* (1960) and Eugen Kogon in his *Der SS-Staat* (1947; *The Theory and Practise of Hell*, 1950), although as Shalamov observes, "there were no gas furnaces in Kolyma. The corpses wait in stone, in the permafrost." It should be remembered that Shalamov was not there for one year, like Bettelheim, or seven years, like Kogon, but seventeen years.

"SENTENTIOUS"

The key to the unique tone in these stories can be found in the story entitled "Sententsiya" ("Sententious"), which describes a prisoner on the verge of death who gradually revives. The evolution of feelings that pass through his semiconscious mind (he is the story's narrator) is of extraordinary interest. At the beginning he is a walking dead man, one of those who were called *Musselmänner* in Nazi concentration camps, "wicks" in the Soviet camps. The narrator observes, "I had little warmth. Little flesh was left on my bones, just enough for bitterness--the last human emotion; it was closer to the bone." His greatest need is for forgetfulness and sleep. Later he improves, and he notes, "Then something else appeared--something different from resentment and bitterness. There appeared indifference and fearlessness. I realized I didn't care if I was beaten or not." As he steadily improves there is a third stage: fear. Then a fourth stage follows: "Envy was the name of the next feeling that returned to me. I envied my dead friends who had died in '38. I envied those of my neighbors who had something to chew or smoke." The narrator says bitingly that after this point, the feeling of love did not return:

> Love comes only when all other human emotions have already returned. Love comes last, returns last. Or does it return? Indifference, envy, and fear, however, were not the only witnesses of my return to life. Pity for animals returned earlier than pity for people.

The passage suggests that the evolution of feelings did not stop there, but continued. It gives a valuable insight into Shalamov's own attitudes. The narrator of the story has to learn language and individual words all over again. Each thought, each word "returned alone, unaccompanied by the watchful guards of familiar words. Each appeared first on the tongue and only later in the mind."

BITTERNESS AND HUMOR

Henceforth, this particular bitterness would stay with Shalamov as a substrate; in the foreground or almost hidden in the background, it provides his unique tone. John Gland has noted that Shalamov's tone sometimes seems neutral, distant, or passive; yet it is never truly neutral. Usually it is closer to the bitterness described above: a dark, profoundly reverberating irony that no other author has expressed as well as Shalamov and is "closer to the bone."

Shalamov's range often goes beyond this. He can surprise with his sense of humor. His description of the visit of an American businessman, Mr. Popp, to the Soviet Union, the hasty preparation of the authorities to receive him, and his meeting with the "Commandant" of a hotel, Tsyplyakov, are as funny as Mikhail Zoshchenko at his best. The variety of people in Shalamov's stories is great. He describes naïve people, such as the young peasant Fedya in "Sukhim paikam" ("Dry Rations"); the omnipresent criminals; religious fanatics; Esperantists' heroic officers from World War II, such as "Pugachov," who were swept into the camps in 1945 and died attempting to escape; bureaucrats; guards; doctors; women; and the most ordinary people. Like Solzhenitsyn, he is particularly good at describing the special kind of meanness, or sadism, of one person

toward another, cultivated by the totalitarian system and by the widespread presence of informers and spies. Even prisoners trying to recruit other prisoners for escape attempts were likely to be hired informers.

"AN EPITAPH"

Some of the stories are especially effective because of the variety and solidity of the characters. There is not only a single protagonist and a few other one-dimensional characters used as foils but also the unexpected breadth of real life. In the story "Nadgrobnoe slovo" ("An Epitaph"), a group of prisoners fantasize about what they will do when they leave prison and return to normal life. No two dreams are the same. One peasant wants to go to the Communist Party headquarters, simply because there were more cigarette butts on the floor there than he had seen anywhere else: He wants to pick them up and then roll his own cigarette. The last words are given to a person hitherto silent who slowly, deliberately, expresses unrelieved hatred: 'As for me,' he said in a calm, unhurried voice, 'I'd like to have my arms and legs cut off and become a human stump--no arms or legs. Then I'd be strong enough to spit in their faces for everything they're doing to us.'"

CHEKHOVIAN TRAITS

There is real artistry in these stories, and it is of an unexpected, nontraditional kind. Shalamov has been compared to Chekhov ("the Chekhov of the camps"), and although the comparison is apt there are real differences between the two writers. Both show economy, sparingly sketch in a background, and lead toward a single dramatic point or realization at the end. Shalamov's stories, however, are less obviously fictional than Chekhov's. Although Shalamov uses a variety of narrators in the stories, a majority have a speaker who resembles Shalamov himself. There is an air of casualness about the stories, both old-fashioned and at the same time extremely modern. Far more frequently than with Chekhov, the reader is unsure of the direction in which a narration is leading, although usually the story has a hidden but inexorable direction. At the end of the story "Perviy zub" ("My First Tooth"), a storyteller tries out several alternate versions of a story on a listener; the technique is similar to that used by Akira Kurosawa in his film *Rashomon* (1950). The story ends:

"I don't like that variation either," I said.

"Then I'll leave it as I originally had it."

Even if you can't get something published, it's easier to bear a thing if you write it down. Once you've done that, you can forget. . . .

As an ending this is disarming, seemingly casual, although the sharp edge of irony should not be missed. Shalamov sometimes says that he wants nothing more than to forget; often when he describes an experience he will admit that he simply did not care what would happen. These attitudes are incorporated into the subject matter of the stories. However, Shalamov the writer, the artist, remembers and cares intensely. Western readers often miss the deeply understated irony in these passages: It is unique, subtle, and extremely powerful.

Shalamov's stories have interested many readers because of their unusual subject matter. On the verge of nonfiction, they are invaluable as documents. Their greatest value, however, is probably in their original use of form and their artistry. Stories such as the allegorical "Domino" ("Dominoes") and "Zagavor yuristov" ("The Lawyers' Plot") achieve a concentrated depth of meaning that is truly remarkable. Like Elie Wiesel, Shalamov is a survivor and a witness who also happens to be an excellent artist. By his own admission, he subordinates art to the truth of experience, yet his art only gains from this.

OTHER MAJOR WORKS

POETRY: *Shelest List'ev*, 1964; *Tochka kipeniia: Stikhi*, 1977.

NONFICTION: *Ocherki prestupnogo mira*, n.d.

BIBLIOGRAPHY

Boym, Svetlana. "Banality of Evil,' Mimicry, and the Soviet Subject: Varlam Shalamov and Hannah Arendt." *Slavic Review: Interdisciplinary Quarterly of Russian, Eurasian, and East European Studies* 67, no. 2 (Summer, 2008): 342-363. Using Arendt's theory of the banality of evil and other concepts of totalitarianism and terror, Boyn analyzes Soviet accounts of the gulag, including *Kolyma Tales*. Argues that Shalamov's prose mimics the Soviet discourse and technology of the gulag.

Conquest, Robert. *Kolyma: The Artic Death Camps*. New York: Viking Press, 1978. An excellent source of background information about the Kolyma concentration camp, facilitating better understanding of Shalamov's stories. Contains frequent references to, and quotes from, Shalamov.

Glad, John. "Art Out of Hell: Shalamov of Kolyma." *Survey* 107 (1979): 45-50. Seeing Shalamov's stories in the Chekhovian tradition, Glad discusses Shalamov's struggle with the authorities and his contribution to the camp literature as a lasting document of human courage.

_____. Foreword to *Graphite*, by Varlam Shalamov. New York: W. W. Norton, 1981. Glad describes the conditions in Kolyma and the Soviet penal system. He sees the uniqueness of Shalamov's stories in their being a bridge between fact and fiction. However, their artistic quality, especially their pantheistic surrealism, makes them true works of art.

_____. Foreword to *Kolyma Tales*, by Varlam Shalamov. New York: W. W. Norton, 1980. Similar to Glad's article in *Survey*.

Golden, Nathaniel. *Varlam Shalamov's "Kolyma Tales": A Formalist Analysis*. New York: Rodopi, 2004. Uses neoformalist theory to analyze eleven of the tales. Includes discussion of the stories' narrative structures, points of view, characterizations, ideas, and motifs and of Shalamov's literary techniques.

Hosking, Geoffrey. "The Ultimate Circle of the Stalinist Inferno." *New Universities Quarterly* 34 (1980): 161-168. In this review of the Russian edition of *Kolyma Tales*, Hosking discusses several stories and the overall significance of Shalamov as a witness of crimes against humanity. He also compares similarities and differences between Shalamov and Aleksandr Solzhenitsyn as writers of camp literature.

Toker, Leona. "Samizdat and the Problem of Authorial Control: The Case of Varlam Shalamov." *Poetics Today* 29, no. 4 (Winter, 2008): 735-758. In the former Soviet Union, samizdat was a system for reproducing and distributing literature that had been outlawed by the government. Toker explains why Shalamov, who became famous because of the clandestine publishing of his works, nevertheless disliked samizdat.

_____. "A Tale Untold: Verlam Shalamov's 'A Day Off.'" *Studies in Short Fiction* 28 (Winter, 1991): 1-8. A discussion of some aspects of Shalamov's modernist techniques, comparable to the works of Ernest Hemingway and Vladimir Nabokov, as embodied in his story "A Day Off." Claims that Shalamov's work is part of the tradition that presents the darkest side of experience against the belief in the ultimate triumph of humanist values.

_____. "Testimony as Art: Varlam Shalamov's 'Condensed Milk.'" In *The Russian Twentieth-Century Short Story: A Critical Companion*, edited by Lyudmila Parts. Brighton, Mass.: Academic Studies Press, 2010. Provides a critical reading of this story.

_____. "Toward a Poetics of Documentary Prose--From the Perspective of Gulag Testimonies." *Poetics Today* 18 (Summer, 1997): 187-222. Places documentary prose into a nonmarginalizing perspective by constructing a paradigm of narrative modes based on the chronological sequence of events in the narrative. Discusses the clash between the rhetorical principles of "defamiliarization" and the "economy of effort" in documentary prose by a brief analysis of Varlam Shalamov's story "Berries."

_____. *Towards the Ethics of Form in Fiction: Narratives of Cultural Remission*. Columbus: Ohio State University Press, 2010. Focuses on narrative structure and its connection to a writer's moral vision in several works of literature, including "The Artist of the Spade" by Shalamov. Compares this story to Franz Kafka's "A Hunger Artist."

John Carpenter
Updated by Vasa D. Mihailovich

ANDREI SINYAVSKY

Born: Moscow, Soviet Union (now in Russia); October 8, 1925
Died: Fontenay-aux-Roses, France; February 25, 1997
Also known as: Abram Tertz

PRINCIPAL SHORT FICTION

Fantasticheskie povesti, 1961 (*Fantastic Stories,* 1963; also as *The Icicle, and Other Stories,* 1963)
Kroshka Tsores, 1980 (novella; *Little Jinx,* 1992)

OTHER LITERARY FORMS

Before his arrest in 1965 for smuggling "anti-Soviet propaganda," Andrei Sinyavsky (ahn-DRAY sihn-YOV-skee) was a senior research associate at the Gorky Institute of World Literature in Moscow and had become a well-known literary critic, focusing primarily on modern Russian literature. After emigrating to Paris in 1973, he published more criticism as well as book-length literary essays. Except for the literary essay *Chto takoe sotsialisticheskii realizm* (1959; *On Socialist Realism,* 1960), the works that led to his arrest were fiction: two novels and some half-dozen stories. All appeared in the West under the pseudonym Abram Tertz. He also wrote a book of aphorisms, *Mysli vrasplokh* (1966; *Unguarded Thoughts,* 1972), and the nonfiction works *Soviet Civilization: A Cultural History* (1990) and *The Russian Intelligentsia* (1997).

ACHIEVEMENTS

Andrei Sinyavsky's literary efforts served as a daring challenge to the tenets of Socialist Realism, the doctrine that was supposed to guide Soviet authors in their choice of subject matter, as well as in their treatment of it. His essay *On Socialist Realism*, written in 1956, at the height of the post-Stalinist thaw, contained an attack on the very conjunction of the words "socialist" and "realism," as well as a historical analysis of the manner in which the doctrine had harmed Soviet literature. His own underground fiction was both antisocialist, in his effort to include a religious dimension antithetical to Marxism, and antirealistic with a strong inclination toward the fantastic and the grotesque. The consequences of writing in isolation, as well as of determinedly breaking with the dominant tradition, sometimes show--he occasionally seems to be trying too hard for effect or to make a point--but Sinyavsky nevertheless stands as a writer who helped undermine the influence of Socialist Realism.

Along with his fellow writer Yuli Daniel he also helped popularize the very notions of samizdat (self-publishing) and *tamizdat* (publishing "there," or abroad). Despite the government's persecution of these two authors, many others throughout the 1960's and 1970's came to write outside the permissible norms--sometimes circulating their work privately, sometimes attempting to publish outside the Soviet Union, and sometimes simply writing "for the drawer." Sinyavsky's example did much to help a clandestine Soviet literature flourish during a trying period. In 1978, Sinyavsky received the Bennett Award from the Grolier Club.

BIOGRAPHY

By the time he was in his early forties, Andrei Donatovich Sinyavsky had achieved a large measure of success within Soviet society. Born and reared in Moscow, he attended Moscow University, from which he received the Soviet equivalent of a doctorate in 1952. His thesis was on Maxim Gorky, often considered the "father" of Socialist Realism. He then received a position at the Gorky Institute of World Literature, a branch of the Soviet Academy of Sciences; during the next dozen years, he published several studies on Gorky and also wrote about twentieth century poetry. At the end of the 1950's, he began to publish reviews in the prestigious literary journal *Novy mir*, aligning himself with those struggling for greater artistic freedom through his attacks on some of the more conservative writers. Still, his name was not widely known until he published the introductory essay to a major 1965 collection of Boris Pasternak's poetry (translated in *For Freedom of Imagination*, 1971).

Later that same year, much to the surprise of nearly everyone, he and a close friend, Yuli Daniel, were arrested; employing the pseudonyms Abram Tertz (the rogue hero of a thieves' song once popular in Odessa) and Nikolai Arzhak, respectively, each had smuggled out stories to the West that were seen by the authorities as examples of "anti-Soviet propaganda." Their trial, in February, 1966, was significant in that it was the first time that Soviet writers were actually convicted of a crime on the basis of their literary works. It also marked the end of the fitful liberalizing tendencies that had characterized the years since the death of Joseph Stalin in 1953 and the imposition of a harsher regime that was to force many writers into exile.

As it turned out, Sinyavsky's life prior to his arrest was more complex than it might have appeared on the surface. Although he grew up as a believer in the ideals of the revolution that brought the Communists to power in the Soviet Union, his faith was shaken by the arrest of his father in 1951 for political activities that predated the Revolution of 1917 and by efforts of the secret police, beginning in 1948, to involve him in a plot that would somehow compromise a friend, Hélène Peltier-Zamoyska, daughter of the French naval attaché in Moscow. He managed to resist, but the machinations continued for several years; later, Peltier-Zamoyska served as the courier for bringing the manuscripts of "Abram Tertz" out of the Soviet Union. In 1955, Sinyavsky wrote the first of his underground works, the story "V tsirke" ("At the Circus"). Then in 1956, the year that is generally regarded as marking the height of the post-Stalinist "thaw," he composed both his essay *On Socialist Realism* and his first novel, *Sud idzie* (1960; *The Trial Begins*, 1960), which can be seen as a literary illustration of the writing that Sinyavsky advocates in the essay. Over the next several years, he continued to compose the works that made Abram Tertz a well-known figure in the West and a wanted man in the Soviet Union.

Sinyavsky eventually served five and one-half years of a seven-year term (and Daniel four of the five years to which he had been sentenced). While in prison, Sinyavsky continued to write, sending out his works in letters to his wife: *Golos iz khora* (1973; *A Voice from the Chorus*, 1976), *Progulki s Pushkinym* (1975; *Strolls* with *Pushkin*, 1993), and *V teni Gogolya* (1975; in Gogol's shadow). He was allowed to emigrate in 1973 and became a professor of Russian literature at the Sorbonne. Remaining active in the literary world, Sinyavsky began his own journal, *Sintaksis*, and wrote the autobiographical novel *Spokoynoy nochi* (1984; *Goodnight!*, 1989). His works remained sufficiently controversial in the Soviet Union that he could be published there only well into the period of glasnost; in 1989, he was allowed to visit the country to pay respects upon the death of Yuli Daniel. His Russian citizenship was restored in 1990. Sinyavsky died of cancer in France in 1997.

ANALYSIS

Andrei Sinyavsky's short fiction resembles his longer work in both its themes and its manner. While for the most part less overt in their political message than the novels, the stories contain heroes who are equally alienated--from society, from themselves, or from both--and who seem trapped in an existence from which they would like to escape. Elements of fantasy abound; in some cases the stories verge on science fiction, while in others the emphasis is more on extreme psychological states. The plots, to the extent that they can be discerned at all, are usually fairly straightforward. Interpretation, however, can be difficult; sometimes a given scene may be viewed as fantastic, as reflecting a character's mental aberration, or as purposefully ambiguous. The first-person narrators are often not helpful in this regard, and situations may appear to be allegorical or metaphorical representations of themes that are not mentioned directly within the works. In short, Sinyavsky is demanding of his readers.

"AT THE CIRCUS"

"At the Circus" stands out from the other stories: It predates them by several years and is also the most conventional in form. The narrator has a distinctive voice, but for once he is not a chief figure within the story itself. Still, the tale offers an early glimpse into some of Sinyavsky's concerns. The hero, Kostia, is a ne'er-do-well who dreams of achieving the skill of those he admires at the circus. During a botched burglary, he kills the very magician he has admired, is sentenced to twenty years of hard labor, and then is

himself killed during an attempt to escape. Kostia is the first of Sinyavsky's many outsiders, those who feel in some way oppressed and want to escape into new lives; indeed, dreams of, or efforts at, getting away from ordinary life lie behind all the major events. Despite the third-person narration, Sinyavsky often limits the perspective to that of Kostia; the narrow focus and the frequent absence of conventional transitions pull the reader deep into the protagonist's psyche, so that his distorted outlook becomes the norm for the world of the story. The narrative, as well as the settings and the subject matter, thus emphasizes the sense of oppression and enclosure; nearly all Sinyavsky's stories seem, in this way, to be claustrophobic.

"TENANTS"

"Kvartiranty" ("Tenants"), composed in 1959, is perhaps among his most obscure stories. The setting of "Tenants," a Russian communal apartment, is sufficiently realistic, but the narrator turns out to be a house sprite. His addressee--not interlocutor because he does not say a word--is Sergei Sergeevich, a drunkard and writer who now lives within the apartment. The story is

Andrei Sinyavsky (AP Photo/ITAR-TASS)

open to a variety of interpretations: It can be seen as a genuine fantasy or, less likely, as the drunken hallucinations of Sergei Sergeevich. The tales related by the house sprite are themselves fantastic, filled with references to literature or writers, and at first seem to be of little purpose. Eventually, though, certain themes emerge. The house sprite points to the prevalence of evil; not only do the names often contain hidden references to the devil or various spirits but also relatively mundane occurrences, such as a spat in the communal kitchen, lead to dire consequences. Many of the figures in the story have been driven out of one existence into another; even water nymphs and wood sprites have been forced from the country to the city. Ultimately, though, "Tenants" concerns the writer: the threats to his well-being, his position as an outsider, and his (perhaps unfulfilled) obligation to deal with the evil around him.

"You and I"

"Ty i ya" ("You and I") is arguably even more resistant to any single interpretation. Much of the work employs a second-person narrative, with the "You" of the title addressed directly. This individual is named Nikolai Vasilyevich (the first name and patronymic of Nikolai Gogol, who, along with Fyodor Dostoevski, clearly influenced this and other works by Sinyavsky) and apparently suffers from a persecution mania. After an opening scene at a party, he hides out in his apartment, refusing to have contact with others until he eventually slashes his throat. The true mystery of the story, though, is the identity of "I," who plays a direct role in the fate of "You." Some critics have seen "You and I" as describing a single individual who suffers from schizophrenia as well as paranoia; others believe that the relationship is between the author and his character or between a godlike figure and the individual (there is sufficient evidence to support all these views).

Despite the purposeful complexity of the narrative--which includes disjointed descriptions of wildly different events taking place simultaneously throughout the city--it is possible to discern several of Sinyavsky's major concerns in "You and I." Part of Nikolai Vasilyevich's paranoia is based on a fear of women; the erotic scenes that are sprinkled throughout the stories, beginning with "At the Circus," not only serve to violate one

of the restrictions of Socialist Realism but also portray sex in a less than flattering manner. The perception of the outside world recalls that of the house sprite in "Tenants": Evil forces threaten "You" and promise to drive him out of his refuge. Most crucially, though, Sinyavsky again raises the question of the responsibility of the creator, the "I," and of his relationship to the world around him.

"The Icicle"

"Gololeditsa" ("The Icicle"), written in 1961, is both the longest of Sinyavsky's early stories and one of the richest. The narrator abruptly achieves the power to see into the future and the past. He finds out that the woman he loves, Natasha, will be killed by a falling icicle in a specific place in Moscow at a certain time. He attempts to flee the city with her, but on the way he is arrested by the authorities and questioned about his magical powers. Natasha returns to Moscow and is killed by the icicle, at which point the narrator loses his special gift.

The topic allows Sinyavsky to display fully his talents as a writer and to probe his most deeply felt ideas. The narrative is fast-paced and almost jaunty; while some old-fashioned suspense makes the work gripping, Sinyavsky imparts a special air by interspersing the sad and at times tragic events with comic interludes. Particularly effective is his portrayal of Colonel Tarasov, the interrogator, whose naïve efforts to obtain politically useful predictions allow Sinyavsky to satirize the mentality of those in power under Joseph Stalin (the story is subtly but clearly dated at the very end of Stalin's reign). Most striking, though, are the meditations that arise from considering the effects of being able to see endlessly into the past and the future; besides the more obvious question of how a knowledge of the future would affect an individual's actions in the present, Sinyavksy considers the meaning of death, experiments with converting time into space (so that the present self represents a simultaneous amalgam of past and future selves), and suggests that an individual with special knowledge or powers has some degree of moral responsibility for others.

"Pkhentz"

"Pkhentz" appeared in the West in 1966, later than the other "fantastic stories," and has been widely seen as an allegory for the situation of the writer in Soviet Russia. Only little by little does it become clear that the narrator of the story is an alien creature, stranded on earth, who has wrapped his body and put on a disguise to hide his true identity. In some ways, his dilemma resembles that of Sinyavsky before his arrest: the creature's pseudonym resembles Sinyavsky's real name, and he too has a fear of discovery. More broadly, though, "Pkhentz" is concerned with the threat of persecution and mockery directed by society toward the one who is different and also with the alienation of the outsider, which here is presented through the revulsion that the alien feels toward such basic human activities as sex and eating. It is one of Sinyavsky's simplest, most direct, and yet most powerful stories.

LITTLE JINX

Little Jinx was written after Sinyavsky's emigration and is generally referred to as a novella, though it is no longer than "The Icicle." The story is dedicated to E. T. A. Hoffmann and inspired by his *Klein Zaches, Genannt Zinnober* (1819; *Little Zaches, Surnamed Zinnober*, 1971). Sinyavsky replaces Hoffmann's good fairy with a pediatrician, Dora Alexandrovna, who cures the stuttering that afflicts the narrator Tsores (Yiddish for grief; he is also sometimes called Sinyavsky). Tsores achieves a gift with words, but he also unintentionally causes the deaths of each of his five half-brothers. Here, it becomes possible to discern a clear direction in Sinyavsky's short fiction; even more clearly than in "Pkhentz," he is writing simultaneously about himself (this story was originally intended to serve as an episode in his autobiographical *Goodnight!*) and more broadly about the condition of the writer, particularly in a totalitarian society. Thus, the story is both about isolation on the one hand and about moral responsibility and guilt on the other; like so many of the earlier heroes, Tsores/Sinyavsky finds that the role of creator becomes an obligation and incurs inescapable burdens--such is the dilemma with which Tertz/Sinyavsky has had to cope as well.

OTHER MAJOR WORKS

LONG FICTION: *Sad idzie*, 1959 (in Polish; *Sud idyot*, 1960; as Abram Tertz; *The Trial Begins*, 1960); *Lyubimov*, 1963 (in Polish; *Lyubimov*, 1964; as Tertz; *The*

Makepeace Experiment, 1965); *Spokoynoy nochi*, 1984 (*Goodnight!*, 1989).

NONFICTION: *Istoriya russkoy sovetsky literatury*, 1958, 1961; *Chto takoe sotsialisticheskii realizm*, 1959 (as Abram Tertz; *On Socialist Realism*, 1960); *Pikasso*, 1960 (with I. N. Golomshtok); *Poeziya pervykh let revolyutsii, 1917-1920*, 1964 (with A. Menshutin); *Mysli vrasplokh*, 1966 (as Tertz; *Unguarded Thoughts*, 1972); *For Freedom of Imagination*, 1971 (essays); *Golos iz khora*, 1973 (*A Voice from the Chorus*, 1976); *Progulki s Pushkinym*, 1975 (*Strolls with Pushkin*, 1993); *V teni Gogolya*, 1975; *"Opavshie list'ya" V. V. Rozanova*, 1982; *Soviet Civilization: A Cultural History*, 1990; *Ivan-durak: Ocherk russkoi narodnoi very*, 1991 (*Ivan the Fool: Russian Folk Belief--A Cultural History*, 2007); *The Russian Intelligensia*, 1997.

BIBLIOGRAPHY

Carrington, Ildiko de Papp. "Demons, Doubles, and Dinosaurs: Life Before Man, the Origins of Consciousness, and 'The Icicle'." *Essays on Canadian Writing* 33 (1986) 68-88. A useful study of Sinyavsky's story.

Dalton, Margaret. *Andrei Siniavskii and Julii Daniel: Two Soviet "Heretical" Writers*. Würzburg, Germany: Jal-verlag, 1973. Along with a discussion of the other works that Sinyavsky wrote prior to his arrest, this study contains a detailed story-by-story analysis of the six stories from that period. Throughout, Dalton pays special attention to the unusual literary devices that often make the works difficult to interpret. Contains notes and a bibliography.

Durkin, Andrew R. "Narrator, Metaphor, and Theme in Sinjavskij's *Fantastic Tales*." *Slavic and East European Journal* 24 (1980); 133-144. Durkin divides the six early stories into three pairs for the purposes of analysis, but his goal is to discern the thematic concerns and formal devices that link all the stories. He emphasizes the role of art and of the artist, as well as the theme of escape, or liberation.

Fenander, Sara. "Author and Autocrat: Tertz's Stalin and the Ruse of Charisma." *The Russian Review* 58 (April, 1999): 286-297. Discusses Sinyavsky in his role as both cultural critic and provocateur Abram Tertz. Argues that by turning the discredited Joseph

Stalin into a double for himself, Sinyavsky/Tertz reveals both the artistry of Stalinism and the mythical privileged place of the writer in Russian culture.

Frank, Joseph. "The Triumph of Abram Tertz." In *Between Religion and Rationality: Essays in Russian Literature and Culture*. Princeton, N.J.: Princeton University Press, 2010. A brief biographical and critical discussion of the events of Sinyavsky's life and the nature of his fiction. Notes the importance of his trial for having his works published outside the Soviet Union. This essay originally appeared in a slightly different form in the June 27, 1991, issue of *The New York Review of Books*.

Haber, Erika. "In Search of the Fantastic in Tertz's Fantastic Realism." *Slavic and East European Journal* 42 (Summer, 1998): 254-267. Shows how the presence of an eccentric narrator who often plays a double role as both character and narrator, creating a highly self-conscious text, is a basic feature of Tertz's fantastic realism. Argues that his narrators at times contradict and even oppose the characters and events they describe, thereby creating a tension between the content of the stories and the manner of their presentation.

Kolonosky, Walter. "Andrei Sinyavsky: Puzzle Maker." *Slavic and East European Journal* 42 (Fall, 1998): 385-388. Compares Sinyavsky's works to puzzles; his pieces are not simply read, but contain historical references, allegorical links, language peculiarities, grotesque allusions, and autobiographical asides that require interpretation.

_____. "Inherent and Ulterior Design in Sinyavsky's 'Pxenc.'" *Slavic and East European Journal* 26 (1982): 329-337. Accepting the notion that "Pkhentz" is, on one level, a work of scientific fiction, Kolonosky claims that it is primarily an allegory about faith, and he traces examples of Christian symbolism within the story.

_____. *Literary Insinuations: Sorting out Sinyavsky's Irreverence*. Lanham, Md.: Lexington Books, 2003. An examination of the satire, playfulness, and provocative writing in Sinyavsky's works. Includes discussion of his novella *Little Jinx* and the short stories "You and I," "At the Circus," "Graphomanics," "The Tenants," and "The Icicle."

Lourie, Richard. *Letters to the Future: An Approach to Sinyavsky-Tertz*. Ithaca, N.Y.: Cornell University Press, 1975. Lourie devotes a separate chapter to the *Fantastic Stories*; his analyses are distinctive both for his critiques of certain stories (he believes that only "The Icicle" and "Pkhentz" are totally successful) and for his efforts to show their relationship to other works in Russian literature. Includes notes, bibliography, and an index.

Morsberger, Grace Anne. "'The Icicle' as Allegory." *Odyssey* 42 (1981): 15-18. A short but interesting study of the story.

Nepomnyashchy, Catharine Theimer. "Andrei Donatovich Sinyavsky (1925-1997)." *Slavic and East European Journal* 42 (Fall, 1998): 367-371. Claims that Sinyavsky's works have been misunderstood; challenges the characterization of him as a political dissident and argues for a view of his texts as works that engage fantasy and encourage the fanciful.

_____. "Andrei Sinyavsky's 'You and I': A Modern Day Fantastic Tale." *Ulbandus Review* 2, no. 2 (1982): 209-230. Notes Sinyavsky's flaunting of his literary antecedents (E. T. A. Hoffmann, Nikolai Gogol, Fyodor Dostoevski). Prefers to view the story not so much as a study in mental disorder as "a realized metaphor--a literal working out of the vision of the artist as God" and thus as a tale combining both the biblical and the fantastic.

_____. "Sinyavsky/Tertz: The Evolution of the Writer in Exile." *Humanities in Society* 7, no. 314 (1984): 123-142. After providing a brief overview of Sinyavsky's career during his first decade in the West, the author goes on to detail Sinyavsky's concerns with the role of the writer in relationship to reality and society at large. Concludes with a discussion of *Little Jinx*.

_____. "The Writer as Criminal: Abram Tertz's 'Pkhents.'" In *The Russian Twentieth-Century Short Story: A Critical Companion*, edited by Lyudmila Parts. Brighton, Mass.: Academic Studies Press, 2010. A prominent Sinyavsky/Tertz scholar analyzes one of his short stories.

Peterson, Ronald E. "The Writer as Alien in Sinjavskij's 'Pkhens.'" *Wiener Slavistischer Almanach* 12 (1982): 47-53. Examines the autobiographical element in the short story "Pkhentz."

Pevear, Richard. "Sinyavsky in Two Worlds: Two Brothers Named Chénier." *The Hudson Review* 25 (1972): 375-402. Pevear contrasts Sinyavsky and Yevgeny Yevtushenko in an effort to elucidate Sin-yavsky's views about the tasks of the writer. Contains a thoughtful analysis of "The Icicle."

Barry Scherr
Updated by Vasa D. Mihailovich

ALEKSANDR SOLZHENITSYN

Born: Kislovodsk, Soviet Russia (now in Russia); December 11, 1918
Died: Moscow, Russia; August 3, 2008

PRINCIPAL SHORT FICTION

Dlya pol'zy dela, 1963 (*For the Good of the Cause,* 1964)
Dva rasskaza: Sluchay na stantsii Krechetovka i Matryonin dvor, 1963 (*We Never Make Mistakes,* 1963)
Krokhotnye rasskazy, 1970
Stories and Prose Poems by Alexander Solzhenitsyn, 1971
Rasskazy, 1990

OTHER LITERARY FORMS

Although Aleksandr Solzhenitsyn (ahl-yihk-SAHN-dehr sohl-zeh-NEET-sihn) is best known for his novels and his multivolume historical-artistic investigation of the Soviet prison system, *Arkhipelag Gulag, 1918-1956: Opyt khudozhestvennogo issledovaniya,* 1973-1975 (*The Gulag Archipelago, 1918-1956: An Experiment in Literary Investigation,* 1974-1978), in which inset tales figure notably, he also wrote independent short fiction, prose poems, narrative poetry, screenplays, essays, biography and autobiography, and drama. His novella *Odin den' Ivana Denisovicha* (1962; *One Day in the Life of Ivan Denisovich,* 1963) was adapted for American television. Solzhenitsyn was awarded the Nobel Prize in Literature in 1970, but Soviet authorities blocked a reception ceremony. His *Nobelevskaya lektsiya po literature 1970 goda* (*The Nobel Lecture,* 1973), was published in 1972.

ACHIEVEMENTS

Seldom has a writer emerged from total obscurity and risen so meteorically in such a short time as did Aleksandr Solzhenitsyn, achieving in little more than a decade world fame and winning the Nobel Prize. He accomplished all this by adhering to the nineteenth century realistic tradition and also by bringing new elements into Russian literature. His greatest successes lie in the genre of the novel, but he was as forceful in his nonfiction writings, especially in his *Gulag Archipelago* trilogy. Even his prose poems or miniature stories are comparable to the best in their genre. Through his artistic achievements, resistance to tyranny, and personal courage, he became the conscience not only of Russian people but also of all humankind and one of the greatest writers in Russian literature.

BIOGRAPHY

Aleksandr Isayevich Solzhenitsyn grew up fatherless and poor in Kislovodsk. He received his his degree in mathematics from the University of Rostov in 1941, having also studied literature by correspondence from Moscow University. After four years of unbroken service as a frontline artillery officer, he was sentenced in 1945 to eight years of hard labor in the gulag, the Soviet prison system, for criticizing Soviet leader Joseph Stalin in a private letter. Inexplicably exiled to Kazakhstan from 1953 to 1956, Solzhenitsyn recovered from a near-fatal cancer, taught mathematics and physics in a high school, and began to set his prison experiences down as fiction. Rehabilitated in 1956, he moved to Ryazan, near Moscow, where he continued to write. The publication of his novella *One Day in the Life of Ivan Denisovich* marked a brief thaw in Soviet literary restrictions under the government of Nikita S. Khrushchev in 1962. Upon the retightening of censorship,

Solzhenitsyn's work was banned from publication in the Soviet Union. After being expelled from the Soviet Writers' Union in 1969 and barred from formal acceptance of the Nobel Prize in Literature he had won in 1970, Solzhenitsyn was ejected from the Soviet Union in 1973. He settled in Vermont with his second wife and children. In his later years, Solzhenitsyn experienced some misgivings in the West because of his uncompromising stand against the regime in his country and his "conservative" views on the future of Russia. He retired from public life, spending all his time writing the *Red Wheel* novels. Solzhenitsyn returned to Russia and lived on an estate outside Moscow until his death on August 3, 2008, at the age of eighty-nine.

ANALYSIS

Aleksandr Solzhenitsyn initially responded to his prison and labor camp experiences by in easy-to-memorize poetry and later in tiny self-contained prose poems, written down in the 1950's and assembled as a rough set around 1962, although not published at that time in the Soviet Union. Shortly after his initial success in the journal *Novy Mir* with *One Day in the Life of Ivan Denisovich*, Solzhenitsyn also published there his short stories "Incident at Krechetovka Station," "Matryona's House," and "For the Good of the Cause" in 1963. Like "The Easter Procession," "The Right Hand" never appeared in the Soviet Union until the end of glasnost in the late 1980's, although "Zakhar the Pouch" was published in *Novy Mir* in 1966 and was the last of Solzhenitsyn's works printed publicly in the Soviet Union. Each of these short pieces contains the germ of a larger work to come, just as each of the individuals or groups named in the titles of the stories reflects one facet of Solzhenitsyn's overriding theme of his country's agony under Communism.

The essence of Solzhenitsyn's message lies in his peculiarly Russian view of shared suffering as vital, even necessary, to human spiritual survival. To this end, he announced in his Nobel lecture that only art, only literature, can bridge the immense gulfs of time and space between human beings, bringing experiences of those faraway others close enough so that their lessons may help overcome evil. Although Solzhenitsyn did not complete large-scale treatments of all the themes presented in his short fiction, the individualization of experience he began with Ivan Denisovich, the lowly camp inmate whose shining humanity enables him to survive, clearly emerges from the prose poems and the short stories, its successive stages mirroring Solzhenitsyn's own existence in Joseph Stalin's prison system.

"INCIDENT AT KRECHETOVKA STATION"

"Incident at Krechetovka Station" draws heavily upon Solzhenitsyn's wartime experience. Set in the critical autumn of 1941, this story defies all the conventions of Soviet war literature, in which the cliché of patriotic self-sacrifice predominates. Its protagonist, Lieutenant Zotov, an assistant transit officer, is sympathetically portrayed in sharp contrast to the self-serving functionaries around him, who collectively form the story's antagonist, the "system," which is to blame for categorically condemning both the guilty and the innocent.

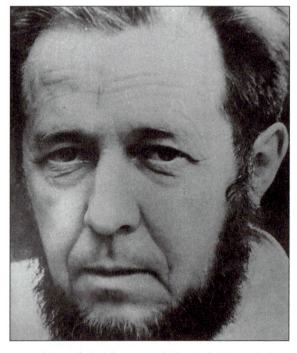

Aleksandr Solzhenitsyn (©The Nobel Foundation)

"Incident at Krechetovka Station" opens in cold, pouring rain with one of Solzhenitsyn's typically abrupt laconic dialogues which achieve a forceful immediacy. Zotov, a youngish man isolated by the war from his family, has gentle features that toughen as he self-consciously straightens his glasses. He observes the misery of the wretched civilians who clutter the station, but he submerges his sympathy for them in his devotion to Marxism. Soon, however, Zotov is miserable himself, distressed by a growing suspicion that the war is not proceeding in tune with Communist Party propaganda.

For more than half of the story, Solzhenitsyn shuttles between the chilly "present" and events in Zotov's past, gradually hinting at the shattering perception Solzhenitsyn himself had grasped as a youth: the vast gap between Communism's promises and reality. Zotov haltingly approaches the truth through chance encounters with other actors in the drama, first in a few poems from line officers critical of their leadership, then in the hunger and cold of the old people and the children in the town. Solzhenitsyn characteristically allows Zotov to linger over the predicament of starving Russian soldiers being repatriated, like Ivan Denisovich, to Stalin's labor camps, their only crime being their surrender to the German army. Lonely and often despairing, Zotov tries to take refuge in his cheap volume of *Das Kapital*, but somehow he cannot finish it. Distracted by the pain of the war's victims, which his heart sees, and by his revulsion at those who prey on them, which his Communist glasses cannot quite shut out, Zotov is disturbed time and again, finally by an "incident" in the bedraggled person of Tveritinov, a former actor trying to find the military detachment from which he had somehow become separated.

Tveritinov strikes up an acquaintance with Zotov, and, as they reminisce about prewar times, the actor's rich voice and winning manner create a mood that for the first time warms the dreary little station with the ceaseless rain beating down on its roof. Solzhenitsyn characteristically insinuates a darker undercurrent when they speak of 1937. Zotov associates that year only with the Soviet involvement in the Spanish Civil War, but Tveritinov, older, recalls an entirely different side to it--the height of Stalin's terrifying purges; his moment of silence, eyes downcast, reveals far more than any speech.

The rapport is suddenly shattered when Tveritinov mistakenly uses the pre-Communist name for Stalingrad. Zotov, struck by the horrifying possibility that he may be harboring an enemy of the state, deceitfully leads the actor into the arms of the security police. Not long after, when Zotov inquires about Tveritinov, he is ominously warned not to look into the matter further. This "incident" at apparently insignificant Krechetovka Station is Solzhenitsyn's metaphor for his country's wartime tragedy. So caught up in Communist zeal that they are able to see the world as Zotov at first did, only through a point of view that obliterates their vital connection to the rest of humanity, Solzhenitsyn's countrymen were being forced to share a perverted brotherhood of opportunism and betrayal, brutality, and inhumanity. As a measure of Solzhenitsyn's sharply ironic message in this story, the "incident" at Krechetovka Station remains Zotov's torment forever.

"THE RIGHT HAND"

In "The Right Hand," a miniature forerunner of *Rakovy korpus* (1968; *Cancer Ward*, 1968), Solzhenitsyn ruthlessly depicts what Zotov might have become if he had not experienced that cruel enlightenment. The story not only excoriates a state-run hospital system that dehumanizes the very patients it purports to serve but also unveils the devastating fate of those whose Party blinders are not removed until it is too late. Having served Communism faithfully, a new patient, clearly terminal, is hypocritically refused admittance to a cancer clinic on a technicality, and this denial of every Party ideal he has slavishly followed snaps his last thread-thin hold on life.

"MATRYONA'S HOUSE"

Like the narrator of "The Right Hand," himself a sufferer, the man who tells the story of "Matryona's House" recently emerged from the crucible of the prison system. All he wants at the outset is to lose himself in the heart of Russia, yearning for the peace of its countryside to restore his soul. Like Solzhenitsyn himself, he takes a position as a mathematics teacher in a shabby ancient village, living in a large old ramshackle house with a sick and aged peasant woman named Matryona. Matryona owns few things, and what she does have is as decrepit as her cockroach-ridden kitchen: a lame cat, a marginal garden, a dirty white goat, and some stunted house plants. Although she had worked on the collective farm for twenty-five years, bureaucratic entanglements have choked off her dead husband's pension--she herself is entitled to nothing--and she is almost destitute. Meager as her life is, however, Matryona's goodness sustains both herself and her lodger, who comes to prize her smile even more than the bit of daily bread they share.

In a strange though altogether convincing way, Matryona's very generosity is responsible for her death. She had loved one of the villagers deeply and waited three years for him to return from World War I. Thinking him dead then, she married his brother, and when the first man returned, he cursed them both. After Matryona's six children died in infancy, she reared one of the daughters of her former sweetheart as her own, and now, feeling she has not long to live, Matryona allows the girl and her friends to dismantle the top part of her house for its lumber. In struggling to help pull the heavy timber sledge over a railroad crossing, Matryona is killed by a speeding train.

For Solzhenitsyn, generosity, purity of heart, goodness, and love, the best qualities of the Russian folk, are as endangered under Communism as they had been under the czars. Now it may even be worse; Matryona's village has become wretchedly poor, with women instead of horses plowing the kitchen gardens, and the system that promised so much offers only corruption, lackadaisical confusion, and mistrust, racing carelessly over people like Matryona on its way to some future too obscure to believe. However, one of the hallmarks of Solzhenitsyn's fiction is the simple "and yet" that illuminates an otherwise hopeless life; "and yet," he says, Matryona, poor in all but spirit, is the one righteous person without whom not a village or a city or the world can stand. Matryona is the personification of the mystical regeneration held inviolate in the Russian people that Solzhenitsyn instinctively sought upon his release and found intuitively in her. Like the old caretaker of a tatterdemalion monument to a forgotten battle in "Zakhar the Pouch," Matryona's stubborn, patient self-sacrifice restored Solzhenitsyn's faith in humanity at a time when he had learned its opposite all too well.

"FOR THE GOOD OF THE CAUSE"

In his political polemic of the early 1960's, "For the Good of the Cause," Solzhenitsyn again pits genuine human affection against villainous bureaucracy. Students of a provincial technical college have helped build themselves a badly needed building, but Party officials usurp it, with the resulting disillusionment wrenching the consciences of director and teachers and breaking the will of many of the students. Their helpless, bitter frustration at official hypocrisy underlies the actions of the vicious hoodlums, inhuman products of a system Solzhenitsyn feels they eventually will indiscriminately trample down, who aimlessly harass "The Easter Procession" in Solzhenitsyn's last short story.

Solzhenitsyn's short fiction resembles an Easter procession of his own, advancing from the Good Friday of the repatriated Soviet prisoner of war through loving recognition of the healing goodness in the peasants Matryona and Zakhar and a clear-eyed estimate of perversion of an honest teacher's responsibility to his students, finally arriving at the realization that the Soviet system and its creatures contain the seeds of universal destruction. The only hope Solzhenitsyn can see lies in the willing acknowledgment of the bond between human beings that springs from the Christian consciousness that all people share their fellows' suffering. In Solzhenitsyn's short fiction, his overture to a powerful literary and spiritual mission, readers recognize that, however separated they are in time and space, his is the voice of their brother.

OTHER MAJOR WORKS

LONG FICTION: *Odin den' Ivana Denisovicha*, 1962 (novella; *One Day in the Life of Ivan Denisovich*, 1963); *Rakovy korpus*, 1968 (*Cancer Ward*, 1968); *V kruge pervom*, 1968 (*The First Circle*, 1968); *Avgust chetyrnadtsatogo*, 1971, expanded version 1983 (*August 1914*, 1972, expanded version 1989 as *The Red Wheel*); *Lenin v Tsyurikhe*, 1975 (*Lenin in Zurich*, 1976); *Krasnoe koleso*, 1983-1991 (includes *Avgust chetyrnadtsatogo*, expanded version 1983 [*The Red Wheel*, 1989]; *Oktiabr' shestnadtsatogo*, 1984 [*November 1916*, 1999]; *Mart semnadtsatogo*, 1986-1988; *Aprel' semnadtsatogo*, 1991).

PLAYS: *Olen'i shalashovka*, pb. 1968 (*The Love Girl and the Innocent*, 1969; also known as *Respublika truda*); *Svecha na vetru*, pb. 1968 (*Candle in the Wind*, 1973); *Dramaticheskaya trilogiya-1945: Pir Pobediteley*, pb. 1981 (*Victory Celebrations*, 1983); *Plenniki*, pb. 1981 (*Prisoners*, 1983).

SCREENPLAYS: *Tuneyadets*, 1981; *Znayut istinu tanki*, 1981.

POETRY: *Etyudy i krokhotnye rasskazy*, 1964 (translated in *Stories and Prose Poems by Alexander Solzhenitsyn*, 1971); *Prusskie nochi*, 1974 (*Prussian Nights*, 1977).

NONFICTION: *Les Droits de l'écrivain*, 1969; *A Lenten Letter to Pimen, Patriarch of All Russia*, 1972; *Nobelevskaya lektsiya po literature 1970 goda*, 1972 (*The Nobel Lecture*, 1973); *Solzhenitsyn: A Pictorial Autobiography*, 1972; *Arkhipelag GULag, 1918-1956: Opyt khudozhestvennogo issledovaniya*, 1973-1975 (*The Gulag Archipelago, 1918-1956: An Experiment in Literary Investigation*, 1974-1978); *Iz-pod glyb*, 1974 (*From Under the Rubble*, 1975); *Pis'mo vozhdyam Sovetskogo Soyuza*, 1974 (*Letter to Soviet Leaders*, 1974); *Amerikanskiye rechi*, 1975; *Bodalsya telyonok s dubom*, 1975 (*The Oak and the Calf*, 1980); *Warning to the West*, 1976; *East and West*, 1980; *The Mortal Danger: How Misconceptions About Russia Imperil America*, 1980; *Kak nam obustroit' Rossiiu?: Posil'nye soobrazheniia*, 1990 (*Rebuilding Russia: Reflections and Tentative Proposals*, 1991); *Russkii vopros*, 1994 (*The Russian Question: At the End of the Twentieth Century*, 1994); *Invisible Allies*, 1995; *Dvesti let vmeste, 1795-1995*, 2001.

MISCELLANEOUS: *Sochineniya*, 1966; *Six Etudes by Aleksandr Solzhenitsyn*, 1971; *Mir i nasiliye*, 1974; *Sobranie sochinenii*, 1978-1983 (10 volumes); *Izbrannoe*, 1991; *The Solzhenitsyn Reader: New and Essential Writings, 1947-2005*, 2006 (Edward E. Ericson, Jr., and Daniel J. Mahoney, editors).

BIBLIOGRAPHY

Bloom, Harold, ed. *Aleksandr Solzhenitsyn*. Philadelphia: Chelsea House, 2001. A collection of critical essays representing the spectrum of opinion on Solzhenitsyn's work.

Emerson, Caryl. "The Word of Aleksandr Solzhenitsyn." *The Georgia Review* 49 (Spring, 1995): 64-74. A critical overview of Solzhenitsyn's achievement. Discusses why the Russian literary world has been so inescapably political for most of the nation's history--and thus why Solzhenitsyn understood that to be a Russian writer is to be more powerful than a holder of a political post.

Ericson, Edward E., Jr. *Solzhenitsyn and the Modern World*. Washington, D.C.: Regnery Gateway, 1993. An examination of the reputation of Solzhenitsyn in the West that tries to clear up previous misunderstandings. Argues that Solzhenitsyn has never been antidemocratic and that his criticisms of the West have been made in the spirit of love, not animosity.

_____. *Solzhenitsyn: The Moral Vision*. Grand Rapids, Mich.: William B. Eerdman's, 1980. An analysis of Solzhenitsyn's work from the perspective of his Christian vision. After a discussion of Solzhenitsyn's theory of art as enunciated in his Nobel Prize lecture, Ericson provides chapters on the major novels, as well as the short stories and prose poems.

Ericson, Edward E., Jr., and Alexis Klimoff. *The Soul and Barbed Wire: An Introduction to Solzhenitsyn*. Wilmington, Del.: ISI Books, 2008. After a biographical survey that traces the evolution of Solzhenitsyn's literary career, the majority of the book provides analyses of almost all of his fiction, as well as other works. Includes examinations of of "Incident at Krechetovka Station," "Matryona's Home," and the short stories of the 1990's.

Feuer, Kathryn, ed. *Solzhenitsyn*. Englewood Cliffs, N.J.: Prentice-Hall, 1976. A collection of thirteen essays. The articles illuminate Solzhenitsyn as a writer, which, in turn, inform readers' understanding of his works, including short fiction. In this connection, Robert Louis Jackson's "'Matryona's Home': The Making of a Russian Icon" offers some keen interpretations of this story.

Kobets, Svitlana. "The Subtext of Christian Asceticism in Aleksandr Solzhenitsyn's *One Day in the Life of Ivan Denisovich*." *Slavic and East European Journal* 42 (Winter, 1998): 661-676. Discusses Christian asceticism in the novella. Notes visual images, linguistic formulas, and conventional symbols in the text that give the book a religious dimension.

Lottridge, Stephen S. "Solzhenitsyn and Leskov." *Russian Literature Triquarterly* 6 (1973): 478-489. In this comparative essay, Lottridge examines Solzhenitsyn's debt to one of Russia's greatest storytellers, Nikolai Leskov. Describes the connection between the two authors in Solzhenitsyn's creation of "Christian" and righteous characters, especially in "Matryona's Home," and in the use of *skaz* technique.

Ragsdale, Hugh. "The Solzhenitsyn That Nobody Knows." *The Virginia Quarterly Review* 71 (Autumn, 1995): 634-641. Discusses the story "Matryona's Home" as an account of the author's return from his first exile in the gulag. Shows how the story is also a statement of the code of values of the Slavophile creed and an allegorical history of Russia in fictional form.

Saur, Pamela S. "Solzhenitsyn's 'Matryona's Home.'" *Explicator* 62, no. 2 (Winter, 2004): 118-121. Explores the details of Soviet life and institutions in this short story, discussing the story's setting, description of poverty, and depiction of inequality and class privilege.

Scammel, Michael. *Solzhenitsyn.* New York: W. W. Norton, 1989. This exhaustive but lively biography deals with practically all important aspects of Solzhenitsyn's life. Unfortunately, his works, especially the short fiction, are not discussed at great length.

_____, ed. *The Solzhenitsyn Files.* Chicago: Edition q, 1995. A carefully edited documentation of Solzhenitsyn's struggles with Soviet literary and political authorities.

Thomas, D. M. *Alexander Solzhenitsyn: A Century in His Life.* New York: St. Martin's Press, 1998. An imaginative, well-documented, and at times combative biography of Solzhenitsyn. Includes discussion of his return to Russia in 1994.

Zekulin, Gleb. "Solzhenitsyn's Four Stories." *Soviet Studies* 16, no. 1 (1964): 45-62. In this compact and authoritative essay, Zekulin discusses "Matryona's House," "Incident at Krechetovka Station," "We Never Make Mistakes," and "One Day in the Life of Ivan Denisovich," which Zekulin treats as a short story rather than as a novella.

Mitzi M. Brunsdale
Updated by Vasa D. Mihailovich

T

Jun'ichirō Tanizaki

Born: Tokyo, Japan; July 24, 1886
Died: Yugawara, Japan; July 30, 1965

PRINCIPAL SHORT FICTION

"Kirin," 1910

"Shōnen," 1910

"Shisei," 1910 ("The Tattooer," 1963)

"Hōkan," 1911

"Akuma," 1912

"Kyōfu," 1913 ("Terror," 1963)

"Otsuya goroshi," 1913

"Haha o kouruki," 1919 ("Longing for Mother,"
    1980)

"Watakushi," 1921 ("The Thief," 1963)

"Aoi Hano," 1922 ("Aguri," 1963)

"Mōmoku monogatari," 1931 ("A Blind Man's
    Tale," 1963)

"Ashikari," 1932 (English translation, 1936)

"Shunkinshō," 1933 ("A Portrait of Shunkin," 1936)

Hyofu, 1950

"Yume no ukihashi," 1959 ("The Bridge of Dreams,"
    1963)

Yume no ukihashi, 1960

Kokumin no bungaku, 1964

Fūten rōjin nikki, 1961-1962 (serial), 1962 (novella;
    Diary of a Mad Old Man, 1965)

Tanizaki Jun'ichirō shu, 1970

Seven Japanese Tales, 1981

The Gourmet Club: A Sextet, 2001 (Anthony H.
    Chambers and Paul McCarthy, translators)

OTHER LITERARY FORMS

For Western readers, Jun'ichirō Tanizaki (joo-nee-chee-ro tahn-ee-zahk-ee) is best known for his short stories and short novels. Throughout his career, however, he was a prolific writer of plays, essays, and translations. Many English readers favor his long novel *Sasameyuki* (1943-1948, serial, 1949, book; *The Makioka Sisters*, 1957) as his best work. It is the story of a family's efforts to arrange a marriage for Yukiko, the third of four daughters in a respectable Ōsaka family. Tanizaki has written a number of plays, and also noteworthy are his two translations into modern Japanese of Murasaki Shikibu's *Genji monogatari* (c. 1004; *The Tale of Genji*, 1925-1933, 1935). Tanizaki's first translation, published from 1936 through 1941, was restricted by the severe censorship during the time of the war with China; his later translation, published from 1951 through 1954. was in more liberal and colloquial language.

ACHIEVEMENTS

The modern Japanese writers most commonly suggested as comparable to Jun'ichirō Tanizaki for the quality of their fiction are the 1968 Nobel Prize-winner Yasunari Kawabata and Yukio Mishima. It is widely believed that Tanizaki was Kawabata's chief rival for the Nobel Prize that year. Mishima's easier fiction attracts more readers but cannot match Tanizaki's more innovative complexity. From his earliest years, however, Tanizaki has had his detractors because many found his youthful "demoniac" works offensive. Throughout his career, for that matter, his frank portrayal of unconventional, even bizarre sexual and marital relationships among his characters caused consternation. In spite of such reservations, Tanizaki was elected to the Japanese Academy of Arts in 1937. He was awarded the Mainichi Prize for Publication and Culture for *Sasameyuki*, 1943-1948, 1949 (*The Makioka Sisters*, 1957) and the Asaki Culture Prize and Imperial Cultural Medal, both in 1949. These are the most important awards that a Japanese writer can receive.

BIOGRAPHY

Jun'ichirō Tanizaki was born in Tokyo on July 24, 1886, the son of a man who owned a printing establishment. He attended the Tokyo Imperial University, studying classical Japanese literature, but he had little interest in attending lectures and did not earn a degree. Even at the university, he wrote stories and plays for small magazines, some of them serialized; indeed, he continued to be productive throughout his life. In his early years, he was noted for dissolute habits, and some readers blamed him for what they believed was his worship of women. His three marriages were unconventional, the experiences of which some critics believe are hinted at in his short fiction. The suggestion is made occasionally that Tanizaki's moving from Tokyo to the Kansai after the earthquake of 1923 contributed to changes in his writing, but changes in phrasing, characterization, or dialogue in these different years are not easy to see in English translations. As one reviews the publications of his life, one finds no time when he was unproductive. In fact, he continued writing to the time of his death, on July 30, 1965, in Yugawara.

ANALYSIS

The dominant theme in Jun'ichirō Tanizaki's best work is love, but few writers so successfully explore this universally preferred topic with such unconventional revelations. Commentators often identified his earliest writings as "demoniac"; his later work they might have characterized as "sardonic." As labels prove to be insufficient for most good writers, however, one must struggle to understand Tanizaki's probing style as he uncovers complicated motives for lovers, spouses, family members, and friends, who continually surprise one another. In addition, as one finishes reading Tanizaki's works of fiction, most characteristically one finds oneself more than a little uncertain as to how things really work out. The dispute, the rivalries, or the resentments always seems resolved or brought to a close; most commonly, though, readers find themselves needing to fill in indeterminate gaps using their own imaginations. This challenge, in fact, contributes to much of the pleasure in reading Tanizaki's fiction.

"THE TATTOOER"

In his early sensational tale "The Tattooer," the exceptional tattooer, Seikichi, behaves much like a sadist in his attitudes toward some of his customers, as he revels in the excruciating pain they endure for the honor of having such an artist adorn their bodies. He outdoes himself in embellishing the back of a beautiful young woman with a huge black widow spider. Readers are told that "at every thrust of his needle Seikichi . . . felt as if he had stabbed his own heart." After he assures the woman that he has poured his soul into this tattoo and that now all men will be her victims, she accepts this prophecy, turns her resplendently tattooed back to him, and promptly claims the tattooer himself as her first conquest.

"TERROR"

With similar emphasis upon intimate revelation of pain, and with similarly ambivalent implications for the suffering endured, in "Terror," a young man describes his peculiar phobia for riding in a train or any other vehicle. For the occasion in the story, he must travel by train to take a physical examination for military duty. His nervous trembling almost drives him mad and certainly drives him to excessive alcoholic consumption. With the combination of neurotic fearfulness and drunkenness, he seems unlikely to pass his physical; the reader, however, hears a doctor reassuring the young man: "Oh, you'll pass all right. A fine husky fellow like you." Such openendedness in Tanizaki's short fiction seems practically his trademark.

"THE THIEF"

The probing into the psychology of nonconforming personalities also reveals itself in "The Thief." In this story, a young man shares the discomfort and embarrassment with his university dormitory roommates as one by one they admit their shame at having suspected the narrator as the perpetrator of recent thefts. Readers can hardly avoid sympathizing with the young man as he reveals his private thoughts about the unfortunate, painful admissions by others who suspect and distrust him. Then one suddenly discovers that this sensitive young man, in fact, truly is the thief. In fact, the thief boasts that, with an outward show of innocence, he can deceive not only roommates and readers but also himself.

"AGURI"

In the story "Aguri," Tanizaki goes further, with his presentation of a self-conscious narrator brooding over his fears and inadequacies. The middle-aged Okada, accompanied by his slim, shapely mistress on a shopping trip, describes in extravagant detail how he is wasting away physically while the young woman, Aguri, craves the most expensive luxuries. As in "The Thief," the narrator of this story carries the reader along with him in his imagination, momentarily at least, with a painful scene of ruinously expensive purchases for Aguri, followed by Okada's fainting embarrassingly in public from weakness. Almost before one realizes the change, however, the reader learns that these disasters were merely an imagined vision. The man and woman end up making modest purchases and with no physical collapse.

"A BLIND MAN'S TALE"

In "A Blind Man's Tale," Tanizaki offers what might be his boldest experiment in narrative point of view. A blind masseur, while massaging a nobleman, recalls the insight he gained thirty years before into a complicated series of events in sixteenth century Japanese history. What he knows he learned largely through the experience of serving as masseur for a beautiful noblewoman. The blind man depends upon his own intuition, overheard conversations, and confidential hints. His story not only opens up multiple perspectives on historical events, interesting for their own sake, but also leaves readers pondering choices in judging these acts as honorable, cowardly, or opportunistic.

"ASHIKARI"

In "Ashikari" the author appeals to easy emotionalism by beginning with a sentimental narrator taking a walk, visiting the Shrine of Minase and then, in the evening, enjoying the moonlight on the river. His detailed observations of ancient scenes and nostalgic thoughts about the past are accompanied by recitation of favorite verses, Chinese and Japanese. He also composes verses of his own, reciting them aloud while admiring the moonlight. Soon, however, this simple sentimentalism gives way.

The brash visitor, Serizawa, who appears suddenly, dominates the scene from this point. Serizawa tells the story of his father's love for the elegant widow Oyu, a woman surrounded by symbols of refinement. This leads to the self-sacrificing of both the father and Oyu's younger sister Oshizu, who marry but remain chaste in respect for the love between Oyu and the father. The three of them remain close companions in this setting for two or three years. In retrospect, though, one is left intrigued with the mystery of what kind of satisfaction either the father or the son gained from their limited sharing in the Lady Oyu's aristocratic way of life.

"A PORTRAIT OF SHUNKIN"

"A Portrait of Shunkin" invites attention for another narrative technique favored by Tanizaki, the use of abundant circumstantial detail to lend an initial air of credence to the unusual love story that follows. At the beginning, the narrator gives precise descriptions of a pair of tombstones in a temple graveyard and then of a privately printed biography, containing the only known photograph of the beautiful, blind woman Shunkin, famous for her samisen lessons. With this narrator, however, one discovers Tanizaki's characteristic ambivalence as the storyteller regularly admits uncertainty about how to interpret the evidence he has found. One suspects that Shunkin gained pleasure from tormenting Sasuka, her disciple, who may have been, in effect, her slave, but quite possibly he was also her lover. The most startling event, Sasuka's blinding of himself following the cruel, disfiguring scalding of Shunkin by an assailant, invites a great range of speculation about Sasuka's motives: to preserve the memory of her beauty, to gain a measure of acceptance from her, or to distract her from demanding so much of him because of her own handicaps.

"THE BRIDGE OF DREAMS"

Certainly one of Tanizaki's most difficult tales is "The Bridge of Dreams," the story of a boy's affectionate memories of his mother and stepmother with resulting family complications. The most striking images in Tadasu's few recollections of his mother are of her sitting by the pool soaking her pretty feet in the water and of her permitting him to suckle her breasts at night when they were in bed together. This was when he was nearly five years old. The new mother, who had been a geisha, was chosen for her striking resemblance to Tadasu's real mother. She even took the same name and adopted similar habits as a full replacement. In time, as the boy grew old enough to marry, he had difficulty distinguishing the two mothers in his memory. When the second mother has a son, too, the new baby is sent off for adoption. The narrator even relates that Tadasu sucked the milk from his stepmother's swollen breasts after she had given up the child. Following the deaths of his father and second mother, Tadasu adopted his stepbrother with a vow to protect him from loneliness. In this story, with the powerful emphasis on family protectiveness, readers can hardly avoid pondering the relative gains and losses from the characters' exceptional watchfulness over their loved ones.

DIARY OF A MAD OLD MAN

Another excellent comic representation of obsessive love reveals itself in Tanizaki's novella *Diary of a Mad Old Man*. In this story, Utsuki, a sickly old man, age seventy-seven, fits into the traditional family pattern as the unchallengeable head of the family, whose word is law. The narrative comes across mostly through the old man's notes in his diary. Tanizaki leaves indeterminate the private thoughts of Utsuki's wife and grown children, but they know of his squandering wealth and affection on his daughter-in-law, the scheming Satsuko. The family had been suspicious of her as a bride for the son, Jokichi, right from the start, because of her background as a lowly cabaret dancer. In fact, as the story begins, Jokichi has already lost interest in her anyway, and Satsuko is visited frequently by another young man, Utsuki's nephew, Haruhisa. Nevertheless, the old man's dotage reveals itself in expensive gifts for her, including a cat's-eye ring costing three million yen, the plan to enshrine her footprints on his gravestone, and niggardliness toward his own children. One's disgust for the old man grows with the combination of abundant references to Utsuki's medicines, drugs, and treatments, and Satsuko's obvious contempt for him. After Utsuki boldly kisses her on the neck one time, she tells him that she felt as if she had "been licked by a garden slug." Near the end, the narrative trails off with a long series of notes attesting the failing health of an apparently dying man. Then, in the final entry, one reads that Utsuki recovered enough to supervise excavation of the garden to construct a swimming pool for his darling Satsuko. Even in his last years, Tanizaki never lost his ability to catch his readers off guard.

OTHER MAJOR WORKS

LONG FICTION: *Itansha no Kanashimi*, 1917; *Chijin no ai*, 1924-1925 (serial), 1925 (book) (*Naomi*, 1985); *Kōjin*, 1926; *Tade kuu mushi*, 1928-1929 (serial), 1936 (book) (*Some Prefer Nettles*, 1955); *Manji*, 1928-1930; *Yoshinokuzu*, 1931 (*Arrowroot*, 1982); *Bushōkō hiwa*, 1931-1932 (serial), 1935 (book) (*The Secret History of the Lord of Musashi*, 1982); *Sasameyuki*, 1943-1948 (serial), 1949 (book) (*The Makioka Sisters*, 1957); *Shōshō Shigemoto no haha*, 1950 (*The Mother of Captain Shigemoto*, 1956); *Kagi*, 1956 (*The Key*, 1960).

PLAYS: *Aisureba koso*, pb. 1921; *Okumi to Gohei*, pb. 1922; *Shirogitsune no yu*, pb. 1923 (*The White Fox*, 1930); *Mumyō to Aizen*, pb. 1924; *Shinzei*, pb. 1949.

NONFICTION: "In'ei raisan," 1934 ("In Praise of Shadows," 1955); *Bunshō tokuhon*, 1934; *Kyō no yume, Ōsaka no yume*, 1950; *Yōshō-jidai*, 1957 (*Childhood Years: A Memoir*, 1988).

TRANSLATION: *Genji monogatari*, 1936-1941, 1951-1954 (of Murasaki Shikibu's medieval *Genji monogatari*).

MISCELLANEOUS: *Tanizaki Jun'ichirō zenshu*, 1930 (12 volumes); *Tanizaki Jun'ichirō zenshu*, 1966-1970 (28 volumes).

BIBLIOGRAPHY

Chambers, Anthony Hood. *The Secret Window: Ideal Worlds in Tanizaki's Fiction*. Cambridge, Mass.: Harvard University Press, 1994. Contains chapters on "ideal worlds" and the short stories "A Portrait of Shunkin" and "The Bridge of Dreams." Includes notes and bibliography.

Gessel, Van C. *Three Modern Novelists: Soseki, Tanizaki, Kawabata*. New York: Kodansha International, 1993. Concentrates on Tanizaki's handling of the theme of modernism. With detailed notes but no bibliography.

Golley, Gregory L. "Tanizaki Junichiro: The Art of Subversion and the Subversion of Art." *The Journal of Japanese Studies* 21 (Summer, 1995): 365-404. Examines the "return to Japan" inaugurated by Tanizaki's novel *Some Prefer Nettles*. Discusses themes and images in the work and suggests that Tanizaki's traditionalist fiction both championed and undermined the idea of an essential Japanese traditional culture.

Ito, Ken K. *Visions of Desire: Tanizaki's Fictional Worlds*. Stanford, Calif.: Stanford University Press, 1991. Contains chapters on his handling of the "Orient" and the "West," on his treatment of the past, and his short stories "The Vision of the Blind," "Fair Dreams of Hanshin," "Writing as Power," and "A Mad Old Man's World." Includes notes, bibliography, and a section on names and sources.

Lippit, Noriko Miuta. *Reality and Fiction in Modern Japanese Literature*. White Plains, N.Y.: M. E. Sharpe, 1980. Considers the struggle of several Japanese writers to define the function of art and literature both socially and personally. The sections on Tanizaki deal with his aesthetic preference for fantasy and complex structure, with a comparison to Edgar Allan Poe.

Long, Margherita. *This Perversion Called Love: Reading Tanizaki, Feminist Theory, and Freud*. Stanford, Calif.: Stanford University Press, 2009. Examines sexual perversion in Tanizaki's short novels and other writings from the 1930's, comparing his depiction of perversion and the possibility of love with the theories of Sigmund Freud.

Rubin, Jay. *Injurious to Public Morals: Writers and the Meiji State*. Seattle: University of Washington Press, 1984. In this unusual approach, the author tackles censorship in Japan and analyzes the relationship between writers and the government. The sections on Tanizaki, an apolitical period writer, suggest how censorship affected his early career. Contains interesting discussions of the bans on his short stories. Includes chronology, notes, a bibliography, and an index.

Suzuki, Tomi. *Narrating the Self: Fictions of Japanese Modernity*. Stanford, Calif.: Stanford University Press, 1996. The epilogue, "Tanizaki's Speaking Subject and the Creation of Tradition," is especially useful. Includes notes and bibliography.

Ueda, Makoto. "Tanizaki Jun'ichirō." In *Modern Japanese Writers and the Nature of Literature*. Stanford, Calif.: Stanford University Press, 1976. Discusses Tanizaki as one of the eight major writers who make up the bulk of modern Japanese fiction familiar to Western readers. Provides an introduction to major literary theories underlying Japanese novels and stories. Supplemented by source notes, a bibliography, and an index.

Walsh, Reuben. "Japanese Female Sadism: A Comparative Reading of Junichiro Tanizaki's 'Tattoo' and Hitomi Kanehara's 'Snakes and Earrings.'" In *The Short Story*, edited by Ailsa Cox. Newcastle, England: Cambridge Scholars, 2008. Compares Tanizaki's short story with a story by another Japanese writer.

Wasserman, Kimberly. "Tanizaki's 'The Tattooer.'" *The Explicator* 60, no. 2 (Winter, 2002): 84. A critique and interpretation of this short story. Compares the image of the spider in "The Tattooer" with creatures in Japanese and Greek mythology and with the Marquis de Sade's philosophy of eroticism.

Yamanouchi, Hisaaki. *The Search for Authenticity in Modern Japanese Literature*. Cambridge, England: Cambridge University Press, 1978. Discusses twelve modern Japanese writers, analyzing the ways each dealt with the difficult personal, social, and intellectual questions in art. The sections on Tanizaki focus on the concept of eternal womanhood in his works. Includes notes, a bibliography, and an index.

David V. Harrington
Updated by Shakuntala Jayaswal

TATYANA TOLSTAYA

Born: Leningrad, Soviet Union (now St. Petersburg, Russia); May 3, 1951

PRINCIPAL SHORT FICTION

Na zolotom kryl'tse sideli, 1987 (*On the Golden Porch*, 1989)

Sleepwalker in a Fog, 1992

White Walls: Collected Stories, 2007

OTHER LITERARY FORMS

Tatyana Tolstaya (tah-TYAH-nah tohl-STI-yah) is known primarily for her short fiction, but she has also written a novel, *Kys* (2001; *The Slynx*, 2003) and essays. *White Walls*, a volume of her collected stories, appeared iin 2007.

ACHIEVEMENTS

When her first collection of short stories was published in the United States in 1989 as *On the Golden Porch*, Tatyana Tolstaya was acclaimed by critics as an original and important new voice in Soviet literature. Her second book, also a group of stories, published in 1992 as *Sleepwalker in a Fog*, was generally conceded to be a worthy successor to her well-received first collection. Among those who paid enthusiastic tribute to Tolstaya were the American poet laureate Joseph Brodsky and Helena Goscilo, a prominent Slavist known especially for her contributions on Slavic women authors.

BIOGRAPHY

Tatyana Tolstaya was born in Leningrad, in the former Soviet Union, on May 3, 1951, the daughter of Nikita Tolstoy, a professor of physics, and Natalia Lozinskaya. Her great-granduncle was the writer Leo Tolstoy, and her grandfather, also a writer, was Alexei Tolstoy. Tolstaya was graduated from Leningrad State University in 1974 with a degree in languages and literatures. She worked as a junior editor in the Oriental literature department of a publishing house in Moscow and later held various positions in American universities, including the University of Richmond, the University of Texas at Austin, Texas Tech University in Lubbock, Skidmore College, and Princeton University. In May, 1974, she married Andrei Lebedev, a professor of philology; they settled in Moscow with their two sons. In the early 1990's, they moved to the United States, where they gained permission to reside. She later returned to Russia, spending part of the year there and the rest lecturing at a university in the United States. In Russia, she cohosted a television program, *The School for Scandal*, on which she interviewed political and cultural figures. Tolstaya's short stories have been published in several Soviet journals, as well as in *The New Yorker*.

ANALYSIS

The title of Tatyana Tolstaya's story "Na zolotom kryl'tse sideli" ("On the Golden Porch") comes from an old Russian counting song that names several different unrelated persons, including a czar, a king, and a cobbler. This is an appropriate title for the first collection because the collection comprises stories about all sorts of people--a five-year-old girl and her nanny, a little boy in love with a beautiful neighbor, an old woman who still dreams of joining her first lover, a desperate young woman who traps a coarse and insensitive man into marriage, a shy fat man who dreams his life away--to mention only a few of the disparate and varied characters. The stories have some elements in common. Similar settings, themes, and styles give the stories more unity and connection with one another than the nursery-rhyme title might suggest. A similar kind of variety, as well as unifying elements, characterize the stories in *Sleepwalker in a Fog*.

The stories are all set in Moscow or Leningrad, with an only slightly less frequent setting being the dacha, or country summer home, so often found in Russian literature. More particularly, the stories repeatedly contrast the cramped, drab, and dismal environments of late twentieth century Soviet citizens with the idyllic life in rural surroundings. There are exceptions to the idyllic quality of the dacha settings, but the connotation is always consistent with relaxation, plenitude, and natural beauty.

Tolstaya seems to have particular favorites among the kinds of characters she portrays: innocent though sometimes mischievous children; hardworking and loving elderly people, especially women; and a distinctive group of weak, deluded, and disillusioned persons of less determinate age but all suffering from vulnerability, deprivation of one sort or another, and a strong tendency to mix dreams and fantasy with harsh reality.

While there is not a totally cheerful story in the two collections, there is much that is joyful, merry, tender, and humorous. The stories are not tightly plotted. Incidents and events are used to reveal characters' interactions, situations, and conditions. Tolstaya seems to be more concerned with evoking moods and portraying unforgettable characters, whether they be a child dreaming of running away with a beautiful woman who betrays him, an old nanny who spends her life living for others, a weak and ineffectual librarian who longs for love, or a no-longer-young woman who traps a man into a loveless marriage. In fact, every principal character in her collections has a story that lifts each of them out of the ordinary into the realms of brilliant, rich imagination.

Tolstaya has been lauded again and again as one of the most original and impressive Soviet writers of the late twentieth century. Her use of multivoiced narrators has been cited, as has her ability to combine sadness with humor, tenderness with cruelty. Her tendency to use objects in anthropomorphic ways has also been praised: Gardens wave handkerchiefs, cabbage soup talks to itself, dresses tuck up their knees inside dark trunks, and a lamp shade is young and skittish. The metaphor of dream is one of Tolstaya's most distinctive devices. It appears in almost all of her stories; some of them consist almost entirely of dreams. The

overall effect is evocative, evanescent, wry, and sometimes bizarre. Her stories have a natural, conversational style, whether in the narrator's voice, in the talk among characters, or even in a character's monologue. Tolstaya's themes reveal her special concerns: the dreadful contrasts between the disappointments and failures of everyday life and the joyful life of the imagination, between reality and fantasy, and between dreams and nightmares.

For the reader delighted with Tolstaya's prose of the 1980's and early 1990's, unfortunately, there is little to add. One story from the 1990's, "Siuzhet" (1992; the story), is not considered to be of the same, high artistic quality as her earlier prose. In 1988, she began residence in the United States with tours of teaching and duties as writer-in-residence in many American universities. She applied for, and was granted, the proper documents for remaining in the United States with her husband and younger son, who joined her. Like Aleksandr Solzhenitsyn, she has found in the New World both a new audience and a new outlook on her ideas. She published articles in *The New Republic* (May 27, 1991) and the *Wilson Quarterly* (Winter, 1992) which expressed her opinion of literary life in Russia. Such a self-conscious, Western reorientation may have been an inevitable result of emigration. Still, the accomplishments already made by Tolstaya stand on their own merit, both in Russia and in the West. In a world of conservative views on gender and nationality, Tolstaya has found a useful flashpoint, literature, where she can meld together articles of faith and pure fantasy, challenging reality and collective consciousness, artistically and, thus, substantively.

ON THE GOLDEN PORCH

Three stories in Tolstaya's first collection exemplify both the similarities and contrasts in her writing. One is set in Leningrad, the other two in a dacha. All three stories are told from the point of view of a child, one of Tolstaya's favorite narrative forms. This method allows her to use a fluid, rambling conversational style, laden with images and strong feeling. In all three stories, the nature of childhood, which is not entirely innocent, is contrasted with cruel betrayals by adults, indeed, by life. The differences, however, are what make each story distinctive and memorable in its own way.

The title story of the first collection alludes to a Russian counting rhyme in its title. Beginning with a brief poetic description of childhood as a garden, it shifts to the less idyllic aspects of childhood and uses several images of blood to convey the cruel and frightening side of that period. For example, a beautiful neighbor sells strawberries, her fingers red with berry blood. The narrator recalls how the same beautiful neighbor once smiled about her red hands after she had just killed a calf, and thus the contrast is established. The child narrator's fears are expressed in fantasies about her mother crawling over broken glass to steal a strawberry runner. Uncle Pasha, the scary neighbor's elderly, meek, henpecked husband, an accountant, runs every day to catch the commuter train to Leningrad. With his black cuff protectors and his scurrying to and from his job in a smoky basement, Uncle Pasha inevitably reminds one of Nikolai Gogol's Akaky Akakyevich. Uncle Pasha's house, however, is an Aladdin's cave of treasures, which are described in fantastic terms. With abrupt speed, the accountant grows old, and his treasure-filled room is now seen with the adult eyes of the narrator as filled with trash and rubbish, tacky, worn, cheap, and fake. Uncle Pasha freezes to death on the porch. Juxtaposed against the picture of him face down in the snow are white snow daisies growing between his still fingers.

"LOVES ME, LOVES ME NOT"

"Liubish'--ne liubish'" ("Loves Me, Loves Me Not"), the first story in the collection, is also told by a child, a five-year-old who resents having to be taken to the park by Maryvanna, an old servant, whom the child hates because of her ugliness, her poverty, and her endless boring reminiscences. The old woman appears to be harmless, but the poems that she recites to the child are filled with frightening images that express night fears of monsters and other threatening creatures that never appear in the daytime. The child's occasional bouts of flu give rise to a different kind of fantasy, fever dreams of banging red drums, a round loaf of bread running along an airfield with a nasty smile, tiny planes like bugs with claws. A flea market provides another setting for fantastic people and objects. In contrast to Maryvanna, who personifies the self-absorption and silly, scary kind of adult, there is Nanny Grusha, who is

too old and feeble to go out but who understands the child's anxieties and suffering and weeps compassionate tears with wordless love.

"DATE WITH A BIRD"

"Svidanie s ptitsei" ("Date with a Bird") is another story set in the country, told by a detached and omniscient narrator who observes the boyish play and infatuation with a beautiful woman named Tamila. Petya, the narrator, is completely captivated by her stories and her possessions--a ring in the form of a snake, a squashed silver toad, a black robe with a red dragon on the back. Petya vows to himself that he will marry Tamila and lock up Uncle Borya in a tower because he teases and torments the boy with ridicule and nagging. The contrast between the two male figures, the boy and the man, is sharply drawn. Between them is the seductive enchantress. Frightened by a nightmare, Petya wakes up and goes to the room where his grandfather has lain ill for a long time; he is dead. Petya runs to Tamila's dacha and there encounters a final betrayal and disillusionment.

"PETERS"

Another group of stories illustrates the capacity to dream and apprehend fantasy on a somewhat more adult level. Among these stories, "Peters" serves as an outstanding example. Abandoned by his parents, Peters is brought up by his grandmother, is never allowed to play with other children, and imagines his scoundrel father living on a tropical island. He attends a library school and goes to work in a library after his grandmother dies. Fat and clumsy, Peters lives in fantasies about beautiful ladies and love. When Faina begins her employment in the library, Peters's dreamworld becomes connected to the real world, a trick that Tolstaya often plays on her characters. Then Peters happens to overhear Faina call him "a wimp . . . an endocrinological sissy," and he realizes that his youth is over. Nevertheless, when spring comes, he falls in love with Valentina, a young woman whom he happens to see buying postcards. He imagines that he might be able to astonish and impress her if he knew German; then, in a restaurant, he is picked up by a "flying flower" named Peri, who steals his money. Peters continues to live as in a dream, sleeping through several years of marriage to a stern, unfeeling woman who eventually abandons him. Now old, Peters feels stirring within him a re-newed sense of life. Now he neither desires nor regrets but is simply grateful for life, though it is slipping past him indifferently, treacherously, mysteriously. Still, he sees it as "marvelous, marvelous, marvelous," and with these significant words, the book ends.

SLEEPWALKER IN A FOG

In the title story of *Sleepwalker in a Fog*, Tolstaya blends several of her characteristic devices and por-traits. Denisov is one of her favorite types: middle-aged, pensive, fearful of dying and being forgotten. His fiancé, Lora, is thoughtless, talkative, and affectionate. With her in a cramped communal apartment lives her gentle widower father, a retired zoologist who is a bit strange but harmless. In her incessant, mindless chatter, Lora provides a considerable amount of humor in the story, while Papa, laboring over scientific articles for children, is the source of an anxious kind of pathos, wandering every night in his sleep.

Denisov, tormented by doubts and despair, lives in a constant round of visions, nightmares, and dreams. Thus he, too, like the old somnambulist, walks through his troubled life in confusion, his waking life a dream. The story takes a bizarre turn as Denisov, attempting to do a favor for a young couple, looks up his comrade Bakhtiyarov, who is relaxing at the Woodland Fairy restaurant. There, events turn nightmarish, as Denisov envisions his friend Makov frozen to death on a moun-taintop, while Bakhtiyarov teases and taunts Denisov, who slips into a state resembling the kind of rational illogic that one experiences in dreams. When he wakes up, he finds that everyone has gone. He calls Lora, who thinks that he has gone out of his mind when he tells her that he was locked in a fairy tale. She herself is in the middle of her own nightmare; having taken Papa to a healer in the country, she left him there, and he ran off in his sleep. The story ends in a poetic passage in which Denisov imagines the old man running through the night, through the forest, up and down hills, in the moonlight, smiling, fast asleep.

"MOST BELOVED"

One of the longer works in Tolstaya's second collec-tion, "Samaia liubimaia" ("Most Beloved"), is set, like many of her stories, in Leningrad and at the dacha. It is a vivid, poignant account of the narrator's recollections

of Zhenechka, the woman who has worked for the family as nurse and governess for as long as the chil-dren can remember. She has always been there.

The narrator recalls especially the first summer morning at the dacha, when Zhenechka would walk through the house, distribute presents, clear the desk, and get organized for the daily lessons, much resented by the children. Zhenechka is implacable, having taught their mother, and before that, having been their grandmother's childhood friend. Zhenechka wears a hearing aid on her chest that chirrs like a nightingale. Walking with a limp, she wears an orthopedic shoe. She never takes off her amber necklace because she be-lieves that some sort of healthful electricity emanates from it. She is strict, loving, devoted. Once, Zhenechka gives one of the girls a box, on the cover of which she has written, "Don't wish to be the prettiest; wish to be the most beloved."

The motif of gift giving is present throughout the story. Tolstaya uses this theme as a very effective way of characterizing Zhenechka. As the children grow up, she continues to bring presents when she comes to visit the family, which is all that she has left in the world. Aging, Zhenechka has become tiresome and boring, endlessly retelling her stories of bygone days. Inter-spersed with incidents from Zhenechka's last years are brief recollections of the first child she ever took care of, a little deaf boy, and of the only love in her life--"short, stunted, meager."

The story closes with a brief description of the de-serted dacha, slowly deteriorating as the grasses take over the path, the mold blooms on the porch, and a spider spins the keyhole shut. The children have all grown up; Zhenechka has died. Although the narrator speaks of the old nurse's wish to be the most beloved as being naïve, the implication is clear that she really was just that. The greatest gift was herself, in her un-thinking, simple, and total love.

"THE MOON CAME OUT"

"The Moon Came Out" is another story about an elderly figure, this time one named Natasha, born fifty years earlier. The story begins with childhood memories of a dacha near Leningrad, of games played to incantations such as "The moon came out behind the cloud." The parents, breaking all the rules, died, but Grandmother hung on to life. Natasha's adolescence is described in Tolstayan fashion, with nightmarish images of filth and horror. There is a brief interlude when Konovalov is attracted to Natasha, but she feels unworthy and retreats into a world of dreams, which the author describes with images of flowers, wind, sleepy forests, bears, and friendly old women--images straight out of the Russian fairy tales on which Tolstaya draws so frequently and effectively.

Natasha becomes a teacher of geography and never mentions the world in her mind, Queen Maud Land. Natasha lives in a communal flat, crowded, dismal, full of daily humiliations. She goes to Moscow once and falls in love with bearded, joyful Pyotr Petrovich, who has come into the city to shop for his family. As he leaves on the train, quite unaware of Natasha's short-lived devotion, she feels old age gripping her firmly by the shoulder.

"LIMPOPO"

Stories in which cruelty and death are themes include "Sarafim," about a misanthrope who kicks a small dog to death, and "Heavenly Flame," about a pointless practical joke played on a man awaiting death in a sanatorium. These themes are also fully expressed in "Limpopo," again a combination of burlesque and fantasy, reality and ridicule, revolving around the narrator's friends, Judy, from Africa, and Lyonechka, a poet who fights for truth. The dismal lives of Soviet citizens under the rule of the Communist Party are described with all the bite and snap of satire, with macabre humor and bitter irony. The political undertones are clearly present but under the guise of weird and grotesque incidents, such as an inexplicable massacre of innocent people by soldiers of "their own side." This story is Tolstaya's richest in terms of wild fancy; a large group of precisely and concisely delineated characters; a plot of complex and enigmatic events; and numerous and widely ranging literary allusions to Dante, the Old Testament, Russian fairy tales, Don Juan, Alexander Pushkin, Dr. Doolittle, Søren Kierkegaard, and Homer, to mention only a few.

OTHER MAJOR WORKS

LONG FICTION: *Kys*, 2001 (*The Slynx*, 2003).

NONFICTION: "In a Land of Conquered Men," 1989; "Intelligentsia and Intellectuals," 1989; "Apples as Citrus Fruit," 1990; "President Potemkin," 1991; *Pushkin's Children: Writings on Russia and Russians*, 2003 (essays).

BIBLIOGRAPHY

Chitnis, Rajendra A. "Subverting Realism: Tat'iana Tolstaia, Dušan Mitana." In *Literature in Post-Communist Russia and Eastern Europe: The Russian, Czech, and Slovak Fiction of the Changes, 1988-1998*. New York: Routledge Curzon, 2005. Examines Tolstaya's short fiction and works by other writers who, during and after the collapse of communism, rejected the politicization of literature and redefined the purpose and nature of writing.

Gifford, Henry. "The Real Thing." *The New York Review of Books* 36 (June 1, 1989): 3-5. Contains a review of *On the Golden Porch* and of three books on contemporary Soviet fiction, including *Balancing Acts* by Helena Goscilo, cited below.

Goscilo, Helena, ed. *Balancing Acts: Contemporary Stories by Russian Women*. Bloomington: Indiana University Press, 1989. Includes Tolstaya's story "Peters," with commentary by Goscilo.

_____. *The Explosive World of Tatyana N. Tolstaya's Fiction*. Armonk, N.Y.: M. E. Sharpe, 1996. A critical review of Tolstaya's œuvre, covering her entire career to the date of publication.

_____. *Heritage and Heresy: Recent Fiction by Russian Women*. Bloomington: Indiana University Press, 1988. Includes three stories by Tolstaya, all published in *On the Golden Porch*, with commentary by Goscilo.

_____. "Monsters Monomaniacal, Marital, and Medical: Tat'iana Tolstaya's Regenerative Use of Gender Stereotypes." In *Sexuality and the Body in Russian Culture*, edited by Jane Costlow et al. Stanford, Calif.: Stanford University Press, 1993. Discusses Tolstaya's symbolism and sound sources in her prose.

_____. "Tatyana Tolstaia's 'Dome of Many-Colored Glass': The World Refracted Through Multiple Perspectives." *Slavic Review* 47 (Summer, 1988): 280-290. A detailed scholarly analysis of Tolstaya's stories. Includes explanatory and reference footnotes, several of them in Russian and untranslated.

Greber, Erica. "Carnivalization of the Short Story Genre and the Künstlernovelle: Tatiana Tolstaia's 'The Poet and the Muse.'" In *The Russian Twentieth-Century Short Story: A Critical Companion*, edited by Lyudmila Parts. Brighton, Mass.: Academic Studies Press, 2010. Provides a critical reading of this story.

Hamilton, Denise. "A Literary Heiress." *Los Angeles Times*, May 12, 1992, p. E1. An interview story that provides a brief biographical sketch of Tolstaya's life. Tolstaya contends that she often distorts reality so that it comes back stronger than before and closer to the truth; discusses her collection *Sleepwalker in a Fog*.

Ljunggren, Anna, and Kristina Rotkirch, eds. *Contemporary Russian Fiction, a Short List: Russian Authors Interviewed by Kristina Rotkirch*. Translated by Charles Rougle. Chicago: Northwestern University Press, 2008. Includes an interview with Tolstaya, in which she discusses her works.

See, Carolyn. "In the Russian Tradition." *The Los Angeles Times Book Review*, January 19, 1992, 3. A review of *Sleepwalker in a Fog*. Suggests that the point of the stories is their timelessness; calls them elegant, overwritten mystical tales that are everything that communism was not.

Sutcliffe, Benjamin M. "Perestroika and the Emergence of Women's Prose: Liudmila Petrushevskaia, Tat'iana Tolstaia, and Women's Anthologies." In *The Prose of Life: Russian Women Writers from Khrushchev to Putin*. Madison: University of Wisconsin Press, 2009. Examines how Tolstaya and five other women writers used images of daily life to depict women's experience in Russia from the 1960's through the early twenty-first century.

Trosky, Susan M., ed. *Contemporary Authors* 130. Detroit: Gale Research, 1990. Includes a brief personal history of Tolstaya, a concise summary of her career, and a short general description of her characters.

Wisniewska, Sophia T. "Tat'iana Tolstaia." In *Russian Women Writers*, edited by Christine D. Tomei. New York: Garland, 1999. A critical biography of Tolstaya describing her contribution to Russian literature.

Natalie Harper
Updated by Christine D. Tomei

LEO TOLSTOY

Born: Yasnaya Polyana, Russia; September 9, 1828
Died: Astapovo, Russia; November 20, 1910
Also known as: Lev Tolstoy

PRINCIPAL SHORT FICTION

Sevastopolskiye rasskazy, 1855-1856 (*Sebastopol,* 1887)

Semeynoye schast'ye, 1859 (novella; *Family Happiness,* 1888)

Smert' Ivana Il'icha, 1886 (novella; *The Death of Ivan Ilyich,* 1887)

Kreytserova sonata, 1889 (novella; *The Kreutzer Sonata,* 1890)

The Kreutzer Sonata, The Devil, and Other Tales, 1940

Notes of a Madman, and Other Stories, 1943

Tolstoy Tales, 1947

Tolstoy's Short Fiction, 1991, 2d. ed. 2008

Divine and Human, and Other Stories, 2000

OTHER LITERARY FORMS

Leo Tolstoy (TOHL-stoy) is most famous as the author of two superb novels, *Voyna i mir* (1865-1869; *War and Peace,* 1886) and *Anna Karenina* (1875-1878; English translation, 1886). He wrote one other full-length novel, *Voskreseniye* (1899; *Resurrection,* 1899), and a number of shorter novels, such as *Destvo* (1852; *Childhood,* 1862), *Otrochestvo* (1854; *Boyhood,* 1886), *Yunost'* (1857; *Youth,* 1886), *Kazaki* (1863; *The Cossacks,* 1872), and *Khadzi-Murat* (1911; *Hadji Murad,* 1911). His fiction tends to overshadow his achievement as a dramatist; his plays include *Vlast tmy: Ili, "Kogotok uvyaz, vsey ptichke propast,"* (pb. 1887, pr. 1888; *The Dominion of Darkness,* 1888; better known as *The Power of Darkness,* 1899) and *Plody prosveshcheniya* (pr. 1889; *The Fruits of Enlightenment,* 1891).

ACHIEVEMENTS

Leo Tolstoy is one of the undisputed titans of fiction, recognized by friend and foe alike as a great artist and man. He is Homeric in the epic sweep of *War and Peace* and *Anna Karenina*; in his stress on the primacy of human beings' senses and physical acts; in the clarity, freshness, and gusto with which he presents his world; in his celebration of nature's processes, from brute matter to the stars; and in his union of an omniscient perspective with a detached vision. Unlike Homer, however, he often shows war as wanton carnage resulting from the vainglory and stupidity of a nation's leaders.

While most critical evaluations of Tolstoy's writings are highly laudatory, he has been reproached by some interpreters for his disparagement of science, technology, and formal education; his hostility to aesthetics and the life of the mind; and most of all for his insistence, in his later works, on dictating programs of moral and religious belief to his readers. As a writer, his greatest achievement was to convey an insight into the living moment that renders with unequaled verisimilitude the course of human passions and the pattern of ordinary actions, enabling him to present a comprehensive, coherent, and usually convincing sense of life. His influence, while not as pervasive as that of his rival Fyodor Dostoevski, is evident in the works of Maxim Gorky, D. H. Lawrence, Ernest Hemingway, Giuseppe Tomasi di Lampedusa, Ignazio Silone, Isaac Babel, Mikhail Sholokhov, Aleksandr Solzhenitsyn, and Boris Pasternak when he composed his novel, *Doktor Zhivago* (1957; *Doctor Zhivago,* 1958).

BIOGRAPHY

Count Leo Nikolayevich Tolstoy was born on September 9, 1828, to a retired army officer, Count Nikolay Ilyich Tolstoy, and a wealthy princess, Maria Nikolaevna Bolkonskaya, who was descended from Russia's first ruling dynasty. His birthplace was a magnificent estate 130 miles south of Moscow, Yasnaya Polyana (serene meadow). Throughout his life, particularly from the late 1850's, when he settled there, this beautiful manorial land, featuring an avenue of lime trees and several lakes, was a romance he kept reinventing, lodged at the center of his self. He disliked urban civilization and industrialization, instead preferring with increasing fidelity the rural simplicities and patriarchal order that had governed the lives of his ancestors and that gave him commanding knowledge of the ways of the landowners and peasants who dominate his writings.

Tolstoy's mother died when he was two, his father when he was nine. He was lovingly brought up by an aunt, Tatyana, who became the model for Sonya in *War and Peace*, just as his parents sat for the portraits of Nicholas Rostov and Princess Maria in that novel. Aunt Tatyana both built the boy's confidence and indulged all his wishes, inclining him to extremes beginning in childhood. He largely wasted several years at the University of Kazan in drinking, gambling, and wenching, then joined an artillery unit in the Caucasus in 1851. That same year, he began working on his first, short novel, *Childhood*, to be followed by *Boyhood* and *Youth*. These works are thinly disguised autobiographical fictions, which unfold a highly complicated moral consciousness.

As a writer, Tolstoy is an inspired solipsist, identifying all other humans in examining his flesh and spirit. His art is essentially confessional, representing the strenuous attempt of a complex and exacting man to reconcile himself with himself. His diary, which he began in 1845, reveals what was to be an inveterate thirst for rational and moral justification of his life. It includes a list of puritanical Rules of Life, which he would update during the tormented periods of guilt that followed his lapses. The biographer Henri Troyat called him "a billy-goat pining for purity." The demands of his senses, mind, and spirit were to contest one another in his character as long as he lived.

Tolstoy served bravely in the Crimean War until 1856, also writing his *Sebastopol* stories as well as a number of other military tales. When he returned to European Russia, he found himself lionized as his country's most promising young author. He passed the years 1856-1861 shuttling between St. Petersburg, Moscow, Yasnaya Polyana, and foreign countries. His two trips abroad disgusted him with what he considered the selfishness and materialism of European bourgeois civilization. In 1859, he founded a school for peasant children at Yasnaya Polyana; in 1862, he launched a pedagogical periodical there; both followed a Rousseauistic model that glorified children's instincts, ignored their discipline, and insisted that intellectuals should learn from the common people instead of vice versa.

In 1862, the thirty-four-year-old Tolstoy married the eighteen-year-old Sophia Andreyevna Behrs. Family life became his religion, and the union was happy for its first fifteen years, producing thirteen children. He dramatized the stability of marriage and family life in *War and Peace* (written 1863-1869), which his wife was to copy out seven times. Sophia efficiently managed Yasnaya Polyana, often served as Tolstoy's secretary, and nursed him through illnesses. She never recovered from the shock she received, however, a week before their wedding, when he insisted she read every entry of his diary, which recorded not only his moral struggles but also seventeen years of libidinous conduct.

Unhappy times followed the composition of *War and Peace*: the deaths of Aunt Tatyana, a favorite son, and several other relatives; quarrels with Sophia; illness; and depression. *Anna Karenina* (written 1873-1877) is a more somber and moralizing book, with the certainty of death hovering over it, and with sexual passion both given its due and dramatized as destructive to happiness. The male protagonist Levin's search for faith is a pale outline of Tolstoy's own spiritual journey, which next led him to write, between 1879 and 1882, an account of his emotional and ethical pilgrimage entitled *Ispoved'* (1884; *A Confession*, 1885).

Shortly after finishing *Anna Karenina*, Tolstoy suffered a shattering midlife crisis that brought him close to suicide. Even though he had much to value--good health, a loving wife, family, fame, wealth, genius--life nevertheless seemed to him a cruel lie, purposeless, fraudulent, empty. For answers, he turned to philosophers, to educated people, and finally to the uneducated but religious peasants whose faith made their lives possible, and he decided to become a religious believer, although rejecting most ecclesiastical dogma.

A Confession is the best introduction to the spiritual struggle that Tolstoy was to wage for his remaining thirty years, which he spent in a glaringly public retirement. Trying to live up to his principles of purity and simplicity, he stripped his personal demands to the barest necessities; dressed and often worked as a peasant; published doctrines of moral improvement in both tracts and tales; signed over to his wife the right to manage his copyrights, as well as his property; and renounced (not always successfully) almost all institutions, his title, concert-and theater-going, meat, alcohol, tobacco, hunting, and even sex. He became the high priest of a cult of Christian anarchy, professing the moral teachings of the Gospel and Sermon on the Mount while rejecting the divinity of Christ and the authority of the Church, which excommunicated him for blasphemy in 1901.

Some typical titles of Tolstoy's didactic last years are *V chom moya vera* (1884; *What I Believe*, 1885), "Gde lyubov', tam i Bog" ("Where Love Is, God Is") and "Mnogo li cheloveku zemli nuzhno?" ("How Much Land Does a Man Need?"). His best-known narrative was the tendentious three-part novel *Resurrection*, which is as long as, but far inferior to, *Anna Karenina*. Its protagonist, Nekhlyudov, experiences remorse after having seduced a peasant woman and expiates his transgression by adopting a moral life. Of greatest interest to literary critics is the book-length essay, *Chto takoye iskusstvo?* (1898; *What Is Art?* 1898), in which Tolstoy rejects all art based on other than gospel ethics and concludes that only the Old Testament's story of Joseph and primitive popular art will satisfy his standards.

Even in his doctrinaire phase, however, Tolstoy managed to produce great stories and novellas, particularly *The Death of Ivan Ilyich*, "Khozyain i rabotnik" ("Master and Man"), and *The Kreutzer Sonata*. He also wrote a powerful naturalistic tragedy, *The Power of Darkness*, which featured adultery and infanticide in a somber peasant setting. By contrast, *The Fruits of Enlightenment* is a satiric, farcical comedy revolving around the foibles of the gentry and the land hunger of the peasantry.

Tolstoy's last years were often mired in squabbles with his wife and some of his children, intrigues concerning his legacy, and bitter enmity between Sophia Tolstoy and his chief disciple, Vladimir Chertkov, who became Tolstoy's close confidant. By 1909, the marriage had become extremely stressful, with Countess Tolstoy repeatedly threatening suicide. On November 9, 1910, Leo Tolstoy, driven to distraction, fled his wife and family; on November 13, he was taken ill with what became pneumonia, at the rail junction of nearby Astapovo, and died in the stationmaster's bed there on November 20. His death was mourned as a loss in every Russian family.

Analysis

Leo Tolstoy's ego embraces the world, so that he is always at the center of his fictive creation, filling his books with his struggles, personae, problems, questions, and quests for answers, and above all with his notion of life as an ethical search as strenuous as the pursuit of the Holy Grail. He does not try to puzzle or dazzle; his work is not a clever riddle to be solved or a game to be played but a rich realm to be explored. He disdains the kind of exterior purism practiced by Gustave Flaubert and Henry James, among others, which concentrates on the inner lives of individuals--although he is superbly skilled at psychological perception. His aim, rather, is to discover, as far as he can, the essential truth of life's meaning, the revelation to be gained at the core of the vast mesh of human relations. What energizes his work is his conviction that this truth is good, and that, once discovered, it will resolve the discords and conflicts that plague humanity.

In Tolstoy's art, the natural, simple, and true is always pitted against the artificial, elaborate, and false; the particular against the general; knowledge gained from observation against assertions of borrowed faiths. His is the gift of direct vision, of fundamental questions, and of magical simplicity--perhaps too simple, as a distinguished historian of ideas has indicated. Isaiah Berlin, in a famous essay titled "The Hedgehog and the Fox," sees Tolstoy as torn between his pluralism (the fox, perceiving reality as varied, complex, and multiple) and monism (the hedgehog, reducing life's fullness to one single truth, the infinity of sensory data to the finite limits of a single mind). Tolstoy, Berlin concludes, was a pluralist in his practice but a monist in his theory, who found himself unable to reconcile the foxiness of his multifarious awareness with his hedgehog-like need to discover one all-embracing answer to its myriad problems.

"THE RAID"

Tolstoy's first stories are set in the Caucasus, where he spent the years 1851 to 1854, with many of the officers and soldiers whom he met serving as thinly disguised models. In "Nabeg: Razskaz volontera" ("The Raid: A Volunteer's Story"), he poses several problems: What is the nature of courage? By what tests does one determine bravery or cowardice? What feelings cause a man to kill his fellow? The first-person narrator discusses these questions with a Captain Khlopov (derived from a Captain Khilkovsky in Tolstoy's diary) and illustrates different types of courage among the military characters. Tolstoy deflates warfare, emphasizing ordinary details and casual, matter-of-fact fortitude rather than dashingly proud heroism. His

Leo Tolstoy (Library of Congress)

descriptions of nature are simple, concrete, and expert. The story's most powerful scene has a dying young ensign pass from carefree bravado to dignified resignation as he encounters his end.

SEBASTOPOL

The element of eyewitness reportage is carried over from the Caucasian tales to the three sketches in *Sebastopol*, which are fiction passing as war dispatches. Tolstoy took part in the Crimean War (1854-1856) as a sublieutenant, with Russia fighting a complex series of actions against a multiple enemy composed of not only Turkish but also some British, French, and Sardinian troops. While aggressively patriotic, Tolstoy was appalled by the disorganization of his country's military forces, with the average Russian peasant soldier poorly armed, trained, and led, while many company commanders nearly starved their men by pocketing much of the money allocated for their food.

"Sevastopol v dekabre" ("Sebastopol in December") has no characters and no particular topography. The first-person narrator constructs a guidebook homily out of lived experience, familiarly addressing readers, inviting them to listen to his frontline experiences as he wanders from Sebastopol's bay and dockside to a military hospital filled with shrieking, often multilated soldiers. The narrator tells readers:

> . . . you will see war not as a beautiful, orderly, and gleaming formation, with music and beaten drums, streaming banners and generals on prancing horses, but war in its authentic expression--as blood, suffering and death.

Tolstoy concludes this sketch with a stirring salute to the epic heroism of Sebastopol's residents and Russian defenders. A somber awareness of death's imminence, as the surgeon's sharp knife slices into his patients' flesh, pervades the sketch.

In "Sevastopol v mae" ("Sebastopol in May"), Tolstoy sharply denounces the vainglory of militarism, stressing the futility of the fighting and the madness of celebrating war as a glorious adventure. The passage describing the death by shellfire of an officer is a superb tour de force, with the author using interior monologue to have the lieutenant crowd his many hopes, fears, memories, and fantasies into a few seconds. The speaker comes to consider war as senseless, horrifying, but also--given human nature--inevitable. He concludes that the only hero he can find is the truth. This is perhaps the finest of Tolstoy's military tales, anticipating the battle and death scenes of *War and Peace*.

In the third narrative, "Sebastopol in August," Tolstoy uses well-developed characters to unify an episodic plot. He focuses on two brothers whose personalities contrast but who are both killed in action. He also strikes a note of shame and anger at Russia's abandonment of the city and the consequent waste of many thousands of lives. He celebrates, however, the quiet heroism of countless common soldiers who risked and often met death with calm nobility.

"Two Hussars"

Before Tolstoy began *War and Peace* in 1863, he wrote a number of long stories that he called *povesti*, defined as "a literary narrative of lesser size than a novel." Their compass is usually too small to accommodate the didacticism that his longer works absorb painlessly. One successful story that avoids moralizing is "Dva gusara" ("Two Hussars"). Its first half is devoted to the officer-father, the second to his son. Twenty years apart, they enact the same sequence of card playing, drinking, and philandering, in the same small town, meeting the same people. Their characters, however, differ drastically. The father is gallant, generous, honorable, and charming; the son is mean, cold, calculating, and cowardly. The father's temperament is natural and open; the son's is contrived and devious, corrupted by decadent society. As always with Tolstoy, he gives his allegiance to the authentic and intuitive, while sardonically scorning the artificial and scheming.

Family Happiness

In *Family Happiness*, Tolstoy treats a problem to which he was to return throughout his career: the place of women, both at home and in society. He had courted a much younger and very pretty girl, Valerya Arseneva, but had become irritated by her fondness for high society and had broken off the relationship. He transforms the experience into a narrative by the young woman, Masha, in the fashion of Charlotte Brontë's novel *Jane Eyre* (1847), which he had read and admired. Now married and a mother, Masha recalls in the story's first half her courtship by a man who knew her

dead father, considered himself her guardian as she grew up, and was thirty-five to her seventeen when they married. Tolstoy magnificently captures the rapturous chemistry of first love as the girl awakens to womanhood. By the story's second half, however, her husband undermines Masha's dreams of romantic happiness as she becomes addicted to the whirl of urban high society, driving her husband into rural retreat and seclusion. Toward the end, at home in the country after disillusionments in the city, she and he agree to a different sort of marriage than they envisioned at its start, basing it not on passion but on companionship and parenthood. Tolstoy has here sounded some of his most pervasive notes: Sophistication is evil, simplicity is good; the city is decadent, the country is healthy; and romance is dangerous, often a "charming nonsense," while marriage, though a necessary institution, should never be sentimentalized.

"Strider"

The story now called "Kholstomer" ("Strider") was originally translated into English as "Kholstomer: The Story of a Horse" because Tolstoy modeled his equine, first-person narrator on a horse by that name celebrated for his enormous stride and speed. The author humanizes his outcast animal, which is consistently stigmatized as a piebald and a gelding, in a keenly compassionate manner, with Strider's sorrowful life made a parable of protest against unjust punishment of those who are somehow different: "He was old, they were young. He was lean, they were sleek; he was miserable, they were gay; and so he was quite alien to them, an outsider, an utterly different creature whom it was impossible for them to pity." Strider's victimization by greedy, selfish owners enables Tolstoy to lash the evils of private property, using an equine perspective to expose its immorality.

The second phase of Tolstoy's production of short fiction follows his two great novels and the tremendous spiritual crisis chronicled in *A Confession*. It was an extremely profound change for an author. The sublime artist came to repudiate almost all art; the nobleman now lived like a peasant; the wealthy, titled country gentleman sought to abandon his property, preaching humility and asceticism; the marvelous novelist and story writer preferred the roles of educational reformer, religious leader, social sage, and cultural prophet. Tolstoy's artistic instincts, however, refused to atrophy, and he managed to create different yet also masterful works, less happy and conventional; uncompromising; sometimes perverse; always powerful; preoccupied with purity, corruption, sin, sex, and death. His late stories express his Rousseauistic hostility to such institutions as the state, which forces citizens to pay taxes and serve in the military; the church, which coerces its communicants by fear and superstition; private property, whereby one person owns another; and modern art, which is elitist. The creative gold nevertheless continues to flow from Tolstoy's pen, despite his moralistic resistance to aesthetics, in such novellas as *The Death of Ivan Ilyich* and *The Kreutzer Sonata* and the story "Master and Man."

THE DEATH OF IVAN ILYICH

The Death of Ivan Ilyich, perhaps his finest story, was Tolstoy's first published work after his conversion. It is more schematic and deliberate than the earlier tales, more selective and condensed in the choice of descriptive and analytic detail. It is a parable of a life badly lived, with Tolstoy here allying his highest art with an exigent passion for establishing the most profound and encompassing truths.

Ivan Ilyich is a cautious, correct, typical representative of his social class. He has achieved success in his profession of judge, in love, in marriage, in his family, and in his friendships, or so appearances indicate. However, when he reviews his past, confronted with the inescapability of a cancer-ridden death, he slowly arrives at the realization that he has led a life of selfishness, shallowness, smugness, and hypocrisy. Significantly, his surname, Golovin, is derived from the Russian word for "head." He has excluded any deep feelings, as he has lived according to principles of pleasantness and propriety, conforming to the values of his upper-middle-class social sphere in his striving for status, materialism, bureaucratic impersonality and power, decorous appearance, and pleasure.

In part 1, which begins with the announcement of Ivan Ilyich's death, Tolstoy's tone is caustically satiric. Ivan's wife, Praskovya Fedorovna, defines the nature of his loveless home life, grieving formally for her loss and accepting colleagues' condolences while really concerned with the cost of the grave site and the possibility of increasing her widow's pension. Ivan Ilyich, however, deserves no better. He is shown as a prisoner of his cherished possessions who wanted Praskovya primarily for her property, secondarily for her correct social position and good looks. The density of things dominates Ivan Ilyich's feelings and conduct, pain and pleasure, happiness and misery. His highest moment comes with the furnishing of a new house; and his fall comes from reaching to hang a drape when he is on a ladder. Symbolically, his fall is one from pride and vanity.

The physicians enter to examine Ivan Ilyich's bruised side. They pursue their profession much as he does, from behind well-mannered, ritualistic masks. Ivan Ilyich soon discovers that not only his doctors but also his wife, daughter, colleagues, and friends all refuse him the empathy and compassion that he increasingly needs; they act on the same principle of self-interested pleasure that he has followed. As his physical suffering grows, he experiences the emotional stages that modern psychology accepts as characteristic of responses to lingering terminal illness: denial, loneliness, anger, despondency, and finally acceptance. He begins to drop his protective disguises and to realize that his existence has consisted of evasions of self-knowledge, of love, of awareness of the deepest needs of others. His fall into the abyss of death thus brings him to spiritual birth.

At the nadir of Ivan Ilyich's suffering, partial grace comes to him through the care of his servant, Gerasim. He is, like Platon Karataev in *War and Peace*, one of those simple, spontaneous, kindly souls whom Tolstoy venerates. In contrast to the sterile pretensions of Ivan Ilyich's social circle, Gerasim, modest and strong, personifies the Tolstoyan principle of living for others. He is in every sense a "breath of fresh air," showing his master unstinting compassion as he exemplifies the health of youth and naturally loving behavior.

Inspired by Gerasim's devotion, Ivan Ilyich becomes capable of extending compassion to his wife and son. When his condition takes a final, fatal turn, as he feels himself slowly sucked into the bottom of death's sack, he comes to the realization that his life has been trivial, empty, worthless. Two hours before his death, he stops trying to justify it and instead takes pity on his wife, son, and himself. He dies loving rather than hating, forgiving rather than whining, at last surrendering his egoism. Both the story and Ivan Ilyich's life thus end on a note of serenity and joyous illumination. Tolstoy shows that profound consciousness of death can bring one to the communion of true brotherhood. Through his relentless pain, Ivan Ilyich discovers the truth about himself, akin to Prince Andrey in *War and Peace*.

THE KREUTZER SONATA

The Kreutzer Sonata, like *The Death of Ivan Ilyich*, is a condensed masterpiece of harrowing intensity, a poem of the poignant pains of the flesh. Tolstoy presents the nature of marriage more directly and comprehensively than any other writer. In *Family Happiness*, he tries to define its benefits and banes; in *War and Peace*, he celebrates it; in *Anna Karenina*, he upholds yet also questions it; in *The Kreutzer Sonata*, he denounces it vehemently. Though he previously advocated marriage as the morally and socially legitimate release for sexual needs, by the late 1880's, his new views on morality, as well as his own increasingly burdensome marriage, caused him to equate sexuality with hostility and sinfulness and to regard sexual passion as degrading, undermining human beings' spiritual self.

The novella's protagonist, Pozdnyshev, confesses on a train journey that he murdered his wife on suspicion--groundless, as circumstances indicate--of her adultery with an amateur violinist with whom she, a pianist, enjoyed playing duets--such as Ludwig van Beethoven's "Kreutzer Sonata." In the spring of 1888, a performance of this work did take place in Tolstoy's Moscow residence. He proposed to the great realistic painter also present, Ilya Repin, that the artist should paint a canvas, while he would write a story, on the theme of marital jealousy. While Tolstoy fulfilled the bargain, Repin did not. The tale was submitted to the state censor in 1888; Czar Alexander III, who read a copy, issued an imperial banning order. Sophia Tolstoya thereupon removed some of the story's sexual explicitness, and the czar permitted its publication, in bowdlerized form, in 1891. Not until the 1933 Jubilee Edition of Tolstoy's works was the text issued in its original form. However, even in its toned-down version, it aroused a storm of controversy among readers.

Pozdnyshev relates his conduct to a lightly sketched narrator. His dramatic monologue is powerful and polemical, although his arguments are often exaggerated and inconsistent. The point of his narrative is that sex is sinful, that those who submit to its drives often become vicious and, in Pozdnyshev's case, murderous. Even in marriage, the protagonist insists, sex is ugly, repulsive, and destructive. Despite the deranged character of Pozdnyshev and the manifest injustice of many of his views, the story is disturbing, forceful, and gripping, as he shows how his sexual lust degraded his character and ruined his marriage. Some critics have interpreted the structure of the tale as equivalent to the sonata form, falling into three movements with a slow introduction and the final chapter as a coda. Tolstoy was himself an accomplished pianist.

In a long, uncompromising afterword to the story, Tolstoy addresses the controversy it caused and clearly links Pozdnyshev's views--but not his pathological personality--to his. He argues that carnal love lowers human beings to animalistic conduct, advocates chastity within as well as outside marriage, denounces society for featuring erotic allure, and dismisses marriage itself as a trap for humanity's finest energies. Men and women should replace conjugal relations "with the pure relations that exist between a brother and a sister." Only thus would they behave as true Christians. Tolstoy thus dismisses sex as relevant--let alone fundamental--to human behavior. Rather, he regards it as a diabolic temptation sent to divert human beings' purpose from seeking the kingdom of God on earth.

"MASTER AND MAN"

In his moralistic monograph *What Is Art?* Tolstoy asks for writing that is easily understandable, whose subject matter is religious, whose situations are universal, whose style is simple, and whose technique is accessible. None of his successful works embodies these criteria more faithfully than "Master and Man," which is essentially a morality play based on the New Testament. The master is Vasíli Andréevich Brekhunov: selfish, overbearing, coarse, rich, rapacious, the biblical gatherer of wealth who neglects his soul. The servant is Nikíta, a reformed drunkard, who is humane, sensitive, skilled in his work, strong, meek, kindly, rich in spirit though poor in pocket. The contrast between them is stark, with Tolstoy stressing the unambiguous and heavily symbolic nature of the story: two opposed sorts of men, two opposed sets of moral values, and the conversion of the master to the ethics of his man. The man of flesh and the man of spirit join in the journey of life and the confrontation with death.

Brekhunov, a merchant proud of his ability to drive a hard bargain, sets off with Nikíta on a business trip to make a down payment on a grove. He can consider nothing but his possessions and how to increase them; his relationships to others are governed by materialistic calculations. On their trip, the pair find themselves immersed in a raging snowstorm, which obliterates all landmarks and turns the landscape into a perilous Wood of Error, a moral Wasteland, through which they must make life's passage. Tolstoy masterfully uses the storm for its emblematic qualities. It "buries" the travelers in snowdrifts, is cold like death, turns the substantial into the spectral, and vice versa. They lose their way as Brekhunov insists on movements to the left because men find their reward only on the right hand of God. As Brekhunov urges his horse away from the sled, after having (temporarily) deserted Nikíta, he can only come around in a circle to the same spot, marked by wormwood stalks--wormwood being identified with sin and punishment in Revelation. He is ritualistically confronted with himself in the person of a horse-thief, for Brekhunov has been cheating Nikíta of his wages and has stolen a large sum of money from his church to buy the grove.

Nikíta accepts his master's wrong turns without anger or reproof, resigns himself to the snowstorm, and patiently prepares to wait it out when they are forced to settle down for the night in their sled. Around midnight, ill-clad and half-frozen, meekly awaiting likely death before morning, Nikíta asks his master to give the wages owed him to his family and to "Forgive me for Christ's sake!" Finally, moved to pity by Nikíta's words, Brekhunov opens his heavy fur coat and lies down on top of his servant, covering Nikíta with both his coat and body as he sobs.

Just before dawn Brekhunov has a visionary dream, in which "it seemed to him that he was Nikíta and Nikíta was he, and that his life was not in himself but in

Nikíta." He wonders why he used to trouble himself so greatly to accumulate money and possessions. At noon the next day, peasants drag both men out of the snow. Brekhunov is frozen to death; Nikíta, though chilled, is alive.

Some critics have faulted the story's ending because Tolstoy has inadequately prepared the reader for Brekhunov's sudden adoption of Christian humility, brotherhood, and self-sacrifice; he has previously shown not the slightest inclination toward moral regeneration. Be that as it may, most of the tale is enormously impressive in the power of its sensuous description as the snowstorm isolates the couple from ordinary existence, strips them of external comforts, exposes them to the presence of death, and forces them to encounter their inmost selves.

Tolstoy's celebration of Brekhunov's redemption through fellowship is his answer to a universe that he has feared all of his life as he confronts the horror of nonexistence conveyed by death. Master and man--or man and man, or man and woman--should cling to each other, love each other, forgive each other. Will such conduct vault their souls into immortality? Tolstoy desperately hopes so.

OTHER MAJOR WORKS

LONG FICTION: *Detstvo*, 1852 (*Childhood*, 1862); *Otrochestvo*, 1854 (*Boyhood*, 1886); *Yunost'*, 1857 (*Youth*, 1886); *Kazaki*, 1863 (*The Cossacks*, 1878); *Voyna i mir*, 1865-1869 (*War and Peace*, 1886); *Anna Karenina*, 1875-1877 (English translation, 1886); *Voskreseniye*, 1899 (*Resurrection*, 1899); *Khadzi-Murat*, wr. 1904, pb. 1911 (*Hadji Murad*, 1911).

PLAYS: *Vlast tmy: Ili, "Kogotok uvyaz, vsey ptichke propast,"* pb. 1887, pr. 1888 (*The Dominion of Darkness*, 1888; better known as *The Power of Darkness*, 1899); *Plody prosveshcheniya*, pr. 1889 (*The Fruits of Enlightenment*, 1891); *I svet vo tme svetit*, pb. 1911 (*The Light Shines in Darkness*, 1923); *Zhivoy trup*, pr., pb. 1911 (*The Live Corpse*, 1919); *The Dramatic Works*, pb. 1923.

NONFICTION: *Ispoved'*, 1884 (*A Confession*, 1885); *V chom moya vera*, 1884 (*What I Believe*, 1885); *O zhizni*, 1888 (*Life*, 1888); *Kritika dogmaticheskogo bogosloviya*, 1891 (*A Critique of Dogmatic Theology*,

1904); *Soedinenie i perevod chetyrekh evangeliy,*
1892-1894 (*The Four Gospels Harmonized and Translated,* 1895-1896); *Tsarstvo Bozhie vnutri vas,* 1893
(*The Kingdom of God Is Within You,* 1894); *Chto takoye iskusstvo?* 1898 (*What Is Art?* 1898); *Tak chto
zhe nam delat?,* 1902 (*What to Do?,* 1887); *O Shek-
spire i o drame,* 1906 (*Shakespeare and the Drama,*
1906); *The Diaries of Leo Tolstoy, 1847-1852,* 1917;
The Journal of Leo Tolstoy, 1895-1899, 1917; *Tolstoi's
Love Letters,* 1923; *The Private Diary of Leo Tolstoy,
1853-1857,* 1927; *"What Is Art?" and Essays on Art,*
1929; *L. N. Tolstoy o literature: Stati, pisma, dnevniki,*
1955; *Lev Tolstoy ob iskusstve i literature,* 1958; *Last
Diaries,* 1960; *Tolstoy's Letters,* 1978 (2 volumes; R.
F. Christian, editor).

CHILDREN'S LITERATURE: *Azbuka,* 1872; *Novaya azbuka,* 1875 (*Stories for My Children,* 1988); *Russkie
knigi dlya chteniya,* 1875; *Classic Tales and Fables for
Children,* 2002 (includes selections from *Azbuka* and
Novaya azbuka).

MISCELLANEOUS: *The Complete Works of Count Tolstoy,* 1904-1905 (24 volumes); *Tolstoy Centenary Edition,* 1928-1937 (21 volumes); *Polnoye sobraniye sochinenii,* 1928-1958 (90 volumes).

BIBLIOGRAPHY

Bayley, John, ed. Introduction to *The Portable Tolstoy.*
New York: Viking, 1978. Bayley has written a discerning introduction to this collection of the shorter
fiction and has compiled a comprehensive chronology and select bibliography. This anthology
omits the long novels but does excerpt *Childhood,
Boyhood,* and *Youth*; also included are *A Confession*
and *The Power of Darkness.*

_____. *Tolstoy and the Novel.* London: Chatto &
Windus, 1966. Influenced by Henry James's organic
conception of the novel, Bayley concentrates on a
trenchant analyses of *War and Peace* and *Anna Karenina.* He also perceptively examines *Family Happiness, The Kreutzer Sonata,* and *The Devil.*

Berlin, Isaiah. "The Hedgehog and the Fox" and "Tolstoy and Enlightenment." In *Russian Thinkers.* New
York: Viking, 1978. The first essay is a famous analysis of Tolstoy's philosophy of history; the second
focuses on his indebtedness to Jean-Jacques

Rousseau. Both are eloquently written by a distinguished historian and philosopher.

Christian, R. F. *Tolstoy: A Critical Introduction.* Cambridge, England: Cambridge University Press, 1969.
Christian is a leading Tolstoyan who is knowledge-
able about his subject's sources and influences,
writes clearly, and provides particularly helpful interpretations of *Family Happiness* and *The Kreutzer
Sonata.*

Freeborn, Richard. "The Long Short Story in Tolstoy's
Fiction." In *The Cambridge Companion to Tolstoy,*
edited by Donna Tussing Orwin. New York: Cambridge University Press, 2002. An examination of
The Death of Ivan Ilyich, The Kreutzer Sonata, and
Father Sergius, which Freeborn argues were Tolstoy's best works of the 1880's and 1890's. This
companion to Tolstoy also includes essays about
Tolstoy as an artist, public figure, and writer of popular literature; the development of the styles and
themes of his works; Tolstoy's aesthetics; and his
depiction of women, sexuality, and the family.

Jahn, Gary R. *The Death of Ivan Ilich: An Interpretation.* New York: Twayne, 1993. After providing a
summary and critique of previous criticism on Tolstoy's most famous story, Jahn examines the context
of the story within other works by Tolstoy to argue
that the story is an affirmation of life rather than a
document of despair.

Orwin, Donna Tussig. *Tolstoy's Art and Thought, 1847-
1880.* Princeton, N.J.: Princeton University Press,
1993. Divided into three parts, which coincide with
the first three decades of Tolstoy's literary career,
Orwin's study attempts to trace the origins and
growth of the Russian master's ideas. After focusing
on Tolstoy's initial creative vision, Orwin goes on to
analyze, in depth, his principal works.

Reyfman, Irina. "Female Voice and Male Gaze in
Leo Tolstoy's *Family Happiness.*" In *Mapping
the Feminine: Russian Women and Cultural Difference,* edited by Hilde Hoogenboom, Catharine Theimer Nepomnyashchy, and Reyfman.
Bloomington, Ind.: Slavica, 2008. An analysis
of *Family Happiness* that focuses on Tolstoy's
depiction of gender.

Simmons, Ernest J. *Introduction to Tolstoy's Writings.* Chicago: University of Chicago Press, 1968. Simmons, who died in 1972, was the dean of Russian literature studies in the United States and wrote a two-volume biography of Tolstoy. This book is compact, well organized, comprehensive, and reliable.

Steiner, George. *Tolstoy or Dostoevsky: An Essay in the Old Criticism.* 2d ed. New Haven, Conn.: Yale University Press, 1996. This welcome reappearance of a classic study of the epic versus the dramatic, first published in 1959, carries only a new preface. In it, however, Steiner makes a compelling case for the reprinting, in the age of deconstructionism, of this wide-ranging study not just of individual texts, but of contrasting worldviews.

Tolstoy, Leo. *Tolstoy's Short Fiction: Revised Translations, Backgrounds and Sources, Criticism.* 2d ed. Edited and with revised translations by Michael R. Katz. New York: Norton, 2008. A compendium of materials by and about Tolstoy. Features twelve works of Tolstoy's short fiction, including "Sevastopol in December," *The Death of Ivan Ilych, The Kreutzer Sonata,* "Master and Man," and *Father Sergius.* The "Backgrounds and Sources" section contains primary source documents that describe Tolstoy's creative process, such as two of his memoirs, excerpts from his diary for 1855, and selected letters from 1858 through 1895. "Criticism" provides twenty-three essays, including six essays written for this edition, that analyze Tolstoy's use of language and specific themes and motifs in the individual works. Four of the essays are written by literary critics Mikhail Bakhtin and John Bayley and writers Vladimir Nabokov and Donald Barthelme.

Wasiolek, Edward. *Tolstoy's Major Fiction.* Chicago: University of Chicago Press, 1978. Having written a superb study of Fyodor Dostoevski's fiction, Wasiolek has composed an equally first-rate critique of Tolstoy's. He concentrates on thorough analyses of ten Tolstoyan works, including *Family Happiness, The Death of Ivan Ilyich,* and "Master and Man." His is a close and acute reading, influenced by Russian Formalists and by Roland Barthes. A twenty-page chronicle of Tolstoy's life and work is illuminating.

Gerhard Brand

IVAN TURGENEV

Born: Orel, Russia; November 9, 1818
Died: Bougival, France; September 3, 1883

PRINCIPAL SHORT FICTION

Zapiski okhotnika, 1852 (*Russian Life in the Interior,* 1855; better known as *A Sportsman's Sketches,* 1932)
Povesti i rasskazy, 1856
First Love, and Other Stories, 1989

OTHER LITERARY FORMS

In addition to *A Sportsman's Sketches,* Ivan Turgenev (tur-GYAYN-yuhf) published several other short stories and novellas individually. His main literary contribution, however, was his novels, some of which are among the best written in Russian, especially *Ottsy i deti* (1862; *Fathers and Sons,* 1867). He also wrote poems, poems in prose, and plays, one of which, *Mesyats v derevne* (pb. 1855, pr. 1872; *A Month in the Country,* 1924), is still staged regularly in Russian theaters.

ACHIEVEMENTS

Ivan Turgenev's opus is not particularly large, yet with about four dozen stories and novellas and his brief novels, he became one of the best writers not only in Russian but also in world literature. Turgenev was a leading force in the Russian realistic movement of the second half of the nineteenth century. Together with Nikolai Gogol, Fyodor Dostoevski, Leo Tolstoy, and

Anton Chekhov, he built the reputation that Russian literature enjoys in the world. Perhaps more than other writers, he was responsible for acquainting foreign readers with Russian literature, and because he spent most of his adult life abroad, he was an esteemed figure in the international literary life.

Turgenev was also instrumental in arousing the sensitivity and consciousness of his compatriots because he dealt with such burning social issues as the plight of Russian peasantry in *A Sportsman's Sketches*; the "superfluous man" in Russian society in "The Diary of a Superfluous Man"; the fixation of Russians with revolution in *Rudin* (1856; *Dimitri Roudine*, 1873; better known as *Rudin*, 1947); the decaying nobility in *Dvoryanskoye gnezdo* (1859; *Liza*, 1869; better known as *A House of Gentlefolk*, 1894); and the age-old conflict between generations in *Fathers and Sons*.

Turgenev also excelled in his style, especially in the use of the language. Albert Jay Nock called him "incomparably the greatest of artists in fiction," and Virginia Woolf termed his works as being "curiously of our own time, undecayed and complete in themselves." His reputation, despite some fluctuations, endures.

BIOGRAPHY

Ivan Sergeyevich Turgenev was born on November 9, 1818, in the central Russian town of Orel, into a small gentry family. His father was a loving, easygoing country squire, while his mother was an overbearing woman of whom Turgenev had many unpleasant memories. He spent his childhood at the family estate, Spasskoe, which he visited every summer even after the family moved to Moscow. He received tutoring at home and later was graduated from the University of St. Petersburg in 1837. He continued his studies in Berlin, acquiring a master's degree in philosophy. His stay in Berlin marks the beginning of a lifelong shuffle between his homeland and the European countries, especially France, Germany, England, and Italy. On one visit to France, he met a French woman, Pauline Viardot, with whom he had a close relationship the rest of his life despite her being married. After serving briefly in the Ministry of Interior, he lived the remainder of his life off his estate income following his parents' death.

Turgenev started to write early, and in 1843, at the age of twenty-five, he published a long narrative poem, *Parasha*, written in imitation of Alexander Pushkin. He soon abandoned poetry for prose, although his reverence for Pushkin and the poetic slant remained constant in his writings. His stories about the dismal life of Russian peasants were much more successful, attracting the attention of readers and critics alike. When the collection of those stories, *A Sportsman's Sketches*, was published in 1852, his reputation as a promising young writer was firmly established. A successful play, *A Month in the Country*, added to his reputation. As his reputation grew, he became friends with many leading writers and critics--Vissarion Belinsky, Nikolai Nekrasov, Tolstoy, Aleksandr Herzen, Dostoevski, and others--but these friendships were often interspersed with heated arguments and enmity. Because of his connections in Europe and a pronounced liberal outlook, he was summoned on several occasions before the investigation committees back in Russia. He was always exonerated, however, and he continued to travel between Russia and Europe.

Turgenev never married, but he had several affairs, while Viardot remained the love of his life, and he was thought to have been the father of a son born to her. His steady stream of successful novels and stories enhanced the esteem in which he was held both at home and abroad. At the same time, he carried on a spirited debate with Russian intellectuals, advocating liberal reforms in Russian society, especially those concerning the plight of peasants, many of whom were still kept as serfs. When they were liberated in 1861, it was believed that not a small merit belonged to Turgenev and his efforts toward their emancipation.

Toward the end of his life, Turgenev kept writing and publishing, though at a slower pace. He also worked on the preparation of his collected works and continued to live in a ménage á trois with Viardot and her husband. During his last visit to Russia in the summer of 1881, he visited Tolstoy at Yasnaya Polyana. His health began to deteriorate in 1882, and, after several months of a serious illness, he died at the Viardots' estate in Bougival, near Paris, on September 3, 1883. As his friend Henry James wrote, "his end was not serene and propitious, but dark and almost violent." Turgenev's body was taken to Russia, where he was buried with great honors in St. Petersburg.

ANALYSIS

The reputation of Ivan Turgenev as a short-story writer is based in equal measure on his stories about Russian peasant life and on stories about other segments of society. Although differing greatly in subject matter and emphasis, they nevertheless share the same mastery of storytelling and style and language. Turgenev wrote stories about the peasants early in his career, revealing his familiarity with life in the countryside and his preoccupation with liberal causes. As he grew older and traveled to Europe, his horizons expanded, and he became more interested in topics transcending his provincial outlook. His acquired cosmopolitanism was also reflected in his turning toward personal concerns of love, alienation, and psychological illumination of his characters. The last story that he wrote, "Klara Milich" ("Clara Milich"), takes him to the realm of the fantastic and supernatural, to life after death, and even to the bizarre twists of the human mind.

A SPORTSMAN'S SKETCHES

Turgenev's stories about Russian peasants are contained primarily in his collection *A Sportsman's Sketches*. As the title implies (the accurate translation is "notes of a hunter"), the twenty-five tales are more like notes and sketches than full-blown stories with plot and characterization. It is one of the few examples in world literature where the entire collection of separate and independent stories has a thematic unity; another example of this unity is Isaac Babel's *Konormiia* (1926; *Red Cavalry*, 1929). The unifying theme is the hard life of Russian peasants--many generations of whom had lived as serfs for centuries--and the neglect of their well-being on the part of their owners. Despite its innocuous title, chosen to mislead the censors, the collection provoked admiration, as well as heated debates. It is credited with speeding up the process of the serfs' emancipation.

The stories are set in the countryside around Turgenev's family estate at the middle of the nineteenth century. They are told by the same narrator, a landowner, in fact the thinly disguised author himself.

Ivan Turgenev (Library of Congress)

During his tireless hunting trips, Turgenev met various characters, mostly peasants, many of whom told him stories. The authentic human quality of the settings and marvelous characterization, rather than the social message, make the stories enduring literature.

The author approaches his characters with an open mind. He observes their demeanor "with curiosity and sympathy" and listens to their concerns and complaints without much comment, with a few questions for his own clarification. He refrains from passing judgment and avoids social criticism or satire. Through such unobtrusiveness, he gains the characters' confidence and allows them to talk freely, making the stories more believable. More important, he does not idealize the peasants; instead, he attempts to penetrate the crust of everyday appearances.

The woman in the story "Ermolai i mel'nichikha" ("Yermolai and the Miller's Wife"), whose freedom had been bought by her husband, talks nonchalantly about her hard lot and the lack of love in her life. However, beneath her story, the reader senses deep melancholy and hopelessness, reinforced by the author's remark to his hunting companion, "It seems she is ailing," and by the companion's retort, "What else should she be?" The burly, taciturn forest warden in the story "Biriuk" ("The Wolf"), who lives alone, excels in protecting the forest from the poachers, and he is feared and hated by the peasants, who are not above stealing wood from the landowner. He cannot be bribed and plays no favorites, finding the only pleasure in doing his job. However, when he catches a poor peasant trying to fell a tree, he lets him go because it is hunger that drove him to thievery. In one of Turgenev's best stories, "Zhivye Moshchi" ("A Living Relic"), a young woman, dying of a fatal illness, gives the impression of total helplessness, yet she is nourished until her untimely death by her naïve religion and love of life. In all these stories, appearances are deceiving and the observer-narrator is able to get to the core of his characters.

Not all characters have an adversarial relationship with their fate. The two friends in "Khor'i Kalynich" ("Khor and Kalynich") epitomize the two halves of a Russian character. Khor is a practical, down-to-earth man who has found success in life. Kalynich is a sensitive soul living in unison with nature, a dreamer who revels in simple pleasures, without worrying about more complex aspects of life. The doctor in "Uezdnyi lekar" ("The Country Doctor"), called to the sickbed of a young girl, falls in love with her, and his love is returned, but he realizes that he cannot save the young girl. He finds solace in the discovery that the girl has satisfied her own craving for love in the last moments of her life. Thus, the results are not as important as the efforts to avoid or alleviate the blows, no matter how unsuccessful the efforts may be.

Peasants are not the only characters drawing the author's attention. The landowners, who wield the power of life and death over their serfs, also appear in several stories. For the most part, they are depicted with much less sympathy and understanding, despite the author's own social origin. In "Dva pomeshchika" ("Two Landowners"), both characters show negative traits: One, a major-general, is a social clown; the other is an insensitive brute who thinks that a peasant will always be a peasant and who uses a homespun "philosophy" that "if the father's a thief, the son's thief too . . . it's blood

that counts." The author seems to be saying that, with such a negative attitude, no improvement of the peasants' lot is possible. "Gamlet Shchigrovskogo uezda" ("Hamlet of the Shchigrovsky District") offers an even stronger castigation of the serf-owning class. Here, an intelligent and sensitive landowner fails to find understanding among his peers for his attempts to improve the lot of everybody. In a Dostoevskian fashion, he is forced to act like a buffoon in hopes of gaining attention that way. Turgenev's position here sounds very much like a sharp satire against the existing state of affairs, but, as mentioned, he abstains from open and direct criticism, thus making his points even more effective.

Not all of the stories in *A Sportsman's Sketches* are bleak or hopeless. The two best stories of the collection are also the most positive. In "Bezhin lug" ("Bezhin Meadow"), Turgenev relates his evening encounter with five young boys taking care of the horses in the countryside. Sitting by the fire in the evening, they tell one another fantastic stories to amuse and even frighten one another. The narrator is impressed by the boys' natural demeanor, straightforwardness, bravery, and, above all, rich imagination of which the folktales are spun. The author seems to imply that the future of the country is secure if judged by the young who are to inherit it.

The second story, "Pevtsy" ("The Singers"), is even more uplifting. In another chance encounter, the narrator stumbles across an inn in the barely accessible backwoods. He is treated with a singing competition among the inn patrons unlike any other he had experienced. Turgenev uses the diamond-in-the-rough theme to show where the real talent can be found. As the narrator leaves the inn, he hears the people's voices calling each other from one hill to another--a possible explanation of where the marvelous singers learn how to sing. These stories, along with a few others, strike a balance between the negative and the positive aspects of the life depicted in the book.

Surrounded and suffused by nature, Turgenev reacts to it by stating his position concerning human beings in nature. He expresses his admiration for nature by using strikingly detailed descriptions, emphasizing colors, sounds, and scents. His subtlety of observation is complemented by genuine lyricism and careful use of a melodic, rhythmical language. Despite these ornamental features, however, the reader is tempted to view the author's notion of nature as being rather unfeeling and indifferent toward humankind, in the best tradition of Georg Brandes's theory of *la grande indifférante*. A closer look, however, reveals that nature in Turgenev's works shows the difference in degree, not in kind, and that for him, humankind is a part of nature, not outside it. Only in unison with nature can human beings fulfill their potential, in which case nature is not indifferent but, on the contrary, very helpful, as seen in the example of the singers in the aforementioned story.

Other artistic merits of these stories (which Turgenev was able to maintain throughout his writing career) can be found in his careful and delicate choice of suggestive and descriptive words; in the sketchy but pithy psychological portraiture; in the uncomplicated plot structure, consisting usually of an anecdote or episode; in the natural, calm, matter-of-fact narration; and in the effective imagery that is not strained or artificial. Superior craftsmanship goes hand in hand with the "social message" here, preventing the stories from being dated or used for inartistic purposes.

"The Diary of a Superfluous Man"

The second group of Turgenev's tales strikes an altogether different path, although a kinship with his earlier stories can be easily detected. Among many stories outside the cycle of *A Sportsman's Sketches*, eight deserve to be singled out, either for the significance of their contents or for their artistic merit, or both. An early story, "Dnevnik lishnega cheloveka" ("The Diary of a Superfluous Man"), despite its relative immaturity, has a significance that surpasses its artistic quality. It is here that Turgenev coined the phrase "a superfluous man," which would reverberate throughout Russian literature of the nineteenth and twentieth centuries. Even though the superfluous man theme had been used before Turgenev by Pushkin's Eugene Onegin in the novel in verse by the same name and by Mikhail Lermontov's Pechorin in *Geroy nashego vremeni* (1840; *A Hero of Our Times*, 1854), it was Turgenev who made the phrase a literary byword. The story presages Dostoevski's *Zapiski iz podpolya* (1864; *Letters from the Underworld*, 1913; better known as *Notes from the Underground*).

Turgenev's "superfluous man" is a young scion of erstwhile wealthy landowners, who writes a diary knowing that he will soon die of a disease. To compound his misery, he is rejected in his love for a beautiful neighbor. The excessive introspection of the "hero" and his inability to cope with reality make this story primarily a psychological character study and not a social statement, as some of Turgenev's works of the same kind would become later.

"Mumu"

Perhaps the best known of Turgenev's stories, "Mumu" comes the closest in spirit to the collection *A Sportsman's Sketches*. A deaf-mute servant loses the girl he loves when he is forced into marrying another woman. Later, he is ordered to kill his beloved dog because its barking is disturbing his mistress's sleep. Drawing the character of the insensitive mistress after his mother, Turgenev castigates the insensitivity of the entire serf-owning class. The story does not sink into sentimental bathos primarily because of the remarkable characterization of the servant as an ultimate sufferer, underscoring the proverbial capacity for suffering of an entire nation. Moreover, by arousing overwhelming pity for the deaf-mute, Turgenev clearly places the blame for this human and social injustice at the door of the unfeeling gentry.

"King Lear of the Steppes"

"Stepnoi Korol' Lir" ("King Lear of the Steppes") is another story that in its countryside setting shows kinship with *A Sportsman's Sketches*. However, it is entirely different in the subject matter, spirit, and atmosphere. In a takeoff on William Shakespeare's tragedy, the story shows children behaving toward their father in a similar manner. The atmosphere here, however, is typically Russian. Harlov, a descendant of a Russianized Swedish family, suffers the same indignity and ingratitude at the hands of his daughters as does Shakespeare's King Lear, and Harlov takes similar revenge upon his daughters, but the tragedy is not relieved or ennobled. Turgenev shows a fine sense for plot, and the dialogues--more excessive than usual for him--are in line with the dramatic nature of its model. Artistically, this story is almost a masterpiece, keeping the reader in suspense until the end.

"ASYA"

Love is an overriding theme in Turgenev's later stories. "Asya" ("Asya") and "Pervaya lyubov" ("First Love") are the best representatives of Turgenev's love stories. Both are told in the first person, tempting one to attribute to them autobiographical character, which may not be totally unjustified "Asya" is set in a German town where the narrator (perhaps Turgenev) comes across two compatriots, a brother and a sister.

As the story unfolds, the narrator is increasingly attracted to the woman and develops genuine feelings of love, yet he is unable to declare his love openly, vacillating constantly until every chance for consummation is lost. Turgenev was known to have been indecisive in his love affairs, as illustrated by his strange attachment to the Viardot couple. Seen from that angle, the autobiographical element becomes very plausible, but there is more to the story than simply Turgenev's indecisiveness. At this stage of his development, Turgenev had published only one book of short stories and one novel, and he was beset by doubts and indecision, not only in his love relationships but also in his literary aspirations, all too similar to those of the narrator in "Asya." As he himself said:

There are turning points in life, points when the past dies and something new is born; woe to the man who doesn't know how to sense these turning points and either holds on stubbornly to a dead past or seeks prematurely to summon to life what has not yet fully ripened.

The story reflects the wrenching doubts and soul searching of the protagonist, which did not enable him to take a resolute stance toward the young woman, who herself was searching for a more assuring love. Thus, the love between Asya and the narrator was doomed to failure almost before it began. The two part, and the only thing left is a bittersweet memory of what might have been.

Perhaps Turgenev was not yet ready to give the story the adequate treatment that it deserves. This is evidenced in the fact that Asya, wistful and charming though she may be, is not developed fully as a character. Turgenev will return soon to a similar theme and develop it to the fullest in his novel *A House of Gentlefolk*. It is also worth mentioning that "Asya" is another example of the theme of the superfluous man, which started with "The Diary of a Superfluous Man."

"FIRST LOVE"

"First Love" is a better love story because both the plot and the characters are more fully developed. It involves a rivalry between a young man and his father, vying for the affection of the same woman, Zinaida. In Turgenev's own admission, the story is autobiographical; as he wrote about it in a letter, "It is the only thing that still gives me pleasure, because it is life itself, it was not made up. . . . 'First Love' is part of my experience." Aside from this candid admission, the story has a wide appeal to all, both young and old; to the young because the first love is always cherished the most (the only true love, according to Turgenev), and to the old because it offers a vicarious pleasure of a last triumph.

It invariably evokes a bittersweet nostalgia in everyone. It also presents a plausible, even if relatively uncommon, situation. Turgenev controls with a sure hand the delicate relationships among the three partners in this emotional drama fraught with the awakening of manhood in an adolescent, with the amorous playfulness of a young woman who is both a temptress and a victim, and with the satisfaction of a conquest by a man entering the autumn of his life. Similarly, the author handles tactfully a potentially explosive situation between the loving father and adoring son, producing no rancor in aftermath. The story is a throwback to Romanticism, which had already passed in Russian literature and elsewhere at the time of the story's publication. The story ends in a Turgenevian fashion--unhappily for everyone concerned. All these attributes make "First Love" one of the best love stories in world literature.

"THE SONG OF TRIUMPHANT LOVE"

Twenty years later, Turgenev would write another love story, "Pesn' torzhestvuiushchei liubvi" ("The Song of Triumphant Love"), which differs from "First Love" in many respects. It again deals with a love relationship in a ménage à trois (it seems that Turgenev was constantly reliving his own predicament with the Viardot couple), but the similarities stop there. The setting is in sixteenth century Ferrara, and the male characters--members of ancient patrician families--are on equal footing, even if one is a husband and the other a suitor. The ending is much more than unhappy: It is downright tragic. What makes this story decisively different from other love stories by Turgenev is the introduction of a supernatural element manifesting itself in the woman's conceiving, not by intercourse, but by the platonic desire and the singing of a song by the unsuccessful suitor.

"The Song of Triumphant Love" marks the transition to a more esoteric subject matter in Turgenev's writing. He had written fantastic stories before ("Prizraki," or "Phantoms"), but in the last decade of his life, he employed the supernatural with increasing frequency. In "Stuk . . . stuk . . . stuk . . . " ("Knock . . . Knock . . . Knock . . . "), he deals with a suicidal urge that borders on the supernatural. In his last story, "Clara Milich," he tells of a man who has fallen in love with a woman after her death. Turgenev believed that there is a thin line dividing the real and the fantastic and that the fantastic stories people tell have happened in real life. As he said, "Wherever you look, there is the drama in life, and there are still writers who complain that all subjects have been exhausted." Had he lived longer, most likely he would have tried to reconcile real life with so-called fantasy and the supernatural.

OTHER MAJOR WORKS

LONG FICTION: *Rudin*, 1856 (*Dimitri Roudine*, 1873; better known as *Rudin*, 1947); *Asya*, 1858 (English translation, 1877); *Dvoryanskoye gnezdo*, 1859 (*Liza*, 1869; also as *A Nobleman's Nest*, 1903; better known as *A House of Gentlefolk*, 1894); *Nakanune*, 1860 (*On the Eve*, 1871); *Pervaya lyubov*, 1860 (*First Love*, 1884); *Ottsy i deti*, 1862 (*Fathers and Sons*, 1867); *Dym*, 1867 (*Smoke*, 1868); *Veshniye vody*, 1872 (*Spring Floods*, 1874; better known as *The Torrents of Spring*, 1897); *Nov*, 1877 (*Virgin Soil*, 1877); *The Novels of Ivan Turgenev*, 1894-1899 (15 volumes).

PLAYS: *Neostorozhnost*, pb. 1843 (*Carelessness*, 1924); *Bezdenezhe*, pb. 1846, pr. 1852 (*A Poor Gentleman*, 1924); *Kholostyak*, pr. 1849 (*The Bachelor*, 1924); *Zavtrak u predvoditelya*, pr. 1849, pb. 1856 (*An Amicable Settlement*, 1924); *Nakhlebnik*, wr. 1849, pb. 1857, pr. 1862 (*The Family Charge*, 1924); *Razgovor na bolshoy doroge*, pr. 1850, pb. 1851 (*A Conversation on the Highway*, 1924); *Mesyats v derevne*, wr. 1850, pb. 1855, pr. 1872 (*A Month in the Country*, 1924); *Provintsialka*, pr. 1851 (*A Provincial Lady*, 1934); *Gde tonko, tam i rvyotsya*, wr. 1851, pr. 1912 (*Where It Is Thin, There It Breaks*, 1924); *Vecher v Sorrente*, wr. 1852, pr. 1884, pb. 1891 (*An Evening in Sorrento*, 1924); *The Plays of Ivan Turgenev*, pb. 1924; *Three Plays*, pb. 1934.

POETRY: *Parasha*, 1843; *Senilia*, 1882, 1930 (better known as *Stikhotvoreniya v proze*; *Poems in Prose*, 1883, 1945).

NONFICTION: "Gamlet i Don Kikhot," 1860 ("Hamlet and Don Quixote," 1930); *Literaturnya i zhiteyskiya vospominaniya*, 1880 (*Literary Reminiscences and Autobiographical Fragments*, 1958); *Letters*, 1983 (David Lowe, editor); *Turgenev's Letters*, 1983 (A. V. Knowles, editor).

MISCELLANEOUS: *The Works of Iván Turgenieff*, 1903-1904 (6 volumes); *The Essential Turgenev*, 1994.

BIBLIOGRAPHY

Allen, Elizabeth Cheresh. *Beyond Realism: Turgenev's Poetics of Secular Salvation*. Stanford, Calif.: Stanford University Press, 1992. Argues that readers should not turn to Turgenev merely for transparent narratives of nineteenth century Russian life. Attempts to expose the unique imaginative vision and literary patterns in Turgenev's work. Discusses Turgenev's development of narrative techniques in *A Sportsman's Sketches*, analyzing several of the major stories, such as "Bezhin Meadow" and "The Singers."

Bloom, Harold. *Ivan Turgenev*. Philadelphia: Chelsea House, 2003. Collection of critical essays about Turgenev's works, including two that pertain to the short fiction: "The Literary Apprenticeship: Pushkin, *A Sportsman's Sketches*," by Richard Freeborn, and "Turgenev's 'Mumu' and the Absence of Love," by Edgar L. Frost.

Brodianski, Nina. "Turgenev's Short Stories: A Reevaluation." *Slavonic and East European Review* 32, no. 78 (1953): 70-91. In this brief but thorough and stimulating study, Brodianski examines Turgenev's short stories in general; their themes, structure, and psychological illumination of characters;

his philosophy (as much as there is of it); and his literary theories about the short story. Inasmuch as it reevaluates some long-standing opinions about Turgenev, it serves a good purpose.

Brouwer, Sander. *Character in the Short Prose of Ivan Sergeevic Turgenev*. Atlanta: Rodopi, 1996. Examines several stories, including "The Dog," "Mumu," and "Bezhin Meadow," to discuss Turgenev's creation and use of characters.

Gregg, Richard. "Turgenev and Hawthorne: The Life-Giving Satyr and the Fallen Faun." *Slavic and East European Journal* 41 (Summer, 1997): 258-270. Discusses Hawthorne's influence on Turgenev. Comments on the common motif that their "mysterious" stories shared--the uncanny spell, curse, or blight. Argues that Turgenev's explicit admiration for those works of Hawthorne in which this motif is found attests a bond of sympathy between the two writers.

Kagan-Kans, Eva. "Fate and Fantasy: A Study of Turgenev's Fantastic Stories." *Slavic Review* 18 (1969): 543-560. Kagan-Kans traces Turgenev's treatment of fantasy and supernatural elements in his stories, as well as the role of fate and dreams. She also examines Turgenev's relationship with other writers, especially the Romantics, and their influence on him as evidenced in individual stories, especially those dealing with fantasy and the supernatural.

Knowles, A. V. *Ivan Turgenev*. Boston: Twayne, 1988. An excellent introductory study, with a biographical sketch and chapters on the start of Turgenev's literary career, the establishment of his reputation, his first three novels, his later novels, his letters, his final years, and his place in literature. Includes chronology, notes, and an annotated bibliography.

Lloyd, John Arthur Thomas. *Ivan Turgenev*. 1942. Reprint. Port Washington, N.Y.: Kennikat Press, 1973. A practical, compact biography, tastefully illustrated, treating Turgenev's life and works in a lively, succinct manner. Tends to cling to traditional views about Turgenev, which is useful for comparative purposes.

Magarshack, David. *Turgenev: A Life*. London: Faber & Faber, 1954. An illustrated biography by Turgenev's translator. Concentrates on the events that shaped Turgenev's life, his relationships with Russian and foreign writers, and the factual circumstances surrounding his works. A useful introduction to Turgenev and his opus.

O'Bell, Leslie. "The Pastoral in Turgenev's 'Singers': Classical Themes and Romantic Variations." *Russian Review* 63, no. 2 (April, 2004): 277-295. An analysis of "The Singers" from *A Sportsman's Sketches*. O'Bell criticizes the use of the pastoral mode in the story and discusses its structural organization and depiction of village life between the Slavophiles and Westernizers.

Platonov, Rachel S. "Remapping Arcadia: 'Pastoral Space' in Nineteenth-Century Russian Prose." *Modern Language Review* 102, no. 4 (October, 2007): 1105-1121. Examines several works of Russian pastoral literature, including *A Sportsman's Sketches*, to define and analyze the concept of "pastoral space."

Seeley, Frank Friedeberg. *Turgenev: A Reading of His Fiction*. New York: Cambridge University Press, 1991. Seeley prefaces his thorough study of Turgenev's fiction with an outline of Turgenev's life and a survey of his poetry and plays. This volume incorporates later findings and challenges some established views, especially the traditional notion of the "simplicity" of Turgenev's works. Seeley stresses the psychological treatment that Turgenev allotted to his characters.

Sheidley, William E. "'Born in Imitation of Someone Else': Reading Turgenev's 'Hamlet of the Shchigrovsky District' as a Version of *Hamlet*." *Studies in Short Fiction* 27 (Summer, 1990): 391-398. Discusses the character Vasily Vasilyevych as the most emphatic and the most pathetic of the Hamlet types in *A Sportsman's Sketches*. Contends that in a striking flash of metafictional irony, Vasily recognizes himself as the walking embodiment of the Hamlet stereotype. Sheidley points out the different implications of the Hamlet character in Elizabethan tragedy and the nineteenth century character sketch.

Waddington, Patrick, ed. *Ivan Turgenev and Britain*. Providence, R.I.: Berg, 1995. Collection of essays on Turgenev's reputation in England and in America, including reviews by distinguished critics, such as

Frank Harris, Virginia Woolf, and Edmund Gosse. Waddington provides a comprehensive introduction, explaining the historical context in which these reviews appeared. With extensive notes and bibliography.

Yarmolinsky, Avrahm. *Turgenev: The Man, His Art, and His Age*. New York: Orion Press, 1959. Reprint. New York: Collier, 1962. Another reliable shorter biography, useful as an introduction to Turgenev. As the title implies, it touches on all important stages in his life and discusses his works as to their geneses, their salient features, and their overall significance for Turgenev and for Russian and world literature. Concludes with a useful chronology and a good bibliography.

Vasa D. Mihailovich

V

Luisa Valenzuela

Born: Buenos Aires, Argentina; November 26, 1938

OTHER LITERARY FORMS

In addition to her novellas, which have been included in collections of her short stories, Luisa Valenzuela (vah-lehn-ZWAY-lah) is the author of several novels, including *Hay que sonreír* (1966; *Clara,* 1976), *Como en la guerra* (1977; *He Who Searches,* 1979), *Cola de lagartija* (1983; *The Lizard's Tail,* 1983), *Novela Negra con Argentinos* (1990; *Black Novel with Argentines,* 1992), *Realidad nacional desde la cama* (1990; *Bedside Manners,* 1995), and *La travesía* (2001). She also has published a collection of essays, *Peligrosas palabras* (2001), and the nonfiction book *Acerca de Dios, o aleja* (2007).

ACHIEVEMENTS

Luisa Valenzuela won a Fulbright Fellowship in 1969 to attend the University of Iowa Writers' Workshop. She also received the Instituto Nacional de Cinematografía Award in 1973 for her first novel, *Clara,* and a John Simon Guggenheim Memorial Fellowship in 1982.

BIOGRAPHY

Born in Buenos Aires in 1938 to a physician father and a prominent writer mother, Luisa Valenzuela grew up in Belgrano, where she had an English tutor and later attended Belgrano Girls School and then an English high school. She received her B.A. degree from the University of Buenos Aires and then wrote for a prominent Argentine magazine. She also worked with Jorge Luis Borges at the National Library of Argentina.

In 1958, Valenzuela went to Paris to become a correspondent for the Argentine newspaper *El Mundo.* While in France she became involved with the structuralist literary theory group known as Tel Quel, returning to Buenos Aires with her husband and her daughter in 1961. After her divorce, she attended the University of Iowa Writers' Workshop on a Fulbright grant in 1969. In 1975, she returned to Buenos Aires and joined the staff of the journal *Crisis.* She has conducted writing workshops and taught Latin American literature at universities in the United States.

ANALYSIS

Luisa Valenzuela has become the darling of feminist critics, making a place for herself as a female writer who has exposed and challenged the Hispanic sexist world, which has historically discriminated against women; typically she relates domestic sexual domination and abuse alongside political repression and torture. The fact that Valenzuela was highly influenced by the psychoanalyst Jacques Lacan during her period of schooling in France has also provided critics with a ready-made set of critical terms with which to approach her fiction.

In many ways Valenzuela's work is a conventional extension of the Magical Realism that characterized writers of the so-called Latin American boom, such as Jorge Luis Borges, Julio Cortázar, and Gabriel García Márquez. Making use of folklore from South America, as well as modern anthropology and psychoanalysis, Valenzuela creates hallucinatory worlds of sadistic men and repressed and autistic women. However, Valenzuela is more a stylist than a political philosopher, focusing on how the story is told rather than what it says. It is in "the articulation between the narrated anecdote and the style of narration" that the secret of the text resides, says Valenzuela.

"I'M YOUR HORSE IN THE NIGHT"

"De noche soy tu caballo" ("I'm Your Horse in the Night") opens mysteriously with the young female protagonist being awakened by her doorbell, concerned it might be some threatening "them." However, it is an equally mysterious and unidentified "him" that she meets "face to face, at last." He embraces her and pulls out "potential clues" that elude her, such as a bottle of liquor and a phonograph record. The song they listen to is "I'm Your Horse in the Night," which she translates slowly to bind him into a spell, telling him he is the horse of the spirit who is riding her. He tells her, however, that she is always getting carried away with esoteric meanings, and that she is his horse as a sexual creature only.

The phone wakes her up and a voice says that the man, Beto, has been found dead in the river, his body decomposed after six days in the water. When the police arrive, she says they will not find anything, for her only real possession was a dream and "they can't deprive me of my dreams just like that." The police want to know where the mysterious man is, but she will say only that he abandoned her. Insisting that even if they torture her she will not tell them her dreams, she says, "The man simply vanished. I only run into him in my dreams, and they're bad dreams that often become nightmares."

The story is about the interrelationship between dream and reality in which the sexual encounter is dreamy while its aftermath is frighteningly real. "I'm Your Horse in the Night" sets up several typical Valenzuela dichotomies. Even as the horse is the nightmare

horse of myth, it is a cultural sign of female submission. While the sexual union is romantic and erotic, it is also a primal animal encounter. Basically, this is a story about the objectification of woman's desire for transcendence above the ordinary world of "mere facts."

"UP AMONG THE EAGLES"

"Donde viven las águilas" ("Up Among the Eagles") is one of Valenzuela's most straightforward philosophical fantasies, presenting her treatment of the split between the sacred and the profane in a relatively uncluttered way. The basic situation of the story is that of a young woman who has gone into the country, "up among the eagles," where the people speak a strange language whose meaning they themselves have forgotten. They speak her language only when dealing with trivial matters of everyday reality; otherwise, their world focuses on the sacred, for which they use a language of silence.

The people have no concept of time as a linear progression, living instead in the realm of mythic time of eternal recurrence. The woman secretly takes Polaroid photographs of herself, a sequence that reflects her existence in the realm of linear time. She fears that if the people find the photos they will either abominate her for being susceptible to age or adore her as if she were like a statue, forever captive and contained.

The story ends with her taking the last photo on her roll of film, hoping to recover her being. However, the picture "gradually reveals the blurred image of a stone wall." She climbs a mountain to reach the city of the dead where she will put the successive faces of her photos on the mummies there so she will be free to go down, taking with her her last photo, in which she is herself and she is stone. The basic dichotomy is between mutable flesh and the transcendence of ultimate desire.

"OTHER WEAPONS"

Called by feminist critics a landmark in Latin American feminine literature for its critique of Western patriarchal practices, "Cambio de armas" ("Other Weapons") is a depiction of woman as wife-whore-slave in the extreme, for the female in the story is reduced to total passivity by torture at the hands of her male master. In an almost autistic state of isolation, her consciousness effaced, the woman feels completely isolated in time and space, cut off from the past, with no hope for a future.

"Other Weapons" falls within a tradition of sadistic Bluebeard stories, stories in which a powerful male figure uses the woman as a sex object, keeps her shut off from the world and imprisoned within herself. The story is told in a fragmentary fashion, in third person but from the woman's perspective, as she haltingly tries to "find herself out." Complete with whips and voyeuristic peepholes where the man's colleagues can watch the man sexually dominate the woman, "Other Weapons" is a paradigm of the sadistic male who uses the phallus as a weapon to subdue the woman.

The final revelation of the story comes when the man tells her that she was a revolutionary who had been ordered to kill him but was caught just when she was aiming at him. He says everything he did was to save her, for he forced her to love him, to depend on him like a newborn baby. "I've got my weapons, too," he repeats over and over. However, when he starts to leave, she remembers what the gun is for, lifts it and aims. Called by feminist critics a horrible symbolic embodiment of the "happy" housewife, the woman in the story reflects the common Valenzuela theme of equating marriage law with political imprisonment.

"SYMMETRIES"

Valenzuela has said that "Simetrías" ("Symmetries"), the title story of her 1993 collection, is like a symmetrical counterpart to the earlier story "Other Weapons." Both stories reflect Valenzuela's insistence that political aggression mirrors sexual aggression. The story is told as a series of monologues that alternate back and forth between the torturer and the tortured. The other significant symmetry in the story takes place in time, alternating between a story that takes place in 1947, which involves a woman becoming obsessively fascinated with an orangutan in a zoo, and one in 1977, which recounts the parallel obsession that a man has with his tortured female victim.

In the first story, the woman's husband, a colonel in the army, becomes so jealously infuriated because of her infatuation with the animal that he kills it. In the second story, the colonel is sent away on a mission by his superiors so that the woman with whom he has become so involved can be destroyed. At the end of

"Symmetries," the two stories and the two time periods become one; the bullet that kills the orangutan and the one that kills the torturer's beloved victim seems to be the same. When the woman returns to the zoo and the man returns to the prison and they find the objects of their obsessive desires dead, "they both find a thread of terror creeping up their spine and they find a hatred that will grow with the days."

OTHER MAJOR WORKS

LONG FICTION: _Hay que sonreír_, 1966 (_Clara_, 1976); _El gato eficaz_, 1972; _Como en la guerra_, 1977 (_He Who Searches_, 1979); _Libro que no muerde_, 1980; _Cola de lagartija_, 1983 (_The Lizard's Tail_, 1983); _Novela Negra con Argentinos_, 1990 (_Black Novel with Argentines_, 1992); _Realidad nacional desde la cama_, 1990 (_Bedside Manners_, 1995); _La travesía_, 2001.

NONFICTION: _Peligrosas palabras_, 2001 (essays); _Acerca de Dios, o aleja_, 2007.

BIBLIOGRAPHY

Bach, Caleb. "Metaphors and Magic Unmask the Soul." _Americas_ 47 (January/February, 1995): 22-28. Notes that Valenzuela is distressed by the cultural banality that is common the world over. Argues that her prose involves the reader by posing questions rather than suggesting simplistic solutions. Maintains her books are not for the lazy reader.

Díaz, Gwendolyn. _Women and Power in Argentine Literature: Stories, Interviews, and Critical Essays_. Austin: University of Texas Press, 2007. Examines how the works of Valenzuela and fourteen other Argentine women writers depict the effects of power as it is used by or against women. The chapter about Valenzuela features an overview of Valenzuela's life and works, an interview with her, and two of her short stories that demonstrate her treatment of power: "Tango" and "The Key."

Hart, Stephen. "'Art in the Gerund' in the Work of Luisa Valenzuela." _Journal of Iberian and Latin American Studies_ 14, no. 2/3 (August/December, 2008): 87-92. Analyzes Valenzuela's fiction, arguing that it can be read as a more "empirically grounded" rewriting of some of the ideas she explores in "Other Weapons." Focuses on the combination of politics and wordplay in her work, demonstrating how many of the short stories and novels use "phonetic coincidence" to engender meaning, with the language sometimes becoming one of the protagonists in the plot.

Logan, Joy. "Southern Discomfort in Argentina: Postmodernism, Feminism, and Luisa Valenzuela's *Simetrías*." *Latin American Literary Review* 24 (July-December, 1996): 5-17. Argues that in the fairy-tale section of *Symmetries*, Valenzuela's critique of Western patriarchal practices is most clear. Claims that the collection is a textual performance of the interplay between postmodernism and feminism.

Magnarelli, Sharon. "Simetrías: 'Mirror, Mirror, on the Wall. . . .'" *World Literature Today* 69 (Autumn, 1995): 717-726. Argues that the collection *Symmetries* is organized around motifs of language and power. Analyzes "Tango," "Transfigurations," and the title story "Symmetries" in terms of the motif of parallel situations and responses.

Marting, Diane. "Female Sexuality in Selected Short Stories by Luisa Valenzuela: Toward an Ontology of Her Work." *Review of Contemporary Fiction* 6 (Fall, 1986): 48-54. Discusses how three stories from *Strange Things Happen Here* treat female sexuality in terms of figurative and mimetic modes of narration.

_____. "Gender and Metaphoricity in Luisa Valenzuela's 'I'm Your Horse in the Night.'" *World Literature Today* 69 (Fall, 1995): 702-708. A survey and critique of previous interpretations of the story, accompanied by a close reading in which Marting ar-

gues that the story criticizes the man for his retrograde treatment of the woman who loves him.

Morello-Frosch, Maria. "'Other Weapons': When Metaphors Become Real." *Review of Contemporary Fiction* 6 (Fall, 1986): 82-87. Discusses the story "Other Weapons" as one in which the protagonist creates her own vision of the world in opposition to the political establishment. Argues that the story presents sexual and political repression in terms of communication with one's past.

Rubio, Patricia. "Fragmentation in Luisa Valenzuela's Narrative." *Salmagundi*, nos. 82/83 (Spring/Summer, 1989): 287-296. Argues that the objective of Valenzuela's writing is not the mimetic representation of reality but the creation of a fictive world that witnesses its own mutation. Discusses Valenzuela's use of the fragment and the various acts of fragmentation in her fiction.

Valenzuela, Luisa. Interview by Marie-Lise Gazarian Gautier. In *Interviews with Latin American Writers*. Elmwood Park, Ill.: Dalkey Archive Press, 1989. In this composite interview, Valenzuela discusses rebellion and freedom in her work, the effect of censorship, writers who have influenced her, the relationship between fantasy and reality in her fiction, and her interest in magic. Valenzuela says she prefers the short story over the novel.

_____. "Writing with the Body." In *Word: On Being a [Woman] Writer*, edited by Jocelyn Burrell. New York: Feminist Press, 2004. Valenzuela is one of the contributors who describe what it means to be a woman writer.

Charles E. May

Mario Vargas Llosa

Born: Arequipa, Peru; March 28, 1936

Principal short fiction

Los jefes, 1959 (*The Cubs, and Other Stories*, 1979)
Los cachorros, 1967 (novella; *The Cubs*, 1979)

Other literary forms

Although Mario Vargas Llosa (YOH-sa) began his literary career as a short-story writer, he is best known for his longer fiction. He has written several novels, which range from works based on personal experience, such as *La ciudad y los perros* (1962; *The Time of the Hero*, 1966), to historical and political novels, such as *La guerra del fin del mundo* (1981; *The War of the End of the World*, 1984) and *La fiesta del Chivo* (2000; *The Way to Paradise*, 2003), to novels dealing with sexual obsession, such as *Elogio de la madrastra* (1988; *In Praise of the Stepmother*, 1990). Throughout his novels, nonconformity and criticism of the authoritarian established order are central themes. Vargas Llosa has published a vast amount of literary criticism, primarily dealing with the novel form and major novelists, such as Gabriel García Márquez, Gustave Flaubert, and Victor Hugo. He has written three plays and published a memoir, *Pez en el agua* (1993; *A Fish in the Water: A Memoir*, 1994).

Achievements

Mario Vargas Llosa is internationally acclaimed as a novelist and as a literary critic, considered one of the most significant and influential Latin American writers. His works have been translated into thirty-three languages. He has won numerous prizes for his fiction, including the Peruvian National Prize (1967), the Prince of Asturias Prize (1967), and the Miguel de Cervantes Prize (1994). He also has received many awards and recognitions, including election as a Miembro de la Academia Peruana de la Lengua (1975), the Peruvian Medalla de Honor del Congreso (1982), the French Legion of Honor (1985), the titles of Honorary Fellow of the Modern Language Association of America and Honorary Member of the American Academy and Institute of Arts and Letters (1996), the Gold Medal of the Pan American Society (1988), the Golden Palm Award of International Arts Relations (INTAR) Hispanic American Arts Center of New York (1992), and member of the Real Academia Espanola (1994). Vargas Llosa has been awarded honorary doctorates from many universities throughout the United States, Latin America, Europe, and Australia. He has received many invitations to teach as a visiting professor. Vargas Llosa is also highly respected for his work in journalism.

Biography

Jorge Mario Pedro Vargas Llosa was born in Arequipa, Peru, on March 28, 1936. He is the son of Ernesto Vargas Maldonado and Dora Llosa Ureta. At the time of his birth, his parents were already separated; he lived with his mother and her family. Vargas Llosa attended elementary school at several different schools because the family moved frequently. When he was ten years old, his parents reconciled, and he saw his father for the first time. The family lived in Lima, Peru, where, Vargas Llosa attended the Colegio La Salle. When he was fourteen, because of his father's influence, he became a student at the military academy Colegio Militar Leoncio Prado. Before graduating, he withdrew from the school and completed his secondary studies at the Colegio San Miguel in Piura. His father disapproved of Vargas Llosa's decision to leave military school.

In 1953, Vargas Llosa began studying literature and law at the Universidad Nacional Mayor in San Marcos. He also began writing fictional stories, often imitating the authors he was reading. The discord between him and his father intensified as Vargas Llosa pursued a career in literature.

In 1955, Vargas Llosa married Julia Urquidi. To support himself and his wife while continuing his studies, he worked as a journalist for *Turismo*, *Cultura Peruana*, and *El Comercio* and as a news editor for Radio Central, and he held various other jobs. In 1957, with his short story "El desafío"("The Challenge"), he won a contest for Peruvian stories sponsored by the *Revue française*. The prize was a two-week trip to Paris. In 1959, he received a Javier Prado fellowship to study at the Universidad Complutense in Madrid. He also won the Leopoldo Alas (Spain) prize for his short-story collection *The Cubs, and Other Stories*. In 1971, he was awarded a Ph.D. with honors. He moved to Paris, where he worked at a Berlitz language school.

In 1963, Vargas Llosa published his first novel, *The Time of the Hero*, for which he received the Crítica Española prize. During the period from 1963 through 2006, he consistently published highly acclaimed novels and lectured and taught at universities throughout the Americas and Europe. In 1964, he divorced Urquidi and in 1965 married his cousin, Patricia Llosa. They have two sons and a daughter. In 1993, he obtained Spanish citizenship.

In the 1980's, Vargas Llosa became politically active in Peru. In 1987, he was involved in the Movimiento Libertad, which opposed nationalization of banking in Peru. In 1990, he was a candidate for president of Peru. After losing the election, he returned to his literary career. In 2009, he published *El Viaje a la Ficción*. He settled in London but has continued to return to Peru for three months each year. He has maintained an important role as a writer, a literary critic, a lecturer, and a teacher.

ANALYSIS

Mario Vargas Llosa wrote almost all of his short stories between 1953 and 1957. This was at the beginning of his career as a writer of fiction, when he was learning his craft and developing his style and voice. During this time, he was reading obsessively and approaching the novels he was reading almost as textbooks that would teach him to write. He often imitated the style of the writers he especially liked. His short fictions shows the influence of those of William Faulkner, Henry Miller, and Ernest Hemingway in their structure, in

their use of brief and precise description, and in their energy. Influences of André Malraux and the French existentialists are apparent in the philosophical ambience of the stories. All of the stories are told from a male viewpoint, the main characters are young males, and the stories chronicle their camaraderie and their efforts to establish their identity and to conquer the obstacles of living.

Although these influences are readily apparent, the stories are Vargas Llosa's own; they are not mere imitations. He has embedded his stories in the Peruvian culture in which he grew up. The stories derive from his own experiences as a child and as a young man. The four stories "Los jefes" ("The Leaders"), "El desafío" ("The Challenge"), "Día domingo" ("On Sundays"), and "Los cachorros" ("The Cubs") are accounts of the lives of young males coming of age and the special world in which they live. The dominant features of these stories are the importance of the barrio (neighborhood) in the individual's life and the machismo of Peruvian culture. These stories depict a world of youth that has its own rules, ideals, and standards of social interaction. It is a world full of discovery and adventure and separated from that of adults and closed to them.

Three stories-- "El hermano menor" ("The Younger Brother"), "Un visitante" ("A Visitor"), and "El abuelo" ("The Grandfather")--take place in the adult world rather than the special barrio world of the young. "The Younger Brother" is a story belonging to the tradition of the Peruvian story of rape of a country girl and class injustice. "A Visitor" is also set in the country and deals with betrayal and injustice. "The Grandfather" is a curious story in which Vargas Llosa attempts to write in the fashion of Edgar Allan Poe and Paul Bowles.

Gossip plays an important role in the stories of Vargas Llosa. There is almost always a character who sees or overhears something and tells the barrio or the town about it. Gossip either moves the plot along, as in "A Visitor," or solves a problem, as in "Dia dimanche" ("On Sundays").

The short fiction of Vargas Llosa previews his longer fiction. The themes explored in the short stories reappear more fully developed in his novels and novellas. The themes of injustice, betrayal, and police and military oppression and corruption recur in *The Time of the Hero*, *La casa verde* (1965; *The Green House*, 1968), and *Conversación en la catedral* (1969; *Conversation in the Cathedral*, 1975) and play an important role in *¿Quién mató a Palomino Molero?* (1986; *Who Killed Palomino Molero?* 1987). The barrio plays a significant role in *Travesuras de la niña mala* (2006; *The Bad Girl*, 2007).

"On Sundays"

"On Sundays" depicts the barrio world of young men coming of age and trying to establish their identity. The male mentality of the barrio is one of brotherhood and machismo. Being the best at sports, able to drink the most beer and going steady with the right girl are all important. Entering into a steady relationship with someone is a decision for both the young men and the girls of the barrio. Whom someone goes with tells who the person is. Opinions of others and impressions made count for everything. The young men live in an existentialist world. Each one creates himself by his actions, and it is only his actions that convince others of his identity. The lives of the young men are dominated by an uneasy mix of camaraderie and competition. They belong to a gang, a sort of "brotherhood," in this case the Hawks; yet they constantly challenge each other. A challenge made must be taken; to decline is, in existentialist terms, an act of bad faith.

The intrigue of the story portrays Miguel, in love with Flora but desperately shy about telling her, faced with thwarting a plot by Rubén and his sister Martha to get Flora for Rubén. Miguel first challenges Rubén to a beer-drinking match, which results in a tie. Then they compete swimming in a cold and rough sea. The loser will stop pursuing Flora. Rubén wins swimming competitions and is the stronger swimmer. However, he gets a cramp, and Miguel saves him. The fog hides them from the other young men. They say nothing of what happened--only that Miguel won. However, Rubén adds that in a pool he would have won. Miguel looks forward to meeting Flora at Salazar Park that evening. Melanés will have told everyone that Miguel won and Flora will be eager to go steady with him.

In addition to recounting the action of the story, Vargas Llosa presents a detailed exploration of Miguel's reactions--emotional, physical, and mental--to what happened to him. Vargas Llosa describes Miguel's fear of talking to Flora, which results in all sorts of uncomfortable physical sensations. He describes the anguish and pain Miguel experiences swimming in the cold water and his determination not to give up. Vargas Llosa also fleshes out his story with precise and detailed descriptions of the avenues the Hawks walk along, the beach, the beach house with its slippery stairs, and the churning and dangerous sea.

"The Challenge"

"The Challenge" is a dark presentation of the machismo mentality of the young men of the barrio. The story portrays the serious conflict between members of different gangs. The characters appear to be slightly older than those of "On Sundays." The action of the story is a knife fight between Justo and the Gimp. It is night and difficult to see the fighters. Vargas Llosa describes in great detail the fighters as they move about, coming together and drawing away from each other. The fight is almost a ritualistic dance; it is filled with suspense and tension and yet also has a beauty created by the description of the fighters' agility and grace. Justo is killed and ceremoniously carried off by his comrades in a mock funeral procession. The story has a lyrical quality, and the descriptions that transform the fight into a dance give the story a musical accompaniment.

Mario Vargas Llosa (AP Photo/Scanpix/Fredrik Persson)

The character of Leonidas adds an atmosphere of fatality and of acceptance of the harshness of life. Leonidas does not belong there; he is an old man. While Vargas Llosa gives clues as to the identity of Leonidas, Vargas Llosa reveals only at the very end of the story that Leonidas is Justo's father.

"THE CUBS"

Based on a newspaper story Vargas Llosa had read of a child being emasculated by a dog in the Andes, "The Cubs" investigates the effects on the life of a boy who has suffered such mutilation. Cuellar is the new student at the Champagnat Academy; the other boys are excited to meet him at the beginning of the narrative. They wonder what he is like, if he will fit in. They discover that Cuellar's father is rich and that Cuellar is a good student; nevertheless, Cuellar fits in. Soccer is the most important element in the boys' lives, and Cuellar is a good soccer player. The schools dog Judas escapes from his pen and attacks Cuellar, emasculating the boy in the shower. Cuellar is in fourth grade. As he grows older and sex and girls replace soccer, Cuellar becomes distanced from the group. He cannot participate; he is different from others; he has lost his place in the barrio. His friends try to include him, but they are incapable of feeling he is one of them. As the story progresses, he becomes more and more distanced from them. They marry, have children, grow old, build summerhouses. Cuellar can find no place for himself. He eventually dies in an automobile wreck, apparently a suicide. Vargas Llosa's method of narration is particularly interesting in this story. The barrio becomes the narrator, as he switches the narration from one character to another, sometimes even within a sentence.

"A VISITOR"

"A Visitor" recounts the police's betrayal of a Jamaican who has been in jail and has agreed to help the police capture Numa, a wanted man. Vargas Llosa does not explain why the police are looking for Numa nor why the Jamaican has been in jail. Numa may be an outlaw or he may be a revolutionary. However, the reader is led to surmise that Doña Merceditas is the reason for the Jamaican having been incarcerated. After the Jamaican is let out of jail, he goes to the isolated inn of Doña Merceditas. On his way, he tells everyone that he is going to kill her in order to bring Numa to the inn. Numa comes as expected, but he brings friends with him, who are waiting in the woods. The Jamaican has won his freedom by setting the trap for Numa. He expects to leave with the police, but there is no horse for him, and the lieutenant kicks him away as they ride off. He is left there as Numa's friends approach and Doña Merceditas laughs loudly. Vargas Llosa begins his story with a long description of the harshness and barenness of the area where the inn is located and of the thick woods behind it. The physical description sets the tone of the story and gives it an ambience of danger and betrayal.

OTHER MAJOR WORKS

LONG FICTION: *La ciudad y los perros*, 1962 (*The Time of the Hero*, 1966); *La casa verde*, 1965 (*The Green House*, 1968); *Conversación en la catedral*, 1969 (*Conversation in the Cathedral*, 1975); *Pantaleón y las visitadoras*, 1973 (*Captain Pantoja and the Special Service*, 1978); *La tía Julia y el escribidor*, 1977 (*Aunt Julia and the Scriptwriter*, 1982); *La guerra del fin del mundo*, 1981 (*The War of the End of the World*, 1984); *Historia de Mayta*, 1984 (*The Real Life of Alejandro Mayta*, 1986); *El hablador*, 1987 (*The Storyteller*, 1989); *¿Quién mató a Palomino Molero?*, 1986 (*Who Killed Palomino Molero?*, 1987); *Elogio de la madrastra*, 1988 (*In Praise of the Stepmother*, 1990); *Lituma en los Andes*, 1993 (*Death in the Andes*, 1996); *Los cuadernos de don Rigoberto*, 1997 (*The Notebooks of Don Rigoberto*, 1998); *La fiesta del Chivo*, 2000 (*The Feast of the Goat*, 2001); *El paraíso en la otra esquina*, 2003 (*The Way to Paradise*, 2003); *Travesuras de la niña mala*, 2006 (*The Bad Girl*, 2007).

PLAYS: *La señorita de Tacna* pr., pb. 1981 (*The Young Lady from Tacna*, 1990); *Kathie y el hipopótamo* pr., pb. 1983 (*Kathie and the Hippopotamus*, 1990); *La Chunga*, pb. 1987 (English translation, 1990); *Three Plays*, pb. 1990; *El loco de los balcones*, pb. 1993.

NONFICTION: *La novela en América Latina: Dialogo*, 1968; *Literatura en la revolución y revolución en literatura*, 1970 (with Julio Cortázar and Oscar Collazos); *La historia secreta de una novela*, 1971; *Gabriel García Márquez: Historia de un deicidio*, 1971; *El combate imaginario*, 1972; *García Márquez y la problemática de la novela*, 1973; *La novela y el problema de la expresión literaria en Peru*, 1974; *La orgía perpetua: Flaubert y "Madame Bovary,"* 1975 (*The Perpetual Orgy: Flaubert and "Madame Bovary,"* 1986); *José María Arguedas: Entre sapos y halcones*, 1978; *La utopia arcaica*, 1978; *Entre Sartre y Camus*, 1981; *Contra viento y marea, 1964-1988*, 1983-1990 (3 volumes); *A Writer's Reality*, 1991 (Myron I. Lichtblau, editor); *Fiction: The Power of Lies*, 1993; *Pez en el agua*, 1993 (*A Fish in the Water: A Memoir*, 1994); *Making Waves*, 1996; *Cartas a un joven novelista*, 1997 (*Letters to a Young Novelist*, 2002); *Claudio Bravo: Paintings and Drawings*, 1997 (with Paul Bowles); *El lenguaje de la pasión*, 2001 (*The Language of Passion: Selected Commentary*, 2003); *La verdad de las mentiras*, 2002; *La tentación de lo imposible: Victor Hugo y "Los miserables,"* 2004 (*The Temptation of the Impossible: Victor Hugo and "Les Misérables,"* 2007); *Wellsprings*, 2008; *El Viaje a la Ficción*, 2009.

BIBLIOGRAPHY

Booker, M. Keith. *Vargas Llosa Among the Postmodernists*. Gainesville: University Press of Florida, 1994. An in-depth look at Vargas Llosa's development as a writer of fiction. Applies the theories of postmodernist literary criticism to his work.

Castro-Klaren, Sara. *Understanding Mario Vargas Llosa*. Columbia: University of South Carolina Press, 1990. Analyzes Vargas Llosa's fiction in its relationship to Peruvian culture; also treats the political aspects of his work.

Kerr, R. A. *Mario Vargas Llosa: Critical Essays on Characterization*. Potomac, Md.: Scripta Humanistica, 1990. Good for understanding the importance of Vargas Llosa's early short stories in regard to his novels. Kerr presents a thorough analysis of characters in the major novels.

Muñoz, Braulio. *A Storyteller: Mario Vargas Llosa Between Civilization and Barbarism*. Lanham, Md: Rowman & Littlefield, 2000. Discusses the role of the writer in Latin America. Considers Vargas Llosa as a writer and a political activist. Analyzes his fiction from a sociotheoretical viewpoint.

Vargas Llosa, Mario. *A Writer's Reality*. Boston: Mariner Books, 1992. Vargas Llosa's ideas on the writer's mission, how fiction is created, and the place of Peruvian history and culture in his fiction.

Shawncey Webb

W

WANG ANYI

Born: Nanjing, China; March 6, 1954

OTHER LITERARY FORMS

Wang Anyi has written the novels *Chang hen ge* (1996; *The Song of Everlasting Sorrow,* 2008), *Tao zhi yao yao* (2004), and *Bian di xiao xiong* (2005). Her travelogue *Mu nü tong you mei li jian* (mother and daughter traveling together in America), was published in 1986; addressed to a Chinese audience, this book is essentially derived from notes and observations written during the author's tour of the United States. She also has published the nonfiction collection *Years of Sadness: Autobiographical Writings of Wang Anyi* (2009).

ACHIEVEMENTS

Wang Anyi first started publishing her work in November, 1976; in less than a decade, she had already been recognized as a prolific writer of substantial achievement. Her short story "Ben ci lie che zhong dian zhan" ("Destination") was chosen for the Chinese National Award for Short Stories in 1982, and her novellas *Lapse of Time* and *Baotown* won the National Award for Short Novels in 1983 and 1986, respectively. *Baotown* was the topic of a seminar hosted by the Writers' Association of Shanghai shortly after its publication in 1985. The Three Loves Trilogy, three novellas published in 1986 and 1987, has attracted attention as a controversial work because of its depiction of illicit or extramarital love affairs--a sensitive issue that, in China, is considered to be a "forbidden territory." Wang's novel *The Song of Everlasting Sorrow* was a best seller in China and was adapted as a television series, stage play, and film; the book received the Mao Dun Literary Award and is considered by many critics to be the most influential work written in China in the 1990's.

BIOGRAPHY

Wang Anyi was born in Nanjing in 1954. Her mother, Ru Zhijuan, is an accomplished writer whose career began in 1947. Thanks to her cultured family background, Wang was exposed to music, art, and literature as a child. She finished her junior high school education in 1969, the third year of the Cultural Revolution, a period during which a cataclysmal chaos extended throughout China as civil and human rights were severely restricted by the Communist regime.

In 1970, like many other teenagers across the Chinese nation, Wang was sent to a rural area in the province of Anhui to join a production brigade as a "young intellectual" (high school graduate) to be "re-educated by the poor and lower-middle peasants." In 1972, however, she managed to find a position in the orchestral troupe of the Xuzhou City Commission for Literature and Arts in the province of Jiangsu; it was during this period that she started writing. In 1978, as the political climate began to change for the better, Wang was transferred to Shanghai, where she started working in the editorial department of *Childhood* magazine. In 1980, she enrolled in the Fifth Annual Writers' Workshop hosted by the Writers' Association of China. Upon graduation at the end of the year, Wang returned to her editorial work and emerged rapidly as an important writer. In 2001, Wang was elected chairperson of the Shanghai Writers' Association.

ANALYSIS

Wang Anyi's career coincides with an important historical juncture in contemporary Chinese literature. Prior to the death of Mao Zedong and the fall of the Gang of Four in 1976, Chinese writers were required to play a subservient role and serve the immediate interests of the government. After the introduction of economic reforms in 1978, however, a relatively ameliorated environment allowed writers to pursue authentic and diversified means of expression with a certain amount of liberty. Wang is one of the young writers who seized such an opportunity. Although she once regarded herself as independent of literary movements, she admits that she has benefitted from trends such as the Literature of Wound, the Literature of Transvaluation, the Literature in Search of Roots, and the Quest for Urban Awareness. These tendencies are evident in her works, but her style is peculiarly her own, and in the end, they also culminate in a uniquely lyrical form of humanistic expression.

"AND THE RAIN PATTERS ON"

Representative of Wang's short stories is "And the Rain Patters On," which is reminiscent of the Literature of Wound, a groundbreaking literary trend that has as its theme the injuries, injustices, sufferings, and aftermaths of the Cultural Revolution. In this story, meticulously crafted from lyrical flashbacks, symbols, and motifs, Wenwen, a woman sent to the countryside as an "educated youth," returns to Shanghai and finds herself to be a spinster and out of place in a world being transformed by modernity. Unable to catch up with the latest fashions, she finds romance to be elusive. While her family has been trying to arrange for her to meet and date a marriageable man, Xiao Yan, she dreamily yearns for a relationship that would somehow be different. One rainy night, after missing the last bus home, she is given a ride on a bike by a man about

Wang Anyi (Xinhua/Landov)

whom she feels ambivalent. The man is simply an ordinary good Samaritan who happened to pass by, but Wenwen is touched by his casual remark about the beauty of street lamps in the rain and by his account of his having been saved by another good Samaritan. She begins to hope and even trust that she will run into this stranger again. Claiming that she has found a boyfriend, Wenwen rejects Xiao Yan, though to the chagrin of her family it is clear that she is simply daydreaming. Toward the end of the story, the narrator asserts that there are many pleasures in life, and dreaming is one of them; one has to insist on believing that dreams will come true, or else life would be unbearable. Encouraging and disturbing at the same time, this message exemplifies the tensions between the ideal and the real, and the conflicts between the inner life and the outer world. "And the Rain Patters On" also typifies Wang's persistent efforts to juxtapose idealistic yearnings and realistic pressures, combining these opposites into a new humanism through lyrical expression and psychological representation.

"DESTINATION"

Such efforts can be found in most of the short stories in *Lapse of Time*, such as in "Destination," an award-winning story. Because of the mundane pressures of life in Shanghai, Chen Xin is confronted with his family's suggestion that he arrange to marry any woman who has a room to offer as dowry. Realizing, however, that "ahead of him there would be another ten, twenty, and thirty years" and that "he must give his future some serious thought," Chen Xin refuses to compromise and is embroiled in a familial conflict, which is left unresolved at the end of the story. In spite of this conflict, the story contains an important touch of humanism as the family, fearing that he may commit suicide, comes searching for him after he has disappeared into the streets for the entire night after a quarrel. Finally, Chen Xin is described as being reconciled to the thought that he will be in search of his true destination--a paradox typical of Wang's fiction in that her protagonists are deprived materialistically and yet remain spiritually unvanquished.

"THE BASE OF THE WALL"

Whether consciously or otherwise, in many of her stories Wang's new humanism focuses on the pervasive phenomenon of alienation under the socialist regime, though in an existential manner she decides that her protagonists are capable of rising or staying above the mire. For example, in one of her most triumphant stories, "The Base of the Wall," A'nian (the son of a working-class family) chooses to befriend and assist Duxing (the daughter of a supposedly antireactionary family from the other side of the broken wall) after he has had a glimpse, through a diary that he has stolen, into the inner life of the sensitive, intelligent, and ostracized "class enemy" whom he and the other kids used to abuse. By eliminating the bigotry from the children of his own neighborhood and by bringing children from both sides of the wall closer to one another, A'nian has dismantled the barrier arbitrarily set up to pit one part of humanity against another.

LAPSE OF TIME

All the above themes--tensions between the ideal and the real, conflicts between the inner life and the outer world, the paradox between spirituality and materiality, and the triumph of humanism over alienation

under socialism--are explored to a fuller extent in *Lapse of Time*. The novella is a series of sketches chronicling the awakening, growth, and transformation of a housewife during the Cultural Revolution. Duanli, a college graduate, is married to Wenyao, the son of a Shanghai businessman. At the beginning of the Cultural Revolution, the properties of the family are seized by the Red Guards. Wenyao is a superfluous man incapable of meeting the new challenges of life; his brother, Wenguang, for fear of being implicated, distances himself from his father. The responsibility of caring for the family of nine falls on the shoulders of Duanli, who finds it difficult to cope with poverty. No longer a "bourgeois lady of the house," she learns the meaning of life anew, starting from the basics of survival. Gradually, Duanli has in effect become the "guardian" of the household. Upon restitution and the return of the family properties after the Cultural Revolution, fortune again seems to smile on the family, and everyone feels complacent and justified in demanding a better life to make up for the losses of the fateful decade. Duanli, who has become a practical person, feels the same and quits working, but after two years of tiresome and unauthentic social life, she is troubled by the loss of her sense of vitality previously gained from the fateful decade. In the end, she decides to resume her job at the factory, not only to fight boredom but also to continue with her search for the meaning of life and to prevent life from lapsing into oblivion. Full of details about quotidian struggles and the sordid nature of life in contemporary China, the novella most likely will pluck at the heartstrings of millions of readers who, having emerged from a decade of hardships, find themselves entrenched in a series of struggles not only to achieve a better economic life but also to establish a significance for themselves.

BAOTOWN

Whereas *Lapse of Time* enlarges on urban consciousness as a condition for the definition of humanity in an alienated society, *Baotown* is an attempt to explore the historical, cultural, and symbolic dimensions of humanity in a rustic and remote corner of rural China. The legend of King Yu of Xia (c. 21-16 B.C.E.), the tamer of the great flood and the founder of the first dynasty in Chinese history, is invoked, somewhat ironically, in the preface in order to situate Baotown in a mythical and historical context. A folk ballad on numbers, which contains quasi-nonsensical cliché references to random events in Chinese history, recurs throughout the story as a leitmotif. The nonlinear plot is constructed intricately around an odd assortment of two dozen characters, four of whom are responsible for the major event in the history of Baotown. The first of these is Picked-Up. Having been reared by his "aunt," an unmarried woman who claims that she picked him up as a baby from the street, he runs away and settles in Baotown to cohabit with, and slave for, a widow, but he is despised by the community. The second is Bao Fifth Grandfather, an old man who has become an "end-of-the-liner" upon the death of his grandson and only descendant. He is befriended by Dregs, the third character and the youngest son of Bao Yanshan. This little boy, in the end, loses his life for the sake of Bao Fifth Grandfather during a flood, but his body is salvaged by Picked-Up. The fourth character is Bao Renwen, a young man whose aspiration to be a writer is fulfilled when he provides a written account about the accident for broadcast on radio. Unknowingly, he not only immortalizes Dregs but also helps to create a sense of importance for Bao Yanshan and to dignify Picked-Up. Written with a mixed sense of humor, irony, satire, sympathy, and lament, *Baotown* is a dazzling work thanks to its technical experimentation and its penetration into the human psyche as it is shaped by the historical and cultural conditions of China. The mythmaking process occurring in both the preface and the conclusion of the novella is especially thought-provoking.

THREE LOVES TRILOGY

While *Baotown* was still arousing much enthusiasm among its readers, Wang moved on to transcend herself even further by turning out the controversial Three Loves Trilogy in 1986 and 1987. These three novellas share the common theme of unorthodox love, but each work has its unique focus. In *Love on a Barren Mountain*, which deals with extramarital love and sex, Wang focuses on the intensity of an obsessive relationship between a talented but superfluous man and a seductive woman of questionable reputation. They can each be described as married to the right person of their choice, until their fatal encounter tells each of them that the

other could have been a better match. It is a poignant tragedy of desire which ends in the lovers' suicide, though death itself does not seem to constitute a real resolution. The omniscient narrator is careful not to take a judgmental stand, as if to suggest that love of such intensity is beyond any ordinary sense of right and wrong or good and evil.

The second book in the trilogy, *Love in a Small Town*, deals with the strange relationship between two dancers of a sleazy troupe. Both performers have been deformed as a result of improper training, the woman being larger and the man smaller in size than normal. Their relationship is full of sadomasochistic contradictions: They both hate and crave each other so intensely that if they are not trying to beat each other's brains out, they are burning with desire for each other. They are condemned to a relationship that amounts to mutual punishment and destruction through either sexual contact or physical combat. Such a consuming affair drags both parties deeper and deeper into a quagmire. Eventually, actually contemplating suicide, the woman, who has been evading the man for a long period, decides to satiate her desire for the last time as if she were going to die in a battle. Miraculously, this last union makes the woman pregnant and gives her the courage to live for herself and her twins as an unmarried mother and an outcast, whereas the man sinks so low that he becomes a good-for-nothing gambler and alcoholic. The solution to the contradictions in the story is therefore polarized between the rise above and the fall below the line that sets humanity apart from bestiality. In this stunning story, which reads like a parable if not a pathological case study, it seems Wang is raising the question of what to do with the inherent deformity or deficiency of human nature itself.

The third novella of the trilogy, *Brocade Valley*, differs sharply from the other two books because the focus here is on an extramarital relationship that is the result of phantasmagoria. In the story, an editor takes part in a conference held in the Lushan Mountains, a scenic tourist resort. With household chores behind her, she is distanced from her contempt-breeding husband, who has become all too familiar. Surrounded by men of talent, she feels that she has fallen in love with a writer who she thinks is also in love with her. Although the romantic scenery intimates that the romance is real, nothing has actually transpired. Returning to her life of daily routines, for a while she hopes that the "romance" will materialize even if it entails a terrible scandal, but finally she is reconciled to the thought that it would suffice only to have a wonderful impression of the valley. This dreamy story is a subtle exploration of the distinctive nature of feminine desire and sexual difference in the context of married life in contemporary China. At issue is not whether the woman and her husband love each other, but rather how love itself can stay uncontaminated by the practical concerns of everyday life and survive the wear and tear of familiarity.

The three stories of the trilogy are independent of one another but also interrelated. They constitute a progression toward the resolution of the question of love, sex, and marriage on psychological rather than moral grounds. In these stories, every single character has gone on trial; although in the end no one really triumphs, readers begin to sense that Wang's examination of the characters' innermost thoughts, feelings, desires, and secrets, however perverse, has sharpened and deepened their understanding of humanity itself. As none of the characters is given a name, the trilogy seems to be inviting readers to witness the introspections of the characters themselves and, in the process, start an introspection of the anonymous man and woman within the reader's own psyche.

XIANGGANG DE QING YU AI

The development of Wang's short stories can be divided into three periods. The writings of the first two periods are represented respectively in *Lapse of Time* and the Three Loves Trilogy. In 1996, Wang edited ten of her stories written in the 1990's into a collection entitled *Xianggang de qing yu ai* (love and sentiment in Hong Kong). The collection signifies the climax of Wang's short-fiction writing. The collection contains the love stories "Miaomiao," "'Wenge' yishi" (anecdotes of the 'Cultural Revolution'), and *Xianggang de qing yu ai*, as well as the critically acclaimed novellas *Beitong zhidi* (a land of tragedy), *Shushu de gushi* (our uncle's story), and *Shangxin Taipingyang* (sadness for the Pacific).

In this collection, Wang continues her quest for the meaning of love. In "Miaomiao," a cleaning maid in a small-town hotel has the daring spirit to adopt the dress style of the big city and explore the meaning of sex and love; ironically, her fashionable dress is seen as "backwardness" in the town and she is repeatedly used and abandoned by men as an object of sex. It does not matter what sexuality means: beauty or adultery. Miaomiao is left with unspeakable loneliness. In "'Wenge' yishi" it is not sexual desire or love but a shared sense of loneliness that binds a couple together. *Xianggang de qing yu ai*, a story of an old rich Hong Kong businessman and his young mistress from mainland China, examines the idea that the balance in a relationship between a man and a woman depends on equal exchange. Spiritual needs can be exchanged for financial independence. The relationship between the businessman and young woman is sincere but businesslike.

In China, Wang is also known as a regional writer. The majority of her stories are set in Shanghai. In her earlier writings, Shanghai was largely portrayed as a land of exquisite culture and taste, new trends, and passionate love. However, in *Beitong zhidi*, Shanghai becomes a nightmarish labyrinth of alienation and persecution for outsiders. Liu Desheng, a peasant from Shangdong, misreads the market when he attempts to sell bags of ginger in Shanghai. Apart from his business failure, he completely loses his bearing in Shanghai. Groping his way in the maze of residential lanes, he is seen as an alien and chased as a "criminal." He is eventually cornered by a mob and the police at the top of a building from which he accidentally falls to his death. Such a sense of alienation worms its way into the story *Shushu de gushi* as the corroding power of melancholy. The uncle, who has become alienated from his wife and his environment, becomes a source of alienation with the rise of his fame and power. His son is so estranged from him that he attempts to kill him. In *Shangxin Taipingyang*, individual melancholy gains historical and global significance. Melancholy becomes a distinctive mode of narration. It adds sobriety and multiple layers of depth to an otherwise simple story.

Having grown up privileged and yet given opportunities to experience and sympathize with the conditions of the deprived in both urban and rural China during a tumultuous age, Wang is a dynamic and conscientious writer equipped with a wide variety of technical resources, including lyricism, cinematic flashes, and psychological realism. Assessing her own career, she has stated that the overall theme that she has been attempting to formulate, after much rational deliberation, is that humankind's greatest enemy is itself. According to this proposition, Wang believes that a human being has to struggle against not only the world outside but also, more important, the self within. Furthermore, she observes that such a struggle is by definition a solitary and lifelong campaign, but in the sense that it is experienced by all human beings on different battlefronts, it is also a collective endeavor that can be shared. The short stories and novellas analyzed above certainly bear out her characterization of the human struggle. Her preoccupation with such a struggle offers a unique humanistic vision perfectly adapted to the social, political, historical, and cultural conditions of contemporary Chinese literature.

OTHER MAJOR WORKS

LONG FICTION: *Chang hen ge*, 1996 (*The Song of Everlasting Sorrow*, 2008); *Tao zhi yao yao*, 2004; *Bian di xiao xiong*, 2005.

NONFICTION: *Mu nü tong you mei li jian*, 1986; *Piaobo de yuyan*, 1996; *Years of Sadness: Autobiographical Writings of Wang Anyi*, 2009.

BIBLIOGRAPHY

Hung, Eva. Introduction to *Love in a Small Town*. Hong Kong: Chinese University of Hong Kong, 1988. Contains an overview of Wang's life and career up to 1987, focusing on her views of women and the authorities' condemnation of the sexuality in the Three Loves Trilogy.

_____. Introduction to *Love on a Barren Mountain*. Hong Kong: Chinese University of Hong Kong, 1991. An informed discussion and analysis of the backgrounds, issues, themes, and techniques of the three novellas in the Three Loves Trilogy both individually and as a progression. Argues that

Wang has adopted a woman-centered attitude in her treatment of relationships between men and women.

Kinkley, Jeffrey. Preface to *Lapse of Time*. San Francisco: China Books and Periodicals, 1988. An introductory overview of Wang's short fiction translated for collection in *Lapse of Time*. Focusing on the humanism by which Wang's works are informed, Kinkley provides brief but useful analyses of their historical background and social contexts, as well as Wang's motivations, preoccupations, themes, techniques, and style.

Leung, Laifong. "Wang Anyi: Restless Explorer." *Morning Sun Interviews with Chinese Writers of the Lost Generation*. New York: Sharpe, 1994. An insightful interview revealing how Wang searches for new subjects and different styles in fictional representation.

Li Ziyun. Preface to *Best Chinese Stories, 1949-1989*. Beijing: Chinese Literature Press, 1989. An extremely useful analysis of the development of short fiction as an engaging art form in the postliberation era. Major trends, along with representative authors and works, are identified and discussed in the context of the political movements in contemporary China.

McDougall, Bonnie S. "Self Narrative as Group Discourse: Female Subjectivity in Wang Anyi's Fiction. In *Fictional Authors, Imaginary Audiences: Modern Chinese Literature in the Twentieth Century*. Hong Kong: Chinese University Press, 2003. An analysis of fiction by Wang and other contemporary Chinese writers. Argues that, although these writers' fictions are not reliable portraits of Chinese life, their works can reveal insights into the writers and their audiences.

See, Carolyn. "Cultural Evolution." Review of *Baotown*, by Wang Anyi. *Los Angeles Times*, January 14, 1990, p. 1. Discusses *Baotown*, Wang's fictional account of her exile to a small village during the Chinese Cultural Revolution of the 1970's. Examines the quality of stubbornness and curiosity that underlies the survival of the workers and peasants there.

Tang Xiaobing. "Melancholy Against the Grain: Approaching Postmodernity in Wang Anyi's Tales of Sorrow." In *Chinese Modern: The Heroic and Quotidian*. Durham, N.C.: Duke University Press, 2000. Examines the origin and content of Wang's tales of sorrow, most notably her critically acclaimed novella *Shangxin Taipingyang*, an imaginative rewriting of an earlier, simpler short story. Argues that this rewriting is motivated by an unresolvable sadness, a global desolation that lies at the heart of Wang's melancholy imagination.

Wang Anyi. "Biographical Note--My Wall." In *Lapse of Time*. San Francisco: China Books and Periodicals, 1988. Wang identifies the wall separating the neighborhood of the deprived from the neighborhood of the privileged (she grew up in the latter) as the spiritual source of her art. Wang explains how, because of the symbolic impact of the wall, she can be likened to an acrobat walking a tightrope both in her life and in her fiction.

Zhang, Xudong. "Shanghai Nostalgia: Mourning and Allegory in Wang Anyi's Literary Production in the 1990's." In *Postsocialism and Cultural Politics: China in the Last Decade of the Twentieth Century*. Durham, N.C.: Duke University Press, 2008. Examines the depiction of Shanghai in Wang's works and how this representation reflects cultural and political developments in China during the 1990's.

Zhong, Xueping. "Sisterhood? Representations of Women's Relationships in Two Contemporary Chinese Texts." In *Gender and Sexuality: Twentieth-Century Chinese Literature and Society*. Edited by Tonglin Lu. Albany: State University of New York Press, 1993. A detailed comparison of Wang's "Brothers" with Jiang Zidan's "Waiting for the Twilight."

Balance Chow
Updated by Qingyun Wu

ZOË WICOMB

Born: Namaqualand, Cape Province, near Vredendal, South Africa; November 23, 1948

PRINCIPAL SHORT FICTION

You Can't Get Lost in Cape Town, 1987
The One That Got Away, 2008

OTHER LITERARY FORMS

Zoë Wicomb has written two novels, *David's Story*, published in 2000, and *Playing in the Light*, which appeared in 2006. She also has written essays about South African literature and culture.

ACHIEVEMENTS

The works of Zoë Wicomb have been translated into German, French, Swedish, Dutch, and Italian. Her short stories have appeared in various anthologies and journals, including *The Penguin Book of Contemporary South African Short Stories* (1993) and *The Heinemann Book of South African Short Stories* (1994). *The One That Got Away* and *Playing in the Light* were shortlisted for the Commonwealth Prize. *David's Story* won the South African M-Net Fiction Award. Wicomb served on the judging panel of the International IMPAC Dublin Literary Award in 2010.

BIOGRAPHY

Zoë Wicomb was born November 23, 1948, near Vredendal, in the area known as Namaqualand in the Cape Province of South Africa. Her mother, Rachel, died when Wicomb was young, and she was raised by her father, Robert, who was a schoolteacher. She was encouraged to speak English rather than Afrikaans, "even though no one within two hundred miles spoke it," and she attended English-speaking schools in Cape Town. She studied at the University of the Western Cape, which at that time was the university designated for those classified as "Coloured." She earned her degree in 1968, and in 1970 she moved to England. She studied further at Reading University, taught school, married artist Roger Palmer, and moved to Glasgow with him and their daughter, Hannah. In Glasgow, Wicomb studied for her M.Litt. degree at the University of Strathclyde, and she eventually serving as writer-in-residence. She was one of the founding editors of the *Southern African Review of Books*. In 1990, she returned to South Africa and taught English at the University of the Western Cape for a few years before coming back to Glasgow, where she took a position teaching creative writing and postcolonial literature at the University of Strathclyde.

ANALYSIS

Numerous scholarly articles and dissertations have been written about Zoë Wicomb's collection *You Can't Get Lost in Cape Town*. Wicomb has noted, though, that she felt "somewhat paralyzed" by the reaction to the work, both "a little put out by its reception as autobiography" and distressed by the "excessive praise because by the time I saw it in print, I knew it to be stylistically flawed, a rather overwritten book." Bharati Mukherjee, among others, would disagree, having called the collection "superb" with "vigorous, textured, and lyrical" writing. In the introduction to an Italian edition, Dorothy Driver heralded the collection as "without precedent."

Although Wicomb may not have intended her first collection to be read as autobiography, there are many similarities between Wicomb and her character, Frieda Shenton, as outlined by Carol Sicherman. Sue Marais notes that the collection may appear autobiographical, but she asserts that Wicomb is writing against the traditional "misguided reception" of black women's writing as autobiographical or having social or anthropological value more than literary or artistic value.

YOU CAN'T GET LOST IN CAPE TOWN

You Can't Get Lost in Cape Town consists of ten stories that trace the life of Frieda Shenton from childhood under apartheid to exile in England and back to Africa.

"BOWL LIKE HOLE"

In the opening story, young Frieda's father is called upon to translate for Mr. Weedon, the English-speaking manager, and the Afrikaans-speaking workers at the gypsum mine. Wicomb captures many details of life under apartheid with her sparse prose. When he returns, her father reports that Mr. Weedon pronounced the word "bowl" like "hole," not like "howl." Her parents "had been so sure" of the pronunciation, but as her mother indicates, "he's English, he ought to know." Frieda's mother is preoccupied with needing to "check the pronunciation of every word she had taken for granted," but Frieda knows that "unlike the rest of us," her mother would adopt the change quickly and "say bowl like hole, smoothly, without stuttering."

"WHEN THE TRAIN COMES"

In the third story, Frieda and her father are waiting at the station for the train that will take her away to school in the city. She will be among the first nonwhite students there. Her mother died sometime in the intervening years, and Frieda's father raised her as best as he could. Frieda recalls his awkward explanation of menstruation when she turned fourteen, but she had already begun her periods long before and informed him that there were disposable supplies now available. Frieda is awkward and self-conscious at the train station, equally annoyed at the rambunctious boys and flirty girls on their side of the tracks and at the fact that the white people are waiting across the way on a real platform.

"YOU CAN'T GET LOST IN CAPE TOWN"

In the title story, Frieda has found love with an English student named Michael, but, given the difference in their race, she has kept it a secret. She recalls the vitriol from her aunts toward one of her cousins who was dating white men, not to mention the additional outrage they expressed that she was dating poor white men. When Frieda finds herself pregnant, she and Michael discuss getting married, which would involve leaving South Africa for the United Kingdom, but Frieda decides instead to get an abortion. The procedure, illegal at that time, is done in a small dark room by a woman of questionable credentials. When Frieda arrives, the woman asks her, "You're not Coloured, are you?" Frieda is surprised by the "absurd" question and wonders how the woman will perform the operation with "such defective sight" until she realizes that her diction and accent do not match her skin tone for the woman. Frieda thinks that she has "drunk deeply of Michael, swallowed his voice as [she] drank from his tongue." She asks herself if he has swallowed hers, and her answer is that she does not think so. Wicomb paints a sad story of love not being enough to overcome all problems for Frieda.

THE ONE THAT GOT AWAY

The One That Got Away finds Wicomb again exploring themes of identity and exile, with a variety of characters, some of whom appear or are at least mentioned in multiple stories. Although the stories feature a variety of different characters, all of them are set in Cape Town, Glasgow, or both. Gwen Vredevoogd welcomed Wicomb's return to the short-story genre, noting that it "seems to suit her writing style, which combines economy with depth and eschews cleverness for its own sake." Wicomb's second collection reflects the changes in South Africa and elsewhere in the two decades since her first stories were published. The way the book is published even signals some of the changes: *You Can't Get Lost in Cape Town* was published with a glossary; *The One That Got Away* does not have a glossary, although in some passages, one might have been appreciated. As one reviewer noted, Wicomb's stories center on characters who are "translating experience from one culture to another, both cultures likely foreign to the reader."

"BOY IN A JUTE SACK HOOD"

Grant Fotheringay, professor of history, finds himself "at a loose end," having finished his recent monograph, "the fruit of four years' research and painful writing" and "only three months late," and finally dealing with the fact that his partner Stella has left him. It is disclosed that Grant has lived in South Africa since 1984, when he accepted a teaching position there, not aware of the boycott against South African universities at the time. In this story, he befriends a young boy, Samuel, who is the son of the gardener and accompanies his father to work on Saturdays. They begin spending their Saturdays together, with Samuel reading Grant's books and interviewing him on historical topics over lunch. Some of Grant's friends find this relationship inappropriate, but what is really inappropriate is how Grant asks Samuel to do some household chores. Samuel begins spending his time elsewhere, and after

several weeks Grant finally asks Samuel's father where he is. Excuses are made, and Grant's late, unwrapped Christmas gift of a thesaurus is refused, as it turns out his father got Samuel one.

"THE ONE THAT GOT AWAY"

Drew and Jane, who have lived together for some time, have gotten married recently. This was done partly to appease Jane's mother, Grace. Drew, an artist, has had an idea for a secret gift for Jane that involves going to Glasgow. He sees getting married as way to justify a trip. Being married seems to change the dynamics of their relationship in ways Jane did not expect. She did not understand why "they couldn't carry on as they were," when they had "poked fun at the idea of a honeymoon." Once they are in Glasgow, though, Jane finds she is "irritated with herself for expecting Drew to behave as if they are on honeymoon." Now that they are married, Jane reasons, she has to "put up with Drew rushing about the place, leaving her to her own devices." Drew's quest to create the secret gift leads to a number of misunderstandings, including one involving their room not being cleaned and Jane's inability to express this to Mrs. Buchanan, who runs the inn. In an unexpected twist, the end of the story reveals an unidentified first-person narrator who is a friend of Drew and has written all that came before as a short story. Drew is not as impressed as the author had hoped: Drew is surprised that one event, discussed during an "idle chat," has been woven into an "elaborate story," with him and Jane serving as characters. Drew's comments to his friend indicate that the storyteller may have taken great liberties with Jane's personality in particular. With this clever turn, Wicomb reminds the reader of the limits--and possibilities--of fiction.

"THERE'S THE BIRD THAT NEVER FLEW"

Drew and Jane return in this story, although this one reflects Jane's point of view. One day during the Glasgow trip, Jane does some sightseeing and is enthralled by the Doulton Fountain. She is filled with questions, and although she tends to avoid analysis of art (she recounts the line that Drew has her perform at exhibitions, where she claims that she knows nothing about art, and "what's more, I don't even know what I like"), she is drawn to the sculpture. Normally she finds frustrating the fact that questions, as opposed to answers, are "all that matters" in art appreciation. As the story unfolds, the reader learns more about Jane's mother's disapproval of her relationship with Drew, Jane's relationship with her in-laws, and her relationship with Drew. Questions she asks herself about the sculpture and her appreciation of it, along with things she recalls Drew saying about art, are all applicable to their relationship. Jane discovers a number of details as she looks closely at the sculpture, and she returns the next day "whilst Drew again charges about the city" to study it further. It is poignant that she has such a personally significant and enlightening experience connected to art, but without Drew, and it is perhaps telling that she later discovers she has lost her wedding ring in the fountain.

"Friends and Goffels"

Wicomb again explores difficult relationships, this time between two old school friends, one of whom left South Africa for Glasgow years ago and married a Scotsman. Julie and her husband Alistair have come to visit, and Dot reminisces about the bonds between the girls at school and the sadness she feels now that her old friend Julie has disappeared. Although the two might have grown apart anyway, Dot blames Alistair. The visit takes a turn for the worse when Dot and Alistair have a huge argument at dinner. Dot sits up alone in the kitchen, crying and upset, and eventually returns to bed. Later, Julie awakens and makes tea in the kitchen. As she recalls the events of the evening, which are similar but not exactly as Dot described, she laments the changes that she sees in Dot and in her hometown. However, she just can't accept that they won't be friends forever. She sends Dot a text message at 3 a.m., which blames excessive drinking for the earlier altercation, and implores Dot that they "all try to be more tolerant." It seems at first that Dot is upset by the method of communication, but as the story ends, she makes clear that "she'll have no truck with wishy-washy tolerance." The story is a painful reminder that memories can be deceiving, that time and distance can change people and relationships, and that sometimes individuals are the last to recognize the changes in themselves.

Other major works

long fiction: *David's Story*, 2000; *Playing in the Light*, 2006.

Bibliography

Gaylard, Rob. "Exile and Homecoming: Identity in Zoë Wicomb's *You Can't Get Lost in Cape Town*." *ARIEL: A Review of International English Literature* 27, no. 1 (January, 1996): 177-189. Provides extensive literary analysis of the collection.

Marais, Sue. "Getting Lost in Cape Town: Spatial and Temporal Dislocation in the South African Short Fiction Cycle." *English in Africa* 22, no. 2 (October, 1995): 29-43. Provides extensive literary analysis of the collection *You Can't Get Lost in Cape Town*.

Meyer, Stephan, and Thomas Olver. "Zoë Wicomb Interviewed on Writing and Nation." *Journal of Literary Studies* (June 1, 2002). Wicomb discusses the "tyranny of place" in her writing and elaborates on the stylistic processes in her writing.

Mukherjee, Bharati. "They Never Wanted to Be Themselves." *The New York Times Book Review*, May 24, 1987, p. 7. Review of the collection *You Can't Get Lost in Cape Town*, with analysis of Wicomb's writing.

Sicherman, Carol. "Zoë Wicomb's *You Can't Get Lost in Cape Town*: 'A New Clean Voice.'" In *Nwanyibu: Womanbeing and African Literature (Selected Papers of the Seventeenth Annual Meeting of the African Literature Association)*, edited by Phanuel Akukbueze Egejuru and Ketu H. Katrak. Trenton, N.J.: African World Press, 1997. Provides extensive literary analysis of the collection.

Vredevoogd, Gwen. "Zoë Wicomb, *The One That Got Away*." *Library Journal* (June 1, 2009): 95. Brief but insightful review of the collection.

Elizabeth Blakesley

X

Xu Xi

Born: Hong Kong, crown colony of Great Britain (now China); 1954
Also known as: Sussy Chako; Sussy Komala; Xu Su Xi

PRINCIPAL SHORT FICTION

Daughters of Hui, 1996 (as Sussy Chako; as Xu Xi, new edition, together with novel *Chinese Walls,* 2002)

History's Fiction: Stories from the City of Hong Kong, 2001

Overleaf Hong Kong, 2004

OTHER LITERARY FORMS

Xu Xi (shew shee) is a successful novelist and writer of well-regarded and influential essays, particularly on the Chinese experience in the diaspora and under colonialism. Attesting to her growing international readership, by 2010, three of her four novels were republished for a wider audience. The first, *Chinese Walls* (1994), came out again in a paperback volume in 2002 with the author's first short-story anthology *Daughters of Hui.* Her essays were collected with short stories in *Overleaf Hong Kong.* Xu Xi's subsequent essays, collected in *Evanescent Isles* (2008), which are highly autobiographical at times, were received positively. Xu Xi has been a coeditor, with Hong Kong's Lingnan University's English professor Michael "Mike" Ingham, of literary anthologies. All center on the experience of Hong Kong encountered across different literary genres and by a diverse range of writers.

ACHIEVEMENTS

One of Xu Xi's early short stories, "The Yellow Line," won selection for broadcasting by the British Broadcasting Company (BBC) World Service's Short Story Program in 1981. "Blackjack" won the *South China Morning Post* annual short-story contest for 1992. Xu Xi earned a New York Foundation of the Arts fiction fellowship and numerous appointments as writer-in-residence in places as diverse as the Anderson Center in Minnesota, Chateau de Lavigny in Switzerland, the Jack Kerouac Project of Orlando, Kulturhuset USF in Norway, and Lingnan University in Hong Kong. In 2004, her undergraduate alma mater, State University of New York (SUNY) College at Plattsburgh, awarded Xu Xi the Distinguished Alumni Award.

In 2005, Xu Xi's short story "Famine" won the Cohen Award of *Ploughshares* magazine and the prestigious O. Henry Award. "Famine" was selected for *The O. Henry Prize Stories of 2006,* edited by Laura Furman. In 2007, Xu Xi's novel *Habit of a Foreign Sky* was shortlisted for the first Man Asian Literary Award.

Xu Xi was elected by her fellow faculty to chair the master of fine arts program in writing at Vermont College in 2009. In honor of her trailblazing work in English, in 2010, Xu Xi was appointed writer-in-residence at the City University of Hong Kong to guide its new M.F.A. program of Asian Writing in English.

BIOGRAPHY

In 1954, Xu Xi was born Sussy Komala, with the Chinese name of Xu Su Xi, the first child of two Indonesian-born Chinese immigrants in Hong Kong, then a colony of Great Britain. Her father was wealthy at first, trading in manganese ore from his native Indonesia. Her mother, a pharmacist, could afford the life of a socialite and did not need to work. Soon, the family grew by two more girls and one boy.

At eight years old, Xu Xi loved to write stories and read. She went to an English-language school in Hong Kong, and even though her parents spoke Cantonese and their native Indonesian, the girl preferred to read and write in English. In 1965, her father's fortunes collapsed. The family had to economize, and eventually her mother returned to work as pharmacist. At fourteen, Xu Xi fought with her mother over her desire to enroll in the arts rather than the science stream of Hong Kong's equivalent of high school. However, the girl lost and changed to science. Nevertheless, when Xu Xi went to college abroad, at State University of New York at Plattsburgh, she graduated with a bachelor of arts in English in 1974.

Returning to Hong Kong, Xu Xi began a career in marketing and advertising, working for Cathay Pacific. She married an Englishman and later divorced. She published her first short stories, such as "The Sea Islands," in Hong Kong literary magazines. Her decision to write in English rather than Cantonese was a bold expression of her international aspirations as writer. Somewhat prematurely, her "Letter from Hydra, Greece" announced her complete dedication to writing. She followed up this decision by enrolling in and graduating from the University of Massachusetts at Amherst with an M.F.A. in fiction in 1985, choosing the pen name of Sussy Chako. Xu Xi became a U.S. citizen in 1987.

She reentered the corporate world in the United States, while married to her second husband, an American, before moving to Hong Kong to work for Federal Express in 1992. "Blackjack" was the winning short story of 1992 for the leading Hong Kong English newspaper. She published her first novel, *Chinese Walls*, and her first collection of short stories, *Daughters of Hui*, with a small Hong Kong publisher. The critical success of her second novel, *Hong Kong Rose* (1997), persuaded her to give up her business career. She changed her nom de plume to Xu Xi, under which she published her subsequent work, beginning with her short-story collection *History's Fiction* and her novel *The Unwalled City* (2001).

Divorced again, Xu Xi launched an independent global existence as a writer and a teacher of writing, which keeps her traveling to the Untied States, Europe, and Hong Kong. On the strength of her ongoing publications and republications of short stories, novels, essays, and coedited anthologies, Xu Xi became a faculty member of the M.F.A. program in writing at Vermont College and was elected chair in 2009. She has continued to work as a writer-in-residence for other institutions. In 2010, Xu Xi launched the new M.F.A. program of Asian Writing in English at City University of Hong Kong.

ANALYSIS

With a wide range of characters, dramatic situations, and settings, Xu Xi's short stories generally focus on female protagonists, who must come to terms with a decisive issue in their lives. In most cases, Xu Xi's central characters are Chinese, mixed-race Asian women, or Eurasian women, whose often diverse ethnic background influences their situation in either a subtle or a profound way. This immediately raises the issue of hybridity, as contemporary literary critics call it, making less simple the question of the protagonist's ethnic characterization. In turn, many of Xu Xi's women protagonists find themselves in troubled romantic relationships with men of an Asian, Eurasian, European, or European American background, highlighting as central to her writing the issues of ethnic heritage and interracial liaisons.

Many of Xu Xi's short stories are set directly in Hong Kong, and almost all contain a link to that city. For short stories taking place on a Greek island, in the United States, or in European capitals, this link commonly derives from the protagonist's birth and upbringing in Hong Kong. Thus the world often is seen through the eyes of a Hong Kong woman, providing a fresh perspective.

The dramatic conflicts of Xu Xi's short stories vary widely but tend to focus on the personal and its encounter with the outside world, especially the contemporary history of Hong Kong. Many stories focus on a personal struggle of the woman protagonist. This can be triggered by a crisis in her love relationship, by an understanding of her personal and professional identity, by an encounter with something new, or by a problem related to the protagonist's artistic endeavors. Xu Xi's occasional male protagonists experience this also.

Generally written from a third-person narrative viewpoint, with the occasional first-person narrator, Xu Xi's stories are told subjectively. Her prose privileges the protagonist's view. In turn, the reader realizes that Xu Xi's protagonists can be rather unreliable, idiosyncratic, often rebellious, and sometimes self-destructive characters.

Even though there are definite autobiographical elements in Xu Xi's fiction, including many of her short stories, it would be wrong to read them as revelations of the author's personal life. Instead, the reader may feel reminded of the way in which the unnamed Chinese woman writer in "Pineapple Upside Down Bird" admits to collecting as character sketches the personalities and experiences of many of the people she encounters. Xu Xi's fiction is full of traces of the fates of real people, including her own, yet the author's creative imagination has altered, recombined, and refashioned them to produce poignant fiction.

A Chinese woman from Hong Kong, educated in the English language and in the United States, Xu Xi has chosen to write in English, which represents a powerful decision. When she began to write short stories in the late 1970's, her choice was shared by few others in Hong Kong, among them Agnes Lam and Louise Ho. By 2010, more Asians, such as Chinese novelist Ha Jin, have followed her example.

Xu Xi (AFP/Getty Images)

DAUGHTERS OF HUI

Xu Xi's first collection of short stories, with the opening text a novella, is united formally by the fact that the protagonists are daughters of Mr. Hui, a dissident Chinese poet exiled to Hong Kong. All the daughters are somewhat unconventional, with two of them leading deliberately oppositional lives.

"Loving Graham" is the first-person account of a rebellious Ms. Hui. She has terminated both her marriages, to a Chinese and then an American, through affairs with her husbands' best friends. Xu Xi paints a forceful picture of an unapologetically willful woman rejecting social conventions and traditional sexual roles. Through her past passionate liaison, when she was between husbands, with Englishman Graham, Ms. Hui proves incorrect her last husband's claim that she cannot enjoy sexual love. Weakly, Graham gives her up, however, for convention's sake.

"The Stone Window" is a gothic tale primarily set on a Greek island, where the mysterious Philomena Hui has stopped to paint. Philomena is not related to Mr. Hui's daughter, Sai Yee, who shares her last name, even though the two women occasionally appear, and finally disappear, as mysterious doubles. Sai Yee marries the Englishman Ralph Carder, who, like her, has bought one of Philomena's paintings. At the story's end, she has left him, perhaps because Ralph had an affair with Philomena.

"Valediction" is written in form of a moving letter by the troublemaking younger sister to her elder one, who committed suicide in London six years ago. In powerful prose, the short story reveals that it was the older, apparently more conventional sister who ended her life when the cheating of her French husband became unbearable. In contrast, the wild younger sister finds the means to survive.

HISTORY'S FICTION

Xu Xi's second collection of short stories contains two of her award-winning early ones. "The Yellow Line" established Xu Xi's literary fame in Hong Kong with a bitter story of an underprivileged, abused six-year-old Chinese boy, who finds unexpected pleasure traveling the new Hong Kong subway to the next, more affluent neighborhood station. As his domestic situation becomes unbearable, the boy steps into the path of an oncoming train, straight across the yellow line marking the danger zone. The story made urban progress a double-edged sword that raised expectations that sometimes were thwarted cruelly and led to more despair.

"Blackjack," selected as story of the year for 1992 by Hong Kong's *South China Morning Post*, presents an allegory on the future of Hong Kong after its handover to mainland China in the story's future. Just as the unnamed Chinese woman protagonist could not predict the outcome of her blackjack play at a casino in Atlantic City, neither losing nor winning much, so she is unafraid of Communist China's imminent rule over Hong Kong. Rejecting the relative safety of staying in America as a naturalized citizen, she returns to her native Hong Kong. With its pragmatic, cautious optimism, the story captured the mood of many Hong Kong readers.

"Democracy" thoughtfully reflects on democratic versus autocratic leadership. It begins in 1966, when some rioting erupted in Hong Kong over public-ferry fare increases by the colonial authorities. Sixteen-year-old middle-class Girl Guide Patricia Chow is vexed by the unexpected announcement that her company's captain, in this Hong Kong equivalent of America's Girl Scouts, is to be elected rather than appointed. Surprisingly, she is elected over her politically ambitious, working-class rival Maria Cheung. A friend of Patricia explains the girls' votes by pointing out that Patricia cares for them and their wishes, while Maria pursues only her agenda. At a reunion of some of the classmates in 2001, Patricia's friend Yin-Fei is running for a Hong Kong party demanding more democracy. This links the past to the present.

OVERLEAF HONG KONG

Among the eleven splendid short stories in this collection is "Famine," the story that won for Xu Xi the O. Henry Prize. The death of her parents finally frees the fifty-one-year-old Chinese woman protagonist to leave behind Hong Kong and her job as an English teacher. Collecting her accumulated savings, she flies business class to New York City, enjoying her opulent in-flight meal, lavishly described to set the theme of the story. In New York, she stays at the Plaza Suite and books dinner for one at the fashionable Lutèce restaurant. Her

unexplained solitary presence startles other guests, who finally assume she must be the famous hat designer Kwai-sin Ho. Mischievously, the narrator lies that she is the designer's estranged twin sister. By ordering the most expensive wine on the menu, she indulges in a meal costing thousands of dollars.

As the narrator luxuriates in her suite, she remembers a lifetime of deprivation under her working-class parents, who eked out a living in Hong Kong and saved money all their lives. In a grand gesture embracing the surreal, the narrator orders a sumptuous meal delivered to her suite to entertain all her imaginary guests, ranging from her friends and her colleagues to her students, acquaintances, and finally her parents. In her imagination, all converge on the feast laid out by her, and so she overcomes her fear of opulence and death. "Famine" is a finely crafted story, celebrating a woman's final independence and long-repressed indulgence into physical pleasure. There is an air of tragedy, too, as her desire to share this freedom is fulfilled only in her imagination.

OTHER MAJOR WORKS

LONG FICTION: *Chinese Walls*, 1994 (as Sussy Chako; as Xu Xi, new edition, together with the short-story collection *Daughters of Hui*, 2002); *Hong Kong Rose*, 1997 (as Sussy Chako; as Xu Xi, 2004); *The Unwalled City*, 2001; *Habit of a Foreign Sky*, 2007.

NONFICTION: *Evanescent Isles*, 2008.

EDITED TEXTS: *City Voices*, 2003 (with Mike Ingham); *City Stage*, 2005 (with Ingham); *Fifty-Fifty*, 2008.

BIBLIOGRAPHY

Greenlees, Donald. "Publishing Comes of Age at Last in Asia." *International Herald Tribune*, November 9, 2007, p. 1. Uses the occasion of Xu Xi's novel *Habit of a Foreign Sky* being shortlisted for the first Man Asian Literary Award to comment that her fiction, like that of fellow Hong Kong-based and other Asian writers, is becoming more recognized by major international publishers.

Ingham, Michael. Preface to *Chinese Walls and Daughters of Hui*, by Xu Xi. Hong Kong: Chameleon Press, 2002. An introduction to Xu Xi's work, which discusses Xu Xi's choice of English for her fiction, her key themes and concerns, the differences in the marketing of her writing, and the different daughters of patriarch Hui. Author also coedited anthologies with Xu Xi.

Lai, Amy. "'Disappearing with the Double': Xu Xi's 'The Stone Window.'" In *Asian Gothic*, edited by Andrew Hock Soon Ng. Jefferson, N.C.: McFarland, 2008. An academic article that places Xu Xi's short story in the tradition of the gothic tale and applies psychoanalysis and feminist theory to show how the author's use of the double empowers female characters to escape the male gaze by disappearing from the text.

Weisenhaus, Doreen. "Asia's Writers Turning to English to Gain Readers." *The New York Times*, December 25, 2001, p. E2. Sees Xu Xi as trailblazer for Asian writers, not just those from Hong Kong. Praises Xu Xi's choice to write fiction in English for immediate access to a wide global readership. Comments on Xu Xi's relative previous isolation as an English-language fiction writer from Hong Kong during the late 1970's and 1980's.

R. C. Lutz

Z

Yevgeny Zamyatin

Born: Lebedyan, Russia; January 20, 1884
Died: Paris, France; March 10, 1937
Also known as: Evgenii Zamiatin; Evgenii Ivanovich
Zamiatin

Other literary forms

The most important work of fiction by Yevgeny Zamyatin (yehv-GAY-nee zuhm-YAHT-yihn) was his novel *My* (1952; *We,* 1924), which was written in 1920-1921. A satirical examination of a future utopian state, the novel affirms the timeless value of individual liberty and free will in a world which places a premium on conformity and reason. This work exerted a significant influence on George Orwell's *Nineteen Eighty-Four* (1949). Zamyatin also wrote plays, adaptations, and film scenarios. His early dramatic works are historical plays--*Ogni svyatogo Dominika* (wr. 1920, pb. 1922; *The Fires of Saint Dominic,* 1971) and *Attila* (wr. 1925-1927, pb. 1950; English translation, 1971)--while a later work, *Afrikanskiy gost* (wr. 1920-1930, pb. 1963; *The African Guest,* 1971), provides a comic look at philistine attempts to cope with Soviet reality. The author's most successful adaptation for the screen was a version of Maxim Gorky's *Na dne* (pr., pb. 1902; *The Lower Depths,* 1912), which Zamyatin transformed into a screenplay for Jean Renoir's film *Les Bas-fonds* (1936; *The Lower Depths,* 1937).

Achievements

Although Yevgeny Zamyatin is best known in the West for his novel *We,* it was his short fiction that was most influential in the former Soviet Union, since *We* was not published there until 1987. In his short fiction, Zamyatin developed an original prose style that is distinguished by its bold imagery and charged narrative pacing. This style, along with Zamyatin's writings and teachings about literature in the immediate postrevolutionary period, had a decisive impact on the first generation of Soviet writers, which includes such figures as Lev Luntz, Nikolay Nikitin, Venyamin Kaverin, and Mikhail Zoshchenko. In addition, Zamyatin's unswerving defense of the principle of artistic and individual freedom remains a vivid element of his literary legacy.

Biography

Yevgeny Ivanovich Zamyatin was born on January 20, 1884, in Lebedyan, a small town in the Russian heartland. The writer would later point out with pride that the town was famous for its cardsharps, Gypsies, and distinctive Russian speech, and he would utilize this spicy material in his mature fiction. His childhood, however, was a lonely one, and as the son of a village teacher, he spent more time with books than with other children.

After completing four years at the local school in 1896, Zamyatin went on to the *Gymnasium* in Voronezh, where he remained for six years. Immediately after he was graduated, Zamyatin moved to St. Petersburg to study naval engineering at the Petersburg Polytechnic Institute. Over the next few years, Zamyatin became interested in politics and joined the Bolshevik Party. This political involvement led to his arrest late in 1905, when he was picked up by the authorities who were trying to cope with the turbulent political agitation that swept the capital that year. Zamyatin spent several months in solitary confinement, and he used the time to write poetry and study English. Released in the spring of 1906, Zamyatin was exiled to Lebedyan. He soon returned to St. Petersburg, however, and lived there illegally until he was discovered and exiled again in 1911.

By this time he had been graduated from Petersburg Polytechnic Institute and had been appointed a lecturer there. He also had made his debut as a writer: in 1908, he published the story "Odin" ("Alone"), which chronicles the fate of an imprisoned revolutionary student who kills himself over frustrated love, and in 1910, he published "Devushka," another tale of tragic love. Although neither work is entirely successful, they both demonstrate Zamyatin's early interest in innovative narrative technique. A more polished work was *A Provincial Tale*, which Zamyatin wrote during the months of renewed exile in 1911 and 1912. Zamyatin's penetrating treatment of ignorance and brutality in the Russian countryside was greeted with warm approval by the critics. On the other hand, his next major work, *A Godforsaken Hole*, provided such a sharp portrait of cruelty in the military that the publication in which the story appeared was confiscated by the authorities.

In 1916, Zamyatin departed Russia for Great Britain, where he was to work on seagoing icebreakers. His experience abroad provided the impetus for two satires on the British middle class, *The Islanders* and "Lovets chelovekov" ("The Fisher of Men"). Zamyatin returned to Russia after the abdication of Czar Nicholas in 1917 and embarked upon a busy course of literary endeavors. The period from 1917 to 1921 was a time of remarkable fecundity for the writer: He wrote fourteen stories, the novel *We*, a dozen fables, and a play. This body of work evinces an impressive diversity of artistic inspiration. Zamyatin's subjects range from the intense passions found in rural Russia ("Sever," "The North") to the dire conditions afflicting the urban centers during the postrevolutionary period ("Peshchera," or "The Cave"; "Mamay"; and "Drakon," or "Dragon") to ribald parodies of saints' lives ("O tom, kak istselen byl inok Erazm," or "How the Monk Erasmus Was Healed").

In addition to his own literary creation, Zamyatin dedicated himself to encouraging the literary careers of others. He regularly lectured on the craft of writing to young writers in the House of Arts in Petrograd, and he took part in numerous editorial and publishing activities. Among those whose works he helped to edit were Anton Chekhov and H. G. Wells. For many of these editions, he also wrote critical or biographical introductions, and such writers as Wells, Jack London, O. Henry, and George Bernard Shaw received Zamyatin's critical attention. As a result of this editorial work and his involvement in such literary organizations as the All-Russian Union of Writers, which he helped to found, Zamyatin's own productivity began to decline after 1921, particularly his prose.

At the same time, Zamyatin found himself in the awkward position of having to defend himself against those who perceived something dangerous or threatening in the ideas his work espoused. In his prose fiction and in numerous essays, Zamyatin consistently articulated a belief in the value of continual change, innovation, and renewal. Seizing upon the thermodynamic theory of entropy--the concept that all energy in the universe tends toward stasis or passivity--Zamyatin warned against the dangers of stagnation in intellectual and artistic spheres. Exhorting writers to be rebels and heretics, he argued that one should never be content with the status quo, for satisfaction with any victory can easily degenerate into stifling philistinism. By the same token, Zamyatin denounced conformist tendencies in literary creation and decried efforts to subordinate individual inspiration to predetermined ideological programs.

Given the fact that one of the ideological underpinnings of the new Soviet state was a belief in the primacy of the collective over the interests of the individual, Zamyatin's fervent defense of individual freedom could not help but draw the attention of the emerging establishment. The writer was arrested in 1922 along with 160 other intellectuals and became subject to an order for deportation. Without his knowledge, and perhaps against his will, a group of friends interceded for him and managed to have the order withdrawn. After Zamyatin's release in 1923, he applied for permission to emigrate, but his request was rebuffed.

During the latter half of the 1920's, the political climate in the Soviet Union became more restrictive, and Zamyatin was among a number of talented writers who were singled out for public denunciation and criticism. He found that the doors to publishing houses were now closed to him and that permission to stage his plays was impossible to obtain. Zamyatin did not buckle before the increasingly vituperative attacks directed toward him. Indeed, he had once written that "a stubborn, unyielding enemy is far more deserving of respect than a sudden convert to communism." Consequently, he did not succumb to pressure and make a public confession of his "errors," as some of his fellow writers were forced to do. On the contrary, he stood up to this campaign of abuse until 1931, when he sent Joseph Stalin an audacious request for permission to leave the Soviet Union with the right to return "as soon as it becomes possible in our country to serve great ideas in literature without cringing before little men."

With Gorky's help, Zamyatin's petition was granted, and he left the Soviet Union with his wife in November, 1931. Settling in Paris, he continued to work on a variety of literary projects, including translations, screenplays, and a novel entitled *Bich bozhy* (1939; the scourge of God). Because of his interest in film, he envisioned a trip to Hollywood, but these plans never materialized. He died on March 10, 1937.

ANALYSIS

Perhaps the most distinctive feature of Yevgeny Zamyatin's short fiction is its charged, expressive narrative style. The writer characterized the style of his generation of writers in a lecture entitled "Contemporary Russian Literature," delivered in 1918. Calling the artistic method of his generation "neorealism," he outlined the differences between neorealist fiction and that of the preceding realist movement. He states:

By the time the Neorealists appeared, life had become more complex, faster, more feverish. . . . In response to this way of life, the Neorealists have learned to write more compactly, briefly, tersely than the Realists. They have learned to say in ten lines what used to be said in a whole page.

During the first part of his career, Zamyatin consciously developed and honed his own unique form of neorealist writing. Although his initial experimentation in this direction is evident in his early prose works (and especially in the long story *A Provincial Tale*), this tendency did not reach its expressive potential until the late 1910's, when it blossomed both in his satires on British life and in the stories devoted to Russian themes. The stories *The Islanders* and "The Fisher of Men" provide a mordant examination of the stifling philistinism permeating the British middle class. The former work in particular displays the tenor and thrust of Zamyatin's satiric style. The first character introduced into the tale is a minister named Vicar Dooley, who has written a *Testament of Contemporary Salvation*, in which he declares that "life must become a harmonious machine and with mechanical inevitability lead us to the desired goal." Such a vision raises the specter of death and stasis, not energy and life, and Zamyatin marshals his innovative narrative skills to expose the dangers that this vision poses for society.

THE ISLANDERS

One salient feature of Zamyatin's style is the identification of a character with a specific physical trait, animal, or object that seems to capture the essence of the character being depicted. Through this technique, the writer can both evoke the presence of the character by mentioning the associated image and underscore that character's fundamental personality type. What is more, once Zamyatin has established such an identification, he can suggest significant shifts in his characters' moods or situations by working changes on the associated images themselves. In *The Islanders*, this technique plays a vital role in the narrative exposition, and at times the associated images actually replace a given character in action. Thus, one character's lips are compared at the outset of the story to thin worms, and the women who attend Dooley's church are described as being pink and blue. Later, a tense interaction between the two is conveyed in striking terms: "Mrs. Campbell's worms twisted and sizzled on a slow fire. The blues and pinks feasted their eyes." Similarly, the central protagonist is compared to a tractor, and when his stolid reserve is shattered by feelings of love, Zamyatin writes that the tractor's "steering wheel was broken." Through this felicitous image Zamyatin not only evokes his hero's ponderous bulk but also suggests the unpredictable consequences which follow the release of suppressed emotion.

As striking as his satires on British conservatism are, however, it is in the stories that he wrote on Russian subjects that Zamyatin attained the apex of his vibrant expressionistic style. In his lecture on contemporary Russian literature, he spoke of his desire to find fresh subjects for literary treatment. Contrasting urban and rural settings, he declared: "The life of big cities is like the life of factories. It robs people of individuality, makes them the same, machinelike." In the countryside, Zamyatin concludes, "the Neorealists find not only genre, not only a way of life, but also a way of life concentrated, condensed by centuries to a strong essence, ninety-proof."

"THE NORTH"

As if to illustrate this premise, in 1918 he wrote the long tale entitled "The North." This story celebrates the primal forces of nature: In a swift succession of scenes, Zamyatin depicts a passionate yet short-lived affair between a true child of the forest--a young woman named Pelka--and a simple fisherman named Marey. Pelka is perhaps the closest embodiment of the ideally "natural" character in all of Zamyatin's works. She talks with the forest creatures, keeps a deer for a pet, and loves with a profound passion that cannot understand or tolerate the constraints imposed by civilized man. Sadly, her brief interlude of love with Marey is threatened by his foolish obsession with constructing a huge lantern "like those in Petersburg." Marey's desire to ape the fashions of the city destroys his romantic idyll with Pelka. After she vainly tries to stir Marey's emotions by having a short fling with a smug, callous shopkeeper named Kortoma, Pelka engineers a fatal encounter between herself, Marey, and a wild bear: The two lovers die at the hands of the natural world.

To illuminate this spectacle of extraordinary desire and suffering, Zamyatin utilizes all the tools of his neorealist narrative manner. Striving to show rather than describe, Zamyatin avoids the use of such connectors as "it seemed" or "as if" in making comparisons; instead, the metaphorical image becomes the illustrated object or action itself. Especially noteworthy in "The

North" is Zamyatin's use of charged color imagery. By associating particular characters with symbolic visual leitmotifs, the writer enhances his character portrayals. Thus, he underscores Pelka's naturalism by linking her to a combination of the colors red (as of flesh and blood) and green (as of the vegetation in the forest). Zamyatin compared his method to Impressionism: The juxtaposition of a few basic colors is intended to project the essence of a scene. At times, Zamyatin allows the symbolic associations of certain colors to replace narrative description entirely. Depicting the rising frenzy of a Midsummer Night's celebration, Zamyatin alludes to the surging flow of raw passion itself when he writes: "All that you could see was that . . . something red was happening."

Zamyatin's attention to visual detail in "The North" is matched by his concern with auditory effects. He thought that literary prose and poetry were one and the same; accordingly, the reader finds many examples of alliteration, assonance, and instrumentation in his work. He also gave careful consideration to the rhythmic pattern of his prose, revealing a debt to the Russian symbolist writers who emphasized the crucial role of sound in prose. Seeking to communicate his perceptions as expressively and concisely as possible, he tried to emulate the fluidity and dynamism of oral speech. One notes many elliptical and unfinished sentences in Zamyatin's prose at this time, and his narratives resemble a series of sharp but fragmentary images or vignettes, which his readers must connect and fill in themselves. Zamyatin explained: "Today's reader and viewer will know how to complete the picture, fill in the words--and what he fills in will be etched far more vividly within him, will much more firmly become an organic part of him."

"IN OLD RUSSIA"

Zamyatin's other works on the deep recesses of the Russian countryside reflect his calculated attempt to evoke deep emotions and passionate lives in elliptical, allusive ways. The story "Rus" ("In Old Russia"), for example, is narrated in a warm colloquial tone in which the neutral language of an impersonal narrator is replaced by language that relies heavily on the intonations and lexicon of spoken Russian. This technique, called *skaz* in Russian, was popularized by writers such as Nikolay Leskov and Alexey Remizov, and Zamyatin uses it to good effect in this tale. His narrator's account of the amorous activities of a young married woman named Darya is accented with notes of sly understanding and tolerance. As the narrator describes her, Darya cannot help but give in to the impulses of her flesh. At the very outset, she is compared to an apple tree filling up with sap; when spring arrives, she unconsciously feels the sap rising in her just as it is in the apple and lilac trees around her. Her "fall," then, is completely natural, and so, too, is the ensuing death of her husband only a few days later. Again, Zamyatin's narrator conveys the news of the husband's death and the gossip that attended it in tones of warm indulgence. In the deep backwaters of Russia, he indicates, life flows on; such events have no more lasting impact than a stone that is dropped into a pond and causes a few passing ripples.

"THE CAVE" AND "MAMAY"

While Zamyatin was drawn to rural Russian subjects, he did not ignore urban themes: Two of his most striking works of 1920-- "The Cave" and "Mamay"--exhibit his predilection for expressive imagery and his nuanced appreciation of human psychology. In "The Cave," Zamyatin depicts the Petrograd landscape in the winters following the Russian Revolution as a primordial, prehistoric wasteland. This image dominates the story, illustrating the writer's own admission that if he firmly believes in an image, "it will spread its roots through paragraphs and pages."

While the overarching image of Petrograd's citizens as cave dwellers creates a palpable atmosphere of grimness and despair in "The Cave," the images with which Zamyatin enlivens "Mamay" are more humorous. This story continues a long tradition in Russian literature of depicting the life of petty clerks in the city of St. Petersburg. The protagonist here is a meek individual who bears the incongruous name of Mamay, one of the Tatar conquerors of Russia. Mamay's wife is a stolid woman so domineering that every spoonful of soup eaten by Mamay is likened to an offering to an imperious Buddha. The sole pleasure in little Mamay's life is book collecting, and it is this mild passion that finally stirs the character into uncharacteristic action. He had been gathering and hiding a large sum of money

with which to buy books, and at the end of the story he discovers with dismay that his stockpile has been destroyed by an enemy. Enraged, he is driven to murder. This contemporary Mamay, however, is only a pale shadow of his famous namesake: The intruder proves to be a mouse, and Mamay kills it with a letter opener.

"A STORY ABOUT THE MOST IMPORTANT THING"

Zamyatin's pursuit of a charged, expressive narrative manner reached a peak in the early 1920's, and in at least one work, "Rasskaz o samom glavnom" ("A Story About the Most Important Thing"), the writer's ambition resulted in a work in which stylistic and structural manipulation overwhelms semantic content. Zamyatin creates a complex narrative structure in which he shifts back and forth among three plotlines involving the life of an insect, revolutionaries in Russia, and beings on a star about to collide with the Earth. The tale forcefully conveys the writer's sense of the power of the urge to live and procreate in the face of imminent death, but in certain passages, his penchant for hyperbole and intensity of feeling detracts from the effectiveness of the work as a whole.

"THE FLOOD"

Later in the decade, however, Zamyatin began to simplify his narrative techniques; the result can be seen in the moving story "Navodnenie" ("The Flood"), perhaps the finest short story of this late period. Written in 1928, "The Flood" reveals how Zamyatin managed to tone down some of his more exaggerated descriptive devices, while retaining the power and intensity of his central artistic vision. One finds few of his characteristic recurring metaphors in the story, but the few that are present carry considerable import. The work's central image is that of flooding, both as a literal phenomenon (the repeated flooding of the Neva River) and as a metaphorical element (the ebb and flow of emotions in the protagonist's soul). The plot of the story concerns a childless woman's resentment toward an orphaned girl named Ganka, who lives in her house and has an affair with her husband. Sofya's rising malice toward Ganka culminates on a day when the river floods. As the river rises and a cannon booms its flood warning, Sofya feels her anger surging too: It "whipped across her heart, flooded all of her." Striking Ganka with an ax, she then feels a corresponding outflow, a release of tension.

Similar images of flooding and flowing accompany So-fya's childbirth, the feeding of her child, and the rising sensation of guilt in her heart. In the final scene of the story, the river again begins to flood, and now Sofya feels an irrepressible urge to give birth to her confession. As she begins to reveal her murderous secret, "Huge waves swept out of her and washed over . . . everyone." After she concludes her tale, "everything was good, blissful . . . all of her had poured out."

The recurring water images link all the major events in "The Flood," and Zamyatin achieves further cohesiveness through additional associations such as birth and death, conception and destruction. The tight austerity of his later fiction endows that body of work with understated force. The writer himself commented on the conscious effort he made to achieve this kind of effective simplicity: "All the complexities I had passed through had been only a road to simplicity. . . . Simplicity of form is legitimate for our epoch, but the right to simplicity must be earned."

The oeuvre that Zamyatin left behind provides an eloquent testament both to the man's skill as a literary craftsman and to the integrity and power of his respect for human potential. His innovations in narrative exposition exerted a palpable influence on his contemporaries, and his defense of individual liberty in the face of relentless repression holds timeless appeal for his readers.

OTHER MAJOR WORKS

LONG FICTION: *My*, wr. 1920-1921, pb. 1927 (corrupt text), 1952 (*We*, 1924); *Bich bozhy*, 1939.

PLAYS: *Ogni Svyatogo Dominika*, wr. 1920, pb. 1922 (*The Fires of Saint Dominic*, 1971); *Blokha*, pr. 1925, pb. 1926 (*The Flea*, 1971); *Obshchestvo pochetnikh zvonarei*, pr. 1925, pb. 1926 (*The Society of Honorary Bell Ringers*, 1971); *Attila*, wr. 1925-1927, pb. 1950 (English translation, 1971); *Afrikanskiy gost*, wr. 1929-1930, pb. 1963 (*The African Guest*, 1971); *Five Plays*, pb. 1971.

SCREENPLAY: *Les Bas-fonds*, 1936 (*The Lower Depths*, 1937; adaptation of Maxim Gorky's novel *Na dne*).

NONFICTION: *Gerbert Uells*, 1922 (*H. G. Wells*, 1970); *Kak my pishem: Teoria literatury*, 1930; *Litsa*, 1955 (*A Soviet Heretic*, 1970).

MISCELLANEOUS: *Sobranie sochinenii*, 1929 (collected works); *Sochineniia*, 1970-1972.

BIBLIOGRAPHY

Balina, Marina, Helena Goscilo, and Mark Lipovetsky, eds. "*Fairy Tales for Grown-Up Children*: Yevgeny Zamyatin." In *Politicizing Magic: An Anthology of Russian and Soviet Fairy Tales*. Evanston, Ill.: Northwestern University Press, 2005. An excerpt from Zamyatin's collection of fairy tales is among several stories in a section of this anthology devoted to "fairy tales in critique of Soviet culture." In his introduction to this section, Mark Lipovetsky explains how Zamyatin was the first Soviet writer to discover the "antitotalitarian" potential of the fairy tale genre, using it as a form of protest against the Soviet government.

Billington, Rachel. "Two Russians." *Financial Times*, January 5, 1985, p. I8. Discusses Zamyatin's *The Islanders*. Notes that the anti-British story helped to make Zamyatin's name in Russia.

Brown, Edward J. "Zamjatin and English Literature." In *American Contributions to the Fifth International Congress of Slavists*. Vol. 2. The Hague, Netherlands: Mouton, 1965. Brown discusses Zamyatin's interest in, and debt to, English literature stemming from his two-year stay in England before and during World War I.

Cavendish, Philip. *Mining the Jewels: Evgenii Zamiatin and the Literary Stylization of Rus'*. London: Maney, 2000. A thorough study of the folkloric and religious background of Zamyatin's sources of inspiration. Traces his attempts to reconcile the folkloric tradition and the vernacular through his artistic expression. In the process, Zamyatin drew from the past and from the language of the Russian people, creating literature that is basically modernistic.

Collins, Christopher. *Evgenij Zamjatin: An Interpretive Study*. The Hague, Netherlands: Mouton, 1973. In this ambitious study, Collins advances a rather complex interpretation of Zamyatin's works, primarily his novel *We*, on the basis of Carl Jung's concepts of the conscious, unconscious, and individualism.

Mihailovich, Vasa D. "Critics on Evgeny Zamyatin." *Papers on Language and Literature* 10 (1974): 317-334. A useful survey of all facets of criticism of Zamyatin's opus, in all languages, through 1973. Good for gaining introductory knowledge of Zamyatin.

Quinn-Judge, Paul. "Moscow's Brave New World: Novelist Zamyatin Revisited." *The Christian Science Monitor*, April 4, 1988, p. 8. A brief biographical background to accompany a story about the publication of Zamyatin's antitotalitarian novel *We* in Moscow.

Richard, D. J. *Zamyatin: A Soviet Heretic*. London: Hillary House, 1962. A brief overview of the main stages and issues in Zamyatin's life and works, paying some attention to his short fic-

tion. An excellent, though truncated, presentation of a very complex writer.

Shane, Alex M. *The Life and Works of Evgenij Zamjatin*. Berkeley: University of California Press, 1968. The most comprehensive work on Zamyatin in English, covering, exhaustively but pertinently, his life and the most important features of his works, including short fiction. Using secondary sources extensively, Shane chronologically analyzes Zamyatin's works in a scholarly but not dry fashion and reaches his own conclusions. Supplemented by an extensive bibliography of works by and about Zamyatin.

Julian W. Connolly
Updated by Vasa D. Mihailovich

Zhang Jie

Born: Beijing, China; April 27, 1937

Principal short fiction

Ai, shi bu neng wangji de, 1980 (*Love Must Not Be Forgotten*, 1986)
Fangzhou, 1983 (*The Ark*, 1986)
Zumu lu, 1985 (*Emerald*, 1986)
Zhang Jie chi, 1986
As Long as Nothing Happens, Nothing Will, 1988
Yige zhongguo nuren zai Ouzhou, 1989
You Are a Friend of My Soul, 1990
Shi jie shang zui teng wo de na ge ren qu le, 1994

Other literary forms

Besides her short stories, Zhang Jie (jong jay) has written novels, poetry, screenplays, and literary criticism. She has also published her experience abroad in a book entitled *Zai na lü cao di shang* (1983; on a green lawn). Although no major collections of her poetry and critical essays have been published, her novels *Chenzhong de chibang* (1981; *Leaden Wings*, 1987; better known as *Heavy Wings*, 1989) and *Zhi you yi ge taiyang* (1988; only one sun) have been quite successful.

Achievements

Although Zhang Jie started writing fiction in her early forties, she has become one of the best-known Chinese women writers in the modern world. Her first novel *Heavy Wings* won the Mao Dun Literary Award in 1985 (an award granted once every three years), and it has been translated and published in a dozen countries: Germany, France, Sweden, Finland, Norway, Denmark, Holland, Great Britain, the United States, Spain, Brazil, and the Soviet Union. Her third novel, *Wu zi* (1998; without words), earned Zhang another Moa Dun Literary Award in 2005, making her the first writer in the prize's history to receive two awards. Zhang, however, is better known as a short-story writer. In 1978, she began publishing numerous stories and subsequently won various prizes. Two collections of her stories, *Love Must Not Be Forgotten* and *As Long as Nothing Happens, Nothing Will*, are widely studied in European and American college classrooms. *As Long as Nothing Happens, Nothing Will* won Italy's Malaparte Literary Prize, an award that has been won by famous writers, such as Anthony Burgess and Saul Bellow.

Zhang's work has received considerable critical attention both in China and abroad. A feminist writer, she has forged a distinctive style that blends well her utopian idealism with social reality in her exploration of women's problems concerning love, marriage, and career. A social critic, she exposes China's hidden corruption and stubborn bureaucracy and vehemently champions the causes of democracy and reform through her literary forms. For her integrated concern for women and society, Zhang can be compared with Western writers, such as Doris Lessing, Marge Piercy, and Ursula K. Le Guin. Her sentimental idealism and militant tone, however, have sometimes irritated critics and readers.

In her biographical note, "My Boat," Zhang made a modest statement:

> A life still unfinished, ideals demanding to be realized. Beautiful, despondent, joyful, tragic. . . . All manner of social phenomena weave themselves into one story after another in my mind. . . . Like an artless tailor, I cut my cloth unskillfully according to old measurements and turn out garment factory clothes sold in department stores in only five standard sizes and styles.

Although her statement applies to most of her stories, a few, with skillful innovations, cannot be judged by any "old measurements."

BIOGRAPHY

Zhang Jie was born in Beijing, China, on April 27, 1937. During the War of Resistance against Japan, her father left, and her mother, a teacher, brought her up in a village in the province of Liaoning. From childhood, she showed a strong interest in music and literature, but she was encouraged to study economics in order to be of greater use to the new China. After she was graduated from the People's University of Beijing in 1960, she was assigned to one of the industrial ministries. Her novel *Heavy Wings* and the short story "Today's Agenda" definitely benefit from her acquaintance with industrial management and bureaucracy. Later, Zhang transferred to the Beijing Film Studio, where she wrote the screenplays *The Search* and *We Are Still Young*. She started to write fiction at the age of forty, which

coincided with the end of the Cultural Revolution. In 1978, her story "The Music of the Forest" won a prize as one of the best short stories of the year. In 1979, she won the Chinese national short-story award again for "Who Lives a Better Life." Meanwhile, her story "Love Must Not Be Forgotten" became widely read and controversial. With the success of her stories, Zhang became a full-time fiction writer. In 1985, she gained additional prestige by winning the Mao Dun Literary Award for *Heavy Wings* and the National Novella Award for "Emerald;" when a subsequent novel, *Wu zi*, garnered the Mao Dun Literary Award in 2005, Zhang became the first writer to receive two of these prizes.

Zhang, who actively participates in international creative activities, traveled to West Germany and the United States and was a visiting professor at Wesleyan University from 1989 to 1990. She has been a council member of the Chinese Writers' Association and the deputy chairperson of the Beijing Writers' Association.

Zhang is known as a determined woman and a political activist. She took part in many political movements and joined the Chinese Communist Party at an early age. Although she mercilessly dissects the cause of China's backwardness and attributes it to feudal ideology, as well as to the corruption of the Communist Party, she firmly defends the socialist system as that best suited to China. In spite of her support for socialism and genuine Marxism, however, she is often criticized inside China for her liberal tendencies. She proudly admits that she loves to read Western novels, particularly those of the eighteenth and nineteenth centuries. Like Dai Houying, Wang Anyi, and other contemporary Chinese writers, she believes that the humanism in classical Western literature is something that Chinese people should learn and promote. She was influenced by Western Romanticism, as well as social critical realism. She stresses love and sacrifice, conscience and responsibility in all her writings.

Zhang Jie is a pioneering feminist writer. She has one daughter and was divorced twice because she could not tolerate men who attempted to dominate women. From her bitter experience of social discrimination against women, especially those who are divorced or unmarried, Zhang attacks male supremacy and patriarchal ideology in Chinese social structure, as well as in the consciousness or subconsciousness of every man, villain or hero. She staunchly insists on a woman's right to remain single and not to be discriminated against. Like early feminist writers in the West, however, she denies a woman's sexuality in order to achieve female autonomy.

Zhang Jie is fully aware that fiction writing in China is never separated from political reality. Partly because of her age and frail health and partly because of political risk, she envisages herself as an old, tattered boat sailing in the raging sea:

> . . . I renovate my boat, patch it up and repaint it, so that it will last a little longer: I set sail again. People, houses, trees on shore become smaller and smaller and I am reluctant to leave them. But my boat cannot stay beached for ever. What use is a boat without the sea?
>
> In the distance I see waves rolling toward me. Rolling continuously. I know that one day I will be smashed to bits by those waves, but this is the fate of all boats--what other sort of end could they meet?

Analysis

Zhang Jie writes on a variety of themes and subjects, ranging from Chinese political and economic reform to an individual's daily problem (such as Professor Meng's obsession with finding a bathroom abroad), from an unmarried girl's idealistic pursuit to a divorced woman's alienation and hard struggle, and from doctors' housing problems to intellectuals' vicissitudes. Her short fiction, written in a vigorous, fresh, romantic style, can be divided into three groups: feminist stories, social stories, and fabulous animal stories.

"Love Must Not Be Forgotten"

"Ai, shi buneng wangj de" ("Love Must Not Be Forgotten") and the novellas *Zum lu* (*Emerald*) and *Fangzhou* (*The Ark*) represent the best in the first group. "Love Must Not Be Forgotten" portrays a thirty-year-old woman who wonders whether she should accept a marriage proposal. Like Ding Ling's Sofia, in her "The Diary of Miss Sophia," the protagonist finds her tall, handsome suitor to be a philistine who lacks spiritual substance and intelligence. Encouraged by the example of her mother, a

widow who has lived all of her life in platonic love with an ideal man who has married another woman out of moral responsibility, she decides to remain single rather than waste her life in a loveless marriage. Although Zhang emphasizes love above all else in the story, she has said that "it is not a love story, but one that investigates a sociological problem." In the light of Chinese society by the end of the 1970's, the story obviously protests discrimination against "old women"--that is, either women from the countryside who return there "educated" or professional women who fail to find men whom they can admire. To Zhang, love is actually the spiritual and creative pursuit of the self. By insisting on love, she strongly rejects the increasing commercialism and demoralization of Chinese society. As a feminist story, "Love Must Not Be Forgotten" explores the female tradition through the mother-daughter relationship and advocates female autonomy by setting women free from marriage-bound traditional life. Zhang is brave enough to declare in the story that "a solitary existence" may manifest a "progress in different aspects of social life such as culture, education and taste."

Zhang Jie (Sophie Bassouls/Sygma/Corbis)

Emerald further creates the image of a strong single woman. The story involves two women's sacrifices for an incompetent man named Zuowei. When Linger is in college, she falls in love with Zuowei. She nurses him when he suffers tuberculosis, helps him catch up in his studies, rescues him from a whirlpool, and serves as his scapegoat in his political crisis. When Linger is labeled a rightist and is sent to reform in a remote area, however, Zuowei abandons her and marries Beihe. Linger has an illegitimate son by Zuowei, and, in spite of humiliation and ostracism, she bravely brings him up in the role of father-mother. Although Beihe has a so-called happy marriage, her husband weighs upon her like a burden. The story begins with Beihe's scheming to make use of Linger, a brilliant mathematician, to support her husband as a newly promoted head of a computer research group; it ends with Linger's agreement to join the group, not as a sacrificial act for any man, but for the needs of society, as well as for her own self-fulfillment. As a result of being abandoned twenty-five years earlier, Linger remains active and intellectually keen, whereas Beihe is dragged down by a dull married life. In spite of Beihe's realization of the slave/master relationship between man and woman, husband and wife, there seems to be no escape for her. Through the characterization of Linger, Zhang further stresses the correlation between female self-fulfillment and liberation from marital bondage.

The Ark exposes prejudices against women at all levels of leadership, especially man-created obstacles, such as political discrimination against, and sexual harassment of, single women. The story portrays a community of spinsters and divorcées who struggle desperately for equality with men in work, human respect, and professional advancement. Not even one man appears to be free from patriarchal influence. The only hope is pinned on a little boy who lives in the community of women and shares their feelings and language.

Although Zhang wrote these three stories separately, they become particularly significant when viewed together. Through her use of an eccentric, idealistic mother who passes the message of life to her daughter, Zhang shows how an individual woman can achieve autonomy by flouting social codes. By using two boats to embody women running on opposite life tracks, Zhang breaks through the traditional jealous relationship between two women in love with one man to achieve a mutual understanding and a new female consciousness. By employing the image of the ark to represent the women's community, she demonstrates how female collective power, drawn from women's shared suffering, is needed to confront the combined patriarchal forces and transform the existing society.

"WHAT'S WRONG WITH HIM?"

"What's Wrong with Him?," "The Other World," and "Today's Agenda" are Zhang stories on social subjects. The title of the first story should have been "What's Wrong with Her?," "What's Wrong with Them?," "What's Wrong with Me?," and ultimately "What's Wrong with the Society?" Unlike her earlier stories, Zhang here discards the conventions of narrative strategies. The story contains no unifying plot, chronological order, or psychological details. What links all characters and phenomena together are the theme of madness and the space of a mental hospital. The pervasiveness of madness reminds the reader of Lu Xun's "Kuangren riji" ("The Diary of a Madman"). Unlike Lu Xun's madness, however, which is Kafkaesque paranoia caused by fear of persecution, Zhang's madness is schizophrenia, developed from repression of perversion or violence. Repressing his rage at the authority's corruption, Grandpa Ding turns to burning a tract of cotton that he has grown and becomes a Peeping Tom. Driven by insomnia and political discrimination, Doctor Hou Yufeng engages himself in a bloody fight with his roommate, a young carpenter, and finds his freedom only in becoming a madman. In order to get a decent room for receiving his foreign friends, a doctor in an eight-square-meter cell dreams day and night of a larger room. Finally, he finds three big rooms in his imagination and goes to the leadership to offer his two imaginary rooms for those in extreme want of housing.

This world of madness is patriarchal. Though women are not Zhang's sole concern, the exposure of sexual discrimination pervades the story. She perceives that men want to marry not women but vaginal membranes and that men call any woman of independent thought "neurotic." A sexually objectified woman is passed like a ball from a former convict to a thief, to a rogue, and then to a nameless ugly man. The specter of the victim leads her mad daughter to rape the father.

To heighten the madness, Zhang adopts violent verbal expressions, weird imagination, and stylistic fragmentation. For all these features, her self-image of a "witch" is recognized by Chinese critics. Xu Wenyu actually pictures her as a witch spitting incantations and says that "there must be something wrong with her." Zhang is indeed mad; her madness lies in her unscrupulous power to snap off the evil of socialist China and penetrate into its dark consciousness.

"THE OTHER WORLD"

"The Other World" is a humorous satire reminiscent of Mark Twain's *The Prince and the Pauper* (1881), only more savage and absurd. The protagonist, Rong Changlan, is an unknown painter. When his talent is discovered by a foreigner and he is invited to go abroad, he is showered with overwhelming attention from politicians, writers, painters, reporters, and women. Because of Yi Yang, a conventional painter, Rong's authorization to go abroad is revoked, and he suddenly becomes a nobody again. Upon returning to the country, he finds countless lice and their eggs in the seams and throughout the fibers of his clothes, which obviously stand for corruption, nepotism, and hypocrisy at large in Chinese society.

When reading "The Other World," one is completely unaware of its narrator. In the absence of a narrator, irony functions as the most effective weapon. Yi Yang appears as the most ardent supporter of young artists such as Rong Changlan. Knowing that Rong cannot drink, Yi Yang offers him one drink after another until Rong gets drunk, barking at the dinner table like a dog. Consequently, Mrs. Hassen revokes her invitation to Rong because of his deceptive (Rong had told her that he does not drink) and barbarous behavior. Comrade Ke, the Communist Party authority of the International Cultural Exchange who first insisted on accompanying Rong abroad, now imposes on Mrs. Hassen a delegation of three--Ke, Ke's son, and Yi Yang.

Another melodramatic device in the story is Zhang's use of comic-strip characters. Through this device, Zhang lashes out most fiercely at conventional women. Unlike her other stories, "The Other World" contains not even one positive image of women throughout the whole farce. Women writers and reporters, in order to go abroad by marrying Rong, fight bloodily. More absurd, a woman who calls herself Yu Ping comes to the hotel to force Rong to admit that he is the father of her illegitimate child. When the woman is challenged, she suffers an epileptic seizure.

The title of the story "The Other World" is particularly significant. The city, full of corruption and absurdity, is the other world to Rong Changlan. He is fooled by this world and finds his freedom again upon his abandonment by the city. In Zhang's view, Rong Changlan is an artist with a soul. His painting *A Ruined Pagoda* reminds the reader of T. S. Eliot's vision of the wasteland. Europe, which could have been the other world of artistic inspiration for artists such as Rong Changlan, is abused as the other world that only spurs Chinese selfishness and political corruption. To some extent, the story is also a caricature of the demoralized China, following its open-door policy.

"TODAY'S AGENDA"

"Today's Agenda" is a satirical story against bureaucracy. Jia Yunshan, the bureau chief, cannot have breakfast because of the irresponsibility of the Water Bureau. When he drops dead at his routine meeting, readers learn that the day's agenda concerned the building of a new block of flats for high-ranking intellectuals and the tracing of a robbery case that took place during the Cultural Revolution. After tedious trivial arguments over Jia's funeral expense and fighting for the position left by the dead man, the new cabinet continues to dwell on the old questions. The old agenda of the *bureau* remains forever today's agenda. In this story, Zhang uses a repetitive narrative structure to echo its thematic monotony and tediousness. Although it is a good story, probing problems in the process of China's industrial reform, for a more artistic and insightful treatment of the subject one must read her novel *Heavy Wings*.

"NOBBY'S RUN OF LUCK" AND "SOMETHING ELSE"

Among Zhang Jie's fabulous tales, "Nobby's Run of Luck" and "Something Else" are the most significant. The former portrays the life of Nobby, a prodigious circus dog. Nobby not only can do arithmetic, algebra, geometry, and trigonometry but also has all the noble qualities: He remains a bachelor in order to devote all of his energy to the circus show, he is never arrogant and domineering, and he shares any extra food with his colleagues. However, when Nobby loses his mathematical brilliance as a result of constant political slandering, he is kicked around. He suffers from insomnia and eventually finds consolation in the majestic scene of the sea and the waves. The story ends with Nobby swimming into the ocean, in spite of the calling of love from Feiffer, a female dog. The reader is left to ponder whether Nobby drowns himself or commits a symbolic action to submerge into the world of nature and imagination.

"Something Else" is the story of a cat and his master, a bully. The cat is fed the heads and tails of fish eaten by the master and is beaten and kicked at the master's will. Even so, the cat thinks that he should stay with the master and be content because the neighbor is rumored to eat cats and because the grass is not always greener on the other side.

These two well-written fables are also political satires. Nobby's luck can be everybody's fate, particularly that of an intellectual in China, while the cat's philosophy reveals an enslaved psychology and a conservatism that hold back the nation from rebelling against its tyranny and catching up with the Western world.

Other major works

LONG FICTION: *Chenzhong de chibang*, 1981 (*Leaden Wings*, 1987; better known as *Heavy Wings*, 1989); *Zhi you yi ge taiyang*, 1988; *Wu zi*, 1998; *She Knocked at the Door = Qiao men de nu hai*, 2005; *Zhi zai*, 2006.

NONFICTION: *Fang mei sanji*, 1982; *Zai na lü cao di shang*, 1983; *Zongshi nanwang*, 1990.

Bibliography

Bailey, Alison. "Travelling Together: Narrative Technique in Zhang Jie's *The Ark*." In *Modern Chinese Women Writers: Critical Appraisals*, edited by Michael S. Duke. Armonk, N.Y.: M. E. Sharpe, 1989. Bailey analyzes Zhang Jie's narrative technique according to Western theories and compares her "narrated monologue" with European writers of the nineteenth century. Bailey believes that Zhang's effacement of the narrator ensures the reader's identification with, and sympathy for, the three unconventional single women in the story.

Dillard, Annie. *Encounters with Chinese Writers*. Middletown, Conn.: Wesleyan University Press, 1984. Dillard, in her chapter on Zhang Jie, vividly presents her, to Chinese and Americans, as a woman and a writer, through different images of the author. Dillard believes that Zhang always retains her trim bearing, while in China she is considered a nonconformist in dressing; Dillard also observes Zhang's conservative reactions to political issues, as well as to sexual allusions, while in China she is actually a most controversial, outspoken writer in both the matter of love and the question of political reform. The gap between the two images of Zhang points to the cultural and political distance between the United States and China.

Elder, Richard. "Chinese Lessons: *Heavy Wings*." *Los Angeles Times Book Review*, December 10, 1989, 3. A review of *Heavy Wings*. Notes that the book is a panorama of small plots, vignettes, and sketches; argues that it is propagandistic, much of it reading like a fictionalized pamphlet.

Feldman, Gayle. "Zhang Jie: A Chinese Novelist Speaks." *Publishers Weekly* 230 (August 8, 1986): 27-28. Discusses the limitations of Zhang's writing in China before 1978. Notes Zhang is a controversial figure, both for her subject matter--women's status in China--and for her use of "Western" writing techniques.

Hsu, Vivian Ling. "Contemporary Chinese Women's Lives as Reflected in Recent Literature." *Journal of the Chinese Teachers' Association* 23, no. 3 (1988): 1-47. Hsu analyzes several of Zhang Jie's stories about women. She particularly notes the two women's realization of their enslaved status in relation to the man whom they love in *Emerald*.

Kenney, Michael. "Stories from China Make Sense of the Nonsensical." *The Boston Globe*, August 9, 1991, p. 47. A review of *As Long as Nothing Happens, Nothing Will*. Argues that the value of the stories in the collection is that they reveal the nonsensical that lies behind the apparent orderliness in China. Asserts that the compression of the short-story form here is heightened by the concreteness of the Chinese language.

Louie, Kam. *Between Fact and Fiction.* Sydney, N.S.W.: Wild Peony, 1989. In chapter 5, "Love Stories: The Meaning of Love and Marriage in China, 1978-1981," Louie treats Zhang's story "Love Must Not Be Forgotten" as a social commentary against the background of China's present problems concerning love and marriage. He points out that the story aims at China's problem of "old maids" and that Zhang's shouting at the end of the story is truly significant because her heroine remains single, "in defiance of aspersions inevitably cast upon her desirability." Louie also discusses love stories by other Chinese writers published in the early 1980's. Includes an excellent bibliography.

Zhang, Jie. "My Boat." *Chinese Literature*, Summer, 1985, 51-54. Zhang Jie provides autobiographical information, as well as her views on literature in relation to life, society, and the self. She believes that it is quite tragic for Chinese writers that the Chinese cannot separate fiction from real politics, thus persecuting writers endlessly.

Zhang, Jingyuan. "Breaking Open: Chinese Women's Writing in the Late 1980's and 1990's." In *Chinese Literature in the Second Half of a Modern Century: A Critical Survey*, edited by Pang-yuan Chi and David Der-wei Wang. Bloomington: Indiana University Press, 2000. Includes information about Zhang, placing her within the broader context of Chinese women writers.

Qingyun Wu

MIKHAIL ZOSHCHENKO

Born: Poltava, Russia; August 10, 1895

Died: Leningrad, Soviet Union (now St. Petersburg, Russia); July 22, 1958

PRINCIPAL SHORT FICTION

Rasskazy Nazara Ilicha, gospodina Sinebryukhova, 1922

Uvazhaemye grazhdane, 1926

Nervnye lyudi, 1927

O chem pel solovei: Sentimentalnye povesti, 1927

Siren' tsvetet, 1929

Lichnaya zhizn', 1933

Golubaya kniga, 1935

Russia Laughs, 1935

The Woman Who Could Not Read, and Other Tales, 1940

The Wonderful Dog, and Other Tales, 1942

Scenes from the Bathhouse, and Other Stories of Communist Russia, 1961

Nervous People, and Other Satires, 1963

A Man Is Not a Flea: Stories, 1989

The Galosh: And Other Stories, 2000

OTHER LITERARY FORMS

Although the fame of Mikhail Zoshchenko (mee-kah-EEL ZAWSH-chin-kuh) rests almost entirely on his short stories, he produced a few works in other genres that are often discussed as important facets of his opus, most notably longer stories (*povesti*), which are almost invariably treated as short novels outside Russia. Two of these, *Vozrashchennaya molodost'* (1933; *Youth Restored,* 1935) and *Pered voskhodom solntsa* (1943, 1972; *Before Sunrise,* 1974), show a different Zoshchenko from that seen in his short stories--an author who is attempting to rise above the everyday reality of his stories. The first of these novels is a variation on an age-old theme--a desire to regain lost youth, with a humorous twist in that the old professor renounces his restored youth after failing to keep up with his young wife. In *Before Sunrise,* Zoshchenko probed deeper into his own psyche, trying to discover his origins, going back even to the prenatal time. In order to achieve this, he employed the psychoanalytical methods of Sigmund Freud and Ivan Petrovich Pavlov, which were and still are a novelty in Russian literature. His other longer stories (a few occasional pieces written at the behest of Soviet authorities in order to conform to the political trends of the time) and playwriting attempts do not enhance his stature; on the contrary, they detract from his reputation so much that they are generally ignored by critics and readers alike.

ACHIEVEMENTS

Mikhail Zoshchenko was fortunate to enter literature in the 1920's, when Russian writers were relatively free to choose their subject matter and to express themselves. His kind of writing--humorous stories and satire--seems to have been possible only in that decade. One of Zoshchenko's most significant achievements is making his brand of humor and satire unmistakably his, not an easy task in a nation known for its exquisite sense of humor. With an ear to the ground, he demonstrated an infallible understanding of human habits and foibles. He was able to see humor in almost every situation, although his humor is often suffused with sadness deriving from the realization that life is not as funny as it often seems. He frequently spoke for the Soviet people when they were not permitted to speak freely, yet he did it in such a way that it was very difficult to pin on him a political bias or hidden intentions until very late in his career. Just as important was his ability to reproduce the language of his characters, a curious concoction of the language of the lower classes and the bureaucratese of political parvenus trying to sound politically sophisticated or conformist. As a consequence, his several hundred short stories serve as a gold mine for the multifaceted study of the Soviet people in the first decades after the revolution. In this respect, Zoshchenko's writings resemble those of Damon Runyon, Edward Lear, and perhaps Art Buchwald. That he was able to achieve all this without sinking to the level of a social or political commentator of the period reveals his artistic acumen, which has not been equaled before or after him.

BIOGRAPHY

Mikhail Mikhailovich Zoshchenko was born on August 10, 1895, in Poltava, Russia, to a lower-gentry, landowning family. His father was a painter of Ukrainian origin, and his mother was a Russian actress. Zoshchenko was graduated in 1913 from a high school in St. Petersburg, the city where he spent most of his life;

one of the worst grades he received was in Russian composition. Later, he studied law at the University of Petersburg. World War I interrupted his studies, and he volunteered for service in the czarist army, became an officer, and was injured and gassed in 1916. In 1917, he volunteered again, this time for the Red Army, although his military duties were limited because of his former injuries. After the revolution, Zoshchenko settled in St. Petersburg (later Leningrad), trying several professions and not settling on any of them until he decided to be a freelance writer. For short periods of time he was a railroad ticket agent, a border-guard telephone operator, an instructor in rabbit and poultry raising, a militiaman, a census taker, a detective, a carpenter, a shoemaker, a clerk-typist, and a professional gambler, among other professions. This plethora of jobs served Zoshchenko later as a source of material for his stories; it also explains the authenticity of his fiction, as well as his deep understanding of human nature. In 1921, he joined the famous literary group of writers calling themselves the Serapion Brothers, who gathered periodically to discuss their own works. His affiliation with this group would have far-reaching effects on him, lasting long after the group had ceased to exist. Being apolitical and having as its main goal the purely artistic improvement of its members, the society contributed significantly to the development of Russian literature at that time; it also left a stigma on its members, however, that would especially haunt Zoshchenko two decades later.

Zoshchenko wrote his first story in 1907 but did not publish anything until 1921. His first book, a collection of short stories, was published in 1922. He immediately became one of the most popular Soviet writers, publishing several additional collections and hundreds of stories. He continued as a freelance writer in the 1930's, his output unabated and his reputation high. However, the new political and cultural climate, manifested especially in the demand on writers to follow the dictates of Socialist Realism, forced him to alter his style. His fiction from that time consequently suffered in quality. He tried his pen in new genres, such as psychological and documentary fiction, with varying success. During World War II, he was active during the siege of Leningrad and was decorated for his performance. Later, he was evacuated to Alma-Ata, where he spent the rest of the war, mainly writing *Before Sunrise*. In 1946, the enmity between Zoshchenko and the Soviet regime, which had been simmering below the surface throughout his writing career, burst into the open when the party cultural czar, Andrei Zhdanov, viciously attacked him, together with the poet Anna Akhmatova, for their "antisocial" and "dangerous" writings. The attack meant removal from the literary scene--a punishment from which Zoshchenko never fully recovered. He disappeared until Joseph Stalin's death in 1953, and even then he was able to publish only a few anemic stories, from which the old spark and power were gone. He died in Leningrad on July 22, 1958. Since then, his reputation has been restored, and his stories are republished regularly. His works, though somewhat dated, are still held in high esteem, especially among literary critics.

ANALYSIS

A typical Mikhail Zoshchenko story is a four- to six-page sketch about a seemingly unimportant event in the lives of ordinary Soviet citizens. Most of his stories take place in Leningrad, and most of his characters come from the lower-middle class--managers, clerks, workers, artists--and the intelligentsia of both sexes, although peasants often appear as well. The episodes usually involve an exaggerated conflict in which the characters reveal their thoughts and attitudes about everyday reality. This dramatic conflict is presented in humorous tones that endear the characters to readers; its resolution makes readers chuckle, sometimes laugh aloud, but it seldom leaves them bitter, angry, or demanding decisive action.

This outward innocence, however, quickly dissipates after a closer look at the characters and their vexing problems. Readers realize that the author does not always mean what he says and does not say what he means, and that much more lurks beneath the surface. In the story "Spi skorei" ("Get on with the Sleeping"), for example, a traveler has difficulties finding a suitable room in which to sleep, and when he does, his problems begin to unfold: A window is broken and a cat jumps in because it mistakes the room for a rubbish dump, a pool of water lies in the middle of the floor,

there is no light ("you're not thinking of painting pictures in it?" he is asked both innocently and sarcastically by the innkeeper), the traveler has to use a table-cloth for a blanket and slides down the bed as if it were an iceberg, and, finally, the room is infested with bedbugs and fleas. At the end of the story, a woman's passport is returned to him by mistake. This comedy of errors, neglect, and incompetence is mitigated by the traveler's last words that the passport's owner "proved to be a nice woman, and we got to know each other rather well. So that my stay at the hotel had some pleasant consequences after all."

THE HUMORIST

The inconveniences portrayed in Zoshchenko's tale are not tragic but rather amusing, and the author's habit of soothing conclusions--whatever their motives--tends to smooth over the rough edges. In "Melkii sluchai iz lichnoi zhizni" ("A Personal Episode"), the protagonist, after realizing that women no longer notice him, tries everything to become attractive again, only to discover that he has grown old. It is all lies and Western nonsense, anyway, he consoles himself. "Semeinyi kuporos" ("The Marriage Bond") shows a young wife who leaves her husband following a fight; after failing to find a suitable place to live, she returns to him. The author again moralizes, "There is no doubt, though, that this question of living accommodation strengthens and stabilizes our family life. . . . The marriage bond is rather strong nowadays. In fact very strong."

The husband in the story "Rasskaz o tom, kak zhena ne razreshila muzhu umeret'" ("Hen-Pecked") falls ill and is about to die, but his wife will not let him die, as they have no money for a funeral. He goes out and begs for money and, after several outings, regains his health. "Perhaps, as he went outside the first time, he got so heated from excitement and exertion, that all his disease came out through perspiration." In another story, "Bogataia zhizn'" ("The Lucky Draw"), a married couple win a huge sum in a lottery but become very unhappy because they have nothing to do afterward. In "Administrativnyi vostorg" ("Power-Drunk"), an assistant chief of the local police is so overzealous in his off-duty efforts to punish a poor woman who allowed her pig to roam the streets that he arrests his own wife because she interceded for the woman.

In story after story Zoshchenko makes seemingly insignificant events so important to his characters that they find in them the moving force of their lives. The reader, however--usually a person who has been exposed to such chicanery at one time or another--cannot help but understand that there is something basically wrong with one's life when such trivial events, against which one feels so helpless, are often repeated in various forms, that such occurrences are not really trifles, and that the primary aim of Zoshchenko's satire is not only to amuse or to exercise social criticism but also to point, rather subtly, at the philosophical meaning of existence.

SOCIAL SATIRIST

Zoshchenko's reputation primarily as a social satirist is still perpetuated by both the connoisseurs of his stories and the Soviet authorities who condemn him, the former saying that Zoshchenko's criticism of the Soviet reality is justified and the latter that it is too harsh and ideologically motivated, even if sugarcoated with humor. There is no doubt that such an interpretation of his approach to reality is possible. Bureaucrats in particular are singled out for scorn. In "Koshka i liudi" ("The Stove"), a committee in charge of maintenance for an apartment building refuses to repair a fuming stove, pretending that nothing is wrong, even though one of them falls unconscious from the fumes. In "Bania" ("The Bathhouse"), checks for clothing are issued after the clothes are taken away, wrong clothes are returned, and there are not enough buckets. In the story "Butylka" ("Bottle"), a bottle lies broken on the street and nobody picks it up. When a janitor sweeps it aside, he is told by the militiaman to remove it altogether. "And, you know," the author chimes in, "the most remarkable thing is the fact that the militiaman ordered the glass to be swept up."

In perhaps Zoshchenko's harshest criticism of bureaucracy, "Kamennoe serdtse" ("A Heart of Stone"), a director demands of his business manager a truck for his personal needs. When the manager tells him that no truck is available, the director threatens to fire him, but the manager retorts, "Now, if you were a product of the old order, an attitude like that toward your subordinate would be understandable, but you are a man of the proletarian batch, and where you got a general's tone like

that I simply can't understand." Nevertheless, the director succeeds in getting rid of the stubborn manager. The not-so-subtle implication here is that the revolution has changed little and that vulgarity (*poshlost'*) is as strong as ever. In all such stories, the bureaucrats, who seem to run the country, are satirized for their unjustified domination and mistreatment of their fellow citizens.

Seen through such a prism, Zoshchenko's attitude toward social problems in his country two decades after the revolution can be seen as direct criticism. In fact, Zhdanov used exactly such an interpretation to attack Zoshchenko in 1946 for his alleged anti-Soviet writings. Singling out one of the stories written for children, "Prikliucheniia obeziany" ("The Adventures of a Monkey"), Zhdanov excoriated the author for writing that a monkey, after escaping from a zoo in Leningrad during the war and experiencing many troubles with human beings, decides to return to the zoo because it is easier for him to live there. The question of whether Zoshchenko wrote this story simply to amuse children or as an allegory of the inhumane (or perhaps too human) conditions in the Soviet society remains unanswered. It is quite possible that the author meant to say the latter. However, he refused to admit political ulterior motives or an ideological slant in his writings:

> Tell me, how can I have 'a precise ideology' when not a single party among them all appeals to me? . . . I don't hate anybody--there is *my* precise ideology. . . . In their general swing the Bolsheviks are closer to me than anybody else. And so I'm willing to bolshevik around with them. . . . But I am not a Communist (or rather not a Marxist), and I think I never shall be.

If one is to believe his words, one must assume that the political or ideological criticism was not foremost on his mind. As for social criticism, he saw no crime in it; on the contrary, he believed that it was his duty to try to remedy ills and shortcomings by poking fun at them, as all satirists have done throughout history.

IMMORALITY

It is more likely that Zoshchenko was primarily interested in criticizing the morals of his compatriots, and in this respect he is no better or worse than any other moralist. He himself said that for the most part he wrote about the petty bourgeoisie, despite the official claims that it no longer exists as a separate class: "For the most part I create a synthetic type. In all of us there are certain traits of the petty bourgeois, the property owner, the money grubber. I write about the petty bourgeoisie, and I suppose I have enough material to last me the rest of my life." When some of the stories containing such criticism are examined, it is hard to disagree with Zoshchenko and even harder to see them as simply political criticism of the new regime. It is the moral behavior of his characters rather than what the government tells them to do that fascinated Zoshchenko.

As a natural satirist, he was attracted mostly to the negative traits in human nature. Foremost among these traits is marital morality or, rather, the lack thereof. Infidelity seems to be rampant among Zoshchenko's marriage partners and, what is even more interesting, they have few qualms about it. In one example of a marital merry-go-around, "Zabavnoe prikliuchenie" ("An Amusing Adventure"), three couples are intertwined through their infidelity, somewhat incredibly, to be sure, but in a way symptomatic of the loosening of moral fiber within Soviet society. Dishonesty and cheating also seem to be rampant. In "Ne nado spekulirovat" ("The Greedy Milkwoman"), a young milkmaid, eager to pocket a large reward, recommends her husband to a widow seeking a new husband, mistakenly believing that after the marriage ceremony things will return to normal. The husband, however, likes the new arrangement and refuses to return to his lawful wife. Hypocrisy is revealed by workers who praise a deceased fellow worker even though they had not said a kind word about him when he was alive in "Posledniaia nepriiatnost" ("A Final Unpleasantness"). Bribery is still abundant despite the official disclaimers, and thievery seems to be as common as winter snow. In two stories, "Telefon" ("The Telephone") and "Dobrorozhelatel," the occupants of an apartment building are called away on urgent business only to find upon their return that their apartments have been robbed and ransacked. In "Akter" ("The Actor"), a reluctant actor is robbed right on the stage by fellow performers who pretend that their crime is part of the play.

Zoshchenko hints at an explanation for such behavior in the persistent discrepancy between the ideal and the real, between official facade and reality, and between appearance and substance. Another explanation can be found in the perpetual clash between an individual and the collective. In a charming one-page sketch, "Karusel'" ("The Merry-Go-Round"), the author destroys the myth that everything can be free in a society by having a young fellow ride a wooden horse, simply because it is free, until he almost dies.

Another likely explanation can be found when untenable living conditions require several people to share not an apartment but a single room: Those who live in the room are packed like sardines; all the tenants rush to the scene whenever even the smallest incident happens, and the room's occupants have completely lost any sense of privacy. How, it is implied, can a man preserve his own dignity and respect for others when he is given a bathroom for an apartment, in which his wife, a small child, and a mother-in-law struggle to live while thirty-two other tenants use the same bathroom ("Krizis"; "The Crisis"); or when the tenants collectively pay the electricity bill until they almost come to blows because some use more and some use less electricity ("Letniaia peredyshka"; "Electricity in Common")? Similarly humiliating struggles are presented in "Istoriia bolezni" ("History of an Illness"), in which a man prefers to be ill at home rather than in a hospital because there he is thrust in the same bathtub with an old, deranged woman and contracts whooping cough while eating from the same plate that the sick children next door have used. Regardless of whether the Soviet citizens will ever learn to adjust to this omnipresent communal life, they are paying a terrible price in over-wrought nerves and general misanthropy.

Perhaps the best explanation for the immorality portrayed in Zoshchenko's stories, however, is simply the imperfection of human nature. Many of Zoshchenko's characters display the same weaknesses found in all ages and societies, which a political system can only exacerbate. His characters are egotistical and selfish to the core, as in the story "Liubov'" ("Love"), in which a young man declares his undying love for a girl on a night stroll, but when they are attacked by a robber he protests when the girl is not robbed at all.

Zoshchenko's characters are also often insensitive toward one another: A man on a train mistreats his woman companion; when people protest, he is surprised, saying that it is only his mother. Other characters are greedy, taking advantage of others; an innocent man is arrested by the secret police, and his relatives sell all of his possessions, even his apartment allotment; he returns, however, in a few hours. In another story, "Vodianaia feeriia" ("A Water Ballet"), when a man comes to a city, all of his acquaintances pay him a visit mainly to take a bath in his hotel. The characters are jealous (an illiterate woman finally agrees to learn how to read only after she stumbled upon a fragrant letter her husband had received from a teacher urging him to arrange for his wife's reading classes), and they are vain (a woman defends her moonshining husband before the judge but balks when the husband reveals that she is older than he). All these traits demonstrate that Zoshchenko's characters are normal human beings sharing weaknesses and problems with people everywhere.

One can read into these traits the corroding impact of a repressive governmental system. Most likely, however, these characters would behave the same way regardless of the system under which they lived, nor does Zoshchenko believe them to be beyond salvation. In one of his best stories, "Ognibol'shogo goroda" ("Big-City-Lights"), a peasant father visits his son in Leningrad with the intention of staying there permanently. When everyone makes fun of his peasant ways, however, the old man becomes irritated and starts to cause problems for everyone, until one day he is treated with deep respect by a militiaman. This causes the old man to change his ways, and he returns happily to his village. In the words of an intellectual in the story, "I've always been of the opinion that respect for individuals, praise and esteem, produce exceptional results. Many personalities unfold because of this, just like roses at daybreak." Whether Zoshchenko is revealing his naïveté here or is adding a didactic touch to mollify the ever-present censors is immaterial; in these few words he diagnoses one of the gravest ills of any totalitarian society.

THE ABSURD AND GROTESQUE

There is another strain in Zoshchenko's storytelling that, again, sets him apart from other humorists and satirists: his penchant for the absurd and grotesque. Many of his characters and situations lead to a conclusion that in essence life is absurd more often than one thinks. As a result, some of his stories are paragons of an absurd set of circumstances that no one can fathom or untangle. In "Ruka blishnego" ("My Brother's Hand"), for example, a nice person, wishing to shake hands with all people, finds out belatedly that one person who was extremely reluctant to shake hands is a leper. The best story depicting this absurdity shows a shipwrecked man during the war unknowingly holding on to a floating mine, happy about his salvation and making plans about his future ("Rogul'ka"; "The Buoy"). The pessimism and pervasive sadness of Zoshchenko's fiction break through in stories such as these despite the humor, proving the old adage that often there is only one step between laughter and tears.

There are other facets of Zoshchenko's short-story repertoire that are less significant, including stories that are simply humorous without any pretense or deeper meaning, parodies of other famous literary pieces, and stories showing the Russians' veneration of everything foreign. They contribute to a multicolored mosaic of a life rich in human idiosyncrasies, in emotions and weaknesses, in lessons for those who need or seek them, which offers plain enjoyment to connoisseurs of good literature. In this respect, Zoshchenko made a significant contribution to the wealth of both Russian and world literature, ranking among those first-rate humorists and satirists--Nikolai Gogol, Nikolay Leskov, and Anton Chekhov--who influenced him.

OTHER MAJOR WORKS
LONG FICTION: *Vozvrashchennaya molodost'*, 1933 (*Youth Restored*, 1935); *Pered voskhodom solntsa*, 1943, 1972 (*Before Sunrise*, 1974).

BIBLIOGRAPHY
Carleton, Gregory. *The Politics of Reception: Critical Constructions of Mikhail Zoshchenko.* Evanston, Ill.: Northwestern University Press, 1998. An in-depth look at Zoshchenko's work.

Domar, Rebecca A. "The Tragedy of a Soviet Satirist: Or, The Case of Zoshchenko." In *Through the Glass of Soviet Literature*, edited by E. J. Simmons. New York: Columbia University Press, 1953. Domar begins her essay by discussing Zoshchenko's excommunication from literary life by the Soviet government in 1946, then proceeds with an analysis of his stories and other works. Her conclusion is that conflict with the authorities was inevitable given the nature of Zoshchenko's satire, and that satire cannot survive in a totalitarian atmosphere, such as that of the Soviet Union. Domar considers the breaking of Zoshchenko's spirit a heavy loss for Russian literature.

Hicks, Jeremy. *Mikhail Zoshchenko and the Poetics of "Skaz."* Nottingham, England: Astra, 2000. *Skaz* is a type of Russian literature in which the written narrative seeks to imitate a spontaneous oral account through its use of slang, dialect, and the idiom of the character who is telling the story. Hicks defines the term and devotes chapters 4 through 6 to an examination of Zoshchenko's use of *skaz* in some of his short stories, including "A Bathhouse" and "A Classy Lady."

Kaminer, Jenny. "Theatrical Motifs and the Drama of Everyday Life in the 1920's Stories of Mikhail Zoshchenko." *Russian Review* 65, no. 3 (July, 2006): 470-490. An analysis of Zoschenko's use of theatrical elements in his depiction of everyday life. Discusses his opinion of the "performance" of daily life in the Soviet Union in the 1920's. Examines the boundaries between the public and the private in his stories.

Livers, Keith A. "Mikhail Zoshchenko: Engineering the Stalinist Body and Soul." In *Constructing the Stalinist Body: Fictional Representations of Corporeality in the Stalinist 1930's*. Lanham, Md.: Lexington Books, 2004. Analyzes Zoshchenko's stories and other works to describe his use of corporeal imagery as a means of both promoting and resisting the concepts of a Soviet utopia and an ideologically pure Soviet body politic.

McLean, Hugh. Introduction to *Nervous People, and Other Satires*. New York: Random House, 1965. McLean attributes Zoshchenko's popularity with Soviet readers to his making their hard life easier to bear through laughter. Life had not changed at all in Soviet society, and Zoshchenko capitalized on that in his stories.

Mihailovich, Vasa D. "Zoshchenko's 'Adventures of a Monkey' as an Allegory." *Satire Newsletter* 4, no. 2 (1967): 84-89. Mihailovich's contention is that this seemingly innocuous story published in 1946 is anything but that. This story is basically anti-Soviet, and the authorities' alarm about it was justified, from their point of view, leading directly to Zoshchenko's ostracism and the end of his career.

Milne, Lesley. *Zoshchenko and the Ilf-Petrov Partnership: How They Laughed.* Birmingham, England: Centre for Russian, University of Birmingham, 2003. Analyzes the comic and satiric works of Zoshchenko and his contemporaries Ilya Ilf and Evgeny Petrov.

Monas, Sidney. Introduction to *Scenes from the Bathhouse, and Other Stories of Communist Russia*. Ann Arbor: University of Michigan Press, 1961. An informative introduction to the stories. Monas makes some interesting remarks about Zoshchenko, including comments about his lack of development as a writer.

Scatton, Linda H. *Mikhail Zoshchenko: Evolution of a Writer*. Cambridge, England: Cambridge University Press, 1993. Examines Zoshchenko's life and career.

Titunik, Irwin R. "Mikhail Zoshchenko and the Problem of *Skaz*." *California Slavic Studies* 6 (1971): 83-96. Titunik examines the *skaz* technique as individualized speech and describes how Zoshchenko practiced it differently from other writers, leading to the conclusion that there are no safe assumptions about *skaz* and that it will continue to be evaluated by critics.

Von Wiren-Garczynski, Vera. "Zoshchenko's Psychological Interests." *Slavic and East European Journal* 11 (1967): 3-22. Zoshchenko's interest in psychological problems was brought on by his own neurasthenia and by his desire to understand the domain of the subconscious. Von Wiren traces the results of his exploration in *Youth Restored, Before Sunrise*, and some of the short stories. She believes that

Zoshchenko would have developed into a much deeper writer had his career not been cut short.

Zholkovskii, A. K. "'What Is the Author Trying to Say with His Artistic Work?' Rereading Zoshchenko's Oeuvre." *Slavic and East European Journal* 40 (Fall, 1996): 458-474. Examines the thematic unity of Zoshchenko's serious and comical texts, discussing the central theme of fear. Argues that Zoshchenko's anxieties focus on the violation of the social being's personal boundaries.

_____. "Zoshchenko's 'Electrician': Or, The Complex Theatrical Mechanism." In *The Russian Twentieth-Century Short Story: A Critical Companion*, edited by Lyudmila Parts. Brighton, Mass.: Academic Studies Press, 2010. Provides a critical reading of this story.

Vasa D. Mihailovich

RESOURCES

TERMS AND TECHNIQUES

Aestheticism: The European literary movement denied that art needed to have any utilitarian purpose and focused on the slogan "art for art's sake." The movement was predominant in the 1890's and had its roots in France. The doctrines of aestheticism were introduced to England by Walter Pater and can be found in the plays of Oscar Wilde and the short stories of Arthur Symons. In American literature, the ideas underlying the aesthetic movement can be found in the short fiction of Edgar Allan Poe.

Allegory: A literary mode in which characters in a narrative personify abstract ideas or qualities and provide a second level of meaning to the work. Two famous examples of allegory are Edmund Spenser's *The Faerie Queene* (1590, 1596) and John Bunyan's *The Pilgrim's Progress from This World to That Which Is to Come*, Part I (1678). Modern examples may be found in Nathaniel Hawthorne's story "The Artist of the Beautiful" and the stories and novels of Franz Kafka.

Allusion: A reference to a person or event, either historical or from a literary work, which gives another literary work a wider frame of reference and adds depth to its meaning. For example, Sylvia Townsend Warner's story "Winter in the Air" gains greater suggestiveness from the frequent allusions to William Shakespeare's play *The Winter's Tale* (pr. c. 1610-1611, pb. 1623), and her story "Swans on an Autumn River" is enriched by a number of allusions to the poetry of William Butler Yeats.

Ambiguity: Refers to the capacity of language to suggest two or more levels of meaning within a single expression, thus conveying a rich, concentrated effect. Ambiguity has been defined by William Empson in *Seven Types of Ambiguity* (1930) as "any verbal nuance, however, slight, which gives room for alternative reactions to the same piece of language." It has been suggested that because of the short story's highly compressed form, ambiguity may play a more important role in this genre than it does in the novel.

Anachronism: An event, person, or thing placed outside--usually earlier than--its proper historical era. William Shakespeare uses anachronism in *King John* (pr. c. 1596-1597, pb. 1623), *Antony and Cleopatra* (pr. c. 1606-1607, pb. 1723), and *Julius Caesar* (pr. c. 1599-1600, pb. 1623). Mark Twain employed anachronism to comic effect in *A Connecticut Yankee in King Arthur's Court* (1889).

Anecdote: The short narration of a single interesting incident or event. An anecdote differs from a short story in that it does not have a plot, relates a single episode, and does not range over different times and places.

Antagonist: A character in fiction who stands in opposition, or rivalry, to the protagonist. In William Shakespeare's *Hamlet, Prince of Denmark* (pr. c. 1600-1601, pb. 1603), for example, King Claudius is the antagonist of Hamlet.

Anthology: A collection of prose or poetry, usually by various writers. Often serves to introduce the work of little-known authors to a wider audience.

Aphorism: A short, concise statement that states an opinion, precept, or general truth, such as Alexander Pope's "Hope springs eternal in the human breast."

Aporia: An interpretative point in a story that basically cannot be decided, usually as the result of some gap or absence.

Apostrophe: A direct address to a person (usually absent), inanimate entity, or abstract quality. Examples are the first line of William Wordsworth's sonnet "London, 1802," "Milton! Thou should'st be living at this hour," and King Lear's speech in William Shakespeare's *King Lear* (pr. c. 1605-1606, pb. 1698), "Blow, winds, and crack your cheeks! rage! blow!"

Appropriation: The act of taking over part of a literary theory or approach for one's own ends, for example, male critics using the feminist approach.

Archetypal theme: Recurring thematic patterns in literature. Common archetypal themes include death and rebirth (Samuel Taylor Coleridge's *The Rime of the Ancient Mariner*, 1798), paradise-Hades (Coleridge's "Kubla Khan," 1816), the fatal woman (Guy de Maupassant's "Doubtful Happiness"), the earth goddess ("Yanda" by Isaac Bashevis Singer), the scapegoat (D. H. Lawrence's "The Woman Who Rode Away," 1925), and the return to the womb (Flannery O'Connor's "The River," 1953).

Archetype: This term was used by psychologist Carl Jung to describe what he called "primordial images," which exist in the "collective unconscious" of humankind and are manifested in myths, religion, literature, and dreams. Now used broadly in literary criticism to refer to character types, motifs, images, symbols, and plot patterns recurring in many different literary forms and works.

Architectonics: A term borrowed from architecture to describe the structural qualities, such as unity and balance, of a work of literature. If the architectonics are successful, the work will give the impression of organic unity and balance, like a solidly constructed building in which the total value is more than the sum of the parts.

Asides: In drama, short passages generally spoken by one dramatic character in an undertone or directed to the audience, so as not to be heard by other characters on stage.

Atmosphere: The mood or tone of a work; it is often associated with setting but can also be established by action or dialogue. The opening paragraphs of Edgar Allan Poe's "The Fall of the House of Usher" (1839) and James Joyce's "Araby" (1914) provide good examples of atmosphere created early in the works and which pervade the remainder of the story.

Ballad: Popular ballads are songs or verse that tell dramatic, usually impersonal, tales. Supernatural events, courage, and love are frequent themes, but any experience that appeals to ordinary people is acceptable material. Literary ballads--narrative poems based on popular ballads--have frequently been in vogue in English literature, particularly during the Romantic period. One of the most famous is Samuel Taylor Coleridge's *The Rime of the Ancient Mariner*.

Black humor: A general term of modern origin that refers to a form of "sick humor" that is intended to produce laughter out of the morbid and the taboo. Examples are the works of Joseph Heller, Thomas Pynchon, Günter Grass, and Kurt Vonnegut.

Broadside ballad: A ballad printed on one side of a large, single sheet of paper and sung to a popular tune. Dating from the sixteenth century in England, the subject of the broadside ballad was a topical event or issue.

Burlesque: A work that, by imitating attitudes, styles, institutions, and people, aims to amuse. Burlesque differs from satire in that it aims to ridicule simply for the sake of amusement rather than for political or social change.

Canon: The standard or authoritative list of literary works that are widely accepted as outstanding representatives of their period and genre. In recent literary criticism, however, the established canon has come under fierce assault for its alleged culture and gender bias.

Canonize: The act of adding a literary work to the list of works that form the primary tradition of a genre or literature in general. For example, a number of stories by female and African American writers previously excluded from the canon of the short story, such as Charlotte Perkins Gilman's "The Yellow Wallpaper" (1892) and Charles Waddell Chesnutt's "The Sheriff's Children (1899)," have recently been canonized.

Caricature: A form of writing that focuses on unique qualities of a person and then exaggerates and distorts those qualities in order to ridicule the person and what he or she represents. Contemporary writers, such as Flannery O'Connor, have used caricature for serious and satiric purposes in such stories as "Good Country People" (1955) and "A Good Man Is Hard to Find" (1955).

Character type: The term can refer to the convention of using stock characters, such as the *miles gloriosus* (braggart soldier) of Renaissance and Roman comedy, the figure of vice in medieval morality plays, or the clever servant in Elizabethan comedy. It can also describe "flat" characters (the term was coined by E. M. Forster) in fiction who do not grow or change during the course of the narrative and who can be easily classified.

Chronicle: The precursors of modern histories, chronicles were written accounts of national or world events. One of the best known is the *Anglo-Saxon Chronicle*, begun in the reign of King Alfred in the late ninth century. Many chronicles were written in Elizabethan times, and these were used by William Shakespeare as source documents for his history plays.

Classic/Classicism: A literary stance or value system consciously based on the example of classical Greek and Roman literature. While the term is applied to an enormous diversity of artists it generally denotes a cluster of values, including formal discipline, restrained expression, reverence of tradition, and an objective rather than subjective orientation. Often contrasted to Romanticism.

Climax: Similar to crisis, the moment in a work of fiction at which the action reaches a turning point and the plot begins to be resolved. Unlike crisis, this term is also used to refer to the moment in which the reader's emotional involvement with the work reaches its highest point of intensity.

Comic story: Encompasses a wide variety of modes and inflections, such as parody, burlesque, satire, irony, and humor. Frequently, the defining quality of comic characters is that they lack self-awareness; the reader tends not to identify with them but perceives them from a detached point of view, more as objects than persons.

Conceit: A type of metaphor that makes highly intellectualized comparisons between seemingly disparate things. It is associated with the Metaphysical poets and the Elizabethan sonneteers; examples can also be found in the poetry of Emily Dickinson and T. S. Eliot.

Conflict: The struggle that develops between the protagonist and another person, the natural world, society, or some force within the self. In short fiction, the conflict is most often between the protagonist and the self or the human condition.

Connotation/Denotation: Denotation is the explicit, formal definition of a word, exclusive of its emotional associations. When a word takes on an additional meaning, other than its denotative one, it achieves connotation. For example, the word "mercenary" denotes a soldier who is paid to fight in an army not of his own region, but connotatively a mercenary is an unprincipled scoundrel who kills for money.

Conte: French for tale, a conte was originally a short adventure tale. In the nineteenth century, the term was used to describe a tightly constructed short story. In England, the term is used to describe a work longer than a short story and shorter than a novel.

Crisis: A turning point in the plot, at which the opposing forces reach the point that a resolution must take place.

Criticism: The study and evaluation of works of literature. Theoretical criticism, as for example in Aristotle's *Peri poētikēs* (c. 334-323 b.c.e.; *Poetics*, 1705), sets out general principles for interpretation. Practical criticism (Samuel Taylor Coleridge's lectures on William Shakespeare, for example) offers interpretations of particular works or authors.

Deconstruction: A literary theory, primarily attributed to French critic Jacques Derrida, which has spawned a wide variety of practical applications, the most prominent being the critical tactic of laying bare a text's self-reflexivity, that is, showing how it continually refers to and subverts its own way of meaning.

Defamiliarization: A term coined by the Russian Formalists to indicate a process by which the writer makes the reader perceive the concrete uniqueness of an object, event, or idea that has been generalized by routine and habit.

Dénouement: Literally, "unknotting"; the conclusion of a drama or fiction, when the plot is unraveled and the mystery solved.

Detective story: The "classic" detective story (or "mystery") is a highly formalized and logically structured mode of fiction in which the focus is on a crime solved by a detective through interpretation of evidence and clever reasoning. Many modern practitioners of the genre, however, such as Raymond Chandler, Patricia Highsmith, and Ross Macdonald, have placed less emphasis on the puzzlelike qualities of the detective story and have focused instead on characterization, theme, and other elements of mainstream fiction. The form was first developed in short fiction by Edgar Allan Poe, and has been used by Jorge Luis Borges.

Deus ex machina: A Latin term meaning "god out of the machine." In the Greek theater, it referred to the use of a god lowered out of a mechanism onto the stage to untangle the plot or save the hero. The term has come to signify any artificial device for the easy resolution of dramatic difficulties.

Device: Any technique used in literature in order to gain a specific effect. The poet uses the device of figurative language, for example, while the novelist may use the devices of foreshadowing, flashback, and so on, in order to create a desired effect.

Dialogics: The theory that many different voices are held in suspension without merging into a single authoritative voice. Developed by Russian critic Mikhail Bakhtin.

Didactic literature: Literature that seeks to instruct, give guidance, or teach a lesson. Didactic literature normally has a moral, religious, or philosophical purpose, or it will expound a branch of knowledge (as in Vergil's *Georgics*, c. 37-29 b.c.e.; English translation, 1589). It is distinguished from imaginative works, in which the aesthetic product takes precedence over any moral intent.

Diegesis: Refers to the hypothetical world of a story, as if it actually existed in real space and time. It is the illusory universe of the story created by its linguistic structure.

Doggerel: Strictly speaking, doggerel refers to rough and jerky versification, but the term is more commonly applied to worthless verse that contains monotonous rhyme and rhythm and trivial subject matter.

Doppelgänger: A double or counterpart of a person, sometimes endowed with ghostly qualities. A fictional doppelgänger often reflects a suppressed side of a character's personality, as in Fyodor Dostoevski's novella *Dvoynik* (1846; *The Double*, 1917) and the short stories of E. T. A. Hoffmann. Isaac Bashevis Singer and Jorge Luis Borges, among other modern writers, have also employed the doppelgänger with striking effect.

Dream vision: An allegorical form common in the Middle Ages, in which the narrator or a character falls asleep and dreams a dream that becomes the actual framed story. Subtle variations of the form have been used by Nathaniel Hawthorne in "Young Goodman Brown" (1835) and by Edgar Allan Poe in "The Pit and the Pendulum" (1842).

Dualism: A theory that the universe is explicable in terms of two basic, conflicting entities, such as good and evil, mind and matter, or the physical and the spiritual.

Eclogue: In Greek, the term means literally "selection." It is now used to describe a formal pastoral poem. Classical eclogues are constructed around a variety of conventional themes: the singing match, the rustic dialogue, the lament, the love lay, and the eulogy. During the Renaissance, eclogues were employed as veiled satires.

Écriture Féminine: French feminist Hélène Cixous argues for a unique female kind of writing, which in its fluidity disrupts the binary oppositions of male-dominated cultural structures.

Effect: The total, unified impression, or impact, made upon the reader by a literary work. Every aspect of the work--plot, characterization, style, and so on--is seen to directly contribute to this overall impression.

Elegy: A long, rhymed, formal poem whose subject is meditation upon death or a lamentable theme; Alfred, Lord Tennyson's *In Memoriam* (1850) is a well-known example. The pastoral elegy, such as Percy Bysshe Shelley's *Adonais: An Elegy on the Death of John Keats* (1821), uses a pastoral scene to express grief at the loss of a friend or important person.

Emotive meaning: The emotion that is commonly associated with a word. In other words, the connotations of a word, not merely what it denotes. Emotive meaning is contrasted with cognitive or descriptive meaning, in which neither emotions nor connotations are involved.

Epic: Although this term usually refers to a long narrative poem that presents the exploits of a central figure of high position, the term is also used to designate a long novel that has the style or structure usually associated with an epic. In this sense, for example, Herman Melville's *Moby Dick: Or, The Whale* (1851) and James Joyce's *Ulysses* (1922) may be called epics.

Epiphany: The literary application of this religious term was popularized by James Joyce in his book *Stephen Hero* (1944): "By an epiphany he meant a sudden spiritual manifestation, whether in the vulgarity of speech or of gesture or in a memorable phase of the mind itself." Many short stories since Joyce's collection *Dubliners* (1914) have been analyzed as epiphanic stories in which a character or the reader experiences a sudden revelation of meaning.

Episode: In Greek tragedy, the segment between two choral odes. Episode now refers to an incident presented as a continuous action. In a work of literature, many discrete episodes are woven together to form a more complex work.

Epistolary fiction: A work of fiction in which the narrative is carried forward by means of letters written by the characters. Epistolary novels were a quite popular form in the eighteenth century. Examples include Samuel Richardson's *Pamela: Or, Virtue Rewarded* (1740-1741) and *Clarissa: Or, The History of a Young Lady* (1747-1748). The form has not been much used in the twentieth century.

Essay: A brief prose work, usually on a single topic, that expresses the personal point of view of the author. The essay is usually addressed to a general audience and attempts to persuade the reader to accept the author's ideas.

Essay-sketch tradition: The first sketches can be traced to the Greek philosopher Theophrastus in 300 *b.c.e.*, whose character sketches influenced seventeenth and eighteenth century writers in England, who developed the form into something close to the idea of character in fiction. The essay has an equally venerable history, and, like the sketch, had an impact on the development of the modern short story.

Euphony: Language that creates a harmonious and pleasing effect; the opposite of cacophony, which is a combination of harsh and discordant sounds.

Exemplum: A brief anecdote or tale introduced to illustrate a moral point in medieval sermons. By the fourteenth century these exempla had expanded into exemplary narratives. Geoffrey Chaucer's "The Nun's Priest's Tale" and "The Pardoner's Tale" from *The Canterbury Tales* (1387-1400) are exempla.

Existentialism: A philosophy and attitude of mind that gained wide currency in religious and artistic thought after the end of World War II. Typical concerns of existential writers are human beings' estrangement from society, their awareness that the world is meaningless, and their recognition that one must turn from external props to the self. The novels of Albert Camus and Franz Kafka provide examples of existentialist beliefs.

Exposition: The part or parts of a work of fiction that provide necessary background information. Exposition not only provides the time and place of the action but also introduces readers to the fictive world of the story, acquainting them with the ground rules of the work. In the short story, exposition is usually elliptical.

Expressionism: Beginning in German theater at the start of the twentieth century, expressionism became the dominant movement in the decade following World War I. It abandoned realism and relied on a conscious distortion of external reality in order to portray the world as it is "viewed emotionally." The movement spread to fiction and poetry. Expressionism influenced the plays of Eugene O'Neill, Tennessee Williams, and Thornton Wilder and can be found in the novels of Franz Kafka and James Joyce.

Fable: One of the oldest narrative forms. Usually takes the form of an analogy in which animals or inanimate objects speak to illustrate a moral lesson. The most famous examples are the fables of Aesop, who used the form orally in 600 *B.C.E.*

Fabliau: A short narrative poem, popular in medieval French literature and during the English Middle Ages. Fabliaux were usually realistic in subject matter, bawdy, and made a point of satirizing the weaknesses and foibles of human beings. Perhaps the most famous are Geoffrey Chaucer's "The Miller's Tale" and "The Reeve's Tale" from *The Canterbury Tales* (1387-1400).

Fabulation: A term coined by Robert Scholes and used in contemporary literary criticism to describe novels that are radically experimental in subject matter, style, and form. Like the Magical Realists, fabulators mix realism with fantasy. The works of Thomas Pynchon, John Barth, Donald Barthelme, and William H. Gass provide examples.

Fairy tale: A form of folktale in which supernatural events or characters are prominent. Fairy tales usually depict a realm of reality beyond that of the natural world and in which the laws of the natural world are suspended.

Fantastic: In his study *Introduction à la littérature fantastique* (1970; *The Fantastic: A Structural Approach to a Literary Genre,* 1973), the critic Tzvetan Todorov defines the fantastic as a genre that lies between the uncanny and the marvelous. Whereas the marvelous presents an event that cannot be explained by the laws of the natural world and the uncanny presents an event that is the result of hallucination or illusion, the fantastic exists as long as the reader cannot decide which of these two applies. Henry James's *The Turn of the Screw* (1898) is an example of the fantastic.

Figurative language: Any use of language that departs from the usual or ordinary meaning to gain a poetic or otherwise special effect. Figurative language embodies various figures of speech, such as irony, metaphor, simile, and many others.

Fin de siècle: Literally, "end of the century"; refers to the last decade of the nineteenth century, a transitional period in which artists and writers were aware that they were living at the close of a great age and deliberately cultivated a kind of languor, world weariness, and satiety. Associated with the period of aestheticism and the Decadent movement exemplified in the works of Oscar Wilde.

Flashback: A scene that depicts an earlier event; it can be presented as a reminiscence by a character in a story, or it can simply be inserted into the narrative.

Folktale: A short prose narrative, usually handed down orally, found in all cultures of the world. The term is often used interchangeably with myth, fable, and fairy tale.

Form: The organizing principle in a work of literature; the manner in which its elements are put together in relation to its total effect. The term is sometimes used interchangeably with structure and is often contrasted with content: If form is the building, content is what is in the building and what the building is specifically designed to express.

Frame story: A story that provides a framework for another story (or stories) told within it. The form is ancient and is used by Geoffrey Chaucer in *The Canterbury Tales* (1387-1400). In modern literature, the technique has been used by Henry James in *The Turn of the Screw* (1898), Joseph Conrad in *Heart of Darkness* (1899, serial; 1902, book), and John Barth in *Lost in the Funhouse* (1968).

Framework: When used in connection with a frame story, the framework is the narrative setting, within which other stories are told. The framework may also have a plot of its own. More generally, the framework is similar to structure, referring to the general outline of a work.

Gendered: When a work is approached as thematically or stylistically specific to male or female characteristics or concerns, it is said to be "gendered."

Genre study: The concept of studying literature by classification and definition of types or kinds, such as tragedy, comedy, epic, lyrical, and pastoral. First introduced by Aristotle in *Poetics*, the genre principle has been an essential concomitant of the basic proposition that literature can be studied scientifically.

Gothic genre: A form of fiction developed in the late eighteenth century which focuses on horror and the supernatural. Examples include Matthew Gregory Lewis's *The Monk: A Romance,* (1796 also published as *Ambrosio: Or, The Monk*), Mary Wollstonecraft Shelley's *Frankenstein* (1818), and the short fiction of Edgar Allan Poe. In modern literature, the gothic genre can be found in the fiction of Truman Capote.

Grotesque: Characterized by a breakup of the everyday world by mysterious forces, the form differs from fantasy in that the reader is not sure whether to react with humor or horror. Examples include the stories of E. T. A. Hoffmann and Franz Kafka.

Gynocriticism: American feminist critic Elaine C. Showalter coined this term for her theory that women read and write differently than men do because of biological and cultural differences.

Hasidic tale: Hasidism was a Jewish mystical sect formed in the eighteenth century. The term "Hasidic tale" is used to describe some American short fiction, much of it written in the 1960's, which reflected the spirit of Hasidism, particularly the belief in the immanence of God in all things. Saul Bellow, Philip Roth, and Norman Mailer have been attracted to the genre, as has the Israeli writer Shmuel Yosef Agnon, who won the Nobel Prize in Literature in 1966.

Hegemony: Italian critic Antonio Gramsci maintains that capitalists create and sustain an ideology to support their dominance or hegemony over the working class. By maintaining economic and cultural power, capitalists receive the support of the working class, who adopt their values and beliefs, and thus control the ideology or social consciousness that in turn controls individual consciousness.

Historical criticism: In contrast to formalist criticism, which treats literary works as self-contained artifacts, historical criticism emphasizes the social and historical context of literature and allows itself to take into consideration the relevant facts and circumstances of the author's life. The method emphasizes the meaning that the work had in its own time rather than interpreting it for the present.

Hyperbole: The term is Greek for "overshooting" and refers to the use of gross exaggeration for rhetorical effect, based on the assumption that the reader will not be persuaded of the literal truth of the overstatement. Can be used for serious or comic effect.

Imagery: Often defined as the verbal stimulation of sensory perception. Although the word betrays a visual bias, imagery, in fact, calls on all five senses. In its simplest form, imagery re-creates a physical sensation in a clear, literal manner; it becomes more complex when a poet employs metaphor and other figures of speech to re-create experience.

In medias res: Latin phrase used by Horace, meaning literally "into the midst of things." It refers to a literary technique of beginning the narrative when the action has already begun. The term is used particularly in connection with the epic, which traditionally begins *in medias res*.

Initiation story: A story in which protagonists, usually children or young persons, go through an experience, sometimes painful or disconcerting, that carries them from innocence to some new form of knowledge and maturity. William Faulkner's "The Bear" (1942), Nathaniel Hawthorne's "Young Goodman Brown" (1835), Alice Walker's "To Hell with Dying" (1967), and Robert Penn Warren's "Blackberry Winter" (1946) are examples of the form.

Interior monologue: Defined as the speech of a character designed to introduce the reader directly to the character's internal life, the form differs from other monologues in that it attempts to reproduce thought before any logical organization is imposed upon it. An example is Molly Bloom's long interior monologue at the conclusion of James Joyce's *Ulysses* (1922).

Interpretation: An analysis of the meaning of a literary work. Interpretation will attempt to explicate the theme, structure, and other components of the work, often focusing on obscure or ambiguous passages.

Irrealism: A term often used to refer to modern or postmodern fiction that is presented self-consciously as a fiction or fabulation rather than a mimesis of external reality. The best-known practitioners of irrealism are John Barth, Robert Coover, and Donald Barthelme.

Lai/Lay: A song or short narrative poem. The term was first applied to twelfth and thirteenth centuries French poems and to English poems in the fourteenth century that were based on them, including Geoffrey Chaucer's "The Franklin's Tale" (1387-1400). In the nineteenth century, the term was applied to historical ballads, such as Sir Walter Scott's *The Lay of the Last Minstrel* (1805).

Legend: A narrative that is handed down from generation to generation, usually associated with a particular place and a specific event. A legend may often have more historical truth than a myth, and the protagonist is usually a person rather than a supernatural being.

Leitmotif: From the German, meaning "leading motif." Any repetition--of a word, phrase, situation, or idea--that occurs within a single work or group of related works.

Literary short story: A term that was current in American criticism in the 1940's to distinguish the short fiction of Ernest Hemingway, Eudora Welty, Sherwood Anderson, and others from the popular pulp and slick fiction of the day.

Local color: Usually refers to a movement in literature, especially in the United States, in the latter part of the nineteenth century. The focus was on the environment, atmosphere, and milieu of a particular region. For example, Mark Twain wrote about the Mississippi region; Sarah Orne Jewett wrote about New England. The term can also be used to refer to any work that represents the characteristics of a particular region.

Logocentrism: Jacques Derrida argues that all Western thought is based on the quest for a nonexistent "transcendental signifier," a sort of primal origin that makes ultimate meaning possible. The Western assumption of some ultimate center, that it calls God, reason, truth, or essence, is what Derrida calls Logocentrism.

Lyric short story: A form in which the emphasis is on internal changes, moods, and feelings. The lyric story is usually open-ended and depends on the figurative language usually associated with poetry. Examples of lyric stories are the works of Ivan Turgenev, Anton Chekhov, Katherine Mansfield, Sherwood Anderson, Conrad Aiken, and John Updike.

Lyrical ballad: The term is preeminently associated with William Wordsworth and Samuel Taylor Coleridge, whose *Lyrical Ballads* (1798), which drew on the ballad tradition, was one of the seminal books of the Romantic age. *Lyrical Ballads* was a revolt against eighteenth century poetic diction; it was an attempt to create a new kind of poetry by using simple language and taking as subject the everyday lives of common folk and the strong emotions they experience.

Malaprop/Malapropism: A malapropism occurs when one word is confused with another because the two words have a similar sound. The term is derived from the character Mrs. Malaprop in Richard Brinsley Sheridan's *The Rivals* (1775), who, for example, uses the word "illiterate" when she really means "obliterate" and mistakes "progeny" for "prodigy."

Märchen: German fairy tales, as collected in the works of Wilhelm and Jacob Grimm or in the works of nineteenth century writers, such as Novalis and E. T. A. Hoffmann.

Marginalization: The process by which an individual or a group is deemed secondary to a dominant group in power and thus denied access to the benefits enjoyed by the dominant group; for example, in the past women were marginalized by men and nonwhites were marginalized by whites.

Medieval romance: Medieval romances, which originated in twelfth century France, were tales of adventure in which a knight would embark on a perilous quest to win the hand of a lady, perform a service for his king, or seek the Holy Grail. He had to overcome many obstacles, including dragons and other monsters; magic spells and enchantments were prominent, and the romance embodied the chivalric ideals of courage, honor, refined manners, and courtly love. English romances include the anonymous *Sir Gawain and the Green Knight* (fourteenth century) and Sir Thomas Malory's *Le Morte d'Arthur* (1485).

Memoir: Usually written by a person prominent in public life, a memoir is the authors' recollections of famous people they have known and great events they have witnessed. Memoir differs from autobiography in that the emphasis in the latter is on the life of the authors.

Metafiction: Refers to fiction that manifests a reflexive tendency, such as Vladimir Nabokov's *Pale Fire* (1962), and John Fowles's *The French Lieutenant's Woman* (1969). The emphasis is on the loosening of the work's illusion of reality to expose the reality of its illusion. Such terms as "irrealism," "postmodernist fiction," and "antifiction" are also used to refer to this type of fiction.

Metaphor: A figure of speech in which two dissimilar objects are imaginatively identified (rather than merely compared) on the assumption that they share one or more qualities: "She is the rose, the glory of the day" (Edmund Spenser). The term is often used in modern criticism in a wider sense to identify analogies of all kinds in literature, painting, and film.

Metonymy: A figure of speech in which an object that is closely related to a word comes to stand for the word itself, such as when one says "the White House" when meaning the "president."

Minimalist movement: A school of fiction writing that developed in the late 1970's and early 1980's and that Roland Barthes has characterized as the "less is more school." Minimalism attempts to convey much by saying little, to render contemporary reality in precise, pared-down prose that suggests more than it directly states. Leading minimalist writers are Raymond Carver and Ann Beattie. A character in Beattie's short story "Snow" (in *Where You'll Find Me*, 1986) seems to sum up minimalism: "Any life will seem dramatic if you omit mention of most of it."

Mise en abîme: A small story inside a larger narrative that echoes or mirrors the larger narrative, thus containing the larger within the smaller.

Modern short story: The modern short story dates from the nineteenth century and is associated with the names of Edgar Allan Poe (who is often credited with inventing the form) and Nathaniel Hawthorne in the United States, Honoré de Balzac in France, and E. T. A. Hoffmann in Germany. In his influential critical writings, Poe defined the short story as being limited to "a certain unique or single effect," to which every detail in the story should contribute.

Monologue: Any speech or narrative presented by one person. It can sometimes be used to refer to any lengthy speech, in which one person monopolizes the conversation.

Moral tract: A propaganda pamphlet on a political or religious topic, usually distributed free. The term is often associated with the Oxford Movement in nineteenth century England, which was a movement to reform the Church of England.

Motif: An incident or situation in a story that serves as the basis of its structure, creating by repetition and variation a patterned recurrence and consequently a general theme. Russian Formalist critics distinguish between bound motifs, which cannot be omitted without disturbing the thematic structure of the story, and unbound motifs, which serve merely to create the illusion of external reality. In this sense, motif is the same as leitmotif.

Myth: An anonymous traditional story, often involving supernatural beings or the interaction between gods and human beings and dealing with the basic questions of how the world and human society came to be as they are. Myth is an important term in contemporary literary criticism. Northrop Frye, for example, has said that "the typical forms of myth become the conventions and genres of literature." By this, he means that the genres of comedy, romance, tragedy, and irony (satire) correspond to seasonal myths of spring, summer, autumn, and winter.

Narrative: An account in prose or verse of an event or series of events, whether real or imagined.

Narrative persona: Persona means literally "mask": It is the self created by the author and through whom the narrative is told. The persona is not to be identified with the author, even when the two may seem to resemble each other. The narrative persona in Lord Byron's *Don Juan* (1819-1824), for example, may express many sentiments of which Byron would have approved, but he is nevertheless a fictional creation who is distinct from the author.

Narratology: The theoretical study of narrative structures and ways of meaning. Most all major literary theories have a branch of study known as narratology.

Narrator: The character who recounts the narrative. There are many different types of narrators: The first-person narrator is a character in the story and can be recognized by his or her use of "I"; third-person narrators may be limited or omniscient. In the former, the narrator is confined to knowledge of the minds and emotions of one or, at most, a few characters. In the latter, the narrator knows everything, seeing into the minds of all the characters. Rarely, second-person narration may be used. (An example can be found in Edna O'Brien's *A Pagan Place*, 1973.)

Novel: A fictional prose form, longer than a short story or novelette. The term embraces a wide range of types, but the novel usually includes a more complicated plot and a wider cast of characters than the short story. The focus is often on the development of individual characterization and the presentation of a social world and a detailed environment.

Novella, novelette, Novelle, nouvelle: These terms all refer to the form of fiction that is longer than a short story and shorter than a novel. Novella, the Italian term, is the term usually used to refer to American works in this genre, such as Joseph Conrad's *Heart of Darkness* (1899, serial; 1902, book) and Henry James's *The Turn of the Screw* (1898). *Novelle* is the German term; *nouvelle* the French; "novelette" the British. The term "novel" derived from these terms.

Objective correlative: A key concept in modern formalist criticism, coined by T. S. Eliot in *The Sacred Wood* (1920). An objective correlative is a situation, an event, or an object that, when presented or described in a literary work, expresses a particular emotion and serves as a precise formula by which the same emotion can be evoked in the reader.

Oral tale: A wide-ranging term that can include everything from gossip to myths, legends, folktale, and jokes. Among the terms used by Saith Thompson to classify oral tales (*The Folktale*, 1951) are märchen, fairy tale, household tale, *conte populaire*, novella, hero tale, local tradition, migratory legend, explanatory tale, humorous anecdote, and merry tale.

Oral tradition: Material that is transmitted by word of mouth, often through chants or songs, from generation to generation. Homer's epics, for example, were originally passed down orally and employ formulas to make memorization easier. Often, ballads, folklore, and proverbs are also passed down in this way.

Oriental tale: An eighteenth century form made popular by the translations of *Alf layla wa-layla* (fifteenth century; *The Arabian Nights' Entertainments*, 1706-1708) collected during the period. Oriental tales were usually solemn in tone, contained little characterization, and focused on improbable events and supernatural places.

Other: By a process of psychological or cultural projection, an individual or a dominant group accuses those of a different race or gender of all the negative qualities they themselves possess and then respond to them as if they were "other" than themselves.

Oxymoron: Closely related to paradox, an oxymoron occurs when two words of opposite meaning are placed in juxtaposition, such as "wise fool," "devilish angel," or "loving hate."

Parable: A short, simple, and usually allegorical story that teaches a moral lesson. In the West, the most famous parables are those told in the Gospels by Jesus Christ.

Paradox: A statement that initially seems to be illogical or self-contradictory yet eventually proves to embody a complex truth. In New Criticism, the term is used to embrace any complexity of language that sustains multiple meanings and deviates from the norms of ordinary language use.

Parataxis: The placing of clauses or phrases in a series without the use of coordinating or subordinating terms.

Parody: A literary work that imitates or burlesques another work or author for the purpose of ridicule. Twentieth century parodists include E. B. White and James Thurber.

Periodical essay/sketch: Informal in tone and style and applied to a wide range of topics, the periodical essay originated in the early eighteenth century. It is associated in particular with Joseph Addison and Sir Richard Steele and their informal periodical, *The Spectator*.

Personification: A figure of speech which ascribes human qualities to abstractions or inanimate objects, as in these lines by W. H. Auden: "There's Wrath who has learnt every trick of guerrilla warfare,/ The shamming dead, the night-raid, the feinted retreat." Richard Crashaw's "Hope, thou bold taster of delight" is another example.

Plot: The sequence of events in a play or story and how those events are connected in a cause-and-effect relationship. There are a great variety of plot patterns, each of which is designed to create a particular effect.

Point of view: The perspective from which a story is presented to the reader. In simplest terms, it refers to whether narration is first person (directly addressed to the reader as if told by one involved in the narrative) or third person (usually a more objective, distanced perspective.)

Portmanteau words: The term was coined by Lewis Carroll to describe the creation of a new word by telescoping two existing words. In this way, "furious" and "fuming" can be combined to create "frumious." The works of James Joyce, as well as Carroll's *Through the Looking Glass and What Alice Found There* (1871), provide many examples of portmanteau words.

Postcolonial: A literary approach that focuses on English-language texts from countries and cultures formerly colonized or dominated by America, the British Empire, and other European countries. Postcolonialists focus on the literature of such countries as Australia, New Zealand, Africa, and South America, and such cultural groups as African Americans and Native Americans.

Postmodern: Although this term is so broad it is interpreted differently by many different critics, it basically refers to a trend by which the literary work calls attention to itself as an artifice rather than a mirror held up to external reality.

Prosody: The study of the principles of verse structure. Includes meter, rhyme, and other patterns of sound, such as alliteration, assonance, euphony and onomatopoeia, and stanzaic patterns.

Protagonist: Originally, in the Greek drama, the "first actor," who played the leading role. The term has come to signify the most important character in a drama or story. It is not unusual for a work to contain more than one protagonist.

Pun: A pun occurs when words that have similar pronunciations have entirely different meanings. The result may be a surprise recognition of an unusual or striking connection, or, more often, a humorously accidental connection.

Realism: A literary technique in which the primary convention is to render an illusion of fidelity to external reality. Realism is often identified as the primary method of the novel form; the realist movement in the late nineteenth century coincided with the full development of the novel form.

Reception theory: Theorist Hans Robert Jauss argues that since readers from any historical milieu create their own criteria for judging a text, one should examine how a text was received by readers contemporary with it. Since every period creates its own "horizon of expectation," the meaning of a text changes from one period to another.

Reminiscence: An account, written or spoken, of remembered events.

Rhetorical device: Rhetoric is the art of using words clearly and effectively, in speech or writing, in order to influence or persuade. A rhetorical device is a figure of speech, or a way of using language, employed to this end. It can include such elements as choice of words, rhythms, repetition, apostrophe, invocation, chiasmus, zeugma, antithesis, and the rhetorical question (a question to which no answer is expected).

Rogue literature: From Odysseus to William Shakespeare's Autolocus to Huckleberry Finn, the rogue is a common literary type. He is usually a robust and energetic comic or satirical figure whose roguery can be seen as a necessary undermining of the rigid complacency of conventional society. The picaresque novel (*picaro* is Spanish for "rogue"), in which the picaro lives by his wits, is perhaps the most common form of rogue literature.

Romance: Originally, any work written in Old French. In the Middle Ages, romances were about knights and their adventures. In modern times, the term has also been used to describe a type of prose fiction in which, unlike the novel, realism plays little part. Prose romances often give expression to the quest for transcendent truths. Examples of the form include Nathaniel Hawthorne's *The Scarlet Letter* (1850) and Herman Melville's *Moby Dick* (1851).

Romanticism: A movement of the late eighteenth and nineteenth centuries which exalted individualism over collectivism, revolution over conservatism, innovation over tradition, imagination over reason, and spontaneity over restraint. Romanticism regarded art as self-expression; it strove to heal the cleavage between object and subject and expressed a longing for the infinite in all things. It stressed the innate goodness of human beings and the evils of the institutions that would stultify human creativity.

Saga: Originally applied to medieval Icelandic and other Scandinavian stories of heroic exploits and handed down by oral tradition. The term has come to signify any tale of heroic achievement or great adventure.

Satire: A form of literature that employs the comedic devices of wit, irony, and exaggeration to expose, ridicule, and condemn human folly, vice, and stupidity. Justifying satire, Alexander Pope wrote that "nothing moves strongly but satire, and those who are ashamed of nothing else are so of being ridiculous."

Setting: The circumstances and environment, both temporal and spatial, of a narrative. The term also applies to the physical elements of a theatrical production, such as scenery and properties. Setting is an important element in the creation of atmosphere.

Shishōsetsu: Literally translated as "I novel," *shishōsetsu* is a Japanese genre, a form of autobiographical or confessional writing used in novels and short stories. The protagonist and writer are closely identified. The genre originated in the early part of the twentieth century; a good example is *An'ya Koro* (1921-1928; *A Dark Night's Passing*, 1958) by Shiga Naoya.

Short story: A concise work of fiction, shorter than a novella, that is usually more concerned with mood, effect, or a single event than with plot or extensive characterization.

Signifier/Signified: Linguist Ferdinand de Saussure proposed that all words are signs made up of a "signifier," which is the written mark or the spoken sound of the word, and a "signified," which is the concept for which the mark or sounds stands.

Simile: A type of metaphor in which two things are compared. It can usually be recognized by the use of the words "like," "as," "appears," or "seems": "Float like a butterfly, sting like a bee" (Muhammad Ali); "The holy time is quiet as a nun" (William Wordsworth).

Skaz: A term used in Russian criticism to describe a narrative technique that presents an oral narrative of a lowbrow speaker.

Sketch: A brief narrative form originating in the eighteenth century, derived from the artist's sketch. The focus of a sketch is on a single person, place, or incident; it lacks a developed plot, theme, or characterization.

Story line: The story line of a work of fiction differs from the plot. Story line is merely the events that happen; plot is how those events are arranged by the author to suggest a cause-and-effect relationship.

Stream of consciousness: A narrative technique used in modern fiction by which an author tries to embody the total range of consciousness of a character, without any authorial comment or explanation. Sensations, thoughts, memories, and associations pour out in an uninterrupted, prerational and prelogical flow. Examples are James Joyce's *Ulysses* (1922), Virginia Woolf's *To the Lighthouse* (1927), and William Faulkner's *The Sound and the Fury* (1929).

Structuralism: Structuralism is based on the idea of intrinsic, self-sufficient structures that do not require reference to external elements. A structure is a system of transformations that involves the interplay of laws inherent in the system itself. The structuralist literary critic attempts, by using models derived from modern linguistic theory, to define the structural principles that operate intertextually throughout the whole of literature, as well as principles that operate in genres and in individual works.

Style: Style is the manner of expression, or how the writer tells the story. The most appropriate style is that which is perfectly suited to conveying whatever idea, emotion, or other effect that the author wishes to convey. Elements of style include diction, sentence structure, imagery, rhythm, and coherence.

Subjective/Objective: Terms used in critical theory. Subjective refers to works that express the ideas and emotions, the values and judgments of the authors, such as William Wordsworth's *The Prelude* (1850). Objective works are those that appear to be free of the personal sentiments of authors, who take a detached view of the events they record.

Supplement: A term used by Jacques Derrida to refer to the unstable relationship between the two elements in a set of binary opposites. For example, in the opposition between truth and lies, although Western thought assumes that truth is superior to lies, closer study reveals that so-called lies frequently reveal profound truths.

Symbolism: A literary movement encompassing the work of a group of French writers in the latter half of the nineteenth century, a group that included Charles Baudelaire, Stéphane Mallarmé, and Paul Verlaine. According to Symbolism, a mystical correspondence exists between the natural and spiritual worlds.

Synesthesia: Synesthesia occurs when one kind of sense experience is described in terms of another. Sounds may be described in terms of colors, and so on. For example, these lines from John Keats's poem "Isabella," "O turn thee to the very tale,/ And taste the music of that vision pale," combine the senses of taste, hearing, and sight. Synesthesia was used especially by the nineteenth century French Symbolists.

Tale: A general term for a simple prose or verse narrative. In the context of the short story, a tale is a story in which the emphasis is on the course of the action rather than on the minds of the characters.

Tall tale: A humorous tale popular in the American West; the story usually makes use of realistic detail and common speech, but it tells a tale of impossible events that most often focus on a single legendary, superhuman figure, such as Paul Bunyan or David Crockett.

Technique: Refers both to the method of procedure in creating an artistic work and to the degree of expertise shown in following the procedure.

Thematics: According to Northrop Frye, when a work of fiction is written or interpreted thematically, it becomes an illustrative fable. Murray Krieger defines thematics in *The Tragic Vision* (1960) as "the study of the experiential tensions which, dramatically entangled in the literary work, become an existential reflection of that work's aesthetic complexity."

Theme: Loosely defined as what a literary work means, theme is the underlying idea, the abstract concept, that the author is trying to convey: "the search for love," "the growth of wisdom," or some such formulation. The theme of William Butler Yeats's poem "Sailing to Byzantium" (1928), for example, might be interpreted as the failure of the attempt to isolate oneself within the world of art.

Tone: Strictly defined, tone is the authors' attitude toward their subject, their persona, themselves, their audience, or their society. The tone of a work may be serious, playful, formal, informal, morose, loving, ironic, and so on; it can be thought of as the dominant mood of a work, and it plays a large part in the total effect.

Trope: Literally "turn" or "conversion"; a figure of speech in which a word or phrase is used in a way that deviates from the normal or literal sense.

Vehicle: Used with the term "tenor" to understand the two elements of a metaphor. The tenor is the subject of the metaphor, and the vehicle is the image by which the subject is presented. The terms were coined by I. A. Richards. As an example, in T. S. Eliot's line, "The whole earth is our hospital," the tenor is "whole earth" and the vehicle is the "hospital."

Verisimilitude: When used in literary criticism, verisimilitude refers to the degree to which a literary work gives the appearance of being true or real, even though the events depicted may in fact be far removed from the actual.

Vignette: A sketch, essay, or brief narrative characterized by precision, economy, and grace. The term can also be applied to brief short stories, less than five hundred words long.

Yarn: An oral tale or a written transcription of what purports to be an oral tale. The yarn is usually a broadly comic tale, the classic example of which is Mark Twain's "Jim Baker's Bluejay Yarn" (1879). The yarn achieves its comic effect by juxtaposing realistic detail and incredible events; tellers of the tale protest that they are telling the truth; listeners know differently.

Bryan Aubrey
Updated by Charles E. May

BIBLIOGRAPHY

THEORETICAL AND CRITICAL DISCUSSIONS OF
SHORT FICTION

Aycock, Wendell M., ed. *The Teller and the Tale: Aspects of the Short Story*. Lubbock: Texas Tech Press, 1982. A collection of papers presented at a scholarly conference focusing on various aspects of short fiction, including its oral roots, the use of silences in the text, and realism versus antirealism.

Bader, A. L. "The Structure of the Modern Short Story." *College English* 7 (1945): 86-92. Counters the charge that the short story lacks narrative structure by contrasting the traditional "plotted" story with the "modern story," which is more suggestive, indirect, and technically patterned.

Baker, Falcon O. "Short Stories for the Millions." *Saturday Review*, December 19, 1953, 7-9, 48-49. Argues that as a result of formalist New Criticism, the short story has begun to ignore entertainment value and the ordinary reader.

Baldeshwiler, Eileen. "The Lyric Short Story: The Sketch of a History." *Studies in Short Fiction* 6 (1969): 443-453. A brief survey of the lyrical (as opposed to the epical) story from Ivan Turgenev to John Updike. The lyric story focuses on internal changes, moods, and feelings, using a variety of structural patterns depending on the "shape of the emotion itself."

Bates, H. E. *The Modern Short Story: A Critical Survey*. Boston: The Writer, 1941, 1972. A history of the major short-story writers and their work since Edgar Allan Poe and Nikolai Gogol. More focus on English and European short-story writers than most histories.

Bayley, John. *The Short Story: Henry James to Elizabeth Bowen*. New York: St. Martin's Press, 1988. A discussion of some of what Bayley calls the "special effects" of the short-story form, particularly its relationship to poetic techniques and devices. Much of the book consists of analyses of significant stories by Henry James, Ernest Hemingway, Rudyard Kipling, Anton Chekhov, D. H. Lawrence, James Joyce, and Elizabeth Bowen.

Benjamin, Walter. "The Storyteller: Reflections on the Words of Nikolai Leskov." Reprinted in *Modern Literary Criticism: 1900-1970*, edited by Lawrence Lipking and A. Walton Litz. New York: Atheneum, 1972. Benjamin claims that the art of storytelling is coming to an end because of the widespread dissemination of information and explanation. The compactness of a story precludes analysis and appeals to readers through the rhythm of the work itself. For the storyteller, the old religious chronicle is secularized into an ambiguous network in which the worldly and the eschatological are i nterwoven.

Bonheim, Helmut. *The Narrative Modes: Techniques of the Short Story*. Cambridge, England: D. S. Brewer, 1982. A systematic and statistical study of the short-story form, focusing on basic short-story techniques, especially short-story beginnings and endings. Argues that a limited set of techniques is used repeatedly in story endings. Discusses open and closed endings and argues that dynamic modes are more apt to be open, while static ones are more apt to be closed.

Boulanger, Daniel. "On the Short Story." *Michigan Quarterly Review* 26 (Summer, 1987): 510-514. A highly metaphoric and impressionistic study of the form, focusing primarily on the detached nature of the short story. Claims that there is a bit of Pontius Pilate in the short-story writer, for he or she is always removed from the tragic outcome. Points out how there are no class distinctions in the short story and no hierarchy.

Bowen, Elizabeth, ed. *The Faber Book of Modern Short Stories*. London: Faber & Faber, 1936. Bowen suggests that the short story, because it is exempt from the novel's often forced conclusiveness, more often approaches aesthetic and moral truth. She also suggests that the short story, more than the novel, is able to place the individual alone on that "stage which, inwardly, every man is conscious of occupying alone."

Brickell, Herschel. "What Happened to the Short Story?" *The Atlantic Monthly* 188 (September, 1951): 74-76. Argues that many contemporary writers have succeeded in breaking the short story away from its formal frame by drawing it nearer to poetry.

Brown, Suzanne Hunter. "The Chronotope of the Short Story: Time, Character, and Brevity." In *Creative and Critical Approaches to the Short Story*, edited by Noel Harold Kaylor, Jr. Lewiston, N.Y.: Edwin Mellen Press, 1997. A survey and analysis of the frequent critical assumption that short stories deal with characters as eternal essence and that novels deal with characters who change over time. Argues that Mikhail Bakhtin's concept of "chronotrope," a literary work's projection of time and space, will help develop a generic theory of the short story that considers both historical and technical factors.

_____. "Discourse Analysis and the Short Story." In *Short Story Theory at a Crossroads*, edited by Susan Lohafer and Jo Ellyn Clarey. Baton Rouge: Louisiana State University Press, 1989. A helpful analytical survey of the research being conducted by psychologists into the nature of discourse, storyness, and cognitive response to narrative.

Cortázar, Julio. "Some Aspects of the Short Story." *Arizona Quarterly*, Spring, 1982, 5-17. Cortázar, an Argentine writer and notable practitioner of the short story, discusses the invariable elements that give a good short story its particular atmosphere. He compares the novel and the short story to film and the photograph; the short story's most significant element is its subject, the act of choosing a real or imaginary happening that has the mysterious property of illuminating something beyond itself.

Cox, Alisa, ed. *The Short Story*. Newcastle, England: Cambridge Scholars, 2008. A collection of essays that provides a critical international overview of short fiction. Includes A. L. Kennedy's reflections on writing short stories, a discussion of the contemporary short story sequence, an essay pondering a definition of the short story, and analyses of stories by Italo Calvino, Jorge Luis Borges, Anita Desai, Martin Amis, Ray Bradbury, and others.

Dawson, W. J. "The Modern Short Story." *North American Review* 190 (December, 1909): 799-810. Argues that a short story must be complete in itself and consist of a single incident. The finest writing in a short story, Dawson maintains, is that which takes the reader most quickly to the very heart of the matter at hand.

Eichenbaum, Boris. *O. Henry and the Theory of the Short Story*. Translated by I. R. Titunik. Ann Arbor: University of Michigan, 1968. Originally published in 1925, this essay is a good example of the early Russian Formalist approach to fiction through a consideration of genre. Eichenbaum poses a generic distinction between the novel and the short story. Short stories are constructed on the basis of a contradiction, incongruity, error, or contrast and, like the anecdote, build their weight toward the ending.

Eldred, Janet Carey. "Narratives of Socialization: Literacy in the Short Story." *College English* 53 (October, 1991): 686-700. Based on the critical assumption that all fiction historicizes problems of socialization. Argues that the short story is a narrative of arrested socialization that ends with characters between two cultures who find their own speech inadequate but their new language problematic.

Elliott, George P. "A Defense of Fiction." *Hudson Review* 16 (1963): 9-48. Elliott, himself a short-story writer, discusses the four basic impulses that mingle with the storytelling impulse: to dream, to tell what happened, to explain the sense of things, and to make a likeness.

Ermida, Isabel. *The Language of Comic Narratives: Humor Construction in Short Stories*. New York: Mouton de Gruyter, 2008. Analyzes how humor works in short fiction, examining short stories by Dorothy Parker, Graham Greene, Woody Allen, David Lodge, Evelyn Waugh, and other English and American writers.

Farrell, James T. *The League of Frightened Philistines and Other Papers*. New York: Vanguard Press, 1945. Ridicules the short-story handbooks published in the 1920's and 1930's and claims that in many contemporary short stories the revolutionary point of view appears more tacked on than integral to the story.

Ferguson, Suzanne C. "Defining the Short Story: Impressionism and Form." *Modern Fiction Studies* 28 (Spring, 1982): 13-24. Argues that there is no single characteristic or cluster of characteristics that distinguishes the short story from the novel. Suggests that what is called the modern short story is a manifestation of impressionism rather than a discrete genre.

_____. "The Rise of the Short Story in the Hierarchy of Genres." In *Short Story Theory at a Crossroads*, edited by Susan Lohafer and Jo Ellyn Clarey. Baton Rouge: Louisiana State University Press, 1989. A historical and critical survey of the development of the English short story, showing how social factors influenced the rise and fall of the form's prestige.

FitzGerald, Gregory. "The Satiric Short Story: A Definition." *Studies in Short Fiction* 5 (1968): 349-354. Defines the satiric short story as a subgenre that sustains a reductive attack upon its objects and conveys to its readers a significance different from its apparent surface meaning.

Fonlon, Bernard, "The Philosophy, the Science, and the Art of the Short Story, Part II." *Abbia* 34 (1979): 429-438. A discussion of the basic elements of a story, including character and conflict. Lists elements of intensity, detachment, skill, and unity of effect. Primarily presents a set of rules aimed at inexperienced writers.

Friedman, Norman. "Recent Short Story Theories: Problems in Definition." In *Short Story Theory at a Crossroads*, edited by Susan Lohafer and Jo Ellyn Clarey. Baton Rouge: Louisiana State University Press, 1989. A critical review of major short-story critics, including Mary Rohrberger, Charles May, Susan Lohafer, and John Gerlach. Argues against those critics who support a deductive, single-term, mixed category approach to definition of the form. Urges that what is needed is a more inductive approach that follows the principle of suiting the definition to the facts rather than trying to suit the facts to the definition.

_____. "What Makes a Short Story Short?" *Modern Fiction Studies* 4 (1958): 103-117. Makes use of neo-Aristotelian literary theory to determine the issue of the short story's shortness. To deal with the problem, Friedman argues, one must ask the following questions: What is the size of the action? Is the action composed of a speech, a scene, an episode, or a plot? Does the action involve a change? If so, is the change a major one or a minor one?

Gerlach, John. "The Margins of Narrative: The Very Short Story, the Prose Poem, and the Lyric." In *Short Story Theory at a Crossroads*, edited by Susan Lohafer and Jo Ellyn Clarey. Baton Rouge: Louisiana State University Press, 1989. Explores the basic requirements of a story, focusing particularly on two minimalist stories by Enrique Anderson Imbert and Scott Sanders, as well as a short prose poem by W. S. Merwin. Argues that point, not mere length nor fictionality, is the principal constituent of story.

Gordimer, Nadine. "South Africa." *The Kenyon Review* 30 (1968): 457-461. Gordimer, a Nobel Prize-winning writer, argues that the strongest convention of the novel, its prolonged coherence of tone, is false to the nature of what can be grasped as reality in the modern world. Short-story writers deal with the only thing one can be sure of--the present moment.

Görtschacher, Wolfgang, and Holger Klein, eds. *Tale, Novella, Short Story: Currents in Short Fiction*. Tübingen, Germany: Stauffenburg, 2004. Reprints the papers delivered at the Tenth International Salzburg Conference, which focused on the short fictional forms of the tale, novella, and short story. Among the topics discussed are the influence of English short fiction on historical texts, such as *The Arabian Nights' Entertainments*; theoretical issues, including the aesthetic principles of compactness and brevity; and analyses of contemporary short fiction from Australia, Africa, the United States, Great Britain, and Ireland.

Gullason, Thomas A. "Revelation and Evolution: A Neglected Dimension of the Short Story." *Studies in Short Fiction* 10 (1973): 347-356. Challenges Mark Schorer's distinction between the short story as an "art of moral revelation" and the novel as an "art of moral evolution." Analyzes D. H. Lawrence's "The Horse Dealer's Daughter" and John Steinbeck's "The Chrysanthemums" to show that the short story embodies both revelation and evolution.

_____. "The Short Story: An Underrated Art." *Studies in Short Fiction* 2 (1964): 13-31. Points out the lack of serious criticism of the short story, suggests some of the reasons for this neglect, and concludes with an analysis of Anton Chekhov's "Gooseberries" and Nadine Gordimer's "The Train from Rhodesia" to disprove the charges that the short story is formulaic and lacks life.

Hanson, Clare, ed. Introduction to *Re-Reading the Short Story*. New York: St. Martin's Press, 1989. Claims that the short story is a vehicle for different kinds of knowledge, knowledge that may be in some way at odds with the "story" of dominant culture. The formal properties of the short story--disjunction, inconclusiveness, and obliquity--connect with its ideological marginality and with the fact that the form may be used to express something suppressed or repressed in mainstream literature.

_____. *Short Stories and Short Fictions, 1880-1980*. New York: St. Martin's Press, 1985. Argues that during this period, the authority of the teller, usually a first-person "framing" narrator who guaranteed the authenticity of the tale, was questioned by many modernist writers, Argues that the movements from "teller" to indirect free narration, and from "tale" to "text," were part of a more general movement from "discourse" to "image" in the art and literature of the period. Includes chapters on Rudyard Kipling, Saki, W. Somerset Maugham, James Joyce, Virginia Woolf, Katherine Mansfield, Samuel Beckett.

_____. "Things out of Words: Towards a Poetics of Short Fiction." In *Re-Reading the Short Story*, edited by Clare Hanson. New York: St. Martin's Press, 1989. Argues that the short story is a more literary form than the novel. Maintains that short stories are framed, an aesthetic device that gives a sense of completeness that in turn allows gaps and absences to remain in the story; thus readers accept a degree of mystery or elision in the short story that they would not accept in the novel.

Hardy, Sarah. "A Poetics of Immediacy: Oral Narrative and the Short Story." *Style* 27 (Fall, 1993): 352-368. Argues that the oral-epic episode clarifies basic characteristics of the short story: It gives the reader a way to understand the density of meaning in the short story and provides a paradigm of the short-story audience as that of a participating community.

Hedberg, Johannes. "What Is a 'Short Story?' and What Is an 'Essay'?" *Moderna Sprak* 74 (1980): 113-120. Reminds readers of the distinction between the Chekhovian story (lack of plot) and the Maupassantian story (anecdotal and therefore commercial). Discusses basic characteristics of the essay and the story; maintains they are similar in that they are both a whole picture in miniature, not merely a detail of a larger picture--a complete work, not an extract.

Hendricks, William O. "Methodology of Narrative Structural Analysis." In *Essays in Semiolinguistics and Verbal Art*. The Hague, Netherlands: Mouton, 1973. Structuralists, in the tradition of Vladimir Propp and Claude Levi-Strauss, usually bypass the actual sentences of a narrative and analyze a synopsis. This essay is a fairly detailed discussion of the methodology of synopsizing (using William Faulkner's "A Rose for Emily" as an example), followed by a brief discussion of the methodology of structural analysis of the resultant synopsis.

Hesse, Douglas. "A Boundary Zone: First-Person Short Stories and Narrative Essays." In *Short Story Theory at a Crossroads*, edited by Susan Lohafer and Jo Ellyn Clarey. Baton Rouge: Louisiana State University Press, 1989. Argues that the precise boundary point between essays and short stories does not exist. Analyzes George Orwell's essay "A Hanging" as a short story and William Carlos Williams's short story "Use of Force" as an essay. Discusses essays and stories that fall in a boundary zone between essay and story.

Hicks, Granville. "The Art of the Short Story." *Saturday Review* 41 (December 20, 1958): 16. Maintains that the focus of the contemporary short story is an emotional experience for the reader rather than character or plot.

Holloway, John. "Identity, Inversion, and Density Elements in Narrative: Three Tales by Chekhov, James, and Lawrence." In *Narrative and Structure: Exploratory Essays*. Cambridge, England. Cambridge University Press, 1979. Holloway looks at stories in which almost nothing happens. He says there is a distinctive kind of narrative episode introduced by an item that is then followed by another item in inverse relationship to the first, which cancels it out and brings the reader back to where he or she started.

Howe, Irving. "Tone in the Short Story." Sewanee Review 57 (Winter, 1949): 141-152. Maintains that because the short story lacks prolonged characterization and a structured plot, it depends mostly on tone to hold it together.

Ibáñez, José R., José Francisco Fernández, and Carmen M. Bretones, eds. *Contemporary Debates on the Short Story*. New York: Peter Lang, 2007. Collection of critical essays about short fiction, some of which are written from the perspectives of globalization and deconstructionism. Includes a discussion of dissent in the modern Irish short story; an overview of short fiction, including a historical overview of the mystery story; and analyses of short fiction by Wyndham Lewis, Henry James, Salman Rushdie, and Judith Ortiz Cofer.

"International Symposium on the Short Story" in *Kenyon Review*. Contributions from short-story writers from all over the world on the nature of the form, its current economic status, its history, and its significance. Part 1, vol. 30, no. 4 (1969): 443-490 features contributions by Christina Stead (England), Herbert Gold (United States), Erih Koš (Yugoslavia), Nadine Gordimer (South Africa), Benedict Kiely (Ireland), Hugh Hood (Canada), and Henrietta Drake-Brockman (Australia); part 2, vol. 31, no. 1 (1969): 58-94 contains comments by William Saroyan (United States), Jun Eto (Japan), Maurice Shadbolt (New Zealand), Chanakya Sen (India), John Wain (England), and Hans Bender (Germany) and "An Agent's View" by James Oliver Brown; part 3, vol. 31, no. 4 (1969): 450-502 features Ana María Matute (Spain), Torborg Nedreaas (Norway), George Garrett (United States), Elizabeth Taylor (England), Ezekiel Mphahlele (South Africa), Elizabeth Harrower (Australia), Mario Picchi (Italy), Junzo Shono (Japan), and Khushwant Singh (India); part 4, vol. 32, no. 1 (1969): 78-108 includes Jack Cope (South Africa), James T. Farrell (United States), Edward Hyams (England), Luigi Barzini (Italy), David Ballantyne (New Zealand), and H. E. Bates (England).

Jarrell, Randall. "Stories." In *The Anchor Book of Stories*. New York: Doubleday, 1958. Jarrell's introduction to this collection focuses on stories as being closer to dream reality than the waking world of everyday life. He argues that there are basically two kinds of stories: stories in which everything is a happening (in which each event is so charged that the narrative threatens to disintegrate into energy), and stories in which nothing happens (in which even the climax may lose its charge and become one more portion of a lyric continuum).

Jouve, Nicole Ward. "Too Short for a Book." In *Re-Reading the Short Story*, edited by Clare Hanson. New York: St. Martin's Press, 1989. An impressionistic, noncritical essay about story length. Discusses *The Arabian Nights' Entertainments* as an archetypal model standing behind all stories, collections of stories, and storytelling. Makes a case for collections of stories that stand together as organic wholes rather than single individual stories that stand alone.

Lewis, C. S. "On Stories." In *Essays Presented to Charles Williams*. Grand Rapids, Mich.: Wm. B. Eerdmans, 1966. Although stories are series of events, this series, or what is called plot, is only a necessary means to capture something that has no sequence, something more like a state or quality. Thus, the "means" of a story is always at war with its "end"; this very tension, however, constitutes the story's chief resemblance to life: "We grasp at a state and find only a succession of events in which the state is never quite embodied."

Lohafer, Susan. "A Cognitive Approach to Story-Ness." *Short Story* (Spring, 1990), 60-71. A study of what Lohafer calls "preclosure," those points in a story where it could end but does not. Studies the characters of such preclosure sentences--where they appear and what they signal--as part of a more general effort to clarify what constitutes story-ness.

_____. *Coming to Terms with the Short Story*. Baton Rouge: Louisiana State University Press, 1983. A highly suggestive theoretical study of the short story that focuses on the sentence unit of the form as a way of showing how it differs from the novel.

_____. "Interdisciplinary Thoughts on Cognitive Science and Short Fiction Studies." In *The Tales We Tell: Perspectives on the Short Story*, edited by Barbara Lounsberry, et al. Westport, Conn.: Greenwood Press, 1998. A brief summary of psychological approaches to cognitive strategies for reading short fiction. Makes a number of suggestions about the future of short-story criticism based on the cooperation between narrative theorists and cognitive scientists.

_____. "Preclosure and Story Processing." In *Short Story Theory at a Crossroads*, edited by Susan Lohafer and Jo Ellyn Clarey. Baton Rouge: Louisiana State University Press, 1989. Analyzes responses to a story by Kate Chopin in terms of identifying those sentences that could end the story but do not. This essay is a continuation of Lohafer's study of what she has defined as preclosure in short fiction.

_____. "Preclosure in an 'Open' Story." In *Creative and Critical Approaches to the Short Story*, edited by Noel Harold Kaylor, Jr. Lewiston, N.Y.: Edwin Mellen Press, 1997. Presents the results of an experiment in preclosure studies in which 114 students were asked to read Julio Cortázar's story "Orientation of Cats" and report on their understanding of it. Lohafer asks the students to identify points at which the story might have ended, a preclosure procedure that makes them more aware of reading tactics and their inherent sense of story-ness.

_____. *Reading for Storyness: Preclosure Theory, Empirical Poetics, and Culture in the Short Story*. Baltimore: Johns Hopkins University Press, 2003. Lohafer discusses many of the literary theories presented in her previous articles, arguing that "imminent closure" is the defining trait of the short story. She demonstrates her theories by analyzing stories by Kate Chopin, Katherine Mansfield, Julio Cortázar, Raymond Carver, Bobbie Ann Mason, Ann Beattie, and other writers.

_____. "Why the 'Life of Ma Parker' Is Not So Simple: Preclosure in Issue-Bound Stories." *Studies in Short Fiction* 33 (Fall, 1996): 475-486. In this particular experiment with student reaction to preclosure markers in a story by Katherine Mansfield, Lohafer is interested in showing how attention to preclosure encourages readers to temporarily suppress their ready-made concepts and engage their story competence.

March-Russell, Paul. *The Short Story: An Introduction*. Edinburgh: Edinburgh University Press, 2009. Historical overview of short fiction, defining its origins, the concept of the well-made story, the short story cycle, and specific types of stories, such as ghost stories and modernist, postmodernist, minimalist, and postcolonial short fiction.

Marcus, Mordecai. "What Is an Initiation Story?" *The Journal of Aesthetics and Art Criticism* 14 (1960): 221-227. Distinguishes three types of initiation stories: those that lead protagonists only to the threshold of maturity, those that take the protagonists across the threshold of maturity but leave them in a struggle for certainty, and decisive initiation stories that carry protagonists firmly into maturity.

Matthews, Brander. *The Philosophy of the Short-Story*. New York: Longmans, Green, 1901. An expansion of an 1882 article in which Matthews sets himself forth as the first critic since Edgar Allan Poe to discuss the "short-story" (Matthews contributed the hyphen) as a genre. By asserting that the short story must have a vigorous compression, must be original, must be ingenious, must have a touch of fantasy, and so on, Matthews set the stage for the subsequent host of textbook writers on the short story.

Maugham, W. Somerset. "The Short Story." In *Points of View: Five Essays*. Garden City, N.Y.: Doubleday, 1958. As might be expected, Maugham's preference is for the well-made story exemplified by Guy de Maupassant's "The Necklace." Most of the essay, however, deals with biographical material about Anton Chekhov and Katherine Mansfield.

May, Charles E. "Artifice and Artificiality in the Short Story." *Story* 1 (Spring, 1990): 72-82. Discusses the artificial and formalized nature of the endings of short stories, arguing that the short story is the most aesthetic narrative form. Discusses the ending of several representative stories.

_____. "Metaphoric Motivation in Short Fiction: 'In the Beginning Was the Story.'" In *Short Theory at a Crossroads*, edited by Susan Lohafer and Jo Ellyn Clarey. Baton Rouge: Louisiana State University Press, 1989. A discussion of how short fiction moves from the "tale" form to the "short story" form through motivation by metaphor in "The Fall of the House of Usher," "Bartleby the Scrivener," "The Legend of Sleepy Hollow," and "Young Goodman Brown."

_____. "The Nature of Knowledge in Short Fiction." *Studies in Short Fiction* 21 (Fall, 1984): 227-238. A theoretical study of the epistemological bases of short fiction. Argues that the short story originates as a primal mythic mode that develops into a metaphoric mode.

_____. "Obsession and the Short Story." In *Creative and Critical Approaches to the Short Story*, edited by Noel Harold Kaylor, Jr. Lewiston, N.Y.: Edwin Mellen Press, 1997. An examination of the common charge that the short story is unhealthily limited and obsessed. Discusses the origins of the relationship between psychological obsession and aesthetic unity in the stories of Edgar Allan Poe, Nathaniel Hawthorne, and Herman Melville. Attempts to account for this relationship as a generic characteristic of the short story.

_____. "Prolegomenon to a Generic Study of the Short Story." *Studies in Short Fiction* 33 (Fall, 1996): 461-474. Tries to lay the groundwork for a generic theory of the short story in terms of new theories of this genre. Discusses the short story's historical focus on the strange and unexpected and the formal demands made by this thematic focus. Argues for a mixed genre theory of the short story that can account for the form's essential, as well as historically changing, characteristics.

_____. "Reality in the Modern Short Story. *Style* 27 (Fall, 1993): 369-379. Argues that realism in the modern short story from Anton Chekhov to Raymond Carver is not the simple mimesis of the realistic novel but rather the use of highly compressed selective detail configured to metaphorically

objectify that which cannot be described directly. The result is a "hyperrealism" in which story is unified by tone and meaning is created by aesthetic pattern.

_____. *The Short Story: The Reality of Artifice*. New York: Routledge, 2002. A historical survey of the short story, tracing its origins in the tales of Geoffrey Chaucer and Giovanni Boccaccio through the nineteenth century and its contemporary renaissance.

_____. *Short Story Theories*. Athens: Ohio University Press, 1976. A collection of twenty previously published essays on the short story as a genre in its own right.

_____. "A Survey of Short Story Criticism in America." *The Minnesota Review*, Spring, 1973, 163-169. An analytical survey of criticism beginning with Edgar Allan Poe and focusing on the short story's underlying vision and characteristic mode of understanding and confronting reality.

_____. "The Unique Effect of the Short Story: A Reconsideration and an Example." *Studies in Short Fiction* 13 (1976): 289-297. An attempt to redefine Edgar Allan Poe's "unique effect" in the short story in terms of mythic perception. Maintains that the short story demands intense compression and focusing because its essential subject is a manifestation of what philosopher Ernst Cassirer calls the "momentary deity." A detailed discussion of Stephen Crane's story "An Episode of War" illustrates the concept.

McSweeney, Kerry. *The Realist Short Story of the Powerful Glimpse: Chekhov to Carver*. Columbia: University of South Carolina Press, 2007. Focuses on the short fiction of five writers--Anton Chekhov, James Joyce, Ernest Hemingway, Flannery O'Connor, and Raymond Carver--to argue that the realist realist short story is a "glimpse--powerful and tightly focused, into a world that the writer must precisely craft and in which the reader must fully invest."

Menikoff, Barry. "The Problematics of Form: History and the Short Story." *Journal of the Short Story in English*, no. 2 (1984): 129-146. After a brief introduction discussing how the short story has been neglected, Menikoff comments briefly on the importance of Charles E. May's *Short Story Theories* (1976) and then discusses essays on the short story that appeared in *Critical Survey of Short Fiction* (1981) and a special issue of *Modern Fiction Studies* (1982).

Miall, David. "Text and Affect: A Model for Story Understanding." In *Re-Reading the Short Story*, edited by Clare Hanson. New York: St. Martin's Press, 1989. A discussion of what readers are doing in emotional terms when they read, using the defamiliarization model of the Russian Formalists. Focuses on three aspects of emotion: self-reference, domain crossing, and anticipation. Basically determines that whereas literary texts constrain response by means of their shared frames and conventions, their affective responses are highly divergent.

Millhauser, Steven. "The Ambition of the Short Story." *The New York Times Book Review*, October 5, 2008, p. 31. Discussion of the short story's essential characteristics and how the form differs from the novel.

Moffett, James. "Telling Stories: Methods of Abstraction in Fiction." *ETC* 21 (1964): 425-50. Charts a sequence covering an "entire range" of ways in which stories can be told, from the most subjective and personal (interior monologue and dramatic monologue) to the most objective and impersonal (anonymous narration). Includes examples of each type.

Moravia, Alberto. "The Short Story and the Novel." In *Man as End: A Defense of Humanism*. Translated by Bernard Wall. New York: Farrar, Straus & Giroux, 1969. Moravia, who wrote many novels and short stories, maintains that the basic difference between the two is that the novel has a bone structure of ideological themes whereas the short story is made up of intuitions of feelings.

Munson, Gorham. "The Recapture of the Storyable." *University Review* 10 (Autumn, 1943): 37-44. Maintains that the best short-story writers are concerned with only three questions: whether they have found a "storyable" incident, how they should cast their characters, and who would best tell their story.

Oates, Joyce Carol. "Beginnings: The Origin and Art of the Short Story." In *The Tales We Tell: Perspectives on the Short Story*, edited by Barbara Lounsberry, et al. Westport, Conn.: Greenwood Press, 1998. Defines the short story as a form that represents an intensification of meaning rather than an expansion of the imagination. Briefly discusses the importance of Edgar Allan Poe's aesthetic and Mark Twain's oral tale to the development of the American short story.

_____. "The Short Story." *Southern Humanities Review* 5 (1971): 213-214. Maintains that the short story is a "dream verbalized," a manifestation of desire; its most interesting aspect is its "mystery."

O'Connor, Frank. *The Lonely Voice: A Study of the Short Story*. 1963. Reprint. Hoboken, N.J.: Melville House, 2004. O'Connor, an accomplished master of the short-story form, presented his observations of the genre in this study. The introductory chapter contains extremely valuable "intuitive" criticism. O'Connor maintains that the basic difference between the novel and the short story is that in the latter readers always find an intense awareness of human loneliness. He believes that the protagonist of the short story is less an individual with whom readers can identify than a "submerged population group," that is, someone outside the social mainstream. The remaining chapters of the book treat this theme in the works of Ivan Turgenev, Anton Chekhov, Guy de Maupassant, Rudyard Kipling, James Joyce, Katherine Mansfield, D. H. Lawrence, A. E. Coppard, Isaac Babel, and Mary Lavin.

O'Faoláin, Seán. *The Short Story*. New York: Devin-Adair, 1951. This book on the technique of the short story claims that technique is the "least part of the business." O'Faoláin illustrates his thesis that personality is the most important element in short fiction by describing the personal struggles of Alphonse Daudet, Anton Chekhov, and Guy de Maupassant. He does his duty to the assigned subject of the book by also discussing the technical problems of convention, subject, construction, and language.

O'Rourke, William. "Morphological Metaphors for the Short Story: Matters of Production, Reproduction, and Consumption." In *Short Story Theory at a Crossroads*, edited by Susan Lohafer and Jo Ellyn Clarey. Baton Rouge: Louisiana State University Press, 1989. Explores a number of analogies drawn from the social and natural sciences to suggest ways of seeing how the short story is different from the novel: The novel has a structure like a vertebrate, whereas the short story is like an animal with an exoskeleton; the novel is a macro form, whereas the short story is a micro form.

Overstreet, Bonaro. "Little Story, What Now?" *Saturday Review of Literature*, 24 (November 22, 1941): 3-5, 25-26. Overstreet argues that as a result of a loss of faith in the old verities of the nineteenth century, the twentieth century short story is concerned with psychological materials, not with the events in the objective world.

Pain, Barry. *The Short Story*. London: Martin Secker, 1916. Pain claims that the primary difference between the short story and the novel is that the short story, because of its dependence on suggestive devices, demands more of the reader's participation.

Palakeel, Thomas. "Third World Short Story as National Allegory?" *Journal of Modern Literature* 20 (Summer, 1996): 97-102. Argues against Frederic Jameson's claim that Third World fictions are always national allegories. Points out that this claim is even more damaging to the short story than to the novel because the short story is the most energetic literary activity in the Third World. He argues that Jameson's theory cripples any non-Western literature that tries to deal with the psychological or spiritual reality of the individual.

Pasco, Allan H. "The Short Story: The Short of It." *Style* 27 (Fall, 1993): 442-451. Suggests a list of qualities of the short story generated by its brevity, such as the assumptions of considerable background on the part of the readers and that readers will absorb and remember all elements of the work. Claims that the short story shuns amplification in favor of inference, that it is usually single rather than multivalent, that it tends toward the general, and that it remains foreign to loosely motivated detail.

Patrick, Walton R. "Poetic Style in the Contemporary Short Story." *College Composition and Communication* (1957): 77-84. Argues that the poetic style appears more consistently in the short story than in the novel because metaphorical dilations are essential to the writer who "strives to pack the utmost meaning into his restricted space."

Penn, W. S. "The Tale as Genre in Short Fiction." *Southern Humanities Review* 15 (Summer, 1981): 231-241. Discusses the genre from the perspective of structure. Primarily uses suggestions made by Jonathan Culler in *Structuralist Poetics* for constructing a poetic persona in the lyric poem, what Culler calls an "enunciative posture," that is, the detectable or intuited moral relation of the implied author to both the world at large and the world he or she creates. Develops two kinds of tales: the radical oral and the exponential oral.

Perry, Bliss. *A Study of Prose Fiction*. Boston: Houghton Mifflin, 1920. Perry claims that the short story differs from the novel by presenting unique and original characters, by focusing on fragments of reality, and by making use of the poetic devices of impressionism and symbolism.

Pickering, Jean. "Time and the Short Story." In *Re-Reading the Short Story*, edited by Clare Hanson. New York: St. Martin's Press, 1989. Discusses the distinction between the short story as an art of revelation and the novel as an art of evolution. General implications that derive from this distinction are that short-story writers do not need to know all the details of their characters' lives and that the short story is doubly symbolic. Structure, theme, characterization, and language are influenced by the short story's particular relation to time as a moment of revelation.

Poe, Edgar Allan. Review of *Twice-Told Tales*. *Graham's Magazine*, May, 1842. The first critical discussion of the short story, or the "tale" as Poe terms it, to establish the genre as distinct from the novel. Because of its sense of totality, its single effect, and its patterned design, the short story is second only to the lyric in its demands on high genius and in its aesthetic beauty.

Pratt, Mary Louise. "The Short Story: The Long and the Short of It." *Poetics* 10 (1981): 175-194. A theoretical discussion of the form. Presents eight ways that the short story is better understood if its dependence on the novel is understood.

Prince, Gerald. *A Grammar of Stories: An Introduction*. The Hague, Netherlands: Mouton, 1973. An attempt to establish rules to account for the structure of all the syntactical sets that readers intuitively recognize as stories. The model used is Noam Chomsky's theories of generative grammar.

_____. "The Long and the Short of It." *Style* 27 (Fall, 1993): 327-331. Provides a definition of the short story as "an autonomous, short, fictional story written in prose and offered for display." Admits that such a definition has limited usefulness but argues that this is characteristic of generic definitions; maintains that texts belong not to one but to an indefinitely large number of textual families and use an indefinitely large number of clusters of features.

Pritchett, V. S. "Short Stories." *Harper's Bazaar* 87 (July, 1953): 31, 113. In Pritchett's opinion the short story is a hybrid, owing much to the quickness and objectivity of the cinema, much to the poet and the newspaper reporter, and everything to the "restlessness, the alert nerve, the scientific eye and the short breath of contemporary life." He makes an interesting point about the collapse of standards, conventions, and values that has so bewildered the impersonal novelist but has been the making of the story writer.

Reid, Ian. *The Short Story*. London: Methuen, 1977. A brief study that deals with problems of definition, historical development, and related generic forms. Offers a good introduction to the short story as a genre.

Rohrberger, Mary. "Between Shadow and Act: Where Do We Go from Here?" In *Short Story Theory at a Crossroads*, edited by Susan Lohafer and Jo Ellyn Clarey. Baton Rouge: Louisiana State University Press, 1989. A thought-provoking review of a number of modern short-story critics and theorists, largely by way of responding to, and disagreeing with, the strictly scientific and logical approach to definition of the form suggested by Norman Friedman. Also includes a restatement of the view that Rohrberger enunciated in her earlier book on Nathaniel Hawthorne, in which she argued for the essentially romantic nature of the short-story form.

_____. *Hawthorne and the Modern Short Story: A Study in Genre*. The Hague, Netherlands: Mouton, 1966. Attempts a generic definition of the short story as a form that derives from the Romantic metaphysical view that there is more to the world than can be apprehended through the senses. Nathaniel Hawthorne is the touchstone for Rohrberger's definition, which she then applies to twentieth century stories by Eudora Welty, Ernest Hemingway, Sherwood Anderson, William Faulkner, and others.

Ruthrof, Horst. "Bracketed World and Reader Construction in the Modern Short Story." In *The Reader's Construction of Narrative*. London: Routledge & Kegan Paul, 1981. Discusses the "boundary situation" as the basis for the modern short story. In the pure boundary situation, the reader's act of bracketing transforms the presented crisis into the existential experience of the reading act.

Scott, A. O. "A Good Tale Isn't Hard to Find." *The New York Times*, April 5, 2009, p. WK1. Discussion of the remarkable durability of the short story, suggesting that it may be poised for a resurgence at the end of the first decade of the twenty-first century.

Shaw, Valerie. *The Short Story: A Critical Introduction*. London: Longman, 1983. A discussion of the form that primarily focuses on British writers, with one chapter on the transitional figure Robert Louis Stevenson. The rest of book deals with the patterned form to the artless tale form, with chapters on character, setting, and subject matter. Shaw argues that the short story cannot be defined by unity of effect or by a history of its "favorite devices and eminent practitioners."

Siebert, Hilary. "'Outside History': Lyrical Knowledge in the Discourse of the Short Story." In *Creative and Critical Approaches to the Short Story*, edited by Noel Harold Kaylor, Jr. Lewiston, N.Y.: Edwin Mellen Press, 1997. A discussion of how readers of short stories must often shift from expectations of a revealed, discursive meaning typical of prose to a gradually apprehended suggestive meaning typical of lyric poetry.

Stanzel, Franz K. "Textual Power in (Short) Short Story and Poem." In *Modes of Narrative: Approaches to American, Canadian, and British Fiction*, edited by Reingard M. Vischik and Barbara Korte. Wursburg, Germany: Konigshausen and Neumann, 1990. Argues that the short story and poetry, which at the beginning of the twentieth century were far apart, have come closer together in both form and content. Suggests some of the similarities between the two forms, such as their focusing the reader's attention on beginnings and endings and their insistence on close readings of the structure of each line and sentence.

Stevick, Philip, ed. *Anti-Story: An Anthology of Experimental Fiction*. New York: Free Press, 1971. An influential collection of contemporary short fiction with a helpful introduction that characterizes antistory as against mimesis, reality, event, subject, the middle range of experience, analysis, and meaning.

Stroud, Theodore A. "A Critical Approach to the Short Story." *Journal of General Education* 9 (1956): 91-100. Makes use of American New Criticism to determine the pattern of the short story, that is, why apparently irrelevant episodes are included and why some events are expanded and others excluded.

Suckow, Ruth. "The Short Story." *Saturday Review of Literature* 4 (November 19, 1927): 317-318. Suckow strongly argues that no one can define the short story, for it is an aesthetic method for dealing with diversity and multiplicity.

Sullivan, Walter. "Revelation in the Short Story: A Note of Methodology." In *Vanderbilt Studies in Humanities*, edited by Richard C. Beatty, John Philip Hyatt, and Monroe K. Spears. Vol. 1. Nashville, Tenn.: Vanderbilt University Press, 1951. The fundamental methodological concept of the short story is a change of view from innocence to knowledge. This change can be either "logical" (coming at the end of the story) or "anticipated" (coming near the beginning); it can be either "intraconcatinate" (occurring within the main character) or "extra-concatinate" (occurring within a peripheral character). Thus defined, the short story did not begin until the final years of the nineteenth century.

Summers, Hollis, ed. *Discussions of the Short Story*. Boston: D. C. Heath, 1963. The nine general pieces on the short story include essays by Edgar Allan Poe and A. L. Bader; excerpts of books by Ray B. West, Seán O'Faoláin, and Brander Matthews; a chapter each from Percy Lubbock's *Craft of Fiction* (1954) and Kenneth Payson Kempton's *The Short Story* (1947); and Bret Harte's "The Rise of the Short Story." Also includes seven additional essays on specific short-story writers.

Szávai, János. "Towards a Theory of the Short Story." *Acta Litteraria Academiae Scientiarum Hungariae, Tomus* 24 (1982): 203-224. Discusses the Giovanni Boccaccio model as a genre that gives the illusion of reflecting reality directly and spontaneously, whereas it is actually a complex, structured entity that both retains and enriches the basic structure of the story. The enrichment resides, on the one hand, in the careful preparation of the point and its attachment to a key motif and, on the other, in the introduction of a new dimension in addition to the anecdote.

Todorov, Tzvetan. "The Structural Analysis of Literature." In *Structuralism: An Introduction*, edited by David Robey. London: Clarendon Press, 1973. The "figure in the carpet" in Henry James's stories is the quest for an absolute and absent cause. This cause is either a character, an event, or an object; its effect is the story readers are told. Everything in the story owes its existence to this cause, but because it is absent, the reader sets off in quest of it.

Trask, Georgianne, and Charles Burkhart, ed. *Storytellers and Their Art*. New York: Doubleday Anchor, 1963. A valuable collection of comments on the short-story form by practitioners from Anton Chekhov to Truman Capote. Noteworthy in part 1 are "Definitions of the Short Story" and "Short Story vs. Novel."

Trussler, Michael. "The Short Story: Interview with Charles May and Susan Lohafer." *Wascana Review* 33 (Spring, 1998): 14-24. Interview with two well-known theorists of the short story, who discuss reasons for past critical neglect of the form, conditions of the recent renaissance of interest in the form by both critics and general readers, unique generic characteristics of the short story, and current and future trends in the short story and theoretical approaches to it.

_____. "Suspended Narratives: The Short Story and Temporality." *Studies in Short Fiction* 33 (Fall, 1996): 557-577. An analysis of the critical view that the short-story form focuses on atemporality. Synthesizes a number of theories that emphasize short fiction's focus on existential confrontations while refusing to mitigate such experiences with abstraction, context, or continuity.

Wain, John. "Remarks on the Short Story." *Journal of the Short Story in English* 2 (1984): 49-66. Wain, himself a short-story writer, argues that the short story is a form of its own, with its own laws and logic, and that it is a modern form, beginning with Edgar Allan Poe. He observes that the novel is like a painting, whereas the short story is like a drawing, which catches a moment and is satisfying on its own grounds. He says there are perfectly successful short stories and totally unsuccessful ones, and nothing in between.

Welty, Eudora. "The Reading and Writing of Short Stories." *The Atlantic Monthly*, February, 1949, 54-58; March, 1949, 46-49. An impressionistic but suggestive essay in two installments that focuses on the mystery of the story and the fact that one cannot always see the solid outlines of the story because of the atmosphere that it generates.

West, Ray B. "The Modern Short Story and the Highest Forms of Art." *English Journal* 46 (1957): 531-539. Describes how the rise of the short story in the nineteenth century was a result of the shift in narrative view from the "telescopic" (viewing nature and society from the outside) to the "microscopic" (viewing the unseen world of inner motives and impulses).

Wharton, Edith. "Telling a Short Story." In *The Writing of Fiction*. New York: Charles Scribner's Sons, 1925. Wharton maintains that the chief technical difference between the novel and the short story is that the novel focuses on character while the short story focuses on situation, "and it follows that the effect produced by the short story depends almost entirely on its form."

Williams, William Carlos. *A Beginning on the Short Story: Notes*. Yonkers, N.Y.: The Alicat Bookshop Press, 1950. In these notes from a writers' workshop session, Williams makes several interesting, if fragmentary and impressionistic, remarks about the short-story form: The short story, as contrasted with the novel, is a brushstroke instead of a picture. Stressing virtuosity instead of story structure, it is "one single flight of the imagination, complete: up and down." It is best suited to depicting the life of "briefness, brokenness, and heterogeneity."

Winther, Per, Jacob Lothe, and Hans H. Skei, eds. *The Art of Brevity: Excursions in Short Fiction Theory and Analysis*. Columbia: University of South Carolina Press, 2004. Collection of essays, including some written by noted short-story theorists, such as Mary Rohrberger, Charles E. May, Susan Lohafer, and John Gerlach. Some of the essays examine reasons for readers' neglect of short stories. Other essays analyze short fiction by Robert Olen Butler, Chris Offutt, James Joyce, Sarah Orne Jewett, Linda Hogan, Flannery O'Connor, Eudora Welty, William Faulkner, and Herman Melville; Danish short stories from the 1990's; and works by Australian writers.

Wright, Austin. "On Defining the Short Story: The Genre Question." In *Short Story Theory at a Crossroads*, edited by Susan Lohafer and Jo Ellyn Clarey. Baton Rouge: Louisiana State University Press, 1989. Discusses some of the theoretical problems involved in defining the short story as a genre. Argues for the formalist view of a genre definition as a cluster of conventions.

_____. "Recalcitrance in the Short Story." In *Short Story Theory at a Crossroads*, edited by Susan Lohafer and Jo Ellyn Clarey. Baton Rouge: Louisiana State University Press, 1989. A discussion of stories with endings that resist the reader's efforts to assimilate them and to make sense of them as a whole. Such final recalcitrance, Wright claims, is the extreme kind of resistance that the short story has developed to thwart final closure and reduce the complexity of the story to a conceptual understanding.

AFRICAN SHORT FICTION

Balogun, F. Odun. *Tradition and Modernity in the African Short Story: An Introduction to a Literature in Search of Critics*. New York: Greenwood Press, 1991. In part 1 of this study, Balogun conducts a general survey of African short fiction, discussing its themes, structure of irony, linguistic characteristics, and other components. Part 2 provides a close reading of short stories by two African writers--Chinua Achebe and Taban lo Liyong.

Gaylard, Gerald. *After Colonialism: African Postmodernism and Magical Realism.* Johannesburg: Wits University, 2006. Gaylard describes how two genres of fiction--postmodernism and Magical Realism--provide reflections on and responses to colonialism in Africa. He argues that genres such as Magical Realism, which allow writers freedom and release, provide African writers a sense of liberty in an era of colonization and assimilation.

MacKenzie, Craig. *The Oral-Style South African Short Story in English: A. W. Drayson to H. C. Bosman.* Atlanta, Ga.: Rodopi, 1999. Examines a particular type of South African short story known as the fireside tale, the *skaz* narrative, or the oral-style story, which has its origin in nineteenth century hunting and camp-fire tales. Focuses on the stories of A. W. Drayson and Herman Charles Bosman but also discusses works by other South African writers.

AFRICAN, INDIAN, AND CARIBBEAN SHORT FICTION IN ENGLISH

Fallon, Erin, et al., eds. *A Reader's Companion to the Short Story in English.* Westport, Conn.: Greenwood Press, 2001. Produced under the auspices of the Society for the Study of the Short Story, this collection of essays, aimed at the general reader, provides brief biographies of numerous writers and analyses of their short fiction. Some of the writers examined are Chinua Achebe, Margaret Atwood, Morley Callaghan, Angela Carter, Janet Frame, Mavis Gallant, Nadine Gordimer, Elizabeth Jolley, Alice Munro, R. K. Narayan, Jean Rhys, Salman Rushdie, and Olive Senior.

Hunter, Adrian. *The Cambridge Introduction to the Short Story in English.* Cambridge, England: Cambridge University Press, 2007. Hunter begins his literary history in the nineteenth century, describing the form and cultural context of short fiction from that time until the late twentieth century. He discusses the works of Charles Dickens, Thomas Hardy, Rudyard Kipling, Joseph Conrad, James Joyce, Virginia Woolf, Katherine Mansfield, Samuel Beckett, Frank O'Connor, Seán O'Faoláin, Elizabeth Bowen, V. S. Pritchett, Angela Carter, Ian McEwan, Chinua Achebe, James Kelman, Alice Munro, and others.

Malcolm, Cheryl Alexander, and David Malcolm, eds. *A Companion to the British and Irish Short Story.* Malden, Mass.: Wiley-Blackwell, 2008. Collection of essays focusing on British and Irish short fiction from 1880 to the present day. Includes discussions of detective and crime stories, ghost stories, science-fiction tales, and gay and lesbian short stories, as well as women's writing. Analyzes the work of Rudyard Kipling, Robert Louis Stevenson, Thomas Hardy, Joseph Conrad, Saki, James Joyce, D. H. Lawrence, Virginia Woolf, Katherine Mansfield, Frank O'Connor, Liam O'Flaherty, Elizabeth Bowen, Ben Okri, Salman Rushdie, Hanif Kureishi, Alan Sillitoe, and John McGehern, among others.

ARABIC SHORT FICTION

Akers, Deborah S., and Abubaker A. Bagader, eds. and trans. *Oranges in the Sun: Short Stories from the Arabian Gulf.* Boulder, Colo.: Lynne Rienner, 2008. Following Akers's introduction, in which she discusses the origins and development of the short story in the Arabian Gulf region, this volume contains a selection of short stories that have been translated into English. These stories are written by authors from Saudi Arabia, Yemen, Oman, the United Arab Emirates, Bahrain, Qatar, and Kuwait.

Chorin, Ethan, comp. and trans. *Translating Libya: The Modern Libyan Short Story.* London: Saqi , in association with London Middle East Institute, School of Oriental and African Studies, 2008. Curious about the lack of "place" in Libya's contemporary short fiction, Chorin compiled and translated this collection of stories that mention Libyan cities and landmarks. He interprets the stories to describe their common characteristics and their depiction of the Libyan psyche, economy, and the status of women, minorities, and immigrants.

Hafez, Sabry. *The Quest for Identities: The Development of the Modern Arabic Short Story.* San Francisco: Saqi, 2007. Analyzes work by Yusuf Idris, Abd al-Rahman al-Sharqawi, Edwar al-Kharrat, and other contemporary authors to determine if the short story genre provides readers with a wider understanding of Arabic culture. Examines how writers in one Arabic-speaking country have influenced writers in another.

Shaheen, Mohammad. *The Modern Arabic Short Story: Shahrazad Returns*. 2d ed., rev. and expanded. New York: Palgrave Macmillan, 2002. The first part of this study provides an extensive analysis of contemporary Arabic short fiction, comparing it to classic Arabic storytelling and discussing the shared use of myth and folklore in Arabic short stories and poems. Part 2 features a selection of short stories that have been translated into English,

Yazici, Hüseyin. *The Short Story in Modern Arabic Literature*. Cairo: G. B. O., 2004. A literary historical survey of Arabic short fiction written in the nineteenth and twentieth centuries.

BRAZILIAN SHORT FICTION

Balderston, Daniel, ed. *The Latin American Short Story: An Annotated Guide to Anthologies and Criticism*. Westport, Conn.: Greenwood Press, 1992. Organizes the enormous body of short-story anthologies from the nineteen countries of Spanish America and Brazil for systematic study. The main section comprises annotated listings of 1,302 short-story anthologies; a second section comprises annotated bibliographies of criticism of the short story. Includes bibliographical references and an index.

Echevarría, Roberto González, and Enrique Pupo-Walker, eds. *The Cambridge History of Latin American Literature*. 3 vols. New York: Cambridge University Press, 1996. Volume 3 covers Brazilian literature. Includes bibliographical references and an index.

Foster, David William, ed. *Handbook of Latin American Literature*. New York: Garland, 1992. Offers separate essays on the literature of all Latin American countries, including French and Creole Haiti and Portuguese Brazil, written by scholars who focus on dominant issues and major movements, figures, and works, with emphasis on sociocultural and interpretive assessments. Includes bibliographical references and an index.

Jackson, K. David, ed. *Oxford Anthology of the Brazilian Short Story*. New York: Oxford University Press, 2006. Contains a selection of short stories published from the 1880's through the late twentieth century, including works by Joaquim Maria Machado de Assis, Jorge Amado, Clarice Lispector, and João Guimarães Rosa. A lengthy introductory essay, "World World Vast World of the Brazilian Short Story," provides background information about the history and development of this genre in Brazil .

Lopes, M. Angélica, ed. *The Brazilian Short Story in the Late Twentieth Century: A Selection from Nineteen Authors*. Lewiston, N.Y.: Edwin Mellen Press, 2009. An introductory essay to this anthology provides an overview of Brazilian fiction and of sociopolitical developments in this nation from the late nineteenth through the twentieth century. In addition, each story is accompanied by a brief biography of the author and a bibliography of his or her works.

CARIBBEAN SHORT FICTION

Arnold, A. James, Julio Rodríguez-Luis, and J. Michael Dash, eds. *A History of Literature in the Caribbean*. Philadelphia: J. Benjamins, 1994. A historical and critical look at literature from this region. Includes bibliographical references and an index.

Bloom, Harold, ed. *Caribbean Women Writers*. Philadelphia: Chelsea House, 1997. A thorough examination of contemporary, female Caribbean authors who write in English, including Jean Rhys, Jamaica Kincaid, Beryl Gilroy, and Edwidge Danticat. Includes bibliographical references and an index.

Dvořák, Marta, and W. H. New, eds. *Tropes and Territories: Short Fiction, Postcolonial Readings, Canadian Writing in Context*. Montreal: McGill-Queen's University Press, 2007. Examines contemporary short fiction written in Canada and the Commonwealth, including works by Native Canadians, Maoris, and writers Katherine Mansfield, Janet Frame, Alice Munro, Mavis Gallant, R. K. Narayan, and David Malouf, among others. Two of the essays provide general analyses of short fiction from South Asia and Australia, while another discusses Caribbean diasporic writing.

Evans, Lucy, Mark McWatt, and Emma Smith, eds. *The Caribbean Short Story: Critical Perspectives*. Leeds, England: Peepal Tree Press, 2011. Collection of twenty-five original essays that examine the significance of short fiction to Caribbean culture of the

twentieth and twenty-first centures. Some of the essays discuss the publishing histories of island-spe-
cific literary cultures; genre, narrative, and orality in
Caribbean short fiction; and the sociopolitical contexts of short stories from this region.

Foster, David William, ed. *Handbook of Latin American Literature*. New York: Garland, 1992. Offers
separate essays on the literature of all Latin American countries, including French and Creole Haiti
and Portuguese Brazil, written by scholars who
focus on dominant issues and major movements,
figures, and works, with emphasis on sociocultural
and interpretive assessments. Includes bibliographical references and an index.

CHINESE SHORT FICTION

Chiang, Sing-chen Lydia. *Collecting the Self: Body and
Identity in Strange Tale Collections of Late Imperial
China*. Boston: Brill, 2005. A Freudian interpretation of short-story collections by Pu Songling and
two of his contemporaries. Examines how the era's
"strange tales" about ghosts, animal spirits, gods,
monsters, and other supernatural phenomena were a
means of writing about suppressed cultural anxieties, gender issues, and the authors' self-identity.

Huters, Theodore, ed. *Reading the Modern Chinese
Short Story*. Armonk, N.Y.: M. E. Sharpe, 1990.
Collection of essays analyzing six contemporary
short stories, including works by Mao Dun, Lao
She, Xiao Jun, and Sui Tuo.

CUBAN SHORT FICTION

Alvarez, José B IV. *Contestatory Cuban Short Story of
the Revolution*. Lanham, Md.: University Press of
America, 2002. Examines countercultural narratives
written by Cuban writers after that nation's revolution. Alvarez provides a historical and cultural context for these stories and a history of the short story
in Cuba. He also discusses homoeroticism in Cuban
short fiction and the works of the *novísimos*, writers
born after the revolution whose works began to appear in the late 1980's.

Whitfield, Esther. "Covering for Banknotes: Books,
Money, and the Cuban Short Story." In *Cuban Currency: The Dollar and "Special Period" Fiction*.
Minneapolis: University of Minnesota Press, 2008.
After the collapse of the Soviet Union in the 1990's,
Cuba instated the U.S. dollar as domestic currency,
the country was opened to foreign markets, and the
nation's culture boomed. Whitfield examines the
impact of these developments upon Cuban literature, devoting a chapter to short fiction's depiction
of money and cross-cultural economic relations.

INDIAN SHORT FICTION

Bande, Usha, and Atma Ram. *Woman in Indian Short
Stories: Feminist Perspective*. Jaipur, India: Rawat,
2003. Examines women writers' depiction of the
"new woman" in Marathi, Hindi, Punjab, and Indian-English short stories published from the mid-
1940's through the late 1990's.

Daiya, Krishna. *Post-Independence Women Short Story
Writers in Indian English*. New Delhi, India: Sarup
and Sons, 2006. Provides an overview of the works
of women short-story writers, analyzing the themes,
characterization, and styles of their stories. Assesses
the status of the short fiction genre and describes the
contributions of women's short fiction to the genre
and to Indian literature. Some of the writers whose
works are analyzed are Shashi Deshpande, Anita
Desai, Jhumpa Lahiri, Githa Hariharan, and Ruth
Prawer Jhabvala.

Mehta, Kamal, ed. *The Twentieth Century Indian Short
Story in English*. New Delhi, India: Creative Books,
2004.Collection of essays analyzing short-fiction by
Indian writers, including R. K. Narayan, Raja Rao,
Gautam Bhatia, Jhumpa Lahiri, and Salman
Rushdie. Includes an introductory essay chronicling
the emergence and growth of the Indian short story
in English.

Melwani, Murli. *Indian English Stories: From Colonial Beginnings to Post-Modern Times*. Calcutta:
Sampark, 2007. Charts the historical development
of the Indian short story in English. Includes discussions of short-story writers, including Raja Rao, R.
K. Narayan, and Ruth Prawer Jhabvala.

Prasad, Amar Nath, and S. John Peter Joseph, eds. *Indian Short Stories in English: Critical Explorations*. New Delhi, India: Sarup, 2008. Collection of more than twenty critical research papers analyzing the works of short-story writers, including Mulk Raj Anand, R. K. Narayan, Raja Rao, Shashi Deshpande, Rusking Bond, Vishnu Prabhakar, Jhumpa Lahiri, and Sarah Joseph. Also provides a historical overview of the Indian short story in English.

Ramanan, Mohan, and P. Sailaja, eds. *English and the Indian Short Story: Essays in Criticism*. New Delhi, India: Orient Longman, 2000. Collection of essays examining the short-story genre in India and its relationship to the English language and to English-language literature. Some of the essays discuss the impact of colonialism on Indian short fiction, how English has shaped Indian short-story writing, and the Indian diaspora; other essays provide feminist perspectives of short stories by women writers.

JAPANESE SHORT FICTION

Katō, Shūichi. *A History of Japanese Literature*. 3 vols. Tokyo: Kodansha International, 1979. A wide-ranging study that pays special heed to the sociohistorical background of Japan's literary development. A good counterbalance to Donald Keene's literary history.

Keene, Donald. *Seeds in the Heart: Japanese Literature from the Earliest Times to the Late Sixteenth Century*. New York: Henry Holt, 1993.

_____. *World Within Walls: Japanese Literature of the Pre-Modern Era*. New York: Holt, Rinehart and Winston, 1976.

_____. *Dawn to the West: Japanese Literature in the Modern Era*. New York: Columbia University Press, 1984. A three-volume English-language history of Japanese literature up to Yukio Mishima written by a leading scholar.

Tsuruta, Kinya, and Thomas Swann, eds. *Approaches to the Modern Japanese Short Story*. Tokyo: Waseda University Press, 1982. An immensely useful critical study of thirty-four stories by Japanese writers.

LATIN AMERICAN SHORT FICTION

Balderston, Daniel, ed. *The Latin American Short Story: An Annotated Guide to Anthologies and Criticism*. Westport, Conn.: Greenwood Press, 1992. Organizes the enormous body of short-story anthologies from the nineteen countries of Spanish America and Brazil for systematic study. The main section comprises annotated listings of 1,302 short-story anthologies; a second section comprises annotated bibliographies of criticism of the short story. Includes bibliographical references and an index.

Brushwood, John S. "The Spanish American Short Story from Quiroga to Borges." In *The Latin American Short Story: A Critical History*, edited by Margaret Sayers Peden. Boston: Twayne, 1983. Argues that Horacio Quiroga was the first Spanish American writer to pay close attention to how a story is created. Provides a historical survey of Spanish American short fiction, in which the late 1920's and early 1930's were characterized by innovative narration, a movement to regionalism took place in the mid-1930's, and a return to innovation and cosmopolitanism characterized the early 1940's.

Del George, Dana. *The Supernatural in Short Fiction of the Americas: The Other World in the New World*. Westport, Conn.: Greenwood Press, 2001. Describes how cultural encounters between European and indigenous societies and between "scientific materialism" and "premodern supernaturalism" resulted in the creation of new narrative forms, including supernatural short fiction.

Echevarría, Roberto González, and Enrique Pupo-Walker, eds. *The Cambridge History of Latin American Literature*. 3 vols. New York: Cambridge University Press, 1996. Volume 1 covers the period from discovery to modernism, volume 2 covers the twentieth century, and volume 3 covers Brazilian literature. Includes bibliographical references and an index.

Erro-Peralta, Nora, and Caridad Silva-Núñez, eds. *Beyond the Border: A New Age in Latin American Women's Fiction*. Pittsburgh, Pa.: Cleis Press, 1991. Covers works by Latin American female writers. Includes bibliographical references.

Foster, David William, ed. *Handbook of Latin American Literature*. New York: Garland, 1992. Offers separate essays on the literature of all Latin American countries, including French and Creole Haiti and Portuguese Brazil, written by scholars who focus on dominant issues and major movements, figures, and works, with emphasis on sociocultural and interpretive assessments. Includes bibliographical references and an index.

Lindstrom, Naomi. "The Spanish American Short Story from Echeverria to Quiroga." In *The Latin American Short Story: A Critical History*, edited by Margaret Sayers Peden. Boston: Twayne, 1983. Discusses the first Latin American short story, Estaban Echeverría's 1838 "The Slaughtering Grounds." Chronicles the movement from Romanticism to realism and naturalism and then to modernism. Notes that while Edgar Allan Poe and Guy de Maupassant were not taken so seriously elsewhere, they were taken more seriously in Latin America, where readers see these writers as providing channels to alternate realms of experience.

McMurray, George R. "The Spanish American Short Story from Borges to the Present." In *The Latin American Short Story: A Critical History*, edited by Margaret Sayers Peden. Boston: Twayne, 1983. Discusses Jorge Luis Borges as a writer who ushered in a new literary era in South America and describes the shift to political and social problems during the 1950's. Argues that the most talented Spanish American writer since Borges is Julio Cortázar from Argentina. Also examines works by José Donoso and Carlos Fuentes.

Ocasio, Rafael. *Literature of Latin America*. Wesport, CT: Greenwood Press, 2004. Examines Latin American literary production from colonial times to the twenty-first century.

Partnoy, Alicia, ed. *You Can't Drown the Fire: Latin American Women Writing in Exile*. Pittsburgh, Pa.: Cleis Press, 1988. Covers twentieth century female writers whose works have been translated into English. Includes bibliographical references.

Plimpton, George, ed. *Latin American Writers at Work*. New York: Modern Library, 2003. A compilation of conversations and anecdotes with contemporary Latin American authors that provides a glimpse into their literary ideas.

Smith, Verity, ed. *Encyclopedia of Latin American Literature*. Chicago: Fitzroy Dearborn, 1997. Contains entries on writers, works, and topics relating to the literature of Latin America, including survey articles on all the continent's countries. Includes bibliographical references and an index.

Swanson, Philip. "Culture Wars: Ways of Reading Latin American Fiction." In *Latin American Fiction: A Short Introduction*. Malden, Mass.: Blackwell, 2005. Offers relevant information to better understand contemporary Latin American fiction.

RUSSIAN SHORT FICTION

Connolly, Julian. "The Russian Short Story, 1880-1917." In *The Russian Short Story: A Critical History*, edited by Charles A. Moser. Boston: Twayne, 1986. Most of this essay focuses on Nikolai Leskov, Anton Chekhov, Maxim Gorky, Ivan Bunin, and Leonid Andreyev. Connolly briefly discusses the Symbolist movement's influence on Russian literature at the end of the nineteenth century.

Cornwell, Neil, ed. *The Society Tale in Russian Literature: From Odoevskii to Tolstoi*. Atlanta, Ga.: Rodopi, 1998. Collection of essays about the Russian "society tale," a genre of nineteenth century short fiction that examined the individual in relation to his or her society. Focuses on the development of this genre from around 1820 until later in the century, when the genre was subsumed by the realist novel. Some of the writers whose works are examined are Alexander Pushkin, Leo Tolstoy, Vladimir Odoevskii, and Maria Zhukhova.

Kagan-Kans, Eva. "The Russian Short Story, 1850-1880." In *The Russian Short Story: A Critical History*, edited by Charles A. Moser. Boston: Twayne, 1986. Focuses primarily on Ivan Turgenev, Leo Tolstoy, Fyodor Dostoevski, and the radical, populist, and feminist writers of the period. Representative stories of the writers are discussed and analyzed in terms of their contributions to the form and their relationship to, or reflection of, Russian social life at the time.

May, Charles E. "Chekhov and the Modern Short Story." In *A Chekhov Companion*, edited by Toby Clyman. Westport, Conn.: Greenwood Press, 1985. A detailed analysis of Anton Chekhov's influence on the development of the modern short story. Isolates Chekhov's most important innovations in the form and then shows how these elements have been further used and developed by such modern writers as Katherine Mansfield, Ernest Hemingway, Bernard Malamud, Raymond Carver, and others.

Moser, Charles A. ed. *The Russian Short Story: A Critical History*. Boston: Twayne, 1986. Surveys the development of the Russian short story from 1830 to 1980. Analyzes the works of short-story writers, including Alexander Pushkin. Argues that the short story might have developed as a genre that combined prose and verse.

Neuhauser, Rudolf. "The Russian Short Story, 1917-1980." In *The Russian Short Story: A Critical History*, edited by Charles A. Moser. Boston: Twayne, 1986. Discussion of postrevolution writers in Russia, such as Yevgeny Zamyatin, as well as the influence of Russian Formalist critics and writers, such as Viktor Shklovsky and Boris Eikhenbaum. A brief discussion of Isaac Babel is included here, although his influence on the short story as a form should probably receive more attention than this. Separate sections are devoted to Russian literature and World War II, the thaw after the death of Joseph Stalin, the woman question, and science prose and village prose.

O'Toole, L. Michael. *Structure, Style, and Interpretation in the Russian Short Story*. New Haven, Conn.: Yale University Press, 1982. An analysis of a few major stories by Nikolai Leskov, Nikolai Gogol, Alexander Pushkin, Maxim Gorky, Ivan Turgenev, and Anton Chekhov in terms of the Russian Formalist theories of Viktor Shklovsky, Boris Eikhenbaum, Boris Tomashevsky, Mikhail Bakhtin, and Vladimir Propp and the structuralist theories of Roland Barthes and Tzvetan Todorov. The introduction provides a general methodological introduction to interpretation through structural analysis.

Parts, Lyudmila, ed. *The Russian Twentieth-Century Short Story: A Critical Companion*. Brighton, Mass.: Academic Studies Press, 2010. Collection of essays analyzing short stories by Anton Chekhov, Ivan Bunin, Isaac Babel, Vladimir Nabokov, Varlam Shalamov, and other writers. Parts's introduction discusses the short story as "the genre of cultural transition."

Terras, Victor. "The Russian Short Story: 1830-1850." In *The Russian Short Story: A Critical History*, edited by Charles A. Moser. Boston: Twayne, 1986. Points out that 1830 was a watershed in the history of Russian literature in that it marked the end of the golden age of poetry and the shift to prose fiction, particularly short fiction. Discusses the Romantic origins of short fiction in Russia with Alexander Pushkin, the transition to psychological realism with Mikhail Lermontov, the significant contributions of the stories of Nikolai Gogol, the transition to the so-called natural school, and the early works of Fyodor Dostoevski and Ivan Turgenev.

SHORT FICTION IN TAMIL

Gros, François. *Deep Rivers: Selected Writings on Tamil Literature*. Translated by M.P. Boseman, edited by Kannan M. and Jennifer Clare. Berkeley: Tamil Chair, Department of South and Southeast Asian Studies, University of California, 2009. Includes an essay entitled "Tamil Short Stories: An Introduction."

SHORT FICTION IN URDU

Suhrawardy, Shaista Akhtar Bano. *A Critical Survey of the Development of the Urdu Novel and Short Story*. Karachi, Pakistan: Oxford University Press, 2006. Part 3 focuses on the Urdu short story. After a brief history of the short story in European literature, Suhrawardy chronicles the development of Urdu short fiction from the 1870's through the present day, including discussions of women short-story writers, modern short fiction, and the future of the Urdu novel and short story.

SOUTHEAST ASIAN SHORT FICTION

Chee, Tham Seong, ed. *Essays on Literature and Society in Southeast Asia.* Singapore: Singapore University Press, 1981. Many of the essays cover the development, impact, and relevance of the short story in select Southeast Asian nations.

Davidson, Jeremy, and Helen Cordell, eds. *The Short Story in South East Asia: Aspects of a Genre.* London: School of Oriental and African Studies, University of London, 1982. One of the first sustained literary studies of the short story in Southeast Asia. Provides a good historical introduction to the topic, with bibliography and notes for each essay.

Patke, Rajeev S., and Philip Holden, eds. *The Routledge Concise History of Southeast Asian Writing in English.* New York: Routledge, 2010. Discusses short stories written in English from the Philippines, Malaysia, and Singapore. A subchapter discusses fiction by nonnative writers that is set in Southeast Asia.

Smyth, David. *The Canon in Southeast Asian Literatures.* Richmond, England: Curzon Press, 2000. Collection of essays that discuss the importance of short stories for the literary canon of select Southeast Asian countries and their relevance in that nation's literary tradition and culture.

Yamada, Teri Shaffer, ed. *Modern Short Fiction of Southeast Asia: A Literary History.* Ann Arbor, Michigan: Association for Asian Studies, 2009. Excellent collection of eleven outstanding essays that cover the development of the short story in almost every Southeast Asian nation and discuss key authors and exemplary texts. Very informative, with a concise introduction by the editor.

_____. *Virtual Lotus: Modern Fiction of Southeast Asia.* Ann Arbor: University of Michigan Press, 2002. The best introduction to the topic. Gives both a concise, critical overview of the development of the short story and a well-chosen sample of stories for every Southeast Asian country but Timor-Leste.

SOUTH KOREAN SHORT FICTION

Holstein, John, trans. *A Moment's Grace: Stories from Korea in Transition.* Ithaca, N.Y.: Cornell University East Asia Program, 2009. The stories, published from 1936 through 1999, depict how South Koreans were affected by the country's modernization, including its liberation from Japan in 1945 and the Seoul Olympics of 1988. Includes a chapter that provides background about the political and social context of these stories.

TYPES OF SHORT FICTION

THE HYPERSTORY

Coover, Robert. "Storying in Hyperspace: 'Linkages.'" In *The Tales We Tell: Perspectives on the Short Story*, edited by Barbara Lounsberry, et al. Westport, Conn.: Greenwood Press, 1998. A discussion of the future of the short story in computerized hyperspace as a form that is nonsequential, multidirectional, and interactive. Discusses linked short fictional pieces in the past in the Bible, in medieval romances, and by Giovanni Boccaccio, Miguel de Cervantes, and Geoffrey Chaucer.

May, Charles E. "HyperStory: Teaching Short Fiction with Computers." In *The Tales We Tell: Perspectives on the Short Story*, edited by Barbara Lounsberry, et al. Westport, Conn.: Greenwood Press, 1998. Describes HyperStory, a computer program developed by the author, which teaches students how to read short fiction more carefully and thoughtfully. Uses Edgar Allan Poe's "The Cask of Amontillado" as an example; attempts to explain, with the help of student comments, the success of the program.

MAGICAL REALISM

Benito, Jesús, Ana Ma Manzanas, and Begoña Simal. *Uncertain Mirrors: Magical Realisms in U.S. Ethnic Literatures.* New York: Rodopi, 2009. Examines Magical Realism in comparison to other literary movements, such as postmodernism and postcolonialism, Studies the use of Magical Realism in works by various authors, discussing how these writers represent themselves and their characters.

Bowers, Maggie Ann. *Magic(al) Realism.* London: Routledge, 2004. Serves as a helpful introduction to the Magical Realism movement. Bowers provides an overview of the genre and a close examination of the genre's connections with postcolonialism.

Faris, Wendy B. *Ordinary Enchantments: Magical Realism and the Remystification of Narrative*. Nashville, Tenn.: Vanderbilt University Press, 2004. Faris discusses key components of Magic Realist fiction and explores the work of authors from around the world. Each chapter focuses on a different aspect of Magical Realism, ranging from studies of narrative structure to the representation of women. Examines the importance of the Magical Realism tradition and its greater cultural implications.

Gaylard, Gerald. *After Colonialism: African Postmodernism and Magical Realism*. Johannesburg: Wits University, 2006. Gaylard describes how two genres of fiction--postmodernism and Magical Realism--provide reflections on and responses to colonialism in Africa. He argues that genres such as Magical Realism, which allow writers freedom and release, provide African writers a sense of liberty in an era of colonization and assimilation.

Hart, Stephen, and Wen-chin Ouyang, eds. *A Companion to Magical Realism*. Rochester, N.Y.: Tamesis, 2006. Collection of essays providing a close examination of the Magical Realism genre. Essayists trace the genre's history, its common symbols, and the politics of representation in close readings of texts, including works by Gabriel García Márquez, Jorge Luis Borges, and Isabel Allende.

Hegerfeldt, Anne C. *Lies That Tell the Truth: Magic Realism Seen Through Contemporary Fiction in Britain*. New York: Rodopi, 2005. Hegerfeldt discusses the debate over the definition of the genre and gives in-depth analyses of literary techniques employed often in Magical Realism.

Schroeder, Shannin. *Rediscovering Magical Realism in the Americas*. Westport, Conn.: Praeger, 2004. Examines works of Magical Realism in North and South America, paying special attention to North American Magical Realists. Schroeder acknowledges that the genre is often associated primarily or only with Latin and Central American writers and confronts this assumption with discussion of often neglected Magical Realist writers.

Takolander, Maria. *Catching Butterflies: Bringing Magical Realism to Ground*. Bern, Switzerland: Peter Lang, 2007. Takolander, like other scholars of Magical Realism, discusses the debate over how the genre should be defined, as well as its inception and its influence around the world. By examining historical context, Takolander attempts to provide answers to questions about the genre's presence, dominance, and influence in the literary world.

Zamora, Lois Parkinson, and Wendy B. Faris, eds. *Magical Realism: Theory, History, Community*. London: Duke University Press, 1995. Collection of essays about developments in the Magical Realism movement in art, literature, and other media.

FOLKTALES AND FAIRY TALES

Ashliman, D. L. *Folk and Fairy Tales: A Handbook*. Westport, Conn.: Greenwood Press, 2004. Ashliman provides readers with a history of fairy tales and folktales, examines the definitions of these genres, and explores some examples of each type of tale.

Bettelheim, Bruno. *The Uses of Enchantment: The Meaning and Importance of Fairy Tales*. New York: Alfred A. Knopf, 1977. This book discusses the tradition of and patterns present in fairy tales, then gives extensive analyses of well-known fairy tales, including "Hansel and Gretel," "Little Red Riding Hood," "Snow White," "Goldilocks and the Three Bears," "The Sleeping Beauty," and "Cinderella."

Bottigheimer, Ruth B. *Grimms' Bad Girls and Bold Boys: The Moral and Social Vision of the Tales*. New Haven, Conn.: Yale University Press, 1987. Bottigheimer discusses the fairy-tale tradition, including specific patterns of the characters' speech, how they endure punishment, their struggle for power, and the value systems implicit in these tales.

Georges, Robert A., and Michael Owen Jones. *Folkloristics: An Introduction*. Bloomington: Indiana University Press, 1995. Defines folklore as a historical tradition, focusing on its role in various cultures, in human psychology, and as a historical science.

Jones, Steven Swann. *The Fairy Tale: The Magic Mirror of the Imagination*. New York: Routledge, 2002. Provides a history of the fairy-tale genre, awarding special attention to the roles of men and women in fairy tales of the past and describing how those figures influenced more contemporary stories.

Leeming, David Adams, ed. *Storytelling Encyclopedia*. Phoenix, Ariz.: Oryx Press, 1997. Provides a general discussion of the storytelling tradition and a look at a number of countries and their specific cultural contributions to the tradition. In addition, there are brief entries regarding the most popular people and theories related to the oral and written traditions.

Propp, Vladimir. *Morphology of the Folktale*. Edited by Svatava Pirkova-Jakovson, translated by Laurence Scott. Bloomington: Indiana University Research Center, 1958. All formalist and structuralist studies of narrative owe a debt to this pioneering early twentieth century study. Using one hundred fairy tales, Propp defines the genre itself by analyzing the stories according to characteristic actions or functions.

_____. *Theory and History of Folklore*. Minneapolis: University of Minnesota Press, 1984. This collection of Propp's essays expands on his theory of the narrative that he presented in *Morphology of the Folktale*.

Tatar, Maria. *Off With Their Heads: Fairy Tales and the Culture of Childhood*. Princeton, N.J.: Princeton University Press, 1992. Tatar examines how important writers in the fairy-tale tradition revised these stories in order to be more didactic for children. She argues that the typical portrayal of children in fairy tales is problematic, especially since the contemporary target audience of fairy tales is children.

Thompson, Stith. *The Folktale*. New York: Dryden Press, 1946. Discusses the nature, theories, and form of the folktale and presents a varied collection of international tales. Selected are tales from many categories, such as the complex and the simple tale.

Warner, Marina. *From the Beast to the Blonde: On Fairy Tales and Their Tellers*. New York: Farrar, Straus and Giroux, 1994. Warner studies the characters whose role is the telling of fairy tales and analyzes gender roles, specifically those of women, including the typical portrayals of daughters, mothers, stepmothers, brides, and runaway girls

Zipes, Jack. *Fairy Tales and the Art of Subversion: The Classical Genre for Children and the Process of Civilization*. New York: Routledge, 1991. Zipes focuses on the didactic function of fairy tales, ranging from the work of the Grimm brothers to later fairy tales. He argues that the primary function of fairy tales is to instill morals and lessons in their child readers.

_____. *Fairy Tale as Myth, Myth as Fairy Tale*. Lexington: University Press of Kentucky, 1994. Examines the history of the fairy tale and its rise as the genre preceding the folktale. Discusses many well-known fairy tales and their role in society.

SHORT FICTION AND WOMEN

Bande, Usha, and Atma Ram. *Woman in Indian Short Stories: Feminist Perspective*. Jaipur, India: Rawat, 2003. Examines women writers' depiction of the "new woman" in Marathi, Hindi, Punjab, and Indian-English short stories published from the mid-1940's through the late 1990's.

Bloom, Harold, ed. *Caribbean Women Writers*. Philadelphia: Chelsea House, 1997. A thorough examination of contemporary, female Caribbean authors who write in English, including Jean Rhys, Jamaica Kincaid, Beryl Gilroy, and Edwidge Danticat. Includes bibliographical references and an index.

Brown, Julie, ed. *American Women Short Story Writers: A Collection of Critical Essays*. New York: Garland, 2000. Collection of essays that analyze short fiction by nineteenth and twentieth century women writers, ranging from serious works of literature to popular tales about "sob sisters." Some of the writers whose works are examined are Lydia Maria Child, Elizabeth Stoddard, Louisa May Alcott, Ellen Glasgow, Edith Wharton, Eudora Welty, Dorothy Parker, Joyce Carol Oates, and Denise Chávez.

Burgin, Mary. "The 'Feminine' Short Story: Recuperating the Moment." *Style* 27 (Fall, 1993): 380-386. Argues that there is a connection between so-called feminine writing that focuses on isolated moments and the concerns of women who have chosen the short story as a form. Claims that the twentieth century epiphanic short story is a manifestation of women's tradition of temporal writing as opposed to the spatial writing of men.

Daiya, Krishna. *Post-Independence Women Short Story Writers in Indian English*. New Delhi, India: Sarup and Sons, 2006. Provides an overview of the works of women short-story writers, analyzing the themes, characterization, and styles of their stories. Assesses the status of the short-fiction genre and describes the contributions of women's short fiction to the genre and to Indian literature. Some of the writers whose works are analyzed are Shashi Deshpande, Anita Desai, Jhumpa Lahiri, Githa Hariharan, and Ruth Prawer Jhabvala.

Erro-Peralta, Nora, and Caridad Silva-Núñez, eds. *Beyond the Border: A New Age in Latin American Women's Fiction*. Pittsburgh, Pa.: Cleis Press, 1991. Covers works by Latin American female writers. Includes bibliographical references.

Hanson, Clare. "The Lifted Veil: Women and Short Fiction in the 1880's and 1890's." *The Yearbook of English Studies* 26 (1996): 135-142. Argues that British women writers in the early modernist period chose the short story to challenge the existing dominant order. Shows how this challenge is embodied in such stories as Charlotte Mew's "Mark Stafford's Wife" as an encounter, presented in iconic, painterly terms, between a male protagonist and a woman, who is then unveiled.

Harde, Roxanne, ed. *Narratives of Community: Women's Short Story Sequences*. Newcastle, England: Cambridge Scholars, 2007. Collection of essays analyzing women's roles in domestic, social, and literary communities and how they attain their identities in these communities. Some of the writers whose works are examined are Sandra Cisneros, Margaret Laurence, Salwa Bakr, Mary Caponegro, Gloria Naylor, Elizabeth Gaskell, Virginia Woolf, Alice Munro, and Maxine Hong Kingston.

Harrington, Ellen Burton, ed. *Scribbling Women and the Short Story Form: Approaches by American and British Women Writers*. New York: Peter Lang, 2008. Collection of essays providing feminist analyses of short fiction by British and American women, focusing on how this genre "liberated" women writers in the period from 1850 through the late twentieth century. Some of the women writers whose works are analyzed are Rebecca Harding Davis, Louise May Alcott, Kate Chopin, Katherine Anne Porter, Flannery O'Connor, Cynthia Ozick, and Lydia Davis.

Palumbo-DeSimone, Christine. *Sharing Secrets: Nineteenth-Century Women's Relations in the Short Story*. Madison, N.J.: Fairleigh Dickinson University Press, 2000. Palumbo-DeSimone contradicts the criticism that many short stories by nineteenth century women writers are framed around a "seemingly meaningless incident," arguing that these stories are detailed, meaningful, and intricately designed works of serious fiction.

Partnoy, Alicia, ed. *You Can't Drown the Fire: Latin American Women Writing in Exile*. Pittsburgh, Pa.: Cleis Press, 1988. Covers twentieth century female writers whose works have been translated into English. Includes bibliographical references.

PERSONAL ACCOUNTS BY SHORT-FICTION WRITERS

Allende, Isabel. "The Short Story." *Journal of Modern Literature* 20 (Summer, 1996): 21-28. This personal account of storytelling makes suggestions about the differences between the novel and the short story, the story's demand for believability, the story's focus on change, the story's relationship to dream, and the story as events transformed by poetic truth.

Bailey, Tom, ed. *On Writing Short Stories*. 2d ed. New York: Oxford University Press, 2011. In addition to containing a sampling of some classic short stories, this book also features a section in which short-story writers discuss some basic issues regarding the definition and form of these works. These writers include Francine Prose, who explains what makes a short story, and Andre Dubus, who explores the "habit of writing." Bailey also contributes an essay about character, plot, setting, time, metaphor, and voice in short fiction.

Barth, John. "It's a Short Story." In *Further Fridays: Essays, Lectures, and Other Nonfiction, 1984-1994*. New York: Little, Brown, 1995. A personal account by a "congenital novelist" of his brief love affair with the short story during the writing of *Chimera* (1972) and the stories in *Lost in the Funhouse* (1968).

Blythe, Will, ed. *Why I Write: Thoughts on the Craft of Fiction*. Boston: Little, Brown, 1998. A collection of essays by various authors about writing fiction. The essays most relevant to the short story are those by Joy Williams, who says that writers must cherish the mystery of discovery in the process of writing; Thom Jones, who discusses his passionate engagement in the writing of short stories; and Mary Gaitskill, who calls stories the "rich, unseen underlayer of the most ordinary moments."

Burgess, Anthony. "Anthony Burgess on the Short Story." *Journal of the Short Story in English*, no. 2 (1984): 31-47. Burgess admits that he disdains the short story because he cannot write it. He says that the novel presents an epoch, while the short story presents a revelation. Discusses different types of stories, distinguishing between the literary short story, which is patterned, and the commercial form, which is anecdotal.

Charters, Ann, ed. *The Story and Its Writer: An Introduction to Short Fiction*. 6th ed. Boston: Bedford/ St. Martin's, 2003. A collection of classic short stories, with commentaries by their authors and other writers that analyze the works and describe how the stories were written. Includes appendixes chronicling storytelling before the emergence of the short story and the history of the short story.

Gioia, Dana, and R. S. Gwynn, eds. *The Art of the Short Story*. New York: Pearson Longman, 2006. This anthology includes an "author's perspective" from each of its fifty-two authors, in which the writers comment on the aims, context, and workings of their short stories. For example, Sherwood Anderson and Raymond Carver provide advice on the craft of writing; Margaret Atwood discusses Canadian identity; Alice Walker writes about race and gender; and Flannery O'Connor explains the importance of religious grace in her work. Some of the other authors included in the anthology are John Cheever, Albert Camus, F. Scott Fitzgerald, Ernest Hemingway, Anton Chekhov, James Joyce, Jorge Luis Borges, William Faulkner, Chinua Achebe, Ha Jin, Sandra Cisneros, and Gabriel García Márquez.

Iftekharuddin, Farhat, Mary Rohrberger, and Maurice Lee, eds. *Speaking of the Short Story: Interviews with Contemporary Writers*. Jackson: University Press of Mississippi, 1997. Collection of twenty-one interviews with short-story writers, such as Isabel Allende, Rudolfo A. Anaya, Ellen Douglas, Richard Ford, Bharati Mukherjee, and Leslie Marmon Silko, and short story critics, such as Susan Lohafer, Charles E. May, and Mary Rohrberger.

Lee, Maurice A., ed. *Writers on Writing: The Art of the Short Story*. Westport, Conn.: Praeger, 2005. A collection of essays in which short-story writers from around the world discuss their craft and analyze stories and types of short fiction. Some of the contributors include Amiri Baraka, Olive Senior, Jayne Anne Philips, Janette Turner Hospital, Ivan Wolfers, Singapore writer Kirpal Singh, and Ivan Wolfers.

Mandelbaum, Paul, ed. *Twelve Short Stories and Their Making*. New York: Persea Books, 2005. These twelve stories by contemporary writers have been selected to illustrate six elements of the short story: character, plot, point of view, theme, setting, and structure. The book also includes individual interviews with the twelve authors in which they describe their writing processes and the challenges they faced in composing their selected stories. The featured writers include Elizabeth Tallent, Charles Johnson, Allan Gurganus, Ursula K. Le Guin, Jhumpa Lahiri, Sandra Cisneros, and Tobias Wolff.

O'Connor, Flannery. "Writing Short Stories." In *Mystery and Manners*, edited by Sally and Robert Fitzgerald. New York: Farrar, Straus & Giroux, 1969. In this lecture at a southern writers' conference, O'Connor discusses the two qualities necessary for the short story: "sense of manners," which writers get from the texture of their immediate surroundings, and "sense of mystery," which is always the mystery of personality-- "showing how some specific folks *will* do, in spite of everything."

Senior, Olive. "Lessons from the Fruit Stand: Or, Writing for the Listener." *Journal of Modern Literature* 20 (Summer, 1996): 40-44. An account of one writer's development of the short story as a personal engagement between teller and listener. Discusses the relationship between the oral tradition of gossip and folklore and the development of short-story conventions. Claims that the short story is a form based on bits and pieces of human lives for which there is no total picture.

Turchi, Peter, and Andrea Barrett, eds. *The Story Behind the Story: Twenty-six Writers and How They Work*. New York: W. W. Norton, 2004. The stories in this collection were written by faculty members in the writing program at Warren Wilson College, including Antonya Nelson, Margot Livesey, David Shields, C. J. Hribal, Andrea Barrett, Steven Schwartz, and Jim Shepard. Accompanying each story is a brief essay in which the writer describes how his or her story was created.

Wright, Austin. "The Writer Meets the Critic on the Great Novel/Short Story Divide." *Journal of Modern Literature* 20 (Summer, 1996): 13-19. A personal account by a short-story critic and novelist of some of the basic differences between the critical enterprise and the writing of fiction, as well as some of the generic differences between the short story and the novel.

Charles E. May
Updated by Rebecca Kuzins

GUIDE TO ONLINE RESOURCES

Web Sites

The following sites were visited by the editors of Salem Press in 2011. Because URLs frequently change, the accuracy of these addresses cannot be guaranteed; however, long-standing sites, such as those of colleges and universities, national organizations, and government agencies, generally maintain links when sites are moved or updated.

African Literature and Writers on the Internet

http://www-sul.stanford.edu/depts/ssrg/africa/lit.html

This page is included in the Africa South of the Sahara Web site created by Karen Fung of Stanford University. It provides an alphabetical list of links to numerous resources about Chinua Achebe, Ben Okri, Ngugi wa Thiong'o, Chimamanda Ngozi Adichie, and other African writers; online journals and essays; association Web sites; and other materials. It also contains a link to the full text of Joseph Conrad's novella *Heart of Darkness*.

Bibliomania: Short Stories

http://www.bibliomania.com/0/5/frameset.html

Among Bibliomania's more than two thousand texts are short stories written by American and foreign writers, including Anton Chekhov, Maxim Gorky, and Nikolai Gogol. The stories can be retrieved via lists of titles and authors.

Books and Writers

http://www.kirjasto.sci.fi/indeksi.htm

A broad, comprehensive, and easy-to-use resource about hundreds of authors throughout the world, extending from 70 B.C.E to the twenty-first century. Books and Writers contains an alphabetical list of authors with links to pages featuring a biography, a list of works, and recommendations for further reading about each author; each writer's page also includes links to related pages in the site. Although brief, the biographical essays provide a solid overview of the authors' careers, their contributions to literature, and their literary influence.

A Celebration of Women Writers

http://digital.library.upenn.edu/women

An extensive compendium of information about the contributions of women writers throughout history. Users can obtain biographical and bibliographical information about African, Latin American, Russian and other women writers by using the Browse by Country feature, or they can browse by the writers' names, ethnicities, and centuries in which they lived.

The Latin American Short Story:
A Cultural Tradition

http://www.yale.edu/ynhti/curriculum/
units/1987/1/87.01.08.x.html#b

This page is included in the Web site for the Yale-New Haven Teachers Institute and contains a lesson plan for teaching students about the Latin American short story. In addition to listing the plan's objectives and strategies, this page provides a historical overview and reading lists for both teachers and students of works by Jorge Luis Borges, Gabriel García Márquez, and other writers.

LiteraryHistory.com

http://www.literaryhistory.com

An excellent source of Web-based academic, scholarly, and critical literature, providing numerous pages about specific eras and literary genres, including individual pages for eighteenth, nineteenth, and twentieth century literature and for postcolonial literature. These pages contain alphabetical lists of authors that link to articles, reviews, overviews, excerpts of works, teaching guides, podcast interviews, and other materials.

Literature: What Makes a Good Short Story

http://www.learner.org/interactives/literature

Annenberg Learner.org, a site providing interactive resources for teachers, contains this section describing the elements of short fiction, including plot construction, point of view, character development, setting, and theme. It also features the text of "A Jury of Her Peers," a short story by Susan Glaspell, in order to illustrate the components of short fiction.

LitWeb

http://litweb.net

LitWeb provides biographies of more than five hundred world authors throughout history that can be accessed via an alphabetical listing. The pages about each writer contain a list of his or her works, suggestions for further reading, and illustrations. LitWeb also offers information about past and present winners of major literary prizes.

The Modern Word: The Libyrinth

http://www.themodernword.com/authors.html

The Modern Word provides a great deal of critical information about postmodern writers and contemporary experimental fiction. The core of the site is "The Libyrinth," which lists authors for which there are links to essays and other resources. There are also sections devoted to Samuel Beckett, Jorge Luis Borges, Gabriel García Márquez, James Joyce, Franz Kafka, and Thomas Pynchon.

The Short Story Library at American Literature

http://www.americanliterature.com/ss/ssindx.html

A compilation of more than two thousand short stories that can be accessed via alphabetical lists of story titles and authors. Although the majority of the authors are American, the site also features English translations of stories by Anton Chekhov, Nikolai Gogol, Alexander Pushkin, and Gabriel García Márquez.

Voice of the Shuttle

http://vos.ucsb.edu

The most complete and authoritative place for online information about literature. Created and maintained by professors and students in the English department at the University of California, Santa Barbara, Voice of the Shuttle is a database with thousands of links to electronic books, academic journals, association Web sites, sites created by university professors, and many, many other resources about the humanities. The page entitled "Literatures Other than English" offers a gateway to information about the literature of numerous countries and world regions, including Africa, Arabic-speaking nations, China, Russia, Japan, and Korea.

Voices from the Gaps

http://voices.cla.umn.edu

This site from the English department at the University of Minnesota is "dedicated to bringing together marginalized resources and knowledge about women artists of color," including women writers. Users can retrieve information by artists' names or by a selection of keywords, including Africans, Belizeans, Caribbean, Jamaicans, and many other nationalities.

ELECTRONIC DATABASES

Electronic databases usually do not have their own URLs. Instead, public, college, and university libraries subscribe to these databases, provide links to them on their Web sites, and make them available to library card holders or specified patrons. Readers can check library Web sites or ask reference librarians to check on availability.

Bloom's Literary Reference Online

Facts On File publishes this database of thousands of articles by renowned scholar Harold Bloom and other literary critics, examining the lives and works of great writers worldwide. The database also includes information on more than forty-six thousand literary characters, literary topics, themes, movements, and genres, plus video segments about literature. Users can retrieve information by browsing writers' names, titles of works, time periods, genres, or writers' nationalities.

Literary Reference Center

EBSCO's Literary Reference Center (LRC) is a comprehensive full-text database containing information from reference works, books, literary journals, and other materials. Its contents include more than 34,000 plot summaries, synopses, and overviews of literary works; almost 100,000 essays and articles of literary criticism; about 180,000 author biographies; more than 683,000 book reviews; and more than 6,200 author interviews. It also contains the entire contents of Salem Press's MagillOnLiterature Plus. Users can retrieve information by browsing a list of authors' names or titles of literary works; they can also use an advanced search engine to access information by numerous categories, including authors' name, gender, cultural identity, national identity, and the years in which he or she lived, or by literary title, character, locale, genre, and publication date.

Literary Resource Center

Published by Gale, this comprehensive literary database contains information on the lives and works of more than 135,000 authors from Gale reference sources in all genres, all time periods, and throughout the world. In addition, the database offers more than 75,000 full-text critical essays and reviews from some of Gale's reference publications, including *Short Story Criticism*; more than 11,000 overviews of frequently studied works; and more than 300,000 full-text short stories, poems, and plays. Literary Resource Center also features a literary-historical time line and an encyclopedia of literature.

MagillOnLiterature Plus

MagillOnLiterature Plus is a comprehensive, integrated literature database produced by Salem Press and available on the EBSCO host platform. The database contains the full-text of Salem's many literature-related reference works, including *Master Plots* (series I and II), *Cyclopedia of World Authors*, *Cyclopedia of Literary Characters*, *Cyclopedia of Literary Places*, and *Critical Surveys of Literature*. Among its contents are critical essays, brief plot summaries, extended character profiles, and detailed setting discussions about works of literature by more than eighty-five hundred short- and long-fiction writers, poets, dramatists, essayists, and philosophers. It also features biographical essays on more than twenty-five hundred authors, with lists of each author's principal works and current secondary bibliographies.

NoveList

NoveList is a readers' advisory service produced by EBSCO Publishing. The database provides access to 155,000 titles of both adult and juvenile fiction, including collections of short fiction. Users can type the words "short story" into the search engine and retrieve more than fourteen thousand short-story collections; users can also search by author's name to access titles of books, information about the author, and book reviews.

Short Story Index

This index, created by the H. W. Wilson Company, features information on more than 76,500 stories from more than 4,000 collections. Users can retrieve information by author, title, keyword, subject, date, source, literary technique, or a combination of these categories. The subject searches provide information about the stories' themes, locales, narrative techniques, and genres.

Rebecca Kuzins

TIMELINE

c. 2000 B.C.E.	The main portion of the poem *Gilgamesh* (*Gilgamesh Epic*, 1917), is written on cuneiform clay tablets. This epic recounts the exploits of Gilgamesh, the legendary king of Uruk and the first literary hero.
c. 430	Liu Yiqing composes *Shi-shuo xinyu* (*A New Account of Tales of the World*), a collection of stories about famous statesmen and military figures and one of the earliest surviving works of Chinese short fiction.
15th century	*Alf layla wa-layla* (*The Arabian Nights' Entertainments* 1706-1708; also known as *A Thousand and One Nights*) is published. This collection of stories from Persia, Arabia, India, and Egypt was handed down orally for hundreds of years before it was compiled and presented in written form.
1686	Ihara Saikaku publishes the work considered his masterpiece, *Kōshoku gonin onna* (*Five Women Who Loved Love*, 1956), a collection of five scandalous love stories.
1766	Chinese writer Pu Songling publishes the work on which his literary reputation rests, *Liaozhai zhiyi* (*Strange Stories from a Chinese Studio*, 1880), a compilation of 431 stories.
1834	*Pikovaya dama* (*The Queen of Spades*, 1858) by Russian writer Alexander Pushkin, is published. This complex story, one of the most well-known in short fiction, uses an omniscient narrator to present the points of view of six characters.
1842	"Shinel" ("The Overcoat," 1923), Nikolai Gogol's tale of a poor and hapless civil servant and his new coat, is published. This story will influence many other writers and will help shape the direction of Russian short fiction.
1852	Ivan Turgenev publishes *Zapiski okhotnika* (*Russian Life in the Interior*, 1855; better known as *A Sportsman's Sketches*, 1932), considered by some critics to be the greatest book of short stories ever written.
1870	Brazilian writer Joaquim Maria Machado de Assis publishes his first short-fiction collection, *Contos fluminenses*.
1886	Leo Tolstoy publishes the novella *Smert' Ivana Il'icha* (*The Death of Ivan Ilyich*, 1887).
1894-1914	Sholom Aleichem's collection *Tevye der Milkhiger* (*Tevvye's Daughters*, 1949) is published. Writing in Yiddish, Aleichem recounts tales of Jewish life in czarist Russia.

1904	Anton Chekhov dies. Often described as the greatest short-story writer ever, Chekhov created the modern short story with works characterized by almost scientific objectivity, irony, the evocation of a single dominant mood, and relatively insignificant action.
1921	Chinese writer Lu Xun publishes his longest and most important work of short fiction, *Ah Q zheng zhuan* (*The True Story of Ah Q*).
1933	Russian writer Ivan Bunin wins the Nobel Prize in Literature.
1935	The Akutagawa Prize, a Japanese literary award presented semiannually, is established in honor of Ryūnosuke Akutagawa, whose numerous short stories include "Rashōmon" (1915). The prize is most often awarded to short stories or novellas.
1936	*Bannen*, the first short-fiction collection by Japanese writer Osamu Dazai, is published.
1941	Kimitake Hiraoka begins using the pseudonym Yukio Mishima, under which he will write more than eighty short stories, as well as novels, plays, and other works.
1944	Jorge Luis Borges establishes his reputation as the most important short-fiction writer in Latin American history with the publication of *Ficciones, 1935-1944*. These and other stories by the Argentinean writer eschew realistic depiction of external Latin life in favor of imaginative tales about universal themes appealing to more intelligent readers.
1950	"Young prose" and "village prose" emerge as new short-fiction genres in the Soviet Union.
1962	Nigerian writer Chinua Achebe publishes *The Sacrificial Egg, and Other Stories*.
1966	Israeli writer Shmuel Yosef Agnon is one of two writers to receive the Nobel Prize in Literature. Agnon is best known for his more than two hundred short stories.
1967	Guatemalan writer Miguel Ángel Asturias is awarded the Nobel Prize in Literature.
1975	*Todos los cuentos de Gabriel García Márquez*, the collected stories of Colombian writer Gabriel García Márquez, are published and will be translated into English nine years later.
1977	Alejo Carpentier wins the Premio Miguel de Cervantes. The works of this Cuban-born writer include a short-story collection, *Guerra del tiempo* (1958; *War of Time*, 1970).
1987	Nigerian writer Ben Okri receives the Commonwealth Writer's Prize for the African region for *Incidents at the Shrine* (1986), his first short-fiction collection.

1996	The publication of *McOndo*, a collection of Latin American short fiction, ushers in a new style of writing that will continue into the twenty-first century. Proponents of *McOndismo* criticize the Latin Boom writers for exploiting Magical Realism, and they are preoccupied with popular culture, fast food, television, films, and the Internet.
1997	Chinese-born writer Ha Jin wins the PEN/Hemingway Award for his first short-story collection *Ocean of Words: Army Stories*. Jin will go on to write other award-winning works of short fiction.
2000	The first Caine Prize, which annually recognizes the best work of African short fiction, is presented at the Zimbabwe Book Fair. The winner is Leila Aboulela of Sudan for her story "The Museum."
2001	V. S. Naipaul, a writer born in Trinidad and Tobago who has published several short-story collections, receives the Nobel Prize in Literature.
2002	*Virtual Lotus: Modern Fiction of Southeast Asia,* edited by Teri Shaffer Yamada, is published. This anthology features English translations of short stories from this region.
2005	Japanese writer Haruki Murakami receives the Frank O'Connor International Short Story Award for his collection *Blind Willow, Sleeping Woman*. The prize, inaugurated in 2005, is named in honor of Irish writer Frank O'Connor.
2008	Ezekiel Mphahlele, considered the most significant black South African writer of the twentieth century, dies in Pretoria. His oeuvre includes five short-fiction collections.
2009	Daniyal Mueenuddin receives the Story Prize for *In Other Rooms, Other Wonders*.
2010	Mario Vargas Llosa of Peru receives the Nobel Prize in Literature.

Rebecca Kuzins

MAJOR AWARDS

CAINE PRIZE FOR AFRICAN WRITING

The Caine Prize is awarded annually for the best original short story by an African writer published in English, and it is given to writers residing in African countries or elsewhere. The prize was first presented in 2000.

2000: Leila Aboulela-- "The Museum"--Sudan

2001: Helon Habila-- "Love Poems"--Nigeria

2002: Binyavanga Wainaina-- "Discovering Home"--Kenya

2003: Yvonne Adhiambo Owuor-- "Weight of Whispers"--Kenya

2004: Brian Chikwava-- "Seventh Street Alchemy"--Zimbabwe

2005: S. A. Afolabi-- "Monday Morning"--Nigeria

2006: Mary Watson-- "Jungfrau"--South Africa

2007: Monica Arac de Nyeko-- "Jambula Tree"--Uganda

2008: Henrietta Rose-Innes-- "Poison"--South Africa

2009: E. C. Osondu-- "Waiting"--Nigeria

2010: Olufemi Terry-- "Stickfighting Days"--Sierra Leone

THOMAS PRINGLE AWARD

This annual award, administered by the English Academy of South Africa, is presented on a rotating basis for literary works, including short stories. This list includes only those authors who have received this award for short stories.

1969: Nadine Gordimer

1979: J. A. Maimane

1981: Andre Lemmer

1982: Greg Latter

1984: Sheila Roberts

1988: Rose Zwi

1990: Patrick Cullinan

1992: Andries Walter Oliphant

1994: Ivan Vladislavic

1996: Peter Merrington

1998: Lerothodi La Pula

2000: Evan Kaplan

2002: Dan Wylie

2004: Ananda Cersh

2006: Ken Barris

2008: David Medalie

THE BEST AMERICAN SHORT STORIES

Published annually since 1915, *The Best American Short Stories* includes the best stories that were published in American or Canadian magazines during the year. Selection for the volume is considered a high honor. This list includes only the authors who are featured in *Critical Survey of Short Fiction: World Writers*.

The Best American Short Stories, 1997: Selected from U.S. and Canadian Magazines, *edited by* **E. Annie Proulx, with Katrina Kenison**

Jin, Ha-- "Manners and Right Behavior: Saboteur"

The Best American Short Stories, 1999: Selected from U.S. and Canadian Magazines,
edited by **Amy Tan, with Katrina Kenison**

Jin, Ha-- "In the Kindergarten"

The Best American Short Stories, 2000: Selected from U.S. and Canadian Magazines,
edited by **E.L. Doctorow, with Katrina Kenison**

Jin, Ha-- "The Bridegroom"

The Best American Short Stories, 2001: Selected from U.S. and Canadian Magazines,
edited by **Barbara Kingsolver, with Katrina Kenison**

Jin, Ha-- "After Cowboy Chicken Came to Town"

The Best American Short Stories, 2008: Selected from U.S. and Canadian Magazines,
edited by **Salman Rushdie, with Heidi Pitlor**

Mueenuddin, Daniyal-- "Nawabdin Electrician"

FLANNERY O'CONNOR AWARD FOR SHORT FICTION

Established in 1983, the University of Georgia Press presents this award to writers for an outstanding collection of short stories or novellas. The prize is named for the esteemed short-story writer and novelist Flannery O'Connor. This list includes only the winners who are featured in *Critical Survey of Short Fiction: World Writers.*

1997: Ha Jin--*Under the Red Flag*

PEN/O. HENRY AWARD

The O. Henry Awards, published each year in a volume entitled *Prize Stories*, were established in 1919; in 2009, prize officials partnered with the PEN American Center and the prize was renamed the PEN/O. Henry Award. The annual volume of prize-winners features stories written in English that were published in American and Canadian magazines. This list includes only the authors who are featured in *Critical Survey of Short Fiction: World Writers.*

2006
Xu Xi-- "Famine"

2008
Ha Jin-- "A Composer and His Parakeets"

2009
Ha Jin-- "The House Behind a Weeping Cherry"

JUROR AWARD

Daniyal Mueenuddin-- "A Spoiled Man"

STORY PRIZE

Established in 2004, the Story Prize award honors the author of an outstanding collection of short fiction that is written in English and initially published in the United States. This list includes only the winners who are included in *Critical Survey of Short Fiction: World Writers.*

2009: Daniyal Mueenuddin--*In Other Rooms, Other Wonders*

COMMONWEALTH AWARDS

COMMONWEALTH SHORT STORY COMPETITION

The Commonwealth Short Story Competition aims to promote new writing for radio. The prize has been awarded since 2008 and is funded and administered by the Commonwealth Foundation and the Commonwealth Broadcasting Association. Competition for the prize is open to all citizens of the Commonwealth countries.

2008

Overall Winner: Julie Curwin-- "World Backwards"--Canada

Regional Winner, Africa: Taddeo Bwambale Nyonda-- "Die, Dear Tofa"--Uganda

Regional Winner, Asia: Salil Chaturvedi-- "The Bombay Run"--India

Regional Winner, Europe: Tania Hershman-- "Straight Up"--England

Regional Winner, Pacific: Jennifer Mills-- "Jack's Red Hat"--Australia

2009

Overall Winner: Jennifer Moore-- "Table Talk"--England

Regional Winner, Africa: Kachi A. Ozumba-- "The One-Armed Thief"--Nigeria

Regional Winner, Asia: Manasi Subramaniam-- "Debbie's Call"--India

Regional Winner, Caribbean Alake Pilgrim-- "Shades"--Trinidad and Tobago

Regional Winner, Pacific: Terri-Anne Green-- "The Colour of Rain"--Australia

2010

Overall Winner: Shachi Kaul-- "Retirement"--India

Regional Winner, Africa: Karen Jennings-- "From Dark"--South Africa

Regional Winner, Canada and Europe: Melissa Madore-- "Swallow Dive"--Canada

Regional Winner, Caribbean: Barbara Jenkins-- "Something from Nothing"--Trinidad and Tobago

Regional Winner, Pacific: Jena Woodhouse-- "Praise Be"--Australia

Special Prize, Science, Technology and Society: Anuradha Kumar-- "The First Hello"--India

Special Prize, Story for Children: Iona Massey-- "Grandma Makes Meatballs"--Australia

Anietie Isong Special Prize for a Story from Nigeria: Shola Olowu-Asante-- "Dinner for Three"--Nigeria

COMMONWEALTH WRITERS' PRIZE

Established in 1987, this prize recognizes the best works of fiction written by an established writer from the Commonwealth countries. Only one work of short fiction has received the prize:

1987: Olive Senior--*Summer Lightning, and Other Stories*--Jamaica

INDIAN AWARDS

JNANPITH AWARD

Any Indian citizen who writes in any of the official languages of India is eligible for the Jnanpith Award. Before 1982, the awards were given for a single work by a writer; since 1982, the prize has been presented for a lifetime contribution to Indian literature. This listing cites only the prize-winning authors whose works include short fiction.

1966: Tarashankar Bandopadhyaya
1967: Kuppali V. Puttappa
1970: Viswanatha Satyanarayana
1973: Gopinath Mohanty
1974: Vishnu Sakharam Khandekar
1975: P. V. Akilan
1976: Ashapurna Devi
1977: K. Shivaram Karanth
1978: Sachchidananda Hirananda Vatsyayan (pseudonym Ajneya)
1979: Birendra Kumar Bhattacharya
1980: S. K. Pottekkatt
1981: Amrita Pritam
1983: Masti Venkatesha Iyengar

1984: Thakazhi Sivasankara Pillai
1985: Pannalal Patel
1986: Sachidananda Roautroy
1987: Vishnu Vāman Sgurwādkar (pseudonym Kusumāgraj)
1989: Qurratulain Hyder
1994: U. R. Aranthamurthy
1995: M. T. Vasudevan Nair
1996: Mahasweta Devi
1999: Nirmal Verma and S. Gurdial Singh
2000: Indira Goswami
2002: D. Jayakanthan
2005: Kunwar Narayan

INTERNATIONAL AWARDS

FRANK O'CONNOR INTERNATIONAL SHORT STORY AWARD

Named in honor of Irish writer Frank O'Connor, this award is presented annually for a collection of short stories. The award was inaugurated in 2005.

2005: Yiyun Li--*A Thousand Years of Good Prayers*--China/United States
2006: Haruki Murakami--*Blind Willow, Sleeping Woman*--Japan
2007: Miranda July--*No One Belongs Here More than You*--United States

2008: Jhumpa Lahiri--*Unaccustomed Earth*--United States
2009: Simon Van Booy--*Love Begins in Winter*--England
2010: Ron Rash--*Burning Bright*--United States

FRANZ KAFKA PRIZE

This international prize honors writer Franz Kafka by presenting an award to a writer for lifetime achievement. First presented in 2001, the prize is cosponsored by the Franz Kafka Society and the city of Prague, Czech Republic. This listing cites only the prize-winning authors whose works include short fiction.

2001: Philip Roth--United States
2002: Ivan Klíma--Czech Republic
2003: Péter Nádas--Hungary

2006: Haruki Murakami--Japan
2008: Arnošt Lustig--Czech Republic
2009: Peter Handke--Austria

JERUSALEM PRIZE FOR THE FREEDOM OF THE INDIVIDUAL IN SOCIETY

The Jerusalem Prize is a biennial literary award presented to writers whose works have dealt with themes of human freedom in society. This listing cites only the prize-winning authors whose works include short fiction.

1965: Max Frisch--Switzerland
1969: Ignazio Silone--Italy
1971: Jorge Luis Borges--Argentina
1973: Eugene Ionesco--Romania/France
1975: Simone de Beauvoir--France
1981: Graham Green--England
1983: V. S. Naipaul--Trinidad and Tobago/England

1985: Milan Kundera--Czech Republic/France
1993: Stefan Heym--Germany
1995: Mario Vargas Llosa--Peru
1999: Don DeLillo--United States
2001: Susan Sontag--United States
2003: Arthur Miller--United States
2009: Haruki Murakami--Japan

MAN BOOKER INTERNATIONAL PRIZE

Established in 2005, this award is presented biennially to a living author of any nationality for fiction published in English or generally available in English translation. The first four winners have all written short fiction.

2005: Ismail Kadaré--Albania
2007: Chinua Achebe--Nigeria

2009: Alice Munro--Canada
2011: Philip Roth--United States

NEUSTADT INTERNATIONAL PRIZE FOR LITERATURE

Awarded biennially since 1970, this award, sponsored by the University of Oklahoma, honors writers for a body of work. This listing cites only the prize-winning authors whose works include short fiction.

1970: Giuseppe Ungaretti--Italy
1972: Gabriel García Márquez--Colombia
1976: Elizabeth Bishop--United States
1980: Josef Škvorecky--Czechoslovakia/Canada
1984: Paavo Haavikko--Finland
1986: Max Frisch--Switzerland

1988: Raja Rao--India/United States
1998: Nuruddin Farah--Somalia
2000: David Malouf--Australia
2002: Álvaro Mutis--Colombia
2006: Claribel Alegría--Nicaragua/El Salvador
2008: Patricia Grace--New Zealand

NOBEL PRIZE IN LITERATURE

Awarded annually since 1901, this award is generally regarded as the highest honor that can be bestowed upon an author for his or her total body of literary work. This listing of winners includes only authors whose works include short fiction.

1904: José Echegaray y Eizaguirre--Spain
1905: Henryk Sienkiewicz--Poland
1907: Rudyard Kipling--England
1909: Selma Lagerlöf--Sweden
1910: Paul Heyse--Germany
1912: Gerhart Hauptmann--Germany
1913: Rabindranath Tagore--India

1916: Verner von Heidenstam--Sweden
1917: Henrik Pontoppidan--Denmark
1920: Knut Hamsun--Norway
1921: Anatole France--France
1922: Jacinto Benavente--Spain
1923: William B. Yeats--Ireland
1924: Władyslaw Reymont--Poland

1925: George Bernard Shaw--Ireland
1926: Grazia Deledda--Italy
1928: Sigrid Undset--Norway
1929: Thomas Mann--Germany
1930: Sinclair Lewis--United States
1932: John Galsworthy--England
1933: Ivan Bunin--Russia
1934: Luigi Pirandello--Italy
1938: Pearl S. Buck--United States
1939: Frans Eemil Sillanpää--Finland
1944: Johannes V. Jensen--Denmark
1946: Hermann Hesse--Switzerland
1947: André Gide--France
1949: William Faulkner--United States
1951: Pär Lagerkvist--Sweden
1954: Ernest Hemingway--United States
1955: Halldór Laxness--Iceland
1957: Albert Camus--France
1958: Boris Pasternak (declined)--Russia
1961: Ivo Andrić--Yugoslavia
1962: John Steinbeck--United States
1964: Jean-Paul Sartre (declined)--France
1965: Mikhail Sholokhov--Russia

1966: Shmuel Yosef Agnon--Israel;
    Nelly Sachs--Sweden
1967: Miguel Angel Asturias--Guatemala
1968: Yasunari Kawabata--Japan
1969: Samuel Beckett--Ireland
1970: Aleksandr Solzhenitsyn--Russia
1972: Heinrich Böll--Germany
1973: Patrick White--Australia
1974: Eyvind Johnson--Sweden
1976: Saul Bellow--United States
1978: Isaac Bashevis Singer--United States
1982: Gabriel García Márquez--Colombia
1983: William Golding--England
1988: Naguib Mahfouz--Egypt
1989: Camilo José Cela--Spain
1991: Nadine Gordimer--South Africa
1994: Kenzaburō Ōe--Japan
1998: José Saramago--Portugal
2000: Gao Xingjian--China
2001: V. S. Naipaul--Trinidad and Tobago/England
2007: Doris Lessing--England
2008: J. M. G. Le Clézio--France/Mauritias
2009: Herta Müller--Germany
2010: Mario Vargas Llosa--Peru

JAPANESE AWARD

AKUTAGAWA PRIZE

The Akutagawa Prize is a Japanese literary award presented twice a year, once in January and again in July. The prize, established in memory of the writer Ryūnosuke Akutagawa, has been awarded since 1935 to the best serious literary story published in a newspaper or magazine by a new or rising author. This list only includes those authors covered in *Critical Survey of Short Fiction.*

January 1958: Kenzaburō Ōe-- "Shiiku" ("The Catch")

LATIN AMERICAN/SPANISH LANGUAGE AWARDS

JUAN RULFO PRIZE FOR LATIN AMERICAN AND CARIBBEAN LITERATURE

The Guadalajara International Book Fair presents its annual literary award to a writer from the Americas who writes in Spanish, Portuguese, French, or English. Award organizers include Mexico's National Council for Culture and Arts and the University of Guadalajara. This listing cites only the prize-winning authors whose works include short fiction.

1992: Juan José Arreola--Mexico
1994: Julio Ramón Ribeyro--Peru
1996: Augusto Monterroso--Guatemala
1997: Juan Marsé--Spain
1999: Sergio Pitol--Mexico

2001: Juan García Ponce--Mexico
2002: Cintio Vitier--Cuba
2003: Rubem Fonseca--Brazil
2004: Juan Goytisolo--Spain
2010: Margo Glantz--Mexico

MIGUEL DE CERVANTES PRIZE

The Miguel de Cervantes Prize, or Premio Miguel de Cervantes, established in 1976, is awarded annually to honor the lifetime achievement of an outstanding writer in the Spanish language from any Spanish-speaking nation. This listing cites only the prize-winning authors whose works include short fiction.

1977: Alejo Carpentier--Cuba
1979: Jorge Luis Borges--Argentina
1980: Juan Carlos Onetti--Uruguay
1987: Carlos Fuentes--Mexico
1989: Augusto Roa Bastos--Paraguay
1990: Adolfo Bioy Casares--Argentina
1991: Francisco Ayala--Spain
1993: Miguel Delibes--Spain
1994: Mario Vargas Llosa--Peru

1995: Camilio José Cela--Spain
1997: Guillermo Cabrera Infante--Cuba
1999: Jorge Edwards--Chile
2000: Francisco Umbral--Spain
2005: Sergio Pitol--Mexico
2006: Antonio Gamoneda--Spain
2009: José Emilio Pacheco--Mexico
2010: Ana María Matute--Spain

RUSSIAN AWARD

RUSSIAN LITTLE BOOKER PRIZE

Established in 1992, the Russian Little Booker Prize is an annual award for a nominated genre of writing. As of 2011, only one prize had been awarded for short fiction.

1993: Victor Pelevin--*Shii fonor* (*The Blue Lantern, and Other Stories*)

CHRONOLOGICAL LIST OF WRITERS

This chronology lists authors covered in this subset in order of their dates of birth. This arrangement serves as a supplemental time line for those interested in the development of short fiction over time.

Born up to 1850

Pu Songling (June 5, 1640)
Ihara Saikaku (1642)
Nahman of Bratslav, Rabbi (April 4, 1772)
Pushkin, Alexander (June 6, 1799)
Gogol, Nikolai (March 31, 1809)
Turgenev, Ivan (November 9, 1818)
Dostoevski, Fyodor (November 11, 1821)
Tolstoy, Leo (September 9, 1828)
Leskov, Nikolai (February 16, 1831)
Machado de Assis, Joaquim Maria (June 21, 1839)
Hearn, Lafcadio (June 27, 1850)

Born 1851-1900

Aleichem, Sholom (March 2, 1859)
Chekhov, Anton (January 29, 1860)
Gorky, Maxim (March 28, 1868)
Bunin, Ivan (October 22, 1870)
Quiroga, Horacio (December 31, 1878)
Lu Xun (September 25, 1881)
Zamyatin, Yevgeny (January 20, 1884)
Tanizaki, Jun'ichirō (July 24, 1886)
Agnon, Shmuel Yosef (July 17, 1888)
Pasternak, Boris (February 10, 1890)
Akutagawa, Ryūnosuke (March 1, 1892)
Babel, Isaac (July 13, 1894)
Zoshchenko, Mikhail (August 10, 1895)
Kawabata, Yasunari (June 11, 1899)
Borges, Jorge Luis (August 24, 1899)
Asturias, Miguel Ángel (October 19, 1899)

Born 1901-1920

Carpentier, Alejo (December 26, 1904)
Narayan, R. K. (October 10, 1906)
Shalamov, Varlam (July 1, 1907)
Guimarães Rosa, João (June 27, 1908)

Dazai, Osamu (June 19, 1909)
Onetti, Juan Carlos (July 1, 1909)
Bombal, María Luisa (June 8, 1910)
Mahfouz, Naguib (December 11, 1911)
Cortázar, Julio (August 26, 1914)
Rulfo, Juan (May 16, 1918)
Arreola, Juan José (September 21, 1918)
Solzhenitsyn, Aleksandr (December 11, 1918)
Mphahlele, Ezekiel (December 17, 1919)

Born 1921-1930

Endō, Shūsaku (March 27, 1923)
Gordimer, Nadine (November 20, 1923)
Donoso, José (October 5, 1924)
Mishima, Yukio (January 14, 1925)
Sinyavsky, Andrei (October 8, 1925)
Lispector, Clarice (December 10, 1925)
García Márquez, Gabriel (March 6, 1927)
Fuentes, Carlos (November 11, 1928)
Achebe, Chinua (November 16, 1930)

Born 1931-1940

Naipaul, V. S. (August 17, 1932)
Ōe, Kenzaburō (January 31, 1935)
Vargas Llosa, Mario (March 28, 1936)
Rasputin, Valentin (March 15, 1937)
Zhang Jie (April 27, 1937)
Desai, Anita (June 24, 1937)
Head, Bessie (July 6, 1937)
Ngugi wa Thiong'o (January 5, 1938)
Valenzuela, Luisa (November 26, 1938)
Oz, Amos (May 4, 1939)
Mukherjee, Bharati (July 27, 1940)

Born 1941-1950

Dovlatov, Sergei (September 3, 1941)
Senior, Olive (December 23, 1941)

Aidoo, Ama Ata (March 23, 1942)
Allende, Isabel (August 2, 1942)
Cliff, Michelle (November 2, 1946)
Rushdie, Salman (June 19, 1947)
Wicomb, Zoë (November 23, 1948)
Murakami, Haruki (January 12, 1949)

Born 1951 and Later

Tolstaya, Tatyana (May 3, 1951)
Xu Xi (1954)

Wang Anyi (March 6, 1954)
Jin, Ha (February 21, 1956)
Okri, Ben (March 15, 1959)
Chandra, Vikram (July 23, 1961)
Mueenuddin, Daniyal (April, 1963)
Alarcón, Daniel (1977)
Adichie, Chimamanda Ngozi (September 15, 1977)

INDEXES

CATEGORICAL INDEX

SUBJECT INDEX

All personages whose names appear in **boldface** *type in this index are the subjects of articles in* Critical Survey of Short Fiction, Fourth Revised Edition.